GENEALOGICAL ABSTRACTS from Early NEW HAMPSHIRE NEWSPAPERS

Volume I

by Scott Lee Chipman

Farmer's Weekly Museum, Walpole (1797-1810)
Gilmanton Rural Museum, Gilmanton (1800)
Gilmanton Gazette, and Farmers' Weekly Museum, Gilmanton (1800)
Democratic Spy, Gilford (1829-1830)
The Strafford Republican, Gilford (1831)
Exeter Federal Miscellany, Exeter (1799)
Political Banquet and Farmer's Feast, Exeter (1799)

HERITAGE BOOKS
2008

HERITAGE BOOKS
AN IMPRINT OF HERITAGE BOOKS, INC.

Books, CDs, and more—Worldwide

For our listing of thousands of titles see our website
at
www.HeritageBooks.com

Published 2008 by
HERITAGE BOOKS, INC.
Publishing Division
100 Railroad Ave. #104
Westminster, Maryland 21157

Copyright © 2000 Scott Lee Chipman

All rights reserved. No part of this book may be reproduced or transmitted in any form or by any means, electronic or mechanical, including photocopying, recording or by any information storage and retrieval system without written permission from the author, except for the inclusion of brief quotations in a review.

International Standard Book Numbers
Paperbound: 978-0-7884-5000-6
Clothbound: 978-0-7884-1550-0

To Milli, who nudged me along when I needed it.

TABLE OF CONTENTS.

Preface vii

Guidelines for the Researcher ix

Abbreviations, Symbols, and Notes xi

Section 1
    Abstracts from the *Farmer's Weekly Museum*, Walpole..................... 1
    An overview of the *Farmer's Weekly Museum* 336
    Geographic distribution of events 337
    Mortality statistics 344
    Miscellaneous statistics 345

Section 2
    Early Newspapers of Gilmanton, N.H. 347
    Gilmanton Rural Museum 348
    Gilmanton Gazette, and Farmers' Weekly Museum 349

Section 3
    Early Newspapers of Gilford, N.H. 351
    Democratic Spy 352
    The Strafford Republican 356

Section 4
    Some Early Newspapers of Exeter, N.H. 359
    Exeter Federal Miscellany 361
    Political Banquet and Farmer's Feast 364

Section 5
    Footnotes 366
    Additions 374

Guide to using the Index to Persons 375
    Index to Persons 376

PREFACE.

"The price of the Farmer's Weekly Museum, which has a wider circulation than any other village paper in the United States, is one dollar and fifty cents, annually, exclusive of postage," so states an advertisement from this newspaper, in the issue of 23 Jan. 1798. A few weeks earlier, the paper gave itself a promotion, stating that "The Farmer's Museum is read by more than two thousand individuals, and has its patrons in Georgia, and on the banks of the Ohio." This might not sound like a large number of readers, but the 1800 census statistics show us just how tiny the country's population was. The *Farmer's Weekly Museum* issue of 19 May 1801 gives us some population statistics gathered from that recent census: New York City was the largest city in the United States with around 60,000 people, and Boston was a distant fourth with a mere 26,000 souls! Later issues of this paper occasionally gave other statistics, such as that of Springfield, Mass. which had a population of about 1900 people! Viewed from this angle, the *Farmer's Weekly Museum*, published in the small village of Walpole, N.H. from 1797 to 1810, is more significant than otherwise might be presumed.

As stated above, the newspaper had readers spread over a large geographical area, and this is reflected by the vast quantity of genealogical information found within the paper. A great many of the early inhabitants of the Walpole area migrated from the Connecticut River Valley in Connecticut and Massachusetts, followed the river to the north, and settled along the river in New Hampshire and Vermont. In addition to local information, thousands of vital records from the far-removed older towns to the south of Walpole, and to the east, were printed in this paper. The quantity of vital records recorded in the paper varied over the years; there were periods of "dry spells," where very few marriages or deaths were reported, but at other times, the quantity of information is enormous. While transcribing some death notices from this newspaper, I found a record of a relative of mine, an elusive character by the name of Zebulon Marsh of Portsmouth, N.H. Heretofore, I have found very little information regarding this man—I had never been able to ascertain his age, other than knowing that he was above 45 years of age, as stated in the 1800 census of Portsmouth. And much to my amazement, his death notice was recorded in the *Farmer's Weekly Museum* printed at Walpole, located on the opposite side of the state from Portsmouth. In that record, we find that Zebulon died in March, 1806, aged 76, thus his year of birth was near 1730. But the example of Zebulon's notice is not unusual; there are a great many vital records recorded here from distant locales such as Portsmouth.

Reading this newspaper was at times rather difficult—in addition to the small print used in this paper, and the fading of some of the text, the researcher is reminded that in the time span of this paper, the letter "s" had two basic forms: firstly, the letter was used in the style as we know it today, but secondly, the form of the letter also appeared as something which resembled the letters "f" or "f." These latter cases were not the letter "**f**," but were actually archaic forms of the letter s, which began to be replaced by the modern version in the late 1700's. However, the archaic form of this letter was used by the *Farmer's Museum* throughout its life span, up until its demise in 1810. Only upon close inspection to the trained eye can the differences between these two characters be distinguished, however when the print is small and faded, sometimes even that is impossible. This was the case with a few surnames that I was unfamiliar with, and in situations of this sort, I have left the surname questionable. Such is the ambiguous example of a man named Isaac who died at New Ipswich in 1806; his last name could have been JOFES, or JOSES. Frequently there was no set pattern used by the Printer—he often seemed to select the style at random, but there was one situation where there was usually some consistency: that is where a word had two cases of the letter *s* within it, such as the word "Federalists;" in an example found within this newspaper, the first *s* was usually of the old style, and the succeeding one was of the new style, thus "Federaliſts."

During my research of old newspapers along the way, I have stumbled across rare issues of uncatalogued and / or unmicrofilmed New Hampshire newspapers stored in various locales. Fearing that we may lose even these remnants to time and neglect, I decided to include some of these abstracts in this volume, thus a small percentage of the book pertains to papers from other parts of the state.

The fact that this book is completed is a major miracle—the project was started several years ago, but had to be set aside at various times for various reasons. The latest hurdle was caused by the catastrophic failure of my old computer, a prehistoric dinosaur by today's standards. The old rattletrap served me well in years past, as slow as it was, for it created my previous publications of the *New England Vital Records from the Exeter News-Letter* series (published by Picton Press of Camden, Maine.) But last summer it finally malfunctioned late into this project. When the new computer was put into service, and the old files were loaded into it, numerous technical problems arose; countless hours were spent diagnosing the problems and resolving them. Much of the software and hardware then had to be modified, including many computer programs which I had written years ago for the indexing portion of the *Exeter News-Letter* project. I had to consult my old computer manuals (which had a good layer of dust accumulated upon them), and hone-up on my computer knowledge which had become very rusty over time. I pray that all the glitches were found and corrected.

The creation of the Index to Persons has been one of the most time-consuming tasks in preparing this volume. Though the total number of names included within this volume is somewhere between 19,000 and 20,000, the "raw quantity" of names presented here is of secondary importance. The major complication has been sorting out all the variations of surname spellings, grouping the similar names together, and creating cross-reference statements for those names in the index. Including the data from this volume and from the *Exeter News-Letter* project, the number of names contained within the computer databases is approaching 100,000; the number of surnames alone tallied up so far is about 7500, and of this total, about 2200 of them are variations of spellings of the main group. Much of the surname work in this volume was created using information from the other databases, and thus the management of all this information has been especially challenging. The researcher is strongly encouraged to read the "Guide to using the Index to Persons" located herein, in order to understand some of the special circumstances which apply to some of these surnames.

Scott Lee Chipman

Portland, Maine
December 1999

GUIDELINES FOR THE RESEARCHER.

In the days before instant communication, news was transmitted across the country at a much slower rate, sometimes taking weeks or months to travel around. The mail system was primitive—very different from the one that we know today. The information was gathered by the proprietor of a newspaper through various methods; letters received by him through private correspondence (such as lists of marriages performed by local ministers), articles copied over from other newspapers printed in various regions of the United States and Europe, and news of local events spread by word-of-mouth.

Newspapers were tiny in size, as compared to their modern counterparts. Paper was scarce, and typically a single issue of a newspaper was comprised of only one large sheet, printed on both sides, folded in half, and thus resulted in a total of four printed pages. Space was at a premium—reports of the European wars and "Domestick" political events frequently crowded out much of the local or regional news. The printers squeezed a great deal of information into a small space. Though when times were quiet in Europe and Philadelphia (and later Washington, D.C.) the printer found space to chronicle items of more local significance.

The newspapers of the early 1700's were primarily read by the "elite;" the printed material primarily consisted of information useful to merchants, politicians, etc. In an evolutionary process, by the late 1700's/early 1800's, newspapers became more accessible and useful to the average person, as more information which reflected a broader range of the population was being printed.

The researcher should consider the above mentioned particulars, and others explained below, as these circumstances impacted how useful old newspapers can be as a research tool:

Geography. As was the case with most newspapers of the era, those included in this volume frequently chronicled an event that happened in a certain town, but the state in which the event occurred was not given. This can be challenging to the researcher, as so many towns in the several states of New England and New York have the same name. Consider the death notice recorded in the *Farmer's Weekly Museum* of Walpole, N.H. from the issue of 21 July 1801: "At Springfield, Mr. Rufus Stebbins, aged 31." There were three towns of significance named Springfield within the viewpoint of Walpole in that era, those in New Hampshire, Vermont, and Massachusetts. The closest town by that name to Walpole is Springfield, Vt., and one might assume that he died there, yet by studying the other death notices clustered around the record in the above example, we see a few towns whose names offer a clue: Southborough, Gloucester, and Boston—towns more unique to Massachusetts. Perhaps we can now assume that Mr. Stebbins died in Springfield, Mass.; however, because so many of these notices were mixed together, the researcher is advised to investigate further, cases such as this.

Occasionally, a newspaper printer would interpret in his own way, that a news event occurred in a certain state, and would then insert (in parenthesis) the state in which he assumed the event occurred. This introduces a possibility of error. Such is the example of the death of Rev. Justus Mitchell, who died in early 1806; in one death notice he was listed as having died in "Canaan, (C.)," the "Connecticut" portion having been added by a printer somewhere along the way. Yet a few weeks later his death notice states that he died in "New-Canaan, (N.Y.)." The second notice does not indicate that this was a correction to the first notice—it only shows that in this second notice, a printer inserted his own assumption that the event happened in the state of New York, thus further research would be needed to determine just where the event occurred.

Spelling. While much of the spelling of the printed material in these old newspapers is more or less consistent, the variations in spelling of surnames is entirely another matter. Consider the example from the Walpole, N.H. *Farmer's Weekly Museum* news account of a man arrested for murder at Wilbraham, Mass.: his name appears in various articles as James *Halligan,* James *Hilligan,* and James *Hallighan.* While much of the Index to Persons included herein compensates for the variations, undoubtedly some surnames have slipped through and remain scattered about. Also consider that in the era when these newspapers were published, hand-written correspondence was a frequent source of information. This method introduced several variables for the accuracy of the relayed information: the clarity of the penmanship of the correspondent, and the ability for the newspaper editor to decipher the correspondent's handwriting, the spelling habits of that correspondent, or, if the proprietor of the paper heard of a news event through word-of-mouth, he introduced his own spelling quirks as yet another variable when the news was set into print.

Ages / Dates. With the size of the text in many of the newspaper articles being very tiny, and the print faded, some of the numerical characters have been difficult or impossible to decipher. It is possible to misinterpret a 3 for an 8, a 5 for a 6, etc. Where this is the case, many of the numbers have been left as questionable or left blank altogether. Even when the print is clear and the numbers unquestionable, consider that the printer who set the type may have copied the numbers over from another newspaper with tiny print, thus another possibility of error.

In the death notices, the ages given for persons were perhaps frequently estimated, rather than based on fact.

Frequently, dates given are structured as "on the 15th inst.," or "on the 23d ult.," but consider that the transmission of news was slow; communication over a few hundred miles may have taken several days or weeks, thus the meaning of "inst." or "ult." could become meaningless, but despite this, the printers copied over from other papers what they read.

Letters left at the Post Office. Periodically newspapers would advertise a list of letters remaining at the local Post Offices. Generally speaking, the Postmaster submitted a quarterly list to the newspaper. To have had a particular name on that list of unclaimed letters does not necessarily indicate that the person moved away, or died. It was simply a list of letters that had accumulated during the previous quarter. Before the days of free postal delivery, a person had to travel to the post office (sometimes which was a great distance away over primitive roads), pay the postage due, and collect their mail. A trip to the post office might have been an rare event, to coincide with a trip "into the village" to purchase supplies.

Advertisements. Many advertisements offer only a glance of the economic class or occupation of the person posting the advertisement, though some offer important information such as those describing a runaway spouse or apprentice. Advertisements generally were posted for a three week minimum run. In this volume nearly all advertisements were reviewed, and generally speaking, the first advertisement in the run was summarized. The exceptions to this are the advertisements published by the newspaper itself, or of its affiliated bookstore, which generally had some sort of advertisement posted every week; these were not summarized or indexed.

Abbreviations, Symbols and Notes.

Adm./ Adm^x.—Administrator / Administratrix.
adv.—advertisement, advertised.
Æ. / Æt. / æ. —Latin *aetatis*, "at the age of."
a.k.a.—also known as.
C.—the printer frequently used this as an abbreviation of Connecticut.
inst.—instant; of the present or current month. (e.g., if the date of the issue is 23 June, and the event occurred on the "14th inst.," it is the equivalent of 14 June.)
mer.—merchant.
Ms.—In the days before the use of zip codes, this was an abbreviation of Massachusetts. The state of Massachusetts previously included in its territory, the District of Maine, before Maine become a separate state in 1820. A particular death notice found in a *Farmer's Weekly Museum* issue in 1799 contains a record from Berwick, *Ms.* (now the town of Berwick, Maine).
[sic]—Latin term meaning *thus*; usually (but not always) used after a word or phrase suspected of being erroneous, but where the information has been copied over verbatim. The cases range anywhere from simple spelling mistakes to gross errors of dates or ages. An example of where this is *not* used to signify a mistake, but only to emphasize that the record was copied verbatim, can be found in the summary of an item from the *Farmer's Weekly Museum* issue of 25 Feb. 1799, where two persons were named in a legal notice, one man was named Joseph *Pierce*, the other John *Peirce*. With so many spelling variations seen in the old newspapers, the use of this notation has been kept to a minimum. As an example of spelling variations, printers could identify someone with the title of "Mr." in one paragraph, while several of the following occurrences would be "mr."
ult.—ultimo; of the month preceding the current one. (e.g. if the date of the issue is 23 June, and the event occurred on the "14th ult.," it is the equivalent of 24 May.)
V.—the printer frequently used this as an abbreviation of Vermont.

- ¶ indicates that a news item was transcribed verbatim in its entirety. Usually followed immediately by the page / column notation indicating where the item was copied from.
- † indicates that a news item was not transcribed verbatim, but only summarized, due to space restrictions. Usually followed immediately by the page / column notation indicating where the item was copied from. Frequently the news items were only brief articles, and the important facts were abstracted and presented in summary form. However, if the article was of great length and contained too many details to be transcribed, the diamond symbol " ♦ " is noted at the end of the summary, to alert the researcher that the original issue (or a microfilm copy) should be consulted for further information.
- [*page column*] — in the event that the researcher must consult the original news item, included herein is the page / column where it can be located. For example, ¶ [4c] indicates that the material was copied verbatim from the fourth page, third column, while † [3a] shows that the news item was summarized from an article appearing on the third page, first column.

Vol. V (No. 209) Tuesday, 4 April 1797.

† [1b] Legal notice concerning a petition by Jacob Copeland, Agent for Stoddard, N.H., regarding business involving town boundaries, etc.

¶ [1b] ELOPEMENT. Whereas Polly, my wife, has eloped from my bed and board, and refuses to return and live with me, this is therefore to forbid all persons harbouring or trusting her on my account, as I will not pay any debt of her contracting after this date. [signed] John Stockbridge. Unity, Feb. 7, 1797.

† [2d] Bryan Stewart, who claimed to belong to Pluckimin, New Jersey, was arrested at New York City for passing counterfeit bills to Mr. William Kimberley. ♦

† [2d] Account of an unusual "find" in a well dug by Samuel Lane, Esq. at Burlington [Vermont—Ed.], near the Onion River. ♦

† [3d] Advertisement of John Newhall, who "has lately come from Lynn" [Mass.—Ed.] and is involved in the shoemaking business at Claremont, N.H., "a few rods north of Park's tavern."

† [3d] Adv. by Samuel Ashley, Jr., offering a farm for sale at Claremont, N.H. ♦

† [3d] List of letters remaining in the Post Office at Walpole, 1 April 1797, as compiled by David Carlisle, Jr., Postmaster:

James Allen,	Walpole.	J.C. Chamberlain, Esq., 2.	Alstead.
Miss Achsah Clark,	"	Jeremiah Higby,	"
Edward Coney,	"	Elisha Kingsbury,	"
Danforth Clarke,	"	Col. Joseph Burt,	Westmoreland.
David M. Foster,	"	Nathaniel Fisk,	"
Samuel March,	"	Eldad Garnsey,	Westminster, Vt.
Samuel Morrison,	"	John Tuttle, Esq.,	" "
Daniel Marsh,	"	Robert Hale,	Chesterfield.
Hephzibah Reed,	"	Ezekiel Pease jun.,	Andover, Vt.
Simon Taylor, two,	"	Alex. Cochran,	Londonderry, Vt.
Mrs. Bingham,	Alstead.		

¶ [3d] DIED.

CONNECTICUT.—At Lebanon, Mrs. Sarah Brown, relict of Capt. Ebenezer Brown, aged 100 years and two months; at Hartford, Mrs. Lydia Shepherd, relict of Mr. Timothy Shepherd, aged 77; Col. Samuel Talcot, aged 86; at Windham, Mrs. Zeruviah Fitch, consort of Deacon Eleazer Fitch, aged 77; Mr. Oliver Allen, aged 20; At Watertown, Mr. Ethel Porter, merchant, aged 31.

MASSACHUSETTS.—At Boston, Mr. Thomas Fleet, printer, aged 65; at Westminster, Lieut. Samuel Gerrish, aged 57; at Sturbridge, Deacon Joshua Harding, aged 71; at Shrewsbury, Mr. Timothy Bragg, aged 46; at Milton, Mrs. Ann Crehore, wife of Mr. William Crehore, aged 70.

NEWHAMPSHIRE.—At Rindge Mr. Barnabas Barker, aged 75; at Portsmouth, the Hon. John Shurburne, Esq. aged 77; at Hinsdale, Mr. Aaron Wright, aged 69.

Vol. V (No. 210) Tuesday, 11 April 1797.

† [1a] List of letters remaining in the Post Office at Charlestown, N.H., 1 April 1797, as compiled by Samuel Crosby, Postmaster:

Oliver Ashley,	Claremont.	Jon. Grout,	Charlestown.
George Atkins jun.,	Charlestown.	Nathaniel Holloway,	"
Eusebius Ball,	Rockingham, Vt.	Samuel Stone,	Claremont.
Solomon Davis,	Chesterfield.	Thankful Taylor,	Langdon.
John Downer,	Sharon.	George Westgate,	Plainfield.
Josiah Dudley,	Newport.	John Westgate	"

† [1b] Adv. by Tisdale Cobb, Westmoreland, N.H., who found a watch in the road.

† [3c] News items dated at Middletown, Conn., 14 March: 1) lightning strike "on Saturday" at a house in Haddam, Conn., instantly killing Mr. James Tyler. 2) The account of the death of Ed. Reding's wife, who was caught in a storm in an unspecified town and supposedly died of exposure. ♦

† [3d] Legal notice adv. by Samuel Slade, Executor of the estate of John Slade, late of Alstead, N.H., deceased, dated at Alstead, 11 April 1797.

=== ¶ [3d] DIED. ===

VIRGINIA.—At Richmond, Francis Lightfoot Lee, Esq; aged 63.
MARYLAND.—At Summer Hill, near Annapolis, John G. Worthington, Esq; aged 32.
PENNSYLVANIA.—At Carlisle, Mr. William Haslet, aged 100 years and 9 months.
NEWJERSEY.—At Burlington, Richard Brooke Roberts, Esq. of Southcarolina, Major in the infantry of the United States; at Cranberry, Rev. Gilbert Snowden, aged 32.
NEWYORK.—At Albany, Mr. John Shepherd; at Stillwater Mrs. Hindman, aged 107; at Kinderhook, Henry C. Van Schaack, Esq. aged 28; at Newyork, John Woods, Esq. Counsellor at Law, aged 65.
VERMONT.—At Brattleborough, Mr. Joseph Herrick, aged 77; at Putney, Mr. Prentiss Willard; at Pownal, of the small pox, Mrs. Sarah Clark, aged 39.

Vol. V (No. 211) Tuesday, 18 April 1797.

† [3b] News item dated at Middletown, Conn., regarding the fire which destroyed the house belonging to Mr. Daniel Starr of Middletown. ♦
† [3c] Item dated at Hallowell [District of Maine—Ed.] regarding a mob which broke open the jail in Pownalborough, and freed a number of prisoners who were held on the battery and robbery of a Mr. Truman, the event having occurred "last summer." 1 ♦
† [3c] Account of the discovery of the body of Lieut. Jonathan Barns, of Brookfield, [Mass.], who supposedly died in a fall from a fence about the 20th of March, 1797. ♦
† [3d] Legal notice adv. by Josiah Dana, & Co., requesting the settlement of debtors by 15 May 1797, "at which time they intend to discontinue business at, and remove from, *Westminster*." The type of business is not specified.
† [3d] Advertisement by Thomas and Isaac Redington, merchants at Walpole, N.H.

=== ¶ [3d] DIED. ===

CONNECTICUT.—At Litchfield, widow Gillet, aged 95; at Scituate, Mr. Caleb Cushing, aged 42; at Glastenbury, Mrs. Catharine Easton, wife of Mr. Timothy Easton, aged 58.
RHODEISLAND.—At Smithfield, David Harns, Esq; aged 64.
MASSACHUSETTS.—At Boston, Col. Andrew Symmes, aged 6[3?].—Miss Jane Rand, aged 20. Mr. Edward Brattle Oliver, aged 84; at Salem, widow Ruth Kimball, aged 69; at Boxford, Deacon John Chadwick, aged 76; at Brookfield, Mrs. Nancy Reed, wife of Mr. Cheney Reed, aged 24; Mrs. Patience Banister, wife of Mr. Solomon Banister.
NEWHAMPSHIRE.—At Hollis, Mr. Oliver Lawrence, aged 70; at Portsmouth, Mrs. Rebecca Foster, aged 41; at Newcastle, widow Mary Bell; at Salisbury, Mrs. Fellows, wife of Mr. Adonijah Fellows.
In this town, April 13th, Miss Polly Fay.

Vol. V (No. 212) Tuesday, 25 April 1797.

¶ [2d] SOUTHCAROLINA. Charleston, March 27. Amons Cadet was killed the evening before last, in a pugilistical combat with a brother Frenchman.
† [2d] News from the Collector for the port of Charleston, S.C. regarding a vessel supposed to be a French Privateer, seen off the coast by "Capt. Andrew Young, commander of the sloop Betsey of Falmouth, in the state of Massachusetts, now employed in the coasting trade of this state."
† [3d] Jether Bailey adv. farms for sale at Springfield, Vt. & Westmoreland, N.H. ♦
† [3d] Legal notice advertised by Josiah Hart, Adm. of estate of Job Johnson, late of Charlestown, [N.H.], deceased.
† [3d] Legal notice advertised by Samuel Garfield, Adm. of estate of John Harris, late of Langdon, [N.H.], deceased.

=== ¶ [3d] DIED. ===

MARYLAND.—At Baltimore, Daniel Dulany, Esq; Barrister at Law, aged 76.
CONNECTICUT.—At Windham, Mr. Samuel Badger, aged 87; at Middletown, Capt. Timothy Starr, jun. aged 44; at Redding, Mr. Ebenezer Couch, aged 87; at Litchfield, Mrs. Sarah Reeve, consort of Tappan Reeve, Esq; at Newlondon, Jeremiah Miller, Esq; aged 77; at Norwich, Capt. Jeremiah Harris, aged 52; at Easthaddam, Samuel Huntington, Esq; aged 73.

MASSACHUSETTS.—At Concord, Doct. Joseph Lee, aged 81; at Andover, Mr. Houghton, paper maker.
VERMONT.—At Williamstown, Mr. Sampson Howe, aged 81.

Vol. V (No. 213) Tuesday, 2 May 1797.

† [2a] A short biography of Alexander Selkirk, "the original Robinson Crusoe," born in 1676, describing his time spent marooned on an island in the South Seas. The article mentions that his chest and musket "are now in the possession of his grand nephew, John Selkirk, weaver, at Largo," Scotland. ◆

† [3d] Public notice from the General Court [N.H.] concerning a petition for a proposed toll bridge across the Connecticut River, near Brattleboro, Vt. This legal notice mentions Lieut. Josiah Hastings' ferry at Chesterfield, N.H., and reference is made to another petition made by Rufus Graves.

† [3d] Adv. by William Fitch & Co., Walpole, N.H., regarding "Hatting Furs."

† [3d] Legal notice adv. by Samuel Guild & Rufus Guild, Adm's. of the estate of Jesse Guild, late of Charlestown, N.H.

=== ¶ [3d] DIED. ===

CONNECTICUT.—At Norwich, Samuel Leffingwell, Esq; aged 75, Mr. Joseph Kelly, aged 67; at Hartford Rev. Elhanan Winchester, preacher of Universal Restoration, aged 46

MASSACHUSETTS.—At Boston Mr. Richard H. Warren, son of the late Maj. Gen. Jos. Warren, aged 27; at Andover, Mr. Stephen Cummins, aged 40; at Beverly, Mr. Samuel Woodbury, aged 50, Widow Elizabeth Higinson, aged 82, Mrs. Hannah Bachelder, aged 57, wife of Josiah Bachelder, Esq; at Petersham, Mr. John [Bouker? or Booker?], aged 90; at Northampton, Mr. Jonathan Strog, aged 88.

VERMONT.—At Bennington, Mrs. Sally Hubbel, wife of Mr. Aaron Hubbel, aged 30; At Castleton, Mrs. Mary Merrill, aged 71.

NEWHAMPSHIRE.—At Hollis, Mr. Oliver Lawrence aged 70; at Amherst, Mr. Ebenezer Holt, aged 18.

Vol. V (No. 214) Tuesday, 9 May 1797.

† [3a] Account of the trial of a female slave owned by Mr. Eccleston of Kent County, Maryland, for the murder of three of his children. The article also mentions the late Mr. Bowers of the same county, who was apparently a former owner of this slave.

† [3d] Advertisement by Robert & Joshua Davis, Jr., merchants in the "south end Boston," sellers of Potash Kettles.

† [3d] Caleb Johnson, owner of a "variety store" at Walpole, advertises an extensive inventory of his wares.

=== ¶ [3d] DIED. ===

CONNECTICUT.—At Newlondon, Mr. Patrick Robertson, aged 47.

MASSACHUSETTS.—At Quincy, Mrs. Hall, mother of President Adams, aged 85; at Grafton, Mr. Phineas Leland, Jun. aged 21; at Charlton, Mr. Joseph Parker, aged 65; at Worcester, Mrs. Martha Adams, widow, in an advanced age.

NEWHAMPSHIRE.—At Amherst, Mrs. Boutell, consort of Mr. Caleb Boutell, aged 3[1?]; at Portsmouth, Mr. William Marston, aged 22.

Vol. V (No. 215) Tuesday, 16 May 1797.

† [3b] Mr. Samuel Moore, Collector of Revenue of the U.S., assaulted and robbed on the bridge between Boston and Charlestown, [Mass.]. ◆

† [3d] Advertisement by John A. Perkins, merchant in English & India Goods, dated at Newport, 9 May 1797.

† [3d] Stephen Parker advertises a stray mule, dated at Charlestown, [N.H.].

† [3d] Public notice that the Partnership of *Evans, Leonard and Co.* is dissolved, and stating that settlement of accounts be made with Eliphalet Felt. The notice is advertised by *Leonard & Felt*, and is dated at Rockingham [Vermont—Ed.], 10 May 1797.

Vol. V (No. 216) Tuesday, 23 May 1797.

† [1a] Adv. by John Carlisle, dated at Walpole 15 May 1797, stating that "he is about to relinquish the business of Shoemaking" and requests settlement of accounts by 1 June.

† [1b] Adv. of "Doctor Lee's True Billious Pills . . . sold by Jonathan Lee, opposite Bellow's Tavern in Walpole Village, or at John Hubbard's Apothecary Store; and at Samuel Crosby's Apothecary Store in Charlestown."

† [2d] Frank, a slave owned by Capt. William Brown, executed [4 April 1797] for a robbery at St. Mary's, Georgia. Article dated at Savannah, 14 April. ♦

† [3a] John Shreeve won a foot race held in Eastern New York; article dated at Poughkeepsie, 12 April. ♦

¶ [3b] RUTLAND, VERMONT, May 15. EXTRAORDINARY BIRTHS. At Christmas last, the wife of John Smith, a journeyman carpenter and wheelwright, at Westbury, Wilts, was delivered of twins, making nine children she has had at four births, and all within six years; it is perhaps, still more remarkable, that the first five chidren were born within thirteen months. She brought forth once three at a birth, and at the other times twins; the three were born alive, but did not long survive—the other six are now all hearty and well with their prolifick mother.

† [3b] Two girls playing near a saw mill wheel were crushed to death at Gilmanton, N.H., [21 April 1797] ; one was a daughter of Mr. Gale, the other a daughter of Mr. Jewett; article dated at Concord, N.H. ♦

† [3d] Reward offered for a lost mare, owned by Abel Walker, dated at Langdon, N.H.

====== ¶ [3d] MARRIED. ======

At Boston, Mr. Isaiah Thomas, jun. Printer, of Worcester, to Miss Mary Weld, of Boston.

At Rutland, (Ver.) on Sunday evening the 7th instant, by the Rev. H. Ball, Mr. Asher Southworth, to the agreeable Miss Sally Hore, both formerly of this town

====== ¶ [3d] DIED. ======

CONNECTICUT.—At Newlondon, Mrs. Catharine Brooks, wife of Mr. James Brooks; at Stonington, Mrs. Abigail Swan, wife of Mr. George Swan, aged 44.

RHODEISLAND.—At Providence, Mr. Joseph Crawford, merchant; at Smithfield, Mr. Preserved Harris, aged 81.

MASSACHUSETTS.—At Boston, Capt. Enoch House, aged 53; at Charlestown, Mr. James Reed, aged 29; at Pepperelborough, Mr. George Jewett, aged 30; at Athol, Deacon Jesse Kendal, aged 70; at Bridgwater, Mrs. Susannah Kingman, wife of Capt. Ezra Kingman, aged 36.

NEWHAMPSHIRE.—At Haverhill, Miss Polly Boynton; at Dunbarton, drowned, Mr. James Heywood, aged 22, formerly of New Ipswich; at Stratham, Mr. Stephen Piper, aged 64.

Vol. V (No. 217) Monday, 29 May 1797.

† [3d] Adv. of Humphrey Sullivan, a Tailor at Alstead, N.H. "near General Shepard's."

====== ¶ [3d] DIED. ======

NEWYORK.—At Livingston Manor, Walter Livingston, Esq; aged 67.

CONNECTICUT.—At East Windsor, Mrs. Unice Payne, wife of Mr. Solomon Payne, aged 35.

RHODEISLAND.—At Providence, Mr. Samuel Pool, aged 75; at Newport, Miss Rebecca Sanford, aged 58; at Bellingham, Elder Noah Alden, aged 72.

MASSACHUSETTS.—At Boston, Capt. David Brace, aged 62; at Salem, William Vans, Esq; at Newbedford, Mr. Robert Bennet; at Marblehead, Mrs. Elizabeth Bowen, consort of Nathan Bowen, Esq; aged 35.

VERMONT.—At Rutland, Mrs. Hepzibah Whipple, wife of Benjamin Whipple, Esq; aged 69; at Hampton, Mr. Peter Cristy, aged 47, Mrs. Beaman, consort of Samuel Beaman, Esq.

NEWHAMPSHIRE.—At Concord, Mr. John Herrick, aged 16, son of Lieut. Asa Herrick; at Bow, Deacon James Buswell, aged 57; at Dover, Mrs. Samuel Emerson, of Poland; at Surry, Mr. William Barron, aged 67.

Vol. V (No. 218) Monday, 5 June 1797.

† [1a] Adv. of "The Poetical and Miscellaneous Works of James Elliot, citizen of Guilford, Vermont, late a noncommissioned officer in the Legion of the United States. ♦

† [1b] Adv. for the settlement of accounts with Caryl & Chandlers, dated at Chester, [Vermont—Ed.], 3 May 1797.

† [3b] Indian attack in Washington County, Georgia, where one Mr. Brown was killed and his wife and children forced to flee; article dated at Savannah, Ga. ♦

† [3d] Notice of Hosea White, an "indented boy" between 16 and 17 years old who ran away from Sardis Miller on 21 May 1797; reward 3 cents; dated at Alstead, [N.H.—Ed.]

† [3d] Six cents reward offered for return of Arter Williams, an "indented boy" who ran away from his master, Othniel Williams; dated at Chester, [Vermont—Ed.] 30 May 1797.

† [3d] Adv. regarding stray livestock at the property of Edward Crandall, dated at Surry, 30 May 1797.

† [3d] Legal notice concerning the insolvent estate of Joseph Rounsevel, Esq., late of Washington, Cheshire County, N.H., deceased, whereby Azariah Faxon, Ebenezer Jaquith, and Ephraim Farwell were appointed Commissioners; dated 19 May, 1797.

===== ¶ [3d] DIED. =====

PENNSYLVANIA.—At Philadelphia, William Allibone, Esq;

MASSACHUSETTS.—At Boston, Mrs. Mary Lewis, aged 49, wife of Mr. Thomas Lewis, Ephraim May, Esq; aged 60; at Cambridge Thomas Lee, Esq; aged 60; At Dedham, Doct. John Sprague, sen. aged 78; at Northborough, Dea. Paul Newton, aged 79; at Grafton, Dea. Joseph Meriam, aged 88; at Petersham, Mr. Jerathmeel Wilder, aged 76; at Orange, Capt. Benjamin Mayo, aged 46; at New Braintree, Mr. Ephraim Woods, aged 85.

VERMONT.—At Fairfax, Miss Sally Page, aged 19, daughter of Mr. Phineas Page, formerly of Charlestown, (N.H.)

NEWHAMPSHIRE.—At Swanzey, Mr. Benjamin Brown, aged 86.

Vol. V (No. 219) Monday, 12 June 1797.

† [3d] Adv. by Mr. Hubbard, who proposes to open a school at Walpole, N.H. ♦

===== ¶ [3d] DIED. =====

PENNSYLVANIA.—At Philadelphia, Joshua Howell, Esq; aged 72.

NEWYORK.—At Newyork, Mrs. Mary Wycoff, aged 46; at Bloomingdale, Charles Ward Apthorp, Esq; aged 73.

CONNECTICUT.—At Bethel, Deacon Benjamin Benedict, aged 84; at Newlondon, Miss Elizabeth Latimer, aged 69; at Norwich, Capt. Timothy Parker, aged 60; at Lyme, Capt. Seth Higgins, aged 35; at Weathersfield, John Robbins, Esq; aged 81.

MASSACHUSETTS.—At Charlestown, Mrs. Elizabeth B[-]s[--]am,[2] widow, aged 72; At Petersham, Miss Polly Doolittle; At Hadley, Hon. Eleazer Porter, Esq; At Newburyport, Mr. Henry L. Tracy, aged 20.

Vol. V (No. 220) Monday, 19 June 1797.

† [1a] Notice of a celebration of the Jerusalem Lodge in Putney, [Vt.—Ed.], to be held at the house of William Stephenson, with a sermon to be delivered by Brother Aaron Leland; adv. by Nathaniel Blanchard, Secretary.

† [3b] Account of Mr. John Millen, of Savannah, Ga., who was aboard the ship Diana, when it was seized by a French Privateer and taken into the port of Brest, France; Millen was kept as a British prisoner with several other passengers, but released and returned to Savannah. ♦

† [3c] Mr. Archibald Carr arrested for killing a man with a sword cane, at Dumfries, [Virginia?—Ed.]; article dated at Alexandria, Va.[3] ♦

† [3d] Celebration of the Franklin Lodge, as advertised by A. Hedge, Secretary, dated at Hanover, [N.H.]

† [3d] Reward offered by John Chapin for a stray horse, dated Lyme, [N.H.], 11 June.

† [3d] Adv. by Caleb Johnson, dated at Walpole 17 June, offering rum for sale.

† [3d] Notice adv. by Josiah Gates, requesting settlement of accounts for "Ferriage", dated at Walpole 15 June.

===== ¶ [3d] DIED. =====

GEORGIA.—At Litchfield, Mrs. Mary Jane Gunn, aged 31, wife of the Hon. James Gunn, Senator in Congress.

NEWYORK.—At Newyork, M[r.] Zacheriah Russell.

CONNECTICUT.—At Norwich, Miss Sophia Rogers, aged 22.

MASSACHUSETTS.—At Boston, Mrs. Catharine Welsh, aged 69, wife of Mr. James Welsh; at Sherburne, Doct. William Jackson, of Boston; at Salem, George Williams, Esq. aged 67; at Dedham, Mrs. Catharine Barnard, aged 95; at Beverly, Mr. John Lovett, aged 80; at Northfield, Mr. Asa Briggs, aged 25; at Milton, Mrs. Lucy Vose, aged 60; at Western, [sic] Mrs. Lydia Jones, of Hinsdale, N.H. relict of the Hon. Daniel Jones, Esq. aged 55; at Warwick, Deacon James Ball, aged 66; at Spencer, Mrs. Rebekah Barnes, wife of Lieut. David Barnes, aged 56.

VERMONT.—At Hinsdale, 4 the consort of Judge Bridgeman, aged 57.

NEWHAMPSHIRE.—At Keene, Mr. Seth Heaton, aged 86; at Lyme, Col. Thomas Gilbert, aged 53; at Temple, Deacon John Craggin; at Concord, Mr. John Herrick, aged 16.

Vol. V (No. 221)   Monday, 26 June 1797.

===== ¶ [3d] DIED. =====

SOUTHCAROLINA.—At Dafusky Island, James Priolare Fraser, Esq; Barrister at Law, of the Inner Temple, London.

MARYLAND.—At Baltimore, Thomas Dewall Montville, Esq; of St. Domingo.

CONNECTICUT.—At Groton, Lieut. Stephen Morgan, aged 26; at Watertown, Mr. John Judd, aged 98.

MASSACHUSETTS.—At Boston, Mr. Edward Waine aged 57; at Newburyport, Mrs. Sibyl Farnham, aged 79, relict of Daniel Farnham, Esq; formerly of that place.

NEWHAMPSHIRE.—At Portsmouth, Capt. William Gerrish.

Vol. V (No. 222)   Monday, 3 July 1797.

† [3d] List of letters remaining in the Post Office at Walpole, 1 July 1797, as compiled by David Carlisle, Jr. "D.P.M."

Thomas Sparhawk, Esq.	Walpole.		Mr. Azariah Faxon,	Washington.
Col. Josiah Goldsmith,	"		Col. Abijah Wheeler,	Temple.
Mr. John Ellis, jun.	"		Mr. Ephraim Adams,	Sullivan.
Mr. Thomas Moor,	"		Mr. Shearman Cooper,	Croydon.
Mr. Asel Bliss,	"		Mr. Jesse Lane,	Newport.
Miss Phebe Gray,	"		Mr. Thomas Dunshee,	Jaffrey.
John Chamberlain, Esq.	Alstead.		Mr. Abiel Briggs,	Putney, (Vt.)
Mr. John Noyes,	"		Mr. Jacob Benton,	Rockingham, (Vt.)
Mr. Solomon Davis,	Chesterfield.			

† [3d] Adv. regarding stray horses, posted by Jonathan Royce, dated Walpole 28 June.

===== ¶ [3d] DIED. =====

CONNECTICUT.—At Preston, Mrs. Elizabeth Baldwin, aged 79; at Norwich, Mrs. Carpenter, wife of Mr. Joseph Carpenter; at Newlondon, Nathaniel Shaw Woodbridge, Esq. aged 26; at Greenfield, 5 Mr. Daniel Bulkley, aged 78.

VERMONT.—At Charlotte, Mrs. Irene Gillet, aged 26, consort of the Rev. Mr. Gillet; at Poultney, Mr. Thomas Goodwin—he was found by the side of this team, which he had been driving, just expiring; at Sudbury, Mrs. Mary Wood, aged 41, consort of Mr. Abel Wood.

Vol. V (No. 223)   Monday, 10 July 1797.

† [3b] In a paragraph entitled "Incidents at Home," a short item includes the following news: "In Canada, two M'Lanes, and a Thomas Butterfield, late an infamous Justice in Vermont, have been apprehended, and are now in irons in Quebec, for traitorous practices against the Government . . ." 6

† [3c] Account of the ordination of Rev. Mr. John Kimball, at Acworth, N.H. 14 June.

† [3d] Jemima Blake, of Keene, N.H., petitions the Superior Court of Judicature for divorce from Obadiah Blake, Jr., yeoman, to whom she was married 10 August 1774, by

the Rev. Edward Goddard. The groom was stated to have been "then of Keene" at the time of marriage, and has been absent for over three years.
† [3d] Reward offered by William Dunton, Dorset, [Vt.], for two mares, strayed or stolen from Pawlet, Vt.
† [3d] Zenas Newell requests all accounts to be settled, dated Springfield, [Vt.?—Ed.] 29 June 1797, "or they may expect cost and trouble."
===== ¶ [3d] DIED. =====
MARYLAND.—At Baltimore, Mr. George Hunter, aged 66.
PENNSYLVANIA.—At Philadelphia, James Reidle, Esq.

Vol. V (No. 224) Monday, 17 July 1797.

† [1a] Jason Wetherbe offers sundry items for sale at Bellows Falls, Vt., though the advertisement is dated at Rockingham, Vt., 1 July 1797.
† [2c] John M'Carrel alias Robert Brown arrested for the murder of Andrew Conrow, who was killed in a shallop near Philadelphia, and one John Rolley / Roley was mortally wounded. ♦
† [3a] Remarkable account of Mr. Nathan Whitemore, of Oxford, [prob. *Mass.*—Ed.] who was struck by lightning near the Mohawk River, but survived and continued on his journey. ♦
† [3d] Adv. by Jesse Smith, stating "that he has lately set up the Tailoring Business in Newport, near the Meetinghouse." Dated at Newport, 6 July 1797.
† [3d] Reward offered by Marcian Williard, for a lost mare; dated Charlestown, 13 July.
† [3d] Adv. for a stray horse, found by Caleb Winn, dated at Chester, [Vt.] 17 July.

Vol. V (No. 225) Monday, 24 July 1797.

† [3a] Remarkable "find" by Mr. Allen Taylor, grocer, in the city of New York. ♦
¶ [3d] DIED. At New Providence, His Excellency Governour Forbes, of an epidemick.
† [3d] Nicanor Townsley adv. his "Cabinent Making Business" at Walpole.
† [3d] Adv. by J.B. Wheeler and William Hall, Jr., of *Wheeler & Hall*, requesting settlement of accounts; also adv. English & West India goods for sale, dated at Grafton.
† [3d] Lime offered for sale by Thomas White, dated at Cavendish, [Vt.], 15 July 1797.

Vol. V (No. 226) Monday, 31 July 1797.

† [1a] Adv. for "The Algerine Captive, or, the Life and Adventures of Doctor Updike Underhill; six years a prisoner among the Algerine," to be published at Walpole.
† [3b] Murder-suicide of John Quigley and wife at "Bucklestown;" article dated at Martinsburg, Virginia, 6 July. ♦
¶ [3c] SPRINGFIELD, MASSACHUSETTS, July 25. THUNDER STORM. [. . .] At Monson the lightning struck the House of Mr. Richard Lull, and entering a chamber, where a son of Mr. Lull, and Mr. Timothy Harris of Strafford, were lying on a bed, it killed the latter instantly, and burnt and wounded the former in a most shocking manner, but he is recovering.
† [3d] Adv. of goods for sale at Oliver Johnson & Co., Westmoreland, N.H.
† [3d] Adv. of *Bonney & Henry*, who set up a Card Manufactory at Charlestown, [N.H.]
===== ¶ [3d] DIED. =====
CONNECTICUT.—At New Fairfield, Mr. Benjamin Taylor, aged 78.
MASSACHUSETTS.—At Boston, Mrs. Abigail Parkman, wife of Mr. Elias Parkman; the Hon. Caleb Davis, Esq, aged 50; at Charlestown, David Wood, Esq. aged 87; at Newton, Mr. Reuben Esty, aged 34; at Southam[p]ton, Mrs. Ruth White, consort of the Hon. Phillip White, Esq.
NEWHAMPSHIRE.—At Lempster, Mr. Robert Roundye, aged 92; formerly of Windham, Connecticut.

Vol. V (No. 227) Monday, 7 Aug. 1797.

† [3d] Copy of a petition to the General Court of New Hampshire, by Isaac Hubbard, of Claremont, N.H., for a privilege of setting up a ferry across the Connecticut River

"over that part of said river which lies between the south line of Claremont aforesaid and three miles north of said line, or to Sumner's south line . . . "

† [3d] Adv. of a stray mare found by Mayhew Hasham, dated Westmoreland, 5 Aug.

† [3d] James Titus adv. for a Journeyman Clothier, dated at Rockingham, [Vt.] 4 Aug.

Vol. V (No. 228) Monday, 14 Aug. 1797.

† [3b] A short notice dated 23 July [at New York], stating that a Mr. Young, "the person who killed Berwick the Deputy Sheriff, was convicted of murder."

† [3b] Extract of a letter under the Albany head, concerning the "Canada plot," which mentions that a reward was offered "for an Esquire Smith, formerly of Lenox, but now resident in Vermont"—and a reward of one hundred pounds was offered for apprehending a Mr. Marvin. See also the notice in 10 July 1797 [3b] contained herein.

† [3c] Account of a major fire at Albany, [N.Y.—Ed.], "which broke out in a stable belonging to the widow A. Bradt, in Montgomery street . . . "

† [3d] Request of debt settlements, by Thomas S. Fullerton, dated Chester, [Vt.] 5 Aug.

† [3d] Notice of a public auction to be held 21 Aug. in Charlestown, [N.H.], at the dwelling house of "Jonathan Holten, D.S."

† [3d] Public notice that the copartnership of Nathaniel Cummings and Ebenezer Hills, a.k.a. *Cummings & Hills*, is dissolved; dated at Washington, N.H. 8 Aug. 1797. An advertisement following this notice indicates that they occupied a Fulling Mill.

† [3d] Adv. of a new clothing business to be operated by Daniel Edwards; dated at Washington, N.H. 9 Aug. 1797.

† [3d] Legal notice concerning the insolvent estate of Tower Hill, "so called," late of Charlestown, [N.H.], deceased; Willard Hastings and Jesse Healy were appointed Commissioners of said estate.

====== ¶ [3d] DIED. ======

At St. Thomas's, (*West Indies*) Mr. John Bellows, son of Colonel John Bellows of this town, aged 24.

PENNSYLVANIA.—At Philadelphia, James Searle, Esq; formerly a respectable merchant of that city, and a Member of Congress under the Confederation.

Vol. V (No. 229) Monday, 21 Aug. 1797.

† [3b] An article dated Hartford, Conn., at the "Prison of Newgate, July 18th, 1797," describing a bizarre event in which Loudon Doney, a prisoner confined there, cut off his fingers and otherwise mangled his hand, his objective being to maim himself to the point of not being able to work. ♦

† [3b] Gruesome account of a Mr. Wadsworth, about 70 years of age, of Becket, [Mass.], who was gored to death by a bull, "on Tuesday morning last." The article is dated at Stockbridge, 7 August. ♦

¶ [3b] WORCESTER, August 9. We are informed that a very severe thunder storm was experienced, the last Sabbath, in the northeasterly part of this county. At Northborough, a Mr. Hopkinson, from Rochester, riding in a sulkey was killed instantaneously by the lightning. His horse was also killed, his carriage shattered to pieces, and of an umbrella, which he held over him, the wood and silk were entirely consumed, and the metal melted. Two or three other persons, and horses were struck down; but recovered. One man remained senseless several minutes. [*see also issue of 28 Aug. 1797*]

† [3d] Account of a flash flood at Walpole, N.H., which damaged much property, and destroyed a "fulling mill, belonging to Mr. Sikes in the north part of the town." 7

¶ [3d] TAKE NOTICE. All persons indebted to Frederick W. Geer of Boston, for crossing the bridge over Bellow's Falls, are desired to make immediate payment to Solomon Hapgood, tender of the gate. Rockingham, August 18, 1797.

† [3d] Legal notice regarding a petition by Josiah Hart, Guardian to Charlotte, [Hisley?], Samuel, Almon, Polly, and Clarissa, minor children of Job Johnson, late of Charlestown, N.H., deceased. The notice was posted by Samuel West, Attorney for the Guardian, and concerns property inherited by the minor children.

† [3d] Adv. by Joseph S. Stearns, who simply states "Cash given for oats." Dated at Claremont, [N.H.] 18 Aug. 1797.

Vol. V (No. 230) Monday, 28 Aug. 1797.

† [3a] Joshua Knight, a poor and infirm man of Somerset County, Maryland, murdered there by four slaves [on 16 July]; article dated at Easton, Maryland, 1 Aug. ♦

† [3c] The body of John Hoxey, of Stockbridge, Mass., discovered in a brook at West Stockbridge "on Thursday morning last," supposedly a victim of his own insanity; the article is dated at Stockbridge, 14 Aug. ♦

† [3c] Extensive article regarding the death of Mr. Parker Hopkinson, about 25 years of age, of Rochester, N.H., who was killed by lightning at Northborough, Mass. on the 6th of August. The article stated that his parents "live at Exeter." In the same lightning strike, Mr. Joshua Barnard of Leicester, Mass., was injured, and Mr. Levi Barnard of Northborough was a witness to the event. ♦

† [3d] Public notice by Sam. Crosby, Collector of the Revenue for the Second Division, District of New Hampshire, regarding licences for retailers of liquor, etc.

† [3d] Adv. for settlement of debts, by Caleb Johnson, Walpole, 28 Aug. 1797.

† [3d] Legal notice dated 7 July, 1797, regarding the insolvent estate of John Simon, Esq., late of Andover, [Vermont], deceased. Moses Warner, Augustus Pease, and Christopher Martin appointed Commissioners of said estate.

===== ¶ [3d] DIED. =====

In London, Gustavus Vassa, the African, well known to the publick, for the interesting narrative of his life.

GEORGIA.—At Savannah, Mr. Titus Powers, printer, formerly of Middletown, (Con.)

PENNSYLVANIA.—At Philadelphia, Mr. Nathaniel Dickinson, printer, late of Northampton, (Mass.) aged 24.

CONNECTICUT.—At Stamford, the Hon. James Davenport, a Representative in Congress; from the State of Connecticut.

NEWHAMPSHIRE.—At Hanover, on the 21st instant a son of Mr. Jedediah Baldwin, aged 14 months.

Vol. V (No. 231) Monday, 4 Sept. 1797.

¶ [3c] *Rockingham*, (Ver.) *Aug.* 28, 1797. "Sally Stearns, a young woman about eighteen, having been in a state of melancholy, for sometime, got up from her bed, on the night of the 21st inst. and made for Saxton's river, where it is supposed she went in at the head of the falls, near Clark's Mills, so-called, and was drowned. Search was made for her on the 22d to no purpose, and on the 23d she was found. The Jury of inquest was called and brought in a verdict that she had risen from her bed in a state of derangement and got into the river.—She has left aged parents and a number of brothers and sisters to mourn her untimely death."

† [3c] Two legal notices concerning the insolvent estate of Prentice Willard, late of Putney, Vermont, deceased. Michael Gilson, Reuben Attwater, and Samuel Pratt, Innholder at Westminster, appointed Commissioners over said estate; Stephen R. Bradley and Mindwell Willard administrators. These notices dated at Westminster, 17 April 1797.

† [3d] Adv. by *Bellows & Stone*, of the goods carried at their store in Walpole, N.H.

† [3d] Phinehas Parker advertises his clothing business at Claremont., N.H.

† [3d] Legal notice by Esther Farnsworth, administratrix of the estate of Simeon Farnsworth, late of Washington, [N.H.], dated there, 22 Aug. 1797.

† [3d] Notice of inspection for the fifth Brigade of Militia of New Hampshire, Amasa Allen, Gen. of Brigade, dated at Walpole, 28 Aug. '97

† [3d] Adv. of property for sale by Timothy Miner, of Lempster, N.H., presumably a Tanner by occupation; dated at "Lemster", 1 Sept. 1797.

Vol. V (No. 232) Monday, 11 Sept. 1797.

† [3b] Account of the death of Mr. Stephen Lefevre, who resided between Elizabethtown and Rahway, New Jersey; he died as a consequence of eating mushrooms. ♦

† [3d] Adv. for a mare taken up by Jonathan Fletcher, dated at Walpole, 9 Sept. '97.

¶ [3d] DIED.

In England, Edmund Burke, Esq; the Orator and Statesman—Charles Marklin, Esq; member of several literary societies, and author of several of the most popular Farces.
PENNSYLVANIA.—At Philadelphia, Doct. Jacob Thompson. Capt. John Mease, jun.
NEWYORK.—At Greenfield, Mr. Rirchard [sic] Waterman, aged 91.
CONNECTICUT.—At Newlondon, Mrs. Bridget Harris, aged 83; At Lyme, Mrs. Miriam Burnham, wife of Capt. Joseph Burnham.
VERMONT.—At Rockingham, Mrs. Lucretia Sanderson, consort of Captain David Sanderson.

Vol. V (No. 233) Monday, 18 Sept. 1797.

† [3c] William Noyes, "nearly 23 years of age," died from injuries he suffered when he was thrown from his horse, and was cut with his scythe. The article is dated at Newburyport, Mass., 31 Aug., and states that the accident occurred "on Monday last," at "Newtown" [Newton, N.H. ?]. ♦
† [3d] Adv. by Oliver Hall for settlement of debts, dated at Charlestown, [NH] 13 Sept.
† [3d] Legal notice by John Farnsworth, Adm. of estate of Thomas White, late of Claremont, deceased, dated 24 Aug. 1797.
† [3d] John Carlisle adv. for a journeyman shoemaker, and an apprentice shoemaker, dated at Walpole, 15 Sept. '97.
† [3d] Simeon Latham, Postrider, requests settlements of debts, dated at Springfield, [Vermont], 1 Sept. 1797.

¶ [3d] DIED.

PENNSYLVANIA.—At Philadelphia, Mr. William Pinkerton, Mr. Joseph Fisher, Mr. E.C. Boyson.
MASSACHUSETTS.—At Boston, Mr. Robert Jenkins, merchant, Mr. Charles Simpson, aged 55, Mrs. Lydia Green, Mrs. Sally Tufts, Miss Hannah Miller.
NEWHAMPSHIRE.—At Hanover, Mr. John Merrill, aged 21, only son of deacon Abel Merrill, of Newbury, (Vt.) Miss Laura Jones, aged 22.

Vol. V (No. 234) Monday, 25 Sept. 1797.

† [3a] Extensive article contained under the head "New York," concerning an account of the brig Polly, of New York, Capt. M'Lean, which was attacked by a privateer [in Honduras?]; the vessel and all aboard were saved, except the boatswain, John Hill. ♦
† [3d] Job Chamberlain adv. a mare taken up on his property; Westmoreland, 22 Sept.
† [3d] Sylvester Skinner adv. his new clothing business at Surry, N.H., 17 Sept.

Vol. V (No. 235) Monday, 2 Oct. 1797.

† [3b] Account of a robbery at the home of Mr. Jonathan Meredith, at Philadelphia. ♦
† [3d] Runaway notice of Deborah Brown, who "eloped . . . and neglects to return" to her husband Daniel Brown, dated at Charlestown, [N.H.] 18 Sept. 1797.
† [3d] Adv. of lime for sale, by *Brooks & Green*, Westmoreland, 30 Sept 1797.
† [3d] Partnership of Azariah Faxon and James Faxon dissolved; dated at Washington, [N.H.], 11 Sept. 1797.
† [3d] Joseph Sweetser offering a farm for sale at Swanzey, [N.H.], and a store for sale in Marlborough, [N.H.]; notice dated at Marlborough, 27 Sept. 1797.

Vol. V (No. 236) Monday, 9 Oct. 1797.

† [3d] Announcement by Abner Felt that he will quit his "Postriding business at the close of my present year," dated at Andover, [Vt.—Ed.] 7 Oct. 1797.
† [3d] Adv. by Daniel Williams, dated at Alstead 2 Oct. 1797, stating that "he has repaired his works, and is now carring on the Clothier's Business, in its various branches, at his Mills in the west part of Alstead . . . "
† [3d] Edward Perry adv. for a Colt which was lost or stolen from the pasture of Howard Reed in Langdon; the notice was dated at Westmoreland, 7 Oct. 1797.

† [3d] List of letters remaining in the Post Office at Charlestown, N.H., 30 Sept. 1797, as compiled by S. Crosby, Postmaster.

John Baxter,	Surry.	Enos Kellog,	Lebanon.
Benjamin Baxter,	Alstead.	John Lampson,	Charlestown.
Charles Bowen, Jr.	Charlestown.	Elias Lyman,	White River.
Daniel Chandler,	Lebanon.	James Ralston,	Lebanon.
Jeremiah Dudley,	Newport.	Job Simons, two,	Newlondon
Major Evans,	Stoddard.	Joseph Simons,	Hancock.
Jno. Grove, Jr.	Charlestown.	William Stevenson,	Swanzey.

† [3d] List of letters remaining in the Post Office at Walpole, 30 Sept. 1797, as compiled by David Carlisle, Jr., Postmaster.

Peter Frink,	Walpole.	Capt. Jonathan Far,	Chesterfield.
Beriah Clap,	"	Isaac Randall,	Alstead.
Mr. Buckston,	"	Nabby Brigham,	Fitzwilliam.
William Fessenden, two,	"	John Whitney,	Rindge.
John S. Hutchins,	"	John Newhall,	Claremont.
John Wheator,	Chesterfield.	Philip Smith,	Washington.
Moses Smith,	"	Thomas Cimbal,	Pittsford, Vt.

===== ¶ [3d] DIED. =====

GEORGIA.—At Savannah, Mr. Samuel McMurray, a native of Canada.

MARYLAND.—At Baltimore, Mr. James Angel, formerly a printer in that city.

PENNSYLVANIA.—At Philadelphia, Mr. Lyman Cady, printer, late of Windsor, Vermont.

NEWYORK.—At Newyork, Andrew Onderdonk, Esq; one of the Senators of that State.

MASSACHUSETTS.—At Boston, Jonathan Amory, Esq; aged 71.

Vol. V (No. 237) Monday, 16 Oct. 1797.

† [3d] Adv. by Jonathan Williams stating that "he is carrying on the Clothier's Business at the works that were formerly occupied by Mr. Griffith, near the Meeting House in Springfield." The notice is dated at Springfield, [presumably *Vermont*—Ed.] 9 Oct. 1797.

† [3d] Obadiah Seely requests settlements of debts for subcribers of the *Newhampshire and Vermont Journal*.

Vol. V (No. 238) Monday, 23 Oct. 1797.

† [2d-3a] Account of the attempted murder of Mrs. Van Inwagen, wife of David Van Inwagen, by a slave who was owned by her father-in-law. The event occurred 18 Sept. 1797, at Peenpack, Ulster County, New York. Article dated Goshen, 28 Sept. ♦

† [3d] Adv. of a lottery offered by the Fourth Class of Dartmouth College; Jonathan Freeman, Michael M'Clary, and William A. Kent, Managers.

† [3d] Adv. by N. Wetmore Washburn, regarding "English & West India Goods" for sale at the Store of Mr. Samuel Pratt in Westminster; dated there 21 Oct. 1797.

† [3d] Caleb Johnson requests settlement of debts; payment to be made to Thomas C. Drew; dated at Walpole, 23 Oct. 1797

† [3d] Legal notice regarding the estate of Daniel Whipple, late of Walpole, deceased; Martha Whipple and Daniel Grout, Admin.; dated at Walpole, 17 Oct. 1797.

† [3d] Isaac Redington adv. a heifer which strayed on his land; dated Walpole, 21 Oct.

† [3d] Six Pence reward offered for Miles Hall, an "indented apprentice to the Printing Business," between 17 and 18 years old, who ran away from Luther Pratt; dated at Troy, [N.H.] 3 Oct. 1797.

===== ¶ [3d] DIED. =====

DELAWARE.—At Newcastle, his Excellency Gunning Bedford, Esq; Governour of Delaware.

Vol. V (No. 239) Monday, 30 Oct. 1797.

† [1d-2a] Extensive biography of Edward Drinker, a centenarian who recollected the time when Philadelphia was inhabited by Indians and a few white settlers. Drinker was born in a small cabin there 24 Dec. 1680, though his parents came from Beverly, Mass. Much of the article describes his vitality in his old age, up to the time of his death on 17 Nov. 1782, aged 103. ♦

† [2c] Two articles contained in the news from Savannah, Georgia, regarding Privateering ♦ : 1) Robert Ploughright committed to jail in Savannah for not having a copy of his commission. 2) garbled account of a series of events at sea, involving Joseph Moffay of Maryland, William Cowel / Cowell of North Carolina, Capt. Callaghan of the schooner *Exuma*, Capt. Ewing, late master of the schooner *Grace*, of Washington, North Carolina, Mr. Armour, owner of the *Grace*, Edward Potter, apprentice of N.C., and Charles Langley, "a boy of Boston."

† [2d] Account of a wild animal shot by James Bartram, Jr., of Danbury, Conn. ♦

† [3b] Account of the death at Bridgewater, Mass. of Nathan Kingman, aged 12, eldest son of Capt. Ezra Kingman; the boy died from injuries received when he was run over by a cart, 19 Oct. 1797. ♦

† [3d] Notice by W.K. Atkinson, dated at Walpole 28 Oct. 1797, warning trespassers not to cut any more timber from his land in Walpole and Westminster.

† [3d] Stray cow on James Chandler's property; dated at Alstead, 26 Oct 1797.

† [3d] Notice of a horse, belonging to Phinehas Willard, strayed or stolen from a pasture owned by Mr. Jabez Walker in Charlestown, [N.H.]; dated there 27 Oct. 1797.

† [3d] Notice of a stray mare found by William Slade, dated at Alstead, 27 Oct. 1797.

===== ¶ [3d] DIED. =====

VIRGINIA.—At Norfolk, after a short illness, Louis Etienne Duhall, Vice Consul of the French Republick at that Place, and lately at Baltimore.

CONNECTICUT.—At Coventry, Mr. Ushall Green, aged 102—his father was in Cromwell's army, and fought eleven pitched battles, and brought a sword to this country which he wore in those engagements.

Vol. V (No. 240) Monday, 6 Nov. 1797.

† [3b] Account of a tornado which struck the 8th of October in several towns near Danbury, Conn., destroying much property and injuring several people, *viz.*: Mr. James Northrop and his daughter in the parish of Ridgebury ♦ ; Mr. Benjamin Crosut and wife, of Long Ridge, "much bruised by the fall of their house, but likely to recover"; also Mrs. Sherman and child, of Ridgebury, "were buried in the rubbish of her house, but drawn out without much injury."

† [3d] William Pierce adv., for sale or rent, "an excellent stand for a Tradesman or trader, lying a few rods north of Mr. Joseph Bellows' Tavern, in Walpole Village . . . "; also a request for all those in debt to him to settle; dated at Walpole 6 Nov. 1797.

† [3d] Adv. of *Francis Brown & Co.*, Hartford, Ct., regarding crockery and glassware.

† [3d] Levi Prentiss requests settlement of debts, dated at Newport, 23 Oct. 1797.

† [3d] Notice of a stray heifer found on property of Thomas Smith; location not given.

† [3d] Bartholomew Gilman requests settlement of debts, dated at Newport, 16 Oct. '97

Vol. V (No. 241) Monday, 13 Nov. 1797.

† [3b] Bizarre account of the suicide on the 20th of Oct., at Rehoboth, Mass., of Martha Burr, wife of Mr. Elisha Burr, and daughter of Col. Peleg Gardner, of Swanzey. This insane woman tried several times to choke herself to death, and once swallowed a spoon which stayed lodged in her stomach for 186 weeks. ♦

† [3d] Martha Whipple advertises a lost heifer; dated at Walpole, 10 Nov. 1797.

Vol. V (No. 242) Monday, 20 Nov. 1797.

† [2a-b] Confusing article dated 7 Sept., contained in the collection of news dated at Paris, France, regarding the crew list of the ship *Mary*, of Boston, bound from Ports-

mouth, N.H. to London, England. The ship was intercepted by the French and taken to Nantz, on a charge that the crew list did not match up to the actual crew. The muster roll produced by the Captain is transcribed here: ♦

    John Choathe, Captain, Charlesto[w]n, Mass.
    William Curtis, first Mate, Marblehead, Mass.
    William Chardall, second Mate, Marblehead, Mass.
    Isaac Waeldin, Seaman, Marblehead, Mass.
    Thomas Ireland, Seaman, Charlesto[w]n, Mass.
    James Hyot, Seaman, New York.
    George Johnson, Seaman, Marblehead, Mass.
    William Colley, Seaman, Marblehead, Mass.
    John Hazard, Seaman, Boston, Mass.

† [3b] Adam Kapple, an inhabitant of Albany, N.Y., committed to jail on a charge of "being a principal agent in setting the late fire."

¶ [3b] PHILADELPHIA, PENNSYLVANIA, November 6. One day this week, John Curtis, bookbinder, out of spite of his wife, retired into the yard back of his house, and drank off two phials of laudanum, which very shortly terminated his existence. It seems he had frequent differences with his wife, and that this is not the first attempt to so singular revenge.

† [3b] Fire destroyed the house of Mr. Moses Savory at Newburyport, Mass., and two unnamed apprentices to Mr. Savory perished in the flames. ♦

† [3d] Six Pence reward offered for Ora Rugg, an apprentice boy 18 years old who ran away, on Nov. 6th, from Ebenezer Crehore; notice dated at Walpole, 15 Nov. 1797.

===== ¶ [3d] DIED. =====

NEWHAMPSHIRE.—At Cornish, Mr. John Smith late of Chester, Vermont.

Vol. V (No. 243) Monday, 27 Nov. 1797.

† [3d] William Balloch adv. a farm for sale in Surry, N.H.; dated there 25 Nov. 1797.
† [3d] William Ramsey adv. his "Wheel Making Business," situated "about two miles south east of the Meeting House in Walpole;" dated at Walpole 22 Nov. 1797.
† [3d] Stray steer found by Thomas Bellows; dated at Walpole 24 Nov. 1797.
† [3d] Josiah Hart, Guardian of the children of Job Johnson, deceased, granted license to sell Johnson's property in Charlestown, N.H.

Vol. V (No. 244) Monday, 4 Dec. 1797.

† [3a] Account of the murder of Peter Smith, second son of Peter Smith, Esq., of Charleston, S.C., by one Peter Bennoit. ♦
† [3c] Adv. of Almanac for sale at the bookstore of David Carlisle, Jr., Walpole, N.H.
† [3c] Notice of unpaid highway taxes on Nonresident Proprietors' land in Croydon, N.H., as compiled by Ebenezer Winter, Collector, 22 Nov. 1797. Delinquent property to be sold at public auction at Croydon, 15 Feb. 1798, "at the Dwelling House of Edward Hall, jun. Innholder . . ."

	No.	Div.	R.	D.	C.
Daniel Chase, Jr.	46	2	100		40
Rev. Mr. Persons, timber	6				5
Solomon Lealand,	28	1	100		40
Jonathan Aldrich,	36	2	100		40
Solomon Chase,	57	1	100		40
	45	2	100		40
Benjamin Wood,	16		60		24
Ebenezer Rawson,	7		60		24
Daniel Putman, 1/2	54	2	100		20
Luke Drewry, } South half paid,	76	1	100		40
Joseph Merriam,	27	1	100		40
	6		100		40

	No.	Div.	R.	D.	C.
Governour's Farm,			500	2	
Ebenezer Waters,	56		60		24
John Whipple,	12	2	100		40
Caleb Chase,	49		60		24
James Taylor,	22		100		40
Ephraim Sherman, }	46		60		24
Meadow, }	13				5
James Whipple,	42		60		24
John Holland,	76		60		24
Thomas Danney,	40	1	100		40
	9		60		24
William Wait,	61		60		24

† [3c] Thomas Moors adv. stray sheep on his property; dated at Walpole, 30 Nov. '97.

† [3d] The copartnership of Job F. Brooks and Thomas R. Green, a.k.a *Brooks & Green*, dissolved; notice dated at Westmoreland, 28 Nov. 1797. Immediately following this notice, and with the same date and place, Thomas R. Green advertises English and West India Goods for sale.

† [3d] Thomas Rand adv. his "Tailoring and Habit Making Business," Alstead, 20 Nov.

† [3d] Elenor M'Lauthlin petitions for divorce, on reasons of cruelty and adultery, from her husband Thomas M'Lauthlin, late of Londonderry, N.H., yeoman, who abandoned her in May, 1794. They were married 26 Dec. 1782, though the location is not stated; the petition is dated at Londonderry, 14 Sept. 1797. Though these events occurred in Rockingham County, N.H., the Superior Court of said county ordered this legal notice to be published specifically in the *Farmer's Weekly Museum*. Curiously, no newspapers in Rockingham County were ordered to post this notice, which may suggest that this missing husband was thought to have been in, or had connections to, the Walpole area.

† [3d] Adv. for "Moor's School, in the vicinity of Dartmouth College," [Hanover, N.H.]

† [3d] John Olive takes in a stray heifer; dated at Charlestown, [N.H.], 27 Nov. 1797.

† [3d] William Jeudevine adv. stray sheep; dated Charlestown, [N.H.] 9 Nov. 1797.

Vol. V (No. 245) Monday, 11 Dec. 1797.

† [3c] Account of a murder—suicide at New York City, involving Ferdinand Leowenstern and Elizabeth Folkenhan, said to have been disappointed lovers." ♦

† [3d] Stephen Prentiss, Jun. advertises his Chair Making and Painting Business," at a "shop on the Main Street in Walpole," dated at Walpole, 5 Dec. 1797.

† [3d] William Butterfield advertises for his horses, which strayed or were stolen from the stable of Benjamin Baxter in Alstead; notice dated at Walpole, 9 Dec. 1797.

===== ¶ [3d] DIED. =====

NEWHAMPSHIRE.—At Rindge, Mr. Thomas Hale, Aged 28, formerly of this town. In this town, the Widow Elizabeth Parker, aged 72.—Capt. David Carlisle, aged 56.

Vol. V (No. 246) Monday, 18 Dec. 1797.

† [3c] Lengthy account, contained under the Newburyport dateline, of a shipwreck found at a place called Bantry Bay, presumably in foreign waters. The *Two Sisters*, bound to Bristol, Rhode Island, was struck by lightning in early August 1797, and a solitary survivor, Samuel Tucker, of "Marblehead, N.E.," was found on board several days later, suffering from exhaustion and dehydration. The ship was owned by Mr. Mozely, of Rhode Island, and the Captain, who perished, was named Gilbert, "belonging to Nantucket." ♦

† [3d] Extensive property for sale at Clarendon, [Vt.—Ed.], offered by Ezra Crary; dated at Clarendon, 5 Dec. 1797.

† [3d] Stray heifer found by Timothy Grannis; dated at Claremont, 8 Dec. 1797.

===== ¶ [3d] DIED. =====

At Bath, in England, John Vassal, Esq.; formerly of Cambridge, Mass.
NEWJERSEY.—At Morristown, Mr. T. Peck, aged 90.

CONNECTICUT.—At Middletown, Rev. Ebenezer Frothingham, aged 81; at Litchfield, his Excellency Oliver Wolcott, Esq. governour of the state of Connecticut, aged 71.—Honourable Andrew Adams, Esq; chief Judge of the Superiour Court, aged 81.

MASSACHUSETTS.—At Boston, Mr. Isaac Larkin, jun. editor of the Chronicle, aged 26; at Weston, Honourable Samuel Phillips Savage, Esq; aged 79; at Dorchester, Mr. Nathaniel Tileston, aged 61; at Warwick, Mr. Daniel Green, aged 99; at Sturbridge, Mr. Benjamin Hyde, aged 74; at Princeton, Dr. Reuben Walker, aged 30.

Vol. V (No. 247) Tuesday, 26 Dec. 1797.

† [3b] Robert Maxwell, Esq., Sheriff of Washington District, South Carolina, dangerously wounded in an assassination attempt. ♦

† [3d] West Bonney requests those indebted to himself or to H. Leonard to settle their debts. Bonney also adv. for two apprentices, one for Card Making and the other for the Blacksmith business; dated at Charlestown, [N.H.], 18 Dec. 1797.

† [3d] Salt for sale, by *Oliver Johnson & Co.*; dated at Westmoreland, 19 Dec. 1797.

===== ¶ [3d] DIED. =====

In Derby, in England, Joseph Wright, Esq. aged 63, a celebrated painter.

In Jamaica, Rev. Joshua His de Cordova, aged 78.

At Quebec, on the 17th of October, the Most illustrious and Right Rev. Jean Francois Hubert, aged about 59, late Bishop of Quebec.

MARYLAND.—At Baltimore, Mr. Thomas E. Clayland, aged 25, one of the proprietors of the Baltimore Telegraph.

RHODEISLAND.—At [P]rovidence, Henry Ward, Esq; aged 65; for 40 years Secretary of Rhodeisland.

MASSACHUSETTS.—At Sharon, Rev. Philip Curtis, aged 81; at Bernardston, Dr. Polycarpus Cushman, aged 47.

NEWHAMPSHIRE.—At Hampton Falls, Rev. Samuel Langdon, D.D. aged 75.

Vol. V (No. 248) Tuesday, 2 Jan. 1798.

† [3b-3c] Account of the arrest at Norfolk, Va., of one Captain Robinson, charged with passing counterfeit notes at New York City. ♦

† [3d] James Whitelaw of Ryegate, Vt., Surveyor General of the State of Vermont, publishes a notice regarding property owners and their taxes due.

† [3d] Advertisement by *Bliss & Horswill*, Cabinet and Chair-Makers, from Boston, stating that they "have taken up a stand in Charlestown, opposite Mr. Oliver Hall's Store." Dated at Charlestown, [N.H.], 26 Dec. 1797.

† [3d] Zebediah Fitch, Jr., adv. a lost pocket book; dated at Claremont, 28 Dec. 1797.

† [3d] Adv. of the Pearl Ash Works of Moses Johnson at Keene, dated 23 Dec. 1797.

Vol. V (No. 249) Tuesday, 9 Jan. 1798.

† [3d] Joseph C. Strong, Physician and Surgeon, advertises that he has lately come to Charlestown, [N.H.] and set up practice there, and is located "at Captain Porter's, Charlestown street . . . "; dated 6 Jan. 1798.

† [3d] One cent reward offered for return of William Tappan, an apprentice boy from Northampton, Mass., about 18 years old, who ran away from Jed. Baldwin "on a stormy sabbath day, about the 26th of November last." Notice dated Hanover, N.H., 9 Jan. '98.

† [3d] List of letters remaining at the Post Office in Walpole, N.H., 1 Jan. 1798, as compiled by David Carlisle, Postmaster:

Aaron Allen,	Walpole.	Seth Geary, two	Alstead.
Jonathan Austin,	"	Seth or Loved Geary,	"
Richard Billins,	"	Maj. Jno. R. Hale,	Chesterfield.
Joseph Baloule,	"	Simon Willard,	"
John Ellis, jun.	"	Maj. Jabez Parson,	Colbrook.
Daniel Joslin,	"	David Danforth,	Washington.
John Ruggles,	"	Hon. Lemuel Holmes, Esq.,	Surry.
Silas Niles,	"	Elijah Phelps,	Lanesborough.
William Park,	Claremont.	Shearman Cooper,	Croydon.
Sewall White,	"	Simeon Smith,	Lambstown.
Josiah Fuller,	Westmoreland.	Oliver Whitney,	Clarendon, Vt.
Robert B. Parkman,	"	Jared Farnam,	Salsbury, Vt.

† [3d] Adv. of goods for sale by William Page, and a request for settlement of debts; dated at Bellowsfalls, Rockingham, [Vt.], 26 Dec. 1797.

† [3d] List of letters remaining at the Post Office in Westminster, [Vt.], 1 Jan. 1798, as compiled by Eleazer May, Postmaster:

Doct. Boaz Searle,	Wardborough.	Daniel Field, Esq.	Chester.
Samuel Barnard,	Townsend.	Jane Forbes,	Rockingham.
Jabez Biglow,	Westminster.	Otis Hayward,	Townsend.
Gilbert Evans,	Rockingham.	Jedediah Johnson,	Westmoreland.
Thomas S. Fullerton,	Chester.		

=== ¶ [3d] DIED. ===

RHODEISLAND.—At N. Kingston, Mr. Brown, aged 17, by an excess of bleeding from an accidental wound in the thigh, from a discharge of a musquet at Newport; Mr. Solomon Southwick, Esq; aged 66, formerly Editor of the Newport Mercury.

Vol. V (No. 250) Tuesday, 16 Jan. 1798.

† [3b] Extract of a letter, under dateline of Hartford, Conn., from Robert Folger, Captain of the Ship *John*, of Boston, which "got on this shoal on the 22d inst." [?22 Dec. 1797—Ed.], and became trapped in ice. The location is not specified, though mention is made that the ship left Hamburgh on the 25th of Oct. Many passengers were trapped on board, and "My third officer Wm. Swain, of Nantucket, with six young men, were lost in the ice on the 21st inst. in trying to save the crew of a sloop that was sinking." ♦

† [3d] Adv. of a house, barn, and small shop for sale by Thomas Baker, the property "lying on the Main Street, a few rods south of General Benjamin Bellow's Seat." Baker

also requests settlements of debts "as he shall discontinue business in this place in a very few weeks." Notice dated at Walpole, 16 Jan. 1798.

† [3d] Levi Prentiss offers property for sale at Reading, Vermont: "Terms of payment may be known by applying to John Stimson living on the premises . . " ; advertisement dated at Newport, N.H., 25 Dec. 1797.

Vol. V (No. 251) Tuesday, 23 Jan. 1798.

† [3d] Adv. regarding the "Country Business" of *George Williams, & Co.*, Watertown, Mass., being closed; request for settlement of debts through Henry or John Williams, at Watertown, or Timothy Williams, No. 12 Long Wharf, Boston.

† [3d] Moses Johnson advertises goods for sale at his store in Walpole, formerly occupied by Caleb Johnson.

† [3d] Adv. for "An Inaugural Dissertation or the Production of Animal Heat," by Lyman Spalding, on sale by the author, Hanover, [N.H.]

† [4d] Account of the death of John Tatson, "an Indian native of Lyme," who froze to death while drunk. ◆

===== ¶ [3d] DIED. =====

PENNSYLVANIA.—At Philadelphia, the Rev. Jacob Duche; at East Notingham, Dr. Adam P. Boyd, aged 24.

CONNECTICUT.—At Newlondon, Mr. John Weeks, aged 114. He married his tenth wife when 106, she was only 16.

MASSACHUSETTS.—At Boston, Miss Margaret Sherburne, aged 53; at Roxbury, Mr. James Howe, aged 51.

NEWHAMPSHIRE.—At Keene, Mr. David Foster, aged 42.

Vol. V (No. 252) Tuesday, 30 Jan. 1798.

† [3b] John Hauer, Charles M'Manus, and Francis Cox arrested near Harrisburgh, Penn., for the murder of Mr. Francis Shitz, and the attempted murder of his brother, Peter Shitz. ◆

¶ [3c] GREENFIELD, MASSACHUSETTS. January 24. MELANCHOLY. We learn that Capt. Daniel Phelps, of Lebanon, (N.H.) with his wife and only daughter, being on their way to Strafford, (Con.) in a sleigh, took to the river in Sunderland, on Saturday last, for the purpose of performing part of their journey on the ice, having proceeded as far as Hockonhom Ferry, near Northampton, the sleigh and horses suddenly went through the ice; and immersed the unfortunate passengers in the wat[e]ry element: Mr. Phelps was taken up after being much exhausted in the struggle to keep above the ice, but sad to relate, his wife and daughter were drowned. Mrs. Phelps was carried under the ice by the current; his daughter was taken up without any remains of life. The horses, sleigh, and about 1000 dollars in cash were entirely lost. [*see issue of 6 May 1799*]

† [3d] List of letters remaining at the Post Office in Charlestown, N.H., 22 Jan. 1798, as compiled by Samuel Crosby, Postmaster:

Enos Kellog,	Lebanon.	Daniel Hawkins,	Winchester.
Daniel Chandler,	"	Dr. Samuel Hamilton,	Dublin.
Abijah Chandler,	"	James Leash,	Littleton.
James Ralston,	"	Jacob Steward,	Claremont.
Jonathan Fish,	Springfield, (Vt.)		

===== ¶ [3d] DIED. =====

SOUTHCAROLINA.—At Charlestown, Arch Brown, Esq; aged 46.—David D. Stole, aged 35, M.L.

CONNECTICUT.—At Thompson, Gen. Daniel Larned; at Windham, Mr. Isaac Bingham, aged 89.

Vol. V (No. 253) Tuesday, 6 Feb. 1798.

† [2c] Extensive account of the sinking, in the area of the Bahamas, of the *Speedwell* of Charleston, [S.C.—Ed.], John Brownlow, master. Brownlow, crew, and passengers survived in their "lifeboats" for about two weeks before reaching Nassau, having only

once in that time found a small island with water and a meager amount of food. ♦

† [2d] Mr. William Compton, of Archstreet, drowned "on Wednesday last," when the stage he was riding in fell through the ice while crossing Gun Powder creek. The article is contained in the news dated at Philadelphia, Penn., 19 Jan. 1798.

† [2d-3a] Execution on 6 Jan. 1798, at Reading, Penn., of Benjamin Baily, convicted of the murder of Job Falhaffer, a pedlar. ♦

¶ [3b] LANSINBURGH, NEW YORK, January 9. On Saturday the 30th ult. as Mr. William Hickok of Burlington, (Vermont) and Mr. Benjamin Franklin Pierce, a young gentleman of liberal education, of that place, were skating upon the ice in Burlington Bay, being side by side, the ice suddenly broke, and they both disappeared. Mr. Pierce was taken up, after being under water three quarters of an hour; Mr. Hickok after an hour and a half: every assistance to restore them to life, proved ineffectual.

† [3b] A child of Mr. Oliver Wheaton bitten by rabid dog at Stockbridge, Mass. ♦

† [3c-3d] Account of the funeral of Abner Cheney, preceptor of the "publick school" at Charlestown, N.H., where he died 11 Nov. 1797. Cheney was born in Milford, Mass., 10 Nov. 1765, son of Ebenezer Cheney. ♦

† [3d] Notice of Aseneth Whitney, wife of "——— Whitney," who ran away from her husband with two small children; dated at Westminster, 3 Feb. 1797 [sic]. This notice appears slightly altered in subsequent issues; the notice in 20 Feb. 1798 gives the husband's name as Asa Whitney, and the date was corrected to read 3 Feb. 1798.

Vol. V (No. 254) Tuesday, 13 Feb. 1798.

† [3a] Account of a fire at the home of William S. Sears, in Mamakating, which burned his disabled wife and claimed the life of "her child two years old," on the 4th of January, 1798; article contained in the news dated at New York City. ♦

† [3b-3c] Fire damages a ship in Salem, Mass. harbor, on 5 Feb., and one Duncan, caretaker of a vessel, was killed in the fire. ♦

† [3d] Thomas Smith, Postrider, informs his customers that he will close his business on the 20th of March next, and requests settlement of accounts. "Those who do not attend to this request will, after that time, find their accounts as follows, (viz.) Walpole, Surry, Alstead, Langdon and Ackworth, with *John C. Chamberlain*, Esq; Charlestown, with *B. West*, Esq; Claremont and Cornish, with *George B. Upham*, Esq; Croydon, Newport, Unity and Lemster, with *C. Ellis*, Esq; Washington, with *Thomas Penniman*, Esq." The notice is dated at Surry, 1 Feb. 1798.

===== ¶ [3d] DIED. =====

MASSACHUSETTS.—At Boston, Miss Julia Wadsworth Knox, daughter of Gen. Knox, aged 14.

Vol. V (No. 255) Tuesday, 20 Feb. 1798.

† [2c] Brief news accounts from Kingston, Jamaica, including a confusing notice of a skirmish on the 19th of December, 1797, between an American brig from New York, the *Nancy*, and a French privateer. A Capt. Aylward was dangerously wounded, and Mr. Casey (second officer) died of his wounds. ♦

¶ [2c] WASHINGTON, MARYLAND. January 20. "Yesterday morning the wife of Mr. Mathew Hart of this city, was found dead. It is by many supposed that she fell from her chair, into the fire, and having no one to help her, was burnt to death; whether this was the case or not, I will not pretent to determine—but it is a fact she was found dead on the hearth, and was suffered to lay full seven hours after she was found: and although her death was known, with the circumstances of the appearance, to one of the magistrates of the city—yet no steps have been taken to make examination or inquiry— she was suffered to lay like a dead horse—to be eaten by dogs—(she is not yet buried) —It is not shameful that circumstances of this kind should happen within the United States; among people who think they are the most civilized of any in the world. In a state, the most free of any in the Union, were it not for the slaves.

† [2d-3a] Bizarre account of the suicide, dated at New York City, of Daniel Chaplin, a native of Connecticut, "who has been a schoolmaster for some time past in Sussex." Chaplin was arrested on suspicion of robbery, but was discharged, and soon after cut

his own throat. The scene was witnessed by the wife of one Joseph Craven, who was so traumatized that she died soon after. ♦
† [3d] Notice regarding Scottish inheritence, in "Ross Shire", of Joseph McKenzie and his heirs, who have disappeared. McKenzie was stated to have left Parsley, Scotland for America in 1774, was in New Hampshire in 1778, and it "was supposed that he was at Hartland in the county of Windsor, State of Vermont, in 1795." Request for information posted by Robert Pagan, Esq., of Saint Andrews, New Brunswick; William Page, Esq., of Charlestown, N.H., listed as a contact "for further information."
† [3d] Maria Winchester, Executrix of the Will and Testament of "Elhanan Winchester, late of Philadelphia, deceased, Clerk," requests that a copy of said Will be recorded in the Cheshire County, N.H. Probate Office.

===== ¶ [3c] DIED. =====

MASSACHUSETTS.—At Boston, Mrs. Catherine Webber, aged 77.—Mr. Stephen Noyes late of Newbury port, aged 22; at Holden, Mrs. Mercy Perry, widow, aged 93; at Upton, Mr. [Hillel?] Baker, [s]on of Capt. Thomas Baker, aged 37.

Vol. V (No. 256) Tuesday, 27 Feb. 1798.

† [3d] Letter from Joseph Burt, Westmoreland, N.H. 22 Feb. 1998 [sic] to Oliver Johnson, late of Westmoreland, "Defunct," exposing Johnson's attempt to fool the public into believing that Johnson had been robbed and murdered by one Pike. The letter mentions that Mrs. Johnson "and ten likely children" were convinced of his murder, and that Pike is in jail, but gives no clue to the whereabouts of Johnson.
† [3d] Cushman Smith offers "one Potatoe reward" for the return of Joseph Watherton, an apprentice boy about 14 years old; dated at Surry, [N.H.], 7 Feb. 1798.
† [3d] Advertisement by Jonathan Robinson of Surry, [N.H.], who offers to purchase "good House Ashes," and also has rum for sale; dated 26 Feb. 1798.

===== ¶ [3d] DIED. =====

CONNECTICUT.—At Newlondon, Mrs. Catharine Ayer, aged 75.

Vol. V (No. 257) Tuesday, 6 March 1798.

¶ [3d] Dr. Kinsman of Newbury, Vermont, has to deplore the loss of an excellent wife. This Lady was daughter of the Rev. Mr. Farrand of Canaan, Connecticut; and died in child birth, on the ninth ultimo. [. . .]
† [3d] Adv. by Gamaliel Fenton regarding his Bell Foundry in Walpole; Fenton also manufactured "Town Clocks," and in the same ad, offers a farm for sale in Walpole.
† [3d] David Carlisle requests immediate settlements of debts; adv. posted by his attorney, Roger Vose; dated at Walpole, 5 March 1798.

Vol. V (No. 258) Tuesday, 13 March 1798.

† [1a] Isaiah Thomas advertises books for sale at his bookstore in Walpole.
† [3b-3c] Brief mention in the news dated at Bennington, Vt., of a Mr. Scott who was stabbed three times, presumably at Salem, N.Y, by one Holmes, who was committed to jail. Another paragraph relates the melancholy news of an unnamed infant who was killed in a sleighing accident at "Newlebanon."
† [3d] Thomas Fessenden offers a farm for sale at Walpole, dated 13 March 1798.
† [3d] Legal notice regarding the estate of Capt. Jonas Butterfield, late of Westmoreland, deceased; Ezra Pierce, Administrator.
† [3d] Public notice by Peter Bonney, dated at Charlestown, [N.H.], 12 March 1798, regarding his note for $120 to Thomas M'Gloughlan, which was dated 22 July 1797 and witnessed by Augustus Brown.

Vol. V (No. 259) Tuesday, 20 March 1798.

† [3b] Brief mention, under the New York dateline, that Mr. Jesse Putnam, of Boston, was arrested in Paris in Nov. 1797, along with Mr. J.B. Murray of New York City and several other Americans. They were later released.

† [3c] Account of a robbery at the store of Moses Johnson, Keene, N.H., on 14 March, by one Peter Hoar, of Keene. ◆
† [3d] Public notice that the Copartnership of *Oliver Johnson & Co.*, of Westmoreland, N.H., is dissolved, and debtors requested to make payment to David Sherwin; dated at Westmoreland, 12 March 1798.
† [3d] Two cents reward offered by Timothy Bullock, for the return of Polly Doyle, a runaway apprentice about 16 years old; dated at Westmoreland, 8 March 1798.
† [3d] Thomas Russell advertises a mare which strayed or was stolen from the stable of "Landlord Johnson" in Walpole; dated at Plainfield, 23 [sic] March, 1798.
† [3d] List of "delinquent Proprietors and owners of the common and undivided land in the town of Acworth . . . " as a consequence of a special tax which was imposed in Sept. 1797; the property still in default by 3 May 1798 to be auctioned off at the house of Mr. Galen Allen, Innholder at Acworth. This list, dated at Acworth, 29 Jan. 1798, was compiled by "Fred. Locke, Prop's. Col."

Col. Sampson Stodard,	Ephraim Adams,	Ben. Byam,
Wm. Stacy,	Reuben Kellecutt,	Jos. Pierce,
John Byam,	Augustus Blanchard,	Wm. Pierce,
Reuben Gould,	James Rogers,	Ben. Butterfield,
Oliver Pierce,	David M'Gregor,	Ben. French,
Sam. King,	James M'Gregor,	Matthew Thornton,
Jacob Farmer,	James M'Gregor, jun.	Robert Fletcher,
Eben. Gould,	James Miltemore,	Sam. Cummings,
David Brown,	Alex. Clark,	Moses Parker,
Moses Estabrooks,	Thomas Craige,	Nat. Butterfield,
Sampson Stodard, Jun.	Jon. Gilmore,	Wiseman Clagget, Esq.
Vryling Stodard,	Daniel M'Fee,	Maj. John Wentworth,
Jona. Blanchard,	Ed. G. Lutwyche,	Hon. [B.?] Atkinson, Esq.
Wm. Thomson,	Sam. French,	Hon. Jam. Nevins, Esq.
Tim. Dustin,	Stephen Powers,	Peter Levius,
Oliver Farwell,	Wm. Roby,	Rev. Eben. Bridge,
Oliver Farwell, jun.	Jon. Hardy,	Col. Jon. Greely,
Nat. Gearfield,	Thos. Blanchard, jun.	Lt. John Parker,
John Hardy,	David Burge,	George Jaffrey, Esq.
James Blanchard,	Sam. Barron,	

===== ¶ [3d] MARRIED. =====

NEWHAMPSHIRE.—At Hanover, on the eighth instant, Mr. Benjamin True, Printer, to Miss Betsey Kimball, daughter of Capt. Stephen Kimball, both of that place.

Vol. V (No. 260) Tuesday, 27 March 1798.

† [3a] Brief account under the dateline of Savannah, of an Indian who raped the wife of John Hilton in Jackson County, Georgia, on the 5th of Feb. ◆
† [3b] Three men committed to jail in New Brunswick on a charge of mutiny on board the British Frigate *Hermoine*, viz.: William Bridgstock, a native of New York; Johannes Williamson, a Swede, and Michael Campbell, an Englishman. ◆
† [3d] Adv. by *Bellows & Stone*, regarding the business of "rearing Horses." Also Clover and herds grass seed on sale at their store, and a request for settlement of debts; dated at Walpole, 26 March 1798.

Vol. VI (No. 261) Tuesday, 3 April 1798.

† [1a] Joseph Burt, Nat. Estabrooks, and Caleb Aldrich, Jr., Commissioners of the insolvent estate of John Mitchel, late of Westmoreland, deceased, request creditors to bring in their claims to "the house of the widow Pheby [sic] Mitchel, in Westmoreland," on specific dates through September next.
† [3d] Items for sale by Justin & Elias Lyman, who also "continue to transact Commission Business as usual; dated "Hartford, March 13th, 1798."
† [3d] Ephraim Carpenter and Abel Walker, Commissioners of the estate of Abner Cheney, late of Charlestown, [N.H.], deceased, represented insolvent, advertise that

they will attend to the business of said estate on specific dates at the "house of Ephraim Carpenter, Esq. innholder Charlestown."
† [3d] Garden seeds for sale at John Hubbard's Apothecary Store; Walpole, 30 Mar. '98.

Vol. VI (No. 262) Tuesday, 10 April 1798.

† [2d-3a] Gruesome account of the insurrection of slaves aboard the ship *Thomas M'Quay*, of Liverpool, Capt. M'Quay; a portion of the crew which escaped and drifted in a boat for 38 days. Several of the passengers resorted to cannibalism by casting lots, but those eventually died of insanity; three survivors reached Barbadoes. ♦

† [3d] List of letters remaining at the Post Office in Walpole, 1 April 1797 [sic], as compiled by David Carlisle, Postmaster:

Wm. Barnard, to the care of J. Barnard	Walpole.	Moses Weswill,	Westmoreland.
Joseph Barnard,	"	Elijah Holbrook,	Alstead.
Wm. Mills,	"	Seth Geary,	"
Jona. Lee,	"	Sam. Hutchinson,	"
Jona. Forbes,	"	James Wilson,	Francistown.
Joseph Falee,	"	David Willey,	"
Jona. Falfett, Esq;	"	Jesse Walker,	Putney, (Vt.)
Charles Fowler,	"	Lovel Stevens,	Claremont.
Col. Joseph Burt,	Westmoreland.	Moses Smith,	Chesterfield.
Mrs. Maria Winchester,	"	Charlotte Reed,	Langdon.
Experience Storrs,	"	James M'Curdy,	Surry.
Alph. Moore, Esq;		Daniel Hawkins,	Winchester.
		Stephen Holbrook,	Sutton.

† [3d] Help Wanted: Journeyman Hatter. Apply to Mr. Royal Craft, Rutland, or Zerah Willoby, Cambridge, Franklin County [Vermont—Ed.]; dated 1 April 1798.

Vol. VI (No. 263) Tuesday, 17 April 1798.

† [3d] Adv. by Stephen Holman, offering a large farm for sale at Walpole, containing 223 acres, situated "about three miles south of the street, on the road leading to Westmoreland." Dated at Walpole, 7 April 1798.

¶ [3d] DIED.

MASSACHUSETTS.—At Boston, John Clarke, D.D. of an apoplectic fit, with which he was seized in the pulpit, while delivering his sermon, aged 43; at Worcester, Major Charles Chandler, aged 43.

Vol. VI (No. 264) Tuesday, 24 April 1798.

† [3d] Jasper Murdock and Mills Olcott, Norwich, Vt., offer 75,000 acres of land for sale in Vermont and New Hampshire.
† [3d] List of letters remaining at the Post Office in Westminster, as compiled by Eleazer May, Postmaster:

Rozel Closen,	Rockingham, (Vt.)	Polly Ball,	Westminster.
Elijah Knight,	"	Nat. Dumbolton,	Thomlingson.
John Blancher,	Andover.	Abraham Powers,	Bridgwater.
Ira Bun,	Windsor.	Willard More,	Putney.

Vol. VI (No. 265) Tuesday, 1 May 1798.

† [3d] Samuel Stone, Adm. of the estate of James Nevin, of Portsmouth, deceased, advertises the sale of land belonging to said estate, in Acworth, Lempster, and New Grantham. Notice dated at Claremont, 23 April 1798.
† [3d] Elisha Kingsbery, Bill Blake, Isaac Randal, and David Buckman advertise for a pair of horses wanted at the Paper Mill in Alstead; dated there 26 April 1798.
† [3d] Petition of Betsy Gorton of Brattleboro, Vermont, for divorce from her husband, Jonathan Gorton, who abandoned her and two small children in March 1793. Jonathan

Gorton, of "Brattleborough" and Betsy Wells were married 12 April 1791 "by Gardner Chandler, Esq; then a Justice of the Peace in and for Windham County . . . "

† [3d] Petition of Mary Day, Westminster, Vt., for divorce from her husband John Day, to whom she was married 27 Feb. 1791, he "then of said Westminster." Mary Day accused her husband of adultery with one Sally Earl, "whom he took with him when he deserted, and has since constantly bedded and boarded, as husband and wife, with the said Sally, by whom he has had several children . . . "

Vol. VI (No. 266) Tuesday, 8 May 1798.

† [3c] Mr. Hubbard advertises "that he intends to open his subscription school on the 14th instant." Notice dated at Walpole, 7 May 1798.

† [3d] Extensive property for sale at Colrain, Hampshire County, Mass., owned by "John Chandler and Brothers." Dated 21 March 1798.

Vol. VI (No. 267) Tuesday, 15 May 1798.

† [3d] A proprietor of the township of Dalton, N.H., advertises that Dalton "is now offered the public for settlement . . . the proprietor may be found at Walter Bloss's, Innkeeper on said premises" at Windsor, [Vermont—Ed.]; dated 26 April 1798.

† [3d] Notice by John Perkins requesting settlement of debts; dated Newport, 15 April.

Vol. VI (No. 268) Tuesday, 22 May 1798.

† [3d] Adv. by David Brown, Secretary of the Jerusalem Lodge of Free Masons in Chesterfield, regarding an upcoming celebration, including a discourse to be delivered by "brother Joab Young." Dated at Westmoreland, "May 9, A.L. 5798."

† [3d] Public notice by Ezekiel Colburn, Secretary of the Olive Branch Lodge of Free Masons, regarding a celebration. "Rev. Samuel Whiting, a brother, will preach a sermon on the occasion." Dated at Chester, [Vermont—Ed.].

† [3d] Ezekiel Colburn, Attorney for "the old Partnership of Charles and Samuel Chandler and Co." requests settlement of debts. Dated at Chester 18 May 1798.

Vol. VI (No. 269) Tuesday, 29 May 1798.

† [1d] Reward offered by John Garfield for a mare which strayed or was stolen from the pasture of Capt. John Willard in Charlestown; dated there 15 May 1798.

† [3d] Adv. by Isaiah Thomas, who informs the public that his Bookselling and Printing Business will be carried on in the future under the name of *Thomas & Thomas*, Isaiah Thomas and Alex. Thomas. Adv. dated Walpole May 1798.

† [3d] Extensive property at Westmoreland, including several mills, to be sold by Thomas Mc'Neil; dated at Westmoreland, 28 May 1798.

† [3d] Zenas Newell offers a farm for sale "in Springfield," dated there 21 May 1798.

Vol. VI (No. 270) Tuesday, 5 June 1798.

† [3b] Extensive account of an explosion, 19 March 1798, caused by two careless boys setting fire to a barrel of gunpowder, at a store owned by Evan Francis, at Hutchcraft's mills, on Stoner [Creek], Bourbon county, Kentucky. The store was destroyed, along with two adjacent houses, and the two unnamed boys were killed. Three other persons later died of injuries, *viz.*, Mrs. Francis (formerly Todd), Joseph Willis "late from Maryland," and a daughter of Mr. Francis. Miss Polly Stewart was injured, as was a daughter of Stephen Radcliff. ♦

† [3d] Adv. of goods for sale by *Bellows & Stone*, Walpole, N.H., 4 June 1798.

† [3d] Moses Johnson offers goods for sale, Walpole, N.H., 4 June 1798.

† [3d] Ebenezer Farnsworth offers one cent reward for David Weed, a 13 year-old boy who ran away "on a Sabbath day." Dated at Charlestown, [N.H.—Ed.], 15 May 1798.

† [3d] John Bennet, of Brattleborough, Vt., petitions for divorce from his wife, Lydia (Elliot) Bennet, to whom he was married 3 Feb. 1791. Bennet claims that Lydia absconded on 14 Jan. 1794, and eloped with one Philip Paddleford, late of Brattle-

borough, "and with him, the said Paddleford, hath lived in open adultery, and hath fled with the said Paddleford to parts unknown . . . "

===== ¶ [3d] DIED. =====

At Petersburg, in Russia, Stanislaus, late king of Poland.
Pennsylvania.—At Philadelphia, Miss Mary Connelly, aged 13; Mr. Coshman Polack.
Massachusetts.—At Boston, Mr. John Owen, aged 63.—At Roxbury, Mr. Joseph Williams, aged 90.—At Newburyport, Mrs. Elizabeth Wood, aged 88.—At Newbedford, Mrs. Deborah Church.—At Lancaster, Capt. Ephraim Carter, aged 56.—At Gloucester, Maj. Frederick Gilman.—At Scarborough, [District of Maine—Ed.] Mr. William Plummer, aged 72.
Newhampshire.—At Lebanon, Mrs. Sally Hough, aged 20.—At Hanover, Miss Sukey Smith, aged [12?].

Vol. VI (No. 271) Tuesday, 12 June 1798.

† [3d] Elisha Ayres advertises a cow which was lost or stolen; dated at Rockingham, [Vermont—Ed.], 6 June 1798.
† [3d] Elijah Kilburn advertises a pocket book which he lost between Claremont meeting house and "landlord Henry's in Charlestown; dated Walpole 11 June 1798.

===== ¶ [3d] DIED. =====

In Halifax, Novascotia, Jonathan Sterns, Esq; Solicitor General, aged 47.
NEWJERSEY.—At Newark, Wynant Van Zandt.
NEWYORK.—At Newyork, Captain James Kidney, aged 30.
RHODEISLAND.—At Portsmouth, Capt. George Scott.
MASSACHUSETTS.—At Worcester, Mr. John Noyes, aged 69.

Vol. VI (No. 272) Tuesday, 19 June 1798.

¶ [3a] WORCESTER, May 30. A few days ago, as Mr. Edward Kitfield, of Manchester, and his wife, were riding home from Salem, in a chaise, the bits having accidentally worked out of the horse's mouth, so that they could not command him, they threw themselves from the chaise when it was going with rapidity, and were so much injured that Mr. K. died in a few hours, and his wife's life was despaired of. The horse finally stopped in a yard, without injuring the carriage.
¶ [3c] ACCIDENT. The following melancholy accident happened a few days since at Antrim in this State. As a Mr. Knight was felling a tree, two of his sisters were approaching the spot where he was at work at the time he had cut the tree nearly through. They were at that moment in a safe situation, and he requested them to stand where they were. But, perhaps from an idea of greater safety, one of the sisters immediately ran towards the place where Mr. Knight stood, in the way of the falling tree, and was crushed to death.

===== ¶ [3c] DIED. =====

Pennsylvania.—At Philadelphia, Nathan Bryan, Esq; Representative in Congress, from Northcarolina.
Newyork.—At Newyork, William Seton, Esq; aged 55; Mr. Samuel Akerly; Mr. Samuel Sparhawk, aged 54.
Connecticut.—At Hartford, Mr. Horace Austin; Mrs. Elizabeth Clark.
Massachusetts.—At Boston, Mrs. Sally Knoulton, aged 18—At Roxbury, Joseph Williams, Esq; aged 90—At Danvers, Mr. John Dodge, aged 60—At Boxford, Mr. Asa Gould, aged 26—At Berwick, Hon. Humphrey Chadbourne, Esq; aged 82—At Portland, Mrs. Greela Wild, aged 80—At Scarborough, Mr. William Plummer, aged 7[2?]—At Colrain, Mr. Robert Miller, aged [59?]
Newhampshire.—At Portsmouth, Mr. Joseph Hill, aged 19; Mrs. Mary Humphreys, aged 55; Mr. Daniel Humphreys, aged 28; Mr. Jonathan Marden.

† [3d] Thomas Bliss, John W. Horswill, B.G. Watkins, and Micah Brown, a.k.a. *Bliss, Horswill, Watkins, and Brown*, of the "Cabinent Business" at Charlestown, N.H. and

Woodstock, Vt., dissolve their copartnership, and request settlements of accounts. Bliss to remain in the business at Charlestown, and Brown to continue on likewise at Woodstock. Dated at Woodstock, 4 June 1798.

† [3d] A list of persons to be distributors of Stamps, and Collectors of the Revenue upon the same, per an Act of Congress laying duties on parchment, paper, etc.

Geo. Hough, printer, Concord, N.H.	Daniel Adams, physician, Keene, N.H.
James Jewett, mer., Dover, N.H.	Andrew S. Crocker, Esq., Haverhill, N.H.
Robert Fletcher, Esq., Amherst, N.H.	John Rogers, Esq., Plymouth, N.H.
Samuel Crosby, Esq., Charlestown, N.H.	

Vol. VI (No. 273) Tuesday, 26 June 1798.

¶ [3d] DIED.

Newyork.—At Newyork, Nathaniel Hazard, Esq;—At Hudson, David Smith, Esq;—At Kinderhook, Isaac P. Van Volkenburgh, Esq;

Massachusetts.—At Boston, Mrs. Abigail Romney, aged 75; Mr. Benjamin Colman; Mrs. Elizabeth S. Conant, aged 24—At Northbridge, Mrs. Maria Bullard, aged 29—At Westspringfield, Mr. Abel Morsey, aged 42—At Franklin, Mrs. Lydia Peck, aged 2[5?]—At Lee, Miss Anner Bassett, aged 18—At Newbedford, Lieut. Joseph Ayers.

Vermont.—At Westminster, Miss Polly Moore, aged 14—At Putney, Miss Rebekah Hide, aged 17.

Vol. VI (No. 274) Tuesday, 3 July 1798.

¶ [3a] CARLISLE, PENNSYLVANIA, June 14. Committed to the jail of this county on Monday last, a certain Sarah Clark, on suspicion of being the person who has poisoned the family of John Carothers, Esq; in the lower settlement, of which Mr. Carothers and his wife have died, and several of the family now very ill. In our next we expect to give a more particular account of this dreadful catastrophe as well as of the female monster who perpetrated it. 8

† [3d] Advertisement of various goods for sale at *Bellows & Stone*, Walpole, 2 July 1798.

† [3d] James Titus advertises for a Journeyman Clothier, and also requests settlement of debts, Rockingham, [Vt.], 2 July 1798.

Vol. VI (No. 275) Tuesday, 10 July 1798.

† [3d] Letters remaining at the Post Office in Walpole, N.H., 1 July 1798, as compiled by David Carlisle, Postmaster:

Thomas Sparhawk, Esq;	Walpole.	Stephen Bennet, 2	Walpole.
Stephen Smith,	"	John Stroad,	Dublin.
Jonathan Lee,	"	Seth Britton,	Westmoreland.
Dr. K. Farnam,	"	Widow Kesia Stone,	"
Samuel Wires,	"	Isaac Prouty,	"
Dr. Jesse Kittredge,	"	Jonathan R. Hale, 2	Chesterfield.
James Lewis,	"	Asahel [Britton?],	"
John Lyon,	"	Samuel Choat,	Rockingham.
Benjamin Beal,	"	James Miller,	Chester.
Edward Watkins,	"	Daniel Moody,	Unity.
Mess. Gay and Stetson, 2	"	Simon Hough,	Richmond, M. 9
John March,	"	Salmon Chandler,	Swanzey.

† [3d] Letters remaining at the Post Office in Charlestown, N.H., 2 July 1798, as compiled by Samuel Crosby, Postmaster. Appended to said list of letters, is a note inserted by the Postmaster: "N.B. Any persons living in the towns, through which Mr. Brooks of Alstead carries the Walpole papers, may be supplied with papers from Philadelphia, Newyork, or Boston, by applying at the Post Office in Charlestown."

Aaron Alexander,	Plainfield.	Abraham Folsom,	Meredith.
Jonathan R. Hale,	Chesterfield.	Samuel Pratt,	Charlestown.

Jonathan Holten,	Charlestown.	Lemuel Peters, Richmond.
William Henry,	"	Jabish Parsons, Coldbrook.
Ebenezer Hitchcock,	Weathersfield, Vt.	Jonathan Thompson, Wallingford, Vt.

===== ¶ [3c] DIED. =====

Connecticut.—At Newlondon, Daniel Shaw, aged 56; Mrs. Elizabeth Warner, aged 46—At Preston, Mr. Ephraim Tucker, aged 72.

Massachusetts.—At Boston, Rev. Jeremy Belknap, D.D., aged 54; Captain Samuel Moore, aged 45; Mrs. Lucretia Stoddard, aged 56—At Petersham, Benjamin Chandler, aged 79.

Vol. VI (No. 276) Tuesday, 17 July 1798.

† [3d] Reward of $150 offered for the return of Joseph Pinnock, "of Strafford," who escaped the jail in Chelsea, Orange County, Vermont, 25 June 1798. Pinnock "confined on an information for murder; he is about thirtyfive years of age, dark complexion, light blue eyes, rather of a down look, long dark hair; he is about six feet high, stout built, wore while in jail a blue coat, blue striped overhalls; supposed to have rode away a light dapple grey horse." Dated at Chelsea, 26 June, 1798, by "Perly Chandler, Gaoler."

===== ¶ [3d] DIED. =====

Newjersey.—At Newark, Philip P. Kiarney, Esq.
Newyork.—At Newyork, Mr. Andrew Turnbull, aged 54.

Vol. VI (No. 277) Tuesday, 24 July 1798.

† [3a] Account of the murder of a Mrs. Perkins, "a woman in years" who attempted to aid a woman who refused to sell liquor to two drunkards in Philadelphia. ♦

† [3d] Adv. by Amasa Allen, who carries "New & Fashionable Goods," at Walpole.

† [3d] Moses Johnson adv. commodities at his store in Walpole, 24 July 1798.

† [3d] Legal notice regarding the last will and testament of Joseph Fox, Jr., late of Boston, Mass. Said will brought to Cheshire County, N.H. Judge of Probate by Joseph Fox, Esq., of Fitchburg, Mass., and the "court of probate" to be held at the house of Samuel Grant, Innholder, of Walpole, on the 23d of August next.

† [3d] Wheat, "which was brought from over the mountain," for sale by Alexander Watkins, dated at Walpole 24 July 1798.

† [3d] Amos Butterfield offers property for sale in Claremont, dated 24 July 1798.

† [3d] One cent reward offered by Levi Green, for the return of Kincaid Read, an apprentice boy about 16 years of age who ran away 8 July 1798; dated at Westmoreland, 16 July 1798.

Vol. VI (No. 278) Tuesday, 31 July 1798.

† [3c] A notice that Thomas and Isaac Redington plan "to discontinue their mercantile business in Walpole," and request settlement of debts by Sept. 1st next; dated Walpole, 30 July 1798.

† [3d] Legal notice regarding a petition by Nathaniel Hall, Innholder, and Jonathan Chase, Jr., Merchant, both of Cornish, N.H., who were appointed guardians of "Jonathan Chase, of said Cornish, gentleman, lunatic."

† [3d] Abel Walker adv. a stray mare on his property, Langdon, N.H., 25 July 1798.

===== ¶ [3c] DIED. =====

At Fort Royal, Martinico, Capt. Turell Bass, a few year's since resident at this place, Aged 23.

MAINE.—At Portland, Mrs. Rebecca Thurlow, aged 55; Mrs. Mary Maria Arnold, aged 22.

PENNSYLVANIA.—At Philadelphia, Mr. Adam Both, aged 103.

Vol. VI (No. 279) Monday, 6 Aug. 1798.

† [3c] "An excellent stand for a Tanner, in Alstead, about forty rods from the Meeting House," for sale by Aaron Stearns; dated at Walpole, 4 August 1798.

† [3c] Reward offered for Thomas Scofield's horse, dated Springfield, 19 July 1798.
===== ¶ [3c] DIED. =====
In London, Mr. William Jenkins, a clerk in the bank, aged 31. This gentleman measured the extraordinary height of seven feet nine inches.
At Martinique, Master James Allen, aged 14, son of Joseph Allen, Esq; of Worcester. MASSACHUSETTS.—At [Rutland?], Colonel John Read, aged 35.

Vol. VI (No. 280)   Monday, 13 Aug. 1798.

† [1c] Advertisement for *Abram & Ebenezer Stearns*, offering cash for butter, and also requesting settlements of debts; dated at Chesterfield, 23 July, 1798.
† [3a] Murder-suicide of Madam and Monsieur Gardie, at New York City. ♦
† [3b] A son of Mr. James Davidson killed by a falling tree at Woodbury, Conn., on the 8th of July. The article is contained under the news dated at Hartford. ♦
¶ [3d] MELANCHOLY ACCIDENT. At Northfield, in this state, as a Mr. George Hancocks was driving a load of hay into his barn; in his hurry endeavouring to shelter it from an impending shower, and the passage between the entrance of the barn and the wheel being narrow, he was unfortunately crushed to death. What adds a pang to the feelings of his friends, the youth, scarce twenty one years of age, was to have been soon married to a deserving young woman, who now mourns the untimely fate of an expected partner and esteemed friend.
† [3d] Samuel Mead and Elisha Kingsbery announce that their copartnership, *Mead & Kingsbery*, is dissolved. Kingsbery "continues to do business in this Store and Oil Mill in Alstead; dated there 13 June 1798.
† [3d] Adv. of a horse found by Asel Griswold, dated at Walpole 11 Aug. 1798.

Vol. VI (No. 281)   Monday, 20 Aug. 1798.

¶ [2d] BOSTON, MASSACHUSETTS. August 11. A man was found dead yesterday near the dock. The depositions before the Coroner, say he must have been dead from six to ten days. The overseers ordered him to be buried on Bird Island.—While a Mr. James Dill, and four others, were digging the grave and Mr. Dill was bringing a large stone to place on the coffin, a sudden explosion of thunder was heard, and sharp lightning seen, but without any rain; when Dill was killed instantly, and Mr. Ludden, the sexton, knocked down, and did not recover until three quarters of an hour after.
† [3d] A lost colt advertised by Isaac Temple, dated at Alstead 13 Aug. 1798.
† [3d] Elkenah Lincoln advertises a blacksmith shop for lease; Westmoreland, 17 Aug.
===== ¶ [3c] DIED. =====
PENNSYLVANIA.—At Philadelphia, Col. James Innes, American Commissioner for the settlement of claims of British subjects against American citizens.

Vol. VI (No. 282)   Monday, 27 Aug. 1798.

† [3d] Advertisement of a proposal by Moses Johnson for a cattle drive from Keene to Boston; dated at Keene 25 Aug. 1798.
† [3d] Advertisement by the Armoury Department, Springfield, Mass., for men experienced in making small arms; posted by Ashley Colton, for David Ames, Supervisor.

Vol. VI (No. 283)   Monday, 3 Sept. 1798.

† [2a] Extensive biography of Major General John Fiske, who was born in Salem, Mass., 10 April 1744. The article also contains genealogical information concerning his father, Samuel Fiske, minister at Salem, Mass., and several other family members. This article is concluded in the issue of 10 Sept. 1798 [1a-2b]. ♦

Vol. VI (No. 284)   Monday, 10 Sept. 1798.

† [3c] An unnamed man from New Salem, Mass. injured at Watertown, Mass., when he jumped from a window after waking from a dream. Article contained under the dateline of Brookfield, [Mass.—Ed.] ♦

† [3c] Reward offered by Daniel Chapman for return of a pocket book which he lost between Walpole and Keene; dated at Keene, 6 Sept. 1798.
† [3c] Legal notice regarding the estate of Abner Harris, late of Chesterfield, deceased; Abner Harris, Jun., Executor. Dated at Chesterfield, 25 Aug. 1798.

Vol. VI (No. 285) Monday, 17 Sept. 1798.

† [3d] Gurdon Huntington and John Livingston, Jun., adv. to hire several men experienced in the gunsmith business; dated Walpole, 15 Sept. 1798. A similar request appears in the next adv., by Amasa Allen, Samuel Grant, and Joseph Barnard, dated Walpole, 25 Sept. 1798. The latter ad also requests Journeymen Blacksmiths.
† [3d] Moses Potter advertises a lost horse, dated at Richmond, 14 Sept. 1798.

Vol. VI (No. 286) Monday, 24 Sept. 1798.

† [2d] The British Schooner *Saucy George*, Capt. Burns, accidentally exploded in the harbor of Charleston, South Carolina. The Captain, Mr. George Kern (passenger), Mr. John Robinson (pilot), and two others were missing and presumed dead. Messrs. Henderson, Patterson, Hunter and M'Kellar were supposed to be mortally wounded. The body of one Lowry, seaman, of the schooner, was "found in the river." ♦
† [3b-3c] Article describing the opening of the new bridge at Bellow's Falls, [Vt.]; Messrs. Miles and Greene, architects, and Frederic W. Geyer, Esq., proprietor.
† [3d] Benjamin Cutter adv. for a Journeyman Blacksmith, dated at Jaffrey, 13 Sept.

=== ¶ [3d] DIED. ===

Northcarolina.—At Edenton, James Wilson, Esq. one of the Associate Judges of the S.C.U.S.
Pennsylvania.—At Philadelphia, Benjamin F. Bache, printer of the Aurora.
Newyork.—At Newyork, Mrs. Todd, and Miss Charlotte Todd. Thomas Greenleaf, printer of the Argus. A[?] Van Hook.
Connecticut.—At Newlondon, Hon. Joshua Colt.

Vol. VI (No. 287) Monday, 1 Oct. 1798.

¶ [3a] MONTEGO BAY, [WEST INDIES] August 4. On Sunday the 21st ult. was executed at Savanna la Mar, pursuant to his sentence, Samuel Graham, for the murder of a negro man his own property.
† [3d] List of letters remaining at the Post Office in Keene, N.H., 30 Sept. 1798, as compiled by Daniel Adams, Postmaster:

Daniel Perin,	Alstead.	Joseph Worster,	Ashby.*
Levi Warren,	"	Abraham Morrison,	Stoddard.
John Steward,	Rindge.	Clement Daniels,	Barrington, N.H.
Simeon Russell,	"	Rev. Laben Ainsworth,	Jaffrey.
Edward Look, 2	"	Joshua Hale,	Walpole.
Cornelius Sturtevant, 2	Keene.	Andrew Seaton,	{ Hancock, Hillsborough Co., N.H.
Elisha Briggs,	"		
Daniel Webster,	"	Samuel Choat,	{ Rockingham, Bellows's Falls, Vt.
Peleg Sprague, Esq;	"		
Maj. Daniel Gould,	Lyndeborough.	Nathan F. Glosson,	New Marlborough.
Abigail Church,	Barrington, N.H.		
Benjamin Merrfeild, 10 or Phillip Britton,	} Surry.		* [perhaps Ashby, *Mass.*—Ed.]

† [3b-3c] In the various news items contained in the "Incidents at Home" column under the head of Walpole, the final item describes the death of Dr. Elihu H. Smith, a benevolent physician of New York City, who died of the prevailing fever there. ♦
† [3c] William Todd offers reward for this lost mare, dated at Keene, 20 Sept. 1798.
† [3d] Legal notice regarding the estate of Mr. Waighstell Field, late of Winchester, N.H., deceased, Anna Field, administratrix. Dated at Winchester, 22 Sept. 1798.
† [3d] Maria Winchester offers a small farm for sale, "in Westmoreland, on the Surry side." Also for sale, at her dwelling house in Walpole, "Universal Dialogues, by the late

Elhanan Winchester. . . " Dated at Walpole, 29 Sept. 1798.
† [3d] Ruggles Woodbridge offers reward for his stolen mare; dated at South Hadley, 24 Sept. 1798.

Vol. VI (No. 288) Monday, 8 Oct. 1798.

† [1a] Frederick W. Geyer posts a notice concerning his new bridge at Bellow's Falls.
† [3d] Josiah Carter, Jr. and Jotham Johnson advertise a request for a cargo of mules, dated at "Lancaster and Leominster," Mass., 3 Oct. 1798.
† [3d] Ephraim Hawkins and Daniel Hawkins, jun. found a lost mare, dated at Winchester, 17 Sept. 1798.
† [3d] A mare strayed or was stolen from Alexander Watkins; dated Walpole, 5 Oct.

Vol. VI (No. 289) Monday, 15 Oct. 1798.

† [1c] List of letters remaining at the Post Office, in Walpole, N.H. 1 Oct. 1798, as compiled by John Hubbard, Postmaster:

Jonas Butterfield,	Westmoreland, N.H.	Ezekiel Graves,	Walpole.
Caleb Butterfield,	" "	Rev. Levi Lancton,	Alstead.
Edward Esty,	" "	Jonas Newton,	"
Dr. Isaac Story,	" "	James Hall,	Pawlet, Vt.
Asa Sibley,	Walpole.	Henery Scovil,	Surry, N.H.
Leonard Herrington,	"	Anna Spence,	Claremont.
John Kilburn,	"	Col. Edward Buckman,	Lancaster, N.H.
Ebenezer Ruggles,	"	Asaph Drake,	Bellow's Falls.

† [1c] List of letters remaining at the Post Office, in Westminster, Vt., 1 Oct. 1798, as compiled by Eleazer May, Postmaster:

Dr. Benjamin Morgan,	Wilmington, Vt.	John Pierce,	Westminster, Vt.
Joseph Ellis,	Newfane, Vt.	Moses Chidester,	Fairfield, Vt.
Esther Meech,	Westminster, Vt.	John Dunlap,	Rockingham, Vt.
John Wiswell,	"	George Caldwell,	" "
John Rice,	"	Benjamin Armington,	Chester, Vt.
Joseph Parmenter,	"	Dudley Thomas,	Westmoreland, N.H.

† [3d] Thomas Edwards offers five cents reward for the return of Dick Simon, "an indentured Indian Boy," who ran away 27 Sept. 1798; dated at Keene, 9 Oct. 1798.

Vol. VI (No. 290) Monday, 22 Oct. 1798.

† [3a] Account of the trial of Matthew Lyon, for sedition, at the Circuit Court of the United States, "which sat at Rutland," Vermont. ♦
† [3d] *Stevens & Parmelee* adv. for an ox which was "lost out of a drove at Redington's tavern in Walpole . . . " Dated at Claremont, 19 Oct. 1798
===== ¶ [3d] DIED. =====
In Newyork, of the [yellow—Ed.] fever, on the 21st ult. Mr. Benoni Cole, aged 23, late of Chesterfield.

Vol. VI (No. 291) Monday, 29 Oct. 1798.

† [3c] Jonathan Muzzy adv. a fulling mill for sale in Alstead, "lately occupied by the subscriber. For particulars, inquire in Keene of Capt. Warner, or of Gideon Griggs in Alstead, near the premises." Dated at Alstead, 24 Oct. 1798.
† [3c] John Brooks "informs those who recieve the Farmer's Museum of him weekly" to settle their accounts. Dated at Alstead, 27 Oct. 1798.
† [3d] Ebenezer Temple, Guardian of Joseph Sweetser, of Marlborough, advertises a legal notice concerning Sweetser; dated there 18 Oct. 1798.
† [3d] Alexander Watkins advertises for a horse which strayed or was stolen from the pasture of Roger Fenton, in Walpole; dated there 27 Oct. 1798.
† [3d] Legal notice concerning the estate of William Barker, late of Marlborough, [N.H.—Ed.]; James Brewer, Thomas Tolman, and Francis Goodhue, jun., appointed

Commissioners over said estate, which was "reprensented insolvent." Business regarding said estate to be attended to at the house of Mr. James Robertson, Innholder in Fitzwilliam.

Vol. VI (No. 292) Monday, 5 Nov. 1798.

† [3c] Account of many slaves killed by a lightning strike at the plantation of Mr. Henry Middleton, in South Carolina. ◆
† [3d] Samuel W. Thurber adv. a notice concerning two notes against him, given "for cattle and grain, payable in three years from the date"; one note was given to Col. Ebenezer Stevens of Kingston, dated 6 July 1796, the other to Nathan Huntley, jun. of Marlow. Said notes now held by one Joseph Huntoon.
† [3d] Legal notice regarding the insolvent estate of Philip Nours, late of Langdon, deceased; James Egerton, Abel Walker, and Samuel Kingsbery appointed Commissioners of said estate. Business concerning said estate to be conducted at the house of Capt. Elijah Putnam of Langdon. Notice dated at Langdon, 29 Oct. 1798.

===== ¶ [3c] DIED. =====

Massachusetts.—At Shrewsbury, Mrs. Mary Jones, aged nearly 105 years. Her maiden name was Mary Richardson. She was born at Woburn, January 10th, O.S. 1694. Her first husband was Henry Baldwin, Esq. of Pelham, N.H. by whom she had three children, who lived to settle in the world, and left families. Her second husband was Col. Jones of Hopkinton, who died about the year 1772, since which time she remained a widow. She enjoyed a good degree of health, until within a few weeks of her death. The serenity of mind, and quietness of temper, which she possest [sic] to an uncommon degree, doubtless contributed to her great age.

Vermont.—At Westminster, of the Iliac passion, Miss Polly Avery, daughter of Mr. Samuel Avery, of that place. If gentleness of manners, if modest merit, and unsullied purity of mind, claim the tribute of friendship, the memory of Miss Avery will always be in bloom. Her soul was the soil of benevolence, and every virtue sprang spontaneous there.

Newhampshire.—At Washington, Miss Polly Shiplie, after a short, but very severe fit of sickness, aged [18?]

Vol. VI (No. 293) Monday, 12 Nov. 1798.

† [2d] Miss Russel, "of Dartmouth," killed by a jealous admirer, one Bembridge, who attempted to also take his own life. (News under dateline of Halifax, Nova Scotia.) ◆
† [2d-3a] Maria Hornby, "a passenger from Cork," drowned when a boat overturned near Hampton Roads, Va.; Capt Keckwith, of the *Iris*, and several of the crew, were saved. Article contained under the dateline of Norfolk, Va., 16 Oct. ◆
† [3d] Agnes Lakin petitions for divorce from her husband, William Lakin, "late of Hancock, in the County of Hillsborough, now living as it is reported, in Whites Creek, in the State of New York." They were married "upwards of fourteen years since past," but the husband absconded nine years ago, and about seven years ago, committed adultery with an unknown woman, who he then married. This petition was delivered to the Superior Court of Judicature, "holden at Keene, within, and for said County of Cheshire, on the third Tuesday of October, A.D. 1798." The location of Mrs. Lakin's residence is not given.

Vol. VI (No. 294) Monday, 19 Nov. 1798.

¶ [3a] NEWBURYPORT, MASSACHUSETTS, October 26. SUICIDE. Last Monday evening, one Benjamin Silsby, who put up at a tavern in Kennebunk, after smoking a cigar in the forepart of the evening, stepped out, and not returning, was supposed to have gone to a neighbour's house and was thought no more of. The next morning the landlord, rising soon after day, discovered a person who was found to be Silsby, hanging by the neck in the necessary house. The spectacle was truly horrid ! The verdict of the jury was "Deliberate suicide."

¶ [3c] MEDEAN MADNESS. The wife of Mr. James M'Donald, of Whitestown, (Mohawk county, Newyork state) lately got so enraged with her infant child, that she threw it into the fire, and burnt it to death !—For which monstrously inhuman and barbarous act, she is condemned shortly to end her days in the same awful manner !

† [3c] Robert and Joshua Davis, jun., announce that their copartnership is dissolved, dated at Boston 12 Nov. 1798.

† [3c] Jonathan Royce adv. for a lost cow; dated [Walpole—Ed.] 10 Nov. 1798.

Vol. VI (No. 295) Monday, 26 Nov. 1798.

¶ [3a] NOVEMBER 12. A most melancholy catastrophe occurred on Saturday afternoon about three o'clock. One of the Elizabeth Town ferry boats, with twenty four passengers, going from Newyork, was struck by a flow of wind off Bergen point at the moment of tacking and instantly upset.—The following persons were unhappily drowned—Benjamin Bonnel, Esq. of Chatham, Chatfield Hodges, David D. Tuttle, James Carter, Abigail Maxfield, and her infant, Mrs. Moor, Mrs. Carter, Mrs. Ann Smith. [. . .]

† [3d] Nathan Estabrook adv. a lost mare on his land; dated Westmoreland, 20 Nov.

† [3d] Legal notice regarding the estate of Capt. David Carlisle, late of Walpole, deceased, John Carlisle, Administrator.

===== ¶ [3d] DIED. =====

At Richmond, Mr. Daniel Cass, aged 74.

"On the first of November, Daniel Ripley, a lad of about thirteen years of age, in attempting to cross Ashuelot river in Winchester, a little above the new dam, near the furnace, when the current, being very rapid, swept him over, and he was unfortunately drowned. He has not been heard of since, though great exertions have been made to find him."

Vol. VI (No. 296) Monday, 3 Dec. 1798.

† [1a] Legal notice by "Samuel Stevens, R.P." stating that "a special Court of Probate will be held at the dwelling house of Samuel Grant in Walpole," in consequence of the fact that "settlement of many estates of Persons deceased, have been for some years unnecessarily delayed, by Executors and Administrators, to the prejudice of heirs, creditors, and all concerned."

¶ [2a] BELFAST, IRELAND. September 21. The following persons have been discharged from the Postlethwait prison ship, having found security to transport themselves to America: Charles Develin, John Service, Tristrim Moor, John Caldwell, Hugh Boyd, James Wallance, (Hollywood) John Quinn, Samuel Boner, Alexander Clandinnan, William Lowry, James Hamilton, William Shaw and David Shaw.

† [3d] Legal notice concerning the insolvent estate of John Graves, Esq. late of Walpole, deceased. Levi Hooper, Jonathan Hall, Jr., and Elisha Hall, Commissioners of said estate, advertise a meeting regarding estate business, to be held at the house of the widow Lydia Graves at Walpole; dated at Walpole 3 Dec. 1798.

Vol. VI (No. 297) Monday, 10 Dec. 1798.

† [3d] William Raymond offers reward for a mare which strayed or was stolen "from the subscriber, in Dublin . . . " Adv. dated at Weathersfield, 18 Nov. 1798.

† [3d] Luther Very requests of his customers "who take the Farmer's Museum of him weekly," to pay their subscriptions for the next six months. Dated Winchester, 4 Dec.

† [3d] Elisha Huntley requests persons who have demands against the estate of Nathan Huntley, Jr., late of Marlow, deceased, "to exhibit them to the subscriber, immediately, for settlement. Dated at Marlow, 6 Dec. 1798.

===== ¶ [3c] DIED. =====

In Packersfield, after a long illness, Reverend Jacob Foster, in the 67th year of his age.

Vol. VI (No. 298) Monday, 17 Dec. 1798.

† [3d] Abram and Eben. Stearns announce that their Copartnership will be dissolved on 21 Feb. 1799, and offer their store for sale; dated at Chesterfield, 10 Dec. 1798

† [3d] *Bellows & Stone* announce that "they have removed from the store adjoining Bellows's tavern, to the store lately occupied by Messrs. Thomas and Isaac Redington," and also present a sample of their goods for sale. Dated at Walpole, 15 Dec. 1798.

† [3d] Adv. of goods for sale by Amasa Allen, Merchant; dated Walpole 17 Dec. 1798.

† [3d] Thomas C. Drew, Josiah Bellows, and Oliver Sparhawk, Commissioners to the insolvent estate of Elhanan Winchester, late of Hartford, Conn., clerk, deceased, announce a meeting regarding estate business to be held at the house of Samuel Grant in Walpole; dated Walpole, 5 Dec. 1798.

Vol. VI (No. 299) Monday, 24 Dec. 1798.

No items of significance contained within this issue.

Vol. VI (No. 300) Monday, 31 Dec. 1798.

† [3d] Legal notice regarding the estate of Hannah Howard, late of Surry, deceased, as advertised by Joshua Flint, Administrator. Dated at Surry, 28 Dec. 1798.

† [3d] Thomas White wishes to exchange Lime for Grain, delivered at Mr. Jonathan Hubbard's, Charlestown," dated at Cavendish, 27 Dec. 1798.

† [3d] David Griffin adv. a stray steer which he found; dated Walpole, 17 Dec. 1798.

Vol. VI (No. 301) Monday, 7 Jan. 1799.

† [3b] Account of a fire at Newport, Rhode Island, which consumed the houses of Mr. Thomas George, Mr. J. Shaw, and Mr. J. Southwick, and other buildings. One Frederick Hoofman, a stranger, perished in the fire at a blacksmith's shop. ♦

† [3c] Account of local fires, one "at Newport" [presumably N.H.—Ed.] which burned the house of Mr. Buel "last week." Also, the store of Col. William Page at Rockingham, [Vt.—Ed.] burned "on Saturday evening." ♦

† [3c-3d] Description of the new bridge over the Conn. River at Bellow's Falls, and an elegant structure recently constructed, being the property of F.W. Geyer, Esq. ♦

† [3d] Letters remaining at the Post Office in Walpole, N.H., 1 Jan. 1799, as compiled by John Hubbard, Postmaster:

Billens Babcock,	Middlebury, Vt.	John Wait,	Walpole, N.H.
Lucy Boyd,	Walpole, N.H.	Otis Doolittle,	Hinsdale, N.H.
Rufus Caryl,	Chester, Vt.	Moses Willard,	Unity, N.H.
Nabby Carter,	Walpole, N.H.	Isaac Woodworth,	Chelsea, Vt.
Capt. Oliver Clap,	"	Capt. David Sanderson,	Bellows falls Walpole
Henry Foster, two	"	Henry Scovel,	Walpole, N.H.
Augustus Gallat,	"	Jonathan Lund,	Milford, N.H.
Thomas Hibberd,	"	Alpheus Moore,	Westmoreland.
Ebenezer Ruggles,	"	John Davis,	Stoddard.

† [3d] Jonathan Hubbard advertises a stray cow which he found; dated Charlestown, [N.H.—Ed.] 19 Dec. 1798.

† [3d] Stephen Dexter and David Dexter dissolved their Copartnership, and request settlement of debts; dated at Claremont, 4 Jan. 1799.

† [3d] List of nonresident owners of land in Springfield, N.H., who have not paid their taxes for the year 1798. Delinquent property to be sold at public auction the 31st of January next at the house of Samuel Clay, Innholder of Springfield. List compiled by Nathaniel Clark, Collector, and dated Springfield 18 Dec. 1798.

	No.	Qty.	Highway	C.
James M'Gregore Esq.	29	192	48 cts.	14 cts.
Ann Ordway	7	96	24	7
Do.	6	96	24	7
Do.	5	96	24	7
[T]homas Thompson, Esq.	8	96	24	7
Do.	9	96	24	7
Moses Webster	6	96	24	7
Ebenezer Fry	7	50	12	4
Capt. Matt. Pettingale	44	192	48	14
Do. half lot	48	96	24	7
Do. half lot	38	96	24	7
Lt. John Sweat Plat	5	96	24	7

Vol. VI (No. 302) Monday, 14 Jan. 1799.

† [3d] Elijah Page adv. a reward for the return of a stallion and a mare stolen from him "in Walpole," dated at Walpole, 11 Jan. 1799.

† [3d] List of nonresident owners of land in Croydon, N.H., who have not paid their taxes for the year 1798. Delinquent property to be sold at public auction on the 11th of March next, at the house of Edward Hall, Jr., Innholder at Croydon. List compiled by Edward Hall, Jr., Collector, and dated 27 Dec. 1798. The notice in the newspaper gives a confusing tax breakdown of each owner; the transcription below thus contains only the name of the property owner, and excludes the remainder of the tax data.

Samuel Chase	Antipas Holland	Benjamin Wood
Daniel Chase	Thomas Denny	Jonas Brown
Moses Chase	William Wait	Dudly Chase
Moses Whipple	Marsh Chase	Josiah Peas

Delinquent taxpayers of Croydon, N.H. (*continued*) :

Joseph Vinson	James Mc'Clanen	Luke Drury
Samuel Chase, Jr.	Rev. Mr. Parsons	Governor's farm
Samuel Ayers	Solomon Lealand	Daniel Read
Joseph Whipple	Jonathan Aldrich	Samuel Dudly
Ephraim Sherman	Solomon Chase	
John Holland	Silas Warren	

† [3d] Moses Johnson advertises to purchase "Salts of Lye;" dated Keene, 14 Jan. 1799.

Vol. VI (No. 303) Monday, 21 Jan. 1799.

† [1c] Moses Johnson advertises to purchase "good house ashes," which may be delivered at his "Potash Manufactory." Dated Keene, 7 Jan. 1799.

† [3d] Legal notice regarding David Rice, yeoman, guardian of Joel Reed, minor, both of Princeton, Worcester County, Mass., in a petition to the Superior Court of Judicature for Cheshire County, N.H., to obtain authorization to sell the minor's right to land in Cheshire County. Several pieces of property are described, including one which states that said Joel Reed is heir to land "undivided and in common with one Alpheus Reed of Westmoreland;" also a reference to a deed to another tract of land in Westmoreland, "executed by Micah Reed to Thomas Reed, grand parent of said minor." ♦

† [3d] Daniel Newcomb offers for sale "The farm lately owned by Major Eames, near the Meeting House in Keene." Dated at Keene, 16 Jan. 1799.

† [3d] Moses Todd and John Emerson dissolved their Copartnership, *Todd & Emerson*, on the 16th of Jan. 1799; dated at Rindge, one day later.

† [3d] H. Leonard advertises "Warrented Axes" that he is "making, as usual, in Charlestown," [N.H.—Ed.]. Dated 19 Jan. 1799.

† [3d] Oliver Hastings advertises a notice regarding the estate of Jonathan Hastings, late of Chesterfield, deceased. Dated at Chesterfield, 28 Dec. 1798.

Vol. VI (No. 304) Monday, 28 Jan. 1799.

† [2a] An article summarizing Acts and Resolves passed at a session of the General Court, holden at Concord, Nov. 1798. A few of said acts pertain to specific individuals:
    1) An act, to restore Nathaniel Dodge to his law.
    2) An act, to alter the name of Raby, to the name of Brookline.
    3) An act, enabling Randolph Freeman, to assume the name of Payton.
    4) An act, to authorize the Guardians of Jonathan Chase, Esq. to sell real estate.
    5) An act, granting a ferry to Tilton Bennett.
    6) An act, granting a ferry to Salah Howe.

† [3d] William Page informs the public that his store at Bellow's Falls was destroyed by fire, and requests settlement of accounts; also various goods advertised for sale. Dated at Bellows' Falls, 21 Jan. 1799.

† [3d] Thomas K. Green requests his customers to settle their debts; dated at Westmoreland, 21st Jan. 1799.

Vol. VI (No. 305) Monday, 4 Feb. 1799.

† [3d] Sarah Learned, Executrix of the estate of Joshua Learned, deceased, advertises land for sale in Marlborough, N.H. belonging to said estate. "For further particluars inquire of the subscriber, at Cambridge, Samuel Learned, of Watertown, Commonwealth of Massachusetts, or of Jesse Hunting, near the premises." Dated at Cambridge, 15 Jan. 1799.

† [3d] John Brooks informs those "who have hitherto taken the Farmer's Museum of him, that from the present week, Capt. Nathan Fay will bring them the papers weekly, on the same rout[e] and at the same price as before . . . " and requests his former customers to settle their accounts. Dated 2 Feb. 1799.

Vol. VI (No. 306) Monday, 11 Feb. 1799.

† [3d] The Copartnership of *Pratt & Pierce* "is by mutual consent, this day, dissolved. All persons, therefore, indebted to the late said firm, are requested, on account of the intended removal of Mr. Pratt, to settle immediately." Dated Marlborough, 30 Jan. 1799.

Vol. VI (No. 307) Monday, 18 Feb. 1799.

† [3b-3c] Sleighing accident at Wilsborough, Clinton County, [N.Y.], involving John Manning, Esq. of Duanesborough and a Mrs. Campbell, "an aged lady of Argyle," both returning home from a journey to Canada. Article contained under the head of Albany, New York. ♦

† [3d] Rufus Graves advertises a Tan Yard for sale "situate in Hanover, within a few rods of Dartmouth College." Dated at Hanover 9 Jan. 1799.

† [3d] Announcement that the Copartnership of *Allen & Dorr* will be dissolved on the 1st of May next, but the business will be conducted afterwards by Joseph Dorr. Dated at Keene, 18 Feb. 1799.

Vol. VI (No. 308) Monday, 25 Feb. 1799.

† [3a] Two accidental deaths recorded under the dateline of Danbury, [Conn.—Ed.], 11 Feb. 1799: Mr. John Dunning, in the 60th year of his age, found dead on 16 Jan. in a well at Brookfield. Also, a son of Mr. Thomas Boughton, of Ridgbury, in the 11th year of his age, killed by a runaway horse. ♦

† [3b] Sad account of a fire at Barnstable, Mass., which claimed the lives of two sons of a Mr. Harthaway. The father lost his sight in the fire in attempting to save his boys. ♦

† [3d] Samuel Cobb, M.D., requests delinquent accounts to be settled. Dated at Springfield, 1 Feb. 1799.

† [3d] Legal notice regarding Josiah Willard, Administrator de bonis non of the estate of Josiah Willard, Esq. late of Winchester, deceased; dated Keene, 13 Feb. 1799.

† [3d] List of nonresident owners of land in Packersfield, 11 Cheshire County, N.H., who have not paid their taxes for the year 1798. Delinquent property to be sold at public auction on the 6th of May next, at the house of Josiah Melvin, Esq., Packersfield. List compiled by Thaddeus Barker, Collector, and dated 5 Feb. 1799. The notice in the newspaper gives a breakdown of each owner's lot size, range location, etc; the transcription below contains only the name of the property owner, and excludes the remainder of the tax data.

Aaron Felt	Bezaleel Spaulding	Samuel Brown
Isaac Appleton	Abraham Shelden	Col. Bauldings heirs
Benjamin Adams	Alexander Rolston	William Thompson
Oliver Scripture	Benjamin Clark	
James Scripture	Azel Shelley	

† [3d] Legal notice regarding demands on the estate of Daniel Rindge, late of Portsmouth, Esquire, deceased; Joseph Pierce, Executor, or "in the absence of said Joseph Peirce [sic] from Portsmouth, persons having business with him as Executor are notified to apply to John Peirce, Esq." Dated at Portsmouth, 11 Feb. 1799.

† [3d] *Bellows & Stone* announce that their Copartnership will be dissolved on 1 April next, and request settlement of accounts. 12 Dated at Walpole, 23 Feb. 1799.

Vol. VI (No. 309) Monday, 4 March 1799.

† [3c] Fire destroys the house and most contents belonging to Mr. Charles Kidd, "of Chesterfield," [prob. *Mass.*—Ed.] on 30 Jan. 1799. Mrs. Kidd, "who had for some months been confined by sickness, and the daughters" were forced to flee. The article is contained under the dateline of Northampton, Mass. ♦

† [3d] Isaac Abbot requests his debtors to settle their debts; dated Chesterfield, 25 Feb.

† [3d] Eliphalet Fox offers a horse for sale, dated at Walpole, 1 March 1799.

Vol. VI (No. 310) Monday, 11 March 1799.

† [3c] Extensive account of the robbery and murder, 3 Jan. 1799, of William Ireland, an old man of 70 years or upwards, who had no family but his wife and a few slaves. "Mr. Ireland the person murdered, was one of the first settlers in the upper end of Iredell county, and by industry and economy, having no children, was supposed to possess a large sum of money, which was luckily lent out." Lewis Collins and William Owen were arrested for the murder of Mr. Ireland. This article is contained under the dateline of Salisbury, South Carolina, but this was probably an error of *North* Carolina. ♦

† [3d] The house of Mr. Abel Jacobs, at Thompson, Conn., "was struck and much injured by lightening," 9 Feb. 1799. Item contained under dateline of Hartford, Conn.

† [3d] John Pierce adv. a house, barn, and one acre of property for sale, "right opposite the Meetinghouse in Westminster"; dated there 12 March 1799.

† [3d] Ranna Cossit offers a farm for lease at Claremont, and land lots for sale at Haverhill, N.H.; dated at Claremont, 6 March 1799.

Vol. VI (No. 311) Monday, 18 March 1799.

† [2d] Account of the murder of a Mr. Todd, in or near Baltimore, Maryland. ♦

† [3d] Levi Prentiss, of Newport, N.H. offers a large farm for sale at Reading, Vt.; adv. dated Newport, N.H. 8 March 1799.

Vol. VI (No. 312) Monday, 25 March 1799.

¶ [3b] LANCASTER, [Pennsylvania—Ed.], March 2. On Wednesday night as Miss Cooper, an amiable young lady of about twenty years of age, was returning from singing school in a sleigh with her two brothers—the sleigh, in passing by a waggon, upset, and Miss Cooper was almost instantaneously killed. This melancholly accident happened on the Turnpike, about twelve miles from *Lancaster*.

† [3d] Legal notice regarding the insolvent estate of Abel Dunbar, late of Springfield, N.H., husbandman, deceased. Jedediah Philbrick, Samuel Powers, and Ebenezer Fletcher were appointed Commissioners over said estate, and advertise meetings to be held at the house of Edward Hall, Jr., Innholder at Croydon, and at Mr. David Bean, Innholder at Springfield.

† [3d] Hezekiah Austin found a lost horse; notice dated at Charlestown, 11 Mar. 1799.

Vol. VII (No. 313) Monday, 1 April 1799.

† [1c-d] Biographical sketch of John Trumbull, Author of *M'Fingal*, "who was born in the town of Waterbury, in Connecticut, in the year 1749 or 1750." ♦

† [3c] Brief account of a fire which destroyed the mill, "with a considerable quantity of grain" belonging to Messrs. Hoag and Sons, at Starksborough, [Vt.—Ed.], 22 Feb. 1799. The article is contained under the dateline of Vergennes, Vermont.

† [3d] Luther Very requests that his customers pay up; notice dated 29 March 1799.

¶ [3d] MARRIED.]—At Braintree, Ms. Mr. Stephen Thayer to Miss Sarah Thayer.—At Barrington, Mr. Miller, aged 71, to Mrs. Bicknack, aged 71.—At Albany, N.Y. Mr. Jacob Ten Eyck, of Cocymans, to Miss Axa Cleaveland.—At Boston, Mr. Nathaniel W. Carnes to Mrs. Dolly Wellman.—At Leominster, Ms. Mr. John Maynard to Miss Sophia Carter. —At Haverhill, Ms. Mr. Barnabas Bradbury to Miss Mehitable Bradley.

¶ [3d] DIED.]—At Middletown, Con. General Comfort Sage, aged 67; and his consort, Mrs. Sally Sage, aged 66; within a few hours of each other.—At Hebron, Mr. Oliver Phelps, aged 55.—At Hartford, Mrs. Seymour, Mrs. Lockwood.—At Providence, R.I. Mr. Charles Estabrooks, aged 90.—At Cambridge, Ms. Mr. William Boyes, aged 25.—At Boston, Mrs. Hannah Haskell, aged 22; Mr. William Sylvester, aged 29; Mr. John Innis, aged 43; Mrs. Hannah Chapman, aged [71?]; Mrs. Francis Botang, aged 53; Mrs. Elizabeth Farnum, aged 27; Mrs. Salona Jeffery; Dr. William Boyes, aged 25; Mrs. Cecelia Horn, aged 23; Apollos Leonard, aged 54.—At Philadelphia, Mr. Mordecai Lewis, aged 51.

Vol. VII (No. 314) Monday, 8 April 1799.

† [1c-2a] Extensive biography of Dr. Timothy Dwight, "the accomplished President of a Connecticut Seminary," who was born in Northampton, Mass., in May 1752. ♦
† [3d] Samuel Salter of Walpole advertises property for sale at Westmoreland "near the baptist Meeting House," dated 4 April 1799.
† [3d] List of letters remaining in the Post Office at Walpole, N.H., on the first day of April, 1799, as compiled by John Hubbard, Postmaster:

Capt. Simon Baxter,	Surry, N.H.	Elijah Pease,	Andover, Vt.
Jacob Brandegee,	Castleton, Vt.	William Ramsey,	Walpole, N.H.
Isaac Bullard,	Walpole, N.H.	Sylvanus Sampson,	Chesterfield, N.H.
Dr. John Field,	Surry, N.H.	Samuel West, Esq.	Walpole, N.H.
Isaac Gates,	Acworth, N.H.	Thomas Wilder,	Lempster, N.H.
Vriling Lovell,	Rockingham, Vt.	Jesse Willcox,	Newport, N.H.
Joshua Osgood,	Sullivan, N.H.	Daniel Williams,	Alstead, N.H.

† [3d] List of letters remaining in the Post Office at Charlestown, N.H., on the first day of April, 1799, as compiled by Samuel Crosby, Postmaster:

William Baker	Charlestown, N.H.	Josiah Raymond,	(supposed) Acworth.
Isaac Butterfield,	Westmoreland, N.H.	Widow Hepzibah Reed,	(supposed) Walpole.
Thomas Colcord,	Springfield, Vt.	Isaac Smith,	Springfield, Vt.
Joseph Ellis,	" "	Josiah Stevens, Esq.	Newport.
Isaac H. Ely,	Charlestown, N.H.	Samuel S. West,	Acworth.
Daniel Graves,	Springfield, Vt.	John White,	Westmoreland.
Jonathan Gliden, Esq.	Unity	Capt. Ebenezer Wheelwright,	Newport.

¶ [3d] MARRIED.]—At Lee, N.H. Capt. John F. Parrot to Miss Hannah Parker.—At Marshfield, Mr. Abner Williamson to Mrs. Sally Thomas.—At Danvers, Mr. Charles W. Symonds to Miss Content Purington.—At Bridgton, Mr. Joseph Fitch to Miss Sally Knap; Mr. Simeon Burnham to Miss Lucy Smith.—At Otisfield, Mr. Thomas Peabody to Miss Polly Read.

¶ [3d] DIED.]—At Berwick, Ms. 13 Hon. Benjamin Chadbourne, Esq. aged 82.—At Rehoboth, Rev. John Hix, aged [88?].—At Plymouth, Mr. Nathaniel Morton, aged 91.—At Foxborough, Mr. John Everett, aged 63.—At Marshfield, Mr. Samuel Little, aged 74.—At Dorchester, Mr. Isaac Davenport, aged 69.—At Boston, Mr. William Sylvester, aged 29; Mrs. Hannah Chapman, aged 71; Mrs. Sarah Skinner, aged 85; Mrs. Anna Joy, aged 33.—At Marblehead, Mrs. Tabitha Green, aged 25.—At Cape Elizabeth, Capt. Samuel Skillings, aged 96.—At Wiscassett, Miss Betsey Precy, aged 57.

Vol. VII (No. 315) Monday, 15 April 1799.

† [1a] Josiah Bowtell, involved with "House, Sign, or Carpet Painting," informs the public that "he has recovered his health, in so great a measure, that he is now able to pursue his business . . ." Dated at Charlestown, 2 April 1799.
† [1b-c] Biography of Col. David Humphreys, who was born at Derby, Conn., "about the year 1752 or 53." ♦
† [1a] Isaac Butterfield found a pair of lost oxen; adv. dated Westmoreland, 9 Apr '99.

Vol. VII (No. 316) Monday, 22 April 1799.

† [1a] Justin & Elias Lyman advertise items for sale, dated at Hartford, [Conn.—Ed.] 30 March 1799, where they also "continue to transact Commission Business; also the boating business up and down Connecticut River as usual; likewise they have coasting vessels that will constantly ply between this, New York and Boston."
† [3d] John Harper advertises a farm for sale; dated at Charlestown, 4 April 1799.
† [3d] List of letters remaining in the Post Office at Westminster, Vt., on the first day of April, 1799, as compiled by Eleazer May, Postmaster:

Samuel Avery,	Westminster, 2	John Gilman,	Rockingham, 2.
William Bemis,	"	John Palmer,	Guildford [sic].

List of letters at the Post Office, Westminster, Vt. (*continued*) :

Thomas Barron,	Westminster	Joseph Parmerter,	Westminster.
Thomas Fuller,	"	John Lock,	"
Levi Goodridge,	"	Noah Wiswall,	"

† [3d] Aaron Matson, Isaac Baker, and Elisha Huntley, Selectmen of Marlow, N.H., post notice that Mary Sawyer, a pauper, "has eloped from her bed and board, appointed her." Dated at Marlow, 10 April 1799. [*see also issue of 29 April 1799.*]

Vol. VII (No. 317) Monday, 29 April 1799.

† [1c-d] An "American Biography" of Dr. Elihu Hubbard Smith, Physician, a native of Litchfield, Conn. ♦

† [2d] Article containing an update of the insurrection in Pennsylvania, dated at Philadelphia, 10 April, which chronicles the arrest of John Fries, John Everhard, and Jacob Huber. ♦

† [3b] Extract of a letter from a gentleman at Savannah, mentioning that Captain Stephen Colver, "has been continually engaged since my arrival at this place, in making preparations for raising the wrecks in this river." The editor inserted a footnote, claiming that Colver "is a native of Connecticut, and is the inventor of the machines for cleaning docks, rivers, &c, &c. which have been used in this place with success, and perhaps we may add, that he is one of the first mechanical geniuses in this country. These wrecks were sunk by the British during the late war, and were a great obstruction to the navigation of Savannah river."

† [3b] Mr. John Woodruff, in his 24th year, died from injuries received when he was thrown from his horse, at Morristown, New Jersey. ♦

† [3d] Brief article describing a fire which destroyed the "valuable dwellinghouse" of T. Chapman, Esq. of Greenfield, Mass.

¶ [3d] Died, lately, at Baltimore, after a short illness in the night, an elderly inhabitant, aged 86 years, and one the very same night; his daughter, one of his grand daughters, and one of his great grand daughters, also died; and to render the whole still more extraordinary, his wife was delivered of a son on the same night.

¶ [3d] Died, in October, 1797, in a small village, near Bergen, in Norway, Joseph Surrington in the 160th year of his age. He retained the perfect use of his senses until the last hour of his life. The day before he died, he assembled his family and divided his property amongst them. He had been several times married, and left behind him a young widow and several children. His eldest son is 103, and his youngest nine years of age.

¶ [3d] Last week, a daughter of Mr. Simon Willard, of Lancaster, was accidentally shot by a younger brother, who had just prepared his gun for game; after having adjusted the flint, and shut the pan, being full cocked, it unfortunately went off; the contents entered just under the eye, and instantaneous death was the consequence.

† [3d] Legal notice regarding the estate of Jean Rogers, late of Acworth, deceased, Jonathan Rogers and John Rogers, Administrators; dated Acworth, 20 April 1799.

† [3d] Elisha Huntley and Isaac Baker post notice that Caroline Sawyer, a pauper, "eloped from her bed and board, provided her by the town of Marlow." Dated at Marlow, 23 April 1799. 14

¶ [3d] Whereas my Wife Betsey, has eloped from my bed and board, and refuses to return, I therefore forbid all persons harbouring or trusting her on my account, for I will not pay any debts of her contracting after this date.

                                                        his
                                     Stephen X Lang.
Wendal, April 14th, 1799.   mark

¶ [3d] MARRIED.]—At Northampton, Capt. Antipas Brigham to Miss Julia Whitney.—At Reading, Dr. Nahum Fay, of Boston, to Miss Mary Putnam, of the former place.—At Dorchester, Mr. John Beadle to Miss Sukey Wilson.—Mr. James Cristie, of Norfolk, V. to Miss Esther Mosely.—At Bedford, Mr. Bradley Bowers to Miss Fanny Lane.

¶ [3d] DIED.]—Boston, Mrs. Mary Lowell, aged 84. Mr. Nathaniel Torrey, aged 32. Mrs. Alice Whittemore, aged 56. Mr. Nicholas Ferriter, aged 58. Mrs. Rhoda Davis, aged 40. Timothy Newell, Esq. aged 81.—Salem, Mrs. Elizabeth Derby, aged 64.—New York, Col. William Duer.—Sutton, Matt. Harvey, Esq. aged 50.—Concord, Mr. Isaac Abbot, aged 51.—Berwick, Mrs. Ch. Key, aged 95, she had eight brothers and sisters, four of whom are deceased, whose ages were 98, 95, 65, and 60—the four living 88, 83, 81, 79.—At Pomfret, C. Capt. William Cargill, of Northumberland, in this state, aged 40.—Portsmouth, Mrs. Rousselet, aged 35. Mr. William Yeaton, aged 63.—Machias, Mr. James Avery, aged 40.—Charlton, Caleb Ammidown, Esq. aged 62.—Marblehead, Mrs. Mary Orne, relict of the Hon. Azor Orne, Esq. aged 58.

Vol. VII (No. 318) Monday, 6 May 1799.

† [3a] Various news reports contained under the dateline of Philadelphia, Penn., 17 April, including an item relating to the insurrection in that state:

"A detachment of Cavalry under the command of Lieutenant Melbecke, arrived in town from Northampton, yesterday morning, with the following prisoners who have been lately lodged in jail:

Jacob Kline, G. Getman, A. Breish, C. Stock, V. Kuder, John Kline, W. German, John Getman, Jacob Huber, Fred. Hainey, John Huber, D. Kline, John Smyer, D. Swartz, John Kyser, Peter Keiser, Henry Stekler, A. Stalneaker, H. Shiffert.

Judge Peters, and Colonel Nichols, the Marshal, arrived with the detachment, which left Allentown early on Wednesday morning, when the cavalry were paraded and ready to march, but it was not positively known where, although it was conjectured towards Reading, which it was supposed would be taken in the route home. The artillery and infantry had moved on the day before." 15

† [3b-c] Description of a fire at Philadelphia, giving the names of owners and occupants of the many building destroyed. ◆

¶ [3d] HARTFORD, CONNECTICUT. April 29. The remains of Mrs. Phelps, who was drowned in Connecticut River, between Northampton and Hadley on the 20th of January 1798, were on Monday last found on the bank of the river, at East Windsor. They were carried to Stafford and decently buried. [*see issue of 30 Jan. 1798*]

¶ [3c] PORTSMOUTH, NEW HAMPSHIRE. April 9. DIED, At Kittery, (Mass.) Mr. James Hanscom, by the bite of a mad dog, which he received about three weeks previous to his death. The bite was in his finger; it had healed entirely up, and he attended to his carpenter's work as usual, without feeling any injury from the place infected, until a few days before his death, when he complained of his hand and arm feeling strangely; symptoms of the hydrophobia soon succeeded, and increased with such violence that he sprang in a second of time directly through a glass window, and carried casement, sash and glass out with him.

We hear that a Mrs. Hanscom, cousin to the above man, was bitten by the same dog, and also many cattle, swine, dogs, sheep, &c. One excellent fat ox, six hogs, some sheep and other creatures are already dead. Several dogs have run mad and been shot in the above town within ten days.

¶ [3d] MARRIED.]—At Philadelphia, Mr. Henry Sweitzer, to Miss Polly Kugler.—At Westford, Ms. Capt. Joseph Swasey, to Miss Polly Stoddard. At Lenox, Capt. Denison, to Miss E. Hide.—At Medford, Mr. Samuel Gray, of Salem, to Miss Mary Brooks.—At Lynn, Mr. Nathaniel Maffay [or *Massay*?], to Miss Elizabeth Mansfield.—At New York, [?]. 16 Mr. S. Murgatroyd, to Miss. Gouverneur.—At Dedham, Mr. Isaac Felton, to Miss Ann Richards.

¶ [3d] DIED.]—At Paris, Thomas Muir, the celebrated Scotch revolutionist.—At London, 30th Dec. Thomas Boylston, Esq. aged 78, a native of Boston.—At Pomfret, C. Capt. Amasa Sessions, aged 84.—At Salem, Capt. William Goodhue, aged 84. Mrs. Sarah Pope and her daughter, Mrs. Ann Cheever, Mrs. Abigail Hewster.—At Foxborough, Dr. Joshua Wood, aged 74.—At Mansfield, Mrs. Abigail Leonard, aged 77. At Tiverton, Mrs. Sarah Bowen, aged 91, for many years a public speaker, among friends. At Foxborough, Lt. S. Billings, aged 40. At Barnstable, the Hon. Daniel Davis, Esq. aged 86. At Worthington, Rev. Nathan Fenn, aged [50?]. At Guilford, C. Mrs. Sarah Bray.

Vol. VII (No. 319) Monday, 13 May 1799.

† [3a] Article dated at Smithfield, North Carolina, describing a vessel built by Messrs. William and Henry Guy, far up the Neuse river in that state. ♦

¶ [3b] PHILADELPHIA, PENNSYLVANIA. April 26. The Grand Jury of the Circuit Court of the United States, now sitting in Philadelphia, have found bills against the following persons:

FOR TREASON.—John Fries, Frederick Heany, Anthony Stahler, Conrad Marks, John Gettman, Valentine Kuder, David Shaefer, Jacob Klien and Philip Disk.

FOR MISDEMEANOR.—Morris Llewellyn, James Jackson, George Britson, Samuel Young, and Artchibald Mentges.

† [3b] Article under the dateline of Hartford, Conn., 6 May 1799, regarding the drowning of six persons at Wilbraham, Mass., viz. "Gurdon Bliss, Leonard Bliss, and their Sister—a daughter of Dr. Merrick, Catherine Warrener, all of Wilbraham, and Guy Johnson, of Tolland." The event occurred "on Monday last." ♦

† [3c-d] An item contained in the *Incidents at Home* column: "The massacre, which took place on board the ship Ocean, a short time since, has received confirmation strong. After an engagement of many hours with two French privateers, a French brig hove in sight, to which the Ocean struck. She was then boarded, and Capt. Kemp was immediately murdered, and a general massacre of the crew took place. Three of our countrymen escaped by concealing themselves in the hold, and were the only persons who were saved from the swords of this piratical and merciless banditti."

† [3d] Legal notice posted by Daniel Farr, Executor of the estate of Deacon Daniel Farr, late of Chesterfield, deceased. Dated at Baltimore, Vermont, 7 May 1799.

¶ [3d] MARRIED.]—At Philadelphia, Mr. William Innes, to Miss Isabella Innes of that city; Mr. Samuel Dewers, to Miss Eliza M'Kean both of that city.—At Boston, Edward St. Loe Livermore, Esq. of Portsmouth, N.H. to Miss Sarah Crese Stackpole, daughter of Mr. William Stackpole, of Boston; Mr. Benjamin Sumner, housewright, to Miss Sarah Clough; Mr. Charles Hallowell, to Mrs. Lois Miller.

¶ [3d] DIED.]—In England, Vice Admiral Thompson, the Earl of Essex.—In France, Rear Admiral Richery, aged 41.—At Rome, French General Rey, of wounds he received at the taking of Naples.—At Newport, R.I. Major John Breeze, British Consul.—At Ipswich Mass. Rev. John Cleveland.—At Salem, Mr. S. Symonds, aged 87.—At Concord, Mass. Major Abishai Brown, aged 53.—At Cambridge, Mass. widow Marsa [sic] Nutting, aged 99.—At Lyme, Con. Matthew Griswold, Esq. aged 84, formerly governor of that state. At St. Johns, N.B. Mrs. Mary Bliss, aged 40, daughter of the Hon. John Worthington of Springfield, Mass.—At Boston, Mr. Ezekiel Tileston, formerly of Dorchester; Mrs. Mary Shattuck, aged 78; Mrs. Anna English, aged 42. At Northborough, Mass. Mr. Samuel Allen, aged 79. At Spencer, Mr. William Green, aged 83. At Westmoreland, N.H. Mr. Nehemiah Howe, aged 33.

Vol. VII (No. 320) Monday, 20 May 1799.

† [3a-b] Account of fire "on Saturday morning last," under dateline of Boston, 13 May, which destroyed many houses: "Mr. John Jarvis owned eight; Mr. Abraham Adams, two; Mrs. Hannah Hunt, one; Miss Inches, one; and Miss Polly Yorkus one.—Messrs. Merckell, Cole, Childs, T. Pease, junr. Wheelwright, Kenny, Graupner, J. Mitchel, J. Brewer, L.D. Goy, H. Fulerton, S. Adams, and Mrs. Hunt, were the occupants."

† [3d] Article regarding rabid dogs in the vicinity of Claremont, N.H., including the mention of an unnamed child "bit in Cornish, about two months ago, we hear is dead."

† [3d] Isaac Foster posts a legal notice stating that he has been appointed Guardian over Walter Himes, of Acworth; dated there 15 May 1799.

† [3d] *Hayward & Daniels* announce that their Copartnership is dissolved; dated at Westmoreland, 15 March 1799.

¶ [4d] In the Wilmington Advertiser, of the 29th ult. a negro man, named Phil, and *aged one hundred and thirty two years*, is advertised as *running* away from his master. He is described to be about five feet, eight inches high, has a good set of teeth, &c. It is supposed he will try to get his *wife* with him.

¶ [3d] MARRIED.]—At Boston, Mr. Thomas Otis, to Miss Charlotte Downes. Mr. Francis Barrett, to Miss Maria F. [Pallucar?]=At Baltimore, Philip Moore, Esq. to Miss Delia Hall.—At Newyork, Mr. John Hunter to Miss Elizabeth [Desbrosses?]

¶ [3d] DIED.]—At Bridgwater, Mrs. Elizabeth Mitchell, aged 65.—At Fairfield, Mrs. Sarah Squire, aged 43.—At Spencer, Mr. William Green, aged 83. In prison, at Newyork, Col. William Duer, aged 54.—At Savannah, Mr. George Lamb, aged 29.—At Newport, R.I. John Breese, Esq. his Britannic Majesty's vice consul for Rhode Island.—At Hingham, Mrs. Anna Thaxter, aged 80.—At Boston, Miss Fanny Hovey, aged 21, daughter of Doctor I. Hovey, of Berwick, (Me.) Capt. Joseph Loring, aged 48. Mrs. Isabella Wallace, aged 44. Mrs. Elizbaeth M'Ellory, aged 90. Mr. James Cutter, aged 32. Mrs. Sarah Low, aged 26. Mrs. Charlotte Fosdic, aged 32. Mr. Thomas Adams, late editor of the Chronicle, aged 41. Mrs. Elizabeth Clark, aged 54.

Vol. VII (No. 321) Monday, 27 May 1799.

† [3a] A brief notice of a "Quarry of Plaister of Paris" discovered on the farm of Mr. John Dill, in York county, about ten miles from Carlisle, Pennsylvania.

¶ [3a] KEENE, NEW HAMPSHIRE, May 18. On Friday morning, 10th inst. about sunrise, Mr. John Converse, of Marlborough, in this county, was found hanging by a rope which was fastened to the top of a loom in one of the rooms in his house. He was a man of respectability and a good neighbour—about 60 years of age. A jury of inquest was summoned—their verdict, insanity. He has left a wife and several children.

† [3c] Petition, dated 7 Feb. 1799, to the Supreme Court of Judicature of Vermont, (Windham County,) by Anna Blanchard of Rockingham, Vermont, for divorce from her husband, William Blanchard, Jr. of Rockingham. Mrs. Blanchard claimed that her husband "hath consorted with divers women of loose and vicious character—more especially with one Martha Adams, commonly called Pat Adams, with whom he has lately fled in company, and now lives in open barefaced adultery, and hath ever since the month of March last past totally abandoned your Orator . . . " William and Anna Blanchard were married 20 March 1790, by Jahiel Webb of Rockingham, Justice of the Peace for Windham County.

† [3c] Petition for divorce, dated 25 Jan. 1799 at Wilmington, Vt,. to the Supreme Court of Judicature of Vermont, (Windham County,) by Anna Wood, "now wife of Benjamin L. Wood, late of Marlborough," Vermont. Mrs. Wood claimed her husband abandoned her more than [three?] years ago and fled to parts unknown, and had not supported "his infant child by said marriage." The petitioner also stated that she was the daughter of Ameriah Parks, late of Marlborough, deceased, and refers to his estate "not yet being settled and divided according to law." Benjamin L. Wood and Anna Parks were married 4 Dec. 1794 by Rev. Hezekiah Taylor, minister of the gospel in Newfane, Vt.

† [3c] Petition for divorce, dated 24 Feb. 1799 at Marlborough, Vt., to the Supreme Court of Judicature of Vt., (Windham County,) by Deliverance Wright, "now wife of John Wright late of said Marlborough." Mrs. Wright stated that they were married 17 Sept. 1781 in Boylston, Mass. by Rev. Ebenezer Morse, and that her husband abandoned her more than three years ago, and believed that Mr. Wright had left Vermont.

† [3d] Thomas C. Drew offers reward for a plough which was stolen from "the tavern, formerly occupied by Mr. Johnson" in Walpole; dated 25 May 1799.

† [3d] Cornelius Sturtevant offers printing press for sale; dated Keene, 27 May 1799.

† [3d] Announcement of a Masonic celebration at Chester, Vt., by Ezekiel Colburn, Secretary, with Br. Joab Young and Br. Martin Field expected to speak.

¶ [3d] Notice is hereby given by the Subscriber to those who owe him or have settlements to make with him, that he resides at the house of Capt. J. Holton, in Charlestown, where he will be happy to attend upon them. As the place is of public notoriety, none can execuse [sic] themselves from not knowing where to find him. Should this notice be neglected, they may probably be called to his head quarters in a very disagreeable manner.

Caleb Hunt.

N.B. The creditors of the subscriber are notified that he is already committed, and intends no escape.

Charlestown, May 24, 1799.

¶ [3c] MARRIED.]—At Beverly, Capt. Wallis to Miss Sarah Adams.—At Pepperell, Mr. Henry Bass, jun. of Boston, to Miss Eliza Bullard, of the former place.—At Boston, Charles Paine, Esq. to Miss Sally Cushing. Mr. Alexander Lovett to Miss Hannah Williston. Mr. Willard Clark to Miss Nancy Gould.

¶ [3c] DIED.]—At New Boston, Mr. Solomon Dodge aged 51.—At Philadelphia, Sharp Delary, Esq.—At Bradford, Mass. Mrs. Martha Thurston.—At Cohasset, Mr. William Whittington, aged 80.—At Grafton, Mass. Mr. Joseph Willard, aged 79.—At Leicester, Mrs. E. Livermore, aged 78.—At Haverhill, Col. David Hobart, aged 76. At Cambridge, Miss Sarah Tappan. At Boston, Mr. John Sturgis aegd [sic] 42.

Vol. VII (No. 322) Monday, 3 June 1799.

† [2c-d] Account from Baltimore, Md. of a "poor disconsolate woman, seemingly delirious, with a beautiful female infant, about five months old," who jumped off a wharf with her child, but both were rescued and brought to the house of Godfrey Hartung. The woman later committed suicide, and was "said to be the wife of a man named Boice, who sailed from this port about 18 months since, and the reason assigned for the above melancholy accident, is the report of his loss at sea. Mrs. Hartung, at present has the child under her protection." Article contained in Baltimore dateline, 17 May. ♦

† [3d] Isaac Abbot adv. goods for sale at his store in Chesterfield, dated 27 May 1799.

¶ [3d] MARRIED.]—At Dorchester, Mr. Joshua Vose, of Boston, to Miss Betsey Lovell, of the former place.—At Newton, Mr. Philip Peak, of Boston, to Miss Catharine Clous, of the former place.

¶ [3d] DIED.]—At Lexington, on the 19th inst. Miss Abigail Fisk, aged 19 and on the 22d Miss Mary Fisk, aged [24?] daughters of Doct. David Fisk—Two very promising young persons.

Vol. VII (No. 323) Monday, 10 June 1799.

† [3d] Poem contained in the *Incidents at Home* column, in reference to a notice published in a Boston paper "of the 5th inst.," regarding the runaway notice of Delia, the wife of Thomas Williams, a black man.

† [3d] Account of the ordination of Rev. Josiah Prentice, at Northwood, N.H., 29 May 1799. Sermons presented by Rev. Mr. Lanckton of Alstead, Rev. Mr. Smith of Gilmanton, Rev. Mr. Coe of Durham, Rev. Mr. Upham of Deerfield, Rev. Mr. Hazeltine of Epsom, and Rev. Mr. Colbee of Pembroke.

† [3d] Adv. by John Hubbard, regarding his Apothecary Store in Walpole, N.H.

† [3d] Ephraim Lane offers grist and saw mills for sale at Walpole, dated 8 June 1799.

† [3d] Elisha Kingsbery offers one cent reward for the return of Horace Taylor, "an indented boy" who ran away 2 June 1799.

¶ [3d] MARRIED.]—At Augusta (Georgia) Doct. M. Burke, of Savannah to Miss Betsey Elbert, daughter of the late Gen. Elbert.—At Philadelphia, Captain John Henry, of the 2d regiment of artillerists and engineers, stationed at Fort Jay, to Miss Sophia Duche, daughter of the late Rev. Jacob Duche, of Philadelphia.

¶ [3d] DIED.]—At Baltimore, Col. Joshua Stevenson, at an advanced age. At Kent, (Maryland) John L. Wilmer, Esq. aged 52. At Richmond, (Virginia) Captain Daniel Pierce, of Pembroke, Mass.

Vol. VII (No. 324) Monday, 17 June 1799.

† [2d] Account of a gunpowder explosion at the store owned by Mr. Henry Fulton, of Harrisburgh, 17 Virginia, on the 14th of May 1799. ♦

† [3d] Announcement by Gurdon H[u]ntington, Secretary of the Masonic Lodge in Westmoreland, of a upcoming festival, with Rev. Mr. Wood, of Chesterfield and Br. B. White to speak. Dated at Walpole, 11 June "5799."

† [3d] Thomas Slader and Samuel Finlay appointed guardians over William Lyons of Acworth, N.H.; dated there 12 June 1799.

† [3d] Advertisement by Thomas K. Green, merchant, dated Westmoreland, 10 June.

¶ [3d] DIED.]—In Newjersey, Michael D. Henry, Esq. attorney and counsellor at law, of Newyork. At Newyork, Mrs. Terentie Varrick, wife of Mr. Abraham Varrick. At East Windsor, (Con.) William Wolcott, Esq. aged 88. At North Bolton, Mr. John Daniels, aged 60. At Stamford, Rev. Dr. Eben. Biddle, aged 84. At Boston, Mr. Charles Baxter, aged 31; Mr. John Gardner, aged 58; Mrs. Johama [sic] Cunningham, aged 73. At Brimfield, (Mass.) Mr. Noah Hitchcock, aged 84. At Dorchester, Mr. Abner Clapp, aged 65. At Roxbury, Mass. on the 7th inst. His Excellency Increase Sumner, Esq. Governour of that Commonwealth, in the 53d year of his age.

Vol. VII (No. 325) Monday, 24 June 1799.

† [2d] Descriptive account of the suicide of Mr. Peter Benicue, Innkeeper at Baltimore, Maryland, on the 4th of June 1799. ◆
† [3a] Murder-suicide of Mr. Treadwell Jackson and wife, "near Brooklyn, Longisland," on the 6th of June 1799. Article contained under the dateline of New York. ◆
† [3a] Scant account of the loss of the *Ontario*, of New York, Captain Wheaton, which ship was wrecked on or near the Cape of Good Hope, but the crew was all saved. Article contained under the New York head, dated 11 June. ◆
† [3a] Chronicle of the fateful voyage, and bare survival of the crew of the *Speedwell*, Capt. Howland. The home port is not specified, though the article is contained in the New York news. The ship had been on a voyage for two years, returning from the Faulkland Islands with seal skins and oil, but wrecked "when she went on the west bank, near the Light House." ◆
† [3d] Moses Johnson adv. goods for sale at his "store in Walpole, and in Keene."
† [3d] Joshua Hale proposes to hold a meeting "at the house of Thomas Redington, Innholder, in Walpole," regarding the problem of certain persons who had constructed dams on the Connecticut River, which "wholly stop[p]ed the course of Salmon and Shad." Notice dated at Walpole, 22 June 1799. In the following week's issue, a duplicate notice appears at [1a], though the name of Asa Gage also appears with the name of Joshua Hale.

Vol. VII (No. 326) Monday, 1 July 1799.

† [3d] Reward offered for the return of Pardon Smith, who broke jail at Providence, Rhode Island, 18 June 1799. Smith was about 28 years old, a native of Smithfield, and was convicted of conterfeiting. The notice contains a description of the prisoner. ◆

¶ [3d] MELANCHOLY ACCIDENTS.

Last Saturday, as a young man by the name of Fisher was prying up the stump of a tree, in Keene, with a lever, it suddenly lost its hold and bounded against his breast, which put an immediate end to his existence.

At Hanover, we learn, that as a Mr. Russell was driving a refractory bull in his pasture, the bull suddenly made at him and after parrying for some time ineffectually, the butting of his horns, he struck them into the abdomen of Mr. Russell, and his bowels, came out of the wound. Surgical assistance was immediately administered; but with what success we have not yet learnt.

In this town, on Sunday last, a number of persons went to the river to bathe. Among the rest was Mr. George Burt, of Petersham, Massachusetts, about eighteen years of age. Not being apprised of the depth of the water, he jumped from the boat and soon sunk. The panic which such an accident generally occasions rendered every attempt to save his life abortive. A few hours after his body was found, and on the next day interred in the village burying ground.

¶ [3d] DIED.]—At Limerick, Joseph Gilpatrick Esq. At Kennebunk, Dr. Edward Watts, of Portland, aged 63. At Dover, Col. Benjamin Titcomb. At Canterbury, Deacon David Morrill, aged 65. At Portsmouth, Miss Sarah Lunt, aged 3[0?]. At Shrewsbury, Widow Lois Wheeler, aged 89. At Holden, Mr. John Abbot, aged 61. At Standish, Dr. Isaac S. Thompson. At Newyork, Mr. Stephen Woollis, aged 70, Comedian.

Vol. VII (No. 327) Monday, 8 July 1799.

† [3d] Josiah Fay offers reward for a mare which was lost or stolen "out of Judge Burt's pasture, near Bellows's Falls, in Westminster." Dated at Windsor, 7 July 1799.

† [3d] List of letters remaining in the Post Office at Walpole, N.H., on the first day of July, 1799. This notice does not contain the name of the Postmaster. However, in the following week's issue, this list is duplicated, and includes the name of the Postmaster, Alex. Thomas:

Dr. Lyman Spalding,	Walpole.	Samuel Slade,	Alstead.
Silas Newcomb, four,	"	William Crosby, Esq.	Milford, N.H.
Joab Pond,	"	Jotham Shephard,	"
Martin Jenison,	"	Elijah Pease,	Andover, Vt.
David Hogg,	"	Thomas Goldthwait,	Dalton, N.H.
Jeremiah Ballard,	Unity.	Joshua Osgood,	Sullivan.
Eli Partridge,	Chesterfield.	Simon Bullard,	Dublin.
Silvanus Sampson,	"	S.S. Roby,	Westmoreland.
Moses Smith, Esq.	"	Solomon Wilon [sic]	Chester, Vt.
Experience Storrs,	Westmoreland.	Jacob Brendegee,	Castleton, Vt.
Jonathan Winchester,	"	Gilbert Evans,	Rockingham, Vt.
Benjamin Baxter,	Alstead.	David Chase,	Dartmouth, N.H.

† [3d] Daniel Whipple found a lost horse "about a mile from Carpenter's tavern, on the road to Walpole street." Notice posted at Walpole, 6 July 1799.

¶ [3d] MARRIED.]—At Boston, Mr. Amasa Davis, Jun. to Miss Hannah Moore; Mr. Daniel Cole, to Miss Betsey Woods, of Groton. At Concord, N.H. Dr. Richard Hazeltine, to Miss Phebe Carter.

¶ [3d] DIED.]—At Altona, in Germany, Dr. John Augustus Unzer, a celebrated physician, aged 71:—At Plymouth, Mass. the Rev. Doct. Chandler Robbins, aged 60.—At Boston, Mrs. Mary Tufts, aged 7[?].

Vol. VII (No. 328) Monday, 15 July 1799.

† [2c] Account of an assassination attempt on John Arbuckle, an inhabitant of Petersburg, Virginia, by one Zachariah Tatum, "of Chesterfield." Arbuckle's wound supposed to have been mortal; article contained under the Petersburg head, 25 June. ◆

¶ [2d] NEWLONDON, CONNECTICUT, July 3. On Sunday last Henry Avery, son of Elder Christopher Avery, of Stonington, fell into Lantern Hill pond and was drowned. His body was taken up a few hours after, and buried the next day, when a sermon was delivered on the subject by Elder Paul Parks. Master Avery was a promising young man, being upwards of six feet in height, though not fifteen years of age until the 4th inst.

¶ [3a] GREENFIELD, MASSACHUSETTS. July 8. *Another sad warning to Fishermen.* Saturday about 11 o'clock, Mr. George Darling of Gill, was accidentally drowned.—Mr. Darling was fishing with a scoop net, from Rocky Island, in Montague Falls; the pole of his net accidentally striking a ladder which was placed against the dam above the rocks, occasioned his being instantly swept on, and all the exertions of the people present to save him were ineffectual. Mr. Darling was in the 39th year of his age, and has left a wife and seven children to lament his untimely death.

† [3d] Alexander Ralston advertises for his lost colts, dated at Keene, 10 July 1799.

† [3d] William Wilson found a mare; notice dated at Langdon, 10 July 1799.

¶ [3d] MARRIED.]—At Salem, Thomas Cushing, Esq. of Newton, to Miss Catharine Sewall Pynchon Orne. At Boston, Jonathan David, Esq. to Miss Mary Amory, youngest daughter of the late Thomas Amory, Esq.

Vol. VII (No. 329) Monday, 22 July 1799.

† [3d] Thomas Bliss advertises for a journeyman Cabinent maker; dated at Charlestown, [N.H.] 10 July 1799.

† [3d] List of nonresident taxpayers of Newport, N.H., for the year 1798, as compiled by Isaac Newton, Collector, 18 July 1799. Delinquent property to be auctioned off 17 Sept. next, at the house of Levi Prentiss, Innholder at Newport. Only the names of the property owner(s) are given here; the table in the newspaper includes tax data such as number of acres taxed, highway rate, etc.: Jere. Clement (5 lots), Ambros Coset and John Blodget, Sam. Crain's heirs, Thomas Bole's heirs (3 lots), and Josi[ah] Buel Jr.

Vol. VII (No. 330) Monday, 29 July 1799.

† [3d] Thomas Bellows found a stray cow; dated at Walpole, 27 July 1799.
† [3d] Moses Burt adv. a mare which strayed onto his property; dated Walpole 18 July.
† [3d] Daniel Caldwell offers reward for return of a stolen mare; dated Henniker 20 Jul.
† [3d] Samuel Joslyn offers for sale a farm "within thirty rods of the Meetinghouse, in Springfield, Vermont." Dated Springfield 29 July 1799.

¶ [3d] MARRIED.]—At Boston, Mr. Johnson Jackson to Miss Polly Nowell.—In this town, on Sunday, the 14th inst. Mr. David Stone to Miss Frances Bellows.

¶ [3d] DIED.]—At Salem, Capt. John Hodges, aged 76.—At Boston, Mrs. Ellen Brown, aged 69.—Mr. Andrew Green, aged 48.

Vol. VII (No. 331) Monday, 5 Aug. 1799.

† [3b] Account of the execution, at New York, of Joseph Perkins, a private in the first regiment of Artillerists and Engineers, who was shot 22 July 1799 for desertion. ♦
† [3c] Account of the sinking of a boat in the [Merrimack] river, at Haverhill, Mass., and the near drowning of Samuel Page and Dudley Bradley. ♦
† [3d] William Stephenson offers property for sale at Putney, Vermont, "which is now occupied as a Tavern." Advertisement contains description of property and location; dated at Putney 20 July 1799.
† [3d] Job Joslin offers a grist mill for sale at Putney, Vt.; dated there 2 July 1799.

Vol. VII (No. 332) Monday, 12 Aug. 1799.

† [1b] Notice by *Marsh & Oakes* that their Copartnership is dissolved by mutual consent; dated Rockingham, 3 Aug. 1799.
† [3b] News update, dated at New York 1 Aug., concerning the fate of the schooner *Nautillus*, "from this port to Curracoa." The schooner was overtaken by privateersmen, who murdered Capt. Dixon and several of the crew. The captain "had a family in Newyork."♦
† [3c] Obituary of John S. Sparhawk, A.M., who died at Andover, Mass. 29 July 1799, the son of Hon. Thomas Sparhawk, Esq. "of this town." ♦
† [3c] John Duncan posts notice that he was appointed guardian for Isaac Duncan of Acworth, N.H; dated there 9 Aug. 1799.
† [3d] Thomas Atker adv. the new "Walpole Bridge Hotel," at Bellows Falls, "lately built by F.W. Geyer, Esq."; dated at Walpole 5 Aug. 1799.
† [3d] Adv. by Jacob Marston of Montreal, who offers vast tracts of land for sale in Canada. John Hubbard, Esq. of Walpole also named as an informant.

¶ [3c] MARRIED.]—At Windham, C. Mr. William Pierce, of this town, to Miss Abigail Brewster, of the former place.

¶ [3c] DIED.]—At Rockingham, on the 7th inst. Mrs. Mary Whiting, the amiable consort of the Rev. Samuel Whiting. [. . .] Her conjugal affection, and her parental tenderness, endear her memory to her bereaved husband and children. [. . .]

Vol. VII (No. 333) Monday, 19 Aug. 1799.

† [1b] Public notice that Josiah Marsh has petitioned the General Court of N.H. for a "priviledge of erecting and maintaining a ferry at any suitable place, within four miles and a half mile, from the south line of Westmoreland, extending northerly" on the Connecticut River.

† [3b] Account of a fire at the home of Messrs. Abel and David Hammond, at Winchester, N.H., which destroyed the house and all contents, and killed a child two years old. "Old Mrs. Hammond" was badly burned, and her daughter, 18 years old, escaped. This event occurred 1 Aug. 1799, and is contained under the Keene head. ♦
† [3b] Daniel Thurber, aged about 14, son of Mr. Hezekiah Thurber, drowned in a pond at Richmond, N.H., "on Sunday morning last." The paragraph is contained under the Keene head, dated the 10th of August. ♦
† [3d] Amos Shepard requests all his debtors to pay up; dated Alstead, 14 Aug. 1799.
† [3d] List of nonresident proprietors and owners of land in Unity, N.H., with outstanding highway taxes for the year 1798, as compiled by Daniel Bingham, Collector. Delinquent property to be sold at auction 8 Oct. next, at the house of Abner Chase, Innholder at Unity. The notice in the newspaper gives a breakdown of each owner's lot size, range location, etc; the transcription below contains only the name of the property owner, and excludes the remainder of the tax data. The tax list specifically identifies these as "Original Prop[r]ietors Names."

John Sherburn	Daniel Moulton	Ebenezer Stephens
William Buswell	Samuel Colcord	Benning Wentworth
James Bean	Capt. John Judkins	Cornelius Clough
Thomas Scribner	John Lad	Samuel Judkins
Philip Huntoon	John Webster	"Proprietors' Lot"
Nathaniel French	Daniel Lad	Benjamin Huntoon

Vol. VII (No. 334) Monday, 26 Aug. 1799.

† [3d] Notice to Retailers and Carriage owners, posted by Samuel Crosby, "Collector of the Revenue, second Division, District of Newhampshire." Dated at the Office of Inspection, Charlestown, N.H., 15 Aug. 1799.
† [3d] Anthony Atwood, Postrider, adv. his delivery of newspapers; dated at Chester, [Vermont—Ed.], 9 Aug. 1799.
† [3d] William Lyons claims an appeal through the courts, regarding his being put under guardianship of Thomas Lader and Samuel Finlay, both of Acworth; dated there 19 Aug. 1799.
† [3d] Phinehas Parker adv. his "Clothier's Business," stating that he employed Mr. Stratton, who worked for him the past." Dated at Claremont, 15 Aug. 1799.
† [3d] Thomas Kimball adv. for his lost horse; dated Chester, [Vt.—Ed.] 16 Aug. 1799.
† [3d] Thomas & Isaac Redington request debtors to pay up; dated Walpole, 26 Aug.
† [3d] Moses Johnson "informs his friends and the public, that, as he is about closing his business in this town," and requests settlement of accounts; dated Walpole, 16 Aug.
¶ [3d] DIED.]—At Charlestown, on the evening of Friday last, much lamented, Col. Samuel Hunt.

Vol. VII (No. 335) Monday, 2 Sept. 1799.

† [1c-2a] Biography of Lemuel Hopkins, Physician and Poet, who was born in Waterbury, Conn., about 1755 or 56. ♦
† [3b] Brief account of the wreck of the Schooner *Patty,* "of Yarmouth," which was driven ashore in North Carolina. The vessel presumably drifted for a long time, as "every soul on board perished, and the bones of several persons were found in the hold. The article is contained under the head of Wilmington, N.C. ♦
† [3c] Mr. John Duncan, who lodged at the Greenwich Hotel, was robbed and beaten in New York City. Article contained in the New York news, under date of 19 Aug. ♦
† [3d] An amendment to the petition of Elizabeth Bingham, of Marlow, N.H., who petitioned the Court in May 1796 for divorce from her husband, Ripley Bingham, "late of said Marlow, yeoman," to whom she was married in Jan. 1781. The petitions claimed that he committed adultery and abandonment, the latter accusation stating that he had been absent "for the space of three years."
† [3d] Legal notice regarding the estate of Capt. Nathaniel Huntoon, late of Unity, NH, deceased, Charles Huntoon & Jonathan Glinden,[17A] Executors; dated Unity 16 Aug.
† [3d] *Bellows & Stone* request settlement of debts, and also make a reference to a cattle drive later in the fall. Dated at Walpole, 2 Sept. 1799.

¶ [3d] Whereas Mary, my wife, has eloped from my bed and board, and refuses to live with me, and has for more than three years now last past, refused to perform the duties of a wife; these are, therefore, to forbid all persons, harbouring or trusting her on my account, as I will not pay any debts of her contracting after this date.
Levi Davis.
Rockingham, August 26, 1799.

¶ [3d] DIED.]—At Philadelphia, Mrs. Maria Whiting, wife of Mr. George Whiting of that city.—At Newyork, I.A.B. Rozier, late consul of the French Republic at Newyork. —At Hartford, Capt. Ebenezer Barnard, aged 73.—At Sandisfield, Ms. the Rev. Ebenezer Mills, in the 90th year of his age.—At Boston, Mr. William Miller, aged 60.

Vol. VII (No. 336) Monday, 9 Sept. 1799.

† [3c] Account of the "Native Heroism" of Captain Charles Blunt, of the *Dianna*, [of Portsmouth, N.H.?] who outwitted French privateers in the Caribbean.◆
† [3d] Public notice stating that Frederick William Geyer and others have petitioned the General Court of New Hampshire, in order to form themselves into a Society for the purpose of erecting and constructing a Turnpike Road.
† [3d] A farm offered for sale, presumably in Walpole; informants are John Cross of Walpole and Jesse Streeter of Surry. Dated at Walpole 3 Sept. 1799.

¶ [3d] DIED.]—In this town, Miss Sukey Redington, aged 20.

Vol. VII (No. 337) Monday, 16 Sept. 1799.

† [3a] The body of Mr. James Reid, "a native of Maryland, and lately a resident of Newbern" discovered near Greenville, N.C.; supposed to have died of accidental death after appearing "for some days past to labour under a considerable derangement of mind. Article dated at Greenville, N.C., 26 July. ◆
† [3b] Two unnamed women killed in a tornado at Livermore, Maine; article dated Portland, "Massachusetts," 28 Aug. ◆
† [3d] Legal notice regarding the insolvent estate of Lucy Smith, late of Plainfield, N.H.; Isaac Williams, William Deen, and Job Stephens appointed Commissioners; dated at Plainfield 12 Aug. 1799.
† [3d] Moses Johnson adv. that he "is about to remove his whole stock in trade from Walpole to Keene, withing a few weeks . . . "; dated at Walpole 16 Sept. 1799.

Vol. VII (No. 338) Monday, 23 Sept. 1799.

† [1c-2a] Biography of Joel Barlow, Poet, who was born in Reading, Conn. ◆
† [3b] Account of the murders of Johnson and M'Farland, travellers killed "twelve miles west of the Muskingum." Article dated 19 August, Washington, Kentucky. ◆
† [3c] Brief paragraph mentioning the prevailing fever in Hartford, Conn., where "Mr. John Thomas and James Tupe, a foreigner, both died on Tuesday last." Article dated 9 Sept. 1799 at Hartford.

¶ [3c] NEWBURYPORT, MASSACHUSETTS. Sept. 18

Extract of a letter from Moses Brown, Esq. Commander of the United States' ship Merrimack, to Mr. William Bartlett, of this town, dated Aug. 20, '99.

"I suppose you will have heard of the fate of your ship Rose, ere you receive this—but perhaps not particulars. The inclosed list of killed, wounded, &c. is handed me by a Mr. Starks, as an authentic account. Capt. Chase behaved with the greatest bravery and conduct; but at last was overpowered and boarded.

"Capt. Chase, of the ship Rose, owned by Mr. W. Bartlet, of Newburyport was taken the beginning of the present month (Aug.) by the privateer L'Egypt Conquise, and after a brave defence of one hour and a half, was obliged to submit to superior force.

List of killed and wounded.

Killed—Benj. B. Dennison, mate; John Tyler, Samuel Foot, and Samuel Williams— the last of whom was shipped in Surrinam.

Wounded—Capt. Chase, slightly; Abel Hale, John Whiting,[18] Samuel Hopkinson, Francis Hill, Johnson Brockins, Moses Currier, Richard Long, Samuel Pearson, Wm.

Reed, Samuel West, Smith Adams, Thomas Kennison, Joseph Norton; John Stone, and a Dutchman, all doing well, except Hale and Whaling [19] [sic], who were severely hurt.

"Capt. Chase engaged 30 Americans from Cayenna to ship on board his vessel but they afterwards declined shipping. Capt. Chase is of opinion, that had they been in his ship he should have carried the privateer, as he had hulled her dangerously, before he was wounded."

¶ [3c] Account of lightning strikes in the vicinity of Leominster, Mass.: house of Mr. David Stearns of Milford struck. // Two cows belonging to Deac. David Wilder struck and killed. // "A girl by the name of Polly Stone, about twelve years of age, was struck down and not perceived to breath for twelve or fifteen minutes—she then revived after bleeding and is like to get well." // Lightning also struck the house of Mr. Eleazer Bullard, of Holliston. Article dated at Leominster, 19 June.

¶ [3d] We are informed that the following melancholy accident happened at Chesterfield on the 11th ult. A daughter of Mr. Elijah Burk, of that town, about eight years old, endeavouring to climb over a fence, her cloth[e]s caught, which precipitated a [loft?] upon her that put an immediate period to her existence.

¶ [3d] Public notice stating that Josiah Stevens and others have petitioned the General Court of N.H. to form themselves into a "Body Corporate" for the purpose of building a Turnpike road from Cornish Bridge to Amherst, N.H.

¶ [3d] Capt. Daniel Livermore and Joseph Lunt named on a list of nonresident owners of land in Springfield, N.H. who have not paid their County and Highway taxes for the year 1799. Delinquent property to be sold at public auction on the 2d of Dec. next, at the house of Samuel Clay, Innholder at Springfield. This list was compiled by Nathaniel Prentice, Collector, and dated 9 Sept. 1799. The notice in the newspaper gives a breakdown of each owner's lot size, lot number, etc.

¶ [3d] Stephen Thornton adv. his two mares that strayed; dated Acworth, 20 Sept.

¶ [3d] Runaway notice regarding Huldah Rice, wife of James Rice, dated Rockingham, 19 Sept. 1799.

¶ [3d] MARRIED.]—At Northampton, Ms. Mr. Noah Edwards, aged 77, to Mrs. Elizabeth Wright, aged 74.—At St. Johns, No. 3, Lt. Col. Thomas [Desbrisay?], of the Royal Artillery, to Miss Anna Bytes, daughter of the Rev. Dr. Bytes.

¶ [3d] DIED.]—At New Orleans, his Excellency Governour Gayoso.—At Newyork, Dr. Elisha Perkins, inventor of the celebrated Metallic Points.—At Salem, Elias Hasket Derby, Esq. aged 60.—At Windsor, Vt. Mrs. Hannah Thompson, aged 74.—At Woodstock, Vt. Dr. Standish Day.—At Boston, Caleb Hopkins, Esq. aged 73.—At Quincy, Mrs. Sarah Shaw, aged 75.

Vol. VII (No. 339) Monday, 30 Sept. 1799.

¶ [3a] FRANKFORT, KENTUCKY, August 22. By a gentleman who arrived in town last evening, we are informed, that those villains who broke the Danville jail (the Harps,) have added two more murders to thier [sic] black catalogue of crimes, since our accounts of last week, they went into a house belonging to a Mr. Graves, killed him and his son, and took their bodies from the house and threw them over the fence in some weeds, where they were found two or three days after, by the smell.

¶ [3c] An item, contained in the "Incidents at Home" column, mentioning a duel at Bristol, Penn., fought between Capt. Johnson and Lieut. Sharpe, of the 10th U.S. Regiment, in which the latter was killed and the former badly wounded.

¶ [3d] Legal notice regarding the insolvent estate of Dr. Ebenezer Wright, late of Plainfield, N.H., deceased. Charles Spalding, Joseph Kimball, and Lemuel Wellman appointed Commissioners over said estate; notice includes a schedule for meetings to be held at the house of Martha Wright in Plainfield. Dated at Plainfield, 24 Sept. 1799.

¶ [3d] Public notice from the General Court stating that John C. Chamberlain, and others, have petitioned said Court to form a Society for the purpose of building a Turnpike from Charlestown to Surry.

¶ [3d] William Heywood, Jun., adv. for his pocket book which he lost between Haverhill and Charlestown, [N.H.—Ed.], which contained a deed of a hundred acres of land in Lunenburg, Vt., signed by Jonathan Grout of Charlestown; dated Ch'stown 26 Sept.

¶ [3d] Elisha Eldredge advertises for his lost steer; dated Walpole, 30 Sept. 1799.

† [3d] List of letters remaining at the Post Office in Walpole, N.H., 30 Sept., 1799:

Danforth Clark,	Walpole.	Noah Sabin, 3d	Chesterfield.
Apollos Gilmore,	"	Moses Smith,	"
Gilbert Griswold,	"	James Roberson,	"
Orange Graves,	"	Aaron Farr,	Hinsdale.
Elijah Page,	"	Ebenezer Palmer,	Alstead.
William Lock,	"	Jno. & I. Roberson,	Surry.
Lazarus Warren,	"	Dr. John Longley,	Langdon.
Seth Briton,	Westmoreland.	John Waters, Esq.	Brookline, Vt.
Josiah Dodge, two,	"	Edward Stevens Esq.	"Newhampshire, up Connecticut river."]
Lt. John Chamberlain,	"		
Abiather Lincoln,	"		
David Lyon,	"	Capt. Jasiah [sic] Robbins,	Alstead.
Samuel Johnson,	"	Richard Ward,	Chester, Vt.
Abiather Shaw,	"	Eleazer Jackson Esq.	Chesterfield.

† [3d] Announcement that the copartnership of *Bellows & Stone* is dissolved, and that David Stone will carry on the business; dated at Walpole, 25 Sept. 1799.

Vol. VII (No. 340) Monday, 7 Oct. 1799.

† [3b] Article dated at Newbern, N.C., stating that "Gen. Dearborne of Massachusetts, arrived a few days ago at Shell Castle," with frames to construct a new light house on Cape Hatteras.

† [3b] A person calling himself Samuel Johnson arrested at Pittsburg, Penn., for burglary at the house of Mr. Thomas Bracken, but "on examination" this person was discovered to be a female, named Sarah Johnson, who was the mother of five children. Johnson was suspected to have been involved with a gang of horse thieves. ♦

¶ [3b-c] AMERICAN HEROISM. New York, Sept. 20. The ship Planter, Captain John Watts, of Richmond, on her passage to London, on the 10th of July, in lat. 29 2, long. 17 30, was chased by a lofty ship, with national colours, carrying 22 guns, twelves, nines and sixes, with small arms in the tops, and full of men. At four P.M. the Planter, finding she could not outsail her, had already for action, all her small sails down, courses up, boarding netting spread, &c. &c. At half-past five, she lay by for her, all hands giving 3 cheers. The privateer then bore down under the starboard quarter of the Planter, and fired one shot into her, which the latter, rounding to, immediately returned with a broadside. The action then commenced, and continued with a constant fire for two glasses and a half, when the privateer sheered off to repair damage, and in about one glass returned with the bloody flag hoisted, to board the Planter, who however, being in readiness, bore upon her with well directed broadsides of langrage and grape shot, which must have made great havock among the crowded decks of the enemy. This action continued three glasses, when the privateer sheered off, and stood to the southwest.

In this honourable instance of American bravery and skill, the passengers, Mr. M'Kennon and Mr. Hodgson, and Mrs. McDowell and Miss Mary Harley, participated equally with the crew; the former standing at their quarters with small arms, and the ladies conveying cartridges from the magazine to the deck, and afterwards humanely attended the wounded.

The privateer on sheering off, was seen heaving the dead bodies overboard in abundance. The Planter was prodigiously damaged in the hull and rigging, carried 12 ninepounders and six sixpounders, and 43 men.

The following is the list of killed and wounded:

Killed.—John Leetch, Samuel Hoffman, William Johnston, William Chester.

Wounded.—W. M'Kennon, passenger, Daniel Comb, 2d mate, D. Gordon, seaman, Henry Mason, do. William Bagnale, do. Goodwin Hill, do. John Brown, do. John Barrow, do.

These particulars are extracted from a letter written by Captain Watts, dated off Dover, July 15, and published in the London Star of July 18.

† [3d] Aaron Hutchinson, Esq. of Lebanon, N.H., offers two farms for sale, one the "late residence of Jacob Choate" in Enfield, N.H., the other "now occupied by Richard C. Everett, Esq." in Lancaster, N.H.

† [3d] Ebenezer Smith, of Durham, N.H., offers reward for his horse which strayed or was stolen; dated at Durham, 27 Aug. 1799.

† [3d] Legal notice regarding a lawsuit by Mary Cook of Shirley, Mass., against Sawtell Holden "late of Wardsborough North District," Windham County, Vt., "but now absconded to parts unknown."

¶ [3d] MARRIED.]—At Sturbridge, Mas. the Rev. Zenas Lockwood Leonard, to Miss Sally Fisher, second daughter of Deacon Henry Fisher, of that town.

¶ [3d] DIED.]—At Paris, France, the celebrated Beaumarchais.—In Savannah, Dr. Willson Goodwin.—On Staten Island, Capt. Ebenezer Messey, of the 2d U.S. regiment of artillerists.—At Fayette, Lieut. David Thompson, of the 2d U.S. regiment of artillerists; an officer universally beloved, and much respected.—At Hamilton, N.Y. Dr. Jonas Dix, formerly of Keene.—At Chester, Vt., Mr. John Lockwood, son in law to the Rev. Aaron Leland, aged 18.

Vol. VII (No. 341) Monday, 14 Oct. 1799.

¶ [2d] NORTHCAROLINA. *Raleigh*, September 17. We learn that the yellow fever is in Newbern—a person direct from that place informs us, that on Tuesday and Wednesday last, inclusive, 16 persons died. Mrs. Craddick has lost during the last week, the whole of her children, five in number—The inhabitants are flying in every direction. We hear also that the same disease is raging violently in Washington.

† [3a] Extract of a letter from a passenger aboard the ship *Mary Ann*, Capt. Knowles Adams, describing the capture of that ship by the French. The letter was dated at Cadiz, 30 July 1799, and printed under the New York head. ♦

† [3a] Account of the Connecticut trial of Isaac Williams, convicted of accepting from the French Republic, "a commission and instructions to commit acts of hostility and violence against the King of Great Britain and his subjects." ♦ Also a mention that the libel trial of Charles Holt, printer of the *Bee*, was postponed. These news items printed under the Hartford, Conn. heading.

† [3b] Sad account, contained under the news dated at Brattleborough, Vt. 7 Oct., of the death "on Tuesday evening last" of Betsey Ward, five year-old daughter of Abigail and the late Samuel Ward of Guilford, Vt. The child's clothes caught fire while she was tending her younger brother. The article also refers to the death of Samuel Ward two years previous. ♦

† [3c] Chronicle of a fire at the home of Mr. Asa Stebbins "of Deerfield" [probably *Mass.*—Ed.] on 29 Sept., in which the widow Cook, aged between 70 and 80, an occupant of the kitchen chamber, perished in the flames. The article is contained in the second paragraph of the news dated at Brattleborough, Vt., which begins in the previous column. ♦

† [3d] List of letters remaining at the Post Office in Westminster, Vt., 1 Oct. 1799, as compiled by Eleazer May, Postmaster:

>Rev. Asaph Rice Westminster, New England.
>Russel Underwood, Putney.
>Capt. Jesse Wilcox, Junr., Newport, New Hampshire.
>William Howard, Andover, Vermont.
>Lydia Barns, Westminster.
>John Currier, Junr. Kingston, N.H.
>Joshua Varney, Starkborough, Vt.
>Jabez Pain, Westminster.
>David Stickney, Grafton, Vt.
>Capt. Bissee, Randolph, Vt.

===== ¶ [3d] **MARRIED.** =====

Southcarolina.—At Charleston, Mr. William Watson to Miss Elizabeth Smith.

Newjersey.—At Princeton, Mr. Gabriel Jameson, to Miss Sally Thompson.—At Hopewell, Mr. Benjamin Burroughs, to Miss Sally Burroughs. Near Cranbury, Mr. Samuel Graves, to Miss Elizabeth Sylvester. At Cranbury, Mr. Andrew Vankirk, to Miss Catharine Hartupie.

Newyork.—Mr. John Arden, to Miss Mary Arden.
Rhodeisland.—At Providence, Mr. Hezekiah Harding, to Miss Sally Seamons: Mr. Thomas Caperhaum, to Miss Sally Black.

=== ¶ [3d] DIED. ===

In England, Rt. Hon. Earl Howe, Admiral of the fleet, and General of the Marines. Sir Peter Parker succeeds him.

Georgia.—At Savannah, Mr. Thomas Bailey, attorney at law, of Baltimore, Maryland.

Southcarolina.—At Charleston, Dr. Stephen Dickson, Fellow of the College of Physicians of Ireland, formerly State Physician of Ireland, and Professor of the Practice of Medicine in the University of Dublin; Mr. John Bennett, a native of Rhodeisland, aged 33; Mrs. Harriet Luscomb, lately from London, aged 28; Mr. Custeen Winn, in the 16th year of his age; Mr. John Singleton, much lamented; Mr. [Avris?] Ezell, aged 21; Mr. Alexander Steward Frink, a native of Preston, Connecticut; Mr. Matthew Jarman, aged 20, a native of Great Britain; Mrs. Jane Morrison, aged 31, she arrived from England about ten months ago. Mr. Horatio Gates Hall, a native of Maryland, and lately from Philadelphia, on his way to Georgia; Mr. Samuel Robinson, a native of Ireland. At Georgetown, Mrs. Elizabeth Dupre, a truly pious and religious lady.

Pennsylvania.—At Philadelphia, Mr William Weatherstine, in the 19th year of his age.

Newyork.—At Newyork, Mr. Robert Forster, late clerk in the office of the Commercial Advertiser; Mr. John Rogers; Miss Ann Field; Mr. John Riches; Mr. John Abernethy; Mr. Christopher [Beckman? or Beekman?], late clerk in the Post Office; At Poughkeepsie, Mr. Jeremiah Smith, of Newyork. At Rome, Mr. Zenas Gillet, of Hebron, Connecticut.

Connecticut.—At sea on board the United States brig Southcarolina, Mr. William Blodget Frink, aged 19, a native of Preston in this state.—At Hartford, Mrs. Sarah Hyde, wife of Mr. Ezra Hyde, aged 59.—At Bethlehem, Mr. Joshua Gitteau, aged 81.— At Coventry, Deacon Nathaniel Eells, aged 50.—At Newhaven, Mrs. Susannah Bonticou, aged 60.—Mr. Peter De Witt, aged 36.

Rhodeisland.—At Providence, Mrs. Sarah Geoffray, aged 31.

Massachusetts.—At Boston, Mr. John Morret, aged 68. Mrs. Mary Vaughan, aged 73; Mr. Ebenezer Blanchard, aged 33.

In this town on Saturday last, Mr. Ethan Griswold.

Vol. VII (No. 342) Monday, 21 Oct. 1799.

† [3b-c] Extract of a letter, dated 29 Sept. from aboard the ship London Packet, to the ship's owner, Mr. H. Goldsborough, of Baltimore, Md., describing an attack on the ship by a French privateer. One Mr. Lindsay, second mate, was killed and Capt. Anderson was wounded. The article is printed under the news dated at Baltimore. ◆

¶ [3d] Ran away from me the subscriber, on the 13th inst. my son, Elijah Randal in the fourteenth year of his age, all persons are forbid trusting or harbouring him on my account, as I will pay no debt of his contracting after this date.

Amos Randal.
Springfield, October 15, 1799.

=== ¶ [3d] MARRIED. ===

Massachusetts.—At Lancaster, Mr. Daniel G. Wheeler of Worcester, to Miss Eliza D. Sweetser of Lancaster. At Worcester, Rev. Leonard Woods, of Newbury, to Miss Abigail Wheeler, of Worcester.

=== ¶ [3d] DIED. ===

Connecticut.—At Farmington, Mr. Joseph Woodruff, in the 84th year of his age.

Massachusetts.—At Boston, Mr. Benjamin Cobb, sen. aged 74. Samuel Wells, Esq. aged 74. At Westborough, Mr. Warban Maynard, aged 20. At Cummington, Mr. William Ward, aged 65. At Southborough, Mrs. Ann Newton, aged 67. At Sturbridge, in a fit, Mr. James Shannon, a native of Ireland.

Vol. VII (No. 343) Monday, 28 Oct. 1799.

† [3b] Account of a ferry which sank in the river at Albany, N.Y., in which eight persons were drowned, viz.: "a Mr. Brooks, a Mr. Peter Ostrander, a Mr. Hagarty, and

two brothers, I. and N. Smith, all of Greenbush and Schodac—a young man of the name of Williams, from Cheshire, in Massachusetts, and the two ferrymen, one named William Lawrence, the other a Negro man belonging to Mr. Abraham Bloodgood." Rev. Mr. Comfort, Mr. Brooks (brother to the one that drowned) and a Mr. Salisbury were saved. ◆

† [3d] Legal notice regarding the insolvent estate of Levi Haskel, physician, late of Westmoreland, N.H., deceased. John Wheeler, Jr., Joseph Buffum, and David Hutchins were named Commissioners; the notice gave a schedule of estate business which was to be conducted "at the dwelling house of the widow of the deceased." Notice dated at Westmoreland, 20 Oct. 1799.

† [3d] One cent reward offered for Simon Powers, a seventeen year-old "indented boy" who ran away from James Meachem, Jr., on "the fourteenth instant," though the notice is dated 13 Oct. 1799, at Charlestown, [N.H.]

† [3d] William Lyons advertises two farms for sale at Acworth, N.H., and also posts a notice stating that "the Honourable Superior Court has liberated the subscriber from having guardians over him," and requesting his creditors to "have patience with him for a few days, and he will pay them honourably." Notice dated at Acworth, 26 Oct. 1799.

===== ¶ [3d] MARRIED. =====

Massachusetts.—At Boston, Mr. Dexter Dana, merchant, to Miss Sally Windship; Mr. William Jenks, of Cambridge, to Miss Betsey Russell, of Boston. At Littleton, Sampson Tuttle Esq. aged [62?], to Miss Rebecca Trowbridge, aged 19.

Vermont.—At Hartford, Mr. Robert Harn, to Miss Betsey Marsh, youngest daughter of Joseph Marsh, Esq. At Concord, Mr. Timothy Edson, of Charleston, S.C. to the amiable Miss Betsey Weatherby, daughter of Capt. Samuel Weatherby.

===== ¶ [3d] DIED. =====

Connecticut.—At Hartford, Capt. William Bull of Litchfield, aged 55. Mr. Isaac Tucker, aged [81?]. Widow Hannah Watson, aged 72. At Newhaven, Stephen Ball, Esq. aged 73.

Massachusetts.—At Boston, Mr. Archimedes Dickson, aged 35; Miss Lilley Field, aged 14; Mr. Samuel D. Phipps, aged [16?]. At Topsham, [*District of Maine*—Ed.], Mr. John Orr, aged 103. At Waltham, Mrs. Margaret Boies, wife of Mr. John Boies, aged 60.

Newhampshire.—At Cornish, the Hon. Moses Chase, aged 72. At Alstead, Mr. Isaac Caady, aged 69.

"Departed this life, on the 16th of October instant Mrs. Leland, the consort of the Rev. Aaron Leland, of Chester, V. By her death her surviving partner sustains the loss of an incomparable blessing of human life; her only surviving son, the loss of a kind and exemplary parent." [. . .]

Vol. VII (No. 344) Monday, 4 Nov. 1799.

† [3b] Account of a fire [22 Oct.] in Nantucket which broke out in Mr. Isaac Folgier's shop, which was destroyed, along with property belonging to Mr. Sylvanus Coffin.

† [3b] Brief article accounting the capture, by a French frigate, of vessel commanded by Capt. Pedrick, who was bound to Cayenne from Marblehead, [Mass.]. The article is printed under the head of news dated at Salem, Mass. ◆

† [3d] Henry Fitch offers a reward for the return of his lost mare, which strayed from Gen. Bellows' pasture in Walpole; notice dated at Walpole, [21?] Nov. 1799.

† [3d] Nathaniel Vilas adv. livestock which strayed onto his land; Alstead, 26 Oct. '99.

===== ¶ [3c] MARRIED. =====

Southcarolina.—At Charlestown, [sic] Nicholas Cruger, jun. Esq. of the Island of St. Croix, to Mrs. Anna Heywood, relict of the late Daniel Heywood, Esq.

Rhodeisland.—At Newport, Caleb Gardner, Esq. to Miss Mary Collins, daughter of the late Gov. Collins.

===== ¶ [3c] DIED. =====

Southcarolina.—At Charleston, Miss Nancy Murray, lately from New York.

Maryland.—At Georgetown, Mrs. Thomas, aged 107.

Newyork.—At Newyork, on the 13th inst. of the prevailing epidemic, Dr. William

Walton Winans, of Staten Island, aged 30: and on the 18th inst. of the same disease, Mrs. Mary Winans, the amiable consort of the above gentleman, aged 27.

Massachusetts.—At Boston, John Webb Checkley, Esq. Mrs. Hulda Archibald. At Salem, Mrs. Elizabeth Whittemore, aged 52.

Newhampshire.—At Portsmouth, Mr. Noah Paul at Kittery, Mr. Daniel Knight, aged 43. [20]

¶ [3d] **Ten Dollard Reward.**

Deserted from his furlough, Anson Parker, a private in the 16th U.S. Reg. of Infantry. He was born in Coventry, in the county of Tolland, and state of Connecticut, aged 21 years and 4 months. Six feet half inch high, brown complexion, grey eyes, and brown hair. Whoever will apprehend said Parker, and confine him in any prison within the United Sates, and give me or any officers in the line information of the same, will render his country a service, and he entitled to the above reward, and and [sic] all necessary charges paid.

Israel E. Trask, *Captain,*
In the 16*th U.S. Reg. commanding at the Rendezvous in Westminster, (Ver't). Nov. 2d,* 1799.

Vol. VII (No. 345) Monday, 11 Nov. 1799.

† [2d] Joshua Butt and Henry [Spieres?] murdered near Southampton Court House, Virginia, by slaves they had purchased. Article dated at Norfolk, Va., 22 Oct. ♦

† [2d] Account of the arrest at Petersburg, Va. of two brothers named Rowles, butchers, who "insulted several magistrates." ♦

† [2d] Remarkable account of the loss of the schooner Violet of Baltimore, Md., John Conway, master, who with some of the crew survived several weeks in the open Atlantic. The Violet was hit by a waterspout and upset; the crew managed to save the lifeboat and a few provisions, and rowed for 700 miles before being rescued by a British ship. Three of the crew died of dehydration, viz.: James Montgomery, John Brown, and John Campbell. A brief account of this story is also mentioned in the "Naval Affairs" at [3b] in this same issue. ♦

† [3a] Article regarding the disappearance of Mr. Jonathan Smith, "a respectable clerk in the Bank of the United States" [at Philadelphia—Ed.] ♦

¶ [3a] PENNSYLVANIA. *Pittsburg,* Oct. 16. The following melancholy accident, we are informed, happened on Thursday night of last week: two families from near Bedford, of the name of Whestone, removing to the westward, had stopped at the house of Mrs. Lockwood on the Laurel Hill, Glade road, but as her house was small she could not accommodate them all with lodging, a number of them went to sleep in the waggons; during the night a large tree fell across the waggons, killed six persons, and dangerously wounded seven.

† [3a] Account of a bear which attacked and wounded a Mrs. Miller, but the lady was rescued by Joshua Gidney, Esq., at Waterborough, Queen's County. The article is dated at St. Johns, New Brunswick, 8 Oct. 1799. ♦

† [3b] William Bently, "of Hoosick, a man nearly 70 years of age," arrested for the murder of his wife, and brought to jail at Troy, N.Y. Bently was formerly a Baptist minister. ♦

† [3b] Account of a storm at Black Rock, Fairfield, Conn., which damaged a store owned by Mr. John Wheeler, and occupied by Mr. Benjamin Perry. The article was dated at Newfield, Conn., 23 Oct. ♦

† [3b] Fire destroyed the barns owned by Mr. Chadwick and Capt. Lander, at Salem, Mass., on 4 Nov. 1799. ♦

† [3d] Anthony Atwood requests his newspaper subscribers to pay up; dated Chester, [Vt.—Ed.] 11 Nov. 1799.

† [3d] Luther Cook posts a notice regarding his horse which was stolen "from the house of John Potters in Swanzey." Notice dated at Richmond, 2 Nov. 1799. ♦

† [3d] Daniel Whipple adv. a heifer which strayed onto his land; dated Walpole 8 Nov.

===== ¶ [3d] **MARRIED.** =====

Massachusetts.—At Boston, Mr. Nathaniel Chandler to Miss Welthy Lummas; Mr. Thomas Seward, to Miss Sukey Faxon. At Portland [*District of Maine*—Ed.], Mr. Samuel Todd, to Miss Sally Shaw. At Westspringfield, Mr. Hosea Parsons, to Miss

Sally Upham; Mr. Elias Russell, to Miss Lucinda Colley. At Beverly, Mr. Ebenezer Francis, of Boston, to Miss Elizabeth Thorndike.

===== ¶ [3d] DIED. =====

Pennsylvania.—At Philadelphia, Mr. John Olden, an opulent merchant; Mr. Joseph Dewees, aged 19.

Newyork.—At Newyork, Mr. Joseph Lockwood, keeper of the Coffee house; Mr. Thomas Alden, sen. At Poughkeepsie, Capt. Abraham Swartout. At his seat on Longisland, Jonathan N. Havens, Member of Congress.

Connecticut.—At Mansfield, Rev. J. Storrs, aged 63.

Massachusetts.—At Boston, Miss Sarah Kelknap; 21 Mr. Jacob G. Cowes, aged 45. At Worcester, Dr. John Green, aged 63; Mr. Robert Gray, aged 64. At Oxford, Mrs. Hannah Meriam, in the 71st year of her age.

Newhampshire.—At Fitzwilliam, Mrs. L. Wright, aged 28.

In this town, on Monday last, Master John Davis, son of Mr. Aaron Davis of Surry, in the fifteenth year of his age. He had been an apprentice in the office of the Farmers' Museum about eight months; and though deprived of the advantages of an early education, had exhibited such marks of genius and attention to business, as promised to render him a useful member of society [. . .]

Vol. VII (No. 346) Monday, 18 Nov. 1799.

† [1d] Josiah Haskell adv. items which he lost between "Carpenter's Tavern and Walpole street." Notice dated 4 Nov. 1799, though the town is not specified.

† [3b] Account of the suicide attempt of George Storer, a "transient insane person" at Strafford, Conn. Storer was said to be a native of Boston, and resided several years in Hartford, where he was employed as a taylor. ♦

† [3b-c] Account of piracy and murder aboard a schooner from Philadelphia or Baltimore, Capt. Willen, bound for St. Thomas. Apparently the captain was dangerously wounded, and Mr. Saunders (the supercargo) was murdered. At least two sentences are chopped off the bottom of [3b]. ♦

† [3d] Notice posted by John Jenison, stating that he has been appointed guardian for Constantine Gilman of Walpole; dated at Walpole 12 Nov. 1799.

† [3d] Samuel Quinton adv. a stray steer on his land; dated Walpole, 15 Nov. 1799.

† [3d] Adv. by David Stone, merchant, dated at Walpole, 15 Nov. 1799.

===== ¶ [3d] MARRIED. =====

Massachusetts.—At Hopkinton, John Harris, Esq. Attorney at Law, to Miss Mary Poor. At Framingham, after eleven years in courtship, William Gleason, Esq. to Miss Ruthy Cloyes.

Newhampshire.—At Amherst, Jeremiah Mason, Esq. Attorney at Law, of Portsmouth, to Miss Mary Means, of Amherst. At Newipswich, Mr. Josiah Bellows, 2d, of this town, to Miss Lydia Preston, of Newipswich.

===== ¶ [3d] DIED. =====

At Valence, in France, where he was a prisoner, Sept. 1, Pope Pius VI, (formerly Cardinal Brasche) born in 1717, and elected Pope, 15th Feb. 1775—one of the wisest and best of men.

Pennsylvania.—At Philadelphia, Lieut. George Price, late Commander of the U.S. Cutter, General Greene.

Newyork.—On Longisland, Capt. William Wade, formerly of the British army.

Massachusetts.—At Boston, Widow Mary Loring, aged 61; Mrs. Abigail Dawson, in the 35th year of her age. At Charlestown, Mr. David Townsend. At Concord, J. Barrett, Esq., aged 65. At Newburyport, Mr. Eleazer Hudson, aged 62. At Sutton, Mr. Ezekiel Cole, aged 76.

Newhampshire.—At Concord, Mrs. Clarissa M'Farland, wife of Rev. Asa M'Farland.

Vol. VII (No. 347) Monday, 25 Nov. 1799.

† [1c] Isaac Baker posts a notice that he has been appointed guardian to James Munsell, of Marlow, N.H.; dated at Marlow 15 Nov. 1799.

† [2d] Account of the murders of the wife and child of Moses Stegall, a Mr. Love, and

a Mr. Johnson, all committed by Micajah Harp and Wiley Harp, brothers. The article is dated at Knoxville, *Kentucky*, 18 Sept., but owing to several other locations named within the article, these events can be presumed to have occurred in *Tennessee*. ♦
† [3a] A brief article describing a duel at Powles Hook, N.Y. between Mr. John Provost and Mr. Cadwalader R. Colden. ♦
¶ [3a] A Mr. Van Zant of Hope (Niagara) lately shot a Mr. Harris, for unlawful intimacy with his wife. Pursuit was making for Mr. Van Zant. 22
† [3b] Robert Pollard, a soldier of the revolution, killed in an accident by being run over by a wagon, between Vauxhall and Newark. Article dated at Elizabethtown, N.J. ♦
† [3d] Advertisement by Moses Johnson, who states that he is "determined to remove his goods in Walpole by the 15th of December." Also a description of his goods for sale at his store in Keene.

===== ¶ [3d] MARRIED. =====

Rhodeisland.—At Newport, Mr. W.S. Burling, merchant, of Newyork, to Miss Eliza Earl, of Newport.
Massachusetts.—At Boston, Don Juan Stoughton, Consul of Spain for the Eastern States of America, to Madam Anna de Neusville, of Cambridge; Mr. William [?] merchant, of Portland, to Miss Sally Brooks, of Boston. At Bridgewater, the Rev. William Briggs, of Old York, to Miss Betsey Hudson, of Bridgewater.

===== ¶ [3d] DIED. =====

At Cadiz, Mr. Yanardi, American Consul.
Northcarolina.—At Edenton Hon. James Iredell, Associate Judge of the United States Court.
Pennsylvania.—At Philadelphia, Lieutenant Huger, quartermaster to the marine corps, aged 25.
Connecticut.—At Newlondon, Mr. James Miller, aged 43. At Easthartford, Mr. David Wells, aged 36. At Brandford, Mr. Ralph Isaacs, aged 58.
Massachusetts.—At Quincy, James Apthorp, Esq. aged 68. At Sheffield, Maj. Gen. John Ashley, jun. aged 63. At Worcester, Capt. Thomas Stowell, aged [44?]. At Holden, Mr. Richard Flagg, aged 92. At Leominster, Lieut. David Johnson, aged 84.
Vermont.—At Westminster, Mrs. Susannah Burt, (of a consumption,) wife of Mr. Leonard Burt, aged 32.—At Hartford, Mr. Samuel Cone, aged 34. At Charlotte, Mr. John Tharp, a very respectable citizen.

Vol. VII (No. 348) Monday, 2 Dec. 1799.

¶ [3c] John Pastona, the Portugese, has been convicted at New York, of the murder of Mary Ann de Caestro. 23
† [3d] Benjamin Williams adv. a stray steer on his land; dated at Rockingham, 5 Nov.
† [3d] Jabez Sarjeant and Solomon Willson post notice that they have been appointed Guardians to Willard Chandler, of Chester, Vt.; dated at Chester 23 Nov. 1799.

===== ¶ [3d] MARRIED. =====

Massachusetts.—At Boston, Lieut. Cotton Thayer, to Miss Abagail Treat. At Ipswich, Mr. John Dean of Hamilton to Mrs. Sally Harris, of the former place: Capt. John D. Farley, to Miss Mary Swett. At Gloucester, Mr. John Scott, Merchant, of Boston, to Miss Harriet Pearce.

===== ¶ [3d] DIED. =====

Pennsylvania.—At Philadelphia, in the Hospital, Hannah Lewis, a native of Pennsylvania, and for 17 years a patient of the Hospital.

Vol. VII (No. 349) Monday, 9 Dec. 1799.

† [3c] Robbery of Mr. B. M'Cabe, by one John Dorsey, on a sloop in the Hudson River. Article contained under the New York header. ♦
¶ [3d] A violent thunder gust did considerable damage lately, at Knoxville, Tennessee. Several gentlemen travelling to that place, on the east side of the Cumberland mountain, received considerable hurt by the lightning. They were thrown from their horses, and Mr. Moses Fiske, who went from this quarter in spring last, had his horse killed. He received by the shock, a small injury.

† [3d] William Page appointed administrator to the estate of John Duncan, late of "Newgrantham," N.H. The notice is dated at Rockingham [Vt.—Ed.] 2 Dec. 1799. Also, a notice by Convers Johnson and William Huntington, who were appointed Commissioner's of Duncan's insolvent estate.

† [3d] Harvey Elkins advertises that he had "purchased the whole stock in trade, now in Moses Johnson's Store at Walpole. Dated at Walpole, 8 Dec. 1799.

Vol. VII (No. 350) Monday, 16 Dec. 1799.

† [3d] Advertisement by Asa Willcox, who is in the business of making and grinding malt. Dated at Surry, 6 Dec. 1799. ♦

† [3d] William Henry, Jr., adv. a heifer which strayed onto his property; dated at Charlestown, [N.H.] 16 Nov. 1799.

===== ¶ [3d] DIED. =====

Newhampshire.—At Westmoreland, Widow Sarah Cummings, aged 93. In this town, Mrs. Mary Wolcott, wife of Mr. Roger Wolcott, aged 47.

Vol. VII (No. 351) Monday, 23 Dec. 1799.

† [3d] William Page adv. that "his Flour Mills at Bellows Falls are now completed for operation . . . " Dated at Rockingham, 23 Dec. 1799.

† [3d] Legal notice regarding the insolvent estate of Josiah Willard, late of Charlestown, N.H., deceased. Abel Walker, Ephraim Curtis, and Asahel Hunt, Commissioners of said estate, posted this notice to announce estate business to be conducted at the house of Joseph Allen, innholder at Charlestown; dated 20 Nov. 1799.

† [3d] Adv. by Thomas Wilder, who "wishes to purchase a quantity of Horses' manes and tails for which he will pay any kind of goods; dated at Lempster, 19 Dec. 1799.

† [3d] Walter Himes offers a farm for sale at Acworth, N.H.; dated there — Dec. 1799.

Vol. VII (No. 352) Monday, 30 Dec. 1799.

† [3d] John Hubbard requests his debtors to pay up; dated Walpole, 25 Dec. 1799.

† [3d] Legal notice regarding the estate of Eli Darling, late of Croydon, N.H., deceased. Isaiah Hayward, Peter Barton, and Elisha Patridge were appointed Commissioners over said estate, and announce that estate business will be conducted at the house of Edward Hall, Jr., Innholder at Croydon. Dated Croydon, 25 Dec. 1799.

† [3d] Russel Bisset, Capt. 2d Regt. of Infantry, advertises for recruits of said regiment; dated at Westminster, Vt., 21 Dec. 1799.

† [3d] Nathaniel Sikes requests his debtors to pay up; dated at Walpole, 27 Dec. 1799.

Vol. VII (No. 353) Monday, 6 Jan. 1800.

¶ [3d] On the 26th ult. at Concord, Ms. Samuel Smith was executed pursuant to his sentence for burglary. He was born in Connecticut, and was in the 56th year of his age, and by his own confession had been a notorious offender.

† [3d] List of letters remaining at the Post Office in Charlestown, N.H., 1 Jan. 1800:

Samuel Burr,	Rockingham, Vt.	Messrs. M'Farlin and Moor,	Antrim.
Jotham Britton, two,	Springfield, Vt.	Epaphras Matson,	Charlestown.
West Bonny,	Charlestown.	Abner Mourton,	"
Robert Blair,	Becket, Vt.	Col. Peter Page,	"
Isaac Bidwell,	Wethersfield, Vt.	Joseph Payment,	Acworth.
William Divol,	Charlestown, N.H.	Robert Anel, or } John Adkins,	Charlestown.
John W. Hall,	" "		
Samuel Hunt, Jr. Esq.	" "	Josiah Rich,	Claremont.
Elihu Lyman,	" "	John Willards, Esq.	Charlestown.

† [3d] List of letters remaining at the Post Office in Walpole, N.H., 1 Jan. 1800, as compiled by Alexander Thomas, Postmaster:

Walter Brock, Esq.,	Barnett, Vt.	Charles Church, (2)	Westmoreland, N.H.
Nathan Bundy, Jr.,	Walpole, N.H.	Joseph Dorr,	" "
John Emery, (2),	" "	George Dorr,	" "
Henry Foster,	" "	Moses Dorr, Esq.	" "
Jones Fairbank,	" "	Alpheus Moor, Esq.	" "
Roger Fenton,	" "	John Robins,	" "
Joseph Gilman,	" "	Experience Storrs,	" "
Josiah Griswold,	" "	Solomon Davis,	Chesterfield, N.H.
Joseph Heaton,	" "	Eleazer Jackson,	" "
John Livingston, Jr.	" "	Roswell Shirtliff,	" "
Stephen Mellish,	" "	Amos Kimball,	Chester, Vt.
Samuel Monson,	" "	James Rogers,	" "
Silas Newcomb,	" "	Luther Oliver,	Alstead, N.H.
Josiah Parks,	" "	Lieut. Edward Waldo, and } Joshua Gilman,	" "
Elijah Page,	" "		
Wm. Page, Esq.(4)	Bellows Falls, Walpole	Wm. Page, Jun.	Rockingham, Vt.
Socrates Swift,	" " "	Capt. David Sanders,	" "
West W. Sampson,	" " "	William Tubbs,	Marlow, N.H.
Abednego Bell,	Newcastle, N.H.	Walter Ward,	Lem[p]ster, N.H.
Luke Cass,	Richmond, N.H.		

====== ¶ [3d] MARRIED. ======

At Salem, Mr. Benjamin Crombie to Mrs. Betsey Gr[ave?].—At Boston, Mr. Martin Burr, to Miss Eunis Turner.—At Scituate, Mr. Nathaniel Ells, to Miss. Abigail Turner.

Vol. VII (No. 354) Monday, 13 Jan. 1800.

† [3d] Stephen Austin, Nathan Cram, and Peter Peirce listed in a notice of delinquent [nonresident?] taxpayers in the town of Washington, N.H., as reported by Ebenezer Spaulding, Collector. The notice, concerning taxes not paid for the year 1798, contains the categories of lot number, range number, etc. [see also issue of 11 Aug. 1800.]

† [3d] Moses Johnson posts an advertisement regarding his "potash manufactory" at Keene, dated 10 Jan. 1799.

† [3d] Adv. by Amasa Allen, requesting payment of debts; dated Walpole 10 Jan. 1799.

Vol. VII (No. 355) Monday, 20 Jan. 1800.

† [1b-c] Lengthy account of one Elizabeth Woodcock, of Impington, [England—Ed.], who was buried under the snow on the 2d of Feb., 1799, and was taken up alive after eight days. ♦

† [3a-b] Extensive article describing the death of Juliana Gilmore Sands, who was found in a well at New York City, and one Levi Weeks arrested as a suspect in her

murder. She was the daughter of a Quaker minister who recently died in England; her infirm mother resided at New Windsor [N.Y.] ♦

† [3d] Legal notice regarding a requested new trial for Caleb Hunt of Stoddard, N.H., who was involved in a conflict with the proprietors of Marlow, N.H.

† [3d] Elkanah Phelps posts a notice regarding a cattle drive; dated at Windsor, Vt., 20 Dec. 1799. However, a similar adv. which appears in the issue of 17 Feb. 1800 [3d] names an additional subscriber to this notice, *Isaac Green*.

† [3d] Benjamin Bellows posts a notice of a meeting at Major William Todd's, Innholder at Keene, regarding business for the third Turpike Road; dated Walpole, 20 Jan.

===== ¶ [3d] MARRIED. =====

Massachusetts.—At Boston, Mr. P.A. Von Hagen, jun. to Miss Lucy Ballard; Mr. John Bellows, formerly of this town, to Miss Betsy Emes; Capt. Meletiah Bourne of Boston, to Miss Ruth Lambert of Scituate. At Salem, Capt. Addison Richardson, to Miss Anstis Blanchard.

Newhampshire.—At Keene, Col. Joseph Kimball, of Plainfield, to Mrs. Rebekah Goodenow. At Newipswich, David Everett, Esq. of Boston, to Miss Dorothy Appleton.

===== ¶ [3d] DIED. =====

Newjersey.—At Newark, Mr. Aaron Pennington.

Massachusetts.—In Boston, Samuel Gridley, Esq. aged 66; Mrs. Mercy Scilly, aged 22; Mr. Richard Corning, aged 32; Dr. William Boyd, aged 23; Mr. James Dakin, aged 30; Mr. John Weare, aged 71; Miss Mary Smith, aged 84. At Marblehead, Mrs. Eliza Lewis. At Stockbridge, Rev. Joshua Paine, aged 64.

Newhampshire.—At Dover, Mr. Josiah Folsom, aged [21?].

Vol. VII (No. 356) Monday, 27 Jan. 1800.

¶ [3c] An editor of a Southcarolina paper, thus notices the death of an aged man of colour: "Died at Manchester, Essex county, 24 Plato Whipple, aged 103, one of God's images in Ebony."

† [3c] Brief mention of Mr. John Ashley, "an industrious and respectable farmer" at W. Springfield, Mass., who donated several thousand dollars for the support of a minister.

¶ [3d] DIED.]—At Alstead, N.H. Dr. Daniel Ferrin, for many years a respectable physician in that place.

Vol. VII (No. 357) Monday, 3 Feb. 1800.

† [3d] Thomas Whiting offers land for sale at Wardsborough, Vt.; dated Alstead 24 Jan.

† [3d] Adv. for a new Post Rider to replace Capt. Fay who carried the newspapers.

¶ [3d] DIED.—At Lancaster, (Pennsylvania,) Gen. Mifflin, late Governor of the state of Pennsylvania.

Vol. VII (No. 358) Monday, 10 Feb. 1800.

† [1a] Josiah Stevens posts a notice concerning a meeting at the house of Stephen Dexter, Innholder at Claremont, regarding business of the Second N.H. Turnpike. Dated at Claremont, 18 Jan. 1800.

† [3c] Suicide of Capt. Henry Porter at Haverhill, Mass., about the 15th of Jan., 1800. ♦

† [3d] Adv. for several lots of land for sale in Winchester, N.H., mentioning one tract which borders on land owned by Zechariah Field. The adv. refers to John Follet of Winchester as a point of contact, or the subscriber, Solomon Vose, "in Northfield."

Vol. VII (No. 359) Monday, 17 Feb. 1800.

† [3a] Account of the gruesome murder, 24 Jan. 1800, of Martha M'Beath, committed by her husband Andrew M'Beath, who "is now in Newcastle goal." The article is dated at Wilmington, North Carolina, 29 Jan. 1800.

¶ [3b] MASSACHUSETTS. *Portland*, Feb. 3. On Wednesday last, Mr. James Libby, of Gorham, in driving a team down a hill near Falmouth meeting house, accidentally slipped under the sled, and was instantly killed.—On Thursday, a Mr. Rand, who had been digging the grave for the deceased, in crossing the road where some teams were passing, slipped down by one of them, which went over both of his legs and crushed them to pieces—His life is despaired of—The many accidents of this nature, it is hoped will render people more careful. 25

¶ [3d] DIED.—At Charleston, Southcarolina, Governour Rutledge; W.R. Davis. Maryland, Upton Sheridan, Esq. At Philadelphia, Mr. Abraham Lott, Printer. At Boston, suddenly, Mr. John Skillings, aged 54. On board ship Portsmouth, Dr. Joshua Gee Symmes, chief Surgeon.—At Mendon, Dr. Eber Keyes, aged 41—At Sutton, Polly Mills, aged 10, Daughter of Rev. Edmund Mills.

Newhampshire.—At Claremont, Mr. Harry Crampton, in the 21st year of his age. His disposition was amiable, his abilities good, and his deportment manly and obliging; he was highly esteemed while living, and greatly lamented in death.

Vol. VII (No. 360) Monday, 24 Feb. 1800.

† [3a-c] Lengthy accounts of the arrest and execution [at Charleston, S.C.?] of Thomas Nash, alias Jonathan or Nathan Robbins. Nash was a seaman aboard the British frigate *Hermione*, and was charged with piracy and murder. He claimed his name was Robbins, and that he was born in Danbury, Conn., but the Selectmen of that town, Eli Mycot, Ebenezer Benedict, Justus Barnun, and Benjamin Hitchcock, who "are from forty five to fifty seven years of age," stated that "there has not been nor now is any family known by the name of Robbins within the limits of said town." Major Taylor, late town clerk of Danbury, aged 56, also certified that no person by the name of Robbins ever resided in or was born in Danbury, during his term as town clerk from 1771 to 1796. Nash later confessed to his true identity, and stated that he was born in Waterford, Ireland. ♦

† [3d] Legal notice regarding the insolvent estate of Jonathan Chase, Esq. late of Cornish, N.H. Moody Dustin, William Breck, and Samuel Fiske were appointed Commissioners over said estate, and posted notice of meetings to be conducted at the house of Sarah Chase, the decedent's widow. The notice was dated at Claremont, 17 Feb. 1800, with an addendum by Sanford Kingsbury, Administrator, dated at Cornish the same day.

===== ¶ [3d] DIED. =====

Newyork.—At Albany, Mr. Nathaniel Locke, formerly of Boston.

Connecticut.—At Newlondon, Mr. Freeman, aged 81.

Massachusetts.—At Boston, John Winthrop, Esq. aged 53; Mr. Moses Newhall, aged 24. At Wells, 26 Mrs. Wells, wife of the Hon. Nathaniel Wells. At Charlestown, Mr. Roswell C. Smith, aged [21?].

Vol. VII (No. 361) Monday, 3 March 1800.

† [3d] Adv. for the sale of the town of Pierpont, *Newconnecticut* [Ohio—Ed.]. The adv. gives an extensive description of the area, and was placed by Pierpont Edwards, and mentions that a survey of said town has been made by John Starke Edwards. The adv. is dated at "Newhaven," 19 Feb. 1800.

† [3d] Adv. by David Stone, lately of the firm of *Bellows & Stone*, requesting settlement of debts, and also items for sale; dated at Walpole, 22 Feb. 1800.

† [3d] Adv. by *Thomas & Thomas*, owners of this paper, requesting settlement of debts.

† [3d] Nathan Fay [formerly a Post Rider—Ed.] announces that "he shall recommence his route on Monday next."

===== ¶ [3d] MARRIED. =====

In this town, Mr. Calvin Ripley, to Miss Sally Bellows.

===== ¶ [3d] DIED. =====

Massachusetts.—At Boston, Mr. George Spriggs, aged 47; Mr. Richard M. Adams, aged 21. At Hardwick, Mrs. Greele, aged 56. At Greenfield, Mr. David Wells, aged 74. At Haverhill, Mr. John White, aged 75.

Rhodeisland.—At Providence, Capt. Paul Allen, aged 58.

Vol. VII (No. 362) Monday, 10 March 1800.

¶ [3a] *List of Officers and Men wounded and missing by the action of the 1st of February 1800, on board the U.S. ship Constellation, of 38 guns, Thomas Truxton, Esq. Commander, with a French National ship of 54 guns.*

Mr. James Jarvis, midshipman, missing who was in the maintop, went overboard with the mainmast.

William Lightfoot,		Killed
John Robinson,	Seaman.	do.
John Smith,	do.	do.
Thos. Stephenson,	Old [Seaman].	do.
John Williams,	Seaman.	do.
John Willson,	do.	do.
James Foster,	do.	do.
Emmanuel Manna,	do.	do.
Robert Smith,	do.	do.
Emmanuel Drift,	do.	do.
William Powel,	Old [Seaman].	do.
Joseph Grower,	Seaman.	do.
Christopher M'Cormick,	Midshipman	do.

Mr. A. Shirly, 2d lieutenant, slight wound in the leg.
Mr. P.C. Wederstrand, midshipman, slight wound in the head;
Mr. R. Warren, midshipman, slight wound in the head;
Mr. F. Comerford, master's mate, slight wound in the head;
John Highland, quarter gunner, shot through the back;
James Rodgers, sergeant of marines, slight wound on the arm;
Jonathan Bell, sailmaker's mate, fractured leg;
John Hoxse, seaman, arm shot off, and wounded in the side;
William Musgrove, seaman, fractured thigh;
James Carter, seaman, wounded in the thigh and side;
Ephraim Jabins, seaman, wounded in the the arm;
Benjamin Bradford, seaman, arm shot off—died;
Antonio Poyntz, seaman, slight wound on the head;
Edward Hallman, seaman, wound in the arm and knee;
George Matthews, old seaman, fractured thigh;
John Logan, old seaman, fractured leg;
Thomas Fitzgerald, old seaman, gluteus maximus muscle badly wounded;
Charles Lewis, old seaman, shot through the arm;
John Baptist, boy, leg shot off;
Philip Smith, boy, wound in the back of the neck;
Cader Branton, marine, wound in the neck;
William Small, marine, shot through the thigh;
William Howell, old seaman, slight wound in the thigh;
George Carson, marine, shot through the hand;

ISAAC HENRY, *Surgeon.*

Feb. 3, 1800.

¶ [3b] *From Gale's Raleigh (N.C.) Register*, Jan. 28. "On Thursday se'night Col. John Sheppard was murdered by his brother, who struck him on the head with an axe at the house of Robert White, Esq. in Glasgow county ! —Both the brothers were intoxicated !"

† [3d] Ebenezer Brewster advertises several pieces of property for sale in the vicinity of Hanover, N.H. Dated at Hanover 26 Feb. 1800.

===== ¶ [3d] **MARRIED**. =====

At Boston, Daniel Newcomb, Esq. of Keene, to Mrs. Hannah Goldthwait of Boston.

===== ¶ [3d] **DIED**. =====

At Quebec, Major George L. Hamilton, of the Royal Artillery, aged 47.
At Honduras Bay, Capt. Joseph Brown, of Portsmouth, aged 36.

Southcarolina.—At Charleston, Mr. Alexander Alexander, aged 52.

Massachusetts.—At Boston, Mrs. Abigail Bender, aged 81; Miss Prudence Bell, at Bedford. Mrs. Susannah Hall, aged 63, wife of Ebenezer Hall, Esq.

Newhampshire.—At Dover, Mr. Samuel Place. At Portsmouth, Mr. Peter Babb, sen.

Vol. VII (No. 363) Monday, 17 March 1800.

† [1b] David Stone requests settlement of outstanding debts; dated at Walpole 22 Feb.

† [2d] Under an article entitled "Female Intrepidity," the wife of Samuel Dille exhibits her bravery by shooting two bears. The article is dated at Washington, North Carolina; Samuel Dille and wife lived "on Wills Creek, a branch of the Muskingum." ♦

† [2d-3b] Extensive account given by Dr. Ed. Stevens, a passenger aboard the schooner *Experiment*, regarding an attack on that vessel by a large number of "barges, manned with negroes and mulattoes." Though not specifically identified, several points of reference mentioned in this letter indicate that this attack probably took place off the west coast of Haiti. The letter is dated at Leogane [prob. *Haiti*—Ed.] 2 Jan. 1800, the day after the attack. The *Experiment* was part of a convoy, along with the *Mary*, and the *Daniel and Mary*. The *Mary* was commanded by Capt. Chipman, who was murdered by the pirates. ♦

† [3c] Article describing the political flavor of a proposed newspaper at New York City, to be published by William Cobbett, "who not long since published a paper in Philadelphia."

† [3d] Editor's acknowledgement of Peter Quince, Esq., a correspondent. ♦

† [3d] Public notice of a meeting regarding the Green Mountain Turnpike Company, held at Salmon Dutton's Esq., Cavendish, Vt. The notice was signed by Peter Read, *Moderator*, and Asa Wheeler, *Clerk*.

===== ¶ [3d] MARRIED. =====

From the Trenton Federalist. At Middletown (Monmouth) on the 5th instant, Thomas Tilton, in the 70th year of his age, to Mary Lucar, in her 13th year. She is the daughter's daughter of Thomas Tilton's former wife; so that this husband and wife were at least half grandfather and half granddaughter.

At the same place, a few weeks since, John Lucar, the brother of the above mentioned bride, to his half aunt, Catharine Clinton, widow, and daughter of Thomas Tilton, the above mentioned bride's groom.

===== ¶ [3d] DIED. =====

Connecticut.—At Stratford, Mr. Thaddeus Birdseye, aged 47.

Massachusetts.—At Boston, Mr. John [Blake?], aged 8[0?]; Mr. Philip Rose, aged 27; Mr. Jonathan Loring, aged 55. At Cambridge, Mr. Samuel Whittemore, aged 79. At Brookline, Mrs. Mary Easterbrooks.

Vol. VII (No. 364) Monday, 24 March 1800.

† [1c] Notice of delinquent proprietors and land owners in the town of Unity, N.H., as compiled by Moses Willard, *Collector*. Property to be auctioned off 15 May 1800 "at the dwelling house of Jonathan Gliddin, in said Unity." The notice contains a breakdown of lot size, location, etc., though the owners' names only are given here:

William Buswell	Edward Fifield	Benjamin Huntoon
Samuel Dearborn	Nathaniel French	Thomas Scribner
John Mason	Benning Wentworth	

†[3d] Legal notice regarding the insolvent estate of Doctor Daniel Perin, late of Alstead, N.H., deceased. The notice was posted by John C. Chamberlain, Oliver Shepard, and Joshua Shepard, Commissioners of said estate, and a includes a schedule of business meetings to be held at the dwelling house of Rebeka Perin, widow.

† [3d] Notice regarding the estate of Amariah Rockwell, late of Langdon, N.H., deceased; posted by Andrew French, Executor, and dated at Walpole, 20 March 1800.

===== ¶ [3d] DIED. =====

Massachusetts.—At Shrewsbury after a lingering illness, Mr Thomas H. Kemble, son of Mr. Thomas Kemble of Boston, aged 27; a worthy man, and a faithful friend [. . .]

Vol. VII (No. 365) Monday, 31 March 1800.

† [3d] Article describing a fire which destroyed the house belonging to Moses Warren, at Acworth, N.H., 17 March 1800. Mr. Warren, his mother, wife, and several children survived the fire. ♦

¶ [3d] Take Notice. All persons indebted to Moses Johnson for Goods purchased at his Store in Walpole, are informed that their demands are left with the subscriber and they are hereby requested to call and settle the same.

Francis Gardner.

Walpole, March 31, 1800.

Vol. VIII (No. 366) Monday, 7 April 1800.

¶ [3b] *Extracts from Coit's Marine List.* Arrived at N. York, sloop Polly, captain Cotron from N. Carolina, came passenger captain Doan, of the sloop Chester, belonging to Seabrook,27 bound for Martinique, laden with cattle, &c. who unfortunately on the 16th February was compelled to abandon his vessel and take to his long boat, in which condition he remained for three days, when he was fortunately taken up by the schooner Federalist, and carried into North Carolina; during which time, his mate and one man died through the intense coldness of the weather.

† [3d] List of letters remaining in the Post Office at Walpole, N.H., on the first day of April, 1800, as compiled by Alexander Thomas, Postmaster:

E. Adams,	Langdon	Elisha Lyman,	Walpole.
Sally Armstrong,	Chesterfield.	James Lewis,	"
Alvin Burt,	Walpole.	Stephen Mellish,	"
Samuel Burr,	Rockingham.	Theophilus Olcott,	Springfield.
Hannah Bingham,	Gilsum. 2.	Mrs. Chloe Perkins,	Walpole.
Capt. B. Caryl,	Chester.	Nathaniel Partridge,	Chesterfield. 2.
Dr. M. Dudley,	Westmoreland.	Eli Partridge,	" 2.
Philip Davis,	Rockingham.	Widow Dorothy Parker,	Litchfield.
John C. Dana,	Walpole.	Edward Ruggles,	Walpole.
Amelia Granger,	Shipton.	James Rogers,	Chester.
Lieut. William Hall,	Grafton.	Moses Smith,	Chesterfield.
Seth Hall,	Westmoreland.	Roswell Shirtliff,	"
Lieut. Augustus Hall,	"	Benjamin Thomson,	Gilsum.
Timothy Lovell,	Rockingham.	Samuel Whitney, Jun.	Rockingham.

† [3d] List of letters remaining in the Post Office at Westminster, Vt., on the first day of April, 1800, as compiled by Eleazer May, Postmaster:

Worthington Holten,	Westminster	Gabriel B. Gibson,	Chester.
Nathaniel Holten,	"	William Page, Esq.	Rockingham.
David Fisk,	"	Samuel Emery,	"
John Lock,	" 2.	William Simons,	"
John Thompson,	"	Daniel Farrand, Esq.	"
Samuel Brisk,	"	Miss Hannah Whitney,	Hartland.
Waitstill Ranney,	Chester.		

¶ [3d] One Cent Reward. Runaway from the subscriber on the 23d inst. an indented Apprentice Boy, named Benjamin Lyon, eighteen years of age, his right leg is crooked. Whoever will return said runaway shall be entitled to the above reward, and no charges. All persons are forbid harbouring or trusting him on my account.

Phineas Parker.

Claremont, March 5, 1800.

† [3d] Calvin Hall advertises for a mare which strayed or was stolen in Claremont, N.H. The notice was dated at Newport, 2 April 1800.

===== ¶ [3d] DIED. =====

Connecticut.—At Eastwindsor, Mr. Caleb Barstow, ship carpenter, aged 53, late of Providence. At Weathersfield, Mr. H. Crane, aged 52.

Massachusetts.—At Boston, Miss Betsy Weld, aged 20, daughter of Mr. Benjamin Weld. Mrs. Sarah Langford.

Vol. VIII (No. 367) Monday, 14 April 1800.

† [3d] Advertisement by N. Wetmore Washburn, who "informs the public that he will carry on the weaving business the following season . . . " Westminster, 4 Apr. 1800
† [3d] Legal notice posted by Calvin Chamberlain, Administrator for the estate of William Chamberlain, late of Rockingham, Vt., deceased.
† [3d] A legal notice posted by Samuel Bellows, who was appointed Guardian over Peter Bellows of Charlestown. The latter was "adjudged by the Selectmen of said Charlestown, to be incapable to take care of himself." Dated Charlestown 7 Apr. 1800. 28

Vol. VIII (No. 368) Monday, 21 April 1800.

† [2d] Account of the trial at New York City of Levi Weeks, charged with the murder of Juliana Elmore Sands. Weeks was found not guilty. ♦
† [3d] Amos Shepard offers a farm for sale at Alstead, "which Ensign Nathaniel Cooper now improves." Advertisement dated at Alstead 8 April 1800.

===== ¶ [3d] MARRIED. =====

Massachusetts.—At Worcester, Mr. Daniel Greenleaf, Printer, to Miss Polly Chamberlain. At Boston, Dr. Thomas Danforth, to Miss Elizabeth Bowers.
Newhampshire.—At Portsmouth, Mr. Edward Co[ ]n 29 to Miss Hannah Seward.

===== ¶ [3d] DIED. =====

At Newlondon, Con. Mr. T. Gould, aged 68. At Bolton, Mr. Jesse Walcott aged 66. At Westmoreland, Mrs. Lydia Dorr. At Hanover, Capt. Simeon Curtis aged 80. At Candia, Mr. Simeon Poor, aged 28. At Exeter, Mrs. Morrison, aged 74.
At Putney, Vt. on the 10th inst. Mrs. Mary Sabin, the amiable and pious consort of the Hon. Noah Sabin, Esq. with whom she lived sixty three years, five months and thirteen days; aged eighty-eight years and three months.—She calmly bade adieu to this terrestrial scene in full assurance of enjoying that rest which is reserved for the peculiar people of God, leaving a tender and affectionate husband, six children, fifty three grand children, and forty eight great grand children, to imitate her piety, and lament her loss.
At Newport, N.H. Mrs Amy Buel, wife to Mr Aaron Buel, in the 55th year of her age.

Vol. VIII (No. 369) Monday, 28 April 1800.

† [3b] Summary of the trial of Charles Holt, editor of the *Bee*, who was convicted of printing seditious libel against the government of the United States. Article contained under the news dated at Hartford, Conn. ♦ 30
† [3b] Elias Bolton, "a transient person," while in a drunken state, swallowed laudanum thinking it was liquor and soon died [12 April 1800—Ed.] The event occurred at the store of Dr. Oliver Fiske, at Worcester, Mass. ♦

===== ¶ [3d] MARRIED. =====

At Rindge, Rev. Reuben Emerson, of Westminster, Ver. to Miss Persis Harden.

===== ¶ [3d] DIED. =====

At Halifax, N.S. Joseph Peters, Esq. Deputy Post Master General.
Massachusetts.—At Westborough, Capt. Jonathan Fay. At Bolton, Mr. Jesse Walcutt, aged 66.
Newhampshire.—At Keene, Peleg Sprague, Esq. Mr. Reuben Fenno, of Westmoreland.

¶ [3d] Ten Dollars Reward. Deserted from this Rendezvous on the 15th inst. Samuel Coffrin, 31 regularly enlisted a soldier in the Infantry of the United States. He was born in Hillsborough, Newhampshire, aged 18 years and four months, five feet four inches and one-fourth of an inch high, dark complexion, blue eyes and brown hair. Whoever will apprehend said deserter and deliver him to any officer in the line, shall be entitled to the above reward, and all necessary charges paid.

Israel E. Trask, *Capt. of the*
15th Reg't of Infantry

Rendezvous at Westminster, April 17, 1800.

Vol. VIII (No. 370) Monday, 5 May 1800.

¶ [2c] PENNSYLVANIA. *Philadelphia*, April 16. CIRCUIT COURT OF THE U. STATES. The Grand Jury have returned the following bills true:— [32]

John Fries, Anthony Stahler, Conrad Marks, Philip Desh, Jacob Klein—Treason.
Jacob Eyreman—Prison Breach and Conspiracy.
The defendants have been arraigned, and plead—Not Guilty. We understand, Mr. Lewis and Mr. Dallas are assigned as counsel for Fries; and that Stahler, Desh and Klein have applied to the Court, that Mr. Ross and Mr. Hopkinson may be assigned as their counsel.
Henry Huber—Treason.
Abraham Samsel, Peter Hundsberg, Abraham Shantz, alias Jans, alias Johnson, Geo. Mumbower, Henry Mumbower, Peter Hager, Peter Gable, Jacob Gable, Danl. Gable, Henry Smith, Valentine Kuder—Conspiracy to obstruct the execution of a law of the United States, &c.
John Everbardt, John Huber, Christopher Sax, John Klein jun. Danl. Klein, John Klein, Adam Briech, Geo. Gettman, Wm. Gettman—Conspiracy, Rescue, and Obstruction of Process.

† [2d-3a] Extensive accounts of the trial of one Thomas Cooper, who was indicted for a libel against the President of the United States, and involving certain hand bills "printed in Northumberland county, in this state . . . " Presumably, the county referred to here is in Pennsylvania. The article is a continuation of trials held at the U.S. Circuit Court in Philadelphia. ◆

† [3a] Account of the trial of "Joseph Berouse, or [Bursa?], Peter Peterson, or La Croix, and Joseph Baker, or Boulanger, indicted for piracy and murder, in having on the 12th day of September last, on board the schooner Eliza, Capt. Whelen, of Philadelphia, rose on the officers of said schooner, and, after barbarously murdering Charles Key, supercargo, Thomas [Cross?], mate, and Jacob Schuster, seaman, took possession of the vessel." [33]

¶ [3b] Newlondon, Connecticut, April 9. SHOCKING ! In the month of Jan. last, Capt. Stephen Strickland of Susquehanna, in journeying to this town, of which he was a native, stopped at a public house in Waterbury. While at dinner a quarrel took place between an American and an Irishman in an adjoining room; the landlord being lame, requested Capt. S. to endeavur to part them; and while he was attempting it, a brother of the Irishman struck him a blow on his head with a heavy stone, which fractured his skull, and rendered him immediately senseless. Two weeks elapsed before Capt. S. was able slowly to proceed on his journey and he remained in an invalid state until the 4th inst. when he died among his relatives at Lyme, aged 38 years. He has left a wife and seven children at Susquehanna, to lament their loss, and weep over his unfortunate destiny.
The culprit is imprisoned at N. Haven for trial.

¶ [3b] April 23. [New London, Conn.—Ed.] CASUALTIES. On Thursday last a fine child, aged 6 years, son of Mr. Wm. Hargill, of this city, was accidentally run over by a loaded cart, and almost instantly killed.
Last week Mr. Elisha Fox of Montville, driving a team down a steep hill, sitting on the tongue of the cart, unfortunately fell off; when one of the wheels ran over his body; and put a period to his life in a few minutes. He was aged about 60 years.

† [3b] Cornelius Smith, "a stranger," apprehended at New Haven, Conn., on a charge of counterfeiting. ◆

† [3b-3c] Fire destroys the house of Mr. Holgate at Milton, Vermont, and one of his children and a maid were killed in the blaze, 3 April 1800. The wife of Mr. Holgate was later charged with setting the fire. The article is dated at Vergennes, Vt., 10 April. ◆

¶ [3d] **Take Notice.**   I the subscriber, do forbid all persons medling, or taking, or having any thing to do with Samuel Cofren, lately advertised as a deserter from the rendezvous at Westminster on their peril, for he is bound apprentice to me, and is not eighteen years of age.

Alpheus Bugbee.

Putney, April 28, 1800.

† [3d] Samuel West, Clerk to the Proprietors of the third Turnpike Road in N.H., posts a notice stating that a meeting regarding said highway will be held at the house of Dr. Thomas Edwards in Keene. The notice is dated at Keene, 1 May 1800.

==== ¶ [3d] MARRIED. ====

At Newburyport, Mr. Richard Pike, to Miss Sarah Boardman. At Salem, Mr. Wm. B. Parker, to Miss Abigail Watson. At Boston, Capt. Reuben Carver, to Mrs. Sarah Kelsa; Mr. Charles Clement, to Miss Dolly Quincy. At Springfield, Rev. Augustus Rowland, of Windsor, C[onn.] to Miss Frances Bliss.

==== ¶ [3d] DIED. ====

At Newburyport, Moses Frazier, Esq. aged 58. At Knoxville, Hon. Wm. Blount, aged 56, formerly Governor of Tennessee. At Springfield, Mrs. Ann Chapin, aged 43. At Hollis, Mr. Moses Thurston, aged 80. At Boston, Mr. Thomas Richardson, aged 33; Mr. James Dunlap, aged 34. At Portsmouth, Mrs. Abigail Elliot, aged 79; Mrs. Hart; Mr. Charles Waters.

Vol. VIII (No. 371) Monday, 12 May 1800.

† [2d-3a] Extensive account of the capture by pirates of the American schooner *Mary*, off the coast of Haiti, on the 2d of March 1800. The schooner's captain, Israel C. Anthony, of Charleston, [S.C.—Ed.] was the sole survivor, the rest of the crew having been murdered. The captain reached safety a few weeks later, and reported his account to Robert Richie, Consul of the U.S. In an article following the account of the *Mary*, William Ridg, "late supercargo of the schooner John, of Philadelphia," recounts a similar fate to the vessel to which he belonged. The *John*, John Prior, master, was captured by pirates opposite the east end of the island of Gonaives, on the 5th of April 1800. ♦

==== ¶ [3d MARRIED. ====

At Barnstable, Mass. Mr. Lemuel Bradford, of Portland, to Miss Hitty Hinckley, of Barnstable. At Hingham Rev. Peter Whitney, to Miss Jane Lincoln. At Newton, Mr. Thomas Hastings, merchant, to Mrs. Elizabeth Jackson, of Cambridge. At Boston, Mr. Elijah Williams, to Miss Rebecca Armstrong.

==== ¶ [3d DIED. ====

In Scotland, J. Anderson, a tinker, aged 114. At Boston, Capt. Mungo Mackay, jun. aged 35; Mr. Aaron Mclintock, aged 33; Capt. Hezekiah Welch, aged 71. At Medford, Ebenezer Hall, Esq. aged 63. At Salem, Mr. Joseph Bowditch, aged 42. At Alstead, Mr. Jonas Newton, aged 56.

Vol. VIII (No. 372) Monday, 19 May 1800.

==== ¶ [3d] MARRIED. ====

At Watertown, Dr. Walter Hunnewell, to Miss Susan Cook. At Cambridge, Mr. Samuel Morse of Boston, to Miss Eliza Barnard. At Salem, Mr. Samuel Chever, to Miss Hannah Clark. At [Boston? or Bolton?], Capt. John Powell, to Miss Susannah King of Portsmouth.—Mr. Daniel Packard to Miss Agnes Orr.—Capt. Israel Loring to Miss Sally Lebay.—Mr. William Whall, jun. to Miss Maria Jane Stokes.

==== ¶ [3d DIED. ====

At Charleston, S.C. Mrs. Frances Bass wife of Capt. J. Bass. At Campas, in Hungary, a Shepherd, aged 126. He never ate meat, subsisting entirely on milk butter, and cheese. At Philadelphia, Tench Francis, Esq. Purveyor of the United States, aged 69.

Vol. VIII (No. 373) Monday, 26 May 1800.

¶ [2d] We learn that Maj. Wm. Kersey, of the third United States regiment, was killed in a duel on the 11th of March last, at the Natches, by Lieutenant Marks of the same regiment. Mr. Kersey was a subaltern in the New Jersey line during the Revolution was and had risen from an ensign in 1779 to the command of a battalion.

† [3d] Moses Johnson advertises a pocket book which he lost between Charlestown and Keene, containing "several notes of hand against Charles Purkens . . . one note against Major Asa Bullard . . . an order on the County Treasurer, for fourteen dollars, in

favour of Solomon Morse, one receipt against Messrs. Nathan Frazier and Co. . . . " Dated at Keene, 22 May 1800.

† [3d] Samuel Crosby, Clerk, advertises that Mr. Abner Morton has taken management of Charlestown Academy.

¶ [3d] Obadiah Wells offers two cents reward for the return of "an indented apprentice boy, named Abel Hubbard, 19 years of age," who ran away "on the 2d inst." Dated at Charlestown, 17 May 1800.

===== ¶ [3d] MARRIED. =====

Massachusetts.—At Boston, Mr. Benjamin Proctor, to Miss Betsey Lane.
At Leominster, Mr. Israel Nichols, Jun. to Miss Esther Gowing.

===== ¶ [3d DIED. =====

In England, Dr. Warton, "the late elegant poet and judicious critic."—Thomas Cotton, aged 105. He attended the Fish market at Liverpool for 40 years.

Massachusetts.—At Leominster, of a dropsy, on Saturday evening, the 17th of the present month Mr. Abijah Wilbur, aged 23 years, fifer in the company under the command of Capt. J. Tillinghast in the 16th Regiment of the army stationed at Oxford.

At Boston, Mrs. Thankful Helpman, in the 63d year of her age. Madam Mary Gorham, aged 83.

At Malden, Capt. Andrew Gardner of Boston, Æt. 73. At Ipswich, Mr. Joseph Goodhue, Æt. 69

Vol. VIII (No. 374) Monday, 2 June 1800.

† [3b] Account of damage from high winds to a "manufactory for making of Duck" at Lexington, Ky. in late April 1800, where one Mr. Banton was injured. ♦

¶ [3b] DUEL. A letter from Baltimore states, that a duel was fought on Monday morning between captain Edwards and lieutenant Lewis, both of the Marines, in which the former was mortally wounded.

† [3d] Stephen Bowker adv. a stray colt which he found; dated Westmoreland 24 May.

† [3d] Moses Willard, Collector, posts a notice of delinquent taxpayers for proprietors and land owner in the town of Unity, N.H., regarding highway taxes for the year 1799. Property still in delinquency by 15 Sept. 1800 to be auctioned off at the house of Joseph Whiston, Innholder of Unity. Given here is a list of delinquent taxpayers; consult the original advertisement for a breakdown of lot number, lot size, etc.:

William Buswell	Nathaniel French	Benjamin Huntoon
John Mason	Benning Wentworth	Thomas Scribner
Edward Fifield		

===== ¶ [3d] MARRIED. =====

At Leominster, Mr. Israel Nichols, to Miss Esther Gowing. At Portsmouth, Mr. Richard Tucker, aged 63, to Miss Mary Abbot, aged 61; Mr. Samuel Davis to Miss Elizabeth Pitman. At Kittery, Mr. Michael Kennard, to Miss Nabby Mason. At Townsend, Mr. Uriah Searls, to Miss Nabby Giles. At Dracut, Mr. Warren Parker, to Miss Betsy Frye of Andover. At Claremont, Mr. Benjamin Grandey, to Miss Susannah Leet.

===== ¶ [3d] DIED. =====

At Portsmouth, Miss Nancy Haslet, aged 19; Miss Abigail Trefethen, aged 60. At Sterling, Mrs. Sarah Smith, aged 47. At Concord, Mrs. Rebecca Greene, aged 46.

Vol. VIII (No. 375) Monday, 9 June 1800.

† [3d] Advertisement of a festival to be held "by the Brethren of Jerusalem, Golden Rule and Olive Branch Lodges," at brother Bullard's Hall in Walpole. The notice was posted by G. Huntington, D. Leavitt, and M. Field, "Masters of the said Lodges." Also mentioned is a sermon to be delivered by Rev. Dan Foster of Charlestown.

† [3d] Legal notice regarding the estate of William Long, late of Rockingham, Vt., deceased. William Stearns, Calvin Webb, and Joshua Hale appointed Commissioners of said estate; included is a schedule of estate meetings to be held at the house of Quartus Morgan, Innholder of Rockingham. The notice is dated at Rockingham, 8 May 1800.

An identical notice appears in the issue of the week following, but in the issue of 23 June 1800, this notice was altered slightly, to indicate that the estate was insolvent.
† [3d] Legal notice regarding the insolvent estate of Obadiah Lamb, late of Westminster, deceased. Ephraim Ranney, jun. and Eldad Hitchcock appointed Commissioners of said estate; business meetings to be conducted at the dwelling house of Mr. Gideon Warner in Westminster. Notice dated at Westminster, 30 May 1800.

===== ¶ [3d] MARRIED. =====

At Boston, Mr. Silas Penniman, of Boston, to Miss Cynthia Stimpson, of Charlestown. 34

===== ¶ [3d] DIED. =====

At his estate near Kobrin in Russia, suddenly, Prince Italisko, Count Suwarrow Rimniski, who had extracted that debt from so many thousands.
At Bilboa, Mr. James Briton of Marblehead. On his passage from Demarara, for Newhaven, Capt. Russel Hubbard, of Boston. At Vergennes, Daniel Alderman, Esq. aged 42.

Vol. VIII (No. 376) Monday, 16 June 1800.

¶ [3a] Norfolk, Virginia, May 27. Yesterday morning Mr. Thorndick, surgeon of the United States frigate Congress, was found dead in his birth; having his throat cut in a shocking manner.
† [3b] Account of a conflict between Mr. Thomas Field, Editor of the *Republican*, and Mr. Thomas Cross, the latter having assaulted the former. Cross was killed, and Field gave himself up to authorities. The event occurred at "Petersburg" [*Virginia* ?—Ed.] about the middle of May 1800, and the letter was sent to the Editor of a Philadelphia paper, the *Aurora*. ♦
¶ [3c-d] The following advertisement, which appears in a Southcarolina paper, sounds somewhat oddly to northern ears. "Having hired my carpenter fellow, Beaufort, to my son, James Bullock, and he having run away, I will give ten dollars reward on his delivery in gaol or to me, M. Bullock." If the blackamoor is wise he will beware of the heels and horns of his old and young master.
† [3d] Extensive advertisement of goods for sale at David Stone's store in Walpole.
† [3d] Legal notice regarding the insolvent estate of Jonas Newton, late of Alstead, deceased. Oliver Sheperd and Thomas Taylor appointed Commissioners of said estate; business meetings to be conducted at the house of Mary Newton, widow of the deceased. Notice dated at Alstead 29 May 1800.
† [3d] George Sparhawk adv. a stray mare which he found; dated Walpole, 12 June.

===== ¶ [3d] MARRIED. =====

At Salem, Mr. J. Burnham to Mrs. B. Pitman. At Roxbury, Mr. Daniel Weld, of Boston, to Miss Hannah Williams. At Boston, Mr. John Chandler of Petersham, to Miss Elizabeth Greene, daughter of Mr. Benjamin Greene; Christopher Seton, Esq. of the island of Tobago, to Miss P. Wentworth Butler, of Hingham.

===== ¶ [3d] DIED. =====

At Trinadad, Mr. John Scott, of Boston, merchant, aged 23. At Philadelphia, Capt. Robert Jackson, of Boston, aged 27. At Quincy, Rev. Anthony Wibird, Senior Pastor of the Congregational Church in that town, aged 72. At Vergennes, Vt. Mrs. Nancy Woodbridge, consort of Hon. Enoch Woodbridge, Esq.

¶ [3d] Whereas Abigail, my wife, has eloped from my bed and board, and refuses to return and live with me, this is to forbid all persons harbouring or trusting her on my account, as I will not pay any debts of her contracting after this date.

Walter Himes.
Acworth, June 6, 1800.

Vol. VIII (No. 377) Monday, 23 June 1800.

† [2c-d] Article dated at Martinsburg, Virginia, describing a duel fought near Harper's Ferry, between Lieut. Swan and one Elliot. ♦

† [2d] Account of a rabid fox which attacked Mr. Ephraim Sayers, of Washington County, Penn., 11 May 1800. Sayers was crossing "the South mountain" in company with one George Watt when attacked. "Mr. Sayers is now lying under the care of doctor Hamilton, in York county, Marsh creek settlement." The article is contained under the Philadelphia news. ♦

† [3b] Article regarding Lucy Day, "a lewd woman" who was under the guardianship of the selectmen of Freeport, Maine, but who ran away. The woman then accused three soldiers at "Fort Sumner" of rape. The article is dated at Portland, Maine. ♦

† [3d] Legal notice regarding the insolvent estate of Reuben Fenno, late of Westmoreland, N.H., deceased. Joseph Burt, Joseph Buffum, and Nathaniel Fisk, appointed Commissioners of said estate; business meetings to be conducted at the house of widow Fanny Fenno at Westmoreland. Notice dated there 13 June 1800.

===== ¶ [3d] MARRIED. =====

At Salem, Mr. James Gavet, to Miss Abigail Duparr. At Bradford, Mr. Samuel Stillman Jackson, to Miss Polly Merrill. At Newburyport, Mr. Samuel Lord Dexter, to Miss Mehitable Hoyt, of Hamstead. At Middleborough, Mr. Kimball Pratt, aged 65, to Miss Martha Morse, aged 16.

===== ¶ [3d] DIED. =====

At Newyork, Gen. John Lamb, aged 67. At Weathersfield, Con. Mr. Daniel Willard, aged 67. At Worcester, Mrs. Eliza Wheeler, consort of Mr. Daniel G. Wheeler, aged 26. At Tewksbury, Eliphalet Hunt, aged 26. At Sea, Mr. Allen Breed, of Davners. [sic] 35 At Marblehead, Mr. Sylvester Stevens. At Scituate, Mr. Elisha Randall aged 83. At Newburyport, Mr. Samuel Williams, aged 21. At Stockbridge, Mrs. Caswell, wife of Mr. Ezra Caswell. At Barnstable, Mrs. Nabby Stimpson, aged 23. At Dracut, Capt. Stephen Russell, aged 28. At Buckston, 36 Mrs. Mary Barns, aged 29.

Vol. VIII (No. 378)   Monday, 30 June 1800.

† [2d-3a] Extensive account of the fate of the British armed brig *Swallow*, Stephen Bourdett, master, which sank after a storm in the Atlantic. A few of the crew survived in a lifeboat for many days without provisions, but only the captain and one other survived to reach New York, after being picked up by the schooner *William*, Jeremiah Goodrich, master. Only one of the *Swallow's* crew was specifically named, Robert Dickie, who died aboard the *William*. The article is contained in the New York news. ♦

† [3a] Another account of a shipwreck contained under the New York news, as given by the two survivors, Thomas White and John Drown, of the schooner *Industry*, of Boston. The vessel sank somewhere in the West Indies, on the 27th of May 1800; the two survivors swam "to a Spanish settlement" and were eventually picked up by the *Minerva*, which was en route to Baltimore. Capt. Shubal Coin is mentioned in this article, but the sentence structure does not clarify whether he was the captain of the *Industry* or the *Minerva*. ♦

† [3a] Account given by Dr. Tilton, late surgeon of the ship Ariel, Capt. Coats, from Canton to Philadelphia, which was captured by French privateers, 5 May 1800. Capt. Coats and "Mr. Burger, of this city" were both shot, but whether they died of their wounds is not clear. The article is contained in the New York news. ♦

† [3a] Account of the capture of three American vessels by French privateers: 1) an unnamed vessel commanded by Capt. Tappan, of Newburyport, 2) the ship *Mac*, Capt. Ingalls, bound from Greenock to Charleston, and 3) the *Mermaid*, of New York, Capt. Farrier. ♦

† [3d] Advertisement by *William Fitch & Co.*, dated at Rockingham, 23 June 1800, requesting "Lambskins with the wool on, also for all kinds of Hatting Furs."

Vol. VIII (No. 379)   Monday, 7 July 1800.

¶ [3b] Lexington, Kentucky. June 3. Two Indians have killed in a barbarous manner, James Johnston, living on Lynn Camp Creek.—We also learn, that they have killed two men at the lower end of Powell's valley, and not far from thence two boys.

† [3d] Peter Fletcher advertises a farm for sale in Springfield, [Vt.—Ed.]; dated at Springfield 5 July 1800. Benjamin Bowker of Springfield named as a point of contact.

† [3d] List of letters remaining at the Post Office in Walpole, N.H., 1 July 1800, as compiled by Alex. Thomas, Postmaster:

Mrs. Sally Armstrong,	Chesterfield, N.H.	Samuel Mott,	Rockingham.
Isaac Butterfield, Esq.	Westmoreland, N.H.	James Parker,	Andover, Vt.
Dr. Chancy C. Chandler,	Andover, Vt.	Levi Williams,	Walpole.
Amos Cumings,	Walpole, N.H.	Peleg Sanford,	Walpole. 3.
Asa Fisher,	" "	Samuel Walker,	Walpole.
Samuel Fales,	" "	Joshua Wood,	Alstead.
David Ferrin, Esq.	Rockingham, Vt.	Dr. Samuel Cutler,	Rockingham, Vt.
William Graham,	Walpole, N.H.	Job F. Brooks,	Westmoreland.
Samuel Gerould,	Stoddard, N.H.	Henry Fitch,	Walpole.
Moses Hale,	Alstead, N.H.	Capt. Simon Baxter,	Surry.
Capt. Jonathan Hall,	Walpole, N.H.	Abner Felt,	New Andover, Vt.
Jonathan Lee,	" "	Ephraim Towner,	Newport, N.H.
James Marr,	Alstead.	Gardiner Towne,	Stoddard, N.H.

===== ¶ [3d] MARRIED. =====

At Gloucester, Capt. Solomon Allen, jun. to Miss Nabby Flowers. At Rowley, Mr. Benjamin Bishop, jun. to Miss Betsy Chaplain; Mr. Peabody Dole, to Miss Lydia Nelson.

===== ¶ [3d] DIED. =====

In England, William Cowper, Esq. Æt. 69, one of the most chaste, and el[e]gant of the English Poets. At Topsfield, Mr. John Conant, Æt. 32. At Danvers, Mr. Jno. Brown, Æt. 68. At Beverly, Mrs. Mary Curtis, Æt. 74. At Lynn, (drowned,) Mr. Nathaniel Fuller, Æt. 40. On board the ship Antelope, from the Havannah, Mr. Charles Goodwin chief mate—lamented by all who knew him. He lived but for others; he died the sport of fortune's wretched power—not will he be forgotten, until virtue and benevolence shall cease to be revered.—In Grenada, Mr. James Findlay, Editor of the Grenada Gazette.

Vol. VIII (No. 380) Monday, 14 July 1800.

† [1a] A list of persons who have not paid their 1797 highway tax for the town of Newport, N.H., as compiled by Uriah Willcox and Reuben Bascom, Selectmen, and Solomon Dunham, Collector. Property still in delinquency by 2 Sept. 1800 to be auctioned off at the house of Jesse Wilcox, jun., Newport.

	No. Div.	No. Lot.	No. Acres.	Value. D. C.	Tax. D. C.
John Blodgett, Ambrose Cossett, }	5	58	80	100	17
Thomas Boles,	3	53	100	100	17
Thomas Boles,	4	9	100	100	17
Thomas Boles,	5	24	100	100	17
Henry Stevens,	4	40	30	60	11
Jeremiah Clements, original proprietor, }	5	42	80	80	14

† [3d] A list of letters remaining at the Post Office in Charlestown, N.H., 1 July 1800, as compiled by Samuel Crosby, Postmaster: [37]

Daniel Adams,	Langdon.	Lieut. John Hastings,	Charlestown.
Caleb Allen,	Charlestown.	Col. George Kimball,	Eaton, L. Canada.
Isaac Bidwell,	Weathersfield, Vt.	Russel Mason,	Weathersfield, Vt.
Samuel Burr,	Rockingham, Vt.	Seth Phelps,	Chester, Cheshire County [38]
Sarah Cass,	Springfield, Vt.		
Sarah Cady,	Alstead.	Elisha Petty,	Springfield, Vt.
Phineas Caal,	Cornish.	John Prentiss,	Wendell.
William Divol,	Charlestown.	Hepzibah Reed,	Charlestown.
Peter Davis,	Unity.	Daniel Safford,	Springfield, Vt.
Samuel Gaskill, Esq.	Richmond.	Isaac Tower,	" "
James Hall,	Springfield, Vt.	Joshua Whitney,	Wendell.
Jona. R. Hale,	Chesterfield.	Joshua Wood,	Alstead.

===== ¶ [3d] MARRIED. =====

At Concord, Mr. Oliver Brewster, of Boston, merchant, to Miss Mary Jones, of the former place.
  At Baltimore, Capt. Sothod, of Boston to Mrs. Speck.
  At Roxbury, Capt. Joseph Curtis to Miss Bethiah Parker.
  At Philadelphia, on Saturday evening the 28th ult. [sic] by the Right Rev. Doctor White, Mr. William Duane, to Mrs. Margaret Harman Bache, relict of the late Benjamin F. Bache ! ! !

===== ¶ [3d] DIED. =====

At Newyork, Capt. Thomas Brown of the ship Albemarle. At Wilbraham, Mr. Abdiel [Boomis ? or Loomis ?], Æt. [30?]. Mr. Joel Stebbins, Æt. 48. At Springfield, Mrs. Hannah Day, Æt. 87. In Europe, the celebrated Mallet du Pan. In Ireland, W. Spillard, the pedestrian traveller, who traversed so great a part of the American continent. At Malden, Mr. Joseph Barrett. At Boston, Mrs. Mary Howe, aged 38, wife of Mr. John Howe, Jun. At Lem[p]ster, Mrs. Rachel Hurd, aged 51, consort of Capt. Shubael Hurd.
  Of the scarlatina, in this town, on Wednesday last, much lamented, Miss Polly Sikes, aged 15, daughter of Mr. Nathaniel Sikes [. . .]

Vol. VIII (No. 381) Monday, 21 July 1800.

† [3b] Account of a rape committed on a girl in New York City by one Kroucher; the suspect also had connections with Juliana Sands, who was previously murdered. ♦
¶ [3b] Lansingburgh, New York, July 1. MELANCHOLY ACCIDENT. The following melancholy accident happened in Troy, on Friday last:—A person having dropped his shoe into a well near Mr. Ashley's tavern, which had been covered and unused for some time, persuaded Master Jack Tillman, a young lad about fourteen years of age, son of the late Christopher Tillman, Esq. of this village, to descend into the well to fetch it up. A stick was tied on the end of a rope for the purpose, on which he placed his feet, and was lowered down; but as he approached the bottom, he was almost instantaneously suffocated with the dead air, and dropped from the rope. A Mr. Jesse Benham, who has attended the ferry at Troy, inconsiderately went down after him, and met with a like fate. The water in the well not being more than a foot in depth, the bodies were soon taken up, but every attempt to reanimate them proved ineffectual. While we sympathise with the repectable and numerous connections of the former, and most sincerely regret his premature death, our sensibility must be peculiarly awakened at the fate of the latter, who has left a wife and several children to lament an irreparable loss.
  † [3c] Samuel Lord, twelve year-old son of John Lord, Esq., of Berwick, [Maine—Ed.], saved a person from drowning. The article is dated at Newburyport, Mass. ♦
  † [3d] Daniel Farrand announces that he has removed from Newbury, [Vt.—Ed.] to Rockingham, Windham County, and "has left his unfinished business, in the counties of Caledonia, and Orange, with Benjamin Porter, Esq., of Newbury, who will attend to the collection and adjustment of their demands." Dated Rockingham, 15 July 1800.
  † [3d] List of letters remaining at the Post Office in Westminster, Vt., 1 July 1800, as compiled by Eleazer May, Postmaster:

Lieut. James Dill,	Westminster, 2.	John Dam,	Westminster.
Jonathan Goold,	"	Thomas Duglass,	"
Jacob Lang,	"	Solomon Goodall,	Jamaica.
James Mardeen,	"	Bailey Rawson,	Townsend.
Thaddeus Hurlburt,	"	Miles Putnam,	Grafton, 2.

† [3d] "Jessemiah" Kitteridge requests all outstanding debts to be paid up. In the following week's issue, his name has been changed to Jesseniah Kitteridge. The notice is dated at Walpole, 18 July 1800.
  † [3d] John Sinkler finds a lost note in Winchester; advertisement dated 21 July [1800.]

Vol. VIII (No. 382) Monday, 28 July 1800.

† [3c] Legal notice regarding Phinehas Chapin, of Newport, N.H., who was appointed guardian of Abigail Goodwin, Molly Goodwin, "Rhode" Goodwin, Ruth Goodwin, and

Israel Goodwin, minors and heirs of Theophilus Goodwin, late of Newport, deceased. Chapin requests that the heirs' property in Newport be sold for their support.

† [3c] Elisha W. Barber offers a farm for sale in Fairfield, Vt.; adv. dated 15 July 1800.

† [3d] Legal notice regarding the insolvent estate of Benjamin Peterson, late of Claremont, N.H., deceased. Ambrous Cosset, Sanford Kingsbury, and Hezekiah Roys were appointed Commissioners of said estate; business meetings to be held at the house of Dr. Thomas Sterne, Innholder in Claremont. Adv. dated Claremont, 30 June.

† [3d] Legal notice regarding the insolvent estate of William Whiting, late of Claremont, N.H., deceased. Ezra Jones, Hezekiah Rice, and Jonathan Fisher appointed Commissioners; business meetings to be conducted at the house of Stephen Dexter, Innholder at Claremont. Adv. dated at Claremont 30 June 1800.

† [3d] Adv. regarding the proposed "third Turnpike Road" in N.H., which will pass from Bellows' Falls to the Massachusetts line. One point of reference named is Millican's Tavern in Jaffrey, which was near the proposed route. The notice was posted by Samuel West, Clerk.

===== ¶ [3d] ORDAINED. =====

At New Hampton, Rev. Salmon Hebard.

===== ¶ [3d] MARRIED. =====

At Portsmouth, the Hon. James Sheafe, Esq. Senator of the United States, for this State, to Miss Polly Fisher, daughter of John Fisher, Esq. of London.

At Marlborough, Mr. Samuel Thurston to Miss Sally French.

===== ¶ [3d] DIED. =====

At Scarborough, the 4th inst. of canine madness, a son of Mr. Enoch Berry, aged 10 years. This boy was bitten in April last by a cat, which at the time was supposed to be affected with canine madness and was immediately killed on that account. The wound was perfectly healed in a few days, and the boy was apparently well till Tuesday the 1st inst. when he complained of the wounded hand's paining him. The symptoms of madness soon after begun—he refused all foods except apples, which he bit at, and ate without touching them with his hands. Water was offered him, and the physician ordered it poured out before him, but he turned from it with disgust, and was greatly agitated when he saw it. He tried to bite everything which came in his way, and once fastened his teeth on his father's arm, took out a piece of the sleeve of his coat and shirt, but fortunately did not touch the flesh. He had his senses perfectly at intervals, knew his friends, but was all the time in the greatest agonies. There was no great variation in his symptoms, excepting only that they grew stronger, and his horror became more extreme, till Friday evening, when he expired in the most excruciating tortures.

At Keene, Mr. Charles Fitch, formerly of this town.—At Brookline, Mrs. Abigail Pierce. At Quincey, the Rev. Anthony Wibird, sen. At Hopkinton, Mr. Samuel Gage. At Exeter, widow Sarah Nelson. At Packersfield, Mr. Caleb Goodenow, aged 20.

Vol. VIII (No. 383) Monday, 4 Aug. 1800.

† [3d] Legal notice by Henry Fitch, Administrator of the estate of Charles Fitch, late of Walpole, deceased. Dated at Walpole, 26 July 1800.

† [3d] Darius Smith proposes to carry newspapers into several towns in Vermont; advertisement dated at Westminster, 4 Aug. 1800.

† [3d] Jonathan Royce posts a notice for his lost pocket book; dated Walpole, 2 Aug.

† [3d] Richard Kelly adv. for a lost hat, which he supposed someone took "at the Hall of Major Bullard, in Walpole . . . " Dated at Walpole, 27 July 1800.

† [3d] Abraham Byington adv. help wanted for "one or two journeymen at the joiner's business," dated Rockingham 24 July 1800.

===== ¶ [3d] MARRIED. =====

At Milton, Mr. Samuel Billings, of Boston, to Miss Hester Hill, of Milton. At Boston, Mr. John Haynes to Miss Mary Hall.

===== ¶ [3d] DIED. =====

At Croydon, Mr. Jonah Stow, aged 53.

Vol. VIII (No. 384) Monday, 11 Aug. 1800.

† [2d-3a] Extensive account of the death of Hugh Case, a lad about 13 years of age who was fatally burned in an explosion of a wine barrel, on the 21st of July. The article is dated at Hartford, Conn., but the event occurred at "Messrs. Mills & Ives' Store in W. Simbury." Also involved in the fire, but not injured, were Mr. Daniel Case 2d, and Mr. Samuel Palmer. The lad was "son to the widow Elizabeth Case of this society," though the context of this statement is unknown. ♦

† [3d] Chronicle of the death, 20 July 1800, at Stockbridge, Mass., of Sally Parker, daughter of Mr. Benjamin Parker, about 10 years of age. The girl's foot was caught in her horse's saddle straps, and she was dragged to her death. ♦

† [3d] A very lengthy account of the slow death of Asa Felton, of Danvers, Mass., who was bitten by a rabid dog in May, 1793. For five years thereafter he maintained good health, but then later suffered through the end stages of the hydrophobia. He died in the 42d year of his age, leaving a wife and six children. ♦

† [3d] Levi Green, Guardian to Lucy Wheeler ("a lunatic person" of Westmoreland, N.H.,) petitions the Superior Court of Judicature, Cheshire County, N.H., in order to receive authority to sell real estate belonging to said Lucy for her support.

† [3d] Two lists of delinquent taxpayers for land in Washington, N.H.:

> 1) A list for "the nonresident proprietors and land owners in the town of Washington, who have not paid their taxes for the year 1798." Peter Pierce and Stephen Austin are named in this list, which was made by Jeremiah Bacon, Azariah Faxon, and Ephraim Farvell, Selectmen of Washington. [39]

> 2) A list of outstanding taxes due for the year 1799, as made by David Danforth and Jonathan Clarke, Selectmen of Washington, and reported by Ebenezer Spaulding, Collector: Moses Man, Enoch Houghton, John Weatherington, Thomas Packer, Esq., Peter Peirce, William Bartlate, and Elnathan Blood.

† [3d] Recruitment notice by Seymour Renick, 2d Lieut. 2d U.S. Reg. Infantry, regarding rendezvouses in Vermont, Massachusetts, and Connecticut.

===== ¶ [3c] MARRIED. =====

At Boston, Capt. Melzer Joy, to Miss Mary Eliot, of [Fairfield?]; John W. Gurly, Esq. to Miss Grace Stackpole. At Sutton, Mr. Joseph Farnsworth, or Miss Asenath Waters.

===== ¶ [3c] DIED. =====

At Augusta, Georgia, Commodore Oliver Bowen. At Boston, Mr. William Cuttler; Mrs. Mary Cushing, aged 25. At Newtown, Mr. William Park, aged 83. At Salem, Mr. George Ireland, aged 25. At Salisbury, Mr. Samuel Pike, aged 40. At Portsmouth, Mr. Sullivan Holman, aged 40.

Vol. VIII (No. 385) Monday, 18 Aug. 1800.

† [1b] Josiah Whitney advertises for several ship carpenters and axe men, for work in Georgia. "Apply to Josiah Whitney at Bullard's Tavern, Walpole, Newhampshire, on the 18th instant; 19th at Dickinson's, Brattleborough, Vermont; 20th, at Hunt's, Northfield, Massachusetts; 23d, at Forbes's, Westborough."

† [3d] David Drury of Weston, Vermont, offers a farm for sale; dated Weston 28 July.

† [3d] Amasa Allen requests outstanding debts to be paid, and also advertisement of items for sale; dated Walpole, 12 August 1800.

† [3d] Notice by Samuel Crosby, Collector of the Revenue, for the 2d division, District of New Hampshire, regarding licenses for liquor sales and certificates for carriages.

† [3d] Isaac Temple adv. that he found a lost mare; dated Alstead 15 Aug. 1800.

Vol. VIII (No. 386) Monday, 25 Aug. 1800.

† [3b] Account of the death at Westmoreland, N.H. of Mr. Josiah Briggs, who presumably was struck in the head while clearing logs, and died instantly. Briggs was between 65 and 70 years of age, and left "an aged widow and 13 children to lament his

untimely exit." The article is dated at Keene, 16 August, but the event occurred on "Tuesday last." ♦

¶ [3c] At Hanover, the dysentary attended with a fever, has swept off many of its inhabitants. The disorder is confined chiefly to children, but in some instances it has proved mortal in adults. A day has been set apart by the inhabitants of those parts of the town where it has raged with the most violence, for the purpose of fasting and prayer. The Hon. Jonathan Freeman Esq. we learn, lies dangerously ill of the disorder. A similar kind of sickness is said to be prevalent in Norwich, V. in the vicinity of Hanover.

† [3d] Robert Duncan, Proprietors Collector, posts a notice that a new tax was voted on certain tracts of land in New Grantham, N.H. Dated there 18 June 1800.

===== ¶ [3d] MARRIED. =====

At Philadelphia, Capt. Marsh Clare, of Boston, to Miss Mary L. Fallon, daughter of the late doctor Jones Fallon of Southcarolina. At Barnstable, Ebenezer Gay, Esq. of Boston, to Miss Mary Alline Otis, of the former place.

===== ¶ [3d] DIED. =====

At Charleston, Southcarolina, Mr. Micah Johnson, printer, formerly of Northampton, Mass. At Philadelphia, Mr. John Drinker. At Boston, Col. Marston Watson, aged 45. Mr. James Tilden, aged 20; Mr. Isaac Bowers Clarke, aged 21. At Northampton, Master Phillip Strong, youngest son of his Excellency Governor Strong.

¶ [3d] TAKE NOTICE. Ran away from me the subscriber, the seventeenth instant, an apprentice boy, named John Davis, indented to me by the town of Swanzey, about nineteen years and three months of age. Whoever will take up said boy, and return him to me, shall have one cent reward, and no charges paid. All persons are forbid harbouring or trusting said boy, as they would wish to escape the penalty of the law.

Jesse Stearns.

Walpole, August 18, 1800.

¶ [3d] A Lost SON. A Boy, named Moses Nichols, in the fifteenth year of his age, son to the subscriber, was on the 27th of July last seduced to leave his home, by a very vicious fellow, named George Nichols, of about nineteen years of age. Said Moses has worked at the shoemaking business, had on, when he went away, a brown coat, light coloured jacket, darkish trowsers, half boots; is light complexioned, and has blue eyes, has a scar on one ancle [sic] caused by a scald. If any person can discover said boy and send, by letter, to the post office in Plymouth, Newhampshire, directed to the subscriber, he shall be handsomely rewarded.

Moses Nichols.

Thornton, August 12, 1800.

Vol. VIII (No. 387) Monday, 1 Sept. 1800.

¶ [3a] Charleston, Southcarolina. Aug. 5. Yesterday, 15 dwelling houses were destroyed by fire, on the west side of King Street. The fire began by accident.—Mr. and Mrs. Miller, were drawing rum by candle light, which caught the rum, communicated the fire to a keg of gun powder, killed Mr. and Mrs. Miller, and occasioned the calamity. The principal sufferers are Mrs. Brunson—Messrs. Miller, Wills, Turner, Vaughan, Pelot, Lewin, M'Millan, Keels, Gray, Presly, Simmons, Crawford, Singleton, M'Cracken, Phillips, and Wells.

† [3d] Public notice stating that Solomon Robbins, of Westmoreland, N.H., has petitioned the General Court of New Hampshire, for the right to construct a bridge across the Connecticut River within the bounds of Westmoreland.

† [3d] Notice concerning the "Second Turnpike Road in Newhampshire," posted by the Directors of said Corporation: Phineas Williams, James Bingham, David Heald, Oliver Holmes, Daniel Warner, William Sweetser, and John M'Neal. The advertisement also mentions Josiah Stevens, Esq., Treasurer of said Corporation.

===== ¶ [3d] DIED. =====

At Coventry, (Con.) Mr. Benjamin Grover, aged 50. In Canada, Jean Baptiste Boucher, Esq. Sieur de Nivorville, Proprietor of Chamblee, aged 86. In Ireland, Miss Marston, aged 100. At Rutland, Mr. Thomas Wood aged 94.

Vol. VIII (No. 388) Monday, 8 Sept. 1800.

† [3d] Legal notice regarding the insolvent estate of Levi Edgell, late of Westminster, deceased. The notice was posted by Eldad Hitchcock, Esq. and Gideon Webster, Commissioners, and dated at Westminster, 2 Sept. 1800.

† [3d] Advertisment by "Mr. Blakmer" which proposes a new dancing school at Walpole, dated 8 Sept. 1800.

† [3d] Notice regarding contracts for the construction of the "3d Newhampshire turnpike road," as posted by John Bellows, Amasa Allen, Lockhart Willard, Benjamin Prescott, and Nathan Meriam. The meetings to be held at the following locations: Samuel Grant, *Walpole*; Davis Carpenter, *Walpole*; Stephen Chase, *Keene*; Thomas Edwards, *Keene*; Benjamin Longley, *Marlboro'*; ———— Danforth, *Jaffrey*; Benjamin Prescott, *Jaffrey*; and Nathan Meriam, *New Ipswich*.

===== ¶ [3d] MARRIED. =====

At Boston, Mr. Robert Harrington, of Lexington, to Mrs. Elizabeth Renous of Boston. —Capt. James Whalon Jun. to Miss Margery Blanchard Baxter.

===== ¶ [3d] DIED. =====

At Boston, Col. Marston Watson, in the 45th year of his age.. At Guilford, (Conn.) widow Mary Norton, of a cancer, supposed to be 105 years and 9 months old. At Charleston, (S.C.) the Hon. John Rutledge.—At Coventry, Mr. David Hibbard, in the 85th year of his age. At Hartland, Mr. Abel Moses, in the 25th year of his age.

Vol. VIII (No. 389) Monday, 15 Sept. 1800.

† [1b] Advertisement of pamphlets for sale by "Mr. Darius Smith, who distributes the Farmer's Museum south and west of Walpole, in the State of Vermont."

† [3b-c] Article describing the capture of Rosewell Bingham, alias Robert Beerman, Levy Stephens, and Ephraim Fitch, counterfeiters, captured in Philadelphia. ♦

¶ [3c] Hartford, Connecticut, Sept. 8. Friday the 29th ult. a daughter of Mr. Joshua Woodworth, of Coventry, about four years old was killed suddenly by a twin brother of hers accidentally turning over a wheel with a sharp spindle, as they were playing together. The spindle pierced through her breast into her stomach several inches, of which wound she died in about ten minutes, to the inexpressible grief of her parents.

† [3d] Mr. Joseph Hitsell robbed in New York City. ♦

Vol. VIII (No. 390) Monday, 22 Sept. 1800.

† [3b-c] Extensive article relating the wounds received by Captain Bradford and Mr. John Boyler, who were wounded in an attack by a French privateer off the coast of Portugal or Spain, 8 July 1800. Bradford and Boyler were taken to a hospital in Lisbon, Portugal, where the Captain had a leg amputated. The news was relayed by Mr. Charles Finley, who was aboard the *Industry*. ♦

† [3c-d] Gruesome account of the murder of a son of Mr. Bixby of Winchendon, Mass. The son was killed by one Robbins, who was "subject to temporary fits of insanity" and was in the employ of the elder Bixby. The article is contained in the news dated at Worcester, 17 Sept., the event having occurred "last week." ♦

† [3d] Sad account of the death of Ruth Higgens, a young daughter of Mr. Isaac Higgens of Brattleboro', Vermont. The girl was crushed to death by a cart wheel passing over her, "on Tuesday last." The article is dated at Brattleborough, 13 Sept. ♦

† [3d] Legal notice regarding the estate of Amariah Rockwell, late of Langdon, N.H. deceased; notice posted by Andrew French, Executor; dated Walpole, 17 Sept. 1800.

† [3d] A legal notice regarding the estate of Samuel Chase, Esq., late of Cornish, N.H., deceased. The notice was posted by the subscriber, March Chase, Executor of said estate, but the sentence structure within the notice is confusing, and perhaps implies that there were two men by the name of March Chase: "All persons having demands against the estate of said deceased, are requested to exhibit the same to March Chase in said Cornish, or to the subscriber, in Sutton, in Worcester county, and commonwealth of Massachusetts . . . " The notice is dated at Cornish, 11 Sept. 1800.

¶ [3d] DIED.

At Bridgewater, Dr. Elisha Tillson, aged 36. At Portland, Mrs. Beersheba Henderson, aged 40. At Easton, (Penn.) Rev. Jacob V. Baskir[k?] aged 62. At West Springfield, Miss Parnel M. Merrick, aged 22. At East Hartford, Mrs. Mabel Bidwell, aged 87. At Hopkinton, Mr. Samuel Walker, aged 44. At Salisbury, Mr. Moses Rowell, aged 68. At Portsmouth, Mr. Thomas Preist, aged 47. Mr. John Beck, aged 76. At Boston, Mr. Joseph Hussey, merchant, aged 60. Mr. Benjamin Jennings, aged 86. At Roxbury, Mr. Joseph Ruggles, 3d, aged 28. At Wardsborough, Vt. Mr. Joseph Chamberlain, aged 38, formerly of Charlestown.

Vol. VIII (No. 391) Monday, 29 Sept. 1800.

† [2c-d] Extensive account of the murder of Capt. John Patterson, of Dinguidsville, Buckingham County, Virginia. Patterson was killed by his slave; the article is dated at Richmond, Va., 5 Sept. ♦

† [3a] Peter Legaux, of Springfield, Penn., cultivates wine. ♦

† [3d] Legal notice regarding the insolvent estate of Prince Atwood, late of Putney, Vt., deceased. Christopher Ormsbee and Aaron Martin were appointed Commissioners of said estate; business meetings to be conducted at the house of Mr. Abial Briggs in Putney. The notice is dated at Putney, 3 Sept. 1800.

¶ [3d] TAKE NOTICE. Whereas Meriam, wife of the subscriber, has left my bed and board and otherwise conducted herself in an improper manner, this is to caution all persons not to harbour or trust her on my account, as I will pay no debts of her contracting after this date.

Stephen Fisk.

Walpole, Sept. 25, 1800.

Vol. VIII (No. 392) Monday, 6 Oct. 1800.

† [3d] Notice by the Third New Hampshire Turnpike Corporation, regarding a meeting to be held at the house of Dr. Thomas Edwards, Keene, N.H.; notice posted by John Bellows, *President*.

† [3d] List of letters remaining at the Post Office, Walpole, N.H., 1 Oct. 1800, as compiled by Alex. Thomas, Postmaster:

Isaac Abbot,	Chesterfield.	J.R. Hale,	Chesterfield.
Mr. Alexander, merchant	Winchester.	Thomas Howe,	Westmoreland.
Luther Adams,	Rockingham.	Mrs. Chloe Hall,	"
Job F. Brooks,	Westmoreland.	Hercules Hayward,	Surry.
Increase Blake,	Walpole.	Lieut. E.A. Hall,	Westmoreland.
Joseph Buffum,	Westmoreland.	Samuel Johnson,	Alstead.
Wm. Coolidge,	Surry.	Oliver Lovel, Esq.	Rockingham.
Edward Crandal,	Keene.	Elijah Norris,	Surry.
Jeremiah Dudly,	Newport.	Phinehas Parker,	Claremont.
John Dana,	Walpole.	Asa Pemberton,	Westminster.
Solomon Davis,	Chesterfield.	Nathan Smith,	Walpole.
Mrs. Patience Estabrooks,	Walpole. 2.	Abel Stockwell,	Chesterfield 2.
Capt. N. Estabrooks,	Westmoreland.	Cushman Smith,	Surry.
Abner Felt,	Andover.	Experience Storrs,	Westmoreland.
Roger Fenton,	Walpole.	Capt. I.E. Trask,	Westminster.
Capt. T.K. Green,	Westmoreland.	Gardiner Towne,	Stoddard.
Mr. John Goldsmith,	Walpole.		

¶ [3d] MARRIED.

At Portsmouth, Oliver Crosby, Esq. of Dover, to Miss Harriot Chase.

At Amherst, the Rev. Jesse Appleton, of Hampton, to Miss Elizabeth Means, of the former place.

¶ [3d] DIED.

At Lancaster, Hon. John Sprague, Esq. Chief Justice of the Court of Common Pleas for the County of Worcester. At Princeton, Deac. Adonijah Howe, aged 63. At

Newport, Mr. Henry Barber, printer and editor of the Newport Mercury. At Washington, the Rev. George L[eslie?], in the 73d year of his age, and 51st of his Ministry. At Deerfield, the Hon. David Sexton, Esq. one of the members of the Senate of that Commonwealth. At Newburyport, Mrs. Mary Bond, consort of Doct. John Bond of that place.

Vol. VIII (No. 393) Monday, 13 Oct. 1800.

† [3d] Legal notice regarding the insolvent estate of Nathaniel Fisher, late of Newport, N.H., deceased. Jesse Lane, Samuel Hurd, and Reuben Bascom were appointed Commissioners; business meetings to be conducted at the house of Jesse Wilcox, Jun., Innholder at Newport. Notice dated at Newport, 2 Oct. 1800.

† [3d] A public notice stating that the Partnership of *Grant and Fessenden* is dissolved; dated at Walpole, 9 Oct. 1800.

===== ¶ [3d] MARRIED. =====

At Boston, by the Rev. Dr. West, Mr. Joseph Richards, to Miss Alice Winchester Lovring.

At Acworth, on Tuesday last, Mr. Levi Turner, to Miss Delia Currier.

===== ¶ [3d] DIED. =====

At Boston, Mr. Robert Lamb, aged 52. At Newport, William Gibson, Esq. of Georgia, Æt.51. At Newyork, Mr. John Drake, merchant; Mr. John Mercereau, merchant. At Boston, Mrs. Hannah Jackson, Æt. 58. Mrs. Mary Winslow aged 44. Mr. Francis Andrews aged 35, a native of England. At Newport, after an illness of a few hours, Mr. Henry Barber, aged 53, Editor of the Newport Mercury.

Vol. VIII (No. 394) Monday, 20 Oct. 1800.

† [2c] Account of the execution of James Allen and John Watson, found guilty by a British court martial for the murder of Capt. Pigot, of the *Hermoine*. Thomas Nash, Irishman, *alias* Jonathan Robbins, was connected with this mutiny. The article is dated at Portsmouth, England, 18 Aug. ◆

† [2d] Account of the murder of Miss Elvey Garthright, "not more that 18 years of age," of Henrico County, Virginia. Miss Garthright was murdered en route from her sister's (the wife of Mr. John Carter,) to her aunt's, Mrs. Whitlock. The article is dated at Richmond, Va., 16 Sept. 1800. ◆

† [2d-3a] Detailed account of the brig *John*, Capt. Atkins, which was wrecked by heavy seas, 15 Sept. 1800, en route from Lisbon to Philadelphia. The ship was carrying part of the crew and passengers of the *Orion*, Capt. Bunker, of and for New York, which previously had sprung a leak and sank. Mr. and Mrs. Gibson and [their?] two children (passengers,) Capt. Bunker, and "two boys belonging to Capt. Atkins," were among the survivors. These souls spent seven days floating on wreckage before they were picked up by a passing schooner. The article is dated at Philadelphia, 7 Oct. ◆

† [3d] Recruitment notice posted by William Laidlie, Lieut. 2d. Regt. U.S. Infantry, Commanding at Westminster Rendezvous, dated Westminster 11 Oct. 1800.

† [3d] Jacob Pierce adv. for a missing horse, dated at Walpole 18 Oct. 1800.

===== ¶ [3d] MARRIED. =====

At Boston, Dr. Robert Fennelly, to Miss Eliza Hilt;—Dr. Amos Bancroft, of Weston, to Miss Sarah Bass;—Mr. Ralph Abrams, to Miss Mehitable Welch.

At Concord, Mr. Abraham Butterfield, merchant, to Miss Mary Cordia.

At Hamilton, Mr. Jacob Berry, of Salem, to Miss Lavinia Cutler, of the former place.

At Newport, Capt. Nathan Fay of Alstead, to Miss Margery Newton of the former place.

At Alstead, Mr. Horatio Cooper to Miss Eliza Gale.—Mr. Willard Moore of Acworth to Miss Polly Fish.

===== ¶ [3d] DIED. =====

At Amherst, N.H. Mr. Joseph Prince, aged 50. At Albany, Mr. Herman Brimmer of Boston, merchant, aged 63. At Westmoreland, on the 5th inst. Mrs. Lucy Temple, consort of Mr. Archelaus Temple, aged 61.

Vol. VIII (No. 395) Monday, 27 Oct. 1800.

¶ [3b] Salem, Massachusetts. Oct. 13. On Wednesday evening last, a melancholy accident happened at Beverly:—Two soldiers returning from the muster at Danvers, stopped at the house of a Mr. Morgan, and previous to going in, determined to Salute him; one of the muskets was loaded with two balls and three buck shot, and a double charge (it was a borrowed one) the charge passed through the house, and wounded Mr. Morgan in the leg, in such a shocking manner, that it has since been amputated. The great number of disasters arising from the foolish custom of saluting, (as it is called) ought to deter honest and sober people from practising it.

† [3c] Editorial comments made in reference to the marriage announcement of Mr. Moses Davis, Editor and Printer of Dartmouth Gazette, to Miss Nancy Fuller, daughter of the Rev. Caleb Fuller. ◆

† [3d] Death notice of Abijah Whiting, Esq., Counsellor at Law, "in about the 33d year of his age." The article is dated at Salem, "West Jersey" 6 Oct. 1800. ◆

† [3d] Zebulon Cutting posts an advertisment regarding notes lost "in Newport, between the dwelling houses of Daniel Dudley, jun. and Lieut. John Pike . . . " One note was signed by William Eastman, and dated at Grantham 5 Feb. 1800, the other signed by Jonas Cutting, dated at Newport 14 March 1800.

† [3d] Joel Holton, jun. informs the public that "he is now carrying on the Clothier's Business at the place formerly owned by Thomas Binney, about a mile distant from the meeting house, in the east parish." The adv. is dated at Westminster, 22 Oct. 1800.

† [3d] Samuel Cobb adv. for a stray colt which he found; dated Westmoreland, 21 Oct.

† [3d] Joel Ranney adv. for a stray mare on his property; dated Westminster, 23 Oct.

Vol. VIII (No. 396) Monday, 3 Nov. 1800.

† [2c] Extensive description of the skeletal remains of a prehistoric animal discovered on the farm of a Mr. Masten, Ulster County, N.C.

† [3b] Lengthy account of the loss of the ship *Hope*, Elihu Doty, Master, of New Bedford. The ship was caught in a hurricane, 7 Sept. 1800, en route from Wilmington, N.C. to "Jamacai." John Bolter, seaman, was washed overboard; the remaining crew saved their souls by lashing themselves to what remained of the ship. They drifted with no food and little water until the 17th Sept., when they were picked up by the *Mercury*, Capt. Jacob Treadwell of Portsmouth, where they arrived on 2 Oct. Mark Lamb, seaman, died from a sickness 3 Oct., and Robert Collet, the 2d mate, "died previous to the gale." ◆

† [3d] Zacheus Hale Loomis, Musician, informs the public that "he has taken lodging at Mr. Noah Sabin's in Brattleborough. He wishes to engage at all assemblies and halls from Deerfield to Walpole, or within twenty miles east and west." Dated at Brattleborough 22 Oct. 1800.

† [3d] Levi Pierce and David Stone announce "that all connexion between them in Business was dissolved by mutual consent, on the 20th instant." Dated 29 Oct.

† [3d] Adv. by *Stone & Bellows*, regarding merchandise at the stores in Walpole and Rockingham.

† [3d] Legal notice regarding the insolvent estate of Nehemiah Allen, late of Londonderry, Vermont, deceased. Samuel Arnold, Rufus Thayer, and Amos Cook named Commissioners; business meetings to be conducted at the house of John Miltemers, Innholder at Londonderry; notice dated at Londonderry 10 Oct. 1800.

† [3d] James Voyer, of Quebec City, Notary Public, offers land for sale in Dorset, Que.

¶ [3d] Run away from the subscriber an apprentice boy, thirteen years old, by the name of John Gass. Said boy is light complexioned had on when he went away, a white hat, brown coloured coat, blue jacket and tow tanner's trowsers. Whoever will take up said boy and return him to me, shall receive one peck of potatoes reward, and no charges.

Daniel Wheelock.

Claremont, Oct. 20, 1800.

===== ¶ [3d] **MARRIED.** =====

Mr. Charles Hayden, of Easton, to Miss Anna Williams, of Weymouth. Mr. John Bois, of Waltham, to Miss Mercy Hichborn, of Boston.

═══ ¶ [3d] DIED. ═══

At Westmoreland, Mr. Warren Butterfield, aged 21, son of Maj. Isaac Butterfield.

Vol. VIII (No. 397) Monday, 10 Nov. 1800.

† [3d] William Cobbett, who formerly printed a paper in Philadelphia, entitled the Porcupine, and who is now in London, is about to resume its publication in the latter place, under the same title. His works for which he issued proposals some time since will issue from his press in February next.

† [3d] John Snow adv. a stray heifer on his property; dated Walpole, 4 Nov. 1800.

═══ ¶ [3d] MARRIED. ═══

At Westminster, Vt., Major John H. Buel, of the 2d U.S. Regiment of Infantry, to Mrs. ——— Metcalf.

═══ ¶ [3d] DIED. ═══

At Charleston, S.C. Mr. Joseph Butman, of Marblehead.   At Salem, Mr. Matthew Mansfield, aged 74.—At Boston, Capt. William Whitwell, aged 37; Mr. John Innis, aged 22; Mrs. Sophia Trask, aged 42, wife of Mr. Jonathan Trask.—At Mendon, Master Levi Rawson, Jun. aged 15.—At Hartford, Mr. William Burr, merchant, aged 53.   At Suffield, Gideon Granger, Esq.

¶ [3d] **Thirty Dollars Reward.**

Deserted from this Rendezvous of the 2d U.S. Regiment of Infantry, John Butler, an enlisted soldier, 20 years old, five feet, six and a quarter inches high, sandy hair, which he wears untied, blue eyes, florid complexion, was duly enlisted on the 21st October, 1800.

William Smith, a man duly enlisted on the 28th Oct. last, twenty five years old, five feet and eight inches high, was born in the town of Barre, in the Commonwealth of Massachusetts, dark hair, dark eyes, and dark complexion.

Robert Facey, duly enlisted on the 24th July, 1800, at Westminster, twenty four years old, five feet, six and three quarters inches high, was born at sea, has an impediment in his speech, brown hair, blue eyes, florid complexion, has a sore on his right leg.

The above three men deserted from this rendezvous on the night of the 4th inst. Whoever will apprehend them, or any individual of them, shall receive ten dollars for each, or thirty dollars for the three with all necessary charges.

WILLIAM LAIDLIE, Lieut.
2d Regt. U.S. Infantry, Commanding at Westminster Rendez.

Westminster, 5th Nov. 1800.

Vol. VIII (No. 398) Monday, 17 Nov. 1800.

† [2d-3a] Account of a prison break by 15 inmates at the State Prison in or near Philadelphia, Penn.   The assistant keeper, Noah Gardner, was over-powered, as was Capt. Pray, who was twice stabbed, but survived. The prisoners were James Runnels, John Sullivan, William Bedford, James Crispin, Richard Shapley, David Read, John Bradley, John Page, James Stanford, Charles Mosier, John H. Bay, John Smith, Alpheus Vincent, William Murdock, and Lewis Taylor. ◆

† [3a] Mr. Greenleaf Clark, son of Jonathan Clark, Esq., of Portsmouth, N.H., badly injured in an accident involving a cannon at a celebration, around the 30th of October, 1800. The accident resulted in the amputation of part of his arm; the article is contained in the news dated at Portsmouth, 4 Nov. 1800.

† [3a] Account of the ordination of Rev. Johnathan [sic] Stickney, pastor of the Congregational Church and Society at Raymond, N.H. ◆

† [3c] Legal notice regarding a petition by Sanford Kingsbery of Claremont, Esq., Administrator of the estate of Jonathan Chase, late of Cornish, deceased. The petition involved certain conveyances of land, viz. to Jacob Whipple for land in Cornish; to David Thompson for land in Alstead; to John S. Orcutt, for land in Alstead; to Samuel Beckwith, for land in Cornish (called the M'Clintock lot); to Andrew Beckwith, for land

in Alstead, and to Aaron Willard, for land in Hartland, Vermont. ♦

† [3d] Joshua Smith posts a notice stating that he "is about to discontinue business in the mechanical line," and requests settlements of accounts. Dated Langdon, 12 Nov.

Vol. VIII (No. 399) Monday, 24 Nov. 1800.

† [3c] Detailed account of the drowning of Mrs. Eleanor Fisk, wife of Mr. Ichabod E. Fisk of the Isle of Mott, on the 5th of Oct. 1800. The woman was canoeing with her son, when the canoe was upset by a whirlpool. The article is dated at Vergennes, Vermont, 30 Oct. 1800.

¶ [3d] Run away from the subscriber on the 15th Oct. last, an indented apprentice, by the name of John Hannas, 18 years of age. Whoever will take up and return said runaway, shall be entitled to two cents reward and no charges; and all persons are forbid harboring or trusting said servant on my account.

Josiah White.
Charlestown, Nov. 15, 1800.

===== ¶ [3d] MARRIED. =====

At Acton, Rev. Nicholas B. Whitney, of Hingham, to Miss Anna Adams, daughter of the Rev. Moses Adams, of the former place.

At Boston, Rev. E. Whitcomb, of Pepperelborough, to Miss Eliza Ruggles.—Mr. Ebenezer Preble, merchant, to Miss Abigail Torrey, of Lancaster.—Mr. Thomas Perkins, to Miss Ann D. Powell.

In this town, Mr. Henry Fitch to Miss Frances Gage.

===== ¶ [3d] DIED. =====

At the Havannah, Mr. William Adams, of Boston, a very respectable and enterprizing young man. At Newburyport, Mr. William Cheever, aged [28?]. At Madbury, Solomon Emerson, Esq. aged 91. At Yarmouth, Hon. David Thacher, Esq. aged 71. At London, Hon. John Chandler, aged 80, formerly of Boston.

Vol. VIII (No. 400) Monday, 1 Dec. 1800.

† [2d-3a] Updated account of a battle at sea, lat. 22° 50', long. 51°, between the U.S. Frigate *Boston*, Capt. Little, and the French National Corvette, *Le Berceau*, on the 12th of Oct. 1800. The Corvette was brought to Boston as a prize; the casualties aboard the *Boston*, viz.—"William Ford, John Higgins, Mathias [Josey?], and William M'Kee, seamen, killed.—Mr. Samuel Young, purser, Thomas Hartley, and Nathaniel Dill, seamen, wounded, since dead: Mr. J.M. Haswell, midshipman, George Groom, Gavon Walkinshaw, Francis Rice, John Runlet, Francis Francis, John Alfred, and John Collins, wounded and likely to recover." ♦

† [3c] The body of Mr. Alexander Catlin, Jr., of Burlington, Vt., aged 26, discovered near the shore of the lake at Charlotte, Vt. Catlin drowned on the 25th of Sept., on his passage to St. John's; his body was conveyed to Burlington and interred there 31 Oct. "with Masonic honours," and a sermon was delivered by Rev. Mr. Sanders.

¶ [3c] Brattleborough, Vermont, Nov. 15. We learn from Grafton, Mass. that on Monday night last, James Burt, a likely young man, aged about 19 years, shot a ball through his body from a gun. He was found dead in a corn barn the next morning. Cause unknown.

† [3d] One cent reward offered by Matthew Miller, Jr., for the return of a runaway "indented apprentice," named James Shafter White, who ran away 23 Nov. 1800. The notice is dated at Rockingham, 24 Nov.

† [3d] Adv. for *Henry Bass & Co.*, Boston, regarding furs and grindstones.

† [3d] Stephen Johnson requests that his outstanding accounts be settled; dated Walpole, 28 Nov.

† [3d] Ashur Southard posts and adv. that he "has opened a House of Entertainment, in Westminster, Vermont, on the east side of the street, nearly opposite the meeting house . . . " Dated at Westminster, 28 Nov. 1800.

† [3d] The copartnership of John Reed and William Wyman, a.k.a. *Reed and Wyman*, is dissolved by mutual consent; outstanding debts to be paid to John Reed, Westminster. Notice dated at Westminster, 26 Nov. 1800.

† [3d] Charles Howland adv. a stray ox found on his land; dated Walpole, 24 Nov.
† [3d] Ebenezer Cole adv. a stray heifer found on his land; dated 25 Nov. [at Walpole?]
† [3d] John Gilmore adv. stray animals found on his land; dated Rockingham, 26 Nov.

===== ¶ [3d] MARRIED. =====

At Pembroke, Mr. David Cross, to Miss Olive Kimball.
At Concord, Mr. Joseph Sherburne, to Miss Dorcas Hall.
At Springfield, Mr. Jacob Perkins, to Miss Lucy Berry. Mr. Oliver Chapin, to Miss Ellis Bush.
At Newyork, Mr. Peter A. Mesier, to Miss Mary Van Wyck.
In this town, Mr. Aaron Allen, jun. to Miss Catharine Salter. Mr. Jacob Lock, to Miss Fanny Wier.

===== ¶ [3d] DIED. =====

At Shrewsbury, Hon. Artemas Ward, Esq. late Chief Justice of the court of common pleas for the county of Worcester. At Dover, Mr. Caleb Hodgdon jun. aged 33. At Rome, N.Y. Benjamin Huntington, Esq. At Voluntown, Mr. John Gordon, aged 96. At Washington city, Jonathan Jackson, Esq.

Vol. VIII (No. 401) Monday, 8 Dec. 1800.

† [3b] Brief account of a fire at the store of Maj. David Smith, and the adjoining house of Mr. Levi Smith, at Springfield, Mass., 17 Nov. 1800.
† [3d] Joel Turner adv. a stray colt on his property; dated Acworth, 1 Dec. 1800.
¶ [3d] Take Notice. William Page informs his customers, that they may pass Walpole Bridge to his Mills, free from toll, during sleighing. Bellows' Falls, December 1, 1800.

===== ¶ [3d] MARRIED. =====

At Northampton, Mr. Elisha Parsons, jun. to Miss Phebe Hurlburt. Mr. David Wells, to Mrs. Edmonds.
At Easthampton, Mr. Sylvester Lyman, to Miss Naomi Janes.
At Newburyport, Capt. Samuel Prince, of Boston, to Miss Sarah Stickney, of the former place.
At Rye, Lieut. Amos Garland, to Miss Olive Jenness.
In this town, Oliver Sparhawk, Esq. Clerk of the Court of Common Pleas for the County of Cheshire, to Miss Hannah Whitney.

===== ¶ [3d] DIED. =====

At Warwick, R.I. John Holden, Esq. aged 100. At Boston, Mrs. Sarah Thayer, aged 103.

Vol. VIII (No. 402) Monday, 15 Dec. 1800.

† [3d] Advertisement regarding the Green Mountain Turnpike Road, leading from Rockingham to Clarendon, for shares to be sold. Salmon Dutton of Cavendish, *Treasurer*, William Page of Rockingham, and Stephen Clark of Mountolly "are authorized by said corporation to dispose of shares to those who wish to take them."
† [3d] Asahel Hunt adv. a cow which strayed on his land; dated Charlestown 12 Dec.

===== ¶ [3d] MARRIED. =====

At Wrentham, Mr. William Brown, to Miss Peggy Shepard.
At Acworth, Mr. Thomas Mitchell, to Miss Nancy Mitchell.

===== ¶ [3d] DIED. =====

At Newyork, Charles Adams, Esq. second son of the President of the United States.

Vol. VIII (No. 403) Monday, 22 Dec. 1800.

† [3c] Legal notice regarding a petition by Hannah (Warren) Brown, of Charlestown, N.H., for divorce from her husband Bowes Brown, to whom she was married 24 Nov. 1795, at Townsend, Mass., by Rev. Samuel Dix, settled minister at Townsend. Mrs. Brown claimed that her husband deserted her 1 Aug. 1796, and went to parts unknown, leaving her with a small child.
† [3c-d] Extensive lists of "resident and non resident proprietors, and owners of rights, lots, and parcels of land" who had delinquent taxes outstanding in the 54th District,

Cheshire County, N.H., resulting from the Direct Tax of 1798. (Said tax was payable on 8 Jan. 1800.) The towns covered in this district were Newgrantham, Plainfield, and Springfield, N.H.; delinquent property to be auctioned off in March 1801 at the houses of Capt. Reuben Hoit, Springfield, Amos Spaulding, Newgrantham, and Nathan Gates, Plainfield. The lists printed in the newspaper give a breakdown of lot size, lot number, etc., though only the names of the delinquents are transcribed in the lists herein.

Delinquents' Names, Newgrantham, N.H.

Theodore Atkinson, Jr.	George Field	Elias Jones
Martin Ashley	David Field	Gad Lyman
Theodore Atkinson	Seth Field	Phinehas Lyman
Lt. Samuel Ashley	Jonathan Hunt	James Nevens
Lois Butler	Benjamin Hall	Proprietors Land
Oliver Barret	Abigail Hall	William Pulfry
Moses Balding	Samuel Hunt	Medad Pomeroy
Benjamin Barret	Capt. Samuel Hunt	Elijah Stebbins
Oliver Doolittle	John Hunt, Jun.	Eliakim Stebbins
Jeremiah Davis, Jun.	Jonathan Hawk	Thomas Williams
Samuel Dickinson	Moses Hawk	Elijah Williams, Jr.

Delinquents' Names, Plainfield, N.H.

Zebina Curtis

Delinquents' Names, Springfield, N.H.

Sarah Dunbar	James M'Gregore	Benjamin Conner
Joseph Slack	John Patch	John T. Gilman
John Hall	Jacob Quimby	John Jewett
Robert Heath	Daniel Rogers	Simeon Ladd
& Wm. Evans	Jonathan Smith	William Rowell
Edmond Leavitt	Thomas Thompson	Philip White
Joseph Lunt	Moses Webster	John Wendal
Benjamin Lamson	Ann Ardway	

¶ [3d] Whereas Lucy, my wife, has eloped from my bed and board, and refuses to live with me after the manner of man and wife; this is to forbid any person or persons harbouring or trusting her on my account; as I will not pay any debt of her contracting after this date.

Thomas Whiting.

Langdon, December 10, 1800.

Vol. VIII (No. 404) Monday, 29 Dec. 1800.

† [3d] Notice by Asa Wheeler, Clerk of the Green Mountain Turnpike Company, announcing a business meeting to be held at the house of Salmon Dutton, Cavendish.

===== ¶ [3d] MARRIED. =====

At York, Mr. John Young, aged 83, to Miss Naomi Hill, aged 75, after 38 years' courtship and cohabitancy ! ! Well done, ye old and faithful servants: your offspring has been numerous ! your love constant ! and your vows unbroken [. . .]

===== ¶ [3d] DIED. =====

At Strafford, Vt. Nicholas Gilman, Esq. At Peachham, Vt. Widow Patience Willey, aged 83. At Keene, Jeremiah Stiles, Esq. aged 56. At Westminster, Vt. Mrs. ——— Kittredge. At New Milford, Rev. Nathaniel Taylor, aged 79.

Vol. VIII (No. 405) Monday, 5 Jan. 1801.

† [2c-d] Two slaves, the property of Mr. Cregmiles, "of the thirteen mile house," sentenced to be burned alive for the murder of William Maxwell, ship carpenter. The article is dated at Charleston, South Carolina. ♦

† [3b] Article summarizing Acts passed by the General Court at Concord; those which relate to specific individuals: 1) to alter the name of Walter Little; 2) to alter the name of Ariel Jacobs; 3) empowering C.M. Wentworth to hold real estate; 4) to empower Mary Ramsay to sell land; 5) granting ferry to S. Far and E. Hildrith.

† [3d] Samuel Patch posts a public notice stating that an auction to sell land in Ludlow, Vermont is to be held at the house of Simeon Patch. Notice is dated at Ludlow, 23 Dec. 1800.

† [3d] List of letters remaining at the Post Office in Walpole, 5 Jan. 1801, as compiled by Alexander Thomas, Postmaster:

David Adams,	Walpole.	Charles Howland,	Walpole.
Mr. Alexander,	Winchester.	Seth Hall,	Westmoreland.
Joseph Adams,	Rockingham.	Elijah A. Hall,	Westmoreland.
Miss Dianthe Aldrich,	Westmoreland.	Hugh Henry,	Acworth.
Alvin Burt,	Walpole.	Joshua March,	Walpole.
Timothy Butterfield,	Westmoreland.	Ebenezer Ruggles,	Walpole.
William Barran, jun.	Surry.	Samuel Scott,	Walpole.
Ralph Butterfield,	Walpole.	Dr. Joseph Stowel,	Winchester.
Aaron Bailey,	Westmoreland.	Ebenezer Stone,	Westmoreland.
Oliver Goodale,	Walpole.	Clement Trowbridge,	Westmoreland.
David Gilman,	Walpole.	Samuel Whiting,	Langdon.
Stephen Griswold,	Walpole.		

† [3c] Extensive lists of resident and non resident owners of land who had delinquent taxes outstanding in the 50th District, Cheshire County, N.H. [resulting from the Direct Tax of 1798.—Ed.] The towns covered in this district were Charlestown, Langdon, and Acworth, N.H., and the list was compiled by Jonathan Grout, Collector of the 50th Collection District. Delinquent property to be auctioned off in March 1801 at the house of Ephraim Carpenter, Esq., Charlestown. The lists printed in the newspaper give a breakdown of lot size, lot number, etc., though only the names of the delinquents are presented in the lists herein.

Names of Owners, or Superintendants:

Charlestown, N.H.	Daniel Barker	Thaddeus Gleason
" "	Benjamin Cloys	Robert Henry
" "	Elihu Dickerson	John Hastings, jun.
" "	Isaac H. Ely	Alpheus Wadkins
" "	Rufus Guild	
Langdon, N.H.	Apollo Gilmore, [of?] Acworth	Asa Holden
" "	Thaddeus Gleason	Samuel Kingsbury
Acworth, N.H.	John Albra	Israel Foster
" "	Theodore Adkinson	Solomon Gee
" "	Ephraim Adams	Gilbert How
" "	Spencer Brown	Samuel Hogg
" "	Nathaniel Butterfield	Samuel Jones
" "	David Brown	James Leslie
" "	Ebenezer Bridge	Frederick Locke
" "	Edward Clifford	James McGregory
" "	Benjamin Clifford	Richard McAllister
" "	James Davidson	John Reid
" "	Peter and Josiah Ewens	Woodward A. Silsby
" "	Samuel French	Lazel Silsby
" "	Samuel Fitch	Retire Trask

Names of nonresidents owning lands:

Charlestown, N.H.	Peter Gilman Berdeaus, in France, House Lot, }
" "	Jonas Park, occupant.
" "	Asa Porter, Newbury, Vermont.
Landgdon, N.H.	Edward Perry, Westmoreland.
Acworth, N.H.	David Coffin, Whitestown
" "	Frederick French, Dunstable
" "	George Jeffrey
" "	William Hogg, New Boston; Simeon Ingols, occupant
" "	John Pinkerton, Londonderry
" "	Sampson Stoddard
" "	Matthew Thornton
" "	Major Wentworth

Vol. VIII (No. 406) Monday, 12 Jan. 1801.

¶ [3a] Castine, Maine. Nov. 28. Drowned, On Saturday last, at a place called Fog Island, in Penobscot Bay, Mr. Nathaniel Shelton, Polly Shelton, his wife, Alexander Hall, a black man, Judea Shelton, daughter of Mr. and Mrs. Shelton, and two young lads, viz. William and Jeremiah Shelton. Mr. Shelton was removing his family in a boat by water from Deer Isle to Fog Island, and had on board a yoke of cattle. The boat had nearly reached the shore, when the cattle broke from their confinement and upset her. Mr. Cutter, who was likewise on board at the time the disaster took place, was the only person who escaped with life. He however, was severely wounded in attempting to reach the shore, which after much difficulty he attained.

† [3c] Barn belonging to Mr. George Smith destroyed by fire [25 Dec. 1800—Ed.] at Partridgefield [now Peru, Mass.—Ed.]. Article dated at Pittsfield, Mass. 30 Dec. ♦

¶ [3c] Brattleborough, Vermont. Dec. 27. Tuesday, the 3d inst. the Rev. Aaron Crosby of Dummerston, set out on a mission to the Oneida Indians, with whom he proposes to spend the winter. His acquaintance with their language, manners, and many of their persons, obtained while a missionary among them, fomerly, joined with his pious zeal, it is hoped, will render his labours among them acceptable.

¶ [3c] January 3. FIRE. The dwelling house of Dr. Isaac Hurlburt, of Northfield was consumed by fire on the 16th ult.

† [3c] Account of the death of Mr. Whitney at Chesterfield, who was shot by a hunter [11 Jan. 1800 ?—Ed.]. Whitney "has left a wife and family to lament him." ♦

† [3d] List of letters at the Post Office, Charlestown, N.H., 3 Jan. 1801, as compiled by Samuel Crosby, Postmaster:

Moses Chase, Esq.	Bradford, N.H.	Nathaniel Hall,	Cornish.
Ebenezer Corbin,	Charlestown.	John Marsh,	Weathersfield, Vt.
David [Chassin ?] 40	Claremont.	Levi Nichols,	Springfield, Vt.
Sarah Cass,	Springfield, Vt.	Nahum Rice,	Charlestown, N.H.
Noah Damon,	Weathersfield, Vt.	Jonathan Steele,	Weathersfield, Vt.
John Goldsmith,	Charlestown, N.H.		

† [3d] List of letters remaining at the Post Office at Westminster, Vt., 1 Jan. 1801, as compiled by Eleazer May, Postmaster:

Jonathan Gould,	Westminster, 2.	Roger Clark,	Rockingham.
Abraham Spencer,	"	James Marsh,	"
Sally Chandler,	"	Dr. Joseph Seagraves,	Chester.
Thomas Baldwin,	"	Aaron Bascom,	"
John Lock,	"	Joseph Hartwell,	"
Noah Wiswall,	"	Dr. Abraham Hedge,	"
Moses Thurston,	"	John Jacobs	Londonderry.
Jabez Paine,	"	Capt. Jonathan Adams,	Springfield, 2.

List of letters at the Post Office, Westminster, Vt., *(continued)* :

Thomas Holmes,	Westminster.	Levi Nichols,	Springfield.
Alpha Kingsly,	"	Obadiah Joy,	Putney.
Gen. John Fuller,	Rockingham.	Luther Winslow,	Colchester.

† [3d] Nathaniel Sikes requests all outstanding accounts be settled by the first of Feb. next. The notice is dated at Walpole, 9 Jan. 1801.

† [3d] List of nonresident owners of land in Croydon, N.H., who had delinquent taxes for the year 1800. The list was compiled by Samuel Marsh, Jun., *Collector*; property still in delinquency by 1 April 1801 to be auctioned off at the house of Mr. Emerson Hall, Innholder at Croydon. The list printed in the newspaper contains a breakdown of lot number, lot size, etc., though the summary presented below contains only the names of the owners:

Samuel Chase	James Whipple	Governor's Farm
Daniel Chase	Thomas Denna	John Whipple
Moses Chase	Ephraim Sharman, jr.	James Richardson
Moodey Chase	March Chase	Samuel Cummings
Moses Whipple	Phinehas Leland	John Holland
Joseph Vinson	Daniel Chase, jr.	Ebenezer Waters
Samuel Chase, jun.	Solomon Chase	Solomon Leland
Samuel Ayers	John Downing	Luke Druary
Joseph Whipple	Joseph Miriam	
Ephraim Sharman	Jona. Chase's heirs	

¶ [3d] MARRIED.

At Suffield, on Thursday evening, the 1st inst. by the Rev. Ebenezer Gay, Mr. Thaddeus Leavitt, jun. to the amiable and accomplished Miss Jemima Loomis.

At Haverhill, N.H. Pelatiah Mills Olcott, Esq. of Hanover, to Miss Sarah Porter, daughter of Col. Porter.

In this town, on the 4th inst. Roger Vose, Esq. attorney at law, to Miss Rebecca Bellows, daughter of Col. John Bellows.

Vol. VIII (No. 407) Monday, 19 Jan. 1801.

¶ [1d] MARRIED.

At New-york, John Rodman, Esq. to Miss Harriet Fenno, daughter of the late Mr. John Fenno.

¶ [1d] DIED.

At Watertown, Mrs. Ruth Hunt, widow of the late John Hunt, Esq. of the same place, in the 85th year of her age [. . .]

At Trenton, N.J. Mrs. Amy Hunter aged 74. At Portsmouth, Mrs. Anna Giles, aged 28. Miss Elizabeth Ross, aged 19. At Dover, Miss Lydia Libbey. Miss Polly Hayes. At Bennington, Mr. Thomas Henderson, aged 66. At Brattleborough, V. Mrs. Catherine Smith, aged 49. At Barrington, Mr. Silas Drew. At Waltham, Mr. Josiah Whitney, aged 70.

Bill of mortality in Salem, in 1800.

Inhabitants reckoned at 10,000. Deaths 157, of whom 79 were males and 78 females —Whites 143, black 14.—Of consumption, Dysentary, and Throat Distemper, 72 of the above number.

¶ [3d] MARRIED.

At Springfield, Mr. Asa Caswell to Miss Asenath Morgan.

At Northborough John Winslow, Esq. attorney at law, to Miss Susan [Ball? or Dall?].

¶ [3d] DIED.

At New Bedford, Sylvanus Sisson, aged 15 years. The melancholy event which caused his death is related to us as follows: That on the afternoon of the 27th ult. he was alone in the blacksmith's shop, engaged in an attempt to draw the charge from a gun which had been some time loaded, and could not be fired off—that he had taken out the shot, and laid them by; and it is supposed dropped in a hot iron to burn out the wadding and powder; when the gun went off, and distressing to ad, the contents were discharged through his head—he lingered till the morning of the 31st, and then departed this life, a striking instance of the uncertainty of its duration.

Vol. VIII (No. 408) Monday, 26 Jan. 1801.

† [3d] A petition by Sanford Kingsbury, Esq., Administrator for the estate of Jonathan Chase, Esq., late of Corinth, deceased, regarding real estate conveyed from Chase to Isaac Morgan of Claremont.

===== ¶ [3d] MARRIED. =====

At Danvers, Mr. John P. Osborne, to Miss Ann H. Oliver, of Salem.
At Boston, Mr. Joshua Ross, to Miss Mary Eayrs.
At Hartford, Mr. Samuel Ledlie, to Miss Abigail Kilbourne.   Mr. Isaac Niles, of Colchester, to Miss Almira Willy, of Chatham.

===== ¶ [3d] DIED. =====

At Washington, Gustavus Scott, Esq. one of the city commissioners.   At Salem, captain John Clarke, aged 82.   At Oxford, Lt. John Nichols, aged 91.

Vol. VIII (No. 409) Monday, 2 Feb. 1801.

No items of significance contained within this issue.

Vol. VIII (No. 410) Monday, 9 Feb. 1801.

† [3d] Abraham Holland requests all outstanding accounts to be settled; the notice is dated at Walpole, 30 Jan. 1801.

===== ¶ [3d] MARRIED. =====

At Barnstable, Holmes Allen, Esq. to Miss Lucy Lawrence.
At Boston, Mr. James Phillips, to Miss Mary Tilden.
At Brookline, Mr. John Peck, to Miss Eliza Gilman.
In this town, Richard W. Fenton, to Miss Lese [sic] Harrington.

===== ¶ [3d] DIED. =====

At Boston, Mr. James Thompson, aged 69.   At Roxbury, James Magee, Esq. aged 51.
At Acworth, on Sunday the 25th ult. Mrs. Joanna Carlton, aged [20?], the amiable consort of Mr. Willard Carlton. By her death, her surviving partner sustains the loss of an incomparable blessing of human life [. . .]
At Plainfield, N.H. on the 13th ult. Enoch Stone, son of Abel Stone, Esq. aged 22. He died on the road to one of the neighbours, it is supposed by a fit of the apoplexy. Being a twin, he has left his mate with his parents to lament his loss.

Vol. VIII (No. 411) Tuesday, 17 Feb. 1801.

===== ¶ [3d] MARRIED. =====

At Concord, Rev. Roswell Messinger, of York, to Miss Mary Brown.
At Newcastle, Mr. Hall Jackson Locke, to Mrs. Abigail Amazeen.

===== ¶ [3d] DIED. =====

In Newjersey, Mrs. Ann Hutchinson, aged 101 years, 9 months and 7 days. Descendants 375. She lived to see three centuries.
At Leominster, Mr. Josiah Fairbanks, aged 16.[41]   At Portsmouth, Capt. James Miller, aged [81? or 82?].   Mr. John Banfil, aged 99.   At Springfield, Mrs. Martha Hitchcock, aged [71? or 74?].

Vol. VIII (No. 412) Tuesday, 24 Feb. 1801.

¶ [2d] There are now living in the town of New-Milford (Con.) two persons who have seen three centuries, being born in the 17th, lived through the 18th, and now see the 19th. One is Mr. Nodine, born at New-Rochelle, state of New-York, of the French protestants who settled there. The other is Mrs. Heames who emigrated thither from the state of Rhode-Island. The husband of her youth died there seven years ago aged 94 or 5. The living of the above persons has been always coarse and simple, and for many years they have been town's poor. They are now able to walk with considerable firmness and the powers of their minds are not wholly abated.

¶ [2d-3a] Norwich, Connecticut, Feb. 4. We learn that Josiah Meigs, Esq. late professor of Mathematics in Yale College has set off with his family for Georgia, for the purpose of superintending a newly incorporated college in that state, of which he has been chosen President, with a salary of 1500 dollars per annum, to be augmented if necessary.

Mr. Peirpont Bacon, who lately died at Colchester, has left the whole of his property, amounting to Thirty Thousand Dollars, to the first society of that town, for the support of a school. By the terms of the will no part of this fund can be appropriated to the erecting or repairing of any building.

† [3d] Levi Prentiss advertises farms for sale in Reading, Vt., and Croydon, N.H., and also a "Hatter's shop, adjoining Capt. Jesse Wilcox's land in Newport, N.H." The ad is dated at Claremont, 10 Feb. 1801.

¶ [3d] Wanted, by the 1st of April, a Journeyman TANNER and CURRIER. One that can be well recommended, may find employment for six or eight months, and good encouragement, by applying to

Philip Davis

Rockingham, Feb. 19, 1801.

¶ [3d] **Ten Dollars Reward.**

Deserted from Fort Wolcott, in the harbour of Newport, JOSEPH BURNAM, a private in the 2d Regiment of Artillerists and Engineers, aged 28 years, 5 feet 9 inches high, dark eyes, light, short curled hair, fair complexion, stout and well made, born at Hampton Falls, in the state of Newhampshire, by trade a blacksmith; enlisted at Oxford, Massachusetts, in June, 1800—he had a furlough (which has expired) to go to Newbury, state of Vermont. The above reward, and reasonable expenses will by paid for apprehending said deserter and delivering him at the above post, or to any military officer in the service of the United States.

William MacRea, *Major*
2d Regt. Artillertists and Engineers.

Newport, Feb. 6, 1801.

Vol. VIII (No. 413) Tuesday, 3 March 1801.

† [3c] Brief article, dated at Keene, N.H., regarding a counterfeit bill passed there by "A Person who calls himself Theophilus Curwin, from some part of Connecticut." ♦

† [3d] *Stone & Bellows* inform the public "that they are about to discontinue business in this place" and request settlement of accounts. The notice is dated Walpole, 2 March.

† [3d] Amasa Allen requests settlement of accounts; dated Walpole, 2 March.

===== ¶ [3d] MARRIED. =====

At Milton, Mr. Ebenezer Spaulding, of Chelmsford, to Miss Eunice Jones.
At Hallowell, Mr. Nathan Bachelder, to Miss Nancy Rollings.
At Dover, Mr. Joseph Hard, to Miss Mary Flint.
At Portsmouth, Mr. Moses Brown, to Miss Susannah Sumner.
At Long-Island, Mr. William Coffin, to Miss Susannah Graves. It is said to have been a dead match.

===== ¶ [3d] DIED. =====

At Shrewsbury, Ms. Mrs. Meriam Harrington, aged 88. At the Island of Tortola, Mr. Elijah Cooper, printer, aged 24, formerly of Boston. At Newport, the Hon. Mrs. Lucia C. Grattan, widow of the late Col. Grattan. At Keene, Mrs. Roxana Blake, aged 30. Mr. Gershom Howe, aged 35. At Salem, Mrs. Sarah Webb, aged 36.

Vol. VIII (No. 414) Tuesday, 10 March 1801.

† [3d] Samuel West, *Proprietors' Clerk*, posts a notice regarding a meeting of the Third New Hampshire Turnpike Road to be held at the house of Thomas Edwards, Innholder

at Keene. The notice is dated 28 Feb. 1801.

† [3d] Moses Willard, *Collector*, posts a short list of "delinquent proprietors and owners of land in the town of Unity," N.H., regarding unpaid highway taxes for the year 1800. Property still in delinquency by 15 June 1801 to be sold at auction at the house of Jonathan Glidden in Unity. The "Original Proprietor's Names" appearing in the list are Thomas Clouge, Moses Sleeper, and John Webster. The list printed in the paper also contains information regarding lot size, valuation, etc.

† [3d] Notice regarding the [insolvent?] estate of Zebulon Cuttin, [sic] late of Newport, N.H., deceased. Jesse Lane, Samuel Church, and John Cutting were appointed Commissioners; business meetings to be conducted at the house of Jesse Wilcox, Jun., innholder at Newport. The notice is dated at Newport, 24 Feb. 1801.

¶ [3d] The subscriber is requested by Capt. Frederick Williams of Digby, in Novascotia, county of Annapolis, to notify the heirs of Thomas Crane, who went from Newhampshire at the beginning of the American war, and resided in Digby, who was frozen to death about nine years since; and who left two improved Farms of 400 acres each, and some other property which may be had by immediate application to said Williams. Crane left a wife and three children very poor. The subscriber presumes the printers in Newhampshire and Vermont will publish this notice gratis.

William Page.

Rockingham, Feb. 28, 1801.

Vol. VIII (No. 415) Tuesday, 17 March 1801.

† [3d] Public notice stating "that the copartnership of Caryl and Chandler was, by mutual agreement, dissolved, on the 2d day of October last. Also, the company of Benjamin and Amos Caryl was in like manner dissolved on the 1st of January last . . . " Benjamin Caryl carries on business in Chester, Vt. "at his new Store a few rods west of the south meeting house in Chester . . ." The notice is dated at Chester, 9 March 1801.

===== ¶ [3d] MARRIED. =====

At St. Albans, Col. Levi House, to Miss Nabby Torry. Mr. Seth Pomeroy, to Miss Olive House.

At Alstead, Mr. Wm. Chene, to Miss Triphene Hatch.

===== ¶ [3d] DIED. =====

At Lunenburg, on the 1st inst., the Rev. Zabdiel Adams, pastor of the Church in that town, in the 6[?]st year of his age, and the 37th of his ministry. At Worcester, Mr. Nathaniel Chandler, aged 51. At Grafton, Mr. Ebenezer Wheeler, aged 85. At Lincoln, Mr. Peter Sylvester, 88.

Vol. VIII (No. 416) Tuesday, 24 March 1801.

¶ [3d] Whereas, Anna my wife has behaved in a very unbecoming manner, and hath absented herself from my bed and board; all persons are forbid trusting her on my account, as I shall pay no debts of her contracting after the date hereof.

David Fish.

Acworth, 20 March 1801.

===== ¶ [3d] MARRIED. =====

At Concord, Mr Nathan Abbot Jun. of Concord to Miss Rhoda Bricket, of Pembroke. Mr. Amos Brown, to Miss Nancy Eastman. At Portsmouth, Mr. James Grant, to Miss Mercy Tetherly.

At Charleston, S.C. John Grochan, Esq. to Miss Adelle de Grasse, daughter of the late Count de Grasse.

At Marblehead, Mr. Edward Loring, of Boston, to Miss Frances Greely, of the former place.

===== ¶ [3d] DIED. =====

At Hanover, Mr. Charles Parks, aged 25. At Piermont, Dr. Thomas Russel, aged 73. In Virginia, Mr. James Madison, father of James Madison, Esq. Secretary of State. At Westfield, Gen. Warham Parks. At Charlestown, Dr. John Peters, aged 55. At Salem, Mr. George C. Ward, of Sanbornton, N.H. At Malden, Rev. Eliakim Willis.

Vol. VIII (No. 417) Tuesday, 31 March 1801.

† [3d] Joseph Bliss offers a tavern for sale, "at Haverhill Corner, in the County of Grafton, within twelve rods of the Court House and Academy . . . " Adv. dated at Haverhill, N.H. 23 March 1801.

† [3d] Thomas L. Chandler, [post rider—Ed.], declares that "his last paper will come on the 14th of April next" and requests that subscriptions to the *Farmers' Museum* be paid up. Dated at Chester, [Vermont—Ed.] 25 March 1801. [42]

Vol. IX (No. 418) Tuesday, 7 April 1801.

† [3a] Account of the capture, by a French privateer, of the brig *Traveller*, of Boston, Capt. George Lee, Master. The brig was en route from Lisbon to Calcutta, and was captured off the west coast of India, 29 Oct. 1801. Lee returned to Boston via the ship *Aurora*, and the account is contained in the news dated at Boston, 28 March. ♦

† [3c] Agricultural item regarding potatoes grown by Mr. Joseph King of Rutland, [Mass.—Ed.] in the year 1799; article dated at Brookfield, Mass.

† [3d] List of letters remaining in the Post Office at Walpole, N.H., 1 April 1801, as compiled by Alexander Thomas, Postmaster:

Isaac Butterfield, Esq.	Westmoreland	Elijah Knights,	Rockingham.
Martin & Isaac Butterfield	Westmoreland	James Knap,	Walpole.
Nathan Bundy,	Walpole.	Joseph Locke, Esq.	Walpole.
John M. Caswell,	Walpole.	James M'Curdy,	Surry.
Jonathan Clark,	Washington.	Eruel Mack,	Surry.
Mr. —— Esterbrooks,	Westmoreland.	Elisha Mack,	Westmoreland.
Joshua Emery,	Walpole.	William Ramsey,	Walpole.
Samuel Emery, Jun.	Rockingham.	David Sharon,	Westmoreland.
Adonijah Fasset,	Winchester.	Asil Streeter,	Walpole.
Thomas K. Green,	Westmoreland.	Ebenezer Stearns,	Chesterfield, 2.
Elijah A. Hall,	Westmoreland.	Col. —— Smith,	Surry.
Ebenezer Harvey,	Chesterfield.	Alvin Simons,	Weston.
Gurdon Huntington,	Walpole.		

¶ [3d] The public is wrongly informed in regard to the conduct of Anna Fish, by said David Fish.—My conduct, if ever unbecoming, was when my name was Anna Hardy, in setting my affections on the worthless Fish; so worthless that he had neither bed nor board for me, nor credit for me to get trusted on. I therefore forbid all persons trusting him on my account, as I will not pay any debts of his contracting after this date.

Anna Fish.

Acworth, March 26, 1801.

† [3d] Legal notice regarding Elizabeth Kitteridge, Adm. of the estate of Stephen Kitteridge, late of Walpole, husbandman, deceased; dated Walpole, 30 March 1801.

===== ¶ [3d] MARRIED. =====

At Winchester, Mr. Asa Alexander jun. to Miss Nabby Alexander. At Portland, Edward Preble Esq. to Miss Mary Deering. At Baltimore, Mr. Moses P. Lancaster, late of Boston, to Miss Betsey Miller. At Wilmington, (Delaware) Mr. Henry King, Jun. of Boston, to Miss Eliza Sharp, of that place.

===== ¶ [3d] DIED. =====

At Milford, N.H. Mr. Stephen Burnham, aged 90. At Newlondon, [43] Mrs. Sally F. Green, aged [22?]. At Rye, Mr. Paul Seavey, aged 61. Mrs. Nancy Jenness, aged 28. At Old Town on Penobscot River, ORONO, chief of the Penobscot tribe of Indians, aged 113. At Athens, Mrs. Rebekah Walker aged 58. At Albany, Mrs. Van Rensselaer, consort of the Hon. Lieut. Governor.

Vol. IX (No. 419) Tuesday, 14 April 1801.

† [3d] Adv. by William Lyons regarding the discovering of a sum of money near his house. Also a description of a note which he lost; said note was signed by Levi Hayward, March 1799, for the sum of eight dollars. Adv. dated Acworth, 1 Apr. 1801.

† [3d] List of letters remaining at the Post Office in Westminster, Vt., 1 April 1801, as compiled by Eleazer May, Postmaster:

Dr. Edward R. Cambell,	Westminster	Timothy Fisher,	Waltham.
Jabez Pain,	"	Martin Field,	Chester.
Asa W. Burnap,	"	Richard King,	Chester.
Widow Badger,	"	Elanar Ranson,	Westmoreland.
Daniel Putnam,	Grafton.	Sally Cooper,	Rockingham.
Stephen Greenleaf,	Windham County	Abiel Evans,	Athens.
Benjamin Stone,	Brookline.	Merrel Rendall,	Chester.

===== ¶ [3d] MARRIED. =====

At Claremont, Mr. John Temple, to Miss Hannah Redfield. Mr. Zina Redfield, to Miss Tryphena Sims.

===== ¶ [3d] DIED. =====

In England, Dr. Herschell, the celebrated astronomer, and discoverer of the new planet Georgium Sidus.

Vol. IX (No. 420) Tuesday, 21 April 1801.

The third and fourth pages of this number are missing from the microfilm. No items of any significance are seen in the first two pages of this issue.

Vol. IX (No. 421) Tuesday, 28 April 1801.

¶ [1a] ONE CENT REWARD. Run away from the subscriber on the evening of the 1st inst. a boy named JOHN ROBERTS, thirteen years old. All persons are forbid harbouring or trusting him on my account.

Corinth, April 9, 1801.   Moody Chace.

† [3c] Account of the death of a child, aged three, who burned to death at Danville, Vt. The child was in a sugar camp, where two sons of Thomas Dow, Jr., were gathering sap. The article seems to state that this child was also the son of Dow. ♦

¶ [3c] On Saturday last, a Mr. Noah Morrison, supposed to be about 30 years of age, was found dead in a brook in Ryegate. The cause of his death is unknown; but from appearances, the jury, which sat upon his body, were of opinion that being insane, or taken in a fit, he fell into the brook, and was drowned; of course, they reported "accidental death."

† [3d] Description of a work regarding a "European Gazetteer" to be published by Rev. Jedidiah Morse of Charlestown and Rev. E. Parish of Newbury, and to be printed by Mr. Samuel Etheridge at Charlestown, though the state is not specifed.

† [3d] *Stephens & Parmelee* post a notice stating that they have lost "sundry notes." Adv. dated at Claremont, 15 April 1801.

† [3d] Abner Royce adv. for a colt which he found; dated 27 April [at Walpole ?].

† [3d] Edward Livingston adv. 43,000 acres for sale on the west side of Lake Champlain; Livingston to be at the house of Judge Hierne, Willsborough, [N.Y.—Ed.] on 1 July. The adv. is dated at New York, 21 April 1801.

† [3d] Advertisement listing several tracts of land for sale in Vermont, posted by Daniel Boardman of New York City, and Elijah Boardman of New Milford, Conn. The tracts of land and the persons to contact are given here, though the adv. gives a more detailed description of lot size and lot location:

Location of land:	Informant:
Wolcott, Vt.;	Mr. Rowell Wells, of Waterbury, Vt.
Montgomery, Vt.;	Mr. Bradley Barlow, Merchant, of Fairfield, Vt.
Hinesburgh;	Mr. Erastus Bostwick, of Hinesburgh.
Shrewsbury;	Mr. Jeffery A. Barney, of Shrewsbury
Westhaven, "original right of Joseph Everish;"	Mr. William Wyman of Westhaven.

===== ¶ [3d] MARRIED. =====

At Stockbridge, Mr. Ebenezer Watson, of Newyork, to Miss Frances P. Sedgwick, daughter of Theodore Sedgwick, Esq.

===== ¶ [3d] DIED. =====

At Haddam, Mrs. Clarissa Rogers, aged 29. At N. Yarmouth, Jonas Mason, Esq. aged 93. In Jamaica, Mr. Samuel Cheney, jun. of Boston.

Vol. IX (No. 422) Tuesday, 5 May 1801.

===== ¶ [3d] MARRIED. =====

At Albany, Goldsborough Banger, jun. Esq. to Miss Maria Jay, eldest daughter of His Excellency Gov. Jay.

===== ¶ [3d] DIED. =====

At Petersburg, Virginia, a lady of extreme beauty and general deportment, who passed there as the wife of a Mr. William Hastings, lately from Boston; but whom H. (otherwise, it is said, Armstrong, a European) said, was not his wife, but the wife of one Cotteri[c?] whom she deserted, and that she was the daughter of a respectable clergyman in England, named Monroe. At Boston, Mr. John Morrison, Æt. 26. Mrs. Nancy Hearsey, Æt. 31. Mrs. Hannah [Neal? or Neat?], Æt. 57.

Vol. IX (No. 423) Tuesday, 12 May 1801.

¶ [3d] Run away from the subscriber, an apprentice boy, eighteen years old, by the name of David Brown. Said boy is light complexion, and curled hair, had on when he went away, a new felt hat, dark coloured coat, white jacket, and gray trowsers. Whoever will take up said boy, and return him to me, shall received one dollar reward, and no charges. All persons are forbid trusting, harbouring, or employing said boy.

Erastus Newton.

Newport April 17, 1801.

† [3d] Benjamin Baxter offers land for sale in Marlow; dated Alstead 7 May 1801.

¶ [3d] For sale, twelve acres of land, with a house and barn, and shop, and fulling mill, and good set of tools, and an excellent place of custom, and priviledge for other mills lying on the county road that leads to Dartmouth College, about two miles above Cornish bridge, will be sold on the most reasonable terms.

William Bryant.

Cornish, May 1th, [sic] 1801.

† [3d] John Salsbury advertises for his lost mare; dated Charlestown, 7 May 1801.

† [3d] A legal notice from John Bellows, Amasa Allen, and Lockhart Willard, the Directors of the Third New Hampshire Turnpike, regarding the route of the proposed road, "laid out and designated through and over lands belonging to the following persons, viz."

Joshua Hale	Ebenezer Crehore	Timothy Harvey
Thomas & Isaac Redington	Barnabas Willey	William Lincoln
Josiah Bellows	Elijah Mason	Aaron Lombard
The heirs of the estate of John Crafts deceased.	Benjamin Bellows	Phineas Farrar
	Stephen Bowker	Phillips Sweetser
William Pierce	Cheever Fowler	Isaac Cummings
Calvin Ripley	Oliver Wright	William Tenney Jr.
Caleb Bellows	Abel Allen	Levi Gates
Stephen Johnson	Benjamin Merrifield	John Penhallow
Eliphalet Fox	William Coolidge	Oliver Wright
Joseph Heaton	Amasa Carpenter	Moses Tucker
Horace Floyd	Stephen Griswold Jr.	Jonadab Baker
Josiah Richardson	Stephen Griswold	William Tenney
Apollos Gilmore	John Houghton	Jonathan Capron
Noah Heaton	Stephen Chase	Solomon Davis
Alexander Watkins	Stephen Easty	Bery Spalding
Aaron Hodgkins	Jonathan Dwinnell	Israel Whitcomb

Proposed Third New Hampshire Turnpike (continued):

Aaron Allen	William William [sic]	Simon Piper
Asa Sibley	Daniel Newcomb	Silas Fife
Manoah Drury	Alexander Ralston	Daniel Emery
Jonathan Jenison	Thomas Baker	Laban Ainsworth
Nathan Bundy Jun.	Josiah Willard	Roger Gilmore
Ebenezer Eaton	Samuel Heaton	Arthur Taylor
The heirs of Daniel Whipple	Zacheus Farnsworth	Benjamin Haywood
Davis Carpenter	Joseph Brown	

===== ¶ [3d] DIED. =====

At Boston, Capt. Francis Butler, Æt. 62. Mrs. Silence Revere, Æt. 46 years. Mrs. Hannah Ford. Mrs. Elizabeth Austin, wife of the Hon. Benjamin Austin, aged [85?] years. Mrs. Elizabeth Lamson, Æt. 68.

Vol. IX (No. 424) Tuesday, 19 May 1801.

¶ [3d] An unfortunate accident took place at Newport, Newhampshire, the 7th instant. A little girl of seven years old, daughter of Jesse Lane Esq. of that place, in following her brother who had gone to work, fell into the river, attempting to cross on a log, and was drowned before her brother who heard her fall could discover her, she was taken from the water, after lying about 30 minutes, and every exertion made to restore her, but without effect. Newport, May 9th, 1801.

Vol. IX (No. 425) Tuesday, 26 May 1801.

† [3d] Legal notice from "The Commissioners in a commission of Bankruptcy" in regards to a case involving Jonathan Winship of Cambridge, Mass., Trader.
† [3d] Antipas Marble advertises for his lost colt; dated at Cornish, 15 May 1801.
† [3d] Farm for sale in Newport, as advertised by Caleb Ellis and Jesse Willcox, Jr., "in Newport."
† [3d] John Hubbard adv. medicines for sale at his Walpole store; dated 12 May.

Vol. IX (No. 426) Tuesday, 2 June 1801.

† [1b] Adv. for a book entitled "The American Herbal, Or Materia Medica," offered for sale by Capt. Luke Brown, Westminster; Dr. John Campbell, Putney, Mr. Simeon Colbey, Dummerston, Dr. Geo. H. Hall, Brattleborough, or Mr. John Prentiss, Keene.
† [3c-d] Extensive and gruesome account of the supposed suicide of Elizabeth Fales, and the attempted suicide of Mr. Jason Fairbanks, at Dedham, Mass.; the two "had for a considerable time entertained an attachment towards each other." ♦ 44
¶ [3d] ONE CENT REWARD. Run away from the subscriber, an indented boy, named John Cohoon, about fourteen years of age; Whoever will take up said boy, and return him to the subscriber, shall have the above reward, and no charges paid. All persons are forbid harbouring or trusting said boy if they would avoid the penalty of the law.
Azariah Dickersan.
Walpole, May 25th, 1801.
† [3d] Joseph Bellows, Jr. advertises goods for sale at his store, which was "lately occupied by *Bellows and Stone.*" Adv. dated at Walpole, 1 June 1801.
† [3d] James Freeman adv. to purchase "twelve or fourteen of the first rate saddle horses . . . delivered at his dwelling house in Cornish, within twenty days, for which he will pay goods in Portsmouth . . . " Dated at Cornish, 22 May 1801.
† [3d] David Wells adv. to hire a journeyman chair maker; dated Westminster 26 May.
† [3d] Notice by Nathaniel Sikes and Orange Graves, a.k.a. *Sikes and Graves*, requesting settlement of debts; dated at Walpole 30 May 1801.

Vol. IX (No. 427) Tuesday, 9 June 1801.

† [3a] Brief account of a ferry which overturned at New York City [18 May 1801—Ed.], in which seven persons were drowned, including Mr. Charles Holmes, merchant. ♦

† [3a] News dated at Troy, N.Y., of the attempted murder of Dr. Edward Davis, of Stillwater, who received several shots in the abdomen, 14 May 1801. Dr. Loudon of Troy removed several slugs from Davis. ♦
† [3a] Cyrus Emly, a black man, was convicted of the murder of Humphrey Wall; the brief account of this trial is dated at Trenton, N.J., 2 June 1801. ♦
† [3b] Several accounts dated from Leominster, Mass. of a severe thunderstorm which struck a large area of N.H. and Mass., [29 May 1801—Ed.]: Mr. Holbrook's barn was blown down in Ashburnham; // Betsey Clerk, about 16 years of age, was killed while milking cows in a barn in Fitzwilliam; ♦ // also, "In Rindge, a Thomas Wetherbee, aged about 50 years was killed by the fall of a tree."
¶ [3b] Burlington, Vermont, May 28. Died on Tuesday last, Mrs. Bostwick, wife of Mr. Arthur Bostwick of Jericho. Mr. Bostwick had left her alone only a few minutes before her death, in apparent good health, but on returning found her lifeless on the floor.
† [3b-c] A young son of Capt. James Richardson of Weathersfield, [Vt.—Ed.] survived an accident at his father's saw mill. The article is dated at Windsor, 1 June 1801. ♦
† [3d] Samuel Farwell adv. a reward for his stolen horse; dated Westminster, 30 May.

===== ¶ [3d] MARRIED. =====

At Baltimore, Mr. Marcea H. Duval, ae. 17, to Mrs. Dorothy Allen, 30.
At Windsor, Vt. Mr. John Cook, to Miss Betsey Baldwin.
At Newmarlborough, Mr. Peter Phelps, of Chesterfield, to Miss Sukey Stickney, of the former place.
At Boston, Mr. Josiah Crossman, to Miss Marsa Hodges.
At Norton, Hon. Jabez Bowen, of Providence, to Miss E. Leonard, daughter of the Hon. G. Leonard, Esq.
At Durham, Mr. Samuel Odiorne, to Miss Olive Thomas.
At Portsmouth, Mr. John Melcher, to Miss Polly Flagg.

===== ¶ [3d] DIED. =====

At Portsmouth, Miss Mary Evans, ae. 27. Mrs. Mary Jackson, ae. 45. At Greenfield, Mr. Samuel Wells, ae. 71. At Hebron, Mr. Daniel Ingram, ae. 77. At Fitchburgh, Miss Susannah Brown. At Bermuda, whither she had retired with her husband for the restoration of her health, Mrs. Bingham, consort of the Hon. Wm. Bingham, of Philadelphia. At Canterbury, Mr. Peleg Brewster, ae. 84. At Salem, Mrs. Mehitable Mottey, ae. 60. At Woodstock, Vt. Mrs. Molly Ransom, ae. 60. At Boston, Miss Hannah Holbrook, ae. 33. Mrs. Sarah Nutt, ae. 50. Mrs. Mary H. Rowan.
On the 16th of March last, at Argentile, in the district of Montreal, Mrs. Elizabeth Hutchins, aged [24?].
At Westmoreland, on the 4th inst., Major Isaac Butterfield, in the 60th year of his age. His remains were interred on Sunday, and followed to the burying ground by a numerous and respectable procession from several of the towns in the vicinity of Westmoreland. His death was occasioned by an injury he received some days previous, by the kick of a horse.

Vol. IX (No. 428) Tuesday, 16 June 1801.

¶ [3c] Keene, New Hampshire, May 30.

ACCIDENTS.

On Wednesday last, a son of Capt. White, of Charlestown, aged 17, was drowned in Connecticut river. He was rowing the ferry boat, when the stay of the oar broke, and he plunged backwards into the river. His body was taken up on the morning following.
At the raising of the Meetinghouse of New Braintree, on the 13th inst. a young man by the name of Wanup fell from the top of the the [sic] belfry, which instantly put a period to his existence.

† [3d] Gideon Handerson adv. a lost colt; dated Claremont, 28 May 1801.
† [3d] Daniel Newcomb, Treasurer of the Third New Hampshire Turnpike, advertises a notice regarding said road; dated at Keene 6 June 1801.

====== ¶ [3d] MARRIED. ======

At Farmington, Dr. Abner Hart to Miss Almira Thompson.

At Boston, Mr. Jeremiah Bumstead to Miss Sarah Crosswell. Mr. Daniel P. Colesworthy to Miss Anna Collins. Mr. David Greene to Miss Bethiah Hopkins. Mr. Nathaniel Elsworth to Miss Betsey Harrison. Mr. Charles Sprague to Miss Margaret Pearson.

At Beverly, Mr. Robert Rantoul to Miss Joanna [Levett? or Lovett?]

At Roxbury, Col. Isaac S. Gardner to Miss Sarah Spooner.

At Falmouth, Mr. Daniel Hardy to Miss Hannah Marston.

At Portland, Mr. Ebenezer Sumner to Miss Henrietta Lowther.

At Quincy, Mr. Thomas Pratt to Miss Sarah Thayer.

====== ¶ [3d] DIED. ======

At Newburyport, Mr. Enoch Gerrish. At Bristol, Capt. Benj. Smith, Æ. 32. At Cambridge, Samuel Jenks Esq. Æ. 70. At Palmer, Deacon Thomas King, Æ. 83. At Westspringfield, Mr. Israel Lanckton. At New Bedford, by lightning, Mr. Peleg Huttleson. At Greenfield, Mr. Samuel Wells, Æ. 71. Widow Mary Cary, Æ. 64. At Marblehead, Mrs. Mary Bowen, Æ. 43. At Salem, Mr. Ramsdell, Æ. 35. At Boston, Mr. Samuel Whitwell, Æ. 84. Widow Joanna Fiars, Æ. 51. At Portsmouth, Samuel Cutts, Esq. Æ. 74.

Vol. IX (No. 429) Tuesday, 23 June 1801.

† [3d] Nathaniel Vilas adv. a stray mare on his property; dated Alstead 15 June 1801.

† [3d] Extensive account of the funeral of Lieut. William Laidlie, of the 2d U.S. Infantry, formerly of New York, aged about 27. Laidlie died at Westminster, Vt., 15 June 1801. ◆

====== ¶ [3b] MARRIED. ======

At Boston, Samuel Howard, Esq. to Miss Betsey Prince. Mr. William Averill to Miss Eunice Mahew.

At Charlestown, Ms. Mr. John Southack, to Miss Jane Barnes.

At Portsmouth, Capt. Wm. Cox to Miss Phebe Harslet. Mr. Joseph Walker to Miss Sally Brewster.

At Fitchburg, Mr. Levi Farwell, to Miss Betsey Carter.

At Providence, Capt. Solomon Tyler, to Miss Lorany Mason.

At Newburyport, Mr. Isaac Alden to Miss Hannah Pike.

At Newyork, Mr. John Thorburn, to Miss Eleanor Marr.

====== ¶ [3b] DIED. ======

At Windsor, Mr. James Langworthy, ae. 40; and his son, Jonathan Langworthy, ae. 17;—Mrs. Mary Hubbard, ae. 78;—Mr. Adams, in an advanced age.—At Claremont, Mrs. Elizabeth Spaulding, wife of Mr. Abel Spaulding, in the 39th year of her age.—At Lancaster, Penn. Frederick Augustus Muhlenberg, Receiver General of the Land Office. —At Dummerston, Mr. James Larrabee, ae. 34.—At Lancaster, Penn. John Wilkes Kittera, Esq. formerly Speaker [45] of the House of Representatives of the U. States.—At Detroit, Jam. Wm. Winston, of the U.S. cavalry.—At Keene, Mrs. Elizabeth Wright, ae. 89, descendants 94.—At Portsmouth, Mr. David Call, ae. 77.—At Woodstock, Mrs. Morse, ae. 99, grandmother of Rev. J. Morse, of Charlestown, descendants 315.—At Rochester, N.H. Mrs. Elizabeth Knight, ae. 78.

Vol. IX (No. 430) Tuesday, 30 June 1801.

† [2a] Account of an unusual lightning strike near the houses of Thaddeus Gage and Jeremiah French, at Sanbornton, N.H., 29 May 1801. ◆

† [2d] A child of Mr. Jacob Wilcox, 10 months old, of Berlin, Conn., scalded to death on the 3d of June 1801; the article is dated at Hartford, Conn. ◆

† [3a-b] Account of a lightning strike near the house of Mr. Charles Willard, in Tinmouth, 5 June 1801. The article is dated at Rutland, Vermont.

† [3c] Elijah Hall offers two farms for sale at Waterford, Vermont; dated 11 June 1801.

† [3c] A notice regarding a Note, dated 23 March 1801, given by John Perkins to

Thomas Way. The advertisement does not mention any town, and is not dated.
† [3d] Advertisement of goods for sale at the store of Joseph Bellows, Jr., Walpole.
† [3d] Legal notice regarding the insolvent estate of Maj. Isaac Butterfield, late of Westmoreland, N.H., deceased. Nathan Babbit, Joseph Buffum, and William Hutchins appointed Commissioners; the adv. also contains a schedule of estate business meetings to be conducted at the house of the Widow Hannah Butterfield in Westmoreland.
† [3d] The copartnership of John B. Wheeler and William Hall, Jr., is dissolved; notice dated at Grafton, 17 June 1801.
† [3d] The copartnership of David Stone and Roswell Bellows, a.k.a. *Stone and Bellows*, is dissolved; the notice was dated at Walpole, 30 June.

===== ¶ [3d] MARRIED. =====

At Boston, Thomas Lane, Esq. merchant, of London, to Miss Elizabeth Appleton. Mr. Archelaus Goddard, to Miss Betsey Low.
At Brookfield, Joseph Cutler, of Boston, to Miss Phebe Ward.

===== ¶ [3d] DIED. =====

At Hartford, Lynde Lord, Esq. ae. 68. At Putney, Vt. John Griffin, Esq. ae. 48. At Greenfield, Mrs. Allen.—At Westerly, R.I. Rowse Babcock, late President of the Westerly Bank. At Andover, Mr. Daniel Page, ae. 69.—At Medford, Mrs. Sarah Kennedy, ae. 30. At Newcastle, Capt. John Simpson, ae. 79. At Portsmouth, Mr. Samuel Doe, ae. 28. At Northwood, Mrs. Susannah Clark, ae. 51. At Alexandria, V. Capt. Philip Magruder, ae. 38. Mr. Robert Allison.
At Sutton, Mrs. Siley Barton. At Bolton, Mr. James Townsend, ae. 68. At Newyork, John Smith, Esq. late lieut. Col. com. of the first legion in the service of the United States. At Hartland, V. Mr. Elisha Marsh jun, ae. 35.

Vol. IX (No. 431) Tuesday, 7 July 1801.

† [3a-b] Detailed account of the murder of Mr. John Clark of Northumberland county, Penn., by a man who called himself Thomas Morgan, a Connecticut man about 20 years of age. ♦
¶ [3b] On Saturday a Duel was fought, opposite Trenton, on the Pennsylvania shore, by Washington Morton and David S. Jones, both of this [46] city.—Mr. Jones was shot through the lower part of his body. The wound is said not to be of a dangerous nature.
¶ [3c] Peacham, Vermont, June 18. "Newbury, June 15th, 1801. On Monday last, Gideon Currier, aged 22, son of Mr. Ezra Currier of Ryegate, and a boy aged 10 years, son of Mr. Timothy Townsend, of Groton, were crossing Connecticut river, in a canoe, and had nearly reached the opposite shore, where two young men were bathing. In this situation they commenced sporting, in which the canoe was accidentally overset, and as neither could swim, both were drowned."
† [3c] Rev. Levi Pillsbury ordained at the church in Winchendon, [Mass.—Ed.]. ♦
† [3d] Legal notice regarding the insolvent estate of Thomas Field, late of Claremont, deceased. James Corbin, Joel Richards, and Shaler Towner appointed Commissioners, and the notice includes a schedule of estate business to be conducted at the house of Theophilus Clark, innholder at Claremont; dated at Claremont 29 June 1801.
† [3d] Walter Bingham offers "two stands of clothiers Works for sale, one in Charlestown, N.H., the other in Claremont, N.H. Adv. dated at Charlestown, 2 July.
† [3d] List of letters remaining at the Post Office in Walpole, N.H., 3 July 1801, as compiled by Alex. Thomas, Postmaster:

Miss Sally Armstrong,	Chesterfield.	Ephraim Mahurin,	Westmoreland.
Joseph or Caleb Aldrich,	Westmoreland.	Elisha Mack,	"
Willard Butterfield,	"	Rev. Allen Pratt,	"
Mariot Black,	Walpole (?)	Nathaniel Partridge,	Chesterfield.
John Cheney,	"	Alvin Robeshaw,	Walpole.
Patience Esterbrook,	"	Lydia Robbins,	Westmoreland.
Roger Fenton,	"	Miss Lucinda Rugg,	Charlestown.
Eliphalet Fox,	"	Amos Stearns,	Chesterfield.
"Asahel Good or Goodrich,"	"	Timothy Skinner,	Westmoreland.
Adonijah Houghton,	"	Miss Ruth Temple,	"

List of letters at the Post Office, Walpole, N.H. (*continued*) :

Elijah [A.?] Hall,	Westmoreland.	Clement Trowbridge,	Westmoreland.
Joshua Hall,	"	John White,	Walpole, 2.
Thomas Jenison,	Walpole.	Elijah Wollage Esq.,	Westmoreland.
Barnard Kimball,	Rockingham.	Joseph Wheeler,	", 2.
John Lovell,	Walpole.	Samuel Whiting,	Langdon, 2.

===== ¶ [3d] MARRIED. =====

At Belchertown, Ms. the Rev. Asa M'Farland of Concord, N.H. to Miss Nancy Dwight of Belchertown.
At Hartford, Mr. J. M'Cracken, to Miss Rebecca Hopkins.
At Hingham, Mr. Thomas Andrews to Miss Hannah Cushing.
At Boston, Mr. William Ward to Miss Mary Bennett.

===== ¶ [3d] DIED. =====

At Windsor, V. Miss Polly Story, ae. 18.   At Hanover, Mr. Ephraim Simonds, ae. 25. At Epsom, the hon. John M'Clary, ae. 82.   At Glastenbury, Capt. Timothy Hale, ae. 74. At Hartford, Mr. John [Kopple?], ae. 44.   At Bo[s?]ton, Miss Ann Lowder, ae. 84.—Mr. William Lovett, ae. 28.   At Bangor, Mrs. Mary Treat, ae. 44.   At Ipswich, Capt. Jeremiah Staniford, ae. 79.   At Lancaster, the Rev. Josiah Bridge, of East Sudbury, in the 62d year of his age, and 40th year of his ministry.   At Roxbury, Mr. James How, ae. 24.   At Salem, Mrs. Eunice Deland, ae. 45.   At Newbury, Rev. Abraham Moor, ae. 32. At Newburyport, Mrs. Elizabeth Fo[?]er. 47

Vol. IX (No. 432) Tuesday, 14 July 1801.

† [1b] Advertisement by "D. & T. Carlisle" requesting help wanted, perhaps for apprenticeships; dated at Walpole 8 June 1801.
† [2a] Summary of Acts passed at a Session of the Honourable General Court, begun and holden at Hopkinton, June 1801. A few of these acts pertain to specific individuals: 1) "An act authorizing Zaccheus Wright, Esq. to convey certain Lands therein mentioned, 2) An act authorizing Miriam Pillsbury to convey certain lands therein mentioned, 3) An act authorizing Shadrack Dodge the exclusive right of keeping a ferry over Connecticut river from the mouth of Amonusuck river, four miles up said river, as that tends," and 4) An act altering the name of John Hogg and others, to the name of Raymond.
† [3d] Detailed account of the suicide [9 June 1801—Ed.] of the wife of Mr. John Culler, an insane woman, of Montpelier, Vt. ♦
† [3d] Joseph Allen adv. for his lost mare; dated at Charlestown, N.H. 10 July 1801.
† [3d] Joseph Burt adv. for his lost mare; dated at Westmoreland, 1 July 1801.

===== ¶ [3d] DIED. =====

At Wethersfield, on the 3d of June, in the 68th year of his age, Capt. James Mitchell. On the 10th of the same month two of his sons, viz. James, aged 27, and Stephen, aged 20, on their passage from Savannah to Baltimore, were swept from the deck of their vessel in a storm and perished in the sea.

Vol. IX (No. 433) Tuesday, 21 July 1801.

† [2c] Account of the murder of Capt. Jonathan Phillips, an officer of the Revolutionary War, by his brother Samuel Phillips, "at Maidenhead." The article is dated at New Brunswick, New Jersey, 2 July 1801. ♦
¶ [2d] Hallowell, Maine, July 3. MELANCHOLY ACCIDENT. Mr. Eliphalet Rowel and Mr. Abraham Weston, both of Livermore, on Monday last were falling trees with a company, and by some unlucky event, with a tree Mr. Rowel was killed dead on the spot; Mr. Weston was so wounded that he survived but a few hours. The former leaving a wife with five small children, with feelings impossible to express, and whose afflictions seem insupportable.
On the same day, Mr. Joseph Tuck, of Fayette, being at the same business, and at the distance of five miles from the others, a tree falling from where it was lodged, broke his thigh and considerably fractured the bone.

We are informed of five more being killed much in the same manner, at no great distance, and all very lately.

¶ [2d] Newburyport, Massachusetts, July 7. MELANCHOLY EVENT. Yesterday two sailors having hired a horse and chaise rode out to Amesbury, and we are informed, they were upset twice and broke the top of their chaise. On their return, at the head of State-street, they again upset, a splinter entered the side of one of them, and penetrating to his heart, instantly put an period to his existence. The other was last evening in too high a state of intoxication to give any accurate information respecting his unfortunate companion, but it is said he belonged to Kennebeck, and that his name is Joseph Harford. He is supposed to be about 30 years of age. The survivor received some slight bruises, but none dangerous.

¶ [3c] A fire lately took place in the house of Capt. Nathan Smith of Stonington, and two young lads, one a son of Capt. Smith, and the other of Mr. Thomas Butler, were so horridly burnt before assistance could be given them, that they expired soon after.

† [3d] The Copartnership of Elisha Kingsbury, Isaac Randal, Bill Blake, and David Buckman, is dissolved; the "business will in future be carried on, by Kingsbury, Randal, and Blake," a.k.a. *Elisha Kingsbury, & Co.* The notice also advertises for a journeyman paper maker.

† [3d] A list of letters remaining at the Post Office in Putney, Vermont, 1 July 1801:

Col. Joseph Burt,	Westmoreland.	Clark Harwood,	Putney.
Barnabas Thurbur,	Putney.	Moses Gilbert,	"
David Gilbert,	"	Elijah Robinson,	Townsend.
Peter Derry,	Brookline.	Jotham Lord,	Putney or Westmoreland.
Rufus Huntly,	Putney.		

===== ¶ [3d] MARRIED. =====

At Portsmouth, Mr. Samuel Balch to Miss Hanna [sic] Whidden.
Mr. Mark Leighton to Miss Deborah Seavey.
At Hallowell, John Davis Esq. of Augusta, to Miss Nancy Cutler.
At Salem, Mr. Benjamin Archer to Miss Margaret Rider.
Mr. Benjamin Wardwell to Miss Dolly Moulton.

===== ¶ [3d] DIED. =====

DROWNED.—In Conventry pond, last Monday evening, James Buell, son of Mr. Solomon Buell, of Rutland, Vermont, aged 13 years. He was a grandson of the Hon. Judge Root, and had lived in his family about five years.

At Lime, Mrs. Lucy Latham, Æ. 62. Mrs. Elizabeth Cutting. At Montpelier, by the fall of a tree, Capt. Samuel Robinson. At Keene, (N.H.) Maj. Josiah Willard, Æ. 64. At Providence, Mr. John Green, Æ. 67. At Boston, Mr. Joseph Barrell jun. At Dover, Mrs. Mary Bragg, Æ. 59. At Rochester, Mrs. Mary Knight, Æ. 33. At Salem, Capt. Thomas Mason, Æ. 78. Miss Sophia Plummer. At Goshen, Deacon Thomas Brown, Æ. 61. At East Haddam, Mr. Josiah Whiley. At Morristown, New Jersey, Col. William de Heart, an officer in the late revolutionary army. At Sterling, Deacon Ebenezer Buss, Æ. 78. At Southborough, Mrs. Dinah Stow, Æ. 72. At Springfield, Mr. Rufus Stebbins, Æ. 31. On board the frigate, United States, Thomas Holland, of Windham, Æ. 22. At Ballstown Springs, Maj. John Rowe, Æ. 64, of Gloucester. At Boston, Mr. Timothy Robertson, Æ. 65. Mr. John Revere, Æ. 63.

At Swansey, The Rev. John Mason, ae. [35? or 85?]. Mr. Job Mason, ae. 75. At Portsmouth, Mr. Geo. Dame, ae. 74.

Vol. IX (No. 434) Tuesday, 28 July 1801.

¶ [3d] It is said that a child was killed by lightning in Jaffrey last week.

† [3d] Legal notice stating that Willard Butterfield is appointed Administrator of the estate of Maj. Isaac Butterfield, late of Westmoreland, N.H.

===== ¶ [3d] DIED. =====

Mr. William Dowst, who lately died at Salem, was a man of uncommon size and strength. He was nearly 7 feet high, and weighed 300 weight. [. . .] ♦

In this town, Miss ——— Smith, of Amherst.

Vol. IX (No. 435) Tuesday, 4 Aug. 1801.

† [1c-d] A copy of a letter to President Thomas Jefferson, from several merchants of New Haven, Conn., who opposed the removal of Elizur Goodrich, Esq. from the office of Collector for the District of New Haven, and the appointment of Samuel Bishop, Esq. to fill his vacancy. The merchants considered Bishop too infirm to perform his duties, as it is stated that "Samuel Bishop, Esq. will be seventy-eight years old in November next." Jeremiah Atwater, Elias Shipman, Abraham Bradley, Abel Burnett, and 80 other unnamed persons signed the letter, along with Isaac Beers, President of the Bank, and of the Chamber of Commerce of New Haven. Elias Shipman, President of the New Haven Insurance Company, along with Beers, "certify that the signers of the foregoing Remostrance are the owners of more than 7-8ths of the navigation of the port of New Haven."

† [3d] William Minard adv. a mare found; dated at Rockingham, 29 July 1801.

===== ¶ [3d] MARRIED. =====

At Hinsdale, The Hon. Lewis R. Morris Esq. to Miss Ellen Hunt.
At Norwich, The Hon. John Allen Esq. of Litchfield, to Miss Ursula M'Curdy.
At Providence, Nicholas Brown Esq. to Miss Mary [B.?] Steele.
At Baltimore, Mr. Alexander Martin, printer, to Miss Mary Rogers.

===== ¶ [3d] DIED. =====

At Greenfield, Mrs. Patience Bell, ae. 34. At Gloucester, David Plummer Esq. ae. 63. At Hampton, Mrs. Sarah Toppan, mother of the Hon. Christopher Toppan Esq. ae. 96. At Watertown, Mr. Zachariah Mills, ae. 36. At Boston, Capt. Jeremiah Hill, ae. 45. Mrs. Nabby Lillie, ae. 32. At Newbury Mr. Seth Plummer, ae. 65. At Newburyport, Mrs. Hannah Noyes, ae. 62. At Durham, Ezekiel Leathers, aged 101 years.
At Portsmouth, Mr. George Dome,[48] ae. 75. At Lancaster, Dr. John Cleverly, ae. 73. At Dover, Mr. Daniel Libbey.

Vol. IX (No. 436) Tuesday, 11 Aug. 1801.

† [3c] Death of Lockwood Curry, at Sheshequin, Penn., who was mistaken for a deer and shot 7 July 1801 by a fellow hunter, a son of Joseph Smith. Curry was the son of William Curry, and in the 19th year of his age

¶ [3b] Hartford, Connecticut, August 3. On Sunday the 26th ult. Mr. Chester Peak was accidentally drowned in Connecticut river, near East Windsor. He was 26 years of age, and has Parents living in Pomfret, in Vermont.

¶ [3c] We learn that a melancholy accident happened at Grafton the last week. As a Mr. Joseph Thacher was felling trees in the woods, one of them descended in such a direction as to fall on both his thighs, and broke them. A surgeon was immediately sent for, and we learn that one of them was amputated, and that he expired instantly at the close of the operation.

† [3d] A legal notice regarding contested property in Lunenburg, Vermont, by one Ben. West, attorney. The land was sold by Joseph Russel of Boston, 24 Jan. 1795, who is since deceased, but later investigation showed Russel was not the legal owner. ♦

¶ [3d] TAKE NOTICE. Whereas Benjamin Smart of Unity did obtain by fraud, of me the subscriber, two notes of hand; one for one hundred dollars, the other for fifty; all persons are forbid purchasing said notes, as I am determined not to pay them.

Aaron Chase.
Lempster, July 28, 1801.

† [3d] Adv. of a farm for sale, where Mr. Norman resides, at Westminster.

===== ¶ [3c] MARRIED. =====

At Concord, Ms. Mr. Paul Adams to Mrs. Rebecca Cargill. At Salem, Mr. Nathaniel Hathorne to Miss Eliza Manning. At Chesterfield, Mr. John Putnam to Miss Mary Converse.
In this town, Mr. William Gage to Miss Sally Hooper.

===== ¶ [3c] DIED. =====

At Greenfield, Mrs. Severance. At Westfield, Mr. Moses Stebbins. At West-Springfield, Mrs. Mary Leonard, ae. 52. At Petersham, Dr. Ephraim Whitney, of Brattleboro' V. æ. 73. At Portland, Mrs. Dorothea Vaughan. At Newton, Miss Caroline Crane, and the same day her mother, Mrs. Susannah Crane, æ. 60. At Boston, Moses Parsons Esq. Widow Mary Sumner, æ. 66. In England, Brigadier General Arnold. At Keene, Mr. David Balch, æ. 61. At Philadelphia, Alexander Wilcocks Esq. At Alstead, on the 29th ult. Richard Page Hale, son of Moses Hale Esq. in the 16th year of his age. On the 30th, Mr. John Procter, æ. 72.

Vol. IX (No. 437) Tuesday, 18 Aug. 1801.

===== ¶ [3d] MARRIED. =====

At Marshfield, the Rev. William Montague, of Dedham, to Miss Jane Little. At Portsmouth, Mr. Jabez Colbert to Miss Abigail Stoodley. At Rockingham, V. Mr. Roswell Bellows, of this town, to Miss Martha Lovell. At Westminster, Mr. Marmaduke Wait, Lieutenant in the 16th regiment, U.S. to Miss Amelia Heileman, eldest daughter of Dr. John F. Heileman.

===== ¶ [3d] DIED. =====

At Boscawen, Mr. Jeremiah Carter—At Schenectady, Jonathan Edwards, D.D. president of Union College.—Hartford, Mr. Rhoderick Olcott, æ. 35. At Newlondon, Mr. Samuel Caulkins, æ. 62. At Havanna, Mr. Richard Salter jun. of Boston, æ. 21. At Boston, Mr. Samuel Pope, æ. 34. Mrs. Jane Nottage, æ. 77. Miss Mary Bacon, æ. 35. Mr. William Colman, æ. 53. Mr. Joseph Payson, æ. 60. Mr. Benj. Bigelow, æ. 42. Mrs. Lydia Lewis, æ. 35. Mr. John Dennett, æ. 60. At Charleston, S.C. on the 25th inst., Mr. Elisha H. Waldo, late of Brookfield, æ. 28.

Vol. IX (No. 438) Tuesday, 25 Aug. 1801.

¶ [3b-c] THE WRECK. It is now ascertained, that the wreck of a vessel, mentioned in the Centinel of the 1st instant, as having been towed into Nantucket, is the wreck of the schooner Sally, which was owned by Mr. Edward Stevens, a planter of Midway, in Georgia. He purchased the vessel at Killingworth, in Connecticut, the last autumn, and took her new from the stocks. On the 7th of April, Mr. Stevens, with his lady, and a number of their friends, embarked in this vessel at Newport, in Georgia, for Newyork. On the 13th, a tremendous gale of wind was experienced on the southern coast, which continued, with various degrees of severity, until the 26th. Within this period, it is probable, the vessel overset, and the passengers and crew lost. The names of the captain and of the seamen are unknown. An unusual interest is taken in the loss of nine passengers, whose friends, in Georgia and Connecticut, must deeply feel and lament this affecting catastrophe.

Mr. Edwards was a sensible, amiable and pious man. Mrs. Sarah Stevens was a woman of modest and intrinsic merit. Both were esteemed as valuable members of the church and society at Midway. Doctor Lathrop Holmes, of Woodstock, in Connecticut, was endeared to his friends, by his amiable disposition and gentle manners; to society, by his integrity and benevolence; and to the church, by his judicious counsels and exemplary life. Mrs. Sarah Holmes, the Doctor's lady, was a woman of rare accomplishments, intellectual, moral and religious, by her native vivacity, tempered and regulated by religion; by her instructive conversation, and by her pre-eminent piety, she at once conciliated general esteem, adorned the Christian profession, and was signally useful in the circle of her acquaintance. Mrs. Mary Stevens, and Miss Nancy Sumner, estimable sisters of Mrs. Holmes; Mr. James Stacy, a worthy man, with two children, of about nine and seven years of age, the one a nephew, and the other a neice of Mr. Stacy, (all belonging to Midway) complete the list of passengers, who, by this ship wreck, were, doubtless buried in the ocean.

In the cabin were found a silver scissors-chain, marked Sarah Stevens, and a cotton handkerchief, marked Sarah Holmes—relics, which friendship will long preserve, and often lave with tributary tears. [49]

† [3c] Article describing the death of Mr. Benjamin Ropes, aged 19, son of Mr. Samuel Ropes, "and second officer of the ship Bellisarius." Ropes was killed in an accident on the ship, in Salem, Mass., 4 Aug. 1801. ◆

¶ [3d] By a late Washington paper, we learn that Mr. Lemuel Hedge, who formerly went from this quarter, and late of Georgetown, on the 5th inst. put a period to his existence by hanging. No previous act led his friends to suspect his intentions. He is said to have been highly respected as a preceptor of youth, and universally beloved by his acquaintance.

¶ [3d] Ordained at Portland, Mr. Benjamin Titcomb of the Baptist Society.

¶ [3d] TAKE NOTICE. Whereas my wife Bethiah, owing, as I suppose to the advice of some other person, has left my bed and board, and taken with her an only child about eight months old, this is to warn all persons from harbouring or trusting them on my account, as I shall pay no debts of her contracting after this date, and as I am ready to receive her if she will return to me.

Aaron Philips.
Westmoreland, August 20, 1801.

† [3d] A notice from the firm of *John B. Wheeler & Co.*, stating an intention to close the business, and requesting settlement of accounts. Signed by John B. Wheeler, William Hall, Jr., and Daniel Wheeler. Dated at Townsend, 19 Aug.

† [3d] Legal notice regarding the insolvent estate of Samuel Chase, Esq., late of Cornish, deceased. Nathaniel Hall, Innholder at Cornish, and March Chase appointed Commissioners; dated at Cornish 21 Aug. 1801.

===== ¶ [3d] MARRIED. =====

At Portsmouth, Mr. James Roach to Mrs. Mary Mendum.
At Charlestown, Mr. Earl Sturtevant to Miss Mary Le Mercier.
At Ashburnham, Capt. George R. Cushing to Miss Catharine Willard.
At Boston, Col. James Robertson, of Lynn, to Mrs. Jane Gay. Mr. Joseph Shed sen. to Mrs. Martin. Mr. John P. Schott jun. to Miss Hannah Meinzes. Mr. Wm. Blackstock to Miss Eliza Maxwell.
At Dover, Dr. Richard C. Shannon to Miss Mary Tebbetts.

===== ¶ [3d] DIED. =====

At Bethlem, C. Mrs. Elizabeth Egleston, æ. 85. At East Hartford, Mrs. Leurenda Kilborn, æ. 45. At Southington, Capt. John Clark, æ. 65. At Bozrah, C. Mrs. Phebe Hough, æ. 75. At Lancaster, Upper Coos, Mrs. Betsey Baker, æ. 46. At Hanover, Mrs. Tisdale. At Rutland, V. Mr. Trobridge Maynard, æ. 32. At Keene, Mr. Elisha Briggs jun. æ. 27. At Springfield, Mrs. Martha Wells, æ. 90. At Northampton, Mrs. Pomeroy, wife of Capt. Seth P. Miss Jane Lyman.

Vol. IX (No. 439) Tuesday, 1 Sept. 1801.

† [1c] Legal notice regarding the insolvent estate of Arnold [50] Clark, late of Lempster, N.H., deceased. Elisha Huntley, Rufus Huntley, and Jacob Shaw appointed Commissioners; meetings to be conducted at the house of Elisha Huntley, innholder at Marlow; dated 24 Aug.

¶ [3c] Hanover, Newhampshire, Aug. 22. Mrs. Sarah Goodale, wife of Mr. Bartholomew Goodale of Strafford, Vt. aged 49, put an end to her existence by hanging herself. She had been unwell for several days, but was getting better—and ate breakfast with her famiy the morning before the horrid act was committed. She was found suspended by a skein of yarn fastened to a peg in the barn. A jury of Inquest was summoned, whose verdict was Melancholy Insanity.

† [3d] Philip Davis offers a farm for sale at Rockingham, Vermont; dated there 28 Aug.

===== ¶ [3d] MARRIED. =====

At Concord, John Brodhead, president elder in the Methodist Connection, to Miss Mary Dodge.
At Boston, Mr. Stephen Turner to Miss Nabby Cooper. Mr. John W. Jones to Miss Ann Joyse. At Brookfield, Mr. Thomas Haskins to Miss Eliza Foxcroft.

===== ¶ [3d] DIED. =====

At Amherst, Miss Eunice Pettingall, æ. 20. Widow Bethiah Phelps, æ. 63. Miss Martha Upham, æ. 25. At Leominster, Widow Sarah Divol, æ. 83. At Hanover, on the morning of Commencement Day, Miss Hannah Brewster, daughter of General Brewster. At Randolph, V. Mr. Alvin Fish. At Wethersfield, Mrs. Honor Belden, æ. 70. At Waterbury, Mr. David Taylor, æ. 64. At Louisville, G[eorgia—Ed.]. General

James Gunn.   At Glastenbury, Mrs. Mary Howe.   At Boston, Miss Hannah Bass, æ. 61.   Mr. William Barber, æ. 32.   Mrs. Priscilla Broaders, æ. 45.   Mrs. Elizabeth Gordon, æ. 68.   Mrs. Hannah Fudge, æ. 32.

Vol. IX [51] (No. 440) Tuesday, 8 Sept. 1801.

¶ [3d] In a late Boston paper actually occurs the following marriage. Mr. John Thing to Miss Betsey Calfe. This young lady probably is of opinion that it is better to be any *Thing* than a *Calf*.

† [3d] Brief article describing a large estate left by Robert Randall, who died at New York on 5 June 1801, for the purpose of creating an asylum for disabled seamen. ♦

† [3d] Adv. of medicine for sale at John Hubbard's Apothecary Store, Walpole.

===== ¶ [3d] MARRIED. =====

At West Springfield, Mr. Daniel Moffatt jun. to Miss Huldah Clough.   At New Bedford, Mr. Jacob Barker to Miss Eliza Hazzard.   At Charlestown, Ms. Rev. Micah Stone, of Brookfield, to Miss Sarah Wood.

===== ¶ [3d] DIED. =====

At Statesburg, S.C. Dr. Timothy Pierce, formerly of Litchfield, C. æ. 24.   At Norwich, Miss Rocksiney Wells. Widow [Parterrill?], æ. 73.   At Woodstock, Widow Elizabeth Saunderson, æ. 89.   At Windsor, Mr. Edward Smith, æ. 77.   At Chester, Mrs. Rebecca Mills, æ. 36.   At Hartford, Mrs. Abigail Hunt, æ. 70.   At Peterborough, Dr. Kendall Osgood, æ. 45.   At Charlestown, Mrs. Sarah Hager, æ. 44.   At Boston, Capt. Judah Delano, æ. 49.   Mrs. Mary White, æ. 74.   Mr. William Moore, æ. 65.   At Surrinam, Hall Tufts Esq. late Captain in the army of the United States.   At Dorchester, Mrs. Hannah Tileston, æ. 30.   At Watertown, Mrs. Mary Bemis, æ. 71.   At Westborough, Mrs. Hannah Parkman, æ. 85.   At Albany, Mrs. Mary Warner, æ. [24?].   At Windsor, Mr. Edward Smith, æ. 77.   At Wells, Mrs. Hannah Gilman.   At Peacham, Mrs. Olive Chamberlin.   At Portsmouth, Mr. Charles Caverly.   At Amherst, Miss Lydia Lane, æ. 17.

At Putney, of a cancer, Mr. ——— Goodwin, late innkeeper in that place.

Vol. IX (No. 441) Tuesday, 15 Sept. 1801.

† [3b] Detailed account of the drowning of the four year-old son of Mr. William Rogers, in or near Hudson, N.Y., 13 Aug. 1801, and the near drowning of the father. The article was copied from the *Balance*, published at Hudson. ♦

† [3b] Account of multiple drownings, 24 July 1801, "near Franklin," in an article dated at Cincinnati, 29 July 1801. David Buchanan and Robert Buchanan (brothers) both drowned while attempting to save John Potts, who also drowned. ♦

† [3c] Lightning strike at the house of Mr. Joel Perham, at Athens, Vt., 25 Aug. 1801, causes substantial damage, and seriously injures an 18 year-old son of Mr. Perham's. ♦

¶ [3d] A Mrs. *Chestnut*, of Chilicothe, N.W.T. [52] has lately been delivered of three girls, and a boy; three were still born and the last died soon after the birth. All these circumstances, added to the singularity of the name, we think will induce some wit to *crack* a joke upon the occasion.

† [3d] Agrippa Warren adv. a stray horse; dated at Walpole, 14 Sept. 1801.

===== ¶ [3d] MARRIED. =====

At Newbury, Mr. Stephen Coffin to Miss Nancy Morland.
At Hingham, Mr. Welcome Lincoln to Miss Susannah Gill.
At Lancaster, Mr. Wm. Wilder, of Portland, to Miss Nancy Beaman.
At Boston, Mr. Oliver Fuller to Miss Abigail Learned.
Mr. Elijah Bicknel to Miss Sally Moore.
Mr. Samuel Ames, of Providence, to Miss Ann Checkley.

===== ¶ [3d] DIED. =====

Drowned at Cornish, September 2d, Spencer Jaquish, æ. 15.   At Norwich, Mrs. Naomi Fisk, æ. 21.   At Rumney, Miss Betsey Haines, æ. 18.   At Lancaster, N.H. ——— Varnum, Esq. æ. 60.   At Lebanon, Mr. Azariah Bliss, æ. 88.   At Lime, Mrs. Laycount, æ. 47.   At Greenfield, a child of Thomas Dickman, printer.   At Amherst, Miss Lydia Lane, æ. 17.   At New-York, Mr. John Franklin, æ. 70.   At Hartford, Mrs.

Abigail Hunt, ae. 70.   At Providence, Mr. Job Danforth, jun.   At Dover, Mrs. Lydia Gray, ae. 35.   At Cape Francois, Mr. Molineux Leach, of Boston.   At Cambridge, Mr. Nathaniel Jarvis.   At Boston, Mrs. Betsey Pratt, ae. 18.   Mr. Wm. Tolley.   Mr. David Hollis, ae. 44.   Miss Mary Ann Smith, ae. 29.   Mr. Francis Archibald, ae. 78.   Mr. James Wall, ae. 64.   On Thursday evening, Col. Roberts, of Marlboro.' He was riding in a chaise between Marlboro' and Keene, and, it is supposed was taken suddenly by a stroke of apoplexy, which put an immediate period to his existence.
At Newport, Rev. Abraham M[inis?] Esq. ae. 23.   At Topsfield, Mrs. Mehitable Dexter, ae. 81.   At Salem, Mrs. Cox, ae. 84.   At Portland, Maj. Thomas Fosdick, ae. 45. At Dover, Mrs. Gray, consort of the Rev. Robert Gray.   At Hubbardston, Rev. Nathaniel Parker, in the 20th year of his ministry, ae. 59.   At Sutton, Capt. Samuel Sibley, ae. 79. At Springfield, Miss Margaret Wardwell, ae. 24.   At Blanford, Reuben Atwater Esq.

Vol. IX (No. 442) Tuesday, 22 Sept. 1801.

¶ [2a] Windsor, Vermont, Sept. 15.   We hear from Rutland, that a young man of the name of Strong, riding swiftly through Rutland street, on Tuesday evening last, rode against a cow, when his horse falling violently on him, bruised him so badly that he was taken up speechless and expired in a few hours after. He was brother to the young man who was killed last year at the raising of a barn in that town.
We learn from Cavendish, that one evening last week, a Mr. Israel Dwinnell, in returning from one of his neighbor's to his own house, the evening being very dark, was suddenly inclosed in the embraces of a Bear; being very much dissatisfied with his situation, he endeavored to extricate himself by exerting all the strength of which he was capable. After two or three struggles, he disengaged himself from the Bear, who finding she was likely to lose her prey, struck the man with one of her claws in the side of his face, which very much scarified and injured him, but not so much but that he is likely to recover.
† [2a] Suicide attempt of Thomas Pilsbury, of Lyman, N.H., who cut his own throat rather than appear at Plymouth Court. The article is dated at Hanover, N.H., and mentions that "He was alive on Tuesday morning—He has a wife and family." ♦
† [3a-b] Thomas Shelden, Prison-Keeper at the Prison of Newgate, describes an attempted jail-break, 7 Sept. 1801, by one Millard, "a noted villain." The article is dated at Hartford, Conn. ♦
† [3d] Peter Fletcher requests all outstanding debts to be settled; dated Alstead 14 Sept.

======= ¶ [3d] MARRIED. =======

At Hopkinton, Levi Israel W. Kelly to Miss Rebecca Fletcher.   At Plymouth, Mr. David Hazeltine, to Miss Mary Ward.   At Coventry, Mr. Apollos Fitch to Miss Cybele Edgerton.   At East Haddam, Mr. Robert Hosmer to Miss Nancy Chapman.
In this town, Mr. Solomon Godfrey, to Miss Mary Jenison.

======= ¶ [3d] DIED. =======

At Albany, the Hon. Robert Yates, Esq. late chief justice of the Supreme Court of the State of Newyork.   In North Carolina, Gen. Joseph M'Dowell late member of Congress from that state.   At Concord, Mrs. Nancy M'Farland, ae. 23, consort of the Rev. Asa M'Farland.   At Boscawen, Deacon Joseph Atkinson, ae. 83.   At Longmeadow, Mrs. Root, ae. 81.   At Amherst, Mrs. Hannah Upham.   At Portsmouth, Mrs. Dorothy Deering, ae. 43.   Miss Elizabeth Babb, ae. 18.
Croydon, August 26, 1801.   This day was found dead on the mountain, near Benjamin Cutting's, Mr. Moses Cummings. A jury of inquest was summoned, whose verdict was an accidental death. He was 76 years of age.
At Alstead, on the 16th instant, Mrs. Lydia Higbee, consort on the Rev. Jeremiah Higbee in the 38th year of her age. Her disorder was a cancer in her breast, which caused her for three months past the most excruciating pain, which she bore with Christian fortitude, and died in full assurance of a better life beyond the grave; thus in the midst of her usefulness she is taken from her family , left her husband to lament the loss of a kind companion, three children, an affectionate and tender mother, the church of Christ an exemplary member, and all her neighbours, and acquaintances, a pattern of piety and benevolence.

Vol. IX (No. 443) Tuesday, 29 Sept. 1801.

† [3d] Legal notice regarding a petition by Eliza Horn of Dover, N.H., for divorce from her husband William Horn. The two were married 1 Jan. 1772 at Dover; Eliza claims neglect and cruelty, and that more than three years ago her husband committed adultery with a Miss Newton, late of Alstead, N.H., and that these two had left for parts unknown.

† [3d] Legal notice regarding the insolvent estate of Asa Lyman Towner, late of Newport, deceased. Jesse Lane, Joseph Bascom, and Samuel Hurd appointed Commissioners over said estate; business meetings to be conducted at the house of Capt. Jesse Wilcox jun. in Newport. Notice dated at Newport 8 Sept. 1801.

† [3d] Adv. of goods for sale at the store of Joseph Bellows, Jr., Walpole, N.H.

===== ¶ [3d] MARRIED. =====

At Weymouth, Rev. Joshua Cushman, of Weymouth, to Miss Lucy Jones.

At Springfield, Mr. Hubbard Bliss, to Miss Emily Hitchcock.

At New York, Wm. Nelson, Esq. to Lady Catherine Duer, relict of the late Wm. Duer Esq. and daughter of the Earl of Sterling.

At Bernardston, Mr. James Couch to Miss Mehitable Alexander, whose ages together amount to one hundred and sixty-six years.

===== ¶ [3d] DIED. =====

At Worcester, Mr. William Parker, ae. 78. Miss Jerusha Stowell, ae. 65. At Boston, Miss Elizabeth Hall, ae. 78. At New-York, Mr. John Byrne. At Boston, Mrs. Catharine Smith, ae. 69. At Dover, Mr. Joshua Hartford. Mr. James Chase. Mrs. Kenney. At Somersworth, Mrs. Rollins. At Block-Island, Mr. Thomas Paine, ae. 24. At Chelsea, V. Mrs. Oaks, ae. 32. Benjamin Troop, Esq. ae. 27. Mr. Stephen Boardman, ae. 29. At Strafford, Mr. A[s?]pha Day, ae. 30. At Concord, Mr. Edward Abbot, ae. [71?]. At Alstead, very suddenly, Mrs. Eunice Williams. At Portsmouth, Mr. Richard Downe, ae. 64. At Leominster, Mrs. Mary Wilder, ae. 84.

Vol. IX (No. 444) Tuesday, 6 Oct. 1801.

† [2a] Detailed account of the trial of William Lathrop, for the rape of Anna Makens in April 1801, at Tioga Point. Lathrop hailed from Duchess County, N.Y.; the trial was held at Wilkes-Barre, Penn. ♦

† [2d-3a] Extensive article describing the murder-suicide of a family near Hurley, New York, in early Sept. 1801. The wife of Mr. Josiah Deo (formerly the wife of Zachariah Huffman) murdered two of her children by her first husband, and an infant daughter of the present marriage, then cut her own throat. ♦

† [3b] Rev. Mr. Smilie ordained at the Congregational Church, Springfield, Vt.

† [3d] List of letters in the Post Office, Walpole, N.H., 1 Oct. 1801, as compiled by Alex. Thomas, Postmaster:

Jarept Aldridge,	Westmoreland.	William Pierce,	Waltham, Vt.
William Cooledge,	Surry.	William Ramsey,	Walpole.
Edward Dame,	Goshen.	Samuel Rodes,	on the Turnpike, N.H.
Jonathan Fletcher,	Walpole.	Jabez Shapley,	Cornish.
Asahel Harvey,	Surry.	Dr. Samuel Skinner,	Packersfield.
Seth Hall,	Westmoreland.	Experience Storrs,	Westmoreland.
Thomas Jenison,	Walpole.	Joshua Stetson,	Walpole.
John Lovel,	"	Rev. Abraham Wood,	Chesterfield.
Sheffield Patridge,	Chesterfield.		
Capt. Enoch Page,	"Newport or elsewhere."		

† [3d] List of letters in the Post Office, Charlestown, N.H., 1 Oct. 1801, as compiled by S. Crosby, Postmaster:

Edward Cook,	Springfield, Vt.	Nathaniel Huntoon,	Charlestown.
Joseph Darruh,	Charlestown.	Joshua Knapp,	Springfield, Vt.
Capt. Hezekiah Emerson,	Goshen.	Ezra Kilburn,	Charlestown.
Simeon Hunt,	Newport, Vt.	Darius Whitman,	Springfield, Vt., three

† [3d] Augustus Mowry adv. for his coat, which was lost "between Bellows's falls and Col. Hunts' tavern in Charlestown"; dated at Putney, 28 Sept. 1801.
† [3d] Nathaniel Woods adv. for a pocket book, which was lost "between general Bellows's and Capt. James Bancroft's in Rockingham"; dated at Packersfield, 6 Oct. 1801.

===== ¶ [3c] MARRIED. =====

At Concord, Mr. Simeon G. Hall to Miss Sally Hardy.
At Boston, Mr. Charles Coffin to Mrs. Ann Waters, of Portsmouth.
At Easthampton, Mr. Amos Tinker to Miss Bathsheba Clap.
At Springfield, Mr. David Walker, to Miss Violet Morgan.

===== ¶ [3c] DIED. =====

At Philadelphia, Dr. David Jackson.—At Chelsea, V. Mrs. Oaks, ae. 52.—Benjamin Throop Esq. ae. 27.—Mr. Stephen Boardman, ae. 29.—At Newlondon, of a rapid decline, Charles Smith Esq. of Righgate, Great Britain, ae. 27.—At Brookfield, Joseph Reed Esq. ae. 70.—At South Hadley, Miss Sally Taylor.—At Springfield, Mr. David Bliss, ae. 16.

Vol. IX (No. 445) Tuesday, 13 Oct. 1801.

† [1c] Adv. by *D.&T. Carlisle*, for apprentices in the "Printing Business," dated at Walpole, 6 Oct. 1801.
† [3a] Comical article describing a runaway notice from a newpaper printed at Halifax, N.C., which notice was posted by Allese Simpson, of Bertie County. Mrs. Simpson offered a reward for the return of her husband, who ran away from her and married Charity O'Daniel, of Halifax County. ♦
† [3d] Thomas Nichols adv. for a steer found on his land; dated Walpole, 7 Oct. 1801.

===== ¶ [3d] MARRIED. =====

In Boston, Mr. John Goodwin, to Miss Mary Munroe; Mr. Geo. James, to Miss Susannah Mollett.—At Newburyport, Benjamin Moody Esq. to Miss Elizabeth Coffin.—At New Jersey, Mr. Nicholas Dubois to Miss Betsey Ryall.—At Suffield, Mr. Enoch Pease, to Miss Elizabeth Walker.

===== ¶ [3d] DIED. =====

At Hetzendorf, in Germany, Maximilian Francis Xavier.—Joseph, Elector of Cologne, ae. 45. His personal property, estimated at 18 millions, he has bequeathed to the Archduke Ferdinand.—In Ireland, Lord Rosimore.—At Philadelphia, Herman Stump, Esq.; Mr. John Harrison.—At New York, Mr. Ch. Watkins.—At Dedham, Mrs. Elizabeth Eaton, ae. 58.—At Charlestown, Miss Lydia Foster.—At Cohasset, (suicide) Capt. Amos Lincoln.—At Salem, Mr. Philips, ae. 35: and 5 Children.—At Watertown, Dea. Daniel Whitney.—At Boston, Mr. Samuel Townsend, ae. 57.; Mrs. Catharine Kendall, ae. 32.—At Hollis, N.H. Rev. Daniel Emerson, ae. 85.—At Barre, Rev. Josiah Dana.—At Stoughton, on Wednesday last, Dea. Daniel Marsh, ae. 90, formerly of Boston.—At Leicester, Mrs. Martha braige, [sic] ae. 74.; Suddenly, Mrs. Washburn.—At Worcester, Mr. William Parker, ae. 78.; and in a fortnight after his wife Elizabeth Parker, ae. 84.—At New York, Mrs. Helen Depeyster, ae. 28.—At Wethersfield, Mr. Joseph Adams, ae. 46.—At Wilkinsonville, after a short illness, Col. David Strong, of the 2d U.S. regiment.

Vol. IX (No. 446) Tuesday, 20 Oct. 1801.

¶ [2a] A person by the name of Wilson, who was driving a team of 5 horses, from Baltimore to Kentucky, was on Tuesday last struck with lightning, and himself and horses instantly killed.
¶ [3b-c] Keene, New Hampshire, Oct. 3. An unhappy incident occurred at Swanzey on Wednesday morning last. It being training day, several young soldiers assembled early to honour some new made under officers, when one of them, Mr. Levi Warren, a youth of about 20, was instantly killed by the bursting of his piece. His companions cautioned him against loading so deep, and when he fired, fearing some accident, stepped a few paces back—The deceased tho't not of danger, and probably felt

ambitious to make the loudest report. The numerous accidents which occur from the imprudent use of fire-arms, ought to deter others from such dangerous experiments.

† [3d] Adv. by William Pierce, who has recently opened a tavern in Walpole, "formerly occupied by Caleb Johnson, and known by the name of the Village Hotel." Dated at Walpole, 20 Sept. 1801.

† [3d] Ebenezer Goodhue offers a farm for sale at Westminster, Vt.; dated 20 Oct. 1801.

† [3d] Philip Sweetser, Clerk of the Board of Directors of the Third New Hampshire Turnpike Corp., adv. a business meeting to be held at Wells' Inn, Keene, N.H.

† [3d] John French offers one cent reward of Chester Reed, a runaway indented boy, aged 19 years, who absconded 16 Oct. 1801; dated the next day at Langdon, N.H.

† [3d] Josiah Hendee adv. a lost mare found on his land; dated Walpole 10 Oct. 1801.

===== ¶ [3d] MARRIED. =====

At Hopkinton, Capt. Stephen Herriman to Mrs. Sarah Silver. This captain it would seem, is determined to be *in cash*. At Halifax, Vt. Mr. Cyrus Newton to Miss Sabra Crane.—At Acworth, Mr. Elisha Parks to Miss Mindwell Grout, daughter of Daniel Grout, Esq.—At Springfield, Dr. Elihu Dwight of South Hadley, to Miss Lydia White.—In this town, Mr. Burt, to Miss Hannah Gage.

===== ¶ [3d] DIED. =====

At Loftus Heights, Capt. William P. Smith, of the 3d Regiment, United States Army.—At Spencer, Mr. Abijah Bisco, candidate for the Ministry, æ. 32.—At Worcester, Mrs. Olive Fiske, æ. 32.—Miss Betsey Tower, æ. 18.—At Concord, Mrs. Sarah Abbot, æ. 45.—At Northfield, Mrs. Eunice Lyman, consort of Capt. Seth Lyman, æ. 60.—At Leyden, widow Freedom Allen, æ. 69.—At Burlington, Vt. Mr. William Moore, æ. 64.—At Onondaga, Sheldon Logan, Esq.—At Wilbraham, Mr. Ezra Barker, æ. 79.—At Springfield, many children.—At Dummerston, Mrs. Stearns, wife of Dr. Samuel Stearns, L.L.D.—At Hollis, N.H. the Rev. Daniel Emerson, in the 85th year of his age, and 48th of his ministry.—At Kennebunk, Rev. Daniel Little, æ. 77.—At Boston, Mrs. Elizabeth Hinckley, æ. 28.

Vol. IX (No. 447) Tuesday, 27 Oct. 1801.

¶ [3c] Mr. Wheeler, of Dorset, Vermont, being on a visit to his daughter in Salem, Washington County, and partaking of some refreshment, which was prepared for him and of which he partook with his usual appetite, and apparently in perfect health, suddenly dropped from his chair and in less than four minutes breathing his last.

¶ [3c] A lad seven years old, son of Mr. Oliver Nelson, of Stockbridge, fell from off a bridge, and was drowned; six days after, the body had not been found.

¶ [3c] Mr. Theophilus Ingles, of Lynn, while on board brig Traveller, setting up the starboard foretopmast back shroud, fell to the deck and opened his scull [sic]; he survived the fall but three hours.

¶ [3c] The clothes of a child, daughter of Mr. John Housan, of Rome, New York, about three years old, accidentally took fire, and before any person could get to her assistance, burnt her in such a horrid manner that she expired in a few hours after. [. . .]

¶ [3c] Woodstock, Sept. 30. On Tuesday the 29th inst. Mr. Israel Williams, of this town, having with the assistance of another person, raised upon his shoulder a large stick of wood, about 12 feet in length, and then finding it too heavy to attempt removing it further, threw it down suddenly, when, to his great surprise, his little son, near seven years old, had unexpectedly proceeded behind him, within reach of the stick, which crushed him to the earth and put an end to his mortal existence in less than half an hour!

† [3d] List of letters remaining at the Post Office, Westminster, Vt., 1 Oct. 1801, as compiled by Eleazer May, Postmaster:

Ephraim Spencer, Jr.	Westminster.		Timothy Parker,	Grafton.
Widow Badger	"		Samuel Davis,	Windham.
Catherine Clark	"		Noah Jones,	Waltham.
David Gilbert,	"		John Willington,	Grafton.
Caleb Whitney,	"		Dr. Abraham Hedge,	Chester.
Benjamin Nichols,	"		Samuel Howard,	Londonderry.

¶ [3d] On the 5th of September, the house of Colonel Cooly at Pittsford, Vermont, was destroyed by fire, with most of the furniture; the fire was communicated by the heat of the oven to a beam or joist.
¶ [3d] The house of Marcus Quincy of Sharon was consumed, on the 7th instant, with all its contents.
† [3d] Levi Hayward adv. a lost horse; dated at Acworth, 14 Oct. 1801.
† [3d] Jaazaniah Barrett adv. a mare found; dated at Richmond "15, 10 Month, 1801."

===== ¶ [3d] MARRIED. =====

At Providence, Mr. Elisha Dyer, mer. to Miss Frances Jones.—At Gloucester, Mr. Benj. Kenthough, mer. to Mrs. Lucy Foster.—At boston, [sic] Mr. Jabez Perkins, to Miss Betsy Jarvis.

===== ¶ [3d] DIED. =====

In Germany, Field Marshal Lascy, the oldest of the Austrian Generals.—At Nottingham, (N.J.) Mr. Aaron Wright, a very respectable member of the Society of Friends.—At Newport, Mrs. Stiles, widow of the late President Stiles, of Yale College, æ. 87.—At Alstead, Mr. Joseph Yeomans, æ. 28.

Vol. IX (No. 448) Tuesday, 4 Nov. 1801.

† [2d] Account of two house fires at Portland, Maine (District of Massachusetts), the buildings being occupied by Mr. Samuel Mayo and Capt. Thomas Robinson. ♦
† [3b] A brief mention of the execution, at Three Rivers, Canada, of "Charles Prenouveau, otherwise Laurent Houle, aged 18 years, for the murder of Judith Houle." The article expands in detail upon the murderous assault of this woman, who died of her injuries 6 June 1801. Part of this article originated in the the *Quebec Gazette*.
¶ [3b] At Salem, a daughter of Mr. Yell, burnt to death—the mother left her in bed with another child, while she went to fetch milk; in her absence it quit the bed, went to the fire, which caught her linen and night gown, and was burnt to such a degree, that she expired in a few hours after.
¶ [3b] Drowned at Hog Island, James Barton, jun. Æt. 16, son of Captain James Barton. This accident was occasioned by four persons, who were on a party of pleasure in a sail boat, impruden by getting on board a float which the young man took off to them, to carry them on shore, which immediately upset.
¶ [3b] Mr. Benjamin Hollister, of Oblong, town of Amenia, Newyork, went from his house, with his waggon partly loaded with timber, and his horses taking a sudden start, threw him out of it, and broke his neck, and otherwise bruised him in a shocking manner. He was discovered in a few minutes, and taken up dead; he was 74 years of age.
¶ [3c] ORDAINED. At Waitsfield, (Ver.) Rev. William Salsbury.
† [3d] A notice by petitioners for a proposed turnpike road from Sugar River Bridge, in Claremont, to Keene; business meeting to be held at the house of Capt. John Willard, Charlestown, N.H. The petition was signed by Benjamin West, John Willard, and E. Burroughs; dated at Keene, 27 Oct. 1801.
† [3d] Adv. for a pair of stray steers found by Benj. Eddy; dated at Walpole 31 Oct.

===== ¶ [3c] MARRIED. =====

At Rochester, Mr. Jer. Berry, æ. 80, to Mrs. Dorothy Emerson, æ. 75.—At Croydon, Mr. Simeon Dwinel to Miss Sally Hayward.
At Westminster, Mr. Thomas Ranney, æ. 81. to Mrs. Desire Rowson, æ. 71.

===== ¶ [3c] DIED. =====

At Onondaga, Sheldon Logan, Esq. first Preceptor of Chesterfield Academy.—At Surry, Mrs. Munro, æ. 76—she left 11 children, 56 grand children, and 6 great grand children.—At Keene, after a long and painful illness, Mrs. Mary Cooke, consort of Noah Cooke, Esq.—At Demerara, Capt. Joseph Parker, of Blue Hill.
In this town, on Wednesday last, Deacon Benjamin Foster, æ. 94—for many years a pensioner on the bounty of Gen. Bellows, of this town.

Vol. IX (No. 449) Tuesday, 10 Nov. 1801.

† [3a] Brief article describing the jail-break, 26 Oct. 1801, at Northampton, Mass., of James Roberts and Jonathan Hasbrook, "otherwise called Cornelius Hasbrook," both serving time for counterfeiting, and of Stephen Rust, confined for horse stealing.

† [3b] Under the heading "Incidents at Home," a brief mention is made of the fire which destroyed the printing office of Messrs. Chipman & Fessenden, at Vergennes. ♦

† [3c] Legal notice regarding the estate of Benjamin King, late of Croydon, deceased. Levi Follet, William Williams, and A. Batchelle appointed Commissioners; business meetings to be conducted at the house of Benjamin Barton, Esq., Croydon. Notice dated at Croydon, 22 Oct. 1801.

† [3d] Samuel Burroughs adv. for his lost livestock; dated at Alstead, 9 Nov. 1801.

¶ [3c] Whereas Sarah my wife behaves herself in an unbecoming manner by not doing her duty as a wife, and squandering my property, I therefore forbid all persons trading with, trusting, or harbouring her on my account as I will pay no debt of her contracting after this date. I likewise forbid all persons from receiving or concealing any of my property that she may attempt to offer, as they would avoid the penalty of the law.

Abijah Beard.

Grafton, November 9, 1801.

===== ¶ [3c] MARRIED. =====

At Providence, Mr. Charles J. Air, of South Carolina, to Miss Rebecca Power; Mr. Stephen Hopkins, to Miss Nancy Brownell.—At Newburyport, Capt. Edmund Bartlett, to Miss Zilpha H. Gerrish.—At Salem, Capt. John Prince, to Miss Martha Derby, daughter of the late E. H. Derby, Esq.—At Beverly Dr. J. Jackson, of Boston, to Miss Elizabeth Cabot, of Beverly.—At Springfield, Rev. Andrew Lee, to Miss Abigail Smith.

===== ¶ [3c] DIED. =====

At Hartford, Mr. Timothy Shepherd, ae. 59.—At Taunton, Mr. Apollos B. Leonard, ae. 27.—At Worcester, Miss Catharine Keys, ae. 71.—At Norfolk, (Virginia,) Mr. Justinian Holden, mer. ae. 34, formerly of Boston.—At Dennis, Jonathan Howes, Esq. formerly a Member of the General Court.—At Lynn, Mrs. Lucy Collins, ae. 51, wife of Mr Zachariah Collins.—In Pennsylvania, Major Gen. Henry Taylor.—At Exeter, (N.H.) last Friday, Miss Abigail Odlin, ae. 18.—At Billerica, Mrs. Polly Parker, ae. 28.—At Salem, on Monday, Mr. Weld Gardner, mer. ae. 56, son of the late Samuel Gardner, Esq. deceased. By his death the following Legacies become due, given by Mr. Geo. Gardner, deceased, brother of Mr. W. Gardner, in 1773. The town of Salem, for the benefit of the poor, £ 400 (?)—Harvard College, for the education of poor scholars, £ 1333 —The Marine Society, to be improved by them according to their discretion for the benefit of superannuated seamen, £ 2000.—At Wilmington, (Middlesex County) Mrs. Abigail Butters, ae. 90—The longevity of the family to which that deceased belonged, is well worthy notice. She was the last of ten children, born of Abraham and Sarah Jaquith, of the said Wilmington; whose ages at their decease were as follow:—Abraham 88; John 77; Adford 80; Ebenezer 86; Benjamin 85; Sarah 84; Mary 86; Elizabeth 70; Abigail 90; and Hannah, 82; amounting to EIGHT HUNDRED AND TWENTY EIGHT YEARS !

Vol. IX (No. 450) Tuesday, 17 Nov. 1801.

† [2c-d] Account of the capture of the *Molly*, a U.S. ship, at Algeziras, Spain, by either a French or Spanish force; the captain was John Miller, and Mr. John Gibson was Supercargo. ♦ 53

¶ [3b] Boston, Massachusetts, November 11. At the Supreme Judicial Court held lately at Cambridge, one Jacob Azott Lewis, an East-Indian, was convicted of a rape on Lydia Heald, an infant of ten years, daughter of Capt. John Heald, of Carlisle. The fellow was a servant of Mr. Lewis, of Dorchester; about eighteen years of age. At the same court several foreigners were convicted of various larcenies.

† [3d] Legal notice regarding a petition of divorce by Mary Nichols, of Swanzey, N.H., from her husband Nathaniel Nichols, to whom she was married 14 March 1777. Mrs. Nichols claims that her husband "left her with six children; and for more than six years last past, has totally neglected to contribute in any degree, towards the support of his

said wife or children; although it hath been and now is in his power to do so."

† [3d] John Temple of Claremont adv. for a lost pocket book, containing several notes signed by Ambrose Redfield, Eleazer Baldwin, Peter Martin, Peter Fletcher, Timothy Fisher, Timothy Greenleaf, Benjamin Alder, John Chaffin, and Seth Putnam, and a note endorsed by Samuel Stone. Adv. dated at Claremont 25 Oct. 1801.

† [3d] Asael Goodridge adv. a lost heifer; dated at Walpole 13 Nov. 1801

† [3d] John Bellows adv. a lost steer found on his land; dated at Walpole 14 Nov. 1801.

Vol. IX (No. 451) Tuesday, 24 Nov. 1801.

¶ [3b] New York, New York, Nov. 7. Timothy Parks, who was imprisoned at Albany, upon suspicion of being the murderer of Lyman Parker, who was shot in that city on the night of the 21st September, was convicted last week in the Supreme Court, and sentenced to be executed on the 11th Dec. next.

George Morrison, alias George Fleming, and Benjamin Nicholson, who had been convicted of Grand Larceny, in Albany, were sentenced to the State-Prison; the former for four, and the latter for five years.

On Wednesday last, as the sloop Washington was coming from Newburgh to this city, a man by the name of Brandel was knocked overboard by the jibing of the boom, and before any assistance could be given, he went down. It is said he lived in Schenectady, and has left a wife and four children. He was on his way to this city, with a considerable sum of money by him, to pay for some land which he had purchased. He was a native of Ireland.

† [3d] Royal Shaw adv. for a lost steer which he found; dated Claremont 16 Nov. 1801.

===== ¶ [3d] MARRIED. =====

At Newport, Major William M'Rea, of the second United States regiment, to Miss Mary Champlin.—Captain Elihu Smith, of New Bedford, to Miss Mary Slocum.—At Salem, Mr. John Eveleth, to Mrs. Elizabeth Burill.—At Boston, Mr. William Wilson, of Portland, to Miss Rebecca Goddard.

===== ¶ [3d] DIED. =====

In England, Mr. Gilbert Wakefield, a celebrated writer and critic.—At Roxbury, Miss Arabella Pomroy.—At Boston, Mr. Nathaniel Patch, an eminent broker; Mr. Henry Coats, a native of England; Mr. Stephen Emery, ae. 53.

Vol. IX (No. 452) Tuesday, 1 Dec. 1801.

¶ [3b] Windsor, Vermont Nov. 24. Drowned, in a mill-pond, in this town on Saturday last, Mr. Abel Blood. He has left a widow and family to lament the irreparable loss.

On the evening of the 30th Oct. the house of Mr. Rebis, of Dearing, (N.H.) took fire, and was soon reduced to ashes, with a child 9 years old. The fire was supposed to have been communicated from an oven.

† [3d] Legal notice stating that Simeon Brooks, Jr. and Patience Marvin were appointed Executors of the last will and testament of Giles Marvin, late of Alstead, N.H.

===== ¶ [3c] MARRIED. =====

At Watertown, Mr. Daniel Scudder, merchant of Boston, to Miss Sally Weld, of the former place.—At Beverly, Mr. Barnabas Dodge, jun. of Hamilton, to Miss Peggy Dodge.—At Salem, Capt. George Nichols, to Mrs. Sally Peirce.—At Woodstock, Mr. Josiah Jaquith, to Miss Anna Holt.—At Windsor, Mr. Ebenezer Shead, to Miss Fanny Bannister.—Mr. Phineas Farrand, of Enfield, (N.H.) to Miss Polly Spencer.

Singular marriages.—Yesterday, se'nnight was married at Filey, R. Shepherd, Esq. of Lebderston Hall, near Scarboro' aged 81, to Mrs. Ann Watson, aged 24. By this union the bridegroom becomes brother to his son, and uncle to his grandson; the father and son having married two sisters.—Some days since was married at Frome, Mr. John Cooke, aged 71, to Mrs. Pope, who, on the morning of the tender sacrifice to Love and Hymen, attained her eighteenth year.—Lately, at Blackness Castle, P. Potter, aged eighty-seven, to Mrs. Rebecca Halwell, aged eighty-eight; the bridegroom about a fortnight before, had the misfortune to lose his third wife.—At Wentor, Salop, Richard Finch, aged seventeen, to Mrs. Ann Wicley, aged eighty-nine.

[London Pap.

¶ [3c-d] DIED.

At Portsmouth, Miss Hannah Huse, ae. 90.—At Charleston, (S.C.) after a short illness, the Right Rev. Robert Smith, Bishop of S. Carolina, ae. 73; of which 47 years were devoted to the duties of minister of St. Philips Church.—At Palmea, Mrs. Rebecca M'Lanathan, wife of Mr. John M'Lanathan, and daughter of the Rev. Moses Baldwin.—At Leominster, Mrs. Deborah Legate, ae. 57, of deserved memory, late consort of Thomas Legate, Esq.—At Oakham, Dr. Spencer Field, ae. 47.—At Portland, Mrs. Mary Gardner, of Freeport, ae. 86.—At Hanover, the 19th inst. Deacon Samuel Barstow, ae. 92 years and nine months.

Vol. IX (No. 453) Tuesday, 8 Dec. 1801.

¶ [3c] On Wednesday last, was drowned in Half Moon pond, in the town of Washington, Mr. Benjamin Wheeler, aged 23 years. He was skating with another person and fell in. Assistance was given immediately to get out the body but not timely enough to save his life.

† [3d] Account of a duel fought at New York, between Capt. George I. Eacker, and Mr. P. Hamilton, aged 20, eldest son of General Hamilton. Hamilton later died of his wounds. ♦

† [3d] Legal notice from Windsor County (Vt.) Court, regarding Alpheus Cheney, late of Hartford, Vt., "an absconding or concealed Debtor." Thomas W. Pitkin, a Trustee of Cheney's, was summoned to answer unto William Burtch of Hartford, concerning financial obligations. ♦

Vol. IX (No. 454) Tuesday, 15 Dec. 1801.

¶ [3c] We hear from Peru, State of Newyork, a lad about seventeen, son of Mr. James Hall, formerly of this town; accidently [sic] slid from the top of a rock; descended 127 feet, the whole not more than ten feet slopewise, fell on a rock, then arose on his feet, took up his hat, walked 100 rods before he knew he was hurt; he is now well. We had this intelligence in a letter from the parents of the fortunate lad.   Croydon, Nov. 18.

† [3c] A news item regarding the use of "Kine-Pox" for the innoculation against Small Pox; Dr. Jonathan Moor's new treatment was given to four patients, viz. Dr. Joseph Goodhue, Mr. E. Burr, Mr. E. Parker and Mrs. Rice; art. originated at Putney, Vt. ♦

† [3d] Reward offered by Oliver Taylor for return of his stolen mare; dated Goshen, Mass., 2 Nov. 1801.

† [3d] Adv. by John C. Farrell, who claims to have a cure for cancer and rheumatism; he has taken up residence at the house of Mr. Ithamer Allen, Wardsboro, Vt.

† [3d] A notice from Edmund Brewster, Librarian, regarding the Walpole Library.

¶ [3d] *John Casper Wersing,* DISTILLER.

If John C. Wersing, who formerly lived at Hooks Town, near Baltimore, be living, he is hereby informed, that his Sister from Germany, has arrived in this country, and is now residing at Trenton, New-Jersey. Any person who can give information of said Wersing, will oblige a distressed Family.   John A. Werner.

¶ [3d] MARRIED.

At New-Gloucester, Mr. Eleazer A. Jenks, editor of the *Portland Gazette,* to Miss Clarina P. Greenleaf.—At Newport, (N.H.) Mr. Hubbard Newton, to Miss Abigail Lyon.—At Lemster, Capt. Erastus Newton of Newport, to Miss Betsey Beckwith.—At Enfield, (C.) the Rev. John Willard, to Mrs. Hannah Fisk.

Mr. Joseph Demond of Rutland, V. to Miss Sally Gage, of this place.

¶ [3d] DIED.

At Windham, Mrs. Hannah Sawyer, ae. 85. Her descendants, from 34 marriages, have been 57 grand-children—and 81 great-grand-children.—At Cumberland island, Oct. 25, Charles Jackson, Esq. formerly of Massachusetts.

In the West-Indies, Capt. George Taber, of New-Bedford.—At Boston, Mr. Alexander Mackay, mer. ae. 54.—At Nassau, Mr. John Owen, assistant editor of the Bahama Gazette.—At Schenectady, Mr. John Taylor, Professor of Learned Languages in Columbia College.

Vol. IX (No. 455) Tuesday, 22 Dec. 1801.

† [3d] Joseph Nutt adv. for a lost colt; dated at Newport, 11 Dec. 1801.
† [3d] E. Minor adv. for lost heifers; dated at Rockingham, 15 Dec. 1801.

Vol. IX (No. 456) Tuesday, 29 Dec. 1801.

† [3c] Deacon Nathaniel Brown's barn burned at Alstead, 16 Nov. 1801. ♦
† [3d] Mr. Washburn's house burned at Westminster, 25 Dec. 1801. ♦
† [3d] List of nonresident owners of land in Springfield, N.H. who have not paid their highway and county taxes for the year 1801, as compiled by Osgood Taylor, Collector. Property still in delinquency 1 March 1802 to be auctioned off at the "house of Lieut. Daniel Noyses in Springfield." The list includes the name of the owner, lot number, number of acres, and the highway and county amount due; the owner's names are given as follows, viz. Ann Ordway, Lt. John Sweet, James M'Gregore Esq., James Brown, and Joshua Clement.
† [3d] A notice from Asa Wheler, *Clerk*, and Salmon Dutton, *Treasurer*, regarding the annual meeting of the Green Mountain Turnpike Company to be held at the house of Joseph Green in Mountholly; dated at Cavendish 19 Dec. 1801.

===== ¶ [3d] MARRIED. =====

At Suffield, Mr. Timothy Ashley to Miss Polly Wyman.—At Westfield, Mr. Aaron Broad jun. to Miss Sabra Sanderson.—At Keene, Mr. John W. Stiles, of Templeton, Mass. to Miss Mary Maccarty, only daughter of Dr. Thaddeus Maccarty, of the former place.

===== ¶ [3d] DIED. =====

In England, O'Brien, the Irish giant; he was 8 feet 6 inches in height.—In Germany, a Woman, aged 102, who had 19 husbands and who bred up 27 children.—In Worcester, Mr. Ebenezer Willington, æ. 85; Mrs. Sarah Gay, wife of Mr. John Gay, æ. 68. —In Springfield, Mrs. Anna Munn, æ. 28.—In Amherst, N.H. John Shepard, Esq. æ. 72; Mrs. Elizabeth Watson, æ. 35, consort of Mr. John Watson; Captain Thomas Whiting, æ. 27.—In Boston, Mrs. Fanny Boardman; Mrs. Eunice Purkitt, æ. 44.—At Surry, of the Small Pox, Mr. Thomas Smith, æ. 63.—At Winchester, Mrs. Sarah Conant, æ. 35.

Vol. IX (No. 457) Tuesday, 5 Jan. 1802.

† [1c] John West adv. books for sale at his bookstore in Boston, Mass.
† [3b] Fire destroys the Druggist and Dry Good Store of Dr. Samuel Willard, at Strafford, Conn., 23 Dec. 1801; item contained under news dated at Springfield, Mass.
† [3b-c] Article describing a fire at a coalpit, in Leominster, Mass., at which Ebenezer and Silas Stewart were tending. One of these brothers, aged 17, was killed by the fire, the other badly burned. ◆
† [3c] Two cases of multiple births mentioned in an article relating to that subject: 1) The wife of Mr. Joel Baker, of New Paltz, Ulster County, gave birth to two sons and a daughter, "on the evening of the 8th instant." 2) The wife of Aaron Bower, "of New-York" was delivered of two sons and a daughter, on the "26th ult."
† [3c] News item describing the ordination of Rev. Andrew Yates "as colleague pastor with the Rev. Eliphalet Williams, D.D., of East Hartford." ◆
† [3d] Legal notice regarding the insolvent estate of Samuel Willard, late of Charlestown, N.H., deceased. Samuel Crosby, Rowell Hunt, and Jesse Healy appointed Commissioners over said estate; notice dated at Charlestown, 28 Dec. 1801.
† [3d] A. Bullard adv. a pair of saddle bags "left in the house of the subscriber," which included "one handerchief marked Joseph Tobey." Dated at Walpole, 4 Jan. 1802.
† [3d] List of letters remaining at the Post Office, Walpole, N.H., 31 Dec. 1801, as compiled by Alex. Thomas:

Joseph Aldridge,	Westmoreland	Ruel Mack,	Surry.
Hannah Atherton,	Chesterfield	Ichabod Onion,	Rockingham.
William Cooledge,	Surry.	William Pierce,	Waltham.
Abiather Dean,	Westmoreland.	Sheffield Partridge,	Chesterfield.
Polly Dean,	"	William Ramsey,	Walpole.
Roger Farnam,	Walpole.	Joel Ranna,	Westminster.
Lemuel Holmes, Esq.	Surry.	Asahel Shirtleff,	Chesterfield.
Calvin Holmes,	Hinsdale mills.	Samuel Skinner,	Packersfield.
Ephraim Lane,	Walpole.	Samuel Whiting,	Langdon.
Dr. Isaac Monro,	Surry.		

===== ¶ [3d] MARRIED. =====

At Princeton, Doctor Martin Howe, of Barre, to Mrs. Eunice Russell, of Princeton.—At Newport, Captain Wm. Ryon, to Mrs. Ann Davis; Mr. Isaac Fish, to Miss Sally Barker; Mr. John Hull, to Miss Lydia Codding—At Boston, Mr. Wm. Ritchie, mer. to Miss Jane Leach.—Mr. Joseph Leach, of Lancaster, to Miss Rebecca Flagg.

===== ¶ [3d] DIED. =====

At Kingston, Massachusetts, Dec. 8th, Mr. Ebenezer Cobb, aged 107 years, 8 months, and 6 days; having lived in three Centuries. He was born in Plymouth, on the 22d of March, 1694. He was ten years cotemporary with Peregrine White, of Marshfield, the first son of New-England, who was born aboard the May-flower, in Cape-Cod harbour, Nov. 1620, and who died July 22, 1704. His occupation in life, was among "the chosen people of God," in cultivating the earth. His mode of living was plain and simple, never varying from that substantial frugality which characterized the husbandman at the beginning of the last Century. Only twice in his life, and then it was to gratify his brethreen on a Jury, did he substitute an enervating cup of tea, in place of the invigorating bowl of broth, or the nutritive porringer of milk—He was of a moderate stature, expanded in chest, stooping in attitude, of a fair and floried countenance. He never used glasses, but for several years could not see to read; and the latter part of the time could descern objects but very imperfectly. The loss of his sight took him off from his labour, which his other faculties would have permitted him to pursue. He enjoyed life in his old age, and the last year of it, declared his attachment to it to be the same as at any former period. The powers of his mind remained unbroken, as was evident, not only from his remembrance of the events of the last Century, but from his quick recollection of the transactions of the last year, month or day. He entered into the spirit of passing events, and in addition to pertinent remarks would often display fallies [sic] of wit and humour. To the writer of this article, lately remarking to him upon his expected dissolution, he shrewdly replied, "*it is very rare that persons of my age die."* As a professing Christian he did not display his piety in affecting to despise the world; or in bestowing hard names upon its objects or rational pleasures; but enjoyed his daily bread with a cheerful and grateful heart, and seemed to derive pleasure even from that comparative importance which arose from the multitude of his years. Industrious in his occupation, honest and upright as a citizen, and hoping in the promise of the gospel, he was neither transported with joy, nor depressed with fear at the approach of Death.—His posterity were not very numerous being 185, of which five were great great grand children.

At New London, Mr. James Harris, ae. 81.—At Concord, Mrs. Mary Minot, wife of Dr. Timothy Minot, ae. 70.—At Burlington, (V.) Mr. Levi Allen, ae. 58.—At Washington, Miss Jane Gardner.—At Petersham, Mrs. Sarah Clark, ae. 61.

Vol. IX (No. 458) Tuesday, 12 Jan. 1802.

† [3d] James Bayley, Postrider, informs his customers that he will no longer deliver the *Farmer's Museum* due to ill health; dated at Athens, 11 Jan. 1802.
† [3d] Bankruptcy notice pertaining to William Todd, of Boston, Mass., Trader.
† [3d] List of letters remaining at the Post Office in Westminster, Vt., 1 Jan. 1802, as compiled by Eleazer May, Postmaster:

Joseph Hamblen,	Westminster	Peter Perfett,	Westminster.
John Holten,	"	Amos Hail,	Waltham.
Richardson Crook,	"	Ephraim Smith,	Grafton.
Urial C. Hatch,	"	Peter Pettengill,	"

† [3c-d] Extensive obituary of George Richards Minot, Judge of Probate for Suffolk County, Mass.; born in Boston, Dec. 1758; died "the 2d instant."

===== ¶ [3c] MARRIED. =====

At Brookfield, Mr. Calvin Gilbert, aged 17 to Miss Theodosia Barret, aged 15.—At Endfield, [sic] Mr. Elisha Kibbe, aged 70, to Miss Polly Ayres, aged 20.

===== ¶ [3d] DIED. =====

In South-Carolina, Hon. Ephraim Ramsay, one of the Associate Judges of South-Carolina, ae. 35.—At Portsmouth, Hon. Geo. Jaffrey, ae. 84.—In Boston, John Sweetser Esq. ae. 75.—At Northampton, Mrs. Phebe Strong, ae. 84.—At Providence, Mrs. Elizabeth Sterry, ae. 94.—At Granby, Mr. Samuel Hays, ae. 72.—At Boylston, Rev. Ebenezer Morse.—At Cambridge, Mrs. Ann Mason, ae. 71.—In Boston, Miss Joanna Buckley, ae. 64.—Mrs. Elizabeth Taylor, ae. 92; Miss Eliza Brooks, ae. 19.

On Sunday evening at Westminster, Mrs. Bradley, consort of Gen. S. R. Bradley.

Vol. IX (No. 459) Tuesday, 19 Jan. 1802.

† [3b] Fire destroys the store "owned by Major John Page, and occupied by Mr. Jacob abbot [sic], of Hallowell."
¶ [3b] Geoege [sic] Robinson, son of James Robinson of Barre, Massachusetts accidentally overset a kettle of boiling water on him, which scalded him to such a shocking degree that he expired in a few hours.—It is supposed that the father of the child is at, or near the city of Washington.
¶ [3b] Mr. John Gray, of Peterborough who was employed in shingling a house accidentally fell from the staging, and striking the frozen ground with the back of his head, expired instantly—he was about 50 years of age.

===== ¶ [3d] MARRIED. =====

In Boston, Mr. Caleb D. Champney, to Miss Hannah Lombard; Mr. Ezra Dyer, to Miss Nancy Jennings.

===== ¶ [3d] DIED. =====

At Salem, Widow Mary Ann Richardson, from Boston.—At Albany, Lucas Van Veckten, Esq. ae. 78, of [Watervliet?].—At Newton, Mr. Joshua Flagg, ae. 81.—In Prince George's county, Maryland, a man by the name of Riddle, at the age of 105 years, having been for many years totally blind and deaf.—In Caroline county, Maryland, Mrs. Mary Beachamp, at the advanced age of 119 years; she possessed to the last an unusual retention of all her faculties.—At Guadaloupe, Mr. Henry Wilder, of Concord, (Mass.) ae. 20.—At Boxford, Mrs. Abigail Foster, ae. 70.—In Martinique, Mr. Alexander Shapleigh, of Portsmouth, by the bite of a shark, his head being completely separated from the body.

† [3d] List of letters remaining at the Post Office in Charlestown, N.H., 11 Jan. 1802, as compiled by Sam. Crosby, Postmaster:

Miss Abigail Bedel,	Charlestown.	George Nye,	Springfield, Vt.
Joshua B. Elderkin, 2.	"	William Neal,	Unity.
Thomas Cook,	Springfield, Vt.	Elder Stephen Place,	Springfield, Vt.
James Converse,	Weathersfield, Vt.	Lieut. Nathan Parks,	
Dean Carlton,	Acworth.	2d Regiment of Artil-	
Major John Gill,		lerists and Engineers,	Charlestown.
Lieut. Asahel Powers or Samuel Hoar,	} Springfield, Vt.	William Rhodes,	Charlestown.
		Major Josiah Stevens,	Newport.
Jacob Glidden,	Unity.	Joseph Wilson,	Charlestown.
Dr. Oliver Hastings,	Charlestown.	Josiah Wetmore,	"
Joseph Lorkwood, 54	Springfield, Vt.		
Lieut. Jesse Lull,	Charlestown.		
Alexander M'Kenzie, Esq. of London, to the care of James Lee, Esq. at Charlestown, N.H.			

Vol. IX (No. 460) Tuesday, 26 Jan. 1802.

† [3c] Brief account of the ordination, at Gray, Maine, of Mr. Thomas Barnes, over the Universal United Churches and Societies of Falmouth, New Gloucester and Norway. ♦
† [3c] List of letters remaining at the Post Office in Bellows's Falls, Vermont, 1 Jan. 1802, as compiled by William Page, Postmaster:

> Frederick Hall, Grafton.
> Abner Stow, Rockingham.
> Hannah White, Rockingham.

¶ [3d] Runaway from the subscriber, on the night of the seventh instant, an indented boy, by the name of Joseph Lee; said Boy was about nineteen years of age. All persons are hereby forbid trusting or harbouring said Boy on my account; whoever will take up and return said Boy, shall have one dollar reward, no charges paid.

STEPHEN HURD.
Newport, Jan. 7th, 1802.

===== ¶ [3d] DIED. =====

At Brookfield, Mr. Wheat Gilbert, merchant.—In Haverhill, Mrs. C. Emerson, ae. 100.—In Boston, Miss Sarah Thacher, eldest daughter of the Rev. Dr. Thacher, ae. 20.—At Chester, Vt. Mrs. Abigail Sargeant, ae. 84.—At Swanzey, Mrs. Rachael Thompson, ae. 54.—At Packersfield, Miss Lucy Hale, daughter of Mr. Ambrose Hale, of Stoddard, ae. 19.—At Lemster, (N.H.) Jan. 2, 1802, Capt. John Way, ae. 69.—At Northampton, Mr. Ithamar Clark, ae. 86.—At Wakefield, Mrs. Piper, consort of the Rev. Asa Piper.—At Londonderry, Mrs. Lucy Danforth, ae. 41.

Vol. IX (No. 461) Tuesday, 2 Feb. 1802.

† [3b] Remarkable account of a Mr. Moore, who was buried in a collapsed well at Brooklyn, N.Y., but survived. ♦
† [3b] Obediah Houghton, aged 13 years, drowned in a pond at Leominster, Mass. ♦
† [3c] Accounts of several fires set by an arsonist in Boston, one of which claimed the life of a four year-old child of Mr. S. Goff, 17 Jan. 1802.
† [3d] Peter Lukin offers large tracts of land for sale in Canada; dated at Montreal, 23 Dec. 1801. John Hubbard of Walpole, N.H. named as a point-of-contact.
† [3d] John Jeffries and Jeremiah Libbey appointed Executors of the last Will of Hon. George Jeffrey. This legal notice was dated at Portsmouth, N.H., 4 Jan. 1802.
† [3d] David Robbins, who "wishes to quit farming," offers his farm for sale at Montpelier, Vt.; dated there 18 Jan. 1802.

† [3d] "Abrm. Holland" intends "to dispose of a large portion of his notes and book-accounts," and requests all outstanding debts to be settled; dated Walpole 26 Jan.
† [3d] *Burroughs & Griswold* post an advertisement regarding a road "from Mr. Redington's Tavern to Surry, N.H., and also mentioning that the Small Pox has been "intirely [sic] removed from the public road through Surry." Dated at Walpole, 26 Jan.

===== ¶ [3d] MARRIED. =====

At Providence, Capt. Moses Adams, to Miss Susannah Pope, daughter of the late Dr. John Pope, of Boston.—At Hardwick, Mr. Stephen Nye, to Miss Lois Marrick.—At Westborough, Mr. Jonathan Forbes, Jun. to Miss Esther Chamberlain.

===== ¶ [3d] DIED. =====

In [P]rovidence, at an advanced age, William Wheaton, Esq. formerly Sheriff of the county of [P]rovidence.—At Haverhill, Mrs. C. Emmerson, ae. 100.—At West Hampton, Miss Lydia Chapman, daughter of Mr. David Chapman, ae. 45. Her clothes accidentally took fire, which was the cause of her death.—At Yarmouth, Dea. Josiah Thacher, ae. 69.

At Hanover, (Mass.) after a short illness, Mrs. Rebecca Mellen, wife of the Rev. John Mellen, ae. 75.

Vol. IX (No. 462) Tuesday, 9 Feb. 1802.

† [3d] Joel Smith adv. goods for sale or barter; dated at Langdon, 8 Feb. 1802.
† [3d] **Take Notice.** The subscriber being about to leave this state soon, calls on all indebted to him to make immediate settlement, or, they must settle with his Attorney.

John Hubbard.
Walpole, Feb. 8, 1802.

===== ¶ [3d] MARRIED. =====

In Boston, Mr. Daniel Taylor Lewis, to Miss Elizabeth V. Greenwood, daughter of Mr. Nathaniel Greenwood.

At Charlestown, Mass. Mr. Ebenezer Larkin, to Miss Mary Howe.

At West-Springfield, Mr. Benjamin Ashley, Jr. to Miss Sally White.

===== ¶ [3d] DIED. =====

In Boston, Miss Nancy Emerson, ae. 20, late of Royalston; Mr. Joseph Howe, Jun. ae. 23; Mr. John G. Fudger, mer. of Gloucester, (Cape-Ann.)

At Paris, Madam Choiseul, widow of the celebrated Minister of that name, and mother of the Duke.

In Ireland, Sir John Parnell, late Chancellor of the Irish Exchequer, and grandson of the poet Parnell.

At Westfield, Rev. Noah Atwater, ae. 50.—At East-Windsor, Mr. Josiah Wolcott, ae. 84.—At East-Hartford, Miss Margaret Pratt, ae. 73.—At Brattleboro' Widow Dameris Briggs, ae. 77.—At Rutland, V. Miss.55 Lydia Chipman, ae. [37?].—Of the Small-pox at Surry, on Friday evening last, Mr. David Lewis.

Suicide, At Turner, Maine, Mr. Caleb Blake, worth 5000 dollars, he is said to have hung himself lest he should some time or other come to want.

Vol. IX (No. 463) Tuesday, 15 Feb. 1802.

¶ [3a-b] DEDHAM COURT. Messrs. D. Sisk, L. Whiting, R. Farrington, E. Fairbanks, jun. N. Davis and S. Gay were indicted for the rescue of Jason Fairbanks, and tried the last week at Dedham. Messrs. Farrington and Whiting were acquitted. Sisk, Fairbanks and Davis were convicted. The two former were sentenced to four months imprisonment, the latter two. Gay is absent. Stephen Fairbanks was indicted but discharged on account of his youth. A bill was also found against the two negroes (Cotton and Hampson,) but they were admitted as evidence. Dukeham was admitted as an evidence and afterwards discharged. A bill was found against the Deputy Jailer; and a bill against Dr. Kittridge for perjury. Trial postponed.

† [3d] Legal notice regarding the insolvent estate of Willard Moore, late of Putney, Vt., deceased. James Fitch and David Leavitt appointed Commissioners over said estate;

business meetings to be conducted at the house of John Campbell, Esq., of Putney. Notice dated at Putney 11 Jan. 1802.

¶ [3d] MARRIED.

At Middlebury, V. Mr. Jacob Sherill to Miss Jerusha Huntington.
At Ipswich, Mr. Joseph Hale, to Miss Hannah Swazey.

¶ [3d] DIED.

At Hartford, Widow Dorcas Brown, ae. 95, formerly of Boston.—In Boston, Mr. John Blanchard, merchant, ae. 32; .Mrs. Ann James, ae. 47; Mrs. Huldah Adams; Mr. Stephen Oliver, ae. 50.—At Philadelphia, Mr. John Henry Tudor, ae. 20, second son of the Hon. William Tudor, Esq.
At Canterbury, Elisha Payne, Esq. ae. 44.—At Hanover, N.H. Dr. Ephraim Woolson, ae. 61.—At Holderness, N.H. the 2d inst. Madam Jane Livermore, wife of the Hon. Samuel Livermore, lately a Senator of the United States.
At Keene, of the small pox, Mrs. Mary Hobart.—At Andover, Mass. the Hon. Samuel Phillips, Esq. lieutenant Governor of that Commonwealth.
Mr. Constantine Gilman, late of this town.

Vol. IX (No. 464) Tuesday, 23 Feb. 1802.

† [3c] Account of the fire which destroyed the house of Mr. Samuel Cleaveland, at Hanover, N.H. The five children, home alone, and ranging from 18 months to 9 years of age, all survived. ♦
† [3d] Thomas & Isaac Redington post a notice requesting settlement of debts; dated at Walpole, 20 Feb. 1802.

¶ [3d] MARRIED.

The Rev. Jacob Abbot, of Hampton Falls, N.H. to Miss Catharine Thayer.
At Boston, Mr. Benjamin Lindsey, printer, to Miss Elizabeth Woods; Mr. Henry Jones, to Miss Sally Eyars.

¶ [3d] DIED.

At Baltimore, Mr. Benj. Levy, ae. 76.—At New York, widow Hopkins, ae. 93.—At New-Haven, Mr. Eben [Humpherwille?], ae. 77; Mr. Eben. Parmelee, ae. 64; Mr. Saml. Hall, bookbinder, ae. 41; Mrs. Lyd. Trowbridge, ae. 73.—At Lunenburg, Mrs. Abiah Woods, ae. 78, formerly of Boston.—At Taunton, 8th inst. in consequence of a fall from his horse, Capt. Jonathan Ingoll, ae. 8[1?].—At Darby, in Connecticut, in Sept. last, Mrs. Hannah Clark, ae. 91. The lineal descendants of this lady, were 333, viz. ten children, sixty two grand children, two hundred and forty two great grand children, and nineteen great great grand children !
At Lempster Capt. Samuel Nichols ae. 58.

Vol. IX (No. 465) Tuesday, 2 March 1802.

† [3c] Amos Shepard announces that he is now in copartnership with Samuel Hutchinson, and adv. a list of goods offered for sale by *Shepard & Hutchinson.* 55A
† [3c] James Knapp posts an adv. for an apprentice carpenter and house joiner; dated at Walpole, 1 Mar. 1802.
† [3d] Davis Carpenter found a lost pocket book; dated at Walpole, 18 Feb. 1802.

¶ [3c] MARRIED.

At Alstead, a few days since, Captain Daniel Williams, to Miss Cynthia Delano.
At Lenox, (Mass.) Rev. Jeremiah Atwater, President of the College in Middlebury, to Miss Clarissa Storrs.

¶ [3c] DIED.

At Gloucester, R.I. Mr. Benedict Arnold, ae. 51; a worthy member of the Society of Friends.—At Nantucket, Abner Coffin, Esq. ae. 49, Register of Probate and Notary Public for the County of Nantucket.—
In this town, on Wednesday the 24th inst. Col. Christopher Webber.

Vol. IX (No. 466) Tuesday, 9 March 1802.

† [3d] Legal notice regarding a petition by Orpah Coombs of Charlestown, N.H., who requests a divorce from Oliver Coombs, to whom she was married 7 July 1788. Mrs. Coombs claims her husband abandoned her in Feb. 1797, leaving her with three children. Notice dated at Charlestown, 17 Oct. 1801.

† [3d] Solomon Godfrey and Levi Childs announce that their copartnership is dissolved; dated at Walpole, 5 March 1802.

===== ¶ [3d] MARRIED. =====

At Jaffrey, Mr. Joel Kingsbury of Keene, to Miss Olive Adams, of the former place.

In Keene, Mr. Comfort Hamilton, of Brookfield, to Miss Charity Carpenter—"*Charity begins at home;*" Mr. Silas Nourse, to Miss Rebecca Carpenter.—At Littleton, Mr. Amos Towne, to Miss Betsy Wright, daughter of Lt. James Wright.

At Temple, Newhampshire, by the Rev. Noah Miles, Major Amos Heald of Chester, Vermont, to the amiable Miss Lydia Edwards of that town.

===== ¶ [3d] DIED. =====

At Baltimore, Mrs. Ann Eleanor Williamer, aged *one hundred and three years, 3 months, and fourteen days* !—At Charlestown, Mrs. Joanna Hurd, ae. 65.—At Boston, in the 74th year of his age, Mr. Thomas Bulfinch, M.D.—

At Marlow, on the 1st inst. Mrs. Elizabeth Gale, in the 78th year of her age.

At Georgetown, Mrs. Rebecca Stoddert, the wife of the late Secretary of the Navy.— At East Haddam, Mr. Zephaniah Andr[u?]s, ae. 71.—At Worcester, Mr. Daniel Johnson, ae. 74.—At Lunenburg, Mrs. Abiah Wood, ae. 78, formerly of Boston.—At Milton, Mr. Ebenezer Tucker, ae. 72.—At Dorchester, Miss Rebecca Blackman, ae. 77.—At Charlestown, Mrs. Sarah Bradstreet, ae. 84.—

Vol. IX (No. 467) Tuesday, 16 March 1802.

† [2d] Tragic account of the death of the wife of Rufus Herick, of Norwich, Chenango County, N.Y., who died in early Oct. 1801 from wounds received from being gored by a cow. On the 12th of Dec. following, three children of Rufus Herick where killed in a fire which destroyed their house. (News under the dateline of Whitestown, N.Y.) ♦

† [3a] Brief account of a fire which destroyed the new house, furniture, and tools belonging to Mr. Joseph Tucker, Carpenter, "in Lynn-street," [Boston, Mass.—Ed.]

† [3a] Account of several shipwrecks, including one which claimed the schooner *John*, Capt. Harrison, from New York for New Orleans, "wrecked on Shoal-Harbor, near Middletown" in the storm of 22 February. Capt. Harrison and David Morris, (pilot) were found dead on the beach. Also, the brig *Dove*, Capt. Hubbard, of Marblehead, [Mass.—Ed.] from the Bay of Honduras, put into Savannah, in distress.

† [3d] Samuel Allen posts a notice that he "purposes to close his administration on the estate of John Brockway, late of Surry, deceased . . . " Dated at Surry, 15 March 1802.

† [3d] Legal notice regarding the estate of Hon. Samuel Chase, Esq., late of Cornish, N.H. Nathaniel Hall and March Chase, Commissioners, post a schedule of business meetings to be held at the house of Nathaniel Hall, Innholder in Cornish.

===== ¶ [3d] MARRIED. =====

At Beverly, Mr. John Thistle, aged 18 to Miss Mehitable Clarke, aged 38. [. . .]—At Newport, Mr. John Stranton, jun. to Miss Ruth Hart; Mr. Israel Lorning, of Washington, mer. to Mrs. Frances Dean.—At Boston, Mr. Cyrus Baldwin Wilson, to the agreeable Miss Jane Livermore Lassly.

In this town, Dr. Joshua Crane to Miss Sally Giddings.

===== ¶ [3d] DIED. =====

At Bridport, Mr. Adonijah Rice, ae. 88, the first male child born in Worcester, Ms. after that place was settled by the English.—At Philad. Mr. John Lynn, ae. 84, a respectable member of the Society of Friends.—At Boston, Mr. Samuel Morris, ae. 71; Miss Susan Geyer, eldest daughter of Frederick Wm. Geyer, Esq. ae. 33.—At New York, whilst on a visit, Mr. Wm. Frobisher, jun. of Boston, ae. 39.—At Chelmsford, Dr. Timothy Harrington, an eminent physician.

At Waterbury, Vt. Mrs. Thankful Crosby, ae. 44; she has left a large family of children to deplore the loss.
At Alstead, March 6th, Mr. Joseph Hatch, ae. 84, left 128 grand and great grand children.
In this town, Mr. Shubael Geer, one of the town's poor.

Vol. IX (No. 468) Tuesday, 23 March 1802.

† [3c] Adv. by Amasa Allen listing goods for sale, but due to financial trouble, will close his business on the 20th of May next; dated at Walpole 17 March 1802.

† [3c] Samuel Crosby adv. for a lost cow, branded "S.C. & N.H." Dated Charlestown, N.H., 16 March 1802.

† [3d] Legal notice regarding the insolvent estate of Maj. Isaac Butterfield, late of Westmoreland, deceased. Nathan Babbit, Joseph Buffum, and William Hutchins appointed Commissioners. Dated at Westmoreland, 10 March 1802.

† [3b-d] Several lists of delinquent taxes owed by "proprietors and owners of land in New Grantham, N.H., for the years 1797, 1799, and 1800, compiled by James Smith and Willard Marcy, Collectors. The lists contain the names of the proprietors, and the rates for road, county, and state taxes for the first, second, and third hundred [acre] lots; the lists for 1797 and 1799 indicate that these proprietors were "nonresidents." The summary given herein contains the proprietor's name, and whether tax was owed for that year (those delinquent for any given year are indicated by an "x.")

Original Proprietor	1797	1799	1800	Original Proprietor	1797	1799	1800
Elisha Alexander [56]	x	x	x	John Hunt, jun.	x	x	x
Martin Ashley [57]	x	x	x	Capt. Jonathan Hunt	x	x	x
Lt. Samuel Ashley	x	x	x	Capt. Samuel Hunt [58]	x	x	x
Theodore Atkinson, Esq.		x	x	Lt. Samuel Hunt	x	x	x
Benjamin Barrett	x	x	x	Elias Jones	x	x	x
Oliver Barrett	x	x	x	Josiah Jones	x	x	x
Martha Belding	x	x	x	Gad Lyman	x	x	x
Moses Belding	x	x	x	James Nevins, Esq.			x
Lois Butler	x	x	x	Mrs. Packer	x	x	x
Seth Catlin	x			William Palfrey [59]	x	x	x
Nathaniel Dickenson	x		x	Samuel Partridge	x	x	
Samuel Dickenson	x		x	Medad Pomroy	x		x
Lucius Doolittle	x	x	x	Thomas Rockwood	x	x	x
Oliver Doolittle	x	x	x	Elijah Stebbens [60]	x	x	
James Dwyre [61]		x	x	Joseph Stebbins [62]		x	x
George Field	x	x	x	James Stoodley [63]	x	x	x
Seth Field, Esq.	x	x	x	James Stoodley, Esq. [64]	x	x	x
Bunker Gay	x	x	x	Oliver Warner	x	x	x
Benjamin Hall, Esq.	x	x	x	Samson Willard [65]		x	x
Benjamin Hall, Jr. Esq.	x	x	x	E. Williams, jr.	x	x	
Moses Hawk	x	x	x	E. Williams, Esq. [66]	x	x	
Arad Hunt	x	x	x	Thomas Williams [67]			x
Elisha Hunt		x	x	Thomas Williams, Esq. [68]	x	x	x
John Hunt	x	x	x	T. Williams, jr. [69]	x	x	

===== ¶ [3b] MARRIED. =====

At Alstead, Mr. James Blake to Miss Esther Randal; Mr. Augustus Johnson to Miss Jerusha Randal; Mr. Joel Sartell of Langdon, to Mrs. Sally Bennett of Alstead.—At Dover, Mr. Stephen Hale of Gerry, to Miss Sukey Waldron.—At Rutland, V. Samuel Prentiss, Esq. to Miss Chloe Wells.

===== ¶ [3b] DIED. =====

At New-York, Mr. John Ward Fenno, late proprietor and editor of the United States Gazette, ae. 24.—At Portsmouth, Mr. Thomas Sherburn, ae. 75.—At Rutland, V. Mr. Joshua Pratt.

At Brooklyn, Con. Mr. Daniel Tyler, ae. 101.—At Kittery, Maj. Samuel Leighton, ae. 60.

At Alstead, widow Jerusha Crane, ae. 77.

Vol. IX (No. 469) Tuesday, 30 March 1802.

† [3d] Legal notice from Joanna Willard, Adm^x for the estate of Samuel Willard, late of Charlestown, N.H., regarding a license to sell real estate; dated there 29 March 1802.

===== ¶ [3d] MARRIED. =====

At Worcester, Jos. W. Rose, Esq. of Martinique, to Miss Harriet Paine, daughter of Wm. Paine, Esq.

===== ¶ [3d] DIED. =====

At Newton, Mr. William Hope, late of Great Britain, ae. 50.

At Bridgewater, the 12th inst. the Rev. John Porter, in the 87th year of his age, and 62d of his ministry.—At Boston, Mrs. Dolly Bacon, the amiable and virtuous consort of Mr. Josiah Bacon.—Miss Rebecca Sumner Perkins, daughter of Mr. James Perkins, ae. 20.

At Bradford, Mrs. Hannah Tenney, ae. 102 years, 11 months and 7 days; descendants 147.

Vol. IX (No. 470) Tuesday, 6 April 1802.

† [3d] Legal notice from Andrew French, Executor of the estate of Amariah Rockwell, late of Langdon, N.H.; dated at Walpole, 2 April 1802.

† [3d] List of letters remaining at the Post Office in Charlestown, N.H., 1 April 1802, as compiled by Samuel Crosby, Postmaster:

Jennison Bernard,	Springfield, Vt.	Ruth Grant,	Charlestown.
Jeremiah Ellis,	" "	Caleb Hunt,	"
Ziba Ellis,	" "	Benjamin Jones,	"
Joshua, Wm. or Jno. Knapp,	" "	Widow Mary Larcom,	"
		Doct. Edmond Pelouze,	"
Jesse Lanksford,	" "	Edward Richards,	"
Levi Nichols,	" "	William Rhoades,	"
Hugh Smith,	" "	Joseph Wilson,	"
Amos Stone,	" "	Timmoth [sic] George,	Weare, N.H.
Isaac Fisher,	Charlestown, N.H.	Daniel Moore,	New London, N.H.

† [3d] List of letters remaining at the Post Office in Walpole, N.H., 31 March 1802, as compiled by A. Thomas, Postmaster. A footnote following the list informs the public that "the Post-Office is now in the possession of Mr. Gurdon Huntington, at the South end of the Street where they will, in future, please to apply for letters."

John Brooks,	Walpole.	Samuel Nutting,	Walpole.
Roswell Baldwin,	"	Nathan Smith, 2.	"
Deacon Roger Farnham,	"	Elisha White,	"
Benj. M. Floyd,	"	John White,	"
Elisha Griswold,	"		

===== ¶ [3c] MARRIED. =====

At Alexandria, Michael Sherman, aged *ninety seven years and four days*, to the amiable and accomplished Miss Eliza Poindexter, aged *fourteen*.

At Winslow, (M.) Mr. John Parshley, of Bath, to Miss Tevasia Clarke.

===== ¶ [3d] DIED. =====

At Albany, Alexander Spencer, Esq.—At Lunenburg, Widow Martha Fessenden, ae. 81.—At Philad., an Indian Chief, of the Shawnese Tribe.

Vol. IX (No. 471) Tuesday, 13 April 1802.

† [3d] Daniel Newcomb, Treasurer of the Third New Hampshire Turnpike, posts a notice regarding shares to be sold at the house of Thomas Wells, in Keene, N.H.

† [3d] Brief mention of a marriage, with poetry attached, of Mr. Joseph Rose, "of Antigua," to Miss Harriet Paine, "of Worcester."

===== ¶ [3d] MARRIED. =====

At Northampton, Mr. John Edwards, to Miss Polly Baral.

In Vermont, by the Hon. G. Olin, C. Nicholas, Esq. to Miss Lydia Pope; and by C. Nicholas, Esq. Hon. G. Olin, to Miss Deborah Pope. *This was one good turn for another.*

===== ¶ [3d] DIED. =====

At Byefield, Mr. Tho. Lull, ae. 77.—At Worcester, Mr. Silas Metcalf, ae. 36, formerly of Keene.

At Salem, Mrs. Catharine Andrews, ae. 53.—At Westerly, Col. Joseph Noyes, ae. 75.—At Newport, Mrs. Phila Townsend, ae. 55.—At Falmouth, (M.) Capt. Jona. Armstrong, ae. 66.—At Scituate, Mr. Israel Turner, ae. 56.

At Demerara, Joseph Leavitt, ae. 18.—In England, the Rt. Hon. Ld. Graves, Admiral of the White.—In Ireland, the Earl of Clare, Ld. Chancellor.—

Vol. IX (No. 472) Tuesday, 20 April 1802.

† [3b-c] Suicide at Great Barrington, Mass. of Rebecca Turner, aged about 68, an insane woman who hung herself at the house of her son, Edward Turner. ♦

¶ [3c] GENUINE PATRIOTISM. On Monday the 5th inst. Col. Benjmain Day, of West-Springfield, in the 93d year of his age, went to Town-Meeting, and gave in his vote, in his own hand writing, for Governor Strong.

† [3c] Account of a fire which destroyed the house of Mr. Ichabod Warner at Bernardston, 26 March 1802. News item copied from the *Greenfield Gazette.*♦

† [3d] Adv. of hymns for sale at Mr. Hinds in Walpole; dated 19 April.

† [3d] Legal notice by Joseph Chapman, Executor of the estate of Capt. Benjamin Chapman, late of Plainfield, [N.H.—Ed.], deceased; dated at Cornish, 20 April 1802.

===== ¶ [3d] MARRIED. =====

At Newton, Mr. Luther Coolidge, of Watertown, to Mrs. Louisa Patterson, of Lunenburg.—

===== ¶ [3d] DIED. =====

At Boston, Mrs. Olive Carol, wife of Mr. Lawson Carol, ae. 26; Miss Abigail Boyd, ae. 72; Mrs. Mary Otheman; Mr. William Skinner, ae. 58; Miss Elizabeth Pearsons, ae. 70.—At Worcester, Mrs. Dorothy Allen, consort of Joseph Allen, Esq. ae. 45.

At Woburn, in Great Britain, March 2d, the most Noble Francis Duke of Bedford, ae. 37.—He was the richest peer in England; and the leader of the Whig interest therein. He is succeeded in his titles and estates by his brother Lord John Russell.

At Brookfield, Mrs. Susannah Upham, aged 67.

Vol. IX (No. 473) Tuesday, 27 April 1802.

† [3d] Legal notice regarding the insolvent estate of William Luey, late of Cornish, deceased. James Ripley, Nath. Huggins, and Benjamin Comings appointed Commissioners over said estate; business meetings to be conducted at the house of Widow Sally Luey, in Cornish; dated there 16 April 1802.

===== ¶ [3d] MARRIED. =====

At Middlebury, (Vt.) [70] on the 15th inst. Mr. Daniel Campbell, Merchant, to Miss Dolly Burham of West Haven, niece of judge Painter.—Mr. Augustine Clark Esq. to Miss Irene Miller, Daughter of the Hon. S. Miller, Esq. of Williston, Vermont.[71]—Mr. David H. Griswold, Esq. Attorney at law, to the amiable Miss Polly Nichols, Daughter of Capt. J. Nichols.[72]—At Boston, Mr. Caleb Pratt, of Chelsea, to Miss Mary Lash.—Mr. Joseph Woodcock, to Miss Ann Hatch.—Samuel Weatherbee, Esq. of Vermont, to Miss Hannah Ross.—At Newport, Lt. Pearsons Titcomb, of the U.S. army, to Miss Anne Maria Deladernia.

===== ¶ [3d] DIED. =====

At Norwich, Mrs. Mary Huxley, ae. 58.—At Danvers, Miss Polly Batchelder, ae. 24.—At Westminster, England, His Excellency Wm. Browne, Esq. ae. 65.—late

Governor of Bermudas. Gov. B. was a native of Salem, and descended from one of the most ancient and respectable families that have lived in the town. He was a Justice of the Supreme Judicial Court in 1774, and Colonel of the first regiment in Essex.—

At Westminster, V. very suddenly, Mr. Samuel Cone ae. 77—At Portsmouth, Mr. John Pillor ae. 33—At Gilmantown, Mr. Benjamin Bodge—At Newfane, Mr. Orison Fisher—At Dummerston, V. Major William Miller—Mrs. Tucker—At Northampton, Mrs. Ursula Wright ae. 55—In this town, Samuel Fessenden, Esq ae. 21, son of the Rev. Thomas Fessenden. 73

Vol. X (No. 474) Tuesday, 4 May 1802.

† [3d] Henry Booth adv. for journeyman shoemakers for his employ; dated at Walpole.

===== ¶ [3c] MARRIED. =====

At Portsmouth, Mr. Daniel Shores to Miss Polly Dennett.—Mr. Arthur Melcher to Mrs. Elizabeth Aherman. 74

At Barnstable, Mr. Robert Bacon, of Boston, to Miss Mary Crocker.

At Boston, Mr. Joseph Herrald, of Portsmouth, to Miss Elizabeth Conner, of Boston.

===== ¶ [3c-d] DIED. =====

At Alstead, on the 2d. inst. John Hale ae. 7 years, son of Moses Hale, Esq.

At Falmouth, (M.) Mrs. Barbour, ae. 94.—At Gorham, Rev. Caleb Jewett, ae. 49.—At Lebanon, (C.) Mrs. Sarah Niles, ae. 91, consort of the Hon. S. Niles, Esq. late of Braintree.

At Boston, Mrs. Abigail Cunningham, ae. 75.—Mrs. Anna Cier, ae. 63.

At Wilton, Rev. Mr. Fisk.

At Charleston, John B. Williamson, Esq. formerly manger of the theatre in Boston.

At Gibralter, Gen. Ch. O'Hara, late Governor of that fortress—At New-Milford, Mr. Andrew Nodine, ae. 102.—In Pennsylvania, the Hon. James Moore one of the Associate Judges for the county of Chester.

In South-Carolina, Hon. Edanus Burke ae. 59, one of the Chancellors of the State. He was a native of Galway, in Ireland. As a partiot, he was ardent; as a Judge inflexibly just; as a writer luminous; as a man honest yet eccentric. He was a member of the first Congress under the present Constitution.

At Quincy, Mr. Samuel Spear, ae. 25.—At New-Braintree, Miss Nabby Bigelow, ae. 20.

Drowned, at Miller's Falls, Montague, on Saturday last, a Mr. Day of Chesterfield. He and three others were attempting to run a raft into the canal; when the current of the river forced it over the dam; two saved themselves above by swimming, but Mr. Day who could not swim, went over with the raft. 75

Vol. X (No. 475) Tuesday, 11 May 1802.

===== ¶ [3d] MARRIED. =====

At New-Bedford, Dr. R. Spooner, to Miss Susan Elliot.—At Charlestown, Dr. Caleb Haskell, to Miss Nancy Fox.

At Ipswich, Mr. Amos Choate, to Miss Lucy Smith.

===== ¶ [3d] DIED. =====

At Dover, (D.) James M'Clyment, Esq. ae. 47.—At Norwich, Mrs. Anna Huntington, ae. 34.—At New London, Mr. Turner Miner, ae. 64.—At New Milford, Mr. And. Nodine, ae. 102.—At Alexandria, Joshua Johnson, Esq. Commissioner of Stamps.

At Boston, Mrs. Susannah Hastings, ae. 40.—Mr. John Murdock, ae. 75, late of Newton.—Mrs. Prudence Eayers, ae. 55.—Pompey, ae. 50, a worthy black man.

At Billerica, suddenly, Jonathan Stickney, Esq. ae. 66.—At Scituate, Mr. Stephen Stockbridge, ae. 69.—In England, Mrs. Chapone, well known as the author of letters moral and instructive.—

At Cambridge, Thaddeus Mason, Esq.—At Frankford, P. Dr. Enoch Edwards, ae. 51.—At Greenfield, Mr. Enos Denlo.

At Guilford, Miss Rebecca Lynds, ae. 17.—On Wednesday last, of a consumption, Mr. Silas Baker, ae. 25 years.

At Ipswich, Mrs. Hannah Hovey, wife of Mr. Francis Hovey, and daughter of Mr. Thomas Lewis, of Boston.

¶ [3d] TAKE NOTICE. All persons indebted to the late firm of Ebenezer Senier & Co. for carding wool at their Manufactory in *Claremont*, are requested to make immediate payment to Mr. David Dexter, of said Claremont.

Thos. Ray,
George Booth.

April 28th, 1802.

¶ [3d] Whereas Keziah Darling, my wife, has eloped from my bed and board, I hereby forbid all persons harboring or trusting her on my account, as I will pay no debts of her contracting after this date.

Otis Darling.

Andover, April 29, 1802.

Vol. X (No. 476) Tuesday, 18 May 1802.

† [3a] Sad account of the death of widow Jerusha Brewster, who was poisoned with arsenic, and died at Canterbury, [Conn., 24 March 1802—Ed.]. The son-in-law, James Morse, was accused of murder, but released on lack of evidence. The widow's daughter and two grandchildren were also poisoned, but recovered. ♦

† [3d] Adv. by Charles Sigourney, Jr., late of Boston, now of Hartford, Conn., regarding goods for sale at his wholesale hardware store; dated Hartford, 10 May 1802.

† [3d] Danforth Clark adv. for his lost or stolen horse; dated at Walpole, 15 May 1802.

† [3d] Legal notice regarding the insolvent estate of Capt. Samuel Nichols, late of Lempster, N.H., deceased. James Bingham, David Willey, and Eliot Cary appointed Commissioners over said estate. The notice includes a schedule of business meetings to be held at the house of Jabez Brainer, innholder at Lempster; dated Lempster 6 May.

† [3c-d] Obituary of William Gordon, Esq., of Amherst, Attorney General of New Hampshire, and late Representative of New Hampshire in Congress. Gordon died at Boston, aged 39. ♦

† [3d] Obituary of Hon. John Lowell, Esq., who died at Roxbury, 6 May 1802, in the 59th year of his age; Chief Judge of the First District of the U.S. Circuit Court. ♦

===== ¶ [3d] MARRIED. =====

At Northampton, the Reverend John Pierce, of Brookline, to Miss Lucy Tappan, of the former place.

Vol. X (No. 477) Tuesday, 25 May 1802.

† [2b] Gruesome account of Mrs. Bean's child, mutilated by Russel Bean, who claimed that the child was not his. The article is dated at Jonesborough, Tenn. ♦

† [2c] Account of Horatio Seney, of Church-Hill, Queen Anne's County, Maryland, who fasted for 44 days, and died shortly after. The article is dated at Elizabeth-Town, N.J. ♦

† [2d-3a] Death of Capt. William Everett, 4 May 1802, during a military inspection at Dedham, Mass., being shot by accident by one Private Morse. The captain was a widower, leaving nine children. ♦

† [3c] A Mr. Albertson, blacksmith of New York City, won a lottery. ♦

¶ [3c] Burnt at Croydon, Newhampshire, on the 15 ult. a dwelling house and Joiner's shop, the property of Lt. Dudley Perkins, together with all his furniture, and tools; estimated at 1000 dollars.

† [3c] Legal notice regarding the bankruptcy case against Martin Butterfield, of Westmoreland, N.H., Trader. Samuel West, Joseph Burt, and Ezra Pierce were chosen as Commissioners of Bankruptcy.

† [3d] Legal notice regarding the sale of tracts of land belonging to the estate of Maj. Isaac Butterfield, late of Westmoreland, deceased. Notice posted by Willard Butterfield, Administrator. The notice mentions land previously owned by Oliver Johnson, late of Westmoreland.

† [3d] Adv. by John Livingston, Jr., who makes and repairs muskets; dated Walpole.
† [3d] Azariah Dickerson found a stray cow; dated at Walpole, 24 May 1802.

Vol. X (No. 478) Tuesday, 1 June 1802.

† [3d] Adv. by Asa Bullard, who lost his cow; dated at Walpole, 1 June 1802.
† [3d] Adv. by Samuel West, Proprietor's Clerk, regarding the 3d N.H. Turnpike Corp.

===== ¶ [3d] MARRIED. =====

In this town, Mr. W. H. Whitney, to Miss Clarissa Wolcott.

===== ¶ [3d] DIED. =====

At Charlestown, Mr. Samuel Wier of this town.

Vol. X (No. 479) Tuesday, 8 June 1802.

† [3b] Article describing a prison break, 22 May 1802, at the Penitentiary [Trenton, N.J.?]. Eight prisoners made their escape, viz: Willaim Tabor, John Huffman, John D. Stewart, Joseph Williams, John Smith, Robert Smith, John Frazer and Findley Boss. The ninth, J. Coryell, was shot and wounded. ◆
† [3d] Stephen Johnson adv. drugs and medicines for sale "at the Store formerly occupied by John Hubbard, Esq." at Walpole.
† [3d] Samuel Griffin, Adm., posts a legal notice regarding the estate of Capt. Stephen Bowker, late of Westmoreland, deceased; dated at Westmoreland, 28 May 1802.
† [3d] Thomas Whipple adv. for a lost mare; dated at Hanover, [?] June 1802
† [3d] Obituary of Hon. Benjamin Bellows, Esq. of Walpole, who died "on the morning of Friday last, in the 62d year of his age." ◆

===== ¶ [3d] MARRIED. =====

At West-Springfield, Ms. Mr. David Newhall, *Printer*, of this town, to Miss Sukey Leonard, of the former place.

Vol. X (No. 480) Tuesday, 15 June 1802.

¶ [3a] Boston, Massachusetts, June 9, 1802. On Sunday, last week, at Fort Independence, in confining Thomas Langdon, an Irish laborer, who, we understand, had abused several of the soldiers, he resisted in a desperate manner, and knocked down two or three of the persons who were conducting him to the guard house. At length he was secured; but it was soon afterwards discovered, that he had received a wound, supposed to be with a bayonet. The attention of the Surgeon was unavailing—he died on Tuesday. The usual steps of the law have been taken.
† [3d] Philip Davis adv. help wanted: "a Journeyman, to work at the Boot and Shoe making business." Dated at Rockingham, 8 June 1802.

===== ¶ [3c-d] MARRIED. =====

At Salem, Ms. Mr. James Brooks, to Miss Polly Caldwell.
At Boston, Mr. Putnam Jordan, to Miss Sally Brewer.—Mr. John Gore, to Miss Mary G. Babcock.—Mr. John Rowe Parker, to Miss Catharine Brigden.
At Beverly, Mr. David Larcom, to Miss Elizabeth Haskell.—Mr. Israel Lovett, to Miss Abigail Elliot.

===== ¶ [3d] DIED. =====

In England, at the priory near Derbey, to which he had lately removed, Dr. Darwin, without the least previous indiposition.
In Great-Britain, the Rev. Mr. Nelson, Rector of Burnham Thorpe, and father of the gallant Lord Nelson, æ. 79.—At New-York, Mrs. Sarah Jay, æ. 45, the amiable and much respected wife of Hon. John Jay, late Governor of the State of New-York, and daughter of the late Governor Livingston, of New-Jersey [. . .]
At Kittery, Mr. James Johnson, æ. 9[2?].—At Boston, Mr. Joseph Pitty, æ. 58.—At Newton, Mrs. Anna Bartlett, æ. 81.

Vol. X (No. 481) Tuesday, 22 June 1802.

† [3c] Samuel Thomson adv. two mares lost or stolen; dated at Alstead, 20 June 1802.
† [3c] Ephraim Lane offers a house, barn, grist mill and saw mill for sale "about two miles south of Walpole village." Dated at Walpole 15 June 1802.
† [3d] Detailed adv. by *Bellows & Stone* of goods for sale; dated Walpole 19 June 1802.
† [3d] Thos. & Isaac Redington adv. goods for sale at their store in Walpole "lately occupied by Messrs. Bellows & Whitney." Dated Walpole, 21 June 1802.

===== ¶ [3c] ORDANIED. =====

At Gill, (Massa.) Rev. Jabez Munsel. At Goffstown, (N.H.) Rev. David Lawrence Morrell.—At Henniker, Rev. Moses Sawyer.

===== ¶ [3c] MARRIED. =====

At Portsmouth, Capt. John Paul, to Miss Elizabeth Nelson.
On Saturday evening the 5th inst. was married by the Rev. Dr. Haven, assisted by his colleague, Mr. Daniel Waldron, to Miss Olive Sheafe, the second daughter of Jacob Sheafe, Esq.
At Boston, Mr. Thomas Dean, Printer, to Miss Nancy H. Grubb.

===== ¶ [3c] DIED. =====

At Westhampton, Mr. Tertius Strong.—At Springfield, the Hon. Samuel Lyman.—At Philadelphia, Mr. Robert M'Kean.—At Boston, Mr. Sampson Read, Merchant.
At Fitchburg, of an apoplexy, Mr. Aaron Eaton, æ. 49.—Near Baltimore, Dec. 29, Abigail Cook, æ. 110.
At Westminster, Vt. Mrs. Shipman, wife of Mr. Abraham Shipman, aged 54 years. Her case was attended with circumstances sufficient to excite the curiosity of the faculty. She died on the 15th in the evening, and her dissection was performed on the succeeding day. Mrs. S's. indisposition commenced about 20 years since. In this term she has had two children, the youngest of whom is now sixteen years of age. The size of her body has gradually encreased [sic] since that period. On dissection 32 quarts of water were drawn from her, and a schirrus, weighing eleven pounds, and a quarter, situated in the right hypocondriac, was extracted. The periconeum was entirely consumed, and the reticulum as well as the integuments and intestines, in a state of perfect putridity. During the whole time of her sickness, no cessation of the catamenia, for even a single day, took place.

Vol. X (No. 482) Tuesday, 29 June 1802.

¶ [3a] New York, New York, June 7, 1802. [. . .] On Friday last, as part of the family of Mr. Thomas Leggett, merchant of this city was coming in a boat to town from his farm near Hell-Gate, it upset, and two of his children were unfortunately drowned. The remainder of those who were in the boat, with great difficulty reached the shore in safety.
† [3c] A son of Mr. Nichols, of Preston, Conn., kills a large snake; article dated at Norwich, 16 June 1802.
† [3d] Adv. by Christopher Colt for his crockery and glassware store, "having purchased Francis Brown's stocke in trade." Dated at Hartford, Conn. 9 June 1802.
† [3d] Adv. by *Chapman & Hartwell* of goods for sale at their store in Alstead.
† [3d] Alexander Atcherson found a lost mare; adv. dated at Rockingham 27 June 1802

===== ¶ [3c] MARRIED. =====

In Connecticut, on the [13?]th inst. Mr. John Buckley, Merchant, to Miss Amelia Daggett, daughter of Henry Daggett, Esq. Capt. Abel Denison, to Miss Mary Whetmore; Mr. Samuel Barney, jun. to Miss Sarah Ransom, all of New-Haven.
At New-York, Mr. Samuel Palmer, of Philadelphia, to Miss Elizabeth Allaire, daughter of Mr. Peter A. Allaire, of New-York.

===== ¶ [3c-d] DIED. =====

At Concord, very suddenly, Levi Dearborn, Esq. Representative in the State Legislature, from the town of Rochester.

At Natchez, Gen. John Willis.—At New-Orleans, William Scott, of the United States army.—On the Mississippi, Lieut. Gabriel Jones, of the 4th United States regiment.—At Marlborough, Mrs. Mary Tarlow, Widow, aged 99.—At Acton, Mr. Samuel Jones, æ. 95. He lived with his wife, who survives him, 70 years. Their posterity amount to 119. It is worthy of notice, that, at the time of his death, there were living within one mile of him, three persons upwards of 90, and in that small town nine others upwards of 80 years of age.

At Windsor, Vt. (very suddenly) Mr. Robert Morrison, æ. 56.

Vol. X (No. 483) Tuesday, 6 July 1802.

† [3d] Legal notice regarding a petition by Lucretia Stevens, of Claremont, Guardian of Rachel Stevens, Sarah Stevens, Roxy Stevens, and Fanny Stevens, minors, all of Claremont, to obtain a license to sell real estate for the support of said minors.

† [3d] List of letters remaining at the Post Office in Charlestown, N.H., 1 July 1802, as compiled by Samuel Crosby, Postmaster:

Joshua Atwood,	Lempster.	Mr. Nathaniel Smith,	Charlestown.
Ebenezer Burr,	N. Grantham.	William Thornton,	Charlestown.
Dr. J.B. Bartlet,	Compton, L. Canada	Jona. Twiss,	Springfield, Vt.
Capt. Jesse Churchill,	Washington.	Joseph Wilson,	Charlestown.
Capt. Hezekiah Emerson,	Goshen.	Stephen Whipple,	Langdon.
Joseph Healey,	Washington.	Jotham White, Esq.,	Springfield, Vt.
Gad Sedgwick,	Springfield, Vt.	Newton Whittlesey,	Cornish.
Capt. David Saunderson,	Charlestown.		

¶ [3d] Ranaway from the subscriber some time in the Month of May last, Daniel Whipple, about thirty years of age; and I hereby forbid all persons from harboring or trusting said Daniel Whipple on my account, as I will pay no debts of his contracting.

Samuel Taylor.

Rockingham, July 2, 1802.

===== ¶ [3d] MARRIED. =====

At Scituate, Mr. Loring Jacobs, of Boston, to Miss Mary Simmons of Scituate.—At Providence, Mr. Henry Grew, merchant, of Boston, to Miss Susannah Pittman.

Vol. X (No. 484) Tuesday, 13 July 1802.

† [3b] Adv. of goods for sale by Joseph Bellows, Jr.; dated at Walpole, 12 July 1802.
† [3d] Isaac Blanchard found a stray mare; dated at Westmoreland, 4 July 1802.
† [3d] Samuel Salter found a stray colt; dated at Walpole, 6 July 1802.

===== ¶ [3b] MARRIED. =====

At Keene, Mr. John G. Bond, merchant, to Miss Sally Newcomb, daughter of the Hon. Daniel Newcomb.

At Norfolk, Lt. Krafftzs (son to the Commodore of the Dutch squadron in Hampton Roads) to Miss Dolly Herrman.

===== ¶ [3b] DIED. =====

At Packersfield, Mr. Archelaus Wilson æ. 56.—At Biddeford, of the yellow fever, Mr. Moses Porter, æ. 22.

At Alstead, Ebenezer Greene, æ. 18, son of Mr. Ebenezer Greene, of Wells, Vt.

Vol. IX (No. 485) Tuesday, 20 July 1802.

† [3b] A detailed account of the slow death, at Packersfield, N.H., of Mr. Stephen Beard, aged 30, son of David Beard. The son was bitten in Feb. by a rabid dog, and eventually developed symptons of the Hydrophobia, and died 2 July. ♦

¶ [3c] A duel was lately fought between Gen. Jackson of Georgia, and Col. Robert Watkins. After exchanging five shots the former was wounded, but not mortally.

† [3c] Adv. of goods for sale by Amasa Allen; dated at Walpole, N.H., 19 July 1802.
† [3c-d] Bankruptcy notice regarding Edward Esty, of Boston, Trader, dated 28 June.
† [3d] Notice regarding a meeting of the Seventh New Hampshire Turnpike to be held

at Gen. Shepard's Tavern in Alstead; notice posted by John C. Chamberlain, who was "authorized by said act to call the first Meeting." Dated at Alstead 15 July 1802.

Vol. X (No. 486) Tuesday, 27 July 1802.

† [3a] Summary of a letter from masters and supercargoes of American vessels "detained in the Spanish ports on the Rio de Plata," in regards to the mistreatment of them by the Spanish officials. The letter was signed by Messrs. Thomas O'Reilly, Joseph Russell, William Todd, Jr., Job W. Hall, Titus Conklin, Jonathan Williams, Henry Davidson, Josiah Gould, Lenoard Jarvis, 3d, Daniel Olney, Jonathan Russell, Titus Welles, Robert Gray, Silas Atkins, William Allen, Daniel M'Pherson, Caleb Loring, Isaac Isaacs, Josiah Roberts, Moses Griffin, John Ansley, and John Grant.

† [3c] Rev. John Peak installed "to the pastoral care of the Baptist Church" at Barnstable, [Mass.—Ed.]. ♦

† [3c] Brief account of the ordination of Rev. James Murdoch at Princeton, [Mass.—Ed.]; the brief notice mentions several ministers who officiated, including another Rev. Murdoch, of Bozrah, Conn.

† [3d] Legal notice by John H. Wires, Adm. for the insolvent estate of Samuel Wires, late of Walpole, deceased. Dated at Walpole 23 July 1802.

† [3d] A notice from Daniel Newcomb, Treasurer of the Third New Hampshire Turnpike, regarding shares to be sold at the house of Thomas Wells, Keene, N.H.; dated at Keene 21 July 1802.

¶ [3d] Whereas Nancy Nash, my wife, has eloped from my bed and board, I hereby forbid all persons harboring or trusting her on my account, as I will pay no debts of her contracting after this date.

Abraham Nash.

Sullivan, July 20th, 1802.

===== ¶ [3c] MARRIED. =====

At Keene, N.H. Mr. Samuel Wheelock, of Boston, to Miss Fanny Goodenow.—At Hinsdale, (Ver.) Dr. Charles Blake, of the U.S. army, to the amiable Miss Frances Hunt, Daughter of the Hon. Jonathan Hunt.—At Boston, John Williams, Esq. attorney at Law, to Miss Sally Chamberlain.

At Staten Island, Mr. Journey, aged 80 to Mrs. Cole, aged 60.

A fellow trav'ler and a friend.
Is found towards to Journey's end.
[BALANCE.

===== ¶ [3c] DIED. =====

"At Norwich, England, Mrs. Beaton, æ. 83; commonly called the Free Mason, from the circumstance of her having contrived to conceal herself one evening in the wainscoating of a Lodge room, where she learnt some part of those secrets, the knowledge of which thousands of her sex have in vain attempted to arrive at. She was a very singular old woman, and as a proof of it, she made her heart the sole confident of the secret."—At Gloucester, (Cape Ann) the 15th inst. very suddenly of an internal hemorrhage, Capt. THOMAS ROBERTS, in the meridian of life, highly esteemed and universally beloved, greatly lamented by his family, and all his acquaintance. His activity and prudence, his integrity and benevolence, so uniform and unaffected as demonstrated that the sublime doctrines and maxims of christianity, influenced his heart, directed his conduct, and inspired him with that hope, which constantly supported him with manly courage in every calamitous situation of life, and enabled him to meet death with fortitude, though in an unexpected moment. His death is a great and public loss—He left affectionate parents to bewail the loss of an amiable son.—A wife; the kind and tender husband.—Eight children; a fond parent.—Society a useful member; and the world a real friend to its whole family.—"Thus God destroys the hope of man."—At Perth, Amboy, Nicholas Gouverner, Esq. President of the New York Bank, and one of the most opulent and respectable merchants of that city.—Deaths at Philadelphia, in June, 163: From January to July, 986.—At Winchester, Virginia, Gen. DANIEL MORGAN, the hero of the Cowpens, æ. 66; He was at the siege of Quebec, in 1775, and commanded at the battle of the Cowpens, in which he completely routed and captured a superior force, and for which Congress presented him with a gold medal and Virginia an elegant sword and pair of pistols.—As a politician he was correct, and he was brave as a soldier.

Vol. X (No. 487) Tuesday, 3 Aug. 1802.

† [2d] The Iron Works belonging to Sampson Hunt of Glastenbury consumed by fire [16 July 1802?—Ed.].
¶ [2d] Mr. David Hosley, of Lancaster, while at the raising of a small frame for a Woodhouse and Cornbarn, was killed by the fall of one side of the frame which put an immediate end to his existence. Aged 59.
† [2d-3a] Account of the death of Master Peter Merrill of Bradford, Vermont, who drowned in Wait's River, and the attempted rescue by Master William Baldwin. ♦
† [3a] Notice of the marriage, at Stoughton, of Mr. Sarda Drake to Miss Polly Dreggs, which has poetry included in the notice.
† [3c] Legal notice regarding the insolvent estate of Samuel Wires, late of Walpole, deceased. Micah Read, David Arnold, and Asa Britton appointed Commissioners over said estate; the notice includes a schedule of business meetings to be conducted at the house of Charles Church, Innholder in Westmoreland; dated Westmoreland 2 Aug. [76]
† [3c] Adv. of a paper manufactory under construction by *Kingsbery & Blake*, on the west side of Connecticut River at Bellows's Falls, "near Col. Page's mills." The adv. also states that papermaking will continue as usual on the east side of the river at Alstead, but this addition to the adv. is identified as *Elisha Kingsbery & Co.*
† [3c] Adv. of stray horses found by Hollon Fay; dated at Walpole [?] July 1802.
† [3c] Adv. of stray mare found by Joseph Burt; dated at Westmoreland 24 July 1802.
† [3c] Adv. of stray steer found by Joseph Jones; dated at Walpole 2 Aug. 1802.

===== ¶ [3b] MARRIED. =====

At Gloucester, R.I. Rev. Oliver Dodge, to Miss Sally Williams.—At Hamilton, Capt. Samuel Brown, to Miss Mary Brown.

===== ¶ [3b-c] DIED. =====

At Northwood, N.H. (drowned) two men, twin brothers, of the name of Carr, and Mr. J. Langley, in attempting to save the former. The two Carrs were married in one day to twin sisters, had each a child about 5 months old—they died in each others arms, and were buried in one grave.
At Springfield, Mr. Preserved White ae. 81.—Mrs. Munn ae. 82.—At Portsmouth, Dr. Bracket, President of the N.H. Medical Society and one of the best physicians and greatest ornaments of our country. He was in the 70th year of his age.—In England, Lord Kensington, Member of Parliament.—At Winthrop, (suicide) Mr. Jacob Stanley, ae. 30.—In Boston, Mr. John Hooton, ae. 81.—Mrs. Helen Lovell, ae. 33.—At Spencer, Mrs. Mary Whittemore, ae. [87?]. It is remarkable that the death of this woman was the first instance of mortality which had taken place in the house she died in for sixty years, though occupied as a masionhouse.—At Newbury-Port, Mr. Joseph Kent, ae. 66.—In a paroxysm of derangement, he rode to the bridge on Deer Island, paid his toll, fastened his horse, pulled of his coat, tied his hands with a handkerchief, and leaped from the bridge into the water and drowned. He was a man of considerable property, and has left a respectable family of children to lament his death.—In Boston, on Tuesday, Mr. James Freeland, ae. 64. As a husband, father, neighbor and friend, he was amiable, beneficient and true.—As a christian, exemplary in his whole life [. . .]
At Westmoreland, after a lingering illness, Mr. Ralph Butterfield.

Vol. X (No. 488) Tuesday, 10 Aug. 1802.

¶ [3a] LONGEVITY.—In 1701, died at Smyrna, one Lupazzolo, at the age of 118 years.—He had sixty children by five wives, besides such as were illegitimate. His oldest son died before him, at the age of 85; at which time his youngest daughter was but six years old.

===== ¶ [3d] MARRIED. =====

At Philadelphia, Mr. John Cummins, aged 92, to Miss Catherine Kelchre, aged 28.—In Boston, Mr. Allen Clark, to Miss Mary Jacobs.—William Woodward, Esq. Attorney at

Law, of Hanover, N.H. to Miss Betsey Curtis, daughter of the late Dr. Benjamin Curtis.—At Baltimore, Mr. Nicholas Leake, aged 60, at Miss Hannah Bark, aged 16.

===== ¶ [3d] DIED. =====

In Russia, Admiral Kutusop. His funeral was attended with great pomp; the Emperor followed the body on foot upwards of two miles. The procession was formed of the Marine Cadets, a number of troops, cannon, &c.—At Fredericksburg, Gen. Lewis Littlepage, aged 44. He was appointed first confidential Secretary in the Council of Stanislaus Augustus, late King of Poland, in 1786; and remained in that office, until the partition of that Kingdom by Russia and Prussia.—At Hartford, Mr. Jona. Conklin, aged 74.—At Montville, Mrs. Mary Wheeler, aged 96.—At Marblehead, Mrs. Mary Carney, aged 75.—At Boston, Mrs. Hannah Fessenden.

Vol. X (No. 489) Tuesday, 17 Aug. 1802.

† [3d] Adv. of a stray colt found by Amos Philips; dated at Walpole 12 Aug. 1802.

===== ¶ [3d] DIED. =====

At Springfield, Widow Elizabeth Bliss, æ. 85.—At Alstead, on the 1st inst. Master Leonard Kingsbury, the only son of Lieut. Ephraim Kingsbury in the third year of his age.—Mr. William Cheney æ. [54?].—At Hampton, Mrs. M. Farnham, æ. 75.—At Wolcott, Mr. David Norton, æ. 71.—At Hudson, Mrs. Eliz. Hudson, æ. 73.—At Portland, Miss Eliza Wadsworth, æ. 22, daughter of Hon. Peleg Wadsworth.—In Boston, Arnold Wells, Esq. President of the United States Bank, in Boston, æ. 75.—

In this town, last Saturday, very suddenly, Miss Polly Warren, æ. 22.

Vol. X (No. 490) Tuesday, 24 Aug. 1802.

===== ¶ [3d] DIED. =====

At Chatham, (Con.) Dea. Isaac Smith, æ. 86.—At Salem, Mrs. Margaret Derby, wife of Capt. Samuel Derby.—At Ludlow, Dr. Philip Lyon, of Randolph, Vermont.—At Middletown, Mrs. Mehitable Parsons, æ. 59.—At Bridport, Mr. John Barber æ. 71.— The deaths in the city of New-York, from the 1st to the 8th inst. were 34—mostly children, and none of the fever.

At Aux Cayes, St. Domingo, Bartholomew Dandridge, Esq. Consul of the United States for the southern department of St. Domingo.—At Dover, Mr. Moses Gage.—At Jamaica, Mr. Joseph Blake, jun. of Boston, late from New York.—At Mount Eagle, (Vir.) the Right Hon. and Rev. Brian Lord Fairfax, æ. 76.

Vol. X (No. 491) Tuesday, 31 Aug. 1802.

¶ [2c] Mason, convicted at the late Supreme Court in Dedham, of murder, is to be executed at that place, on Thursday the 7th of October next.

¶ [2c] The ticket, No. 13,433, which drew the highest prize in the South Hadley Lottery, on Monday last, was sold by Mr. John West, and is owned by two gentlemen in Cornhill.

† [2d] Account of a dysentery outbreak at Greenfield, [Mass.—Ed.], claiming several victims, though none are named specifically. ◆

¶ [2d] Rutland, Vermont, July 26, 1802. A few days ago, as Mr. William Welden, of Warren county, (N.C.) was walking near a branch, he perceived a hern seized by a turtle. He hastened to relieve the hern; but on approaching her she darted her bill into the socket of his eye and holding, by the ball, suspended herself and the turtle for some time, by which he has lost the sight of the eye.

¶ [3c-d] MELANCHOLY ACCIDENT. In Worcester, Mas. on Monday last, a son of Mr. Samuel Johnson, about two years and a half old, being at play in the bark house belonging to his tannery, and accidentally left alone for a few minutes, was caught under the wheel of the bark mill, which passed over his head, and instantly put a period to his life.

¶ [3d] A duel was fought in Georgia on the 31st ult. by Peter L. Van Allen, Esq. Solicitor General, and Wm. H. Crawford, Esq. Attorney at Law, in which the Solicitor was killed.

† [3d] Legal notice by Abner Smith, Adm. for the estate of Ornal Clarke of Marlow, deceased; dated at Marlow 31 Aug. 1802.

¶ [3d] Whereas Ellice my wife, has eloped from my bed and board, I hereby forbid all persons harbouring or trusting her on my account, as I will pay no debts of her contracting after this date.

George Lord.

Westminster, Aug. 1st, 1802.

===== ¶ [3d] MARRIED. =====

In Boston, Mr. Lawson Dench, to Miss Mary Stoddard.

===== ¶ [3d] DIED. =====

At Charlestown, on the 27th Aug. Samuel Crosby, Esq. treasurer for the County of Cheshire, aged 46. In the walks of private life and in his public concerns, he displayed all those qualities, which constitute the affectionate friend and useful member of society. [. . .]

In Bristol, by the sting of a bee in the temple, Miss Pierce.—In Worcester, Mrs. Sarah Pierce, æ. 77. She left nine sons and six daughters, all settled in life; and all excepting one daughter, could with ease attend the funeral in seven hours ride. She lived in a married state 57 years; all her sons and three of her daughters attended the funeral. Her grand children and great grand children are very numerous.

In New York, Capt. Christopher Miller. The deaths in New York, from the 8th to the 15th inst. were 11 adults and 43 children of various diseases.

At Baltimore, Miss Maria Skerrett, æ. 20; a young lady of sweet and amiable manners; the *day of her death*, had been but a short time previous fixed on for the *day of her wedding !*—At Northampton, very suddenly, Mrs. Hinckley, aged 44, consort of Samuel Hinckley, Esq. and sister of His Excellency Governor Strong.

In this town, Mr. Jonathan Hall ae. 90. He lived with his wife, who is still alive, 68 years.

In Boston, Mrs. Sarah Davis, aged 79.

Vol. X (No. 492) Tuesday, 6 Sept. 1802. [77]

† [3c-d] Account given by George Dickson, seaman, the solitary survivor of the brig *Mary*, of New York, which ran ashore on an island near Nantucket. The brig was commanded by Capt. Newtus, and was partly owned by a Mr. Penny, Supercargo; both Newtus and Penny drowned. Dickson drifted at sea for four days. ♦

† [3d] Adv. by John Franklin, Clerk of the Connecticut Susquehannah Company, regarding a business meeting to be held on Monday, 6 Sept. "at the Academy at Athens, on Tioga point, Luzerne County." The notice is "[d]ated at Athens, July 1st, 1802." [78]

† [3d] Adv. regarding the purchase of flax-seed at the store of E. Brown, Jr., dated at Westmoreland, 2 Sept. 1802.

===== ¶ [3d] MARRIED. =====

At Marblehead, Mr. Timothy Jones, merchant, of Boston, to Miss Betsy Abrams.

At Roxbury, Capt. Jonathan Dorr to Miss Eliza Smith, daughter of Ralph Smith, Esq.

===== ¶ [3d] DIED. =====

At New-London, Mrs. Jackson, æ. 73. At Lancaster, Penn. George Henry Kepple, Esq. æ. 29, of the *tetanus*.—At Newbury, Rev. Gardner Thurston, Pastor of the Baptist Church in that town.—At Meredith, Maj. Richard Boyington, of the yellow fever which he took at Portsmouth [prob. *Virginia*—Ed.].—At Vergennes, Miss Betsy Young, æ. 15.

In England, Lord Viscount Cullen, æ. 92.—In the West Indies, Rear Admiral Totty.

In Boston, Mr. Jona. Cary, æ. 52, and Mrs. Cary, his wife, æ. 50.

Vol. X (No. 493) Tuesday, 14 Sept. 1802.

† [2c] Brief account of lightning which struck a barn owned by Mr. Harman Van Der Zee, who was injured, and killed a Mr. Zandt; the event occured 26 Aug. 1802 at Coeymans, New York, and the news item is dated at Albany, 30 Aug. 1802.

¶ [2d] An Indian by the name of John [Hewit?] killed a white man of the name of

Harrington, at Buffaloe, Ontario County, N. York, and wounded with his knife two other white men before he was taken.—The Sheriff of Ontario County accompanied by some of the Seneca chiefs, bro't him from the Fort at Niagara, (where he was confined) and lodged him in safety last week in Canadargua Goal. Two years ago this same Indian killed another Indian at Canadargua, named Drunken Joe; but from his powerful strength and activity he escaped from the hand of Justice until now.

† [3d] Extensive account of a duel at Savannah, Georgia, between William Hunter, Esq. and Col. David B. Mitchell, 19 Aug. 1802; Hunter was killed. ♦

† [3d] Joshua Phelps, [Postrider—Ed.] announces that he will "discontinue his route at the last of the present month," and that Mr. Partridge will take his place; dated 13 Sept.

===== ¶ [3d] MARRIED. =====

At Exeter, Rev. William F. Rowland, to Miss Ann Giddings.—At Salem, Mr. John Scobie, mer[chant] to Miss Lydia Maley.—At Portsmouth, Mr. William Clarkson, ae. 55, to Mrs. Matilda Odiorne, ae. 70, after a courtship of 30 days.

Vol. X (No. 494) Tuesday, 21 Sept. 1802.

¶ [3c] APPOINTMENT BY THE PRESIDENT. Dr. Jonathan H. Sparhawk, of this place, to be surgeon's mate to the troops stationed at Fort Wayne, on the Miami.

† [3c] Brief account of the installation of Rev. Hezehiah Packard at Wiscasset, [Maine].

† [3c] Larnard Mann, Clerk of the Seventh New Hampshire Turnpike, announces a business meeting to be held at General Shepard's Tavern, Alstead, N.H.; notice dated at Alstead 13 Sept. 1802.

¶ [3d] Whereas Ruth my wife did on the 7th inst. elope from my bed and board, and clandestinely with the help of others, in my absence, carried away with her securities for money to the amount of one hundred and thirty dollars, and household furniture to a considerable amount. This is therefore to warn all persons against harboring, or trusting her on my account, as I will not pay one cent of her contracting after this date.
Daniel Wheton.
Ludlow, Vt. September 15th, 1802.

† [3d] Ziba Stevens adv. for a lost mare; dated at Claremont 11 Sept. 1802.

† [3d] John Carlisle adv. for two journeymen shoemakers; dated at Walpole 18 Sept.

¶ [3d] Ranaway [sic] from the subscriber, the 15th inst. Calvin Chafee, about twenty years of age; and I hereby forbid all persons from harbouring or trusting said Calvin Chafee on my account, as I will pay no debts of his contracting.
Silas Burk.
Westminster, Sept. 18, 1802.

† [3d] Bankruptcy notice regarding Martin Butterfield of Westmoreland, N.H.

===== ¶ [3c] DIED. =====

At Bermuda, Elizabeth Gillingham, a maiden lady, aged 101 years, 1 month and 5 days. She never took any medicine except herb teas and diet drink, and but little of them.
At Marblehead, Mr. Russell Trevett, ae. 89.—At Chelmsford, Mrs. Mary Stokes, ae. 70.—At Milton, Miss Mary Curtis, ae. 42.—At Middletown, Colonel Matthew Talcott, ae. 89.—At Hartford, Capt. Samuel Marsh, ae. 71.—At Litchfield, Jedadiah Strong, Esq. ae. 64.—At Coventry, Mrs. Phebe Richardson, ae. 69.—At Roxbury, Mr. Thomas Wyman, ae. 74. At Boston, Mr. Henry Davis, ae. 54.—On Monday, August 30th, departed this life, at Hingham, in the 81st year of his age, and the 56th of his Ministry, the Rev. Daniel Shute, D.D. Senior Pastor of the second Church in that town.

Vol. X (No. 495) Tuesday, 28 Sept. 1802.

† [3b-c] Account of a regimental muster held at Walpole, near Capt. Carpenter's Inn, commanded by Col. Caleb Bellows. ♦

† [3d] Legal notice regarding the estate of Samuel Crosby, Esq. late of Charlestown, N.H., deceased. Oliver Hall, William Briggs, and Horace Hall Adminstrators.

† [3d] John Atkinson posts a notice for the stock holders of "the Company for Rendering Connecticut River Navigation by Bellows' falls;" dated at B.F., 24 Sept. 1802.

† [3d] Phillips Sweetser, Clerk of the Board of Directors of the Third N.H. Turnpike, post a notice regarding a business meeting to be held at Wells' Inn, Keene, N.H. Notice dated 16 Sept. 1802.

===== ¶ [3c] DIED. =====

At Salem, on Wednesday the 15th inst. after a long and severe illness, Miss Eunice Richardson—lovely—accomplished—intelligent [. . .]

In this town, Mrs. Hall.

A child of Mr. William Pierce.

Vol. X (No. 496) Tuesday, 5 Oct. 1802.

† [3a] Brief article stating that Rev. Dr. Eliot, D.D., laid the cornerstone of the "New North Meeting House, in this town." ◆

† [3c] Mention-in-passing of a Mrs. Betsey Guest, who was killed by lightning at an unspecified location; the notice was copied from *The Bee*, "of the 21st ult. under its domestic head." The place of publication of the latter paper is not given, but perhaps was the one by that name published at New London, Conn.

† [3d] Announcement that "[a]ll connexion in business between William Page & John Atkinson of New York, at Bellows' Falls" is dissolved; dated at Rockingham 1 Oct. 1802. Included is an adv. of goods for sale by William Page, Jun., Agent for *Bellows' Falls Co.* Whether there was one or two merchants by the name of William Page involved in this adv. is unclear.

† [3d] Legal notice regarding the estate of Hon. Benjamin Bellows, late of Walpole, deceased; Caleb Bellows and Samuel Grant, Administrators; dated at Walpole 4 Oct.

† [3d] Legal notice regarding the estate of Samuel Chase, Esq., late of Cornish, deceased; Mr. March Chase, Executor of said estate. Dated — Sept. 1802.

† [3d] Calvin Chamberlain adv. for a lost horse; dated Westminster, Vt. 28 Sept. 1802.

===== ¶ [3c-d] DIED. =====

In England, the Hon. Isaac Barre, member of the British Parliament; celebrated for the part he took in favour of the American Colonies in 1774, 5, &c. He was blind for several years before his death.

At Acworth, on the 2d inst. Dr. Daniel Grout, in the fortieth year of his age. By this instance most sensibly felt; he has left a widow and orphan, to lament the loss of a tender husband and fond parent, the vicinity that of an able Physician, and Surgeon, and society in general, a worthy citizen.

In this town, Mr. Daniel Whipple.

Vol. X (No. 497) Tuesday, 12 Oct. 1802.

† [2c-d] Article describing the attempted murder of Captain Fuller and family, by their slave who attempted to poison them. This incident occurred in Harman Street, New York City; the victims were dangerously sick but survived. ◆

† [2d] Duel fought 5 Sept. 1802, near Newbern, North Carolina, between Richard Dobbs Spaight, Esq. formerly Governor of that state, and John Stanley, Esq., Senator of the District of Newbern. Spaight died of his wounds. ◆

¶ [3a] Sept. 25. On the 11th inst. Mrs. Martha Bush———,79 of Saybrook, was found drowned in a small brook, where the water was not more than six inchest deep. By what accident is not known.

† [3d] The copartnership of *Bisco & Co.* is dissolved; all outstanding debts to be paid to Daniel W. Bisco; dated Walpole 7 Oct. 1802.

===== ¶ [3d] DIED. =====

At Northampton, on the 2d inst. Mrs. Sally Mills, wife of Mr. Elijah H. Mills, Attorney at Law—and only daughter of the Hon. Ebenezer Hunt, æ. 23.

At Acworth, after thirteen years decriped [sic] and lingering illness, Eliphaz Silsby, aged 43.

In Prussia, Prince Henry, æ. 76, brother of Frederick the Great.

At Charlestown, S.C. Mr. John Wallis. Mr. Michael Makahaly. Mr. Samuel Hart, Printer, from New England.

At Boston, on the 2d inst. Mr. Frederick Gilbert, ae. 36.
At Philad. Gen. Jacob Morgan, ae. 61.
Mrs. Ruth Knox, ae. 52.—Mr. Samuel Watts, ae. 60.—Mr. Caleb Champney, ae. 26.
At Royalton, V. Mr. Ebenr. Herrick.

Vol. X (No. 498) Tuesday, 19 Oct. 1802.

¶ [3a] On Thursday, Ebenezer Mason, was executed at Dedham, for the murder of his brother-in-law, Mr. William Pitt Allen, of Medfield.

† [3d] Legal notice regarding the insolvent estate of Samuel Howe, Jr., late of Westmoreland, N.H., deceased. Nathan Babbit, Job F. Brooks, and William Brittun appointed Commissioners over said estate, and the notice includes a schedule of business meetings to be conducted at the house of Clement Trowbridge, Innholder in Westmoreland. Notice dated at Westmoreland 11 Oct. 1802.

† [3d] Legal notice regarding the estate of Col. Christopher Webber, late of Walpole, deceased; Norman Webber, Administrator; notice dated 15 Oct. 1802. All outstanding debts to said estate were to be paid to Stephen Johnson, Walpole, N.H.

† [3d] Adv. by Joseph Brown, 2d, offering gravestones, hearthstones, etc. for sale. Adv. dated Westmoreland, 14 Oct. 1802.

† [3d] List of letters remaining at the Post Office in Charlestown, N.H., 1 Oct. 1802, as compiled by Frederick A. Sumner, Postmaster:

Abel Parker, Esq.,	Charlestown.	Landlord Parker,	Springfield, Vt.
Mr. John Salisbury,	"	Amos Stone,	" "
Moses Hale,	"	Charles Cowell,	" "
Miss Deidamia Varnum,	"	Jacob Whitcomb,	" "
Jona. Watson,	"	Reuben Bisbee,	Langdon.
Cyrus Perkins,	"	Daniel Barber,	Claremont.
Mr. John Gould,	Springfield, Vt.	Nathl. A. Bowen,	Richmond.
Isaac Smith,	" "	Philip Huntoon,	Unity.

===== ¶ [3d] MARRIED. =====

At Westminster, Vt. William Czar Bradley, Esq. to Miss Sally Richards.

At Worcester, Capt. Thomas Chandler, to Mrs. Eliza Dana, daughter of the late Robert Davis, of Boston. Mr. Joseph Carr, merchant, of Orrington, Maine, to Miss Elmira Barker.

At Albany, Mr. Henry Weaver, to Miss Margaret Ruby [. . .]

===== ¶ [3d] DIED. =====

At Canisteer, Penn. by the bite of a rattlesnake in the leg, James Moore, jun. He died in about 5 hours after he was bitten.

At New Haven on the 9th ult. a son of Mrs. De Witt. He was bitten by a mad dog in June last—no symptoms of the hydrophobia appeared until just before his death—he died in a state of agony not to be described.

Killed at Buckland, the 6th ult. Capt. B. Trow, ae. 39. This accident happened by getting logs down a steep place to his saw mill—he and a brother in law were busily engaged with a log which they had gotten part of the way down the hill, when another started from above; they discovered their danger. Captain Trow attempted to get into the mill for safety, but in crossing some logs he fell, and the log struck on the back part of his head, and crushed it in such a manner, that by the time his brother in law got to him, there was no appearance of life.

Vol. X (No. 499) Tuesday, 26 Oct. 1802.

† [3b] Pirates attempt to capture the American sloop *Astrea*, of New York, Captain Johnson, but the Captain foiled their plan. The event occurred in the vicinity of The Bahamas.◆

† [3d] Polly Whitman adv. for her lost great coat, lost between Charlestown and Walpole. "Whoever finds said coat and will leave the same at the Walpole Bookstore, will oblige a poor girl." Dated 4 Oct. 1802.

¶ [3d] MARRIED.

At Madrid, His Excellency Don Carlos Carracciolo, Ambassador of the King of the Two Sicilies (as proxy of the Hereditary Donna Maria Isabella, Princess of Spain.—At Natchez, Capt. Ferdinand L. Claiborne, late of the United States army, to Miss Magdaline Hutchins, daughter of Col. Hutchins, of the Mississippi Territory. On the day after the marriage Col. H. placed his son-in-law in the lap of ease by giving him a very considerable fortune.

At Windsor, Gen. Caleb Stone, to Miss Abigail Brown, of Worcester, Mass.

¶ [3d] DIED.

In Virginia, Mr. John Ward, sen. in the 104th year of his age. He lived through one Century, and just peeped into two; and was generally a very healthy looking man, till within a few years of his death.

At Georgetown, Maine, John Stinson, Esq. aged 91.—At Bristol, Maine, Capt. James Huston, aged 70.

In Windsor, Mr. Eber West, son of Mr. Gersham West.

On his passage from Boston to Baltimore, Mr. William Dorsey of Maryland.

Vol. X (No. 500) Tuesday, 3 Nov. 1802. [80]

† [1a] Adv. by Charles Sigourney, Jr., "late of Boston," but now a wholesaler of hardware goods at Hartford, Conn.; dated at Hartford 16 Sept. 1802.

† [1c] Adv. by Joseph Brown, 2d, apparently a stonecutter by trade, regarding the sale of gravestones, hearthstones, etc. Dated at Westmoreland, 14 Oct. 1802.

† [1d-2a] Copy of a circular dated at Tripoli [Africa] 9 July 1802, from one William Eaton, regarding the capture of the American brig *Franklin*, Capt. Andrew Morris. The brig was on account to merchants in Philadelphia; the captain and crew were sent to Tripoli.

¶ [3d] On Monday evening the 20th ult. John Williams of Oglethrope [sic] county, (Geo.) his wife and two children, were all found dead with their throats cut from ear to ear. A razor was found in William's hand. From this and other circumstances, the jury gave it as their opinion that the murder was committed by him. (Monitor.

† [3d] Reward offered by Timothy Holton regarding two horses stolen from him. Holton accused Jonathan Little, of Burlington, Vt., age about 23, and a servant boy named Caleb Lewis, age about 17, of the theft. The notice gives a brief physical description of the wanted men. Notice dated at Ellington, Conn., 27 Oct. 1802. ♦

† [3d] Benjamin Carter posts a notice of a missing mare, which strayed or was stolen from a pasture owned by Davis Carpenter, innkeeper at Walpole. Notice dated at Charlestown, 28 Oct. 1802.

† [3d] Probate notice concerning the will of John Temple, "late of the Kingdom of Great Britain, but last a resident of the City of New York, Baronet." The will was presented at the Cheshire County Probate Office.

¶ [3d] DIED.

In Greenfield, a son of Mr. Joel Smith, in the 7th year of his age, and on Thursday, Mrs. Elizabeth Smith, consort of Mr. Joel Smith, in the [42?] year of her age. The son of Mr. Smith, in descending a short hill, fell before the wheel of a cart, which crossed his bowels, and put a period to his existence in about three hours.

In this town, on Sunday morning, after a few days illness, Hon. Thomas Sparhawk, Esq. aged 65 years. He sustained the office of clerk of the court of Common Pleas, for many years in this county, with faithfulness and ability. His general usefulness, and numerous acts of private charity serve better to eulogize his character than columns of newspaper praise, or "sculptured monument or marble bust."

Vol. X (No. 501) Tuesday, 9 Nov. 1802.

† [3a] Account of longevity by a couple named Graham, "now living at Morpeth," [perhaps *England*] the husband is 101 years old, the wife 95. ♦

¶ [3b] DIED.

In this town, Miss Sophia Bellows, daughter of Col. John Bellows, in the 20th year of her age. [. . .]

At Philadelphia, on the 20th of September, in the nineteenth year of her age, Miss Kitty Redman, and on the Saturday following her sister, Miss Elizabeth Redman, in her twenty-first year, daughters of Mr. Jonathan Redman. These lovely sisters fell pray to the ravages of the malignant fever [. . .]

Vol. X (No. 502) Tuesday, 16 Nov. 1802.

¶ [3c] James M'Girk has been executed at the city of Washington persuant to sentence, for the murder of his wife.
† [3d] Legal notice published by Daniel Dwight, "Assignee," regarding the bankrupt estate of Martin Butterfield, trader, of Westmoreland, N.H.

Vol. X (No. 503) Tuesday, 23 Nov. 1802.

† [3a] Account of a fish deposited down the chimney of one Mr. Obed Edson of Richfield, N.Y., during a thunderstorm. ♦
¶ [3b] At the Supreme Court of Ver[mon]t. George Tibbitts and George Whiting [81] were convicted of manslaughter. Peleg Moon and Amos Eldridge of horse stealing. The sentence of the two first is three months imprisonment, and a fine of four hundred dollars each, and five hundred dollars bonds for good behavior for ten years.
† [3b] Account of a well collapse during construction, killing an eleven year-old son of Mr. Lampson, and wounding Mr. Robert Olds. The accident occurred in Poultney, 29 Oct. 1802, and the article was copied from a Vermont newspaper. ♦
† [3c] Adv. that the copartnership of Samuel Grant and Daniel W. Bisco is dissolved by mutual consent. Dated at Walpole 22 Nov. 1802.
† [3d] Adv. by Hugh Henry requesting settlement of debts; dated Acworth 15 Nov.
¶ [3d] TAKE NOTICE. Whereas Lydia, my wife has eloped my bed and board, I hereby forbid all persons harbouring or trusting her on my account, as I shall pay no debts of her contracting after this date.
                                                                                    Theodore Messer.
Lemster, Nov. 9, 1802.

===== ¶ [3b] MARRIED. =====

At Worcester, Mr. D.G. Wheeler, to Miss Eliza Grosvenor.—At Nachez, Ed. Tuvner, Esq. to Miss Mary West.—At Charlestown, Mr. Jotham Johnson, to Miss Susannah Tufts.—At Boston, Mr. William Moore, to Miss Sally M. Rand.—At Haverhill, Mr. Enoch Bradley, jun. to Miss Abigail Hildreth.

===== ¶ [3b-c] DIED. =====

At Haverhill, Mrs. Mary Greenleaf, Æt. 68.—Mrs. Mary Creasy, Æt. 65, and Mrs. Anna Weed. They were all borne together to the grave.—At Halifax, James Clarke, Esq.—At Charlestown, (S.C.) Mrs. Williamson, widow of J.B. Williamson, of the Theatre, and late widow of Mr. Jones, comedian.—At Amherst, Mrs. Thankful Dickinson, Æt. 81.—At Ashby, Mr. Isaac Wyman, Mer., Æt. 34.—At Boston, Mrs. Joanna Smith Bell, Æt. 35.—Mrs. Abigail Amory, Æt. 63.—At Savanna, Mrs. Elizabeth Grafton Seaver, Æt. 24.—Robert Lithgow, Æt. [44?].—At Portsmouth, Dea. Samuel Bowles.—Drowned in the Connecticut river, Mr. Eben Burbank.—At Providence, Mrs. Mehitable Bosworth. Dea. Ephraim Wheaton, Æt.79.
At Rutland, Vt. Mrs. Lucy Webber of this town, æ. 51.
At New Ipswich, Mr. Asa Stratten, of Keene.
At Wiscasset, Joseph Tinkham, ae. 49. Mrs. Elizabeth Wood.—At Northampton, Mr. Samuel Green, ae. 92.—Mr. Joseph Root, ae. 73.—Mr. Timothy Pomroy, æ. 60.—At Lee, (N.H.) Doctor Wigglesworth.

Vol. X (No. 504) Tuesday, 30 Nov. 1802.

† [3a] Account of Mr. Worden, who murdered his own child, at Stonington, Conn. ♦

===== ¶ [3d] MARRIED. =====

At Norwich, Mr. Samuel Whiting, of Albany, editor of the Albany Centinel, to Miss Fanny Leffingwell.

At Portsmouth, Mr. Jostin Washington Street, to Miss Nancy Whidden.

==== ¶ [3d] DIED. ====

Lately, in Prussia, Gen. D'Elsten, Æt.68.—Lieut. Gen. Count de Schwerin, Æt. 83, two of the oldest Generals in the Prussian service.—At Salem, (N.Y.) Rev. James Proudsit, Æt. 71, and 50th year of his ministry.—At Hudson, Mr. Isaac de Forest, Æt.33.—Mrs. Rebecca Powers, Æt. 32.

Vol. X (No. 505) Tuesday, 7 Dec. 1802.

† [3d] Legal notice by Azubah Grout, Admx. for the estate of Doctor Daniel Grout, late of Acworth. Dated 29 Nov. 1802.

¶ [3d] Whereas my wife Sally, has eloped from my bed and board, I hereby forbid all persons harbouring or trusting her on my account, as I will pay no debts of her contracting after this date.

Joseph Steel.

Washington, Nov. 29th, 1802.

==== ¶ [3c] MARRIED. ====

In this town, on Thursday last, by the Rev. Mr. Fessenden, Dr. George Sparhawk, to Miss Polly Allen, eldest daughter of Mr. Aaron Allen.

==== ¶ [3c] DIED. ====

At Keene, Thaddeus [Maccarty?], Esq.—At [Sununty?], G.[82] Samuel Proctor Baillie, Esq. Attorney at Law.—At Savannah, G.[eorgia—Ed.] [M'?]Nicholas Johnson, Printer.—At Botany Bay, the celebrated pickpocket, George Barrington.—At Waterford, N.W.T.[83] Capt. Dean Tyler, formerly of Massachusetts.—Drowned, in Lake Champlain, Edward Sweeney, a native of Ireland, on a visit to his friends in the city of New-York, served in the British army 26 years; and assisted at the battle of Aboukir, in the burial of Gen. Abercrombie; as a certificate from his colonel testified.

Vol. X (No. 506) Tuesday, 14 Dec. 1802.

† [1c] Thomas Moor posts a notice regarding a mare he found; dated Walpole, 4 Dec.

¶ [2c] November 29. On Monday last, a dispute took place on board brig Juliana, at Fell's Point, Baltimore, between John Skinner, an American, and a Spaniard, named Francis Alanzo, when the latter stabbed the former in his left side; the Spaniard was immediately apprehended, and we learn the unfortunate American is in a very dangerous situation.

† [3d] Elisha Kingsbury offers his grist and saw mills for sale; dated Alstead 8 Dec. '02.

Vol. X (No. 507) Tuesday, 21 Dec. 1802.

† [3b] Extensive account of the death of Timothy Hadley, aged about 18, and the serious injury to Charles Ruby, aged 21, both of whom were poisoned by charcoal gas as they slept. Dated at Dunstable, N.H., 13 Dec. 1802. ◆

† [3d] William Page, Jr. offers goods for sale at Bellows Falls, Vt.; adv. dated 16 Dec.

Vol. X (No. 508) Tuesday, 28 Dec. 1802.

† [3c] Petition to the Court of Common Pleas of Cheshire County, by Alexander Watkins, Innholder of Walpole, regarding a road near his house.

† [3d] Probate notice regarding the estate of Hon. Thomas Sparhawk of Walpole.

† [3d] Andrew French, Executor of the estate of Amariah Rockwell, late of Langdon, N.H., posts of legal notice regarding said estate. Dated Walpole, 23 Dec. 1802.

† [3d] Olive Lowell, Admx. for the estate of Samuel Lowell, late of Washington, posts a legal notice regarding said estate. Dated at Washington, 23 Dec. 1802.

† [3d] Legal notice posted by Joanna Willard, Admx. for the estate of Samuel Willard, late of Charlestown, deceased. Dated at Charlestown, 27 Dec. 1802.

† [3d] Legal notice posted by Susannah Harrington, Executrix of the will of Deacon Eli Harrington, late of Alstead, N.H.

Vol. X (No. 509) Tuesday, 4 Jan. 1803.

† [3a] Article contained within the news from Boston describing a hunting accident 11 Dec. 1802 at Abington, Plymouth County, [Mass.—Ed.], whereby Elias Pool was killed by his brother David Pool, and Marlborough Curtis was wounded. Pool was in his 22d year, and left a widow and orphaned child, a mother, and several siblings. ♦

† [3a-b] Extensive article regarding a massive fire at Portsmouth, N.H. in late Dec. 1802, which destroyed about 100 buildings, including many dwellings. The following is a list of "the sufferers." ♦

John Pearse	George Cutts	Enoch Thompson
Nathaniel White	Mrs. Hart	Abel Harris
Stephen Pearse	George Cate	W. and D. Treadwell
William Rice	Peter Pearse	Mrs. Cutts
Samuel Sprague	Neil M'Intire	Mrs. D. Pearse
Rowe and Skeper	Mrs. H. Bowles	James L. Giles
Charles Pierce	Capt. M'Clintock	Samuel Pearse
Samuel Larkin	Cazneau Bayley	Benjamin Brierly
Jacob Walden	N.B. Folsom	George Danie
William Simes	John Frothingham	B. & H. Simes
John Badger	N.S. & W. Peirce	Mrs. Seavy
Mrs. Furniss	"Newhall's estate"	Josiah Dwight
D.R. Rogers	Edward Parry	Richard Evans
Joshua Blake	James Rundlet	Jonathan Goddard
Samuel Haven	Samuel Thompson	Oliver Briard
James Foster	Nath. Dean	Mr. Gordon
Henry Haven	Richard Perry	Judge Pickering
Nathaniel Weare	John Penhallow	Mrs. Nelson
James Henderson	Isaac Smith	John B. Sewall
Jacob Sheafe	Nathan B. Folsom	Peter Pearse, Jr.
Daniel Austin	William Boyd	Daniel Eaton
John Langdon	Mrs. Nutter	Keyron Walsh
——— Coleman	William Hart	Mr. Ball
Mrs. Greenwood	Mary Hardy	H. & D. Penhallow
Mrs. Jenkins	Mr. Hasty	Mr. Beck
Henry Ladd	Mr. Seavy	Eliphalet Ladd
Stephen Little	Jeremiah Libbey	Mr. Rymes
Isaac Stanwood	Ebenezer Chadwick	John Gains
Mr. Noble	Robert M'Cleary	Clement Jackson
William Garland	Benjamin Leverett	Job Harris
Joseph Gavet	John Nelson	Samuel Jones
Benjamin Sweet	William Jones	Mrs. Warner
Theodore Furber	tenant of Mrs. Warner's	Peter Coffin
J. & J. Haven	Custom House	N.A. & J. Haven
John Melcher	Alex. Ewen	Mrs. Winkley
Samuel Hill	Henry Burleigh	Jonathan Clark
Mrs. Simes	J. Shapley	Mr. Nutter
Long & Hamilton	Folsom & Spring	

† [3d] List of letters remaining at the post office, Charlestown, N.H., 1 Jan. 1803, as compiled by Frederick A. Sumner, Postmaster.

Rev. William Farewell, Charlestown, 2
Mrs. Abiah Parker, Claremont, 1
Mrs. Elizabeth Vargason, Claremont, 1
Mr. Jacob Parker, Claremont, 2
Col. Timothy Lovell, Rockingham, 2
Mr. Comfort Wilcox, Lemster, 2
Mr. Israel Danforth, Washington, 1
Mr. Andrew Woodbury, Acworth, 1
Col. Abijah Wheeler, Temple, 1
Mr. Gideon Lee, Worthington, 1
Mr. Nathaniel Hall, Goshen, 1
Mr. Thaddeus Gleason, Charlestown, 1
William Neal, "Charlestown or Unity," 1
Jesse Johnson, Jr., Enfield, 1
Thomas Dana, Springfield, 1
Jesse Lanksford, Springfield, 1

† [3d] Legal notice posted by Lasell Silsby, Executor, and Esther Silsby, Executrix, of the estate of Eliphaz Silsby, late of Acworth, N.H. deceased; dated 27 Dec. 180[2].

¶ [3d] MARRIED.

At Keene, Mr. Joshua Ellis to Miss Rosanna Clark.
In Pennsylvania, Mr. John P. Thomas, editor of the Frederick-Town Herald, to Miss Margaret Holmes.—At Salem, Capt. Nathaniel Silsby, to Miss Mary Crowninshield.

¶ [3d] DIED.

At Cape Francois, Nov. 3, General Le Clerc, Commander in Chief of the French forces there, and brother-in-law to Bonaparte.
At Berbice, Capt. B. Williams of Portland.—At Springfield, suddenly, Mr. Lemuel Newell, Æt. 39.

Vol. X (No. 510) Tuesday, 11 Jan. 1803.

† [3b-c] A bill of mortality for the town of Northampton, Mass., giving a breakdown of deaths in each month of the year 1802, and grouped by age at death. ♦
¶ [3c] Concord, N.H., Dec. 30. *Post Office at Salisbury.* We are informed that Thomas Thompson, Esq. is dismissed as Postmaster at Salisbury, for being a Federal Republican; and Moses Eastman, who lives on another road, is appointed in his stead.
† [3b] Extensive article regarding the death of John Pingry, aged about 20, son of Mr. William Pingry of Bridgewater, N.H. Pingry and his helper, Abner Emmons, were caught in an accident involving a collapsed banking at Bridgewater. [14 Dec. 1802]. ♦
† [3d] Amasa Allen adv. to purchase a large quantity of shingles; dated Walpole 7 Jan.
† [3d] Legal notice posted by Allen Willey, Adm. to the estate of Barnabas Phelps, of Goshen, deceased. Dated at Goshen 25 Dec. 1802.
† [3d] List of letters remaining at the Post Office at Westminster, Vt., 1 Jan. 1803, as compiled by Eleazer May, Postmaster:

Silas Briggs, Westminster.	Aaron Taft, Townsend.
Doct. Edward R. Campbell, Westminster	Joseph Wiswall, Westminster.
John Cole, Jamaica.	John Putnam, Grafton.
Nathaniel Adams, Dummerston.	Josiah Gates, Westminster.

¶ [3d] MARRIED.

At Charlestown, Massachusetts, Mr. Joseph Bellows, jun. of this town, merchant, to Miss Mary Adams, daughter of the late Rev. Zabdiel Adams, of Lunenburg.

¶ [3d] DIED.

At Portsmouth, N.H. Mr. Thomas Simes æ. 42.—Deacon Samuel Bowles.—At Hopkinton, Mr. Edward Northey, Mr. Nehemiah Colby.
From a Savannah paper of Dec. 21.
Died, on Thursday, the 16th inst. at the house of Mr. S. Howard, merchant, in this city, of a pulmonary affection, the Rev. Peter Thacher, D.D. Pastor of the independent Church and Congregation, assembling in Brattle-street in the Town of Boston. His death being announced, the vessels in the harbour exhibiting from their masts their usual signal of grief, united with the city in expressing respect and sorrow for departed worth. [84]

Vol. X (No. 511) Tuesday, 18 Jan. 1803.

† [3c] Brief account of a fire which destroyed the shops of Messrs. Smith & Co., Shipwrights, Mr. Pratt, Joiner, and Mr. Clark, Cooper. The fire occurred "in this town ... on Leach's, late Lyman's wharf." Presumably, this event occurred in Boston, Mass.
† [3c] Fire destroyed the store occupied by Mr. Royal Craft, or Crast, [85] at Schagitcoke point; article dated at Troy [N.Y.—Ed.] 13 Jan. 1803. ♦
† [3d] Legal notice posted by Joel Doolittle, Adm. of the estate of John Doolittle, Esq., late of Westmoreland, deceased; dated there 18 Jan. 1803.
† [3d] Legal notice posted by Oliver Hall, William Briggs, and Horace Hall, Administrators of the estate of Samuel Crosby, Esq., late of Charlestown, deceased.
† [3d] Moses W. Hastings found a stray horse; adv. dated Charlestown, 7 Jan. 1803.

Vol. X (No. 512) Tuesday, 25 Jan. 1803.

† [2d] Account from a group of men who nearly died from thirst and starvation on a voyage, having been driven off an island, perhaps in the Caribbean. The group included Theophilus Bailey, Hadock Hunt, William Bradley, William Roberts, and David King; they belonged to the "fishing smack Greyhound, of New London," which safely arrived in New York. ♦

† [2d] Article dated at Boston, Mass., describing the death of Josiah Winslow, 25, and ——— Hayward, 19, at Easton, Bristol County, Mass. The two men died 17 or 18 Dec. 1802, having suffocated in their bedroom by asphyxiation from charcoal gas. ♦

† [3a-b] Account of a fire at Boston, displacing many persons, including Mr. Bowen, Mr. Doyle, widow Pollard, Mr. Bumstead, Othello Pollard, Mr. Elijah Loring, and Mrs. Burditt. ♦

† [3b] Account of a fire, probably at Charlestown, Mass., affecting Josiah Batchelder, Esq. of Chelsea, Mr. John Hooten, Mr. Libbey, Mrs. Edwards, Mr. Hayden, and Mr. Hall. ♦

¶ [3c] *MELANCHOLY ACCIDENTS.* On the night of the 16th ult. the Greenwich packet boat up[set] in the Delaware, in a violent gale of wind, and Isaac Wheaton, Esq. of Cumberland county, (N.J.) his daughter, a Miss Schillinger, a young lady of Philadelphia, and a young man, were all unfortunately drowned. Mr. Wheaton had been to Philadelphia to purchase wedding clothes for his daughter, who was soon to be married.

¶ [3c] *Woodstock, Jan. 10.* On the evening of Friday the 7th inst. Master Abner Cobb, about five years of age, was found in a lot, mortally wounded on the head—he expired in about 2 hours after he was discover by the family—A sheep which was in the lot, was in the morning discovered to have on its horns and wool marks of blood, and is thought was the destroyer of the child.

† [3d] Extensive account of a miser, Mr. John Little, aged 48, who died recently at Kentishtown, England. ♦

† [3d] Adv. by *T.& I. Redington,* who have various items for sale; dated 25 Jan. 1803. ♦

† [3d] Nathan Bundy, Jr., adv. a stray steer which he found; dated Walpole 24 Jan. '03.

===== ¶ [3d] **MARRIED.** =====

In Claremont, Jude Mills D'Forest, Esq. of Lemington, (Vt.) to miss [sic] Hannah Hitchcock of the former place.—In Windsor, Mr. Seth Silsbury, of Roxbury, Mass. to Miss Betsey Cady of the former place.—In Keene, Mr. William Esty, to Miss Sally Blake.

===== ¶ [3d] **DIED.** =====

At Bolton, of a paralytic shock, Rev. Phineas Wright, aged 50, 18th year of his ministry.—At Newington, N.H. Col. Ephraim Pickering, aged 60.—At Weston, of the Hydrophobia, Mr. John Hobbs, aged 32.—At Sagamore Creek, near Portsmouth, Mr. Benjamin Lear, aged 82. For more than 20 years he lived in a hut, which scarcely anyone would have deemed decent for a barn. [86]—At Philadelphia, Chamless Wharton, of the Society of Friends.—At Medford, Mr. Asa Mason, father of the unfortunate Ebenezer Mason, who was lately executed at Dedham.—At Williamsburg, the [?] inst. Rev. Joseph Strong, in the 74th year of his age, and 51st of his ministry.

At Roxbury, Mrs. Mary Warren, aged 90.—At Boston, Mrs. Christen Andrews, aged 56.—At Worcester, Miss Nancy Leonard Paine, eldest daughter of the Honorable Judge Paine, aged 16.

Died, "at Chester, in Saybrook, (Con.) on the 24th ult. the wife of Mr. John Buckingham, late Innholder there, in the 60th year of her age.—The manner of her death, was to the utmost degree distressing and calamitous.—After being left in her house for a few moments, by her husband, she was heard to cry out—he immediately entered the kitchen, where she had been trying some tallow, and found her standing with her clothes in flames, and the greatest part of them consumed, and her body consequently universally seared.—She appeared then in the full strength of her reason, but could not tell how her clothes were caught by the fire.—In defiance of medical aid, she expired in about four hours during which time she suffered in great distress."

Vol. X (No. 513) Tuesday, 1 Feb. 1803.

¶ [3a] A Duel was fought at Leghorn, [Italy—Ed.] on the 16th of October last, between capt. M'Knight and lieut. Lawson, of the U. States ship Chesapeake, which proved fatal to the former the first fire.

† [3a-b] Extract from a letter dated aboard the U.S. frigate Constellation off Leghorn, [Italy—Ed.], 16 Oct. 1802, describing a sunken boat which belonged to the schooner Enterprise. Mr. Ennis, midshipman, and three other unnamed men drowned. ♦

† [3d] Brief description of a daily newspaper proposed to be published at Charleston, S.C., by Mr. Loring Andrews, "late of Albany."

† [3d] Brief account of a fire which destroyed Col. Huntley's barn at Marlow, N.H.

† [3d] List of nonresident landowners in Charlestown, N.H., who have delinquent taxes for the year 1801; consult this issue for a breakdown of lot number, acreage, etc. The list was compiled by Jonathan Grout, Collector. Those marked with an asterisk (*) have more than one parcel of land identified in the list. [87]

Samuel Hunt *	Moses Wheeler	Samuel Stevens
Moses Wheeler *	Hunt & Weatherbe	William Heywood
Lemuel Hastings *	Peter Labree	John Spafford
Capt. Weatherbe's heirs	Simon Stevens	Seth Walker

===== ¶ [3d] DIED. =====

In this town, Mr. Antipas Harrington, aged 55.—At Newyork, Frances [sic] Lewis, Esq. aged 90.—At Portsmouth, Mrs. Hannah Shores.—In Boston, Mr. Peter Vose, aged 26.

Vol. X (No. 514) Tuesday, 8 Feb. 1803.

¶ [1c] Carlisle, Pennsylvania, Dec. 29. *A Singular Narrative.* A letter dated Canonsburgh, 3d Dec. 1802, written by Samuel Gordon, and directed to Joseph Hays, of this town, contains the following very remarkable circumstances. The facts are stated precisely as we have received them, and the account is corroborated by another letter, received by another gentleman of this town, on the same subject.

The Rev. John Watson, (who had presided over the academy at Canonsburgh, in Washington county) and the Rev. John Moorehead, were married (by Rev. Mr. Marquis) to two daughters of the Rev. John M'Millin, on the same day. Each of those gentlemen had a child born to him on the same day.—They both laboured for a considerable time under a consumptive complaint, both died on the same day, (viz. 1st Dec. 1802) and were both interred on the same day, and in the same grave. And the same minister who married them delivered a very affecting sermon on the occasion.

† [3b] Poem written for a couple, Mr. Seth Paddleford and Miss Patience Moulton, daughter of Mr. Job Moulton, who were recently married. The marriage notice and poem were copied from "a late Peacham paper."

¶ [3c] MARRIED.] At Westmoreland, Mr. John Prentiss, of Keene, to Miss Diantha Aldrich, of the former place.—At Hartford, Mr. Henry Hall Merchant,[88] to Miss Jerusha Kilborn.

¶ [3c] DIED.] At Charlestown, very suddenly, Col. Samuel Heywood, æ. 71.—At Keene, Mrs. Rebecca Ellis, æ. 30.

Vol. X (No. 515) Tuesday, 15 Feb. 1803.

† [1a] Larnard Mann, Proprietor's Clerk, posts a notice regarding a meeting of the Seventh N.H. Turnpike Corporation, to be held at Gen. Shepard's Tavern in Alstead.

† [1c] Nathaniel Sikes and Orange Graves request settlement of debts; dated Walpole 2 Feb. 1803.

† [3d] Samuel Whittle advertises for journeymen wheelwrights under his employ; dated at Walpole, 14 Feb.

Vol. X (No. 516) Tuesday, 22 Feb. 1803.

¶ [3d] DIED.]—At New-Ipswich, Dr. John Preston.—In this town, Harry Bellows, oldest son of Mr. J. Bellows, jun. aged 8.
† [3d] Adv. by *Shepard & Hutchinson*, who offer goods for sale; dated Alstead 10 Feb.
† [3d] *Johnson & Orr* offer goods for sale at their store in Walpole.

Vol. X (No. 517) Tuesday, 1 March 1803.

¶ [3c] MARRIED.—On Wednesday evening last, by the Rev. Thomas Fessenden, Dr. David Taylor of Charlestown, to Miss Mary Redington, of this town.

Vol. X (No. 518) Tuesday, 8 March 1803.

¶ [3d] MARRIED.—At Cornish, the Rev. Joseph Rowell to the amiable Miss Hannah Chase.
† [3d] *Bellows & Stone* offer stone lime for sale at their Walpole store.
† [4d] Bill of mortality for the town of Portsmouth, N.H., as compiled by Lyman Spalding, M.D. The list is categorized by cause / number of deaths.

Vol. X (No. 519) Tuesday, 15 March 1803.

† [3d] Account of the trial regarding the murder of Bernard Mahon, a drunken Irishman, by William Rhoads, "keeper of a tavern on the Lancaster road." The article was copied from another paper, probably from Philadelphia. ♦
† [3d] William Briggs, Attorney, posts a legal notice regarding the estate of William Heywood, Esq. late of Charlestown, deceased.
† [3d] William Henry, Jr. offers farms for sale or lease at Charlestown, N.H.
===== ¶ [3d] MARRIED. =====
At Newburyport, Robert Duning, Esq. to Miss Mary O'Brien.
At Boston, Mr. Solomon Eddy, to Miss Mary Vose.
At Baltimore, Mr. Wm. H. Sewall, to Miss Rebecca B. Lewis.
===== ¶ [3d] DIED. =====
At Natchez, James Campbell, Esq. Attorney at Law.—At Philadelphia, Mr. Robert W. Morgan.—At Middlebury, Vt. Miss Thuril Goodrich, æ. 20.—At Northampton, Mrs. Jemima Gere æ. 23.—At Portsmouth, Mrs. Mary Dillon, æ. 72.

Vol. X (No. 520) Tuesday, 22 March 1803.

† [2d] Account of a duel between Mr. Chapman, of Alexandria, and Mr. Breckenridge from Kentucky. Chapman's wound was apparently mortal. This letter was dated Wilmington, N.C., 16 Feb., and was contained under the New York news.
¶ [3b] MELANCHOLY EVENT. A gentleman from Eastport, Maine, informs us, that on the 24th ult. the house of Mr. Joseph Prince, a respectable merchant, (lately of Newburyport) took fire while the family were asleep, and in a few minutes was entirely consumed with its contents. Mr. Prince, and a son and daughter perished in the fire. He lost his life in attempting to save his children.
¶ [3d] MARRIED—In this town, Mr. Nathaniel Smith to Miss Speedy Goodell.
† [3d] Joseph Dorothy offers a farm for sale at Alstead; adv. dated 15 March.
† [3d] William Weed, Adm., posts a legal notice regarding the estate of David Weed, late of Unity, N.H., deceased.
† [3d] Polly Harwood, Admx., posts a legal notice regarding the estate of James Harwood, late of Unity, N.H., deceased.

Vol. X (No. 521) Tuesday, 29 March 1803.

† [2c-d] An extensive list of Acts passed by the Seventh U.S. Congress; a few of these Acts were passed "for the relief" of specific individuals: Charles Hyde (#1), Henry Messennier (#3), Moses White (#12), and Joshua Harvey (#30).

¶ [3b] The name of *Thomas Paine*, attorney at law in this town, has been altered to *Robert Treat Paine*, by an act of the General Court.

† [3b] Copy of an elopement notice from a Kentucky newspaper, whereby Mary M'Dougle, wife of John M'Dougle, ran away from her husband. Mrs. M'Dougle "went off with Col. Matthew Lyon, who was a member of the last general assembly, from the county of Livingston." Lyon was stated to have been "the celebrated patriot of Vermont." However, a notation made by the editor of the *Farmer's Museum* gives doubt to the identity of the man who called himself Lyon. 89 ♦

† [3d] Caleb T. Barrows offers various items for sale; dated Westmoreland, 24 March.

===== ¶ [3d] MARRIED. =====

At Philadelphia, General William M'Pherson, to Miss Elizabeth White, daughter of Bishop White.
At Boston, Mr. Samuel Waters, to Miss Betsey Eunson.
At Newcastle, Capt. George Kimball, to Miss Lucretia Amazeen.
At New-York, Mr. Mathew Campbell to Miss C. M'Donald.

===== ¶ [3d] DIED. =====

At Bamberg, some time since, Philip Mark, Esq. Consul from the U. States.—At New-Salem, Mrs. Priscilla Foster, consort of the Rev. Joel Foster.—At New York, Mrs. Sarah Bayley.—At Rutland, Vt. Mrs. Mary Bootman, æ. 26.—At Middlebury, Miss Nancy Tuttle, daughter of Mr. Samuel Tuttle, of Monkton.

Vol. X (No. 522) Tuesday, 5 April 1803.

† [3d] David Carter, Proprietor's Clerk, posts a notice regarding a meeting of the Third N.H. Turnpike to be held at the house of Phillip Sweetser, Innholder, in Marlborough. Also a notice posted by Daniel Newcomb, Treasurer of same.

Vol. X (No. 523) Tuesday, 12 April 1803.

† [3b] Extensive account of the robbery of Miss Esther M'Dowell, only child of Dr. John M'Dowell of Kentucky, formerly of Montreal. The robbery was committed by Benjamin Connet, age 22; the article gives a physical description of Connet. 90 ♦

† [3d] Thomas Drew, John Flint, and Levi Allen appointed Commissioners for the insolvent estate of Daniel Whipple, late of Walpole, deceased. This legal notice was dated at Walpole 9 April 1802 [sic].

† [3d] Allen Willey, Adm., posts a legal notice regarding the estate of Barnabas Phelps, late of Goshen, N.H., deceased; dated at Goshen 4 April 1803.

† [3d] William Story, Adm., posts a legal notice regarding the estate of Isaac Weatherby, late of Goshen, N.H., deceased; dated at Goshen 5 April 1803.

† [3d] Legal notice posted by Thankful Fields, Admx. for the estate of Dr. Thomas Fields, late of Claremont, deceased. Notice dated at Newport, 5 April 1803.

† [3d] List of letters remaining at the Post Office at Charlestown, N.H., 1 April 1803, as compiled by F.A. Sumner, Postmaster:

Samuel West, Esq., Charlestown, N.H.
Rev. William Farewell, " "
Mr. William Rhoads, " "
Mr. Joseph Willson, " "
Nath. & Moses Wills, " "
Mr. John Wallace, Acworth, N.H.
Mr. T. Mitchell, " "
Mr. Andrew Grout, " "
Capt. Joseph Gregg, " "
Mr. Nathan Cass, Richmond, N.H.

Mr. Ezekiel Dunbar, New Grantham, N.H.
Elijah Frink, Esq., Lempster, N.H.
Mr. Jonathan Sawyer, Enfield, N.H.
Mr. David Seymour, Springfield, Vt.
Col. John Barrett, " "
Mr. James Whipple, " "
Mr. Joseph Ellis, " "
Mr. Peris Whitcombe, " "
Mr. John Ellison, Chester, Vt.

===== ¶ [3d] MARRIED. =====

At Alstead on the 5th inst. Mr. John Wait to Miss Amy Stone.—At Acworth, Mr. Silsby Stephens to Mrs. Abigail Weatherby.—Mr. Lewis Brigham to Mrs. Susannah Hayward.

====== ¶ [3d] DIED. ======
At Newport, Mrs. Abigail Green.—At Newton, [22?] ult. Mr. Oliver Monrowe.

Vol. X (No. 524) Tuesday, 19 April 1803.

¶ [3a] The nototious George White, known to almost all the prison keepers and thief-takers in the United States, and whom bolts and bars have been but slight obstruction to his escape from prisons and castles, has been apprehended, and is now confined in Taunton goal. He is the ringleader of a gang of thieves; which is now broken up.

† [3a-b] Mrs. Wright, of Stoddard, N.H., in a fit of depression, murdered her youngest child, and attempted murder on two others, 17 March 1803. The article was dated at Amherst, N.H., 31 March. ♦

¶ [3d] RAN AWAY from the subscriber, the 11th inst. Aaron Bennett, about nineteen years old. I hereby forbid all persons from harbouring or trusting said Aaron Bennett on my account as I will pay no debts of his contracting.

STEPHEN BENNETT.

Alstead, April 11, 1803.

Vol. X (No. 525) Tuesday, 26 April 1803.

¶ [3b] A general Court-Martial will be held this day, at Cambridge, for the trial of Lt. Col. Willington, for disobedience of orders, at the parade in Waltham, the last autumn.[91]

† [3d] Obituary of Emily Spencer, "the Venus of England," who died there Æt.36. ♦

Vol. X (No. 526) Tuesday, 3 May 1803.

¶ [3c] Hanover, N.H., April 23. SUICIDE. We hear from Lebanon, that on Saturday last Mrs. Hinckley, wife of Lt. Hinckley of Lebanon, put an end to her existence by hanging—She was found in the chamber suspended by a skein of yarn. We understand that Mrs. Hinckley has been insane for several months past. A rational Mind would not likely commit suicide. Many relatives and friends now mourn that a godly woman has thus ended her life.

¶ [3d] ONE CENT REWARD ! Ranaway from the subscriber, on the Nineteenth of April instant, an indented boy, named Seth Watson, about eighteen years old. Whoever will take up said run-away and return him, shall receive the above reward, but no charges paid. All persons are forbid harbouring said indented boy as they would avoid the penalties of the Law.

BILL BARNES.

Claremont, April 20th, 1803.

Vol. XI (No. 527) Tuesday, 10 May 1803.

====== ¶ [3d] MARRIED. ======

At Alstead, a few days since, Mr. Joseph Farnsworth, merchant, to Miss Patty Shepard.—Dr. Eber Carpenter to Miss Judith Greene.—At Langdon Mr. Asa Carleton to Miss Dorcas Perry.—At Charlestown Mr. Gideon Kidder of Weathersfield, (Vermont) to Miss Fanny Hubbard of the former place.

====== ¶ [3d] DIED. ======

At Alstead, very suddenly, Miss Perses Hatch, daughter of Mr. Phinehas Hatch in the sixteenth year of her age.—At Langdon, Miss Lucinda Prouty aged sixteen years.

Vol. XI (No. 528) Tuesday, 17 May 1803.

† [3b] Article describing the unusual death of Col. Alpheus Moore, aged 38, who died 26 April 1803 at Andover, N.H., on a journey from Peacham, Vt. to Boston. ♦

† [3b] Article dated at Amherst, N.H., describing the remarkable longevity of Mr. Ephraim Pratt, who was born in Sudbury, Mass., of European parents, and who is alive and well, living at Shutesbury, Hampshire County, Mass., aged 117 years. ♦

† [3b] A barn belonging to Mr. I. Shepard is burned at Portsmouth, N.H. ♦
† [3d] Israel Greenleaf adv. a mare which he found; dated Langdon, 10 May 1803.
¶ [3d] **One Cent Reward.** Ran away from me the subscriber a lad of about seventeen years old, by the name of Joseph Burk. Whoever will bring back said boy shall have the above reward and no charges paid; all persons are forbid harbouring or trusting him on my account.

ASA AVRILL.
Westminster, V. May 9, 1803.

===== ¶ [3d] MARRIED. =====

At Hanover, Doct. Joseph Roby, of (N.H.) to Miss Relief Curtis, of Sudbury, (Mass.)—At Vergennes, Robert Bostwith, Esq. to Miss Sybil Geer.—Eleazer W. Keyes, Esq. of St. Albans, to Miss Pamela Allen, daughter of the late Gen. Ethan Allen.—At Chester, Vt. Mr. Levi Bigelow, of Putney, to Miss Nancy Goodhue.—At Thetford, J.H. Palmer, Esq. to Miss Lydia Lomis.—At Northampton, Mr. William Shelden to Miss Sally Holt.

In this town, on Sunday last, by the Rev. Thomas Fessenden, Mr. Levi Brown to Miss Elizabeth Temple.—Mr. David Mead to Miss Esther Bundy.—Mr. Jacob Lock to Miss Polly Muzzy.

===== ¶ [3d] DIED. =====

At Natchez, Mr. Thomas Thursby, mer.—In New Jersey, Isaac Pennington, Esq.—In New York state, Hon. Issac Bloom - chosen lately a member of the 8th Congress.—At Augusta, Mrs. Sarah Whitwell, Æt. 29, wife of Benjamin Whitwell, Esq. of that place, and daughter to the late Judge Sprague, of Lancaster.—At Southampton, the 29th ult. Mrs. Katharine Edwards, relict of the late Dea. Samuel Edwards, Æt. 80 years and three days.—At Northampton, on Thursday last, Mr. Bela Strong, Æt. 83.—On Friday last, Mr. Oliver Parsons, Æt. 43.—At Watertown, on Thursday last, William Hunt, jun. Esq. eldest son of William Hunt, Esq. and Aid-de-camp to Major General Hull, Æt. 24.

Vol. XI (No. 529) Tuesday, 24 May 1803.

† [2d] Article describing the murder of Dr. James Hopkins of Virginia, supposedly by one Lewis M'Queen, a Scotsman. ♦
† [3b] Several sentences issued by the Superior Court of N.H., at Hopkinton: Samuel Clark, George Little, Jacob Hadley, David Pettee, and Jonathan Dow convicted of passing counterfeit bills; Jonathan Eaton, Ephraim Harrington, and John Trask alias John Putnam convicted of horse stealing. ♦
† [3d] Alexander Morrison listed as the solitary nonresident of Wendell, N.H., who had not paid his taxes for the year 1802. In a second notice, Morrison and another tax delinquent, William Ham, are listed for the year 1801; notices posted by John Chase, Collector.
† [3d] Adv. by Joseph Bellows, Jr., offering goods for sale; Walpole, 23 May 1803.

===== ¶ [3d] MARRIED. =====

At Haverhill, (N.H.) James Elliot Esq. of Brattleboro', Vt. to Miss Lucy Dow, of the former place.—At Windsor, Vt. Mr. Alpheus Dunham, of Boston, to Miss Grace Learned, late of New London, Conn.

===== ¶ [3d] DIED. =====

On the Spanish shore, near Natchez, [92] Dr. James Wier, killed in a duel with a Mr. Sargent, of Natchez.—In the Chickesaw Country, the Chief Wolf's Friend, by shooting himself, in a fit of remorse, for having killed a young Indian in a drunken frolick.—At Haddam, on the 14th ult. the Rev. Eleazer May, in the 71st year of his age & 46th of his ministry.

Vol. XI (No. 530) Tuesday, 31 May 1803.

† [2a] Detailed account of the agonizing death of Joseph Gundy, a young man who burned in the explosion of a distillery at Harrisburg, Penn. ♦
† [2c] Extensive article regarding the death of several members of a family fatally burned, the only survivor being Rev. Asa Dunham. The accident occurred at Sha-

mokin, Northumberland County, Penn. ♦
† [3d] Rebeckah Cheney and William Cheney, administrators, post a legal notice regarding the estate of William Cheney, late of Alstead, N.H., deceased; dated 20 May.

===== ¶ [3c-d] MARRIED. =====

At Northampton, Richard E. Newcomb, Esq. of Greenfield, to Mrs. Mary Lyman, youngest daughter to the late Gen. Warren.—At Brookline, by the Rev. Mr. Pierce, Mr. Thomas White, to Miss Rachel Thayer, both of that place.

In this town, on Sunday last, by the Rev. Mr. Fessenden, Mr. Elisha Hooper to Miss Jemima Ormsby.

===== ¶ [3d] DIED. =====

At Detroit, on the [14?]th instant, John F. Hamtramck, Esq. Colonel of the 1st Regiment, in the army of the United States. He was a native of Canada, joined the American Army in 1775, and continued in that service nearly twenty seven years—as a Disciplinarian he was exemplary—As a Gentleman and an officer highly respectable.— Having merited the approbation of General Washington, he received from him the most honourable testimonials.—At Dedham, on the 17th inst. the Rev. Jason Haven, Pastor of the first Church in that town, in the 71st year of his age, and 48th of his ministry.— At Porte de la Ville, (South America) in Oct. last, Mr. Joseph Babcock, jun. of Milton, Æt. 23. - mate of the ship Traveller.—At Savannah, Rev. Mr. Ustic, pastor of the Baptist Church.—At Berlin, C. Miss Sybil Shepherd, Æ 91.—Canterbury, Capt. U. Borwell, Æ 59.—At Gloucester, Mr. Moses Allen, merchant, Æt. 25 - a man highly esteemed by all who knew him.—At Cambridge, Mr. Joseph Perry Æ. [29?].—At Malta, Mr. Cochran, an English gentleman, killed in a duel, by Mr. Bainbridge, a midshipman of the United States frigate New York.—At Curracoa, March 14, Benjamin H. Phillips, Esq. Consul for the United States to that Island.—At Wilmington, N.C. Mr. Matthew Johnson, grocer. —The verdict of the jury was, that his death was occasioned by a wound in the side, with a pen-knife, which was inflicted the evening before by his wife Unity.

DROWNED.] At Exeter, Mr. Joseph Flood; the verdict of the Jury was accidental death.

—Near Hartford, drowned by the upset of a pleasure-boat, Mr. John Foote, a respectable merchant, and Capt. John Watson.

Vol. XI (No. 531) Tuesday, 7 June 1803.

† [2c-d] Account of the capture and escape of outlaws Sam Mason and his sons, in Louisiana. ♦

¶ [3b] Springfield, May 31. SUICIDE. Mr. William Hancock of Enfield, [93] put an end to his existence on Saturday last, by cutting his throat with a razor. This unfortunate man has left a wife and eight children.

† [3d] Adv. by Noble Orr, Secretary, regarding the festival of St. John the Baptist, to be celebrated at the house of brother Alexander Watkins; dated at Alstead, 30 May 1803.

† [3d] Notice posted by Moses Hale, Sealer of Weights and Measures for Cheshire County, regarding Standards for the county; dated at Alstead 30 May 1803.

Vol. XI (No. 532) Tuesday, 14 June 1803.

† [2b] Capt. Herod, while at work in his field, was shot and scapled by Indians, in or near Chilicothe, Ohio, 20 May 1803. ♦

† [3b] Brief notice of a fire which consumed Mr. Lovering's Soap & Candle manufactory, "in Bennet-street," [presumably *Boston, 8 June*—Ed.]

† [3c] Description of spinning houses for linen, operated by Messrs Zebina and Thomas Stebbins, at Springfield, [Mass.—Ed.] ♦

† [3c] Brief item describing the robbery of Nathaniel F. Fosick, of Portland, whose desk was stolen. ♦

† [3d] Mr. Bisco's house at Walpole was damaged by fire. ♦

¶ [3d] DIED.] In this town, on Saturday evening last, Mrs. ——— Carpenter, consort of Capt. Davis Carpenter of this place.

† [3d] Willard Butterfield, Adm., posts a legal notice regarding the estate of Maj. Isaac Butterfield, late of Westmoreland, deceased. Adv. dated there, 1 June 1803.

† [3d] Amos Phillips found a stray mare; dated Walpole, 11 June.
† [3d] Legal notice concerning Azubah Grout, guardian of Nancy Grout, a minor, in regards for a request of Acworth, N.H. property to be sold for the support of Nancy.

Vol. XI (No. 533) Tuesday, 21 June 1803.

¶ [3a] The dwelling house of Mr. Jero. Scripture, in Alford, [94] was destroyed by fire the 25th ult.

¶ [3a] Harris Ramson, has been tried before the Supreme Court, at Portland, and convicted of swindling, in having pretended to have discovered a rich silver mine in Freeport, and thereby defrauding several persons of considerable sums of money, and has been sentenced to be pilloried, imprisoned six months, and fined.

¶ [3c] ACCIDENTS. We learn that Mr. James Ide, of Putney the other day was thrown from his horse and Broke his leg. The bone is said to have penetrated through his stocking and boot, and stuck into the ground two or three inches, and broke off. The lower part of the leg was fractured in many pieces. On Sunday last, after consultation, it was concluded to amputate it, and it was taken off by Dr. Goodhue, a little below the calf.—A similar accident we learn took place a few days since in Rockingham. A Mr. Roundy had a tree fall on his leg in such a manner as to break it, and it is thought it will likewise be amputated.

† [3d] Cady Parks adv. to hire two shoemakers; dated at Bellows Falls, 16 June 1803.
† [3d] John H. Wires adv. for a mare which he found; dated at Walpole, 16 June 1803.

===== ¶ [3c] MARRIED. =====

At Northampton, R.E. Newcomb, Esq. of Greenfield, to Mrs. Mary Lyman.—At Washington, Lt. James Thompson, of the Marines, to Miss Burrows, daughter to Colonel Burroughs.—At Wells, (Maine,) Mr. Jonathan Harding, to Miss Persis Stevens.—At Salem, Mr. Edward Stanley, to Miss Esther Waters.—Mr. John Patterson, to Miss Susannah Eulen.—At Natick, Dr. Uriah Hagar, of Waltham, to Miss Jane Atkins, daughter of Capt. John Atkins, of the former place.—At Boston, Mr. Edmund Tileston, of Dorchester, to Miss Nancy Minns, of Boston.—At West Springfield, Mr. Alford Flower, to Miss Harriot Leonard.

===== ¶ [3c] DIED. =====

At New Boston, Rev. Solomon Moor, Æt. 67, in the 30th of his Ministry.—At Middlebury, Mr. Alexander Osborn, Æt. 60.—At Cornish, Dr. Josiah Goodrich, of Thetford, Vt. aged 30.—At Belville, near Nashville, Capt. Edward Butler, of the 2d regiment of Infantry in the army of the United States.—At West Hampton, Mr. Thomas Elwell, Æt. 50.—Northampton, Mrs. J. Lyman, wife of Gen. Wm. Lyman.—At Greenfield, Mass. Mr. William Wells, Æt. 22.—At Williamsburgh, Deacon Joseph Carey, Æ. 81.—At Milton, Mr. Stephen Bradley, Æt. 33.—England, Mr. William [Forlar?], a Master in the British Navy 40 years. He was master of the Formidable, in Admiral Kepple's engagement; and in 1778, he boasted a title which one of the greatest men of the age would make almost any sacrifice to obtain - he was master of the Ocean.—At Boston, Mrs. Hannah Breed, consort of Mr. William Breed.—Major John Rice, in the 50th year of his age.—Capt. William Downe, aged 48.—At Westford, V. within 10 days of each other, three brothers of the name of Woodruff, all of whom left families.—At Grenada, Mather Byles, aged 39; grandson of the late Rev. Dr. Byles, of Boston, and eldest son of the Rev. Dr. Mather Byles, of N.B.—At Waterford, Richard Wetmore aged 54.—At Canterbury, (Con.) Mr. Moses Bradford, son of John Bradford, aged 22.—Nearly six hundred persons were in the funeral procession.—At Beverly, Mr. William Gallop, jun. formerly of Topsfield, aged 53.

Vol. XI (No. 534) Tuesday, 28 June 1803.

† [1c] Notice of delinquency of road taxes for the year 1801, due from "the Original Proprietors and owners of Land in New-Grantham." Property still in delinquency by 20 Sept. 1803 was to be sold off at public auction at the home of Amos Spalding, New Grantham. The newspaper's list contains a breakdown of rates applied to the "1st, 2d, and 3d 100" acre lots, though only the names of the proprietors are given here:

Delinquent taxpayers, New Grantham, N.H.:

Olive Doolittle	Benj. Hall, jun. Esq.	James Dwyer
Charle[s] Doolittle	William Polfrey	Mrs. Packer
Simeon Alexander	Benjamin Barrett	David Field
Elisha Alexander	Theodore Atkinson, jun.	Daniel Jones
Moses Belding	Phenious Lyman	Josiah Jones
Martha Belding	Hon. James Hevins	Seth Catlin
Benjamin Hall, Esq.	Col. Wm. [Simms?]	John Williams
Bunker Gay	Capt. Sam. Hunt	Nathaniel Dickerson
Rufus Field	Capt. Jonth. Hunt	Col. John Hawks
Arad Hunt	Mrs. Abigail Hall	Moses Hawks
Oliver Barret	Elijah Williams jun.	Samuel Dickerson
Lois Butler	Lt. Sam. Ashley	Rufus Wells
Samuel Patridge	Oliver Ashley	Medad Pomroy
John Hunt, jun.	Capt. Joseph Stebbins	Eben Pomroy
Gad Lyman	Elijah Stebbins	

¶ [2d] Charleston, South Carolina, May 31. William Weathers, for attempting to break into the vaults of the South Carolina Bank, was this forenoon sentenced to stand for one hour in the pillory on the 15th of June; and to be imprisoned for three years, from this day.

¶ [2d] New York, New York, June 16. Mr. James Hughes, of Petersburgh, Virg. who was wounded in a duel with Mr. George Tucker of that place on Sunday the 5th instant died of his wounds on the Tuesday following.

===== ¶ [3c] MARRIED. =====

At Portsmouth, Mr. Reynal M'Cartney, to Miss Olive Swanzey.—At New York, Thomas H. Merry, to Miss Sarah Maria Taylor, both of that place.—Mr. John Barbarie to Miss Ann Van Tuyl, daughter of Mr. Andrew Van Tuyl, all of that city.—At Savannah, Judge Trezevant, of South Carolina, to Mrs. Henrietta Morel, relict of the late honourable John Morel.—At New York, Mr. John G. Carpendee, [95] to Miss Catharine Parsells. —At Salem, Mr. Benjmain Patterson, to Miss Mary Barnes.—At Boston, Mr. Moses Wilson, to Miss Jane Somes.—Mr. John F. Jennison to Miss Nancy Rand.—Mr. William Cook to Miss Susannah Woods.—At Westmoreland, Mr. Joshua Britton, to Miss Kezia Chamberlin.

===== ¶ [3c] DIED. =====

In England, Mr. William Bell.—He was a warm 45 and 92 man; and when Wilkes was sentenced to two years imprisonment, he swore he would neither shave himself, nor change his linen, until the object of this idolatry had regained his liberty; and in the brutal state he actually remained until the period was expired.—In France, at Besancon, where he was confined, Toussaint Louverture, the famous black Governor of St. Domingo.—In England, Lord Henniker.—Mr. James Aiken, Æt. 64, of Drury-lane Theatre.— At Catskill, Rev. David Bobee.—In River la Plate, Mr. Philip Greene, son of Wm. Greene, Esq. of Warwick, (R.I.)—In Demerary, Capt. John Chase, Nathan Briggs, and John Leaman of the sch. Three Brothers, of Wiscasset.—At Nevis, Capt. Hildrop, of Hartford; who was unfortunately shot by a merchant's clerk, in a dispute respecting the delivery of some flour.—The clerk was in custody for trial.—At Charleston, (S.C.) William Lenox, aged 74, an old resepactable inhabitant and Merchant of that city.

In this town, on Wednesday last Mrs. Anna Butterfield, wife of Mr. Amos Butterfield, in the fifty second year of her age.

Vol. XI (No. 535) Tuesday, 5 July 1803.

† [1b] Daniel Kimball, Esq. of Plainfield, N.H. petitions to have recorded in the Probate Office of Cheshire County, N.H., a copy of the will of John Lyon, late of Worcester, Mass., merchant, deceased, regarding Lyon's land in Cheshire County.

† [1c] Amos Butterfield adv. for a mare; dated at Walpole, 25 June 1803.

† [1c] Daniel Webster adv. for standard weights and measures, mentioning the County sealer Moses Hale, Esq., of Alstead. Dated at Keene, 25 June 1803.

† [1d] Samuel Peirce adv. for a lost mare, owned by Dr. Jesse Kettridge of Walpole, dated there 27 June 1803.

† [2b-c] Extensive account of a confrontation involving Joseph Duncan, John Childers, and Stephen Duncan, outlaws, resulting in the death of Mr. Joseph Rayenhill, formerly of Winchester, Va. Rayenhill was assisting the local sheriff in capturing the outlaws, who had evicted James and William Park from their farm near Knoxville, Tenn. The article is dated at Knoxville, 30 May.

¶ [3a] William Conklin has been convicted of the murder of James Limington, at Poughkeepsie, and has received the sentence of death. At the same place, two brothers by the name of Thompson, one 15, the other 16 years of age, were convicted of burglary, and sentenced to confinement at hard labour in the state prison for life. Isaac Cole and William Cole, father and son, have been convicted of larceny at Hudson.

† [3d] Samuel Whittle adv. a stray horse which he found; dated Walpole, 4 July 1803.

† [3d] List of letters remaining at the Post Office, Charlestown, N.H., 1 July 1803, as compiled by F.A. Sumner, Postmaster:

Mr. James M. Warner, Acworth, N.H.		Mr. James B. Harris, Charlestown, N.H.	
Mr. [Harry Bogg?],	"	Doct. Peter Allen,	"
Mr. Thomas Kenney,	"	Mr. Joshua Hovey, Unity, N.H.	
Mr. Samuel Lowell, Charlestown, N.H.		Miss Sally Gilman,	"
Mr. Moses Willard,	"	Mr. Jacob Shaw,	"
Mr. William Armes,	"	Capt. Ezekiel Cook, Springfield, Vt.	
Doct. Peter Allen,	"	Mr. Jacob Stevens, Claremont, N.H.	
Mr. Kendal Bailey,	"	Mr. Oliver Willard, Langdon, N.H.	
Mr. William Rhodes,	"	Rev. Abijah [Winse?], Newport, N.H.	
Mr. James B. Harris,	"	Mr. James Ballock, Cornish, N.H.	

"To a man in Springfield, who carries on the Tinning Business; name not known. Vermont."

===== ¶ [3c] MARRIED. =====

At New-York, Mr. John Martin Baker, sen. of Gibraltar, to Miss Jane Peters.—At Boston, Mr. William Payne, to Miss Lucy Dobell.—Mr. John S. H. Cox, to Miss Nancy Lewis.—At Providence, Capt. Amasa Delano, to Mrs. Hannah Appleton, both of Boston.—At Springfield, Mr. Oliver Allen, to Miss Jane Benton.—At Wiscasset, Mr. Thomas [Nickles?] to Miss Jane Hodge.

===== ¶ [3c-d] DIED. =====

In England, Miss Reynols, a maiden lady.—She has by her will bequeathed 50,000 sterling to government, towards the reduction of the National Debt.—At Alexandria, Mr. William Henry Washington.—He died of a coup de foliel, when performing military duty at Washington.

At Falmouth, Barnstable county, (Mass.) June 7, 1803, the wid. Elizabeth Chadwick, aged 101 years and 3 months.—Early she embraced the Christian Faith [. . .] having been engaged with skill and success, in the practice of midwifery, upwards of 70 years. [. . .] Between the age of 90 and 100 years, being called to her great grand daughter in confinement she rode on horseback at the distance of between three and four miles in haste, and afforded her relief and comfort in the birth of a *great great grand child*. [. . .]

Vol. XI (No. 536) Tuesday, 12 July 1803.

† [3d] Nathan Smith adv. for a stray mare which he found; dated Walpole, 9 July 1803.
† [3d] David Churchill adv. for a stray or stolen mare, missing from Mr. Huestead's property; dated at Westmoreland, 6 July 1803.

Vol. XI (No. 537) Tuesday, 19 July 1803.

¶ [3b] A most melancholy event happened on Sunday in Lynn. Mr. Miles Shory and his wife were instantaneously killed by the lightning. He was found in the entry way, and Mrs. S. close by him—she had a babe in her arms, which sustained no other injury than having its hair a little burnt. A Mr. Newhall, a tenant in the same house, was knocked down, but not hurt. Several other persons were in the house, but received no injury. The Lightning first struck the chimney, and shattered the house considerably.

† [3b] Gruesome account of the death of Mr. William T. Hall, merchant of Rutland, Vt., who was killed by the discharge of a cannon at the Fourth of July celebration at Castleton, Vt. Mr. George Down was dangerously wounded. ♦

† [3d] Adv. by Thomas Redington, Edmund Brewster, and Isaac Redington, who recently opened a country store under the name of *Edmund Brewster & Co.*, at Westmoreland; dated Walpole 19 July 1803.

† [3d] Nicholas and J. Farwell adv. for their boot and shoemaking business; dated at Claremont, 15 July 1803.

† [3d] Timothy Clark of Greenfield, N.H. offers a reward for his stolen mare.

===== ¶ [3d] MARRIED. =====

At Dorchester, Mass. Mr. James Howe, merchant of Boston, to Miss Elizabeth Clap, daughter of the late Ebenezer Clap, Esq. of the former place.—At Newton, on Thursday night, the 23d June, by [Justice?] Fuller, Mr. Thomas Waterman, late Pastor of the Baptist Church in Charlestown, to Miss Elizabeth McNeil.—At Boston, Mr. Job Jackson, to Miss Deborah Nowell.

===== ¶ [3d] DIED. =====

At Newburyport, Hon. Matthew Thornton of Merrimack, N.H. Æt. 88.—At Winchendon, Mr. Elisha Tucker, Æt. 42.—At Menotomy, Mr. Joseph Locke, 3d, Æt. [27?], an industrious and worthy man.—At Fort Independence, Mr. William Arnold, Æt. 26, of the U.S. Artillery.—His death was occasioned by his being burnt in the late fire.—At Salem, Mrs. Mary Dodge widow of the late Mr. James Dodge, of Boston, aged 86.

Vol. XI (No. 538) Tuesday, 26 July 1803.

===== ¶ [3c] DIED. =====

At Hungar Parish, (Virginia) Rev. Dr. M'Crosky.—The vestry of the parish offer the glebe, containing 1600 acres of land, 12 slaves, a brick dwellinghouse, out houses, &c. to any Minister of the Protestant Episcopal Church, who shall be inducted there. By the will of the devisor, this glebe reverts to his heirs, if the parish remains vacant six months, which will expire the 20th October next.—In Greenfield, Mr. Alexander Hamilton, Æt. 28.—Near the mouth of the Connecticut river, Latham Smith, drowned by the upsetting of a boat.—In Dedham Mr. Benjamin Whitney, of Fitzwilliam. He is the person mentioned in our last as having been killed by an explosion in blowing rocks.[96]—At Havanna, in June last, of the prevailing fever, Mr. Edward Jones, jun. of Boston, eldest son of Edw. Jones, Esq.—On his passage from Charleston, to New York, Herbert [Rees?], Esq. of S. Carolina.

Vol. XI (No. 539) Tuesday, 2 Aug. 1803.

† [3d] Shubael Stone of Marlborough, N.H., guardian of John Barker of Marlborough (*non compos Mentis*), petitions the Court of Judicature for authorization to sell land owned by Barker for his support.

† [3d] Legal notice regarding the insolvent estate of Asa Durkee, late of Croydon, N.H., deceased. Benjamin Barker, Administrator, petitioned the Court for license to sell Durkee's estate.

===== ¶ [3d] DIED. =====

At sea, Mr. John [Collin? Coffin?], aged 18, by the sting of a musquetto. [sic]—At Hartford the Rev. Eliphalet Williams, D.D. aged 77 years, and 56 of his ministry.—At Newbury-Port Mr. Samuel Titcomb, aged 87.—At Keene, Mrs. Sally Blake, wife of Capt. Abel Blake, aged 40.—Mr. David Nims, aged 87.—One of the first settlers in Keene, a sensible, worthy man. His descendants are numerous; forty of whom followed him to the grave.

Vol. XI (No. 540) Tuesday, 9 Aug. 1803.

¶ [3a] A labourer, by the name of Mason, was killed on Friday last, by the explosion of a tube, in blowing rocks, on the Dedham turnpike road. This is the second accident of the kind, near the same road. [97]

¶ [3a] Amherst, N.H. July 28. On Friday last, a son of Deac. Ebenezer Woods of Merrimac, about seventeen years of age, was instantly killed by lightning.

† [3a] Noah Lovel, Esq. appointed Postmaster at the new Post Office, Dunstable, N.H.

† [3a] Mr. David Wallingford's clothier's shop, Hopkinton, N.H., burned by arsonist.

† [3b] Article detailing the drowning, 22 July 1803, of Mr. Levi Phelps of Stoddard, at the "Chesterfield long pond." Phelps was 42 years of age. ♦

† [3c] Legal notice regarding property in Cheshire County, N.H.: Lewis R. Morris, Esq. of Springfield, Vt., ". . . Parent and Guardian to Lewis Morris, and Martha Morris, Minors, under the age of twenty one years that said minors are with Jacob Smith and Martha his wife, in right of said wife, Theophilus Olcott, and Lucretia Olcott, tenants in common of certain parcels of land . . . in Charlestown . . . " Morris petitioned the Court for license to sell land for the support of "said Wards."

† [3c] Legal notice regarding sale of property in Cheshire County for the support of Samuel Crosby and Henry Crosby, Minors, of Charlestown, N.H., who were under the guardianship of Ruth Crosby.

† [3d] Adv. by Isaiah Eaton and Benjamin Kindreck, a.k.a. *Eaton & Kindreck*, regarding their Clock-making business. Eaton also states ". . . that he has removed from Walpole to Westminster, (Vt.) near the meeting house . . . "

† [3d] Legal notice regarding the sale of property in Cheshire County for the support of Cynthia Sartwell, Fanny Sartwell, Clarissa Sartwell, and Lucy Sartwell, Minors, all of Charlestown, N.H. Moses Willard Hastings of Charlestown was the guardian, and the notice also mentions one Asa Sartwell as being part owner of the property.

† [3d] Legal notice regarding the insolvent estate of Capt. James Rogers, late of Lempster, N.H., deceased. James Bingham, Samuel Bullard, and Timothy Miner were appointed commissioners of said estate.

===== ¶ [3b] MARRIED. =====

At Mendham, N.J. William Blazer, aged 16, to Miss Catharine Gayden, aged 11 ! ! !

Rutland, Vt. Ebenezer Rollins, to Miss Polly Farmer.—Amherst, N.H. Mr. William Neavens Wheeler, to Miss Hannah Odell.—Newbury Port, Mr. Enoch Titcomb, jun. to Miss Abigail Whitney.—Mr. William R. Woodman, to Miss Catharine Norton.—Mr. Thomas H. Balch, to Miss Aron [sic] Hovey.

===== ¶ [3b-c] DIED. =====

At Keene, N.H. Mr. George Wells, a journeyman printer.—he put an end to his existence by suspending himself by the neck to a tree: he had been deranged in his mind for a considerable length of time.—At Wilmington, Del. John Lee Esq. aged 78.—Smithfield, R.I. Henry Jencks, aged 70.—Nantucket, Hon. Josiah Barker, Esq. aged 75.—New Bedford, William Greenleaf, Esq. aged [80?]—Vassalborough, John Bliss, aged 86.—Belfast, Capt. Jonathan Elwell, jun. aged 65.—Marblehead, William Hayden, aged 82.—Hartford, Mr. Benjamin Rockwell, run over by his team and killed.—Mrs. Sarah Fish, aged 66, and at about the same hour at Enfield, her brother, Capt. Allen Stillman.—Salem, Mr. Benjamin Moses, aged 66.—Capt. Edward Allen, universally lamented.—Scituate, widow Mary Jacobs, aged 98.—Medford, widow Mary Ayres, aged 95.—Charlestown, S.C. Mr. Joachim Hartstene, aged 71.—West Stockbridge, Mr. Nathaniel Rawson, aged 88.—Philadelphia, Mrs. Margaret Stedman aged 76.—At Florence, (in Italy) May 27th, Louis I, King of [?]—to which he was elevated by Bonaparte, in 1801.—At Richmond, (Virg.) Mr. James Thompson Callender, author of the "Prospect before us," and many other libels on the Washington & Adams Administration, & late editor of the Recorder."—He was drowned in James River, in which it was his daily custom to bathe. As there were but three feet of water, where his body was found it is supposed he was affected either by the cramp or a fit.—He was taken up soon after, and some efforts made to recover him but in vain.

Vol. XI (No. 541) Tuesday, 16 Aug. 1803.

† [3c] John Ingalls adv. for a horse which he found; dated Walpole, 14 Aug. 1803.

===== ¶ [3c] MARRIED. =====

At Acworth, Mr. Nathaniel Grout, to Miss Lucinda [Slader?].

¶ [3c] DIED.

At Williamsburg, Capt. Samuel Fairfield, aged 73.—At Wilmington, N.C. Mr. William Harp; aged 102.—At Northampton, Mr. Ansel Goodrich, aged 80.—At Roxbury, Mrs. Catharine Mayo, aged [81?]—At Charlestown, Mr. Joseph Abrahams, aged 53.—At Boston, Mrs. Ursula Wells, aged 66.—At Lansingburgh Mr. James Maulling, aged 75.—At Salem, widow Hannah Grover aged 53.—At Pownal, Mr. John Buck, aged 84.—At New London, Mrs. Amy Brooks, aged 74.—At Hanover, widow Rebecca Parks, aged 82.—At Worcester, Mr. Benjamin Stowell, aged 73.

In this town, on Saturday last, sincerely regretted by numerous relations and friends, Mrs. Frances Stone, consort of Mr. David Stone, in the 23d year of her age.

Vol. XI (No. 542) Tuesday, 23 Aug. 1803.

† [2d-3a] Article detailing the deaths of Roxana Wright, aged 11, and Fanny Wright, aged 8, daughters of Mr. Phineas Wright. The girls drowned in the Ashuelot River, though the town is not named. The article is dated at Keene, N.H., 13 Aug., the event having occurred "on the Friday of last week."

† [3d] Adv. by *Bellows & Stone*, dated at Walpole, regarding goods for sale or purchase.

† [3d] Amasa Allen adv. that he has taken a new partner into his firm, and that his business will henceforth be known as *Amasa & Oliver Allen*. Dated Walpole, 1 Aug.

¶ [3c] MARRIED.

At Acworth, Mr. John Davidson to Miss Abigail [Prouter?]—At Amherst, Mr. Amos Elliot, jun. to Miss Peggy Willey.

In this town, Mr. John Gage to Miss Betsey Merriam.

¶ [3c] DIED.

On the 20th ult. as Mr. Zenas Searl, of Chester was attempting to fasten a pair of Steers to a yoke of Oxen, which were on a cart, the steers immediately started—the chain hitched round his ancle; they dragged him over rocks, &c. with great rapidity. Although assistance was nigh yet their exertions proved ineffectual. They dragged him 100 rods or more, before their speed was mitigated. He was bruised in a shocking manner—deprived of his reason, and expired within about two hours. He was in the 38th year of his age.—He lived respected and died lamented. Mr. Searl, with four of his children have been buried within ten weeks past. He was a worthy member of Church and State, and his death is terribly felt by all his acquaintance.

Vol. XI (No. 543) Tuesday, 30 Aug. 1803.

† [3c] Brief article stating that there have been forty deaths in the town of Cornish, due to the dysentary, within a period of four weeks, most of the victims being children.

† [3c] Moses Hall and Nicanor Townsley report the official measurement along the Turnpike from the bridge at Bellows Falls, "to Stephen Chase's Sign-post in Keene."

† [3d] Abel Johnson and Andrew Tracy, both of Cornish, N.H., and both guardians to the several heirs of Abel Spalding, Jr., late of Claremont, N.H., husbandman, deceased, petition the Court for permission to sell Spalding's property in Claremont for the support of the Wards. Joshua Spalding, Zebina Spalding, Lovell Spalding, and Betsey Spalding were under the guardianship of Abel Johnson. Lebbeus Spalding, Samuel Spalding, and Nancy Spalding were under the guardianship of Andrew Tracy. 98

¶ [3c-d] MARRIED.

At Acworth, Mr. John Grout, to Miss Hannah Stebbins.—At New-York, Major Benjamin Russell, Editor of the Columbian Centinel to Miss Sarah Campbell, of New-York.

¶ [3d] DIED.

At Charlestown, Mrs. Mary West, consort of Benjamin West, Esq. Æt. 52.—At Portsmouth, Mrs. Mary Jackson, aged 37.—At Exeter, Capt. Charles Rundlet, aged 88.—At the city of Washington, Mrs. Lydia Story, late of Charlestown, Mass.—At Alstead, Mrs. Becket, consort of Mr. Becket.—At New Ipswich, after a long and painful illness, Mrs. [Hill?]. 99 —At Newburyport, very suddenly, Mr. Bulkeley Emerson, aged 48.—At Dedham, Mr. Eben. Paul, Æt. 56.

Vol. XI (No. 544) Tuesday, 6 Sept. 1803.

===== ¶ [3c] MARRIED. =====

At Newbury-port, Mr. John Walton Whitecake, to Miss Catharine Wise.—At Beverly, Capt. Thomas [Mesk?], jun. of Marblehead, to Miss Mercy Nichols, of the former place.—At Dorchester, Mr. Josiah Briant, of Lexington, to Miss Sally Withington.—At Boston, Mr. Jacob Endicott to Miss Ruthy Hawkes.—At New-Castle, Del. Mr. William Hazlet, aged 72, to Mrs. [*compare to issue of 20 Sept. 1803*] Rebecca Crawford, aged 36. The strawberry of June and the snow-ball of December.—At Rutland, Vt. Mr. Anthony Goff, of Burlington, N.Y. to Mrs. Martha [Finten?], of the former place.

===== ¶ [3c-d] DIED. =====

In England, Rev. H. R. Courtney, Lord-Bishop of Exeter.——Admiral Sir Achibald Dickson.——Mrs. Pope, of Druryland Theatre.——She had a fit of apoplexy, while [?] for Mr. Cooper's benefit, and soon after, died at an early age.——Mr. Evans, late a celebrated bookseller.——Mr. E. requested in his will, that he might be buried without a coffin or shroud, and that the whole of his funeral expense should not exceed forty shillings.—He left the bulk of his fortune to an acquaintance, though he had a son.——At New-York, Mrs. Dorothy Schmidt, Mr. John Stagg, Æt. 71.——At Westford, (N.Y.) Mr. William Richards, Æt. 42. He went to bed in perfect health. About midnight he waked [sic] his wife and informed her he was dying, and immediately expired. —— At Albany, the 15th inst. Mr. Thomas Otis, of Barnstable, [99A] in this State. He was on a tour to the westward for the recovery of his health.——At Catskill, Col. Hale Æt. 44.——At Brattleborough, Ver. Elenora, daughter of Mr. John Thomas, Æt. 14.—— At Keene, N.H. Mrs. Charity Carter, consort of Mr. Samuel C. Æt. 64.——At Deerfield, the 31st July last, Squire Bishop, son of Mr. Isaac Ball - a promising youth.——At Northampton, Mrs. Sarah Hunt, consort of the Hon. Ebenezer Hunt.——At Plaistow, Mrs. Sarah Gill, consort of Mr. David G.——At Northfield, the 23d inst. Mrs. Lydia Mason, consort of the Rev. Thomas Mason. [. . .] ——At Wiscasset, Mr. Moses Eaton, Æt. 32.——Mrs. Mary [100]

Vol. XI (No. 545) Tuesday, 13 Sept. 1803.

† [2d] Article dated at Washington, D.C. describing the interception by a British ship, of the American sloop *Hiland*, a trader from Philadelphia to Alexandria. The *Hiland's* master was Capt. Hand, and one of his men was impressed by the British ship: "The impressed man's name is Daniel Gitchell, he was born near Philadelphia, and has a family consisting of a wife and children in that city . . . " [101] ◆

† [3a-b] Article describing an explosion aboard the U.S. Frigate, *New York*, off the coast of Sardinia, 25 April 1803. "The Gunner 'Morril,' died the following night, and also a boy Hamilton.—Mr. Shults died in about thirty-six hours. Barrior, captain's clerk, died since our arrival here, (Malta.) Dr. Weems is yet ill though recovering fast, as likewise are Mr. Alexis, midshipman, Kenedy, purser's steward, Mr. Gee, Marine., Mr. Lewis, midshipman, and Mr. Israels, are well." ◆

===== ¶ [3c] MARRIED. =====

At Raymond, Mr. John Leavitt, Æt. 60, to Mrs. Hannah Shannon, Æt. 74 [. . .]

At Washington, Rev. Wm. Clingan, a Baptist Minister of Tanneytown, Maryland, to the widow Sarah Derby.——At Enfield, Rev. Nehemiah Pruden, to Mrs. Sibyl Potter.

===== ¶ [3c] DIED. =====

At Oxford, of the dysentery, three children of Joseph Rawson, jun.——At Vergennes, Mr. Donald M'Intosh, aged 76, a native of Scotland and a brave man.—— Mr. David Tyler, aged 44.—At Hanover, Mrs. Clarissa Bingham, aged 35.——At Pembroke, Rev. Gad Hitchcock, D.D. Senior pastor of the second church in that place, aged 85, and in the 55th year of his Ministry.——At Derryfield, Mrs. Hannah Blodget, aged 77.——At Martinique, Admiral Louis Thomas Villaret Joyeuse, late Captain General of that Island. He commanded the French fleet on the memorable 1st of June, when it was defeated by Lord Howe.——Dr. Isaac Ledyard, Health officer for the port of N. York.—It does not appear by the returns, though his decease was sudden, that he was a victim to the yellow fever.——At Windham, Mr. Zerub Hunewell, Æt. 93.——At Preston, (yellow fever) Mr. Nehemiah Smith, Æt. 37.   At Newbury, Capt. Edmund Little, Æt. 87.——At Salisbury, Lt. Joseph Adams, Æt. 63.——At Nantucket, drowned, Mr. Shubael Coffin.——At Dedham, widow Abigail Doggett, Æt. 76.——At Deerfield, of the small pox which he took in Canada, Mr. Joseph Barnard, aged 64.

Vol. XI (No. 546) Tuesday, 20 Sept. 1803.

† [2c] Article describing the death of William Alton Mitchell, aged 22, who died from burns he received at Bristol, Conn., "last Thursday." The article is dated at Bristol, 5 Sept. Mitchell left a wife and infant son. ♦

¶ [2c] At Southwick of the dysentary, five children of the Rev. Mr. Clinton, all within a space of five days; three children of Saul Fowler, Esq.; three children of Mr. Bill; two children of Shubael Stiles; a child of Mr. Root; a child of Mr. Timothy Noble; a child of Mr. Samuel Owen; a child of Mr. Thomas Hanchett; a child of Mr. Ezra Kent, jun.; Mrs. Hair, aged 85; Mrs. Kent, wife of Mr. Ezra Kent. We are informed that upwards of thirty persons have died of the dysentary in the small town of Southwick, within a few weeks. [101A]

===== ¶ [3a] MARRIED. =====

At Waldoborough, Mr. S. Hardy, aged 69, to Miss Polly Belknap, aged 19.—A difference in their ages of only 50 years.——At New Castle, Del. Mr. Wm. Hazlet, aged 72, to the amiable and accomplished Miss [compare to issue of 6 Sept. 1803] Rebecca Crawford, aged 36.——At Portsmouth, Mr. John Badger, to Miss Elizabeth Stanwood. —At Boston, Rev. Asa M'Farland, of New-Concord to Miss Eliza Kneeland, of Boston.

===== ¶ [3a-b] DIED. =====

At Poughkeepsie, Mr. Samuel Nelson, late of Belfast, Ireland, and editor of the "Northern Star," a spirited revolutionary paper.——At Athens, in New York State, Mr. Thomas Clarendon Villiers, Æt. 29 - well known in Boston as a son of Thespis, and late Manager of the theatre at Charleston. Alas ! poor Yorrick ! He was on a visit to his wife at Albany, took the fever at New York; and was on his passage up the river, when it seized him, and after a conflict of 11 days hurried him to that "bourne from whence no traveller returns."——At Orange, instantaneously killed by the falling of a log upon him, Mr. Samuel Briggs.——Drowned, off Nahant, Mr. John Ballard, and a Mr. Pendleton and son.——At Franklin, Dea. James Metcalf, Æt. 74.—He had just seated himself in the dinner house on his meadow, when he was observed by a small boy to lie down and gape—who informed the other workmen in the meadow, that his grandfather had gone to sleep. No sign of life was discovered after.——At Newburyport, the Right Rev. Dr. Bass, Bishop of the Episcopal Church in Massachusetts, Æt. 78. After two days illness. His remains were entombed yesterday; when a funeral sermon was delivered by the Rev. Dr. Parker of Boston. The Merrimac Humane Society, and St. Peters and St. John's Lodges of masons attended the funeral of the deceased.—At Keene, Mr. Elisha Briggs, Æt. 63.——At Charlestown, N.H. Miss Polly Carpenter, daughter of Ephraim Carpenter, Esq. in the 25th year of her age. [. . .]——At Pittsfield, on the 1st instant, Mr. Z. Stiels, jun. aged 48—after a sickness of 28 years. He has for 12 years past been deprived of the use of his legs, insomuch that he has not been able to walk across the room—has not uttered a loud word for nearly 14 years, and for two years past has been completely deprived of the use of his speech.—At Newburyport, Hon. Theophilus Bradbury, aged 64, for several years a Representative in the Congress of the United States, and late an Associate Judge of the Supreme Judicial Court of Massachusetts.

† [3d] Asa Patridge, Post-rider from Walpole to Cornish, requests his customers to pay up. Notice dated 13 Sept. 1803.

† [3d] William Pierce adv. for a lost horse; dated at Walpole, 20 Sept. 1803.

Vol. XI (No. 547) Tuesday, 27 Sept. 1803.

† [2d-3a] Article describing an accident 26 July 1803, at Grafton, N.H., where Stickney Smart, aged three, son of Mr. Francis Smart, was horribly mangled in a tub mill. The

boy died about a week later. ♦

¶ [3c] TAKE NOTICE. Whereas Rebekah my wife has eloped from my bed and board, and has taken with her my son Joshua; I hereby forbid all persons harbouring or trusting them on my account, as I shall pay no debts of their contracting after this date.

INCREASE BLAKE.

Walpole, Sept. 24, 1803.

==== ¶ [3b] MARRIED. ====

At Westminster, Vt. Hon. Stephen R. Bradley, Senator of the United States, to Miss Malinda [Wills?].

==== ¶ [3b-c] DIED. ====

At Townsend, Vt. Mrs. Martha Prouty only daughter of Col. Amariah Taft, and wife of Mr. Thomas Prouty of Langdon, N.H. in the twenty-ninth year of her age—she went from Langdon, in May last, to visit her parents in Townsend and died on the 10th inst. of the consumption.——In Halloway, Mass. on the 18th May last, Capt. Joseph Lord of Westmoreland, N.H. aged 74——The deaths in Baltimore, the week ending the 12th, were 20 - 8 adults, 12 children.——At Brooklyn, Walter Hubbell, mer. and Mr. Edward Davis, his clerk, both of the yellow fever.——In Philadelphia, John Barry, Esq. for many years a distinguished Commander in the Navy of the United States.—In Newington, Col. Timothy Dame, Æt. 67.—At Albino, near Rome, the Right Rev. the Earl of Bristol, Lord Bishop of Derry, Æt. 73.——At Providence, Mr. William Mumford, aged [25?].

Vol. XI (No. 548) Tuesday, 4 Oct. 1803.

† [2d-3a] Lengthy article describing the interception of the American brig *Gen. Warren*, Capt. Nathaniel Jones, of Portland, Maine, by a British warship. ♦

† [3d] Moses Mead, Jr. adv. for items lost "between Wilcox's Tavern in Surry and Walpole meeting-house." The adv. mentions Elijah Burrough's Tavern.

==== ¶ [3d] DIED. ====

At Clarendon, Vt. Mr. Whitfield Foster, Æt. 59.——At Poultney, Miss Polly Martin, Æt. 20, who went to bed well, and was found dead in the morning.——At Dover, Mr. Wm. Roberts, Æt. 79.——At Suffield, Con. on Sunday the 25th ult., Mr. Seth King late an innkeeper in Boston.——At Conway, Mrs. Abigail Nash, Æt. 94.——At Leyden, Mrs. Hannah Extill, Æt. 86.——At Providence, Hon. John Brown, Æt. 68, universally known for varied extensive usefulness as a merchant and citizen.—At Sneedsborough, N.C. Mr. Charles Jourdan, Æt. 114.

The deaths in Philadelphia the week ending the 22d ult. were 57.

The deaths in Boston the week ending the 24th ult were 12 only.

Vol. XI (No. 549) Tuesday, 11 Oct. 1803.

¶ [3b] Jacob Burke was convicted before the Supreme Court, at Providence, on Monday last week, of a rape on the body of Elizabeth Stafford; and is to be hanged the 11th November.

At the same Court, Capt. Enoch Tower was convicted of murder in the second degree; and sentenced to three months imprisonment, a fine of 500 dollars, and costs of prosecution.

† [3d] Elisha Putnam adv. land and house for sale at Charlestown, N.H.

Vol. XI (No. 550) Tuesday, 18 Oct. 1803.

† [3b] Brief article mentioning the scheduled execution of Caleb Adams, who was convicted at Windham, Conn., for the murder of Oliver Woodworth, a child aged six years. Adams was sentenced to be executed 29 Nov. 1803. ♦ [102]

==== ¶ [3d] DIED. ====

At Elkton, Md. Col. Henry Hollingsworth, one of the Senators of Maryland.——At Conway, Ms. Capt. Abel Dinsmore, aged 65. Going from his house in the afternoon to mill, with two bushels of grain on his horse, and driving also a yoke of oxen; he had proceeded a little more than a mile, when he fell from his horse, and within a few minutes he was taken up, and after a few breaths expired. Since the 4th July have died in Conway 65 persons; four with canker rash, three consumption, remainder of the dysentary. The whole number of deaths since the commencement of the year was 79.——At Colerain, Mr. David Lyons, aged 67; Mrs. Elizabeth Lee, aged 95.——At Greenfield, Mr. Cornelius Post, aged 86.——At Leominster, Mrs. Desire Nichols, aged 76.——At Ward, Dr. Hezekiah Merriam, aged 100 years. He has left a widow with whom he had lived 78 years.——At Northampton, Mr. Benjamin Sheldon, aged 74.—At New York, Mrs. Frances Hodgkinson, a celebrated comic actress on the boards of that city.

Vol. XI (No. 551) Tuesday, 25 Oct. 1803.

† [3d] List of letters remaining in the Post Office in Charlestown, N.H., 1 Oct. 1803:

Mr. Abel Houghton, Springfield, Vt.
Mr. William Gibson, Croydon, N.H.
Mr. James Russel, Unity, N.H.
Mr. Jesse Stearns, Langdon, N.H.
Mr. Levi Spencer, Charlestown, N.H.
Mr. Simeon Bingham, Washington, N.H.
Mr. Moses Thurston, Unity, N.H.
Mr. Joel Smith, Langdon, N.H.
Mr. Benj. Thurston, Unity, N.H.
Mr. Benj. Clough, Unity, N.H.
Mr. Thomas Glidden, Unity, N.H.
Miss Sukey Corey, Claremont, N.H.
Mr. Joseph Willson, Charlestown, N.H.

Mr. James Gurnsey, Charlestown, N.H.
Mr. Reuben Bisbee, Langdon, N.H.
Mr. Wm. Lewis, Marlow, N.H.
Mr. Wm. Dutton, Charlestown, N.H.
Mr. Lemuel Hitchcock, Claremont, N.H.
Mr. Wm. Gibson, Croydon, N.H.
Mr. Thomas Curtis, Winchester, N.H.
Mr. Nath. A. Bowen, Richmond, N.H.
Mr. Phineas Hutchinson, Charlestown, N.H.
Mr. Isaac Merriam, Groton, N.H.
Mr. Samuel Marsey, Wethersfield, Vt.
Miss Sally Rice, Springfield, Vt.
Mr Stephen Arthur Jenesee, Ch'stown, N.H.

† [3d] James Jaquith adv. property for sale at Alstead, N.H., dated 21 Oct. 1803.
† [3d] Isaac Randall adv. for sale one third interest in a paper mill, and other property, at Alstead, N.H.
† [3d] Richard H. Jones and Thomas Bellows, 2d, a.k.a. *Jones & Bellows*, dissolve their partnership, and request outstanding debts to be settled; dated Walpole, 24 Oct. 1803.

Vol. XI (No. 552) Tuesday, 1 Nov. 1803.

This issue is not included on the microfilm.

Vol. XI (No. 553) Tuesday, 8 Nov. 1803.

† [1c] Nathaniel Baker adv. for a stray cow; dated at Walpole, 29 Oct. 1803.
† [3c] Extensive article describing the death of Mr. Seth Walker, of Langdon, N.H., who drowned in his well, 25 Oct. 1803. He was in his 58th year, and left a wife and one son. ♦
† [3d] Adv. of a runaway notice of Joseph Bidwell, of Langdon, N.H., "about 19 years of age, under mental derangement." Bidwell ran away from his parents 13 Oct. 1803. ♦

Vol. XI (No. 554) Tuesday, 15 Nov. 1803.

† [3d] List of delinquent nonresident owners of property in Unity, N.H., as compiled by Noah Ladd, *Collector*. The list includes the lot number, acreage, etc., but only the names of the "Original Proprietors" are given here: John Sherbern, Thomas Clough, Samuel Winslow, T. Atkinson, Esq., John Moulton, Daniel Moulton, John Webster, and B. Wentworth, Esq. ♦

===== ¶ [3d] MARRIED. =====

At Hampton, Charles H. Atherton, Esq. of Amherst, to Miss Mary Anne Tappan, of the former place.
At Dummerston, on the 10th inst. by the Rev. Samuel Mead, Hon. Samuel Stearns, LL. D. to Mrs. Elizabeth Kelley, of that place.
At Fitchburg, Mr. Samuel Dorr to Miss Lucy Fox.
At Boston, Mr. David Wyman, to Miss Sally Cook.

At Barnstable, Mr. Isaac Berry, to Miss Abigail Young.
At Salem, Mr. Joseph Kimball to Miss Fanny Stimpson.

===== ¶ [3d] DIED. =====

At Northampton, Mr. Quartus Pomeroy, Æt. 68.——At Fredericksburg, Hon. Edmond Pendleton.—At Acworth, much lamented, Mr. John Whipple, jun. only son of Mr. John Whipple of Grafton, Mass.—At Aberdeen, Scotland, the celebrated Dr. James Beattie.—At Canajoharry, [sic] Mr. Jonathan Dwight, Æt. 44, formerly of Northampton. —At Boston, Mr. Thomas Bayley, Æt. 25; Mrs. Catharine Adams, Æt. 40, wife of Mr. Samuel Adams.—In Paris, Mr. Alexander Innes, Æt. 88, for many years President of the Scotch College.—At Gloucester, R.I. Capt. Benjamin Wilkinson, Æt. 90. ——At New Bedford, Mr. Elnathan Tuber.——At Cambridge, Miss Priscilla Watson, Æt.[20?]——In Jamaica, much lamented, Mr. John Appleton, Æt. 22, youngest son of the widow Sarah Appleton, of Boston.——At Baltimore, Richard Lawson, Esq. Æt. 54.
At New York, Col. Joseph Fay—Col. S. Bauman, post-master of that city.

Vol. XI (No. 555) Tuesday, 22 Nov. 1803.

† [1a] Jonathan Arms adv. for an apprentice blacksmith; dated Charlestown, 7 Nov.

===== ¶ [3d] MARRIED. =====

At Pembroke, N.H. Mr. Jonathan Freeman, jun. of Hanover, to Miss Mary Whitehouse, of the former place.
At Newburyport, Mr. Robert Harvey, mer. to Miss Rebecca Plummer.
At Portland, Mr. George W. Duncan, mer. to Miss Margaret Weeks.
At Ashby, Mr. Nathaniel Adams, mer. of Boston, to Miss Alice Wyman, of the former place.
At Boston, Mr. Peter Dickerman, to Miss Abigail Lord.
In this town, by the Rev. Mr. Fessenden, Mr. Amos Butterfield, to Mrs. Lusena Brown.
At Albany, Matthias B. Talmadge, Esq. to Miss Elizabeth Clinton, daughter of his Excellency Governor Clinton.

===== ¶ [3d] DIED. =====

At Newburyport, Mrs. Mary [Thurlo?], aged 99 years and four months.——At [Boston?], Mr. Samuel Buck, Æt. 92.——In Trinadad, Mr. Isaac Perkins, of Boston.—At Salem, Mrs. Catharine Pynchon, Æt. 92.——At Roxbury, Mrs. Martha [M'Carty?], Æt. 27.——At Cambridge, Mr. Robert Vose, mer. Æt. 43.—At Boston, Mr. Benjamin Larkin, Æt. 49.——At Ipswich, Mr. William Dodge, Æt. [79?].
At Wetford, (England) Joseph Galloway, Esq. formerly Speaker of the House of Assembly of Pennsylvania.—In Montague, U. Canada, Miss Hannah Arnold, sister of Gen. Benedict Arnold.
In this town, a child of Mr. Josiah Griswold, aged 18 months.

Vol. XI (No. 556) Tuesday, 29 Nov. 1803.

===== ¶ [3d] MARRIED. =====

At Boston, the Rev. Hezek. May, of Marblehead, to Miss Margaret White, of Boston.——Charles Davis, Esq. to Miss Eliza Bussey.
At Salem, Mr. Benjamin Daniels, to Miss Abigail Leach.
At Princeton, Mr. Robert B. Thomas, to Miss Hannah Beaman.

===== ¶ [3d] DIED. =====

In Annapolis, Allen Quinn, Esq. Æt. 77, for 25 years a member of the House of Delegates.——At Salem, Mr. John Bray, Æt. 80.——At Marblehead, widow Rebecca Clark, Æt. 78.——At Barnstable, 2d inst. Mrs. Bathsheba Crocker.—At Concord, universally lamented, Capt. David Wheeler, Æt. 75.——At Woburn, on the 15th inst. of a consumption, Mr. Jacob Goggin, Preacher of the Gospel.——At Boston, Miss Anne Fleet, Æt. 77.——At Wethersfield, Mr. Ebenezer Grant Marsh, Æt. 27.—At Hartford, Mr. Samuel Thompson Baker, Æt. 37.—At Schenectady, Mr. Timothy Treadwell Smith.——At Northampton, Mr. Timothy Wright, Æt. 57.——In Amherst, Ms. since the 1st January last, there have been 49 deaths.

In this town, on Thursday the 14th inst. Frances, daughter and only child of Mr. David Stone, aged six months.—Within the brief term of 18 months, Mr. S. has had to mourn the loss of his amiable partner, a daughter aged about 1 1/2 years, and the infant above mentioned [. . .]

Vol. XI (No. 557) Tuesday, 6 Dec. 1803.

† [3a] The body of Jemima Colby, wife of Mr. Archelaus Colby of Dunbarton, N.H., discovered in Goffstown. Mrs. Colby left her home 6 July 1803 "under symptoms of mental derangement." ♦

¶ [3c] Thomas Moore, Esq. a native of England, and formerly a practitioner of law in the city of New York, fell lately in a duel with lieutenant Buck, of the U.S. army at Natchez.

† [3c] Mr. ———— Baker, aged 30, cordwainer, commits suicide at Hanover, N.J. ♦

† [3d] Stephen Johnson and Noble Orr announce that their copartnership, *Johnson & Orr*, is dissolved. Noble Orr also adv. that he will continue in business.

===== ¶ [3d] MARRIED. =====

At Alstead, on the evening of the 24th ultimo, by the Hon. Amos Shepard, Esq. Mr. John Dinsmoor, to Miss Olive Wardner.—Mr. Ebenezer Severence to Miss Sarah Wardner.

At Acworth, Mr. Stephen Yeomans, to Miss Judith Woodbury.

===== ¶ [3d] DIED. =====

In Cornish, Mr. Abraham Johnson, Æt. 73.——At Grafton, Mrs. Whipple, wife of Mr. James Whipple, Æt. 63.——Mr. Josiah Whipple, son of Mr. James W. Æt. 21; and a child of Mr. Nathaniel Whipple.—Widow Brigham, Æt. 70.——Mrs. Leland, wife of Mr. Phineas L., Æt. 50.—Mrs. Leland, wife of Mr. Daniel L. Æt. 27, and a child of two years. Three children of Mr. Amaziah Haywood.——At Sturbridge, widow Rachel Foster, Æt. 90.——At Warwick, widow Mary Stevens, Æt. 88.——Killed by the kick of a horse at Fitzwilliam, on the 10th ult. Mr. Israel Whitcomb, of Winchendon, Æt. 55.

Vol. XI (No. 558) Tuesday, 13 Dec. 1803.

¶ [3d] ORDINATION.]—On Wednesday, the 28th ult. the Rev. Gideon Burt was ordained to the pastoral charge of the church in Effingham, in this state.

¶ [3d] MARRIED.]—At Brattleboro', Mr. Alfred Bar——103 to Thede Dickerman——Mr. David Horton, jun. to Miss Lucinda Arms.

¶ [3d] DIED.]—At Scipio, N.Y. Gen. Benjamin Ledyard.—A[t] Lime, Mrs. Joanna Shaw, aged 43.—At Brunswick, Va. Mr. John Peeble, aged 111.—At Claremont, Mr. Noah Cook, aged 36.—On the 1st instant, the amiable and much lamented Mrs. Caroline Hubbard, consort of Mr. Isaac Hubbard, and daughter of Major Ezra Jones, in the 23d year of her age.

Vol. XI (No. 559) Tuesday, 20 Dec. 1803.

¶ [3c] Uriel C. Hatch, Esq. is appointed postmaster in Cavendish, Vt.

† [3d] Amos Atwood and Moses D. Brooks announce that their copartnership in trade is dissolved; dated at Lempster, 5 Dec. 1803.

===== ¶ [3d] MARRIED. =====

At Milton, Mr. Isaac Saunderson, to the agreeable Miss Betsey Gill.

Near Fincastle, (Vir.) Major Thomas Lisle, aged 69, to Miss Harriet Huston, aged 21.

In Providence, Mr. Samuel A. [Peak? Peck?], mer. to Miss Sally Lewis, both of Barnstable, Mass.

In Andover, Col. Nathaniel Lovejoy, to Mrs. [Benja?] Woodbridge.

At Charlestown, N.H. Mr. George W. Sumner, of Claremont, to Miss Matilda Hutchins.

In this town, on Wednesday evening last, Mr. Jonathan Holten, of Charlestown, to Miss Nancy Pope.

===== ¶ [3d] DIED. =====

In the Alms-house, at Plymouth, Hannah Barrett. The verdict of the jury of inquest was, that being intoxicated, she attempted to drink water out of a bucket, and was thereby drowned. The bucket contained just water enough to cover her face.——At Boston, on Sunday evening the 11th inst. Mr. Benj. Edes, printer, Æt. 71. He was for many years the editor of a popular paper in that town. Every proper effort peculiar to his sphere of action, was made by him, to aid the accomplishment of the American Revolution; and his exertions were valuable. [. . .]——At New York, Rev. Robert Smith, Æt. 34, of Savannah, (Geo.)——At Providence, Col. Jeremiah Whiting——At Newport, Peleg Clarke, Esq. Æt. 70.——At Newburyport, Deacon Ichabod Atkinson, Æt. 87.——At Boston, Mr. John [Mellus?] Æt. 84.——At Alstead, Mrs. Mary Severence, Æt. [82?].——At Bristol, in England, much lamented, Mr. Edward Breck, of Northampton, Æt. 25.——In Coventry, (Con.) Miss Dinah Jones, Æt. [?]——In East Hartford, Mr. John Pitkin, Æt. 55.——In Providence, Col. Jeremiah Whiting.

Drowned, at Marlboro', John Stone, 4th son of Mr. John Stone, jun. of Dublin, aged 16.

Vol. XI (No. 560) Tuesday, 27 Dec. 1803.

† [2d] Gold discovered on property in Cabarrus County, N.C., owned by Mr. John Reed, a native of Hesse Cassel, in Germany. Article contained in the news dated at Raleigh, N.C.

===== ¶ [3d] DIED. =====

At Northampton, Mr. Jonathan Strong, Æt. 66.——At Dorchester, Mr. Josiah Glover, Æt. 77.——At Boston, Mr. Thomas [Shimmin?], in the 21st year of his age.——Mr. Samuel Thwing, sen. Æt. 60.——Miss Experience Bridge, Æt. 84, sister of the late Rev. Ebenezer Bridge of Chelmsford.——At Acworth, very suddenly of an advanced age, Mr. Thos. Wallace.

Vol. X [104] (No. 561) Saturday, 31 Dec. 1803.

===== ¶ [3d] MARRIED. =====

In Salem, Mr. Nathaniel Cummings, to Miss Mary Putnam.
In Boston, Mr. Andrew Aitchinson, to Miss Sally Langdon.

===== ¶ [3d] DIED. =====

In England, the Marquis of Stafford, Æt. 86. His successor is Earl Gower.——Ralph Griffith, Esq. LL. D. Æt. 83.——the institutor, and for 54 years the conductor of the Monthly Review.

At sea, Dr. James Boyd, late surgeon in the U.S. navy.——In Maryland, Hon. William Vans Murray, late an American Minister in Europe.——At Foster, (R.I.) Mr. Abner Wade was killed by the falling of a sand bank, which buried him seven feet under ground.——At Salem, Ms. Major Samuel Epes, Æt. 56. He was a captain in Lexington battle.——At Amherst, Mr. Benj. Wilkins, Æt. 80.——In New Jersey, James Salter, Esq. Treasurer of that state; who was severely ill treated when the treasury was robbed a short time since.——In Weymouth, Mrs. Mary Ripley, aged 104 years.

In this town, of the canker rash, a child of Mr. Sever.

Drowned between Newhaven and Long Island, Lieut. Joseph Green, late of Hanover, Æt. 49.

SUICIDE.—At Temple, under mental derangement, Mr. Joseph Heald. [105]

Vol. X (No. 562) Saturday, 7 Jan. 1804.

† [1a] Daniel Newcomb, Treasurer, posts a notice regarding the Third N.H. Turnpike.
† [1c] David Carter, Proprietors' Clerk, posts a notice regarding Third N.H. Turnpike.
† [3d] *Roby & Curtis* adv. a farm for sale in Charlestown, N.H.

===== ¶ [3d] MARRIED. =====

In England, Oct. 31, at St. Margaret's church, Westminster, Ashbury Dickins, Esq. late of Philadelphia, to Miss Lilias Arnot, daughter of the late Hugo Arnot, Esq. of Balforino, Scotland.
In South Carolina, Enoch Huntington, Esq. of Norwalk, Con. to Miss Margaretta Dewitt.
At Kennebunk, Mr. Charles W. Williams, to Miss Abigail Lord.
In Springfield, Mr. Henry Brewer, Editor of the Federal Spy, to Miss Lucy [?].
In Portsmouth, Mr. Robert M'Clary, to Miss Sophia Davenport.
In Boston, Capt. Peter Geyer, aged 67, to the amiable and accomplished Miss Polly Sancry, aged 17.
In Salem, Capt. Benjamin Crowninshield, jun. to Miss Mary Boardman.
In this town, by the Rev. Mr. Fessenden, on the 1st inst. Mr. ——— Pease, to Miss Kezia Griffin.

===== ¶ [3d] DIED. =====

In Russia, the Great Dutchess Helena Pawlawna, sister to the Emperor Alexander.
In Savannah, Mr. Thomas Thomas, of Wales.—In South Carolina, William Lee, Esq.—In Maryland, Mr. Benjamin Duvall, Æt. 103.—In New Jersey, Mr. Matthias Luyster.—In Philadelphia, Mr. John Exley, Æt. 73.—In Fitchburg, Mr. Joseph Low, Æt. 39.—In Hubbardston, Mr. Ezra Pond, Æt. 82.—In Amherst, Mr. Benjamin Wilkins, Æt. 80.—In Newburyport, Mr. Stephen Clark, Æt. 82.—In Acton, Col. Edwards.—At Newton, Mr. Samuel Richardson, Æt. 70.—At Sheldon, of the small pox, Maj. Jedidiah Clark, jun.—At Middlebury, Mrs. Esther Boardman, Æt. 40.—In Windsor, Con. Deacon Nathaniel Hayden, Æt. 94.—In Portsmouth, Mr. Thos. Harry, Æt. 44.—Mrs. Catharine Cotton, Æt. 61.—In Boston, Mrs. Elizabeth Rea, Æt. 73.—At Cavendish, Mrs. Hepzibah White, Æt. 53.—At Newport, Rev. Samuel Hopkins, Æt. 83.—At Hartland, Widow Alice Cabot, Æt. 73.—Mrs. Polly Mackenzie, Æt. 28.
Three young children of Mr. Ebenezer Pratt, of Amherst, Mass. were consumed by fire, in the house of their parents, the 22d inst. Both parents were from home, and the house was discovered to be on fire about 8 o'clock in the evening. The house was owned by Gen. Mattoon. [*Cent.*

Vol. X (No. 563) Saturday, 14 Jan. 1804.

===== ¶ [3d] MARRIED. =====

At Cambridge, in Massachusetts, Hon. Thomas Bellows, Esq. of this town, to Miss E. Foster, of the former place.
At Baltimore, Jerome Bonaparte, youngest brother of the First Consul of France, to Miss E. Patterson, of that city.
At Northampton, Mr. Amasa Nims, jun. to Miss Nancy Quin.
At Londonderry, the Hon. John Bell, Esq. of Chester, to Miss Persis Thom, of the former place.
In Philadelphia, Thomas Manners, Esq. Captain in the British 49th regiment, to Miss Mary Rush, daughter of Dr. Rush.
At Boston, Mr. Benjamin True, printer, to Mrs. Maria Gilbert.
At Roxbury, Mr. James Collins, to Miss Eunice French.

===== ¶ [3d] DIED. =====

At Cumberland Island, (Geor.) the Hon. Phineas Miller, Esq. one of the justices of the Inferior Court of Camden County.—At Worcester, Mr. Cornelius Stowell, Æt. 80.—At Jaffrey, suddenly, Mr. David Bailey, Æt. 87.
In Milan, (Cisalpine Republic) Sept. 24, Fontana, the celebrated Naturalist.—In Acton, Col. John Edwards, Æt. 43.—In Boston, Mrs. Abigail Bulfinch, in the 64th year of her age: Widow Violet Greenough, Æt. 76.—At Pelham, Mr. Ebenezer Palmer, aged

about 75: Mrs. Betsey Richardson, wife of Mr. Ezekiel Richardson, Æt. 44: Widow Elizabeth Gibson.—At Alstead, Mrs. Woods, wife of Col. John Woods.

At Somers, Rev. Charles Backus, D.D. Æt. 54.—At Union, Mr. John Laflin, Æt. 105.—At Groton, Capt. Henry Farwell, Æt. 80.—At Middletown, Mr. Stephen Ranny, Æt. 75.

The number of deaths in Concord, during the last year, was 36. 4 of 80 years and upwards, 6 from 60 to 80, 3 from 40 to 60, 5 from 20 to 40, 1 from 10 to 20, & 17 under 10.

Vol. X (No. 564) Saturday, 21 Jan. 1804.

† [3d] Joseph Bellows, jun. adv. for his "Pot Ash works near Mr. Roger Fenton's."

===== ¶ [3c] MARRIED. =====

In this town, Mr. Joel Tinker, to Miss Charlotte Sikes.

At Boston, Mr. Edmund Munroe, to Miss Harriet Downes.

===== ¶ [3c] DIED. =====

At New York, Mr. Daniel Gilman, brother of the Governor of this State, Æt. 34.

At Sturbridge, of the dysentery, Capt. Samuel Hamant, Æt. 65—his wife, Æt. 64—and his son Peter, Æt. 29, all in the short period of nine days.

At Bellows' Falls, Rockingham, of the canker rash, a child of Mr. Morgan.

Vol. X (No. 565) Saturday, 28 Jan. 1804.

===== ¶ [3c] MARRIED. =====

At Dunbarton, Mr. Samuel Sparhawk, of Portsmouth, to Miss Elizabeth M'Kenzie, of the former place.

In Maryland, Mr. John Divers, to Miss Charity Onion.

===== ¶ [3c] DIED. =====

At Westmoreland, on the 4th inst. Mr. Reuben Kendall, Æt. 55.——Mr. John White, Æt. 40.——Of a consumption, Mr. Langdon.——At Newfane, an infant child of Mr. Butterfield.——In Philadelphia, Mr. Zachariah Poulson, sen. printer, Æt. 67.

Vol. X (No. 566) Saturday, 4 Feb. 1804.

† [1b] Adv. by Joseph Swasey, of Ipswich, Mass. regarding a new machine invented for the shelling of indian corn.

===== ¶ [3d] MARRIED. =====

In this town, Capt. Davis Carpenter, to Mrs. Lucy Bowker.

===== ¶ [3d] DIED. =====

At Concord, Mr. Ebenezer Sandborn, Æt. 37.——In Boston, Mr. John Holland, Æt. 77.——Mr. Joseph Curtis, Æt. 73.

Vol. X (No. 567) Saturday, 11 Feb. 1804.

† [3c] A. Southard adv. "that he has taken the TAVERN lately kept by Maj. Bullard, in Walpole;" dated at Walpole, 10 Feb. 1804.

===== ¶ [3b] DIED. =====

At Middlebury, Vt. Samuel Mattocks, Esq. Æt. 65.——At Hamburg, (N.J.) Mr. William Lawrence, Æt. 18.——In Concord, Mass. widow Mary Barrett, Æt. 90.——In Salem, widow Lydia Beckford, Æt. 100 years and five months.

Vol. X (No. 568) Saturday, 18 Feb. 1804.

† [3d] Margaret Williams, of Littleton, N.H., petitions Cheshire County Superior Court, for divorce from Joseph Peters Calvett. Williams and Calvett were married 6 Dec. 1797; Williams claimed that her husband had another wife yet living.

===== ¶ [3c] DIED. =====

At Fort Wilkinson, Capt. George Salmon, of the 2d U.S. regt.——In Hampstead, Dr. John Bond, Æt. 86.——In Andover, wid. Sarah Furbush, Æt. 71.

Vol. X (No. 569) Saturday, 25 Feb. 1804.

===== ¶ [3c] MARRIED. =====

LEAP-YEAR.——Married, at Hartland, Vt. Mr. John Huntington, of Hartford, aged 45, to Miss Laura Burbank, aged 15.

Vol. X (No. 570) Saturday, 3 March 1804.

† [3d] Asahel Hunt posts a notice regarding some items "pawned at the subscriber's in Charlestown." Adv. dated at Charlestown, 2 March 1804.

¶ [3d] DIED.——At Rutland, Vt. Mr. David Smith, postmaster, Æt. 37.——In this town, on Thursday last, at a very advanced age, Mrs. ——— Graves.

Vol. X (No. 571) Saturday, 10 March 1804. [106]

† [3c] Mary Brown petitions the Superior Court of Judicature at Keene, for divorce from Aaron Brown. The two were married 18 Sept. 1794, the groom being a resident of Marlow, N.H.; Brown deserted his wife "upwards of four years ago." The petition is dated at Acworth, 16 Sept. 1803.

† [3d] Nathaniel Emerson, Esq. and others petition the General Court for a Turnpike Road.

† [3d] Arethusa Smith petitions the Superior Court of Judicature at Keene for divorce from Thomas Smith. The two were married 2 Feb. 1787; Smith, "more than five years ago, left [Arethusa] with a family of small children." The petition has no date, nor a place of residence given for the petitioner.

¶ [3c] DIED.—At Bellow's Falls, Rockingham, of the canker rash, Miss Lucinda Morgan, eldest daughter of Mr. Quartus Morgan.

At Canterbury, (Con.) Rev. John Staples, ae. 61.

Vol. XI (No. 572) Saturday, 17 March 1804.

¶ [3c] CAUTION. All persons are hereby forbid harboring or trusting my son Samuel, on my account, as I will pay no debt of his contracting after this date.

JOSEPH BARSTOW.

Cornish, March 3, 1804.

¶ [3b-c] Died in this town on the 11th instant, Caleb Strong Bellows, aged ten years, son of Col. Caleb Bellows.—His death was occasioned by a fall from a horse on the 3d of November last, which threw him with his head against a bar of iron, [. . .]. ♦

Vol. XI (No. 573) Saturday, 24 March 1804.

† [1c] *Shepard & Hutchinson* adv. items for sale "at their store opposite the old Meeting House in Alstead. Dated at Alstead 5 March 1804.

¶ [2c] Kingston, New York, March 10. On Friday evening last, in the late severe snow storm, Mr. Elias Hardenbergh, of Kline Esopus, being on his return home from a neighboring house, left the road, and as no relief could be obtained, he perished.

Mr. Simon Schuyler, of Minden, Montgomery county, also perished in the snow near Schenectady the same evening.

† [3b] Oliver Hastings adv. items for sale at his apothecary store; dated Charlestown, 15 Mar. 1804.

† [3b] Martha Lovell and Vryling Lovell adv. a "farm to be let" in Rockingham. Also, the same individuals offer "a tavern to be let, near the Meeting House in Rockingham." The second adv. is dated at Rockingham 12 March 1804, and located at [3d].

† [3c] Elisha Huntley, David Heald, and Amos Shepard petition the General Court for a Turnpike Road from Cold River to Washington, N.H.

† [3d] *Leverett Tuttle & Co.* adv. plaster of paris for sale; dated Bellow's Falls, Vt.

===== ¶ [3b] MARRIED. =====

At New Haven, Abraham Bishop, Esq. to Miss Betsey Law.

¶ [3b] DIED.

In England, Hon. Wm. Bingham, late a Senator of the United States.

In Jaffrey, N.H. occasioned by her clothes taking fire, Miss Nancy Thorndike Lincoln, Æt. 9.——In Waldoboro', Capt. Charles Sampson, Æt. 63.——In Gloucester, Mrs. Lucy Forbes, wife of Rev. Eli Forbes.——In Boston, Enoch Rust, Esq. Æt. 79; Mr. Andrew Johonnot, Æt. 69.——At Washington, Gen. D. Heister, member of Congress, from Maryland.

Vol. XI (No. 574) Saturday, 31 March 1804.

† [3c] *Kingsbery & Blake* adv. their paper mills in Alstead and Bellows Falls.

† [3d] Adv. by Benjamin W. Morris, recruiting settlers for a new settlement in Lycoming county, Penn., which included numerous mills. "For particulars apply to John Norris, at the Mill on the premises; or Samuel Hunt of Charlestown, N.H. or the Subscriber in Philadelphia."

¶ [3c] MARRIED.

At Platte-Kill, (N.Y.) Mr. Andrew Sutton, to Miss Phebe Garrison [. . .]

¶ [3c] DIED.

At Leghorn, Wm. M. Seton, Esq. mer. of New York.—In England, George Lyde, Esq. formerly of Boston; a gentleman highly esteemed for his virtues.—In Charleston, (S.C.) Elias Houser; he had been in the city 50 years. In South Carolina, Geo. Breaker, Æt. 60; a native of Germany, he had been in America 40 years.—In Tennessee, Jonathan Lawrence, formerly of Norwich, Con.—At Norfolk, James Allison, mer.—In Maryland, Walter Mackall, Esq.—In Pennsylvania, Elder James Bigham, Æt. 67.; ruling elder at Chesnut level.—At Philadelphia, John Vanerd, mer.; Charles Eddy Æt. 50, mer.—At Canandaigua, Lucius Cary, printer.—In Kingston, (Jam.) Mr. Joseph Dean, mer. late of Wilmington, (N.C.) and formerly of Boston.—At Lancaster, (Penn.) Samuel Cocke, Esq. one of the members of the house of Representatives of that state.

Vol. XI (No. 575) Saturday, 7 April 1804.

¶ [3c] DIED.

In this town, Mrs. March, Æt. 65. She was the mother of twelve children, all of whom are living. No deaths had before taken place in the family for 46 years, except those of two grandchildren.

A child of Mr. Amos Phillips.

Lately, in Lithuania, a man, aged 163 years.—This modern Methusaleh, at 89, married a second wife, in the 15th year of her age. He had been a soldier, had been wounded, but never had been sick.—A monument has been raised on his grave. He was eleven years older than *Old Parr*, who died in England, in 1634, aged 152, and who had lived in ten reigns.

In Kingston, (Eng.) Mr. George Gregory, æ. 106, supposed to be the last of the crew of the Centurion, in which Lord Anson circumnavigated the world.

In Falmouth, (N.S.) Mr. Jonathan Masters, aged 70, burnt to death in attempting to save his daughter from the flames of his house on fire; when both father and daughter perished.

At Westminster, (Vt.) on the 1st inst. Mrs. Ruth Hall, the amiable consort of Atherton Hall, Esq. aged 57. [. . .]

At Plainfield, on the 26th of Feb. 1804, of a violent inflammation on the brain, Maj. Joseph Smith, in the 60th year of his age. [. . .]

Vol. XI (No. 576) Saturday, 14 April 1804.

† [3c] Thomas Redington and Isaac Redington announce "that all connexion in Trade under the firm of *Thomas & Isaac Redington*, is this day by mutual consent dissolved." Dated at Walpole, 13 April 1804.

† [3c] Isaac Redington adv. that he continues his business at Walpole; dated 13 April.

† [3c] Joseph Crandal adv. for a lost pocket book, which contains notes of hand, one signed by Aaron Howard, dated Aug. 1803, one against Alexander Howard, dated July

1803, and one signed by Peter Bridget, dated June 1803. Notice dated at Rockingham, 9 April 1804. Two "signatures" appear in this notice, both of them given as *Joseph* Crandal. However, in the two successive issues, the later "signature" was changed to *Jabesh* Crandal.

† [3d] Legal notice regarding the estate of Samuel Willard, late of Charlestown, deceased, by Joannah Willard, adm'x.

† [3d] Nathaniel Sikes and Orange Graves announce that their co-partnership, *Sikes & Graves*, is dissolved; dated Walpole 29 March 1804. A second adv. at [3d] concerns a Walpole farm for sale. "For further particulars inquire of Nathaniel Sikes, living on the premises, or of Thomas C. Drew, of said Walpole." dated 30 Mar. 1804.

===== ¶ [3c] DIED. =====

In Cornish, Miss Sarah Edmister, æ. 32.
In this town, on Monday last, Lieut. Aaron Allen, in the 62d year of his age.

Vol. XI (No. 577) Saturday, 21 April 1804.

† [3d] Simeon Olcott and Samuel Stevens, *Proprietors* of the Charlestown Turnpike Corporation, post a notice regarding a meeting to be held at Isaac Ely's tavern in Charlestown.

† [3d] William Sterne offers his services as physician and surgeon. "He my be found at Mr. Southard's Tavern." Dated at Walpole, 20 April 1804.

===== ¶ [3d] MARRIED. =====

At Washington, Richard Cutts, Esq. a Representative in Congress from Massachusetts, to Miss Paine, of Washington.

===== ¶ [3d] DIED. =====

In Chilicothe, Mr. Henry Abrams, æ. 102.—At East Windsor, Mr. Ebenezer Bissel, æ. 86.—In Boston, Mr. Robert Wyer, in the 36th year of his age.

DROWNED.—At Bellows Falls, on Monday the 16th inst. William Johnson, son of Sylvanus Johnson of Walpole, in the 23d year of his age.—Said deceased had on when drowned, a light grey sailor jacket and trowsers, a blue under jacket, and a silver watch in his jacket pocket:—Any person who may find the body of the deceased, will confer a favor on the afflicted family by giving information. The printers at Brattleboro', Greenfield and Northampton, by giving this a place in their papers, will confer a favor on their afflicted friend,

SYLVANUS JOHNSON.

April 19th, 1804.

Vol. XI (No. 578) Saturday, 28 April 1804.

† [2d] Mr. John Hill, of Bedford County, Kentucky, murdered "by his negro fellow." Article dated at Lexington, 27 March. ◆

¶ [3d] Whereas Chloe my wife has eloped from my bed and board, without any provocation, and taken with her my daughters, Arethusa and Persis—This is to warn and forbid all persons harboring, entertaining or crediting them, or either of them, on my account, as I am determined to pay no debts of their contracting, after this date.

LEVI COLE.

Westmoreland, April 24, 1804.

===== ¶ [3d] MARRIED. =====

At Westminster, Vt. Uriel C. Hatch, Esq. of Cavendish, Vt. to Miss Narcissa Birch.
At Leominster, Abijah Bigelow, Esq. attorney at law, to Miss Hannah Gardner, daughter of the Rev. Francis Gardner.

===== ¶ [3d] DIED. =====

At Acworth, George Duncan, Æt. 16.[107]—In South Carolina, Hon. Thomas Young, of the Senate of the U. States.—At Chilicothe, Henry Abrams, Æt. 102.—At Millstone, N.J. Gen. Frederick Frelinghuysen.—At sea, 25th January, Mr. Thomas White, on board the ship Indus, from Batavia for Boston.

Vol. XI (No. 579) Saturday, 5 May 1804.

¶ [3d] THOMAS LEECH—*Wanted.* If Thomas Leech, a native of the Township of Worsley, near Manchester, in the county of Lancaster, England, (son of John Leech, of the aforesaid Township) will apply at the Printing Office of the Boston Centinel, he will hear of something greatly to his advantage.

N.B. The object of the above is to ascertain whether the said Thomas Leech is living or not, as in case he is, it will be of considerable importance to Simon Hilton and Matthew Hilton, to be informed of it, they being interested in a lease hold Tenement, of which he is the surviving life. May 2, 1804.

† [3c-d] Extensive article describing the accidental death of Abner Lewis, jun., aged 17, son of Mr. A. Lewis, at Dedham. ◆

† [3d] Mr. Holebrook drowned at Bellows' Falls. ◆

===== ¶ [3c] MARRIED. =====

In England, a Mr. Mason, to a Miss Carpenter [. . .]
At Philadelphia, Mr. Robert Stout, to Miss Elizabeth Evans.
At Boston, Mr. Jonathan Harrington, to Miss Lucy Hunewell.
At Mount Vernon, Mr. Josiah Coburn, to Miss Judith Carleton, daughter of Deacon John Carleton.

===== ¶ [3c-d] DIED. =====

At Alstead, on Thursday last, of the phthisis pulmonalis, Mr. Calvin Watts, aged about 23 years. [. . .]

In London, on the 10th March, Lord Camelford, of the wound he received in a duel with his friend Mr. Best. The dispute originated in some alleged remark of Mr. B. respecting his Lordship's mistress.—At Springfield, (Ms.) on the 16th ult. Miss Mary G. Leonard.—At Amherst, Mr. Isaac Kidder.—Mr. Joshua Pettingail.—In Greenland, Rev. Dr. M'Clintock.—At Dorchester, wid. Patience Leeds, Æt. 65.—At Boston, Mr. Abijah Hills, Æt. 50. —At Rutland, Vt. Jonathan Bell, Esq.—In Trenton, Col. William Barrett, Member of the Legislative Council.—In Portsmouth, Mrs. Sarah Pickett, Æt. 64.—In Schenectady, Rev. Dr. D. Romeyn, Æt. 61.—In Portland, Mrs. Mary Bagley, Æt. 66.—At Brookline, Mr. John Heath, Æt. 72.—In Boston, Mr. Samuel Hill, engraver, Æt. 38.—Mr. Joseph Helyer, Æt. 75.—Mrs. Mary Newell, Æt. 81.—At Rutland, Vt. Capt. Jonathan Willard, Æt. 84.—In Portsmouth, Mrs. Ann Sheaffe, Æt. 38.—At Windham, (C.) Shubael Abbe, Esq. Æt. 60.—In Montgomery county, (Penns.) Mr. Christopher Zingler, Æt. 90—and on Monday following, (same county) Mrs. Curry, Æt. 100.—In Philadelphia, Dr. Joseph Pleiffer, Æt. 70; Mr. John Roney, Æt. 60.—At Boxford, Mr. Nathan Wood, ae. 83.—In Utica, (N.Y.) Rev. Bethuel Dodd, Æt. 38.—At Acworth, a child of Mr. James Wallace, aged six months.

Vol. XI (No. 580) Saturday, 12 May 1804.

† [2d] Extensive article regarding trials at the late term of the Supreme Court at Hopkinton, Hillsborough County, with descriptions of the following cases: John Stewart, Timothy Call, David Call, William Gilman, and John Silver, all for forgery; ——— Heath, horse stealing; and John Wilson alias Benson, theft. ◆ 108

† [3d] Legal notice by Caleb Bellows, heir and adm. on the estate of the late Gen. Benjamin Bellows; dated at Walpole, 10 May 1804.

===== ¶ [3d] MARRIED. =====

At Danvers, Mr. Edward Parry, of Portsmouth, to Miss Ruth Collins.
In Providence, Mr. John Pitman Clark, to Miss Mary Pitman.
In Framingham, Mr. John Ttrowbridge, [sic] mer. of Cambridge, to the agreeable Miss Sally Howe, of the former place.
In Boston, Mr. John Sullivan, to Miss Catharine Blair.

===== ¶ [3d] DIED. =====

At Greenland, N.H. Rev. Samuel M'Clintock, D.D. Æt. 72.—At Rindge, Mrs. Anna Chamberlain, widow, Æt. 76.—At Templeton, widow Sarah New, in the 99th year of her age.—At Monticello, Mrs. Eppes, second daughter of the President of the United States.—In Hartford, Hon. Jeremiah Wadsworth, Æt. 60, for many years a member of

Congress.—In Boston, after a lingering illness, Hans Gram, Esq. formerly of Copenhagen, (Denmark)—In Lunenburg county, Virginia, Col. Christopher Robertson, one of the framers of the Federal Constitution.—In Charlestown (Mass.) Mrs. Hannah Runey, Æt. 73: Mr. Nicholas Hopkin, Æt. 79.—In Boston, Mr. Benjamin Eustis, Æt. 84.

FATAL ACCIDENT.—Killed by lightning on the 17th ult. at Cornwall, (Con.) Mrs. Sarah Swift, consort of the Hon. Heman Swift.

At Newport (N.H.) on the 2d inst. the amiable Miss Sible Parmele [. . .].

N. Grantham, May 1, 1804. Last Saturday, a son of Capt. Abner Johnson of this town, aged 11 years, was accidentally killed by the falling of a tree.

Vol. XII (No. 581) Saturday, 19 May 1804.

¶ [3d] DIED.—At Concord, Mr. James Farnum, ae. 65.—In Northampton, Mr. Joseph Hutchings, ae. 78.—In Boston, Mr. James Perkins, merchant, ae. 32.—In Berlin, (Mass.) Dr. Stephen Nurse, Æt. 50.

Vol. XII (No. 582) Saturday, 26 May 1804. [109]

===== ¶ [3d] DIED. =====

In England, General Sir William [?]. His funeral was attended with military pomp [. . .].

At Port [?] (St. Domingo) on the [23d?] of February last, Capt. Timothy Hall, of Cheshire, C. brother of the Rev. A. Hall, of Keene.—At New Grantham, (killed by the falling of a tree) a son of Capt. Abner Johnson, aged 11.—At Portsmouth, (drowned) Miss Nancy [Moses?], aged [?]—(Killed by a fall from the [? ? ?] Moore, aged [18?]—At Hubbardson of the small pox, Capt. Ithamar [? ? ?].

Vol. XII (No. 583) Saturday, 2 June 1804.

Most of the image from this issue of the microfilm is too blurred to read.

Vol. XII (No. 584) Saturday, 9 June 1804.

¶ [3a] On the 22d ult. Mr. Jonathan Laskey, of Lee, in this state, was committed to prison in Dover, for the murder of his son, a child about nine years old. His trial will be in September next.

† [3a] Brief article describing the murder of Richard Adams of Richmond County, Va., who was killed by Jonathan Jarvis, his indentured servant. ♦

† [3a-b] Bizarre account of the suicide of Henry Crimes, of Bath county, Kentucky. ♦

===== ¶ [3d] DIED. =====

At Gloucester County, (N.J.) Mr. John Smith, aged 105.—At Exeter, Mrs. Dorothy Hale, aged [62?].—At Epping, Mr. Jonathan Rundlet, aged 99. His posterity are numerous; 10 children, 60 grandchildren, 180 great grandchildren, and 37 of the fifth generation.

At Claremont, on the 17th of February last, Mr. David Taylor, in the 53d year of his age. He left a wife and nine children to lament the loss of an affectionate husband and tender parent.

SUICIDE.—Mr. Humphrey Thomson, of Topsham, lately put a period to his existence by discharging a musket under his chin. He was 38 years of age. He left a wife in the anguish of indescribable woe, and two young children.

Vol. XII (No. 585) Saturday, 16 June 1804.

† [3d] Adv. of goods for sale by Joseph Bellows, jun.; dated at Walpole, 3 June 1804.

Vol. XII (No. 586) Saturday, 23 June 1804.

† [3b] Accounts of an accident copied from a Hanover (N.H.) paper: Mrs. Pomroy, wife of Major Pomroy of Northampton, and Mrs. Emerson, of Norwich, Vt. and her child, injured when their carriage overturned. ♦

¶ [3b] Last Friday, Mr. Benjamin Kimball, of Lebanon, unfortunately lost one eye and injured the sight of the other, by the accidental discharge of a rock, which he was preparing to blow in pieces.

===== ¶ [3c] MARRIED. =====

In Charlestown, (Mass.) the Hon. John Treadwell, Esq. of Salem, to Miss Hannah Austin, of the former place.

At Charlestown, on the 3d inst. by the Rev. Mr. Foster, Mr. Chester Gaylord, of Hadley (Mas.) to Miss Sidney Dickinson, of Charlestown.

===== ¶ [3c] DIED. =====

At Newton, Mrs. Sally Grafton, wife of Rev. Mr. Grafton, aged 41.—In South Carolina, Hon. Ralph Izard.—At New York, Hon. John Stratton, late member of Congress.—At Boston, Samuel Rogers, Esq. aged 57; Mrs. Mary Mahony, aged 75.—At Holliston, Mrs. Mary Prentiss, relict of the late Rev. Joshua Prentiss, aged 81.—In Charleston, Col. Thomas Sereven, aged 64.—In Shutesbury (Va.) [110] Mr. Ephraim Pratt, aged 117 years.—In Westboro', Mr. John Belknap, aged 101.—In Worcester, Mr. Clare Chandler, aged 60.—In Roxbury, Mr. James Mears, aged 73.—At Keene, Capt. Alpheus Nims, aged 49.—At Vealtown (N.J.) Mr. Samuel Hains.—At Dummerston, of a consumption, Mr. John Wilder, aged 34.

At Acworth, much lamented, Miss Clarry Chatterton, daughter of Mr. Joseph Chatterton, aged 13 years and ten months:—Very suddenly, Mrs. Elizabeth Thornton, consort of Mr. Stephen Thornton, aged 43.

Vol. XII (No. 587) Saturday, 30 June 1804.

¶ [3c] We hear from Westminster, that on the 12th inst. a lad by the name of Burbank, about 16 years of age, having engaged to perform the duties of a soldier in one of the militia Companies in that town for his employer, was unfortunately killed. One of the soldiers who was forward of him accidentally slipped down, and being anxious to save his gun from injury, threw it back; the bayonnet of which entered the eye of this unfortunate young lad, and came out at the back of his head, and he expired instantaneously. [*Worcester paper*].

† [3d] Extensive account of the death of Mr. Phillip Miller, of Lebanon, N.J., who was killed while raising a barn; he left a wife and three children. This article is contained within the death notices. ♦

===== ¶ [3d] MARRIED. =====

At Elizabethtown, (N.J.) on Friday the 1st inst. the Rev. Henry Kollock, Professor of Divinity in the College of New Jersey, to Mrs. Campbell.

At Charlestown, (Mass.) by the Rev. Dr. Morse, Mr. David Devens, merchant, to Miss Abigail Adams, both of that place.

===== ¶ [3d] DIED. =====

At Newark, (N.J.) Mrs. Rachel Budinot, consort of the Hon. Judge Budinot, of that place.—In Salem, Mrs. Jemima [Morona?], aged 82.—In Greenfield, in a fit of the Epilepsy, Azor Smead, Esq. attorney at law, aged 26.—In Windham, Mrs. Anna Elderkin, aged 84.—In Springfield (Mass.) Mr. S. Pepoon, aged 81.—At Worcester, Mr. John Wm. Caldwell, attorney at law, aged 23.—In Beverly, Mrs. Nancy Emerson, consort of Rev. Joseph E.—At Medford, Mrs. M. Billings, aged 79.

Vol. XI (No. 588) Saturday, 7 July 1804.

† [3c] Account of the journey of the Packet *Experiment*, Isaac Riddle, commander, from Bedford, N.H., via the Middlesex Canal, to the arrival at Boston. ♦

† [3c] Detailed account of the murder at Canton, Mass. of Sally Talbot, aged about 14, daughter of Mr. Daniel Talbot, "a respectable yeoman of that town." The suspect was one John Batteas, or Beatis. ♦

† [3d] Extensive detail concerning the death of Capt. Christian Johnson, who died at Lebanon township, N.J., six months after injuring his hand while bridling his horse. ♦

† [3d] Several pieces of property offered for sale at Troy, [Vt.—Ed.], and Peacham, Vt., by William Moore; adv. dated at Peacham, 20 June 1804.

¶ [3d] DIED.

In Geneva, M. Necker, formerly Minister of Finance in France.—In England, Mrs. Morrell, aged 44, a woman well known throughout Great Britain as an extraordinary production of nature, born without arms. She could cut the smallest watch papers and devices, in the most ingenious manner, by means of her toes.—In Springfield, (Mass.) Capt. Thomas Stebbins, aged 77.

Vol. XII (No. 589) Saturday, 14 July 1804.

† [3d] Nathaniel Emerson and James Hopkins, Proprietors of the Stoddard Turnpike Corporation, announce a meeting to be held at John Gibson's tavern, Francistown, N.H.
¶ [3d] CAUTION ! All persons are hereby forbid harbouring or trusting my son, Abel, on my account; as I will pay no debt of his contracting after this date.
ELI SANDERSON.
Springfield, Vt. July 14.

¶ [3c] MARRIED.

At Rumney, (S.C) Rev. Dr. Isaac S. Keith, to Miss Jane Huxham.
At Philadelphia, the Rev. Thomas Sergent, of Maryland, to Miss Helena Barlow.
At New York, Mr. James Waterman, printer, to Miss Hannah Fountain.
In this town, on Monday last, by the Rev. Mr. Fessenden, Mr. Noah Curtis, of Richmond, aged 73, to Miss Jenny M'Cullough, aged 47.

¶ [3c-d] DIED.

In Charleston, (S.C.) Mr. James Patterson, lately from Jamaica.—In Boston, Mrs. Elizabeth Chamberlain, aged 87.—At Marblehead, Mrs. Sarah Frero, aged 71.—In Bolton, (Ms.) Capt. Philip Cooledge, aged 85.—At New Ipswich, Mr. Enos Knight, aged 74.
At Acworth, a child of Mr. Jacob Haywood, aged three years and six months.—Two children of Mr. James Dickey; and a child of Mr. Daniel Campbell, of the canker rash.

Vol. XII (No. 590) Saturday, 21 July 1804.

¶ [3c] On the evening of the 7th inst. at the moving of a barn in Washington, Capt. Samuel Jones was severely wounded. His leg was crushed in a shocking manner, and it was found necessary that amputation should be performed, above the knee, which took place the day after.—It is hoped he will recover.
† [3c] Nathaniel Cross adv. for a colt he found; dated Walpole 18 July 1804.
† [3d] Simeon Olcott, Esq. and others petition the General Court regarding a proposed toll road.

¶ [3c] MARRIED.

At Windsor, Vt. Mr. Joshua Pennyman, of New London, Con. to Miss Clarissa Bates, of Killingworth, Con.
——— Mr. Isaiah H. Carpenter, printer, to Miss Elizabeth Welch.

¶ [3c] DIED.

At Plymouth, the Rev. Nathan Ward, aged 83.—At Concord, Mrs. Elizabeth Dow.—At Royalston, Mrs. Dewey, aged 38.—At Townsend, V. Ephraim Wheelock,[111] Esq. aged 40.—At Albany, Mr. Lewis Barrington, aged 90.—At Marblehead, Mrs. Sarah Frero, aged 71.—At Philadelphia, William Savery, a revered minister of the Society of Friends.—At Springfield, Capt. T. Stebbins, aged 77.—At Charlton, widow Tabitha Green, aged 75.—At Boston, Mr. Thomas Needham, aged 70: Miss H. Luckis, aged 78. —At Gosport, (Isle of Shoals) Josiah Stevens, Esq. aged 61.
We are concerned to state, that a son of Mr. Samuel Gray, jun. of Salem, about 14 years of age, was yesterday afternoon instantaneously killed by lightning. He was returning to town with several others, who had been sailing in the harbour in a pleasure boat, when the fatal stroke cut short the hopes of parents and friends by his death. No other person in the boat received any injury. [*Salem Gazette.*

Vol. XII (No. 591) Saturday, 28 July 1804.

† [3d] Alexander Fish adv. for a lost horse; dated at New Marlboro', 23 July 1804.

¶ [3c] MARRIED.—In this town on Thursday last, by N. Townsley, Esq. Mr. Nathan Daggett, of Westmoreland, to Miss Zeruah Graves.

¶ [3c] DIED.—At Barnstable, Hon. Thomas Smith, Esq. aged 85.—At Cambridge, Mr. Stephen Sewall, aged 71.—In Boston, Mr. Alexander [Steel?], bookbinder, aged 60.—Mr. Andrew Dunlap, brewer, aged 64.—Capt. Samuel Stetson, aged 37. He expired a few minutes after the return of the procession from the interment of his wife.—At Portsmouth, Mr. Caleb Brewster, aged 66.—At Salem, Capt. John Berry, aged 70.—At Brattleboro', Hon. Samuel Knights.—At Milford, Mr. Amos Boutell, aged 61.—At Philadelphia, Ruth Wood, aged 100 years.—In Suffield, Dea. Aaron Phelps, aged 71.—In Keene, Mrs. Elizabeth Blake, aged 83.

In this town, on Thursday last, Mr. Gurdon Huntington, post-master, aged 41.

Vol. XII (No. 592) Saturday, 4 Aug. 1804.

† [3c] Capt. Snow Stetson catches an unusual find, while fishing off Boston. ♦

¶ [3c] DIED.

In Gorham, (Maine) Hon. William Gorham, Esq. aged 62. Judge of Probate and Chief Justice of the Court of Common Pleas for the county of Cumberland.—In Edgecomb, Rev. Benjamin Chapman, aged 46, a minister of that place.—In Haverhill, (suicide) Mr. Daniel Webb, aged 48, a native of England.—In Boston, Mrs. Elizabeth Wells, [sic] aged 39, consort of Arnold Welles, [sic] Esq. and eldest daughter of the late Major General Warren.—At New-Fane, Mr. Thomas Greene, aged 81.—In Woodbridge, Rev. Stephen Rawley, aged 66.—In Bridgewater, widow Mary Orr, aged 80.—In Boston, suddenly, Mr. Peregrine White, of Westmoreland, N.H. aged 36. He was a descendant of, and bore the name, of the first white male child born in America.—In Fairfax, Vt. Dr. Joseph Farnsworth, aged 90.

In this town, on Monday last, Mr. Phinehas Rice, in the 69th year of his age.

Vol. XII (No. 593) Saturday, 11 Aug. 1804.

¶ [2d] Whereas Auphe my wife has eloped from my bed and board, and hath made a practice in so doing, and hath taken two children with her, this is to forbid all persons harboring or trusting her, or any of my children for I will pay no debts of this contracting after this date.

THOMAS DARBY.

Westmoreland, Aug. 9.

Vol. XII (No. 594) Saturday, 18 Aug. 1804.

¶ [2b] Charleston, South Carolina, July 11. Mrs. Micow, wife of Lewis Micow, heretofore a tailor at Cape Francois, now in this city, has lately been informed that her said husband was not massacred at the Cape, as she supposed, but had made his escape in some vessel to one of the Northern States: this is to inform him, should he be still living, that his wife and daughter are in this city, and are anxiously waiting to hear some tidings of him. ☞ The printers in the northern states, will oblige an unfortunate woman, by giving this notice a place once or twice in their publications.

† [2c] Accounts of several lightning strikes in Massachusetts, [on 7 Aug. 1804—Ed.]: 1) Mr. Talbot of Sharon, Mass. died a few days after being struck by lightning at Dedham, Mass. ♦ 2) Several farm animals belonging to Mr. Artemas Bartlett, of Holden, Mass. killed by a lightning strike. 3) Mr. Gregg's barn at Brookline struck and burnt.

† [2c] Rev. Diodate Brockway, of Ellington, Conn., survives a fall 65 feet from a meetinghouse. ♦

¶ [3b] Was drowned lately on the west side of Lake Champlain, after conducting "his own affairs in his own way, unembarrassed by too much regulation, or fiscal exactions," the noted Timothy Call, of money making memory. Having received a collegiate education at a New England university, he prostituted his talents for the above illicit purpose, and came to this untimely end.

† [3d] Apollos Gillmore adv. for a lost horse; dated Walpole, 17 Aug.

===== ¶ [3d] MARRIED. =====

In Paris, (N.Y.) Mr. Francis Amory, mer. of Boston, to Miss Sally Kirkland, sister of the Rev. Mr. Kirkland, of Boston.

At Claremont, Mr. Godfrey Cook, to Miss Abigail Hubbard, of Charlestown.

===== ¶ [3d] DIED. =====

In England, Miss Maria Manson, aged 17:—she hung herself in a fit of love phrenzy: a coroner's jury brought in as verdict that she "died by a visitation of Cupid."

In Philadelphia, from July 28 to August 4, 55: 21 adults, 34 children.—In New York, for the last seven days ending the 4th August, 61.

At Point Petre, Mr. Peyton Randolph Gardner, of Portsmouth, aged 24.—At Enfield, (N.H.) Mr. Alexander Campbell, jun. aged 28.—In Dover, (Del.) Pompey, aged 120.—In Amherst, Captain Ebenezer Boltwood, aged 52.—In Boston, Mrs. Mary M'Cleary, aged 55. On Monday morning last, deeply lamented by the People of his Charge, and by the public also, the Rev. Dr. Simeon Howard, Pastor of the West Church in Boston.

In this town, two infant children of Mr. Phinehas Rice.

Vol. XII (No. 595) Saturday, 25 Aug. 1804.

† [3d] John Hubbard adv. for lost horses; dated at Charlestown, 20 Aug. 1804.

† [3d] Legal notice: Benjamin Palmer, John Prentiss, and John French appointed Commissioners over the insolvent estate of the late John White, of Langdon, N.H. Abel French and Esther White, Administrators.

† [3d] Elisha Kingsbery and Bill Blake announce that their copartnership is dissolved; dated "Alstead & Bellows' Falls, August 20, 1804." In the notice immediately following, Elisha Kingsbery, Isaac Randal, and Bill Blake announce that their copartnership is dissolved; dated at Alstead, 20 Aug.

Vol. XII (No. 596) Saturday, 1 Sept. 1804.

† [3d] Legal notice regarding the insolvent estate of Gurdon Huntington, gent., late of Walpole, deceased. James Campbell, Isaac Redington, and Alex. Watkins named as Commissioners, and Asa Sibley was the Administrator; business meeting to be held at the home of widow Temperance Huntington.

† [3d] Legal notice regarding the estate of Oliver Lovell, Esq., late of Rockingham, deceased; Irena Lovell, Executrix. Dated at Rockingham, 20 Aug. 1804.

===== ¶ [3d] DIED. =====

At Marlow, on the 13th inst. Mr. Solomon Gee, aged 68.—At Sturbridge, Widow Sarah Wilder, aged 90.—At New York, Mr. John Harrison, editor of the New York Museum.—At Northampton, Mrs. Phelps, aged 93: Mrs. Clarke aged 92: Mr. Ethan Marshall, aged 67.—At Berwick, Elder Daniel Libbey, aged 88; descendants 201.—At Windham, Con. Elder Benjamin Lathrop, aged 78: Mr. Seth Palmer, aged 81.—At Michilimakinac, Mathew Henry, Esq.—In Portland, 15th ult. Mr. Samuel Gookin, aged 75; and the next day, Sarah, his wife, aged 73.—At Alstead, on the 22d last month, very suddenly, Mr. Joshua Shepard.

At Hanover, the Hon. Bezaleel Woodward, Esq. for many years Professor of Natural Philosophy, &c. in Dartmouth College, and Judge of the Court of Common Pleas.

At Middleton's Ferry, South Carolina side, in a duel, (with Mr. John Rowe) Mr. William Appling, of Columbia county, Virginia.

Drowned, at Sheshequin on the Susquehannah, on Sunday the 29th July, Miss Cyrene Drown, aged 18; Miss Rebecca Rogers, aged 12, and William Rogers, aged 7 years.

Drowned, in the river Alatamaha, Georgia, Mr. Henry Brazer, late of Worcester, aged 26.

The number of deaths in the city of Philadelphia for the week ending the 11th August, were 79.

Deaths in the city of Baltimore, for the week ending the 13th August, were 28.

In New York, from August 11 to 18th, 77; 22 adults, 55 children, of whom 31 were boys and 24 girls, 43 under two years of age; 30 died of flux, 6 of consumption, 6 of

dysentery, and 6 of small pox; none of the yellow fever.
In Philadelphia, from August 11 to 18th, 57;—20 adults, 37 children.

Vol. XII (No. 597) Saturday, 8 Sept. 1804.

† [2c-d] William Southick of New Salem found guilty of attempting to obtain the prize of the South Hadley Lottery with a forged ticket. ♦
† [2d] Death notice of Mr. Samuel Carlisle, aged 38, who died at Charlestown, N.H. "on Thursday the 6th inst."
† [3d] Elisha Kingsbery offers property for sale at Alstead, N.H.
¶ [3d] DIED.

In Philadelphia, of the cholera Morbus, Maj. General William Irvine, a distinguished officer in the revolutionary war.—Near Elizabeth-town, N.J. Mrs. Sarah Whitehead, aged 103.—At Newfane, Mr. Joseph Hall, aged 71.—At Charlestown, on Thursday morning last, Mr. Samuel Carlisle, æ. 38.

Vol. XII (No. 598) Saturday, 15 Sept. 1804.

† [3b] Rev. James W. Woodward ordained over the "Congregational [112] Church" at Norwich, Vt. ♦
† [3c] Nathaniel Smith adv. for a colt which he found; dated Walpole, 10 Sept. 1804.
¶ [3b-c] MARRIED.

At Brattleboro', Vt. Elijah H. Mills, Esq. attorney at Law, of Northampton, to Miss Harriet Blake, of Boston.
In England, Mr. Jolly, aged 24, to Miss Mary Musgrove, aged 60 [. . .]
¶ [3c] DIED.

At Monson, Mrs. Lucy Hoar, aged 43.—At Wethersfield, Lieut. Jonathan Church, aged 40.—At Charleston, S.C. Rev. Nicholson Waters, aged 65.—Near New York City, Commodore James Nicholson, aged 69.—At Philadelphia, Dr. John Blair Lynn, pastor of the First Congregational Church in that city.—In the city of New York, from August 25 to the 1st inst. 57 persons, 36 of whom were under two years of age.—At Menotomy, Mr. Thomas Hall, aged 44.—At Gloucester, Gen. Eliphalet Davis, aged 48.—At Poughkeepsie, Robert H. Livingston, Esq.—In Kentucky, the Rev. John Gano.—At New Boston, Mrs. Rebecca Cristy, aged 25.—At Ashburnham, Capt. Ebenezer Thomas Adams, aged 48.—At Amherst, Mrs. Rebecca Harvey, aged 65.—At Portsmouth, Mrs. Elizabeth Twiman, aged 84; Mr. Theodore Davis, aged 52.
DROWNED.—In Otter Creek, near Middlebury, Mr. Thomas Hall, of Cornwall, aged 24.

Vol. XII (No. 590) [113] Saturday, 22 Sept. 1804.

† [3d] Stephen R. Whitman adv. medicines for sale, in the shop which he purchased from *Johnson & Orr* in Walpole.
† [3d] Duncan Cook adv. for a journeyman tailor and an apprentice; dated at Charlestown, 14 Sept. 1804.

Vol. XII (No. 600) Saturday, 29 Sept. 1804.

¶ [3c] ORDAINED—At New Salem, the Rev. Warren Pierce.
† [3d] Nathaniel R. Smith adv. for a lost pocket book, taken at Madson's Tavern in Charlestown.
† [3d] Adv. of goods for sale by *Leverett Tuttle & Co.*, dated at Bellows Falls, 19 Sept.
¶ [3c] MARRIED.

At Burlington, Rev. Eliphalet B. Coleman, to Miss Alice Fitch.
At Exeter, Capt. Henry Moore, of Portsmouth, to Miss Ann Odiorne, of Exeter:—Rev. Jacob Cram, of Hampton Falls, to Miss Mary Poor, of Exeter.
At Lancaster, P. Stephen Smith, Esq. to Miss Elizabeth Ruggles. It is worthy of remark that each party entered their *ninety third* year, on the day they approached the altar of Hymen.

In England, Mr. William Arney, at the advanced age of 82, a celebrated Welsh poet, to Miss Ann Francis, aged 16.

In England, Mr. Cook to Miss Mutton. Between the two, a very palatable meal may be prepared.

===== ¶ [3c-d] DIED. =====

In New York, from Aug. 25th to Sept. 1st, 57; 16 adults and 41 children:—from Sept. 1st to 8th, 70: 21 adults and 49 children.

In Philadelphia, from Aug. 25 to Sept. 3, 47; 20 adults and 27 children:—in the succeeding week were 55; 19 adults and 36 children.

In Baltimore, from Sept. 3d to 10th, 21; 8 adults and 13 children.

In Boston, for the week ending Sept. 8th, 15; 8 adults and 7 children.

At Sutton, Mr. James Adams, aged 88.—At Charleston, S.C. Mrs. Mary Pinckney.—At Harwinton, in an advanced age, Mr. Timothy Humason; Daniel Catlin, Esq. aged 47; Widow Abigail Lankton, aged 84.—At Gloucester, Gen. Eliphalet Davis, aged 48.—At Keene, Mr. Luther Bragg, aged 63.—Murdered, in the wilderness not far from Natchez, Mr. Robert M'Alpin, of Georgia.—Murdered, in Charleston, S.C. Mr. James Shaw, factor of that city, by Richard Dennis, jun. The latter has been committed.—In Virginia, Buller Claiborne, Esq.—At Litchfield, Reuben Smith, Esq. aged 68.—At Sandbornton, Capt. Abram Perkins, aged 69. At Henniker, Mrs. Patty Childs, aged 57.—At Hanover, Mrs. Hannah Brewster, consort of General Ebenezer Brewster.—At Boston, Mrs. Hannah Weld, aged 71; Capt. John Palfrey, aged 56; Mrs. Nancy Robbins, aged 84.—At Charlestown, (Mass.) Mrs. Abigail [Bradish?], aged 69.—At Dorchester, Mrs. Elizabeth Kelton, aged 71; Mr. Edward Glover, aged 61.—At Kingston, (N.H.) John Eastman, Esq. aged 60. Engaged in moderate exercise in the field, he fell, and instantly expired.—At Baltimore, suddenly, Nahunt Fay, M.D. of Boston.—In New Jersey, Vincent Dey, aged 28: hung himself in his room; insanity.—In Dresden, (Maine) 10th instant, Hon. Jonathan Bowman, Esq. aged 69; Judge of Probate, and a Judge in the Court of Common Pleas for the County of Lincoln.—In England, Vice Admiral C. Parker, son of Ad. Sir Peter Parker, and distinguished by many gallant actions in the naval service:—the celebrated Admiral Duncan, who defeated Dutch fleet off Camperdown.

On the 10th ult. Capt. Joseph Case, of Anstinsburg, (Ohio) aged 51, in passing a stream near his house, in flood water, fell from his boat, probably in a fit, and was drowned.

Vol. XII (No. 601) Saturday, 6 Oct. 1804.

† [2d-3a] Item of agricultural news, regarding Nathaniel Graves of Westmoreland.

† [3c] Installations: 1) Thomas Jones, late pastor at the Universalist Church in Philadelphia, to the First Christian Independent Society at Gloucester, Mass. 2) Rev. Frothingham to the Second Congregational Church, Lynn, Mass. 3) Rev. Ebenezer Price, at Boscawen.

¶ [3c] TAKE NOTICE. Whereas Lydia, my wife, has eloped from my bed and board, I hereby forbid all persons harbouring or trusting her on my account, as I will pay no debts contracted by her.

ABEL RICE.

Claremont, Sept. 30, 1804.

===== ¶ [3c-d] DIED. =====

In Philadelphia, from Sept. 15 to 22d, 38; 19 adults and 19 children.—In New York, from 15th to 22d Sept. 57; comprising 15 men, 7 women, 15 boys and 14 girls; 11 persons died of consumption, and 6 of the small pox.—New Carlisle, (Penn.) Margaret Hetherington, who gained a livelihood by carrying butter and eggs to Carlisle market, which, during half a century, she attended regularly on foot, twice a week, amounted, in the whole time to nearly 100,000 miles.—In Stockbridge, (Mass.) Mrs. Elizabeth West, consort of the Rev. Dr. West, aged 74; Henry W. Dwight, Esq. aged 47.—On the 27th ult. at his seat in Roxbury, Martin Brimmer, Esq. aged 62.—In Boston, Mr. Samuel Bass, aged 84: Mr. Benjmain Ober—killed by the accidental discharge of a gun: on the 28th ult. while in the act of trying on a pair of shoes, in a store, a Mr. Miles, of Ashfield.—In Savannah, (Georgia) Mr. Peter Johonnot Seaver, mer. aged 34, a native of Boston.—In Charleston, (S.C.) the Rev. George Hartwell, aged 46, a native of Ireland.

At New Bedford, on the 24th ult. the Rev. Joseph Willard, DD. LL D. President of Harvard University—aged 65 [. . .]

Vol. XII (No. 602) Saturday, 13 Oct. 1804.

† [3d] Daniel Spooner adv. "that he now carries on the Hat manufacturing in its various branches, in the shop lately occupied by Richard H. Jones, in Walpole."

Vol. XII (No. 603) Saturday, 20 Oct. 1804.

† [3b] Lengthy account of a severe storm which struck New England. Among the casualties, all aboard a Hallowell Packet, Capt. Weston, which was lost off Capt. Porpoise. "The body of Dr. Appleton, of Waterville, formerly of New Ipswich, his wife and child, have been found."

† [3d] Adv. by Joseph Dorothy and Jacob Pierce who are licensed to build and sell a machine for shelling indian corn; dated at Alstead, 15 Oct. 1804.

===== ¶ [3d] MARRIED. =====

At Boston, Mr. Henry Prentiss, of New Ipswich, to Miss Sally Whipple.

At Marlborough, Mr. George Washington Philips, of Dublin, to Miss Lucinda Bemis, of the former place.

===== ¶ [3d] DIED. =====

At Princeton, Mr. Sadey Mason, aged 76: Capt. Amos Merriam, aged 44.—Killed, at Concord, 114 Grafton county, Mr. Robert Barkley, of Lyman, aged 48, by a fall from a bridge building over the Amonoosick. He has left an afflicted widow and nine children to mourn his loss.—The whole number of deaths in Boston last week, 16; 7 ad, 9 ch.

In this town, on Tuesday last, Capt. John Jenison, aged 60—an honest man, and a good member of society.

Vol. XII (No. 604) Saturday, 27 Oct. 1804.

¶ [3a] An unhappy accident occurred at Leominster week before last at a Regimental review. After the troops were dismissed, a great number of scattering guns were fired, and, as is common, with very little precaution. Mr. Silas Whitney, a Lieut. of a Company from Ashburnham, received the contents of a heavy loaded musket in the groin, and no hopes are entertained of his recovery.—*Keene Sent.*

¶ [3a] At Stoddard, on the 11th inst. Mrs. Betsey Adams, aged 53, wife of Deac. Ephraim Adams, was found hanging by a skein of yarn on one of the pins of a loom in an out house.—The verdict of the Jury, *insanity.*—Mrs. Adams (who has left 7 children to lament her shocking exit) discovered symptoms of a disordered imagination eight or ten weeks ago—but until within six weeks, had been to appearance perfectly free. Since which time, although Deacon Adams was possessed of a handsome interest, she imagined the family were coming to want, and must inevitably perish before the ensuing spring. She was highly respected by her neighbors and acquaintance. [*Keene Sent.*

† [3d] David Cottrell adv. land for sale at Jamaica, Vermont, dated 5 Oct. 1804.

===== ¶ [3d] MARRIED. =====

In Salem, Mr. Jacob Peabody, merchant, to Miss Lucy Manning.

In Providence, Sullivan Dorr, Esq. of Boston, to Miss Lydia Allen, of that place.

===== ¶ [3d] DIED. =====

At Danville, Capt. James Chamberlin.—In Salem, Charles C. Carlton.—In In [sic] Ryegate, Mrs. Sarah Johnson, aged 79.—Jamaica, Hon. Wm. Jackson, Chief Justice.—In Portsmouth, in consequence of a fall, Mr. John Rundlet, aged 17.—In Halifax, Vt. Lieut. Benjamin Rice, aged 80.—In Charleston, S.C. Rev. James Malcomson.—In Easton, Dr. John Kittridge.—At his seat, Pleasant Hill, Charlestown, on the 13th inst. very suddenly, Joseph Barrell, Esq. aged 64.—In Boston, Mrs. Sarah Stimson, aged 70: Mrs. Charlotte Boyer, aged 63.—At New-Milford, N.Y. Col. Isaac Nicolls.—In New York, deaths from the 6th to the 13th inst. 46.—In Connecticut, Rev. Jeremiah Learning, D.D. aged 87.—At Newton, Deacon Jonas Stone, aged 92.—At New Hartford, Mrs. Lucy Jerome, consort of the Rev. Amasa Jerome, and daughter of Lieut. Governor Treadwell, aged 24.—At Leicester, Mr. Thomas Snow, aged 74.—In Reading, Mr. Thomas Rayner, aged 63.—In Charlestown, (Mass.) Mr. John Harris, aged 58.—In Annapolis, (Maryland) Gen. John Hoskins Stone;—in our revolutionary war a distingquished officer, and from '94 to '97 was Governor of Maryland.—In Baltimore, from Oct. 9 to 16th, 27 deaths; 19 adults, 8 children.—In Bedford, on Sunday last, Mrs. Margaret Fassett, aged 50 wife of Mr. Asa F. of Alstead, N.H.—In Milton, 7th ult. Thomas Crane, Esq.—In Boston, Mrs. Mary Harvey, aged 73: 19th inst. Major Christopher Marshall, aged 63.

Executed, at New-Brunswick, pursuant to his sentence for the *murder of his father*, John Pullen.

Vol. XII (No. 605) Saturday, 3 Nov. 1804.

† [3a, 3c] Robbery at the store of Amasa and Oliver Allen, Walpole. ♦

===== ¶ [3c] MARRIED. =====

In this town, Mr. Benjamin Muzzy, to Mrs. Jane Ingalls.

On Thursday morning last, Francis Gardner, Esq. to Miss Peggy Leonard, of West Springfield.

===== ¶ [3c] DIED. =====

At Westminster, Joseph Willard, Esq. aged 84.—At Springfield, Capt. Joseph Lyman, aged 73.—In France, Ad. Latouche Treville, an able office, and, we think, commander of the Toulon fleet.

Vol. XII (No. 606) Saturday, 10 Nov. 1804.

¶ [2d] We hear from Thompson, a town bordering on this County, but in the State of Connecticut, that on Saturday the 15th inst. a dispute arose between Dr. Weaver and a Mr. Starr, at the house of the latter. Mr. Starr, it is said, ordered the Doctor out of his house, but he not going, Starr attempted to push him out, when Starr received a blow from the Doctor, which immediately terminated his existence. The Doctor we learn is committed. [*Worcester paper.*]

† [3b] Adv. of goods for sale by Eben Stearns and John Stearns, a.k.a. *E. & J. Stearns*, who "have taken the Store lately occupied by Messrs. Roby & Curtis." Dated at Charlestown, Nov. 1804.

===== ¶ [3b] DIED. =====

In Loudon, Mr. Jethro Bachelder, aged 81.—At Groton, Deac. Benjamin Bancroft, aged 80.—At New Orleans, Joseph Briggs, Esq. private secretary to Gov. Claiborne.—At Enosburg, suddenly, Rev. Job Swift, D.D. of Addison.—At Brookfield, Mr. Eli Howe, aged 52.—At Sterling, Mrs. Elizabeth Putnam, aged 78.—At Dudley, Abigail Corbin, aged 76.—At Westminster, Mrs. Priscilla Eaton, consort of Major Isaiah Eaton, late of this town, aged 40.—Deaths in New York, for the week ending 17th ult. 39: 10 men, 17 women, 7 boys, and 5 girls.—In New Orleans, Gov. Claiborne's lady and child.—In Philadelphia from the 20th to the 27th October, 42 deaths; 16 adults, and 26 children.—In Baltimore, from the 22d to the 20th October, 21 deaths: 13 adults and 8 children.—In Boston, Mr. Robert Patridge, aged 45.

COMMUNICATION. Died, at Westminster, on the 5th inst. after a short but severe illness, Mrs. Priscilla Eaton, wife of Maj. Isaiah Eaton [. . .]

Vol. XII (No. 607) Saturday, 17 Nov. 1804.

¶ [2b] Raleigh, North Carolina, Oct. 20. A most atrocious and wilful murder was perpetrated in the county of Mecklenburg, in this State, on the 16th inst. on the body of John Cooke, Esq. High Sheriff, whilst in the lawful execution of the duties of his office, by a certain Thomas Jarrel, alias Thomas Fitch Jarrel, by firing a gun at him, the contents of which passed through his head. Unfortunately for humanity and justice, this execrable wretch has made his escape, and it is supposed that he will aim for the State of Tennessee.

¶ [2b-3a] A report of a very distressing nature, has reached us from Niagara—That Judge Cartwright, and a number of the principal Judicial officers of Upper Canada, a short time since, on their passage from Kingston to York, where a court was to be held for the trial of a Messasauga Indian for murder, have all perished—no information having been received of them for 10 or 12 days after their sailing, and parts of a wreck having been discovered on the lake, which it was lear[n]ed was the unfortunate vessel which they were on board of. [*Albany Gazette.*]

† [3c] William Sterne adv. "that he has taken a Store, next door South of Messrs. Bellows & Stone's" where he sells medicines; dated Walpole 16 Nov. 1804.

† [3c] Legal notice regarding a lawsuit: "Aaron Swan, of Lyman, Grafton Co., N.H., vs. Nathan Skerret and Sabin Johnson, both of said Lyman, husbandmen or Gentlemen, Trustees of Timothy Tucker, late of Westmoreland, in our county of Cheshire, now resident in the State of New York, cooper . . . " ♦

===== ¶ [3b] MARRIED. =====

At Charlestown, Mass. Mr. Joseph Cushing, of Amherst, editor of the Farmer's Cabinet, to Miss Rebecca Edmunds, of the former place.

In Old York, Gen. Abiel Wood, of Wiscasset, to Miss Sarah S. Katen, of the former place.

At Hanover, Dr. Eliphalet Lyman, of Stafford, (C.) to Miss Abigail Ripley, daughter of the late Rev. Sylvanus Ripley.

===== ¶ [3b-c] DIED. =====

In London, (England) John Hancock, Esq.—In Nova Scotia, Rev. Joshua W. Weeks, formerly Episcopal Minister at Marblehead.—In Pittsfield, Eli Root, Esq. aged 74.—In Scarborough, Col. Samuel March, aged 76; a very capable and active officer in our revolutionary war.—In New Orleans, Mr. George Cooper, printer, of New Jersey.—In Milton, after a lingering illness, Mrs. Esther Vose.—At Petersham, Mr. Simeon Aldrich, aged 44.—At Leicester, Mrs. Mary Washburn, aged 70.—At Upton, Mr. Moses Partridge, aged 71.—In New York, Mr. William Fitch.—At Merrimac, Jonathan Woods, in the 11th year of his age;—Nathaniel W. Woods, in his 3d year; both son of Deacon Ebenezer Woods:—Also, three daughters of Mr. Benjamin Woods, in their 7th, 5th, and 2d years. All the above mentioned children died between the 11th and 28th ult. with the dysentary. They were the children of brothers whose house were adjoining.—In Baltimore, from Oct. 29 to Nov. 5, 24 deaths; 11 adults, 13 children.—In Philadelphia, from the 27th Oct. to the 3d Nov. 42 deaths; 26 adults, 16 children.—In New York, from the 26th Oct. to the 3d Nov. 42 deaths; of whom 14 were men, 10 women, 13 boys, and 6 girls; by taking laudanum (suicide) one person; *Ten of Small Pox!*—In Providence (R.I.) Mr. Daniel Branch, aged 81.—In Salem, Capt. John Lambert, aged 63.—In Weymouth, Capt. Samuel Arnold.—In Watertown, William Hunt, Esq. aged 54.—In Boston, Major Thomas Fobes, aged 40.

Vol. XII (No. 608) Saturday, 24 Nov. 1804.

† [3d] Bellows & Stone adv. for a lost cow; dated Walpole, 20 Nov. 1804.

===== ¶ [3d] MARRIED. =====

In Baltimore, George Dugan, Esq. to Miss Eliza Chase, daughter of the Hon. Samuel Chase, of that city.

At Keene, Mr. Henry Strong, to Miss Milatiah French. Mr. Henry Bragg, to Miss Polly Felt.

===== ¶ [3d] DIED. =====

At Salisbury, Mrs. Rachel Meloon, aged 94.—At Warner, Nathaniel Beane, Esq. aged 55.—At New Orleans, Mr. Hotchkiss, contractor to the army.—At Hebron, Col. John Peters, aged 86.—At Hopkinton, Mrs. Martha Maxson, aged 100 years, and 14 days.—At Westfield, Mr. Pliny Pomroy, aged 71.—At Philadelphia, Mrs. Mary Hopkinson, aged 87.—In Landigrove, Vt. Mr. Benjamin Archer, formerly of Keene.—In Boston, Ms. Mr. Joseph Houghton, aged 62 ; Col. Robert Longley, aged 72 ; Mrs. Thankful Wheeler, aged 75.—In London, August 24, Mrs. Margaret Arnold, aged 44, widow of Brig. Gen. A. and daughter of the Hon. Edward Shippen, Chief Justice of the state of Pennsylvania.—In Norfolk, Mr. Edward M[iric?], bookseller.—In Baltimore, during the month of Oct. 65 adults, 32 children.—From Nov. 5th to 12th, 11 adults, 8 children.—In Philad. during the month of Oct. 85 adults, 80 children;—from the 3d to 10th Nov. 18 adults, 13 children, total 31.—In New York, during the month of Oct. 119 males (60 men, 59 boys) and 89 females (56 women, 33 girls)—total 208.—In Salem, wid. Bullock, aged 90. In Groton, Hon. Oliver Prescott, Esq. æ. 73.

Vol. XII (No. 609) Saturday, 31 Nov. 1804. [115]

¶ [2c] SUICIDE.—Mr. Perkins, of the Theatre, put a period to his existence yesterday morning, by taking a large quantity of laudanum. This act is said to have been induced by the infidelity of his wife, who has gone away in company with the captain of a vessel. [116]

¶ [2d] Randolph, Vermont, Nov. 19. We hear from Newbury, in this State, that on Tuesday last, as some people were raising a Saw-mill, a Mr. Samuel Meservey fell from the frame, a distance of 18 feet, upon the rocks underneath, which bruised him in such a shocking manner, that he is since dead. And on the next day, a man by the name of Joseph Rowe, fell from the same frame, and nearly the same spot; his head first struck a sharp rock, with such violence that it cracked the skull bone about seven inches, and broke off a piece of it the bigness of a dollar, which was found upon the rock; the skull bone was left entirely bare, the skin being all torn from it—a sight shocking to behold ! He was not dead when our informant left Newbury, and the surgeon even entertained some hopes of his recovery.

† [3a] Unusual item in the garden of Mr. Jonathan Conant, Jr., of Mount Vernon, NH.

¶ [3c] EARLY PARTURITION. A medical friend has communicated to us the following obstetrical incident. Mrs. Eliza Burlingame, wife of Mr. Amasa Burlingame, of Sturbridge, lately became the "living mother of a living son," weighing eight pounds, on the day that she (the mother) was twelve years, six months, and five days old. "*Thy wife shall be a fruitful vine.*" [National Ægis.

===== ¶ [3d] MARRIED. =====

At Plainfield, the Rev. John Lord, of Washington, (N.H.) to Miss Sally Chase, of Cornish. [*compare to the marriage record in 8 Dec. 1804*]

At Hanover, Mr. Eben. Knapp, to Mrs. Irene Wright.—Mr. Thomas Peabody, to Miss Elizabeth Willes—all of Hanover.

In New York, Mr. C.B. Brown, of Philadelphia, to Miss Elizabeth Linn, daughter of Rev. Dr. Linn.

===== ¶ [3d] DIED. =====

At Albany, much regretted, Gen. Philip Schuyler.—At Norwich, suddenly, Deacon Burnet, aged 79.—At Farmingham, [117] Major William Judd, aged 63.—At Hopkinton, Dr. John Clement.—In Georgia, Mr. James Thomas, aged 134; his eye-sight was so little impaired that he could read print, without the assistance of glasses, to the last year of his life.—In Baltimore, Mr. Robert Dew, sen. aged 73.—In Milton, Mr. Vose Crane, aged 74.—In Gloucester, Mr. Wm. Murphy, aged 76.—In North Providence, Mr. Daniel Collier, aged 87.—In New Bedford, Mrs. Abigail Lee, aged 84.—In Boston, Mrs. Francis Gibson, aged 34 : Mr. Thomas Wheeler, aged 73 : Mrs. Catharine Fullerton, aged 33.—In Paris, Gen. Rewbell, one of the Ex-Directors whom his Imperial Majesty, Napoleon I ordered to quit the Directorial throne, on the *pas charge*.—In Baltimore, from the 12th to 18th November, 17 ; 8 adults, 9 children.—In Philadelphia, from 10th to 17th Nov. 38 ; 20 ad. 18 child.—In New York, from the 10th to 17th Nov. 13 men, 6 women, 8 boys, 12 girls ; total 39 : 8 of *small pox !*——In Machias, George Stillman, Esq.—In Salem, Mrs. Eliza Grosvenor, aged 68, widow of the Rev. Ebenezer G. formerly of Harvard, and daughter of the Rev. Peter Clark, of Danvers.—In Portsmouth, Capt. Thomas Dannet, aged 42.

At Charlestown, on the 20th ult. Deacon *John Hastings*, aged 83,—one of the first settlers of that town.

Vol. XII (No. 610) Saturday, 8 Dec. 1804.

¶ [2c] Mr. Charles Prentiss, formerly of Leominister, in Mass. and some time editor of a paper in Baltimore, is about purchasing the establishment of the "Washington Federalist."

¶ [2d] On the night of Saturday the 24th ult. Capt. Joel Hatch, of Strafford, put a period to his existence by cutting his throat.

† [3d] Solomon Bellows adv. for a cow found on his land; dated Charlestown, 3 Dec.

====== ¶ [3c] MARRIED. ======

At Cornish, Doctor Jonathan Badger, of Concord, to Miss Elizabeth Hall, of the former place :—Mr. Joseph Carter, to Miss Margaret Taylor :—Mr. Benjamin Hilliard, to Miss Roxina Hall :—Mr. Israel Hale, to Miss Mary Wood :—Mr. Asaph Bennett, to Miss Sarah Simpson.

At Hartland, Mr. John Hall, of Cornish, to Miss Loisa Morgan.

At Windsor, (Con.) George Bliss, Esq. of Springfield, to Miss Abigail Rowland.

In Charlestown, (Mass.) by the Rev. Dr. Morse, Mr. John Soley, to Miss Rebecca Henley.

At Monkton, Mr. Joseph Turner, to Miss Sally Tuttle :—Mr. Ephraim Bates, to Miss Lucy Turrill.

At Lime, Mr. Lyman Converse, to Miss Polly Kent.

At Plainfield, Rev. John Low, [117A] of Washington, to Miss Sally Chase, of Cornish.

====== ¶ [3c-d] DIED. ======

In England, at a very advanced age, Thomas Brand Hollis, Esq. F.R.S.A.S.—In Albany, the Hon. Philip Schuyler ; a Major General in the revolutionary war, and father to the widow of the late Gen. Hamilton, aged 71 :—A man, eminent for his useful labours, in the military and civil affairs of our country.—In Farmington, (Con.) William Judd, Esq. High Priest of the Grand Chapter of Royal Arch Masons in Connecticut, aged 63 :—The deceased has held a conspicuous station in the political struggles in Connecticut, as one of the leaders of the democratic party in that state :—Independent of his politics, he was an able and useful citizen, and a humane and intelligent man.—Peace to his ashes.—In Danvers, William Shilaber, Esq. aged 70.—In Dorchester, Mr. Edward Holyoke, aged 71.—In Lexington, Mr. Thomas Robbins, aged 82.—In South Kingston, R.I. Mr. Thomas Salter, paper maker, formerly of Worcester.—At Newburyport, Joseph Cutler, Esq. aged 53, cashier of Merrimack Bank.—At Concord, Mr. John Souther, of the dysentery, aged 45.—At Allentown, George Evans, Esq.—At Winchester, Mr. Ebenezer Scott, aged 87.—At Northborough, (Mass.) Mrs. Persis Maynard, consort of Mr. Holland Maynard.—At Windsor, very suddenly, Mr. Ezra Conant, aged 82.—In Frankfort, (Ken.) 9th ult. Gen. John Caldwell, Lt. Gov. of Kentucky : of an inflammation of the brain ; he presided in the Senate on Thursday, and died on Friday.—In Kentucky, Col. James Barbour, aged 72 ; an officer in our revolutionary war.—In Baltimore, Captain James C. Stewart—from the 19th to 26th Nov. 8 ad. 5 chil.—In Philad. from the 24th to 29th Nov. 29 deaths ; 15 ad. 14 chil.—In N. York, from the 18th to 25th Nov. 42 ; of whom 12 were men, 9 boys, 11 women, and 10 girls ; 15 of *small-pox* !

In Carver, 17th Nov. the Rev. John Howland, Pastor of the Church of Christ, in that town, aged 84, and in the 59th year of his ministry [. . .]

It is an ill wind that blows nobody good.—Died, at Stockbridge, on the 30th June last, Mrs. Abia Dean, consort of Mr. Lemuel Dean, aged 44—and on the 27th September, Mr. Nathan Dean, aged 30.—Married, at the same place, on the 4th Nov. Mr. Lemuel Dean, the widower, to Mrs. Abigail Dean, the widow.

Vol. XII (No. 611) Saturday, 15 Dec. 1804.

† [3c] Rev. Ezra Leonard ordained in the Third Parish in Gloucester, Mass. ♦

† [3d] *Chapman & Hartwell* announce that they "being about to close business in this place . . ." request outstanding debts be paid up; dated Alstead, 4 Dec. 1804.

† [3d] Aaron Dean adv. for a lost heifer; dated at Charlestown, 10 Dec. 1804.

====== ¶ [3c] MARRIED. ======

In Lancaster, Hon. Benjamin Goodhue, Esq. of Salem, to Miss Ann Willard, daughter of the late Hon. Abijah Willard.

In Randolph, Vt. Mr. Wm. Bryant, to Miss Annas Spalding, of Plainfield, N.H.

In Boston, John Head, Esq. of Waldoborough, to Miss Sally Ross, of Boston.

====== ¶ [3c-d] DIED. ======

In Darien, (Geo.) Col. A. Thomas. This gentleman was among the many old officers that was removed by Mr. Jefferson—he went to Georgia to strive to accumulate property for his family, a thing he had neglected while in the service of his country, and has fallen a victim to that unhealthy climate.—In Berwick, Mrs. Sarah Lord, aged 89.—In Sturbridge, Mr. John Tarbell, aged 91.—In Barre, Mr. Ezekiel Lee, aged 74.—In Spencer, Mr. Thomas Grout, aged 75.—In Hingham, Mrs. Elizabeth Cushing, relict of the late Mr. Stephen C. aged 80.—In Boston, very suddenly, and deeply regretted, the Right Rev. Samuel Parker, D.D. Bishop of the Protestant Episcopal Church in Massachusetts, in the 60th year of his age.

At Brattleboro', Benjamin Butterfield, Esquire, aged 79.

At Philadelphia, Mr. Adam Gooss, aged 92 years, 6 months and 9 days. He was born at Rosenthal, in Germany, on the 19th May, 1712, and resided in Philadelphia 64 years.—On the day preceding his death, he paid his accustomed visit to his grand and great grandchildren, and appeared to enjoy his usual health, and on the morning following he departed without any apparent indisposition.—During the whole of his long life he was esteemed a man of strict integrity, and was highly respected by his fellow citizens for his amiable and inoffensive deportment.

Vol. XII (No. 612) Saturday, 22 Dec. 1804.

¶ [3c] *Unfortunate accident.*—One day in last week, the house of the Widow Robb, of Acworth, caught fire, and was consumed, with all its contents. What adds to the distress was the melancholy circumstance of her daughter, aged fifteen years, being burnt to death. It was occasioned by the catching of a quantity of flax, brought into the house for the purpose of drying.

¶ [3c] INSTALLED.]—In Albany, (N.Y.) the Rev. John B. Romeyn, to the pastoral charge of the Presbyterian Church, [late under the charge of the Rev. Mr. Nott] in that city. —In Biddeford, (Maine) the Rev. John Turner, pastor over the second religious society in that town. The Rev. Levi Nelson, to the pastoral care and charge of Newent Society, in Lisbon, Con.

===== ¶ [3c] MARRIED. =====

In New York, Mr. George Edward Charles Frederick Meridick Rose Reynolds, to Miss Ellen Hageman. [. . .]

At Cornish, Mr. Nathaniel Huggins, jun. to Miss Sally Stone.

In Lincoln, (Mass.) the Rev. Jonathan French, of Northampton, (N.H.) to Miss Rebecca Farrar, of the former place.

===== ¶ [3c-d] DIED. =====

In Berlin, (Mass.) Mr. Joshua Jewet, son of Mr. Jesse Jewet, aged 22.—In Barbadoes, Rt. Hon. Viscount Proby, son of the Earl of Carysford, Capt. of the British frigate Amelia, of 38 guns ; and a Member of the British Parliament, for Buckingham : He was buried with the honors of war—In Louisiana, Ephraim Kirby, Esq. one of the newly appointed Judges in that Territory : He had been a conspicuous political partizan in Connecticut.—In North Carolina, James Hogg, Esq. : Maj. General M'Clure, formerly a surgeon in the revolutionary army.—In Elizabeth, (N.J.) Mrs. Susan Beasly, aged 23 ; daughter of the Hon. Jonathan Dayton, and wife of the Rev. Frederick Beasly.—In Ballstown, (N.Y.) Mrs. Ball, consort of the Rev. Eliphalet B.—In Hanover, (N.H.) Mrs. Bearce ; Misses Sally & Abigail Bearce, and Alpheus Bearce, the wife and children of Mr. Jonathan B. all of the fever, and within a few days of each other.—In Boston, Mrs. Mary Colson, aged 96.—In New York, Mrs. Jane Le Portevine, aged 102 ; a native of France, and resident in New York upwards of 50 years.—During the month of Nov. there were born, in Newyork city, 128 males, 148 females, total 276—died, 51 men, 48 boys, 46 women, 47 girls, total 192 ; excess of births, 84—During the week ending 8th inst. there died 14 men, 6 women, 13 boys, 6 girls, total 39—Mr. George F. Taderhorst, merchant, late of Hamburg : Mr. W——— [. . .]—In Philadelphia, from the 1st to the 8th inst. 16 adults and 15 children, total 31.—In Baltimore, from 3d to 10th Dec. 9 adults and 8 children.—In Gloucester, the Rev. Eli Fobes, D.D.—In Boston, Mr. Wm. Greenough, aged 58.—In Salem, Mrs. Mary Cheever, aged 80.—In Scituate, Mrs. Eunice Russell, aged 78.—In Newton, Mrs. Elizabeth Cheney, aged 44.

Vol. XII (No. 613) Saturday, 29 Dec. 1804.

† [3a] A summary of Acts recently passed by the Legislature; those listed here relate to specific individuals: 1) An Act to change the name of Nathan Clough. 2) An Act to restore Nathan Puffer to his Law. 3) An Act for a grant of Ferry to Nahum Goodenow. 4) An Act to restore Abiel Eastman to his Law. 5) An Act to authorize John Marsh to collect taxes.

¶ [3b] Lorenzo Dow, the celebrated pedistrian, and itinerant preacher, was lately at the Natchez, holding religious meetings.

¶ [3b] *Fire.*—Accidents occasioned by this element are unfortunately very frequent. On the 1st inst. the house of Mr. J. Moore, jun. of Leyden, was burnt, and his son, of sixteen years of age, perished in the flames.

† [3d] Joseph Bellows, Jr., adv. "to purchase good house ashes, for which he will pay one shilling per bushel, if delivered at his Pot-Ash, near Gilbert Griswold's Tavern . . ." Dated at Walpole, 27 Dec. 1804.

¶ [3d] *TAKE NOTICE.* Whereas Esther, the wife of the subscriber, has eloped from my bed and board without any just provecation, and contracted several debts injurious to the subscriber, this is to caution all persons against harbouring or trusting her on my account, as I shall pay no debts of her contracting.

JONATHAN WILLARD.

Chester, Vt. Dec. 24th, 1804.

===== ¶ [3c-d] DIED. =====

In Tellico, (Tenn.) on the 15th ult. John Worthington Hooker, Esq. Superintendant of the Public Stores at that place, and youngest son of the late Rev. John Hooker, of Northampton.—In South Carolina, Mr. John Robinson, aged 81, a native of Virginia ; left 10 children, 96 grandchildren, and 47 great-grandchildren.—In Charleston, Mr. Duncan Littlejohn, aged 55, a native of Sterling, in Scotland.—In Wilmington, (N.C.) Major Gen. M'Clure.—In Lancaster, (Penn.) Rev. Morgan J. Rhees.—In Norwich, (Con.) Mrs. Fanny, wife of Mr. Samuel Whiting, (Sen. editor of the Albany Gazette) and daughter of Col. Christopher Leffingwell, of Norwich, aged 21.—In Smithfield, (R.I.) Mr. Silas Arnold, aged 48 ; by falling from a mow while foddering his cattle.—In Pembroke, Mrs. Deborah Turner, aged 89.—In Andover, Mr. James Frye, aged 76.—In Gloucester, Mr. John Logan, aged 62.—In Sturbridge, Lieut. John Tarbell, aged 95.—In Boston, Mr. Daniel Crosby, aged 67 : Miss Mary Hood, aged 60.—In Hopkinton, of a cancerous sore, Mrs. Mary Proctor, aged 57.

At Canada, Ytyen-ti Fuhi, aged 102 ; a native of China, brought to America in early youth. He is said to have descended from the race of the ancient Chinese Emperors ; and being of strong powers of mind and body, instituted in Canada a Society, by the name of "ROUSTIGOUCHE," in imitation of those of his own native country, and in Europe ; several branches of which are now in existence in the United States [. . .] ♦

Vol. XII (No. 614) Saturday, 5 Jan. 1805.

¶ [3b] SHOCKING ACCIDENT. At Long-Island, (N.Y.) the house of Mr. Jeffrey Smith has been destroyed by fire.—Mrs. Smith, with three children, who all slept in one bed were burnt to death. Mr. Smith, and the father of his wife, were at New-York at the time of the fire, which took by a spark from the hearth.

¶ [3c] *Accident.*—As Mr. Phineas Holbrook, of Upton, (Mass.) was falling a tree, a limb fell and fractured his skull in such a manner that he died about one o'clock the next morning, in the 22d year of his age.

¶ [3c] On the 22d ult. the dwelling house of Mr. Isaac Maine, of Hartland, was destroyed by fire—furniture mostly saved.

† [3c] Account of the suicide of James Townsend, Esq. of St. Mary's, Georgia, on "the 7th ult." ♦

¶ [3c] Drowned, on Saturday last, between William's Island and Hancock's Wharf, Mr. Henry Davis, of Boston, aged 33.

† [3d] Ordination of Rev. Solomon Allen, late of Northampton, Mass., at a church in Middletown, Conn.

† [3d] Cushman Smith requests all outstanding debtors to pay up; notice dated at Surry, 29 Dec. 1804.

====== ¶ [3d] MARRIED. ======

In Germany, the celebrated dramatic writer, Kotzebue, to Mrs. Von Kersell.

In Berkshire, (Eng.) Mr. Joseph Harliun, to Miss Sally la Croix. The bridegroom was 85 years of age, the bride 83, and the two ladies who officiated as bride-maids above 70; six grand-daughters of the bridegroom strewed flowers before the company [. . .]

In Fitchburg, Z.B. Adams, Esq. attorney at law, to Miss Martha Fox, daughter of Joseph Fox, Esq.

In New Jersey, Mr. Edward Andrews, farmer, (aged 72) to Miss Catharine Budd, late of Sclavonia, (Germany) spinster, aged 22.

====== ¶ [3d] DIED. ======

In Baltimore, from 10th to 17th Dec. 11 adults, 4 children.—In New York city, from 8th to 15th Dec. 12 men, 11 women, 8 boys, 7 girls, total 38; 12 of consumption, 4 of small pox.—In Norwich, (Con.) Mr. Samuel Brown, aged 90.—In Sunderland, Mrs. Elizabeth Barnard, aged 63.—In Portland, Mrs. Rebecca Lewis, wife of Capt. John L. and daughter of the late Rev. Thomas Brown.—In Boston, Col. Jonathan Glover, aged 78; an active revolutionary patriot.—In Camp Claiborne, (N. Orleans) Capt. Aaron Gregg, of the 2d reg't of U.S. infantry ; a valuable and brave officer.—In Bardstown, (Ken.) Mr. Samuel Paul Jones; being in a state of celebacy, and having no relations in the country, he left all his property to be disposed of for the purpose of erecting a place of public worship, for the use of every denomination of christians : his death was occasioned by a cold he caught after having taken a quantity of spirits and brimstone as a remedy for the itch.—In Springfield, (Mass.) Mrs. Sarah Worthington.—In Charlestown, Mrs. Ann Edmonds, aged 62.—In Groton, (Mass.) Mr. Caleb Blood, aged 70.—On the 23d ult. at Westford, (Mass.) Major Asa Bullard, formerly an innkeeper in this town, aged 45.—In Pennsylvania, Gen. Richard Hampton, Adj. Gen. of the militia of that state; he was a native of the West of England.—In Philadelphia, from Dec. 15 to 22d, 27 adults, 19 children, total 46 [. . .]—In Kinderhook, (N.Y.) Peter Van Ness, Esq. for many years a senator in the legislature of Newyork.—In Kingston, (N.H.) Mr. Jonathan F. Sleeper, aged [84?]; formerly one of the instructors of a public school in Boston.—Very suddenly in Norwich, (Ver.) Deac. John Burnap, aged 79.

Vol. XII (No. 615) Saturday, 12 Jan. 1805.

¶ [2d] Kingston, New York, Dec. 29. On Thursday evening last, Mr. Johanne I. Roosa, of Marbletown, his daughter, and another young woman, were fording the Marbletown Creek, and on approaching the west shore, the box of the sleigh gave way, which precipitated them into the water, when Mr. Roosa's daughter was unfortunately drowned.

¶ [3a] During the late distressing fire at St. Thomas, but few lives were lost. A Mr.

Colin, of immense property, distracted by his loss, threw himself into the flames and perished.—A faithful and affectionate servant immediately followed the dreadful example of his master.—*Amer. Daily Adv.*

¶ [3a] *Fire.*—Accidents occasioned by this destructive element continue to reach us by almost every mail.—On the morning of Sunday the [22?]d ult. at about 3 o'clock the house of Wm. Stinson jun. of Dunbarton was consumed by fire with all its contents; the family narrowly escaping the rapid conflagration. The loss is estimated at nearly 8000 dollars.

¶ [3a] On Monday, the 31st ult. at about 6 o'clock, A.M. a house owned by Col. Bradbury Cilley, and occupied by a Mr. Randal, was consumed by fire at Nottingham, with most of its contents.

† [3c] List of nonresident owners of land in the town of Stoddard who are delinquent for taxes in the year 1804, as compiled by Stephen Wright, *Collector*; property to be sold at public vendue at the house of Gardner Towne, Esq., Stoddard. The notice contains a breakdown of lot number, acreage, etc., though only the names are presented here:

Heirs of Col. Stoddard	Jotham Odiorne	Samuel Seaward
Matthew Thornton	Seth Wheeler	Joseph Spaulding
Heirs of Joseph Blanchard	Nathan Whittemore	Charles Lawrance
Roland Cotten [118]	Nathaniel Richardson	Thomas Read's heirs
Joseph Read	Ebenezer Pierce	Ebenezer Parker's heirs
Benjamin Butterfield	Henry Fergesan	
John Dutten	Joseph Warren	

¶ [3c] **MARRIED.**

At Plainfield, Mr. Lathrop Willes, to Miss Triphene Tisdale.
At Hanover, Mr. Edward Brown, to Miss Lucy Ridley.

¶ [3c] **DIED.**

In New Jersey, John Longstreet, Esq. aged 95.—In Portland, Mr. Samuel Pierce, aged 70.—In Haverhill, Mrs. Mary Harrod, aged 81.—In Northampton, Mr. Daniel Clark, aged 92.—In Weston, Enoch Greenleaf, Esq. aged 73.—In Spencer, Deac. Oliver Watson, aged 86.—In Leicester, Wid. Deborah Earle, aged 88.—In Quincy, Mrs. Ruth Penniman, aged 60.—In Sharon, (C.) Mr. Joseph Long, aged 80.—In Boscawen, Mr. Jonathan Dix, aged 95.—In Scott County, (Ken.) of the Hydrophobia, Mr. Jones; who was bitten on the end of his finger, by a mad dog, last Spring.—In North Bolton, (Con.) on the 22d ult. Jonathan Chapman, jun.—his death was occasioned by taking too great a draught of ardent spirits:—On the 30th, Mr. Daniel King; he fell on the crank of a saw-mill and was instantly killed.—In Tolland, (Con.) of a consumption, on the 22d ult. Mrs. Patty West, wife of Dr. Jeremiah West, aged 49.—In Lebanon, his death occasioned by the falling of a tree, Mr. Oliver White, aged 35.—In Alstead, of the small pox, Mrs. Vilas.

Suicide.—At student in Columbia College, of about 18 years of age, lately put a period to his existence by poison.

Vol. XII (No. 616) Saturday, 19 Jan. 1805.

† [3a] Several brief paragraphs describing American losses at Tipoli; casualties included Lieut. Decatur, Lieut. Caldwell, Mr. Dorsey, Capt. Somers, Lieut. Wadsworth (son of Hon. Peleg Wadsworth of Portland, Maine), and Mr. Izard, of South Carolina. ♦

¶ [3a] *Melancholy Accident.*—On the night of the 11th inst. as a Mr. Luther Adams, of Weston, (Ver.) lately residing in this town, was passing through Andover, late in the evening, he missed his way, and, not being able to reach any house, he was found on the next morning lying in the road frozen to death.

¶ [3c] ORDAINED.—To the work of the gospel ministry in Heath, the Rev. Moses Miller. In Salem, on the 11th inst. Mr. Bowles, over the new Baptist Church in that town.

† [3d] Notice from *Bellows & Stone*, regarding outstanding debts; dated Walpole 10 Jan.

¶ [3c] **MARRIED.**

In Cambridge, England, James Gordon, a sergeant in His Majesty's service, to Miss Nancy Pitcher. The young lady had constantly visited the parade, and smitten with his

adroitness and manly appearance, made him an offer of her hand, and a fortune of 5000 pounds sterling, which was accepted [. . .]
===== ¶ [3c-d] DIED. =====

In Fishkill, (N.Y.) William B. Verplank, Esq. aged 34.—In Westmoreland, on the 24th ult. Mr. Benjamin Jones, a native of West Springfield, aged 86.—In Providence, Capt. William Earl, aged 77.—In E. Hartford, Mr. Norman Spencer, burnt to death in a powder mill.—On his passage from Calcutta, Capt. Geo. Lane, of Charlestown, (Mass.) aged 50.—In New Haven, a child, about 3 years old, by carelessly administering to it, through mistake, two tea spoons full of laudanum; it was an only daughter, and lived after the accident but a few hours.—In Savannah, Hon. Joseph Clay, Esq. aged 64, after a life of eminently useful to his relatives, his friends, and his country.—In North Carolina, Rev. Lewis F. Wilson, aged 52; a native of the island of St. Kitts, and minister to the Presbyterian Churches in Concord and Statesville, N.C.—In Baltimore, from 1st to 8th inst. 3 ad. 7 child.[. . .] In Newport, Col. Jabez Champney, aged 78:—Mrs. Lucretia Hooker, aged 73.—In Waltham, Mr. Silas Stearns, aged 71.—In Westhampton, Mrs. Phebe Parsons, aged 73.—In Boston, Mrs. Martha Emmons, aged 40 : Mr. John Brown, aged 49.—In New York, Mr. Thomas Gardner; he served an apprentice ship to the tailor's business, and, by industry and good fortune, is said to have amassed one million of dollars.

At Alstead, in the hospital, at about one o'clock in the morning on the 16th inst. of the small pox, which he took by the natural way, Maj. Elisha Kingsbery, of Alstead. Society has sustained a real loss in the death of Major K. His friends and acquaintance will long have reason to deplore his untimely exit. His age was about — years. [119]

At Shirley, on the 27th ult. Mrs. Sophia Parker, aged 21—having been married only two days.—At Stow, widow Mercy Gordon, aged 88; her sister Abigail Houghton, aged 101; her daughter, Abigail, aged 78;—Mr. Bezaleel Hale, aged 88.—At Topsham, John S. Abbot, A.M. aged 25 formerly of Salem.—At Portsmouth, Mr. John Thomas, aged 40.—At Wiscasset, Deac. Nymphas Stacey, aged 79.—At Pelham, Mr. Theodore Butler, aged 23.—At Concord, widow Kimball, aged 83; widow Elizabeth Locke, aged 71; Mr. Jacob Carter, aged 50.—In Newburyport, Mr. John Stickney, aged [70?]—At Uxbridge, Mr. David Read, aged 96.

Vol. XII (No. 617) Saturday, 26 Jan. 1805.

† [3d] Cady Parks adv. items for sale "At his store West end of Walpole Bridge." Dated at Rockingham, 26 Jan. 1805.

† [3d] Ebenezer White and Joseph Bellows, Jr., adv. to "manufactures of ashes in the United States," regarding patent rights for improvements in "manufacturing pot and pearl ashes."

† [3d] David Carter, Proprietor's Clerk, adv. the annual meeting of the Third Turnpike Road to be held at Sweetser's Tavern in Marlborough; dated there 15 Jan. 1803.
===== ¶ [3c] MARRIED. =====

In Janesburgh, (Vir.) Mr. Andrew Mannis, aged 97, to Miss Fanny Fessenden, aged 17.

In Scarborough, Capt. Roger Libby, aged 75, to Mrs. Hannah Watson, he being her fourth husband.

In Middlebury, (Ver.) Dr. Daniel Campbell, to Miss Betsey Sedgwick, of Williamstown, (Mass.)

It is an approved sentiment that "two heads are better than one." 'Tis hoped the following couple will experience the truth of the maxim.—Married, at Pembroke, Mr. Isaac Head to Miss Sally Head.

At Nashua Village, Dunstable, Mr. Samuel Preston, to Miss Esther Taylor.

At Bellows Falls, Rockingham, V. by the Rev. Mr. Sage, of Westminster, Levi Barnard, Esq. of Lunenburg, V. attorney at law, at Miss Lucy Page, eldest daughter of Col. Wm. Page, of the former place.
===== ¶ [3c-d] DIED. =====

In Portsmouth, Woodbury Langdon, Esq.—In Kentucky, Dr. John M. Lucket, of Louisville, killed in a duel with George Strother, Esq. They were both young men, and very intimate friends. A dispute between them, from firmest friends changed them to bitter foes.—At Hospital Island, (of the small pox) Mr. Elisha Dunham. We understand that there are five or six persons now on the island sick with that malady; and that several persons belonging to the island have been vaccinated to preserve them from the disease.—In Boston, Mrs. Sarah Elliot, relict of the late Mr. Simon Elliot, aged 80.—In Milton, Mr. Ebenezer Swift, aged 80.—In Sumpter District, (S.C) Laurence Manning, Esq. Adj. General of South Carolina, aged 48, eminent for his public services and private worth.—In Windsor, Mrs. Bathsheba Smead, aged 45.—In Southington, (Con.) very suddenly, and within 18 hours of each other, Joseph Gridley, aged 88, and Sarah, his wife, aged 75. They were both interred in one grave.—In Somers, (C.) Reuben Sikes, Esq. aged [73?].—In New Haven, Mr. Moses H. Woodward, printer, aged 44.—In Willsboro' (N.Y.) two small children of a Mr. Adams, burnt to death, in the absence of their parents. Their house and its contents were also wholly consumed. —In Smithfield, by the fall of a tree, which crushed his skull and put a period to his existence in a few minutes, Mr. Ezekiel Aldrich.—In Sterling, (Mass.) Widow Mehitabel Child, aged 73.—In Hanover, of the fever, Miss Lucy Ingalls, aged 18, and Miss Sally Parks, aged 15 : Mrs. Hannah Fuller, aged 64.—In Andover, Ver. Capt. Joseph Sibley, of Sutton, Ms. aged 65.

Vol. XII (No. 618) Saturday, 2 Feb. 1805.

¶ [2c] *Fire.*—On the night of the 3d ult. a gristmill, with two run of stones, belonging to Mr. Andrew Miller, of Ryegate, V. was consumed by fire, together with about 160 bushels of grain. Loss estimated at 1500 dollars.

† [3c] Legal notice regarding the insolvent estate of Major Elisha Kingsbery, late of Alstead, deceased. Moses Hale, J.H. Bingham, and John Prentiss appointed commissioners, and John C. Chamberlain, administrator. Claims of the creditors to be examined at General Shepard's Tavern, Alstead. Dated at Alstead, 25 Jan. 1805.

† [3c] John Hubbard requests all debtors to pay up; dated Charlestown, 28 Jan. 1805.

† [3d] *Burr & Hamilton* adv. a wax-figure museum, opening briefly "at the house of A. Southard" in Walpole; included in the collection is a "striking likeness of Jason Fairbanks, who was executed at Dedham; he is dressed in the same clothes that he wore at the time of his trial; also a likeness of the unfortunate Eliza Fales."

===== ¶ [3b-c] DIED. =====

At Washington, James Gillespie, Esq. member of Congress from the state of North Carolina.—In Boston, on the 21st ult. Hon. Thomas Davis, Esq. aged 48; a man peculiarly dear to his near connexions, greatly esteemed and beloved by a numerous and respectable acquaintance, and whose death is deservedly deplored by all who knew him.—In New York from 5th to 12th Jan. 13 men; 11 women, 7 boys and 9 girls, total 40; of small pox 3, consumption 5, convulsions 6.—In Hallowell, 2d ult. Gorham Dummer, Esq. Attorney at Law, aged 23.—In Kingston, (Plym. county) Mrs. Thankful Adams, wife of Mr. John Adams, aged 89. She had lived with her present husband above 70 years, and has left him a sincere mourner, aged 91, in full exercise of his reason. They have 10 children, (all living in said town) have had 73 grand children, and 52 great-grand-children.—In Salem, Miss Sally Southword, daughter of Capt. G.S. jun. aged 21.—In Bolton, Dr. Samuel Brown, formerly of Boston.—In Holden, Elnathan Davis, Esq. aged 43, a member of the General Court.—In Worcester, Mr. Wm. M'Farland, aged 83.—In Brattleboro', (V.) Mr. Samuel Knight, eldest son of the late Judge Knight, aged 36.—In Newport, (R.I.) Col. Jabez Champlin, aged 73; Mrs. Lucretia Hookey, aged 73.—In Middletown, (R.I.) Mrs. Hannah Bailey, aged 71.—In Wrentham, Mr. Nathaniel Heaton, aged 66.—In Philad. Mrs. Charlotte Lillibridge, aged 28. She died of the small pox, which she took the natural way.—In Concord, Mr. Jacob Carter, aged 50.—In Nottingham, Benjamin Butler, Esq. aged 76.—In Litchfield, C. Mrs. Ruth Kirby,[120] widow of Col. E. Kirby, deceased.—In Rutland, (Ver.) Mr. Amos Himes, aged 60.—In Richmond, (Vir.) Mr. Walker, one of the legislature of the state.——In Kemsville, (Virg.) John Hancock, jun. Esq. formerly a member of the same legislature.—In Goshen, (N.J.) Rev. Nathaniel Ker, aged 68.—In Bridgewater (East Parish) on the 18th ult. Rev. Samuel Angier, aged 62, late pastor of that parish.—In Haverhill, (Mass.) of a paralytic shock, Rev. Hezekiah Smith, D.D. Pastor of a Baptist Church in that town, aged 67.—In Charlestown, (Mass.) Thomas Macdonogh, Esq. aged 65, Consul of his Britannic Majesty, for the Eastern Department of the U.S.—Deaths in Orford, in 1803, 1 adult & 15 children; in 1804, 2 adults and 12 child.; in 34 years, 251 persons.—In Philad. Mr. William Wharton, aged 66.—In New York, of an apoplexy, Mr. Conrad W. Ham, aged 61.

In Rutland, Vt. Mrs. Sarah Andrus, aged [31?].—A child of Capt. William Butman, aged 5 years.

In Alstead, Mrs. Sarah Hatch, aged 85.

Vol. XI (No. 619) Saturday, 9 Feb. 1805. [121]

† [3a] Extensive account of the wreck of the *Hibernia*, near Plymouth, Mass., giving details regarding the failed attempts to rescue the crew, who all but one perished: "Andrew Farriss, master, of Boston; William Payne, First Mate, formerly of Wellfleet, but now of Boston, the only survivor, who was found lashed to the helm, and taken from thence almost lifeless; Joseph Cordis 2d mate, of Charlestown, and the following seamen, viz. James D. Hammond, of Marblehead, Ezra Bicknall, of Weymouth, John Smith of Boston, Samuel Carter, of Philad., John Smith, of Newport, Thomas Brown, of Gloucester, William Howard, boy, of Newyork, and Francis Trask, Cook, of Newburyport . . . " ♦

¶ [3b] *Fire*.—The dwelling house of Mr. Samuel Smith, in the westerly part of Windsor, together with most of his furniture was consumed by fire, on the 25th ult.

† [3c] Dr. S. Reynolds details a surgery performed on a son of Mr. Joseph Earl, aged 18, who was impaled upon a "rakestail." The event occurred in Florida, Montgomery county, though the state is not specified; the article was copied from another newspaper, perhaps from the *Albany Centinel*. ♦

† [3c] Rev. Joseph Stevens Buckminster ordained at Boston. ♦

† [3d] *Thos. & Isaac Redington* request debtors to pay up; dated 7 Feb. 1805.

===== ¶ [3c] MARRIED. =====

In Rochester, on new year's day, Mr. Samuel Berry, aged 83, late post master at Wilksbarre, (ejected from office by the present levelling system) to the widow Dorothy Churchill, of Rochester, aged 77. Fifty of their male descendants (federalists to a man !) were present at the ceremony, which was performed by the Rev. Joseph Clark, a nephew of the bride [. . .]

In Orford, Mr. Abel Curtis, to Miss Lucy [Morey?].

In Harvard, 5th ult. Rev. Thomas Beede, of Wilton, (N.H.), to Miss Nancy Kimball; Mr. John Park, to Miss Nabby Kimball.

In Middlebury, (Ver.) Mr. Robert Torrence, to Miss Sally Clark of Sheffield, Ms.

In Windsor, Mr. Frederick Burnham, to Miss Hannah Mason.

In Norwich, Dan Carpenter, Esq. of Waterbury, to Miss Betsey Patridge.

===== ¶ [3c-d] DIED. =====

In Philadelphia, from 12th to 19th Jan. 20 adults, 11 children, total 31.—In Northampton, Mr. Benjamin Parsons, aged 87 : Mrs. Mary Clark, aged 70.—In Worthington, Nahum Fager, [*compare to issue of 16 Feb. 1805*] Esq. aged 6[—]; one of the first settlers, and much respected through life;—Mrs. Abigail Bigelow, aged 20.——In Shelburn, (county of Hampshire) John Long, Esq. aged [58?], member of the House of Representatives of Massachusetts.—In Dorchester, Mr. Thomas Knox, aged 73.—In Andover, widow Susannah Marshall, aged 90 : widow Bethiah Holt, aged 84.—In Haverhill, Madam Mary Sargeant, aged 72.—In Gloucester, Capt. Benj. Somes, aged 72.—In Watertown, Mr. Thomas Patten, aged 73.—In Bolton, Ms. Miss Sally Sawyer, aged 28 : Miss Lucretia Whitcomb, aged 20.—In Vernon, Hon. John Bridgman, Esq. aged 67; for many years Judge of Probate, and of the County Court.—In Danbury, C. Thaddeus Benedict, Esq. aged 76.—In Huntington, C. Mrs. Sarah Hawley, after an illness of 34 hours, aged 63.—In Hanover, Mr. Thomas Brown, aged 21 : Mr. Jonas Ketcham.—In Surry, Mr. Moses Field, aged 35.

At Grand Ecore, on Red River, Mr. John Hiller, aged 96. He was never sick a day in his life ; small pox, measles, &c. excepted.—For 60 or 70 years he was every day, if not intoxicated, at least, not sober. Let this extraordinary case be no encouragement to tipsers.—In Lebanon, 26th December, Mr. Oliver White, aged 35. His death was occasioned by the fall of a tree which fractured his skull. He survived only 12 hours.—In Boothbay, Mr. Joseph Thompson, aged 82. He had 18 child. 105 gr. ch. and 25 gr. gr. ch.

In Alstead, Mr. Simeon Shepard, in the 21st year of his age.

Drowned.—On Monday morning was taken up, on the north side of Hancock's wharf, Boston, the body of a seaman, who was drowned.—His name is supposed to have been *Libbey.*—Off Marblehead harbour on Saturday, 26th ult. Messrs. *James Felton, Benj. Doak,* and *John Millet.*—They were fishing in a small boat, which sunk.—They were all married men; and it is said have left 11 children.—In North River, by adventuring too far on the ice at New York, three boys living with a Mr. M'Intire. They were found in a frozen state a few days after.

Perished, in one of the late snowstorms, in New York state, two men belonging to Canandaigua, named Robbins and Kennedy.

Vol. XI (No. 620) Saturday, 16 Feb. 1805.

† [3c] Detailed account of the death of a young girl who was tortured by a fiendish schoolmaster, Stephen Arnold, of Burlington, Otsego County, N.Y. The article includes a physical description of Arnold, who absconded to the West. ♦ 122

† [3d] Rev. Sherman Johnson, at Milford, Conn., and Mr. Samuel Merwin, at New Haven ordained at their respective churches.

===== ¶ [3d] MARRIED. =====

In Herkimer, (N.Y.) Mr. Daniel Bellows to Miss Eleanor Sheldon, both of the Little Falls.

At Westmoreland, on the 6th inst. by Joseph Burt, Esq. Mr. Benjamin Snow to Miss Marcy Snow, both of Westmoreland.

In Keene, Deacon James Lanman, to Miss Susanna Goldthwait.

In Rutland, (Ms.) Lovell Walker, Esq. to Miss Eliza Russell.

In Dover, (Eng.) Charles Pritchard, Esq. aged 87, to Miss Charlotte Pursuivance, aged 19 [. . .]

===== ¶ [3d] DIED. =====

In Philadelphia, Mr. George Dowie, a native of Scotland; by the breaking of a blood vessel.—In Utica, Mr. Lemuel George;—while walking in the street, with his face partly covered to evade a storm, he was met by a sleigh, the tongue of which struck him on the breast, and instantly put a period to his life.—In Danbury, Thaddeus Benedict, Esq. aged 76.—In Wells, (Maine) Mr. Joseph Eaton, aged 79.—In Sterling, Captain Ephraim Wilder, aged 72.—In Plymton, [sic] Mr. Philemon Sampson: he accidentally fell into a well, & was drowned.—In Boston, Mr. John Lewis, aged 55; a loaded team of bricks passed over his body.—Mrs. Ann Williams, wife of Mr. Robert W. aged 75.—On Sullivan's Island, S.C. Capt. Simond Tufts, aged 83; he was one of the first naval officers appointed by that State, in the late revolution.—In Virginia, the Hon. James Henry, a member of the old Congress, and late a Judge of the General Court of that State.—In New York, from Jan. 13th to 20th, 53 persons; [12?] of consumptions, 6 of small pox, 3 casualties-the casualties all by fire.—In Providence, Grindall Rawson, Esq. a native of Mendon, (Mass.) aged 36.—In Glastenbury, (Con.) Rev. J. Eells, aged 62.—In Savannah, (Geo.) at a very advanced age, Dr. Noble Wimberly Jones.—Near Fincastle, (Vir.) William Dunkin, aged 124, possessed of all his faculties.—In Northampton, Mrs. Mary Clark, aged 70.—In Worthington, Nahum Eager, [*compare to issue of 9 Feb. 1805*] Esq. aged 65.—In Newton, Mrs. Tabitha Blackington, aged 67.—In Jaffrey, Widow Dorothy Whitcomb, aged 84. She was married at 16; had 16 children, and one of her daughters has 160 grand-children. Her posterity is upwards of 400, who are scattered in New Hampshire, Massachusetts, Maine, Newyork and Canada. Children of the 5th generation are now 10 years of age.—In Philadelphia, from Jan. 26 to Feb. 2, 21 adults, 9 children.—In Germantown, Mr. Justus Fox, type-founder and printer.—In Morristown, (N.J.) Gen. Joseph [Breasley?], aged 93.—In New York, from Jan. 26 to Feb. 2d, 9 men, 13 women, 10 boys and 4 girls; total 36; 5 of small pox, 4 convulsions, 7 consumption;—Hon. John S. Hobart aged 67 ; Judge of the District Court of New York.—At Fort Wolcott, near Newport, Dr. George Dill.—In Cambridge, on Monday last, Thomas Fayerweather, Esq. aged 82.—In Douglass, Mr. Richard Williams, aged 105 years, 8 mo. and 2 days.—In Worcester prison, Mr. Daniel Robbins, a lunatic, aged 33.—In Burlington, (V.) Mrs. Martha Russell, aged 50.—In Northampton, Mr. Daniel Strong, aged 60.—In Windsor, Mrs. Cady, wife of Mr. Thomas Cady.—In Windham, Con. Mr. David Spencer, aged 74.

In Westmoreland, Mrs. Editha Cole, the amiable consort of Deacon Jonathan Cole, aged 76;—one of the first families which settled in that town.

In London, (Eng.) Miss Catharine Tibbets, aged 96; suddenly, of a broken heart—occasioned by not receiving a prompt return of affection from a young Clerk [. . .]

Accident.—On Tuesday last, a washer-woman was found in her chamber, in Middle-street, lying in the fire-place, burnt to death. [*Boston paper.*]

Vol. XI (No. 621) Saturday, 23 Feb. 1805.

¶ [2d] *Fire.*—The dwelling house of Mr. John Scovill, of Clarendon, Vt. was lately consumed by fire. Most of the furniture, and also eighty bushels of grain were also burnt.

† [3c] Article written by Samuel Mead, who states his belief in the vaccination against small pox, when he was in the hospital in Alstead. Harriot Mead, his daughter, was vaccinated by Dr. Sterne, of Walpole. Mead's neighbor, Mrs. Webster, is mentioned as "being extremely sick in it." Several other physicians are mentioned in the article: Drs. Benton, Hastings, Carpenter, Moore, and a Dr. Spaulding of Portsmouth. ♦

¶ [3c] COMMUNICATION. On Thursday the 7th day of Feb. inst. Mrs. Elizabeth Heald, wife of Mr. Josiah Heald, of Chester, (Vt.) being that day, and several days before, in a state of partial delirium, went out of the house, took an axe, and cut off her left hand at the joint of the wrist; surgical aid was immediately obtained, and amputation took place, and symptoms of recovery appear favorable. The respectability of Mr. Heald's family, and the unhappy situation of the woman interest the feelings of all their acquaintance, who sincerely regret the melancholy event.

A FRIEND.

Chester, Vt., Feb. 11th, 1805.

† [3d] Adv. of Dartmouth College land for sale in Lebanon, N.H., mentioning that the property is bounded by farms belonging to Zenas Alden and John Andros, and lands of President Wheelock.

† [3d] List of nonresident proprietors and owners of land in the town of Marlow, N.H., who are delinquent for their taxes in the year 1804. The list was compiled by Amos Gale, Jr., Collector, and the notice gives the acreage and rate, however only the names are given here:

William Towne	Ephraim Adams	Ezra Selden
Daniel Downing's heirs	Jonathan Royce	Daniel Whitmore
Josiah Whitney	John M'Curday	
Benjamin Baxter	Thomas Sabin	

===== ¶ [3c-d] MARRIED. =====

In this town, by the Rev. Mr. Fessenden, Mr. Moses Cutter, of Stockbridge, Vt. to Miss Hannah Webber. . . . Mr. Bradford Chase, of Grafton, (Mass.) to Miss Polly Drury.

In Newark, (N.J.) Rev. John M'Dowell, to Miss Henrietta Kollock, both of Elizabeth-town.—Mr. Ramadow Muscissian, late from Bourdeaux, to Miss Culture, of Springfield, late of St. Croix.

In Lyme, (Con.) Hon. E. Perkins, Esq. to Miss Polly Mumford.

In Westfield, (Mass.) Mr. Lyman Lewis, to Miss Margaret Ashley.

In Wilbraham, (Mass.) Mr. Daniel Ladd, jun. to Miss Hannah Burt.

At Cavendish, Dr. Luther Fletcher to Miss Salome Fletcher.—Mrs. Asa Fletcher to Miss Rebeckah Fletcher. The young gentlemen are sons of Josiah Fletcher, Esq. of Ludlow, and the young ladies are daughters of the Hon. Asaph Fletcher, Esq. of the former place.

In Brookfield, Mr. Medcalf Witherell, to Miss Frances Foxcraft.

At New-Boston, Abraham B. Story, Esq. attorney at law, of Washington, (N.H.) to Miss Letitia Cochran.

¶ [3d] DIED.

In Croydon, on the 11th ult. much lamented by her friends and acquaintance, Mrs. Mary Cooper, wife of Mr. Barna Cooper, aged 36.—In Baltimore, Capt. Jeremiah Yellott.—In Virginia, Capt. Littleton Savage, aged 65.—In London, Dec. 12, Alderman Boydell, aged 87.—In Savannah, (Geo.) John Miller, Esq. Sheriff of Beaufort District, S.C. aged 55.—In New York, Mr. Gabriel W. Ludlow, aged 71 : Mrs. Mary Tare, aged 67:—In New York, for the week ending the 2d inst. 36.—In Springfield, Mrs. Mary Morgan, aged 45 : Miss Delia Bliss, aged 15.—In Northampton, Mrs. Sarah Parsons, aged 38.—In Wilbraham, Mr. Isaac Shepard, aged 46.—In Lyme, after nine hours pain by striking a chissel into his thigh, Mr. Israel Burt, aged 22.—On the night of the 5th inst. frozen to death, in Chatham, (Con.) Mr. Henry Goodall : Being insane and under the care of the town, he was chained to the floor and in the morning was found dead.—By the falling of a tree, in Preston, C. Mr. Patrick Hazard.—In Dover, Capt. Thomas Wentworth.—In Old York, Capt. Edward Smith, aged [71?].—In Portsmouth, Capt. Samuel S. Bailey, aged 30 :—Very suddenly, Thomas Martin, Esq. aged 73.—In Kittery, (Me.) Mrs. Hannah Hammond, aged 95.—In Boston, William Powell, Esq. aged 79.—In New Jersey, Samuel Ogden, Esq. Æt. 72.—In Maryland, John Thomas, Esq. formerly President of the Senate of that State.—In Litchfield, Isaac Baldwin, Esq. Æt. 94; he took his degree in Yale College in the year [1735?] and is said to be the oldest person in Litchfield county.—In Leicester, Mr. Wm. Earle, aged 90 y 10 m.

Vol. XI (No. 622) Saturday, 2 March 1805.

¶ [2b] FIRES.—At Paris, (N.Y.) the house of Mr. Gideon Conde, with its contents, has been consumed:—the large ship chandlery store, occupied by Mr. R. [Tittermafy?], do.—At New London, the dwelling house of Col. W.M. Richards, with its contents. [Col. Cent.

¶ [3d] ORDAINED]—As an evangelist and minister for the next season as a missionary, by the Central and South Association, lately convened at Southampton, Mr. John Dutton, of Hartford, Vt.

¶ [3d] INSTALLED]—To the pastoral care of the church and congregation in Westminster Society, Canterbury, Con. on Wednesday the 6th ult., Rev. Erastus Learned.

The ordination of the Rev. Pliny Dickinson, as colleague with the Rev. Mr. Fessenden, will take place in this town on Wednesday next. 123

¶ [3d] MARRIED]—At Middletown, C. Mr. Justin Lyman, of Hartford, to Miss Frances Goodwin.—In Westminster, Vt. Capt. Bela Clap, of Boston, to Miss Elizabeth Gilbert.

¶ [3d] DIED]—In Wilton, Con. Mrs. Rachael [Betts?] in good health a few days previous to her death, which was occasioned by a fall on the ice, at the advanced age of [102?].—In Salem, Mass. Mrs. Mary Gardner, aged 90.—In Oxford, Widow Elizabeth Kidder, aged 93.—In Sterling, Widow Vashti Prescott, aged 78.—In Coventry, C. Mrs. Priscilla Kingsbury, æ. 85. In Mansfield, Mrs. Mary Chaplin æ. 84.—In Concord, Widow Hannah Lovejoy, aged 90; descendants, 5 ch. 40 gr. ch. 40 gr. gr. ch. and 4 of the 4th gener.

† [3d] Legal notice regarding the estate of Aaron Allen, late of Walpole, deceased; Levi Allen, Executor; dated Walpole, 25 Feb. 1805.

† [3d] Notice by David Carter, Treasurer, regarding the 3d N.H. Turnpike Road.

† [3d] *Leverett Tuttle & Co.* request debtors to pay up; dated Bellows Falls, Vt., 27 Feb.

Vol. XI (No. 623) Saturday, 9 March 1805.

¶ [1d] Danbury, (Con.) Feb. 6. The trial of Eli Lion, who was indicted for the commission of a rape on Mrs. Jerusha Ferriss, of Newtown, came on last week before the Superior Court holden in this town. He was found *Guilty,* and sentenced to be executed on the 3d of July next.

¶ [1d] *From Charleston, (S.C.) Feb. 9.* Pursuant to their sentences, *Joshua Nettles,* for the murder of John Cannon; and *Rich'd Dennis,* jun. for the murder of James Shaw, were executed yesterday in this city.

¶ [3b] ORDINATION. At Manchester, Vt. the Rev. Abel Farley, to the pastoral care of the Congregational Church and Society in that town.

† [3c] Adv. of two lots of land for sale at Pomfret, Vt., one "drawn to the original right of John Williams," the other "to the original right of Isaac Dana." The adv. gives the lot numbers and size; "For farther particulars apply to Rev. Daniel Oliver, Boston, Mr. Richard Lang, Hanover, or at the Walpole Bookstore."

† [3c] Oliver Hall adv. a meeting of the Cheshire Turnpike; dated Charlestown, 7 Mar.

† [3d] List of nonresident proprietors and owners of land who are delinquent for their taxes for the year 1804, as compiled by James Young, Collector for the town of Wendell, N.H. The notice contains a breakdown of acreage, lot number, etc., though only the names are presented here:

Jonathan Herreck	Daniel Lyon	Benjamin Harris [124]
Heirs of Mat. Harvey	Nathaniel Fales, jun.	Benjamin Eale
Charles Church	Moses Eastman	

† [3d] Amos Garnsey, guardian to Stephen Kittridge, Roswell Kittridge, Sukey Kittridge, and Ebenezer Eaton Kittridge, (all minors under 14 years of age), petitions the court to sell the minors' land at Walpole, N.H. for their support. Individuals who bound on said property include "Doctor Kittridge" and Levi Fay.

¶ [4c] *From the* KENNEBEC GAZETTE. LONGEVITY. The following instances of unusual longevity, have been recorded in the American Papers, during the year 1804—to wit:

	Years	Mo.		Years	Mo.
John Quarterman, *Penn.*	108	8	Mrs. Rice, *Marlborough, Mass.*	99	
Samuel Bartow, *Boothbay, Me.*	105		Susanna Robinson, *Dorchester, Mass.*	94	
Ephraim Pratt, *Shutesbury, Mass.*[125]	117		Eleanor Shackford, *Portsmouth, N.H.*	91	
John Belknap, *Wilksboro'*	101		Mildred Frothingham, *Providence*	91	
Dorothy Dusan, *Philad.*	105		Abigail Edwards, *Connecticut*	96	
Ann Baker, *Waterford, Me.*	103		Mary Hastings, *Weston, Mass.*	101	10
Sarah Low, *Fitchburg, Mass.*	93		Mrs. Mason, *Salem, Mass.*	95	
Abigail Stone, *Groton, Mass.*	93		Moses Belknap, *Atkinson, N.H.*	93	
Henry Abram, *Chillicothe*	102		Joseph Farnworth, *Fairfax, Ver.*	90	
George Gregory, *Kingston, Eng.*	106		Susanna Babbridge, *Salem, Mass.*	90	
Jean George, *England.*	110	10	Mrs. Bullock, *Salem, Mass.*	90	
John Stewart, (Col. of the Tinkers) *Aberfeldy, Eng.*	106		Esther Lane, *England,*	105	
			Samuel Brown, *Connecticut*	90	
A Man, in *Lithuania, Poland*	163		Issachar Baker, *York, Maine*	93	
James Thomas, *Georgia, U.S.*	134				
Pompey, (Negro) *Delaware,*	120				
Anthony, (Negro) *Philad.*	105				
Uty-Enti-Fohi, a Chinese, *Canada*	102				
Abigail Houghton, *Stow, Mass.*	101				
Lydia Bickford, *Salem, Mass.*	105				

☞ *Twelve* of whom had the singular felicity of living in THREE CENTURIES.

N.B. Old Parr died in England, in the year 1634, aged 152.

===== ¶ [3c] MARRIED. =====

In Westmoreland, by J. Burt, Esq. Mr. Moses Trist, of Putney, (Ver.) to Miss Clarissa Burt, of the former place.

In Westminster, Mr. Jonas Clark, to Miss Sally Lake.—Mr. Solomon W. Burk, of Woodstock, to Miss Polly Crague.

At Templeton, Simeon Gray, Esq. to Miss Sarah Fitts.—Mr. Jotham Sawyer, to Miss Lucy Fisk.

At Brookfield, Mr. Elijah Davenport, Merchant of Boston, to Miss Susan Ward, daughter of the Rev. Ephraim Ward, of Brookfield.

Text.—'The lion shall *lie down* with the lamb,"—*Improvement.*—Married, in Rutland, (Vermont) Mr. Thomas *Lyon*, to Miss Betsey *Lamb.*

In this town, by the Rev. Mr. Dickinson, Mr. Martin Doyle, to Miss Martha Thompson.

===== ¶ [3c] DIED. =====

In Vienna (Germany) the Countess Zamoiska, sister to the late King of Poland.—She did not leave behind her more property than was sufficient to bestow some legacies to the poor, and the exact amount of what she inherited from her parents.—It is known that her unfortunate brother, King Stanislaus, was equally generous, patriotic, and disinterested; and instead of enriching himself or his relations, lived the last years of his life upon *alms*, at St. Petersburg, where he died a *pauper !*—In England, Mr. George Morland, Æt. 40; a celebrated painter of rural scenes:—The Rev. Samuel Aylcough, Æt. 55; a Librarian of the British Museum, and an eminent compiler.—He was said to have examined more books than any man in England.—The Right Hon. John Howe, Baron Chedworth, Æt. 51;—He was said to have died worth 500,000 *l*. sterling [. . .]

Melancholy.—On Tuesday of last week a child of Mr. Samuel Tuthill, of Westminster, aged four years, fell backwards into a tub of hot water and was scalded in such a shocking manner, that it survived the accident but three days, when it expired.

On Sunday, the 3d ult. Ebenezer Pratt, of South Brimfield, was found on a hay mow in his barn, dead, with his throat cut in a shocking manner. The coroner's inquest brought in a verdict of *"premeditated self-murder."*

Vol. XI (No. 624) Saturday, 16 March 1805.

† [3d] Legal notice regarding the estate of Jonathan Duncan, late of New Grantham, deceased; William Page, Adm.; dated at Bellows Falls, Rockingham, 14 March 1805.

===== ¶ [3b] MARRIED. =====

In Portsmouth, Mr. George Daniels, to Miss Elizabeth Hill.—Mr. George B. Odiorne, to Miss Ruth Kinnear, both of Newcastle.

===== ¶ [3b-c] DIED. =====

In Philadelphia from Feb. 2d to 9th, 19 adults, 12 children, total 31.——In the Genesee country, Mr. Joshua Paul, formerly of Westminster.——In Mendon, Mr. Ebenezer Chapin, aged 90.——In Brookfield, Mrs. Damaris Olds, aged 87. Her descendants are ten children, 79 grand-children, 127 great-grand-children, and one of the fifth generation; making in the whole 217:——Mrs. Mary Richards, aged 35, wife of Mr. Thomas Richards.——In Barre, Mrs. Sarah Jones, aged 82, wife of the late Capt. Wm. Jones, formerly of Barre.——In Rutland, (Mass.) suddenly, Mr. Wm. Bridge, aged 64.— In Sutton, Miss Betsey Gale, aged 40.——In West-Springfield, Mrs. Hannah Burbank, aged 52.——In Pownal, Mrs. Theoda Dimmock.——Found dead, on the 18th ult. in the road between Newington and Portsmouth, Widow Sarah Drisco, of Durham.——In Pomfret, Thomas Barns, Esq. aged 85.——In Hopkinton, Mrs. Sarah Towne, aged 43.— In Concord, N.H. Mr. Jonathan Fisk, aged 22.——In Goshen, Mr. Samuel Mott, aged 66.——In Northampton, Wid. Abigail Lyman, aged 61.——In Syracuse, Lieu. John B. Nicholson, of the United States navy, killed in a duel with Mr. Dehart, also an officer of the United States navy : The parties exchanged three shots, when Mr. Nicholson was shot through the head and expired instantly.——In Philad. from the 9th to 16th Feb. 22 adults, 17 children; total 39.——In Amwel, N.J. Mrs. Naylor, aged 103.——In Haverhill, Mass. Dea. Joseph Eaton, aged 74 : Next day after his funeral, very suddenly, his daughter Mary Eaton : wid. Rachael Bradley, aged 67.——In Reading, Mr. James Hull, aged 77.——In Andover, Capt. Henry Abbot, aged 80.——In Boston, Widow Mary Freeman, aged 66 : Capt. Roger Bartlett, aged 81 : Mrs. Ann M'Million, aged 81 : Mrs. Mercy Gooding, aged 76.——In Woodstock, (N.J.) Mrs. Charlotte Ayers; while standing before the glass, combing her hair, she fainted, fell down, and expired in a few minutes.——In Newport, Mr. Stephen Deblois, aged 70.——In Colchester, of the small pox, Miss Sybel Cook, aged 26, formerly of Preston: Another victim, in the enlightened state of Connecticut, to the Small Pox ! "Tell it not in Gath," &c.——In Dorchester, Mrs. Mary Skinner, aged 70.—In Winchester, (Vir.) Col. Richard Kidder Meade, one of the Aids-de-camp of Gen. Washington.——In Philad. from the 16th to the 23d Feb. 22 adults, 12 children; total 34—6 of small pox, a suicide by laudanum, 8 consumption; 2 casualties, a woman burnt to death by falling into the fire, and a child, whose clothes accidentally caught fire.——In Kittery, of a palsy, Mr. James Paul, aged 56.——In Portsmouth, Mrs. Ann Hoar:—Mrs. Elizabeth Hart, aged 38.—In Gilmanton, Miss Sally James, aged 21.—In Providence, Mr. Archibald Stewart, aged 78 : Mrs. Lydia Williams, aged 64.——In Wickford, Mr. Richard Updike, aged 70.——In New York, in December last, 185 deaths : In January, 217. In the same months the births were 282 and 305.—— In Litchfield, suddenly, of the lock-jaw, Mr. Appleton Kilborn aged 69.—In Hadley, on

the 24th ult. Mrs. Thankful Kellog, [sic] wife of Mr. Gardner Kellogg, [sic] aged 77.——
In Woodbridge, (N.J.) Mr. David Edgar, aged 85.

Suicide.—On Saturday evening, the 16th ult. Joseph King, of Suffield, Con. put a period to his life by swallowing a quantity of laudanum.—In December last, Dr. Erastus King, brother of the deceased, put an end to his life in the same manner.

A man in Brookfield lately put an end to his existence by cutting his throat.

On the 11th of January last was found dead, at the bottom of a well in Barre, the body of Joseph Reynold, of Hanover, N.H. The jury of inquest brought in a verdict "that he came to his death by plunging himself head foremost into said well, and there drowning." To appearance he was a man about 45 years of age, and has left a wife and family to lament his loss—The day previous to his being found in the well, he called at a house where no person was at home except the woman; here he staid until evening. He stated that he was in debt, and that he was going to Canada to get away from his creditors. As he appeared to be insane, the woman was afraid to continue with him alone in the evening, and therefore persisted in his leaving the house, which he did. Next morning the horse was found hitched near the door. This led the family to suppose he had gone on afoot; but an uncommonly disagreeable taste which they perceived in the tea at breakfast, induced them to search the well, where he was found in the astonishment of the family. [*Randolph Paper.*

Vol. XII (No. 625) Saturday, 23 March 1805.

† [1c] Joseph Bellows, Jr. adv. property for sale, "it being the place now in the occupation of Samuel Whittle." Dated at Walpole, 18 March 1805.

† [2c] Article dated at Charleston, S.C., describing the murder of Mr. Daniel Doughty, of Pendleton district. Doughty was claimed to have been poisoned by his wife, his step-father Laban Oakley, and one John Andrews. ♦

¶ [2d] POST OFFICE.——Mr. Thomas Hough, of Lebanon, is appointed postmaster, [vice?] Mr. J. Ralstone, dismissed.

† [3b] Barn and livestock belonging to Ebenezer Thomas, of Plainfield, N.H., struck by lightning on the "8th inst."

† [3b] Rev. Abel Farley ordained at the Congregational Church in Manchester, Vt., and Rev. Samuel Bliss ordained "on the 6th inst. at Congregational Church in Bradford."

† [3c] David Carter, Treasurer, posts a notice regarding the Third N.H. Turnpike Road, and mentions a public auction of shares to be sold at the dwelling house of Phillips Sweetser, Esq., in Marlboro'. Dated Marlboro, 16 March 1805.

† [3d] Legal notice regarding the insolvent estate of Richard Field, late of Claremont, deceased. John Moore, David Buckman, and Thomas Perry appointed Commissioners; examination of claims to be held at Daniel Chase's Tavern, Claremont.

† [3d] Legal notice regarding the estate of Asa Walker, late of Langdon, deceased; James Egerton, Executor.

† [3d] *Bellows & Stone* request debtors to pay up; dated Walpole, 19 March 1805.

===== ¶ [3b] MARRIED. =====

In Boston, Mr. Luther Lapham, to Miss Sophia Dunbar.
In Rutland, (Ver.) Mr. Joseph Harris, to Miss Lucretia Lord.
In Windsor, Mr. Frederick Burnham, to Miss Hannah Mason.
In this town, on Thursday last, Mr. Geo. Cobb, to Miss Sally Chandler.

===== ¶ [3c] DIED. =====

In Natchez, Hon. David Ker, one of the Judges of the Superior Court of the Territory.——In Charleston, (S.C.) the Rev. Abraham Azuby, minister of the Hebrew congregation in that city, aged 67, a native of Amsterdam. ☞ *Error in a late Obituary, corrected.* Mrs. Ruth Kirby's death was mentioned, who we see by the late papers is still living. [126] ——In Sherburne, Mr. Benjamin Kendal, aged 96. The longevity of his family is worthy of notice : His father died in the 95th year of his age, a sister in the 93d, another sister living in her 86th, and a brother in his 81st.——In Salem, Widow Mary Joslin, aged 75.——In Boston, Mrs. Sarah Skinnow, aged 62 : Mrs. Hannah Pope, aged 61, a member of the Society of Friends.——In West Hartford, Mr. Gideon Deming, aged 75.——In Haverhill, Mr. Jacob Wyman, aged 68.——In New York, Dr. Lot Tripp, aged 54, a member of the respectable society of Friends.——In Spencertown, on the

18th Jan. Rhoda, in her 15th year, and on the 28th, Wesley, in his 14th year, children of Mr. Daniel Leonard.——In Goshen, C. Mr. Samuel Mott, aged 66.——In Charlestown, very suddenly, Capt. Noah Porter.—In Watertown, Mr. Amos Hickox, aged 90.——In England, the Marchioness of Rockingham, widow of the late celebrated Marquis.——In Portsmouth, Miss Hannah Langdon Gove, Æt. 14.——In Westminster, (Mass.) Mr. Timothy Fessenden, aged 74.——In Barre, Mrs. Dinah Fay, aged 76.——In Baltimore, much lameneted, Miss Eliza Stickney, late of Worcester, aged 20.——In West Springfield, Mrs. Hutchins, Æt. 55.——In Litchfield, Isaac Baldwin, Esq. aged 94.——In Hudson, Joseph Hamilton, M.D. Æt. 67.——In Claverack, Capt. Casparus Conyne, Æt. 79.——In Providence, Mrs. Esther Angell, Æt. 68 : Suddenly, of the apoplexy, Mrs. Mercy Arnold, aged 68.——In Pomfret, (Ver.) Capt. Thomas Barns, aged 81.——In Mason, Mr. Jason Dunster, aged about 75.—In Milford, Mr. George Barns, aged 72.—In Montague, Rev. Judah Nash, aged 77, and 54th of his ministry.——In Royalton, Mr. Rufus Flagg, aged 62.——In Granville, (N.Y.) on the 24th ult. Capt. Daniel White. He had been unfortunate, and having just returned from his brother, in Connecticut, who had given him means to reinstate himself in the possession of his former property, fell dead instantly, while cheerfully communicating the glad tidings to his son, in the street.——In Charlestown, S.C. Mr. William Mason, a native of Salem, Ms. aged 30.—In Groton, (C.) Elder Park Allen, aged 72.—In Preston, (C.) Mrs. Sarah Crary, aged 85.——Deaths in New York, for the week ending the 9th inst. 8 men, 4 women, 5 boys, 8 girls; total 25.—In Canaan, of a consumption, Jonathan Burrall, Esq.——In Litchfield, Mr. Elisha S. Monger.——In London, the 31st December, George Evans, Baron Carbery of the kingdom of Ireland, aged 39.——In Marietta, Col. Ebenezer Sproat, an officer of distinguished merit in the American revolutionary war.——In Abbeville, (S.C.) Mrs. Margaret Dickson, aged 104 : Until a few days previous to her death, she enjoyed perfect health, and regularly attended divine worship, altho' the meeting house was three miles distant from her home.——In Washington city, on the 6th inst. Col. William W. Burrows, late Colonel Commandant of the Marine Corps.——In Philadelphia, from 2d to 3d inst. 35.——In Gloucester, (N.J.) Maj. Samuel Hugg, a brave and zealous officer in the American revolutionary war.——At Montville, (Con.) the widow Dolly Babcock, and Mr. George Dolebear, both of the *small pox !* ——In Northampton, Mrs. Sarah Storrs, aged 44.——In Newburyport, Mrs. Mary Plummer, aged 27 : Dea. David Perkins, of Thornton, (N.H.)—he fell down dead, while walking in a street.——In Salem, Wid. Hannah Gardner, aged 34.——In Westminster, Mr. John Kendrick, aged about 17.

Vol. XII (No. 626) Saturday, 30 March 1805.

¶ [3b] *New Post-Master.*——Dr. Thomas Hooker is appointed Deputy-Postmaster in Rutland, Vt. in the room of Samuel Prentiss, Esq. resigned.

† [3c] Rev. John Sabin ordained on the 6th inst. at Fitzwilliam.

† [3c] Francis Gardner offers property for sale at Walpole, including a Fulling Mill.

† [3d] Legal notice concerning Asa Sartwell, Cynthia Sartwell, Fanny Sartwell, Clarissa Sartwell, and Lucy Sartwell, minors under age 21, and under the guardianship of Samuel Crosby, Esq., late of Charlestown, deceased. Oliver Hall, William Briggs, and Horace Hall were administrators of Crosby's estate.

† [4b-c] Extensive letter written by Dr. Thomas Welsh to "the President and Members of the Board of Health," regarding his observations of small pox cases among crews and passengers aboard several vessels, and his success with the Kine Pock vaccination. The article was copied from the *Palladium*, which originally, copied it from the letter dated at Boston, 1 March 1805. Dr. Welsh states that he visited vessels anchored near "Rainsford's Island for purification, since the beginning of June, 1804." ♦

1) The brig *Rambler*, Capt. William Gooch, from Martinico, arrived 23 Dec. 1804. Capt. Gooch, and the mate Seth Hatch, had the small pox, but both recovered.
2) Schooner *Polly*, Capt. William Williams, arrived from Philadelphia, with several of the crew infected with the small pox: Lewis Darley (died 6 Feb. 1805); Abijah Dunham (died 8 Jan. 1805); James Snow (died 23 Feb. 1805); and Daniel Parker, who recovered and was discharged from the Hospital, 6 Feb. 1805.

3) Dr. Welsh innoculated the following persons, who all survived the epidemic: Sally Davis, Elijah Davis, and Samuel Davis, "two children in Mr. Spear's family, and James M'Cormick, of the U.S. Revenue Cutter, which then lay at the Island."

===== ¶ [3c] MARRIED. =====

In Portsmouth, Charles Cushing, jun. Esq. of Boston, to Miss Ann Sheafe.
In Pittsfield, (Mass.) Mr. John Breck, of Northampton, to Miss Clarissa Allen.

===== ¶ [3c] DIED. =====

In Calcutta, in Oct. last, Ram Chunder Benorjea, an Hindoo merchant; well know to Americans who have of late years visited that port, as a man of uprightness and integrity; and who transacted the business committed to his care, with fidelity and dispatch : He has left an estate of about 400,000 dollars.—In Baltimore, Mr. Hugh M'Curdy, merchant.—In N. Carolina, Rev. Thomas Hines, a Baptist missionary:—The Newbern Circular, mentioning his death, says—"In the saddle-bags of this pretended servant of God, but disciple of Mammon, were found, his bible, and a complete apparatus for stamping and milling dollars !"—In Hartford, Mrs. Mary Ann Goodrich, consort of Chauncey G. Esq. aged 40.

Vol. XII (No. 627) Saturday, 6 April 1805. [127]

¶ [2d] *Duel.*—Mr. M.G. Lewis, a brother of the late Mrs. Claiborne, fell in a duel fought about the 12th of February, with Mr. Robert Sterry, both of New Orleans.

† [3b] Article detailing the deaths of eight members of the Villeneuve family, at St. Augustin, Quebec, near the city of Quebec. The family was crushed in their home by an avalanche of snow. A woman named Laurencelle, lodging in the house, was also killed. ♦

† [3c] Rev. Jonathan Nye ordained at St. Albans, Vt.

===== ¶ [3c] MARRIED. =====

In Woodstock, (Vermont) Mr. Thomas Randall, to Miss Hannah Field.
In New York, Mr. John Wright, to Miss Elizabeth Quirk. [. . .]

===== ¶ [3c-d] DIED. =====

At Paris, M. Francis Tanoise, clerk in the French Treasury, aged 88. He left behind him no less than ten widows, though he was a bachelor until 1792. In his will he declares he never intended to marry, had not the National Convention passed the law for Easy divorces. He leaves to each of his widows an annuity of 200 livres (50l.) as he says they were all equally dear to him. Not one of them is yet 30 years of age.—In Williamstown, very suddenly, Mr. William Lamb, formerly of Gerry, Ms. aged about 30.—In Washington, (N.H.) on the 21st ult. Mr. Simeon Farnsworth, aged 89 : leaving a wife, 10 children, 68 grand-ch. and 46 gr. gr. ch. making 124 in all : of whom 56 attended his funeral.—At Middleton-point, (C.) Dr. Thomas Barber, aged 64.—In Amherst, Mr. Samuel Whiting, aged 41.—In Haverhill, (Ms.) Jabez Kimball, Esq. attorney at law.—In Pelham, (N.H.) Mrs. Mehitable, wife of Mr. Joshua Atwood, aged 78 : they lived together in the married state above sixty years ; have had 17 children, 68 grand-children, and 12 great-gr. children; total 79. [128] —of these, 13 children, 56 grand-ch. and all their great-gr. children are still living.—In Madbury, (N.H.) Mr. Jacob Joy, sen.—suicide by hanging himself—he was in affluent circumstances, and had an agreeable wife, and several promising children.—At Dracut, Dr. Ebenezer Varnum, Æt. 38.—In Winchester, Mrs. Lydia Woolley, aged 36.—In England, the Most Rev. Father in God, Dr. John Moore, Archbishop of Canterbury, aged 75.—He is succeeded in his dignified office, by Dr. Charles Manners Sutton, late Bishop of Norwich.—In Ireland, the Rt. Rev. and Hon. Dr. Stopford, Bishop of Cork and Ross.—Off the coast of France, drowned, in his endeavors to save the crew of the Doris frigate, Capt. Jervis, of Le Tonnant, of 80 guns, nephew of the Earl of St. Vincent, and Treasurer of Greenwich Hospital.—In Charleston, S.C. Mr. Wm. White, Æt. 54.—In Brookfield, Dr. Wm. Thomas, aged 61 : Mr. Charles Gilbert, aged 27, candidate for the Gospel ministry.—In West Hartford, Mrs. Sarah Trumbull, of Watertown, aged 87.—In Walden, of the dropsy, Mrs. Elizabeth Gilman—Within three years she has been tapped thirteen times, and 70 gallons water extracted.—In Charleston, (S.C.) Mrs. Susannah Wadsworth, aged

72.—In Marietta, (Terr. N.W. of the Ohio) [129] the Rev. Daniel Story, aged 47, Pastor of the Church in that place and its vicinity, and a native of Boston.—In Hinsdale, Dr. Richard Starr, aged 87.—In Gloucester, Capt. Robert Elwell, aged 84.

In Halifax, (Ver.) of a putrid malignant fever, Feb. 16th, Freeman, son of Mr. Abel Scott, aged 4 years ; on the 27th, widow Sarah Scott, aged 59. March 6th, Reuben, son of Mr. Abel Scott, aged 6 years ; on the 9th, Ruby, daughter of Widow Scott, aged 16;— on the 20th, Polly, wife of Mr. Abel Scott, aged 31 ; all residing in one house.—Also, March 3d, Cynthia, daughter of Mr. Thomas Scott, aged 1 year and 10 months. Thus Mr. Scott is left to mourn, not only the death of his worthy and affectionate consort, but the bereavement of all his children, save one little daughter under two years old. Two died previous to this sickness. Also an only surviving and affectionate parent ; an amiable sister, and brother's daughter. The house is left to him desolate.—The scene is mournful.—The change is awfully solemn.—But a few weeks since health and sprightliness beamed in every countenance; love and friendship animated every heart. —They were happy in the company of each other, and in the society of their friends: But, alas ! the sad reverse ! [*Greenfield Gazette*.

In a late paper we noticed the death of Mrs. Jemima Tute. Our more distant patrons and the public should be informed that this respectable matron is the same lady who is celebrated as the "Fair Captive," by Col. Humphreys in his life of General Putnam, and an account of whose sufferings is presented in the appendix of Dr. Belknap's history of New Hampshire.

This lady had been eminently unfortunate in the early parts of her life ; her two first husbands were both killed by the Indians.—On the death of the second, Mr. Caleb Howe, in 1758, she with several young children were carried to a long and cruel captivity among the Indians—but her sufferings and magnanimity are already too well known to require any statement.

Mrs. Howe, on her return from captivity, settled in Hinsdale, where after some years she married Mr. Amos Tute, whom she survived about ten years.

She was among the first settlers of Hindsdale, and lived to see that town from an uncultivated wilderness surrounded with Savages, from whom she was in continual dread of death or slavery of herself or friends, become a continued scene of cultivation and beauty. Many of her children grew up around her in peace, with no fear of the tomahawk or savage foe which they had so severely felt the effect of in their early youth; and repaying her by their kindness and attention the many days and nights of anxiety and terror she had passed for them.—*Reporter.* [130]

WESTMINSTER, VT. APRIL 4, 1805.

"Departed this life, half after three o'clock on Monday morning the 1st inst. Mrs. Margaret Wall, wife of Patrick Wall, Esq. in the 68th year of her age, after three months confinement with a most painful and distressing complaint," [. . .]

Vol. XII (No. 628) Saturday, 13 April 1805.

† [2d-3a] After considerable sniping at Mr. Griswold, the editor of a competing Walpole newspaper, (the *Observatory*,) the editor of the *Museum* states that Griswold will be departing for the Michigan territory "in a few weeks." [131]

† [3c] Asa Evans adv. a reward for items stolen from his store; dated at Peterborough, 9 April 1805.

† [3d] *Webster, Cole & Co.* adv. for their paper mill at Alstead.

===== ¶ [3c] MARRIED. =====

At Rockingham, (Ver.) on Sunday last, by the Rev. Samuel Whiting, Mr. Joseph Weed, to Miss Deborah House.

In Litchfield, Mr. Younglove Cutler, of Watertown, to Miss Anna Woodward, of the former place.

In Wethersfield, (Ver.) Mr. Daniel Lockwood, of Springfield, to Miss Abigail Chillson.

In Castleton, (Ver.) Rev. Mr. Boise, of Tinmouth, to Miss Caroline Cogswell.

In Newburyport, Michael Hodge, jun. Esq. to Miss Mary Johnson.

In Epping, Mr. Henry Gilman, of Exeter, to Miss Nancy Wiggin, of the former place.

¶ [3c] DIED.

In Haverhill, Mr. Nathan Barker, aged 81.—In Portsmouth, Stephen Chase, Esq. aged 61.—At Long-lane, Mrs. Norton, aged 80.—In Sutton, Mrs. Betsey Rich, aged 90, daughter of the Rev. Benjamin Marsh, who was one of the first settlers of the town.—At Sturbridge, Mrs. Deborah Freeman, aged 66.—In Boylston, Mr. Ephraim Beaman, aged 60.—In South Brimfield, Mr. Isaiah Blood, aged 85.—In Claverack, (N.Y.) Lawrence Hogeboom, Esq. aged 68.—In Cincinnati, Major Thomas Doyle, of the U.S. army.—In Salem, Mr. Edward Gray, jun. printer, aged 27.—In Keene, Mrs. Bial Willard, consort of Mr. Josiah Willard, aged 26 : Mrs. Abigail Snow, wife of Dea. Daniel Snow, aged 75.—In Boston, Capt. Benj. Hammatt, aged 93.—In Woodstock, (Con.) on Saturday morning last, Mrs. Morse, mother of the Rev. Dr. Morse, of Charlestown, Mass. in the 81st year of her age : Capt. Wm. Lyon, aged about 62.

In this town, Mr. David Hall, aged 50—a good citizen and a worthy man.

Westmoreland, April 11th, 1805.

Died, in this town, this morning, in a fit of the numbpalsy, the Widow *Hannah Butterfield*, aged 59 years. Her funeral will be attended on Saturday next, at one o'clock, P.M. In Shelburne, V. Mr. Moses Pierson, Æt. 71.

Vol. XII (No. 629) Saturday, 20 April 1805.

† [3a-b] Extensive account of the murder of two children of Asa Lupton, of Hampshire County, Va., by one Isaiah Martin. ◆

† [3d] Adv. by Seth Hall, jun., who is searching for an apprentice to the Clothier's business; also an adv. for "cloth dressed in the neatest manner, and on very short notice, at his works one mile west of Elder Bailey's meeting-house." Dated at Westmoreland, 12 April 1805.

† [4a-b] An extensive article regarding the benefits of a Mineral Spring at Stafford, Tolland County, Conn., Dr. Willard, proprietor. Gen. James Gordon, of Plainfield, Conn., writes that he recalled when Miss Mardenbrough, (daughter of Christopher Mardenbrough, Esq., of St. Christophers island), resided in 1774 with her uncle, Mr. George Wright of Newport, Rhode Island. In 1775, Mr. Wright removed his family to Norwich, Conn., and Miss Mardenbrough, suffering health problems, was sent to the Mineral Spring. ◆

¶ [3c] MARRIED.

In Halifax, Capt. Thomas Farnsworth, to the widow Catherine Wells.

In Greenfield, Mr. Roswell Lombard, of Springfield, to Miss Cornelia Hall, of the former place.

¶ [3c] DIED.

In New York, Mrs. Sarah Alexander, relict of the late Major General Lord Sterling.—In Westminster, (Mass.) Dr. Asa Miles, aged 43.—In Charlton, Widow Susanna Foskett, aged [91?] years and 4 months.—In Canandaigua, Mr. Robert Palsy, an indigent laborer, (suicide) by taking upwards of an ounce of laudanum.—In Stephentown, (N.Y.) on Thursday the 20th ult. Mr. Elisha Bligh, late of Hudson, aged about 24; and a few hours after his eldest brother, Samuel Bligh, jun. both of a consumption.—In Germany, M. Huber, a very celebrated writer, and Editor of the Gazette General: He was appointed by the Elector of Bavaria, Member of the Administration of Bavaria, in Swabia.—In Richmond, (Virg.) Gen. Robert Lawson.—In Baltimore, Capt. John R. Card.—In Sparta, N.Y. Maj. Elias Ogden.—In New Rochelle, (N.Y.) 2d inst. Samuel Pintard, Esq. aged 69, formerly a captain in his Britannic Majesty's 25th regiment of foot: he was a native of New York.—In Northampton, Mrs. Anne Burt, aged 88. In Starksborough, 29th ult. Deacon Abraham Hall, aged 75, a pious, worthy man.—In Saybrook, Mr. Wm. Buck, aged 35.—In Middlebury, Mrs. Azubah Kirby, aged 32.—In Portsmouth, Stephen Chase, Esq. A.M. aged 61.—During the month of March, in Boston, there were *born* 24 males, 35 females, 6 sex not returned; total 76—6 still born—*Died*, 15 males, 13 females, total 28.—In Philadelphia, from March 30 to April 6, 18 adults, 16 children; total 34.—In Newyork, from 30th March to 6th April, 16 men, 11 women, 2 boys, 5 girls; total 34.—In Portsmouth, 11th inst. the Hon. John Pickering, Esq. L.L.D. aged 63.

In this town, an infant child of Mr. Joseph Jones.—On Wednesday morning last, Mr. John Watkins, aged 38.

Vol. XII (No. 630) Saturday, 27 April 1805.

† [3b] The villagers of Lempster, N.H., team up to capture a wolf, who killed several sheep owned by Mr. Freegrace Booth.

† [3b-c] Widow Kendrick and her daughter murdered at their home in Hollis, N.H.; Dr. Lawrence, of Pepperell, was called to the scene. The widow's son was suspected of the murder. Article copied from the *Amherst Cabinent*. ◆ 132

¶ [3d] BIRTH.—At Middleboro, the lady of the Rev. Mr. Girney, of a daughter; after having lived in the married state childless more than seventeen years, and having entered her 48th year.

† [3d] Amos Shepard, John C. Chamberlain, and Nathaniel Emerson, Directors, post a notice regarding a meeting of the Stoddard Turnpike Corporation.

† [3d] William Jennison, Executor, posts a legal notice regarding the estate of John Jenison, late of Walpole, deceased. Dated Walpole, 26 April 1805.

===== ¶ [3c] MARRIED. =====

In Paris, Count Rumford, to the widow of M. Vareefy; by which nuptial experiment he obtains a fortune of 8000 *l*. per annum [. . .]

In Troy, Dr. Moses Hale, to Mrs. Mary Porter.

In New-Lebanon, the Hon. Joseph Jenks, Esq. of Elizabethtown, to Mrs. Hannah Bennit, of the former place.

At Manlius, (N.Y.) Samuel Prescott, Esq. of Chesterfield, (N.H.) Attorney at Law, to Miss Frances Johnson, daughter of Mr. Moses Johnson, late of Keene.

===== ¶ [3c-d] DIED. =====

In Granville, 1st inst. Timothy Robinson, Esq. aged 77.—In Machias, Mrs. Martha Holway, aged 63.—In Marlborough, (Ms.) Capt. Jonathan Weeks, aged 63.—In Wilbraham, at an advanced age, Mr. Oliver Bliss.—In Danbury, (Con.) Mr. John M'Lean, aged 67.—In Great-Barrington, (N.Y.) Mr. William Patterson, aged 89.—In Southington, (Con.) Mrs. Susannah Root, aged 88.—In Hamden, Capt. Alling Cooper, aged 64.—In Windsor, Con. Mr. Jonathan Filly, aged 72.—In Bolton, (Ms.) Obadiah Wheeler upwards of 90 years of age; a respectable member of the Society of Friends.—In West Springfield, 23d March, Mrs. Dorcas Lathrop, wife of Mr. Elijah Lathrop, aged 48.—In Ballston, (N.Y.) on the 10th inst. the Rev. Gamaliel Thatcher.—In Bridgetown, Cumberland County, N.J. on the 1st ult. Lieut. Colonel Eli Elmer. He was a distinguished officer during the Revolutionary War, and won by his good conduct and affable deportment the esteem of all who had the pleasure of his acquaintance. A disciple of the Washington school, he of course fell a victim to the persecuting spirit of the present administration, and was turned out of office soon after Mr. Jefferson was made our President.—In the parish of St. Elizabeth, (Jamaica) Rebecca Miles, aged upwards of 113 years. Her children, grand-children, great-grand-children, and great-great-grand-children, amount to 295; and one of the companies of the regiment of foot militia of that parish, consisting of more than 60 persons of the name of Banks, is composed of her issue, besides a number in other companies. She retained her senses to the last, and was very active as a midwife, going often the distance of ten miles on foot in preference to riding. 133——In Bellpre, (State of Ohio) Feb. 24, Mrs. Abigail Browning, consort of Mr. Wm. Browning, of that place, and daughter of Gen. Rufus Putnam, of Marietta, aged 35.—In England, Sir Richard Pearson, Knt. Lieut. Governor of Greenwich Hospital, who distinguished himself in the American war, in his gallant action of seven hours in the Serapis frigate, against Paul Jones, in the Bon Homme Richard.—In Philadelphia, Mr. William Spotswood, printer and bookseller, formerly a resident of Boston.—In New York, Mr. John Slidell, sen. aged 74 :—From 6th to 13th inst. 46 ; of which number were 13 men, 12 women, 15 boys and 6 girls ; 2 died of small pox, 17 of consumption.—In Providence, Mr. Phineas Brown, aged 84.—In Newbury, (N.H.) Mrs. Jaques, aged 92.—In Newburyport, Widow Hannah Holland, aged 84.—In Plymouth, the 9th inst. Mr. Nehemiah Cobb, aged 51.—In Boston, Mrs. Mary Richards, aged 65 ;—Mr. Daniel Jennings, aged 50.—In Rockingham, (Ver.) 19th inst. of a consumption, much lamented, Mr. John Felt, son of Eliphalet F. aged 22.—In Hartford,

Mr. Francis Rockwell, aged 19.—In Whitestown, (N.Y.) Mrs. Vina Perkins, aged 33.—At Ashley River, Mrs. Mary Frazer, aged 26.—In Brookfield, Mrs. Tamar Hawley, aged 38.—Drowned, from on board the sloop Anna Eliza, near Newberg, Eliphalet Webb.—In Burke, Mrs. Demon : Choaked [sic] by a pea, a child of Mr. Geo. Nichols, 9 months old.—In Scotland, Dr. Robinson, Professor of Natural Philosophy in the University of Edinburgh : Dr. Playfair, ex-professor of mathematics in the same university, has succeeded him.—Dr. Rotheram, professor of Natural Philosophy in the neighbouring university of St. Andrews :—Also, Dr. William Buchan, aged 76.—In England, Sir Gregory Turner;—33,400 guineas were found in his escretoire and chest; —he left 310,000 *l.* in funded property, and landed estate which produced 24,000 *l*, per annum.—In Virginia, Col. Charles Stockley, aged 49.—In Salem, Capt. Ephraim Very, aged 51.—In Cambridge, (Mass.) Mr. Bossenger Foster, sen. aged 63.—In Cornish, (N.H.) Mr. Samuel Reed, aged 84.—In Hartland, (Ver.) Mr. Nathan Harvey, aged 93. —In Weston, (Mass.) Dr. John Clarke, aged 27.—In Boston, Mr. Thomas Brewer, aged [51?] :—Isaiah Doane, Esq. aged 51.—In Medford, Mr. Andrew Hall, aged 43.—In Charlestown, Mrs. Elizabeth Maxwell, aged 24.—In Baltimore, from 1st to 7th inst. 14 adults, 6 children.

Vol. XII (No. 631) Saturday, 4 May 1805.

¶ [3b] *Another instance of Democratic Tyranny.*—John Mann, jun. Esq. a pupil of the Washington school has been removed, by Mr. Granger, from the office of postmaster, at Orford, in this State, and Mr. Stephen Lombard, a devotee to Democracy, appointed in his place.

¶ [3c] *Remarkable increase of Republicanism in the East.* On the 12th inst. the wife of Mr. Roger Phelps, jun. a respectable republican in Hebron, presented him three children (one son and two daughters) at a birth; each weighed 5 lbs. and are all likely to do well. [*Connecticut Courant.*

¶ [3d] J. PHELPS, *Postrider from Walpole to Brattleborough,* informs those persons who live on his route, that he can supply them with either the *Political Observatory, Farmers' Museum,* or *Brattleboro' Reporter,* as they may choose. He trusts that his punctuality and endeavors to serve his customers will procure him liberal patronage. May 4.

===== ¶ [3d] MARRIED. =====

At Bradford, Vt. Col. Dan Shaw, of Lime, to Mrs. Mary Bliss, of the former place.
In Lebanon, Mr. Jabez Baker, to Mrs. Polly Robertson.

===== ¶ [3d] DIED. =====

In New York, Mrs. Experience Noel, Æt. 74 :—From the 13th to 20th April, 16 men, 11 women, 6 boys and 3 girls; total 36—15 of consumption.—In Philadelphia, from 13th to 20th April, 23; 16 adults, 12 children [sic].—In Portsmouth, Mr. Collin Lina Campbell, aged 47 : Mr. Samuel Penhallow, jun. mer. aged 48 : In consequence of a fall from the eaves of a house 12 days before, Jean Baptiste Reynal, aged 41, a native of Brest, who was a glazier on board the Auguste, a 74 in the French Fleet which came into Portsmouth in 1782.—In Hartford, (Con.) Mr. Moses Ensign, aged 73 : Alcis E. Hart, Esq. aged 22.—In Hebron, Mr. Jedidiah Caulkins, aged 40.—In Fairfield, Mr. Ebenezer Hall, aged 82.—In Ludlow, Mrs. Martha Lombard, aged 73.—In Sullivan, Mr. Stephen Brown, Æt. 23.—In Franconia, N.H. (drowned,) Mr. James Sanger, aged 25.—In Quebec, Mrs. Ann Allsop, wife of George A. Esq.—In New Orleans, Capt. Robinson, of the U.S. artillery.—In Knoxville, (Ten.) Mr. George Roulstone, aged 38, editor of the Knoxville Gazette and a native of Boston.—In Maryland, Mr. John Fowler, murdered by his negroes.—In Providence, Mrs. Mary Brown, relict of the late Hon. Obadiah Brown : Christopher Champlin, Esq. aged 76; he was formerly President of the Rhode Island Bank.—In Rochester, (R.I.) Mr. John Andrews, aged 80; he was a member of the Baptist Church upwards of fifty years.—In Marblehead, Mr. Joshua Foster, aged 86.—In Shelburne, 20th ult. widow Martha Ware, aged 81.

In Alstead, on Monday last, Absalom Kingsbery, Esq. aged 74; an affectionate husband, a tender father, a good friend, and a worthy citizen:—a first settler of the town, which he served with integrity and benevolence in various offices;—a lover of his country, and an exemplary christian.—His funeral was attended with due respectability.

Vol. XII (No. 632) Saturday, 11 May 1805.

† [2c-d] In an article dated at Marblehead, (Mass.), 24 April 1805, an extensive account is given of the sinking of the ship *Jupiter*, a trader bound from London to New York, which struck ice and sank in the North Atlantic. The ship had 73 persons aboard; only a yawl and a long boat were available for escape. Eight persons in the yawl were rescued by the schooner *Joanna*, Capt. Henry Quiner. The *Jupiter* sank in 30 minutes, claiming 27 persons; 38 persons were aboard the long boat, which was separated from the yawl in rough seas. In a separate article at [3b], the news arrived that the long boat had been rescued, and some of the passengers were brought to Marblehead by a Capt. John Hammond. ♦ 134

Names of those left at sea in the long boat.

Gilbert I.E. Smissaert, of Amsterdam, cabin passenger
Mr. Ashley, wife and three daughters 135
Mr. Medcalf, wife and infant
Mr. Merritt, wife and apprentice boy
James Trice and mother
Isaac Paine, wife and child
George Slowman
Rachel Luff
Eleazer Wood
Mr. Mitchel and wife
James Williams
Mr. Temple's servant
two Germans, (names unknown)
Thomas Williams, 2d mate
eleven of the crew
one unkown, steerage passenger.

Names of persons in the yawl.

Capt. Richard Law, jun. of New York
Eliab Sturtevant, of New York
George Pierson, of New York, seaman
Hon. Robert Kennedy, cabin passenger
James B. Temple   "   "
John Tappan, of Boston   "   "
James Ilbery, of London "   "
Thomas Trice, steerage passenger

Names of those lost in the ship.

Mrs. and Miss Mirritt
Mr. Beach, wife, and two children
Mr. Giles, wife and seven children
Mrs. Grange
Mrs. Leete and four children
David Brand and two sons
three persons, names unknown,
  [steerage passengers.

† [2d-3a] Mr. Camden, who lived near Lancaster, Garrard County, Kentucky, murdered by Francis Major, who Camden had befriended. ♦
† [3a] Account of the punishment, in the pillory in State Street, Boston, of John H. Nichols, for counterfeiting. Mixed in with "the facts," is much bashing of President Jefferson by the editor; also, in an "editorial," is additional information at [3c].
† [3b] A man who claimed his identity as Martin Scott, of Bennington, Vermont, arrested for counterfeiting at Providence, and taken to Taunton jail. ♦

===== ¶ [3c] MARRIED. =====

In Windsor, Mr. Jeremiah Griswold, to Miss Lucy Darby.
In Brooklyn, (Con.) Mr. George Brinley, mer. of Boston, to Miss Catharine Putnam, daughter of David Putnam, Esq. of the former place.

===== ¶ [3d] DIED. =====

In Portland, Capt. John Thurlo, aged 67.—In Cambridge, Mr. Bossenger Foster, sen.—On the 23d ult. at Fort Knox (Indiana Territory) very suddenly, Capt. Cornelius Lyman, of the U.S. Regt. of Infantry, and formerly of Northampton, aged 47.—He was found dead in his bed, in the morning, without any previous indisposition.—At Pembroke, on the 12th instant, Mr. Samuel Knox, aged 22, son of Mr. John Knox, senior; on the 13th of January last, widow Sarah Holt, in the 88th year of her age—her descendants were 11 children, 98 grand-children, and nearly 200 of the third and fourth generations.—In Kentucky, a Mr. Cambden:—a Francis Major had requested the defunct to hold his horse while he lighted his pipe, and loaded a pistol; which having done, he offered to take from 10 dolls. to 2 pence to shoot the deceased through the head, but which the deceased refused to give; upon which Major shot him through the head.—In New York, from 23d to 30th ult. 14 men, 8 women, 9 boys, and 6 girls; total 37—2 of small pox, 11 of consumptions.—In Portsmouth, Madam Hannah Bracket, aged 70, relict of the late Hon. Joshua Bracket, Esq. M.D.—In Abington, Mr. Jedidiah Beal, aged 88, formerly of Hingham.—In Watertown, Miss Sarah Salter, aged 67.—In Leicester, Mr. Daniel Hubbard, aged 79.—In Peterboro', Mr. John Leathers, aged 52.—In Castleton, Dea. Brewster Higly, aged 70.—In Ballstown, (N.Y.) Mrs. Ruth Baldwin.—In Concord, Mrs. Mary Kimball, aged 64.—In Vergennes, the Hon. Enoch Woodbridge, late chief justice of the state of Vermont.—In Troy, Mrs. Eliza H. Coe, consort of the Rev. Jonas Coe, aged 27.

—In Philadelphia, Mr. Samuel Akerman, printer, of small pox.—In New York, in an advanced age, Mr. Hugh Gaine, a respectable printer and bookseller.—In Swanton, (Ver.) in Feb. last, Mrs. Sally Ripley, the amiable and worthy consort of Deacon Noah Ripley, late of Barre, aged 45.—On his passage from Trinity, to Newburyport, M. France Gallet, a French gentleman.—In Little Cambridge, Miss Anna Dana, aged 73.—In Portsmouth, Capt. Joseph Noble : Mrs. Margaret Howe, aged 48 :—Drowned, from on board the schooner Industry, Mr. Joseph Roach, aged 18.—At Pelham, (N.H.) Mrs. Mehitable Atwood, aged 78, wife of Mr. Joshua Atwood——they lived together in the married state about 60 years, and have had 17 children, 68 grand-children, and 12 great-grand-children.

Departed this life, on the 23d ult. the amiable, and much lamented Mrs. Jones, consort of Mr. Benj. Jones, of Claremont, in the 45th year of her age.—She has left a husband, and thirteen children to lament the loss. [. . .]

MELANCHOLY ACCIDENTS.—On Wednesday, 1st inst. in the afternoon, Mr. David Eckley, son of the Rev. Dr. E. and Mr. John Eddy, brother to Mr. E. of the firm of Dyer & Eddy, all of Boston, with a seaman, whose name is unknown, were unfortunately upset in a boat on their return from the outer harbour, and the latter young gentleman, with the seaman, drowned. Mr. Eckley was fortunately taken up by a fishing boat, at the moment of sinking through fatigue.

On Friday, the 26th ult. the wife of Mr. Abner Gove, of Deering, in this State, was instantaneously killed by lightning, while looking out her window. Another woman, in the room, was knocked down, but recovered.

DROWNED.]—Near Salem, Mr. William Hicks.—In Merrimack river, a Mr. Davison, of Andover, (Mass.)

Vol. XII (No. 633) Saturday, 18 May 1805.

† [2a] Capt. Gage, of the schooner *Industry*, of Hallowell, Maine, aids the ship *Sarah*, Capt. R. Crane, which was in distress in the Atlantic Ocean. The *Sarah* was en route for Philadelphia with passengers from Germany. ♦

† [2b] John Vallier, a free black man, arrested for the murder of Isam Harris, another free black man, at New York City. ♦

† [3c] Baxter Lyon convicted at Ipswich Court for passing counterfeit bills. ♦

¶ [3c] MELANCHOLY ! *Canterbury*, April 16, 1805. "On Sabbath morning, the 14th inst. the body of Mr. John Carter, of this town, was found lifeless, about 50 rods north of his own house. He was returning home from a neighboring town, and it is conjectured he fell from his horse, which caused him to bleed freely at the nose—attempting to proceed home, he fell into a small rivulet, from which thro' weakness, he was unable to extricate himself; he there perished, (aged 54) leaving a wife and seven children to lament their loss."

===== ¶ [3d] MARRIED. =====

In Scituate, Mr. Israel Sylvester, aged 89, to the widow Sarah Totman, aged 70.

In Hampton, (Conn.) John Abbot, Esq. of Westford, (Mass.) to Miss Sophia Moseley, daughter of Ebenezer Moseley, Esq. of the former place.

In Hudson, (N.Y.) Mr. Samuel F. Adams, of Canaan, (Conn.) to Miss Mary

Sampson, daughter of the Rev. Ezra Sampson.

In Rowe, Mr. Amos Gleason, to Miss Lucy Hall.

In Middlebury, Vt. Mr. Horace Loomis, to Miss Mary Chipman.

In Rutland, Vt. Mr. William Fay, printer, to Mrs. Lydia Smith.

===== ¶ [3d] DIED. =====

In England, Jacob Bryant, Esq. aged 89, author of the immortal works on mythology.—In Philadelphia, from 27th April to 4th May, 22 adults, 15 children.—In New York, from 29th April to 7th May, 12 men, 6 women, 6 boys and 6 girls; total 30.—In Troy, Mr. Daniel M'Bride, killed by the splitting of a gun.—In Boston, Capt. John Gray, aged 65 :—M.M. Hays, aged 64 : His remains were conveyed to Newport, to be deposited in the Jewish sepulchre in that city.—In Norwich, Mr. Gamaliel Reynolds, aged 80.—In Ashburnham, Mr. Joseph Whitmore, aged 86.—In Petersham, Dea. Davis Sanderson, aged 90.—In Barre, Major Seth Caldwell, aged 48.—At Loudon Forge, (Penn.) Major General James Chambers.—In Hamilton township, (Penn.) Mr. William Whitney, aged 78.—In Philadelphia, Mrs. Elizabeth Claypoole, aged 88.—In Northfield, Frederick Hunt, Esq. aged 24.—In Lime, Mr. Dan. Shaw, jun. aged 23.—In Hanover, Elias Weld, Esq.—In Canterbury, the 18th ult. Mrs. Whitney, aged 42.—In Providence, Capt. Daniel Bucklin, aged 73.—In Newport, Christopher Champlin, Esq. in the 76th year of his age : for many years an eminent merchant, and President of the Bank of Rhode Island.—In Springfield, (Mass.) the Widow Elizabeth Stebbins, aged 92 : She left of the second generation, 7 ; of the third, 69; the fourth, 125; the fifth, 2.—In Bridgetown, Cumberland county, (N.J.) on the 1st February last, Lieutenant Colonel Eli Elmer. He was a distinguished officer during the Revolutionary War, and won by his good conduct and affable deportment the esteem of all who had the pleasure of his acquaintance:—A disciple of the Washington school, he of course fell a victim to the persecuting spirit of the present administration, and was turned out of office soon after Mr. Jefferson was made our President.—In Hanover, Capt. Joseph Woodward, aged 79.—In Montreal, on Monday, the 29th ult. aged 42, the Hon. John Elmsley, Chief Justice of the Province; universally respected for his talents and private worth.—In Cornish, Mr. Eliphaelt Kimball, aged 74.—In Portsmouth, Mrs. Mary Trusdell, aged 33.

Vol. XII (No. 634) Saturday, 25 May 1805. [136]

† [3b] Review of a new paper entitled *Northern Memento*, printed by Mr. Isaiah H. Carpenter, and published at Woodstock, Vt.

† [3b] Mr. Eben. Daniels of Keene, while "visiting" John H. Nichols in the pillory in Boston, had his pocket picked by one M'Foot, alias Hamilton, who was later captured.◆

† [3d] Legal notice regarding the estate of Absalom Kingsbery, Esq. late of Alstead, deceased; Ephraim Kingsbery, Administrator. Dated Alstead, 22 May 1805.

===== ¶ [3c] MARRIED. =====

In Haverhill, (Ms.) Thomas B. Adams, Esq. of Quincy, to Miss Ann Harrod, of the former place.

In Croydon, Mr. Norman Chapman, to Mrs. Rachel Barton.—Mr. Ebenezer Melendy, to Mrs. Sybil Willard.—Mr. Paul Jacobs to Mrs. Prudence Stow.—Mr. John Allen, to Mrs. Hannah Goldthwait.

In Shirley, Dr. Amos Parker, of Boston, to Miss Elizabeth Whitney, daughter of the Rev. Phineas Whitney.

In Boston, Mr. Samuel Clark, of Newton, to Miss Rebecca P. Hull, 5th daughter of Gov. Hull, of the Michigan Territory.

In Woodstock, Vt. Mr. Alfred Fuller, to Miss Lucena Wyllys.

===== ¶ [3c-d] DIED. =====

In Great Barrington, Mr. Josiah Dewey, aged 44.—In Amherst, Mr. Joel Hagar, aged 52. His death was occasioned by a fall from a chamber floor, which fractured his skull in several directions. He lived but a few hours after the wound.—In England, Lord George Lenox; the Earl of Chatham succeeds him as Governor of Plymouth: Dr. Peter Renaudet, aged 40, highly eminent as a physician : Mr. Wm. Parrington, aged 86, formerly a molecatcher, in which possession he acquired upwards of 2000 *l.*—In Ireland, the Rt. Hon. Clothworthy, Eart Massareene, aged 62.—In Prussia, the Queen Dowager of

Prussia, aged 84.—In Fredericktown, (Md.) George Murdoch, Esq. aged 63, a stedfast friend to his country's happiness.—In Maryland, Thomas Bond, Esq. aged 63.—In Philadelphia, from the 4th to the 11th inst. 21 adults, 13 children.—In New York, from 4th to 11th inst. 13 men, 10 women, 7 boys and 9 girls ; 4 of consumption, but one of small pox.—Mr. Henry Whiteman, aged 79.—In Columbia, (Con.) Mr. Gideon Hoxcy, jun. of Lebanon, aged 24;—he was returning from a militia muster, and was killed almost instantly by the discharge from a gun.—In Bethel, (Maine) Dea. James Grover, aged 76.—In Wrentham, Mr. Jeremiah Day, of an apoplexy, aged 85.—In Dorchester, Mr. Richard Hall, aged 56.—In Bridgewater, Capt. David Kingman, aged 72.—In Lincoln, Mrs. Lydia Babson, aged 62.—In Danbury, Maj. Ezra Starr, aged 52.—In Newtown, Mr. James Blackman, aged 76.—In Framingham, Mrs. Ann Harrington, aged 81, relict of the late Rev. Timothy Harrington, of Lancaster, formerly widow of the Rev. Matthew Bridge, of Framingham.—In Lunenburg, Mr. Joseph Turner, aged 46.—In Greenland, N.H. John J. Toscan, Esq. formerly consul for France.—In Hingham, Mrs. Rachel Garder, aged 71;—She went to bed in perfect health, and was found dead in the morning.—In Boston, Mrs. Elizabeth Davies, aged 80.—In Hartford, Vt. Mrs. Sarah Green, aged 60.—In Swanzey, Deac. Daniel Warner, aged 64.—In Ashburnham, Mr. Joseph Whitmore, aged 85 y. 7 m. and 7 days.—In Richmond, Mrs. Tamson Ballou, consort of Mr. James Ballou, aged 80 : Descendants 165.—In Baltimore, from the 6th to the 13th inst. 10 adults, 2 children.

In Amherst, Mr. *John Penuel Kendrick*, of Holles, aged 30, the unhappy man whom we lately mentioned as having killed his mother and sister in a fit of insanity.

Vol. XII (No. 635) Saturday, 1 June 1805.

† [2d] Storm damage to a store owned by Dr. David S. Brooks, at N. Guilford, Conn. ♦

¶ [3a] On the 8th ult. were executed, near Annapolis, (Md.) pursuant to their sentences, negro *George*, convicted of arson, at the last county court—and negroes *Dennis, Ned, and Kate*, for the murder of their master, Mr. John Fowler, of Perapsco.

¶ [3b] On the evening of the 3d ult. the house of Mr. Aaron Hoppin, of Aurelius, in Cayuga county, was accidentally burnt, and two of his sons, aged 11 and 2, consumed in the flames—owing, it is supposed, to the chimney being built with sticks, a practice too common in new settlements. [*Bee.*

† [3b] David Graham, John Linsley, and a Mr. Gilmore drowned when their boat was upset in a storm on Oneida Lake; also, a boat commanded by Mr. John Graham was set adrift by the storm. Article copied from the *Utica Gazette.* ♦

† [3d] James Johnson adv. that "he has purchased the store lately occupied by *Chapman & Hartwell*, near the Baptist Meetinghouse in Alstead." The adv. contains an extensive list of goods carried at his store. Dated at Alstead, 30 May 1805.

† [3d] *Bellows & Stone* request debtors to pay up; dated 29 May 1805.

† [3d] Seth Hall, jun. adv. for his clothier's business; dated Westmoreland 30 May '05.

===== ¶ [3c-d] DIED. =====

In London, 11th March, Mrs. Hunt, wife of the Rev. J. Hunt, one of the Loyalists who left this country in the revolutionary war.—In Bath, (Eng.) the Hon. Thomas Pownall, formerly Governor of New Jersey, in 1757 Governor of Massachusetts.—In London, Dr. Miller, aged 72; author of several valuable works on medicine.—In England, Elizabeth Clayton, aged 60: this woman, from an early propensity to masculine employments, had worked as a ship carpenter at a dock yard upwards of 40 years, and always in man's apparel : — she used to drink, chew tobacco, and keep company only with the workmen, yet would never enter into the matrimonial state: She was a strong, robust woman, and never permitted anyone to insult her with impunity. —In London, Lord Hawke.—In Paris, Mr. Claude Chappe, inventor and manager of the Telegraphe, aged 40——In Bolton, Mr. Abraham Holman, aged 40.—In Lancaster, Mrs. Sarah Whiting, aged 67.—In Littlehampton, (Eng. Mr. Corney, a farmer; he has left 100,000 *l.* to be distributed amongst his poor relations, to the 3d and 4th generation.—In Charleston, (S.C.) the Rev. Dr. Robert Cooler, late of Pennsylvania.—In Baltimore, Mr. Joseph L'Estrange, aged 77.—In Philadelphia, for the week ending 17th ult. 16 adults, 22 children.—In New York, for the week ending 17th ult. 9 men, 7 women, 6 boys and 4 girls; of consumption 4, of small pox 1:—Mungo Jackson, a black man, aged 110.—In

Cornwall, (Con.) Mr. Solomon Hart, aged 83.—In Worcester, Sylvia, a female African, aged 105.—At South-East, (Con.) Mrs. Sarah Minor, consort of the Rev. John Minor, aged 56.—In Easton, Md. (SUICIDE) Mr. John Hilliard.—In Little Cambridge, Mr. Jonathan Cook, aged 60.—In Raymond, (N.H.) Hon. John Dudley, Esq. aged 80.—Near Portsmouth, of the small pox, Mr. William Hilton, aged 19.—In Greenland, John J. Toscan, Esq. formerly consul from France.

DROWNED.—At the mouth of the Genesee River, N.Y. Mr. Henry Janes, aged about 24, supposed to have been from Northfield, by his papers.

SUICIDE.—At New York, James Asner, Esq. formerly an officer in the revolutionary army, and late brigadier-general of militia for the county of New York; he was also of late superintendant of the state prison.

Vol. XII (No. 636) Saturday, 8 June 1805.

† [2b-c] Farnham Marsh convicted at Circuit Court, Portsmouth, N.H., for passing counterfeit bills. William Perkins and Benjamin Bagley tried "for theft committed on the high seas;" the jury could not agree on a verdict and those two were discharged. ♦

† [3a] Article describing an explosion of a powder mill at Sunnytown, Penn., owned by Mr. Daniel Schmidt. George Weidemeyer and Mr. Barger was killed; Barger left a wife and eight children. Jacob Wagner was fatally wounded, and left a wife and four children. ♦

¶ [3a] We learn from Greensborough, (N.Y.) that on the 18th inst. as Mr. Nathaniel Cary, from Hartland, aged 23, and Mr. Farwell, from Poultney, Vt. aged 28, were conveying a raft down the river, and getting too far into the stream, as the water was very high, they found it impossible to save the raft, and in attempting to swim ashore were both drowned.—The latter has left a wife and two small children to lament their loss.—*Northern Mememto.*

† [3a] Rev. James Arms[t]rong Neal ordained at Greenland, N.H., and Rev. Mr. Bancroft Fowler ordained at Windsor, Vt. ♦

† [3b] Adv. for *Henry Smith & Co.* "at the white store a few doors south of Southard's Inn." Dated at Walpole, 8 Jan. 1805.

===== ¶ [3b] MARRIED. =====

In Halifax, (N.S.) Admiral Sir Andrew Mitchell, K.B. Commander in Chief of His Britannic Majesty's fleet on that station, to Miss Mary Uniacke, eldest daughter of R.J. Uniacke, Esq.—Thomas N. Jeffery, Esq. Collector of His Majesty's Customs, to Miss Martha Maria Uniacke, second daughter of the same gentleman.

In Shrewsbury, (Mass.) Capt. Ashbel Smith, to Widow Azubah Baldwin;—Mr. Asael Allen, to Widow Mary H. Harrington;—Mr. Nymphus Pratt, to Widow Submit Kingsbury, all of Shrewsbury. Comfort and encouragement to Widows.

At Lexington, Mr. Jonathan Wheelock, of Concord, to Miss Sally Munroe, daughter of Col. William Munroe, of the former place.

In Keene, Mr. Caleb Warner, to Miss Priscilla Reed.

===== ¶ [3b] DIED. =====

In England, Mrs. Clarke, widow of the late Capt. Peter Clarke, of the British navy, and niece of the celebrated Dr. Franklin.—In Philadelphia, from the 18th to the 25th May, 12 adults, 18 children.—In New York, from the 18th to the 25th May, 10 men, 7 women, 6 boys and 6 girls : total 39 [sic] : 8 of consumption, 5 convulsions, a suicide.—In Canaan, (Con.) Mrs. Clarinda Prentice, wife of the Rev. Charles Prentice, aged 27.—In Hartford, Mr. Wm. Goodwin, aged 71.—In Fairfield, Mr. Benjamin Banks, aged 104 [*compare to issue of 15 June 1805*].—In Georgetown, (Maine) Mr. John Sewall, aged 89: His posterity are 8 children, all now living : 56 grand-children, 44 of whom are living : and 54 great-grand-children, 52 of whom are still living.—In Boston, Mr. John Short, aged 35 : Miss Sarah Champney, aged 74.—At Raymond, (N.H.) the Hon. John Dudley, Esq. aged 83, formerly a Judge of the Superior Court of New Hampshire.—In Windsor, (Con.) Mrs. Priscilla Loomis, wife of Dea. Amasa Loomis, aged 39.—In Bristol, suddenly, Mrs. Lydia Wolcott, aged 49.—In Concord, (N.H.) George William Livermore, Esq. of Holderness, aged 41.—In New Gloucester, Mr. ———— Ramdell ; he was found dead in the road, about three rods from his horse, with his neck broken, some hairs of the mane in his hand, and the bridle round his foot.—In North Yarmouth, Mr. Benjamin Humphrey, aged 78.—In Watertown, 31st ult. Deacon Jedidiah Lane, aged 74.

ACCIDENT.—As Mr. Ebenezer Wright, of Wethersfield, (Con.) was assisting in rigging a ship, at a wharf in Hartford, he fell from the mast head, and expired in a few minutes—he was in the 40th year of his age, and has left a disconsolate widow and six small children.

DROWNED.—On the 1st inst. about two miles below Newburyport, Mr. Robert Lithgow Murray, aged 26, son of the late Rev. John Murray, of Newburyport; he was upset in a boat, by a violent gust of wind, and sunk immediately.

☞ HUGH GAINE, whose death has been prematurely mentioned of late in almost every paper in the Union, has recently been elected one of the Governors of the New York Hospital.—Cent.

Vol. XII (No. 637) Saturday, 15 June 1805.

¶ [2a] Winchester, Virginia, May 23. On Tuesday the 14th inst. was executed at Fincastle, Bosetourt county, a negro man named Archy the property of *John Sweetzer*, of said county, for perpetrating a rape on the body of his mistress.

===== ¶ [3c] MARRIED. =====

At Acworth, May 19th, Mr. Bela Humphrey, to Miss Rebecca Beckwith.

In Troy, (N.Y.) Mr. Theodore Barnard, formerly of this town, to Miss Lucy Stebbins, late of Deerfield, (Ms.)

At Pittsford, (Vermont) Gordon Newall, Esq. to Miss Nancy Prentiss.

===== ¶ [3c] DIED. =====

In Verdun, (France) James Parry, Esq. aged 36, prisoner of war, well known in Great Britain as ci-devant editor of the Courier.—In Glasgow (Scotland) on the 21st of March last, John Murray, Esq. Consul of the United States.—In Philadelphia, from the 25th May to 1st June, 8 adults, 21 children.—In New York, from May 24th to 1st June, 29 deaths; of consumption 7, of small pox 1.—In East Hartford, Mr. John Reynolds, aged 61, was lately found dead in his bed : Jury's verdict, SUICIDE. Within a few months, many instances of self murder have taken place in various parts of the Union.—In Fairfield, (Con.) on the 19th ult. Mr. Benjamin Banks, aged 102 [*compare to issue of 8 June 1805*].—In East Windsor, Mr. Arodi Wolcott, aged 45 : Mrs. Priscilla Loomis, aged 39.—In Coventry, Widow Margaret Loomis, aged 83.—In Fredericksburg, (Vir.) Thomas Lumford Lornax, Esq. aged 27.—In Richmond, (Vir.) Capt. John Dixon, printer.—In Providence, Mrs. Rachel Martin, aged 87.—In Lancaster, Mrs. Sarah Whiting, aged 67.—In Worcester, Mrs. Elizabeth Stearns, aged 82.—In Farmington, (Conn.) Mrs. Susanna Woodford, late consort of Capt. Wm. W. aged 80. The mother of the deceased lived 101 years. The descendants of the deceased are 13 children, 75 grand-children, and 42 great-grandchildren.—In Wethersfield, Mr. Alexander Rhodes aged 65.—In Litchfield, suddenly, Mrs. Mary Tallmadge, the amiable and esteemed consort of the Hon. Benjamin Tallmadge, Esq. aged 41.—In Newark, (N.J.) Mr. Josiah Beach, aged 64; death occasioned by his cart running over his head.—In New York, Mr. Leonard Kip, aged 80.—In Mifflin county, Penn. the Rev. Mr. Logan. On Sunday the 19th ult. immediately after closing divine exercises, he sunk down in his pulpit and expired.—In Portsmouth, on Saturday last, Mrs. Mary Buckminster, the amiable consort of the Rev. Dr. B. aged 39. She was in the enjoyment of her usual health about three hours previous to her death.—In Morristown, V. (suicide) Mr. John Hoyt, of Randolph. He was found dead, on Sunday morning, the second inst. hanging by a bridle. He fastened his horse near the house before committing the desperate act. About 50 dollars were found in his pocket-book. He bore the character of a remarkable steady, prudent, industrious young man. He was 23 years old, and has parents living in Newton, N.H.

At Acworth, Jan. 8th, Mrs. Polly Humphrey, wife of Mr. Bela H. and daughter of Mr. Ripley Bingham, formerly of Marlow, in the 25th year of her age.

In Westminster, (Ver.) on Saturday last, Dr. William Town, in the 30th year of his age.—Mr. Amasa Soper, aged about 17.

ACCIDENT.—At North Haven, on the 26th ult. Mr. Elijah Atwood, of Mansfield, was instantly killed by the bursting of a gun.

Vol. XII (No. 638) Saturday, 22 June 1805.

¶ [3b] The highest prize in the 7th Class of South Hadley Canal Lottery, was purchased in Worcester, by Mr. Jacob Rich, of Charlton, an industrious farmer.
† [3c] Adv. by *Bellows & Stone*, for West India Goods; dated 25 June 1805.
† [3c] Peter Evans adv. his "Evans's Mill" for sale, (saw and gristmill), "in Rockingham, on William's River, near the Meetinghouse." Dated Rockingham, 13 June 1805.
† [3c] *Amasa & Oliver Allen* adv. goods for sale; dated Walpole, 15 May 1805.
† [3c] Levi Warren adv. "that he has erected a Picking and Carding Machine, near his mills in Alstead, where he will pick and card wood at eight cents per lb."
† [4d] Article describing a patent received by Mr. Isaac Cox, of "Duck Creek X Roads, in Delaware," regarding improvements in the manufacturing of hats.

===== ¶ [3c] DIED. =====

Near Ranelagh, (Ireland) Mrs. Bridget Kavanagh, at the advanced age of 118 years, who left four sons, the eldest of whom is near 100 years of age.—In Lexington, (Ken.) Col. Robert Saunders.—In Philadelphia, from the 1st to the 8th inst. 13 adults, 8 children.—In New York, from the 1st to the 8th June, 34 : 8 men, 12 women, 6 boys, 8 girls; none of small pox.—In New Boston, (N.H.) suddenly, John Cochran, Esq. aged 60.—In Boston, Mrs. Betsey Emes, consort of Maj. Luther Emes, aged [30?]—In Brookfield, (Mass.) Mrs. Mehitable Rice, aged 86.—In Newport, (R.I.) Hon. David Olyphant, Esq.—In Westborough, (Ms.) of a cancer, Mr. Jonathan Forbes, aged 59.—In Newton, (N.J.) Thomas Anderson, Esq. aged [62?]

In Westminster, (Ver.) Mrs. Joanna Chamberlain, aged 34.

SUICIDE.—In New York, by cutting his throat, Mr. Cady M'Cowan.

DROWNED.—On Wednesday, the 29th ult. Caleb Bancroft, a young man in the 21st year of his age, in attempting to swim on a plank (in order to learn), across a mill-pond in Dunbarton, about 5 rods wide; having got about half way across, where the water was 8 or 9 feet deep the plank suddenly turned, and he slipt off. A man and a boy were standing on the shore, but being no swimmers, could afford him no assistance. He was taken out in about half an hour, but too late to be restored to life. A jury of inquest was impannelled whose verdict was "DEATH BY MISFORTUNE." He was interred the next day. He was a young man of promising usefulness, and has left a mother and a number of brothers and sisters to mourn his death. [Concord Courier.

At Saybrook, (Con.) 2d inst. from on board the schooner China, in which vessel he was passenger, Mr. Allen Wells, of the firm of Wells & Kingsbury, Roxbury, Ms.—and son of Mr. Thomas Wells, of Keene, N.H.

On Wednesday last, in the outer harbour, Mr. George Cade, of this town, and Capt. Robert Reed, of Burlington, (Ms.)—They were fishing after Mackarel, and the boat upset by a sudden gust of wind.——Boston paper.

Vol. XII (No. 639) Saturday, 29 June 1805.

¶ [3a] *Fire.*—A house in Surry, belonging to Mr. *John Brockway*, was burnt on the 21st inst. in the evening, with the principal part of its contents.
† [3b] Detailed account of child abuse upon Elizabeth Fulmer, aged 12, an "apprentice" to Samuel Depui. Her cruel master was convicted but given a lenient sentence, causing a public outcry. The case was tried at Easton, Northampton County, Penn. ♦
¶ [3c] The following slur upon a New England editor appears in a Troy paper. The yankee Yorker is informed, however apparent an Hibernianism it may be, that it is an absolute fact, and that its seeming impossibity arises from the change of the names of the place of his residence:

"The Keene (N.H.) paper says, that "old Mr. John Shepherd of Foxborough, (Mass.) is now 101 years old. He was born in Dorchester, where he resided 18 years : He then resided in Stoughton about 10 years ; afterwards in Dedham 15 or 20 years, and in Wrentham 25 or 30 years : He has been many years in Foxborough, and now lives on the same farm where he was born, *from which he* NEVER *removed!*" This beats Paddy's ramble all the way from Cork till Dublin, while at the same time he remained snug in his cabin at dear Carricksargus."

¶ [3c] INSTALLATION. On Wednesday the 12th inst. the Rev. Samuel Sumner was installed at Shrewsbury, Pastor of the Church and People of Bakersfield, (Vermont.) The Rev. Mr. Bascom, of Gerry, introduced the service by prayer; the Rev. Mr. Bancroft, of Worcester, preached from 2 Corin. iii, 10-15. The Rev. Mr. Whitney, of Northborough, made the consecrating prayer;—the Rev. M. Sumner, of Shrewsbury, gave the charge, and the Rev. Mr. Puffer, of Berlin, gave the right hand of fellowship and made the concluding prayer. A respectable audience attended the service with a seriousness and solemnity becoming the occasion.

===== ¶ [3c] MARRIED. =====

In New York, George Hammeken, Esq. Danish Consul for the Eastern States, to Miss Eliza Ogden.

In Augusta, the Rev. Eliphalet Gillet, of Hallowell, to Miss Mary Gurley, of Connecticut.

In Chesterfield, Capt. Abel Blake, of Keene to Mrs. Jemima Hart, of the former place.

===== ¶ [3c] DIED. =====

In Charleston, (S.C.) Mrs. Esther Azuby, relict of the late Rev. Abraham Azuby, aged 50.—In Gerry, Mrs. Sally Bascom, consort of the Rev. Ezekiel Bascom.—In Orford, of a consumption, Miss Polly Gilman, aged 23.—In Trenton, Miss Theodosia Yard, aged 21.—In Danbury, C. Mrs. Anna Weed, aged 60.—In Albany, Mrs. Mary Forman, consort of Dr. William Forman, aged 58.—In Portsmouth, Mr. William Swanson.—In Raymond, Hon. John Dudley, Esq. aged 80, formerly a Judge of the Superior Court.—In Poughkeepsie, (N.Y.) 16th inst. Duncan Ingraham, jun. Esq.—At Mohegan, MARTHA, aged 120. She was widow of Zacarah, one of the Nobility of the Mohegan tribe of Indians, and many years an agent from said tribe to the General Assembly of Connecticut.—In Partridgefield, Mrs. Hepsebah Leland, consort of the Rev. John Leland, of that town.—In Portland, Mrs. Rebecca Clow, aged 87. She was one of the first settlers of that town, and has out-lived all her children, five in number.—Mr. George Tucker, of Milton, aged 56, in attempting to place himself on the tongue of a waggon he was driving through Roxbury, accidentally fell before the wheels, which passed over his body, and instantly terminated his life.—In Berlin, Feb. 25, Frederique-Louisa, Queen of Prussia, of the House of Hesse d'Armstadt, and widow of Frederick-William II, King of Prussia, born Oct. 16, 1751, aged 54.—In England, John Burges, aged 104.—In India, the gallant Major General Frazer, in consequence of a wound received on the 13th November last.—In New York, from the 8th to 15th inst. 13 men, 17 women, 6 boys and 1 girl; of consumption, 10; of small pox, one; suicide, 4 :"It is, (says the N.Y. Gazette) at this hot season, pleasing to remark, that the deaths in this city are almost one third less than during the winter and spring:—The city now contains 80,000 inhabitants, of course it must, considering the few deaths, be considered very healthy."—In Georgetown, (Me.) Mr. John Sewell, aged 89; his posterity are 8 children, all now living; 56 grandchildren, 44 of whom are living; and 54 great-grand-children, 52 of whom are still living.

Vol. XII (No. 640) Saturday, 6 July 1805.

† [2d] Dr. Sotridge murdered by Dr. Hampton "on the bank of the river Ohio, near the mouth of Big Sandy, in Kanhawa Country." The dispute involved the son of Dr. Hampton who married the daughter of Dr. Sotridge. ♦

† [3b] Sally Capron, aged 16, daughter of Capt. Joseph Capron, killed by lightning at Leicester, [prob. Vermont—Ed.] ♦

† [3c] Rev. Stephen Chapin ordained at Hillsborough, N.H.

† [3d] Shepard & Hutchinson adv. goods for sale at their Alstead store; dated 1 July 1805.

† [3d] Legal notice regarding the insolvent estate of Capt. Noah Porter, late of Charlestown, N.H. deceased. John C. Chamberlain, Joseph Roby, and Jason Wetherbe appointed Commissioners.

† [3d] John Barnet adv. for horses found on his property; dated Walpole, 1 July 1805.

† [3d] Legal notice regarding the estate Gurdon Huntington, late of Walpole, deceased; Francis Gardner, Attorney to the Administrator.

¶ [3d] RUN AWAY. From the subscriber, a Negro boy, aged 19 years, stocky built. He carried away with him a drab coloured spencer, waistcoat and overalls. He is supposed to have them on, with other clothing, such as two woolen striped shirts, and one of linen, besides other clothing. Whoever will take up said negro and return him, or give information respecting him, shall be rewarded for their trouble.

N.B. I hereby forbid all persons harbouring or trusting him on my account, as I will pay no debts of his contracting after this date.

JAMES DICKEY.

Acworth, July 1, 1805.

† [2b-c] An account of experiments of small pox innoculations on several persons in Colchester, Conn. Dr. John R. Watrous, of Colchester, was appointed to carry out the experiments; also Dr. Utley and Dr. Noah B. Foote were involved. The house of Capt. Ely Gillet "was made use of for a Hospital." Most of the participants were residents of Colchester; those from neighboring towns are so noted. The article is very lengthy, with details of who participated in the experiment. The names given here appear in the article, regardless of whether they were involved directly in the experiment: ♦

Ely Gillet, jun.	William Shepardson, jun.	Judah Clark
Phebe Gillet, 2d	Nathaniel S. Woodbridge	
William Bramble	Griswold Isham	Civil Authorities (Selectmen, Justices of the Peace)
Isaac Crocker	Benjamin Mather, jun.	
Asa Crocker	Gilbert Cone, of Hebron	
James Sexton, jun.	Ziba Peters, of Hebron	Joseph Isham
Gibbons M. Champlain	Josiah Clark	Henry Champion
Stephen Drinkwater	Sibyl Cook (died)	William A. Morgan
Patty Gillet	Sophia Foote	Roger Bulkeley
Solomon L. Gillet	David Y. Foote	Joel Worthington
Anne Gillet	J. Williams	John Isham
Jeffry Worthington	Ralph Yeomans	Elijah Waterman
Gibbons P. Mather	William Shepardson	I. Lord Skinner

===== ¶ [3c] MARRIED. =====

In Enosburg, Mr. Solomon Williams, of Middlebury, to Miss Cynthia House, of the former place.—In Lee, Obed Hall, Esq. of Bartlett, to Miss Eliza Fox, of the former place.—In Dover, Mr. William Pegin, to Miss Abigail Drew.—In Westmoreland, Dr. Moses Dudley, to Miss Sally Carlisle.—In Marlow, Mr. James Gale, to Miss Phebe Dubbs.—In East Hartford, Mr. Thaddeus Gale, (Medico Electrician) aged 43, to Miss Harriet Bates, aged 11 years. *Dr. G. we understand, in a work published by him a few years since, professes to have made important discoveries in the medical application of his electrick apparatus. We have witnessed the powerful effect of his machine on the systems of others, but the above, if Miss Bates is "troublingly alive all o'er," must have been the severest* SHOCK *he ever communicated.*]—In East Sudbury, Mr. Samuel Elliot, of Brattleboro', to Miss Fanny Foster.—In Cambridge, Mr. Royal Makepeace, to Mrs. Rebecca Vose.

===== ¶ [3c] DIED. =====

In Quebec, Mr. Josiah Hunt, aged 38.—In Alstead, on the 15th May, the widow Rachel Kent, in the 86th year of her age.—In Fredericktown, killed instantaneously by lightning, Mr. Joseph Doll, jun. aged 35.—In Andover, (Ver.) Chloe Felt, aged 12. Her death was occasioned by her falling into the fire in a fit.—In Charlton, (Mass.) Widow Rachel Wheelock, aged 75.—In Morristown, (N.J.) Caleb Russell, Esq. aged 56.—In Preston, (C.) Mrs. Sally Brewster, aged 23.—In New London, Mrs. Elizabeth Lee, aged 78.—In Bedford, (N.Y.) Dr. Stephen Rockwell, aged 35.—In Greenfield, Mr. Eleazer Wells, aged 76.—In Charlotte, Miss Betsey Dutton, aged 18.—In Whiting, Mrs. Lucy Peck, aged 18.—In Dover, Mrs. Abigail Wallingford, aged 74.—In Portsmouth, Mrs. Mary Buckminster.—In West Hartford, Mr. Asa Goodman, aged 66.—In Sunderland, Mrs. Lydia Montague, aged 76.—In Boston, Mr. Gibbs W. Eddy, junior, partner of the firm of Dyer & Eddy, aged 22.—In Boston, Mons. Julien, aged 52, well known to the inhabitants of that town, and to strangers, as the proprietor of a respectable Restorator:—Drowned, in the outer-harbour, Mr. George Sprague, mason.—In Lynn, Mr. Samuel Fordman, aged 42.

Vol. XII (No. 641) Saturday, 13 July 1805.

† [2b] News of the burning of Detroit, Michigan Territory, brought by the schooner *Charlotte*, Capt. Nihen, who arrived at "Fort Erie."
† [2d] A body of an old woman, name unknown, found in the Chicopee River, near Springfield, Mass.; one of her handkerchiefs was marked "A.H," and she may have been from Connecticut. ♦
† [2d-3a] A child of Mr. Moses Dustin, 8 or 9 years of age, was struck and killed by lightning, at Northumberland, N.H. The event occurred "On Saturday last," and the communication is dated at Northumberland, 18 June 1805. ♦
† [3a] A log house belonging to Mr. Zebulun Hunt struck at Bath, [N.H.—Ed.] ♦
† [3a] Lightning strikes the farm of Lt. Henry Fields, at Merrimac, N.H. ♦
† [3d] Goods for sale by James Johnson; dated Alstead, 8 July 1805.

===== ¶ [3c] MARRIED. =====

In Worcester, Luther Lawrence, Esq. of Groton, attorney at law, to Miss Lucy Bigelow.—At Westmoreland, Mr. Phinehas Fusham, of Chesterfield, to the widow Bathsheba Leach, of the former place.—At New Orleans, Edward Livingston, Esq. to Madame Marie-Louise-Magdalene-Valentine-Davezac-Cuffra Moreau, widow of the late Louis Moreau de Lassy [. . .]

===== ¶ [3c] DIED. =====

Suddenly, in Wethersfield, Mr. Richard Robbins, aged 53.—In Hartland, Deac. Jonathan Wilder, aged 66.—In Gerry, Mrs. Sally Bascom, consort of the Rev. Ezekiel Bascom.—In Leicester, Mrs. Alice Adams, consort of E. Adams, Esq. perceptor of the academy, aged 37.—In Worcester, Mr. Asa Flagg, aged 53.—In Charlestown, [137] in the gaol, Mr. Paul Harris.—In Brookfield, Mr. Jonathan Abbot, aged 83.—In Hingham, Mr. Benjamin Thaxter, aged 73.—In Boston, Mr. George Sprague, the eldest son of Mr. Samuel S. of that town, aged 24 : Mrs. Sarah Mulvaney, aged 68.—In Russia, March 20, the Right Rev. Father Gabriel Gruber, General of the Society of Jesuits.—In Jamaica, Mrs. Mills, aged 118 ; she was followed to the grave by 295 of her children, grand-children, great-grand-children, & great-great-grand-children, 60 of whom named Ebanks, belong to the regiment of militia for St. Elizabeth's parish. For 97 years she practised midwifery, during which period it is stated that she ushered 143,000 persons into the world ! She retained her senses to the last, and followed her business until within two days of her death. [138]—Departed this life, at her house in Rowe's Lane, Boston, on Monday morning last, Mrs. Hannah Rowe, widow of John Rowe, Esq. formerly of that town, having nearly completed her 80th year.—In Grafton, Vt. Mr. John Wier, aged 94.—In Edinburgh, (Scotland) Rev. Dr. James Kemp.—In Fryeburgh, Miss Elizabeth Clement Fessenden, aged 17, daughter of the late Rev. and Hon. William Fessenden.

Suicide.—In Charlestown, we understand that Mrs. Arms, a few days since, put a period to her existence by hanging herself. The verdict of the jury of inquest, we understand, was that insanity was the cause. She had hitherto borne a character uniformly exemplary and respectable.—In Pawlet, (Vt.) by laudanum, Mr. Benjamin Sage, of Granville, N.Y. aged about 30. Having suffered himself to be guilty of perjury, by swearing falsely to an account of 40 dollars against a neighbour whom he owed a grudge, he confessed the fact, and the horrors of a condemning conscience hurried him to commit the desperate act.

Accident.—On Friday last, a promising son of Capt. Shubael Hurd, of Lemster, aged 14, was killed instantaneously, by the falling of a lever, while assisting to remove a building. [*Keene paper.*]

Vol. XII (No. 642) Saturday, 20 July 1805.

† [2c] Fire at Portland, Maine, claiming three shops on Union wharf, occupied by Messrs. Wright, taylor, Woodman, hatter, and Harty, blacksmith; other losses suffered by Hon. W. Storer, Mr. R. Boyd, and Capt. D. Smith. The article is dated at Boston 13 July, with the event having occurred "on Monday night last." Also, a fire consumed the house of Mr. Pillsbury, at Haverhill, Mass., on "the 5th inst."

¶ [2d] *Accident.*—The house of Mr. John Buswell, of Rindge, was consumed by fire at midday, on the 8th inst. A few articles only of furniture, clothing and provisions of a large and industrious family, were all that were saved from the flames.

¶ [3c] Whereas Achsah my wife has eloped and left my bed and board, and refuses to live with me any longer, these are, therefore, to caution all persons against trusting her off my account, as I shall pay no debts of her contracting after this date.—All persons are forbid harbouring or employing her as they would avoid the penalty of the law.

SAMUEL CRAM.

Unity, July 11th, 1805.

† [3c] Adv. of goods for sale by *Shepard & Hutchinson*, dated Alstead, 15 July 1805.

† [3d] J. Livingston, jun. adv. for his gun shop; dated Walpole, 19 July 1805.

===== ¶ [3b] MARRIED. =====

In Brattleborough, Mr. Isaiah M. Cole, of Wilmington, to Miss Olive B. Munroe, of Brattleboro'.

===== ¶ [3b-c] DIED. =====

In Montreal, on the 15th ult. Bryce M'Cumming, Esq., who had served his king and country faithfully for 45 years. He died regretted by all who knew him.—In Dover, N.H. Capt. Shadrach Hodgdon, aged 39.—In Charlotte, Mrs. Anna Mead, aged 29.—In Vergennes, Deacon Daniel Horman, aged 55.—In Bethlem, Mrs. Lucy Brace, aged 54.—In Ashby, Mrs. Betsey Wyman, aged 21.—In Merrimack, Rev. Timothy Fuller, formerly pastor of a church in Princeton, (Mass.) aged 66.—In Dunbarton, Mr. Benjamin Lewis, of Milford.—In Claremont, killed by lightning a few days since, two children of a Mr. Thomas ; particulars we have not learned.—In Randolph, Mrs. Tracey, wife of Mr. Timothy Tracey.—In Hingham, Benjamin Thaxter, aged 75.—In Hartland, Col. Edward Swan, aged 58.—In Charlestown, (N.H.) on the 1st inst. Moses Wheeler, in the 85th year of his age. He supported the character of an industrious and honest man through life.—In Jaffrey, suddenly, Mr. James Gowing, aged 69 : In May last, widow Esther Brooks, aged 90 : Also, very suddenly, Mrs. Sally Gilmore, consort of David Gilmore, aged 33 : Mr. Reuben Spaulding, aged 34.——Killed, in Granville county, (N.C.) over a card table, a Mr. Jethro Royster, by another named N. Norwood. —In New York, 36 deaths for the week ending the 5th inst. viz. 12 men, 7 women, 11 boys and 6 girls.—In Seneca, (N.Y.) Rev. Samuel Lacock, aged about 45.—Very suddenly, in Catskill village, Dr. Thomas Thompson, aged 55.—In Great Barrington, Mr. William Morgan, over 70 years of age.—In Troy, Mrs. Delia Maria Hart, consort of Mr. Richard P. Hart, and daughter of James D[ ]le, Esq.[139] aged 22.—In Wethersfield, Miss Polly Carter.—In Hopkinton, of consumption, Mr. Johnathan [sic] B. Storey, aged 26.—In East Haddam, Elder Budge, of Waterford.—In Wrentham, of an apoplexy, Mr. Jeremiah Day, aged 85.—In Tortola, of yellow fever, Mr. Isaac Thomas, of Philad.—In Alexandria, (Va.) 1st inst. Mrs. Jane Fairfax, relict of the late Bryan (Lord) Fairfax, after a short illness.—In Philadelphia, from the 29th June to July 6, 13 adults, 26 children.—In Worcester, William Caldwell, Esq. High Sheriff of the county of Worcester, aged 52.—In Gloucester, on the 4th inst. the Rev. Ebenezer Cleveland, A.M. formerly pastor of a church in that town, in the 80th year of his age. He was born at Canterbury, in Connecticut, on the 25th December, 1725, old style, and received his education at Yale College. He lived 59 years in the matrimonial state with his wife, who died the 25th Dec. last. He was a tender and affectionate husband, a kind and indulgent parent, and a very respectable Minister of the Gospel.—In Cambridge, Mrs. Sarah Frost, widow of the late Deacon Gideon Frost, aged 76.—In Europe, the Rev. Thomas Coke, L.L.D. one of the Bishops of the Methodist Episcopal Church in the United States of America.—In Sunderland, (Mass.) Mrs. Lydia Montague, aged 76.—In Salem, Capt. Ebenezer B. Ward, aged 46 ; Widow Oakman, aged 88.—In Cambridge, Mrs. Mary Ware, wife of the Rev. Henry Ware, and eldest daughter of the Rev. Jonas Clark, of Lexington, aged 43.—In Wrentham, July 11, Mrs. Lydia, wife of the Rev. Elisha Fisk, aged 31.—In Salem, Mrs. Sarah Cushing aged 38.—In Northwood, found dead with his head crushed to atoms by a cart wheel running over, Capt. [Ran?], formerly of Rye.—In Bethlem, (Con.) Mrs. Lucy Brace, aged 54.—In Hebron, C. Mr. John House, aged 90.—In Keene, Major ——— Ingersol, of the United States army.

In this town, very suddenly, after two or three days illness, Mrs. Adams, consort of

Mr. John Adams, aged 43.

Drowned.—In Merrimack, Mr. Timothy Clark jun. of Amherst.—In East Windsor, Andrew Root, aged 18.—In Vernon, a child of Mr. William Howe, aged 12 years.

Suicide.—In France, Mons. Chape, inventor and director of the Telegraph. His reason for self murder was that he was *tired of life.*—In Dublin, Mr. Henry Quin, with a pistol:—He was a gentleman of handsome fortune, and fashionable life.

Vol. XII (No. 643) Saturday, 27 July 1805.

† [2c] Accidents to two children of widow Hamlin, of New York City, both involving skull fractures. ♦

† [2c] Numerous fires caused by drought blacken towns in eastern New Hampshire. The homes of Mr. William Bennett and Mr. Isaac Leathers, "both industrious and worthy citizens" were destroyed in Farmington; a barn belonging to Mr. David Tuttle; one belonging to Mr. Levi Young of Alton; and another, the property of Mr. Benjamin Tricky, of Wakefield. ♦

† [3a] Mr. Henry Edes ordained at the First Congregational Church, Providence, R.I.

† [3b] Daniel Chapman adv. for a mare, lost "from the pasture of Mrs. Sprague, of Keene." Dated at Keene, 12 July 1805.

† [3c] Adv. of goods for sale at the store of Joseph Bellows, jun; dated Walpole 26 July.

† [3c] Legal notice concerning Peter Smith, of Dublin, N.H., Husbandman, who petitions for a divorce from his wife. Smith was married 29 Nov. 1780, by Rev. Reuben Holcomb, to Lucy Willard, "then of Lancaster, in the commonwealth of Massachusetts." Smith claimed that prior to 1784, Lucy "committed adultery, and soon afterwards the said Lucy absconded . . . " ♦

===== ¶ [3a] MARRIED. =====

In Salem, the Rev. Joshua Spaulding, to Miss Elizabeth Bradshaw.—In Dover, (N.H.) Mr. Jonathan Footman, to Miss Sally Hodgdon.—In Newington, the Rev. Enos George, of Barnstead, to Miss Sophia Chesley, of Dover.

===== ¶ [3a-b] DIED. =====

In Staunton, (Vir.) David Rawn, Esq. aged 85, principal Clerk to the office of the Comptroller of the Treasury.—In Halifax county, (Vir.) Dr. Robert Mackey, a native of Pennsylvania, killed by lightning.—In Washington City, much regretted, General Uriah Forrest, clerk of the Circuit Court of the district of Columbia.—In Baltimore, Robert Curson, esq. aged 80.—In New York, the week ending the 13th ult. 59 ; 11 men, 15 women, 18 boys and 15 girls.—In Cranston, (R.I.) Mrs. Amey [Mawper?], aged 81.—In Brookfield, Lieut. Jonathan Abbot, aged 82.—In Shrewsbury, Capt. Isaac Harrington, aged 70.—In Somers, (C.) Mr. John Billing, aged 68.—In Ashburnham, Mrs. Mary Whitmore, aged 87, relict of the late Joseph Whitmore.—In Rutland, (Jefferson county, N.Y.) of Typhus fever, Mrs. Tayle Stanly, Rebecca B. Stanly, and Miss Patty Taylor, all daughters of Mr. Moses Taylor.—In Sheffield, Capt. Ezra Fellows, aged 75.—In Portsmouth, Mrs. Leach, aged 47.—In Harrisburg, (Penn.) Mrs. Elizabeth Simpson, consort of Gen. Michael Simpson, aged 71.—In Cornish, Miss Grata Fitch, aged 16.—In Deerfield, (Ms.) Mrs. Rebecca Sexton, aged 77.—In Rockingham, (Ver.) 21st inst. Mrs. Hannah Benton, wife of Mr. Jacob Benton, in the 70th year of her age.

Major George Ingersoll, whose death we announced in our last, has the following character in the Keene Sentinel:—He was "lately an officer in the U.S. Army, and member of the society of the Cincinnati, aged 51; a man in whom were eminently united the gentleman, the soldier, and above all the christian [. . .] The breaking out of our Revolutionary war soon presented him an opportunity of gratifying his prevailing inclination, and of displaying his superious talents and patriotism [. . .]

Drowned.—In Concord, on the 13th inst. in Merrimack river, George Whitefield Rogers, aged 8 years, the only son of Lieut. Geo. W. Rogers. He, with three other boys about the same age, went into the river to bathe without any older person with them, and neither of them being able to swim, the unfortunate lad, it is supposed, inadvertently stepped into a hole where the water was about 4 feet deep, and could not recover.—In Athen, (Vt.) 4th June, Moses Farrington, an active lad, of 14 years of age, eldest son of Mr. Elijah & Mrs. Elizabeth Farrington. It being training day, he, with some other boys of his age, went to a pond to bathe, and thinking he could swim across the pond, made the attempt ; but being exhausted when about the middle, cried to his companions, who were on shore, to know if he gained any ; and being informed that he did not much, turned to go back, but immediately sunk. No assistance being near, he lay in the water the space of an hour; After which every exertion was made to recover him, but in vain.

Suicide.—By cutting his throat, Mr. Isaac Hornbeck, of Rochester, N.Y. A coroner's inquest was held by a jury of 23, whose unanimous verdict was *insanity*.

Vol. XII (No. 644) Saturday, 3 Aug. 1805.

† [2c] Account of the murder of Capt. William Sterling, by his son-in-law William Sill, of Lyme, Conn. The article is dated at New London, 24 July, the event having occurred "on Monday last." Sterling was about 67 years old. ♦

¶ [2c] In a thunder storm, on the 13th inst. the house of Mr. E. Ives, of Hamden, in this state, [Conn.—Ed.] was struck by lightning, and a daughter of Mr. David Warner, aged 17 years, was instantly killed. Seven other persons were in the room with her, but received no injury.

¶ [3a] A Canandaigua paper mentions, that a man by the name of David Williams, who was lately tried at Cayuge, and convicted, is to be hung in October next, for the murder of Ira Lane.

† [3a] Mr. Nathan Fuller of Amherst, N.H., kills a snake. ♦
† [3b] Rev. Erastus Scranton ordained at North Milford, Conn.
† [3c] Legal notice regarding the insolvent estate of David Hall, late of Walpole, deceased; Thomas Sparhawk, Isaac Redington, and Ephraim Lane, Commissioners; "Lydia Hall, or Levi Allen," Administrators; dated Walpole, 1 Aug. 1805.
† [3d] *Shepard & Hutchinson* request debtors to pay up; dated Alstead, 25 July 1805.
† [3d] Legal notice regarding the insolvent estate of Dr. William Town, late of Westminster, Vt., Isaiah Eaton, Adm. Dated Westminster 30 July 1805.
† [3d] John Kidder found a mare; notice dated at Grafton, Vt., 22 July 1805.

===== ¶ [3b] MARRIED. =====

In Alstead, on Sunday evening last, Mr. Nathaniel Vilas, aged 38, to Miss Lovina Crosby, in the 19th year of her age.
In Keene, Mr. Ebenezer Daniels, to Miss Patty Mann.
In Boston, the Rev. Henry Edes, to Miss Catharine C. May.

===== ¶ [3b-c] DIED. =====

In England, Sir William Pultney, bart. He had a seat in seven successive British Parliaments.—In Charleston, (S.C.) Mr. James West, a native of Ireland, aged 42, a once celebrated comedian.—In Robeson, (N.C.) Mr. William Harrison; shot by a runaway negro, who he mortally wounded.—Near Alexandria, (Vir.) Mr. Isaac Janney, Mr. Robert Lindsey, Mr. Becksmith Koester, and a black man; killed by lightning, at the moment they were stepping on board a boat to go on a party of pleasure.—Near Philadelphia, Mrs. Catharine Heister; supposed to have been murdered by a widow and her son, who were inmates with her, and who have been committed.—In Mendon, Hon. Peter Penniman, aged 77.—In Windsor, C. Mr. Abijah Loomis, aged 49.—In Sherburn, (N.Y.) Mr. ——— Clark; he dropped down and expired instantly, while attending the funeral of his sister.—In New York, from 13th to 20th July, 18 men, 8 women, 21 boys, and 14 girls; of small pox 1; intemperance 1, apoplexy 3; consumption 6, convulsions 5, 4 by drinking cold water, and 16 of flux.—In Lyme, (C.) Capt. Wm. Sterling, aged 67; killed by Mr. Wm. Sill, his son-in-law, who, in a fit of insanity, discharged a loaded gun at him, the contents of which entered his breast.—In Salem, of a violent nervous fever, attended with convulsions, Mr. William Carleton, aged 33, editor of the Salem Register.—In Sullivan, 16th ult. widow Lydia Ellis, aged 85. Mrs. E. was the third woman who moved into that town, at its first settlement.—In England, the Countess Dowager of Masserine; aged 39—In Northumberland, (Penn.) Maj. Henry Antes: he fell 30 feet from a cherry tree, head foremost, and was killed instantly.—In Elizabethtown, N.J. Mr. Izal Johnson; he fell from a load of hay, by the breaking of a rope while in the act of binding it.—In Marblehead, Mr. Ebenezer Clough, aged 74.—In Curracoa, J.C. Holthuysen, Esq. formerly a respectable merchant of New York.—In Averasboro' (N.C.) David Sinclair, an itinerant preacher, hung himself.—In Philad.

from the 13th to 20th ult 17 ad. 42 child. total 59.—In Woodstock, (N.Y.) on the 19th June, a child of Mr. John Hogan, of the dysentery; on the day following a second child died; and while the afflicted parents were attending their two departed children to the grave, a third was snatched away by the disorder.—In Sherburne, (Mass.) 28th ult. Elijah Brown, jun. A.B. aged 24, eldest son of the Rev. Elijah B. of said town.—In Cambridge, Jacob S. Willard, aged 17, son of the late President Willard, and student at the University.—In Halifax, (Ver.) on the 2d ult. Mr. William Willcox, aged 85; has left 9 children, 81 grand-children, and 62 great-grand-children; 10 of which were carried in their parents' arms to the grave, to mourn the loss of an aged and respectful parent.

Suicide.—In Sharon, (C.) Avery Harlow, aged only 12 years, hung himself, in consequence of a gentle chastisement of his father for some misbehaviour.

Accidents.—As Mr. Slaid was returning from Ballstown Springs to his home in Galway, his horse was frightened by the fall of a gun, which he had deposited in his carriage;—in which fright the carriage was upset. Mr. Slaid, as he related, felt considerably shocked by the fall he thereby sustained, but soon recovered, put his carriage in order, and proceeded about two miles from the Springs, to an intimate acquaintance of his in Milton, a Mr. Dibble, where he alighted, accepted an invitation to take tea, and related not only the accident which had befallen him, but entered into familiar conversation on various topics. After tea he invited a daughter of Mr. Dibble's to ride home with him and spend a few days with his family, to which Miss Dibble assented. They had not proceeded a mile when Mr. S. osberved "*I believe I shall not live to arrive at home*"—These words, delivered with a tone of voice that was "never to utter more," shocked Miss Dibble—she cast a look to his face, discovered his situation, and requested him to give her the reins. They were no sooner deposited in her hands that Mr. S. laid his head in her lap and fainted.—He was immediately taken to a Mr. Gregory's inn, and physicians called, who, on examination, found some blood vessels were broken in his head. He continued in a swoon a short time and expired.

Vol. XII (No. 645) Saturday, 10 Aug. 1805.

† [2a] Copy of a letter from Jonathan Cowdery, Esq., Surgeon of the late Frigate *Philadelphia*, now held captive in Tripoli, to a Dr. Mitchell, dated 24 Nov. 1804. ◆

† [2b] Mr. John Peter, an officer of the bank of Columbia, was robbed and shot near Alexandria, though he survived; dated at Georgetown, Maryland, 20 July. ◆

† [3a] Mr. William Howe, about 45 years of age, of Barnard, Vermont, died from a broken neck sustained in falling from a hay wagon. His son was driving the team. ◆

¶ [3a] On Friday the 19th ult. agreeable to sentence, Peter Shaver was executed at Poughkeepsie, in the state of New York, for the murder of his sister, Barbara Shaver.

† [3b] Rev. Asa Eaton, of Christ's Church, Boston, ordained as Priest at New York.

¶ [3c] TAKE NOTICE. All persons having any demands on the subscriber, are requested to call and take their pay, as it is now ready.

JAMES CORBIN.

Newport, July 26, 1805.

† [3c] Silas Dickinson adv. for his new "Clothier's Business on Sackton's river, near Bellows' Distillery." Dated Rockingham, 8 Aug. 1805.

† [3c] Samuel Finley and James Dickey, guardians to Robert Lyon, of Acworth, "Lunatic," petition the Court to sell Acworth property legally owned by Lyon. The bounds of the lot include a reference to a line "formerly between James M'Cluer and William Clark "

† [3d] Asher Southard adv. medicines in his store, "at the sign of the Golden Mortar, next door south of the store of Messrs. Bellows & Stone." Dated Walpole, 26 July 1805.

===== ¶ [3b] MARRIED. =====

In Claverack, (N.Y.) Col. Derick Lane, merchant, of Troy, to Mrs. Angelica Van Rensselaer, widow of the late John R. Van Rensselaer, and daughter of Col. Henry I. Van Rensselaer, of the former place.

In Montague, Mr. Joseph T. Buckingham, printer, of Boston, to Miss Melinda Alvord, of the former place.

At Lime, (N.H.) Mr. Charles Fox, to Miss Peggy Allen.

In Fredericktown, (Maryland) 17th ultimo, George Devil, *bis* *, Esq. to the amiable and agreeable Miss Rebecca Devil - *bis*. [. . .]   * Latin for twice.

===== ¶ [3b] DIED. =====

In Sunderland, (Eng.) Dr. Paley—This very respectable pillar of the church, and ornament of literature, was Archdeacon of Carlisle, Subdean of Lincoln and Rector of Bishop-wearmouth.—In Hillsborough, (S.C.) Major Thomas B. Bowen, a member of the Cincinnati of S.C. and a much respected officer of the Pennsylvania line, during the revolutionary war.—In Philadelphia, from 20th to 27th July, 21 adults and 55 children.—In New York, from 20th to 27th July, 8 men, 14 women, 13 boys and 10 girls; of small pox 1.—In Durham, Con. a child, æ. 4; while at play with several other children round a waggon, the horses started and crushed her to death.—In Framingham, widow Hannah Park, Æt. 70.—In Virginia, the 14th ult. Miss Catharine Storke, daughter of William Storke, Esq. of Beliste. The death of this young lady was occasioned by an accident singular and uncommon; On the 4th July, 1804, in the course of an afternoon's walk, with some ladies of her acquaintance, she pluckt [sic] a head of timothy grass and put in her mouth; soon after, meeting a labourer who had made a little too free with the bottle, and whose deportment was extremely aukward [sic] and ludicrous, occasioned her to laugh, and to swallow the head of the grass whole; and which finally occasioned her death.—In Harrisburg, (Penn.) Gen. John A. Hanna, for several years a member of congress.—In Newport, his Honor Paul Mumford, Lt. Gov. of Rhode-Island, aged 72.—In Scituate, Deac. Samuel Jenkins, aged 97; and on the same day, in Woburn, Mr. Jacob Read, aged 91.—In Newport, (R.I.) on the 26th ult after a long and lingering illness, in the 46th year of his age, Joseph Wiseman, Esq. Vice-Consul from his Catholic Majesty, the King of Spain, to the State of Rhode-Island.—At Providence, of the yellow fever, Mrs. Julia Martin, consort of Mr. John D. Martin, mer. aged 26.—In Ashburnham, Mrs. Whitmore, aged 87, consort of the late Mr. Joseph W.—In Charlestown, (Montgomery county, N.Y.) Mr. Charles H. Van [Ept?], in the 82d year of his age. His death was very sudden.—In Albany, Mrs. Bassett, mother of the Rev. Dr. Bassett : Mrs. Elizabeth Mott, relict of the late Capt. Jesse Mott, of the revolutionary army, aged 52.—In Boston, Mr. George Bright, aged 79.—In Stafford, C. Mr. Joseph [Pasco? or Palco?], aged 80.—In New Haven, C. Mr. Jeremiah Townsend, aged 45.—In London, Sir William Pulteney, of a mortification, after submitting to a surgical operation.—In Bradford, Mr. Joseph Marble, aged 78.—In Boston, Mrs. Margaret Edwards, a native of the county of Hereford, (Eng.) and consort of Mr. Wm. Edwards, aged 33.

Drowned.—Near Salem harbour, Mr. Christopher Crowell, of Salem, aged 56.

Vol. XII (No. 646) Saturday, 17 Aug. 1805.

¶ [3a] On Friday the 26th ult. eight valuable cattle, the property of Mr. Stephen Congdon, of Windham, (Conn.) were killed by lightning.

† [3a] Rev. Benjamin Worcester installed over the church in Fairfield, Vt., and Rev. Perez Lincoln ordained in Gloucester.

† [3a] William Geer and Asahel Hunt adv. for a stolen horse. They believe the thief was Capt. Thomas Norton; the adv. gives a physical description of Norton, stating that he is forty years old. Adv. dated at Charlestown, 12 Aug. 1805. ♦

† [3b] Isaiah Eaton and Benjamin Kendrick, a.k.a. *Eaton & Kendrick*, mutally agree to dissolve their partnership. Eaton adv. that he will carry on the "Gold & Silver Smith Business." Dated at Westminster, 8 Aug. 1805.

† [3b] William Hall, jun., Martin Kellogg, and Daniel Wheeler, a.k.a. *Hall, Kellogg, & Company*, mutually agree at dissolve their copartnership. Hall will continue on the business. Dated at Rockingham, Vt., 6 Aug. 1805. In the adv. immediately following, the same three men dissolve their copartnership *Wheeler, Kellogg, & Company*; Wheeler to carry on that business. The second adv. is dated at Orford, N.H., 6 Aug.

† [3b] Legal notice regarding the estate of Samuel Crosby, Esq., late of Charlestown, deceased; Oliver Hall, William Briggs, and Horace Hall, Adm.

† [3b] Legal notice regarding the insolvent estate of William Henry, Jr., late of Charlestown, deceased; Abel Walker, Benjamin Clark, and Horace Hall appointed Commissioners. Estate claims to be examined at the house of Mr. Isaac H. Ely, inn-

holder at Charlestown. Notice dated at Charlestown, 15 Aug. 1805.

† [3c] Isaac Redington adv. goods for sale, and also request debtors to pay up to his company, *Thos. & I. Redington*. Notice dated at Walpole 12 Aug. 1805

† [3c] Nathaniel Gould adv. that "he has commenced business in the Saddling line, in the shop formerly occupied by Charles Mattoon, under the firm of *Nathaniel Gould & Co*. . . ." Dated at Walpole, 15 Aug. 1805.

† [3d] Legal notice regarding the estate of Giles Marvin, late of Alstead, deceased; Simon Brooks, jun., and Patience Colburn, Executors; dated Alstead, 9 Aug. 1805.

===== ¶ [3a] MARRIED. =====

In Rutland, (Ver.) Mr. Ira Manly, of Dorset, to Miss Dorcas Hale, of Rutland.

===== ¶ [3a] DIED. =====

In Ireland, Rev. Dr. Thomas Bernard. Lord Bishop of Limerick [. . .] aged 87. He was the contemporary and intimate friend of Garrick Burke, Sir Joshua Reynolds, Cumberland and Goldsmith.—Lately in France, the Baron [?] formerly Grand Master of Malta.—In England, the Rev. John Darwin, M.A. brother to the celebrated author of "The Lives of the Plants," [. . .]—In Philadelphia, from 20th July to 2d Aug. 23 adults and 43 chil.—In Hackensack, (N.J.) Col. Nehemiah W[ ]de, [140] aged 46.—In Portsmouth, Mrs. Elizabeth Salter, aged 54 : Deacon Solomon Cotton.—In Charlestown, on the 2d inst, Mr. Wm. Henry.—In Haverhill, Mrs. Mary [Merrill? or Morrill?], aged 85.—In Danvers, Miss Rebecca Judd, aged 94.—In Salem, Miss Hannah [Twiss?], aged 90, for 74 years a school mistress.—In Acton, the 5th inst. Francis Faulkner, Esq. aged 77, after a very active and useful life.—In Quincy, 8th inst. Capt. Seth Baxter, aged 7[?].—In Branford, C. at an advanced age, Dr. Wm. Gould.—In New Haven, of the Dropsy in the *Ovaria*, the wife of Mr. George Peckham.—At Fairview Farm, (York county, Penn.) Mrs. Elizabeth Simpson, aged 72.—In Hartford, Mrs. Sarah [Swetland?], aged 82.—In Georgetown, (Del.) killed by lightning, Dr. Wolfe, of Lewis.—At Ballstown Springs, Mr. David Fonda, merchant, aged 49.—In New York, the week ending Aug. 30, 26 adults, 42 children, total 68.—In Cornish, Miss Susannah [Hagins?], aged 28.—In Windsor, (Vt.) Widow Abigail [Dean?], aged 78.—In Lansingburgh, Mrs. Eliza [Bugbey?].—In Litchfield, (Con.) Mr. Jeremiah Townsend, aged 45.—In Clifton, England, John Fisher, Esq. formerly of Portsmouth.—In Greenland, by a fall from his horse, Mr. Ebenezer Johnson, aged 70. In Quebec, Mr. Duncan Ritchie, printer.—In Hartford, (Vt.) Mrs. Gross, consort of Rev. Mr. Gross.

DROWNED.]—At sea, Mr. Samuel Pickering, of Portsmouth, aged 21.—In Worcester, by accidentally slipping into the river as he was fishing, Mr. John Sparhawk, æ. 19.

Vol. XII (No. 647) Saturday, 24 Aug. 1805.

† [2c] Mr. Enoch M. Lyles, of Alexandria, Va., killed 7 Aug. 1805 in a duel with Mr. John F. Bowie, [*compare to death notices below*] of Piscataway, Maryland. ♦

¶ [3a] A Court martial was sitting at New Orleans on the 1st ult. for the trial of Col. Thomas Butler, at which Lt. Col. Freeman presided. [141]

† [3a] Brig. Gen. Amasa Allen, and Joseph Bellows, jun., Brigade Maj. and Inspector, announce that the Fifth Brigade of N.H. Militia will be inspected and reviewed. Notice dated at Walpole, 23 Aug. 1805.

===== ¶ [3b] MARRIED. =====

In Boston, Mr. George Vose, to Miss Susanna Lewis.
In Springfield, (N.J.) Master Moses Cherry, to Miss Nancy Bodgley, both aged 17.

===== ¶ [3b] DIED. =====

In Maryland, Mr. Enoch M. Lyles, of Alexandria, killed in a duel with a Mr. Bowles [*compare to news item above.*]—In Providence, Messrs. Stephen Russell and Benjamin Tunbridge, of the fever lately there.—In Gloucester, (Mass.) John Gibaut, Esq. Collector of that Port, aged 38.—In Barre, Mr. Robert Nicoll, aged 66.—In Sutton, Mrs. Rebecca Marsh, aged 85.—In Stanburg, (Ohio) Levi Buttles, Esq. late of Connecticut.—In Croydon, Widow Hannah Jiles, in the 94th year of her age ; Deac. John Cooper, in the 81st year of his age.—In England, Joseph Wilkes, Esq. He had a peculiar mode in the formation of roads, of which thirty years experience has fully established the reputation [. . .]—In Philadelphia, Mr. John Thompson, Printer, celebrated for his elegant hot-pressed edition of the Holy Bible.—In Alford, supposed by an apoplectic fit, Mr. Samuel Stevens, aged 25.—In Philadelphia, week ending 10th inst. 17 adults, 41 children.—In New York, accidentally drowned, Wm. Beattie, aged about 19.—In Windsor, (Con.) Miss Sarah Hosford, aged 49.—In Oxford, Widow Abigail Davis, aged 87.—In Wassamasaw, S.C. Maj. Robert Thornley.—In India, (killed) Lt. Col. James Maitland, of the 75th British reg't.—In Halifax, (N.C.) Mr. Abraham Hodge, proprietor of the North Carolina Journal.—In New York, the 14th inst. Frederick Crater. He had been convicted of Grand Larceny, and sentenced the day before to nine years hard labour in the states prison.—At East Sudbury, on the 16th inst. Mrs. Abigail Curtis, aged 73.—In Boston, Maj. Asa Hatch, aged 34.—In Hartford, (Vt.) of consumption, Miss Fidela Rider, aged 15, the seventh child which the parents have buried within two years and 11 months.—In Croydon, Deacon John Cooper, aged 81.—In Topsfield, (Ms.) Mrs. Esther Estey, aged 100.—In Ira, (Vt.) Mr. Samuel Squires, aged 80 ; his aged consort died about three weeks before him : Capt. Joseph Hinds, aged 60.—In Bridport, (Ver.) Miss Sophia Claves, aged 18.—Near London, Arthur Murphy, Esq. an eminent barrister, and dramatic writer.—In Danvers, Miss Rebecca Judd, aged 91.—In Portsmouth, Mr. William Gates, aged 43.

Vol. XII (No. 643) Saturday, 31 Aug. 1805.

† [2b-c] Account of a Spanish galley which intercepted and captured the brig *Success*, Capt. Brum, of New York, somewhere off Cuba. One of the seaman of the brig, Peter Duchemin, escaped. ♦

† [3a] Accounts of the increase of yellow fever at Philadelphia, noting the deaths of "The younger Mr. Bickman," and Mrs. Krist; also, a daughter of Mr. Isaac Hozey was taken ill. Other articles dispute the claim of the yellow fever. ♦

† [3d] Asa Partridge posts a notice, "intending to relinquish the carrying of papers on the route he has rode for two years past, has contracted with Mr. Abel Phelps, of Alstead, to take his place for that purpose on the 28th of September next . . . "

¶ [3d] NOTICE. Those gentlemen who have generally been supplied with papers from the Observatory press on the route lately rode by Mr. Burroughs, are respectfully informed that they may be furnished with the Farmer's Museum, on reasonable terms, by the present postrider.

====== ¶ [3b] MARRIED. ======

In Middleburgh, (Schoharie county, N.Y.) Mr. Peter B. Best, to Miss Catharine Gray [. . .]

In Charlotte county, in Virginia, Mr. Perrin Aldey, aged 105 years, to Mrs. Ann Tankesley, aged 90. She is his third wife and he her third husband.

In New-Fane, (Ver.) Mr. Ebenezer Morse, 2d, to Miss Sally Goodenough.

In Exeter, (N.H.) the Rev. Walter Powars, of Gilmanton, to Miss Elizabeth M'Clure.

====== ¶ [3b-c] DIED. ======

In Poughkeepsie, (N.Y.) Mr. John Copeman, aged 68.—In Charleston, (S.C.) Roger Smith, Esq. aged 60.—In Dummerston, (Vt.) caught between the wallow and main cog wheel, a son of Mr. Josiah Ward. His head was bruised in a shocking manner.—In Kittery, John H. Bartlett, Esq. and Capt. Dennis Fernald, two aged and venerable characters.—In Preston, (Con.) Mr. Zipporam Yarrington, aged 76.—In New Haven, Mrs. Mary Beers, aged 60, consort of Mr. Isaac Beers.—In Norwich, C. Widow Mary Woodbridge, aged 74.—In Hartford, Mrs. Webster, aged 83 : Mr. James Kilbourn, aged 55.—In Orford, Mr. Theodore Andrus.—In Littleton, a man by the name of James Kitteridge, found dead in the road.—In Johnstown, (N.Y.) of the dysentery prevailing there, three sons of Mr. John M. Vain, and all interred in one grave.—In Reading, C. Mr. David Mallory, aged 82.—In Cheraw District, (S.C.) Wm. Falconer, Esq. an eminent attorney at law.—In Hillsborough, Rev. Jonathan Barnes.—In Pembroke, Richard Bartlett, Esq. aged 62.—In South-Hampton, Mrs. Susannah Pilsbury, aged 70.—In Charkoff, (R.) A.F.M. Willich, M.D. author of lectures on "Diet and Regimen," &c. He was Professor of Medicine &c. in the new Russian University of Charkoff, in the Ukraine, 1000 miles South of Petersburg.—In Trenton, Mr. John C. Miller, of Philadelphia, aged 35, formerly in the department of Secretary of State.—The interments in Philadelphia, from the 9th to the 16th August, were 45.—At New York, Mrs. Ann

Anderson, aged 75, formerly of Boston.—The deaths in New York, from the 10th to the 17th inst. were 77, of which 60 were under five years of age.—In Ridgfield, (C.) Deac. Nathaniel Olmstead. The posterity of this aged patriarch amounted to 430.—In Fairfield, C. Mrs. Eunice Burr, aged 75.—In Dorchester, Mr. John W. Billings, aged 74.—In Lexington, Capt. Joseph Smith, aged 62.—In Windham, (C.) Deacon Samuel Bingham, aged 82 : Mr. Joel Manning, aged 49.—In Belchertown, Mr. Ethan Drake, killed by lightning.—In Salem, Mrs. Elizbeth Carlton, aged 33, widow of the late Mr. Wm. Carlton, and proprietress of the *Salem Register*.—In Boston, Mrs. Elizabeth Tuckerman, aged 37.—In Portland, Mrs. Mehitable Preble, aged 77, relict of the late Brig. Gen. Preble, and mother of Commodore Edward Preble. After taking her evening repass, at about 7 o'clock, she retired to her chamber, and before 8 was a lifeless corpse.—In Worcester, Mrs. Caldwell, relict of the late William Caldwell, Esq.—In Bridgewater, (Ver.) Mrs. Mary Denison, aged 59.—In Boston, Maj. Asa Hatch, aged 34.

In this town, on Tuesday last, Mr. Ebenezer Eaton, aged 60 years.

Patricide.—Deliberately shot by his own son, about 23 years of age, on the high hills of Santee, in South Carolina, Mr. Thomas Maples. The abandoned and unhappy wrech was soon taken and committed to jail, and confessed the fact.

Drowned.—At Montville, C. Mr. Richard Miner, aged 68, and at Waterford, Mr. John Weldon, aged 40.—In Farmingham, Mr. Luke Fairbanks, aged 25, and Daniel, his brother, aged 18.—In Winchester, Ezebon Hutchins, aged 14.—In Merrimack River, at Bow, Mr. Moses Noyes, aged about 50.—In Dudley, Ms. Mr. Reuben Burrell, as he was bathing.

Suicide.—At Lexington, (Ken.) on the 20th ult. Mrs. Eve, a widow woman, put an end to her existence by hanging herself. Grief for the loss of her husband and property was the cause of her committing the criminal deed.

Vol. XII (No. 649) Saturday, 7 Sept. 1805.

¶ [3a-b] *Extract of a letter to the Editor from a correspondent at Nashville, Tennessee, dated 8th August.* "Col. Burr arrived here on the first inst. from New Orleans.—We have had two duels at this place within three weeks: The first between Mr. Thomas J. Overton, and Mr. Nathaniel A. M'Nairy; they exchanged a shot, without injury. The other, which happened a few days afterwards, between Mr. Thomas J. Overton, and Mr. John Dickinson, Clerk of the Federal Court for the district of West Tennessee; they exchanged two shots; Mr. Overton was wounded through the left arm, and in the breast, but not dangerously.—Mr. Dickinson was formerly a citizen of Charlestown, N.H.— [. . .].

¶ [3c] *Murder !* —We hear from Ryegate, Vt., that a Mr. Maxfield, of that town, was one evening last week, while in a state of intoxication, beat and bruised in a shocking manner, by his wife and a late emigrant from Scotland; and the next morning was found dead. The murderers have been taken and committed to prison.

† [3c] Adv. of items for sale at the store of Jonathan P. Hall, No. 1 Union St., Boston.

† [3d] Legal notice regarding the estate of Job Johnson, late of Charlestown, deceased, Josiah Hart, Adm.

===== ¶ [3c] DIED. =====

In Groton, (Con.) Mr. Ezra Barns, aged 75.—In Norwich, Rufus Lathrop, Esq. aged 74.—In East Haddam, suddenly, Mr. Caleb Chapman, aged 74.—In Middletown, Mrs. Anna Hall, aged 77.—In Gloucester county, (Vir.) of cholera morbus, occasioned by using an immoderate quantity of ice, William Wischam, Esq.—In Hamilton township, (Penn.) Mrs. Rebecca M'Brien, a native of Ireland, aged 101 years.—In Baltimore, Abraham Van Bibber, Esq. aged 61.—In Woodstock, (N.Y.) three children of Mr. John Hogan, of the dysentery; the last died while the parents were attending the other two to interment.—In Rutland, (N.Y.) Three daughters of Mr. Moses Taylor, by a fever.—In Lime, N.H. Otis Post, only son of Mr. Joseph O. Post, aged 15.—In Cornish, Mrs. Sarah Cummings, aged 59.—In Richmond, Ms. Dr. Beriah Bishop, aged 27.—In Pompey, (N.Y.) Mrs. Amarilla Jerome, aged 38.—In Pomfret, Vt. Miss Abigail Bailey, aged 24.—In Quebec, on the 21st ult. His Excellency Lieut. General Peter Hunter, Lieut. Governor of Upper Canada, and commanding in chief his Majesty's forces in both the Canadas.—The last papers announce the death, at Milan, of His Excellency Charles M.

Talleyrand, Secretary of Foreign Affairs to his Imperial Majesty, Napoleon I.—In Petersburg, (Russia) the celebrated Princess Carjarin, the beautiful favorite of the late Emperor, Paul I. Her interment was attended with great funeral pomp and magnificence:—All the foreign Ministers attended.—Also, at Petersburg, Mr. Fretter, the Hanoverian Ambassador.—In Kentucky, Miss Polly Hinton; maliciously shot by an unprincipled fellow.—In Amesbury, Dr. Aaron Sawyer, aged 76.—In Newburyport, Mrs. Rebecca French, aged 83.

Vol. XII (No. 650) Saturday, 14 Sept. 1805.

¶ [2d] *Murder.*—A murder was lately perpetrated in Perkinsonville, (Vir.) by Edward Jones on the body of John Hill. The latter owed Jones a small sum, which he was either unwilling or unable to pay, and he "therefore slew him."

¶ [3a] *Unfortunate Accident.*—We learn that in Springfield, one day last week, as a Mr. Nichols was running his horse, the horse got the command of the bit, so as to sheer off to one side of the road and run against a tree, causing in a few hours the death of the rider.

¶ [3a] *Lightning.*—On the 13th ult. the house of Mr. Luke Aldrich, of Northbridge, was struck by lightning. Six men and a lad were sitting at dinner. They were all thrown back from the table, and a Mr. Joseph Johnson, of Milford, and a little girl who was in the room, were taken up for corpses. They all, however, survived the shock; Johnson, by the application of cold water, recovered in about three quarters of an hour.

† [3d] Rev. Asaph Morgan ordained at Essex, Vt.

† [3d] Loveil Bowman adv. "that he has just taken the Clothier's Works lately occupied by Mr. Nathaniel Sikes" in Walpole; dated there 9 Sept. 1805.

===== ¶ [3d] MARRIED. =====

In Virginia, the Hon. Thomas Claiborne, late M. of Congress, to Miss Ann Driver.

In Rutland, Vt. Mr. Truman Mead, to Miss Betsey Gould.

In Bennington, Orsamus C. Merrill, Esq. to Miss Mary Robinson, daughter of the Hon. Jonathan Robinson.

In Coventry, Mr. Levi Russell, aged 19, to Miss Sarah Wentworth, aged 60.—In Lee, (N.H.) Robert Parker, Esq. aged 73, to Miss Hannah Chesly, aged 22.

===== ¶ [3d] DIED. =====

In Jamaica, 4th July, on board his Britannic Majesty's frigate Franchise, the Hon. John Murray, captain of that ship.—He was son of the Earl of Dunshore, the last Governor of Virginia under the Royal Government. Capt. M. was a vigilant and meritorious officer, and is much regretted.—In St. Louis, Captain Robert Randall, aged 56, late of Boston. His remains were respectfully interred, and military and masonic honors were performed to commemorate his departed worth.—In New York, from the 24th to 31st Aug. 11 men, 10 women, 16 boys, and 17 girls—total 54—of malignant fever 1.—In Newburgh, (N.Y.) John Skey Eustace, Esq. aged 46. He was aid-de-camp to Gen. Charles Lee, and of considerable merit as an officer during the revolutionary war.—In Clinton, (Me.) Captain Samuel Grant, an officer during the revolutionary war.—The mention in our last of the death of M. Talleyrand, has been contradicted in the Paris papers.—Interments in Boston, from Friday Aug. 30 to Thursday the 5th Sept. following, both included, 43, chiefly children.—In Amesbury, Dr. Aaron Sawyer, aged 76.—In Orangetown, (Me.) John Crane, Esq. aged 61.

Drowned.—At New York, Five apprentices of Mr. M'Intire, stone cutter.—They were on a water frolic when the boat upset.—It is a little singular that three of his apprentices were drowned last winter by falling through the ice.

Vol. XII (No. 651) Saturday, 21 Sept. 1805. [142]

¶ [2d-3a] MALIGNANT FEVER. [. . .] New York. In our last, the returns included the 9th inst. On the 10th *twenty-nine* new cases, and 3 deaths, viz. John R. Jones (a Welshman), Joseph Burling, and John Sykes.—On the 11th, *twelve* new cases, and seven deaths, vix. [sic] Sarah Skillings, (from Philadelphia) Hannah Saltonstall, Patrick Finnick, Thomas Jones, Susannah Wright, and Nancy Prowning.—On the 12th, *twenty three* new cases, and four deaths, viz. Abigail Caywood, Abraham Benenger, jun.

Thomas Thornton Mackaness, (at Greenwich) and Peter Brown. The Board of Health have announced that the fever being now ascertained to be prevalent, no removal of the sick would be enforced.—Every precaution had been taken to guard the city against fire; and every provision made for the comfort and care of the indigent sick. On the 13th, *eleven* new cases, three deaths.

† [3a] Account of the death in Watervliet, N.Y., of Mrs. Nancy Waugh, aged about 36, who was fatally wounded in an accident involving a runaway carriage. She had come from Wilmington, N.C., to recover the health of an only child, a boy aged 11, and to visit her sister, Mrs. Redfield, wife of Mr. Bela Redfield, of Lansingburgh, N.Y. The carriage was driven by Mr. F. Bradley, who, with Waugh's son, survived. ♦

† [3b] Editorial comments regarding the *Troy Gazette*, which has now as a contributor to that paper, Mr. Sterling Goodenow. When this gentleman was associated with the *Farmers' Museum*, he used the pen name of "Hampden."

† [3b] Thomas Dickman, Esq. of Greenfield, Mass., removed from the post office there, and replaced by Mr. Ambrose Ames, formerly a blacksmith. Ames has employed Dea. Proctor Pierce. ♦

† [3b] Elder Paul Davis ordained at New Salem.

† [3c] Amasa Allen's house robbed, and he offers a reward; dated Walpole, 16 Aug.

† [3c] Cornelius Warren turns over his delivery of Walpole newspapers for the towns of Goshen, Fisherfield, Wendal, Sutton, New London, Springfield, New Grantham, Croydon, and Newport, to Mr. Ephraim Fletcher.

¶ [3b] MARRIED.

In Philadelphia, (after a tedious courtship of *ten minutes*) Mr. William Whats, pilot, to Miss Susan House.—In Litchfield, Mr. John Crafts Wright, of Troy, printer, to Miss Mary Bouel Collier, of the former place.

¶ [3b-c] DIED.

In Philadelphia, from August 30th to 6th Sept. 53 adults and 36 children.—In New York, from August 31st to Sept. 7th, 30 adults and 34 children.—In Lancaster, 10th inst. deeply lamented, Samuel John Sprague, Esq. attorney at law, only son of the late Hon. John Sprague, aged 25.—In Brattleboro' (Vt.) Mr. John Thomas—Deaths in Boston week ending 12th inst. 40.—In Cornish, Mr. Wm. Lane, aged 32. In Worcester, Mrs. Betsey M'Farland, aged 41.—Near Chambersburg, (P.) Mr. John Johns, sen. aged 71.—In Castleton, Mrs. Anne Remington, aged 45.—In Poultney, Mr. John Gidins.—In Haddam, said to be in consequence of using a solution for the itch called Dr. Hall's solution, Mr. James Child, aged 22. The composition was Sal ammoniac, and corrosive sublimates.—In Hartford, Mr. Nathaniel Blake, aged 42.—In Norwich, C. Mr. Nathaniel Shipman, aged 82.—In Bellmont, (Vir.) Col. Thomas Lee.—In Dedham, Mr. Jonathan Dean, aged 75.—In Peckskill, N.Y. the 29th ult. Mr. John Thompson, aged 107.—In Sutton, Capt. Moody Morse, aged 87 ; Widow Patience Marble, aged 84.—In Dudley, Mr. John Haskell, aged 83.—In Peterborough, 25th August, Capt. William Alld, in the 82d year of his age. He was a native of Ireland, and came to New England in the year 1737.—

Suicide.—In Pittsfield, Mr. John Foulton, leaving a wife and five or six children.

Drowned.—In Lower Salem, C. Mr. Zadock Reynolds, as he was riding his horse into the pond to wash him.

Vol. XII (No. 652) Saturday, 28 Sept. 1805.

¶ [3a] On Saturday, the 8th inst. the house of Mr. Daniel Jackson, of Canaan, C. accidentally took fire and was wholly consumed with its contents, together with his child of two years old.

¶ [3d] *Record of* DISEASE *and* DEATH. [. . .] New York. In our last we gave the reports to the 17th. On the 18th there were *seven* new cases, and three deaths, viz. Dominick Lively, James Brazer, and Maria Miller. On the 19th, *seven* new cases, and *eight* deaths, viz. John Morevell, John Thomas, Mr. Steward, Lewis Baehr, James Harvey, William Kneeland, Henry Leak, Nancy Sweeney. On the 20th, there were *eight* new cases, and *four* deaths, viz. Caleb Smith, merchant of the house of C.and E. Smith, John Long, Mary Brown, and John Underwood. [*Cent.*

† [3d] Ordained : Rev. Samuel Walker, at the South Society in Danvers; Rev. Perez Lincoln to the first Parish in Gloucester; and Rev. Thomas Cochran at Camden, Maine.

===== ¶ [3d] MARRIED. =====

In this town, on Sunday evening last, by the Rev. Mr. Dickinson, Mr. David Stone, to Miss Hannah Bellows, daughter of Col. John Bellows.

On Thursday evening last, Mr. Andrew Cooke, of Hadley, (Mass.) to Miss Abigail Sparhawk, of this town.

On Thursday se'ennight, Mr. Elisha Hall, 2d to Mrs. Lucinda Badger.

At Bellows Falls, Vt. the 20th inst. Mr. Leverett Tuttle, to Miss Cynthia Page, youngest daughter of Col. William Page.

In Windsor, Joseph Burton, Esq. of Norwich, (Ver.) to Miss Polly Hodgman.

===== ¶ [3d] DIED. =====

In Townsend, Mr. Giles Alexander, aged 63.—Drowned off York harbor, Mr. Elias Damon, and two young men.—At Winchester, August 25th, Mrs. Esther Morse, wife of Mr. David Morse, aged 62.—At Peterborough, 25th of August, Capt. William Alld, in the 82d year of his age. He was a native of Ireland, and came to New England in the year 1737.—At Amherst, N.H. Capt. Levi Adams, aged 41. His death was occasioned by a wound in his bowels from the kick of a horse the Thursday preceeding.—At Newton, Mr. John Kenrick, aged 83.—At Peekskill, on Thursday the 29th ult. in the 107th year of his age, Mr. John Thompson. He was a native of Ireland.—In Danbury, C. Mrs. Susanna Barber, aged 79.—In Sharon, C. at 9 o'clock, A.M. Miss Elizabeth St.John, aged 37—at 3 P.M. Miss Abigail St.John aged 22—on the 10th Mr. Allen Rice St.John, aged 25, all the children of Deacon Silas St.John. The latter and his wife at the same time afflicted with the same malady, and the former not expected to recover.— Mr. John Hoy, aged 70.—In Owego village, Samuel Avery, Esq. aged 76.—Near Quebeck, suicide, M. Robitailie. He borrowed a gun, as he said, to kill a fox, dug his grave, made his coffin, laid himself in it, and then shot himself. He was not found for some days.—In Washington, (district of Columbia) Mr. John Hodgkinson, a celebrated comedian; and who, a few years since, had the management of the Boston Theatre. He died of the yellow fever; having left New York about the time the alarm first became serious.—In Westchester, N.Y. Mr. Thomas Arden, bookseller, of New York.—Mrs. Collins, wife of Mr. Isaac Collins, bookseller, of New York.—Of fever, Mr. Lewis Nichols, book-printer.—Mr. William Young, printer, of the House of Ming & Young, printers of the price Current.—In Henniker, N.H. Capt. Edward Whitman, aged 52.—In Shippensburg, (Pen.) Capt. John Shippen.—Drowned, in a small creek of Merrimack river, in the East parish of Bradford, Mr. Joseph Holden.—On Salisbury Beach, Mr. Nathan Webster, aged 24, of Atkinson.

Vol. XII (No. 653) Saturday, 5 Oct. 1805.

¶ [2d] Ephraim Wheeler, of Windsor, in Berkshire county, has been convicted of a rape on the body of Betty Wheeler, his daughter, a child of 13 years of age, and sentenced by the Supreme Court to suffer death. The particulars are too shocking for general public. 143

¶ [2d] NEW YORK. Our last publication included the report of the 20th inst. On the 21st *eight* new cases were reported, and *two* deaths, viz. James Fitzpatrick, and James Gilchrist. On the 22d Three new cases, and *no death*. On the 23d, *Sixteen* new cases, and *no death*. On the 24th, *Thirty* new cases, and *five* deaths, viz. Grace Sharp, Robinson [Howard?], Mary Dunn, James Kirkwood, & Nicholas ———. In the Hospital at Bellevue last date, 32—of whom 10 were convalescent.

¶ [2d-3a] HEALTH-OFFICE Boston, Sept. 27, 1805. The Board of Health have pledged themselves not to conceal the actual state of the health of the town. They therefore frankly inform their fellow citizens that a death by Malignant Fever occurred this morning. The following are the facts of the case. Mr. James Scobie left New York on Friday, the 13th inst. and arrived here the 16th. While in New York he was necessitated to do business in the infected part of the city.—He underwent much fatigue on Saturday last; and then complained of shiverings and ague. On Tuesday he was visited by Dr. Danforth, his physician; and on Thursday the Doctor reported to the Board his case to be of Malignant Fever of the type of that prevalent in 1798.—This morning, at 4 o'clock, he died; and was immediately interred.—His bedding and wearing apparel were also buried, the house thoroughly aired and purified; and the attendants with him at his decease, removed to a place of safety. The Board have no knowledge of any other case of malignant fever in town. E. Larkin, President. R. Gardner, Secretary.

¶ [3c] We understand that the postmaster-general, Gideon Granger, Esq. is at Suffield, (C.) and dangerously ill of a fever.

† [3c] Ordinations: Rev. Henry Bigelow, at Middletown, Vermont, Mr. Horace Holly in the parish of Greenfield, in Fairfield, and Rev. Alfred Johnson at Belfast, Maine.

† [3d] Leverett Tuttle, David Porter, and Perez Jones announce the dissolution of their partnership, *L. Tuttle & Co.*; dated at Bellows Falls, Vt., 28 Sept. 1805. Tuttle continues on his business of selling goods from the East and West Indies.

===== ¶ [3c] MARRIED. =====

In Castleton, (Vt.) Robert Temple, Esq. attorney at law, to Miss Clarina B. Hawkins.

===== ¶ [3c-d] DIED. =====

In England, Lt. Col. the Hon. Arthur Wolfe, 2d son of the late (murdered) Lord Kilwarden, aged 38.—In Harlington, (England) John Kimpston, aged 111.—In Milan, Locatelli, of Verona, the celebrated sculptor, aged 80.—In Maryland, James Campbell, Esq. aged 70.—In New York, of the fever, Mr. David Dickson : Mr. James Haydock, jun., merchant.—At his country seat, Pascal N. Smith, Esq. President of the Columbian Insurance Office.—Drowned, in Penobscot river, George Darrow.—In Marblehead, Dr. Elisha Story, aged 93.—In Troy, Frederick Selleck, aged [20?] ; Mrs. Sarah Conger, aged 35, and her infant child.—In Pittstown, N.Y. Mr. Peter Van Allen, aged 96.—In Boston, the week ending Thursday the 19th ult. 43, 28 of whom were not over 3 years old.—In Hudson, Mrs. Abigail Armstrong, aged 85.—In Sunderland, (Eng.) Mr. Edward Lawson, Æt. 106, who had been blind three years, but recovered his sight a short time previous to his death.—In Greenwich, (Eng.) Richard Braithwaite, Esq. Admiral of the White ; Mr. Wm. Dodrill, who weighed 406 lbs.—In Portsmouth, Mrs. Abigail, relict of the late Mr. Jacob Sheafe, mer. aged 73.—In Demerara, on his plantation, 26th July, Burrill Carnes, Esq. formerly of Boston.—In Boston, Miss Isabella C. Dana, aged 16, daughter of the late Rev. J. Dana, of Barre.—In Baltimore, Mrs. Elizabeth Toope, aged 111, last Christmas (old style.)—In New York, from 14th to 21st Sept. 36 men, 10 women, 8 boys, and 12 girls ; 66 ; of malignant fever 37, of consumption 7, convulsions 6, dysentery 4.—In Brooklyn, N.Y. Mr. Nathaniel Parsons ; hung himself in a fit of intoxication.—In Whateley, (Mass.) Mr. Joshua Belding, aged 74.—In Buck's county, (Penn.) Mrs. Dorothy Linderman, aged 91, leaving 200 descendants.—In Boston, Mr. Isaac Codman, aged 68.—In Cambridge, Madam Jane Lee, relict of the late Thomas Lee, Esq.—At Holles, the 23d instant, aged 21, Mr. Benjamin Hudson. He was preparing for training—had washed out his gun, and immediately loaded it, and rammed a wet wad excessively hard, and fired.—The wad never moved, but the lower end of the barrel split.—A piece of the barrel went into his body a little above his heart ; on which he ran about three rods, and dropped down dead, without speaking.

Vol. XII (No. 654) Saturday, 12 Oct. 1805.

† [2c] New Jersey Supreme Court orders the execution of Harry Lawrence, "a negro man," who was convicted of poisoning his wife; article under the Philadelphia head. ♦

¶ [2d] Philadelphia, Pennsylvania, Sept. 24. On Saturday last, at Brooklyn, Nathaniel Parson, a rope-maker, hung himself on a poplar tree in John Hasting's nursery. He has left a wife and four children; the former of whom was a witness to the distressing scene.

† [2d] William Shaw, a native of the highlands of Scotland, captures a bear at Delhi, Delaware Co., N.Y., by entering the bear's den. Article dated at Albany, 24 Sept. ♦

¶ [3b] COUNTERFEITERS. By the Peacham paper, we find that Samuel Spring, Russel Underwood, John St. Clair, and John Giles, were severally convicted at the sessions of the Superior Court in Orange County, Ver. of counterfeiting or passing bank bills of the N.H. Bank, payable at Philadelphia, Boston Branch Bank, Providence and Cheshire Bank. They were sentenced to stand in the pillory one hour for two or three successive days:—to receive thirty-nine stripes, and pay fines from 20 to 400 dollars, according to the enormity of their offence. 144

† [3b-c] Isaiah Potter, Thomas Gross, and Ignatus Thompson witness a meteor, while

viewing the Northern Lights, at "Rev. Mr. Gross's house in Hartford, Vt."

† [3c] Notice from Jesse Wilcox, jun., Treasurer of the Croydon Turnpike Road.

† [3d] Auction notice regarding the estate of Absalom Kingsbery, Esq., Ephraim Kingsbery, Executor; dated at Alstead, 4 Oct. 1805.

† [3d] Auction notice regarding the estate of Maj. Elisha Kingsbery, late of Alstead, deceased; Amos Shepard, Administrator de bonis non; dated Alstead 4 Oct. 1805.

===== ¶ [3c] MARRIED. =====

In Boston, Mr. Jonathan Phillips, mer. to Miss Rebecca Salisbury; and Mr. John Tappan, mer. to Miss Sarah Salisbury; daughter of Samuel Salisbury, Esq.

In Groton, (Mass.) John P. Little, Esq. to Miss Mary F. Prescott.

In Plymouth, (Con.) Mr. Daniel Leonard, of West Springfield, to Miss Nancy Fenn.

===== ¶ [3c] DIED. =====

Near Montreal, Antoine Robert la Mouche, aged 106 years, 8 months and 17 days.—In Leedstown, (Vir.) Col. Samuel Turner, of the 51st Regt. aged 39.—In Winchester, (Virg.) by a fall from a horse, Mr. Thomas Brown, aged 23.—In Hillsboro', by a fall from his horse, Capt. Solomon Rhodes.—In Baltimore, from 16th to 23 Sept. 14 adults, 10 children, —8 died of bilious fever, of small pox 1.—In Pennsylvania, Mrs. Dorothy Linderman, aged 91, leaving 200 descendants.—In Fairfield, Rev. Andrew Elliot, aged 62.—In Newburyport, Mr. Wm. Greenough, aged 71 : Mr. Wyatt, aged 84.—In Plainfield, 29th ult. Mrs. Sally Spalding, consort of Capt. Daniel S. aged 35.—In Northboro' (Mass.) Mrs. Hannah Howe, aged 49.—In Bolton, (Ms.) Mr. Joseph Fletcher, aged about 50.—Interments in Boston, from Friday Sept. 27, to Thursday the 3d Oct. following, both included, 42—30 of whom were children.—In New York, Mr. Gerard Smith, aged 94.—In Brooklyn, N.Y. Mrs. Phebe Stout, aged 94.—In Albany, Mr. Silas W. Hawell, and Mr. Ab'm D. Lansing, merchants, of the malignant fever of New York, from which city they had just returned.—In Litchfield, (Con.) Mrs. Elizabeth, consort of the Hon. Oliver Wolcott, aged 39.—In Springfield, (Mass.) Mrs. Temperance, wife of Maj. Thomas J. Douglass, aged 50 : Mr. Marshfield Williston, aged 87 : Mr. David Rider, aged 87.—In Europe, Her Royal Highness Madame the Countess of D'Artois, consort of the second brother of the unfortunate Louis XVI, of France.—In England, Miss Prudence Blood, aged 109.—Mr. Wm. Welch, aged 104.—In Barbadoes, Lieut. General Sir Wm. Myers, Commander In Chief in the British Islands—and Lieut. Col. George Brinley, Commissary General to the British forces in Nova Scotia.—In Warren, (Con.) Capt. Simeon Fuller, aged 72.—In Salem, Mrs. Hannah Torrey, aged 87.—In Boston, Mrs. Christian Armstrong, aged 83.

In Newton, October [2?], Mr. Benjamin Houghton, of Princeton, aged 21 ; his death was occasioned by a small splinter of wood entering the lower part of his little finger, and which in a few days brought on the lock jaw; he died soon after in great agony.

Some days since, we announced the death of Gen. Eustace, in New Jersey. This officer served in the American war, and attained the grade of Major General in the French army of the North, in the early days of ther French Revolution [. . .].

Vol. XII (No. 655) Saturday, 19 Oct. 1805.

† [1c-2a] Extract of a letter, dated at Malta 4 July 1805, from Mr. Pascal Paoli Peck, son of Col. William Peck, of Providence, R.I.; the younger Peck was an officer on board the U.S. brig *Argus*. He related his account of a long journey across the Lybian desert, where his comrades were involved in the disputes in the North African countries. ♦

¶ [2c] Natchez, Mississippi, Sept. 6. DARING OUTRAGE ! We are informed by a gentleman from the neighborhood of Pinckneyville, that a party of armed Spaniards (number not known) entered that place, late on Monday evening last, and forcibly seized and carried off Messrs. Reuben and Samuel Kemper.—When our informant left home he understood that Col. Baker was employed taking depositions respecting this event, for the information of the executive.—

An agent of Mr. Edward Randolph's, who kept a store, at the mouth of Bayau Sarah, has been also driven from thence at an hour's notice. 145

¶ [2c] RECORD OF DISEASE. [. . .] NEW-YORK.—On the 7th inst. there were *nine* new cases, and *four* deaths—viz. Joshua Mackay, Robert Griffith, Richard Tabole and Johannes Christian Bernard. In the Hospital, the 8th, 27—11 convalesent.—During the

week ending 5th Oct. *sixty-two* died of the prevailing fever.
† [2d] Mr. Ebenezer Hoisington, of Windsor, Vt. reaps six ears of corn from one stalk.
† [3b] Edward Savage, James Hildreth, James Burt, Jno. Swartwout, Samuel Crossett, James Glover, P.G. Hildreth, Daniel Sayre, Jos. Annin, W. Mynderse, and Israel Smith claim to have seen a tree of enormous dimensions, at Jefferson, Cayuga County, N.Y. ♦
¶ [3c] INSTALLED.—At Belfast, (Me.) on the 12th ult. the Rev. Alfred Johnson.
† [3c] Stephen R. Whitman adv. for medicines sold at his store; dated Walpole, 9 Oct.

===== ¶ [3c] MARRIED. =====

In [Bury?], (Eng.) after a *tedious* courtship of two days, Mr. James Whittle, farmer, to Miss Alice Horrocks. The united ages of this brace of *tender chickens* are 143 years.—In Northampton, Mr. John [Biege?], of Brattleborough, to Miss Hannah Strong, of Northampton.—In Keene, Mr. Noah Smith, to Miss Nancy Blake.
In Cornish, by the Rev. Joseph Rowell, Thomas Penniman, Esq. of Washington, to Mrs. Zurviah Dudley, of the former place.

===== ¶ [3c] DIED. =====

In England, His Royal Highness, the Duke of Gloucester, &c. He was the last of the four Princes who, with the King of England, composed the Male issue of Frederick, Prince of Wales.—The Rt. Hon. George Busly [Villiers?], Earl of Jersey, Viscount [?] of G. Britain, and Viscount Grandison of Ireland, aged 71.—In Ireland, the Rt. Hon. Parry Yelverton, Viscount Avonmore, Chief Baron of the Court of Exchequer in Ireland.—In St. Domingo His Imperial Majesty Dessalines, Emperor of Hayti.—It is presumed he will be succeeded by Gen. Christophe.—In Charleston, (S.C.) Hon. Wm. Marshall, one of the judges of the Court of Equitty.—Mr. Charles Morgan;—three black persons, in consequence of eating a cake, in which arsenick had been accidentally mixed with the flour; the recovery of 5 others who ate the cake is doubtful.—In New York, at his seat in the Bowery, Petres Stuyvesant, Esq.—In Boston, Mr. Benj. Burt, aged 76.—In Troy, Mrs. Mary Penniman, wife of Mr. O. Penniman.—In Hudson, widow Abigail Armstrong, aged 85.—In Alstead, on the 1st inst. Widow Elizabeth Hartwell, aged 86, formerly of Lunenburg, Mass.—At Wakefield, by the fall of a tree, Mr. John M. Johnson, aged 46.—In Portsmouth, Madam Elizabeth Lowel, aged 97.—In Springfield, Miss Lydia Warner, aged 79.—In Unity, Mr. Amasa Powers, of Woodstock, aged 49 : His death was occasioned by a waggon running over him. In Danbury, Mr. Major Taylor, aged 62.—At South Farms, near Litchfield, Dr. Seth Bird, aged 73, an eminent physician.—In Middlesex, (N.J.) Col. Gershom Dunn.—In Charleston, (S.C.) Major General William Moultrie.

Vol. XII (No. 656) Saturday, 26 Oct. 1805.

¶ [3a] At the last session of the supreme Court of Vermont, Asa Bucknam plead guilty to an indictment charging him with arson, in burning a new building, the property of Levi Barnard Esq. of Lunenburg. The court sentenced him to stand in the pillory two successive days, one hour in each, and to be whipped twenty five lashes; which sentence has been put into execution.
† [3b] Rev. Alvan Somers ordained at the Church of Christ, Spencertown, N.Y.; Rev. Samuel Harris ordained at Windham, N.H.; Rev. Fessenden Smith, formerly of Rowe, "installed to the care of the two Churches and Societies in Mendon."
† [3c] Levi Haward and Willard Carleton dissolve their copartnership, *Levi Hayward & Co.*; dated at Acworth 21 Oct. 1805.
† [3d] Advertisement and promotions for "Dr. Rawson's Anti-Bilious and Stomach Bitters," including a letter from Walter Bingham, dated at Charlestown, N.H., 27 April 1805, stating that ". . . In the month of August the dysentery, with the most alarming symptoms, broke out in this vicinity, and proved uncommonly mortal; there was no family in my neighbourhood, except my own, but had this dreadful malady. I had eight in my family . . . " Also, Dr. John Wilcox, of Vergennes plugged the product, which was offered for sale by I. Thompson of New London.
† [3d] Legal notice regarding the insolvent estate of Jacob C. Jewett, late of Goshen, deceased. Micah Morse, Benjamin Willey, and Hezekiah Emerson appointed Commissioners; claims to be examined at the dwelling house of Daniel True, Goshen. Notice dated at Goshen 18 Oct. 1805.

¶ [3b] MARRIED.

In Lebanon, Mr. Jabez Edwards to Miss Sophia Simonds.—In Lansingburgh, Mr. Sylvanus F. Penniman, bookseller, to Miss Olive Fitch.

At Groton, (Vt.) the 10th inst. by the Rev. Wm. Hall, Mr. David Stickney, aged 73, to the Widow Rachel Putnam, aged 72 [. . .]

¶ [3b] DIED.

In Philadelphia, Mr. Wm. Lancaster, pr.—On his passage from London to Philadelphia, Mr. John Churchman, celebrated for his useful magnetic charts in finding the longitude at sea.—In Woodstock, Vt. (suicide) Jason Richardson, by drowning, aged 44.—In Springfield, Mr. David Nichols, jun. aged 20.—At Berwick, Mrs. Eunice Taber.—In Granby, Mr. John Gifford, in the 95th year of his age.—He has left a widow, aged 88, with whom he lived in a marriage state 70 years and one month.—At Shrewsbury, Mr. Elnathan Allen, aged 77 : Mr. Jonathan Stone, aged 81 : Widow Grace Harrington, aged 86.—At Shelburne, Capt. Lawrence Kemp, aged 71.—In Dover, (Del.) Wm. Killen, Esq. late chancellor of that state, aged 84.—At Shirley, Mrs. Lydia Whitney, aged 56, wife of the Rev. Phinehas Whitney.—At Sturbridge, on the 30th ult. Mr. Daniel Faulkner, jun. aged 45, and on the 1st inst. Mr. Daniel Faulkner, the father, aged 72.—In Kent, (Con.) Mr. Aner Ives, in consequence of a wound by a bayonet from the hand of Zenas Beebe, on a day of Regimental review in Sharon, C.—In Norfolk, (C.) Mrs. Sarah Beach, aged 43.—In New London, Mr. Nathan Miner, aged 51.—In Newburgh, (P.) Maj. Wm. Telford, an old revolutionary officer.—The death of Dessalines, emperor of Hayti, is contradicted.—Suddenly, at Alderney, Lieut. Col. Cuyler, of his Britannic Majesty's 3d Regiment of Foot, son of the late Henry Cuyler, Esq. of the state of New York.

Vol. XII (No. 657) Saturday, 2 Nov. 1805.

† [2d] Article describing hurricane damage in coastal Maine; a Mr. Byeard, at Sedgwick, Maine, was injured, perhaps fatally; also a new house belonging to Messrs. Colby and Bowles was damaged at Blue Hill, Maine. ♦

† [3a] Mrs. Munger, of Duffin's Creek, in the township of Pitcairn, hunts down a bear, which had carried off a sow belonging to her neighbor, Mrs. Woodruff. Article copied from a paper published at York, Upper Canada, located 23 miles from Pitcairn. ♦

† [2b] Rev. William Bascomb ordained at the Congregational Church in Fitchburg, Mass.; Rev. Mr. Chadwick installed over the Congregational Church at Hanover, Mass.; Rev. David Southerland installed at the Congregational Church in Bath, N.H., and Rev. Abner Kneeland installed at Langdon.

† [3c] W.K. Atkinson, of Dover, N.H. offers property for sale at Westminster, Vt., including one farm apparently occupied by Judge Hall.

¶ [3b] MARRIED.

In Brookfield, (Ms.) Mr. David H. Sumner, of Claremont, (N.H.) to Miss Martha B. Foxcroft, of the former place.—In New London, (C.) [Firah?] Isham, Esq. to Miss Sally Starr, daughter of Jonathan Starr, Esq.—In Wethersfield, Mr. Daniel Buck, jun. mer. of Hartford, to Miss Julia Mitchell, daughter of the Hon. S.M. Mitchell, Esq.—In Leominster, (Mass.) Mr. Mark Farley, to Miss Lucretia Gardner, daughter of the Rev. Francis Gardner.—In Portsmouth, Mr. Nathaniel S. Peirce, one of the printers of the New Hampshire Gazette, to Miss Sally Greenough.

At Chester, (Ver.) John P. Williams, Esq. Attorney at Law, to Miss Rachel Dodge, both of that town.

¶ [3b-c] DIED.

In Charleston, (S.C.) Lieut. N. Fanning, commanding officer of Gunboat No. 1 Æt. 51. He was a native of Connecticut, and a good officer.—In Northampton, Deacon Aaron Cook, aged 77.—In Sidmouth, (Eng.) Dr. James Currie, late of Liverpool, physician, and F.R.S.—An author, scholar, and practioner, of great eminence.—In N. Orleans, Lt. Col. Butler, of the U.S. army.—In Pennsylvania, Andrew Robinson, Esq. one of the associate Judges of the county of York.—In N. York, from 5th to 12th Oct. 16 men, 17 women, 14 boys and 8 girls—total 65 [sic] ; of bilious fever 3, malignant fever, 29. typhus fever 1.—In Chelsea, Miss Hannah Floyd, aged 70.—In Menotomy, widow

Mary Frost, aged 88.—In Boston, Mr. John M'Lane, aged 83 ; Mrs. Hannah, consort of the Hon. Joseph Gardner, Esq. aged 81.—In Norwich, (Con.) the Widow Dennis, aged 86.—In Franklin, Rev. John Ellis, aged 78.—In Hartford, (C.) Capt. Jeremiah Taber, aged 83.—In Lyme, C. Mrs. Mary Lee, relict of the late Rev. Joseph Lee, in the 99th year of her age.—In Hermitage, (in Genesee county, N.Y.) Mrs. Stilwell, killed by a tree falling on her as she was riding on a visit to her friends, with a child in her lap, which was also killed.—Her husband, Mr. Samuel Stilwell, was killed just three weeks previous, at the raising of a house.—In Albany, Mr. Ephraim Hunt, aged 46 : He served as an officer in the late revolutionary war, and was a member of the society of Cincinnati.—In Hanover, (N.Y.) Mr. Daniel Tuttle, aged 81.—In Providence, His Excellency Arthur Fenner, Esq. Governor of the state of Rhode Island.—In Paris, the cidevant Duke D'Fitzjames.—In Dublin, Mrs. Mayne, alias Sally M'Lean, a noted Cyptian; she left property to the amount of 4000 *l.*—In New Orleans, Dr. Hull, a surgeon's mate in the U.S. army.—In Dover, (Del.) William Killen, Esq. aged 84, late Chancellor of the state of Delaware.—In Rutland, (Ms.) Dr. John Frink, aged 74, president of the medical society of Worcester county.—In Biddeford, widow Mary Tarbox, aged 94 ; she lived 57 years with her husband ; her descendants were 14 children, 95 grand-children, 313 of the 3d generation; total 423.—In Springfield, (Mass.) Mrs. Experience Bliss, aged 90 ; Mr. Justin Bliss, aged 43.—In Northampton, Mrs. Mary Lyman, relict of the late Capt. Joseph Lyman, aged 74 ; Miss Naomi Bartlett, aged 73.—In Beverly, Sept. 10, after nearly a week's sickness, Mr. Wm. Lovett, aged 27, leaving a widow and two children.—Oct. 14, after a fortnight's sickness, Mr. John Lovett, aged 36, and Oct. 22d, after a fortnight's sickness, his widow, Mrs. Hannah Lovett, aged 35, leaving four orphan children.—In Scituate, Mrs. Barnes, consort of the Rev. Dr. Barnes.—In Quincy, Mrs. Mary Bracket, relict of the late Moses B. Esq. aged 76.—*Interments in Boston, from Friday, Oct. 18, to Thursday following, both included, 24; of whom 17 were adults.*—In England, Lt. Col. Cuyler, eldest son of the late Henry Cuyler, Esq. of Greenbush, (N.Y.)—In Baltimore, from 14th to 21st inst. 14 adults, and 12 children.—In Philad. from 12th to 19th inst. 41 ad. and 18 ch.—Mr. Adam Stricker, aged 56.—In New Haven, Mrs. Jane Noyes, aged 80.—In Shelburne, Capt. Lawrence Kemp, aged 71.—In Provincetown, wid. Elizabeth Newcomb, aged 63.—In Hopkinton, Maj. Thos. Mellan, aged 48.—In Dorchester, Mr. Sam'l Blackman, aged 48. In Dedham, Mr. Wm. Savils, aged 63.—In Salem, widow Osgood, aged 84.—In Reading, Mr. Thomas Stimpson, aged 71.—In Dorchester, Mr. Sam'l Mellish, aged 76.—In Boston, John Cutler, Esq. aged 82 : Mr. Jeffry Richardson, Æt. 63.

Vol. XII (No. 658) Saturday, 9 Nov. 1805.

† [2b] Article describing the collapse of "a great part of the bank under the bluff" into the river at Natchez, Mississippi. No lives were lost, but several persons lost property, including "Mr. Lee, an industrious young man, from Boston, the widow Chisholm, the estate of Daniel Barney, and Mr. John Callender." ♦

† [2b-c] William B. Carpenter and Roswell Carpenter, brothers belonging to Barton, Orleans County, Vermont, arrested 8 Oct. at New London, Conn., for counterfeiting. ♦

¶ [3a] We are sorry to learn that the *Courier of New Hampshire*, a paper lately printed at Concord by Mr. George Hough, and which was the uniform advocate of correct politics and morals, is now discontinued.

¶ [3b] On Saturday morning, the 2d instant, the blacksmith shop belonging to Mr. Samuel Hedge, of Windsor, was consumed by fire.

¶ [3b] Ordained to the pastoral charge of the fifth church and congregation in Gloucester, Rev. David Jewett.

† [3c] Adv. by Benjamin Belcher for the Springfield Furnace "being now in blast," and one by *J.&H. Dwight* who operate at store at Springfield, Mass. Dated 21 Oct.

† [3c] Samuel Finlay and James Dickey, 2d, Guardians of Robert Lyons, "Lunatic," obtain a license to sell property owned by Lyons at Acworth. Property to be sold at auction at Amos Keyes, innholder at Acworth; dated 6 Nov. 1805.

† [3d] Adv. for "Newton's Highly Approved Essence of Peppermint," developed by Israel Newton of Norwich, Vermont.

¶ [3b] MARRIED.

In Claremont, (N.Y.) Peter R. Livingston, Esq. of New York, to Miss Joana Livingston.—In New London, (Con.) Capt. Wm. Harris, to Mrs. Elizabeth Hempstead.—In Dunstable, (N.H.) Major Gen. Stephen Abbot, of Salem, to Miss Mary Badger, of the former place.—In Danvers, the Rev. William Black, of Salisbury, to Miss Mary Wadsworth, eldest daughter of ther Rev. Mr. Wadsworth, of the former place.— In Norton, Mr. Melatiah Everett, attorney at law, to Miss Nancy Shaw.—In Windsor, Mr. Moses Currier, (a Methodist priest) of Hartland, to Miss Charlotte Story:—Mr. Jonas Blanchard, to Miss Nabby Perry.

¶ [3b] DIED.

In Chelsea College, (Eng.) Robert Swinfield, a pensioner, aged 155 years.—and Abrahm Mois, aged 100—both of whom retained their faculties to the last.—In Virginia, Sir P. [Skipwith?], aged 62.—In Norfolk, Rev. John M'Christie, Baptist minister.—In Hamden, (Ct.) Simeon Bristol, Esq. late Judge of New Haven County Court.—In Franklin, (Con.) Rev. John Ellis, aged 78.—In Northampton, Dr. Levi Shepherd.—In Portsmouth, Mrs. Phebe Treadwell, aged 85.—In Scituate, 22d ult. Rachel, the wife of the Rev. Dr. Barnes, aged 78 y. 3 mo.—daughter of the Hon. George Leonard, deceased.—In Boston, Mr. Peter Trott, aged 33.—In New London, Mr. John [Pineveret?], formerly a French Commercial Agent, aged 59 years.—In Windsor, (Vt.) Mr. Isaac Lyon.—In Middlebury, Mrs. Diana Schuyler, aged 24.—In Cornish, Oct. 25, Mr. James Fitch, aged 23.—In Trenton, Mr. Wm. Roscoe, aged 73.—In Danbury, (C.) Mrs. Sarah Crosut, aged 70; instantly killed by a fall from a waggon.—In Hartford, Capt. Jeremiah Taber, aged 84.—At Sullivan, Mr. James Rowe, aged 74; death caused by intoxication.—In Wethersfield, (Ver.) 1st inst. Mr. Thaddeus Bond, in the 89th year of his age, a native of Watertown, (Ms.) and late of Tolland, (C.)—At Newbury, (Ver.) Mr. Charles C. Walker; his death was the consequence of his great joy at the successful amputation of one of his legs, which had been broken.—In Chester, (Ver.) Mrs. Lucy Hazelton, consort of Dr. John Hazelton, aged 40.—In Leonardtown, (Md.) Mr. Samuel Jameson Maginnis, the celebrated puppet-shewman, aged 33.—In New Jersey, Dr. William Delany, of Philadelphia.—In New York, Mr. Henry Piingle [sic], proprietor of the *N.Y. Daily Advertiser.*—In Greenfield, (Ms.) Mrs. Abigail Newton, consort of the Rev. Roger Newton, D.D. aged 67.—In Dedham, 15th ult. Mr. John Ellis, mer.—he completed his 70th year on the day of his death.—In Roxbury, Mr. Samuel Warren, aged 60.—In Ipswich, (Mass.) Mr. James Smith, of Linebrook, aged 66.—In Amherst, (N.H.) Miss Jane Means, daughter of Robert Means, Esq. aged 17.—In Methuen, Mr. Timothy Eaton, aged 70.—In Middlebury, of a consumption, Mr. David Allen, aged 45.—In Addison, Mrs. Louis [sic] Strong, consort of Deac. Oliver Strong, aged 62.—In Fairfield, Major William Buck.—In Williston, Doctor Thomas Benney, aged 66 years, late of Tyringham, (Ms.) He was a distinguished surgeon, and an eminent patriot in the American revolution.—In Thetford, Mrs. Burton, consort of the Rev. Asa Burton, D.D.

Drowned.—At Enfield, Mr. Hewet Stockwell, and Mr. Elijah Fish.

Vol. XII (No. 659) Saturday, 16 Nov. 1805.

† [2d] Fire destroys a hatter shop occupied by Mr. Nathaniel Mower at Worcester; the store of Mr. Daniel Waldo, Jr., and the home of Dr. Dix were saved. [31 Oct.? 1805] ♦

¶ [3a] *Melancholy event.*—On Friday the 1st inst. as a son of Jairus Hall, Esq. of Wilmington, about ten years old, was diverting himself with the body of a cart which had been turned up against the fence in a heedless manner, it fell upon him and fractured his skull in a shocking manner. He expired in about fifteen minutes. [*Brattleboro' Reporter.*]

† [3b] The Committee of Benevolence in Charleston, S.C. requests financial assistance to the widow and infants of Mr. Lunzies, "late apothecary at Cape Francios." ♦

† [3c] Amasa and Oliver Allen offer reward for the capture of Nathan Eldridge, accused in the robbery of their store in Oct. 1804. Eldridge was of Westminster, Vt., but was formerly from Mansfield, Conn., a blacksmith by trade, and about 33 years old. The adv. contains the suspect's physical description, as well as a list of towns in New England and New York where he was known to have connections. ♦ 146

† [3c] David Stone adv. for his store at Walpole; dated 10 Nov. 1805.

¶ [3c] MARRIED.

In Watertown, (Ms.) Mr. James Prentiss, of Boston, to Miss Sophia Mellen.

¶ [3c] DIED.

In Savannah, (Geo.) Capt. Alexander Small, late master of the brig Ruby, of Portland:—Capt. Stephen Brown, late master of the brig Goorge, of Gloucester.—In Lyme, (Con.) in the compass of five days, Mr. John Anderson, his son, his granddaughter, and his gr. grand-child, all under the same roof.—At Enfield, on the 13th of June, Charity, the wife of Mr. John Abbe, aged 67, and on the 17th of October, Mr. John Abbe, aged 66;—Of a consumption, on the 20th instant, Mrs. Abigail Lee, of Colebrook, consort of the Rev. Chauncey Lee, in the 36th year of her age.—At Tolland, very suddenly, the 18th of October, Mr. Thomas Howard, aged 61.—At Wallingford, Doct. Billious Kirtland, in the 44th year of his age.—In Charleston, (S.C.) the 19th ult. Mr. Loring Andrews, late one of the proprietors and editors of the *Charleston Courier*, aged 38. He was born at Hingham, in Massachusetts, and is well known as an able, intelligent and independent Editor; a frank and honest man.—In Pennsylvania, Miss Margaret Dalton, aged 116 years, 8 months & 10 days, a native of Tyrone, Ireland.—In N. York, Mr. Josias Ten Eyck, principal clerk in the post office.—In Dedham, Mrs. Elizabeth Scarborough, aged 81, daughter of the late Hon. Wm. Dudley, Esq. of Roxbury.—At Cambridge, of a consumption, Wm. Watson, jun. A.B. aged 20.—In Charlestown, Ms. Mrs. Helen Lucinda Harris, aged 22, consort of Capt. Thomas Harris, jun.—In Boston, Mrs. Susannah Sohier, aged 74 : Mr. Richard Jennins, aged 48.—In Troy, (N.Y.) Mrs. Catherine Storer, aged 54.—In Montague, Ms. Miss Sally Church, aged 21.—In Chester, Vt. Mr. David Stedman, aged 53.—In Lewistown, (Penn.) Edward M'Carty, Esq. sheriff of Misslin county.—In Lexington, (Ken.) Mr. Patrick Gullion, supposed to be considerably above one hundred years old.—In Princeton, Mrs. Susannah Rolph, aged 80.

In this town, yesterday morning, Mr. Samuel Trott, aged 76.—In the various situations of life he proved a useful member of society, and an honest man.

Vol. XII (No. 660) Friday, 23 Nov. 1805.

† [2c] Execution at Windham, Conn., of Sam Freeman, a mulatto, who murdered Hannah Simons, an Indian woman. Freeman was 25 years old. ♦

¶ [2d] Providence, Rhode Island, Nov. 9. *Accident.*—On Wednesday evening last, Mr. Timothy Thayer fell from the top to the bottom of a pair of stairs in his house, which instantly put a period to his life.—A Coroner's inquest was called the next day, who pronounced that he came to his death by a dislocation of the neck, occasioned by an accidental fall down a pair of stairs.

† [2d] Extensive article detailing the suicide of Deacon Abel Stockwell, aged 60, of Chesterfield, N.H., the 11th of Nov. 1805. ♦

† [2d] Account of the fire which destroyed the home of Mr. Ebenezer Sibley, of Sutton, Mass., 9 Nov. 1805. The article mentions a "maiden sister of Mr. Sibley, living in the house." ♦

† [2d] The oil mill of Samuel Smith, Esq., of Peterborough, N.H., destroyed by fire. ♦

† [2d-3a] A man by the name of Lyon was robbed and murdered at Wilbraham, Mass., 9 Nov. 1805, supposedly by two Irishmen. "Mr. Lyon belonged to Woodstock, (Con.) and was on his way home from the state of Newyork . . . " 147

† [3b] Rev. William B. Wesson ordained 30 Oct. 1805 at Hardwick, Mass.

† [3b] George Dennison, "Black Ball maker," adv. to his creditors, that if they will wait a little longer, they will be paid.

† [3c] Daniel Buck, jun. & Co. adv. the store "near the ferry," Hartford, Conn; 15 Nov.

† [3c] Stephen Stewart adv. for his new and improved fire engine, for which he obtained a patent; dated Walpole, 20 Nov. 1805.

¶ [3b] MARRIED.

In Roxbury, the Rev. Joseph Grafton, Pastor of the Baptist Church in Newton, to Miss Hannah Parker, of the former place.—In Boston, the Rev. Wilkes Allen, of Chelmsford, to Miss Mary Morrill, of Boston.—At Fitchburg, Mr. Samuel Cowdin, to Miss Betsey Goodridge.—At Burlington, Mr. Jesse Hollister, to Miss Clarissa Hurlburt.

—In Chesterfield, Mr. Lemuel Warner, to Mrs. Elizabeth Stone.—In Northfield, Mr. Theodore Henidale, jun. to Mrs. Francis [sic] Lyman.—In Suffield, (Con.) Mr. Asahel Strong, of Northampton, to Miss Aura Ferry.

===== ¶ [3b] DIED. =====

In Savannah, Mr. James Johnston, pilot, a native of Wethersfield, Con.—In Fredericksburg, (Vir.) Hon. Joseph Jones, aged 78, one of the Judges of the General Court of Virginia.—In Boston, Mrs. Sarah Dana, relict of the late Rev. Josiah Dana, of Barre.—In Westmoreland, the 9th inst. Miss Prudence Temple, aged 16.—In Northampton, Mrs. Rachel Parsons, wife of Mr. Joseph Parsons, aged 84.—At Phelps, (N.Y.) Mr. James Robinson, aged 26 : death occasioned by a wound received at a training.—At Geneva, Mr. John M'Curdy.—In Richmond, (Vir.) Henry Benskin Lightfoot, Esq. of the island Antigua.—He was a native of Virginia.—In Attleborough, Wid. Margaret Tingley, aged 90.—In Haverhill, Mr. Nathaniel Clark, aged 77.—In Chesterfield, Mr. John Stephenson, aged 87.

Drowned.—In Monson, on the evening of the 14th ult. Capt. David Hyde, aged 63—He was attempting to cross a bridge which had no railing on the sides, and it being very dark, walked off, and fell into a mill pond.

Vol. XII (No. 661) Tuesday, 3 Dec. 1805.

¶ [2d] Madame Jerome Bonaparte, and child, with her brother, Mr. Robert Patterson, have arrived at Baltimore, from England.

¶ [2d] *Horrible Murder!*—On the night of the 10th inst. a man named Abel Clemmons, at his place of residence upon the lands of Col. George Jackson, near Clarksburg, (Virg.) under circumstances of the most unprecedented cruelty, murdered his wife far advanced in pregnancy, and their 8 small children, the eldest about 12 years old, by striking them on the head with an axe while they were asleep in three separate beds, lying in the same room ! He escaped. [148]

† [3a-b] Article copied from the *Middlebury Mercury*, describing the ordeal of two men lost in a snowstorm in New York State. Mr. Samuel Stone, of the 4th township in St. Lawrence County, and Truman Skeels, son of Mr. Truman Skeels of Chesterfield, set out in early Oct. to survey for a road in St. Lawrence county. Skeels, aged 20, lost his way, and froze to death. ♦

¶ [3b] The two persons who are said to have committed the late murder in Wilbraham, (Mass.) were taken in Rye, about 30 miles from New York. They are both Irishmen, one of the name of James Hilligan, who has been in this country about three years; the other of the name of Dominic Daly, and has been from Ireland only about nine months. The latter says he has a brother and other connexions in Boston.

† [3c] Description of the new bridge at Springfield, Mass; Mr. Walcott, of Windham, Conn. and Mr. Reed, of Harvard, Mass. were the builders.

† [3c] John Bellows adv. for a stray steer on his property; dated Walpole, 27 Nov. '05.

† [3c] Adv. by S. & L. Pulsifer for lost horses; dated Plainfield 20 Nov, though the horses strayed "from the Drove of the subscribers, in Westmoreland."

===== ¶ [3c] MARRIED. =====

In Concord, (Mass.) Mr. John Ballard, jun. mer. of Boston, to Miss Louisa Paine, daughter of the late Maj. Paine.—In Greenfield, Elijah Alvord, Esq. of Greenwich, to Miss Sarah Wells.—At Charlestown, John M. Foster, Esq. attorney at law, to Mrs. Alice Carlisle, relict of the late Samuel Carlisle.—In the society of Westhaven, (Con.) on the 22d Sept. last, Mr. Nathaniel Charter, one of the printers of the *Political Observatory*, to Miss Lovina Trowbridge, daughter of Capt. David T.—In Keene, Dr. J.H. Bradford, to Miss Sally Ralston:—Mr. Thomas P. Batchelder, to Miss Anna Baker.

===== ¶ [3c] DIED. =====

In Columbia, (S.C.) Maj. Joshua Benson, aged 53.—At Rocky Mount, (S.C.) Col. Francis Menther, a native of Deux Ponts, (France)—he served with honour and respectability throughout the American revolution; and for several years since the war, was adjutant-general of the militia of Pennsylvania.—In Lexington, (Ms.) the Rev. Jonas Clark, aged 75.—the fifty-first year of his ministry.—In Roxbury, Capt. Lemuel May, aged 67.—In Boston, Mrs. Elizabeth Vickery, aged 79.—At Halifax, on the 20th Oct.

Miss Lucy Orvis, in her 28th year : on the 23d, Mr. Wm. Willcox, aged 41 : on the 25th, Miss Phebe Willcox, aged 20 : on the 26th, Mrs. Peggy Richardson, consort of Dr. Samuel Richardson, aged 37 : Nov. 6th, Miss Hannah Green, aged 20.—At Rye, Mr. James Perkins, aged 71.—

Drowned.—Near Norwalk, (C.) Mr. Wm. B. St. John, merchant, of that place.—Near Quebec, on the 26th Oct. Mr. Simon Frazer, his nephew, Mr. John M'Millan, Miss Catherine M'Millan, and Joseph Carrier.—In Bolton, (Ms.) Sarah Fry, of the society of Friends, aged 24, wife of Jonathan Fry, and daughter of Robert Earl, of Leicester.

Vol. XII (No. 662) Friday, 6 Dec. 1805.

¶ [3b] The paper mills belonging to Mr. Boies, of Milton, were lately consumed by fire. They were occupied by Tileston & Hollingsworth, whose loss is estimated at 6000 dollars.

† [3c] Rev. Ignatus Thompson ordained at Pomfret.

† [3c] Samuel Bellows adv. a stray mare on his property; dated Charlestown, 1 Dec.

† [3c] Chester Bingham posts a notice for his runaway wife, Deborah, who "behaved herself in a very unbecoming manner." Dated at Chesterfield, 3 Dec. 1805.

===== ¶ [3c] MARRIED. =====

In Barnard, (Ver.) Mr. John Hammond, of Woodstock, to Mrs. Wing, of the former place.—In Portsmouth, Mr. Wm. Yeaton, mer. of Alexandria, (Vir.) to Miss Lucy Chauncey, daughter of the Hon. Charles Chauncey, Esq.—In Georgetown, (Md.) Mr. Peter M[elin?], aged 69, to Mrs. M'Fee, aged 54.

===== ¶ [3c] DIED. =====

In France, Joseph Alex. de Segur, author of the Treatise on Women, and brother to the Chamberlain of Napoleon I.—In Philad. Mrs. Mary, consort of Mr. Thomas Bradford, Editor of the True American.—At Manheim, (Penn.) the Rev. John F. [Ernst?], the Lutheran minister of that town and the adjoing congregation.—In New York, from the 9th to the 16th Nov. 11 men, 14 women, 7 boys and 4 girls—10 of consumption.—In North Providence, Edward Smith, Esq. aged 73 ; late a member of the General Assembly of R.I.—In Essex, (Ver.) Mrs. Sarah, consort of Maj. Lloyd ; the Major is thus a disconsolate widower for the *fifth* time.—In Boston, Mr. Richard Hunnewell, aged 73 : Mr. Isaac Hall, aged 66.—At Peterboro', Mrs. Hannah Porter, aged 56.—In Hartford, Mrs. Maria, wife of Mr. Henry Hudson, and daughter of his Ex. Gov. Trumbull, aged 20.—In Preston, (Con.) Capt. Eleazer Prentice, aged 70.—In Brookfield, (Ms.) Mr. Stephen Martin, aged 71, formerly of Andover.—In Templeton, suddenly, Rev. Ebenezer Sparhawk, aged 67.—In New York, Mr. John Callahan, aged 53 ; the eldest and best pilot of the port of N. York.—In Boston, Mrs. Mary Franck, aged 81.—In Bloomingdale, (N.Y.) Israel Wilkes, Esq. aged 86.

Drowned.—At Enfield Falls, (Con.) Mr. Elijah Fisk, and Mr. Hewett Storkwell ; both young married men.—In New York harbor, Mr. Abraham Osborne, aged 26.

Vol. XII (No. 663) Friday, 13 Dec. 1805.

¶ [3c] DIED.]—In Mifflin county, (P.) Miss Margaret Dolton, aged 116 y. 3 m. and 10 d. —In Sutton, (Mass.) Mr. Jonas Woodward, aged 70 : Mrs. Hannah Morse, aged 52.—In Cooperstown, (N.Y.) Mr. Christopher Babbitt, aged 76.—In Westminster, (Ver.) Mr. Richardson.

SUICIDE.—In Hartwick, (N.Y.) supposed to be in consequence of religious melancholy, Mrs. Holden.

† [3c] List of nonresident proprietors and owners of land in the town of Washington, N.H., who are delinquent on their taxes for the year 1804, as compiled by Ebenezer Jaquith, *Collector.* The notice, dated at Washington 29 Nov. 1805, gives a breakdown of lot number, acreage, etc., though only the names of the owners are presented here:

Thomas Parker	Moses Mann	Benjamin Swett
Peter Peirce	Jacob Chace	Nehemiah Jones
Isaac Davenport	Ebenezer Temple	Jonas Stratton
Stephen Austin	Reuben Brown	Allen & Sowers

† [3c] Joseph Bellows adv. goods for sale; also "Good house ashes will be received at his pot-ash near Gilbert Griswold's Tavern; dated Walpole, 11 Dec. 1805.

¶ [3d] RAN AWAY from the subscriber on the night of the 7th November last, *Samuel Rice*, an indented apprentice, about twenty years of age. All persons are prohibited harbouring or trusting him on my account. Whoever will take up and return said apprentice to me, shall receive one cent reward, but no thanks, nor any charges paid.

SAMUEL BROWN.

Plainfield, N.H. Dec. 3, 1805.

† [3d] Notice from David Carter, Treasurer, regarding the 3rd N.H. Turnpike Road, dated at Marlboro', 2 Dec. 1805.

Vol. XII (No. 664) Friday, 20 Dec. 1805.

¶ [3c] Mr. Deming, late postmaster at Hinsdale, was committed to Pittsfield gaol on suspicion of having robbed the mail of considerable sums of money going from Albany to Messrs. Thomas & Andrews and Mr. John West, of Boston. He has since procured bail in the sum of 2500 dollars.

† [3c] J. Risque, Esq. and Mr. Thomas Beale fought a duel at Fincastle, Va.; Risque was shot in the side, and may recover.

† [3c] Legal notice regarding the estate of Elisha Kingsbery, late of Alstead, deceased; Amos Shepard, "Administrator de bonis non." Dated at Alstead, 13 Dec. 1805.

† [3d] Josiah Bellows, 2d, David Stone, and Joseph Heaton announce the dissolution of Partnership of *Bellows & Stone*, by mutual consent. Also, the copartnership of *Joseph Heaton & Co.*, of Acworth, is likewise dissolved. Dated at Walpole, 19 Dec. 1805.

===== ¶ [3c] MARRIED. =====

In this town, on the 17th inst., by the Rev. Pliny Dickinson, Mr. John H. Perry to Miss Matilda Williams.

===== ¶ [3c] DIED. =====

In Boston, Mr. John Stillman, son of the Rev. Samuel Stillman, aged 33 ; Mrs. Penelope Adams, aged 70.—In Salem, Miss Hannah Bassett, aged 90.—In Harpersfield, Col. Joel Mack, aged 44.—In Hartford, Dr. Asa Hopkins, aged 48.—In Portsmouth, Mr. John Obie, aged 27.—Very suddenly, in Norwich, (C.) Mr. Daniel Huntington, aged 43.—In Lime, Mr. Isaiah Howard, aged 78.—

☞ DEPARTED this life, in the city of Richmond, on Monday the 28th day of October last, the Hon. Henry Benskin Lightfoot, Esq. aged about 58 years, late of the island of Antigua; respected and regretted by all who knew him.

NOTICE.—If Francis Lightfoot, a native of the county of New Kent, and formerly a resident of the state of Virginia, he now living, or has any legal heir or descendant living, either in the United States or elsewhere, by applying either in person or by special agent, and producing sufficient evidence of their being such legal descendant, to William or Nicholas Lightfoot, of the county of James' City, to Gen. or Lightfoot Poindexter, of New Kent, or to James Poindexter, of Powhatan, will hear of something highly important and much to their advantage.

The Printers throughout the United States are requested to insert the above twice in their respective papers, and transmit their accompts to the editor of the Inquirer.

☞ The friends of William Dudly and Chester Dudly his son, living in the state of New York, are hereby informed that each of the above named persons departed this life on the 29th of October, at my house in the county of Dinwiddie, Virginia, and 26 miles south of Petersburgh. There remain in my care 6 mules, several bonds, and some specie. Those who are lawfully empowered to receive the above property are requested to make an immediate demand, and bring with them sufficient evidence that they are the proper persons to whom it should be delivered. A certificate to that effect from Mr. Archibald Gracie, of the city of New York, will afford ample testimony.

THEODORICK WALKER.

Vol. XII (No. 665) Friday, 27 Dec. 1805.

¶ [3c] HORRID MURDER.—We understand that a Mr. Burnham, who was confined in the gaol in Haverhill, in this state, in the same room with two others, Col. Russell Freeman and a Mr. Starkweather, watched his opportunity and stabbed them with a sharp knife which he had kept concealed for that purpose. They are both dead. It is said he made several attempts on his own life, but without effect. [149]

† [3c] Mr. Asaph Mitchel, of Deerfield, Mass., "was fired upon by some assassin in the bushes," while traveling from Deerfield to Sunderland, 13 Dec. 1805. ◆

† [3c] Rev. Cornelius Adams ordained over the church and congregation of Scotland Society at Windham, Conn.

===== ¶ [3c] MARRIED. =====

In Worcester, by the Rev. Mr. Bancroft, Capt. James Rowan, of Boston, to Mrs. Eliza Chandler.

===== ¶ [3c-d] DIED. =====

In Athenrie, (Ireland) Dennis Carrobie, aged 117. He married seven times, had 48 children, 236 grand-children, and 944 great-grandchildren; making a total of 1253 descendants.—In Amherst, (N.H.) widow Hannah Lovejoy, aged 101 y. 7 m. and 13 d. She had 11 children, 51 grand-children, 223 great-grand-children, and 51 of the fourth generation; total 336.—In Amherst, (Mass.) 14th inst. the Hon. Simeon Strong, Esq. one of the Judges of the Supreme Judicial Court of the Commonwealth of Massachusetts, in the 70th year of his age.—In Rockingham, Vt. on the 23d ult. Mr. Job House, aged [52?], formerly of Abington, (Mass.)—In Providence, Ebenezer Thompson, Esq. aged 71; naval officer for Providence district.—In Portsmouth, Mrs. Abigail, relict of the Hon. Judge Pickering, aged [63?]; she was eldest daughter of the late Mr. Jacob Sheafe, mer. of Portsmouth.—In Roxbury, Mrs. Martha Parker, relict of the late Mr. Jeremiah Parker, aged 84.—In Hingham, Mr. Wm. Cushing, jun. pr.[150] Æt. 25.

Vol. XII (No. 666) Friday, 3 Jan. 1806.

¶ [2d] Cooperstown, (N.Y.) Dec. 12. *Suicide.*—On Friday morning last, Mr. Jacob I. Cuyler, of Otsego, in this county, on quitting his bed stepped into blood, with which the floor was nearly covered;—near by lay the lifeless body of his wife, with her throat cut, and her left arm gashed to the bone. We are told that she left the bed, in which she lay with her husband, while he was asleep, and perpetrated the horrid act with a razor. She was about 27 years of age, and respectably connected. We have received no details of the reasons of the rash act but have reason to suppose that religious fanaticism, & some family disagreement, led to the fatal catastrophe.

¶ [3a] A deer was killed, last Sunday, in Scarborough, by a Mr. Coolbroth; the quarters weighed 124 pounds—he was walking with some cattle, within 40 rods of the post-road. [*Portland paper,* Dec. 13.

¶ [3b] *Another murder.*—By the last *Amherst* Cabinet, it appears that on the evening of the 12th ult. Mr. Peier [sic] Severance, of Chester, inhumanly fired at and killed Mr. Benjamin Wicher, of Boscawen, and badly wounded another:—the murderer is committed to Exeter gaol. [151]

¶ [3b] It is said a duel has been lately fought between Major Jackson, and Mr. D.W. Cox, both of Philadelphia;—subject of dispute the President's Message.

† [3c] Barn belonging to Mr. Stoddard burned at Westminster, Vt.

† [3c] Mr. William Joiner of Waitsfield, Vt. suffers a close call by a tree which fell and killed the horse he was riding on. ♦

===== ¶ [3d] MARRIED. =====

In Rutland, (Ver.) Mr. Wm. D. Smith, to Miss Fanny Chipman.—In Royalton, Mr. Ephraim W. Besbee, to Miss Charity Lathrop.—In Brandon, Dr. Joel Green, to Miss Lucy Horton.—In Lunenburg, Mr. James Patterson, of Dunstable, to Miss Sally Stearns.—In Marietta, (Ohio) Mr. Ebenezer Buckingham, jun. to Miss Catharine Putnam, daughter of Gen. Rufus Putnam, all of Marietta.

In Westminster, (Vt.) on Wednesday evening last, by the Rev. Mr. Sage, Mr. John A. Graham, of Chesterfield, to Miss Priscilla Eaton, daughter of Maj. Isaiah Eaton, of the former place.

===== ¶ [3d] DIED. =====

In Paris, (France) Capt. J. Wright, of the British navy—a prisoner in the Temple. The French papers say he committed suicide, after hearing the defeat of the Austrian army. The English papers hint a suspicion that there was some foul conduct in the death of this distinguished officer.—In Savannah, (Geo.) James Todd, Esq. cashier of the Philadelphia Bank.—In Salem, Mrs. Mary Bowditch, Æt. 68.—In Cambridge, Mrs. Ruth Freeman, aged 72.—In Boston, Mr. Alexander Hill, aged 83.—In Hudson, N.Y. Mr. James Ramsey, aged 62.—In Amherst, Dr. Ebenezer Weston, aged 73.—In Plainfield, on the 10th inst. of a lethargy, Widow Sarah Stoddard, aged about 65.—In Salem, Mr. Wm. Gray, sen. aged [78?].—In Lanesboro,' Deac. Ebenezer Buck, aged 89.—In Shapleigh, Mr. John Ham, aged 100 years, 7 m. and 15 d.—In Winchester, Mrs. Mary Bond, Æt. 60.—In Brookline, (suicide) Mr. Dan'l Dascombe.—In Charleston, (S.C.) Mr. Isaac Cohen, aged 70.—In Washington, Capt. Elisha O. Williams. He was much respected and esteemed; and was one of the few remaining officers of the revolution.—In Westerly, (R.I.) Arnold Clark, Esq. cashier of the Washington bank.—In Portsmouth, Mr. Nathaniel Sherburne, aged 70.—In Kittery, Mrs. Marcy Adams, aged 69.

Vol. XII (No. 667) Friday, 10 Jan. 1806.

¶ [3b] *Fire.*—A new house, the property of Capt. David Francis, of Unadilla, (N.Y.) was lately consumed by fire.

† [3c] Ordinations: Rev. Thomas A. Merril at Middlebury, Vt.; Rev. Charles Lowell, at the West Church in Boston; and at Bath, Rev. Wm. Jenks.

† [3d] *Shepard & Hutchinson* request debtors to pay up, with a notation stating that "all persons indebted to said Shepard, for Goods sold at his store in Marlow, by Wm. Lamphier, are requested to make immediate payment. . . " Dated Alstead 3 Jan. 1806.

† [3d] Legal notice regarding estate of Maj. Elisha Kingsbery, dated Alstead 6 Jan. 1806

====== ¶ [3d] MARRIED. ======
At Charlestown, (N.H.) Mr. Willard Glidden, to Miss Polly [Prouty?].—In Boston, Mr. Daniel Greenleaf Wheeler, of Worcester, to Miss Nancy Clap, of the former place.
====== ¶ [3d] DIED. ======
At Montreal, on the 10th ult. of wounds received in the thigh by a stove, on the upsetting of a sloop, in which he was crossing lake Champlain, Noel de Rocheblave, Esq. Member of the Provincial Parliament for the County of [Surry?].—At Alstead, 28th ult. Wid. Abigail Brown, aged 67.—In Saco, (Me.) a Mr. Nathaniel Brooks, aged about 25, of Buxton; was found dead in the road, supposed to have died in a fit : He was seen a few moments previous in apparent good health, driving his team; observing his team stopping in the road, some person went to it, and a few paces behind it found him lifeless.—In Charlton, Mrs. Dorothy Hammond, wife of Lieut. Moses H. in the 45th year of her age.—In Worcester, Lieut. Isaac Willard, aged 81.—In Salem, Mr. Thomas Nichols, aged 60 ; highly esteemed and deeply regretted.—In Salisbury, Captain Benj. Pettingale.—In Hanover, Mr. Hardy, a student in Dartmouth College ; said to be of the hydrophobia.[*see issue of 17 Jan. 1806.*]—In Shelburne, Miss Malinda Wetherly, aged 12, of wound occasioned by the butting of a furious ram.—In Deerfield, Mr. Hilkiah Howes, aged 46.—In Plaistow, Mr. Ebenezer Noyes, aged 88.—In Haverhill, Mrs. Abigail Alexander aged 61.—In Hartwick, (N.Y.) Mrs. Martha Willard, aged 87 ; Mrs. Mary Clinton, aged [57?].—In Bethlem, on the 10th Nov. Wid. Experience Lewis, in the 92d year of her age.—In Litchfield, (Conn.) on the 28th Nov. of a dropsy, Capt. William Stanton, aged 78; "a zealous patriot in the American revolution."—In Saco, (Maine) Wid. Mary Haley, aged 88—she had 11 children, 51 grand-children, 97 great-grand-children, and one of the 4th generation—total 160.—In Lower Paxton, (Penn.), Mrs. Elizabeth Gilchrist, at an advanced age.—In Mecklenburg county, Col. William Davies. —In Franklin, on the 9th ult. Deacon Peter Whiting, aged 59.

Vol. XII (No. 668) Friday, 17 Jan. 1806. [152]

† [3a-c] List of acts passed by the Legislature, held at Portsmouth in Dec. 1805:
1) An act authorizing Stephen Rowe, otherwise Stephen Brown, to assume the name of Stephen Rowe Brown.
2) An act to authorize William Steel to collect certain taxes.
3) An act to disannex a part of the farm owned by Bracket Weeks, from the town of Stratham, and to annex it to Greenland.
4) An act to authorize Isaac Clement to assume the name of Isaac Langdon Clement, and David Clement the 3d, to assume the name of David Smith Clement.
5) An act to vest in Abel Farr the privilege of keeping a ferry over Connecticut river.
6) An act relating to Samuel Blodget regarding a Lottery for locking Amoskeag Falls.
7) An act authorizing the Judge of Probate for the county of Rockingham to reconsider an account of Nathaniel Giddinge, deceased, of his guardianship of his children by his former wife, Anna Giddinge, deceased, exhibited for allowance by Eliphalet Giddinge, admintrator of the estate of the said Nathaniel Giddinge, deceased.
8) An Act to incorporate William Simpson and his associates and their successors, by the name of the Piermont Turnpike Branch.
9) An act granting to Joseph Cooley an appeal from a Judgement recovered against him before a Justice of the Peace in a criminal prosecution.

† [3a] Ordinations : Rev. Evan Bardsly at Shoreham, Vermont, and Freeman Sears, at Natick.

====== ¶ [3d] MARRIED. ======
In Portland, Capt. William Goddard, to Miss Mary Storer, daughter of the Hon. Woodbury Storer.
====== ¶ [3d] DIED. ======
In Washington, suddenly, the principal Osage (Indian) Chief; one of the Chiefs on a visit to the President of the United States.—In East Sudbury, Maj. Daniel Maynard, aged 39.—In Northampton, Mrs. Esther Phelps, aged 75.—In Providence, (R.I.) Mr. Nath'l Gilmore, aged 71.—In North Providence, Mrs. Phebe Treadwell, aged 82.—In

Rowley, Dr. Amos Spofford, aged 52.—In Woodstock, very suddenly, Mrs. Taylor.—In Monson, Rev. Jesse Ives, pastor of the church in that place.—*The death of Mr. Hardy, of Hanover, mentioned in our last, we learn, was not occasioned by hydrophobia, but by an inflammation of the brain, in consequence of intense mental application.*—In Newcastle, (N.Y.) by a fall from his horse, which broke his arm and leg, and shattered his skull so as to cause instant death, Mr. Thomas Blakey, a respectable inhabitant.—In Dorchester, Mrs. Hannah Preston, aged 44.—In Acton, Mrs. Martha Barker, aged 90.—In Northampton, Mrs. Hannah Wait.—In Williamsburgh, Dr. Francis Manton, aged 42.—In Leyden, Mr. William Fisk, an itinerant person, aged 73.—In Bolton, (C.) a son of Mr. Aaron Strong, being the 14th child he has committed to the grave.

Drowned.]—On his passage from Shelburne, for Halifax, George Gracie Esq. a very respectable merchant of the former place.

Vol. XII (No. 669) Friday, 24 Jan. 1806.

† [2c] Fire on Carpenter St., Salem, Mass. destroys houses belonging to Messrs. Edwards, Chaplin, and Lamson, "on Thursday evening last." [under Boston head, 18 Jan.]
¶ [3c] Mr. James Jarvis, a shoemaker, in Maiden-Lane, New York, is the owner of ticket No. 3928, which on Wednesday last, drew *Twenty Thousand Dollars*, in the lottery drawing there.
† [3c] Rev. Elijah Waterman installed at the Presbyterian Church, Bridgeport, Conn.
† [3d] Legal notice regarding estate of Elisha Kingsbery; dated Alstead 17 Jan. 1806. [153]
† [3d] David Carter adv. a notice regarding a meeting of the Third N.H. Turnpike Corporation, to be held at the house of Jacob Danforth, Innholder in Jaffrey; dated Marlboro, N.H. 25 Jan. 1806.
† [3d] Jonathan Grout adv. for lost livestock; dated Charlestown, 13 Jan. 1806.
† [3d] Ezra Kidder requests debtors to pay up; dated Alstead, 18 Jan. 1806.
† [3d] Legal notice regarding the insolvent estate of William Henry, Jr., late of Charlestown, deceased; Abel Walker, Benjamin Clark, and Horace Hall, Commissioners. [154]

===== ¶ [3c] **MARRIED.** =====

In New Orleans, Capt. Stille, of the U.S. army, to Mrs. Gayoso, widow of the late Governor.
In Lebanon, (Con.) Mr. Eliphalet Huntington, to Miss Nancy Clark.
In Boston, Mr. Joseph Bray, merchant, to Miss Frances Eliot.

===== ¶ [3c-d] **DIED.** =====

At the city of Washington, Major Thomas Smith, one of the officers of the Maryland line during the revolutionary war.—In Philadelphia, Mrs. Hannah Hodge, aged 85.—In Montreal, Francis Masson, Esq. employed as a Botanist by his Britannic Majesty, since 1798 in Upper and Lower Canada, where his researches have been employed from Lake Superior to the Gulph [sic] of St. Lawrence.—In Chesterfield, (Mass.) the Rev. Timothy Allen, aged 91.—In Billerica, Mr. John Farmer, aged 70.—In Roxbury, Wid. Elizabeth Bird, aged 88.—At Hartford, (Ver.) Mrs. Polly Clark, wife of Mr. Mosely Clark.—In Windham, Greene county, New York, killed by the fall of a tree, in the 44th year of his age, Mr. Benajah Ticknor, leaving a widow and eight children to lament the loss of a worthy character. It is not a little remarkable that it is less than nine months since the former possessor of the same farm was killed in the same manner.—In Boston, Capt. Nathaniel Curtis, aged 68.

In New Ipswich, Mr. Isaac [Jofes?], aged 25.—In Norwich, C. Miss Fanny Woodbridge.

In Hingham, Miss Charlotte B. Caldwell, aged 19, daughter of William Caldwell, Esq. late of Worcester. [. . .]

Died, in the First Parish in Springfield, (Mass.) in 1805, 23 persons—12 males and 11 females.—Under 5 years of age, 7 : between 10 and 20, 2 : 20 and 30, 2 : 30 and 40, 4 : 40 and 50, 2 : 60 and 70, 1 : 70 and 80, 2 : 80 and 90, 1 : 90 and 100, 2.—Of consumption 5, slow fever 4, dropsy 2, hooping cough 2, apoplexy 1, fits 3, drowned 1, old age 2.—The whole number of souls in the Parish at the last census was about 1900.

Deaths in Orford, in 1805,—6 adults and 10 children. In 85 years, 267—70 of whom were adults.

Vol. XII (No. 670) Friday, 31 Jan. 1806.

† [3b] Fire destroys the store of Messrs. Smith and Hamilton at Tinmouth, Vt., 17 Jan.
¶ [3c] The highest prize in Piscataqua Bridge Lottery, now drawing, was sold by T. Clark, Portland. The number was 9377.
† [3c] Outbreak of rabies at Hartland, Vt., with 13 persons being bitten by dogs, though no persons are specifically named.
¶ [3c] *From a Salem paper of January* 21. *Another Fire !*—About 3 o'clock on Thursday morning last, the tavern house of Mr. Andrew Peabody, in Bradford, was burnt down. Mr. P. had barely time to rescue his wife and children from the flames, by throwing them out of the window into a snow bank. In getting out a desk which contained much value, he was so sorely burnt, and, before he could be got into any house, frozen, that his life was despaired of. His wife and most of his children (Seven in number) were more or less frozen. There are circumstances to justify a suspicion, that the fire originated from malice.
† [3d] Rev. Isaiah Stone ordained at New Boston, N.H.
† [3d] Legal notice regarding Walpole property formerly owned by Samuel Graves, 2d, deceased, mentioning the land bounded by Josiah Griswold, heirs of John Graves, Amos Graves, Elisha Hall, and William K. Atkinson. Notice posted by Darius Graves, Administrator, and dated at Walpole, 27 Jan. 1806.

===== ¶ [3d] MARRIED. =====

In Concord, (Mass.) George B. Upham, Esq. to Miss Mary Duncan.—In Beverly, Daniel Rogers, Esq. mer. of Gloucester, to Miss Phebe Homans, daughter of Maj. Homans, of the former place.

===== ¶ [3d] DIED. =====

In the Moro Castle, (Havanna, Dec. 21) where he had been confined, the celebrated Gen. Bowles. He was reduced to a mere skeleton, and for forty days before his death was under apprehensions of being poisoned.—On the 3d of Nov. last, on his way home from Halifax to the Province of New Brunswick, Samuel Lee, Esq. aged 49, son of the late Dr. Joseph Lee, of Concord, (Ms.) : On the 10th Jan. Mrs. Lucy Lee, relict of the above mentioned Doctor Lee, aged 89.—In East-Haven, (Con.) Mrs. Rebecca Tuttle, aged 87.—In Bath, Dudley B. Hobart, Esq. Collector of that port.—In Kingston, Widow Jane Crawford, aged 76, formerly of Boston.—In Boston, Mrs. Sarah [Leate?], aged 79.—In Portsmouth, Capt. Samuel Parker : Wid. Margaret Noble.—In Rutland, (Vt.) Mr. Silas Willis, aged 86.—In Wallingford, of typhus fever, Mr. Roswell Andress, aged 25 : The funeral was attended on the following Sabbath. On the following Friday, his wife, Isabel Andress, aged 23, of the same fever : the funeral was attended on the next Sabbath.—At Winchester, Mr. Abel Hammond, aged 68.—In Piermont, (N.H.) John Patterson, Esq. aged 94.—In Lebanon, (Con.) Mr. Elisha Doubleday, aged 94; he was the father of twenty-seven children.

Vol. XII (No. 671) Friday, 7 Feb. 1806.

† [2d] Fire at Salem, Mass., consuming a book printing office occupied by Mr. Joshua Cushing, Essex St. Mr. Ashton's house was damaged.
† [2d-3a] Extensive account of the suicide of Pierce Phillips at Tunbridge, Vermont; he claimed to have been from Freetown, Mass., and was between 40 and 50 years of age. ♦
¶ [3b] The dwelling house of Mr. John Fuller, occupied by himself and Mr. Matthew Seymour, in the village of Lansingburgh, lately took fire and was consumed with most of its contents.
¶ [3c] Mr. Jesse Torry, of New Lebanon, has lately discovered on the lands of Mr. Issachar Rowley and the Rev. Aaron B. Bodge, near the Lebanon Springs, an excellent Slate quarry.
† [3c] Rev. David Butler inducted as Rector of St. Paul's Church, Troy, N.Y.
† [3c] Rev. Evan Burdsly ordained at Shoreham, Vermont.
† [3d] Legal notice regarding the estate of Elijah Grout, Esq. of Charlestown, N.H., "he being old, and so deranged in mind that he is incapable of taking care of his estate." Timothy Holden and Benjamin Laberee appointed guardians; dated Charlestown 1 Feb.

† [3d] Cornelius Warren informs his customers that he is unable to perform his newspaper delivery; dated 5 Feb., though the town is not stated.

¶ [3c] MARRIED.

At Charleston, (S.C.) Mr. E.S. Thomas, of Providence, late of the former place, bookseller, to Miss Ann Fonerden of Baltimore.

In Charlestown, on the evening of Thursday, the 23d ult. Mr. Zacheriah Lawrence, to Miss Ama Rice.

¶ [3c-d] DIED.

In Sparta, (Geo.) Capt. Richard H. Carew, aged 77, a native of Norwich, (C.)—Near Savannah, Maj. Lachlan M'Intosh, aged 49; a revolutionary officer.—In Dutch Fork, (S.C.) Mrs. Margaret Scheilley, aged 96, a native of Germany; had been 53 years in America, and 33 years a widow: she had 9 children, 59 grand-children, 171 great-grand-children, and 3 great-great-grandchildren.—In Annapolis, (Md.) Hon. Alexander Contee Hanson, chancellor of the state of Maryland, of an apoplectic fit.—Near Baltimore, Mr. Augustine Rouxelin Denos, Chevalier of the order of St. Louis; he was captain in the French reg't Saintonge, and served under Gen. Rochambeau at the siege and taking of York.—In New York, from the 11th to the 18th Jan. 15 men, 3 women, 3 boys and 8 girls.—In Newport, (R.I.) Mrs. Elizabeth, relict of Col. Edward Cole, aged 78.—In Boston, Richard Codman, Esq. aged 43.—In Norwich, (C.) Mrs. Sarah Bliss, aged 84 ; Mr. Simon Caulkins, aged 71.—In New London, the Hon. Richard Law, Esq. aged 73, Mayor of that city, and U.S. District Judge for the district of Connecticut.—In Sandisfield, Mr. Joseph Wentworth, aged 62; he took supper, went to bed well, and in about 5 hours was dead.—In New Bedford, Col. Thomas Kempton, an aged and respectable inhabitant of that town.—In Buckstown, (Me.) Mrs. Rachel Cottle, aged 60.—In Portsmouth, Capt. Samuel Hall, aged 76 ; Mr. Tobias Melcher, aged 71 ; Capt. Samuel Parker, aged 40 ; Mrs. Partridge, aged 80 ; Mrs. Randall, aged 87.—In Shrewsbury, (Mass.) Mr. Gershom Wheelock, aged [86?] ; Widow Sarah Drury, aged 71.—In Randolph, Col. Seth Turner, aged 78.—In Fredericktown, (Md.) at an advanced age, Mr. Jacob Bierly.—At Hebron, apparently in perfect health three minutes before her dissolution, Mrs. Fuller, aged 57.—At Wintonbury, Mrs. Hannah Mills, aged 89.—At Ashford, Capt. Reuben Marcy, aged 73.—At Norwich, making four persons who have died of fever in the same family within five weeks, Mr. John Bushnell, aged 47, and Mr. John Bushnell, jun. aged 21.—At Redding, Mr. Ephraim Wheeler, aged 90. —In New Haven, Mr. Jacob Pinto, aged 82.—Of a pulmonic consumption, on his passage for his health from Norfolk to Charleston, (S.C.) Rev. Mr. Joseph Washburn, of Farmington, (C.) aged 39, and in the 11th of his ministry.—In Newark, N.J. Mr. Joshua Atwood, aged 95.—At Heath, Ms. Capt. Samuel Hunt, aged 98.

At Acworth, Mrs. Anna Locke, wife of Mr. Frederick Locke, aged 45.

At Langdon, on Sunday last, after a long and lingering consumption, Mrs. Waitstill Kneeland, daughter of Captain Christopher Ormsbee, late of Putney, and consort of the Rev. Abner Kneeland, aged 29.—Also, on the Sunday preceeding, their infant child, aged 14 weeks. What is a little remarkable, her father, sister, child and herself all died on Sunday, and not many hours from the same time of the day. [*Correspondent.*]

At Waterford, (C.) Melon Kelly, of Cape Cod, (Ms.)—If it were fair to hazard a pun on so serious a subject, we might say that, literally, we do not remember to have ever witnessed the occurrence of so *melancholy* an incident.

Drowned.—Lately, in crossing the ferry from Williamsburgh, in Upper Canada, to Louisville, in New York, Doctor *Barber* and a *Mr. Chapman* of Madrid, *Jonathan Alexander* and *Silas Powell*, of Louisville.

Vol. XII (No. 672) Friday, 14 Feb. 1806.

† [2d] Fire claims the lives of four children belonging to Mr. William Fowler, at Marcellus, N.Y., and his wife was seriously burned [17 Jan. 1806?]. ♦

¶ [3b] With deep regret we announce to the public the death of Tarleton Bates, late prothonotary of this county—who fell in a duel with Thomas Stewart, on Wednesday the 8th of Jan. instant. [*Pittsburg Tree.*

† [3c] A detailed Bill of Mortality for Portsmouth, N.H., for the year 1805, compiled by Dr. Lyman Spalding. ♦

† [3c] Notice of a public vendue at Cobb's tavern in Walpole, by Asa Sibley, "V. Master." Dated at Walpole, 8 Feb. 1806.
† [3d] Adv. of goods for sale by Joseph Bellows, Jr.; dated Walpole, 10 Feb. 1806.
† [3d] David Stone adv. goods for sale at his store, which adjoins Cobb's tavern in Walpole, and which previously had been occupied by Joseph Bellows, Jr.; dated 10 Feb.

===== ¶ [3b] MARRIED. =====

Mr. Barza Hayward, of Croydon, to Miss Sukey Adams, of Newport.
Mr. Laban Chamberlin, of Pomfret, (Vt.) to Miss Abigail Mellendy, of Croydon.
At Lyme, (C.) Doctor Samuel Mather, aged 63, to Mrs. Sally Anderson, aged 29.
Mr. Elijah Lathrop, of West Springfield, to Mrs. Peggy Palmer, of Salisbury, C.

===== ¶ [3b-c] DIED. =====

In Russia, count N. Surow, an officer of high celebrity, and brother-in-law to the celebrated Suwarrow.—In Gallicia, the Austrian general Weyrotter. He was one of those sent to conduct the Russian armies to Austria, and is said in the French papers, to have died of a dreadful malady, then raging in the Russian army, not materially different from the antient [sic] *leprosy*.—On the 11th of Dec. 1805, James Allen, of Little Britain, Lancaster county, late of Chester county, Pennsylvania. *The printers in the United States are requested to give this a place in their papers, for the information of an absent heir*.—In Bolton, (Mass.) Mr. Asa Whitcomb, aged about 40.—At Sturbridge, Mr. Ebenezer Clark, aged 50.—In Charlestown, (Ms.) Widow Ruth Harrington, Æt. 70, late of Lexington.—In Portsmouth, Mrs. Phenix, aged 98.—In Portland, in the year 1805, 157 persons.—In Hartwick, (N.Y.) of a cancer in her cheek, Mrs. Anna Hinman, aged 54, leaving nine children.—In Redding, (C.) Mr. Ephraim Wheeler, aged 90.—He has left a widow with whom he lived 67 years.—At Malta, (N.Y.) Mr. Joseph S. Stewart, Æt. 34.—In York, (Me.) Capt. Samuel Bragdon, aged 69.—In Boston, Mrs. Margaret Ballard, aged 85 ; Constant Freeman, Esq. master of the Alms-House, aged 77.—In East Sudbury, Mrs. Tabitha, relict of John Noyes, Esq. deceased, aged 90.—In Lunenburg, a Mr. ———— Knight, aged 24; in attempting to enter the house of one Wm. Kilburn, after having been forbidden, he was pierced through the bowels by a sword, and instantly expired; Kilburn and his wife were the only persons in the house when the deed was perpetrated; he has been committed to gaol.—At Vernon, (Ver.) Mrs. Electa, wife of Doct. Cyrus Washburn, aged 26.—At Dummerston, V. Widow Dinah Sargeant, aged 76.—At Westminster, of the dropsy, Mr. Isaac Green, of Mendon, (Mass.) aged 63 years. He had been up the river to visit a son, and was taken on his return, at Mr. Goodale's tavern, where he languished a week and expired. He has a sister in Charlemont, and kinsmen in Gill, Ms.—At Guilford, Mrs. King, consort of Mr. James K. aged 60.—In Concord, Ms. (drowned) Mr. Ezra Conant; attempting to cut the ice, he fell into the flume, and was drawn under the gate, which was raised in part.—In Swanzey, Mrs. Mary Aldrich, aged 100.—In Danvers, Wid. Sarah Goldthwait, aged 89.—At Southold, (L.I.) Joseph Wickham, Esq. aged 73.—At Ellington, the 27th Jan. Mr. Moses Thrall, aged 72.—In Troy, the Hon. John Bird, Esq. Counsellor at Law, and late a member of the U.S. Congress, aged 37.

At Croydon, Mrs. Lydia Clements, aged 94 years.—Deaths in Croydon, in 1805, 11—5 adults and 6 children.—In 18 years, 186—46 adults and 140 children.

At Plainfield, on the 28th ult. much lamented, Mr. Timothy Swan, aged 57, after a tedious confinement of about ten weeks.

Vol. XII (No. 673) Friday, 21 Feb. 1806.

† [3b] Mr. Jesse Talcott, 36, of Springfield, Mass. commited suicide by hanging himself in a barn. ◆
† [3c] Rev. Samuel P. Robbins ordained at Marietta, Ohio, 8 Jan. 1806, and in Swanzey, N.H., Rev. William M'Culler ordained at the Baptist Church, 12 Feb. 1806.
† [3c] Mr. Quartus Morgan adv. a pocket book which he found; dated at Bellows Falls 19 Feb.

===== ¶ [3c] MARRIED. =====

At Springfield, (Ver.) Mr. Edward Forble, to Miss Kesiah Crofford : Mr. Warden Place, to Miss Eleanor Powers.—At St. Albans, Mr. Henry Gould, of Rutland, to Mrs.

Betsy Keyes, of the former place.

At Alstead, by Moses Hale, Esq. Mr. Richard Page, of Cambridge, (Vt.) to Miss Hannah Straw, of the former place.

===== ¶ [3c] DIED. =====

At Longueil, district of Montreal, Monseigneur Pierre Denaut, Bishop of the Roman Catholic Church of Quebec, aged 63.—Near Niagara Falls, state of New York, on the 2d of Sept. last, Mr. Gershom Beach, on the day he had completed his 77th year. He was one of the first settlers of the town of Rutland, and took an early part in the revolutionary war; was with three of his sons, in the famous battle fought near Bennington.—In Hudson, N.Y. Mrs. Mary Barnard, widow of the late Capt. Joseph Barnard, aged 73.—In Barnard, (Vt.) in consequence of eating a quart of chestnuts the night before, Mr. Stephen Ellis, aged 23.—In Haverhill, (Ms.) Mr. Enoch Marsh, aged 68, one of the twelve children of the late Deacon David Marsh; the other eleven are now living, the eldest of whom is 82 years old.—In Virginia, Ralph Wormeley, Esq. Æt. 64. [*compare to issue of 28 Feb. 1806.*]—In Baltimore, Capt. Enoch Welsh, aged 48.—In Philadelphia, Mrs. C. Graff, aged 78.—In Scituate, Mrs. Lettia Hayden, aged 66;—Mrs. Thankful Bailey, aged 67.—In Gloucester, Capt. Peter Dolliver, aged 79.—In Boston, Mrs. Mary Hammond, aged 73.—In London, Alderman Le Mesurier, M.P.—In Nashville, (Ten.) Ruth Talbot, infant daughter of Capt. Thomas Talbot, aged 11 mo. 22 d. The death of this child was occassioned by the nurse giving it an over potion of laudanum, to keep the child quiet while she went on a party of pleasure.—In Saco, Mr. David Burbank, of Newfield;—he was driving a loaded team into that town, and on descending a hill he slipt and fell, when the sled passing over him injured him so considerably that he expired three days after.—In Newburyport, Capt. Nathan Poor, aged 65;—while attending divine service, in the Rev. Mr. Dana's meeting-house, he was attacked by a fit, and expired in a few minutes.—At Clarendon, (Vt.) Deacon John Cooper, aged 88.—At Middletown, (C.) Mr. John Sage, aged 80.—In Kingston, (N.Y.) Abraham B. Bancker, Esq. in the 51st year of his age;—his death was occasioned by a paralytic stroke.—At Bourdeaux, in France, M. Charles de la Croix, prefect of the Department of Le Gironde.—At Haddam, C. of the palsy, Lieut. Elijah Brainard, aged 72.

In Putney, (Ver.) on the 8th inst. the widow Rebecca Goodhue, aged 82.

DROWNED.—In the Great Pond, in Middleboro', the 8th inst. Nicholas Power and Nathan Bird, drivers of the New-Bedford and Boston Mail Stage, and a young lady, a passenger with them, by the name of Polly Spooner, of N. Bedf.

Vol. XII (No. 674) Friday, 28 Feb. 1806.

† [3c] James Freeman adv. mills for sale at Cornish, N.H.

† [3d] R. Vose adv. a hotel and store for sale at Walpole, where Mr. William Pierce now operates a tavern.

===== ¶ [3c] MARRIED. =====

In Virginia, Mr. Nathaniel Lee, aged 87, (after being three times married, and having 11 children, 49 grand-children, and 10 gr.-grand-children) to the lovely Miss Elizabeth Tucker, aged 19.—At Woodstock, Mr. Elisha Taylor, to the Widow Cheney, of Hartford.

In Unity, Mr. John Bartlett, to Miss Betsey Huntoon.—Mr. Solomon Honey, to Miss Rebekah Huntoon.

===== ¶ [3c] DIED. =====

In New York, from Jan. 25 to Feb. 1, 25 adults and 15 children;—of consumption 8;—adventure 1, a child, to whom an over dose of opium had been given by a person unacquainted with its powers. During the months of January, there died of consumption, 17 men and 14 women.—In Troy, Captain Jeremiah Peirce, aged 63.—In Haddonfield, (N.J.) Mr. John E. Hopkins, aged 68.—In Trenton, Mrs. Phebe Hunewill, aged 72.—In Beverly, (Ms.) Mrs. Anna, wife of Deac. John Dike, aged 53.—In Cambridge, Widow Eunice Hunnewell, aged 66.—In Boston, Mrs. Mary Murdock, aged 69 ; Daniel Sargent, Esq. mer. aged 75 ; Mrs. Jane Hill, aged 78.—At Lempster, Mr. John Abbot, aged 28.—At Weare, on the 20th Jan. last, after a lingering state of debility occasioned by a shock of the numb palsy, Mrs. Lydia Hadley, consort of Capt. Geo.

Hadley, aged 64. She has left a husband and numerous family to lament her inconsolable loss.—At Boushnourville, (Canada) Dr. Wm. Barr, aged 31.—At Burlington, Mr. Oliver Avery, aged 23.—In Northampton, Miss Susannah Clark, aged 49.—At Croydon, Mrs. Clement, formerly of Petersham, aged 94.—At Putney, (Vt.) Widow Rebekah Goodhue, aged 82.—In Providence, Mr. Jonathan Bucklin, aged 93, late of Rehoboth.—In North Providence, Mr. Oliver Carpenter, aged 67.—In Cranston, J. Rice Arnold, Esq. Æt. 55.—At Smithfield, John Fenner, Esq. aged 79.—In Charlestown, (Ms.) Widow Anna Winship, aged 100.—In Wilbraham, Mr. Stephen Bliss, aged 74. After doing a day's work at dressing flax, he went to bed as usual, and by nine o'clock was a corpse.—In Springfield, (Ms.) Mr. Seth Chapin, aged 82 : Very suddenly, also, Col. William Smith.—At Rosegill, (Virg.) Ralph Wormly, Esq. aged 62. [*compare to issue of 21 Feb. 1806.*]—At Deerfield, N.H. Mr. John Neal, aged 84.—In Philadelphia, Col. Thomas Willis, of the 25th regiment of Pennsylvania militia : Mrs. Rebecca Coxe, consort of Tench Coxe, Esq.—In Worcester, Deacon Nathan Perry, aged 88.—In Bradford, Wid. Martha Kimball, aged 78.

Drowned.—At Baltimore, Francis Elwin, a native of Amsterdam : the day after his arrival from Gonaives, (W.I.) he carelessly walked overboard.—In Lamberton, Mr. John Poole, hatter, of Philadelphia ; he deliberately walked into the Delaware.

Vol. XII (No. 675) Friday, 7 March 1806.

† [3b] Dr. Porter of Williamstown, Mass. lost his home by fire, 14 Jan. 1806.

¶ [3b] *Robbery.*—Mr. Ebenezer Crawford, of Guildhall, (N.Y.) while returning from a journey to the westward, was lately attacked, on the shores of Lake Erie, by three villains (one Indian and two white men) armed with pistols and knives, and robbed of about 40 dollars.

† [3c] Account of a fire in Boston "in the Rope Walk" owned by Mr. J. Howe; other rope walks destroyed were owned by Mr. Samuel Emmons, Capt. Penuel B. Rogers, and Mr. Isaac P. Davis. ♦

===== ¶ [3d] MARRIED. =====

In Quebec, Capt. A. Paul, of the Royal Artillery, to Miss Anne Johnson.

===== ¶ [3d] DIED. =====

In Goree, (Africa) Dr. Hast. Handy, formerly of the Maryland.—In Quebec, Mr. John Hill, formerly keeper of the gaol.—In Philadelphia, from the 8th to the 15th Feb'ry, 22 deaths.—In New York, from the 8th to 15th Feb. 27 deaths; of consumption 5; infantcide 1.—In Canandagua, (N.Y.) Mr. Charles M. Connell [*compare to issue of 14 March 1806*], aged 99.—In Tolland, C. Capt. Jabez Edgerton, aged 84.—In Wiscasset, Mr. Robert Foy, aged 86.—In Boston, Mr. Giles Atkins, aged 66 : Mrs. Hannah Cordwell, aged 67 : Mrs. Mary Emmons, aged 70.—In East Sudbury, Widow Abigail [Damon?], aged 97.—In Portland, Mr. Thomas Shed, aged 66.—In Swansey, (R.I.) Hon. Simeon [Porter? Potter?], Esq. aged 91.—In Canterbury, (N.H.) Hon. Abiel Foster, formerly representative in Congress.—In Bridgwater, (N.H.) Mr. James Nelson, aged 77.—In Milford, Lieu. Benjamin French, aged 63.—In Windham, (N.H.) John Nesmith, Esq.—In Portsmouth, Col. Eliphalet Ladd, aged 62 : Mr. Zebulon Marsh, aged 76 : Mr. John Walden, aged 88 : Mrs. Anna Abott, aged 56.—In Greenland, Lieut. David Simpson, aged 78.—In Dracut, Mr. Samuel Blanchard, aged 89.—In Saco, Mrs. Eunice Dearing, aged 86.—In Norwich, (Vt.) Mr. Josiah Goodrich, aged 89.—At Windsor, Mr. Jonathan Willis, aged 48.—In Troy, (N.Y.) Mr. Theral Kilborn, aged 40.—In Windham, (Con.) Mr. Stephen Fitch, aged 94.—In Swansey, Mrs. Sarah Aldrich, aged 100.—At Southington, (Con.) Mr. David Cogswell, aged 81.—At Glastenbury, Mrs. Elizabeth Plummer, aged 73.—At Fort Constitution, Sergeant John Glynn, of the U.S. army, aged 31.—At Newburyport, Mrs. Sarah Little, aged 57.

In Alstead 25th ult. Nathan, son of Mr. Abel Phelps, aged 13 years 8 mo. and 7 days

Drowned.—In Concord, the week before last, Mr. Roland Parker, son of Dr. Isaac Parker, of Hanover, aged 18.

☞ *The Rev. Clergy in this county, and in the towns in the county of Windham in Vermont, which are in this vicinity, are requested to forward (free of postage) a correct list of deaths and marriages, which will find a ready insertion in the Museum.*

Vol. XII (No. 676) Friday, 14 March 1806.

¶ [3b] The day appointed for the execution of Stephen Arnold, for the murder of Betsey Van Amburgh, is the last Friday in May next.

¶ [3c] The wife of Mr. Aaron Fairchild, of Granville, (Mass.) on the 24th ult. was delivered of *three* male children, weighing eight pounds ten ounces each.

† [3c] Rev. Ephraim Putnam Bradford ordained at New Boston, N.H., 26 Jan. 1806.

===== ¶ [3c] MARRIED. =====

In West Springfield, Mr. Dwight Lathrop, mer. of New York, to Miss Lora Stebbins.—In Leicester, the Rev. Ezekiel L. Bascom, of Gerry, to Miss Ruth Myers.—In East Sudbury, Mr. Josiah Bridge, mer. to Miss Irene Morse, daughter of the late Rev. A. Morse.—In Marshfield, Capt. John Thomas, to Miss Lucy Turner.—At Hartland, Mr. Russell Fletcher, of Woodstock, to Miss Rachel Scott, of the former place : Eliakim Spooner, Esq. to Miss Amelia Gilson.

In Unity, Mr. Calvin Nichols, to Miss Sukey Briant.

At Warwick, Mr. Nathan Hastings, to Miss Esther Woodward, of Orange.

In this town, on Tuesday last, by the Rev. Mr. Dickinson, Mr. William Robertson, to Miss Sally Baker.

===== ¶ [3c-d] DIED. =====

In Curracoa, John Lyle, Esq. consul of the U.S.—In Philadelphia, from 15th to 22d Feb. 17 adults and 13 children.—In New York, Col. John Lasher, aged 83—during the week ending 22d Feb. 7 men, 7 women, 3 boys and 4 girls ; of consumption 9.—In New London, Mrs. Rebecca, relict of the late Tim'y Greene, Esq. aged 63.—In New Haven, Mr. Edward Granniss, of hydrophobia ; he was bitten by a mad dog, and in about seven weeks after, he died with all the horrid symptoms accompanying that dreadful disorder.—In Keene, Mrs. Lydia, wife of Capt. George Hadley, aged 64.—In New Ipswich, Dea. Isaac Appleton, aged 74.—In Cambridge, of a nervous fever, Robert Adams, A.B. of Westford.—At Merrimac, Mr. Samuel Chandler, aged 27, killed in unloading a log from a sled.—At Braintree, capt. [sic] Samuel Whitmarsh, aged 73, formerly of Boston.—In Boston, Mrs. Ann Gault, aged 85 : Miss Mary Wakefield, aged 78.—In Demerary, Capt. William Leeds, of New London.—In Bellemont, (N.B.) the Hon. Daniel Bliss, Esq. one of his Britannic Majesty's Counsellors for the Province of New Brunswick, aged 68.—In Savannah, Maj. John Wylde, aged 63.—In Philad. Richard D. Cantillon, Esq. aged 61.—In Fairhill, (Pen.) Mr. James Thomas ; while racing his horse, which run against a sign-post, he was thrown and had his skull fractured.—In Kennebunk, Mr. Aaron Stackpole, aged 37, killed by the fall of a tree.—In Portsmouth, the Rev. Samuel Haven, D.D. aged 79.—In Roxbury, Mr. Samuel Cookson, aged 63.—In East-Windsor, (Con.) very suddenly, Mr. Nathaniel Drake, aged 64 years.—In Barnard, V. Mrs. Phebe Freeman, aged 76. She was one of the first settlers of Barnard, and it its infant state, a mother to its inhabitants.—At Cornwall, (C.) Mrs. Experience Hunt, aged 78.—At Deerfield, Mr. Aaron Arm[ ],[155] aged 57.

Suicide.—The Montgomery Intelligencer informs us, says the Troy Gazette, that on the 10th ult. a young man, about 19 years of age, hung himself in a barn in Utica—and that on the next day a young woman, 3 or 4 miles on this side of Utica, hung herself in a stable.

DIED.]—In Canadaigua, Mr. Charles M'Connell [*compare to issue of 7 March 1806.*], aged 99.—At Lebanon, on the 19th ult. Miss Hannah Aspenwall, aged 21.—At Westborough, Mrs. Lydia Chamberlain, aged 52.—At Sutton, Mr. John Hall, aged 54.—At Leicester, Mr. Jonathan Sargeant, aged 77.—At West Hartford, (Conn.) Mrs. Elizabeth Webster, aged 44 years.

Vol. XII (No. 677) Friday, 21 March 1806. [156]

† [3a-b] A son of Mr. Ezra Whitaker, of Adams, [Mass.], aged 14, died from injuries sustained in being dragged by a frightened horse. ♦

† [3b] Mr. Joseph Mason of Dublin, [N.H.], aged about 57, died from an injury when a limb fell on his head. He left a widow and eight children. ♦

† [3c] Rev. Mr. Hovey ordained at Weybridge, Vermont, 20 Feb. 1806.

† [3d] Asher Southard adv. that he "has again opened the tavern in this village formerly improved by him, and of late occupied by Mr. George Cobb." Dated Walpole, 20 March 1806.

† [3d] Two notices regarding the Third N.H. Turnpike Corp.: 1) Benjamin Prescott and Joseph Frost, Directors, mentioning a meeting to be held at Horace Wells, innkeeper at Keene, and 2) a dispute between D. Carter, Treasurer, and Ephraim Hartwell, Esq.

===== ¶ [3c] MARRIED. =====

At Norwich, Mr. David Newton, jun. to Miss Eliza Partridge ; Mr. Jacob Burton to Miss Betsey Safford ; Mr. Nathan Safford to Miss Anna Hopson ; Mr. Eliphalet Hunt to Miss Lucy Goodrich ; Mr. Roswell Craw to Miss Sally Hammond ; Mr. James Baldwin to Miss Lura Calkins ; Mr. David Ford to Miss Sally Lyman ; Mr. Calvin Johnson, jun'r. to Miss Temper Morse ; Mr. John Burnap to Miss Polly Peak ; Mr. ——— Flint to Miss Olive Smith; Mr. Enoch Thatcher to Miss Laura Bicknell.

===== ¶ [3c-d] DIED. =====

In Waynesborough, (S.C.) Mr. Mackay M'Norvell ; while in the act of discharging the duty of sheriff, he was shot by a Mr. John Randolph.—In Portsmouth, 3d inst. the Rev. Samuel Haven, D.D. aged 79 ; and on the 5th, suddenly, Mrs. Margaret Haven, his consort, aged 60.—In Worthington, Feb. 13, Mr. S. Adams, aged 25. The circumstances of his death were most shocking;—he incautiously placed his left foot in the jaws of a machine used for breaking tanner's bark, to prepare it for grinding, into which he was drawn in the course of eight seconds, and his foot and leg were cut into two inch pieces; during which excruciating operation he thrust his right hand between the two cog wheels, which broke it across at the insertion of the wrist, and severed one finger from it. He survived the shock twelve hours, and expired.—In Holliston, Feb. 21, Mr. Timothy Rockwood, aged [76?].—In Boston, widow Rachel Emmons, aged 75 : the Hon. Shearjashub Bourne, Esq. aged 59.—At Middlefield, (C.) Mr. ——— Curtiss, in consequence of wounds received by the blowing up of the powder mill in Middletown.—In Canaan, (C.) at one o'clock, on Tuesday morning, the 14th ult. the Rev. Justus Mitchell, in the 52d year of his age. He had delivered a Sermon the evening preceeding, apparently in usual health. The spirit of another of the "noblest works of God" has thus ascended to Him from whom it emanated.—In New Brunswick, (N.J.) Col. Ephraim Martin, aged 73.—At Hamden, Mr. David Atwater, aged 82.—At New Milford, Mr. David Canfield, aged 100 years.

Vol. XII (No. 678) Friday, 28 March 1806. [157]

† [1b] Notice of dissolution of partnership between Thomas Redington, Isaac Redington, and Edmund Brewster, a.k.a. *Edmund Brewster & Co.* The business in the future to be conducted by Edmund Brewster and Benjamin Snow, under the firm of *Brewster & Snow*. Dated at Westmoreland, 16 March 1806.

¶ [3b] *Lamentable accident.*—Between one and two o'clock, P.M. on Friday, 21st ult. Mr. Rowland Parker, son of Dr. Isaiah Parker, of Harvard, an amiable youth, in the 19th year of his age, attempting, in company with Captain Edgarton, of Shirley, when returning from Boston, to cross the flood near Price's Bridge, so called, in Concord, was drowned, and capt. Edgarton narrowly escaped. The body was found the Lord's day morning succeeding. [*Leominster paper.*]

¶ [3c] A paper-mill, the property of Mr. Alexander Dunihue, of Castleton, was lately consumed by fire, in Fairhaven, Vt.

¶ [3c-d] COMMUNICATION. On the 8th instant, were consumed by fire, two good barns in Boscawen, twelve tons of hay, some wheat, and some farming utensils.—Property owned by Maj. Enoch Gerrish, of said town.—loss estimated at 600 dollars.—Said barns were burnt by a child's setting shavings on fire under one of them. March, 1806.

† [3d] B. Dudley Emerson offers reward for his horse, stolen from the stable of Capt. John Willard at Charlestown; dated there 27 March 1806.

† [3d] David Stone adv. for flax, and mentions his store at Walpole; dated 27 March.

¶ [3d] ☞ A person, formerly known by the name of *Abigail Foster*, a native of Lyon's Farms, in New-Jersey, but who has not been heard of for some time past, is, if living, desired to return to the place of her nativity, to receive the lawful portion of her father's estate. N.B. The printers throughout the U. States are desired, in the most tender affection, to give this publicity in their respective papers, at least two weeks.

===== ¶ [3d] MARRIED. =====

In Concord, (Ms.) the Rev. Joseph Chickering, of Woburn, to Miss Betsey White.—In Portsmouth, Isaac Lyman, Esq. to Miss Lucretia Pickering.

===== ¶ [3d] DIED. =====

In Great Britain, the Rt. Hon. William Pitt, Æt. 47, Chancellor of the Exchequer, First Lord of the Treasury, Lord Warden of the Cinque Ports, &c. &c. &c second son of the illustrious William Earl of Chatham. He was never married.—In India, the Most Noble Marquis Cornwallis, Governour General of Bengal, Constable of the Tower of London, [. . .] aged about 60. He was on his way to join the army in the interior, when he was taken sick and died.—In Russia, Count Woronzow, the Russian Imperial Chancellor. He had been distinguished for his diplomatic talents.—In Fredericktown, (Md.) Mrs. Alice Fleming, aged 85.—In Gloucester, (Ms.) Mr. Joseph Kilham, aged 101 years.—In Northboro', Mrs. Hannah Fay, relict of the late Mr. Gersham Fay, aged 100 years.—In Reading, Mr. Wm. Prentiss, 6th son of the late Rev. Caleb Prentiss, aged [20?]—In East-Sudbury, after a long and painful illness, Mrs. Fanny Goodenow, wife of Mr. Asel G. aged 46.—In Medford, Mrs. Tabitha Tufts, widow, aged [82?]—In Boston, Mr. John Fleet, printer, aged 71.—In Randolph, (Ver.) Mr. Joseph Griswold, aged 77.—In Shoreham, (Vt.) Mrs. Martha Stewart, aged 59.—In Lyman, (Ver.) Widow Abigail Way, aged 86.—In Peacham, Mr. Ezra Harvey, aged 58.—In Springfield, Dr. Samuel Cobb.—In Wethersfield, Vt. Mrs. Elizabeth Whipple ; Mrs. Plant.—At Fort Constitution, near Portsmouth, Mr. Jacob Frost, of the U.S. army.—In Portsmouth, Mrs. Elizabeth Fall, aged 77 ; Mr. William Nelson, aged 77.—In Litchfield, (C.) Mr. Daniel Begelow, formerly of Hartford, aged 82.—In New-Canaan, (N.Y.) Rev. Justus Mitchell.—At Canterbury, (Con.) Mr. William Ensworth, aged 86.—Near Paris, Gen. Farrand, Ex-Prefect of the department of the Mense, and a member of the legion of honor. [. . .] In Thurlow, (Eng.) Mr. Chick, aged 135 ; he had been upwards of 53 years a school-master in that parish.—In Holt, (Eng.) Mr. John Griffith, farmer, aged 103.—In Sunderland, Mary Farrier, aged 112 ; though infirm and blind, she was greatly celebrated and resorted to, for taking and copying drawings, &c. having the wonderful power of ascertaining clours, &c. by feeling.—In Southampton, (Eng.) Mr. John Tucker, fisherman, aged 131.—In England, Sir Hyde Parker : Alderman Skinner. [. . .] In Bourdeaux, on Christmas eve. Col. Joshua Orne, of Marblehead ; an old officer of the American revolutionary army. His death was caused by a fall in descending the steps from the American Consul's door, in which he received a blow on the head, which killed him instantaneously. Also, in Bourdeaux, on the 9th January, Mr. Peter Gilman, formerly of Boston.—In Halifax, (N.S.) Lt. Gen. Gardner, who had the military command there. He is succeeded by Maj. Gen. Hunter.—In Philad. Mr. Joseph Magossin, mer. aged 71.—In Weare, (N.H.) Mr. Joseph Huse, aged 55.—In Upton, Capt. Samuel Wright, aged 82.—In Worcester, Mrs. Margaret Kingsbury, aged [55?].—In Boston, on Friday last, Miss Mary Thomas, aged [78?].—In Philadelphia, Gen. Thomas Proctor, aged 68.

At Acworth, on the 19th inst. of a consumption, Mrs. Lucinda Grout, consort of Mr. Nathaniel Grout, and daughter of Thomas Slader, Esq. aged 23.

In this town, Mr. Cornelius Warren.

No. 3.—Vol. XIV (Whole No. 679) Friday, 4 April 1806.

† [3a] Brief news item stating that John Tucker, "who has been suspected of signing most of the counterfeit bills" circulating in Massachusetts, is now in a N.H. prison.

† [3c] The wife and three children of Capt. Luke Johnson, of Leominster, Mass., were all bitten by their dog, supposed to have been rabid. Capt. Johnson was away on a journey at the time.

† [3c] Ordinations: Rev. Nathan Waldo, at Williamstown, Vt., 28 Feb. 1806; Rev. Samuel Bascom, 12 March 1806, at Sharon, Vt.

† [3d] Isaac Redington requests debtors to pay up; dated Walpole, 2 April 1806.

¶ [3d] RAN AWAY from the subscriber, the 14th of March instant, an indented apprentice, known by the name of David Thomson, about fifteen years old. All persons are forbid harbouring or trading with him. Whoever will take up and return said apprentice to the subscriber, with sufficient bonds that he shall run away no more, shall have Ten Dollars reward, and no charges paid.

CHRISTOPHER NEWTON.

Newport, N.H. March 14, 1806.

===== ¶ [3c] MARRIED. =====

At Peterborough, Mr. James Cunningham, to Miss Sally M. Cunningham.—At Swanzey, Mr. Josiah Hammond, to Miss Experience Stanley.—At Fitzwilliam, Mr. Benjamin Holbrook, of Swanzey, to Miss Betsey Shearley.

===== ¶ [3d] DIED. =====

At Washington, Gen. James Jackson, a Senator from Georgia.—In Carlisle, (Penn.) Andrew Galbraith, Esq. formerly of the army of the U.S.—In Boston, Mrs. Sarah Powell, aged 73, relict of the late Hon. Jeremiah D. Powell, Esq.—In Deerfield, Mr. Aaron Arms, aged 57.—At Lee, (Con.) Mrs. Thankful West, wife of Deacon Oliver West, aged 70.—In Becket, Mrs. Elizabeth King, aged 62.—In New London, Mr. Isaac Fellows, aged 87.—At Marlboro', 23d ult. suddenly, with the Croup, Mr. Edward Longley, second son of Mr. Benj. Longley, aged [20?].—In Keene, very suddenly, after a very short indisposition, Miss Mary Holbrook, eldest daughter of Mr. Elihu Holbrook, aged 14.

In this town, a child of Mr. Thomas Jenison, æ. [28 mo.?].

☞ The death of Thomas Allen, Esq. of Pittsfield, has been mentioned prematurely in some of the papers. He is still living.

No. 4.—Vol. XIV (Whole No. 680) Friday, 11 April 1806.

¶ [3a] *Atahualpa*, Adams, (late Porter,) from N.W. Coast, arrived Nov. 16. The *Atahualpa*, in June last, on the N.W. coast, was attacked by the natives, and, after an obstinate conflict, in which capt. Porter and nine others were killed, and nine wounded, the Americans succeeded in getting off the ship, though with great difficulty. Nearly 50 of the natives were killed or died of their wounds. Among the killed on board the ship, were both the mates, and Mr. Plumer, of Salem, [*Mass.*—Ed.] captain's clerk, a very worthy and promising young man. Only five persons on board escaped unhurt. [*see also issue of 8 Aug. 1806 herein—Ed.*]

† [3c] Mr. Benjamin Bacon kills two large hogs, at Greenwich, N.Y.

† [3d] Legal notice regarding the insolvent estate of John Adkins, late of Charlestown, deceased; Daniel H. Cone and Nathan Allen, Commissioners. Dated at Charlestown, [12?] Feb. 1806.

¶ [3d] WHEREAS Esther, my wife, on the 23d day of February last, at Princeton, eloped in a private manner, without my knowledge or consent, from the bed and board of the subscriber, late of Chester, in the county of Windsor, and state of Vermont; but now resident of Princeton, in the county of Worcester. This is to forbid all persons entertaining or trusting her on my account, as I will pay no debts of her contracting after this date. Also eloped from my employ, Peter Willard, son of the subscriber, aged about 19 years, who went off about the 20th of last month. All persons are also forbidden trusting said Peter on my account, as I shall pay no debts of his contracting after this date.

JONATHAN WILLARD.

Princeton, April 1st, 1806.

¶ [3d] ☞ Information is wanted of TIMOTHY POWERS, jun. who joined the United States Army, and marched to Georgia in the year 1790, and has not been heard of for several years past. Said Timothy, if living, is informed that his Parents and friends still live in Rockingham, in Vermont, and are very anxious to hear from him. N.B. The Printers in the U. States, and particularly at the Southward, would perform an act of kindness and humanity if they would give the above short notice one or two insertions in their respective papers.

===== ¶ [3d] MARRIED. =====

At Alstead, by the Rev. Mr. Higbee, on the 16th ult. Mr. Jonathan Fisher, jun. to Miss Rebecca Adams.—Mr. Asahel Scripter, of Langdon, to Miss Azuba Tenney, of Alstead.

¶ [3d] DIED.

In Frederickstown, (Maryland) Mrs. Mary Hymes, aged 103 years. During the last forty years, she was scarcely known to have had one hour's sickness. To the very last, she enjoyed all her faculties and activity, and, what is very uncommon, could read the smallest print without the aid of spectacles.—Departed this life, the 17th of march last, at the residence of her son, Dr. James Ewing, in Pittstown, New Jersey, in the 78th year of her age, Mrs. Hannah Ewing, relict of the Rev. John Ewing, D.D. late senior pastor of the First Presbyterian Church in Philadelphia, and Provost of the University of Pennsylvania.—In Boston, the Hon. Joseph Gardner, Esq. aged 92.—In Cambridge, (Ms.) Mr. Stephen Palmer, aged 88.—In Watertown, Mrs. Elizabeth Willington, aged 75.—In Rowley, Mr. Nath'l Bradstreet, aged 67.

In Londonderry, (Ver.) 24th ult. Mr. Patrick Larkin, aged 56. He has left a wife and four children to lament his departure.

N.B. The death of Thomas Allen, jun. Esq. of Pittsfield, is confirmed by our latest papers. He died in Boston, aged 37.

No. 5.—Vol. XIV (Whole No. 681) Friday, 18 April 1806.

† [2d-3a] Mr. Knowlton, Keeper of the lower Toll-House in Roxbury, Mass., thwarted a robbery attempt. ♦

† [3a] Account of a duel fought in the vicinity of Providence, R.I., between S. Elliot, jun., and W. Austin of Boston. ♦

¶ [3c] *Melancholy accident.*—As a son of Mr. James Dunton, of Bolton, (Ms.) aged about 16 years, was drilling in a well in Fitzwilliam, in this state, whilst another person was charging in the same rock, a spark of fire was communicated to the charge, which exploded and entered his body. He expired in a few hours.—Accidents of this kind should excite people to more carefulness in the use of powder.

† [3c] Rev. Samuel Prince Robbins ordained at Marietta, Ohio, 8 Jan. 1806, and at Western, (County of Worcester), Rev. Sylvester Burt, 12 March 1806.

† [3d] *Daniel Buck, Jr. & Co.* adv. goods for sale at Hartford, Conn.; dated 31 March.

† [3d] Asa Willcox and Calvin Hayward offer reward for the capture and return of Cushman Smith of Surry, N.H., previously arrested for counterfeiting. The notice contains a physical description of Smith; dated at Charlestown, 12 April 1806. ♦

† [3d] Thomas Bellows, 2d and Joseph Bellows, Jr., form partnership of *J. & T. Bellows*; dated at Walpole, 15 April 1806.

† [3d] Levi Allen and Calvin Eaton, Executors of the estate of Ebenezer Eaton, late of Walpole, deceased, request debtors to pay up. Notice dated at Walpole 16 April 1806.

¶ [3c] DIED.

Near Fredericktown, (Md.) Mr. James Henderson, sen. aged 74.—In Philadelphia, of a pleurisy, Mr. Elihu Palmer, aged 42, the well known moral and political lecturer;—from the 15th to the 22d ult. 40 adults, and 30 children; from the 22d to the 29th ult. 25 adults, and 17 children.—In New York, from the 22d to the 26th ult. 54; of consumption 11; hanged, one, viz. Francisco Son, pursuant to the sentence for the murder of A. Graham, in June last.—In Boston, Mrs. Elizabeth Jones, wife of Mr. Ephraim Jones, aged 36.—In Newton, Mrs. Polly Harback, aged 72.—In Boxford, Rev. Elizur Holyoke, aged 75.—In Salem, Capt. Thorndike Deland, aged 54 : Mrs. Ame Howard, aged 69.—In Boston, Prince Watts, aged 71, a respectable and honest African. —In Middlebury, (Ver.) on the 29th ult. of a consumption, Mrs. Millicent Goodrich, wife of Mr. Amos Goodrich, aged 34.—At Shoreham, (Vt.) on the 28th ult. Mrs. Sally Willson, consort of Mr. William Willson, in the 30th year of her age.—In Chester, (N.H.) 11th ult. Mrs. Sarah Webster, relict of the late Mr. Ebenezer Webster, of Bradford, aged 82.—In Exeter, 15th ult. Mrs. Love Bartlett, aged 90.—In Dover, Mrs. Rebecca Gage.—In Montville, Joshua Raymond, Esq.—In Philadelphia, Capt. William Keith, aged 69.—In Lancaster, Ms. 3d inst. suddenly, Mr. Benjamin Edgarton, aged 45.—At Enfield, (Con.) Mr. Aaron Pease, aged 88.—At East Hartford, Mrs. Anna Risley, wife of Mr. John Risley, aged 77.—On the 4th inst. at New-Haven, C. departed this life, Mrs. Martha Day, aged 35, the amiable consort of Jeremiah Day, Professor of Mathematics and Natural Philosophy, and daughter of the late Hon. Roger Sherman, of

that place.—In Boston, Mrs. Elizabeth Shelton, aged 69.
SUICIDE.—In Chambersburg, (P.) Mr. Samuel Bell.

No. 6.—Vol. XIV (Whole No. 682) Friday, 25 April 1806.

† [2b] Account of the execution at New York City of Francisco Son, a Portuguese man convicted of the murder of Archibald Graham. ♦

¶ [3b] We are informed by a gentleman from Lyme, that on Wednesday morning last, as Capt. Azariah Whittelsey of Saybrook, with his grandson and one passenger, were crossing the Ferry at that place, the boat upset, and Capt. Whittelsey and his grandson, a lad about 12 years of age, were both drowned—the passenger was saved by timely assistance from the shore. [*Middleton Pap.*

¶ [3b] *Fatal accident.*—On Saturday the 23d ult. one of the Catskill Ferry boats was overset by a squall, and Mr. Samuel Hollenback, aged nearly 60, unfortunately drowned. Two horses were lost at the same time. [*Bee.*]

† [3d] Legal notice regarding the insolvent estate of John Thacher, late of Lempster, N.H., deceased, Peter Thacher, Administrator. Probate Court to be held at Mr. Ely's tavern, Charlestown. The notice is dated at "Hartford", 15 April 1806.

† [3d] James Johnson adv. that he is "about to close business in this town," and requests debts to be settled; also, Johnson adv. for sale or rent the store formerly occupied by *Chapman & Hartwell* in Alstead. "For terms, apply to David Chapman, at Keene, or J.H. Bingham, near the premises." Dated at Alstead, 16 April 1806.

† [3d] Notice regarding the Stoddard Turnpike Corporation; signed by Nathaniel Emerson of Stoddard, Amos Shepard, and Ephraim Kingsbery; dated 15 April 1806.

¶ [3d] WHEREAS Jonathan my husband, late of Chester, but now resident in Princeton, has at divers times abused me, and has frequently forsook the bed, and board, of an innocent and obedient wife, preferring the company of divers lewd women; for the truth of which I appeal to the most respectable inhabitants of Chester : this is, therefore, to forbid all persons (especially lewd women) to harbour or trust my said husband, as I will pay no debts of his contracting after this date.

ESTHER WILLARD.

Chester, April 15th, 1801. [sic]

FIVE DOLLARS REWARD.

WHEREAS my father, Jonathan Willard, has wilfully abused my honoured mother, Esther Willard, at divers times, the circumstances of which I am well acquainted with ; in favour of innocence and virtue, and actuated by filial affection, I have assisted my mother against a father who appears to be destitute of paternal and conjugal affection. If any person will bring my said father to Chester, so that he may be arrested, by due course of law, I will pay the above reward, and all necessary expenses.

PETER WILLARD.

Chester, April 15th, 1806.

====== ¶ [3c] MARRIED. ======

In Concord, (Mass.) Mr. William Abrams, jun. of Boston, to Miss Martha Hunt, of Concord.—At Lynnfield, Mr. Matthew Cox, to Miss Elizabeth Motty, daughter of the Rev. Joseph Motty.

====== ¶ [3c] DIED. ======

At Burlington, (Ver.) on the 26th ult. departed this life, in the [64?]th year of his age, Col. Ebenezer Allen. It is a fact (says the Burlington paper) well known to many of the Revolutionary Heroes of America, that Col. Allen, in 1777, (then a Captain) with only a lieutenant and forty of his "green mountain boys," ascended the horrid precipice of Mount Defiance (nearly opposite Ticonderoga) in the night, surprised, and took the almost impregnable fortress thereon, which was defended by far superior numbers of well disciplined regular British troops, and heavy artillery. This was effected without the loss of a single man. At the celebrated battle of Bennington, in the same year, Captain Allen, with only thirty men, taking the advantage of a natural breastwork of rocks, for a considerable time contended with the front of the main body of Burgoyne's army, and with great slaughter actually caused a temporary retreat.—At Leyden, (Ms.) on the 24th of February last, Mr. Oliver Babcock, in the 84th year of his age, having lived 60 years in wedlock with his wife, (who is yet living) by whom he had 14 children. His descendants amount to 148, viz. 14 children, 86 grand-children, and 48 great-grand-children.—In London, Dec. 12, 1805, Henry Sampson Woodfall, aged 67: who for 40 years conducted "The Public Advertiser," in which the celebrated letters of Junius were originally published.—At St. Thomas, Feb. 14, Mr. William Singleton, a native of Massachusetts : 16th, Mr. Isaac Sloan, of Vermont, both mechanics.—At St. John, (N.B.) Mr. Thomas Walker, aged 87.—Near Baltimore, James Winchester, Esq. late Judge of the District Court of Maryland.—In Southington, (Con.) very suddenly, on the 27th of February last, Mrs. Vashty Tyler, wife of Mr. Asahel Tyler, aged 27 years.— At Guilford, Roger Averill, Esq. post-master.—In Norwalk, (C.) Deac. Nathaniel Benedict, aged 90 ; he has left 91 grand-children, and 88 great-grand-children; the whole number of his descendants now living, are 191.—In Pelham, (N.H.) Mrs. Thankful Church, consort of the Rev. John H. Church, aged 31.—In Leominster, (Ms.) Maj. Metaphor Chase, aged 45.—In Rutland, (Ms.) Mr. Jonas Reed, aged 84.—In Worcester, Mrs. Barnard, aged 67.—In Dana, Mrs. Sarah Johnson, aged 83.—In Middletown, (Con.) Capt. William Haskell, aged 74 : Mrs. Mary Plumb.—In New London, Mr. Isaac Fellows, aged 87. He has left a widow with whom he had lived since marriage upwards of 65 years, without having been absent so long as a week but once during the time.—In Springfield, (Ms.) Mrs. Eunice Chapin, relict of the late Dea. Edward Chapin, aged 78. In the absence of the family, she was probably siezed with a fit of apoplexy : when they returned she was found lying on the fire, into which she had fallen, burned in a shocking manner, and without a symptom of life.—At Wilbraham, 31st ult. Mr. Aquila Caulkins, aged 95, formerly of East Haddam, (C.)—In Brattleboro', Mr. Charles Haywood, aged 82.—Lately died at an obscure lodging at White chapel, in England, aged 91, Richard Weston. His room had not been cleaned for 55 years. One hundred guineas were found wrapped in brown paper, and he died possessed of 30,000 pounds in the funds.

No. 7.—Vol. XIV (Whole No. 683) Friday, 2 May 1806.

† [3a] Account of the death [30 March? 1806] of Mr. Benjamin Leek, of Plattsburg, N.Y., who died from injuries sustained from the fall of a tree. Leek, in his 44th year, left a wife, 3 children, a mother and mother-in-law. Dr. Pomeroy, of Burlington, Vt., attempted to save his life. ◆ Also, a brief mention of another case which Dr. Pomeroy attended to: a son of Mr. Francis Calver of Plattsburg, aged 13 years, was thrown from a horse, and his injuries were probably fatal.

† [3a-b] Gruesome account of the murder of widow Morriset, in Chesterfield County, Virginia, by two slave women. ◆

¶ [3c] On the *first of April*, Mr. David Matteson, of Shaftsbury, killed EIGHTEEN Crows at one shot. [*Bennington paper.*]

† [3c] Death of Mr. Daniel Shove, "of Middlefield," who was killed by the fall of a tree. The article was copied from a Cooperstown paper, presumably *New York*. ◆

† [3c] Rev. Mr. Sturges installed over the Second Society, Bethel, Conn.

====== ¶ [3d] MARRIED. ======

In Pittsfield, (Ms.) Mr. Nathan Appleton, mer. of Boston, to Miss Maria Theresa Gould, eldest daughter of Thomas Gould, Esq.—In Newburyport, the Rev. Jeremiah Chaplain, of Danvers, to Miss Mercy O'Brien.—At Hanover, Mr. Jabez Kellogg, to Miss Ruby Utley.—At Putney, Mr. Joseph Metcalf, to Miss Sally Hutchins.

At Croydon, Mr. John Williams to Miss Sukey Powers ; Mr. James Powers to Miss Huldah Cooper ; Mr. Peter Powers to Miss Lois Sanger Cooper ; Mr. Cyrus Hall to Miss Sally Cutting ; Mr. Noah Lovel, to the amiable Miss Phebe Putnam.

At Newport, Mr. Charles Buel to Miss Lucinda Alden.

====== ¶ [3d] DIED. ======

In Elkridge, (Penn.) Joseph Pierrepoint, aged 86 ; for many years a preacher amongst the Society of Friends.—In Philadelphia, on the 15th ult, Hon. Edward Shippen, late Chief Justice of the Supreme Court of Pennsylvania, Æt. 78.—In Conajoharry, (N.Y.) Col. Myndert Roseboom, aged 71.—In Providence, Maj. Bennett Wheeler, formerly editor of the U.S. Chronicle.—In Northampton, Mrs. Sarah Baker, relict of the late Mr. Samuel Baker, in the 93d year of her age.—In Halifax, in February, Lieut. Gen. William

Gardiner, commanding His Britannic Majesty's forces in Nova Scotia, New Brunswick and their dependencies.—Departed this life, on the 18th ult. aged 77 years, George Pitkin, Esq. of East-Hartford, who was Clerk of the Superior Court more than 50 years. He was a son of the late Governor Pitkin, and highly respected as a virtuous man and good Citizen.—At Plymouth, widow Catharine Clark, aged 62.—At Coventry, Mr. Daniel Badger, aged 64.—At Wethersfield, Mrs. Rebecca Wells, aged 71.—In Reupert, (Ver.) Mr. Selah Stebbins, aged 49.—At Winchester, (N.H.) Mrs. Elizabeth Hurd, aged 78.—In Springfield, (Mass.) Mr. Benajah Stephenson, aged 80.—In Brattleboro', Mr. John Birge, in the 80th year of his age.—At Chesterfield, (Mass.) Rev. Timothy Allen, in the 91st year of his age.—At Preston, (Conn.) Mr. John Partridge, aged 90 years.—At Plainfield, (C.) Mr. Andrew Spalding, aged 86.—At Shrewsbury, (Ms.) widow Sarah Howe, aged 73.—At Acton, Mr. Timothy Brooks, aged 24, son of Mr. Seth Brooks. This is the last of nine brothers and sisters, who have in a few years died of a pulmonic consumption, all of them of an adult age, and in the prime of life. They were healthful when children. Their parents have been and still are persons of good health and constitutions, and educated them in habits of temperance, industry and sobriety. No particular known cause produced the disease in these victims.

At Rockingham, (Ver.) Mr. J. Gilmore, at an advanced age.

No. 8.—Vol. XIV (Whole No. 684) Friday, 9 May 1806.

† [3c] Brief news item stating that the State of Georgia offers a reward "for the detection of one Lewis M'Gahagan, who is supposed, on the 25th of March last, to have murdered John Loudon, Esq. senator for the county of Effingham, in that state. ♦

¶ [3c] Dominick Daley, and James Hallighan, who were confined at Northampton, for the murder of Marcus Lyon of Wilbraham, in Nov. last, have been convicted and sentenced to death. One Busby, an Irishman, and a Mrs. Ellis, at Northampton, in March last, have been tried and acquitted.

¶ [3c] FIRE.]—On the 18th inst. the barn of Mr. O. Blakesly, at Hamden, Con. was destroyed by fire—and two children were burnt to death in it.

† [3d] Nathaniel Holden, Administrator, offers a farm for sale at Charlestown, it being part of the real estate of William Henry, Jr., deceased. Dated April —, 1806.

† [3d] A. & O. Allen offer goods for sale at their Walpole store; dated 8 May 1806.

===== ¶ [3d] MARRIED. =====

At White-Plains, Mr. Isaac Valentine, aged 80 years, to the amiable Miss Fredenburg, aged 18 years.—At Windham, (Conn.) Mr. George W. Webb, to Miss Mary Lee.—At Hampton, Mr. Daniel Martin, of Mansfield, to Miss Betsey Adams.

===== ¶ [3d] DIED. =====

In Constantinople, the Sultana Valide, mother of the Grand Signior. [. . .]—In Quebec, Nathaniel Taylor, Esq. Deputy Secretary and Register of the Province. His public as well as private conduct was without reproach, and gained him the esteem and respect of all who knew him.—In Bridgewater, (Con.) Mrs. Mary, wife of Richard Perkins, Esq. M.D. aged 66.—In Simsbury, on the 24th ult. Mr. John Payson, aged 57. About 7 o'clock he sat down to supper in usual health, and in ten minutes after he was a lifeless corpse. He has left a widow and six children, and an aged mother to lament their loss.—In Hartford, Mr. Thomas Burket, aged [51?].—Deaths of aged people in Wallingford, (C.) within three months: Mr. Joseph Cowles, aged 96 ; Mrs. Hannah Cook, aged 86 ; Mrs. Elizabeth Darrow, aged 97 ; Mrs. Esther Webb, aged 94 ; Mr. John Church, aged 81.—In Charlestown, (Ms.) suddenly, Miss Elizabeth Abraham, aged 72.—At Charlotte, (Ver.) on the 6th ult. the Rev. Walter Farris [compare to the issue of 16 May 1806], in the 39th year of his age, and in the 8th year of his ministry. He has left an amiable wife and five children, a respectable church and society, to lament the loss of a kind husband, an indulgent parent, a faithful minister and charitable neighbour. —In Norwalk, (Con.) in consequence of a fall from a horse, Thomas Belden, Esq. aged 72.—In Danbury, Capt. Thomas Starr, aged 85.—In Sunderland, Mr. Phineas Graves, aged 80.—In Marblehead, Mr. Robert Smith, aged 83.—In Stamford, Mr. Samuel Adsit, aged 84.—In Londonderry, Deac. Samuel Fisher, aged 84.—In Hallowell, Mr. Richard Dummer, aged 84.—At Montague, (Mass.) Mr. Judah Wright, in the 99th year of his age.—In Chester, (N.H.) Mrs. Mary Dearborn, aged 61.—In Kensington, Maj. Joseph

Clifford, aged 73.—In Pittsfield, (Mass.) Mr. Josiah Wright, aged 77.—In Albany, Mr. Geo. Hutton, aged 77 : Mr. Marte Mynderse, aged 79.—At Washington, Dr. Starling Archer, of Virginia, aged 24, late of the Navy, and killed in a duel with Dr. Smith, of the Army. The deceased was mortally wounded the first fire.—In Penobscot, Mr. Sam'l Brown, of Sebesticook, aged 20, killed by the falling of a tree.—In West-Springfield, Mr. Eli Bedortha, aged 30, killed by the falling of a barn frame.—In Boston, Capt. Samuel Treat, aged 55.—In Norwich, (C.) Miss Judith Waterman, aged 86.—At Newburyport, Timothy Dexter, Esq. commonly called Lord Dexter ; a man not more distinguished for his immense riches, than for those mean and grovelling qualities which sunk him to a level with the brutes, and whose ignorance was almost without a parallel in the United States of America. 158—Deaths in Newburyport, (Ms.) during the year 1805, 140 ; of which 71 were males and 69 females. Births, 290. Newburyport, in 1800, contained 5946 inhabitants.—At Barnard, Vt. the Rev. Joseph Bowman, aged 71.—At Winchendon, Ms. Mr. Eliphalet Goodridge, aged 73.—At Westmoreland, Mr. Constant [Chaffe? or Chasse?], æ. 44.—At Groton, C. Mr. Christ'r Brumbly, aged 70.

No. 9.—Vol. XIV (Whole No. 685) Friday, 16 May 1806.

† [3a] Detailed account of the death, [18 April? 1806] of William Johnson, stage driver of Kingston, New Jersey, who attacked Mr. Skillman, a blacksmith. ♦
¶ [3c] Thursday, the 5th June, is assigned for the execution of Daley and Halligan, lately convicted of high-way robbery and murder, in Hampshire county.
¶ [3c] It is stated in the New-York Morning Chronicle, that the senate of that state, have passed a resolve, commuting the punishment of Stephen Arnold, from death to confinement in the state prison for life.
¶ [3c] *Increase and Multiply.*—A remarkable instance of which occured last week in Stoneham—the wife of Capt. Josiah Green, a gentleman about 80 years of age, produced him a child, his daughter a child and his grand daughter a child—all within 48 hours. [*Boston paper.*]

===== ¶ [3c] MARRIED. =====

At Lempster, on the 4th inst. Mr. Byron Beckwith, to Miss Candace [?]. 159

===== ¶ [3d] DIED. =====

In Charleston, (S.C.) Dr. William Dumont, aged 61.—In Litchfield, (Con.) Capt. Elihu Harrison, aged 66.—In Danbury, Mrs. Hannah Andrus, widow, aged 70.—In Hudson, (N.Y.) in the 68th year of his age, Nathaniel Greene, Esq. formerly judge of the circuit court of common pleas in the county of Columbia.—In Georgetown, (Me.) Mrs. Mary M'Cobb, aged 70 years. She was sister to His Excellency, John Langdon, and eldest of the Langdon family.—At Colrain, (Ms.) on the 11th ult. after a long and painful illness, Mr. Stephen Shepardson, in the 46th year of his age.—At Charlotte, (Vt.) on the 6th inst. the Rev. Walter Jarvis [*compare to the issue of 9 May 1806*], in the 38th year of his age.—Suddenly, on the 27th of April last, the amiable Mrs. Lovice Taft, consort of Mr. Willard Taft, of Townsend, (Vt.) in the 36th year of her age.—In Brookfield, (Ms.) by a stone falling on him, Mr. Levi Deball, aged 40.—In Newton, Mrs. Martha, consort of Mr. Jonas Stone, aged 54.—In Quincy, Mrs. Mary Vesey, daughter of the late Rev. Dr. Miller.
At Rockingham, Mrs. Macafee.
At Salisbury, (N.H.) the 2d inst. Mr. Thomas Perrin, aged 73.

ROBERT RANSOM.

A transient person, who called himself Robert Ransom, died of epileptic fits, in the town of Richmond, in the county of Chittenden and state of Vermont, on the 23d April inst. He was by occupation a Limner, and had some trifling materials with him for that business. He was so suddenly deranged by the disorder which caused his death, that no particular information could be obtained from him respecting his former place of residence, but from some observations which he made, those who attended him concluded that he had a wife and one child, living in or near Portsmouth, New Hampshire. [*Burlington paper.*]

No. 10—Vol. XIV (Whole No. 686) Friday, 23 May 1806. [160]

† [3d] *Flint & Alcock* adv. "that they carry on the Saddler's business, in the house of Oliver Shepard jun. in Alstead, near the old meeting house . . . " Dated 20 May 1806.

† [3d] Legal notice regarding the insolvent estate of Cornelius Warren, late of Walpole, deceased; Jonathan Royce, Elijah Burroughs, and William Slade, Commissioners. Dated at Walpole, 22 May 1806. Also, in an appended notice, Moses Hale, Administrator, requests that debtors to Warren's estate to pay up.

† [3d] Amos Shepard and Samuel Hutchinson announce that their copartnership, *Shepard and Hutchinson*, is dissolved. Hutchinson to carry on the business in the future. Dated at Alstead 20 May 1806.

===== ¶ [3c] DIED. =====

At Goshen, 12th inst. Capt. Samuel [Gunnison?], aged 85.—Mrs. Clarisa Humphrey, wife of Mr. Samuel H.

At Claremont, on the 1st inst. after a lingering sickness, Mrs. Hannah Wise, wife of Mr. John Wise, aged 32 years. She has left four small children, and a sorrowful husband to bewail the loss [. . .]

In Cadiz, 9th April, of the wounds he received in the battle off Trafalgar, Admiral Gravina, Commander in Chief of the Spanish fleet.—In Chilmark, (on the island of Martha's Vineyard) the Rev. Zachariah Mayhew, aged 88.—His great-grand-father, grand-father, father, and himself, were missionaries to the aboriginals of that island in succession.—In Danvers, Mr. Gilbert Tapley, aged 85 ; his posterity now living are 72. —In Havana, Nathaniel Fellowes, Esq. mer. late of this town.—At Granby on the 3d inst. Mr. John Holliday, aged 105.—At Mendon, on the 9th ult. Mrs. Thankful Rawson, wife of Mr. Levi Rawson, in the 60th year of her age.—In England, the Earl of Maccartney, a celebrated diplomatic character, aged 69:—Also, the accomplished Duchess of Devonshire.—In Philadelphia, Robert Morris, esq. aged 72 ; whose signal and important services during our revolutionary struggle, will long be remembered with gratitude.—In White Plains, (N.Y.) Edward Thomas, esq.—In Plymouth, (C.) widow Catharine Clark, aged 63 ; she went to bed in good health, and was found dead in the morning.—In Simsbury, Mr. John Payson Æt. 57; he sat down to supper in good health, and in about ten minutes was a lifeless corpse.—In Salisbury, (N.H.) Hon. Ebenezer Webster, aged 68.—In Andover, Mr. Jacob Foster, aged 88.—In Amesbury, Mr. Moses Bagley, aged 91 ; in the whole course of his long life he never was six miles distant from his dwelling, and always enjoyed uninterrupted health.—In Boston, Mr. Daniel Lotty, aged 90.—In London, a man, of the name of Cooper, who had long endured the horrors of a guilty conscience, which he disburdened a few hours before his death, by declaring that he had aided in murdering Mr. Rice, about 40 years ago.—At Brimfield, last Wednesday morning, Mr. Richard Bishop, aged 74. He went to bed in good health, and by 3 o'clock in the morning he died without a struggle or a groan. He has left a numerous family to mourn his departure : 15 children, 53 grand children, and 5 great grand children.—At Waitsfield, (Vt.) on the 23d ult. Capt. John Wells, in the 74th year of his age.

In Charlestown, on the evening of Saturday last, Joseph Allen, esq. of this town, attorney at law, aged 33.

DROWNED.] In Machias river, (Me.) 27th ult. Capt. Stephen Rice, of Annapolis, or Grand Passage, (N.S.); he had been insane at times.

No. 11—Vol. XIV (Whole No. 687) Friday, 30 May 1806. [161]

¶ [3b] Mr. Simeon Butler, a federalist, is removed from the Post Office, at Northampton, to make room for Daniel Wright, Esq. a *warm* Democrat—but *a very moderate man*. [*Greenfield Gaz.*

† [3c] Stephen R. Whitman adv. drugs and medicines; dated Walpole 30 May 1806.

† [3c] Edward Hall, Jr. adv. mills for sale, "lately occupied by Capt. Abijah Hall, in Croydon, lying on the main road, and near the centre of town . . . "

† [3d] *J. & T. Bellows* adv. goods for sale; dated Walpole 30 May 1806.

¶ [3c] MARRIED.

At Turkey-Hill, (Conn.) Mr. Levi Shepherd, to Miss Betsey Hutchins, both of Northampton.—At Marcellus, (N.Y.) the Rev. Caleb Atwater, to Miss Diana Lawrence, daughter of Col. Bigelow Lawrence.—In Gloucester, (Ms.) Dr. John Kittredge, to Mis. [sic] Mary Plummer.

In this town, on Sunday morning last, by the Rev. Mr. Fessenden, Mr. John Dennis, of Woodstock, Vt. to Miss Mary Carlisle, of this town.

¶ [3c] DIED.

In Brunswick, (Germany) William V. Prince of Orange, and son of the late Stadholder of Holland.—In London, Dr. Isaac Mosely, formerly of Connecticut.—In Nassau, (Bahama) Mrs. Susan Powell, aged 104.

In Hudson, (N.Y.) Mr. Daniel Pinkham, in the 72d year of his age.—In Worcester, (Ms.) on the 17th instant, within a few moments of each other, the brothers Lemuel and Luke Rice, the former after a long and distressing debility, aged 66, the latter suddenly without previous complaint or indisposition, aged 61. A solemn and impressive instance of the mortality of man ! —At Northbridge, Major David Batchelder, aged 64.— At Randolph, (Vt.) Col. Israel Converse.—At Barnard, the Rev. Joseph Bowman, aged 72.—In Keene, Mr. Daniel Snow, aged 79.—In Bernardston, on Saturday last, Mr. Ruel Willard, aged 54. He left home in the morning, apparently in good health, to attend to his business, and in a short time after, was found, about half a mile from his house, lying upon the ground—just expiring. It is thought his sudden death was occasioned by a fall from his horse.—In an advanced age, in the gaol of the county of Providence (where he had chosen to remain about 15 years, rather than pay his debts) Abner Lapham, Esq; late of Cumberland.—In Litchfield of a lingering disorder, Mrs. Abigail Skinner, wife of Gen. Timothy Skinner, aged 60 years.—At Stratford, Miss Sophia Stebbins, Æt. 18, daughter of the Rev. Stephen W. Stebbins.—In Colcester, (C.) 7th inst. Mr. Pratt, son of Mr. Daniel Pratt, jun. aged 20 ; on the 9th, Mr. Daniel Pratt, jun. aged 50 ; and on the 10th, Mr. Daniel Pratt, sen. aged 70 ; being father, son, and grand-father.— In Walpole, (Mass.) Mrs. Sarah Palmer, aged 72, relict of the late Rev. Joseph Palmer, of Norton.—At Cranbury, (N.J.) Mr. John Story, in the 91st year of his age.

In Plainfield, (N.H.) Lieut. Daniel Freeman, aged 73. He has left a wife and eleven children.

At Charlestown, on Tuesday last, John Hubbard, Esq. aged about 50 years.

In this town, on Wednesday morning last, of a consumption, Mrs. Phebe Ormsby, consort of Mr. Stephen Ormsby, in the 43d year of her age. She was a kind and affectionate wife [. . .]

SUICIDE.—On Wednesday, the 13th of April, Mrs. Patty Pierson, consort of Mr. Oliver Pierson, of Cazenovia, (N.Y.) and daughter of Mr. Zachariah Fairchild, of Great-Barrington, put an end to her life by discharging the contents of a loaded gun into her breast. She had been previously deranged in her mind, occasioned by sickness and melancholy; and had before made several attempts to destroy herself, but was prevented by the watchfulness of the family. But her perseverance in the horrid design at length got the better of their vigilance. She obtained a two barrelled gun that was loaded in the house, (but cautiously left without priming) and primed it herself with powder, which she had probably carried with her for that purpose for some time; cocked both locks, placed the muzzles just below her left breast, and probably intended discharging both at the same time, but one only went off, and loaded its contents near the shoulder blade, which put an end to her existence, in the 25th year of her age.—Utica pap.

☞ We mentioned, in a late paper, the death of T. Dexter, Esq. of Newburyport. It was taken from a Connecticut paper, and is said to be not true.

No. 12.—Vol. XIV (Whole No. 688) Friday, 6 June 1806.

† [2d] Death of Mr. Isaac Preston at Ashby, Mass., who was found dead in a stream, [11 May 1806]. ♦

† [3a] Rev. and Mrs. Davidson of Carlisle, [Penn.?—Ed.] injured when their chaise was upset by a frightened horse. Mrs. Davidson eventually died of her injuries. ♦

¶ [3b] MARRIED.

In Rowley, (Mass.) Rev. Nathaniel Todd, of Schenectady, (N.Y.) to Miss Elizabeth Green Bradford, eldest daughter of the late Rev. Eben. Bradford, of Rowley.

In Cornish, Doctor Erastus Torrey, to Miss Gratia Chase.

At Washington, on the 2d of April last, Mr. Samuel Warren of this town, to Miss Lucy Proctor, of the former place.

At Alstead, Rev. Abner Kneeland, of Langdon, to Miss Mann, daughter of the late Rev. Mr. Mann, of Alstead.

¶ [3b] DIED.

In Newyork, James Watson, Esq. aged 56.—In Skeensboro', (N.Y.) 11th April, Mrs. Chloe Ormsby, aged 36, wife of Mr. Gideon Ormsby, of Manchester, Vt., and daughter of the Rev. Daniel Barber, of Claremont, (N.H.).—In Londonderry, Deacon Samuel Fisher, aged 84 : Capt. Adam Taylor, aged 69.—In Newburyport, Capt. Lawrence Furlong, aged 72.—In Milton, (Ms.) after a long and tedious sickness, Mr. Elitheia Cain, aged 79.—At Marietta, Hon. Joseph Gilman, late Judge of the Supreme Court of the N.W. Territory, aged 68.—In Providence, Major Daniel Jackson, in the 65th year of his age ; Mrs. Sally Hubbard, wife of Mr. Ezra Hubbard, on her 32d birth day.—In Northampton, Mrs. Lucy Marsh, aged 67.

At Westmoreland, Mrs. Polly Wheeler, wife of Mr. [Carler?] Wheeler, aged 21.

At Alstead, on Tuesday last, Mrs. Higbee, consort of the Rev. Mr. Higbee, of that town.

In Surry, on Tuesday last, very suddenly, Mrs. Susan Bundy, aged about 45, wife of Capt. Elias Bundy, formerly of this town.

SUICIDE.—In Middletown, (Vt.) Mr. Lemuel Stoddard, aged 20 ;—he had for a long time paid his constant addresses to a young girl, and the day had arrived when, with the mutual consent of their parents, they were to be married;—every thing was prepared, and the friends and parents expected to witness a pleasant scene—when the young man related to her, that he doubted the sincerity of her attachment, that her chastity was not inviolate; that a friend had convinced him his suspicions were not groundless ; that he could not marry her without being miserable, nor could he live happy without her.—He then proposed she should depart with him to a better world, where their spirits would dwell together in the same bonds of affection that distinguished them here—She agreed; both swallowed a dose of laudanum—but the girl sickened, and a discharge from the stomach saved her from a dreadful end.—The dose taken by her anticipated companion proved fatal.——In N. Jersey, Mr. Nehemiah, son of Mr. Enoch Williams ; he shot himself while in a state of inebriation.—In Milford, (Con.) Mr. John Adam Hartline, lately from Canada ; reduced from affluence to poverty, he hung himself during a fit of melancholy.—In Middleborough, 25th inst. (by suicide) Deacon Abner Bourne ; of late years he has been zealously engaged as an itenerant [sic] preacher, contrary to the opinion of his friends—He has left an amiable wife and family to lament his melancholy exit.

No. 13.—Vol. XIV (Whole No. 689) Friday, 13 June 1806.

† [3a] Josiah Burnham convicted at Superior Court, Plymouth, N.H., for the murder of Starkweather and Freeman in Haverhill, N.H.; execution set for 15 July 1806. [162]

† [3a] Article describing the fire at a house in Avery's Gore, where a black man and woman lived with their three children. The children burned to death; the identity of the family is not given. ♦

† [3a] Fire destroyed a paper mill at Alstead, owned by Webster Cole and Philip Brown. David Buckman, a neighbor, sounded the alarm, and awoke Alvan Shipman, a workman who was sleeping in the mill. The date given at the close of the article, 16 June 1806, must be incorrect. ♦

† [3a-b] A two year-old daughter of Mr. Phineas Mirick, tanner, of Alstead, fell into a tanning pit, and was discovered lifeless, but was resuscitated, 7 June 1806. ♦

† [3b] James Hilligan and Dominick Daley executed [at Boston?], for the murder of Marcus Lyon, 9 Nov. 1805, at Wilbraham. ♦ [163]

† [3b] Legal notice regarding the insolvent estate of John Abbot, late of Lempster, deceased. Claims to be examined at the house of Jabez Brainard, at Lempster; Issac

Foster and Thomas Slader, Commissioners, and Metalda Keyes, Administrator.
† [3b] Timothy Holden advertises for lost steers; dated Charlestown, 2 June 1806.
† [3b] Sol. Van Rensselaer of Albany, N.Y. adv. for two runaway slaves named York and Ruf. The adv. gives a description of both men. ♦
† [3d] Simon Smith of Plainfield adv. for breeding horses.

No. 14.—Vol. XIV (Whole No. 690) Friday, 20 June 1806.

¶ [2d] *Accident.*—A melancholy accident happened on Friday last, at the new Meeting-house, West-Boston. Mr. Warren Jacobs, a worthy and industrious mason, fell from the stageing, and expired in a few hours from the wounds he received. [*Col. Centinel.*]
† [3a] Account of a severe thunderstorm which struck Hadley, Mass., 1 June 1806, destroying a barn owned by Capt. Moses Kellogg.
† [3b] Rev. Josiah W. Cannon ordained at Gill, 11 June 1806. 164
† [3c] Legal notice regarding the estate of William Henry, Jr.; Nathaniel Holden, Adm.
† [3d] Ezekiel R. Bigelow of Charlestown adv. for a lost mare; dated 16 June 1806.

===== ¶ [3b] MARRIED. =====

At Williamstown, (Mass.) on the 4th May, Mr. John Holmes, of Hanover, to Miss Sally Town, of the former place.—In Keene, Mr. Seth Britt, to Miss Betsey Robinson.—At Wethersfield, (Con.) Capt. Ebenezer Welis, of Brattleboro', Vt. to Miss Mary Chester, daughter of the Hon. John Chester, of the former place.

===== ¶ [3b] DIED. =====

At Hopewell, (N.J.) the Rev. James Ewing, for many years a preacher in the 1st Baptist church of that place.—In New Fairfield, (Con.) on the 9th ult. Mr. John Bradshaw, aged 104 years, 10 months and 20 days.—In Somers, (C.) Wid. Mary Sexton, aged 91 ; she practised midwifery 55 years, and by her records she was at the births of 1000 children ; she was the mother of 11.—In Chelsea, Mr. William Watts, aged 70.—In Vergennes, (Vt.) Mrs. Speedy Fitch, consort of Col. Jabez G. Fitch.—In Woodstock, V. Mr. Stephen Fitch, aged 70.—At Peacham, Mrs. Mary Buswell, aged 71.—In Amherst, by a fall into a well, Mr. Daniel Stevens, aged 84.—In Swanton, Mrs. Arethusa Hubbard, aged 28.—At Chester, 25th April, Mrs. Mary Dearborn, wife of Deac. John S. Dearborn, in the 62d year of her age.—In Georgia, Capt. John Spencer, aged 61 ; an old revolutionary officer.—In Philadelphia, from 30th May to 7th June, 41 deaths.—During last week, in New York, 40 deaths.—In Danvers, Col. Jeremiah Page, aged 83.—In Ipswich, Dea. John Crocker, aged 83.—In Boston, John Avery, Esq. Secretary of the Commonwealth of Massachusetts, aged 67 : Maj. Isaac Winslow, aged 88.—In Hartford, (Con.) on the 28th ult. of a consumption, John Porter, Esq. Comptroller of the Public Accounts of that state, aged 48.—In Danbury, Mr. Nathaniel Benedict, in the 90th year of his age.—At Athens, (Ohio) on the 29th April, in the 90th year of her age, a few years since from the state of R. Island, the Widow Susannah Anthony, long an ornament to religion, and a pattern of female excellence.

No. 15.—Vol. XIV (Whole No. 691) Friday, 27 June 1806.

† [1c-d] Summary of Acts passed by the New Hampshire Legislature at Hopkinton, June 1806. Those Acts which related to individuals are given here:
 1) An Act to authorize John Brooks to assume the name of John Drury Brooks.
 2) An Act to alter the name of Joseph Hogg, Simpson Hogg, and William Hogg.
 3) An Act, to incorporate Joseph W. Pickering and others into a religious society, called and known by the name of *The First Baptist Society in Portsmouth.*
 4) An Act authorizing John March to collect certain taxes.
 5) An Act authorizing the Superior Court to adjust and determine the account of John Mooney, of his administering upon the estate of Stephen Mead, and for other purposes.
 6) An Act, for incorporating William Caldwell and his associates, by the name and style of *The Proprietors of Piscataquog Canal.*
 7) An Act, to restore Eleazer Cummings, Aaron Wheeler, Joel Adams, Nathaniel Prentice, Woodes Lee, Oliver Hosmore, and Nathan Blood, to law, in their certain cases.

† [3b] Samuel Hutchinson adv. goods for sale; dated Alstead 23 June 1801 [sic]. In a second adv., at [3d] additional goods for sale are offered "at the Store lately occupied by Shepard & Hutchinson, in Alstead." The second adv. is dated 11 June 1806.
† [3c] *Wyman & Chapman* adv. their new store in Alstead; dated 25 June 1806.
† [3d] Samuel Ashley adv. for a lost horse; dated Claremont, 16 June 1806.
† [3d] Thomas Thompson and Elijah Hall, Managers, adv. for the Sixth Class of Piscataqua Bridge Lottery tickets. Dated 20 June 1806.

====== ¶ [3a] DIED. ======

In Philadelphia, col. Michael Kitts, of the 50th regimental of Pennsylvania militia, in the 59th year of his age.—In Middletown, (Con.) Mrs. Elizabeth Stone, aged 70.—In Greenfield, (Ms.) Mr. Joseph Hastings, aged 64.—In Richmond, (Vir.) Hon. Geo. Wythe, chancellor of the state. He was one of the few surviving who signed the Declaration of Independence.—In Dublin, on the 16th inst. Col. Abel Wilder, aged 46 years.

No. 16.—Vol. XIV (Whole No. 692) Friday, 4 July 1806.

¶ [2c] On Thursday last six venerable ladies, in good health, sisters of the late Col. Simeon Potter, made a day's visit to Mr. Hopestill M'Neill, of this town, the son of one of them, and the nephew of the others. The eldest is 93 years of age, and the youngest 74. The amount of their ages is 487 years. A seventh sister, in an advanced age, now resides at Bristol, in this State. [*Prov. pap.*
¶ [2c] We learn that two married women were killed by lightning, in Lebanon, York County, Me. on Sunday, the 8th inst. They were both in one house, tho' in separate rooms.
¶ [2d] On the 20th ult. was executed in Wilkes county, Polly Barclay, as an accessary in the murder of her husband. [*Augusta G. paper.*
† [3a] Rev. Joseph Strong ordained at Eastbury, Conn. on the "11th ult."
† [3c] David Taylor adv. for a runaway indented boy named Joshua Blood, aged about 19 years, and offers one cent reward for his return. Dated at Charlestown, 30 June 1806.
† [3c] *E. & J. Stearns* adv. goods for sale; dated Charlestown, 30 June 1806.

====== ¶ [3a] MARRIED. ======

In Portland, (Me.) Rev. Joshua Taylor, to Miss Dorothy Smith.—In Boston, Dr. Edward Jones, physician, lately from London, to Mrs. Ann Pope, widow of the late Wm. Pope, Esq.—Mr. Nathaniel W. Appleton, to Miss Sarah [Wildes?].—Mr. Philip Andrews, to Miss Eliza Stevens.—In Roxbury, (Mass.) William Austin, esq. of Charlestown, to Miss Charlotte Williams.—At Woodstock, (Ver.) Mr. ——— Ripley, to Miss Susanna Cottle.—At Hartland, Mr. Cary Allen, of Woodstock, to Miss Sally Rice.—At Temple, Nathaniel Shattuck, esq. attorney at law, to Miss Mary Wallace, both of Milford.—At Cornish, Mr. Wm. [Butman?], of Barnard, (Vt.) to Miss Olive Heldrith.—At Claremont, on the 8th ult. Mr. Joseph Tyler, to Miss Mary Gideons, daughter of Capt. Gideons, of that place.—At Plainfield, on the 16th ult. Mr. William Grannis, mer. of Claremont, to Miss Melinda Dustin, daughter of Major Moody Dustin, of the former place.

====== ¶ [3b] DIED. ======

In Charleston, (S.C.) Capt. Joseph Doane, aged 45.—In Philadelphia, from the 7th to 14th June, 21 adults and 20 children.—In New York, from the 7th to 14th June, 15 men, 9 women, 11 boys and 16 girls ; of consumption 4, of small pox 3.—In Boston, Mr. John [Blimer?], aged 70 :—Mr. Stephen Cleverly, aged 75.—In Rehoboth, Mrs. Martha Paine, wife of Mr. Jonathan Paine ; she was killed by lightning, the 8th ult.—At Cumberland, Miss Morris, also killed by lightning.—In Hampton, Capt. Caleb Tappan aged 65.—In Walpole, (Mass.) Madam Sarah Palmer, aged 72.—In Chilmark, (Me.) Rev. Zachariah Mayhew, in the 88th year of his age.—In Hartford, (Conn.) Mr. Timothy Steele, aged 70.—In Orange, (Vt.) Mr. Joseph Williams, aged 76 ; he was the first settler in that town.—At Amherst, Wid. Sarah Burditt, aged 94.—At Milford, Mrs. Hannah Howe, aged 51.—In France, Admiral Villeneuve, commander in chief of the combined French and Spanish fleet in the battle off Trefalgar. He was found dead in his chamber, at Morlaix, in the night of the 22d April, where he had just arrived from England. He had given himself five wounds with a knife in his left side.—In Philad. from the 14th to 21st

June, 18 adults and 19 children.—In New York, during the week ending 21st June, 18 adults and 19 children.—In New York, during the week ending 21st June, 8 men, 10 women, 6 boys and 4 girls ; of consumption, 7 ; Mr. Peter Low [*compare to issue of 11 July 1806*], aged 79.—In Albany, Mrs. Sybil, wife of John Kane, Esq. aged 67.—In Ellington, (Con.) Dea. Joseph Kingsbury, aged 85.—In Hollis, (N.H.) 16th inst. Capt. William Tenney, aged 56.—In Manchester, (Ma.) Mr. Aaron Lee, for thirty years town clerk of that place.—In Salem, Mr. William Hilburt, aged 82 ; he was a soldier in the expedition against Louisburg, in 1746.—In Dedham, Mr. Nehemiah Fales.

The death of the late venerable Chancellor Wythe, in Virginia, has been reported to have been by means the most "foul and unnatural." It appears that his nephew, a young man who lived with him, had forged his uncle's name to checks on the bank. To prevent detection, and to anticipate a considerable sum of money which the Chancellor had bequeathed him, he put poison in his coffee, which occassioned his death, not however until after he had discovered the villainy of his nephew, and had altered his will accordingly.

DROWNED.—In Hadley, Mr. Samuel Warner, of Amherst. On the Saturday evening previous to the late eclipse he attempted to pass a stream, on a log, and fell in ; his body was found by some workmen, who went to the stream during the eclipse in order to view that phenomenon in the water.

No. 17.—Vol. XIV (Whole No. 693)   Friday, 11 July 1806.

† [3c] Notice of a meeting at Amos Keyes's tavern, regarding the Charlestown Turnpike Corporation; John Duncan, Josiah White, and Jonathan Spaulding, Directors. Dated at Acworth, 20 June 1806.

† [3d] Jesse Willcox, Jr., posts a notice regarding the Croydon Turnpike Road. Dated at Newport, 27 June 1806.

† [3d] Asahel Hunt adv. for "creatures" he found on his land; dated Ch'stown, 8 July.

===== ¶ [3c] MARRIED. =====

In Boston, Mr. Joseph Newell, mer. of Boston, to Miss Mary Reynolds, of Providence.

At Baltimore, Mr. Reuben Coffin, to Miss Polly Butt. [. . .]

===== ¶ [3c] DIED. =====

In Quebec, Capt. Lamb, of the ship Duke of York. [Quebec paper.]

On Saturday, the [Bonne?] Femme Constantineau, of this city, aged 105. She has left a son aged 72 to lament her memory.   Ibid.

In Philadelphia, Mr. James Ray M'Corkle, merchant and planter of the colony of Surinam. After an absence of several years, in the pursuit of laudable and successful enterprise, he had returned to his affectionate relatives, with an intention of making arrangements for spending the remainder of his days in his native land, and enjoying that independence which he had acquired ; when he was arrested by death, in the prime of his life, and surrendered up his soul to his God. U.S. Gaz.—In New York, Mr. Peter Dow [*compare to issue of 4 July 1806*], of that city, aged 79 years.—In Westfield, C. Deac. Israel Dewey, in the 88th year of his age. He has left an aged consort with whom he had lived 64 years, to bemoan his loss.—In Amherst, widow Lyon, aged 73.—In Ellington, (C.) the 8th ult. Dea. Joseph Kingsbury, in the 85th year of his age, in a fit of the numb palsy, being on his return from Tolland to Enfield.—In Thurlow, (Eng.) Mr. Crick, aged 135. He had been 53 years a school-master in that parish.—In Southampton, (Eng.) Mr. John Tucker, fisherman, aged 131.—Not long since at Winchester, (Eng.) Capt. Hall, of the army, aged 91. He was Surgeon's Mate of the Centurion, and went round the world with Lord Anson, in the year 1740, when the Manilla galleon, Nostra Signora de Cabadonga, was taken. She was the richest prize ever taken, having near a million and a half of dollars on board, and was larger and of more force that the Centurion. Mr. Hall came home Surgeon of her. It was after this voyage, which lasted three years and nine months, that Lord Anson, when he landed on the Point in Winchester, fell upon his knees and offered an ejaculatory prayer to HIM who had preseved him from such imminent dangers. Capt. Fortescue is the only person living who went on that voyage.—In New York, from 22d to 29th June, 39 persons ; 3 of small pox, 1 a suicide.—In Boston, Mrs. Ann Blake, aged 82.—In

Hubbardston, Lt. Benjamin Church, son of Capt. Asa Church, aged 30. His death was occasioned by a fall from the frame of a house.—Also, suddenly, Mr. Nathan Holden : he attended the funeral of his friend, Mr. Church, and went to bed at the usual hour in perfect health—at midnight he was a corpse.—In Lancaster, very suddenly, Deacon [Joseph?] White, aged 53.

DROWNED.]—During the celebration of the 4th inst. about 4 o'clock, P.M. Mr. Ephraim Stearns, jun. 4th son of Dea. Ephraim Stearns, of this town, was drowned in Connecticut river. He was bathing in the river in company with a couple of smaller lads. As soon as information of the unhappy event was communicated to those who were celebrating the day on the common, a party immediately repaired to the place where he was drowned, among whom were several physicians, who made use of the usual means recommended for the resuscitation of drowned persons, but their efforts were ineffectual. The sad ridings were conveyed to the unhappy parents, whose agonizing feelings on this melancholy occasion may be better conceived than expressed. He was in the 19th year of his age.

Drowned, at Barre, Ms. on the 23d inst. Adams Howe, son of Eliphalet Howe, of that town, aged 17 years.

No. 18.—Vol. XIV (Whole No. 694) Friday, 18 July 1806.

¶ [2c] FIRE ! —On the night of the 27th June was consumed by fire, the Hatter's shop of Mr. Christopher Arms of Conway, with all his valuable stock to the amount of 1500 dollars. [*Northampton paper.*]

† [3b] Rev. Daniel Marsh installed at Bennington, Vermont, 3 July 1806, and Rev. Joseph L. Mills ordained at the Congregational Church, Becket, Mass, 5 June 1806.

† [3d] James Norris adv. in regards to his carding machine and gristmill. "The Mills are one mile from the Westerly Meeting-house in Boscawen." Dated Boscawen, 9 July.

===== ¶ [3b] MARRIED. =====

At Hartford, (Conn.) William Woodbridge, Esq. of Marietta, (O.) to Miss Julia Anna Trumbull, daughter of the Hon. John Trumbull, Esq. of the former place.—At Williamstown, (Mass.) Rev. Stephen West, D.D. of Stockbridge, to Miss Elenor Dewey, of the former place.—In Brookline, Mr. Eben. Crafts, of Roxbury, mer. to Miss Sarah H. Spooner.

===== ¶ [3b-c] DIED. =====

In Tennessee, Mr. Charles Dickinson, of Maryland ;—killed in a duel by Gen. Jackson.—In Lexington, (Ken.) Miss Lewis, neice of Col. Burford : killed, while in bed, by lightning, which passed down the chimney and struck one of the foot bed-posts.—In Pennsylvania, Capt. Luke Broadhead. He was in the first Pennsylvania rifle reg't which marched to Boston in 1775.—At Lisle, (N.Y.) on the 6th inst. of a fit of the palsey, Mrs. Elizabeth Hyde, aged 64, consort of Gen. C. Hyde, formerly of Lenox.—In East Sudbury, (C.) Mr. Ebenezer Staples, aged 71.—In Roxbury, (Mass.) Nathaniel Ruggles, A.M. aged 96.—In Palmer, 13th ult. Mrs. Dolly Hamilton, wife of Mr. Joshua Hamilton, in the 27th year of her age, and on the Monday following, John Hamilton, aged 77, who on the Sunday preceeding had attended the funeral of his daughter.—In Ludlow, 4th inst. Mr. Elisha Hubbard, aged 70.—In Bradford, (Vt.) 1st June, Mrs. Mehitabel Mitchell, aged 80.—Killed, suddenly, at Groton, in this state, on the 3d inst. Mr. Enos Buell, by the fall of a tree. In him society have lost a very enterprizing and industrious member, and his wife and six small children a kind husband and a tender parent.—At Plainfield, Mr. Oliver Miner, aged 22.—In Switzerland, Count de Meuron, a Lt. General in his Britannic Majesty's service.—In Brandywine, (Delaware) Mrs. Flankington, killed by lightning; she was riding with her husband, each on horseback, when she was struck dead instantly.—In Philadelphia, from 28th June to 5th July, 15 adults and 14 children.—In New York, during the week ending 5th July, 13 men, 7 women, 14 boys and 7 girls ; one of small pox ; 3 casualties, two men and a child ; one of the men was killed by the going off of a cannon whilst in the act of ramming down the charge ; the other drowned in a brewer's cistern ; the child by falling from a sloop.—In Waterford, (N.Y.) Mrs. Elizabeth Cross, aged 60 ; her death was occasioned by drinking salt-petre, which she mistook for salts.—In Roxbury, Capt. Isaac Sturtevant, aged 66.

At Chester, (Vt.) on the 2d inst. of consumption, Dea. Jonathan Lawrence, in the 52d year of his age.

In this town, on Wednesday last, an infant child of Mr. D.W. [Bisco?].

DROWNED.—In Kennebeck river, Master Samuel Titcomb, son of Samuel T. Esq.—In Raymond, three boys, viz. Daniel Small, 4th, and Henry and Moses Simons.

No. 19.—Vol. XIV (Whole No. 695) Friday, 25 July 1806.

† [2d] Gruesome account of Capt. James Purinton, who murdered his wife and six children, then killed himself. A son, aged 17, escaped, and a daughter survived though was clinging to life when the account was written. The event occurred at Augusta, "Massachusetts" [District of Maine—Ed.], 9 July 1806. Purington was 46 years old, and had recently removed from Bowdoinham, Maine, and was said to have been worried about his poverty. ♦ 165

¶ [3b] *Fire.*—A house and barn, with nearly all their contents, the property of Mr. Samuel Allen, was destroyed by fire, at Manchester, 13th inst.—Supposed to have originated in the barn by a spark from a pipe.—A barn the property of Mr. Clough, took fire and was destroyed by lightning, at Gloucester, 8th inst. [*Col. Centinel.*]

† [3b-c] A Mr. Baldwin arrested for the murder of a lady who refused his intentions. The event occurred in the vicinity of Litchfield, though the state is not identified, nor is the name of the victim given. The article was copied from a "Windham paper."

¶ [3c] On Friday, the day on which John Banks was executed, a Spaniard stabbed a woman in Warren-street, and killed her almost instantly. Capt. Salter fell from the second story of a store in South-street, and was killed on the spot. A man killed his wife by beating her with a pail—And a person, whose name we have not learned, hung himself. [*New York paper, July* 15.]

¶ [3c] The late mails have contained numerous accounts of fatal occurrences, and murders, the "most horrid, foul and unnatural." The last New York paper states that a few days since one *Jesse Wood,* having had a controversy with his son, went home, took his gun, and shot that son dead. [*Cent.*]

† [3c] Nathaniel Grant and John Grant offer property for sale, consisting of "one acre of good land, with a small store and barn on said land well situated for a Trader or Mechanic, nigh the Meetinghouse in Acworth." Dated there, 16 July 1806.

† [3c] Roswell Willard adv. goods for sale at Charlestown, where "he has commenced trade in the store formerly occupied by Doct. Samuel Crosby." Dated 20 July 1806.

===== ¶ [3c] DIED. =====

In Africa, the celebrated traveller, Mungo Park. He was on a second tour of discoveries in Africa. In March, 1805, he landed at Goree, with about 40 attendants, fitted out by the British Government. They ascended the Gambia, and penetraded about 1500 miles into the interior of Africa, to Sago, a walled city, considered the largest in Africa ; where, after the Negro king had shewn him every curiosity, he ordered him and his attendants to be cruelly and brutally murdered. The account of this event has been received from traders who have arrived at Rio Pongus.—In Philadelphia, from 5th to 12th inst. 25 adults and 33 children ; 6 adults of consumption, 15 children of cholera morbus.—In New York, from 5th to 12th inst. 14 men, 8 women, 11 boys and 6 girls ; four persons were permitted to die of small-pox, although experience has established the efficacy of vaccination as an infallible preventative :—Rev. Mr. Pierre Antoine Alvert, rector of the French Episcopal Church du St. Esprit ; he was a native of Lausanne, (Switz.) a sincere and pious christian, a learned and eloquent divine.—In Norwalk, (Conn.) Rev. Dr. Matthias Burnett.—In Methuen, Mr. Asa Messer, aged 67.—In Gloucester, suddenly, Samuel Whittemore, Esq. aged 73.—In Medford, Maj. Ephraim Hall.—In Westerly, (C.) Col. James Rhodes, aged 76.—In Preston, 30th ult. in the 68th year of his age, Nathaniel Lord, esq. son of the late Rev. Hezekiah Lord, a pastor of the second Church in Preston.—In Keene, Thomas Baker, esq. aged 76.

At Rockingham, (Vt.) on the 12th inst. after a long and painful illness, which he bore with uncommon patience and fortitude, Mr. John L. Cutler, son of Dr. Samuel Cutler, aged 18 years.

DROWNED.]—At New Haven, (C.) Mr. Tucker, late of Massachusetts.

No. 20.—Vol. XIV (Whole No. 696) Friday, 1 Aug. 1806.

¶ [2c] Died at Syracuse, [Sicily—Ed.] in February last, Lieut. Joseph Maxwell, of the U.S. Navy.
¶ [2c] Died, suddenly, on the 6th of June, on board the U.S. bomb-ketch Vengeance, Mr. Simeon Smith, Midshipman. Mr. S. was one of the American prisoners in Tripoli, and was on his return to Rhode-Island, of which State he was a native.
¶ [2c] Died, at Syracuse, [Sicily—Ed.] in April last, Lieutenant Seth Carter, commander of Gun-boat No. 10—a native of Rhode-Island; and Mr. Bent, midshipman on board the U.S. cutter Hornet.
¶ [2d-3a] Found dead in Attleborough, on Saturday the 14th ult. (Near the Turnpike road, northward of Israel Hatch's tavern) a man by the name of John Welch, supposed by certain papers to have wrought in the business of printing.—A coroner's jury of inquest was held on the body, whose verdict from evidence produced on examination was, that he died in consequence of fatigue, ill health, want of rest, and falling asleep on the ground.—After which, the body was decently interred.—The clothes, papers, and some money found on the deceased, are left with John Richardson, jun. in said town. [*Dedham Paper.*]
† [3b] Asa Ellis adv. for his new "Store of Dye-Stuffs" at Cambridgeport, Mass, 1 July.
¶ [3b] RAN AWAY From the subscriber on the night of the 19th inst. Theodore Bellows, jr. aged about 19, a small, black-hair'd boy, indented to me for the blacksmith trade. Whoever will return him shall receive *one dollar* reward, without charges.—All persons are cautioned against harbouring, trusting, or dealing with him in any way, and I shall call for damage therefor, and will not pay any expenses for him, or debts of his contracting.

JONATHAN ARMS.

Charlestown, July 21, 1806.
† [3c] Isaac Redington adv. a notice for his debtors to pay up; dated 30 July 1806.
† [3c] William Briggs, Clerk, posts a notice regarding the Cheshire Bridge Corporation, dated 28 July 1806.
† [3c] Samuel Hutchinson adv. goods for sale; dated Alstead, 20 July 1806.

===== ¶ [3b] MARRIED. =====

At Lyme, (Conn.) Mr. Christopher Brockway, to Miss Christiana Chapel, after a fatiguing courtship of three hours.—In New London, Mr. Roswell Williams, of Stonington, to Miss Mercy Gardner.—At Unadilla, (N.Y.) Sherman Page, esq. attorney at law, to Miss Maria Crocker.—At Leominster, (Ms.) Mr. Samuel Salisbury, jun. of Boston, to Miss Nancy Gardner, daughter of the Rev. Francis Gardner, of the former place.—At Greenland, (N.H.) Mr. Timothy Frost, mer. of Kennebunk, to Miss Susan Coffin, of the former place.—In Barnet, (Vt.) Mr. John Spencer to Miss Polly Thurston ; Mr. Joseph Henry, jun. to Miss Patty Hadlock ; Mr. Benjamin Sanborn to Miss Polly Hall; Mr. Daniel White to Miss Rebecca Pierce ; Mr. Joshua Moran to Miss Sally Pierce ; Mr. John Morgan, jun. to Miss Ruth Haseltine ; Mr. Thomas Young to Miss Polly Goodwillie.

===== ¶ [3b] DIED. =====

On the 14th of June last, at Cape Francois, Mr. Charles Harmar, son of Gen. Harmar, of the neighbourhood of Philadelphia.—In Dover, (Delaware) the Rev. Richard Whatcoat, one of the Bishops of the Methodist Episcopal Church.—In Germantown, on the 5th ult. in the 68th year of his age, Maj. John Nice, of the revolutionary army.—At his seat in Carlisle county, Virginia, on the 16th June, Col. James Upshaw, aged 76 years.—In Worcester, (Mass.) Mr. James Trowbridge, aged 89 ; Mr. Walter Tufts, aged 40.—At Poultney, (Vt.) Mr. Wm. Buckland, in the 43d year of his age.—At Colrain, on the 23d ult. Mrs. Boggs, aged 79, relict of the late Mr. James Boggs, formerly from Lansingburgh, (N.Y.) who for more than three years has been in a state of the most surprising degree of insanity and distraction.—In Albany, 16th inst. in the 76th year of his age, Mr. Garrit Van Zandt, an old and respectable citizen of that city.—At Lebanon Springs in the 22d year of her age, Mrs. Henrietta Shepherd, wife of Mr. John Shepherd, of Northampton, and daughter of John Tryon, Esq. of the former place.—In

Hingham, (Ms.) Mr. Joseph Andrews, aged 75.—In Charlestown, Miss Mary Russell, aged 53, daughter of the late Hon. James Russell, esq.
    Drowned, at Harpswell, Mr. John Blake, aged 44.

No. 21.—Vol. XIV (Whole No. 697) Friday, 8 Aug. 1806.

† [2a-b] A very extensive account of the battle aboard the *Atahualpa*, a Boston trading ship which was attacked by natives off the northwest coast of America, probably off present-day British Columbia, 13 June 1805. The Captain and nine of the crew were killed, and nine others wounded. Capt. Porter was taken prisoner by the natives, and died after being tied to a tree for 15 days. The narrative was given by Mr. Joel Richardson, armorer on board the vessel. ♦

Dead.	Wounded.
Capt. Oliver Porter	Ebenezer Baker, seaman
Mr. John Hill, chief mate	Henry Tompson, seaman
Daniel Gooding, second mate	Ebenezer Williams, seaman
John G. Ratstraw, Captain's clerk	Joseph Robinson, carpenter
Mr. Lyman Plumer, seaman *	Thomas Edwards, steward
Peter Spooner "	William Walker
Luther Lapham "	
Samuel Lapham "	
Isaac Sammes, cooper	* nephew of Theodore Lyman, Esq. of Boston, ship's owner.
John Williams, cook	

† [3b] Account of the execution of a slave belonging to Mr. M'Corcle, for the murder of his Mistress, at Lincoln County, Georgia. ♦

¶ [3c] ORDAINED. In Phillipstown, (N.Y.) Mr. John Younglove, jun. pastor of the united congregations of Union village, Union and Stephentown.

===== ¶ [3c] MARRIED. =====

In paris, [sic] Gen. Le Burne, aged 58, to the beautiful Miss Pildmont, aged 15.—In Boston, Mr. James Foster to Miss Sarah Porter ; Mr. Wm. Fenno to Miss Catharine N. Adams.—In Windsor, Mr. Sewall Cutting, to Miss Mary Hunter.—At Hebron, C. Steward Beebe, jun. esq. of Wilbraham, to Miss Sophia Gilbert, daughter of the hon. Judge Gilbert, of the former place.

===== ¶ [3c] DIED. =====

In Kingston, (Eng.) Mr. T. Lloyd, 2d Lieutenant of the Dreadnought man of war. While on a party of pleasure with some brother officers, in the height of good humour he requested his companions to go with him to the churchyard, and see a spot where he should like to have his body interred. They went; and though in apparent good health at the time, he was taken with a complaint in the bowels, died a few hours after, and was interred in the spot he had pointed out, agreeable to his desire.—In Syracuse, Lieut. Joseph Maxwell, of the U.S. navy :—Lieut. Seth Carter, commander of gunboat No. 10, a native of Rhode-Island ; Mr. Bent, midshipman.—On board the U.S. bomb-ketch Vengeance, Mr. Simon Smith, midshipman, a native of R. Island.—In Lexington, (Ken.) Mr. John Falling, killed in an extraordinary duel with Mr. James Vann, his brother-in-law. In consequence of a dispute they agreed to meet half way between their own houses; they met, with their seconds all armed with muskets and pistols. When they appeared in sight of each other, they galloped up so near that their horses heads were touching, when they fired nearly at the same instant. The contents of Vann's musket, 30 rifle bullets, entered the breast of Falling, who fell dead from his horse. Vann's coat sleeve was burnt with the powder of Falling's musket.—Near Baltimore, William, a labouring man. He was killed by the mephitic air of a well, into which he had descended to rescue a fellow labourer whose life he succeeded in preserving. ☞ To prevent similar misfortunes (says the C. Centinel) from the effect of mephitic air, in wells, we offer the following recipe of an eminent writer on the subject : "If any doubt of foul air exists, take one pound flour of sulphur, mixed with one pint spirits of wine, or strong ardent spirits of any kind ; dip in that mixture sheets of paper, set them on fire and throw them into the well ; if they continue to burn, the mephitic air is expelled; then any person may descend with perfect safety."—In New York, killed by a fall from the third story of a ware-house, Capt. Perkins Salter, aged 31, son of Capt. Richard S. of

Portsmouth, N.H. ; this is the third son he has lost by accidental death.—In Philadelphia, from the 19th to 26th July, 22 adults and 35 children : 19 of cholera morbus.—In New York, from the 19th to 26th July, 11 men, 5 women, 11 girls and 18 boys.—In Boston, Mrs. Abigail Monk, aged 85 ; Mrs. Elizabeth Moody, aged 79.—In Salem, Mr. Jonathan Gavett, aged 75.—In Reading, Jonah Freeman, supposed to be 107 years old. When he was upwards of 40 years of age, (a slave) he married a free woman of colour, with whom he lived upwards of 60 years, by whom he had 5 children ; two of them engaged in the American war, and died defending the freedom of that country which had enslaved their father. Previous to this, one of them, by his industry and economy, accumulated property, with which he purchased his father, took a bill of sale of him, and gave him his freedom. Soon after this uncommon proof of filial affection, this benevolent son died and left the whole of his little property to his aged father; by which means the father, as heir to the son, had a legal Bill of Sale of HIMSELF. A singular instance ! perhaps the only one ever known. Jonah has been an exemplary professor of christianity nearly 40 years. He died in the exercise of an unshaken hope, through Christ, of eternal life. "If the SON shall make you free, then shall you be free indeed."—Salem Gaz.—In Northampton, Mr. Nathaniel Day, aged 63 ; Mr. Joel Clark, aged 73.—In Middletown, (Con.) Mrs. Sarah Goodwin, aged 60.—In Groton, (C.) Mrs. Phebe Avery, in the 84th year of her age.—At Reading, Vt. Mrs. Chloe Weld, aged 72.—In Brattleboro', Mrs. Fanny A. Elliot, consort of Mr. Samuel Elliot.—In Portsmouth, Mr. John Williams, aged 74.—In Bedford, Mrs. M'Gregore, consort of the Rev. Mr. M'Gregore, and daughter of the Hon. John Orr, esq. of that place.—At New Boston, in the 44th year of his age, Mr. Thomas Moor.—In Stoddard, in the 40th year of her age, Mrs. Esther Barker, consort of Capt. John Barker.—In Chesterfield, Mrs. Lydia Torrey, in the 44th year of her age.

At Chester, (Ver.) 2d ult. Capt. George Earle, aged 71 ; he was at work in his shop, apparently well, about 5 minutes previous to his death.—On the 14th, Mr. Abel Duncan, aged 56 ; he was taken ill in the morning, and died about two o'clock in the afternoon.—On the 22d, Mr. Jonathan Caryl, aged 76, formerly of Hopkinton, Ms.

In this town, on Tuesday last, the Widow Overlocke, aged 96 years.

SUICIDE.—In Adams, (Mass.) 18th ult. Miss Esther Allen. She hung herself by a skein of yarn. No cause for this act is assigned, unless it be attributed to a gloom fixed upon her mind from observing the eclipse of the sun on the 16th June.

DROWNED.—At Plumb-Island, Mr. John Clark, aged 22.

Died, in Boston, on the 4th inst. Charles Austin, aged 18, son of Benjamin Austin, Esq. and member of the present senior class in Cambridge College ; by the discharge of a pistol from Thos. O. Selfridge, esq. The particulars of this unfortunate and melancholy affair are so variously represented by contradictory reports, that, were it in any respect proper, it would be impossible for us to give a correct detail. We merely understand that a dispute of a personal nature had taken place between the father of the young gentleman deceased, and Mr. Selfridge, and that on the meeting of the two latter in State-street yesterday, about 1 o'clock, the unhappy event ensued which terminated in the death of Mr. Austin, on the spot. Mr. Selfridge has surrendered himself for trial. [Boston pap. Aug. 5.] [166]

No. 22.—Vol. XIV (Whole No. 698) Friday, 15 Aug. 1806.

† [3a] Editorial remarks regarding Selleck Osborn, "editor of a violent paper in Connecticut," who is in Litchfield jail for libelling the character of Julius Deming, a judge of the Superior Court.

† [3b] Legal notice regarding the estate of Ebenezer Eaton, late of Walpole, deceased; Levi Allen and Calvin Eaton, Executors. Dated Walpole, 13 Aug. 1806.

† [3b] Legal notice regarding the estate of David Hall, late of Walpole, deceased; Levi Allen and Lydia Hall, Administrators. Dated Walpole, 13 Aug. 1806.

† [3b] Shubael Conant adv. "that he continues to carry on the goldsmith's business, in all its branches, in his shop a few rods south of Southard's tavern, in Walpole." Dated Walpole 14 Aug. 1806.

† [3b] James Cochran adv. for a journeyman Tailor; dated Walpole, 15 Aug. 1806.

† [3c] John Metcalf adv. a farm for sale or lease at Charlestown, N.H.; dated 12 Aug.

† [3c] Adv. for the Hatfield Bridge Lottery; Samuel Porter, Elijah Dickinson, Isaac Abercrombie, Samuel F. Dickinson, and John Hastings, Jr., Managers. Dated July 1806.

¶ [3b] MARRIED.

At Washington, on the 7th inst. Mr. Daniel Farnsworth to Miss Patty Proctor.

¶ [3b] DIED.

At Westmoreland, on Wednesday last, Major Jason Wait, aged 64 years ; an active and brave officer through the revolutionary war. His funeral will be attended this day, from the Rev. Mr. Pratt's Meeting house, at 2 o'clock, P.M. with Masonic and Military honours.

No. 23.—Vol. XIV (Whole No. 699) Friday, 22 Aug. 1806.

¶ [2d] Mr. Carpenter, late editor of the Charleston Courier, has issued proposals for establishing a semi-weekly paper in New York. To this plan, Mr. Coleman offers his full and unqualified protest.—*Bost. Gaz.*

¶ [2d] *Counterfeiter.*—A fellow by the name of Jesse Richardson, has been committed to gaol in Canadaigua, for passing counterfeit twenty-dollar bills of the U.S. Bank.—*Balance.*

† [3b] Rev. Joseph L. Mills ordained at Becket, Mass., First Congregational Church.

¶ [3b] RAN AWAY. John Brown, an indented servant, 15 or 16 years old, ran away from me last Thursday; had on an old [surtout?], cotton shirt, overhalls, barefoot, &c.—He is in the habit of lying and stealing. Any person that will take him up and secure him shall have 3 cents reward, but no charges paid. All persons are hereby forbid harbouring, secreting or trusting him.

EPHRAIM CARPENTER.

Charlestown, Aug. 17, 1806.

† [3d] Legal notice regarding the estate of David Eaton, late of Sutton, Hillsborough County, N.H., Jonathan Eaton, Administrator.

¶ [3b] DIED.

In Scotland, His Grace John, Duke of Argyll, a Field Marshal, aged 82.—In Savannah, (Geo.) Capt. Thomas Allen, aged 40.—In Wiscasset, (Me.) Mrs. Sarah Hodge, relict of the late Henry Hodge, esq. aged 70.—In Watertown, Widow Rachel Bright, aged 73.—In Boston, Mr. Samuel Fenno, aged 61 ; Widow Martha M'Carney, aged 66 ; Widow Mary [Ozier?], aged 68 ; Thomas Edwards, esq. aged 53.—At Newton, Nathan Goodale, esq. for many years an eminent and respectable merchant at Salem, and of late years Clerk of the District Court of Massachusetts ; a truly honest man, and of universal benevolence.—In Brookfield, (Con.) Capt. Elijah Starr in the 55th year of his age.—In Windham, Mr. Samuel Hovey, aged 90 ; Mr. Roswell Lathrop, aged 55 ; Miss Zeruvia Tilden, aged 69.—In Litchfield, Mr. David Beach, aged 64 ; Mr. Solomon Kilborn, aged 70.—At Rindge, (N.H.) 4th ult. Widow Huldah Haskell, formerly of Lancaster, aged 97.—In England, Charles Francis Sheridan, esq. brother of Richard Briasley Sheridan, M.P.—In New Orleans, 3d July, Lt. Josiah Taylor, of the 2d U.S. Regt. of Infantry.—In Fraquier [sic] county, (Vir.) Charles Marshall, esq. attorney at law.—In Ward, (Ms.) Mr. Benjamin Carter, aged 101 y. 8 m.—In Concord, (N.H.) Dr. Philip Carrigain, aged 59.—In Bedford, Mrs. Emma Goodale, aged 77.—In Flanders, M. Mosment : He had ascended in a balloon, the car of which, from some defect upset, and precipitated him from an immense height to the ground ; where he was found dead, and dreadfully mangled.—In Nassau, Mr. Powell, surgeon in the British navy, of a wound received in a duel with a Mr. Cookley, who fell in the duel.—In Lynchburg, (Virg.) Rev. James Tompkins.—In Richmond, (Vir.) James Lyles, jun. esq.—In Newport, (R.I.) Mrs. Ruth Champlin, wife of Geo. Champlin, esq.—In Bradford, (Ms.) Mrs. Susannah Dowlin, aged 89 ; she had enjoyed good health, and was found dead, sitting by her husband, who did not discover the event until informed of it by his daughter.—In Salisbury, Col. Jonathan Evans, aged 69 ; an officer in our revolutionary struggle, and a firm friend to the interest and welfare of his country.—In Salem, Mr. Benj. Ward, aged 82.—In Portsmouth, Mr. James Grouard, aged 74 ; Mrs. Thankful Shapley, consort of Mr. James Shapley, merchant, and daughter of Richard Champney, esq. in the 45th year of her age.—At Bow, very suddenly, Dea. Isaac White, aged 74.

DROWNED.]—In Acworth, while in the act of bathing, a son of Mr. Stephens, aged about 14 years.

☞ Went from Bolton, (Ms.) in the autumn of 1800, a young man by the name of Aaron Moors, and has not been heard of since. He was then an apprentice to Thomas Rich, shoemaker, of Lynn, and was in the 19th year of his age. If he is living, he would confer an infinite favour upon his afflicted mother, by giving information to Daniel Cooledge, of Walpole, (N.H.) of the place where he now resides.—Other persons acquainted with his present residence, or any particulars concerning him, are requested to transmit information thereof to the same person.

He had a warm propensity for naval business, and it is supposed he is engaged therein. Any masters of vessels that have been acquainted with a person by that name, and would give information of the same, would much relieve the solicitous suspense of his tender mother and only surviving parent of an only child.

☞ Printers throughout the United States, by inserting the above two or three weeks in their respective papers, would confer a favour on those interested therein.

No. 24—Vol. XIV (Whole No. 700) Friday, 29 Aug. 1806.

† [2c-d] Account of the death of Mr. Mason Moseley, who was stabbed by a runaway slave at Edgefield district, South Carolina, 28 July 1806. ◆

† [2d] Mr. John Gromet and wife burned in a fire at Ebenezer, Effingham County, Georgia, 22 July 1806. Mr. Gromet died the next day, and his wife probably will die. ◆

† [3a] Account of a fire at the Twine Manufactory "in Charlestown, occupied by Mr. Bacon." A house adjoining was also burned, which belonged to Mr. Otis Clap. The facility was owned by Messrs. Clap, Bacon, and Geddes. The event occurred "on Monday evening last." ◆

† [3a] A Mrs. Smith and her twenty month-old infant were thrown from a carriage, at Washington, D.C., 10 Aug. 1806. The child was killed instantly, and Mrs. Smith injured. Mr. Smith was not injured; the family resided in Calvert County, Maryland. ◆

¶ [3b] Gun Boat No. 7, commanded by Lieut. Ogilvie, it is said has not been heard of since leaving New York; and it is said there is every reason to believe she is lost with all her crew.

¶ [3c] On Wednesday last, Mr. Charles Martin, living on the plantation of Simon Eaker, in Antrim township, and a Mr. John M'Farlan, of Washington township in this county, fell victims to the imprudence of entering a well on the place of Mr. Eaker, infected with fixed air, or "suffocating choke damp."—*N.Y. pap.*

† [3c] N. Townsley, Secretary, posts a notice regarding the Walpole Mechanic Society.

† [3d] Legal notice regarding the estate of John Hubbard, late of Charlestown, N.H.; Prudence Hubbard and Henry Hubbard, Administrators. Dated [28?] Aug. 1806.

† [3d] Samuel Hutchinson adv. for flax and mustard seed; dated Alstead, 20 Aug.

===== ¶ [3c] MARRIED. =====

At Hampstead, (N.H.) Silas Dinsmore, esq. agent of the United States to the Choctaw tribe of Indians, in the Mississippi territory, to Miss Mary Gordon.

In Albany, Mr. Thomas M'Auley, L.L. Professor in Union College, to Miss Mary Magossin.

===== ¶ [3c] DIED. =====

At New Orleans, on the 11th ult. W.J. Pealert;—His death was occasioned by a wound received from a Spaniard, with whom he had a dispute at a late fire. This premeditated and daring murder was committed in the presence of a large number of citizens. The atrocious villain, shortly after the dispute began, deliberately withdrew and sharpened a large knife ; on his return he gave the Spaniard a fatal stab in the side, which severed one of his ribs ; after which this blood-thirsty murderer made several attempts to stab those who were in the act of apprehending him. This murderer has been tried and acquitted, by a jury composed principally of Spaniards.—In New York, Mrs. Dorothea Price, aged 87.—In Poundridge, (N.Y.) Mr. Daniel Dickson; in a fit of religious frenzy, he killed himself.—In Salem, (N.Y.) Gen. John Williams, formerly member of Congress.—In New Fairfield, (Con.) Mr. Robert Scudder, in the 56th year of his age.—In Salem, (Ms.) Mr. William Patterson, aged 71.—In Belchertown, Mrs.

Pamela, wife of the Rev. Mr. Graves, of Woodstock, (Con.) and daughter of the Rev. Mr. Forward.—At Portland, Salmon Chase, esq. son of Dudley Chase, esq. of Cornish. —In Plainfield, Widow Mary Freeman, aged 67.—In Hartford, Mr. Nathan Whitney, aged 81.—In Richmond, (Virg.) John Pendleton, esq.—In Philadelphia, John Dennis, esq. of Somerset county, Maryland, aged 35, for several years a representative in the U.S. Congress.—In Wardsbridge, (N.Y.) Arthur Parks, esq. aged 70, one of the members of the first Provincial Congress.—In Goshen, (C.) Dr. Joseph North, aged 70. —In Lancaster, (Pen.) Mr. John Albright, printer, in the 66th year of his age, for many years a respectable citizen of that borough.—In Alexandria, Mr. Stephen Parham, a respectable merchant of Norfolk, on his way to the Sweet Springs.—In New London, Mrs. Hannah Chapman, widow of the late Mr. James C. aged 88 ; Miss Hannah Manwaring, aged 56.—In Preston, Mr. Amos [Clift? or Clist?], aged 68 ; Mr. Ichabod Downing, aged 50.—In East-Haddam, Capt. Elijah Atwood, aged 83 ; Widow Esther Isham, aged 78.—At Lyme, Black Point, (drowned) Mr. Joseph Manwaring, aged about 44.—In Royalston, (Ms.) Lt. Samuel Goddard, aged 63.—In Bolton, (Ms.) 21st ult. after a few days illness, the Widow Wheeler, consort of the late Obadiah Wheeler, aged about 80 years. She was a member of the Society of Friends in that place, and an amiable woman.—At Maidenhead, near Trenton, lately, Mr. William Phillips, sen. in the 84th year of his age.—In Hull, (Eng.) John Russell, Esq. a Royal Academician, and portrait painter in crayons to the British King and Prince of Wales. [. . .]—In Philadelphia, during the week ending 16th August, 17 adults and 18 children.—In New-York, during the week ending 16th August, 15 men, 6 women, 19 boys and 21 girls; of cholera 1, consumption 8, whooping cough 7 ;—Col. William Bell, of the revolutionary army.—In Brookfield, (Ms.) Mrs. Bathsheba Bartlett, aged 77.—In Wrentham, Capt. Andrew Gilmore, aged 79.—In Salem, Capt. John Brown, of the health boat, aged 74.—In New York, Aug. 23, 1805, Capt. William Leonard, aged [72?] years ; he was one of the first officers who took up arms in defence of America.—In Hudson, (N.Y.) Mr. Samuel Nichols, aged 83 years.—In Canaan, N.Y. (of [fear?] in travail) Mrs. Warner, wife of Mr. Lupron W. aged 38.—On the 21st ult. of a consumption, at her father's house (Judge Tryon's) in New Lebanon, Mrs. Henrietta Shepherd, wife of Mr. John Shepherd, of Northampton, in the 22d year of her age.

At Alstead, Mrs. Martha Prentice, consort of Nathaniel S. Prentice, esq. aged 70 years. "Blessed are the dead who die in the Lord."

In this town, at an advanced age, the Widow Watkins.—Last week, a son of Mr. Edward Watkins, aged 13 years.—Henry, youngest son of Mr. Philip P. [Bundy?], aged one year and 7 months.

No. 25.—Vol. XIV (Whole No. 701) Friday, 5 Sept. 1806.

† [2b-c] A series of articles describing, with contradictions and doubts, the capture and executions of several Americans at Caraccas [Venezuela], who were involved in disputes in South America. Those named in one of the articles: James Ledlie, Capt. Donahue, and Mr. Lippincott, all of whom had connections to Philadelphia, Mr. George Kirkland, Capt. Gardner, Paul George (son of a rich merchant of Lisbon, and well known in New York), and Mr. Smith, a butcher of New York. Several of those persons had interests in Hayti. In a later news item, the list of those executed was corrected, and included the following names : ◆

James Gardner,	Gustavus Adol. Bengudd,
Charles Johnson,	Miles Hall,
John Farris,	Francis Farguahason
Thomas Donahue,	Thomas Villop,
Daniel Kemper,	Paul P. George.

† [3b] Rev. Daniel Staniford ordained at Boscawen, "20th inst."

† [3c] Samuel Hutchinson adv. goods for sale; dated Alstead 1 Sept. 1806.

† [3d] Legal notice regarding estate of Col. Willard, for land in Putney, Vt.; William Briggs, Administrator; dated Charlestown, N.H. Aug. 1806.

† [3d] James Cunningham adv. for a lost coat and handkerchief; dated Walpole 4 Sept.

===== ¶ [3b-c] MARRIED. =====

On the 10th inst. at the house of Jeremiah Van Rensselaer, jun. esq. at Utica, John A. Schuyler, esq. of New Barbadoes Neck, (N. Jersey,) to Miss Catharine Van Rensselaer, of Claverack, daughter of the late General Robert Van Rensselaer, deceased.— In Charlestown, Ms. Mr. Christopher A. Olney, of Boston, (formerly of Providence, R.I.) to Miss Phebe Trumbull, only daughter of the late Hon. T. Trumbull, esq. of Charlestown.—In Windsor, (Ver.) the Rev. Bancroft Fowler, to Miss Lucia Curtis, daughter of Gen. Zebina Curtis :—Mr. Rufus Norton, to Miss Lucy Smith.—In Keene, Mr. Benj. Bretton, to Miss Relief Durant.

===== ¶ [3c] DIED. =====

In Charlestown, (S.C.) after a few hours illness, Mr. Jones, of the theatre. He had attained a degree of celebrity in his possessions : but to that indulgence which easily besets many it is said he fell a victim.—Mr. Ashur [Bennet?] ; in a fit of insanity he killed himself.—In Virginia, John P. Cocke, esq. high sheriff of Prince George county ; the third person holding the office of high-sheriff who has died in that county within eight months.—In Alexandria, Mr. George Wells, a native of Massachusetts. He had served three years on board the frigate President, as a marine, and had recently been discharged. He was found drowned near one of the wharves.—In Philad. during the week ending 23d inst. 16 adults and 17 children.—In New-York, same week, 17 men, 10 women, 25 boys and 25 girls ; total 76.—In Nahony, (Penn.) Mr. Peter Murir, (suicide)—The coroner's inquest was, that "he hung himself by persuasion of the devil." —In Providence gaol, John Norman ; he was imprisoned for the murder of Toby Miller, and hung himself.—In Marietta, (Ohio) Mrs. Lydia Moulton, aged 83, formerly of Newburyport.—In Hopewell, (N.J.) Mrs. Elizabeth Rose, in the 90th year of her age.—In N. London, Mrs. Anna Stark, aged 85.—In Northampton, Mr. Hains Kingsley, aged 77 ; Mr. Medard Edwards, aged 80.—In Rowley, Mrs. Ann Lambert, aged 82.—In Hartford, (Vt.) the widow Phebe Gross, aged 72.—In Bow, Deacon Isaac White, aged 77.—In Gilmanton, Joseph Parsons, esq.—In Dummerston, (Vt.) Wid. Lucy Cook, aged 81.

No. 26.—Vol. XIV (Whole No. 702) Friday, 12 Sept. 1806.

† [2b-d] A very extensive account of the calamity aboard the ship *Rose-in-Bloom*, which was wrecked in a storm. The ship left Charleston, S.C. 16 Aug. 1806, perhaps bound for New York. Several days later, the ship upset in a gale, and several persons were swept overboard. The survivors were forced to lash themselves with ropes to the weather railing on the stern. There were at least eleven survivors; those that were identified were E.M. Macpherson, Mr. John Rutledge, and Doddridge Crocker. Sometime before the group was rescued, the article identifies a Mr. Booth and Miss McPherson (same as E.M. Macpherson?) who both had survived the initial wrecking of the ship. Those who drowned included Gen. McPherson, Mrs. Booth and son, Mr. Tait (of the house of Tait & Wilson, Charleston) and Mr. Bowesing. The survivors were rescued by a British brig, the *Swift*, Capt. Phelan, an Irishman. The survivors were brought to New York City. ♦

† [3a] Ira Johnson, "lately from Canada," arrested at Lansingburgh for passing counterfeit bills; he was supposed to be connected with Stephen Burroughs.

† [3a] Description of a new paper at New York, published by Mr. Carpenter, lately from Charleston, S.C.

† [3b] David Stone adv. goods for sale; dated Walpole, 10 Sept. 1806.

† [3c] William Poyntell of Philadelphia adv. numerous tracts of land for sale in Pennsylvania; dated Philadelphia, 12 July 1806.

===== ¶ [3b] DIED. =====

In Germany, the celebrated General Melas, commander in chief of the Austrian army in the battle of Marengo.—In England, the Hon. Mrs. Leigh, of Stonely : By her death, an estate, which 60 years since rented at 17,000 *l.* per annum, devolves upon some unknown heir at law. The rents on her estate had not been raised for 60 years.—In Simsbury, (Conn.) Mr. Eliphalet Mitchelson, aged 74.—In Rowley, (Ms.) Mrs. Ann Lambert, aged 92.—In Dorchester, Mr. Samuel Cox, aged 82.—In Topsham, Mrs. Lucy Gould, aged 84.—In Leicester, Mary Bond, aged [87?].—At Marlborough, Simon Howe, aged

84, whose parents lived to the same age, and had six children, four of whom lived to the age of fourscore years and upwards, the other two to the age of threescore and ten.

At Alstead, 30th ult. at the house of Mr. Joseph Putnam, Mrs. Mehitable How, aged 83.

No. 27.—Vol. XIV (Whole No. 703) Friday, 19 Sept. 1806.

¶ [2b] Among other distressing accounts of the damage done at sea, during the *August storms,* is that of the loss of schooner Comfort, from Baltimore for Charleston.—Of 25 souls on board, only six were saved.—Capt. Drummond, her commander, Mr. Archibald Leslie, of Demarara, Rev. Mr. Mercier, of Charleston, were among those who were drowned.—Lt. Henry, was one of the six who were saved, after great sufferings.

† [2b-c] Unfriendly editorial remarks regarding Rev. Stanley Griswold, "an ex-priest of Connecticut," who was appointed Secretary of State of Michigan.

† [2c] Lengthy article describing a conflict between Joseph L. Smith, Esq., a Democrat, and Rev. Judah Champion, a minister of Litchfield, Conn., where he had preached for 54 years. Smith supposedly ordered Rev. Champion from his meeting-house. Rev. Huntington was also involved. ♦

† [2d] Two men, who said their names were Church Wardwell and Samuel Durant, arrested at Portsmouth for passing counterfeit bills from Lincoln and Kennebeck Banks.

† [3b] *Dana & Foxcroft* adv. West India goods for sale; dated Boston, 17 Sept. 1806.

† [3b] Andrew Grout adv. a horse found on his land; dated Acworth, 13 Nov. 1806. [167]

† [3c] Adv. regarding the Amoskeag Canal Lottery, Phillips Payson, Samuel Swan, and Loammi Baldwin, Jr., Managers. Dated at Boston, 16 Aug. 1806.

† [3c] Legal notice regarding the estate auction of William Henry, Jr., deceased, mentioning land adjoining Major Grout's farm. The public vendue to be held at Capt. Hamlin's tavern; Nathaniel Holden, Adm. Dated at Charlestown, 10 Sept. 1806.

† [3c] Frederick A. Sumner adv. "an excellent stand for a merchant, or Mechanic of almost any description, now occupied by James Hunt . . . " Dated Charlestown, N.H. 15 Sept. 1806.

===== ¶ [3a] MARRIED. =====

At Claverack, (N.Y.) on the 27th ult. by the Rev. Mr. [Gebbard?], Mr. Henry Van Valkenburgh, to Miss Anna Van Valkenburgh, daughter of Mr. Barney Van Valkenburgh, both of Kinderhook. [. . .]

In Boston, Mr. William P. Cleveland, Professor of Mathematics, &c. in Brunswick College, (Maine) to Miss Martha Bush, of Boston.

In Hingham, Mr. Thomas C. Cushing, Editor of the Salem Gazette, to Miss Rachel Andrews.

In Windsor, (Ver.) Mr. Nathaniel Bancroft, to Miss Sally Eastman.

In New-Market, (N.H.) Mr. Benjamin Mathes, of Durham, to Miss Comfort Smart, of the former place.

In Albany, William Root, Esq. to Miss Lucretia Star, of Goshen, Conn.

In Amherst, the Rev. Ephraim P. Bradford, of New Boston, to Miss Mary M. Barker, of the former place. Also, at Amherst, Benjamin West, Esq. of Charlestown, to Mrs. Gordon, of the former place, relict of the late Hon. William Gordon, Esq.

At Charlestown, Mr. Roswell Willard, to Miss Elizabeth Taylor.

In Keene, Albe Cady, Esq. to Miss Sarah Warner.

===== ¶ [3a-b] DIED. =====

In England, Arthur Richard Dillon, Archbishop and Duke of Narbonne, President of the States of Languedoc, &c.—In Baltimore, Mrs. Elizabeth Bond, aged 87.—In Herkimer, (N.Y.) Dr. William [Peirce?], aged 73.—In Farmington, Mr. William Whittle; a cart passed over his body.—In Rowley, Capt. Amos Nelson, aged 70.—In Haverhill, (Mass.) Capt. Nathan Bailey, aged 66.—In Hyde Park, (Long-Island) Capt. George Dunbar, aged [66?].—In Waterford, (N.Y.) Mrs. Catharine Wray, in her [69th?] year, widow of the late George Wray, Esq. of Westfield, Washington county.—In Brookfield, Mr. Josiah Lyon, student at law, aged 22.—In Deerfield, Mrs. Abigail Norton, aged 60 ; Mr. John Sheldon, aged 66.—At Orono, Me. on the 7th ult. (drowned) Capt. John Southgate, of Leicester, aged 68.—In Rutland, (Mass.) Samuel Williams, jun. oldest son of Lieut. Samuel Williams, aged 13. He was playing in the barn with the neighbouring boys, and slipped from the haymow on to a fork, which entered his bowels and put an end to his existence.—In Worcester, 9th inst. Mrs. Hannah Bangs, wife of Edward Bangs, esq.—In New London, Mr. Joshua Hempstead, aged 82. His descendants have been children 13—grand-children 69—great-grand-children 65—total 147, of whom 121 are now living.—In Boston, the Rev. Peter Jayne, pastor of the Methodist Episcopal Church, aged 29.—In Brimfield, Mr. Thomas Bliss, aged 64.—In Newtown, (N.H.) Dea. Francis Chase, aged 91. He left 11 children, upward of 80 grand-children, and upwards of 100 great-grand-children.—In Atkinson, Mrs. Hannah Dow, aged 65.—In Cornish, the widow Joanna Jerrel, aged 73.—In Portsmouth, Capt. William Tredick, aged about 64.—On his passage from Eastport to Portland (drowned) Capt. George W. Allan, of Eastport.—In Burlington, (Vt.) 18th ult. very suddenly, Mr. Amos M. Booge, of Georgia, who had for a number of months past driven the mail stage from Rutland to St. Albans.—In Brookfield, (Mass.) Mrs. Bathsheba Bartlet, aged [77?].—In Westfield, Miss Mary Douglass, second daughter of Maj. Thomas L. Douglass, aged 19.—In Randolph, (Ver.) Wid. Lydia Edson, formerly of Strafford, (C.)—In Leominster (Ms.) capt. Joseph Wilder.—At Burlington, (Vt.) Col. Udney Hay.—At Montpelier, David Wing, jun. esq. Secretary of the State of Vermont.—At Woodstock, Mrs. Susannah Richardson, aged 71.—At Hinsdale, Richard Whitney, esq. attorney at law, of Brattleboro', aged 39.—In Hartford (Ver.) Rhoda, wife of Peter Rider, aged 42. Mr. Rider has buried a wife and 8 children within 4 years.

DIED—On Tuesday night, at the mansion-house of Stephen Van Rensselear, Esq. after a lingering illness, which he bore with becoming fortitude and resignation, the honorable William Patterson, one of the associate Judges of the Supreme Court of the United States. In Mr. Patterson his country has lost an able, independent and upright Judge, a real and enlightened patriot, and the state of New-Jersey, one of its most valuable and respectable citizens. [. . .]

No. 28.—Vol. XIV (Whole No. 704) Friday, 26 Sept. 1806.

¶ [2b] UTICA, [N.Y.—Ed] Sept. 2. *Murder and Suicide.*—On Wednesday last, Mrs. Sarah Hallock, wife of Mr. Henry Hallock, of Westmoreland, murdered all her children, four in number, and killed herself. No cause can be assigned for her unnatural and barbarous conduct. In the forenoon she visited one of her neighbors, and was apparently sane, and in good health and spirits.—Mr. Hallock, having been absent the whole day, returned in the evening and found his house deserted—Search was made, and the bodies of his wife and children, mangled and lifeless, were found in an adjoining cornfield. The children were all daughters, the eldest aged seven years, and the youngest an infant of ten months.

† [3a] Extensive account of Richard Devoe, a sailor lad, who was the only survivor from the schooner *Mary*, Seth Wadsworth, Master. The vessel was wrecked in a storm on passage from Curracoa for New York. Devoe was rescued by the *Rose*, Capt. Gardner, from Philadelphia, bound for Cork. ♦

† [3a] Account of the trial of [Lemuel?] Meserve, convicted of horse stealing at Dover, N.H., and sentenced to receive "nineteen stripes on the naked back . . . " ♦

† [3c] Account of lightning damage to a barn belonging to Mr. Isaac [Smith?] and his son-in-law, Mr. Joseph Dodge, at Mont Vernon, N.H., 13 Sept. 1806. ♦

† [3c] Amasa Allen and Oliver Allen adv. that they will be barreling beef; dated Walpole, 10 Sept. 1806.

===== ¶ [3c] MARRIED. =====

At Hoosick, (N.Y.) Mr. Elijah Wales, aged 80, to the amiable and much respected Miss Betsey Noathrut, aged about 17, both of that town.—At Thinebeck, (N.Y.) the Rev. Augustus Wackerhagen of Schoharie, to Miss Mary A. Mayer, of the former place.

At Charlestown, Mr. Noah Dike, to Miss Betsey Huntoon.

===== ¶ [3c] DIED. =====

At his seat in Rocky Mount, (S.C.) 24th ult. of a lingering illness, in the 53d year of his age, Col. Christian [Senf?], Chief Engineer to the State of South Carolina. He was an officer of merit and information, and had served with great applause in the Southern States, as an Engineer, during our revolutionary contest.—In Charleston, in the 58th year of his age, Mr. John Combe.—In Philadelphia, Charles Pettit, Esq. aged 69 ;

formerly of the revolutionary army, and a member of the old Congress, and many years president of the first insurance company in Philadelphia.—On Thursday last, Arthur Parks, Esq. in the 70th year of his age. He was a member of the first Provincial Congress ; a member of the Convention that formed our state constitution, and one of the late convention that amended it. During eleven years he represented the middle district in the senate. He lived and died a warm patriot, an honest man, and a sincere christian.—Orange County Repub. Aug. 14.—In Cayenne, Louise Charlotte Marie Angelique Tacquin, consort of Victor Hughes, French Commissary in that colony, aged 32. She is spoken of as an amiable lady.—In Albany, the Rev. John H. Meier, minister of the Reformed Dutch Church in the city of Schenectady, in the 32d year of his age.— In Charlestown, Montgomery county, Newyork, Mr. Peter S. Chase, of Sutton, Ms. supposed to be about 40 years of age.—At Poughkeepsie, (N.Y.) Albert Livingston, esq. clerk of the county of Dutchess, in the 64th year of his age.—In Gloucester, (N.J.) 8th ult. Thomas Seeds, a native of the county, aged 104 years. It is worthy of remark that there have died in this county three citizens whose ages together amount to upwards of 317, to wit, John Smith, aged about 101, and Aaron Hewit, aged 106, all within the space of two years. Smith was a native of this county, and it is believed Hewit was the same.—In Worcester, (Mass.) Mr. Benjamin Tucker, aged 72.—In Westborough, 14th inst. Mr. Benjamin Chamberlain, aged 28 ; and on the 17th, his father, Mr. Ebenezer Chamberlain, aged 66.—In Canton, Rev. Zachariah Howard, in the 49th year of his age, and 20th of his ministry.—In Beverly, capt. Asa Leach, postmaster.—In Milton, Mr. Nath'l Gay, aged 68.—At Sandy Creek, Elder Edmond Littlefield, aged 50, formerly of Colrain.—In Haverhill, 10th inst. Mrs. Sarah Whiting, aged 83 ; in the evening of the same day, the Widow Lydia Kimball, aged 77.—By lightning, in Templeton, Edward Sawyer, of Templeton, and Seth Kendall, of Athol.

At Claremont 5th inst. Titus [Vespasian?], a man of colour and respectability, formerly of Westfield.

ACCIDENTS.—Capt. Peter L. Van Alen, of Kinderhook, in attempting to ford the creek called Maj. Abram's Kill, in a waggon, was upset and drowned. He has left a very large family. [Hudson Balance.]

On Tuesday evening last, as three men were returning from this town to Rye, the boat was upset a few rods from the beach where they intended to land, and two of them, Joses [168] Brown and James Jenness, were drowned—the other, a black man, was saved. Mr. Brown was a young man of irreproachable character, and has left a amiable partner and numerous friends to lament his untimely fate. [Portsmouth Oracle.]

MURDER.—One day last week (says the Poughkeepsie, N.Y. paper) a horse, which appeared to have been lately killed, was found in the high lands, near Warren's tavern. —On searching further, the body of a man recently murdered, was found covered over with leaves and brush.

No. 29.—Vol. XIV (Whole No. 705) Friday, 3 Oct. 1806.

† [3b] Enos Lovell, S. Goodridge, D. Tuttle and D. Cottrell, all of Grafton, Vt., vouch for Bartholomew Fuller, of Grafton, regarding a giant radish grown in Fuller's garden.

¶ [3b] *Fire.*—On Friday last, the barn of Mr. Stephen Earls, of Gerry, containing 90 bushels of grain, 15 tons of hay, and several farming utensils, were consumed by fire. Loss estimated at 500 dollars.

¶ [3c] ORDAINED.]—At Utica, (N.Y.) Rev. Amos G. Baldwin, to the gospel ministry, at the Episcopal Church.

† [3d] Isaac Redington adv. in regards to outstanding debts; dated 16 Sept. 1806.

† [3d] S. Porter, E. Dickinson, I. Abercrombie, S.F. Dickinson, and J. Hastings, jun., Managers, adv. for the Hatfield Bridge Lottery; dated Hatfield, 18 Sept. 1806.

† [3d] Phillips Payson adv. for Harvard College Lottery; dated Charlestown, 20 Sept.

† [3d] Samuel Hutchinson, of the late firm of *Shepard & Hutchinson*, adv. a notice for outstanding debts; dated Alstead, 25 Sept. 1806.

====== ¶ [3c] MARRIED. ======

In Salem, Rev. Jeremiah Noyes, of Gorham, to Miss Lucy Johnson, daughter of the late Rev. Mr. J. of Harvard.—In Dedham, Rev. Josiah Cannon, of Gill, to Miss Almira

Smith, of N. Marlborough.—In Sandwich, Captain Ansel Bourne, to Mrs. Abigail Parker.—In Bernardston, Mr. Simeon Allen, aged 20, to Mrs. Polly Flagg, aged 40.

===== ¶ [3c] DIED. =====

In Italy, the French General Vallongues; killed by a shell from Gaets, in an attack upon that fortress.—In New Orleans, col. Frederick H. Baron de Weissenfels, aged 78 ; he was a native of Prussia, and a colonel in the American revolutionary army.—In North Carolina, Maj. Thomas Pasteur, of the U.S. army.—In Washington, Mr. Joseph Taylor, formerly of Connecticut, and clerk in the U.S. Treasury department.—In Philadelphia, Mr. Charles C. Barringer, in the 64th year of his age : Mr. Charles Jervis, in the 77th year of his age.—In New York, Hagar Johnson, a black, aged 100.—In Killingly, C. Mrs. Elizabeth, wife of Rev. G. Johnson, aged 31.—In Danbury, Mrs. Lydia Broughton, aged 95 ; her posterity is 115.—In Berkhampsted, (C.) Mr. Joshua Ransom, aged 91.—In New London, Mr. Joshua Hempsted, aged 82. His descendants were 13 children, 69 grand-children, and 65 great-grandchildren; total 147, of whom 121 are living.—At the same place, Mr. William Harvey, aged 101.—In Preston, (C.) Elias Brown, esq. aged 60.—In Uxbridge, (Ms.) Col. Daniel Tillinghast, formerly of Providence, aged 75.—In Acton, Lt. Simon Tuttle, jun. aged 43.—In Pembroke, Mrs. Ruth Cushing, aged 85, consort of the late Josiah Cushing, esq. a lady who through life sustained the first of useful and respectable characters.—In Boston, Capt. Bartholomew Trow, aged 70.—In Springfield, Mr. Reuben Bliss, aged 80 ; Mr. Ebenezer Whitney, aged 61 ; Capt. David Pratt, aged 60.—In Salisbury, Mr. Benjamin Carr, aged [68?].—In Manchester, (Vt.) Mr. Nathaniel Richardson, aged 82.—In Randolph, Zebediah Butler, esq. late of Roxbury.—In Leyden, Ms. Mr. Oliver Babcock, in the 61st year of his age.—In Northwood, 8th inst. the wife of Col. Samuel Johnson.—In Keene, on Friday last, Mr. Jehasophat Grout, aged 53.—In Marlborough, Mr. Timothy Bemis, aged 72. His death was occasioned by a fall from the top of a load of stocks on Wednesday evening, 16th inst.—In Worcester, (Mass.) Mr. Benjamin Tucker, aged 73.

At Alstead, very suddenly, Mr. Benjamin Fay, son of Capt. Nathan Fay, aged 22. He retired in good health, to bed, on Tuesday evening, and was found a corpse the next morning. 169

In New Grantham, on the 16th ultimo, Robert Duncan, esq.

DROWNED.—In crossing Connecticut river, opposite Hartford, John M'Curdy Strong, A.B. a graduate of Yale College, at the late commencement, and son of the Rev. Dr. Strong, of Hartford; an excellent young man.—In Kentoocook [sic] river, on the 8th inst. Mr. Thomas Stewart.

No. 30.—Vol. XIV (Whole No. 706) Friday, 10 Oct. 1806.

† [2a] Mention of a duel fought near Fort Adams, around the 5th of Aug. 1806, between Nathaniel Evans, Esq. and Capt. Richmond, of the U.S. Army, in which Richmond was shot dead. The information was obtained from a private letter from a gentleman in Wilkinson County, Mississippi Territory.

† [2a-b] Account of the murder of a daughter of Rev. John Record, aged about seven, in Williamson County, Tennessee, 18 Aug. 1806. ♦

† [3b] Article detailing the deaths of Mr. Willet and Mr. Hill, by drowning, and a Mr. Filer was in custody as a suspect. All were crew members of Capt. Reed's sloop; the article was copied from the Troy Gazette issue of 30 Sept. 1806. ♦

† [3b] A daughter of Mr. Ebenezer Knapp, aged about 3 years, injured in an accident "on the 18th inst." at New Marlborough; article copied from a Stockbridge paper. ♦

¶ [3b-c] On Monday last Mr. E. Sandford of Montreal being on his return in a canoe from viewing his new lands, on the river Ottawa, unfortunately the canoe overset, by which accident he was drowned. His body was not found on Wednesday. The water where he fell was 80 feet deep.   He was accompanied by Mr. Joseph Shuter, of Montreal, who saved himself by swimming ashore. The oversetting of the canoe was occasioned by Mr. Sandford's standing up in the period of a calm, and taking hold of the mast, he being tired of sitting. Mr. S. was much respected and is no less regretted. *Quebec Gaz. Sept. 15.*

¶ [3c] It is with sorrow we relate that about three weeks since, the dwelling house of Mr. Oliver O'Hara, at Gaspe, accidentally took fire, and was consumed to ashes. Mr.

O'Hara's two children and a female servant unhappily shared the fate of the house. It is said that this melancholy event has affected Mr. O'Hara to a degree of phrenzy. [*Quebec Gaz.*]

¶ [3c] ORDAINED.]—In Cooperstown, (N.Y.) Rev. Willaim Niell.

† [3c] Notice of the 3d N.H. Turnpike Road Corporation, David Carter, Treasurer; dated at Marlboro', N.H. 1 Oct. 1806.

† [3c] John Bellows adv. for stray sheep; dated at Walpole, 10 Oct. 1806.

† [3d] Adv. of land for sale in Willsborough, Essex County, N.Y.; apply to Norman Newel near the premises, or to Samuel Starr at Troy, N.Y.; dated 23 Sept. 1806.

† [3d] Alex. Houston adv. a runaway notice regarding James N. Brown, an indented boy about 19 years of age, who ran away 24 Sept.; dated same day, at Acworth.

===== ¶ [3c] **MARRIED.** =====

By John Wall, esq. on the 18th August, 1806, at Fort Adams, (Mississippi Territory) Lieut. Horatio [?] [170] of the first United States regiment of Infantry, to Miss Hannah Ellis, of Franklin, (Conn.) daughter of Doctor Benjamin Ellis.

In Virginia, Mr. Stephen Cruinfeather, aged 60, to Miss Sally Graham, aged 55. Better late than never.—In Troy, (N.Y.) James Dole, esq. of that village, to Miss Jane M'Creedy, of Albany.—In Cambridge, (N.Y.) Mr. John Lawson, preceptor, to Miss Sally Davis, preceptress, of the academy in that place.—In Lexington, (Ms.) Mr. John Bridge, of Boston, to Miss Mary Bridge, of the former place.—In Hingham, Mr. Thomas C. Cushing, editor of the Salem Gazette, to Miss Rachel Andrews.—In Natick, Mr. Samuel Fish to Miss Nancy Stone.—In Amherst, Dr. Matthias Spalding to Miss Rebecca Atherton.—In Killingly, (C.) Mr. James Cutler, aged 82, to Miss Experience Graves, aged 29.—In Cambridge, (Ms.) James T. Austin, esq. attorney at law, of Boston, to Miss Catharine Gerry, eldest daughter of Hon. Elbridge Gerry, of the former place.—In Keene, Lockhart Willard, esq. to Mrs. Rebeckah Goodenow.—In Alstead, Dr. Thomas D. Brooks to Miss Lucinda Hatch.

===== ¶ [3c] **DIED.** =====

At Dixon's Spring, (Tennessee) 26th Aug. Mrs. Polly Dixon, aged 39 years, the amiable consort of Maj. Timon [sic] Dixon.—In Burlington, (N.J.) Dr. William M'Ilvaine, in the 57th year of his age.—In Winchester, (Vir.) Mrs. Mary Glen, aged 71.—In Philad. from 20th to 27th ult. 10 men, 11 women, 10 boys and 11 girls ; of consumption 4, whooping cough 2, flux infantile 9, small-pox two ! —In Portsmouth, Capt. Thomas Pierce, aged 62.—In Leicester, Capt. Thomas Mower, formerly of Worcester, aged 54.— In Deerfield, (N.H.) Col. Nathaniel White, of Portsmouth, aged 46 ; late aid-de-camp of His Excellency Governor Gilman; a worthy man and an excellent citizen.—In Rowley, Mrs. Chandler, widow of the late Rev. James C. of Rowley ; Lt. Joseph Kilborn, aged 87.—In Salem, Mr. Jonathan Brown, aged 86 ; Mrs. Mary Robie, a descendant of the venerable Governor Bradstreet, of Massachusetts ; she left a name worthy of her descent.—In Hingham, Mrs. Huldah Gardner, aged 75.—In Boston, Mrs. Hannah Kenny, wife of Mr. P.M. Kenny, of the theatre, aged 44 ; Mr. Andrew Turner, aged 83.—In Grenada, August 4, on board the sch'r Mary and Eliz. Lyman Smith, belonging to the State of Vermont.—In Newburyport, Mrs. Elizabeth Pike, aged 72.—In Franklin, Mrs. Elizabeth Thurston, aged 82.—In Waltham, Miss Anna Cushing, daughter of Rev. Jacob Cushing, aged 46.—In Deerfield, Mr. James Childs, aged 26, son of Mr. Amzi Childs ; a graduate at the late commencement at Williams' College.—In Washington, (Con.) the Rev. Jeremiah Day, aged 70.—In Hartford, the widow Alice Caldwell, in the 97th year of her age.—In Ellington, Matthew Hyde, esq. in the 73d year of his age.—In Killingly, Mrs. Elizabeth Johnson, wife of the Rev. Gordon Johnson, of that place, aged 31 years.—In Sherman, Mrs. Catharine Coudrey, consort of the late col. John Coudrey, in the 57th year of her age. In life she was useful ; in death, peaceful and resigned. She had assisted at the births of more than 1400 children, in 19 years, and not a single instance occurred but that the lives of both mother and child were reserved.—In Danbury, Mrs. Lydia Boughton, in the 95th year of her age. She was able, until a few days before her death, to ride abroad on horseback, and retained her mental faculties to the last hour of her life. She was a daughter of the Rev. Seth Shove, who was the first settled minister in that town, in the year 1694. Her posterity were 8 children, 38 grand-children, 68 great-grand-children, and one great-great-grand-child, making in the whole

115.—In Reading (Vt.) of a very lingering consumption, Mrs. Mary Felch, aged 46.—In Townsend (Vt.) Capt. Benjamin Mowdock, in the 39th year of his age. His death was caused by a small wound in his foot by a thistle, which mortified and struck to his vitals.—At Merrimac, Mr. Richard Hale, aged 57.—In Francestown, Oliver Holmes, esq. aged 66.
   At Bernardston, (Mass.) on the 9th ult. Mr. Benajah Skinner, of a putrid fever, aged 35.
   At Tunbridge, (Ver.) Amy, consort of Samuel Tracy, esq. aged 76.

No. 31.—Vol. XIV (Whole No. 707) Friday, 17 Oct. 1806.

† [1d] Gunpowder explosion at the shop of Mr. Charles Deblois, at Quebec, caused by a careless clerk, Mr. Goslin, who was killed. Deblois survived, but was in a critical state. ♦

¶ [1d] *Drowned.*—At Henniker, on Wednesday the 24th day of Sept. in the 35th year of his age, Mr. Nathan Blanchard. He was attempting to cross Contocook River in a small wherry, and overset.—Mr. Blanchard has left a wife and *seven* children, the oldest aged 10 years, and the youngest 2 months to lament his sudden and afflictive death. [*Amherst Cabinent.*

¶ [1d] A Child of Capt. James Francis, of Wethersfield, was last week scalded to death. [*Con. Courant.*]

† [3a] Brief description of a new newspaper to be published in Montpelier, Vt., by Rev. Mr. Brown, of Putney, entitled *The Vermont Precursor.* Also a proposed newspaper, *The North Star,* to be published by Mr. Ebenezer Eaton, at Danville, Vt.

† [3a] Article describing the arrest of Jesse Dutton at Batavia, N.Y., for counterfeiting. Dutton later committed suicide in prison; copied from a Canandaigua paper. ♦

¶ [3b] Last week a son of Capt. Elisha Williams, of Wethersfield, aged 11 years, fell from a Cart, the wheel of which passed over his body, and he almost instantly expired. [*Conn. Courant.*

† [3b] Ordinations: Rev. Henry True, at Union, Maine, and Rev. David T. Kimball, at Ipswich, Mass., 8 Oct. 1806.

† [3c] Legal notice regarding the estate of John Adkins, late of Charlestown, N.H., deceased. Public vendue to be held at the house of Amos Johnson in Charlestown; Amos Johnson and Robert Rand, Adm. Dated at Charlestown, 8 Oct. 1806.

===== ¶ [3b-c] MARRIED. =====

In Kingston, (Upper Canada) by the Rev. Mr. Stuart, Capt. Fuller, of the 41st regiment, to Miss England, daughter of Poole England, esq. and niece of Lieut. Gen. England, Lieut Governor of Plymouth.—In Derby, (Con.) by the Rev. Dr. Mansfield, aged 94, Mr. James Masters, of Schaticook, aged 77, to Mrs. Elizabeth Osborn, of Derby, aged 74.—In Danville, (Ver.) Mr. John Bolton to Miss Cynthia Chamberlin, both of Danville.—In Portsmouth, the Rev. Charles Lowell, of Boston, to Miss Harriot Spence, of the former place.
   At Westminster, (Ver.) Mr. Josiah Demond to Miss Julia Beach.

===== ¶ [3c] DIED. =====

At New-Orleans, the 2d August, the Rev. Father Walsh, vicar general of Louisiana. —In Cumberland Island, (Geo.) John C. Nightingale, esq.—In Philadelphia, during the week ending the 4th inst. 24 adults and 6 children : of consumption 5, small-pox 1.—In Newyork, during the week ending 4th inst. 16 men, 8 women, 12 boys and 11 girls ; of consumption 6, small-pox 1.—In Cherry Valley, (N.Y.) Joel B. Potter, esq. attorney at law, of a typhus fever, after about three weeks illness.—In Baltimore, Maj. David Stoddert, aged 58.—Near Smyrna, (Del.) Col. James Henry, of the continental army in 1775 ; in 1787 he became a zealous advocate for the christian religion, and for several years was a leader of a class of the Methodist Episcopal church.—In Blenham, (N.Y.) in an apoplectic fit, Mr. Caleb Croswell, at an advanced age.—Near New-Haven, (C.) Mr. Joseph Frith, member of the senior class of Yale College, aged 18 ; he was on a gunning party with three of his fellow collegians ; two of whom, on discovering a bird taking wing, fired, and the contents of one of the pieces lodged in the head of young Frith, who survived the accident but a few hours.—In Danbury, (C.) Mrs. [Seran? or Serah?] Nichols, wife of Mr. Ebenezer N. aged 46.—In Lyme, (C.) Josephus Martin, a transient person, generally known by the name of the German Doctor.—In Newburyport, Dea. Richard Smith, aged 89.—In Marshfield, Dea. Thomas Dingley, aged 75.—In Newton, (Ms.) 4th inst. capt. Samuel Jackson, aged 68.—In York, Me. Edward Emerson, aged 79.—In Marlboro' (Mass.) Mr. Timothy Bemis, aged 72 ; by falling from a load of stalks.—In Northumberland, Mr. Nicholas Tillinghast, by the bursting of a blood vessel.—In Newbury, Mr. Tristram Coffin, aged 72.—In Salem, Mr. Jonathan Brown, aged 86 ;—Mrs. Margaret, widow of Mr. G. Lazell, aged 74 ; her mother, Margaret Swasely, is now living at Salem, in the 100th year of her age.—In Canton, John Tant, esq. aged 69.—In Groton, capt. Jephthah Richardson, aged 49.—In Norwich, (N.Y.) Dea. Nathan Foster, late of Rowe, Ms. aged 54.

No. 32.—Vol. XIV (Whole No. 708) Friday, 24 Oct. 1806.

† [3c] George Dutton ordained "the 1st inst." over the 3d society in North Yarmouth.
† [3d] Samuel Hutchinson adv. goods for sale; dated Alstead, 21 Oct. 1806.
† [3d] Joseph Smith, Jr. requests his debtors for newspaper delivery to pay up. Smith states "that the second week in November will complete one year since he has carried them." Dated 17 Oct. 1806.
† [3d] Stephen R. Whitman adv. drugs and medicines for sale; dated Walpole, 23 Oct.
† [3d] Legal notice regarding the estate auction of Elisha Kingsbery, late of Alstead, deceased, mentioning "the priviledge of using and vending in said town of Alstead, Benjamin Tyler's patent Gristmill, 14 years from the 19th day of March 1804." Dated Alstead, 18 Oct. 1806; Amos Shepard, "Administrator de bonis non on said estate."

===== ¶ [3c] MARRIED. =====

At Stillwater, on the 9th inst. by the Rev. Mr. Paige, the Rev. Mr. Walter Fullerton, of Hebron, to Mrs. Martha Gregory, of Milton, eldest daughter of Judge Thompson, of Stillwater.—At Greenbush, Theodore Ross, Esq. of Willsboro', to Miss Eliza Gansevoort, daughter of L. Gansevoort, jun. Esq. of Greenbush.—At Haddam, (Con.) Mr. Parry Dickinson, of Somers, to Miss Clarissa Clark, of the former place.—At Saybrook, (Con.) the Rev. Sala Post, to Miss Frances Hayden.—At Walton, (N.Y.) Col. Erastus Root, of Delhi, to Miss Eliza Stockton, daughter of Mr. Charles W. Stockton, of the former place.

===== ¶ [3c] DIED. =====

In Philadelphia, during the week ending the 11th inst. 25 adults and 6 children ; of consumption 6.—In Newyork, during the week ending the 11th inst. 9 men, 13 women, 11 boys and 7 girls; of consumption 5, small-pox 1.—In Baltimore, in the 72d year of his age, much regretted, Robert Purviance, esq. late collector of the port of Baltimore.—In New-Vernon, (N.J.) Jonathan Hill, esq. aged 84.—In Boston, Mrs. Sarah Russell, widow of the late Mr. Ezekiel Russell, in the 57th year of her age.—In Petersham, Mrs. Alice Mann, aged 58 ; Mr. David Curtis, aged 86.—In Newburyport, Mrs. Abigail Smith, aged 79, relict of Dea. Smith who also died last week.—In Machias, 2d inst. Stephen Smith, esq. collector of the customs.—In Canton, capt. William Bent, aged 69.—In Franklin, 15th inst. the Hon. Jabez Fisher, esq. aged 91.—In Needham, Jonathan Kingsbury, esq. aged 55.—In Randolph, (Ms.) Dr. Ebenezer Alden, aged 51.—In Portland, Wid. Nabby Wiswal, aged 80.—In Poughkeepsie, (N.Y.) after a short but painful illness, Garret B. Van Ness, esq. counsellor at law, in the 33d year of his age.—In East-Haven, (Con.) Rev. Nicholas Street, pastor of the church in that place, aged 77 ; he had been in the gospel ministry 51 years.—In Danbury, Mrs. Lucy Dixon, aged 38.—In Bridgeport, of a wound received by the accidental discharge of a gun, Mrs. Deborah Caldwell, aged 51.—In Weston, Mr. Reuben Judd. This young man, on the evening of the 30th ult. had loaded his musket with a large quantity of powder, and forced in with great violence a wad of wet paper. In discharging it, a piece of the barrel burst off, and struck him over the right eye, which fractured his skull in such a manner that he expired in a few hours.—In Derne, (N.Y.) by the careless discharge of muskets at a military training, Mr. John Barns, and Capt. Brownell.—In Barton, (Vt.) Mr. Nehemiah Young, aged 22. His death was occasioned by the fall of a frame, which put an immediate period to his existence.—In New-London, N.H. of a consumption, Mr. Ezekiel Knowlton, aged 51. He was one of the first settlers of that town, and an exemplary and useful citizen.—In Francestown, Oliver Holmes, esq. aged 66.

At Rindge, Widow Mary Sawtell, aged 78.

At Cornish, suddenly, Widow Chase, relict of the late Gen. Jonathan Chase.
Killed, by the fall of a tree, the 7th inst. Captain Hezekiah Emerson, of Goshen, N.H. He survived about 48 hours.
In this town, on Wednesday last, Captain Levi Hooper, aged 64; an old and respected inhabitant of this place.

No. 33.—Vol. XIV (Whole No. 709) Friday, 31 Oct. 1806.

¶ [1d] *Accident.*—At the review at Hampden, (Me.) on the 23d ult. Mr. James Pomroy, of the artillery, was severely wounded by the accidental discharge of one of the pieces, and is since dead. Two other persons were considerably injured by the same discharge. The frequency of similar accidents should teach caution to our officers of militia.

¶ [3b] *Distressing accidents.*—Expired in about 23 hours, after the accident, Miss Eliza Fox, of South-East, (N.Y.) aged 4 years. She was standing by a fire; and her clothes, being of muslin, caught the flame, and occasioned her death.

In Washington, (Conn.) Mr. Ruggles Beardsley was thrown from his horse and expired in three hours after. He was about 26 years of age.

In Bridgeport, a woman by the discharge of a gun. A young man took it up and not knowing it was loaded, in sport presented and fired it. As she turned to run it went off and the contents were lodged in her back. The young man has been delirious ever since.

In Danbury, Philander Baldwin, about 8 years of age, climbing a chesnut [sic] tree had reached a limb about 40 feet from the ground, when it broke, and he was precipitated head foremost on the rock beneath. There are scarce any hopes of his recovery.

¶ [3b-c] *Shocking Murder.*—Mr. Francis Constable, of [Basteterre?], (St. Kitts) murdered his four infant children, the latter part of August, and then put a period to his own life by taking a large dose of laudanum. He gave as a reason his inability to provide for them so amply as he wished.

† [3c] Ordinations: At Colchester, Conn., West Chester Society, "on the 1st inst." Mr. Ezra Stiles Ely; at Cooperstown, N.Y., Rev. William Neill; at Pawtucket, R.I. Rev. David Benedict, pastor of the Baptist Church.

† [3d] William Whittle adv. that "he has commenced the Wheelwright Business in Westminster, a few rods South of Mr. Wales's tavern . . . " Dated 29 Oct. 1806.

===== ¶ [3c] MARRIED. =====

At Cornish, on the 20th inst. by T. Chase, esq. Mr. Jabez Luther, to Miss Betsey Parkman. Mr. Luther, some years ago, unfortunately lost both his hands, and a part of both arms, by the discharge of a cannon; but being naturally active and enterprising, he soon found means to feed, dress and shave himself; he writes well, and pursues the mercantile business with a success that enables him to meet the expenses of a family, with a good prospect of performing the duties due to Love & mankind. [Com.

===== ¶ [3c] DIED. =====

In London, Mr. Whitfell, one of His Majesty's cooks, who has left property to the amount of upwards of 12,000 l. without any relative to inherit it.—In Paris, Mr. Coulcomb, celebrated for his philosophical attainments, particularly in electricity and magnetism. His funeral eulogium was pronounced at his grave by M. de Lalande, the oldest of the French astronomers.—In Portsmouth, (Virg.) Dr. James Blamire.—In Norwich, (N.Y.) Deac. Nathan Foster, aged 54, late of Rowe, in Hampshire co. Ms.—In Norwich, (Con.) Mr. Wm. J. Cox, aged 70, a native of G. Britain.—In East-Haven, Rev. Nicholas Street, aged 77.—In Tolland, very suddenly, Dr. Jeremiah West.—In Granby, Mr. Silas Holcomb, aged 70.—In Worcester, (Ms.) Mrs. Elizabeth Rowan, aged 28 ; Mr. Ebenezer Barber, aged 57 ; Miss Reed, daughter of Dea. Ebenezer R. aged 35.—In Richmond, (Ms.) Mr. Rufus Gaston, his wife Mary, and his only child, all of consumption.—In Northampton, Mr. Thomas Delano, aged 41.—In Haverhill, Mr. Caleb Cushing, aged 69.—In Petersham, Mr. David Curtis, aged 84.—In Portsmouth, Mrs. Margaret, relict of Dea. Daniel Lunt, aged 86.—In Cavendish, (Vt.) Mrs. Esther Chaplin, aged 69, wife of capt. William Chaplin. They lived together 48 years.

In Newburyport, Mr. Timothy Dexter, aged 60. He styled himself, "Lord Dexter, first in the East." He was a man of large property, and a perfect IGNORAMUS. His follies and eccentricites are proverbial throughout Massachusetts.

In this town, on Saturday morning last, Mr. Ross Burt, second son of Mr. Moses Burt, in the 19th year of his age.

DROWNED.—In Bilboa river, the 19th August, by the oversetting of a passage boat, capt. Archibald Selman, of Marblehead, commander of the brig America.

No. 34.—Vol. XIV (Whole No. 710) Friday, 7 Nov. 1806.

† [2d] Account of a duel fought 10 Oct. 1806, "near the American garrison at Niagara, between William Dixen, Esq. a judge of the district court of Upper Canada, and William Weeks, Esq. a member of Parliament of the same province." Weeks was killed. ♦

† [3b] Account of the capture of the ship *Essex*, Capt. Orne, of Salem, Mass., by an Arabian ship. All the crew was murdered, and the ship sunk. ♦

† [3b-c] Article describing the counterfeiting problem in the U.S., and mentioning that Ira Johnson, who lately escaped from the jail "in this county", was recaptured. Article copied from a Lansingburg [N.Y.] newspaper.

¶ [3c] At the late Superior Court in the County of Grafton, George Wheeler, John Avery, George Downer, and John Trufant, were convicted of uttering and passing counterfeit bank bills, and were punished by fine and imprisonment. At the same court, Ezekiel Flanders was convicted of horse-stealing. [*D. Gaz*.

¶ [3c] *Fire*.—On the 26th ult. the Glass-works at East-Hartford, (C.) belonging to Mr. John Mather, were consumed by fire.

† [3d] Daniel Buck & Co. adv. goods for sale; dated Hartford, Conn., Oct. 1806.

===== ¶ [3c] DIED. =====

In Washington, (Penn.) Mr. John Israel, late editor of the "Tree of Liberty;" in consequence of a mortification from a trifling puncture in one of his fingers.—In Tolland, (C.) very suddenly, the 18th ult. the Hon. Jeremiah West, esq. in the 54th year of his age.—In Deerfield, (Ms.) Wid. Esther Wright, in the 92d year of her age.—In Dorchester, Mrs. Jemima Bailey, aged 72, late of Boston.—In Boston, Mrs. Comfort Hull, aged 66 ; Mrs. Elizabeth Francis, aged 66.—At Spruce head, Penobscot Bay, 1st Sept. last, Mr. John Walton, aged 106. He was born in England, A.D. 1700, under the reign of William and Mary ; always led a temperate life, resided about seven miles from London, was a member of Mr. Whitefield's church till his emigration to America. It is a remarkable fact that he retained his strength and faculties to a very advanced life ; when at the age of 70, being out in the bay, in a small boat with his wife and child, a sudden squall upset the boat, he caught one of them, swam to the shore, returned and took the other, and again reached the shore in safety.—In Carlisle, (Penn.) Capt. Lemuel Gates, of the U.S. regiment of artillery and engineers, aged 48. At the age of nine years he entered the U.S. army, and continued in it during the revolutionary war. In 1797, when the government of this country was [insulted?] by a foreign power, he was appointed a captain in the artillery ; and for several years was commander of Fort Independence, near Portsmouth. As an officer and a gentleman, his conduct uniformly manifested that he was worthy the confidence that was placed in him.—In Kingston, (Jamaica) Catharine Lopez, a black woman aged 135 years.—In Charlestown, (Ms.) Thomas Sparhawk, esq. of Portsmouth, aged 33.—In Salem, Mrs. Ann Savage, aged 40:—By a fall from a house, Mr. Abner Hill, aged 22.—In Lyme, (C.) Mr. Bartemous Thousar, one of the poor, born blind and dumb, aged 56 years.—In Putney, (Vt.) on the 29th inst. Mr. Joel Hunt, aged 39.—In Brattleboro', Mr. Enoch Hotchkiss, aged 75 years, formerly of New-Haven, (C.)—In Keene, Mrs. Pond, wife of Mr. Joab P.

In Cavendish, Calvin Stevens, aged 4 years, killed by the fall of a cart-body.

In this town, a child of Mr. Philemon Lawrence, in the 5th year of his age.

No. 35.—Vol. XIV (Whole No. 711) Friday, 14 Nov. 1806.

¶ [1d] Sunday morning last, the body of Mr. Amasa Joslin, of Schenectady, was found dead on the Schenectady turnpike, about three miles from this city. On information to the coroner, (Mr. E. Dorr) he immediately attended with a jury, to ascertain by what means he came to his untimely death; when it appeared in evidence, that it was occasioned by an accidental fall from his waggon, at about the hour of ten o'clock the preceeding evening, when returning home from this city. [*Albany Gaz.*]

† [2b] Brief account of thunderstorms in the vicinity of Hanover, N.H., mentioning that a barn in Hartland, Vt., owned by Mr. Zebulon Lee, was destroyed.

† [2b] Mr. James Mercer, aged 84, of North Carolina, sentenced to be hung for the murder of his son-in-law. ♦

† [2d-3a] Lieut. John Proctor, 49, of Henniker, N.H., fell 37 feet down his well, but survived. Article copied from the Farmer's Cabinet, [Amherst, N.H.—Ed.] ♦

† [3a] Rev. Abel M'Ewen ordained at Presbyterian Church, New London, "22d ult."

† [3c] Amasa & Oliver Allen adv. goods for sale; dated Walpole, 5 Nov. 1806.

† [3c] Joshua Phelps, who delivers the *Farmer's Museum* on the route from Walpole to Brattleboro, and other Vt. towns, request payment from subscribers.

† [3c] Jonathan Farnsworth adv. a farm for sale at Alstead; dated there 11 Nov. 1806.

† [3c] Legal notice regarding the estate of Absalom Kingsbery, Esq., Ephraim Kingsbery, Executor; dated Alstead, 11 Nov. 1806.

† [3c] John Flint adv. for stray sheep; dated Walpole, 12 Nov. 1806.

† [3d] Legal notice regarding the insolvent estate of Amos Brown, late of Boston, deceased. Ephraim Davis and Ephraim Farwell appointed commissioners. Dated at Washington, [N.H.—Ed.], 1 Nov. 1806.

===== ¶ [3a] MARRIED. =====

In Goshen, (C.) Rev. James Beach, of Winchester, to Miss Hannah Baldwin, of the former place.—In Salem, (Ms.) Rev. Brown Emerson to Miss Mary Hopkins, daughter of the Rev. Daniel Hopkins.—In Beverly, Capt. Freeborn Thorndike. [171]—In Orrington, Allen Gilman, esq. of Bangor, attorney at law, to Miss Eleanor Brewer, daughter of colonel John Brewer, of Orrington.

At Dublin, Luther Farrar, esq. attorney at law, of Norway, (Me.) to Miss Marcy A. Whiting, of New Ipswich.

At Rockingham, Samuel Whiting, esq. attorney at law, to Miss Betsey Chamberlain.

At Grafton, William E. Green, esq. attorney at law, of Worcester, to Miss Lucy Merriam.

===== ¶ [3a-b] DIED. =====

In Newyork, Mr. Lewis Jones, sen. printer.—In Salem, (Ms.) Mrs. Williams, at an advanced age:—Capt. William Patterson.—In Concord, on the 18th October, Mrs. Rebecca Barrett, relict of the late Col. James Barrett, aged 90. Her descendants are 9 children, 3 of them living; 62 grand-children, 45 living; 108 great-grand-children, 86 living; one great-great-grand-child living; total 180, living 135. Her social and religious sentiments and habits were correct and useful, which merited the esteem and friendship of her numerous acquaintance, rendered her mind tranquil, and her future prospects hopeful and joyous.—In Beverly, much lamented, Dea. Robert H. Wood, of Bluehill.—At sea, Hon. Col. Carleton, of the 25th British Light Dragoons, eldest son of Lord Dorchester.—At sea, James Watson, esq. of the island of Antigua.—In Aux. Caves, (Hisp.) Duncan M'Intosh, esq. assissinated lately by some of the blacks there. He is spoken of as a gentleman of unbounded humanity and uncommon beneficence. His death may be considered as one of the many fatal effects of the bloody lessons taught the negroes by their French instructors.—In Smithfield, (R.I.) Mr. Othniel Matthewson, aged CVII.—In Hartford, Mrs. Jennet Collier, aged 74 years.—At East-Hartford, Mrs. Yates, consort of the Rev. Andrew Yates.—On the 22d ult. at Cherry Valley, (N.Y.) in the 22d year of her age, Mrs. Mary Hall, wife of the Rev. George Hall, and daughter of Mr. Henry Deming, deceased, of Wethersfield.—In Boston, Stephen [Bruce?] esq. aged 60.—In Petersham, (Ms.) much lamented Hon. Daniel Bigelow, esq.—In Hubbardston, Mr. Edward Selfridge, aged 71. [172]—In Rutland, Mr. Wm. Browning, aged 85.—In Oakham, Wid. Mary Fitts, aged 83.—In Mendon, Wid. Deborah Chase, aged 83.—In Upton, Mr. Josiah Childs, aged 76.—In Sutton, Mrs. Susanna Haven, aged 90.—In Oxford, Mrs. Bathsheba Crane, aged 65.—In Worcester, Lt. Josiah Pierce, aged 85. He has left 14 children, 77 grand-children, and 35 great-grand-children; —Mrs. Mary Reed, aged 62, wife of Dea. Ebenezer Reed.—In West Springfield, Mr. Isaac Motley, aged 78.—In Middlebury, (Vt.) Mr. Paul Lucas, in the 34th year of his age.—In Orwell, 13th ult. Mr. [Billy Monger?], sen. in the [?]th year of his age, late of Middlebury.—Suddenly, at Crown Point, on the evening of the [14?]th ult. of an apoplectic fit, Mr. Joseph Bostwick, of Bridport, in the 71st year of his age. It is believed he had no warning of his approaching dissolution, being in apparent good health the preceding day, and made no complaint of previous indisposition.—In Cavendish, Mrs. Esther Chaplin, aged 69, wife of capt. William Chaplin.—Killed instantly, at Cavendish, by the fall of a cart body, which he attempted to climb, Calvin Stevens, aged 4 years, son of Mr. Levi Stevens.—In Portsmouth, capt. Edw'd Fernald, aged 48 ; Mr. James Ryon, aged 60 ; Mrs. Fitzgerald, aged 79 ; Mrs. Mary Babb, aged 64.—In Chester, on Sunday the 5th ult. Mrs. Hannah French, aged 83, wife of Maj. Jabez French ; and on Thursday the 9th ult. Maj. Jabez French, aged 86.—In Hampstead, Thomas Mussey, esq. aged 61.—In Keene, after a short illness, much lamented by her relatives and friends, Mrs. Betsey Fisher, consort of Mr. Thomas Fisher, aged 51.—In Keene, Mr. Ebenezer Barden, of Stoddard. He was a close prisoner in the debtors' apartment until removed by the humanity of the jailer to an adjoining chamber, (no person appearing to bail him) where every attention was paid to him by the family.

In Lempster, very suddenly, a daughter of Mr. T. Nichols, aged about 10 years. She was slightly ill the night before her death, but no danger apprehended until morning, when she was found a corpse.

DEATH OF GENERAL KNOX.

WARREN, OCT. 26, 1806.

DEAR SIR.—It is with the deepest regret I have now to inform you that the great and good General Knox departed this life yesterday morning, aged 57. He was confined about six days. It is supposed that the cause of his death was his swallowing a sharp chicken bone, which perforated his bowels and produced a mortification. The event was very sudden and unexpected by his physicians until a short time before his death. It has covered us all with the deepest gloom. [Cent. corresp.]

DIED.—At his house near Smyrna, Kent county, in the state of Delaware, Col. James Henry, greatly lamented by all who knew his virtues. Mr. Henry in politics was of the Washington school. He entered the continental army, in the state of Maryland, at the head of a company in the year 1775.—On the new organization of the army, he returned to civil life. In the year 1787, he became a zealous advocate for the christian religion—he was for several years a leader of a class in the Methodist Episcopal church. —Departed this life, on the 1st inst. in the 47th year of his age, Philip Nicklin, esq. of the house of Nicklin and Griffith, merchants, of Philadelphia.—On the 21st ult. in the 54th year of his age, Israel Whelen, esq. formerly a representative of the city of Philadelphia and district in the Senate of Pennsylvania.—In New London, (C.) Mr. Walter Harris, aged 90.—In Colchester, 22d ult. Ebenezer Lathrop, esq. aged 74 years. Thirty minutes antecedent to his dissolution he was busy about his usual employments, and manifested no signs of indiposition—he entered his house, sat down in a chair, and complained of a nausea, and in a few minutes fell from his chair and instantly expired. —In Brattleboro', 29th ult. Wid. Elizabeth Orvis, aged 89 ; Mr. Edward Stebbins.—In Wardsborough, Miss Sally Dexter, aged 14.

No. 36.—Vol. XIV (Whole No. 712) Friday, 21 Nov. 1806. [173]

† [2c] Account of the trials of several persons at Poughkeepsie, N.Y., in an article copied from the New York Commercial Advertiser: 1) Jesse Wood, for the wilful murder of his son, found guilty, sentenced to be hung 5 Dec. 1806. 2) David Root, guilty of poisoning horses owned by Benjamin B. Adams.♦ 3) Tom, a black man, guilty of assault and battery, sentenced to 10 days in jail. 4) James Van Blarcum and John Thompson; the former found guilty of burning the jail, the latter acquitted.♦ 5) William Gilman indicted by a grand jury for passing counterfeit bills, chiefly of the New Hampshire Bank.

† [2c] George Lamphere and his mother committed to Woodstock jail, charged with physical abuse upon his wife, who died 2 Nov. 1806 from injuries sustained from beatings. Article copied from the *Windsor Post-Boy.* ♦

¶ [2c] *Remarkable Production.* Mr. Seth Munson, of Moretown, raised the last year from one Bean, 2764 Beans. *Windsor Post-Boy.*

† [2c] Description of a large cabbage grown by Mr. Simeon Tracy, of Richmond, Mass.
† [3b] Benjamin Snell shot Michael Tompkins dead, over a dispute, 10 Nov. 1806, at Taunton, Mass.; Snell was arrested. ◆
† [3b] Rev. James Flint ordained at Bridgewater [Mass.—Ed.], 29 Oct. 1806.
† [3c] Daniel Spooner requests all debtors to pay up; dated Walpole, 18 Nov. 1806.

==== ¶ [3b] MARRIED. ====

In Redding, (Steuben county, N.Y.) the 5th ult. Mr. James Ovenshire, to Miss Mary Osgood, both of that town.—At Three Rivers, John Sawers, esq. to Miss Elizabeth M'Pherson, both of Upper-Canada.—At Plymouth, (Vt.) Mr. Elijah Dunbar to Miss Rachel White, both of that place.—In Providence, (R.I.) Mr. John Wheelock, of Eyerlett, in the 50th year of his age, to Miss Lucinda Leonard of Taunton, in the 17th year of her age.—In Goshen, C. Rev. James Beach to Miss Hannah Baldwin.
At Rockingham, (Vt.) Mr. George Wilson to Miss Mary House.
In Charlestown, Mr. Jacob Wright to Miss Dorcas Walker.
In this town, Mr. Ephraim Brown, of Westmoreland, to Miss Mary Huntington.
Dr. Francis Kittridge to Miss Sibel Bundy, daughter of Mr. Asahel Bundy.

==== ¶ [3c] DIED. ====

In Redding, (Steuben county, N.Y.) the 11th ult. Mrs. Mary Ovenshire, mentioned in the above marriage, Æt. 17.—In Quebec, Lt. Col. Mackintosh, of the 2d battalion of the 60th reg't.—Mr. Geo. Pozer, jun.—In Kingston, (N.Y.) 28th ult. the Rev. Thomas Adams, principal of the academy.—Departed this life, at his seat in Baltimore a few days since, Benjamin Bannaker, a man of colour, who has been celebrated for his astronomical knowledge, and other scientific acquirements, in the 70th year of his age. This person affords strong evidence that Nature had not been so partial in her dispensations as some have supposed, and that she sometimes irradiates the minds of those who were *"The sable livery of the burnish'd sun."*—In Virginia, Gabriel Jones, esq. aged 85 ; he was the oldest man in the state, bred to the practice of the law, and for many years stood in the foremost rank of his profession. A certain *great man* once made him a *paper money tender;* "thereby hangs a tale."—In Philad. Mrs. Frances Jollier, aged 96 ; Mrs. Mary Walnut ; Capt. Nathaniel Faulconer, aged 77.—In New-London, David Mumford, esq. aged 78.—In Middletown, very suddenly, Mrs. Ruth Tuell, in the 52d year of her age.—In Boston, Mr. Benjamin Jeffry, aged 79. In Springfield, Abraham Vanhorn, aged 79 ; Mrs. Mabel Ferre, aged 81, wife of capt. Joseph Ferre.—In Exeter, Mrs. Elizabeth, wife of Mr. Henry Ranlet, printer.—Departed this life, on the 3d inst. Mrs. Ann Chadbourn, aged 53, consort of the late Jonathan Chadbourn, esq. and daughter of Samuel Hale, esq. of Portsmouth.—In Keene, Mrs. Betsey, wife of Mr. Thomas Fisher, aged 51.—In Windsor, Mr. Jacob Stowell, aged 70.
In Chester, Vt. Mr. Ricard [sic] Thompson, aged 56, formerly of Rindge.
In Salisbury, on the 6th inst. Mrs. Sukey Eastman, wife of Moses Eastman, esq. aged 29.
In this town, Mary, only child of Mr. Charles Stratton, aged 2 y. 2 mo. and 19 days.

No. 37.—Vol. XIV (Whole No. 713) Friday, 28 Nov. 1806.

† [1d] Rev. Amasa Smith installed "22d ult." at the 2d church, North Yarmouth.
† [3b] Legal notice regarding the estate of John Hubbard, Esq., late of Charlestown, deceased; notice published by Henry Hubbard of Charlestown, and dated 25 Nov. 1806.
† [3b] Legal notice regarding the insolvent estate of Buckminster White, late of Charlestown, deceased. Samuel Prouty, Abel French, and John Sartwell appointed Commissioners, and Henry Hubbard, Adm. Dated Charlestown, 25 Nov. 1806.
† [3c] Jesse Willcox, Treasurer, posts a notice regarding the Croydon Turnpike; dated Newport, 15 Nov. 1806.

==== ¶ [3a] MARRIED. ====

In Paris, H.I.H. Prince Jerome Bonaparte, to H.R.H. the Princess Royal of Wirtemburg ; sister-in-law to the late Princess Royal of Great-Britain, now Queen of Wirtemburg.—In Worcester, Mr. Joshua Blake to Miss Sarah Staunton.—In Portsmouth, Mr. Benjamin Holmes, aged 68, to Miss Nancy Rand, of Rye, aged 24.

¶ [3a-b] DIED.

In Swansea, (En.) Mr. David George; he was in the act of disengaging a sole fish from a net, when the fish made a spring down his throat, and choaked him.—In Charleston, (S.C.) 22d Oct. Mr. Samuel Ham, aged 38, shipwright ; a native of Newhampshire : He had resided for the last 17 years at Charleston, acquired a very handsome property, and is spoken of as a most worthy and useful man, whose death is much regretted.—In Baltimore, during the week ending 8th inst. 9 adults and 13 children.—In Philad. during the week ending 8th inst. 14 adults and 7 children ; of consumption 4.—In New-York, during the week ending the 8th inst. 19 men, 15 women, 11 boys and 8 girls ; of consumption 7 ; small-pox 1.—In East-Hartford, (C.) Mrs. Mary, consort of the Rev. Andrew Yates, aged 30.—In New-York, 11th inst. Mr. Daniel Butler, jun. in the 22d year of his age, son of Dr. Daniel Butler, of Hartford, C.—In Westfield, (C.) very suddenly, Mrs. Abigail Higby, aged 47 years, wife of Mr. Lemuel H.—In Canterbury, very suddenly, Gen. Moses Cleveland.—In Northampton, Mr. Abraham Vanhorn, aged 79 ; Mrs. Mabel Moody, wife of capt. Daniel M. aged 81.—In Ipswich, (Ms.) Mrs. Abigail Galloway, aged 65.—In Roxbury, Mr. Joseph Cranch, aged 60.—In Boston, Mr. Simeon Polley, aged 45.—In Salem, Mr. Thomas Henman, aged 40.—In Sutton. Hon. Amos Singletary, esq. aged 85, a man equally distinguished as a pious & devout Christian and an able Statesman. He early in life made profession of religion, and served as an Elder of the church in Sutton 38 years.—He had a seat in the Provincial Congress 3 years—in the General Court 10 years—in the Senate 4 years—and held a commission as justice of the Peace 27 years. He left 13 children, 73 grand children, and 57 great grand children.—In Worcester, Mr. Reuben Stearns aged [?].— In Augusta, (Geo.) Ralph Emms Elliot, esq. of Beaufort, (S.C.) aged 79.—In Winchester, (Vir.) Edw'd M'Guire, sen. esq.—In Springfield, Mrs. Jemima Cooper, aged 76.—In Great Barrington, 6th inst. Mrs. Mary Potter, wife of Mr. Job Potter, aged 48. —In Brookfield, Wid. Ruth Nickols, aged 75.—In Durham, Oct. 25, Mr. Benjamin Small, aged 94.—At St. Dennis, (Isle of Bourbon) 12th August last, capt. John Williams, jun. late master of the brig Reward, of Salem, and only son of the Hon. John Williams, esq. of Deerfield.—In Newport, (R.I.) Mrs. Hannah, widow of the late Mr. John Goddard, aged 79.—In Lisbon, (C.) Joseph, John, Clarissa, and Philorus Harrington ; their decease was occasioned by their drinking water from a well, into which a bag of arsenic had been thrown by design.—In Woodstock, (C.) 26th ult. Mr. John Torrey, formerly of Boston, hatter, aged 78.—In Rowley, (Ms.) Wid. Sarah Baker, aged 53.—In Lincoln, 9th inst. the Hon. Eleazer Brooks, esq. aged 80 ; an old revolutionary officer and patriotic statesman. —In Orford, Maj. Samuel Todd, aged 52, very suddenly.

In Charlestown, very suddenly, Mrs. Hunt, widow of the late Col. Hunt, in the 66th year of her age.

No. 38.—Vol. XIV (Whole No. 714) Friday, 5 Dec. 1806.

† [3b] Suicide of Mr. Robert Smith, at Louisville, 9 [Nov.?] 1806. ♦

† [3b] Robbery of Mr. Luther Hodgkins of Walpole. ♦

† [3b] Rev. Noah Porter ordained "12th inst." at Farmington, Conn., and Rev. Abraham Bodwell ordained at Sandbornton, "on the 13th ult."

† [3d] Legal notice regarding the estate of John Cutting, late of Croydon, deceased; Moses P. Durkee, Samuel Powers, and Thomas Whipple appointed Commissioners. Claims to be examined at the house of Stephen Eastman at Croydon; dated 26 Nov. '06.

† [3d] Samuel Mills adv. his new bookstore at Burlington, Vt.; dated 3 Nov.

¶ [3b] MARRIED.

In Baltimore, at Zion hill, (Maryland) commodore John Rodgers to Miss Minerva Deniston.—At Woodstock, (Vt.) Mr. David Thompson, preceptor of Randolph Academy, to Miss Irene Case, of the former place.—At Jaffrey, Mr. Daniel Cutter to Miss Sally Jones.—In Groton, (Ms.) Tyler Bigelow, esq. att'y at law of Watertown, to Miss Clarissa Bigelow, of the former place.—In Dracut, Mr. Silas Pierce, of Chelmsford, to Mrs. Hannah Littlehale ; she being his sixth wife.—In Deerfield, (Ms.) Mr. Jesse Morgan, of Conway, to Miss Hannah Stebbins, of the former place.

In this town, on Sunday evening last, Mr. William Wait to Miss Nancy Christy.

¶ [3c] DIED.

In Great-Britain, Earl Clermont, aged 84.—In Lisbon, Mr. Lunardi, a celebrated aronaut.—Near Chilicothe, (Oh.) Rev. Samuel Welsh.—Near Morristown, (N.J.) Mr. Nicholas Comisau, aged 90, a native of France.—In Philadelphia, Capt. Nathaniel Faulconer master war[?], and one of the oldest captains of that [?], aged 77; Mrs. Frances Jollier, aged 96.—In Baldhead, (N.C.) Mr. Henry Long. Being out with his son-in-law, hunting after deer or wild hogs, and the son-in-law seeing the brush move and supposing they contained game, fired, when the whole charge entered the bowels of Mr. Long.—In Salisbury, (C.) on the 30th Oct. the Hon. Joshua Staunton, aged 38 years, late Chief Judge of Chittenden, (Vt.) County Court.—In New-Haven, Capt. Robert Townsend, aged [?]8.—In Reading, (Ms.) Deacon Henry Putnam, aged 51.—In Boston, Widow Louis Clouston, aged 69 ; Mrs. Martha Thwing, relict of the late Dea. James T. aged 68.—In Royalton, (Vt.) 7th ult. Mr. Samuel Cleveland, aged about 77.—In Braintree, the 15th ult. Mrs. Rachel Burke consort of Mr. John Burke, aged [?]5. She was a native of Brookfield, Ms. and a regular member of the church in that town.—In Rutland, much lamented, Miss Lucy Dewing, aged 25.—In Bridgewater, (N.H.) Mr. Samuel Simons, aged [?]7 ; run over by his waggon.—In Durham, Oct. 25, Mr. Benjamin Small, aged 94.—In Portsmouth, Mr. James [Foster?], aged 45 ; Mrs. Abbot, aged 75 ;—Capt. John Yeaton, aged 27.—In Jaffrey, Rebecca, daughter of Mr. Daniel French, aged 2 years. Her death was occasioned by falling into a kettle of boiling water.—In Germany, the hereditary Prince of Brunswick, brother to the English Princess of Wales.—In England, Miss Cholmondeley ; she was riding in a [?]arouche with the Princess of Wales, and Lady Sheffield, when the coach upset and Miss C. dashed against a post, and killed outright. The Princess was much bruised, but not dangerously.—In England, the Rt. Rev. Dr. Horseley, Bishop of St. A[?]ph.—In Canterbury, (C.) Gen. Moses Cleveland, aged 52.—In Portland, 18th [ult.?] Mrs. Jane, relict of the late Hans [Gram?], esq.—In Boston, Mr. Robert Rob[in?]son, aged 67 ; Mr. Joseph Cutler, mer. aged 35 ; Mr. John Muntzenbecher, aged 32.

No. 39.—Vol. XIV (Whole No. 715) Friday, 12 Dec. 1806.

¶ [1d] A black man, named Hardy, was yesterday indicted for the murder of an infant child, by strangling, and throwing it overboard, on Thanksgiving evening, from South Boston bridge. He is to be tried on Friday.—*Col. Cent.*

† [2d] Some farmers in Belpre, Ohio, upon reading in the Walpole and Worcester papers about produce grown in New England, responded by measuring and weighing their own. "Col. N. Cushing, the magistrate, Solomon Monrow, Joseph Kersey, Oliver W. Fuller, and the school master of the place, all, it is presumed, as good and true men as the gentlemen of Grafton, repaired to the garden of Col. Israel Putnam, of this place . . . " to witness the vegetables grown by Putnam.

† [2d] Abraham Barnes planted an apple tree in Warwick 25 years ago, and this year it produced 50 bushel. The news item was copied from the Agricultural Register.

† [3b] Paragraph describing the new African Baptist Meetinghouse in Boston, where Mr. Thomas Paul, "a respectable black," will be installed as pastor. ◆

† [3c] Henry Foster adv. a farm for lease in Walpole, dated there 6 Dec. 1806.

† [3c] Abraham Holland requests debtors to pay up; dated Walpole, 9 Dec. 1806.

¶ [3b-c] MARRIED.

In Boston, Francis D. Channing, esq. to Miss Susan Higginson, daughter of Stephen Higginson, esq.—In Scituate, Dr. Cushing Otis, to Miss Abigail Cushing, eldest daughter of the Hon. Nathan Cushing.—In Keene, Maj. John P. Blake, to Miss Sally Ellis.— Also, Mr. John Hoar, jun. of Westminster, Ms. to Miss Esther Kendall.—At Attakapas, (Louisiana) 27th Sept. His Ex'y Gov. Wm. C.C. Claiborne, to Miss Clarice Duralde, daughter of Martin Duralde, esq.—In Orrington, Allen Gilman, esq. to Miss Eleanor Brewer, daughter of Col. John Brewer.—In Providence, Mr. Richard Salisbury, to Miss Lydia Thurber.

At Newport, Mr. Asa Corbin to Miss Abigail Hurd.—Mr. Stephen Hurd to Miss Abigail Willcox.—Mr. Nathan Call to Miss Hannah Eastman.

¶ [3c] DIED.

In Charleston, (S.C.) Capt. James Payne, commander of the State revenue cutter.—In Virginia, William Lawrence, esq.—In Georgetown, (Colum.) Robert Peter, esq.—In Baltimore, during the week ending the 23d Nov. 14 adults and 10 children.—In Philad. during the week ending the 22d Nov. 19 adults and 9 ch. total 28 ; not more than two of any one disease.—In Newyork, during the week ending the 23 ult. 47, viz. 16 men, 10 women, 18 boys and 8 girls ; —*Consumption*, as usual, claimed the highest number of victims, eight, six of them women, of the ages 22, 23, 35, 43, 45, 47.—In Oxford, (C.) Rev. David Bronson, aged 67 : "*Blessed is he whose sun is set on earth to rise in heaven.*"—In Newhaven, Mr. Stephen D'Wolf, aged 71.—In Goshen, 20th ult. Mrs. Sarah Mills, relict of the late Dea. Joseph Mills, of Norfolk, aged 70.—In Windham, the Rev. Cornelius Adams.—In Glastenbury, 23d ult. Susannah Wheeler, aged 57.—In Bristol, (R.I.) Capt. Benj. Moore, late of New Hampshire.—In Middleborough, (Ms.) Rev. Isaac Backus, aged 82 ; pastor of the first Baptist church in that town ; he had been in the gospel ministry 60 years.—In Scituate, 22d ult. in the 72d year of his age, Doctor Charles Stockbridge, of a dropsy. In the death of this valuable man, science has lost a favourite, society a benefactor, & the commonwealth one of her best citizens. Unambitious, he believed the "post of honour was the private station;" and could never be induced to accept any office or appointment in public life.—In Salem, Mrs. Mary Prince, consort of the Rev. Dr. P. of that place, aged 53.—In Portland, Mr. Frederick Parker, aged 36, a native of Vermont.—In Boston, William Bant Sullivan, esq. aged 25.—In East-Andover, Mr. John Rice, aged 30 ; at Belfast, Mr. Amos Rice, aged 40 ; sons of Capt. Amos Rice, of Northboro'.—In Sterling, Dea. Solomon Jewett, aged 62.—In Oxford, Doctor Simeon Kingsbury, æt. 44.—In Woodstock, (Ver.) Mr. Amos Wheeler.—At Hampstead, Mrs. Mary Goodwin, relict of Mr. Nathan Goodwin, at an advanced age.—At Mont-Vernon, widow Mary Herrick, æt. 71.

At Charlestown, on Thursday, 4th inst. after a long and painful sickness, Mrs. Relief Roby, consort of Doctor Joseph Roby, aged 28 years; also, the 13th ult. Jane, their infant daughter, aged 3 months.

DROWNED.]—In Springfield, (Vt.) Col. J. Barrett, aged 74. The circumstances attending this melancholy event, we learn, are as follow : On Wednesday he attended a turkey shooting at Gen. Morris's Mills, a mile or two from his house, and set out on his return home early at night. It is supposed that, owing to the darkness of the evening, and a snow which was falling at the time, he must have mistaken the road. He was found on Friday in Black river, into which he had fallen from the bank, from 12 to 15 feet. His head appeared to be immersed in water only about a foot deep, and the rest of his body was out.—His remains were consigned to the grave on Monday last, attended by a numerous and respectable procession of mourners and friends.

No. 40.—Vol. XIV (Whole No. 716) Friday, 19 Dec. 1806.

¶ [3b] A duel has been fought near Fort Wilkinson, between Lts. Foster and Arnistead —the latter was dangerously wounded.

† [3b] Ordinations: at Providence, R.I. Rev. Ferdinand Ellis; at Sandbornton, N.H., Rev. Abraham Bodwell; and at Minot, 12 Nov., Rev. Jonathan Scott installed at the First Church.

† [3c] Runaway notice for Asahel Whitney, aged about 17, indented as a wheelwright apprentice to John Willson, 3d, who offers $1 reward for his return; dated at Acworth, 17 Nov. 1806.

† [3d] J. Bellows adv. for debtors to pay up; dated 17 Dec. 1806.

¶ [3c] MARRIED.

In Woodstock, (Ver.) Mr. Elias Thomas to Miss Polly Adams ; Mr. Stetson Randall to Miss Polly Kingsley ; Mr. Jehosaphat Briggs to Miss Betsey Warren.—In Hartland, Mr. John Rice to Miss Nabby Smith.—In Reading, Mr. Jonathan Benjamin, jr. to Miss Hannah Swinnerton.—In Windsor, Mr. Willard P. Hall of Keene, to Miss Betsey Stone ; Mr. Isaac French to Miss Abby Winch.

At Newport, Mr. Samuel Stiles, of Claremont, to Miss Hepsibah Towner, of the former place.

¶ [3c] DIED.

In Edinburgh, (Scot.) John Bell, esq. a celebrated bookseller.—In Clinton, (Up. Canada) Rev. Samuel Covell, of Cheshire, (Mass.) while on a missionary tour among the Indians.—In Fredericktown, (N.B.) Hon. Isaac Allen, aged 65, member of Council, and one of the Judges of the Supr. Court in that province.—In Windham, (C.) Rev. Cornelius Adams.—In Lyme, Mr. David Peck, æ. 87.—In East Haddam, Mr. Sam'l Emmons, aged 79.—In Colchester, C. Eben. Lathrop, esq. brother to the Rev. Dr. Lathrop, of Boston. Thirty minutes antecedent to his dissolution he was busy about his usual employments, and manifested no signs of indisposition; he entered his house, sat down in his chair, complained of a nausea, and in a few minutes fell and instantly expired.—In Lincoln, Ms. Mr. Peter Underwood, aged 78.—In Plymouth, Mrs. Mary Thomas, aged 75. In Middleborough, Rev. Isaac Backus, pastor of the first Baptist church in that town, aged 83. His writings, which are considerably voluminous, contain much ecclesiastical and historical information.—In Beverly, Mrs. Elizabeth Chipman, aged 40.—In Salem, Mr. Henry Jackson, of Boston, aged 33.—In Southampton, 15th Oct. Mr. Job Strong, aged 54 ; on the 16th Nov. Mrs. Eunice Clark, consort of Mr. Selah Clark, aged 91 ; on the 24th, Mr. Gideon Searl, aged 75 ; on the 26th, Mrs. Mary Searl, relict of Mr. Nathaniel Searl, aged 90 ; on the 29th, Mr. Selah Clark, aged 91.—In Northampton, Widow Marcy Hawley, relict of the late Hon. Joseph Hawley, aged 77.—In Templeton, Widow Mary Cobleth, aged 73.—In Princeton, Mr. Samuel Mirick, aged 49.—In Sturbridge, Capt. Comfort Freeman, aged 56.—In Portland, Mrs. Mary Goddard, aged 22, consort of Capt. Wm. Goddard, and daughter of the Hon. Woodbury Storer ; Mr. Frederick Parker, aged 36, a native of Cambridge, Vermont.—In Greenfield, 8th inst. Mrs. Thankful Severance, aged 77 ; on the 9th, David Smead, esq. aged 74.—In Buckland, (Mass.) Joshua, son of Mr. Jotham Forbes, aged 11. As he and two other lads were playing at goal, he and John Porter, one of the lads, left their goals and ran with great violence at each other—as they met, the latter raised his knee, which came in contact with the bowels of his companion—He instantly fell, and cried out, *I am kill'd !*—He soon after began to puke which he did at intervals that and the two following days, when he expired.—In Guilford, Mrs. Prudence Briggs, aged 54.—In Woodstock, (Vt.) Wid. Sarah Hamilton, aged 61.—In Portsmouth, Mrs. M. Lewis, aged 77. In Temple, Mrs. Polly Cutter, wife of Maj. Benj C.—In Hopkinton, Robert Molineux, aged 40, after a painful illness of six years.—In Keene, Miss Rachel Hale, Æt. 23.—In Surry, Mr. Elijah Streeter, aged 31, son of the Rev. Zebulon Streeter.

Drowned.—In Danbury, (C.) by accidentally falling into a well Mr. Henry Fritz, hatter, aged 28 years, lately of Newyork.

No. 41.—Vol. XIV (Whole No. 717) Friday, 26 Dec. 1806.

This issue is missing from the collection.

No. 42.—Vol. XIV (Whole No. 718) Friday, 2 Jan. 1807.

† [1c-d] Extensive account of a robbery and attempted murder of Mr. John Pye, a tavern-keeper at Watervliet, New York. The robber's name was said to be Johnson, who belonged to New Jersey. In a related article at [3a], Johnson was said to be the one who attempted to rob Mr. Painter, of Vergennes. [174] ♦

† [2c-d] Account of a massive fire at Portsmouth, N.H., 24 Dec. 1806, which affected the following persons or businesses : ♦

Benjamin Hill	Robert Harris	Jeremiah Libbey
Daniel Weeks	Edward Cutts	William Walker
Stephen Little	George Cutts	Daniel Brown
Washington Pierce	James Day	B. Weane [or Weare?]
Nathaniel Adams & Son	Christopher Rimes	J. Weane " "
Ebenezer Thompson	Samuel Cotton	Jacob Wendell
Nathaniel A. Haven	John Staples	William Thomas
John Haven	widow Tuttle	Charles Neil
John Rindge	Mark Simes	G. Leavitt
C. Rimes	George Wendell	Capt. Phillips
Abel Harris	Mr. Giles	

† [2d] Francis M'Collister and Luther Calender Parker arrested at Weathersfield, Vt., on charges of counterfeiting; also one Wiswall was taken on the same charge. ♦

† [3a] Smith Williams, Moses Bacon, John Steward, Thomas Smith, and Samuel Tibbetts arrested [at Walpole?] for counterfeiting. The first three were released for want of evidence; Smith and Tibbetts sent to jail in Montreal. ♦

† [3c] Rev. Samuel Veazie ordained at Freeport, Maine.

† [3d] S.R. Whitman adv. drugs & medicines for sale; dated Walpole, 2 Jan. 1807.

===== ¶ [3d] MARRIED. =====

In Northampton, Mr. James Shepherd, 2d to Miss Eliza Phillips ;—Maj. Erastus Lyman, to Miss Rachel Hutchins.—In Castleton, (Ver.) Mr. Daniel Moulton to Miss Roxana Kilbourn, both of that place.—In Norwich, (Vt.) Mr. Alpheus Hatch to Miss Sally Hutchinson ;—Mr. Samuel Hunt to Miss Polly Wilder ;—Mr. Cyrus Patridge to Miss Polly Loveland.

===== ¶ [3d] DIED. =====

In Digby, (N.S.) Isaac Bonnell, esq. aged 70.—At Fort Miller, in the county of Washington, (N.Y.) after a long and tedious illness, in the 78th year of his age, Noah Payne, esq. He has left a numerous offspring, 13 living children and 52 grand children. He was an indulgent husband, kind parent, benevolent to the poor, hospitable to strangers, a true patriot of '76, and upright in all his dealings.—In Cooperstown, (N.Y.) Col. Richard Cary. The Sunday preceding he had the misfortune to fracture one of his legs badly, which, with other bruises, occasioned a fever, which terminated his existence. He was one of the early aids-de-camp to Gen. Washington ; an upright, well-bred, and agreeable gentleman, possessed of wit, genius and humor.—In New Haven, (C.) Mrs. H. Griswold, aged 94.—At Harwinton, C. Mr. Zebulon Culver, of Danbury, aged 90.—In Salem, (Ms.) Mr. Andrew Ward, aged 30. He died, without any previous sickness, as he was sitting at ease in his chair.—At Pawtuxet, Mr. Ezra Dean, aged 89; as venerable in virtue as in years;—Col. Job Randall, aged 63.—In Limington, Mr. Samuel Plaisted, Æt. 87.—In Boston, Dr. William Saxton, aged 62 ; Mr. Joseph Snelling, aged 73 ; Mr. William Groom, aged 74 ; Mr. Patrick Moore Kenny, comedian, aged 44.—In Wrentham, Mrs. Lucy Fisher, Æt. 70.

Erratum.—In our obituary of last week, for *James* Hall, read *Solon* Hall.

No. 43.—Vol. XIV (Whole No. 719) Friday, 9 Jan. 1807.

† [1c] Samuel Hutchinson adv. goods for sale; dated Alstead 10 Dec. 1806.

† [3c] Amos Shepard and Samuel Hutchinson announce the formation of a new business, *Shepard & Hutchinson*, which sells European, East and West India goods, etc.; located near the meetinghouse, Newport, N.H. Dated 1 Jan. 1807.

† [3d] Legal notice regarding the estate of Samuel Wires, deceased. The notice states

that John H. Wires will settle his accounts with the Judge of Probate; dated at Walpole, 7 Jan. 1807.

===== ¶ [3b] DIED. =====

In Quebec, the Hon. Antoine Jucherean Duchesnay, esq. one of his majesty's Executive Counsellors for the Province of Canada, and Colonel of the Beauport division of militia.—In Norwich, C. very suddenly, Maj. Thomas Tracy, aged 38; of the house of Avery & Tracy—In New Haven, (Con.) during the year ending Dec. 31, 1806, 104 deaths; of which 45 were under 5 years of age; 9 from 5 to 30 ; 28 from 30 to 60 ; 11 from 70 to 90, and 6 from 90 to 100 y'rs.—In Mansfield, (C.) Mr. Daniel Howe, aged 67: He was found dead, sitting in a chair, in a small, tight room, over a kettle of burning coals. —In Hartford, C. Mr. Archibald Wells, aged 73.—In Suffield, Mr. Eben. Hathway, aged 84.—In Windham, Mr. Josiah Manning, Æt. 81.—In Oakham, (Ms.) Miss Hannah [Fins?] aged [?]3.—In Holden, Mr. John Perry, aged 75.—In Danvers, Mr. Joseph Endicott, aged 79.—In Boston, Mrs. Amo[zoel?] Boynton, aged 73, widow of the late Dea. Richard Boynton, of Boston ; Mr. James Campbell, aged 49.—In Weybridge, (Vt.) 18th ult. Mr. Roger Wales, aged 17, formerly of Windham, C.—In Woodstock, Mrs. Urania Williams, aged 49.—In Windsor, Mrs. Amy Woods, aged 40.—In Concord, (N.H.) Widow Hanniford, aged 92.—In Portsmouth, very suddenly, Mrs. Ann Waldron, Æt. 84.—In N. Hampton, Mr. Eben. Lovering, aged 87.—In Temple, Mr. Gideon Powers, aged 76.—In Newmarket, capt. Hubartus Neal, aged 89.—In Keene, Mr. Stephen [Eveleth?], aged 37.

In Putney, on the 18th ult. Miss Sally Bigelow, aged 25.

In this town, Mrs. Fanny Charter, consort of Mr. Nath'l Charter, one of the printers of the Political Observatory, in the 20th year of her age.

ACCIDENT.]—On the 22d inst. a child, of about six years of age, son of the widow Coolidge, being at play, in Watertown, with other boys in the Cotton Manufactory, he was unfortunately caught in one of the wheels, and was crushed to pieces in an instant.

No. 44.—Vol. XIV (Whole No. 720) Friday, 16 Jan. 1807.

† [1c] *Nath'l Gould & Co.* adv. that "they have on hand a General Assortment of articles in the Sadlery Line," dated at Walpole, 6 Jan. 1807.

¶ [3b] On the 10th ult. a new and elegant house 44 by 36 feet, was consumed by fire in Guildhall, the property of Noah Sabin, jun. formerly of Brattleboro'.—Loss 1500 dollars. Last spring the same gentleman lost his pearl-ash works, & c. to the amount of 1000 dollars.

¶ [3b] A two-year-old was killed in this town, on the 27th ult. by Mr. John Carpenter, which weighed 922 lbs.—the weight of the hide alone was 123. *Randolph pap.*

¶ [3b] A Medical friend has favoured us with the following very extraordinary *parturient* case *Cooperstown pap.*

> Mrs. Catharine Cross, wife of Ephraim Cross, of this place, on the 22d of March, 1806, was delivered of two children (boys), and on the 9th inst. she was again delivered of three children, (two boys and a girl.) Thus you will discover from the above dates, that she was delivered of FIVE living children within the course of *eight* months and *twenty-three* days.
> *Milford*, 15*th* Dec. 1806.

† [3b] Rev. Samuel P. Williams ordained at the First Church of Christ, Mansfield, CT.

===== ¶ [3b] MARRIED. =====

In Boylston, (Ms.) Mr. Roger Chase, aged 72, to Miss Catharine Clap, Æt. 44.—In Greenfield, (Ms.) Mr. Ira Arms to Miss Sophia Allen.—In Windham, (C.) Mr. John French, mer. to Miss Fanny Allen.—In Charlestown, (Ms.) Henry Adams, esq. to Miss Susan Foster.—In Boston, Ralph Alexander Moorhouse, esq. of Leeds, (Eng.) to Mrs. Taylor, widow of the late Wm. Henry Taylor, esq. of London.

===== ¶ [3b-c] DIED. =====

In Charleston, (S.C.) in the 75th year of his age, Mr. Alexander Robertson, for many years a respectable inhabitant of that city.—At Raleigh, (N.C.) Dec. 27, Mr. Charles Story, comedian, late of the Charleston and Virginia theatres.—In Baltimore, during the week ending 24th ult., 7 adults and 8 children; of consumption 3.—In Philad. Joseph Swift, esq. mer. and an alderman :—Mr. Matthew Hall, for many years an officer of the Customs.—In Philad. during the week ending 27th ult. 14 adults and 11 child.—In Newyork, during the week ending 27th ult. 10 men, 10 women, 8 boys and 7 girls ; one of the latter burnt to death by her clothes taking fire.—In Brunswick, (N.J.) John Dennis, esq. aged 83.—In the Oneida Lake, (N.Y.) drowned, Mr. Mettler, a native of Zurich, Switz.—In Sandy Creek, (N.Y.) Mr. Isaac Cutler, a native of New Hampshire. —In N. York, Mr. Edward Backhouse, cabinet-maker ;—Mr. Christopher Neuswanger, a watchman, stabbed during a riot in that city on Christmas evening : The Irishman who stabbed him, being conscience struck, has made voluntary confession of the crime. [175] —In Hartford, (C.) the Rev. James Coggswell, D.D. aged 87 ; —Mr. Caleb Church, aged 79.—In Granby, Dec. 16, Dea. Elnathan Strong, aged 70.—In East-Hartford, 1st inst. Mrs. Mary A. King, the amiable consort of the Rev. Salmon King, in the 31st year of her age.—In Danbury, Mr. Asa Cummings, aged 45.—In Newport, (R.I.) Mr. Wm. Vernon, mer. aged 87.—In Lewiston, (Me.) Capt. Elisha Lake, aged 85; a veteran of the revolutionary war.—In Biddeford, Mrs. Lydia, relict of the late Benj. Hooper, esq. aged 79.—In Newburyport, in the six religious societies, during the year 1806, the deaths are stated at 118.—In Salem, from Jan. 1, 1806, to Jan. 1, 1807, 200 deaths; 101 males, 99 females; of consumption 40—In Rev. Mr. Worcester's society, in 1804, 1805, and 1806, in each year, [39?].—In Marblehead, in Rev. Mr. Dana's society, in 1806, 54 deaths; 27 males and 27 females.—In Boston, Mr. Joshua Pico, aged 73 ; Widow Rebecca Flagg, aged 68 ; Suddenly, Ebenezer Storer, esq. aged 77.—In Charlestown, Miss Chary Stone, aged 82 ; and at Lynn, Mrs. Dorcas Smith, aged 38, daughters of Mr. Jona. Stone, of Shrewsbury. [176]—In Sterling, Mrs. Phebe Francis, wife of Mr. Nathaniel Francis, aged 75.—At Ward, Dea. Jona. Stone, aged 81.—In Rutland, 5th inst. Mr. Benoni Smith, aged 57.—In Brookline, (N.H.) Dec. 30, Miss Rebecca Wadsworth, aged 46.—In New-Ipswich, Mrs. Mary Bartlett, consort of Maj. Noah B.—At Temple, Mrs. Sarah Wright, wife of Mr. Aaron Wright;—25th ult. Maj. Benjamin Cutter.

In Charleston, (S.C.) Miss Mary Bacot, aged 89.—In Lee, Mrs. Remember Burden, aged 91 y. and 7 m.—In Concord, (N.H.) Widow Hanniford, aged 92.—In Middletown, (N.J.) Mr. John Wall, aged 84.—In Bernardston, Mr. Paul Mendell. He went to bed apparently well and was found a corpse next morning.—In Kingston, (Jamaica) Hugh Lenox, esq. American consul.—In New-York, Mrs. Lydia Sheldon, aged 75.—In Colchester, Mr. Hezekiah Kilbourn, aged 77.—In Southboro', Jonas Ball, esq. aged 71.—In Vassalborough, Mrs. Jane Farwell, aged 65.

In Rutland, (Vt.) Miss Electa Strong, aged 28.—In Windsor, V. Mrs. Amy Woods, aged 40.

On the 16th ult. at Winchester, Capt. John Alexander, aged 58.—On the 4th inst. Capt. Noah Pratt, aged 58.

At Hopkinton, Mr. Robert Molineux, aged 46.

In Croydon, Dec. 21, Widow Sarah Eames, aged about 70 years. Her disorder was of a dropsical nature ; in about 20 months, there were drawn from her 350 lbs. of water, and she at last died of a quick consumption.

At Acworth, Mrs. Polly Keyes, wife of Mr. Amos Keyes, aged 38 years.

In Alstead, Mr. Joel Burroughs, aged 58.—On the 5th inst. Master Thomas Witherbe, aged 10.

In this town, on Tuesday morning last, a child of Mr. Wm. Pierce, aged about one year.

In Charlestown, N.H. Capt. Sylvanus Hastings, aged 87, the first settler in the town.

No. 40.[177]—Vol. XIV (Whole No. 721) Friday, 23 Jan. 1807.

† [3b-c] Account of a fire at the Columbian Museum in Boston. After the fire was extinguished, a wall collapsed "into the Chapel burying ground, and killed six young men, and wounded several others. Those killed are William, son of Capt. Michael Homer, aged 11, a promising youth.—John, son of Mr. Philip Condon, (one of the pressmen employed in the Centinel Office) aged [14?].—Henry Fullerton, aged [20?], an apprentice of Mr. Richard Thayer, housewright.—Isaac Peabody, of Shirley, an

apprentice of Mr. John Leman, blacksmith, aged 15.—Joshua Urann, an apprentice of Mr. [Ayer?], cooper, aged 17.—And James D. Beals, an apprentice of Mr. Jennings, wheelwright, aged [13?]."

† [3c] Rev. Jonathan Scott installed over the first church, Minot, Maine, 12 Nov. 1806. Also, in Guilford, Conn., Mr. Aaron Dutton was inducted over the first church.

† [3c] Rowell Hunt, Treasurer, posts a notice regarding the Charlestown Turnpike Corporation; dated Jan. 1807.

† [3d] *J. & T. Bellows* adv. numerous goods for sale, and also mention the purchase of house ashes "either at their store in Walpole street, or at their Postash works near Gilbert Griswold's tavern." In an attached adv., J.&T. Bellows and David Stone adv. for contracting the transport of pork to Boston. Both adv. dated Walpole, 22 Jan. 1807.

===== ¶ [3c] MARRIED. =====

In Randolph, Leonard Farwell, Esq. to Miss Fanny York.—In Concord, Mr. William Jenness, to Miss Mary George, daughter of David George, esq.

===== ¶ [3c] DIED. =====

In Fredericktown, (N.S.) Hon. Isaac Allen, in the 65th year of his age ; member of Council, and one of the Judges of the Supreme Court in that province; he was formerly of Trenton, N.J. and a Colonel in the British service during the revolutionary war.—In Raynham, (Ms.) Wid. Bathsheba Crane, aged 99. In the same place, a few months since, two sisters, Hannah Keith and Bethiah Robinson, the one about 90, the other 95—they had two sisters born in Salem, who lived, the one to the age of about 90, the other 95.—In Craftsbury, Vt. Rev. Samuel Collins.—At Enfield, (N.H.) 21st Dec. Mrs. Mary Dustin, wife of Rev. Caleb D. aged 22.—At Hatfield, (Ms.) Wid. Mary Smith, aged 79.

At Sutton, 9th inst., Josiah Hildrith, a promising youth of 16 years of age, son of the late Capt. Ephraim Hildrith. His death was occasioned by a fall on the ice, on the 8th, and he died on the 9th.

No. 46.—Vol. XIV (Whole No. 722) Friday, 30 Jan. 1807.

† [1d] Extensive account of a fire which destroyed the house of Lieut. John Pratt at New Ipswich, N.H., 29 Dec. 1806. Pratt and his family survived, including his aged mother. Also residing in the home were Joseph Jeffers, "a foreigner" who rescued a Mrs. Wheeler and one of her sons, but a younger son perished in the fire. ◆

¶ [1d] Drowned, a few days since, near Albany, by a sleigh breaking thro' the ice, Miss Jane Lansing, daughter of S. Lansing, esq. of Albany, aged 16. There were two other young ladies, and one gentleman in the sleigh, at the same time, who escaped drowning.

† [3c] Adv. for an itch ointment made by John Snow, of Keene, and sold by Daniel Brooks, Esq., Westmoreland—Chandler & Bigelow, Putney—Eleazer May, Westminster —Dr. Stephen R. Whitman, Walpole—Maj. S. Hutchinson, Alstead—and Dr. Philip Munroe, Surry.

† [3d] David Carter, Proprietors' Clerk of the N.H. Turnpike Corporation, adv. a meeting to be held at the house of Phillips Sweetser, Esq., Innholder in Marlboro'.

===== ¶ [3c] MARRIED. =====

In Hartford, (C.) the Rev. Amos Basset, of Hebron, to Miss Eunice Pomeroy, daughter of Ralph Pomeroy, esq.—In Boston, Mr. James Stimpson, mer. to Miss Sophia Andrews.—In Andover, Barnard Douglass, esq. of Portland, to Miss Betsey Cummings.

At Claremont, on the 25th inst. by the Rev. Mr. Barber, Mr. John Wise, to the amiable Miss Mary-Ann Stearns, both of Claremont.

===== ¶ [3c] DIED. =====

On the 24th ult. Thomas Faunce, esq. town major and naval officer of the port of Quebec.—His remains were interred with military honours.—In Cooperstown, (N.Y.) Richard Edwards, esq. of an asthmatic disorder. He was interred with masonic and military honours.—In East-Windsor, (C.) Dec. 21st, Mrs. Abigail Lathrop, wife of Mr. Thatcher Lathrop, aged 62 years.—Jan. 9th, Mr. Eliphalet Chapin, aged 65 years.—At Suffield, the 17th inst. Mr. Ebenezer Harmon, in the 80th year of his age.—In Hartford, Mr. Zechariah Sanford aged 70 years.—Departed this life, at West-Hartford, on the 19th inst. after a short but painful sickness, the widow Abigail Wells, aged 69 years, in the pleasing hopes of a blessed immortality. It is worthy of notice, that her husband, Mr. Ashbel Wells, died on the 11th of December last, aged 73 ;—their son, Mr. James A. Wells, 22d February last, aged 47;—and also their son, Capt. Erastus Wells, the 4th of July last, aged 35 years. Such a succession of deaths in one family, in so short a time, is very uncommon.—In the Poor House, in Salem, Widow Whittemore, aged 93.

No. 47.—Vol. XIV. (Whole No. 723) Friday, 6 Feb. 1807.

¶ [3c] FIRE.—The dwelling house of Mr. Ira Gates, of Lebanon, was reduced to ashes on Thursday evening, 22d ult. We understand the fire was communicated by holding a lighted candle under the bed.—H. Gaz.

† [3c] Rev. Silas Parsons ordained at the Congregational Church, Sudbury [Vt.], on the 1st inst. Also, at Westminster, Rev. Mr. Field ordained "21st ult."

==== ¶ [3c] MARRIED. ====

In Springfield, (Ver.) Mr. Roswell Hubbard, to Miss Sally Wilson, of Charlestown, (N.H.)—Mr. Joseph Judivine, of Concord, Vt. to Miss Hannah Powers, of Charlestown.

At Acworth, by the Rev. Mr. Kimball, Maj. Isaiah Eaton, of Westminster, Vt. to Mrs. Azubah Grout, of the former place.

==== ¶ [3c] DIED. ====

In Parsippany, Morris county, N.J. Abraham Kitchel, esq. formerly member of Council from that county in the State Legislature.—In New Germantown, N.J. Walter Kerr Cole, esq. att'y at law.—In Mansfield, (C.) Mr. Joshua Abbe, aged 67. His descendants are ten children, 87 grand children, 117 great-grand children, and 4 great-great-grand children ; in all 218 descendants.—In Bethlem, of consumption, David Leavitt, esq.—In Windham, Capt. Samuel Morgan, aged 73.—In Litchfield, Mrs. Mary [Sanford? or Sanlord?], aged 82.—In Philadelphia, during the week ending 17th ult. 17 adults and 17 children; of consumption 4.—From May 1, 1806, to Jan. 3, 1807, there were 1344 deaths, 729 adults and 615 children—of consumption 168, apoplexy 26, casualties 25, cholera morbus 141, convulsions 68, dysentary 45, of fever 85, but *one* malignant case ; drunkeness 6, palsy 14, hooping-cough 32, small-pox, nat. 18, innoc. 2, suicide 7, worms 45, teething 23.—In New York, David Thompson, esq. aged 38 : harbour-master of the port; supposed to have died in consequence of a wound received in a duel.—In Northampton, Mr. Eliphalet Phelps, aged 54.—In Worcester, Miss Catharine Drowne, aged 70, formerly of Boston.—In Fairfield, (S.C.) Wm. Kirkland, aged 71.—In Middlefield, (C.) Capt. David Coe, aged 93.—In Berlin, C. Dr. James Percival, aged 40.—In Middletown, C. Mrs. Hannah Swaddle, aged 41.

In this town, Mr. John Livingston, sen.

No. 48.—Vol. XIV (Whole No. 724) Friday, 13 Feb. 1807.

¶ [1d] EXTRAORDINARY. A sheep belonging to Mr. Joseph Baker, of Packersfield, was missing immediately after the driving snow storm of the 3d of Dec. last; and on the 2d instant she was discovered, in the snow, which had melted around her, and taken out alive. She must have been buried all this time, (30 days) and existed without any other sustenance than the melted snow, and the turf on which she lay.

† [1d] Gruesome account of the death of Col. Silas Dickerson, who was killed in an accident in his own nail factory at Stanhope, N.J. ♦

† [3a-b] Floods damage the area around Hartford, Conn., destroying the gristmills of Mr. Warburton, A. Buckland, Mr. Rockwell, the powder mill of Mr. John Mather, and a fulling mill of Mr. Wright in Coventry. ♦

¶ [3b-c] Mr. David Whittemore, a native of Thompson, (C.) was murdered at Augusta, (Geo.) on the 19th December, where he had some time resided as a trader and merchant. The perpetrators of this deed of horror, were three men and a woman, the wife of the principal actor; their object was money. One of the men has been caught and confessed the whole.—We trust the remaining culprits will be found.

† [3c] The chocolate mills owned by Ichabod Glover, Danvers, Mass. destroyed by fire.

† [3d] Shubael Conant adv. jewelry and watches for sale; dated Walpole 12 Feb. 1807.

† [3d] Legal notice regarding property in dispute at Concord, Grafton County, N.H.,

formerly owned by John Hubbard, Esq. late of Charlestown, N.H. The land was conveyed by bond to Asa Morse and Farnum Morse, both of said Concord, but Hubbard died before making the deed. Prudence Hubbard and Henry Hubbard, administrators for John Hubbard's estate, petitioned for a license to deed the property to Asa and Farnum.

===== ¶ [3c] MARRIED. =====

At Croydon, Mr. Peter Powers to Miss Louis S. Cooper.—In Keene, Mr. Wm. Whittle, of Westminster, Vt. to Miss Electa Rugg, of the former place.

===== ¶ [3c] DIED. =====

In Lewiston, Capt. Elisha Lake, aged 66, a veteran of the Revolutionary War. He had been helpless and supported by the town for ten years past; and his wife having tied him in a chair as usual, and left him for a moment, on her return found he had fallen with the chair into the fire, and was so burned as to survive but a few hours.—In Ipswich, Mr. William Goodhue, aged 79.—In Craftsbury, Mr. Nathaniel Babcock, aged 76 ; Mr. Jacob White, aged 70 ; both professors of the christian religion.—At Sheldon, Dr. Jabez Fitch, aged 80.—At Vergennes, on the 4th inst. Mr. Humphrey Palmer, in the 67th year of his age.—At Walliston, Mrs. Hannah Wells, aged 100.—At Craftsbury, Rev. Samuel Collins.—In Panton, on the 17th ult. very suddenly, Mrs. Tirzah Curtis, aged 72 years, wife of Mr. Joseph S. Curtis.—At Newmarket, Capt. H. Neal, in the 90th year of his age.—At Northampton, [178] Mr. Samuel Jenness, an useful worthy citizen. —At Stratham, Deacon SAMUEL LANE in the 80th year of his age.—In Portsmouth, Mrs. Esther Hart, aged 61.—In Durham, (N.H.) Miss Margery Sullivan Steele, daughter of Jona. S. Esq. aged 18.—At Salisbury, (N.H.) on the 14th inst. Mr. Thomas Chase, aged 71 years and 8 months.—At Cooperstown, (N.Y.) Richard Edwards, Esq. Att'y at Law, aged 40.—At Franklin, Mr. Samuel Ladd, aged 75.—In Boston, Mrs. Deborah, widow of Mr. Nathaniel Baker, late of that town, aged 74.—At Conway, on the 28th ult. Mr. Thos. Billings, (from Greenfield) aged 72.—His death was caused from a shocking burn which he received a short time previous, by falling from his chair into the fire.—At Deering, Dec. 18, Mrs. Elizabeth Alcock, wife of Hon. Robert Alcock, Esq.

No. 49.—Vol. XIV (Whole No. 725)   Friday, 20 Feb. 1807.

¶ [2d] The house of Michael Sprinkle, of Bedford, Pennsylvania, has been destroyed by fire. Two of his children perished.

† [3a] Farming news regarding Mr. Henry Baker "of Hopewell."

† [3d] Samuel Hutchinson requests all debtors to pay up to the firm of Shepard and Hutchinson (dated Alstead 5 Feb. 1807); also appended to this notice is a similar request for outstanding debts to the Shepard and Lanphier store at Marlow.

===== ¶ [3b] MARRIED. =====

At Hartland, 15th ult. Mr. Sylvester Smith, of Surry, to Miss Rebecca Stevens.
At Wendal, 3d inst. Mr. John Currier to Miss Nancy Pickerman.

===== ¶ [3b-c] DIED. =====

At Guilford, on the 14th inst. Mr. Humphrey Palmer, in the 67th year of his age.—In Portland, widow Abigail Finney, aged 98.—Mr. Ellis Swan, aged 70.—On the 15th of November last, in Laurens district, (S.C.) Mrs. Ann Newby, at the advanced age of 112 years.—Until a few months before her death, she was able to transact the business of her house, she has left her husband, Mr. Robert Newby, only 37 years of age, together with a numerous train of acquaintance, to lament her loss.—At Killingsworth, C. (North Society) on the morning of the 3d ult. after a long and useful life in the office which he sustained and in the faith of a glorious mortality, Deacon Abel Wilcox, in the 75th year of his age, and 34th of his office.—In Hartford, Mrs. Anne Olcott, aged 71 years.—At Warren, Octobert 8th, 1806, Huldah Swift, aged 19 years, also, January 5, 1807, Aner Swift, aged 16 months, daughters of Nathaniel Swift, Esq.—At Providence, Mrs. Arnold, aged 91, widow of the late Christopher Arnold, Esq.—In Scarborough, Mrs. Abigail Taylor, aged 85. Her descendants were 12 children, 67 grand children, 96 great-grand children, and 10 great gr grand children : total 185.—This matron has deserved well of her country.—At Scarborough, Hon. Wm. Thompson, aged 76, Chief Justice of the Court of General Sessions for the county of Cumberland.—At West-

minster, (Vt.) on the 19th ult. widow Anne Goodell, aged 92 years.—In Washington, (N.H.) Miss Charlotte Pollock, aged 40.
† [3b-c] Extensive article detailing the death of Betsey Spear, aged 11 years, 2 months, daughter of David and Mary Spear of Ellington, who fell through the ice and drowned 2 Feb. 1807. ♦

No. 05.[179]—Vol. XIV (Whole No. 726) Friday, 27 Feb. 1807.

† [1d] Gruesome account of the murder of Mrs. Crowell, an old woman about 80 years of age, mortally wounded by her deranged daughter, who was the wife of Mr. Jeduthun Spooner. The event occurred "on the 22d ult." at Hardwick, Mass., and was copied from a Peacham [Vt.] paper. ♦
† [1d] Account of the murder of Mr. James Pollock, son of Justice Pollock, of Ligomer Valley, Westmoreland County, Penn., by two Frenchman, named John Pascal Arnaud and Noel Huguel. ♦
¶ [2c] The grand jury of New York has presented John Foster, (formerly of Taunton) an itenerant preacher as an idle and blasphemous character, pursuing no lawful, regular means of support, and propagating principles wholly repugnant to religion and morality. [180]
† [3b] Rev. Samuel Giles ordained at Milton, Mass.
† [3b] Legal notice posted by Joseph Willard and Rebecca Willard his wife (in her right), regarding an appeal of the estate of Daniel Perrin, late of Alstead, deceased, Ephriam Kingsbery, Adm. William Briggs was the attorney for the Willards.
† [3d] Isaac Redington adv. goods for sale, and also requests debtors to pay up. Dated 25 Feb. 1807.
† [3c-d] List of non-resident proprietors and owners of land in New Grantham, N.H., who have not paid their taxes for the year 1806, as adv. by Richard Gile, *Collector*. All delinquent property to be auctioned off at the house of James Smith, Esq., New Grantham. The list contains a breakdown of lots, and taxes due for road, school, state and county, though only the names are presented here:

Sampson Willard	James Stoodley, Esq.	Capt. Jonathan Hunt
Eleazer Pomroy	Oliver Doolittle	Benjamin Hall, Esq.
Samuel Partridge	Benjamin Barret	Oliver Barret
Arad Hunt	Lois Butler	James Droyse
Medad Pomroy	Elias Jones	Phineas Lyman
Capt. Samuel Hunt	Elijah Stebbin	Bunker Gay
William Syms	Miss Packer	Elisha Alexander
Moses Hawks	Hon. James Nevins	
Simeon Alexander	Moses Belding	

¶ [3b] MARRIED.]—In West Springfield, (Ms.) Isaiah Doolittle, mer. to Miss Susannah Burbank.—At Westminster, (Vt.) on Sunday evening last, by the Rev. Sylvester Sage, Mr. Nathaniel Gould, of this town, to Miss Clarissa Eaton, daughter of Maj. Isaiah Eaton.—In Rutland, Wm. Page, jr. esq. to Miss Mary Boardman, both of Rutland.

¶ [3b] DIED.]—In Montreal, 18th ult. Cornelius Cuyler, esq. late captain in his majesty's army, in which he served near twenty years.—In Craftsbury, (Vt.) Mr. Jacob White, aged 71.—In Rutland, 11th inst. of a consumption, Mr. Judah P. Spooner, printer, aged about 60 years.—At Conway, 28th ult. Mr. Thos. Billings, aged 72. His death was occasioned by a shocking burn.—On the 4th Dec. last, Doctor Calvin Taylor, of the U.S. army, late of Hinsdale, N.H.—In Brattleboro', 5th inst. Mr. Timothy Bebee, aged 70; on the 7th inst. of a dropsy, in the 71st year of his age, Mr. Jesse Frost.—In Barnstable, (Ms.) the Rev. Oakes Shaw, aged 70.—In Williamstown, 13th inst. Rev. Seth Swift.—In Fitchburg, Brig. General James Read, one of the worthies of the revolution.—In Becket, Doct. William Baker, aged 75, late a resident in New-Lebanon, N.Y.—At Packersfield, Mrs. Lydia Edson, aged 77. Her descendants are about 100, scattered over New England.—In Croydon, Mr. Joel Cooper, aged 50.

In this town, on Friday morning last, Henry, child [of] Mr. Thomas Sparhawk, aged 16 mo.

No. 51.—Vol. XIV (Whole No. 727) Friday, 6 Mar. 1807.

† [1a] Adv. for the Amoskeag Canal Lottery; Philips Payson, Samuel Swan, Jr., and Loam. Baldwin, Jr., Managers.
† [1b] Article describing a flood at Patchogue, Long Island, [N.Y.], 2 Feb. 1807, where the family of Charles Swan, Esq. barely escaped. ♦
¶ [1b] *Robbery.*—A Mr. Redding, of Lynn, was robbed on the Salem Turnpike by 3 men, a few evenings since, of several hundred dollars. He was beaten with clubs, until he ceased to make any resistance, and has since been in a state of delirium. [*N.H. Sent.*]
† [2d] The house of Capt. Thomas Lovering at North Hampton, N.H., destroyed by fire, 18 Feb. 1807. The article mentions the distressing situation of Mrs. Brown, a daughter of Capt. Lovering. ♦
† [3b] Legal notice regarding the estate of Asa Walker, late of Langdon, N.H.; James Egerton, Executor. Dated Langdon, 27 Feb. 1807.
† [3b] David Stone adv. goods for sale, and also requests debtors to pay up; dated Walpole, 2 Mar. 1807.
† [3c] Leverett Tuttle requests debtors to pay up; dated Bellows' Falls, 2 Mar. 1807.
¶ [4d] Last week, the widow Margaret Swazey in Salem, finished her hundreth [sic] year, and very lately she was one of the five then living, who were received into the 2d church in that town, in 1737.—She employed the day in which she passed her hundreth [sic] year in weaving tape, a work which has employed her the better part of her life. [*Pallad. Feb.* 20.

=== ¶ [3a] MARRIED. ===

At Springfield, (Vt.) ——— Edwards, Esq. of Connecticut, to Miss Louisa Morris, daughter of Hon. L.R. Morris, Esq.

=== ¶ [3a] DIED. ===

In England, His Grace, the Duke of Richmond, aged 73 : who for many years took an active part in the politics of the British nation [. . .]—In Baltimore, during the week ending the 14th ult. 10 adults and 12 children : of consumption 4.—In Princeton, (N.J.) Rev. Anthony Schmit, a respectable Catholic priest, and formerly a curate at Guadaloupe, aged 75.—In Scott, (C.) Mr. Thomas Bingham, aged 80.—At Hartland, (C.) Mr. Joshua Giddings, aged 88. He was the second residing settler of that town.—In Windham, Mr. Charles Dyer, aged 22 : In attempting to save his dog, which had fallen thro' the ice, Mr. D. broke thro' the ice and was drowned.—In Pittsfield, Mr. Jer. Silvey, aged 78 ; found dead in his barn, supposed to have died in a fit.—In Ashford, Feb. 14, Elder David Bolles, aged 64.—In Scituate, (Ms.) Mr. John Bowker, aged 83.—At Green, 9th ult. Abigail, wife of Mr. Joseph Adams, aged 76 years, late of Uxbridge.—At Pejepscot, Maj. Thomas Finson, aged 52.

At Schaghticoke, yesterday se'nnight, aged 76 years, 11 months and 25 days, Mr. Matthew Webster, father of the senior printers of the Albany Gazette. From early life, he had embraced the religion of the scriptures—and it was ever the man of his counsel ; his hope while living, and his only consolation in death. [*Waterford Gaz. Feb.* 17.

The Rev'd Doctor John Willard was ordained Pastor of the first Church in Stafford, on the 23d day of March, A.D. 1757. His constitution was feeble, yet by his own prudent care, and the good hand of his God upon him, he continued in the ministry almost half a century ; and in life 74 years. For a few weeks, he laboured with a grievous cold ; but his disorder was not alarming till within a few days of his death. When he viewed his case to be dangerous, he was very calm and resigned to the will of heaven ; and with firm hope in the mercy of God and merits of the Redeemer, he fell asleep in Jesus (as we believe) on Monday the 6th of this instant February—and on Thursday following, his funeral was attended by a large concourse of people, and a number of his brethren in the ministry. On that mournful occasion a sermon was delivered by Dr. Williams of Tolland [. . .]

Mr. Willard's immediate father was the Rev. Joseph Willard of Biddeford, in the district of Maine. His grandfather lived and died in Kingston, on the island of Jamaica. His great-grandfather was the Rev. Samuel Willard, formerly President of Harvard College. His younger brother was the late president of that university. [*Conn. Courant.*

At Williamstown, on the 18th inst. the reverend Seth Swift. [. . .]

At Guilford, (Vt.) on the 19th day of February inst. Capt. John Barney, and on the tenth day of the same month his consort, Rebeccah, being each about seventy seven years of age ; and, in good health on the 1st inst. having enjoyed an unusual degree of social felicity in their nuptial relation, for more than 58 years ; forty of which they have lived in the town of Guilford—left to regret their loss, 6 children, 86 Grand children, 55 Great Grand children : deceased in their day, 6 children, 30 Grand children, and 10 Great Grand Children, amounting to 193. Lineal posterity from these two persons in less than 58 years, of which 147 are now living in usual prosperity. [*Brattleboro' pap.*

Melancholy Accident. On Tuesday last, a Mr. Lewis Lawton, son of Josiah Lawton, who lives near the Little Falls, on Mohawk River, fell from a tree which he had ascended, in pursuit of a squirrel, which he had wounded, the distance of 25 feet, and so fractured his skull, that he died within two hours. *Stockbridge Paper.*

Perished in the snow-storm on Friday night the 30th January, at Freehold, Greene co. Mr. Isaac Hall, son of Mr. Hezekiah Hall, of that place, in the 21st year of his age. [*Hudson Paper.*]

The editor of the Portfolio thus prefaces the biographical sketch of the late Deac. E. Storer, which was published in the Boston papers at the time of his late decease [. . .].

No. 52.—Vol. XIV (Whole No. 728) Friday, 13 Mar. 1807.

† [3a] Rev. Aaron Palmer ordained over the Congregational Church in Barre, Vt.

¶ [3b] THIS MAY CERTIFY, THAT Abel Rice, late of Claremont, but now of Norwich, in the state of Vermont, has gained a Bill of Divorce against Lydia Buckman, that adulterous woman, in spite of her master rage, (which was the reason why he did not get it many years ago) at Manchester Court the fourth Tuesday of February last.

(Paid for.)

† [3d] William M'Clintock, Jr. adv. a farm for sale in Charlestown; dated 2 Mar. 1807.

===== ¶ [3a] MARRIED. =====

At Sag-Harbour, (L.I.) Mr. Alden Spooner, editor of the Suffolk Gazette, to Miss Rebecca Jermain.

At Weathersfield, (Vt.) Mr. Darius Jones, mer. to Miss Eliza Hatch, daughter of Reuben Hatch, esq.

===== ¶ [3a] DIED. =====

In Charleston, (S.C.) suddenly, Mr. John Shoemaker, a Polander, patroon of a small Stono schooner—Verdict of the jury, "that he came to his death by voluntarily taking a phial of liquid laudanum, owing to the state of mind, being much agitated for the loss of a valuable watch instrusted to his care, and which was clandestinely taken from him."—In Windham, (C.) Mr. Charles Dyer aged 22 ; in attempting to save his dog, which had fallen through the ice, Mr. D. broke through the ice, and was drowned.—In Barnstable, Rev. Oaks Shaw, pastor of the 2d church of Christ in that town, in the 71st year of his age, and 46th of his ministry.—In Beverly, Dr. Elisha Whitney, aged 59.—In Roxbury, Mr. Nathaniel Felton, aged 93.—In West-Springfield, 21st ult. Miss Sophia Morgan, daughter of Lucas Morgan, Esq. in the 23d year of her age.—In Monson, 17th ult. deacon Abijah Newell, aged 76 ; his descendants are 103, of which 93 are living, 27 in the family of their oldest daughter.—In Westfield, Abel Whitney, Esq. aged 52.—At Wrentham, on the last day of December, Mrs. Esther Holbrook, consort of Mr. Daniel Holbrook, and on the 17th of Jan. Mr. Daniel Holbrook, both aged 78. They lived together 56 years, and within 17 days of each other, took their flight hence to be here no more !

In Litchfield, (Conn.) Mr. Nathaniel Woodruff, aged 79.—At Cornwall, (C.) Mr. Matthew Patterson, in the 62d year of his age.—In Northampton, Mr. Job White, aged 36 :—On the 28th ult. Mrs. Mary Dwight, relict of the late Timothy Dwight, esq. and daughter of the Rev. Jonathan Edwards, formerly minister of Northampton, in the 73d year of her age.—In Leominster, Capt. Thomas Legate, jun. in the 44th year of his age. —In Kittery, Mrs. Ann Gibson, aged 64, daughter of Capt. Stephen Seavey, who survives his daughter, and is near 95 years of age.—In Rutland, (Vt.) Mr. Timothy Cheeney, aged 61 : —Mr. Daniel Greeno, aged 55.—In West-Rutland, Mrs. Deland, wife of Mr. Rufus Deland.—In Windsor, Mrs. Hannah Smith, aged 47 : Mrs. Peggy, consort of Capt. Timothy Lull, aged 72.—In Portsmouth, Mr. Samuel Sherburne, in the 77th year of his age.—In Amherst, Mr. Philo Talbot, aged 84.—In Plymouth, 9th ult. Mrs. Azubah Willoughby, wife of Elder John Willoughby, aged 68,—a person of exemplary life and conversation.—In Washington, Miss Charlotte Pollock, æ. 40.—In Peterboro', Dr. Young, aged 75.—In Thornton, after a long and tedious illness, John Brown, Esq. aged 60 ; —a kind husband and a tender father—a christian, patriout and friend.—At Sturbridge, Maj. Stephen Harding, aged 52.

No. 1.—Vol. XV (Whole No. 729) Friday, 20 Mar. 1807.

† [3b] Fire destroys the house of Mr. Gilbert Griswold, together with the barns and shed; the house was "occupied for a tavern." The event occurred "on Saturday night last [14 March 1807.] ♦

† [3c] Josiah Eaton offers several tracts of land for sale in New Hampshire and Vermont; dated at Walpole, 14 March 1807.

† [3d] Jos. Smith posts a notice stating that he will discontinue his newspaper delivery at the end of March. Notice dated 14 March.

† [3d] Eber Carpenter requests debtors to pay up; dated Alstead, — March 1807.

===== ¶ [3c] MARRIED. =====

In this town, yesterday morning, by the Rev. Mr. Dickinson, Doctor John Brooks, of New-Fane, to Miss Nancy Redington.

Last week, Mr. James Russell to Miss ———— Houghton.

===== ¶ [3c] DIED. =====

In St. Bartholomew's Parish, Charleston, (S.C.) Mrs. Mary Caveneau, late of Cannonsboro', in the 63d year of her age.—Capt. Thomas Ross, of Charleston.—At Nassau, (S.C.) aged 76 years, Benjamin Lord, Sen. Esq. formerly of South-Carolina ; afterwards Surveyor-General of East-Florida, and for the last 21 years, a resident in the Bahama Islands.—At Albany, Mr. Abraham Bloodgood, aged 65 years. Mr. Andrew Brown, merchant, aged 65 years.—Major Garret Groesbeck, aged 65 years.—At New-York, Miss Louisa C. Livingston, daughter of the Hon. Brockholst Livingston, in the 16th year of her [   ]181 in the county of Schoharie, (N.Y.) the Hon. Jonathan Danforth, Esq. one of the judges of the court of Common Pleas.—He was interred in masonic order.—In Greenbush, (N.Y.) very suddenly, as he sat at table, John E. Van Alen, Esq. recently a Representative in Congress from this district.—In Dover, (N.H.) Mrs. Elizabeth Canney, upwards of 90 years of age : she has left an affectionate husband, with whom she lived in the greatest hamony [sic] 71 years and 6 months. In Gilmanton, Mr. Benjamin Mudget ; he slipped suddenly & struck his head against a stone.—In Rye, on the 19th ult Amos Seavey, Esq. aged 86.

No. 2.—Vol. XV (Whole No. 730) Friday, 27 Mar. 1807.

† [2c] Two articles describing the arrest of Jackson Neal and Polly his wife, for counterfeiting, at Marblehead, [Mass.], and a Daniel Howland of Dartmouth, Mass., convicted of passing fake bills received from a noted villian named Jabez Thomas. ♦

¶ [3c] ONE CENT REWARD.

ABSCONDED from the service of the subscriber, on the 7th inst. an indented apprentice to the bookbinding business named Walton Feltch. As he may wish to get employment in some bindery, this is to forbid all persons harbouring or trusting him, as they would avoid legal penalties. The above reward will be given to any person who will return him to the subscriber, but no charges paid.

JUSTIN HINDS.

Walpole, March 25, 1807.

† [3d] Adv. of Dr. Jonathan Moore's ESSENCE OF LIFE, a medicine claimed to cure just about everything. Several physicians in the area approved of its use: Abel Duncan and Samuel Stearns, L.L.D., both of Dummerston; William Town, Westminster; C.W. Chandler, Andover; Abraham Holland, Walpole; Jonathan Badger, Westminster; Nathan Stone, New-Fane; Prescott Hall, Chesterfield; and Charles Blake, Keene.

===== ¶ [3a] MARRIED. =====

At Barre, (Ms.) Mr. Naphtali Wetherel, aged 17, to Miss Mary Casey, aged 15.—In Worcester, Mr. John Curtis to Miss Nancy Stowel.

===== ¶ [3a] DIED. =====

At Washington city, Hon. Abraham Baldwin, member of the U.S. Senate from Georgia.—In Baltimore, Capt. Myers, an old revolutionary officer.—In Herkimer, (N.Y.) Maj. John Hopkins, aged 53, of the revolutionary army.—In East-Haven, (C.) Mr. John Woodward, aged 66.—In Torrington, Samuel Griswold, esq. Æt. 77.—In Lyme, Mr. Joshua Harvey, aged 84.—In New-Gloucester, Rev. Samuel Foxcroft.—In Boston, Rev. Samuel Stillman, D.D., pastor of the first Baptist church in that town, aged 70, and in the 43d year of his ministry. He supported an uncommon popularity till the close of his life. [182]—In Reading, Widow Mary Hartshorn, aged XCIII ; Widow Mary Upton, aged XCVII.—In Spencer, Widow Mehitable Bemis, aged LXXV.—In Paxton, Widow Elizabeth Howe, aged LXXXVII.—In Barre, John Caldwell, esq. aged XCIII.—In Worcester, Mr. Jabez Totman, Æt. XCIX.—In Shoreham, (Vt.) 8th ult. Col. Ephraim Doolittle, Æt. LXXXVI.—In Windsor, of the asthma, Mrs. Elizabeth Elkins, wife of Dea. Jonathan Elkins, aged LXX.—In Shelburne, V. 8th inst. Miss Philenda Minor, aged 20, eldest daughter of Mr. Roswell Minor, of that town.—At St. Albans, Col. Joseph Jones. His death was occasioned by his falling into a vat of hot grains from a distillery.—At Hanover, while on a visit, Deacon ——— Howard, of Thetford, Vt. Without any previous apparent illness, he fell from his chair and expired instantly.—At Fitzwilliam, suddenly, 2d inst. Mrs. Betsey, wife of Maj. Jonas Robeson, aged 29.—In Keene, Mr. John Lamson, printer, aged 43.

In this town, on Tuesday morning, Nathaniel Trowbridge, an infant child of Mr. Nathaniel Charter, aged about 4 m.

Suicides.—We learn by a gentleman from Montreal, that Mr. Monk, nephew of Judge Monk of that city, put a period to his existence, a few days since, by the discharge of a pistol. The charge lodged in his breast, but did not produce immediate death; he, however, survived but a short time. The cause is unknown. [*Worcester paper.*]

On the 1st inst. Mr. Return Strong, aged 52 years, was found with his throat cut and a razor by his side, in his barn, in Pawlet. He had been in a desponding state for a considerable time, and the two last days entirely deranged.

Note: The publication of *The Farmer's Museum* was suspended until 24 Oct. 1808.

Vol. XV (No. 1) [183] Monday, 24 Oct. 1808

† [3d] Rev. Mr. John M. Whitton ordained in Antrim, Mass., and Rev. Mr. Sebastian Streeter ordained at Washington, N.H., over the Universalist Church and Society in Washington and Weare.

===== ¶ [3d] MARRIED. =====

In Northampton, Jonathan H. Lyman, Esq. attorney at law, to Miss Sophia Hinckley.
—In Boston, by the Rev. Mr. Eaton, Shubael Bell, Esq. to Miss Nancy Hughes.

===== ¶ [3d] DIED. =====

In the state-prison, at Charlestown, (Mass.) Major Amos Witter, formerly of Preston, (Con.)—In Hingham, (Mass.) Dea. Joseph Thaxter, aged 85.—In Andover, after a distressing illness, Mr. Nehemiah Abbot, aged 78, one of the Trustees of Philips' Academy.—In Fincastle, (Virg.) Gen. William Mosely, Treasurer of Virginia.—In Philadelphia, during the week ending 8th inst. 36, viz. 20 adults and 16 children : of drunkeness ONE ! small-pox THREE !—In New York, John Murray, Esq. of the house of Murray & Sons, aged 70, President of the Chamber of Commerce, and Director of the National Bank ; highly esteemed as a merchant and a man.—In Oxford, Dea. David Harwood, aged 76, and his wife Rebecca, aged 80.—In Sterling, Mr. Artemas Maynard, aged 73.—In Springfield, (Mass.) Mr. Gordon Chapin, aged 27, of the lock-jaw, by running a nail into his heel.—In Boston, widow Esther Goff, aged 72.—In Hubbardston, Mr. Jonathan Gates, aged 62.—In Plainfield, (N.H.) Mr. Andrew Miner, printer, aged 26.—In Middlebury, (Ver.) Loyal Case, Esq. state's attorney for Addison county.— In Surry, Rev. Zebulon Streeter, aged 80.

DROWNED, in Exeter, on the 14th inst. a Son of the Hon. Jeremiah Smith.

Vol. XV (No. 2) [184] Monday, 31 Oct. 1808.

No news items of significance found within this issue.

Vol. XV (No. 3) Monday, 7 Nov. 1808.

¶ [3c] We learn from Montpelier, that the legislature have passed an act granting a respite of fourteen days in the case of Cyrus B. Dean, who was to have been executed yesterday at Burlington. [*Rut. Her.*

¶ [3c] *Shocking.*—We learn that on Thursday evening, (27th ult.) Mr. Poindexter, who was lately married, and who had resided near the great bridge, was shot through the head during the time he, in company with his wife, were at tea. It is said, this horrid act was perpetrated by one of his own negroes. [*Bost. Rep.*

¶ [3c] A large Bear, weighing ten score, was killed in Temple, (N.H.) the 24th ult. by Major E. Heald.

† [3c-d] Rev. Elisha Rockwood ordained at the church in Westborough, "the 26th ult." Also, Rev. Caleb Berge installed at Gudderhall, N.H.

† [3d] *J.&T. Bellows* offer cash for ashes delivered at their store on Walpole Street, or "at their Pot-Ash works, near Gilbert Griswold's." Dated 4 Nov. 1808.

† [3d] John Langdon offers reward for the capture of Archibald M'Curdey Richards, who stole a large sum of money from Langdon. Dated Goffstown, N.H. 26 Oct. 1808.

===== ¶ [3d] MARRIED. =====

In Virginia, George Hay, Esq. U.S. attorney for the dist. of Virginia, to Miss Eliza Monroe, eldest daughter of James Monroe, Esq. late minister to G. Britain.

In Barnstable, R.D. Shephard, Esq. of New Orleans, to Miss Lucy Gorham, daughter of Edward Gorham, Esq.

In Litchfield, (Con.) Rev. John M. Whitton, of Antrim, (N.H.) to Miss Abbey Morris, daughter of James M. Esq. of Litchfield.

In Boston, Rev. Thomas Skelton, of Foxborough, to Miss Ama Willard, of Ashburnham.

===== ¶ [3d] DIED. =====

In Louisiana, Col. Thomas Hunt, of the 1st regiment U. States infantry.—In Virginia, Dr. John Claiborne, lately a member of congress from that state.—In Richmond, (Virg.) Hon. John Page, late governor of Virginia.—In Philadelphia, during the week ending on the 25th inst. 37 deaths, viz. 21 adults and 16 children ; of consumption 4, small-pox FIVE. !—In Newyork, during the week ending on the 15th inst. 44 deaths, viz. 15 men, 11 women, 6 boys, and 12 girls ; of consumption 8, small-pox ONE !—At Sandy Hill, on 13th inst. on his way from Canada to New York, Archibald M'Neil, Esq. his Britannick majesty's consul general for Louisiana.—In Sutton, (Mass.) Lt. Caleb Chace, aged 86, and his son Nathaniel, aged 57.—In Barre, Mr. Jonathan Fisk, aged 84.—In Worcester, Mr. Phinehas Newton, aged 86.—In Boston, Mrs. Mary Butler, aged 64—Mr. James Allen, aged 70—Mr. Thomas Bell, aged 82—Mr. Daniel [Lillie?], sen. aged 73.—In Chillicothe, (Ohio) Mrs. Putnam, wife of Col. Israel P.—In Baltimore, Mr. William Patterson, jun. of the house of Wm. P. & Sons.—In Albany, Dr. Withelmus Mancius, aged 70 ; he had practised the last 40 years in that city with great credit.—In Waltham, Mrs. Lydia, relict of Mr. Samuel Harrington ; she survived her husband 13 months, who lived in the conjugal state 71 years.—In Lexington, Mrs. Sibil, relict of Thaddeus Bowman, Esq. aged 89.—In Hudson, David Lawrence, Esq. late recorder of that city.—In Plastow [sic], John White, Esq. aged 67.—Mr. Nathaniel Sawyer.—In Rehoboth, Lieut. Elkanah French, aged 80.—In Philadelphia, during the week ending on the 22d ult. 38 deaths, viz. 18 adults, 20 children; of consumption 3, small-pox THREE !—In Newyork, during the week ending on the 22d ult. 29 deaths, viz. 10 men, 7 women, 6 boys, 6 girls : of consumption 7, small-pox TWO !

On Sunday, the 30th ult. at Rockingham, (Vt.) much lamented, Dr. Levi Sabin, aged about 44 years.

Vol. XV (No. 4) Monday, 14 Nov. 1808.

† [3c] Ordinations :Rev. Warren Fay over the church in Brimfield, on the 2d inst.; Rev. Thomas Skelton over the church at Foxborough; and Rev. Sylvester F. Bucklin of the church in Marlborough.

† [3c-d] Asher Miller, Shubael Griswold, and Eli Whitney, committee members, being appointed by the Conn. legislature, post a notice regarding a lock-system for navigation up the Connecticut River beyond the falls at Enfield, Conn. A business meeting to be held at the house of Daniel Abbe, Jr., innholder at Enfield. Notice posted at "Newhaven," 5 Nov. 1808.

† [3d] *Stone & Bellows* adv. goods for sale; dated Walpole, 10 Nov. 1808.

† [3d] S.R. Whitman adv. drugs and medicines for sale; dated 10 Nov. 1808.

† [3d] Legal notice regarding Fila Abbot, "now of Acworth," guardian of Minerva Abbot, Maria Abbot, Elmira Abbot, and Fila Abbot, minors under age 14. The elder Fila petitioned for a license to sell the childrens' property in Lempster for their support; the attorney for Fila Abbot was Fred. A. Sumner. Dated Acworth, 9 May 1808.

† [4b-c] Biographical sketch of Jonathan M. Sewall, Esq., born in Mass. in 1748, the "patriotic poet of Newhampshire," who died "last March." ♦

===== ¶ [3c] MARRIED. =====

At Chelsea, (Mass.) Rev. Joseph Tuckerman to Miss Sarah Cary, daughter of Samuel Cary, Esq.

In Salem, Capt. Oliver K. Wellman, to Miss Ursula M. Draper.

In Portland, Rev. Joshua Taylor, of Monmonth, to Mrs. Hannah Delano.

===== ¶ [3c] DIED. =====

In Brookfield, Hon. Joseph Dorr, Esq. late Judge of Probate for Worcester county, aged 78.—In Cornwall, Mrs. Patience Swift, aged 83.—In Bridgeport, Mrs. Eunice Sterling, aged 83.—In Preston, Rev. Levi Hart, D.D.—In Philadelphia, Lewis Hallam, aged 74, the father of the American Theatre.—In Wilmington, (Del.) Mrs. Elizabeth Baily, aged 36, wife of Dr. Joseph Baily, of that place.—In Leicester, (Mass.) Mr. Benjamin Baldwin, aged 71 ; Mrs. Phebe Henshaw, consort of Wm. Henshaw, Esq. aged 56.—In Surinam, Capt. David Smith, of the Boston-Packet, of Salem.—In Honduras, Capt. Peter Warren, of Portland aged 20.—In Warrenton, (N.C.) Henry L. Chapman,

Esq.—In Philadelphia during the week ending 29th ult. 35 deaths, viz. 14 adults and 21 children; of consumption 4, fever 3, small-pox FIVE.—Robert Loiler, Esq. aged 69, one of the associate Judges for Montgomery county.—In Burlington, (N.J.) Mrs. Hannah, wife of Elias Boudinot, Esq. aged 73.—In Lynn, Capt. William Farrington, aged 74. He lead a company to Lexington battle.

Vol. XV (No. 5) Monday, 21 Nov. 1808.

¶ [3b] We learn by a gentleman from Burlington, Vt. that *Cyrus B. Dean* was executed at that place, on Friday the 11th inst.

† [3b] Dr. Imla Keep robbed at Machias. ♦

† [3d] Remarkable account of a Newfoundland dog who rescued six men from the water after their boat upset. One of those rescued, the dog's owner, was Mr. Cook, a tavern-keeper "in Cleaveland Street." The article was copied from a Quebec paper. ♦

† [3d] Legal notice to the heirs of Aaron Chase of Lempster, posted by Uzzel Hurd, guardian of said Chase, regarding settlement with the Judge of Probate. The notice is dated at Lempster, 10 Nov. 1808. The week following, in the issue of 28 Nov. 1808 [3b], another notice appears in which Hurd petitions the Court for permission to sell Chase's property in Lempster and Unity to settle outstanding debts. Neither this notice nor the previous one states that Chase is deceased.

===== ¶ [3d] MARRIED. =====

In Vergennes, Vt. on the 16th ult. Elkanah Brush, Esq. to Mrs. Lucretia Strong.

In Killingsworth, Sept. 21st. Rev. Hosea Beckley, of Dummerston, Vt. to Miss Lydia Pierson, of the former place.

===== ¶ [3d] DIED. =====

In Boston, Mrs. Sarah Tyng, wife of Hon. D.A. Tyng, Es. [sic] aged 47.—In New Orleans, Mr. Robert Patterson, of Philadelphia.—In Wolfborough, Isaiah Orne, Esq. aged 53—for many years a Representative to the general court of Newhampshire.—In Newburyport, Capt. Richard Greenleaf.—In Bradford, Capt. Thomas Stickney, aged about 70.—In Haverhill, Mass. Lieut. Jeremiah Kimball, aged 74, formerly of Bradford. —In Mendon, Mrs. C. Hastings, wife of Hon. Seth Hastings, Esq.—In Fitzwilliam, Mrs. Elizabeth Reed, wife of Phinehas Reed, Esq. aged 40.

Vol. XV (No. 6) Monday, 28 Nov. 1808.

† [3b] The wife of Mr. David Young, of Athol, saves the family's house and barn from fire, which had been struck by lightning. ♦

¶ [3b] A house, with the contents, valued at 4,000 dollars, belonging to Mr. John Philbrick, of Weare, was destroyed by fire, on the 1st inst. [*Hav. pap.*

† [3c] Samuel Grant, Clerk, posts a notice to the proprietors of the Walpole Village Bridge; dated 21 Nov. 1808.

† [3c] John Duncan, and J.C. Chamberlain, Directors, post a notice to the proprietors of the Charlestown Turnpike Road, and request a meeting to be held at the house of Isaac H. Ely, Charlestown. Notice dated at Acworth, 14 Nov. 1808.

===== ¶ [3b] MARRIED. =====

In Boston, Mr. Ebenezer T. Andrews to Miss Eliza Weld.

In Concord, Mr. Jesse C. Tuttle, printer of the Concord Gazette, to Miss Curviah Abbot.

In Keene, Mr. Edmund Wetherbee, of Surry, to Miss Abigail Wright.

In Claremont, Mr. William Pettigrew, of Weathersfield, to Miss Mary Alden.

In Cavendish, Mr. Aram Thomas to Mrs. Abigail Chapman—Mr. Jonas Spalding to Miss Hannah Woods—Mr. Giles Dolf to Anna Spalding.

===== ¶ [3c] DIED. =====

In Hampstead, (N.H.) the hon. John Calfe, Esq. in the 68th year of his age. Few men have been so much beloved and respected, as this worthy member of society. In the beginning of the late revolutionary war, he sustained a military commission at Greatisland and Ticonderoga.—In Frankfort, (Penn.) the gallant captain Stephen Decatur.—In Guilford, (Vt.) Mrs. Betsey, aged 43, wife of Mr. Manasseh Bixby, jun. of a consumption.—In Milton, (Ms.) Miss Mary Ingersol, aged 57.—In Boston, Mr. William Amory, aged 33.—In Windsor, (Vt.) suddenly Miss Sally Lyman, daughter of Mr. Solomon L. of Weathersfield, aged 18.—In Easthampton, Dr. Hophni Clapp, aged 37.—In Northampton, Deac. Josiah Clarke, aged 87 ; Miss Elinor Clark, aged 51.—In Fitzburg,[185] Mrs. Mary, relict of capt. Cowdin, of Boston.—In Amsbury [sic], Mrs. Betty, wife of Deac. Orlando Sargeant, aged 75.—In Lincoln, Miss Susan Stearns, daughter of Rev. Charles Stearns.

Vol. XV (No. 7) Monday, 5 Dec. 1808.

† [3d] List of non-resident proprietors and owners of land in Springfield, N.H. who have not paid their taxes for the year 1808, as compiled by Reubin Hoyt, Collector. Delinquent property to be sold at public auction at the house of Daniel Noyes, Esq., Springfield. The original list contains a breakdown of Lot No., acreage, etc., but only the owners' names are presented here:

Henry Elkins	John T. Gilman	Simeon Ladd & Lambson
Capt. Stephen Kimball	George Hough	Nehemiah Tilton
Joseph Emery	Simeon Ladd	
Jeremiah Fogg	Col. Aaron Kinsman	

Vol. XV (No. 8) Monday, 12 Dec. 1808.

† [3c] Rev. Timothy Davis ordained at Wellfleet, the 16th ult.
† [3d] Adv. by *J.& T. Bellows* offering goods for sale; dated Walpole, 10 Dec. 1808.
† [3d] Newton Whittelsey offers a small house, blacksmith shop, and two acres of land for sale at Cornish, N.H.; dated there 28 Nov. 1808.

======= ¶ [3c] MARRIED. =======

In Croydon, Mr. Samuel Putnam to Miss Sukey Gibson ; Mr. Nathaniel Cole, of Claremont, to Miss Sally Putnam ; Mr. Robert Hogg, jun. of Springfield, to Miss Huldah Winter ; Mr. Luke Paul, of Newport, to Miss Sally Cooper.

======= ¶ [3c] DIED. =======

In Plainfield, Deacon Ebenezer Cole, aged 82.—In Croydon, Mr. Ezekiel Powers, aged 64, one of the first settlers of the town.—In Portsmouth, Dr. John Jackson, aged 63, after a distressing and lingering illness.—In Greenland, Mrs. Sarah, wife of capt. Joseph Kingsbury, aged 30.—In Rutland, Vt. Mrs. Polly Williams, aged 44, relict of the late hon. Samuel Williams ; Mrs. Mary Trask, aged 62.—In Salisbury, Mass. deacon W. Hacket, aged 70.—In Scotch-plains, N.J. Mrs. Betsey Cotes, aged 98 ; she lived a widow 56 years ; had seen her own family to the 7th generation, and nearly 300 of her own offspring are now living.—In Warwick, R.I. Mr. John Levalley, aged 94.—In Newburyport, Mr. Daniel Pike, aged 57.—In Plymouth, Gen. James Warren, a distinguished revolutionary character.—In Plumbstead, Penn. Mrs. Mary Meredith, aged 100.—In New-Brunswick, hon. George D. Ludlow, Esq. chief justice of the province of New-Brunswick.—In St. Mary's, Dr. Daniel Turner, a native of R. Island.—In Johnson, Col. Daniel Mantor, aged 66.—In Medford, Mr. Gardner Greenleaf, aged 83.—In Leicester, Mrs. Eleanor, wife of Rev. Joseph Emerson, of Beverly.—In Worcester, Mr. Phinehas Ward, aged 79.—In Thetford, Vt. widow Mary Choate, aged 82, formerly of Newburyport.—In Guilford, Con. Mr. Thomas Caldwell, aged 74.—In Middlebury, C. Capt. Ebenezer Smith, aged 79.—In Somers, Mrs. Ann Collins, aged 94.—In Bridgeport, Mrs. Eunice Sterling, aged 88.—In Barkhamstead, Mrs. Experience Slade, aged 80.—In Mansfield, Mrs. Ruth Davis, aged 76 ; Capt. Lemuel Barrows, aged 86.—In Canfield, Ohio, Mrs. Lydia Dodd, aged 74, formerly of Sharon, C.—In Richmond, Vir. Dr. John Gringer.—In Georgetown, Dr. George Weems.—In Baltimore, Mr. Empson Bird, aged 99.—In Wolfborough, N.H. Isaiah Orn, Esq. aged 53.—In Uxbridge, Ms. Mrs. Sarah, wife of Dr. John B. Brown, and daughter of hon. B. Tuft, Esq.—In Salem, Capt. Nathaniel Kinsman.—In Milton, Mrs. Mary Ingersoll, aged 67.

DROWNED.—in lake Champlain, Mr. James Carlton, aged 16, lately of Charlestown, Ms. While passing from Burlington to Peru, his skiff upset.

Vol. XV (No. 9) Monday, 19 Dec. 1808.

† [3d] Philip Bundy offers one cent reward for the return of Flint Russell, an indented apprentice boy aged about 16 years, who ran away Sunday, 11 Dec. 1808. Dated at Walpole, 13 Dec. 1808.

===== ¶ [3d] MARRIED. =====

In Troy, Mr. Lewis Munn to Miss Louisa Weld.
In Litchfield, Aaron Burr Reeve, Esq. to Miss Annabella Sheldon, of Newyork.
In Albany, Samuel Rockwell, Esq. Attorney at law, to Miss Sarah Ann Spencer.

===== ¶ [3d] DIED. =====

In Boston, on Saturday morning, the 10th instant, his Excellency JAMES SULLIVAN, Governour and commander in chief of the commonwealth of Massachusetts, in the 65th year of his age. He was an eminent lawyer, and at different times had sustained the offices of attorney general, judge of probate, judge of the supreme court, member of council, national commissioner, and lastly chief magistrate of the state. His remains were interred on Friday last, with military honours, and other publick testimonials of respect.

In Boston, Mrs. Deborah Stearns, aged 24, wife of Mr. Calvin S. late of this town.—In Worcester, Mr. Daniel Waldo, aged 87.—In Shrewsbury, widow Sarah Wyman, aged 87.—In Easthaddam, Con. Mrs. Hannah Spencer, aged 78 ; Mr. Green Hungerford, aged 93 ; Mr. Joel Spencer, aged 80.—In Granby, Mr. James [Hillyer?] [186] aged 98.—In Danbury, Mr. Daniel Wood, aged 82.—In Greenwich, Mrs. Kezia How, relict of Mr. Issac How, aged 101.—In Westfield, Ms. Hon. Samuel Mather, aged 72.—In England, Mr. Richard Porson, an eminent Greek scholar, and professor of that language in Trinity College ; John Horn Tooke, Esq. aged 72.—In the Mississippi Territory, the Rev. Lorenzo Dow, a celebrated Methodist preacher.

† [3d] ☞ *The Reverend Clergy in the vicinity are requested occasionally to send us by the postriders, and other convenient conveyance, a weekly or monthy register of* Deaths and Marriages *in their respective towns.*

Vol. XV (No. 10) Monday, 26 Dec. 1808.

===== ¶ [3d] MARRIED. =====

In Boston, Mr. William Tuckerman, merchant, to Miss Judy P. Shaw.
In Westminster, Mr. Vine Carpenter to Miss Desire Hall, daughter of Atherton Hall, Esq.
In Randolph, Vt. Capt. Barna Bigelow, merchant, to Miss Lois Griswold.

===== ¶ [3d] DIED. =====

In Brattleboro', Mrs. Abigail, wife of J.W. Blake, Esq. aged 41.—In Somerset, Mrs. Hannah Greenman, aged 91.—In Goshen, Ohio, Rev. David Zeisberger, senior missionary of the United Brethren among the Indians.—In Georgetown, Columbia, [187] Rev. Robert Molyneaux, aged 72, president of the college in that town.—In Portsmouth, Mr. Richard Billings, aged 73.—In Worcester, capt. Ralph Earle, aged 83.—In Boston, Mr. John J. Geyer, aged 51.

Vol. XV (No. 11) Monday, 2 Jan. 1809.

¶ [3b] A house was struck at Tolland, Con. on the 22d ult. by lightning, occupied by Mr. Azel Crandall. The house was very much injured, and a young woman, his daughter, aged 23 years, and who had been married only 3 weeks, was instantly killed by the explosion.

† [3d] Joseph D. Hewitt adv. a correction to an earlier adv. which appeared in the *Vermont Journal*, stating that he had been robbed of his horse and money. The notice is dated at Pomfret, Vt., 13 Dec. 1808. ♦

† [3d] Two legal notices regarding the estates of Palsgrave Wellington and Quincy Wellington, both late of Alstead, deceased; James H. Bingham, Cyrus Kingsbury, and Azel Hatch appointed Commissioners. Claims of both estates were to be examined at the homes of the widows. Both notices dated at Alstead, 26 Dec. 1808.

===== ¶ [3c] MARRIED. =====

In Croydon, Mr. Zebadiah B. Dow, of Claremont, to Miss Asenath Smart.
In Keene, Lt. James Wells to Miss Sally Wilder, daughter of Dea. Abijah Wilder.

===== ¶ [3c-d] DIED. =====

In Kingston, (Jam.) 29th Oct. last Mr. Amos Bigelow, of Weston, aged 22.—In Savannah, Capt. D.N. Cottineau; during the American revolution he commanded the U.S. frigate [Pallis?], under the celebrated commodore John Paul Jones.—In Boston, Mrs. Mary, Widow of the late Mr. Thomas Hudson, aged 89.—In Philadelphia, during the week ending 17th ult. 33 deaths, of consumption 6, of small pox FOUR !—In Newyork, during the week ending 17th ult. 41 deaths, viz. 7 men, 14 women, 14 boys and 6 girls ; of consumption 3, of small pox FOUR !—In Greenbush, (N.Y.) Rev. Timothy Woodbridge, aged 64, pastor of a church in Stephenton.—In Albany, Mr. Philip Wendell, aged 75.—In Smithfield, (R.I.) Mr. Jeremiah Bucklin, aged 70.—In Royalston, Miss Eliza Town, aged 52.—In Newington, (N.H.) Lieut. Nicholas Pickering, aged 81.—In Salem, Hon. John Norris, aged 57, an eminent merchant and an excellent citizen.—In New London, Mrs. Mary Rogers, aged 90.—In Waterford, (Con.) Mrs. Lydia Gorton, aged 96. Mr. John Morgan, aged 70.—In Lyme, Mr. Park Woodward, aged 92 ; Mr. Samuel Lord, aged 71.—In Cornish, the Rev. James Wellman, aged 86.—In Royalton, Miss Martha Morris, aged 13, daughter of Lewis R. Morris, Esq. of Springfield, (Vt.) —In Alstead, Mr. Quincy Wlelington [sic].—In Jaffrey, Mr. Nathan Cutter, jun. aged 24.—In Port St. Mary's, Spain, of a pulmonary complaint, Mr. Charles Frederick Gilman, aged about 21, only son of the Hon. Nicholas G. of this state. His remains were attended to the grave by his countrymen from the neighbouring city of Cadiz.

Vol. XV (No. 12) Monday, 9 Jan. 1809.

† [3d] Brief paragraph describing the fire "[l]ast Saturday" which destroyed the Clover-Mill in Burlington, [Conn.] owned by Bliss Hart, Esq.

† [3d] Ordinations: At the Stone Chapel, Boston, 1st inst., Rev. Samuel Cary, Colleague with Rev. James Freeman; and in Haverhill, Rev. Joshua Dodge at the Congregational Church.

===== ¶ [3d] MARRIED. =====

In Greenfield, Mr. Hooker Leavitt, attorney at law to Miss Nancy Munn.
In Boston, Mr. Joshua Cushing, printer, to Miss Ann Avery.

===== ¶ [3d] DIED. =====

In Andover, Vt. 8th ult. Rev. Nathan Noyes, aged 61.—In England, Dr. James Anderson; well known by his writings on agriculture, political economy, &c. —At Havana, Capt. Frederick Thomas, of Boston.—In Northampton, Mrs. Sarah, relict of Abraham Burbank Esq. aged 65.—In Andover, (Mass.) Dr. Ward Noeys, [sic] aged 78.—In Savannah, Mr. James Johnson, printer, 70.—In Boston, the Hon. Thomas Dawes, senior, aged 78.—In Deerfield, Mr. William Clareck, a state pauper, aged 75. He was a native of France, and was on board the [Viligents?], a French ship of war, captured near Cape Breton, in the year, 1745.—In Putney, Vt. Mrs. Hepzibeth Stevens, aged 67, formerly of Plainfield, (Conn.)—In Huntington, (Vt.) Mrs. Mary Tufft, aged 61, burnt to death by fainting and falling into the fire.—At Montreal, Mrs. Henry, consort of Capt. Henry, late of Windsor, (Vt.)—In Danbury, Con. Mr. Nathaniel Gregory, aged 76.—In Redding, C. Mrs. Mary Burr, aged 94.—In Sutton, Mrs. Lucy King, aged 40, consort of Mr. Jonathan K.—In Sterling, Mr. James Richardson, aged 78.—In Charleston, S.C. Mr. Jacob Cohen, aged 71.—In Newhaven, Con. Capt. Edmund French, aged 68.—In Milton, Mr. Joseph Billings, aged 54.—In Boston, General Henry Jackson, aged 62.

SUICIDE.—On Thursday, a seafaring man, by the name of William Jones, late gunner of the ship Roxana, shot himself in a cellar near the market. 188

Vol. XV (No. 13) Monday, 16 Jan. 1809.

† [3d] Notice of taxes owed by non-resident proprietors and owners of land in the town of Marlow, N.H., for the year 1808, as compiled by Nathan Howard, Collector, and dated at Marlow 2 Jan. 1809. Delinquent property to be sold at public auction at the house of Elisha Huntley, Innholder at Marlow. The list contains a breakdown of acres, land valuation, etc., though only the owners names are presented here:

John Dodge	——— Ellingwood	Samuel Morrison
William Towns	Thomas Hale	Lot Comming
Benjamin Adams	Benjamin Baxter	William Richardson
John Gram	Eli Herington	Jese [sic] Willard
W. True Webster	Jona. Webster	John Spalden
Ralph Hall	John M'Cordy	Timothy Scott
James Ramsey	Ezra Seden	

===== ¶ [3d] MARRIED. =====

At Pittsfield, Jesse Gove, Esq. attorney at law, of Rutland, Vt. to Miss Sophia Ingersol.

In Alexandria, (Virg.) Capt. Charles M'Intire, of Portsmouth, (N.H.) to Miss Sarah Heineman.

In Middletown, Con. Rev. Noah Porter, to Miss Mehitable Meigs.

In Windsor, Mr. Salmon Hale to Miss Lois Smith.

In Guilford, Mr. Abraham Kingsbury, to miss [sic] Sally Palmer. ; Mr. William Shephardson, to Miss Harriot Cambridge ; Mr. Darius Wood, to Miss Sally Marsh ; Mr. Ira Stowell, to Miss Elenor Goss ; Capt. Paul Chase, to Miss Lucy Hyde ; and Mr. William Gregory, to Miss Sally Cutting, and all of Guilford.

===== ¶ [3d] DIED. =====

In Cornish, N.H. Mr. Jonathan Huggins, aged 67.—In Trenton, (N.Y.) Col. Jacob Hochstrasses ; an officer in the patriot army of our revolution, and for several years a member of the N.Y. legislature.—In Preston, Mr. Samuel Leonard, aged 72.—In Lyme, Widow Huntley, aged 70 ; killed by a ram as she was passing through a field.—Mrs. Elizabeth, widow of Mr. Stephen Chapel, aged 77.—In Springfield, (first parish) during the year 1808, 26, viz. 15 ad. 11 ch.—In Portland, during the year 1808, 74, viz. 31 ad. 43 ch. ; 6 drowned and one executed.—In Medford, 31st ult. Mr. Paul Dexter, aged 68.—In Philadelphia, during the week ending 31st ult. 37 ; 17 adults and 20 children ; of consumption 5, and nine sacrificed to the small pox ;—John Nixon, Esq. president of the bank of N. America, aged 76 ; a respectable merchant.—In Boston, Capt. Joseph Moses, aged 74, formerly of Salem.—In Schaghticoke, N.Y. Capt. Hull, of Poultney, Vt.—the loss of a sinch-pin occasioned one of the wheels of his waggon to run off and he was thrown among the horses, and killed instantly.—In Vergennes, Mr. Samuel Welch, aged 20 ; Miss Sally Welch, aged 14 ; and Miss Abby Welch, 12—all children of Mr. Paul W.—they died within a few days of each other.

In Hanover, Ebenezer Scribner, of a putrid fever, aged 19 ; of the same fever on the 16th ult. Elizabeth Scribner.—In Chesterfield, suddenly, on the 5th ult., Capt. Ebenezer Harvey, aged 82.—In Marlboro' N.H. Mr. Josiah Farrar, aged 87.—In Surry, on the 23 ult. Mrs. Elizabeth M'Curdy, aged 85, relict of Mr. Samuel M'Curdy. They were natives of Antrim County, North part of Ireland, and lived together upwards of 60 years. Descendants, 65.

Vol. XV (No. 14) Monday, 23 Jan. 1809.

¶ [3d] LORENZO DOW. A report of the death of this celebrated Methodist apostle, in the Mississippi Territory, being in circulation in the papers, it may gratify his friends to be informed that he has preached in Hudson several times since he is reported to have deceased. [*Hudson Bee.*]

===== ¶ [3d] MARRIED. =====

In Brattleborough, Mr. Peter Houghton, printer, to Miss Isabel Clark.
In Hartland, Mr. Nathaniel Jenny to Miss Sally Cabot.

===== ¶ [3d] DIED. =====

In this town, on the 10th inst. Deac. [Jotham?] White, aged 85, formerly of Leominster, Mass.—In [Croydon?], widow Thankful Powers, in the 85th year of her age; she left 5 children, 68 grand-children, 79 great grand-children, and 4 of the fifth generation ; in all 156.—In Burlington of the Asthma, John Fay, Esq. attorney at law, aged 41.—In Jerico, the Hon. [? ?] one of the judges of the Court of Chittenden County.—In this town, a child of Mr. [Ephraim Drury ?] [?] infant of Mr. Thomas [Swan?].

Vol. XV (No. 15) Monday, 30 Jan. 1809.

† [3d] David Carter, "Pro. Clerk" of the Third New Hampshire Turnpike Corporation, posts a notice regarding a meeting to be held at the house of Phillips Sweetser, Esq., in Marlboro'. Notice dated at Marlboro', 26 Jan. 1809.

Vol. XV (No. 16) Monday, 6 Feb. 1809.

===== ¶ [3b] MARRIED. =====

In Rehoboth, Mr. Simeon Mason, of Swanzey, aged 74, to Mrs. Experience Baker, aged 79.
In Orford, (N.H.) Mr. John Mann 3d, to Miss Martha Phelps, of Chester, Mass.
In Boston, George Sullivan, esq. attorney at law, to Miss Sarah Bowdoin Winthrop, daughter of Thos. L. Winthrop, esq.
In Weathersfield, Mr. Joseph Cutting to Miss Fanny Hatch.
In this town, Mr. Bartlett Bowker, to Miss Hannah Carpenter, daughter of Capt. D. Carpenter.

===== ¶ [3d] DIED. =====

In Prussia, the princess Withelmina, relict of prince Henry of Prussia [. . .] In Boston, Mrs. Elizabeth Lathrop, consort of the Rev. Dr. Lathrop, aged 59. Mr. Edward Saunders, aged 91. Mrs. Sarah Gardner, aged 30. In Concord, on Thursday the 26th inst. Col. Thomas Stickney, in the 80th year of his age. He was nine years old when his father settled in this town, at a time when the country (almost a wilderness) was incessantly overrun by the savages, whose barbarities will scarcely find a parallel in the annals of any nation.

From minutes kept by the Rev. Jeremiah [Higbee?], of Alstead. There died in Alstead during the year 1807, nine adults and eight children. Total 17. In 1808, thirteen adults, seven children. Total 20.

In Rumney, Jan. 11th, Mr. John Haines, aged 85 years and 7 months. He left 2 male children, 20 grand children, 41 great-grand children, and two of the next generation. He had lost 2 children, who died young, 7 grand-children, and fifteen great grand-children, which in aggregate amount to 85 descendants. At his funeral there were present (including his widow) five generations. A short time before he expired he began to sing the 23d Psalm and sung part, when his strength failing he repeated the remainder. [. . .] [*Concord Gaz.*]

Vol. XV (No. 17) Monday, 13 Feb. 1809.

===== ¶ [3d] DIED. =====

In Rye, N.Y. Rev. Evan Rogers, of the Episcopal Church.—In Concord, N.H. Col. Thomas Stickney, aged 80.—In Augusta, Geor. suddenly, George Stepton Washington,

Esq. of Virginia, nephew of the late President Washington, aged 37.—In Fredericksburg, Vir. Charles Yates, Esq. aged 81.—In Boston, Mr. Martin Gay, aged 82 ; Mr. Edward Saunders, aged 91.—In Chelsea, Mass. Mrs. Abigail Cheever, aged 63, wife of Deac. Joshua C.—In Rutland, Vt. Mr. William Hale, aged about 40.—In Gilmanton, N.H. Hon. Joseph Badger, Counsellor for Strafford county.

Vol. XV (No. 18) Monday, 20 Feb. 1809.

¶ [3d] FIRE. On the 21st ult. the house occupied by John Lyle, at Carlisle, Pennsylvania, was destroyed by fire—both Lyle and his wife perished in the flames. It is said they had quarelled the preceding evening, and both went to bed intoxicated. An old woman made her escape, but was considerably burnt. *N.Y. pap.*

† [3d] Legal notice regarding the insolvent estate of Josiah Swett, late of Claremont, deceased. Nathaniel Draper, David Stone, and Dan Baldwin appointed Commissioners; dated at Claremont, 13 Feb. 1809.

===== ¶ [3d] MARRIED. =====

In Springfield, Mr. Lyman Tilden, of Hartford, (Vt.) to Miss Abigail Hearsee, of Springfield.

In Boston, Mr. Ephraim Harris, printer to Miss Lydia Cox.

===== ¶ [3d] DIED. =====

In Grafton, on the 15th inst. Mr. William Wyman, of this town, aged 58, very suddenly of an apoplectic shock.—In Boston, Mrs. Martha Thayer, aged 69, widow of Rev. Ebenezer Thayer, late of Hampton ; Mr. Robert Crocker, aged 42 ; Jeremiah Allen, Esq. sheriff of Suffolk aged 58.—In West-Cambridge, Mr. Thos. W[i]llliams aged 101; retaining the full possession of his intellectual powers, memory, &c. until the last.—In Dorchester, Mr. John White, aged 75.—In Rutland, Mrs. Mary Barker, aged 54.—In Andover, Capt. Benjamin Ames, aged 83 ; he was an officer in the American revolution and commanded a company in the memorable Battle of Bunker's Hill.—In Norridgewock, Col. John Moor, aged 77, being an old revolutionary officer, who commanded the American troops on the left in the battle of Bunker Hill.—In Westmoreland, Dr. Jonathan Knight, aged 87 ; Mrs. Anna Metcalf, aged 83.—Mrs. Martha Hardwick, aged 64.—In West-Hartford, Mr. John Seymour, aged 82. The descendants from him were 14 children, 60 grand-children, 13 great grand-children, in all 93.

Vol. XV (No. 19) Monday, 27 Feb. 1809.

† [3c-d] Account of a snow slide in Quebec, which buried the house of Mr. Alexander Munn, ship-builder. Two children of Munn's were taken from the snow alive. ♦

† [3d] Ordinations: on the 9th inst. Rev. Daniel Lewis at New Gloucester, and Rev. Thomas Holt at Ipswich, to the 2d Church.

† [3d] Legal notice regarding the estate of James Wellman, Esq., late of Cornish, deceased. James Ripley, Ith. Chase, and Caleb Chase, 2d appointed Commissioners; claims to be examined at the house of Wellman's widow. Notice dated at Cornish, 8 Feb. 1809.

===== ¶ [3d] MARRIED. =====

In Boston, George Sullivan, Esq. to Miss Sarah Bowdoin Wentworth.

In Hartland, Mr. William Barrett, to Miss Anny Denison, daughter of Col. George Denison.

In Charleston, Mr. William Powers, printer, of Virginia, to Miss Lucy Stoddard.

In Keene, Mr. Samuel Nevens, of Hanover, to Miss Hannah Wood.

===== ¶ [3d] DIED. =====

In Philadelphia, during the week ending 11th inst. 14 adults, 12 children ; of consumption 6, small-pox three.—In New York, during the week ending 11th inst. 10 men, 7 women, 4 boys, and sixteen girls ; of consumption 6, small-pox 5 !—In Ballston Spa, (Penn.) John B. Ball, Esq. aged 28, att'y at law.—In Gorham, (N.Y.) Mr. Wm. Slosson, of Onondaga ; by poison supposed to have been given by one Gorbet, alias Coombs, who was taken in the act of running off with Slosson's sleigh and horses.—In Stockbridge, Miss Julia West, daughter of the late Dr. West of Tolland, (Con.)—In

Freeport, Rev. Samuel Veazie, aged 30.—In Boston, Mrs. Sarah Cabot, consort of Samuel Cabot, Esq. aged 46 ; very suddenly, Mr. Edward Weld, aged 75.—In Newport, R.I. Mrs. Sarah, wife of Dr. William Read, of Charleston, S.C.—In Wilmington, N.C. Mr. Eben'r Burrill, of Salem, printer ; he drowned himself in a fit of despair.—In Middletown, (Con.) Mrs. Abigail Goodrich, aged 25 ; Stephen Clay, merchant, aged 57.—In East Hartford, Deacon Timothy Cowles, aged 89 ; Mrs. Sarah Mix, aged 84.—In East Windsor, Mr. Elishama Crane, aged 91.—In Amherst, Gen. Zebina Montague, aged 55. —In Sutton, Mrs. Hannah, wife of Mr. Thomas Lovell, aged 81.—In Gerry, Mr. Silas Goddard, aged 27.—In New-Ipswich, widow Margaret Bacon, aged 100 years and six months ; she drank nothing stronger than small beer for fourteen years before her death;—Mrs. Elizabeth Batchelder, consort of Mr. Joseph Batchelder, aged fifty six years.—In Dunstable, Capt. Mathew Chambers, in the 67th year of his age—an officer in our revolutionary army.—In prison, in Paris, the celebrated Marshal Brune ; he had incurred Bonaparte's displeasure, on some account, and was imprisoned.—In Kaskaskias, (Indian. Ter.) Rice Jones, Esq.; deliberately murdered in the street, by Dr. James Dunlap, for the apprehending of whom 500 dls. reward is offered.—In Schoodick, (N.Y.) Robert Woodworth, Esq. one of the judges of the court of common pleas for that county.

Vol. XV (No. 20) Monday, 6 March 1809.

† [3c] Account of a fire "on the 17th instant" at the house of Mr. Asa W. Burnap, Lancaster, Coos County, N.H.; the fire started in a room used as a bookbindery. The article was copied from the "Coos Cour." ♦

† [3c-d] Legal notice regarding the estate of Cornelius Warren, late of Walpole, deceased, Moses Hale, Adm. The probate court for this estate to be held at Pierce's Tavern, Keene. Dated at Alstead, 3 Mar. 1809.

† [3d] Samuel Hutchinson adv. goods for sale in Alstead; dated there 1 Mar. 1809.

† [3d] *Shepard & Hutchinson* adv. books and other items for sale at their store in Newport; dated 1 Mar. 1809.

† [3d] David Stone requests "for the last time" that debtors pay up ; dated Walpole 2 March 1809.

† [3d] Legal notice regarding the estate of Thomas Wallace, late of Acworth, deceased. William Grout, Edward Slader, and Mezalda Keyes appointed Commissioners; claims to be examined at the house of Amos Keyes, Inn-holder at Acworth. Notice dated at Acworth, 23 Feb. 1809.

===== ¶ [3c] DIED. =====

In this town of a scald, a child of Mr. James Hooper.—In Rockingham, Mr. Calvin Eaton, of this town.—In Alstead, Hon. Israel Smith, aged 68 ; —Mrs. Lucy [or Luey?] Brewer, aged about 60.—In Ware, Mass. Rev. Reuben Moss, aged 50.—In Orford, on the 23d ult. Mrs. Lydia Mann, aged 42, consort of Maj. John M. junr.

Deaths in Portsmouth—The whole number of deaths in Portsmouth, N.H. in 1808, were 108—Births 275—Marriages 56.—Number of inhabitants about 7000.

In Newburyport, Mass. 99 deaths—Births, 166 males, and 177 females—total 343— marriages 76.

Vol. XV (No. 21) Monday, 13 March 1809.

† [3d] Legal notice regarding the estate of Hannah Newton, late of Newport, N.H.; John Smith, executor. The estate business to be conducted at the house of Josiah Shepley, Inn-holder at Charlestown.

===== ¶ [3d] DIED. =====

In this place, while on a journey, and very suddenly, Mr. Samuel Bond, of Dummerston, aged 25 years. Intellingence was transmitted to his wife of his illness on the 8th, and she attended his funeral the next morning.—In Barre, (Vt.) Luther Holton, Esq. aged 33.—In Montpelier, Mr. William Hutchins, aged 38.—In Havanna, Mr. Wm. Pierce, of Portland, aged 29.—In Montgomery county, (Mary.) Samuel Turner, Esq, aged 84.—In Worthington, Dr. Moses Brewster, aged 40.—In Hawley, Dr. Daniel Forbes, aged 40.—In Brookfield, Dr. Whitman Gilbert, aged 28.

Vol. XV (No. 22) Monday, 20 March 1809.

¶ [3c] FIRE. On the night of the 1st inst. while the family were absent, the house of Moses Rowles of Dummerston took fire by some unknown means, and was consumed with all its contents. [*Brattleboro pap.*]

¶ [3c] We learn from Chandlersville, that a fire broke out in a large and elegant house belonging to Mr. Gustavus Fellowes, of Roxbury ; and that the house, with all the furniture, and out houses, were consumed. Loss estimated at 6000 dls. [*Col. Cent.*]

¶ [3c] ORDAINED. In North Blanford, (Con.) Reverend Charles Atwater.

† [3c] Rev. Horace Holley installed as pastor at the church on Hollis Street, Boston.

† [3d] William Briggs, Clerk, posts a notice regarding the annual meeting of the proprietors of the Cheshire Bridge to be held at Charlestown. Dated 7 Mar. 1809.

† [3d] Joseph Cobb and Henry Rice, a.k.a. *Cobb & Rice*, adv. "that they have taken the shop west of the Common, near *Mr. Hall's* Chaise shop, where they intend to carry on the blacksmithing business . . . " Dated at Walpole 20 Mar. 1809.

† [3d] Stone & Bellows adv. to purchase tow-cloth. Dated Walpole, 16 Mar.

† [3d] Molly Colby of Sandbornton adv. a notice for her missing husband, Peter Colby, Husbandman, who, "in February, 1808, left his home in Sandbornton, under pretence of going a trading voyage into the state of Vermont, and has not since returned . . . " The notice mentions his "tender offspring." Dated at Sanbornton 26 Jan. 1809.

===== ¶ [3c] MARRIED. =====

In Cornish, Mr. David Huggins to Miss Jerusha Cobb ; Mr. Gilbert Gross to Miss Esther Hilliard.

In Wardsboro' (Vt.) Mr. Aaron P. Perry, to Miss Mary Fay ; Miss Charity Simons, aged 20, to the young and sprightly Mr. David Ward, aged 62 [. . .]

===== ¶ [3d] DIED. =====

In Orford, N.H. Mrs. Lydia Mann, aged 42, consort of Maj. John Mann.—In Richmond, (Vir.) Tylor Braxton, Esq. aged 28.—In Boston, Mr. James Eunson, jun. aged 27 ; Mr. C.W.A. Morton, only son of the hon. [Perez?] Morton, aged 22.—Suddenly, in New-Ipswich, Mrs. Abigail Jones, wife of Mr. Jonas Jones, aged about 65.—In Westmoreland, 2d inst. Mrs. Ester Fuller, wife of Dr. Noah Fuller, aged 69.—In Swanzey, on the 1st inst. Capt. Thomas Warren of Lenox, Berkshire county, Mass. formerly of Townshend, aged 82.—In Herkimer, (N.Y.) Gaylord Griswold, Esq , aged 42.—In Scituate, Mrs. Lucy, wife of Deacon John Ruggles, aged 77.—In Salem, Mrs. Abigail, wife of Deacon Thomas Hartshorn, aged 58 ; Mr. Nathaniel Phippen, jun. aged 44.—In Eastham, Mrs. Freeman, wife of Samuel Freeman, Esq. aged 40.—In Northampton, on Saturday last, Hon. Samuel Henshaw, Esq. Judge of Probate.—In Hartford, on the afternoon of 27th ult. Miss Nancy Bull, aged 28, was seized with the prevailing (spotted) fever, and before the noon of the 28th, was a corpse ; Miss Hannah Bull, aged 32, was seized on the 28th and died the next day (March 1st) just as her deceased sister was going to the grave ; Miss Rebecca Bull, aged 22, was seized March 1st, died in the evening of the same day, and on the 2d was buried in the same grave with her first deceased sister ;—They were the daughters of Joshua Bull, Esq.—Also, between the 28th ult. and 7th inst. there were taken ill and died, Mr. John Dodd, post-master, aged 66 ; his wife Mary, aged 56 ; his oldest son John, aged 43 ; and his nephew, Capt. Josiah Dodd, aged 30 ; and within a few hours of each other, two children of Mr. Joseph Pratt jun. There have been a number of other deaths in Connecticut, of the above afflictive malady.

Vol. XV (No. 23) Monday, 27 March 1809.

† [3c] Samuel Grant and Samuel Sparhawk announce that their copartnership is dissolved; dated Walpole, 24 March 1809.

† [3c] Legal notice regarding the estate of William Wyman, late of Walpole, deceased; Jon. Royce, Stephen Parker, and Bela Frink appointed Commissioners. Claims to be examined at the house of Wyman's widow. Notice dated at Walpole, 24 March 1809.

† [3c] Joshua Phelps, Post-Rider, announces that he has discontinued carrying the newspapers; dated 25 March 1809.

† [3d] Legal notice regarding the estate of John Marvin, late of Surry, deceased; the widow was Carolina Marvin; Jonathan Royce, Adm. Dated 20 March 1809.

† [3d] Legal notice regarding the estate of David Wells, late of Walpole, deceased; Probate Court to be held at Pierce's tavern, Keene; Isaac Redington, Adm. Dated at Walpole, 23 March 1809.

¶ [3c] FIRE !

The School-House, standing near the house of John Russel, Esq. in Cavendish, was lately consumed by fire, together with a considerable quantity of books.

The dwelling-house of Jirah Durkee, at Royalston, (Vt.) has been destroyed by fire.

A house in Harlem, (Maine) occupied by a Mr. Bonny, was consumed with its contents by fire, on the 27th February.—Two children perished in the flames.

===== ¶ [3c] MARRIED. =====

In Croydon, Mr. Daniel Melendy to Miss Sally Powers.

In Salem, Mr. Samuel H.G. Rowley, mer[chant]. of Hanover, (N.H.) to Miss Susan Hopkins.

===== ¶ [3c] DIED. =====

In Johnstown, (Rhode-Island,) Roger Williams, Esq. aged 90, great grand-son of Roger Williams, who was the Founder of the colony of Rhode-Island.—In Woodstock, Mr. Jos. Darling, aged 73.—In Vienna, Mad. Roose, and actress of celebrity ; at whose funeral 10,000 persons, and upwards of 1000 noblemen's carriages, attended.—In East-Haddam, (Con.) Dea. Joseph Beckwith, aged 96.—In Providence, on Thursday last, suddenly, col. Christopher Olney, aged 64 ; John Mason, Esq. aged 67.—In Boston, col. Wm. Scollay, aged 52 ; Widow Elizabeth Warden, aged 77 ; Mrs. Mary, wife of Mr. Benj. Cushing, aged 38.—In Portsmouth, John Penhallow, Esq. aged 85.—In Canandaigua, N.H.[189] hon. Oliver Phelps, aged 60.—In Pittsfield, Ashbel Strong, Esq. counsellor at law, aged 55.—In Sheffield, general Jeremiah Hickok, aged 61.—In Cornish, widow Hulda Hall, relict of Dea. Thomas Hall, aged 86.—In Orford, on the 16th inst. Mr. Abijah Mann, youngest son of John Mann, Esq. aged 18 years.—In Warner, 11th inst. Miss Anna Flanders, of consumption, aged 18.—On the 12th inst. after a long and singular disorder, of four years, Mr. Moses Clark, aged 38. Subsequent to his death the physicians opened and took out of him a hard bony substance that grew in his heart ; his heart on one side had grown fast to the flesh.—In Nottingham-West, Lieut. Reuben Spaulding, aged 82 ; Widow Susanna Spaulding, aged 50.—In Lyndeborough, Mr. Joshua Hadley, aged 71.—In Mount-Vernon, Rev. John Bruce.—In Groton, Feb. 22, Mr. Charles Quails, aged 80. He was a native of Ireland ; during a long absence from his country, he ever maintained this patriotick sentiment—"Should dear Ireland be sunk, many Gentlemen would lose their lives."—In Nantucket, during the short period of 10 months and 24 days, Miss Mary Joy ; Miss W. Joy : Franklin Joy ; Mrs. Kesia Joy, aged 33 ; Miss Eliza Joy.—The wife and children of Capt. David Joy.—In Andover, (Vt.) 13th inst. Mr. [Hart?] Balch, aged 24.—In Keene, Mr. William Goodenow.

Vol. XV (No. 24) Monday, 3 April 1809.

† [2d] Account of a duel fought in Canada between Messrs. Blake and Dix, both of Boston. Dix was shot through the lungs, but the article does not specify if the wound was mortal. ◆

† [3c] Article describing the suicide of William Forrest, a resident of Shippensburg, Penn., who travelled to Virginia in search of a cure for his affliction of "dropsy in the head" which he had suffered for four years. Forrest brought his wife and three children on the journey, but after no cure was found for his ailment, on their return, he took laudanum about the first of March and died in Winchester. [190] The widow and children were lodged at Mr. Farra's inn, Winchester. Forrest was a native of Massachusetts, and a soldier in the revolution. ◆

† [3d] A.&O. Allen adv. "Plaister of Paris" for sale; dated Walpole, 1 Apr. 1809.

===== ¶ [3c] MARRIED. =====

In Cavendish, (Vt.) Mr. Moses Spaulding, late of Jaffrey, N.H. to Miss Persis Chapman.

At Fitchburg, (Mass.) the Rev. Phinehas Whitney, of Shirley, to Mrs. Jane Gaffield.

In Boston, Mr. Samuel G. Snelling, printer, to Miss Susan Alley.
In Cornish, Mr. Oliver Jenks, of Newport, to Miss Lavina Jackson ; Mr. Daniel Vinton, to Miss Huldah Smith ; Mr. Dan Campbell to Miss Abigail Coburn.

===== ¶ [3d] DIED. =====

In Woodstock, Mrs. Scena, consort of Mr. Joseph Barrett.—In Windham, (Con.) of a pleuritick complaint, Mr. Solomon Huntington, aged [91?].—In Stoneham, (Mass.) widow Easter Richardson, aged 100.—In Lyndeborough, Rev. Sewall Goodridge.—In Maure, Counter Admiral Savary, commandant of the French Legion of Honour, who distinguished himself by three descents on Ireland.—In Sterling, Major Andrew Putnam, aged 52.—In S. Carolina, Mr. Benjamin Alston, jun. Esq. of [Waccamaw?], aged 42.—In Bradford, (Vt.) Mr. Benjamin Little, Esq. aged 71.—In Georgetown, (Me.) Mr. Joshua Shaw, Esq.—In Salem, capt. Benjamin West, aged 70.—In Windham, (Con.) Mr. Oliver Dyer, printer, aged 28.—In Marlow, Mrs. Merriam Beckwith, aged 87.—In Shrewsbury, Deacon Jonas Stone, aged 84, a member of the legislature, and a worthy patriot in the American revolution.—In Virginia, Nathaniel Pope, Esq. of Chiltern Farm; killed in a duel.

A short time since we announced the death at Gerry, of Silas Goddard. The afflicted father, Simon Goddard, has in the short space of eleven years, buried, by the all-conquering consumption, a wife and seven children ! ! —Memento mori ! [Worcest. pap.

DROWNED.—off Gloucester, on Sunday morning last, from on board sloop Ranger, on his passage from Portland for Boston, capt. David C. Prince, of Portland. He was struck over board by the boom. Every exertion to save him proved fruitless. He has left a widow and three children, to mourn an irreparable loss ; and a large circle of friends and relatives to lament this bereavement.

† [3d] List of letters remaining at the post office, Walpole, 1 April 1809, as compiled by O. Allen, Postmaster.

Aaron Allen, Walpole.	Daniel Marsh, Walpole.
John Brellan, Surry.	Ephm. Meads, do.
Hannah Boney, Walpole.	Coste Merchaud, do.
Aron Benett, Alstead.	G.W. Nichols, do.
Sewall Benett, Lempster.	Editors P. Observatory, do.
Thos. Craig, Walpole.	Elijah Putnam, Langdon.
Isaac Cunningham, do.	James Prentiss, do.
Polly Eaton, Alstead.	Thomas Russel, Walpole.
Levi Green, Westmoreland.	Aquilla Russell, do.
Justin Hinds, Walpole.	Polly Reed, do.
Sam. Hutchinson, Alstead.	Simeon Smith, do.
Wm. Holbrook, Westmoreland.	Israel Smith, Alstead.
Eleazer Jewett, Langdon.	Israel Smith, do.
John Ingols, Walpole.	Mercy Smith, Walpole.
Deborah Keder, do.	Samuel Turner, do.
Jesse Kittredge, do.	George Willard, Langdon.
John Livingston, do.	

Vol. XV (No. 25) Monday, 10 April 1809.

† [3d] Adv. by the Clothier's Works of *William Bryant & Son*, stating "that they have purchased the place formerly owned by Ezra Cobin, on the Flat, in the north-east part of Cornish." Dated at Cornish, 27 March 1809.

† [3d] Legal notice regarding the estate of Oliver Minor, late of Plainfield, deceased; Daniel Kimball, Adm. Dated at Plainfield, 6 Apr. 1809.

===== ¶ [3c-d] DIED. =====

At Cape May, Jona. Leaming, Esq.—In Waterford, (N.Y.) Mrs. Carey, the wife of Dr. Carey.—In Chatham, Col. John Blague, aged 70.—In Claremont, Mrs. Sarah Jennison, the only daughter of the late Rev. Dr. Fiske, of Brookfield, aged [42?].—In S. Hadley, John Farrah, aged 55, a transient person said to be from Sullivan, (N.H.) In Stockbridge, Widow Sarah Shurtluff, aged 95. In Newburyport, Stephen Cross, Esq. Post-

Master, aged 77.—In Bridgewater, Lieut. Joshua Alen, aged 80.—In Cohasset, Mr. Mordecai Lincoln, aged 90.—In Boston, Mr. Fitch Hall, Jun. mer.—In Staunton, (Vir.) Mr. Leonard Lootz, of the locked jaw, occasioned by a blow or blows upon the back of his head, with a piece of wood, by one John Hagarty who absconded.—In Groton, (Con.) Mrs. Lucy Turner, aged 100 y. 7 m. she retained her memory and reason to her death—In West-Springfield, Mr. John Beach, aged 100 y.—In Salem, Capt. Benjamin West, aged 70.—In Boston, Mrs. Martha Rouseau, aged 50.—In Westmoreland, after 3 1-2 years sickness and confinement, Mr. Artemas Knight, aged 32.—In Putney, Mr. Nathaniel Corbin, jun. aged 17.—In Derryfield, Mr. Samuel Stark, aged 73 ; a noted officer in the old French war.—In Philadelphia, Hon. Thomas Smith, Esq. ; one of the Judges of the supreme court of Pennsylvania.—In Hartford, Mrs. Susannah Grew, wife of the Rev. Henry Grew, aged 29.—In East Hartford, Mr. Benjamin Brown, aged 67.— In West Hampton, Mr. Asa Thayer aged 60.

† [3d] List of letters remaining in the Post Office, Charlestown, N.H., 1 April 1809, as compiled by F.A. Sumner, Postmaster:

S. Adams, Charlestown, N.H.	Amasa Houghton, Springfield, Vt.
Asa Allen, " "	Elijah G. Holden, " "
Mr. Baily, Acworth, N.H.	William Jackson, Unity, N.H.
Polly Barrett, Springfield, Vt.	David Kemp, Charlestown, N.H.
Merril Bates, " "	A. Lockwood, 2 Springfield, Vt.
Simeon Brown, " "	William M'Crae, 191 " "
Abigail Barnard, " "	Joseph Muzzy, Rockingham, Vt.
Elisha Brown, " "	John Nurse, Springfield, Vt.
Samuel Clark, Acworth, N.H.	Jos. Rogers, Charlestown, N.H.
Asa Chandler, Stoddard, N.H.	Mary D. Patson, Springfield, Vt.
Jona. Davis, Alstead, N.H.	Aaron Parks, Charlestown, N.H.
James Fletcher, " "	Nath. Prince, " "
Peter Fletcher, " "	Eben. Stearns, " "
Jona. Glidden, Unity, N.H.	Aaron Spencer, Springfield, Vt.
James Huntoon, " "	Joseph Selden, " "
Louisa Huntoon, " "	Ben. Stearns, Langdon, N.H.
Sam. Hardy, Langdon, N.H.	Chancey Smith, Croydon, N.H.
Caleb Hunt, 2 Lancaster, N.H.	Luther Scofield, Springfield, Vt.
Deborah Hoar, Charlestown, N.H.	James Whipple, " "
Smith Holman, Springfield, Vt.	John Way, Alstead, N.H.

Vol. XV (No. 26) Monday, 17 April 1809.

† [3b] Account of a party of "drunken, patroling soldiers" who harrassed a Capt. House of Enosburgh, Vt., and Mr. and Mrs. Stone of Berkshire, Vt. A Mr. Emmons was one of the party, he being the deputy Custom-house officer in Berkshire. ♦

† [3b] Article describing the robbery of property belonging to Capt. Levi Bigelow, of Derby, Vt., by a group of soldiers. ♦

† [3c] Shubael Conant requests debtors to pay up. Dated 14 April 1809.

† [3c] Adv. of goods for sale by *Samuel Hutchinson* in Alstead, and *Shepard & Hutchinson*, in Newport; dated 10 April 1809.

† [3c] Adv. of a "School for Young Ladies," opening in Claremont, Miss Goodrich, Preceptress. The subscribers of the adv. are Stephen Farley, Samuel Fiske, Linus Stevens, and Daniel Parmelee; dated Claremont, 11 Apr. 1808 [sic].

† [3c] Eliab Sartwell requests debtors to pay up; dated Langdon, 14 April 1809.

† [3c] Ira Eaton adv. for his lost pocket-book, which contained among other items, a note of hand signed by Isaiah Eaton. Dated at Westminster, Vt. 7 April 1809.

† [3d] Abel Cole, Secretary, adv. the annual meeting of the members of the "Band of Military Musick," to be held at Martin Butterfield's in Westminster; dated Westmoreland, 3 April 1809.

† [3d] Legal notice regarding the estate of Quincy Wellington, late of Alstead, N.H., Learnard Mann, Adm. The notice mentions that a meeting is to be held at the house of Josiah Shipley, Charlestown, N.H. Dated 6 April 1809.

Vol. XV (No. 27) Monday, 24 April 1809.

† [1a] Adv. of the "Ladies' Academy", offering instructions by Miss Hayes; dated Walpole, 8 April 1809.
¶ [3a] MELANCHOLY ACCIDENT. We learn that a young man was drowned in Brattleborough, last week. His name and other particulars of this melancholy event, we have not been apprised of.
† [3d] Isaac Redington requests debtors to pay up; dated 21 April 1809.
† [3d] Amos Shepherd adv. property for rent at Alstead; dated there 21 April 1809.
† [3d] Harvey Chase, Clerk, adv. a meeting of the Cornish Turnpike Corporation to be held at the house of John Vinton, in Cornish; dated there 14 April 1809.

===== ¶ [3d] MARRIED. =====

In Boston, Mr. Thomas Vinton, mer. to Miss Elizabeth Oliver, daught. of Rev. Daniel Oliver.
In New York, John Montgomery, Esq. member of congress, from Maryland, to Miss Maria Nicholson, of N.Y.
In Boston, Mr. Joshua Thomas, of Lancaster, to Miss Mary Armstrong.

===== ¶ [3d] DIED. =====

In Greenfield, Mrs. Mary Johnson, wife of Mr. Richard Johnson, aged 74.—In Lyme, Mrs. Debroah Gee, aged 96.—In Rehoboth, Rev. Jacob Hickes, aged 70.—In Truro, 21st ult. Mr. George Laws, aged 89.—In Hardwick, on the 25th of February last, capt. Seth Pierce, aged 62.—In Brookfield, Mrs. Zeriah Bruce, consort of Mr. Roger Bruce, aged 72.—In Belchertown, of a consumption, Mrs. Euncie Phelps, wife of Mr. Abner Phelps ; and youngest daughter of Rev. Justus Forward. The dispensations of Providence have been remarkable towards Mr. Forward's family—of 11 children, 9 have been removed by death, five of which by consumption.—In Westminster, Mr. John Brown, aged 24.—In Lyme, Samuel Mather, Esq. aged 63.—In Groton, Mrs. Lucy Turner, aged 100 years 7 months and 16 days.—In Norwalk, (Middlesex Society,) on the 19th ult. Mr. Moses Bigsbee, aged about 70. He was found dead in his bed.—In Keene, widow Mary Carter, aged [44?].—In Reading, Mrs. Abigail Lucas, aged [57?], wife of Mr. Samuel Lucas.—In Weathersfield, Mrs. Deane, wife of Wm. Deane.—In Royalton, Mrs. Eunice Cole.—In Hardwick, Mrs. Mary Stone, wife of capt. David Stone; and daughter of Doctor Samuel Huntington.—In Morristown, (N.J.) Mr. Joseph Woodman, aged 100 years.—In Norwich, Dr. Rhodolphus Knight, aged 40.—In Easthampton, Mr. Elijah Wright, aged 76.—

Vol. XV (No. 28) Monday, 1 May 1809.

† [3c] Account of two fires in Windsor, Vt., the first one which burned two barns owned by Samuel Shuttleworth, Esq., the other a blacksmith shop owned by Mr. Amos Tinkham. ♦
† [3d] James Cochran and John Maynard adv. their new co-partnership, *John Maynard & Co.* The adv. describes their saddlery business, and is dated [Walpole] 17 April 1809; a second adv. by J[ames]. Cochran requests all persons indebted to *Stewart, Hall & Co.* to pay up.
† [3d] Salma Hale, Secretary, adv. a meeting for the Walpole Mechanick Society, to be held at Mr. Southard's Inn.

===== ¶ [3d] MARRIED. =====

At Jaffrey, Mr Peter Felt, to the widow Mary Gilmore ; Mr. Ira Ingalls to Miss Jerusha Hogg ; Mr. Josiah Ingalls, to Miss Lois Capron ; Mr. Wm. Dutton, to Miss Abigail Smith, of Fitzwilliam.

===== ¶ [3d] DIED. =====

In Alstead, Mrs. Susannah Smith, in the 29th year of her age—triumphant in the faith of the gospel of Christ.—In Marlow, Mrs. Phebe, wife of Mr. Josiah Washburn, aged 84 ; a daughter of Mr. Elijah Huntley, aged 2 years.—In Cornish, Mr. Abel Spalding, aged 81.—In Plainfield, Mrs. Jane Cory, aged 65.—In Springfield, Vt. Mr. Levi Nichols, aged 69.—In England, Dr. French Lawrence, Member of Parliament ; Lord Falkland, killed in a duel with Mr. Powell, an English gentleman—the Hon. Joshua

Upham, chief Justice of the Province of New Brunswick.—In Sarragossa, the celebrated General Palafox, after some days sickness ; he died a few days before the surrender of that city.—In North Yarmouth, Rev. Tristram Gilman, pastor of the first church and congregation in that place, aged 74, and the 40th of his Ministry.—In Worcester, Mrs. Sarah, wife of Mr. William J. Stearns, aged 63.—In Putney, capt. David Moore, aged 66.—In Barrington, Mr. Joshua Foss, in the 100th year of his age. His posterity which are now living, are 7 children, three of which are above 70 years of age, 47 grand children, 95 of the 4th generation, 4 of the 5th generation—27 deceased—Total 180 ! !

Vol. XV (No. 29) Monday, 8 May 1809.

† [3b] Account of the sentences received at Superior Court in Worcester, Mass., by several criminals: 1) Thomas Stearns, for passing counterfeit bills; 2) Joshua Willard, for adultery; 3) Moses G. Bigelow, for forgery; and 4) Thomas Gleason, for theft. ♦

† [3c] A cow belonging to Mr. Thomas Ames of Bridgewater, Mass. calved four calves.

† [3c] Rev. Nath. Kennedy ordained 12 Apr. at the Presbyterian Church, Litchfield.

† [3c] Mathew Miller and S.R. Whitman adv. their new chair-making business, under the name of *Miller & Whitman*, located at Walpole, N.H. and Westminster, Vt.; dated 1 May 1809. In an attached adv., S.R. Whitman requests all debtors to pay up.

† [3d] A.& O. Allen adv. Plaister of Paris for sale; dated Walpole, 5 May 1808 [sic].

† [3d] Legal notice regarding Samuel Chase, appointed guardian to Aaron Chase; dated at Unity, 27 April 1809.

† [3d] Adv. for the Haverhill Academy Lottery; William Tarlton, S.P. Webster, and E. Kingsbury, Jr., Managers; dated at Haverhill, [N.H.] 26 July 1808.

===== ¶ [3c] MARRIED. =====

In Providence, Samuel Eddy, Esq. secretary of R.I. State, to Miss Ann Angell.

In Boston, Capt. Richard P. Beals, to Miss Frances M. Butler.

===== ¶ [3c] DIED. =====

In Franklin county, (N.C.) Mrs. Jane Bledso, aged 92 ; just before her death she requested that, instead of the usual solemnities observed at funerals, a drum should beat and precede her to the grave.—In Philadelphia, during the week ending 22d ult. 29; of consumption 5, of small pox two !—In New York, during the 22d inst. 24 ; of consumption 11.—In Providence, Hon. Darius Sessions, aged 92 ; a venerable statesman, patriot and christian ; Mrs. Susannah, relict of Mr. Constant Bailey, of Newport, aged 84.—In Attleborough, Mr. John Shepherd, aged 105 ; Mrs. Meriam Cobb, aged 92.—In Cornish, (N.H.) April 24th of the consumption, Miss Mary Chase, aged 26 years, daughter of doctor Solomon Chase.—In Danville, Florella Eaton, and Sophronia Eaton, daughters of Mr. Ebenezer Eaton, printer.—In Craftsbury, doctor James Paddock.—In Windsor, doctor Abraham Hedge.—In Westmoreland, on Sunday, the 30th ult. Dr. Noah Fuller, aged 70 years. The death of his aged consort was published in the Museum a few weeks since.—In Chester, N.H. Mr. Jonathan Bell, aged 28.—In Concord, N.H. Mr. Galen H. Fay, aged 29.—In Lancaster, very suddenly, Nathaniel White, Esq.—In Barrington, Mr. Joshua Foss, aged 99 years.—Died, at his seat in Richmond county on the 31st ult. Gen. Henry W. Harrington, aged 61.—He was an active useful officer, and acquired honour in the Revolution which secured to this country its Independence.—In Portsmouth, very suddenly, colonel George Gains, aged 73 ; Mr. Sherman, aged 70.—In Easthampton, Mr. Elijah Wright, aged 76.

We have to announce the death of the Rev. John Smith, D.D. Professor of the learned languages in Dartmouth College; whose literary acquirements, and particularly his improvements in the learned languages, are well known to the publick. [. . .]

Vol. XV (No. 30) Monday, 15 May 1809.

¶ [3c] The Louisville, (Ken.) Gazette of the 12th inst. says "this morning Mr. Benjamin Wilkinson with a hardy band of warriours, hunters, and trappers, all well armed and equipped, for a three years' expedition, left this place for St. Louis, there to join the St. Louis Missouri Company, who intend to push their trade to the river Columbia, and probably in a few years, by that route, to the East Indies."

† [3c] Farming news items copied from a Worcester, Mass. newspaper: 1) "Mr. Phineas

Maynard, of this Town, last month killed a hog which weighed 692 pounds." 2) "A hog lately killed by Mr. Josiah Jones at Stockbridge weighed 636 pounds." 3) "Mr. Nehemiah Ordway, of Southampton, N.H. has an ewe only six years old, which has produced twenty-one lambs."

† [3c] Legal notice regarding the estate of Asa Grant, late of Alstead, deceased; Richard Beckwith, Adm. Dated at Alstead, 12 May 1809.

† [3d] Adv. by Stone & Bellows regarding the purchase of cloth; dated Walpole 9 May.

† [3d] Legal notice regarding a meeting for the estate of Calvin Eaton, late of Walpole, deceased; Nicanor Townsley, Jesseniah Kitteridge, and William Watkins appointed Commissioners. Meeting to be held at the house of Asher Southard, Inn-holder at Walpole. Dated at Walpole, 12 May 1809.

=== ¶ [3c] MARRIED. ===

In Londonderry, N.H. Mr. Alanson Tucker, of Boston, to Miss Eliza Thom.

In Greenfield, Mr. Sargent Straw to Miss Sally Gould.

=== ¶ [3c] DIED. ===

In Brattleborough, (Vt.) Mrs. Carpenter, wife of Mr. Asa Carpenter, of consumption ; Mr. Stephen Bennitt, aged 70.—In New Fane, Mrs. Mary Bell.—In Andover, Vt. Mrs. Mary Brown, the amiable consort of Samuel B. Esq.—In Colrain Mrs. Phebe Workman, aged 77.—In Windsor, Mrs. Jannet M'Collester, aged 47.—In Raleigh, N.C. Mr. Patrick Conway, an Irish merchant ; inhumanly murdered in his store, supposed by one John Owens, a cabinet maker, who is taken up and confined.—In Nantucket, George Folger, jun. Cashier of the Nantucket Bank. In Wilmington, Timothy Walker, Esq. aged 77.— In Boston, Mr. Isaac Watts, aged 61 ; Mrs. Mary Martin, aged 90 ; Dea. Thomas Lewis, aged 60.—In Medford, Miss Sally Condy.—In Bedford, captain Thomas Boies, aged 82.—In Orford, on the 7th inst. Mrs. Mary Pratt, aged 66.—In Lancaster, N.H. very suddenly, Nathaniel White, Esq. aged 57.—Suddenly, in Londonderry, 21st ult. Widow Margaret Evans, aged eighty eight ; also, in the same town, her brother James Alexander, aged eighty, on the 25th ult. with a similar disorder, on his return home from her funeral.—In this town, on Friday evening last, an infant child of Mr. Joseph Bridge.

Vol. XV (No. 31)   Monday, 22 May 1809.

† [1c-d] Extensive account of the single survivor, Thomas Moorhead, of the ship *Acorn*, which was wrecked by a storm in the Atlantic Ocean, 30 Oct. 1808. The rest of the crew died from being washed overboard, exposure, hunger, or thirst; those named were Capt. M'Leod "of Stockton, to which they were bound from America;" the master, Andrew Brass, and John Simpson, a boy; Francis Bradlay (timber-man); Christopher Baly, and Thomas Bales, boys; Thomas Charlton, and the boy Charles English, and William Pearson. Moorhead was "a native of the county of Durham;" no state or country is specified, though presumably it was England. Moorhead resorted to cannibalism in order to survive; he was rescued after being at sea for 51 days. ◆

¶ [3c] As the Rev. Mr. Jackson and his wife were returning from Newark to Bloomfield, (N.J.) on Thursday, May 4, in the evening after dark, the horse left the road, went off a high bank, and Mrs. Jackson was unfortunately killed on the spot. Mr. Jackson received no material injury.

¶ [3c] In Middlefield, N.Y. a son of Mr. Moses Thompson, aged 13, was killed by the wheel of a saw mill.

† [3d] A farm for sale in Langdon, N.H.; apply to Dr. David Taylor, Charlestown, or Isaac Redington, Walpole; dated 19 May 1809.

=== ¶ [3c] MARRIED. ===

In Kinderhook, N.Y. Mr. Arent Von Vleck, to Miss Sally Pruyn :—Two brothers and two sisters of the bridegroom are married to two sisters and two brothers of the bride.

In Boston, capt. Samuel Goldsbury, jun. to Miss Sally Jones.

In Boylston, Nathaniel Woodcock, of Orange, aged 71, to Miss Sarah Fuller, aged 60, of the former place.

=== ¶ [3d] DIED. ===

In this town, Edward, son of Mr. Josiah Bellows, aged 2 years and 6 months, unfortunately drowned in a barrel of water standing near the house. He was not discovered till so late as to render every medical attempt applied, and the means made use of for resuscitation, ineffectual.

Mr. Peter Joslin.

In Westminster, Vt. on Wednesday last, the Hon. Lot Hall, Esq. aged 52, formerly one of the Judges of the Supreme Court. He has left an afflicted family to submit to this dispensation of Divine Providence [. . .]

In Keene, Dr. Daniel Newcomb, aged 24. His death is regretted by a numerous class of relations and friends. He had already attained considerable professional eminence.

Near London, the 19th March last, Hugh Strap, aged 85—the identical personage whom Dr. Smollet has rendered so conspicuously interesting in his Roderick Random. For upwards of 40 years he kept a hair-dresser's shop in the parish of St. Martin-in-the-Fields, where he was buried [. . .] ♦

In Newport, R.I. capt. Joseph Warren, aged 69.—In Boston, Mrs. Mary Cunningham, aged 44, consort of Andrew Cunningham, Esq.—In Newburyport, Walton, son of Rev. Dr. Spring, aged 19.—In Wilmington, Timothy Walker, Esq. aged 77.—In Philadelphia, Miss Sarah Rebecca Coxe, daughter of Tench Coxe, Esq.—In Philadelphia, during the week ending 6th inst. 31 ; of consumption 3, small pox one.—In Cambridge, Mr. George Webber, eldest son of the Rev. President Webber, and a member of the juniour class in the University.—In London, Thomas Holcroft, Esq. aged 61 ; a celebrated literary character, author of Hugh Trevor, the Road to ruin, &c.—In New-London, capt. G. House, of the revenue cutter Argus.—In Rutland, widow Beulah Walker, aged 85.—In Sturbridge, widow Hannah Clark, aged 92.—In Uxbridge, Mrs. Sarah Taft, aged 52, wife of the hon. Bezaleel Taft.

By a passenger in the last Rutland stage we were informed of the recent death of Judge Galusha, of Shaftsbury.

DROWNED.

In Ashuelot River, Keene, on Monday evening, a promising boy, the only child of Mr. Caleb Warner, about 3 years old. Mr. W's house is contiguous to the river, near the mills. After the child was missing an ineffectual search was made, until the next morning, when he was discovered a few rods from the house, near the bank. [N.H. Sent.

Vol. XV (No. 32) Monday, 29 May 1809.

No news items of significance located within this issue.

Vol. XV (No. 33) Monday, 5 June 1809.

† [3b] Rev. Daniel Sharpe ordained over the Baptist Church, Newark, N.J.

† [3c] Samuel Hutchinson, at Alstead, and Shepard & Hutchinson, at Newport, adv. goods for sale; dated 1 June 1809.

† [3d] Samuel Ruggles (formerly *Ruggles & Hunt*) announces that he is "intending to leave his present occupation," and offers drug-store supplies for sale at his store in Boston, located at No. 6 Broad St., in the rooms over Messrs. S.&C. Stearns; dated Boston, 18 May.

† [3d] Adv. by Amos Heald, Secretary, of a Masonic meeting to be held "at the Hall of Brother Aaron Seamans," with sermon by Aaron Leland and oration by Ethan Allen. Dated at Chester, 24 May 1809.

† [3d] Preston Merrifield and Thomas & Thomas announce that their copartnership at Windsor is dissolved, "on the 26th ult."; future business to be conducted by Merrifield; dated 1 June 1809.

† [3d] Samuel Hills adv. for a lost mare; dated at Surry, 27 May 1809.

† [3d] Silas Angiers adv. for a mare which he found; dated Walpole 2 June 1809.

===== ¶ [3b] MARRIED. =====

In Boston, Mr. Lebah Hayden, mer. to Miss Sarah Oliver, eldest daughter of the Rev. Daniel Oliver.

In Killingworth, (Con.) Rev. Joshua Huntington, of Boston, to Miss Susan Mansfield, daughter of Rev. Achilles Mansfield, of K.

In Huntington, Conn. Rev. Reuben Hubbard, to Miss Abigail Mehitable Lester.

In Gilsum, Mr. Asa Mash, to Miss Rhoda Davis, of Sullivan.

===== ¶ [3b] DIED. =====

In Halifax, (N.S.) George Brinley, Esq. commissary general ; a respectable individual; and a native of Boston.—In Stafford co. Vir. John Fitzburg, Esq. aged 83 ; he never experienced an hour's sickness.—In Hampshire co. Vir. col. Moses Rawlings; of the revolutionary army.—In Fredericktown, Mary., Mrs. Margaret, wife of Mr. J.P. Thompson, editor of the Herald.—In Dedham, a young woman who passed by the name of Clarke ; she was left there about a year since by a gentleman, and soon found herself with a helpless infant, deserted, and unprotected in a strange place ; her child lived but a few weeks, and is now joined by its unfortunate mother.—In Boston, Mr. Elijah Vose, [son?] Mr. Bill Vose ; suddenly, capt. John Doggett, aged 35.—In Maryland, hon. James Tilghman, a judge in that state.—In Providence, Hon. Darius Sessions, formerly lieutenant governour of Rhode Island, aged 92.—In Shelburne, the 7th inst. Mr. Roger Haskel, aged 63.—In Colrain, Mr. Thomas Anderson, aged 86.—In Leyden, widow Prudence Hunt, aged 98.—In Cornish, (N.H.) capt. Daniel Putnam, aged 70—formerly one of the officers of the revolutionary army.—In Danbury, (Con.) capt. Noble Benedict, aged 73.—In Salisbury, Mr. George Bissel, aged 93.—In Groton, Mr. Amos Chapman, aged 88.—In Lyme, cap. Gosper Dowzick, aged 85.—In Barrington, Mr. Joshua Foss, aged 100.—In Middletown, Mr. William Marks, aged 78.—In Attleborough, Mass. Mr. John Shepard, aged 105 years ; Mrs. Meriam Cobb, aged 92.—In Hancock, James Hosley, Esq. aged 75.—In New-Ipswich, suddenly, of a lung fever, Mrs. Sibbil Craggin, aged 59, wife of Francis Craggin, Esq.—In Barre, widow Mehitable Lee, aged 71.—In Newport, R.I. Mr. John Pitman, aged 53.—In Portsmouth, Dr. Peter T. Wales, aged 67.—In the city of Albany, Mr. Nathaniel Barney, of the Friend's Society, aged 79.—In Calcutta, J.P. Doncaster, Esq. much regretted; he was well known to most of the Americans who had visited Calcutta.—In New-Castle county, Delaware, Rev. William M'Kennan, aged 90.—At the cantonment, near Fort Adams, capt. Francis Johnson, of the U.S. army.—In New-York, Mr. John Low, publisher of the Encyclopedia.

Vol. XV (No. 34) Monday, 12 June 1809.

¶ [3b] On Sunday night last, eleven fat oxen, belonging to Mr. Benjamin Wilcox, of Westport, were killed by lightning.—The loss is estimated at 1000 dollars. *Ibid.* [192]

¶ [3b] Sentence of death was yesterday pronounced by the honorable Judge Buchanan, on Thomas Burke, who was found guilty at March court last, for committing a rape on a child between the age of ten and eleven years. [*Hagerstown Gaz.*

¶ [3b] FORGERY. George Howell has been sentenced to 14 years imprisonment to the State prison New York, for forging a check on the New York Bank. *Worcester Spy.*

¶ [3b] Capt. Ezekiel Parsons, of Windsor is appointed keeper of the Prison, in that place. [*Windsor pap.*]

† [3b] Rev. Richard Briggs ordained at Mansfield, [Mass.] "24th ult."

===== ¶ [3b-c] MARRIED. =====

In Brattleborough, Mr. Thos. Harris, of Charlestown, Mass. to Miss Abigail Chapin, only daughter of the hon. Oliver Chapin, Esq.—In Pelham, Mr. William M'Fall, aged 100 ! to widow Judith Perkins ! *both paupers* ! —In Ipswich, Mr. Mark Ross, aged 19, to the *blooming* Mrs. Teelock, aged 70 ! —In Fryeburgh, the Rev. Samuel Osgood, of Springfield, to Miss Mary S. Osgood, of Fryeburgh.—In Northampton, Mr. Timothy Dwight, jun. mer. of N. Haven, to Miss Clarissa Strong, daughter of the hon. Caleb Strong, Esq.—In Roxbury, Charles Shepherd, Esq. of Northampton, to Miss Betsey Dow.

===== ¶ [3c] DIED. =====

In Philadelphia during the week ending 27th ult. 43, viz. 25 adults and 18 children ; of consumption 6, small-pox FOUR !—In New York, during the week ending 27th ult. 45, viz. 14 men, 14 women, 8 boys and 9 girls.—In Sharon, Mr. Aaron Fisher, aged 46 ; most deeply lamented ; he died of a cancer.—In Bristol, England, lately, the celebrated Dr. Thomas [Beddoes?].—In New York Quarantine Ground, capt. George Roach, master of brig Hawk, from Havana; shot by his mate : The Coroner has reported the following statement of facts ; "When capt. Roach returned on board, he inquired of the mate if he had performed certain duties as directed, in counting some sticks of logwood; the mate replied that "he had weighed them, but had not taken the count," and declared that he (the captain) had not directed them to be counted. The captain affirmed that he had directed them to be counted, and called the mate a *liar !* The lie was returned; upon which the captain pulled the mate by the nose, and called him a man of *no spirit !* The mate replied, "bring up your pistols and I will convince you that *I am a man of spirit*." The captain immediately brought a pair of pistols out of the cabin, and on presenting one to the mate he said, "There is a loaded pistol for you mine is not loaded ; take your distance !" The mate went forward and said, "capt. are you ready?" The other replied "Fire and be damned." Upon which he did fire, and shot the capt. through the head. The mate was secured in gaol for trial.—In Oswego, (N.Y.) on the 8th of Feb. last, capt. Ebenezer Montague, of Charlemont, in the 40th year of his age.— In South Hadley, Mr. Silas Smith, aged 88.—In Barre, Widow Mehitable Lee, aged 71. —In Lunenburg, Mr. Wm. Jones, aged 73.—In Charlestown, of an apoplexy, Philips Payson, Esq. aged 49.—In Worcester, lieut. James Kennedy, aged 69. This man had well earned the reputation of a veteran. He had served faithfully in the old French and revolutionary wars : In the former of which he had two brothers killed. He outlived nine of eleven successive commanders of the same grade, under whom he had fought.

† [3c-d] Extensive obituary of Mr. Erastus Edgerton, son of capt. Daniel Edgerton, aged 22, who died at Tolland, Conn., 24 April 1809. ♦

Vol. XV (No. 35) Monday, 19 June 1809.

¶ [3a] Capt. Wm. P. Bennett, of the U. States army, who lately ordered his sergeant to enter Canada, and shoot Mr. Underhill, a deserter, and who expressed himself *"proud"* of the cruel murder, has been put under arrest, by col. Simonds, and is to wait further orders at Albany. [*Boston Gaz.*

† [3d] Samuel Grant and Samuel Sparhawk request debtors to pay up; dated Walpole 17 June 1809.

† [3d] Jesse Willcox, Jun., Treasurer, adv. a notice regarding the Croydon Turnpike; dated Newport 3 June 1809.

† [3d] Adv. of a book, "A Brief Sketch of a New System of Orthography," published by Thomas & Thomas. The author was Abner Kneeland of Langdon, N.H.

===== ¶ [3c] DIED. =====

In this town, Mr. John March, aged 72.

In Newbury, Vt. May 30th, Mrs. Prudence Bayley, wife of Gen. Jacob Bayley, aged 84. She was married at the age of twenty, and became the mother of ten children— nine sons and one daughter, of which only four sons survive her. Her husband having obtained a charter of Newbury, and being the principal in settling it, she soon removed to the new settlement, in what was called, the Coos county. In her removal from Hampstead, N.H. seventy miles of the way was a desolate wilderness, the dangers and fatigues of which she bore with fortitude, and even cheerfulness—as she also did the many inconveniences attending the infant settlement—and the still greater calamities of living on the frontier in the revolutionary war. She lived most agreeably with the husband of her youth almost 64 years—whose house has been noted for friendship and hospitality.—Of upwards of an [sic] hundred descendants, nearly seventy children, grand-children, and great-grand-children followed her remains to the house appointed for all the living. In early life she made a profession of cordial attachment to the christian religion [. . .] [*Coos Cour.*

DROWNED.

Near Providence, Mr. *Nathan Allen*, aged 47, *Henry*, his son, aged 13, and *George*, another son, aged 10. Another son on board was saved. He clung to the mast of the boat till assistance was afforded him.

Vol. XV (No. 36) Monday, 26 June 1809.

¶ [3d] UNFORTUNATE AFFAIR. On Monday last as Mr. David Maynard, of Royalton, with two or three other men were felling timber they were cutting into a dry hemlock tree which was leaning against another tree of the same description, the one into which they were cutting broke off near the middle by reason of which the top part was precipitated back towards the stump and struck Mr. Maynard with such violence, that he languished about four hours and expired. Mr. Maynard has left a wife and six small children to lament his untimely exit. [*Windsor pap.*

† [3d] Legal notice regarding the estate of Samuel Huggins, late of Cornish, deceased; Daniel Kimball, Ithamar Chase, and Newton Whittelsey appointed Commissioners; estate business to be conducted at the house of Benjamin Comings, Inn-holder at Cornish; notice dated at Cornish 19 June 1809.

===== ¶ [3d] MARRIED. =====

In Rutland, (Vt.) on Tuesday the 20th inst. Mr. Cheever Felch of this town, printer, to Miss Mary Hale, of the former place.

In Croyden [sic], Mr. Sibley Melendy, to Miss Rhoda Emery ; Mr. Moses Marshall of Unity, to Miss Elizabeth Lamberton, of Croydon.

In Thetford, Doct. Joram Allen to Miss Maria Hinckley, daughter of O. Hinckley, Esq.

===== ¶ [3d] DIED. =====

In Croydon, Mrs. Rachel Powers, wife of Stephen Powers, Esq. aged 68. In Troy, of a lingering disease, John Stoughton, Esq. one of the Judges of the Common Pleas of Rensselaer county, aged 81 years.—In Claremont, Mr. Luther Deane, aged [48?].—In Newport, Mr. Joel Wakefield, aged 45.—In Langdon, (suddenly,) Mr. Joshua Smith, aged 39.—In Boston, James Scott, Esq. aged 68 ; Mrs. Abigail Englesby, aged 64 ; Mary, wife of Mr. Daniel Tuttle, aged 43.—In Roxbury, Mr. John Williams, aged 63.—In Charlestown, Elizabeth Warren, wife of Dea. Isaac Warren, aged 51.—In New-Orleans, lieut. Bowie, of the Light Dragoons, killed in a duel with lieut Hague, of the same corps. The latter is expected to lose a hand, by the wound.—In Newport, Miss Sarah Mumford, daughter of the late Mr. William Mumford, in the 60th year of her age.—In Kingston, (Plym. co.) hon. William Sever, aged 80 ; many years a member of the Executive council of Massachusetts ; a gentleman of distinguished worth, conscientiously uniform in the discharge of the various duties of life.

Vol. XV (No. 37) Monday, 3 July 1809.

† [3c] Adv. by Samuel Hutchinson, at Alstead, and Shepard & Hutchinson, at Newport, dated 26 June 1809.

† [3d] List of letters remaining at the Post Office, Walpole, N.H., 1 July 1809, as compiled by O. Allen, Postmaster:

Joel Bixby, Walpole.	Miss Lucy Mason, Walpole.
Elias Burbank, "	George W. Nichols, "
Capt. Charles Bond, Surry.	Miss Betsey Parmer, "
Jona. Booth, Lempster.	Joseph Smith, Lempster.
John Britton, Surry.	James Smith, Walpole.
David Clark, Walpole.	Ben. Smith, "
Josiah Crosbey, Alstead.	Doct. Geo. Sparhawk 2, Walpole.
Sampson Drewry, Walpole.	John Sartwell, Langdon.
Jona. Davis, Stoddard.	Miss Mary Sparhawk, Walpole.
Miss Lydia Flint, Walpole.	Hon. Amos Shepard, Alstead.
Capt. Peter Fletcher, Alstead.	Samuel Tuttle, Walpole.
Uri Fairbank, Walpole.	David Turner, Walpole.
Ben. H. Floyd, "	William Tuttle, Walpole.
Simoen [sic] Frasure, Alstead.	Thadeus Colburn, Athens, Vt.
Benjamin Gould, Surry.	Amasa Tiffany, Walpole.
Joseph Guild, Walpole.	Mrs. Sally Tiffany, "
Miss Abigail Haynes, Alstead.	Nathan Vilas, Alstead.
Doct. Lewis Johnson 2, Surry.	Thomas & Thomas, Walpole.
Rev. Abner Kneeland, Langdon.	Miss Susan Wright, "
Joseph Mason, Walpole.	Miss Edah Willard, Langdon.
John Marsh, Walpole.	George Willard, Langdon.
Joseph Mason, Jun., Walpole.	Colonel John Wood, Alstead.

† [3d] Legal notice regarding Thomas Whipple, Gentleman, of Charlestown, N.H., Guardian of Huldah Hogg, Jasper Winter, Fila Winter, Daniel Winter, and Garey

Winter, "Children of Heirs of Thaddeus Winter, late of Croydon," yeoman, deceased. Whipple petitioned the Court for license to sell the Heirs' land in Croydon, which bounded on lands of Ebenezer Winter, Edward Hall, and Abijah Powers.

Vol. XV (No. 38) Monday, 10 July 1809.

¶ [3c] A Post-Office has lately been established in Cornish, this state, and Harvey Chase, Esq. appointed Post-Master.

† [3c-d] Obituary of Alexander Thomas, Esq., one of the Publishers of this newspaper, who died 2 July 1809 at Saratoga Springs, where he had gone for his health. Thomas was in his 35th year. ◆

† [3d] Henry Rice adv. for an apprentice blacksmith; dated Walpole 6 July 1809.

† [3d] List of nonresident proprietors and owners of land in New Grantham, N.H., who were delinquent for their taxes in the year 1808, as compiled by Joseph Sargent, Collector. The list contains a breakdown of the number of acres, division, etc., though only the names of the owners are presented here. Note: the heading of the list specifically states that these were the "Names of the original proprietors or owners."

    Elia. Stebbins   David Field   Phin. Lyman
    Samp. Willard   O. Doolittle   Josiah Jones
    Med. Pomroy   Elisha Hunt   Nath. Hall
    Cpt. S. Hunt   Lt. S. Hunt
    Moses Hawks   Jas. Dryen

† [3d] List of letters remaining at the Post Office, Charlestown, N.H., 1 July 1809, as compiled by Fred. A. Sumner, Postmaster:

Samuel Bradford, Acworth.
Samuel Clark, "
Isaac Burbank, Alstead, N.H.
Asa Harrington, " "
Shubel Wardner, " "
Theodore Bellows, Charlestown, N.H.
Phila Boman, " "
David Gay, " "
Deborah Hoar, 2 " "
Jesse Healy, " "
Col. Hubbard, " "
Eliza Holden, " "
Ichabod W. Hart, " "
William Mack, " "
David Parker, " "
Samuel S. West, " "
Daniel Cheney, Fisherfield, N.H.
David Fish, Langdon, N.H.
Daniel Howard, " "

Abner Kneeland, 2, Langdon, N.H.
Lucy Putman, " "
Jinason Barnard, Springfield, Vt.
Jona. Barnard, " "
Merrill Bates, " "
Zeletes Bemis, " "
Samuel Bugbee, " "
Daniel Griswold, " "
Abraham Lockwood, " "
Abraham Lockwood, 2d, Springfield, Vt.
Oliver Person, Springfield, Vt.
John Putman, " "
Simeon Randall, " "
Reuben Sartwell, " "
Isaac Tower, " "
Amos Stow, Society Lands, N.H.
Charles Huntoon, Unity, N.H
Jonah Carter, Weathersfield, Vt.

Vol. XV (No. 39) Monday, 17 July 1809.

† [3c-d] Article describing the explosion at Fort Constitution, Portsmouth, N.H., at the 4th of July celebration, naming several of those killed or wounded. The house belonging to Capt Walbeck (commander of the Fort) was damaged. ◆

    Ephraim Pickering Esq., of Newington, dead.
    A son of Mr. Stephen Paul, of Kittery, aged 14, dead.
    John Mitchell, a lad, dead.
    ———— Trefethen, a lad, dead.
    ———— ————, a man about 18 years of age, spectator, dead.
    Sergeant Albert, dead.
    Peletiah M'Daniels, dead.
    Theodore Witham, of New Gloucester, dead.
    Samuel Stevens, Reo Gamoth, Gideon Gold, Edmund Hurd, John Ricker, and Robert Miller, all wounded, perhaps mortally.

† [3d] Eber Carpenter offers a reward for his lost mare; dated Alstead, 12 July 1809.

===== ¶ [3d] MARRIED. =====

In Medford, Samuel Hinckley, Esq. of Northampton, to Miss Martha Prince, daughter of John Prince, Esq. of Medford.

===== ¶ [3d] DIED. =====

In Middletown, Rev. Enoch Huntington, aged 69.—In New Orleans, Mrs. Elizabeth, wife of hon. Judge Moreau Lislet.—In Beckley, (Penn.) Williams, a noted horse thief.—In Bozrah, (Con.) gen. Elijah Abel, aged 65.—In Hopkinton, (R.I.) Mr. Samuel Marry, aged 90.—In Providence, deac. Edward Thurber, aged 74.—In Germantown, (Penn.) Rev. William Graff, aged 82.—In Greensborough, Roxelana Huntington, aged 20, daughter of Dr. Samuel Huntington; the third daughter deceased, of the same family, in the space of 13 weeks.—In New-Haven, Elisha Fuller, Esq. aged 47.—In Easthampton, deacon Stephen Wright, aged 85.

In Alstead, on the 4th inst. Mr. Gideon Delano, aged 66.

DIED.—In Chester, (Vt.) on the 10th inst. Mrs. Mary Learned, wife of Joseph D. Learned, Esq. in the 21st year of her age. [. . .]

Vol. XV (No. 40) Monday, 24 July 1809.

¶ [3b] A REMARKABLE INSTANCE OF LONGEVITY.

There is now living in Augusta, (Kennebeck) a man by the name of John Gilley, who, by the best information, has attained the extraordinary age of CXIX years. He was born in the county of Cork, in Ireland, and emigrated to this country at about the age of 60. He was a bachelor till between 70 and 80, at which time he married a young woman of about 18, who still lives with him. He has always been a labouring man. Till he married, he was addicted to intemperance, but has since beeen temperate and sober. His living has been upon solid food. He never had any sickness, or suffered pain but from violence of wounds. He retains to this day his faculties of mind, and considerable bodily strength. He is of low stature, perfectly erect, and of a good countenance, though deeply furrowed ; he cuts wood, tends his barn, and performs other light labour, and not unfrequently walks six miles a day. Such were his bodily condition and his habits in 1806, when our informant saw him ; and he has heard of him within a few days, that no apparent changes have taken place in him. [*Salem Gaz.*]

† [3c] Lieutenant George W. Morrison, "late of Madison county," killed in Richmond, Kentucky, by the accidental discharge of his brother's gun. ♦

† [3c] Mr. William Corbin, "a repectable merchant, principal of the house of Messrs. Corbin & Bozworth," of Champlain, [New York], died from injuries [17 June 1809] received from his runaway horse, in the town of Chazy. ♦

¶ [3c] On Sunday the 9th inst. the house of Mr. Samuel Burpy at Templeton was struck by lightning. One of his children was stunned and entirely senseless for about 10 minutes—and Mr. Ephraim Stone, who was in the house received a severe shock. [*Worces. Spy.*]

¶ [3c] DROWNED. In Boscawen, on Saturday, the 7th instant, John Bellings, aged 10 years, son of Mr. Winthrop Bellings, [?] of Boston.

† [3d] Legal notice regarding the estate of Lot Hall, Esq., late of Westminster, Vt., deceased; Polly Hall and Joel Ranney, Executors. Notice dated at Westminster, 20 July '09.

† [3d] Reward offered by Thomas Bellows, Sheriff, for the capture of several escaped prisoners: Ezra Trask, "so famous for breaking gaol," aged about 35, and Rufus Mann, both escaped from the jail in Keene. James Mondell, (age about 23), George Dean, (age about 23), and David Huntly (age about 22) escaped from the jail in Charlestown, N.H. The adv. offers a very brief description of all the escapees except Rufus Mann. ♦

† [3d] C. Felch adv. for two cows which strayed; the livestock had the name of "Asa Hale" branded on their horns. Dated 22 July.

===== ¶ [3d] MARRIED. =====

At New-York, Mr. Noah Totten, Printer, to Miss Maria Stone.

At Middletown, (Con.) Mr. Theodore Bellows, of Charlestown, to Miss Elizabeth Davis, of the former place.

In Portland, Barrett Potter, Esq. to Miss Nancy Storor, daughter of the Honourable Woodbury Storor.

=== ¶ [3d] DIED. ===

In Annapolis, Ben. Ogle, Esq. formerly governour of Maryland.—In New York, Mr. M. M'Pharland, printer.—During the last week 53 persons died in New York, principally children.—In Deerfield, (N.Y.) Isaac Brayton, Esq.—In Packersfield, widow Juda Richardson, relict of the late Thomas Richardson, aged 78.—In Windham, Miss Sally Dole, aged 19.—In Canton, Mr. Silas Case, aged 59.—In England, Lord Dunmore, formerly Governor of Virginia.

In this town, on the 21st inst. Mrs. Ruth Smith, in the 83d year of her age.

DIED.—In Acworth, on the 5th instant, Daniel Grout, Esq. aged 73. He was an affectionate husband, a kind father, a real and social friend, and a worthy citizen, an early settler of the town, which he seved with integrity in various offices [. . .]

Vol. XV (No. 41) Monday, 31 July 1809.

† [3c] Article copied from the Amherst [N.H.] *Cabinet* describing the arrest of several persons charged with passing counterfeit bills: James Cunningham, Philip Emery, Moses Johonnet, and George Clerk, all of Goffstown, James Hervey, of Derryfield, and Mark Jewett, of Hopkinton. Two other men, by the names of Bailey and Whitney, were arrested at Hillsborough for the same offence. ♦

† [3c] Isaac Jennings adv. for a stray horse; dated Walpole, 25 July 1809.

† [3d] Several notices regarding the settlement of accounts for the late firm of *Thomas & Thomas*, due to the death of Alexander Thomas. The surviving partner was Isaiah Thomas of Worcester, Mass., and Thomas K. Thomas was the Adm. of Alexander Thomas' estate. Roger Vose, Esq. of Walpole is also named in the notices regarding the settlement of accounts.

† [3d] Amasa Allen and Oliver Allen announce the dissolution of their copartnership; the mercantile business will be carried on by Oliver Allen. Notice dated at Walpole, 27 July 1809.

Vol. XV (No. 42) Monday, 7 Aug. 1809.

This issue is not included on the microfilm.

Vol. XV (No. 43) Monday, 14 Aug. 1809.

† [1b] Notice to those indebted to *Charles Duncan & Co.* to pay up; dated Alstead, 2 Aug. 1809.

† [1b] Jesseniah Kittredge requests debtors to pay up; dated Walpole 3 Aug. 1809.

† [1c] Adv. by Josiah Eaton, that he has iron ware for sale, cast at "his Furnace near the Gate, on the Turnpike from Walpole to Keene." Dated at Walpole 2 Aug. 1809.

† [1c] Thomas Redington and Moses Fairbanks adv. that they "have formed a connection in business under the firm of *Redington & Fairbanks*." The adv. lists items for sale at their store in Charlestown, N.H. Dated 29 July 1809.

† [1c] Cady Parks adv. items for sale at his store near Walpole Bridge; dated at Bellows' Falls, 3 Aug. 1809.

† [1c] Notice of payment due for those indebted to Isaac Redington, or to *Redington & Seaver*. Dated 5 Aug. 1809.

† [3d] Adv. for the auction of the estate of Alexander Thomas, late of Walpole.

Vol. XV (No. 44) Monday, 21 Aug. 1809.

† [3d] Legal notice from James Campbell, Register of Deeds, that "he will attend to receive Deeds, &c. at the following places, viz. at Mr. J. Shepley's, in Charlestown, . . . and at Mr. Wm. Pierce's, in Keene . . . " Dated at Walpole, 15 Aug. 1809.

† [3d] James Cochran requests debtors to pay up; in the same adv. is a similar notice for Stewart, Hall, & Co. Dated at Walpole, 19 Aug. 1809.

¶ [3c] MARRIED.

In this village, Sunday week, by the Rev. Mr. Fessenden, Oliver Allen, Esq. merchant, to Miss Olive Hoar, both of this village.

In Boston, B.M. Watson, Esq. to Miss Eliza Parsons, daughter of the honourable chief justice.

In Keene, Seth Newcomb, Esq. attorney at law, to Miss Joanna Gardner.

¶ [3c-d] DIED.

In Wilton, N.H. Rev. Jonathan Livermore, aged 80. In Pelham, N.H. Joshua Atwood, aged 86 ; he had by one marriage 17 children.—In Andover, Rev. Jonathan French, aged 70.—At his seat in Lebanon, on the 7th inst. his Excellency Jonathan Trumbull, Governor of the State of Connecticut, in the thirteenth year of his office, aged 69.—In Cassel, (Westphilia) the 29th of May last, the celebrated Swiss Historian, Johannes Von Muller.—In Charleston, (S.C.) Mr. William Stephens, merchant; during a night of excessive heat, he rose from his bed to refresh himself, by sitting at a third story window, from whence, (having fallen asleep) he was precipitated upon the street pavement.—In Virginia, hon. Peter Lyons, aged 75, President of the Court of appeals of that state.—In Rutland, Mass. col. Benj. Hammond, late from Newton, aged 85.—In Westmoreland county, (Penn.) Dr. David Marchand, aged 64.—In Middletown, (Con.) Dr. W.B. Hall, aged 45.—In Brattleboro', Dr. Sam. Stearns, L L. D. a celebrated astronomer [sic].

DIED.—In Charlestown, on the 12th inst. Miss Louisa Hastings, the amiable daughter of Doct. Oliver Hastings, aged 14 years. [. . .]

Vol. XV (No. 45) Monday, 28 Aug. 1809.

† [1b] Auction notice of the estate of Quincy Wellington, late of Alstead, deceased; Larnard Mann, Adm. Dated at Alstead, 8 Aug. 1809.

† [1c] Benjamin Clarke posts a notice that he intends "to discontinue business in this town, by the first day of March next," and requests debtors to pay up; dated Charlestown, 14 Aug. 1809.

¶ [3c] Messrs. Henry Sperry and Samuel Cook, two of the unfortunate men cajoled into the Miranda expedition, captured by the Spaniards, and who have been three years in slavery and chains, in Carthagena, have made their escape and have arrived in Salem, from that port. They left from 25 to 30 still enduring the horrours of slavery; but who, they think, on a proper representation of our government, would be liberated by the Spaniards. [Cent.

† [3d] Convicts sentenced to hard labor at the state's prison at Windsor, by the Supreme Court of Vermont, "now sitting at Woodstock," on the 19th inst.:

1) David Wilbour, Westmoreland, N.H.; for passing counterfeit bills (7 years hard labor.)
2) Samuel Hemenway, Weare, Mass. (6 years hard labor.)
3) Abel Whitman, Cavendish, Vt. (5 years hard labor.)
4) Amos Hartwell, Springfield, Vt. (5 years hard labor.)
5) John Flamagan [sic], a transient person; for stealing (2 years.)

† [3d] Ordinations: 1) Rev. Chester Wright to the Congregational Church at Montpelier, Vt.; 2) Rev. Dyer Burge, to the Congregational Church at Colebrook, N.H. 27 July 1809 ; and 3) at Boothbay, Rev. Jabez Pond Fisher.

† [3d] Legal notice regarding an auction of the estate of Amos Hager, late of Croydon, deceased; Benjamin Barton, Adm. Dated Croydon, 7 Aug. 1809.

† [3d] One cent reward offered by Joshua Cory, for the return of Sarah McIntire, an indented servant who ran away 25 Aug. 1809. Dated Grafton, Vt., 26 Aug. 1809.

¶ [3d] MARRIED.

In Kennebunk, Mr. Wm. Weeks, editor of the New Hampshire Gazette, to Miss Nabby Hubbard, of K.

In Pomfret, Doct. Galen Palmer, of Woodstock, to Miss Polly Howard, of the former place.

In Middlebury, John Willard, Esq. Marshal of the State of Vermont, to Miss Emma Hart.

¶ [3d] DIED.

In England, in June, Daniel Lambert, whose immense bulk has so long attracted publick curiousity in England : He died suddenly in his 40th year ; and weighed 739 pounds, being 151 pounds heavier than Mr. Bright, of Essex. His coffin was eight feet long, and 4 feet 4 inches wide ; he measured three yards four inches round the body, and one yard one inch round the leg. He was rolled to his grave on a car, and the earth cut sloping away to admit it.—In England, Capt. John Sutherland convicted of the murder of his cabin boy—by excessive cruel usage—and stabbing him with a dirk—was executed the 29th of June, at Execution Deck.—He exhibited every mark of contrition and acquiescence in the justice of his sentence;—and was launched into eternity amidst an immense crowd of spectators. Great influence was made to save his life ; but without avail.—In Dover, N.H., a son of capt. Samuel Wentworth, aged 5 years ; he was thrown from a chaise, and though there was not the least vestige of external injury whatever, he lived only 15 minutes after his fall.—In Haverhill, Mr. Peter Niles of Bath.—Having recently experienced what he deemed a disappointment in love he determined to commit suicide—and accordingly arranged his business,—made his will—composed a view of his religious principals, accompanied with addresses to his relatives left orders concerning his funeral, and with great diliberation retired in the afternoon to the edge of the woods, where, as he imagined, he terminated all his woes by a shot of his gun.—In Charlestown, Major Benjamin Frothingham, aged 76 ; —a brave and distinguished officer of the revolutionary army.—In Maloan, N.Y. on the 18th ult. Mrs. Lucy Haswell, consort of Mr. Anthony J. Haswell, in the 30th year of her age.—On the 28th Earl Rockwell, late of Cornwall, Vt. in the 24th year of his age.—In Constable, on Thursday the 3d of August, at 8 o'clock P.M. as Mr. Wm. Wares, Richard Buswell and two others were returning home from their labour, near the line of Canada in a canoe—were suddenly overtaken with a storm of rain, wind and heavy thunder ; the canoe upset—and melancholy to relate, two of the four, viz. Wares and Buswell unfortunately perished in the water. Their bodies were found on the 4th at noon—— they were decently interred on the 5th—a sermon was delivered by the Rev. Elder Rowley, of Grenville. Wares left a wife and four children ; Buswell has a wife and one child in Deerfield, H.H. [193] to lament the loss.—In Vienna, May 31st, Hayden, the celebrated musical composer, aged 79.—In Dresden, (Me.) Mr. Philip Theobald ; descending from a barn chamber on a ladder he slipped off and occasioned his immediate death.—In Augusta, (Maine) (in a fit of apoplexy, without the least warning or previous illness) Solomon Vose, Esq. aged [40?], son of col. Joseph Vose, of Milton.—In Danvers, widow Elizabeth Endicott, aged 91 ; she enjoyed perfect health through life, has left a numerous posterity, and has a brother now living in Danvers, aged 100 years, enjoying good health.—In Cornish, N.H. Mrs. Pike, consort of Mr. Ebenezer Pike.

Vol. XV (No. 46) Monday, 4 Sept. 1809.

This issue is not included on the microfilm.

Vol. XV (No. 47) Monday, 11 Sept. 1809.

† [1a] Legal notice regarding the estate of John March, late of Walpole, deceased; Stephen Johnson, Jonas Hosmore, and Aaron Hodgkins appointed Commissioners; Levi Allen, Adm. Estate business to be conducted at Asher Southard's in Walpole. Notice dated at Walpole, 31 Aug. 1809.

† [1b] E. Carpenter adv. for a lost horse; dated at Charlestown, 28 Aug. 1809.

† [2b] Seneca Page and Harris Covert arrested in New Jersey for passing counterfeit bills of New York and New England banks. Article dated at N.Y.C., 1 Sept.

† [2b-c] Peter Stalcup and John Bingham arrested at Russelville, Kentucky, for the murder of George W. Welch, who they claimed had deserted from the army. ♦

† [2c] Fire destroys the clock factory belonging to Major Timothy Chandler of Concord, N.H., 17 Aug. 1809; the fire spread to barns owned by Mr. Robert Harris, and those were destroyed. Houses owned by Mr. Dustin and Mr. Abbot were spared. A fire in Salisbury, N.H. 16 Aug. 1809 claimed a new house owned by Joseph Noyes. ♦

¶ [2c] TROY, Aug. 25. As a number of men were raising the frame of a large store, twelve belts suddenly fell to the ground and buried the workmen under the timber. Allen Griffin and ——— De Witt were killed on the spot, and fourteen others were wounded, one of whom, Daniel Elliot, is since dead. [194]

† [3d] Cady Parks adv. a lost pocket book which he found; dated Bellows' Falls 6 Sept.

† [3d] Asa Partridge posts a notice that he "expects to discontinue his route with No. 52 of the MUSEUM," and requests debtors to pay up.

† [3d] Samuel Hutchinson adv. for flax seed "delivered at the Oil-Mill, or at his Store in Alstead." In a second adv., *Shepard & Hutchinson* request flax seed delivered to their store in Newport; both adv. dated 5 Sept. 1809.

† [3d] Legal notice regarding the estate of Josiah Robins, late of Brandon, Rutland County, Vt.; J.H. Bingham and Cyrus Kingsbury appointed Commissioners; estate business to be conducted at the house of Eber Church, Alstead, N.H. Dated at Alstead 4 Sept. 1809.

† [3d] Joseph Bridge requests debtors to pay up, and also adv. for an apprentice lad for the hatting business; dated Walpole, 6 Sept. 1809.

† [3d] Abner Porter adv. land for sale in Langdon, formerly owned by Isaiah Porter; dated at Langdon, 9 Sept. 1809.

===== ¶ [3d] DIED. [195] =====

In Hartford, Mr. Thomas Lloyd, aged 73.—In Providence, capt. Nathaniel Packard, aged 80 ; the [oldest?] nautical commander in the town.—In Virginia, [Mr.?] Thomas Trask, aged 102 years. He kept his coffin [?] years ; Mr. Leonard Ballou, a baptist minister of the gospel, aged [60?]. He was found dead under a [tree?] with his bible under his arm.—In Warren, R.I. [Mr.?] Charles Thompson, aged [24?].—In Pawtuxet, [sic] Mrs. Phebe Dean, aged [80?].

Vol. XV (No. 48) Monday, 18 Sept. 1809.

† [3b] Gruesome account of the murder of an infant, nine months old, a son of Mr. Elisha Ward of Reading, [Steuben County?], N.Y., by a young son of Mr. Isaac Baldwin, of Litchfield, Conn. ♦

† [3d] Abraham Holland requests debtors to pay up; dated Walpole 12 Sept. 1809.

¶ [3d] DIED.—In this town, on Friday evening last, a child of Maj. Joseph Bellows, aged 11 months.

Vol. XV (No. 49) Monday, 25 Sept. 1809.
Vol. XV (No. 50) Monday, 2 Oct. 1809.

These issues are not included on the microfilm.

Vol. XV (No. 51) Monday, 9 Oct. 1809.

† [1b] List of letters remaining at the post office in Walpole, N.H., 30 Sept. 1809, as compiled by Oliver Allen, Postmaster:

Nath. Bird,	Walpole	David Griffin,	Walpole	Samuel Turner,	Walpole
Daniel W. Bisco,	"	Nathan Gould & Co.,	"	Roger Vose 2,	"
Reuben Brown,	"	Jonathan Hunting,	"	John Williams,	"
Thomas Bellows, Esqr. 2,	"	Miss Eliza Hill,	"	Peter Dustin,	"
Mrs. Ellen Bellows,	"	David Henry, Jun.	"	Mrs. Abigail Deely,	"
Bill Blake & Co.	"	Samuel Mead,	"	Aaron Bennett,	Alstead
Levi Colby,	"	Daniel Marsh,	"	Nathaniel Evans,	"
Ephraim Cutter,	"	Moses Mead, Jun.	"	James Hoyt 2,	"
Mathew Deekey,	"	Mrs. Rebeckah Miller,	"	Samuel Kidder,	"
Miss Hepzebeth Foster,	"	David Mack,	"	Samuel Leomis,	"
Roger Fenton,	"	Alpheus Paul,	"	Jeremiah Robbins,	"
Samuel Grant 3,	"	Mrs. Hannah Robinson,	"	Mr. Hill,	"
Miss Nancy Graham,	"	Widow Mary Smith,	"	Isiah Hackett,	Westmoreland
William Guile,	"	Oliver Sparhawk 2,	"	Josiah White,	"
Gilbert Griswold,	"	Widow Lois Steel,	"	David Adams,	"

† [1a] Calvin Bemis adv. that he has the kine pox vaccine, and he "will inoculate all persons upon the most reasonable terms." The adv. states that Bemis lives in the house formerly occupied by Mr. Alex. Thomas. Dated at Walpole, 2 Oct. 1809.

† [1a] Nathan Willey adv. for money he found "between the Turnpike Gate, and Capt. Carpenter's in Walpole"; dated there 19 Aug. 1809.

† [1b] Legal noticed regarding the estate of Quincy Wellington, Larnard Mann, Adm. Dated at Alstead, 14 Sept. 1809.

† [3c] Ordinations: in Bernardston, Mass., "on the 20th inst." the Rev. Timothy F. Rogers over the Congregational Church. Also, "in Middletown," Rev. Dan Huntington.

† [3c] List of letters remaining at the post office in Charlestown, N.H., 1 Oct. 1809, as compiled by F.A. Sumner, Postmaster:

Parker Butterfield, Acworth	Howard Reed, Charlestown, N.H.
William Boyd, "	Martin Stevens, " "
John Barnard, Alstead, N.H.	Clarissa Sartwell, Claremont, N.H.
Polly Kemp, " "	Moody Dusten, " "
George Atkins, Charlestown, N.H.	Sally C. Goodenow, Langdon.
Asa Burrows, " "	Joseph Willard, "
George Barnard, " "	Comfort Wilcox, Lempster.
Samuel Chamberlin, " "	Perez Chapen, Newport.
Laura Cheney, " "	Nathaniel Burge, jun., Springfield, Vt.
Francisco Demorasci, " "	Calvin Day, " "
William Fiske, " "	Willard L. Hodgman, " "
Joseph Ford, " "	James Hall, " "
Charlotte Grinnell, " "	David Harlow, " "
Parley Holmes, " "	John Leland, " "
Zacheus Hale, " "	Lemuel Maynard, " "
Deborah Hoar, " "	Joseph Packard, " "
David Judkins, " "	Esther Spencer, " "
Amos Johnson, " "	Roswell Ward, " "
David Putnam, " "	Lemuel Whitney, " "
Bayley Putnam, " "	

† [3d] Joseph Axtell adv. a farm for sale at Grafton; dated there 2 Oct. 1809.

† [3d] Legal notice regarding the estate of John Marvin, late of Surry, deceased; Jonathan Royce, Adm. Estate business to be conducted at the house of Marvin's widow; dated at Walpole 6 Oct. 1809.

† [3d] Legal notice regarding the insolvent estate of Ambrose Cossit, Esq., late of Claremont, deceased. Thomas Warner, Alex. Pukens, and Joel Richards appointed Commissioners. Estate business to be conducted at the house of Theo. Clark, Innholder at Claremont. Dated at Claremont 3 Oct. 1809.

† [3d] Salmon Bellows adv. for a stray heifer; dated at Walpole 6 Oct. 1809.

† [3d] William Hildreth offers reward for his lost oxen; dated at Chesterfield, 5 Oct. '09.

===== ¶ [3c] MARRIED. =====

In Halifax, (N.S.) at the seat of Sir John Wentworth, Bart. Richard Cunningham, Esq. of Windsor, to Miss Sarah Athorp Morton, eldest daughter of the Hon. Perez Morton, of Boston, and neice of Lady Wentworth.

In Lebanon, (Con.) Benjamin Stillman, Esq. professor of chemistry and natural history, in Yale College, to Miss Harriot Trumbull, daughter of the late Governour Trumbull.

===== ¶ [3c] DIED. =====

In Westfield, Asher Eager, Esq. aged 64, one of the representatives of that town to the General Court.—In New London, Mr. Ebenezer Dunton, aged 94.—In Providence, Mr. Lewis Bosworth, aged 64.—In Pawlet, Mr. Aaron Sanford, aged 64.—In Hardwick, Paul Mendell, Esq. aged 86.—In Wilbraham, Dea. Ezekiel Ladd, aged 95.—In Burlington, Mrs. Dorcas Wood, aged 65.—In Marblehead, Mrs. Hannah Cowell, aged 48.—In New York, George Clinton, jun. late a representative in congress from that state.—In Mount Vernon, after a short and distressing illness, Lieut. James Smith, aged 25.

Vol. XV (No. 52) Monday, 16 Oct. 1809.

† [3d] Allan Melvill offers reward for return of merchandise stolen from his store in Boston; dated 9 Oct. 1809.

† [3d] Legal notice regarding the estate of Thomas Wallace, late of Acworth, deceased; Joseph Wallace, Adm. The notice mentions that the estate auction includes the "dwelling house & barn thereon; situated on Charlestown Turnpike road, about 2 miles east of Acworth meeting-house . . . " Dated at Acworth, 6 Oct. 1809.

† [3d] J.P. Batchelder, Physician, informs "the inhabitants of Charlestown, that he has taken lodgings with N. Lovell, Esq. . . . " and mentions that he will also innoculate for the Kine Pox. Dated at Charlestown 12 Oct. 1809.

† [3d] List of nonresident proprietors and owners of land in Springfield, N.H. who are delinquent on their taxes for the year 1809, as compiled by Reubin Hoyt, Collector. The property to be auctioned off at the house of Major J. Quinby, Springfield. The list contains a breakdown of lot number, acreage, etc., though only the names of the property owners are included here:

    Lt. John Swett   Jona. Wilson, Esq.
    Capt. Stephen Kimball   George Hough
    Capt. Wm. Rowell   Maj. James McLure
    Ann Ordway   Simeon Ladd & Lamson

Vol. XVI (No. 1) Monday, 23 Oct. 1809.

† [3c] Article mentioning that Thomas G. Fessenden, Esq., is now the editor of the *Brattleborough Reporter*, and his brother, Mr. W. Fessenden, is the paper's proprietor.

† [3d] An unusual adv. of "Bank Mineral Rod" by Simon Twistum.

===== ¶ [3d] DIED. =====

In Richmond, (Virg.) Maj. W. Armistead; an officer in the revolutionary war;—Mr. Wm. Claiborne, father of the governour of New Orleans Territory.—In Sharon, (N.Y.) Mr. ——— Austin:—[In attempting to drive a bull from an enclosure into which he had broken, he was obliged to beat the stubborn animal severely before he would quit the field.—The next day the young man went to repair the breach in the fence ; the bull no sooner saw him than he began to excite the sand with his feet—roar and make towards him ; and while attempting to drive the bull back, the enraged animal with his horns tore the young man's body in a shocking manner, and then placed himself directly over the mangled victim, and viewed him with a kind of indignant satisfaction, as if conscious of past injury and present revenge ; nor was it in the power of numbers who came to assist the young man to stir the brute from his position ; the body was taken from under him, and he shot before he could be moved.]—In Marlborough, (Mas.) colonel James Wesson, aged 72.—In Newyork, Mr. Lews Jones, jun. printer, aged 31.— In Pittsfield, Mr. Philip Bagley, aged 33, while standing behind the counter, giving the price of goods, he fell and died immediately.—In Keene, on Friday last, Mrs. Mary Wilder, consort of Mr. John Wilder, aged 28.

In this town, on the 13th inst. Harriot, daughter of Mr. Benjamin Muzzy, Æt. 4 y's.

Vol. XVI (No. 2) Monday, 30 Oct. 1809.

† [3c-d] Adv. of a farm for sale by Asahel Hunt; dated Charlestown, N.H. Oct. 1809.

† [3d] Adv. regarding the annual meeting of the Walpole Social Library, S.R. Whitman, Librarian. Dated Walpole 28 Oct. 1809.

† [3d] Legal notice regarding the estate of Calvin Eaton, deceased, mentioning the estate auction at the house of the widow, Comfort Eaton; Josiah Eaton and Levi Allen, Administrators. Dated at Walpole, 27 Oct. 1809.

† [3d] Legal notice regarding the estate of John March, late of Walpole, deceased; Levi Allen, Adm. Dated Walpole, 27 Oct. 1809.

† [3d] Isaac H. Ely adv. for a stray horse; dated Charlestown, 16 Oct. 1809.

† [3d] Adv. for the Haverhill Academy Lottery; S.P. Webster, William Tarlton, and E. Kingsbury, Managers; dated Haverhill 19 Oct.

¶ [3c] MARRIED.

In Alstead, Mr. William Simons, to Miss Huldy Yeomans.
In New Ipswich, Benjamin Champney, Esq. to Miss Rebecca Brooks.
In Concord, William Draper, Esq. attorney at law, of Marlborough, to Miss Eliza Paine, of the former place.
In New York, Mr. William H. Webster, the celebrated Songster and Comedian, to Miss Rebecca Meirckin, of Philadelphia.

¶ [3c] DIED.

At Bluehill, Mass. Ebenezer Floyd, Esq. representative from that town to the state legislature.—In England, Matthew Bolton, Esq. F.R.S. eminent as enterprising and successful in establishing manufactures ; Lord H. Stuart, aged 34 ; Andrew Mackay, L.L.D. F.R.S. In Newman Street, London, Peter Johonnet, Esq. formerly of Boston, New England.—In Boston, Mr. James Muzzy, aged 23.—In Montreal, (Canada) Robert Fletcher, Esq. of Boston, aged 47.

Vol. XVI (No. 3) Monday, 6 Nov. 1809.

† [3c-d] Legal notice regarding the insolvent estate of John Worster, late of Alstead, deceased. Estate business to be conducted at the house of the widow. Larnard Mann, Samuel Kingsbery, and Nathaniel Vilas, Commissioners. Dated Alstead, 28 Oct. 1809.
† [3d] Adv. for *Stone & Bellows*, dated Walpole, 6 Nov. 1809.
† [3d] William Mitchell adv. for a lost pocket book, which he lost between his house and that of Aaron Kemp's, in Acworth. Dated Acworth, 30 Oct. 1809.
† [3d] Adv. for the *New Hampshire Register*, published by George Hough and Daniel Cooledge. The publishers purchased from Samuel Curtis, Esq., of Amherst, all interest in publication of the Register. Dated Concord 18 Sept. 1809.

Vol. XVI (No. 4) Monday, 13 Nov. 1809.

¶ [3b] The house and store of Messrs. Goodale & Holmer, of Jaffrey, were consumed by fire, with their contents, on the 5th inst.
† [3b] Ordinations: 1) "on the 13th ult." Rev. Nathan Felch, Jr., at the Episcopal Church in Bedford, N.Y. 2) Rev. John Laughton, at the Congregational Church in Windham, Vermont.
† [3c] Adv. of axes for sale, by Henry Rice, whose shop is on the west side of the common. Dated Walpole, 11 Nov. 1809.
† [3c] John Denison adv. for items he found on the turnpike between the gate and Southard's tavern; dated Walpole 10 Nov. 1809.
† [3c] Legal notice regarding the insolvent estate of Charles Bowen, late of Charlestown, N.H.; claims to be examined "at Shepley's." John Willard, Roswell Hunt, and Joseph Roley appointed Commissioners. Dated Charlestown 21 Oct. 1809.
† [3c] Legal notice regarding the insolvent estate of Asa Nichols, late of Charlestown, N.H., deceased; Alpheus Nichols, Adm. Nathan Allen, Lewmon Huntley, and William Neal appointed Commissioners. Dated Charlestown, 21 Oct. 1809.
† [3d] Dr. Samuel Lee offers a reward for the capture and conviction of those producing and selling "Dr. Lee's Bilious Pills," of which Lee holds the patent. In the adv., Lee accused one John Crosby of Ashby, Mass. of pirating his patent. Lee resided in the town of Windham, though the state is not specified; Dr. Isaac Thompson of New London is mentioned in the adv., as was Lee's attorney, I. Thompson.

¶ [3b] MARRIED.

In Rutland, Vt. Mr. Abel Page to Miss Zilpha Barnes.
In Pawlet, Joel Doolittle, Esq. of Middlebury, to Miss Sally Fitch.

¶ [3b-c] DIED.

In Acworth, on the 2d inst. the widow Mehitable Smith, aged 85. She was one of the first settlers of the town.
Died in Charlestown on Monday the 6th instant, the Rev. Dan Foster, aged 62 [. . .] For sixteen years he statedly ministered to the church and people of Charlestown [. . .]

Vol. XVI (No. 5) Monday, 20 Nov. 1809.

† [2d-3a] Account of three American ships captured by French Privateers, the *Laconia*, of Portsmouth, (N.H.?), Capt Walker, The *Henrietta*, of Boston, Capt. John Nichols, and the *Resolution*, of New York, Capt. Bunker. The *Resolution* was seized and destroyed, the *Henrietta* was taken as prize, and the *Laconia* was released on ransom. Three crew members of the *Laconia*, Joseph W. Weld and Enoch Haslet (seamen), and Samuel Pray (mate), were held as hostages. ◆

† [3d] Legal notice regarding the estate of Josiah Swett, late of Claremont, deceased; Nathaniel Draper, David Stone, and Dan Baldwin appointed Commissioners. Dated at Claremont, 8 Nov. 1809.

¶ [3d] *Auphea*, My wife, has eloped from my bed and board, and has made a practice in so doing; this is therefor to forbid all persons harbouring or trusting her on my account, for I will pay no debts of her contracting after this date.

THOMAS DARBY.
Westmoreland, Nov. 16, 1809.

===== ¶ [3c] MARRIED. =====

In Croydon, Mr. Isaac Newton, of Newport, to Mrs. Hepzibah Eastman.
In Cornish, Mr. Gridley Dorr, to Miss Roxilana Kimball.
In Boston, J.E. Foxcroft, Esq. of New Gloucester, to Miss Abigail Hammond.

===== ¶ [3c-d] DIED. =====

In New Orleans, Alpheus Roberts, Esq. 2d lieut. of the United States artillery, formerly of Plainfield, N.H.—In Weathersfield, Con. col. John Chester, an officer of great merit in [? ? ?][196]—In Wilbraham, Hon. John Bliss, aged 83 ; late one of the judges of the court of common pleas—formerly a member of the executive council, and for a length of time a member of the senate or house of representatives of the commonwealth.—In Philadelphia, during the week ending 4th inst. 32, viz. 8 men, 10 women, 8 boys and 6 girls, of consumption 6.—In Albany, Mrs. Elizabeth, relict of the late Rev. Joseph Treat, aged [72?].—In Northampton, Mr. Morrise Lamprey, aged 97 y's 10 months.—In Lyme, capt. Abner Lee, aged 83.—In Saybrook, Mr. Benj. Jones, 98.— In Rochefort prison (France) capt. Andrew Tucker of Marblehead, late master of ship William of Newburyport, one of the vessels condemned in France, and her crew imprisoned by our "good ally" Napoleon.—In New York, Joseph Stansbury, Esq. sec'y of the United Insurance Co. aged 59.—In Boothbay, Jonathan Sawyer, Esq. aged 61.— In Cornish, Mr. Moses Parker, of Standish, in crossing Saco river he was thrown from his horse and drowned.

Vol. XVI (No. 6) Monday, 27 Nov. 1809. [197]

† [3d] Edward Slader, Director of the Charlestown Turnpike Road, adv. a meeting to be held at the house of Mr. J. Shepley, Charlestown, N.H. Dated Acworth 16 Nov. '09.
† [3d] List of nonresident proprietors and owners of land in Wendell, N.H., who are delinquent for their taxes in the years 1808 and 1809, as compiled by Samuel Rogers, Collector; land to be auctioned off at the house of Richard C. Rogers, in Wendell. The list contains a breakdown of lot number, acreage, etc., though only the owners' names are presented here:

> Benjamin Brotton, 10 acres, part of a lot that Giles Bartlett formerly owned.
> Charles Emerson.
> Wid. Rebecca Hardy.
> Amos Avery 1 acre arable land formerly owned by John Avery, lying by R.C. Rogers.[198]
> Jere. Kelley 1/2 acre formerly owned by Daniel Moses.

† [3d] Aaron Baker adv. for a tippet which he found; dated Walpole 20 Nov. 1809.
† [3d] "Steppn" (misprint of Stephen?) Rice or J. Maynard & Co. adv. for shoe-thread; dated Walpole 24 Nov. 1809.

===== ¶ [3c] MARRIED. =====

In Litchfield, Conn. Theron Metcalf, Esq. of Dedham, Mass. to Miss Julia Tracy, daughter of the late Hon. Uria Tracy.

In Boston, Mr. Nathaniel H. Wright, printer, to Miss Mary Hudson.

====== ¶ [3c] DIED. ======

In Hartland, col. Uriel Holmes, aged 68.—In Worcester, Mr. Benjamin Whitney, aged 98;—Mrs. Mary, wife of Mr. Alpheus Thayer, aged 29 ; Mr. Oliver Kingsbury, aged 27, formerly of Coventry, Conn. a respectable teacher of youth.—In Chelmsford, Oliver Barron, Esq. aged 77.—In the Alms-house, Boston, Mr. Joshua Curtis, hatter, late of Danbury, Con. in a fit of insanity, he leaped from a second story window, and expired soon after.—In Shelburne, on the 5th inst. the Rev. Bethuel Chittenden, aged 70 years.—On the day of his death, he rode about half a mile, to a place of publick worship, with an intention of preaching and administering the sacrament, and was apparently in as good health as usual, but a moment before he expired. He was a brother of the late Governour Chittenden, and was a man of exemplary piety.—Near Black-River, N.C. Mr. Walter Strachan;—shot by a negro boy :—(The reason assigned by the boy for killing his master was, he was fearful of being punished for some offence committed.)—In Augusta, (Geo.) Mr. David Bull, mer. aged 26, son of Jona. B. Esq. of Hartford, Con.—This is the fifth child Mr. Bull has lost in less than nine moths [sic].—In Philadelphia, during the week ending 11th inst. 50, viz. 28 adults, 22 children ; of consumption 4, whooping cough 5.—In New York, Philo Schofield :—(Killed, by Samuel Hackwood, in an affray which arose from gambling : H. has been sentenced to 14 years imprisonment for manslaughter.)—In Northampton, widow Mary Rust, aged 95.—In Conway (of the spotted fever) Mr. Medad Chittenden, jun. aged 20.—In Tennessee, Gov. Lewis, of Upper Louisiana.

In Langdon, on the 13th inst. of a consumption, Mrs. Prudence Burr, wife of Mr. Laban Burr, aged 30 years.

Vol. XVI (No. 7) Monday, 4 Dec. 1809.

† [2c-d] Account of a fire in Portsmouth, N.H. which destroyed the shop belonging to Messrs. John and Butler Abbot, tanners. ♦

¶ [3a] DISTRESSING. On the 15th ult. a barn belonging to Mr. Abel Larkin, of Lyndeboro', was consumed by fire. Two of his daughters, aged 10 and 6, and a son of Mr. T. Larkin, aged 2, were unfortunately consumed in the flames.

¶ [3c] ORDAINED. In Penobscot, Rev. Philip Spaulding, over the congregational church and society.

† [3d] *Shepard & Hutchinson* request debtors to pay up; dated Newport 21 Nov. 1809.
† [3d] Samuel Hutchinson requests debtors to pay up; dated Alstead 22 Nov. 1809.
† [3d] Meigs Buel adv. for a lost mare; dated Walpole 28 Nov. 1809.
† [3d] Jesse Healy adv. for a stray horse that he found; dated Charlestown 28 Nov. '09.

====== ¶ [3c] MARRIED. ======

In this town, by the Rev. Mr. Fessenden, Mr. Prosper Boothe, to Miss Lucinda Jenison.

In Springfield, (Penn.) Hon. James Lloyd, jun. Esq. of Boston, to Miss Breck, daughter of the late Samuel B. Esq.

====== ¶ [3c-d] DIED. ======

In Portland, Mrs. Mary Merrill, aged 84.—In Farmington, Moses Starling, Esq. Æt. 61.—In Portsmouth, Mons. L. La Tappy, aged 67.—In New Jersey, col. Thomas Dowry. —In Barnstable, Homes Allen, Esq. aged 35.—In Cambridge, Joseph Prescott, aged 21 ; resident graduate at the University.—In Boston, Wm. Cooper, Esq. aged 88 years, 49 of which he was successfully elected Town Clerk, and during that time was never absent at a town meeting ; After a long confinement, Wm. Brown, Esq. aged 77. His early services as a naval commander in the defence of our independence, will long be remembered with gratitude by all the friends of the revolution.

Vol. XVI (No. 8) Monday, 11 Dec. 1809.

† [3c] Joseph Cobb adv. "that he has taken the shop belonging to F.W. Geyer, Esq. at Bellows' Falls, Rockingham" where he carries on boot and shoe-making. Dated Rockingham 6 Dec. 1809.

† [3d] Jessee Wilcox, Jun., Treasurer, posts a notice regarding a public vendue of the

Croydon Turnpike Corporation to be held at Farnsworth's Tavern, Washington, N.H. Notice dated at Newport 6 Dec. 1809.

† [3d] Legal notice regarding John Fay, of Newgrantham, who is under the guardianship of John Brown. The notice is dated 5 Dec. 1809, though no town is identified.

† [3d] Alph. M. Hunt and Lewis Hunt adv. that they have taken the stand recently occupied by Col. Asahel Hunt, where they operate a new tavern. Dated Charlestown 9 Dec. 1809.

Vol. XVI (No. 9) Monday, 18 Dec. 1809.

† [3d] Legal notice regarding the insolvent estate of Henry Allen, late of Charlestown, N.H., deceased; estate business to be conducted at Joseph Allen's Tavern in Charlestown. F.A. Sumner, Enos Stevens, and Jona. Baker appointed Commissioners; Benj. Laberee, Adm. Dated at Charlestown, 18 Nov. 1809.

† [3d] E. Wright, Secretary, adv. a Masonic Festival; dated Charlestown, 12 Dec. 1809.

† [3d] S.R. Whitman, Librarian, adv. a meeting of the proprietors of the Walpole Library to be held at Southard's Tavern. Dated 16 Dec. 1809.

Vol. XVI (No. 10) Monday, 25 Dec. 1809.

† [3d] Capt. S.R. M'Lellan, of the brig Henry, rescues his vessel from French Privateers, who had captured it 6 Nov. ♦

† [3d] Luther Jeudwine adv. for lost horses; dated Charlestown, 12 Dec. 1809.

† [3d] Samuel Hutchinson adv. goods for sale; dated Alstead 18 Dec. 1809.

===== ¶ [3d] DIED. =====

In Croydon, on the 7th inst. Mr. Benjamin Powers, son of Stephen Powers, Esq. first male child born in that town, aged 42.—In Rutland, Mrs. Eunice Pratt, consort of Mr. Nathan Pratt, Jr. aged 25.

Vol. XVI (No. 11) Monday, 1 Jan. 1810.

† [3c] James Cochrane posts a notice that "he is about closing business in this village," and requests debtors to pay up. Dated Walpole, 1 Jan. 1810.

† [3d] List of letters remaining at the Post Office in Walpole, N.H., 1 Jan. 1810, as compiled by O. Allen, Postmaster:

David Aldrich, Walpole	Shubael Conant, Walpole	Benjamin Muzzey, Walpole
Rhoda Avery, "	Josiah Crosby, Langdon	Daniel Markum, "
Job Anger, Acworth	Samuel Edgarton, "	Silas Merrifield, "
Hubard Bellows, Walpole	Eliphalet Dart, Surry	Daniel Marsh, "
Col. C. Bellows, "	Silas Aldrich, Walpole	Cady Parks, "
Titus Brown, Alstead	Isaac Farr, "	Jane Rugg, "
Laban Burr, Langdon	Richard Emerson, Stoddard	Thomas R. Bow, "
Simon Baxter, Surry	Enos Goodale, "	Sartile Prentiss, Alstead
Parker Butterfield, Acworth	Eliphalet Fox, Walpole	Oliver Sparhawk 3, Walpole
Zenas Bingham, Gilsum	Nath. Fay, Alstead	Henry Scovel, "
Elijah Bixby, Walpole	Wm. Marvin, Langdon	Ephraim Sherman, "
Josiah Bellows, "	Levi Green, Westmoreland	Sylvester Smith, Surry
Clark Brown, "	Samuel Hutchinson, Alstead	Mary Thompson, Walpole
Josiah Bellows 2d, 2, Walpole	Jeremiah Higbee, "	Polly Taylor, "
James Campbell, "	Ephraim Kingsbury, "	Joseph White, "
Jesse Carpenter, "	Israel Kent, "	William D. Wheeler, "
John Carlisle, "	John Ingols, Walpole	Edmond Wellington, Alstead
Zachariah Carpenter, "	George Kemball, Langdon	
Elijah Carpenter, "	John Livingston, Walpole	

† [3d] Runaway notice for one John Ball, "supposed to be deranged." Ball was said to be about 35 years old; the notice contains his physical description, as well as a description of the clothing he was wearing when he was last seen, 17 Nov. 1809. "He has left a handsome property in the care of an aged mother; which, with all the trouble of his absence, has brought her to a low state of health." The notice was posted by Bulah Ball, and dated at Langdon, N.H., 28 Dec. 1809.

† [3d] Joseph Bellows, Jun. and Thomas Bellows, 2d, a.k.a. *J.&T. Bellows* post a notice that their copartnership was dissolved 26 Dec. 1809, and that Thomas Bellows, 2d has purchased the stock in trade owned by the company.

===== ¶ [3c] MARRIED. =====

In Acworth, Mr. Jesse Thornton to Miss Betsey Campbell ; Mr. James Southard to Miss Hannah Wilcox ; Mr. Richard Clark of Langdon, to Miss Sally Thornton, of the former place.

===== ¶ [3c] DIED. =====

In Washington, Caleb Swan, Esq. late paymaster Gen. of the United States army.— On his passage from St. Vincents, Mr. Theodore Hart, native of Portsmouth.—Near the Potomac, (Maryl'd side) Mr. Peyton B. Smith, eldest son of Gen. John Smith, representative in Congress from Virginia; killed in a duel by Mr. Joseph Holmes of Winchester, (Virg.)—In Royalton, Mrs. Parkhurst, aged 92, consort of Mr. Joseph Parkhurst.

Vol. XVI (No. 12) Monday, 8 Jan. 1810.

† [3d] List of letters remaining at the Post Office in Charlestown, N.H., 1 Jan. 1810, as compiled by F.A. Sumner, Postmaster:

Asa Harrington, Acworth, N.H.	Mary Griswould, Springfield, Vt.
John Keyes, "Alstead or Langdon"	William Gilkey, " "
Elias Bacon, Charlestown, N.H.	Asa Hooper, " "
Rhoda Castleton, " "	Benoni Lockwood, " "
Nancy Hannars, " "	Amos Randal, " "
Perley Holmes, " "	Jacob Bartlett, Unity, N.H.
Joseph B. Hinds, " "	Jacob Kanady, " "
William Gunnison, Fishersfield, N.H.	James Ladd, " "
William Cheney, Newport, N.H.	Joseph Straw, " "
Ruth Bugbee, Springfield, Vt.	

¶ [3c-d] DIED.

In England, Charles Bourne, Esq.; formerly a colonel in his B.M's service : He distinguished himself during the war with America. In Charleston, Capt. Wm. M. Harris, master of the Spanish brig Felicity : He died of a wound received in his thigh from a large Spanish clasp-knife, but by whom inflicted not known.—Near Manchester, (Virg.) John Steveningham, Esq. aged 50; a native of England.—In Baltimore, General Thomas Sprigg, aged 62.—In Maryland, Miss Harriot, daughter of Wm. Seton, Esq. of N. York, aged 22.—In Philadelphia, Isaac Snowden, Esq. aged 78.—During the week ending 23d ult. 44, viz. 25 adults, 19 ch. ; of consumption 7, apo[p]lexy 3.—In N. York, during the week ending 23d ult. 45, viz. 29 adults, 16 ch. of consumption 10 ; casualties 2, viz. Capt. Garret Barry, choaked in eating, and a child to whom a dose of laudanum was administered by mistake.—In Easton, (Mass.) Rev. William Reed, aged 54, and 26th of his Ministry.—In Dorchester, Widow Elizabeth Roulstone, aged XCVIII.

Vol. XVI (No. 13) Monday, 15 Jan. 1810.

¶ [3c] MARRIED.

In Acworth, Mr. Jeduthan Waldo, of Alstead, to Miss Lucy Markham ; Mr. Manly Humphrey, to Miss Ireana Lastis.
In Alstead, Mr. Moses Miller, to Miss Sally Drury.

¶ [3c] DIED.

In Charlestown, Miss Lucretia M'Carty.—In New Haven, Mr. Caleb Cooper, aged 74.—In Canterbury, widow Dorcas Perkins, aged 70.—In Yarmouth, (Eng.) Mr. Thomas Shatswell, of Salem, aged 28.—In St. Jago de Cuba, Nov. 12, 1809, capt. Jonathan Wiggin, late of Moultonborough, (N.H.) and master of a vessel out of Salem ; he was interred in the Cathedral there.—In New York, during the week ending 30th ult. 49, viz. 14 men, 14 women, 14 boys, and 7 girls; of consumption 12.

Vol. XVI (No. 14) Monday, 22 Jan. 1810.

† [3d] Charles Storer, "Agent of the company for rendering Connecticut River navigable by Bellows' Falls," posts a listing of toll rates for the Bellows' Falls Canal; dated 17 Jan. 1810.
† [3d] Legal notice regarding the estate of Palsgrave Wellington, late of Alstead, deceased, Abigail Wellington, Executrix. Dated Alstead 10 Jan. 1810.
† [3d] Legal notice regarding the estate of Quincy Wellington, late of Alstead, deceased, Larnard Mann, Adm.; dated Alstead 10 Jan. 1810.
† [3d] Elijah Kittredge adv. "that he has commenced the stone cutting business about one mile and a half west of the old meeting-house in Alstead, at Mr. Arad Worster's." Dated at Alstead 13 Jan. 1810.

Vol. XVI (No. 15) Monday, 29 Jan. 1810.

No news items of significance found within this issue.

Vol. XVI (No. 16) Monday, 5 Feb. 1810.

† [3d] Harvey Chase, Clerk, posts a notice regarding the annual meeting of the Cornish Turnpike, to be held at the the house of Eleazer Jackson, Cornish, N.H. Dated there 5 Feb. 1810.

¶ [3d] MARRIED.

In Chelsea, Vt. Mr. S.B. Dana, merchant, to Miss Mittia Caldwell, both of Boston.
In New York, John A. King, Esq. (Son of the Hon. Rufus King) to Miss Mary Ray;—Mr. Nicholas Schroeder, of Germany, to Mrs. Mary Paul, relict of capt. John Paul, of Portsmouth.
In Newburyport, Mr. John L. Shannon, to Miss Sarah F. Blunt.
In Plaistow, N.H. Rev. Ab'm Burnham, of Pembroke, to Miss Mary White.
In Cheshire, Ambrose Kasson, Esq. of Adams, to Miss Laura Hill.

¶ [3d] DIED.

In Germantown, (Penn.) John Johnson, aged 62 ; of the Society of Friends.—In Middletown, (Con.) Mrs. Elizabeth, wife of capt. Comfort Goodwin, aged 38 ; she went to bed in usual health, and was found dead in the morning ;—Mrs. Ruth Jackson, aged 78.—In Pittsfield, Mr. ——— Howard, aged 85.—In Hopkinton, Major Isaac Chandler ;—Major ——— Jones ; deacon Nathan Clements, aged [60?] ; he went to bed in good health, and was found dead in the morning.—In Malden, Mrs. Mary Perkins, aged 91.—In Boston, Mr. Joseph Young, aged 55.—In Hartford, (Mary.) Mr. Wm. H. Wood, aged 40 ; for the last 20 years he had been a preacher in the methodist connexion ; Ann Morgan, aged 93, of the Society of Friends.—In Middletown, (Penn.) Mr. Increase Tilton, aged 96.—In New Germantown, N.J. Dr. Oliver Barnet, aged 66, late marshal of the district of New Jersey.—In Litchfield, Mr. John Wilmot, jun. he accidentally fell under the wheel of a loaded cart, and was crushed to death.—In Woburn, two young men, named Brooks:—froze to death in the woods in the late severe weather.—In Boston, Samuel West, Esq. aged 38, eldest son of the late Rev. Dr. W.— Lately, at the seat of her son, Ebenezer Jackson, Esq. Middletown, Conn. Mrs. Ruth Jackson, relict of the late Gen. Michael Jackson, of Newton, Mass.—In Northampton, Mr. Wm. Stockwell, aged 60 ; Mrs. Patience, wife of Mr. [Moses?] Bartlett. During the last year, 32, 15 under 5 years.

Vol. XVI (No. 17) Monday, 12 Feb. 1810.

This issue is missing from the microfilm.

Vol. XVI (No. 18) Monday, 19 Feb. 1810.

† [1b] Benjamin Rich offers a farm for sale at Claremont, N.H.; dated 31 Jan. 1810.
† [1b] Jesse Wilcox, Jr., Treasurer, posts a notice regarding the Croydon Turnpike; dated at Newport, 6 Feb. 1810.
† [3d] Leverett Tuttle adv. property for sale in Grafton, Vt., he "being out of health," and "wishes to close business for the present." Dated at Grafton, 17 Jan. 1810.
† [3d] Abraham Brown, Jr., adv. that he "has sold his Carding Machine, and is about to leave this place," and requests debtors to pay up. Dated at Walpole 16 Feb. 1810.

Vol. XVI (No. 19) Monday, 26 Feb. 1810.

† [3d] List of non-resident proprietors and owners of land in Unity, N.H., who are delinquent for taxes owed for the year 1809, as compiled by Jeremiah S. Chase, Collector. Delinquent property to be auctioned at the house of Jacob Bartlett in Unity. The heading in the newspaper list specifically states that these persons were the "original proprietors." The list contains a breakdown of lot number, acreage, etc., though only the names of the owners are presented here:

Nathaniel Barre *	Nathaniel French	John Sherburn	
James Bean	Ben. Wentworth	John Moulton	
Cornelius Clough	Isaac Godfrey	Mesheck Wear	
William Long	William Buswell		[* listed twice.

† [3d] Legal notice regarding a conflict in the estate of Absalom Kingsbury, late of Alstead, deceased, Ephraim Kingsbury, Executor. Joseph Willard and Rebecca his wife in her right appealed a decree made by a probate judge regarding said estate.

Vol. XVI (No. 20) Monday, 5 March 1810.

† [3d] Legal notice regarding the estate of Levi Brown, late of Charlestown, deceased; William Bond, John Densmore, and Henry Hubbard appointed Commissioners. Estate business to be conducted at the house of Josiah Shepley, Charlestown. Dated there 2 March 1810.
† [3d] Settlement of debts requested by Isaac Redington, or *Redington & Seaver*; dated at Walpole 3 March 1810.

¶ [3d] DIED.

In Rockingham, Quartus Morgan, Esq. P.M. a very worthy and respectable citizen.

Vol. XVI (No. 21) Monday, 12 March 1810.

† [3c] Paragraph regarding the disputed age of Gov. Langdon, and of his brother Hon. Woodbury Langdon. ♦

===== ¶ [3d] DIED. =====

In Pittsford, Vt. on the 27th ult. Col. Benjamin Conley, an old and very respectable inhabitant of that town.

In Middlebury, on the 8th ult. Mrs. Mary Brooks, aged 82 years, relict of Mr. Benjamin Brooks, formerly of Northfield, Massachusetts.

At Philadelphia, Mr. Charles B. Brown, Editor of the American Register.

Vol. XVI (No. 22) Monday, 19 March 1810.

===== ¶ [3d] MARRIED. =====

In this town, Mr. John Chamberlain of Peterborough, to Miss Lydia Ripley of this town.

In Georgetown, (Col.)[199] Hon. Wm. B. Giles, of the U. States Senate, to Miss Frances Ann Gwynn, eldest daughter of the late Tho's Peyton Gwynn, of Virginia.

In Concord, Mr. Emerson Barrett, to Miss Martha Jones.

===== ¶ [3d] DIED. =====

In Lower Canada, Col. Abraham Cuyler, a native of Albany, and formerly mayor of that city.—In St. Albans, (Vt.) Capt. Wm. Weeks.—In Pittsford, (Vt.) Capt. John Sprague, of Bedford, (Ms.) aged 53, of spotted fever.

In Westford, (Vt.) Capt. Wm. Henry, aged 43 ; leaving a wife and 11 children under 15 years of age.—In Richmond, Deacon John Chamberlain, aged xc.—In Burlington, Mrs. Chloe, wife of Hon. Noah Smith.—In Portsmouth, Thomas Chadbourne, Esq.—In Hillsborough, (N.H.) of consumption, Mr. Jonathan Jones aged 32.—In Rutland, (Vt.) Mrs. Anna Prentiss, consort of Capt. John Prentiss, aged 60. [200]

Vol. XVI (No. 23) Monday, 26 March 1810.

† [3d] Hasadiah Smith adv. land for sale in Acworth; dated there 3 March 1810.

† [3d] A journeyman wheelwright is wanted by *Boothe & Cobb*; dated Walpole 23 Mar.

† [3d] William Briggs, Clerk, adv. the annual meeting of the Cheshire Bridge to be held at Shepley's in Charlestown; dated 20 March 1810.

===== ¶ [3d] DIED. =====

In Virginia, John Henderson, Esq.—In Newton, (N.H.) Rev. Nathan Woodhull, aged 54.—In Townshend, (Vt.) 16th ult. Mrs. Jane Hazelton, aged 103 years, relict of John H. Esq. ; She had seen her descendants to the number of 500, from the first to the 5th degree.—In Petersham, (Worcester county, Ms.) between Feb. 20 and 6th March, 5 deaths, of the *spotted fever*, viz. Phebe, daughter of Mr. James Babcock, aged 12 years; —Mehitable, daughter of Mr. John Negus, aged 14 y's ; Mary, daughter of Mr. Joel Negus, aged 27 months ; Clarissa, daughter of Mr. Caleb Willis, aged 16 years ; Ellen, daughter of Lewis Bigelow, Esq. aged 28 mo's. (The 7th inst. was set apart in Petersham, as a day of fasting, humiliation and prayer, in consequence of the prevalence of the above disease.)

In West Boylston, widow Sarah Goodale, aged 96 ; leaving six children, the youngest aged 60 y. and [120?] grand and great- gr. ch.—In Munson, Mr. Joseph Sessions, aged 25 ; a member of the senior class in Burlington (Vt.) University, and son of Col. Alexander Sessions, of Brimfield ;—The circumstances of his death were melancholy—on the morning of the 7th inst. he unfortunately made a fatal mistake by taking king's yellow instead of sulphur.—In York, (Maine) Rev. Isaac Lyman, aged 85 : To give a general sketch of his excellent character and worth, we might fill this paper with [panegyrick?] and just praises of the reverend Divine.—In Boston, Mr. Thomas Wells, aged 64.

Vol. XVI (No. 24) Monday, 2 April 1810.

¶ [3c] EXTRACTS OF LETTERS. "Barre, [Mass.—Ed.] March 20, 1810. That most dreadful disorder, the spotted fever, rages here in an awful manner, and in the vicinity. In my neighbourhood, four persons were intered yesterday (19th inst.) ; Capt. Jonas Eaton, Edmand Howes, Doctor Burrows, and the only child of Major S. Henry ; the latter, however, of a different complaint. Mrs. Perry attended the funeral of her brother yesterday, was seized with the disorder at nine in the evening, and died at three this morning—Mr. Perry is at this moment in a violent delirium, and not expected to live.—Mr. Thompson was in a very dangerous state through the night, but is a little better this morning. Last evening upwards of fifty cases were reported, and an additional number today. Not less than six or seven physicians, from other towns, are constantly here, but not sufficient to attend all the sick."

† [3d] List of letters remaining at the Post Office in Walpole, N.H., 1 April 1810, as compiled by O. Allen, Postmaster:

Esther Adams, Walpole.	Rebecca Miller, Walpole.	Roger Wolcott, Walpole.
Jesse Barrows, "	Hannah Mason, "	Mary Wyman, "
Susan Bundy, "	James Neal, "	James Edgerton, Langdon.
H. Bellows, "	Arvin Pierce, "	Abner Kneeland, "
D.W. Bisco, "	Solomon Robins, jr. "	James Prentiss, "
Elisha Eldrich, "	Calvin Stone, "	Eliab Sartwell, "
Joseph Fay, "	Steward & Cobb, "	J.H. Bingham, Alstead.
Sally Herbert, "	O. Sparhawk, "	Ebenezer Wilson, "
Jonathan Jenison, jr. "	Daniel Turner, "	
Jane Morison, "	Samuel Turner, "	

† [3d] Legal notice regarding the insolvent estate of Heman Redfield, *Saddler*, late of Claremont, deceased; David Dexter, Thomas Warner, and Theo. Clarke appointed Commissioners. Estate business to be conducted at the house of Daniel Chase, Innholder at Claremont. Dated Claremont 24 March 1810.

† [3c-d] List of non-resident proprietors and owners of land in Washington, N.H., who are delinquent for their taxes due for the year 1809, as compiled by James Faxon, Collector. Public auction for delinquent property to be held at the house of Mr. William Lawrence, Innholder at Washington. The list in the newspaper contains a breakdown of lot number, acreage, etc., though only the names of the owners are presented here:

Doct. Haven,	"Sally & March"	Nathan Carr
Thomas Packerd, Esq.	John Ringe, Esq.	Elnathan Blood
Joshua Pierce	Theodore Atkinson	Benjamin Sweat
Joseph Pierce, Esq.	Peter Pierce	Robert Carr
Capt. Isaiah Kidder,	William Whitimore	David Smiley
Maxwell Lot, 201	Jeremiah Bacon	

† [4a-d] Extensive medical description of the spotted fever, which was raging throughout parts of New England. The report was drawn up by Dr. Samuel Woodward, Physician at "Torringford"; the article mentions Dr. Mason F. Cogswell, of Hartford, and also a Dr. Ricketson. The fever was first reported in the town of Winchester, Litchfield County, Conn., in April 1807. [202]

===== ¶ [3c-d] DIED. =====

In Keene, Alexander Ralston, Esq. aged 64 ; Mrs. Stiles, relict of the late Jeremiah Stiles, Esq. aged 55.—At Oakham, Ms. of the Spotted Fever, Mr. Daniel Estabrooks, jr. and his wife, both buried in one grave.

In Claremont, 16th ult. Mrs. Sophia Redfield aged 22 Years. She was the second wife of Mr. Heman Redfield, who died February 1st, both of a consumption. Their only child Charles—aged 7 months died the 4th ult. Thus in the short term of 6 weeks a young and once healthy family has become extinct.

In Opelousas, (N.O. Terr.) [203] colonel John Thompson, late Register and Commissioner of Land Claims, and one of the Judges of the Superiour Court : He shot himself with a pistol.—In New Orleans, Mr. Michael Rellieux : Reported to be shot in a duel.—Near Natchez, Lieutenant Stephen Rose (of the 3d regt. U.S. inf.) killed by Mr. Andrew

H. Holmes, in a duel, at the first fire, distance 10 steps.—In Richmond, (Virg.) Mrs. Elizabeth, wife of Edmund Randolph, aged 56.—In Lancaster, (Penn.) the wife of Gov. Snyder.—In New York, Mrs. Eliza Laight, aged 84.—In Lyme, (C.) elder Jason Lee.

Vol. XVI (No. 25) Monday, 9 April 1810.

† [3d] Legal notice regarding the estate of Elijah Mason, late of Walpole, deceased, whose personal estate did not cover his debts. Hannah Mason and Levi Allen, Administrators, petitioned the Court for a license to sell Elijah's property (widow's dower excepted). Notice dated 4 April 1810.
† [3d] James Smith adv. a farm for sale at Langdon; dated there 4 April 1810.
† [3d] List of letters remaining at the Post Office in Charlestown, N.H., 1 April 1810, as compiled by F.A. Sumner, Postmaster:

Jonathan Rogers, Acworth.		Abner Kneeland, 2, Langdon.	
Joseph Whitney,	"	John Burroughs,	"
Samuel Bowman, Charlestown.		Simeon Brown, Springfield, Vt.	
Harry Brown,	"	Betsey Bugbee,	" "
Dean Carleton,	"	Jonathan Barnard,	" "
Laura Cheney,	"	Joseph Howe,	" "
Daniel Cone,	"	Lemuel Heywood,	" "
Jerusha Carpenter,	"	Edmond Lee,	" "
Amos Johnson,	"	Jesse Lankford,	" "
Uriah Searl,	"	Stephen Morse,	" "
John Simonds,	"	Sylvester Newton,	" "
Moses Shattuck,	"	Simon Randal,	" "
Levi Spencer,	"	Robinson Smiley,	" "
James Egerton, Langdon.		David Judkins, Unity.	
Polly Fish,	"	John Stoddard,	"

===== ¶ [3c] MARRIED. =====

In Haverhill, N.H. the Hon. Arthur Livermore, Esq. Chief Justice of this State, to Miss Louisa Bliss, of that town.

===== ¶ [3c-d] DIED. =====

In Ridgefield, Con. Mrs. Mary Chambers, aged 89.—In Trumbull, Dr. Miner Higby, aged 32.—In New Haven, Mrs. Hannah Thompson, aged 69 ; Mr. Justus Trowbridge, aged 36.—At sea, Capt. Elisha Atwater, of New Haven—washed overboard with the mate and cook.—In Roxbury, Mr. Elias Bates, aged 98.—In Middletown, Dr. Jehiel Hoadley, aged 66.—In North Stonington, Stephen Hall, Esq. aged 65.—In Windham, Mr. Eliphalet Palmer, aged 85.—In Bensalem, (Penn.) Mrs. Catharine Severns, aged 100, leaving 264 descendants.—In Baltimore, Peter Collins, Esq. aged 57, his Swedish majesty's consul for Maryland.—In Lancaster, (Pen.) Alexander Scott, Esq.—In Philadelphia, Mrs. Sarah, wife of Mr. Richard Thomas, aged 51.—In N. Utrecht, N.Y. Capt. James Apthorp, an officer in his Britannick majesty's service.—In Watervliet, N.Y. Cornelius Gleen, Esq.—In Whitestown, N.Y. of Spotted Fever, Mr. Pardon Powell.—In New York, Lieutenant Winlock Clarke, of the U.S. navy; in stepping from a brig, he fell between the brig and wharf, and drowned—He was a valuable officer.—In Rutland, Vt. on the 29th ult. Mrs. Charity Chipman, wife of G.D. Chipman, Esq. aged 22;—Mild as the breath of Spring, and blameless in her manners, she was beloved in life and is lamented in death.—In Windsor, Vt. suddenly, on the 4th inst. while on a visit, Rev. Joseph Brown, of Springfield formerly minister of Winchendon, Mass.

Vol. XVI (No. 26) Monday, 16 April 1810.

† [3d] Legal notice regarding the sale of the farm of Charles Bowen, late of Charlestown, N.H., deceased. Dated at Charlestown, [6?] April 1810.
† [3d] Amasa Allen requests the return of a "dirt scraper;" dated [Walpole] 14 Apr. '10.
† [3d] Oliver Allen adv. a room for rent for the tayloring business, formerly occupied by James Cochrane; dated Walpole 16 April 1810.

¶ [3d] DIED.

In this town, on the 11th inst. a daughter of Mr. Matthew Dickey, aged 12 years, of the Spotted Fever.

In Alstead, on Friday last, a child of Mr. Sam'l Kingsbury, aged 2 years, of the Spotted Fever.

Vol. XVI (No. 27) Monday, 23 April 1810.

† [3a] Brief article describing two robberies in Vermont, both having occurred 1 April 1810, as copied from the *Danville Star*: 1) Mr. Joseph True, of Wheelock, was robbed of about 1400 dollars, and 2) a horse, saddle and bridle were stolen from Samuel Morrill, Jr., of Danville, by one Benjamin Spencer, of Littleton, N.H. The latter was captured in northern N.H. and brought back to jail in Danville.

† [3d] Abiather Shaw, Secretary, posts a notice of the annual meeting of the "Band of Military Musick," to be held at the tavern of Mr. Brooks, Westmoreland, N.H. Dated there 17 April 1810.

¶ [3d] MARRIED.

In Roxbury, Mr. Wm. Crehore, of Milton, to Miss Sarah Clarke.

In New Orleans, Gen. James Wilkinson, to Mademoiselle Trudeau, handsome, accomplished, rich, and about 26 years of age : The General is about 56.

¶ [3d] DIED.

In Rutland, Vt. on the 11th inst. Mrs. Mary Page, wife of Wm. Page, Jun. Esq. aged 25 years ; a lady of distinguished worth ; endeared to a numerous acquaintance by the most graceful accomplishments, and amiable manners.

In this town, on the 15th inst. a child of Thomas Bellows, Esq. aged about one year.

Vol. XVI (No. 28) Monday, 30 April 1810.

† [1a] Adv. for the Hatfield Bridge Lottery; Samuel Porter, Isaac Abercrombie, Samuel F. Dickinson, Nathaniel Smith, and Medad Dickinson, Managers. Dated at Amherst, Mass., 22 March 1810.

† [2c-d] A brutal "editorial" regarding Stanley Griswold, formerly a minister in Conn., later editor of a competing newspaper in Walpole, but now a Judge of the Supreme Court of Illinois Territory, appointed by James Madison. ♦

† [3d] Ordinations: on the "10th inst." Rev. Daniel Haskell, over the "Calvinistick congregational church" at Burlington, Vt., and on the "20th inst." Rev. Samuel Clark, Jr., over the First Congregational Society, also at Burlington.

† [3d] Joseph Bridge adv. his new hat store, "lately occupied by Messrs. Grant & Sparhawk." Dated at Walpole 27 April 1810.

† [3d] Meigs Buel adv. that "he has commenced the tayloring business, in the Brick Building, over the store of Messrs. Stone & Bellows." Dated Walpole 25 April 1810.

¶ [3d] DIED.

In St. Thomas, Capt. Dummer Freeman, of Portland.—In Rutland, (N.Y.) 22d ult Dr. Richard Perkins, Æt. 44, son of Richard Perkins, Esq. of Bridgewater, (Ms.)—In England at the age of twenty-one, Benning William Bentick Wentworth, Esq. Lieutenant in his Brittanick Majesty's navy, and son of the Hon. Benning Wentworth, late Secretary of the Province of Nova Scotia. The legitimate descendant of the Earls of Stafford, and presumptive heir to the titles and honours of that Earldom, yet this accomplished youth was less distinguished by the adventitious nobleness of descent than by *the true nobility of nature*.

In Charleston, Peter Robut, Esq.—Near Norfolk, Dr. [Burgo?] Godwin.—In Westchester, (N.Y.) Richard Morris, Esq. late Chief Justice of N. York State.—In Swanton, (Vt.) Maj. G.W. Foster.—In St. Albans, (Vt.) Mr. Josiah Brigham. (The St. Albans paper of 5th inst. says, "It is a melancholy reflection that the spotted fever, which is now alarmingly prevalent in this, and more particularly so in some of the neighbouring towns, has already deprived the community of several characters in this vicinity, whose worth and influence were justly considered as essential to the good of society and the prosperity of their fellow citizens.")—In Stoneham, Col. Joseph Bayant aged 80. —In Needham, Dea. Joseph Daniels, aged 74.—In Dedham, Mr. Benj. Dean, aged 93.

Vol. XVI (No. 29) Monday, 7 May 1810.

¶ [3c] A house belonging to Mr. Flint, of Wilton, [204] was lately consumed by fire.

† [3d] Adv. by Francis Wyman, "lately in the employment of Mr. John Gibson," regarding iron and steel products for sale in Cambridgeport, Mass. Dated 23 Apr. 1810.

† [3d] *Stone & Bellows* adv. "that they have got their supply of coarse all tow cloth;" dated Walpole 2 May 1810.

¶ [4d] TWINS. Some time since died in London, two twin sisters, Margaret and Judith Hodges, maiden ladies, aged 53 years. They expired, as they were born, within a few minutes of each other. I have heard of several instances of the death of twins occurring in this manner ; and one of them in which the parties were in different nations. To a philosophical mind a circumstance of this kind affords room for curious speculation.

¶ [4d] LONGEVITY. Helen Gray, a woman who died a few years ago, in England, in the 105th year of her age, had new teeth a few years before her death.

===== ¶ [3d] DIED. =====

In this village, on Saturday, Mrs. Persis Sexton, aged 29 years, wife of Mr. Phinehas Sexton.

Vol. XVI (No. 30) Monday, 14 May 1810.

† [3d] Legal notice regarding the estate of Joshua Smith, late of Langdon, deceased. Sally Smith, Adm^x. for the estate, petitioned for a license to sell real estate to pay debts. Estate business to be conducted at the house of William Pierce at Keene. Dated at Charlestown, 1 May 1810.

† [3d] Legal notice regarding the estate of Elijah Mason, late of Walpole, deceased. Hannah Mason and Levi Allen, Administrators, adv. the public auction of property of Elijah's real estate, consisting of about 70 acres "lying on the Turnpike road near the south end of Walpole;" dated Walpole, 11 May 1810.

===== ¶ [3d] MARRIED. =====

In Windham, (Con.) Dr. Earl Swift, to Miss Laura Ripley.
In Portsmouth, Hon. Richard Evans, to Miss Ann Penhallow.
In Keene, Mr. Wheelock Houghton, of Pittsford, Vt. to Miss Betsey Leonard.
In this town, Mr. Jonathan Cutler, to Miss Phebe Buel.

===== ¶ [3d] DIED. =====

In Philadelphia, Mr. Frederick Shinckle, aged 84.—In Barkhampstead, (Con.) Rev. Daniel Hitchcock, aged 43.—In Hartford, Miss Sarah, daughter of Mr. Nathaniel Patten, aged 17, of spotted fever ; within a few months he has lost two other children, of the same disease.—In Providence, Robert Newell, Esq. aged 60.—In Barre, of spotted fever, Joseph G. son of Dr. Asa Walker, aged 18 months.—In Sturbridge, of spotted fever, Mrs. Nabby and Russel, the wife and son of Mr. Daniel Copeland.—In Rutland, of spotted fever, Hannah M. daughter of Zadock French, aged 18 months.—In Charleston, (S.C.) 21st of April, Mr. Samuel Bird, of Massachusetts; he graduated at Cambridge University last August.—In Baltimore, Rev. Daniel Ruff, aged 64 ; for 35 years a preacher in the Methodist Society.—In Kingston, (N.Y.) Gen. Moses Cantine.

In Hingham, Major General Benjamin Lincoln, late collector of the port of Boston and Charlestown.

In this town, on Thursday last, the widow Graves, aged 72.

Vol. XVI (No. 31) Monday, 21 May 1810.

† [3d] Legal notice regarding the insolvent estate of Rev. James Wellman, late of Cornish, deceased. Daniel Kimball, George Cook, and Moody Hall appointed Commissioners; dated at Cornish 9 May 1810.

† [4d] Humourous news items stating that John Harwood, Jr. and his wife Elizabeth Harwood announce that their copartnership is dissolved. The paragraph was copied from the *Providence Phoenix*.

===== ¶ [3d] DROWNED. =====

In Connecticut River, near White River falls, David Roberts, of Lebanon, and Daniel Davis, of New-Grantham. They were employed in preparing a [raft?].—

While engaged the canoe overset, and threw them into the current. Their bodies have not yet been found.

Vol. XVI (No. 32) Monday, 28 May 1810.

† [3d] C. Felch, Clerk, adv. the annual meeting of the Walpole Fire Engine Company, to be held at M. Butterfield's tavern; dated 26 May 1810.

† [3d] A notice posted that the stores lately occupied by *Shepard & Hutchinson* at Croydon and Newport, will henceforth be known by the name of *Shepard, Hutchinson & Cheney.* Dated Newport 1 May 1810.

† [3d] Legal notice regarding the estate of Asa Nichols, late of Charlestown, deceased, Alpheus Nichols, Adm. The real estate (excepting the widow's dower) to be sold at auction; dated Charlestown 10 May 1810.

† [3d] Caleb Bellows adv. cotton yarn for sale; dated Walpole, 22 May 1810.

===== ¶ [3d] MARRIED. =====

In Hillsborough, on the 6th inst. Doctor Reuben Hatch, of Newport, to Miss Lucy Andrews, of H.

In Alstead, Mr. Willard Harding, to Miss Polly Howard.

In East Greenwich, (R.I.) Mr. Henry Olin, aged XCIII years, to Miss Sally Aylesworth, aged 75.

Vol. XVI (No. 33) Monday, 4 June 1810.

† [3c] Article describing damage from floods in the Walpole area, caused by a rainstorm in late May 1810: In Walpole, a sawmill and mill-dam, belonging to J. Rice Esq., and mill-dams belonging to Messrs. Chase, Fisher, and Mead, were carried off. In Alstead, the tan-works of Mr. Myrick were swept away. In Surry, the malt-house of Mr. Wilcox, and the carding machines and clothiers' works of Mr. Jonathan Locke were destroyed. ♦

† [3c] Adv. for the Ladies Academy at Walpole, Miss Harriot Hayes, Preceptress. Apply to Rev. Pliny Dickinson, Thomas Bellows 2d, or Cheever Felch. Dated Walpole 1 June 1810.

Vol. XVI (No. 34) Monday, 11 June 1810.

===== ¶ [3d] MARRIED. =====

In Exeter, Rev. Ichabod Nichols, of Portland, to Miss Dorothea F. Gilman, Daughter of the Hon. John T. Gilman, Esq.

===== ¶ [3d] DIED. =====

In Fairfield district, (S.C.) Rev. Wm. Rosborough.—In Wilmington, (N.C.) Major Samuel Bloodworth.—In Prince Geo. county, (Md.) Gustavus A. Clagget, Esq.—In New York, Capt. Benj. C. Simmons.—In Hebron, (Con.) Dea. Benj. Buell, aged LXXXIX. —In Northampton, D. Cooley, Esq. of Amherst, (by suicide) aged 60.—In Deerfield, Wm. D. Hornell, aged 19 member of Williams' College, son of Hon. George H. of Canisteo, (N.Y.) : He, with other young men, went in to Deerfield river to bathe, and by exerting himself to preserve the life of a boy who was in danger of being drowned, he lost his own.—In Leominster, 25th ult. Col. Timothy Boutell.—In Worcester, 22d ult. the wife of Mr. E. Smith, of Tolland, (Con.) : They had arrived at Worcester on their way to Boston, when Mrs. S. was seized with a fit of apoplexy, which occasioned her death ; and Mr. S. had the mournful duty to perform of returning with her corpse.—In Palmer's river, (Rehoboth) drowned, Dea. Calvin Jacobs, aged 59, his son Saranus, aged 20, and Wm. H. Pearce, aged 14 : Pearce, while washing sheep in the stream, was overwhelmed by the water, which young Jacobs observing ran to his assistance, but got entangled with P., Mr. J. seeing them struggling and drowning, sprang from a bridge to relieve them, but in the struggle of death they held him to the spot, and the three literally embraced death in each others arms : A boy, who was present, and who narrowly esaped being drowned, relates the tragical story.

In Dummerston, very suddenly of a fit of the apoplexy, Elisha Bigelow, Esq. Attorney at law.

In Alstead, on the 4th inst. Ichabod, son of Mr. Azel Hatch, aged 11 years—of the spotted fever.

Vol. XVI (No. 35) Monday, 18 June 1810.

† [3c] *Shepard, Hutchinson & Cheney* adv. goods for sale at their stores in Croydon and Newport; dated Newport 15 June 1810.

† [3c] List of nonresident owners of land in the town of Croydon who have not paid their taxes for the years 1809 and 1810, [205] as compiled by Samuel Marsh, Collector; delinquent property to be sold at auction at the house of Benjamin Barton, Esq., Innholder at Croydon. The list contains a breakdown of lot number, acreage, etc., though only the names of the owners are presented here:

Name.	For the year 1808.	For the year 1809.
James Wellman	x	x
John Stow	x	x
March Chase	x	
Daniel Chase, jun.	x	
Rev'd Persons	x	
Solomon Chase	x	
Benj. Leland	x	x
Daniel March	x	x
John Downing	x	
Joseph Meriam	x	
Lebeus Chase	x	x
Samuel Paine	x	x
Luke Drury	x	x
Elias Martindale, "Howard lot"	x	x
Rev. Stephen Chase	x	x
Solomon Leland	x	
Nathaniel Hall		x
Asa Coburn		x
Israel Bryant		x

† [3d] List of nonresident proprietors and owners of land in New Grantham, N.H. who are delinquent for their taxes for the year 1809, as compiled by Oliver Dutton, Collector; delinquent property to be sold at auction at the house of Jonathan Spalding, New Grantham. The list contains a breakdown of lot number, acreage, etc., though only the names of the owners is presented here. The last few names in the list (those marked with an asterisk, "*") are persons whose land formerly was situated in Cornish or Croydon, but with changes in town boundaries, were later located within New Grantham:

Oliver Warner	Moses Belding	Hon. Jas. Nevins
Elikim Stebbins	Phinehas Lyman	James Nevins
Eleazer Pomroy	Josiah Jones	R. Dodge, Jr.
Samuel Partridge	Theodore Atkinson, Jr.	
Lucius Doolittle	James Stoodley, Jr.	Samuel Plant *
Medad Pomroy	Bunker Gay	Rev. J. Haven *
James Stoodley, Esq.	John Hunt	Doc. N. Smith *
Oliver Doolittle	O. Baker, Jr.	David Stockwell *
John Harris	Theodore Atkinson, Esq.	Isaac Clement *
Moses Flanders	William Palfrey	Widow Burr *
Abigail Hall	Widow S. Stevens	Ed. Hall *
Benjamin Hall, Esq.	J. Pool	

Vol. XVI (No. 36) Monday, 25 June 1810.

† [3c] Account of a horrid murder committed by one Philips upon his own wife, in the county of Champaign, Ohio. The article is dated at Cincinnati 16 May.

¶ [3c-d] *WHEREAS*, Capt. Elias Bundy, my Husband, has disposed of all my Stock, not even leaving me one cow, and all my farming utensils, and part of my household furniture—he has likewise disposed of all my provision of every kind, not leaving me even one peck of potatoes—he has in addition to this deprived me of the use of my dower by leasing it for the present year—thus I am left poor and wretched without any provision —without a shelter to cover my head; but upon sufferance, whilst the only consolation I received at home, is, his using me very ill by his indecent and unbecoming talk, and abroad by his belching forth his anathemas against me and my children, and threatens to secure the use of my dower to himself yearly.

These are to forbid all persons taking a lease of my dower or trusting him on my account as I will pay no debt of his contracting after this date.

MARTHA BUNDY.

Surry, June 13, 1810.

† [3d] Legal notice regarding the estate of Levi Brown, late of Charlestown, deceased, Lucy Brown, Admx. Brown's real estate to be auctioned at the house of Josiah Shepley, Charlestown. Notice dated 21 June 1810.

† [3d] Notice of the dissolution of the copartnership of *Bill Blake & Co.*; signed by Bill Blake and "CH: Storor" (attorney for John Atkinson). In an attached adv., Bill Blake states that his paper-making and book-binding business will continue; dated Bellows' Falls, 22 June 1810.

† [3d] G. Burroughs, Jr., Auctioneer, adv. that Cheshire Bank Bills will be sold; dated Boston 30 May 1810.

† [3d] William Blanchard adv. for a strayed mare; dated Westmoreland 23 June 1810.

===== ¶ [3c] MARRIED. =====

In Scipio, N.Y. Mr. Jonathan Woodworth, aged 19, to Miss Ellen Cummings aged 11.

===== ¶ [3c] DIED. =====

At the plantation of George Calvert, Esq. Prince George's County, Maryland, negro Jack, in the 120th year of his age. He retained every faculty in a remarkable degree to the last.—In Philadelphia Wm. Ball, Esq. aged 81 : He was an attending member of the Society of Freemasons, upwards of 59 years, and was the first Grand-Master of the Grand Lodge of Pennsylvania ; His remains were interred in masonick form, by the Grand Lodge and the subordinate (14) Lodges in the city.—In N. York, Verdine Elsworth, Esq.—In Long Island, Mr. John Weeks, aged XCI.—In Gloucester, John, son of Col. James Tappan, aged 15 months ; he got at and filled his stomach with dry white beans ; on physical aid being given he brought up twenty-one whole and and a number parts of beans, swolen to an unus[u]al size.—In Charlestown, Joseph Smith, Esq. attorney at law.—In Norfolk, Mrs. West, of the Theatre.

Vol. XVI (No. 37) Monday, 2 July 1810.

† [2c-d] Extensive accounts of several bills lately passed by the N.H. House of Representatives; those which involved specific individuals:

1) A bill to restore Amos Shepherd, Esq. to his law.
2) A bill to disannex Phineas Dinsmore, Israel Hill and Jesse Hill, and their estates in the town of Unity, and to annex said persons to the town of Charlestown.

† [3c] Elias Bundy responds to his wife Martha's "advertisement" appearing in the previous week's issue of the *Museum*, denying all of her accusations. Additionally, this notice states that Martha Bundy was married previously to one Benjamin Isham, with Timothy Isham and an unnamed daughter being children of that marriage. Elias Bundy also stated that a conflict existed between this unnamed daughter and "my own children." The executor of Benjamin Isham's estate was Levi Fuller. The notice is dated at Surry, 28 June 1810. ♦

† [3c] Cornelius Jeudevine adv. a farm for sale in Concord, Vt.; dated 11 June 1810.

† [3d] Legal notice regarding the estate of Francis Goodhue, late of Weathersfield, Windsor County, Vt., Francis Goodhue, Esq., Executor of the will. The latter Goodhue petitioned to have a copy of the will recorded in the probate office of Cheshire County, N.H. Estate business to be conducted at the house of Josiah Shepley, Charlestown, N.H. Dated 10 May 1810.

† [3d] List of letters remaining at the Post Office in Walpole, N.H., 30 June 1810, as compiled by O. Allen, Postmaster:

Shubael Babcock, Walpole	Pearl Parker, Walpole	Josiah Willington, Alstead
Nathaniel Brown, "	Joseph Russell, "	Samuel Edgerton, Langdon
Caleb Bellows, "	Oliver Sparhawk, 2 "	Joseph Nevers, "
Esther Cunningham, "	Thomas & Thomas, 3 "	Miss Tabitha Prentiss, "
Sally Chaffin, "	Joseph Taylor, "	Leonard Reed, "
Davis Carpenter, "	Joseph White, "	Stearns & Edgerton, "
Orpha Darby, "	Darius Graves, "	Obadiah Sartwell, "
Simeon Doggett, "	Samuel Grant, "	Elijah Waldo, "
T.C. Drew, "	Miss Loretho Hynes, "	Miss Phebe Meller, Acworth
Elijah Eldridge, "	Samuel Hutchinson, Alstead	Mrs. Electa Parmerter,
John Johnson, "	Samuel Burroughs, "	[Stoddard.
Rebecca Miller, "	Abigail Hatch, "	John Putnam, Grafton, Vt.
Rebeker Mellens, "	Azel Hatch, "	Sylvester Smith, Surry
Loisia Pierce, "	Joshua Wood, "	

† [3c-d] List of nonresident and owners of land in the town of Marlow, N.H., who are delinquent for their taxes for the year 1809, as compiled by Elliot Cary, Collector. Delinquent property to be auctioned at the house of Gen. Elisha Huntly, innholder at Marlow. The proprietors named are Benjamin Baxter, ——— Ellingwood, and Jesse Willard; the list in the newspaper contains a breakdown of acreage, valuation, etc.

¶ [3c] DIED.—On the 27th ult. of Consumption in Landgrove, Sally Tuthill, consort of Daniel Tuthill, Esq. in the 25th year of her age—with which distressing disorder she continued eleven weeks, and endured it with admirable patience and resignation and has left a disconsolate husband and several children with numerous friends and connections to lament her loss. [. . .]

In Lyndeborough, Mrs. Lydia Chamberlin, aged 20, wife of Mr. John Chamberlin, Jun. late of this town.

In this town, on Friday last, Mr. Asa Griffin, of consumption, aged 38.

† [4c] Extensive account dated at Danville, Vt., of the collapse of a large pond in the town of Glover, 6 June 1810. Local residents had dug a channel from the pond, to increase the water flow to Mr. Wilson's mill in Glover; the hillside collapsed, sending a massive wall of water, 20 feet high, down into the valley, and destroying many thousands of acres of farmland and timber. Mr. Wilson's mill was destroyed. ◆

¶ [4d] *Suicide.* On the 1st instant, Mr. Elijah Rugg hung himself with a bridle on a tree near his own house, in Lancaster, Ms. In the same town, the wife of Mr. Samuel Barrett hung herself with what women generally make use of in such cases—a skein of yarn.

Vol. XVI (No. 38) Monday, 9 July 1810.

† [2b-c] List of Acts passed by the N.H. Legislature, June session 1810; in which persons are specifically named: 1) "An act authourising Robert Murdough & others to assume the name of Newell." 2) "An act authourising Jonathan Cram, 3d, to assume the name of Jonathan W. Cram." 3) "An act authourising Stephen Morse, 3d, to assume the name of Stephen B. Morse." 4) "An act authourising George Ham to assume the name of George Washington Ham." 5) "An act to incorporate Jonathan Shepard, Thomas Means and others by the name of the Milford Cotton and Woollen Manufactory Corporation." 6) An act to incorporate James Parker and others by the name of the Amoskeag Cotton and Woollen Manufactory." 7) An act granting to Jonas Warren and others leave to build a dam and erect mills on Connecticut river, between Littleton in this State, and Waterford in the State of Vermont." 8) "An act to incorporate Charles Cutts & others into a Company by the name of the Portsmouth Insurance Company." 9) "An act granting Arthur Livermore, his heirs and assigns forever, the exclusive right to build and keep a toll bridge over the river between the towns of Plymouth and New-Holderness." 10) "An act authorizing Isaac Smith to review a certain action." 11) "An act to incorporate Israel Aldrich & others by the name of the Pembroke Cotton Factory." 12) "An act in addition to 'an act to incorporate Samuel Blodget, Esq. and others, with

the exclusive right of cutting a Canal by Amoskeag falls.' " 13) "An act authorising John Tibbets to assume and bear the name of John Gerrish Tibbets."

¶ [3a] The meetinghouse in Reading, was consumed by fire, on Monday night last, Doctor Woodbury Mercy, of Windsor, Vt. has been arrested on suspicion of setting it on fire.

† [3c-d] In a continuation of the Elias and Martha Bundy domestic conflict, the Bundys' neighbors join the side of Mrs. Bundy, in her assertion that her husband had left her destitute. The neighbors who signed the notice were Sylvester Smith, Jesse Streeter, Gaylord Willcox, Levi Fuller, Asa Willcox, and Ezra Carpenter. Dated at Surry, 4 July 1810.

† [3d] List of letters remaining at the Post Office in Charlestown, N.H., 1 July 1810, as compiled by F.A. Sumner, Postmaster:

Oliver Brown, Alstead.	Abel Brown, Springfield, Vt.
Enoch Stevens, Acworth.	Charles Dickinson, " "
Joseph Wilson, "	Elias Damon, " "
John Grow, Jr., Charlestown.	John Davis, " "
Jonathan Hubbard, "	Joshua Fowler, " "
Almon Johnson, "	Wales Gould, " "
Egra [206] Merriman, "	Benoni Lockwood, " "
Isaac Pease, "	James Mills, " "
Elizabeth Parker, "	Daniel Martin, " "
Elizabeth Parks, "	Hannah Putnam, " "
Abner Rogers, "	Samuel Shattuck, " "
Jimna Walker, "	Hugh Smith, " "
Ithiel Hoadley, Langdon.	Leonard Walker, " "
Henry Prentiss, "	Cyrus Whitney, " "
Nancy Oaks, Rockingham, Vt.	John Delaware, Unity.
Charles Williams, " "	

† [3d] Legal notice regarding the insolvent estate of Eliphalet Robinson, Jr., late of Claremont, deceased; Alexander Peckens [207], Jennings Ellis, and George Fiske appointed Commissioners over said estate. Estate business to be conducted at the house of Daniel Chase in Claremont. Notice dated 25 June 1810.

† [3d] Eber Carpenter requests debtors to pay up; dated Alstead 3 July 1810.

† [4d] Rev. John Woodbridge ordained Colleague Pastor with Rev. Hopkins over the church in Hadley, on the "20th ult."

====== ¶ [3c] MARRIED. ======

In Woburn, Rev. Timothy Rogers, of Bernardston, (Ms.) to Miss Mary Pierce, of W. daughter of Mr. Jacob P.

In England, Lord James Murrat, to Lady Percy, daughter of the Duke of Northumberland.

====== ¶ [3c] DIED. ======

In Germany, Haydn, the celebrated musical composer : Among his effects lately sold was a parrot which he had taught to sing several Dutch airs.—Near Augusta, (Geo.) Capt. Wm. Green Smith, a native of England ; his horse stumbled, threw him and occasioned his death.—In Southington, (Col.) [208] Edward, son of Mr. Urban Barrett, aged 12 y. ; while ploughing he was killed by lightning, together with a yoke of oxen.— In Mason, (Vt.) Capt. James Scriptor; he went under a tree to avoid a shower, and was killed by lightning.—In Keene, Dr. Obadiah Blake, aged XCI.—In Portsmouth, Capt. Hugh H. Tuttle.—In Deerfield, Mr. John Barns, of New-Salem, drowned.—In Oxford, 5th inst. Dr. Jona. Larned, aged 43, after a short illness of 30 hours ; his death was occasioned by a mortification, which was supposed to originate from the Mumps, with which he was attacked several weeks before.—

In this town, on Tuesday last, a child of Mr. Israel Wightman, aged 2 years.

Vol. XVI (No. 39) Monday, 16 July 1810.

† [3d] A notice stating that the partnership of *Charles Duncan & Co.* is dissolved; signed by Charles Duncan and "Wyman & Chapman." Settlement of claims to be hand-

led by James H. Bingham, Esq., of Alstead, agent for Wyman and Chapman. Dated Alstead 1 July 1810.

Vol. XVI (No. 40) Monday, 23 July 1810.

† [3d] David Taylor offers a farm for sale "near Langdon Meetinghouse," which includes a house used as a tavern. Dated Charlestown, 17 July 1810.

† [3d] Stephen Rice requests outstanding accounts to be settled; also, an adv. by Stephen Rice and Joseph Cobb announcing that "the boot and shoe making business will in future be carried on by Rice and Cobb in the Brick Building, over the Store of Messrs. Redington & Seaver . . . " Dated Walpole 21 July 1810.

† [3d] Silas Angier adv. that a new carding machine "is now erected near Chase's Mills in Walpole . . . "; dated there 19 July 1810.

† [3c-d] Obituary of Samuel Harris, aged 26, an undergraduate of Harvard University, who drowned at Cambridge, Mass. 7 July 1810. ◆

† [3d] A paragraph, mostly of a religious nature, noting the deaths of two persons in Chesterfield, 16 July 1810 : Mr. Isaac Farr, aged 63, died while in the act of sharpening his scythe, and of Albert, the only son of Mr. Isaac Abbot, aged 6, who died a few hours after becoming ill.

† [3d] Thaddeus Osgood offers a note of thanks to those "who have contributed towards assisting the new settlements . . . on the frontiers of our own country and in Canada." Dated Walpole 17 July.

=== ¶ [3c] DIED. ===

In Paris, Paul Benfield, a once-famous Asiatick *nabob*, who brought from the E. Indies a fortune of little less than a million sterling ; he died in very indigent circumstances.—In Kentucky, Wm. Cletter, executed for the murder of Mr. John Farmer.—In Bedford, (Penn.) Mr. David Bacon; shot by an insane person.—In Peterboro', (N.Y.) Col. Joshua Leland, of Eaton; thrown from his waggon, the wheels passing over his neck.—In Charlotte, (Vt.) Mr. Joseph Al[l]en, aged 74; he arose from bed in the morning in apparent good health, dressed himself, & then lay down and expired immediately.—In Torrington, (Con.) Phineas North, Esq.—In Pomfret, (Con.) Barnard Phillips, jun. aged 19 ; he fell 46 feet from the girt of a steeple as he was assisting in raising a tower ; and although he weighed 200 lbs. and nothing intercepted his fall, no bones were fractured or dislocated, but the shock deprived him of all sensibility below his hips; he survived the accident several days.—In Amherst, (N.H.) Mrs. Anna, wife of Hon. J.K. Smith, aged 28.—In Merrimack, Jacob M'Gaw, Esq.

Vol. XVI (No. 41) Monday, 30 July 1810.

¶ [3d] "THE WASHINGTONIAN." The publication of this paper commenced at Windsor, Vt. on Monday last. The correct principles and brilliant talents of the Editor, Josiah Dunham, Esq. promise much support to the cause of Americanism in this part of the country.

† [3d] William M'Clintock, Jr. adv. farms to be auctioned in Charlestown; dated there 20 July 1810.

=== ¶ [3d] DIED. ===

In Newport, July 14, Widow Jane Buel, aged 72 years. She was seized with a fit of apoplexy while about some light work in the kitchen and lived about two hours ; on the 19th inst. a child of Mr. John Hall, aged about 14 months.

Near Natchez, Maj. Elisha Strong of 7th reg't U.S. infantry —In New York Sound, Mr. Nathan Meigs, supposed to have been shot by his own son in a boat, and thrown overboard.—In Roxbury Dexter Wheeler, run over and killed by a loaded waggon.—In Cambridge-Port, Mr. Jonathan Houghton, late a merchant of Boston, aged 66.—In Plymouth, Eng. John [Dogorn?], a pilot of a man of war ; he had been married six months and having returned from sea, without any cause became jealous of his beautiful wife, desired her to go into another room with him, where he deliberately drew a pistol and shot her through the heart.—He afterwards fired another pistol through his own heart, and expired on his wife's body.

Vol. XVI (No. 42) Monday, 6 Aug. 1810.

¶ [3b] On thursday last, a young woman, together with the horse upon which she was riding, was killed by lightning, in Washington, N.H.

† [3d] List of nonresident proprietors and owners of land in Washington, N.H., who have not paid their taxes for the year 1809, as compiled by James Faxon, Collector. Property in default to be auctioned at the house of David Farnsworth, Innholder at Washington. The list contains a breakdown of lot number, size, etc., though only the names of the owners is presented here:

    Th. Packard, Esq.   Theod. Atkinson
    Joshua Pierce   Peter Pierce
    Sally & March   Benjamin Sweatt
    John Rindge, Esq.

===== ¶ [3d] DIED. =====

In this town, on the 2d inst. Mr. Nathan Bundy, aged 67, one of the first settlers of the town.—[Printers in the northern states will confer a favour on the friends of the deceased by publishing this death.]

Vol. XVI (No. 43) Monday, 13 Aug. 1810.

† [1a] Ebenezer Brewer adv. for a pair of oxen which strayed from his pasture in Unity, (though the notice is dated at Claremont), 4 Aug. 1810.

¶ [3b] A young woman in Acworth, of the name of Jerusha Smith, was, on the 2d inst. killed by lightning, while riding on horseback. The horse was also killed.

¶ [3b] FIRE. The house of Mr. Abijah Foster, of Keene, was consumed by fire on the 4th inst. Damage estimated at 2,000 dols.

† [3d] *Hall & Weld* adv. their "Dye Stuff Store" at Boston; dated there August 1810.

† [3d] Samuel Hutchinson requests debtors to pay up; dated Alstead 4 Aug. 1810.

===== ¶ [3d] MARRIED. =====

In this town, Mr. James Crosfield, of Keene, to Miss Eugenia Frink.

In Boston, Mr. Richard Boylston, editor of the Farmer's Cabinet, of Amherst, (N.H.) to Miss Mary Mosely.

Vol. XVI (No. 44) Monday, 20 Aug. 1810.

† [3d] Jonathan Locke, Clothier, who lost his business in the recent flood, adv. that he "has rebuilt his works at Surry, and is now ready to receive cloth for dressing." Dated at Surry 15 Aug. 1810.

===== ¶ [3d] DIED. =====

In Hanover, on Tuesday last, the Hon. John Hubbard, aged 50. Professor of Mathematicks and Natural Philosophy in Dartmouth College ; formerly of this town. Not only the College and his family, but the publick at large have sustained a heavy loss by the death of Mr. Hubbard, a Christian, a scholar and a gentleman. Amiable and engaging in his manners pure and uncorrupt in his life, able and assiduous in his profession, he has left imprinted on the hearts of many friends the remembrance of his worth. With him is lost to the world a fund of science, which he was imparting to others, and thereby multiplying the stock of literature.

In this town, on Tuesday last, Mrs. Buckston, wife of Mr. Jonathan Buckston.— Also, a child of Mr. Jonathan Cutler.

Vol. XVI (No. 45) Monday, 27 Aug. 1810.

† [3d] Account of another flood in the Walpole area, which did much more damage than the one of the previous May. Those whose property was destroyed: Mr. Angier's carding machine, a blacksmith shop owned by Mr. Burbank, a shop owned by Mr. Chase, Mr. Eaton's forge, the dam of Col. Bellows, an oil mill owned by Gen. Shepard in Alstead, the saw mill of Maj. Prentiss at Langdon, and the dam of Dr. Kittredge was swept away. ♦

† [3d] Isaac Redington requests all debtors to him or to *Redington & Seaver* to pay up.

Vol. XVI (No. 46) Monday, 3 Sept. 1810.

¶ [3b] Dr. Woodbury Mercey, of Windsor, who was indicted by the grand jury of that county, for burning Reading meetinghouse, has been tried and acquitted.
¶ [3d] Drowned, at Weathersfield, Vt. on the 22d ult. Gregory Stone, Esq. He was standing on a bridge, viewing the rise of the water during the late freshet, when the bridge was suddenly carried off, and he thrown into the water, from which he could not extricate himself.
† [3d] William Tileston adv. his new dye-stuff store at Boston, opposite Boardman's hat manufactory on Ann Street; dated Boston Aug. 1810.
† [3d] Legal notice regarding the estate of Archibald M'Collom, late of Acworth, deceased; Rebecca M'Collom, Admx. Dated Acworth 20 Aug. 1810.
† [3d] Legal notice regarding the estate of Charles Bowen, late of Charlestown, N.H. Dated there 29 Aug. 1810. Charles Bowen, Adm.
===== ¶ [3d] DIED. =====

In Washington, N.H. on the 19th ult. Mr. John Healy, aged 77. [. . .]
In Croydon, on the 1st ult. the widow Mehetable Haven, formerly the wife of James Haven, aged 77.
In Cornish, 10th ult. Daniel M. aged 18 months, son of Dea. John Chase.
In Fincastle, (Virg.) the person who called himself by the assumed name of Washington, who lately ran off with the wife and child of a Post-master in the State of New York, and for the apprehending of whom a large reward was offered. Not being able to find the bail ordered, he was sent to goal and there committed suicide. The manner of his death involves some mystery. Before the magistrate, and after confinement, he steadily pe[r]sisted in refusing to reveal his name, and after his death it was found he had not only burnt every article of his clothing that could lead to a discovery of his family, but had also burnt a large sum in bank notes, from an apprehension that they might afford some clue to that object. He has left a paper on the subject of his conduct, written in a disguised hand. His very boots were cut in small pieces, lest they should betray him, and his face and body so mangled as to bear no resemblance to their original appearances. 209

Vol. XVI (No. 47) Monday, 10 Sept. 1810.

† [3c] Rev. Clark Brown, formerly minister of Brimfield, Mass., installed over the Congregational Church at Swanzey, N.H. "on Wednesday last."
† [3d] List of nonresident proprietors and owners of land in the town of Wendell, N.H., who are delinquent for their taxes for the year 1810, as compiled by Robert Emerson, Collector. Property in default to be auctioned at the house of R.C. Rogers in Wendell. The list contains a breakdown of lot number, range, etc., though only the names of the owners are presented here:

> Benjamin Broton, ten acres, part of a lot Giles Bartlett formerly owned.
> Charles Emerson
> Widow R. Hardy (two lots).
> Joseph Towne 50 acres part.
> Jeremiah Kelsey jun. (two lots, one formerly owned by D. Moses).

† [3d] *Shepard, Hutchinson & Cheney* adv. to purchase flax seed for their stores in Newport or Croydon; dated Newport 1 Sept. 1810.
† [3d] Adv. for the first meeting of the Cornish Manufacturing Corporation, to be held at the house of Jonathan Chase in Cornish. Signed by Leonard Comings and Ithamar Chase; dated Cornish 30 Aug. 1810.
† [3d] James Campbell, Register of Deeds, adv. that he will attend to his business at Mr. J. Shepley's, Charlestown, and at Mr. William Pierce's in Keene; dated Walpole 30 Aug. 1810.
† [3d] Samuel Turner adv. for a stray mare; dated Walpole 6 Sept. 1810.
† [3d] Benjamin Ranney adv. for a stray mare; dated Westminster, Vt. 8 Sept. 1810.

===== ¶ [3c] MARRIED. =====

In New Orleans, Mr. Alexander Philip Socrates Aemilius Caesar Hannibal Marcelius George Washington Treadwell, to the amiable Miss Carolina Sophia Margaretta Maria Julienne Wortley Montague Joan of Arc Williams ! ! ! ! ! ! !

===== ¶ [3c-d] DIED. =====

In this town, on Thursday last, very suddenly, Capt. John Flint, aged 56, a respectable and useful member of society.

In this vil[l]age, on Wednesday last, Mary, aged 2 years, daughter of Samuel Grant, Esq. She unfortunately fell into a cistern at a neighbouring house, and was drowned. [. . .]

In Alstead, on Wednesday, the 29th of August, Miss Sally Todd, daughter of Mr. Todd of Temple, aged about 40. She was a professor of religion, and was an ornament to it.

In Peachham, Vt. Mrs. Susanna Brooks, Wife of Mr. Daniel Brooks.

Vol. XVI (No. 48) Monday, 17 Sept. 1810.

† [1c] Samuel Hutchinson adv. to purchase flax seed at his Alstead store; dated 1 Sept.

† [3d] Elisha Huntly, Brig. Gen., and Eber Carpenter, Brigade Maj. and Inspector, post the Brigade Orders for upcoming inspections of the Fifth Brigade in the Third Division of New Hampshire Militia. Dated 14 Sept.

† [3d] Edward Hall offers several farms for sale in Croydon, N.H.: 1) the Hagar Farm (so called), 2) a farm formerly occupied by Mr. David Powers, 3) a farm on the Turnpike, near Breck's Store, and 4) the store formerly owned by Mr. Moses Towne. Dated at Croydon 23 Aug. 1810.

† [3d] A paragraph describing the death of Jehiel Farmer, aged 15, who drowned at Walpole, N.H. [9 Sept.?], son of Joseph Farmer of Grafton, Vt.. (Some of the information contained in this article is missing, as part of the article was torn off the page.) ♦

===== ¶ [3c] MARRIED. =====

In Torrington, Con. James Ripley Esq. of Cornish, N.H. to Miss Florella Mills, of the former place.—In Pomfret, Vt. Harvey Chase, Esq. of Cornish, N.H. to Miss Eunice Dana of the former place.

In Newburg, N.Y. Rev. James Matthews of the city of New York, to Miss Charlotte Walsh.

===== ¶ [3d] DIED. =====

In this town, on the 3d inst. Mr. Richard Alexander, aged [81?] years.

In Cornish, [Hannah?] Johnson, aged 14 years, Daughter of Mr. John Johnson. Also William Atwood, son of Mr. Joshua Atwood, aged 2 years.

In Acworth, on the 14th ult. Stephen, son of Mr. John Mitchel aged two years.

In Washington, col. John Whiting, of the 5th reg't U.S. infantry, formerly of Lancaster, (Ms.) aged about [54?].—In Bloomfield, Mr. Jesse Scudder; killed by his horse, which reared and fell upon him.—In Albany, maj. Jacob Right, of N. York ; Mr. John Jones, aged 21, son of Dr. Jones, of N. York.—In Portsmouth, (R.I.) Job [Darsee?], Esq. aged 70.—In Kennebunk, Mrs. Sally Gilman wife of Tristram G. Esq. aged [28?].—In Wrentham, capt. Joshua Grant, aged 70 ; by falling from a hay stack.—In Southampton, Mr. Amos [Barr?], jun. aged 21—drowned.—In Greenfield, Wid. Eunice Loveland, aged 47—suicide.

Vol. XVI (No. 49) Monday, 24 Sept. 1810.

† [1a] Royal Crafts adv. that he transacts financial business at Boston; dated at Boston 17 Aug. 1810.

† [3c-d] Extensive account of the suicide of Samuel Smith of Derby, Vt., 4 Sept. 1810. Smith was formerly of Windsor, but removed to Derby were he was ordained as pastor of the Baptist Church; he left a widow and eight children. ♦

† [3d] *J.&T. Bellows* request debtors to pay up; dated Walpole 22 Sept.

† [3d] Legal notice regarding the insolvent estate of James Hall, late of Alstead, deceased; Simon Brooks, Silas Robbins, and Willard Fairbanks were appointed Com-

missioners. Dated at Alstead 22 Sept. 1810.

¶ [3d] EXPERIENCED NAVIGATOR. Captain Collins, from New York, now in this village, (says the 'Ballston New York Advertiser,') is said to have crossed the Atlantick *one hundred thirty seven times !*—An instance of nautical experience unparalleled, perhaps, in the annals of navigation.

¶ [3d] SAGHARBOUR, *Sept. 1. Shocking Catastrophe.*—The schooner Amanda, Captain Rhodes, of this port, on her passage from Jamaica to New York, was struck with lightning near Cape Hatteras, & one of the masts carried away at the moment that four of the men were on the yards, three of whom went overboard and were lost. It is with regret we have to state that Mr. Stratton Havens, of Shelter Island, mate of the schooner, was one of the persons lost. He has left a young family to lament their irrepairable loss.

At Mamaroneck, Westchester County, N.Y. Sept. 8, Miss Elsia and Miss Ann Titford, daughter of Doctor Isaac Titford, fell from a rock on which they were fishing into a mill pond, and were drowned, no[t]withstanding they were speedily taken out of the water, and the assistance of a medical gentleman, who accidentally passed at the time, was obtained.

===== ¶ [3d] MARRIED. =====

In Grenville, N.Y. Mr. Samuel Batchelder jr. of N. Ipswich, to Miss Mary Montgomery, daughter of John Montgomery, Esq. of Haverhill, N.H.

===== ¶ [3d] DIED. =====

At Washington city, on the 4th inst. Colonel John Whiting, of the United States Infantry, aged about 54. He has left behind him a numerous family to lament [. . .]

In Germany, 19th July, Louise Auguste Withelmine Alnelie, Queen of Prussia [. . .] —On his passage from St. Domingo, to New York, 12th inst. Capt. Wallis Rust, late mate of sch. Polly & Sally, of Boston.—On James Island, (S.C.) James Tood, Esq.—In Maryland, Lieut. John Nicholson, of the U.S. Navy.—In Potts' Grove, (Penn.) 31st Aug. Mr. William Weeks, aged 23, son of Benjamin Weeks, Esq. of Gilmanton, (N.H.)—In Philad. Peter Hoofman, Esq.—In New Ipswich, Hon. Ebenezer Champney, Esq. aged 67.—In Amherst Mrs. Mehetabel Bell, aged 30, wife of the Hon. Samuel Bell.

In Langdon, Mrs. Betsey Wilson, aged 35, wife of William Wilson.

In Alstead, widow Betsey Watts, aged 80.

Vol. XVI (No. 50) Monday, 1 Oct. 1810.

† [3c] Doct. Oliver Hastings adv. goods for sale at his store in Charlestown; also, in the same adv., Solomon Lothrop requests to purchase "fifty smooth shipping horses;" dated at Charlestown 25 Sept. 1810.

† [3c] Amos Graves adv. "that he has lately commenced the Clothing Business near Chase's Mills in Walpole . . . " Dated Walpole 27 Sept. 1810.

† [3d] List of letters remaining at the Post Office, Walpole, N.H. 1 Oct. 1810, as compiled by O. Allen, Postmaster:

David Esty, Westmoreland.	Samuel Foster, Walpole.	Miss Carolina Marvin,
William M. Bully, Walpole.	Francis Gardner, "	[Surry.
Elias Burbank, "	Elihu Hall, "	Sylvester Smith, "
Thomas Bellows, Esq., "	William Jenison, "	Tabitha Prentiss,
Caleb Bellows, "	Luther Knowlton, "	[Langdon.
James Campbell, "	David Manly, "	William Wilson, "
Miss Martha M'Collom, "	Miss Lucy Mason, "	Ellis Pishen, Stoddard.
George Cochran, "	Silas Merrifield, "	Jerusha C. Hutchinson,
Benjamin Davis, Jr., "	Stephen Steward, "	[Alstead.
Hugh Dunche, "	Mercy Smith, "	Elisha Simonds, "
Richard Alexander, "	Zenas Warren, 2, "	Amos Shepherd, 2, "
Sylvester Everett, "	Woolston Brochway, Surry	Isaac Temple, "
Miss Meriam Fletcher, "	Samuel Hills, "	

† [3c] Nealleay Norris posts a notice warning the public not to purchase two notes against him, "which are in the possession of Moses Potter, of Brattleborough." Both

notes were dated 21 Nov. 1809. Notice dated at Windham, Vt. 28 Sept.

† [3d] Legal notice regarding the insolvent estate of Rev. Dan Foster, late of Charlestown, deceased. Jonathan Arms, Obediah Wells, and George Olcott appointed Commissioners. Estate business to be conducted at the house of Josiah Shepley, innholder at Charlestown. Dated there 24 Sept. 1810.

† [3d] List of nonresident proprietors and owners of land in Springfield, N.H. who are delinquent for their taxes due for the year 1810, as compiled by Reuben Hoyt, Collector. Property in default to be auctioned at the house of Col. John Quimby, Springfield. The list contains a breakdown of lot numbers, acreage, etc., though only the names of the owners are presented here:

    Capt. Steven Kimball   Simeon Ladd
    Capt. Wm. Rowell   Capt. Aaron Kinsman
    John Durbern (two lots)   Simeon Ladd & Sampson
    Joseph Lunt   "Haven, Wm. Craft & Co." 210

† [3d] Stephen Steward adv. his "Splitting Machine" for splitting sheep skins; dated Walpole 29 Sept. In an attached "plug," William Fessenden attests to the usefulness of the machine; his endorsement is dated at Brattleborough, 1 July 1810.

† [4c] An unbelievable account, but "certified by several respectable citizens of this county," describing a wager upon one Daniel Pels, who was given 25 cents for swallowing a snake egg. After several hours, Pels vomited up a live snake, with others supposed to be still in his stomach. The event occurred upon a meadow owned by Daniel Thatcher, and the story was coped from the *Trenton True American*. ♦

Vol. XVI (No. 51) Monday, 8 Oct. 1810.

† [3a] Account of a number of citizens who approached a Shaker society at Turtle Creek, accusing them of holding three grandchildren of Col. James Smith, of Kentucky, against their will. The article is dated at Cincinnati, Ohio, 1 Sept. ♦

† [3d] List of letters remaining at the Post Office in Charlestown, N.H., 1 Oct. 1810, as compiled by F.A. Sumner, Postmaster:

John Perkins, Unity.
John Walker, Springfield, Vt.
James Underwood, " "
Isaac Tower, Jun., " "
Thomas Stoddar, " "
Amos Parker, " "
David Putnam, " "
Eli Alead, " "
Julius S. Holden, " "
Jeremiah Ellis, " "
William Cooper, " "
John Brown, " "
Smith W. Babcock, " "
Samuel Clark, Acworth.
Matthew Porter, "
Asa Chandler, Stoddard.
William Cheney, Newport.
Ezra Stowell, New Grantham.

Polly Harding, Langdon.
Laban Burr, "
Samuel Sischo, Fishersfield.
Ephraim Wesson, Claremont.
Ira A. Wheeler, Charlestown.
Simeon Wheeler, "
Samuel S. West, "
Shaler Towner, "
Benjamin Pierce, "
Sukey Kimball, "
Jerusha Carpenter, "
Martha Bellows, "
William Ballow, "
David Burns, "
Amy Atherton, "
Mary Allen, "
Sally Chaplain, Baltimore, Vt.

† [3d] Legal notice regarding the insolvent estate of John Flint, late of Walpole, deceased, Levi Allen, Administrator. N. Townsley, E. Crehore, and William Watkins appointed Commissioners. Estate business to be conducted at the house of Asher Southard, Innholder of Walpole. Notice dated at Walpole 5 Oct. 1810.

† [3d] William Jenison adv. a stray heifer; dated Walpole 4 Oct. 1810.

======= ¶ [3b] MARRIED. =======

In England, Hon. Samuel Hood, son of Admiral Lord Hood, to Charlotte Nelson, neice of the immortal Nelson.—In Stockbridge, Mr. Chester Dewey, P.M. and N.P. in Williams' College, to Miss Sarah Dewey.

In Portsmouth, the Hon. William Eustis, secretary at war, to Miss Caroline Langdon, daughter of the late Hon. Woodbury Langdon, of P.

At Spencer, (Mass.) Rev. Roswell Shurtleff, Professor of Theology, in Dartmouth College, to Miss Ann Pope, of the former place.

At Piermont, N.H. Mr. Reuben Porter, of Hartford, Con. to Miss Mary Swett, of Piermont.

At Lebanon, N.H. Mr. Elisha Parkhurst, of Concord, to Miss Betsy Hall, of Cornish.

At Milford, Penn. Capt. Joseph Weaver, to Miss Kitty Spinner.—A Southern punster says this union indicates the growth of domestick manufactures.

===== ¶ [3b-c] DIED. =====

At Albany, William P. Beers, Esq. Clerk of the City and County of Albany.—In New York, on Wednesday 26th ult. Mr. James Cheetham Editor of the American Citizen.

In Paris, Madame Recamier, equally celebrated for the beauty of her person, symmetry of form, superiour taste, and amiability of character.—In Germany, the Dutchess Dowager of Mecklenberg, Schwerin, aged 79.—In London, Mrs. Jonstone, an actress of the Drury Lane Theatre.—In the streight of Belleitle, on the 24th June last, Walter Phillips, aged 27, oldest son of the late Benjamin Philips, of Lynn.—In S. Carolina, Dr. John R. Lazell, late of Massachusetts.—In N. Jersey, Gen. James Cox, M.C. aged 57.—In Ammonoosuck river, Bath, in Vermont[211] [drowned] Mr. [Legyard Tislot?], a German, aged 44 ; who had escaped death in the sanguinary fields of Germany, and in the perils of the ocean, to meet it in fording an insignificant streamlet.

In Portsmouth, Mr. Richard Champney, merchant, aged 75.—In Gilmantown, Thomas Cogswell, Esq. aged 64.—In Scituate, Hon. William Cushing, aged 77.

Vol. XVI (No. 52) Monday, 15 Oct. 1810.

¶ [3a] JAMES ELLIOT Has purchased and commenced Editor of the Massachusetts Spy, lately owned by Isaiah Thomas, jun. We may now look to the east again for the star. *Letters upon French Influence.*

† [3c] Rev. Ephraim G. Swift ordained, in Colleague with Rev. West, at Stockbridge.

† [3d] *Stone & Bellows* request debtors to pay up; dated 11 Oct. 1810.

† [3d] Joseph Bridge requests debtors to pay up; dated Walpole 13 Oct. 1810.

===== ¶ [3c] MARRIED. =====

In Charleston, (S.C.) Wm. Crafts Esq. to Miss Harriet P. Poaug. In Augusta, (Me.) Mr. Wm. Babcock, mer. to Miss Nancy Babcock.

In Shirley, Hon. James Wilson, Esq. of Peterborough, Member of Congress for N.H. to Miss Betsey Little, daughter of W. Little Esq. of the former place.

===== ¶ [3c-d] DIED. =====

In New York, Oct. 5th, Mr. Solomon Williams, aged 38, of the house of William and Whiting, Booksellers. Mr. Williams was a gentleman of liberal education, of amiable manners, exemplary morals and ardent piety [. . .]

In Philadelphia, from 22d to 29th Sept. forty-seven—Of consumption eight, and Oh ! shame, of Small Pox natural, One ! Two of the deceased were between 90 & 100 years old !—In New York, same time Thirty-two—Consumption five. In New York hospital, Thomas Smith, of Boston, John Turell, N. Hampshire.—In Savannah, Mr. Clifford Hunt, late of Providence, much regretted : Capt. Thomas Newell, aged 66.—In Maidenhead, (N.J.) Mrs. Sarah Scudder.—In Wethersfield, Mrs. Wells, aged LXXXII.—In Cheshire, Mr. Lyman De Wolf, aged 21.—In Oakham, Mr. D. Tomlinson jun. son of Rev. Mr. T. aged 23.—At Sea, Mr. Joseph B. Hart, aged 30, and Mr. Joseph M'Intire, aged 25, both of Portsmouth, (N.H.).—At Sea, [drowned] capt. Thomas Rindge, also of Portsmouth.—In Lynn, capt. Wm. P. Cantisheer, keeper of the poor house.—Topsfield, Mr. Zeb Perkins, aged 70—who for the last nine years of his existence was unable to feed himself, or to move in bed, without assistance !—"*What is man?*"—In Salem, Mr. Parker Lawrence, aged 27, formerly of Epping, by a fall from the staging of a house.

At Barnstable, on the 23d inst. Joseph Otis, Esq. aged 83. This worthy and respectable gentleman was son of the late Hon. James Otis, Esq. of Barnstable, and brother of the distinguished Statesman and Lawyer, of the same name.—Like the other members of his family, he was a zealous and early friend to the Liberties and independence of his country ; and was from the beginning of the revolution, employed in various publick offices, the duties of which he discharged with perfect fidelity.

An Overview of *The Farmer's Weekly Museum*.

The information included within the *Farmer's Weekly Museum* contains a wealth of genealogical data, covering several regions of New England. The goal of this research project was to locate anything of genealogical value—marriage or death notices, legal notices, advertisements from local merchants or farmers, runaway notices, letters remaining at local post offices, or any other news item which might offer a clue to the researcher.

The newspaper had a respectable lifespan, beginning publication at Walpole, N.H. in April of 1793, and continuing until October of 1810. There was a suspension of publication for portions of the years 1807 and 1808. The paper originated under the name of *The Newhampshire and Vermont Journal*, but in April 1797 the name evolved to *The Farmer's Weekly Museum: Newhampshire and Vermont Journal*. In April 1799 the "Newhampshire and Vermont Journal" portion of the title was deleted, and thereafter the paper went through several title changes, but from April 1797 to its demise, always included the "Farmer's Museum" somewhere in the title. The paper went through several proprietors and printers, but the purpose of this work is not to focus on the history of this newspaper. However, it is worthy of note to say that one of the most prominent owners of this newspaper was Isaiah Thomas of Worcester, Mass. and much of the news presented in the *Farmer's Museum* was presumably gathered from his Massachusetts newspapers. An excellent account of this paper's transition from owner to owner is contained in the "History and Bibliography of American Newspapers, 1690-1820," by Clarence S. Brigham, published by the American Antiquarian Society, Worcester, Mass., 1947. This source also contains an inventory of all known issues of this paper known at that time, which will be useful to researchers who need to locate missing issues of this paper.

The *Farmer's Museum* was microfilmed from the collection owned by the American Antiquarian Society, and it is nearly a complete run. In a few instances, the camera was out of focus during the microfilming process, resulting in illegible images of portions of the microfilm, but overall, most of the images are legible. Additionally, a few issues had portions of the original damaged, torn or cut off. There are a few issues missing from their collection, or otherwise damaged, and those are noted here:

21 Apr. 1801 – third and fourth pages missing.
1 Mar. 1803 – third page torn.
7 June 1803 – part of third page is cut.
6 Sept. 1803 – a portion is out of focus, and the fourth column of the second page has been cut.
1 Nov. 1803 – missing.
26 May 1804 – death notices on third page out of focus; mostly illegible.
2 June 1804 – extensive list of marriages and deaths, out of focus.
5 Dec. 1806 – the column of death notices has been cut; several letters unknown.
26 Dec. 1806 – missing.
23 Jan. 1808 – third page partially illegible.
7 Aug. 1809 – missing.
4 Sept. 1809 – missing.
20 Nov. 1809– third page, death notices, partially torn off.
27 Nov. 1809– first page not microfilmed.
12 Feb. 1810 – missing
17 Sept. 1810– third page torn, upper right corner.

The microfilm was produced by Readex Corporation, and is contained on three reels of microfilm. Unfortunately, when this project commenced, I was unable to obtain from my source the first reel of film, which contains the issues from April 1793 through March 1797. However, the second and third reels have been thoroughly investigated, and all items of interest are contained herein, whether presented verbatim or in summary format. Perhaps at a later time, the earliest years could be researched, and presented in a future volume for publication.

The *Farmer's Museum* had a circulation of about 2000, according to an advertisement in the issue of 23 Jan. 1798, which stated that it had "a wider circulation than any other village paper in the United States." The paper was issued weekly, and like most of the newspapers of that time it was printed on a single sheet, on both sides, and folded in half, which resulted in a paper containing four "pages." Frequently reports of the wars in Europe or U.S. politics crowded out any local news—at times the inclusion of any marriage or death notices was meager or nonexistent, but at other times, there are very extensive lists of marriages and deaths.

Oddly, the statistics of "vital records" of marriage and death notices are most frequent, not for New Hampshire, but for Massachusetts. Most notable are the numbers from Boston, but there are also large numbers of events reported from Worcester and Essex counties in Massachusetts, and the Connecticut River Valley in Vermont, New Hampshire, Massachusetts and Connecticut. And in another odd discovery, there are periods of time when significant numbers of deaths were reported from Portsmouth, N.H., located on the opposite side of the state from Walpole. Great numbers of marriages and deaths were also reported from the largest "cities" on the East Coast—New York, Philadelphia, Baltimore, and Charleston, S.C.

There are over one thousand death notices where the cause of death is actually stated—the greatest single cause identified was by drowning, followed by murders and suicides. Epidemics of small pox, yellow fever, etc. also claimed many lives, and numerous accounts of these are included herein. But generally speaking, the average death notice gives the name of the person, their age, and the town that they died in.

The statistics given below represent the total number of "vital records" (i.e. usually a marriage or death notice) relevant to each town, whether the event occurred within a given town, or the person was a resident of that town and the event occurred somewhere else. For example, in the death notice from the issue of 19 Sept. 1806: "At Orono, Me. on the 7th ult. (drowned) Capt. John Southgate, of Leicester, aged 68;" the event has relevance to Leicester, (Mass.), so that town has one event added to its tally, as does Orono, Maine, where the event occurred. However, there are many more thousands of abstracted news items, such as advertisements, letters remaining at post offices, etc., which are not counted in the statistics below.

Connecticut.		E. Hartford	16	Lebanon	8
		E. Haven	4	Lee	1
Ashford	2	E. Windsor	13	Lisbon	4
Barkhampstead	3	Ellington	4	Litchfield	29
Berlin	3	Enfield	14	Lyme	27
Bethel	2	Fairfield	4	Mansfield	8
Bethlehem	6	Farmington	5	Middlebury	2
Bloomfield	1	Franklin	1	Middlefield	2
Bolton	3	Glastonbury	6	Middletown	30
Bozrah	2	Goshen	6	Milford	1
Branford	3	Granby	2	Montville	6
Bridgeport	3	Greenfield	1	New Fairfield	3
Bridgewater	1	Greenwich	2	New Hartford	1
Bristol	2	Groton	11	New Haven	33
Brookfield	2	Guilford	5	New London	45
Brooklyn	2	Haddam	6	New Milford	2
Canaan	6	Hamden	4	Newtown	1
Canterbury	9	Hampton	2	Norfolk	1
Chatham	2	Hartford	78	North Haven	1
Colchester	9	Hartland	3	Norwalk	5
Columbia	1	Harwinton	4	Norwich	32
Cornwall	5	Hebron	10	Oxford	1
Coventry	13	Huntington	2	Plymouth	2
Danbury	23	Kent	1	Pomfret	3
Derby	2	Killingly	3	Preston	17
E. Haddam	13	Killingworth	3	Redding	4

Ridgbury	1			Bowdoinham	1
Ridgefield	2			Bridgeton	2
Roxbury	1	Augusta	7	Bristol	1
Salem	1	Cumberland Co.	1	Brunswick	1
Salisbury	2	Cumberland Isl'd	1	Buxton	3
Saybrook	9	Darien	1	Cape Elizabeth	1
Scott	1	Ebenezer	2	Clinton	1
Sharon	7	Litchfield	1	Cornish	1
Sherman	1	Louisville	1	Deering	1
Simsbury	3	Midway	1	Dresden	2
Somers	6	Oglethorpe Co.	3	Eastport	4
Southington	7	Savannah	30	Edgecomb	1
Stafford	2	Sparta	1	Fairfield	1
Stamford	3	St. Mary's	2	Falmouth	4
Stonington	7	Sununty	1	Freeport	2
Stratford	2	Washington Co.	1	Fryeburg	2
Suffield	11	[not given]	9	Georgetown	4
Thompson	2			Gorham	5
Tolland	10	Georgia totals:	62	Hallowell	5
Torrington	3			Hampden	1
Trumbull	1	*Indiana.*		Harlem	1
Union	1			Harpswell	1
Vernon	2	Fort Knox	1	Hollis	1
Voluntown	1	Kaskaskias	1	Isle Au Haut	8
Wallingford	8			Kennebunk	7
Warren	3	*Kentucky.*		Kittery	12
Washington	2			Lebanon	1
Waterbury	2	Bardstown	1	Lewiston	2
Waterford	6	Bath County	1	Limerick	1
Watertown	3	Bedford County	1	Limington	1
W. Hartford	6	Bourbon County	4	Livermore	3
W. Haven	1	Frankfort	1	Machias	4
Westfield	2	Lancaster	1	Monmouth	1
Weston	1	Lexington	5	New Gloucester	5
Wethersfield	19	Louisville	2	Newfield	1
Wilton	1	Lynn Camp Cr`k	1	Norridgewock	1
Windham	31	Richmond	1	North Yarmouth	3
Woodbridge	1	Scott County	1	Norway	1
Woodbury	1	[not given]	6	Old Town	1
Woodstock	4			Orangetown	1
[not given]	8	*Louisiana.*		Orono	1
				Orrington	2
Conn. totals:	782	Attakapas	1	Otisfield	1
		New Orleans	25	Pejepscot	1
Delaware.		Opelousas	1	Penobscot	1
		[not given]	2	Poland	1
Brandywine	1			Portland	47
Dover	4	*Maine.*		Saco	6
Georgetown	1			Scarborough	6
Lewis	1	Athens	1	Sebesticook	1
New Castle	2	Augusta	7	Shapleigh	1
Smyrna	2	Bangor	2	Spruce Head	1
Wilmington	3	Bath	1	Standish	2
		Belfast	2	Topsham	3
Delaware totals:	14	Berwick	7	Turner	1
		Bethel	1	Vassalborough	2
District of Columbia.		Biddeford	2	Waldoboro	3
		Bluehill	2	Warren	1
Washington	23	Boothbay	2	Waterville	2

Wells	4	Chelsea	4	Lancaster	21
Windham	1	Cheshire	4	Lanesborough	1
Winslow	1	Chester	1	Lee	1
Winthrop	1	Chesterfield	2	Leicester	18
Wiscasset	12	Chilmark	1	Lenox	5
York	8	Cohasset	3	Leominster	18
[not given]	4	Colrain	8	Lexington	12
		Concord	18	Leyden	7
Maine totals:	240	Conway	6	Lincoln	6
		Cummington	1	Littleton	2
Michigan.		Dana	1	Longmeadow	1
		Daniel	1	Ludlow	2
Detroit	2	Danvers	18	Lunenburg	8
		Dedham	25	Lynn	11
Massachusetts.		Deerfield	16	Lynnfield	1
		Dennis	1	Malden	4
Abington	3	Dorchester	27	Manchester	4
Acton	8	Douglas	1	Mansfield	2
Adams	3	Dracut	5	Marblehead	28
Alford	1	Dudley	3	Marlborough	7
Amesbury	4	East Sudbury	5	Marshfield	5
Amherst	18	Easthampton	6	Medfield	1
Andover	21	Easton	5	Medford	14
Arlington	4	Falmouth	1	Mendon	9
Ashburnham	7	Fitchburg	10	Methuen	2
Ashby	4	Foxborough	4	Middleborough	6
Ashfield	1	Framingham	7	Milford	2
Athol	2	Franklin	7	Milton	21
Attleboro	6	Freetown	1	Monson	6
Barnstable	16	Gerry	7	Montague	5
Barre	22	Gill	2	Nahant	2
Becket	3	Gloucester	28	Nantucket	11
Bedford	6	Goshen	1	Natick	2
Belchertown	4	Grafton	8	Needham	2
Berlin	2	Granby	4	New Bedford	15
Bernardston	7	Granville	1	New Braintree	3
Beverly	25	Great Barrington	4	New Salem	1
Billerica	2	Greene	1	Newbury	6
Blandford	1	Greenfield	26	Newburyport	60
Bolton	14	Groton	7	Newton	27
Boston	745	Hadley	6	Northampton	87
Boxford	5	Halloway	1	Northborough	8
Boylston	6	Hamilton	4	Northbridge	2
Bradford	11	Hanover	1	Northfield	7
Braintree	3	Hardwick	5	Norton	3
Bridgewater	11	Harvard	4	Oakham	6
Brimfield	7	Hatfield	1	Orange	4
Brookfield	43	Haverhill	31	Oxford	9
Brookline	6	Hawley	1	Palmer	3
Buckland	2	Heath	1	Paxton	1
Burlington	1	Hingham	19	Pembroke	7
Cambridge	39	Holden	5	Pepperell	1
Canton	4	Hollis	1	Peru	1
Carver	1	Holliston	2	Petersham	20
Charlemont	1	Hopkinton	14	Pittsfield	12
Charlestown	50	Hubbardston	8	Plainfield	1
Charlton	6	Hudson	1	Plymouth	9
Chatham	1	Ipswich	14	Plympton	1
Chelmsford	7	Kingston	2	Princeton	10

Provincetown	1	Westford	4	Barnstead	1
Quincy	12	Westhampton	5	Barrington	2
Randolph	4	Westminster	4	Bartlett	1
Raynham	3	Weston	7	Bath	2
Reading	9	Weymouth	4	Bedford	2
Rehoboth	10	Whately	1	Boscawen	5
Richmond	4	Wilbraham	18	Bow	4
Rowe	3	Williamsburg	4	Bridgewater	3
Rowley	11	Williamstown	5	Brookline	2
Roxbury	40	Wilmington	2	Candia	1
Royalston	4	Winchendon	2	Canterbury	5
Rutland	12	Windsor	1	Charlestown	46
Salem	140	Woburn	6	Chester	7
Salisbury	10	Worcester	90	Chesterfield	16
Sandisfield	2	Worthington	6	Claremont	28
Sandwich	1	Wrentham	9	Concord	40
Scituate	18	Yarmouth	2	Cornish	46
Sharon	2	[not given]	9	Croydon	35
Sheffield	4			Deerfield	3
Shelburne	7	Mass. totals:	2882	Deering	2
Sherborn	3			Dover	29
Shirley	6	*Maryland.*		Dublin	6
Shrewsbury	20			Dunbarton	4
Shutesbury	1	Annapolis	6	Dunstable, see Nashua	
South Hadley	4	Baltimore	52	Durham	4
Southampton	8	Caroline County	1	Enfield	3
Southborough	3	Church-Hill	1	Epping	3
Southwick	11	Easton	1	Epsom	1
Spencer	8	Elkton	1	Exeter	15
Springfield	52	Fredericktown	7	Fitzwilliam	8
Sterling	10	Georgetown	8	Francestown	2
Stockbridge	16	Hartford	2	Franconia	1
Stoneham	2	Kent	1	Gilmanton	10
Stoughton	2	Leonardtown	1	Gilsum	1
Stow	4	Prince Geo. Co.	1	Goffstown	1
Sturbridge	20	Somerset Co.	2	Goshen	3
Sudbury	5	Tanneytown	1	Gosport	1
Sunderland	6	[not given]	22	Grafton	1
Sutton	23			Grantham	2
Swansey	4	Maryland totals:	107	Greenfield	1
Taunton	4			Greenland	6
Templeton	7	*Mississippi.*		Groton	1
Tewksbury	1			Hampstead	9
Topsfield	5	Fort Adams	1	Hampton	6
Townsend	2	Natchez	12	Hampton Falls	3
Truro	1	[not given]	4	Hancock	1
Tyringham	1			Hanover	47
Upton	5	*Missouri.*		Haverhill	7
Uxbridge	5			Henniker	3
Walpole	2	St. Louis	1	Hillsborough	4
Waltham	7			Hinsdale	9
Ward	2	*New Hampshire.*		Holderness	2
Ware	1			Hollis	7
Warwick	4	Acworth	39	Hopkinton	5
Watertown	19	Allenstown	1	Jaffrey	17
W. Springfield	25	Alstead	67	Keene	90
W. Stockbridge	2	Amherst	31	Kensington	1
Westborough	9	Antrim	2	Kingston	3
Westfield	10	Atkinson	2	Lancaster	5

Langdon	12	Sutton	2	N. J. totals:		99	
Lebanon	12	Swanzey	10				
Lee	6	Temple	9	*New York.*			
Lempster	9	Thornton	2				
Lisbon	1	Troy	4	Albany		51	
Litchfield	1	Unity	5	Amenia		1	
Littleton	1	Wakefield	2	Antrim		1	
Londonderry	4	Walpole	172	Aurelius		2	
Loudon	1	Washington	13	Ballston		3	
Lyme	10	Weare	2	Ballston Spa		1	
Lyndeborough	5	Wendell	1	Ballston Springs		3	
Madbury	2	Westmoreland	34	Batavia		1	
Manchester	2	Wilton	3	Bedford		1	
Marlborough	9	Winchester	13	Bloomingdale		2	
Marlow	8	Windham	1	Buffalo		1	
Mason	1	Wolfborough	1	Burlington		1	
Merrimack	9	Woodstock	1	Cambridge		1	
Milford	6	[not given]	6	Canaan		1	
Mont Vernon	2			Canajoharie		2	
Moultonborough	1	N.H. totals:	1506	Canandaigua		6	
Nashua	4			Canisteo		1	
Nelson	7	*New Jersey.*		Catskill		4	
New Boston	7			Cazenovia		1	
New Grantham	1	Amwel	1	Charlestown		2	
New Ipswich	19	Bridgetown	1	Chatham		1	
New London	2	Brunswick	1	Chazy		1	
Newbury	1	Burlington	2	Cherry Valley		2	
Newcastle	5	Cranbury	4	Chesterfield		1	
Newington	5	Cumberland	1	Claremont		1	
Newmarket	3	Elizabeth	1	Claverack		4	
Newport	19	Elizabethtown	5	Coeymans		2	
North Hampton	4	Gloucester	2	Constable		2	
Northfield	1	Gloucester Co.	1	Cooperstown		4	
Northumberland	3	Goshen	1	Crown Point		1	
Northwood	5	Hackensack	1	Deerfield		1	
Orford	8	Haddonfield	1	Delhi		1	
Pelham	8	Hamburg	1	Derne		2	
Pembroke	5	Hanover	1	Eaton		1	
Peterborough	9	Hopewell	3	Fishkill		1	
Piermont	3	Kingston	1	Frankfort		1	
Plainfield	16	Lebanon	2	Freehold		1	
Plaistow	5	Maidenhead	2	Geneva		1	
Plymouth	2	Mendham	1	Gorham		1	
Portsmouth	200	Middlesex	1	Granville		3	
Raymond	5	Middletown	3	Great Barrington		2	
Richmond	3	Morristown	7	Greenbush		3	
Rindge	8	New Vernon	1	Greenfield		1	
Rochester	5	Newark	10	Greensborough		2	
Rumney	2	Newton	1	Hamilton		1	
Rye	9	Nottingham	1	Hanover		1	
Salisbury	5	Pittstown	1	Hartwick		4	
Sanbornton	2	Princeton	2	Herkimer		4	
Somersworth	1	Springfield	1	Hermitage		3	
South Hampton	1	Stanhope	1	Hoosic		2	
Springfield	1	Trenton	8	Hudson		15	
Stoddard	6	Vealtown	1	Hurley		3	
Stratham	2	Woodbridge	1	Johnstown		1	
Sullivan	5	Woodstock	1	Kinderhook		6	
Surry	12	[not given]	26	Kingston		3	

Kline Esopus	1		Sussex	1		Ohio totals:	22
Lansingburgh	5		Syracuse	1			
Lisle	1		Thinebeck	1		*Pennsylvania.*	
Louisville	3		Trenton	1			
Madrid	1		Troy	20		Beckley	1
Malone	2		Unadilla	1		Bedford	3
Malta	1		Utica	3		Brooklyn	1
Mamakating	1		Walton	1		Buck's County	1
Manlius	1		Wardsbridge	1		Cansteer	1
Marblehead	1		Washington	1		Canonsburgh	2
Marcellus	2		Waterford	3		Carlisle	8
Middleburgh	1		Watervliet	3		Chambersburg	2
Middlefield	2		Westchester	2		Chester County	1
Minden	1		Westfield	1		E. Nottingham	1
New Canaan	1		Westford	1		Easton	1
New Lebanon	2		Westmoreland	2		Elkridge	1
New Milford	1		White Plains	2		Fairhill	1
New Rochelle	1		Whitestown	3		Fredericktown	1
New York City	231		Willsboro	1		Germantown	3
Newburgh	2		Windham	1		Hamilton	2
Newcastle	1		Woodstock	1		Harrisburg	4
Niagara	2		[not given]	19		Lancaster	11
Norwich	4					Lewistown	1
Onondaga	2		New York totals:	582		Little Britain	1
Oswego	1					Loudon Forge	1
Otsego	1		*North Carolina.*			Manheim	1
Owego	1					Mecklenburg Co.	1
Paris	1		Averasboro	1		Middletown	1
Peekskill	1		Baldhead	1		Mifflin Co.	2
Peterboro	1		Edenton	2		Montgomery Co.	3
Phelps	1		Glasgow County	1		Nahony	1
Pittstown	1		Granville County	1		New Carlisle	1
Platte-Kill	1		Greenville	1		Newburgh	1
Plattsburg	2		Halifax	1		Northumberland	2
Pompey	1		Iredell County	1		Paxton	1
Poughkeepsie	9		Mecklenburg	1		Philadelphia	144
Poundridge	1		Newbern	2		Pittsburg	2
Redding	3		Raleigh	2		Reading	1
Rochester	1		Robeson	1		Shamokin	1
Rome	3		Sneedsborough	1		Sheshequin	4
Rutland	4		Warrenton	1		Shippensburg	1
Rye	1		Wilmington	8		Sunnytown	3
Sag Harbor	1		[not given]	10		Washington	1
Salem	4					Westmoreland	2
Sandy Creek	2		N. C. totals:	35		York Co.	2
Saratoga Springs	1					[not given]	15
Schaghticoke	3		*Ohio.*				
Schenectady	7					Penn. totals:	238
Schoharie	1		Anstinsburg	1			
Schoodick	1		Athens	1		*Rhode Island.*	
Scipio	2		Belpre	1			
Seneca	1		Canfield	1		Bellingham	1
Sharon	1		Champaign	1		Block Island	1
Sherburn	1		Chillicothe	4		Bristol	3
Skeensboro	1		Cincinnati	1		Cranston	2
Sparta	1		Franklin	3		Cumberland	2
St. Lawrence Co.	1		Goshen	1		E. Greenwich	1
Stephentown	2		Marietta	7		Foster	1
Stillwater	2		Stanburg	1		Gloucester	3

Hopkinton	1	Andover	5	Middlebury	21
Johnston	2	Athens	1	Middletown	1
Middletown	2	Barnard	7	Milton	1
N. Kingston	1	Barnet	7	Monkton	3
Newport	42	Barre	1	Montpelier	4
Portsmouth	2	Barton	1	Morristown	1
Providence	80	Bennington	3	Newbury	7
Smithfield	8	Bradford	3	Newfane	7
S. Kingston	1	Braintree	1	Newport	1
Tiverton	1	Brandon	1	Norwich	19
Warren	1	Brattleboro	33	Orange	1
Warwick	3	Bridgewater	1	Orwell	1
Westerly	4	Bridport	4	Panton	1
[not given]	5	Brookfield	1	Pawlet	1
		Brookline	1	Peacham	7
R. I. totals:	167	Burke	2	Pittsford	4
		Burlington	15	Plymouth	1
South Carolina.		Cambridge	2	Pomfret	7
		Castleton	7	Poultney	6
Abbeville	1	Cavendish	10	Pownal	1
Beaufort	2	Charlotte	7	Putney	15
Charleston	91	Chelsea	5	Randolph	10
Cheraw District	1	Chester	16	Reading	3
Columbia	1	Clarendon	2	Richmond	2
Dafusky Island	1	Concord	2	Rockingham	23
Dutch Fork	1	Cornwall	2	Royalton	8
Edgefield District	1	Coventry	1	Rupert	1
Fairfield	1	Craftsbury	6	Rutland	46
Georgetown	1	Danville	4	Ryegate	3
Hillsborough	1	Derby	1	Shaftsbury	1
Middelton Ferry	1	Dorset	2	Shelburne	3
Nassau	1	Dummerston	12	Sheldon	2
Pendleton Dist.	1	Enosburg	2	Shoreham	3
Rocky Mount	2	Essex	1	Somerset	1
Rumney	1	Fairfax	2	Springfield	16
Santee	1	Fairfield	1	St. Albans	7
Statesburg	1	Georgia	1	Starksborough	1
Sullivan's Island	1	Grafton	13	Strafford	4
Sumpter District	1	Greensboro	1	Sudbury	1
Wassamasaw	1	Groton	2	Swanton	3
Waynesborough	1	Guilford	13	Thetford	5
[not given]	18	Halifax	16	Tinmouth	1
		Hampton	2	Topsham	1
S.C. totals:	132	Hartford	11	Townshend	5
		Hartland	16	Tunbridge	2
Tennessee.		Huntington	1	Vergennes	15
		Ira	3	Vernon	1
Belville	1	Isle La Motte	1	Waitsfield	1
Dixon's Springs	1	Jamaica	1	Walden	1
Jonesborough	1	Jericho	1	Wardsboro	3
Knoxville	7	Landgrove	2	Waterbury	1
Nashville	1	Leicester	1	Weathersfield	14
Tellico	1	Lemington	1	Wells	1
[not given]	3	Londonderry	5	Westfield	1
		Ludlow	2	Westford	2
Vermont.		Lunenburg	1	Westminster	41
		Lyman	1	Weston	1
Addison	2	Manchester	2	Weybridge	1
Alexandria	1	Mason	1	Whiting	1

Williamstown	1	Charlotte Co.	1	Mount Eagle	1
Williston	2	Chesterfield Co.	1	Norfolk	8
Wilmington	2	Clarksburg	2	Perkinsville	1
Winchendon	1	Columbia Co.	1	Petersburg	3
Windham	1	Dinguidsville	1	Portsmouth	1
Windsor	47	Dinwiddie	2	Richmond	17
Wolcott	1	Fincastle	4	Richmond Co.	1
Woodstock	29	Fredericksburg	4	Rosegill	1
[not given]	2	Gloucester Co.	1	Southampton	3
		Halifax Co.	1	Stafford	1
Vermont totals:	705	Hampshire Co.	1	Staunton	2
		Hampton Roads	1	Winchester	7
Virginia.		Henrico Co.	1	[not given]	30
		Hungar Parish	1		
Alexandria	13	Janesburgh	1	Virginia totals:	120
Bellmont	1	Kemsville	1		
Brunswick	1	Leedstown	1		
Bucklestown	2	Lunenburg Co.	1		
		Lynchburg	1		

Causes of Death.

Accidents, unclassified,	20	Croup,	1
Accidents, hunting,	1	Crushed to death,	16
Accidents, saw mill,	1	Dropsy,	7
Accidents, unclassified fall,	37	Drowned,	155
Accidents, fell on ice,	2	Drunk,	2
Accidents, fell off horse,	10	Duel,	33
Accidents, dragged by horse,	3	Dysentery,	20
Accidents, kicked by horse,	2	Epilepsy,	1
Accidents, stone falling,	1	Executed,	40
Accidents, shot,	8	Explosion, unclassified	17
Amputation,	1	Explosion, powder mill,	1
Apoplexy,	12	Fever, unclassified	21
Asthma,	3	Fever, Lung,	1
Avalanche,	2	Fever, Malignant,	35
Balloon accident,	1	Fever, Nervous	1
Bee sting,	1	Fever, Putrid,	2
Burned	56	Fever, Spotted,	31
Cancer	7	Fever, Typhoid,	6
Canker rash	6	Fever, Yellow,	20
Carriage accident,	7	Fit,	1
Choked,	2	Food poisoning,	1
Cholera,	2	Frozen,	10
Concussion,	1	Gored by animal,	4
Consumption,	30	Gun burst,	1

Causes of Death (con't.)

Heart disease,	1	Scalded,	7
Impaled	1	Scarlatina,	1
Inflammation of brain,	1	Shark,	1
Injuries, unclassified,	6	Shot,	9
Killed (mostly foreign countries)	47	Small pox,	19
Lethargy,	1	Snake bite,	1
Lightning,	37	Stroke,	1
Lockjaw,	4	Suffocated	5
Lost at sea,	8	Suicide,	82
Mumps,	1	Tetanus,	1
Murdered,	94	Tornado,	1
Numb Palsy,	3	Tree, killed by falling	23
Palsy,	3		
Pleurisy,	1		
Poisoned,	12	Total number of	
Rabies,	9	deaths specified,	1034
Run over by wagon,	12		

Other Statistics.

A.W.O.L.	1
Advertisements	876
Counterfeiters	41
Fires	308
Freedom notices	1
Jailbreaks	33
Legal notices	244
Letters remaining at post offices	1442
Ministers ordained	136
Missing person notices	4
Persons vaccinated for small pox	42
Persons quarantined	1
Prisoners of war	30
Robberies	16
Runaway notices	76
Ships pirated at sea	22
Shipwrecks	30
Tax delinquencies	684
Vital Records, number of marriages	1236
Vital Records, number of deaths	6318
Vital Records, number of divorces	18

Section 2.

Early Newspapers of Gilmanton, N.H.

Gilmanton Rural Museum (1800)
The Gilmanton Gazette, and Farmers' Weekly Magazine (1800)

Gilmanton Rural Museum.

The *Gilmanton Rural Museum* was "printed and published weekly, by Elijah Russell, near the Academy in Gilmanton," according to a rare copy, that of Vol. I, No. 17, dated 28 Feb. 1800. This was a short-lived paper; the one surviving issue located within the state is at the New Hampshire Historical Society in Concord, N.H. *

Vol. I (No. 17) Friday, 28 Feb. 1800.

† [1a] Runaway notice posted by James Chase, Jr., for one John Kelley, an indented apprentice about 18 years of age, described as 5' 5" in height and of a light complexion. The notice is dated at Gilmanton 6 Jan. 1800, and Chase offered one gill of oats reward for the return of Kelley.

† [1a] Runaway notice posted by Durrel Bean, for one Henry Barter, jr. "an apprentice boy" about 15 years old, described as having dark complexion and dark hair. Barter absconded 2 Jan. 1800; the notice was dated at Gilmanton the same day.

¶ [3c-d] BOSTON, FEB. 17. The following information is given by Capt. Boden, arrived at Baltimore the 6th instant, from Cape Francois, which place he left the 15th ult. "The United States schooner Experiment, Capt. Maley, with a convoy off the east end of Goniaves, in the Bite of Leogane, was attacked about the 10th of January, by 12 of Rigaud's barges; during the action, three of them went on shore and renewed their crews; the day being calm, they had every advantage of the schooner, but after she had sunk 3 of them, the remained sheered off, they however took possession of a northern brig, Captain Chipman, *whom they instantly murdered*; part of the crew saved themelves by jumping overboard—she was soon afterwards retaken by one of Toussaint's barges. Dr. Stephens was on board the Experiment at the time of the engagement."

¶ [3d] PORTLAND, Feb. 3. Last Wednesday, as Mr. James Libbey, of Gorham, was driving his team, with a loaded sled, he unfortunately fell, and the sled went over him, broke several of his bones, and mangled his body in so shocking a manner, that he expired in a few hours.

As a Mr. Rand was returning from digging Mr. Libbey's grave, he stopped to converse with a man whom he met with a team when he accidentally slipped, the sled passed over him, and broke both his legs in such a manner, that it was necessary they should be amputated. He was living last Saturday, but his life was despaired of.

---

* According to the "History and Bibliography of American Newspapers, 1690-1820," by Clarence S. Brigham, (American Antiquarian Society, Worcester, Mass., 1947) this paper was probably established 28 Oct. 1799, and continued publishing for six months. This source's inventory states that Harvard University has the issues of 11 Nov. and 18 Nov. 1799.

The Gilmanton Gazette, and Farmers' Weekly Magazine.

A single issue of *The Gilmanton Gazette, and Farmers' Weekly Magaine,* that of 20 Dec. 1800, exists in the newspaper collection owned by the New Hampshire Historical Society in Concord. It was another short-lived Gilmanton paper, and was published by Dudley Leavitt and ——— Clough. They may have acquired ownership of a print shop which was owned by Elijah Russell, named above. In the last column of the fourth page of the issue of 20 Dec. 1800, Dudley Leavitt advertised that he will put out for collection those debts owed "to Elijah Russell, for papers printed in Gilmanton."

Vol. I (No. 17) Saturday, 20 Dec. 1800

† [3d] Legal notice from the Superior Court of Strafford County: "Samuel Shepard of Gilmanton in the county aforesaid, Guardian of Jonathan Bachelder, of the same Gilmanton, husbandman, who is represented and adjudged so far an ideot [sic] as to be incapable of taking care of himself or estate; that the personal estate of said Bachelder is insufficient to discharge his debts, and that it is necessary to sell a part or whole of his real estate for that purpose.—Wherein your petitioner prays this honourable Court to authorize and empower him to sell so much of the real estate of said Bachelder not exceeding the sum of six hundred dollars, as will be sufficient to discharge said Bachelder's debts."

¶ [3d] *Please to take Notice.* The Season is now arrived when the interest and the Donations to Gilmanton Academy is become due, and a considerable part of the Preceptor's last year's Salary remains unpaid for want of money in the Treasury to discharge it. Those therefore who have made Donations are requested to make immediate payment of the interest to the Subscriber—and those who have given their obligations for the donations of others, and for the purchase of the Academy Lands are hereby notified, that they must be punctual in the payment of their interest, or they will be called upon in another way,

By STEPHEN MOODY, *Treasurer,*
Gilmanton, Dec. 16th, 1800.

¶ [3d] Stray sheep, came into the enclosure of the Subscriber some time last Summer, two white, and one black sheep, marked with Spanish Brown Paint. The owner may have them again by proving property and paying charges.

NOAH DOW.
Gilmanton, Dec. 20, 1800.

¶ [3d] Stray ram, came into the enclosure of the Subscriber about the first of last July, a large white ram, having no artificial mark. The owner may prove property, pay charges, and take him away.

NATHANIEL PIPER.
Gilmanton, Dec. 20, 1800.

¶ [4b] The first Printing-press erected in America, was at Cambridge, by Mr. Samuel Green, in the year 1638. The first work printed, was the Freeman's Oath—the next, an Almanack, made for New England, by mr. Peirce, mariner.—and then the Psalms newly turned into [?].

The Gilmanton Gazette, and Farmers' Weekly Magazine (con't.)

¶ [4d] TAKE NOTICE. To be sold, at public auction, by virtue of a license from the Judge of Probate of Wills, &c. for the county of Strafford, on Monday the twenty-second day of December next, at two of the clock in the afternoon, so much of the Real Estate of Benjamin Page, deceased, as will raise the sum of one hundred and sixty dollars, to be sold at the house of Richard Boynton, Esq. innholder in Meredith. Conditions of sale to be made known at time and place of sale.
SARAH PAGE, Administratrix.
Meredith, Nov. 29, 1800.

¶ [4d] Stray sheep, came into the enclosure of the Subscriber about the first of September last, three sheep. The owner is desired to take them away, after proving property and paying charges.
JOSEPH JONES.
Gilmanton, Dec. 6, 1800.

¶ [4d] STATE OF NEW HAMPSHIRE, STRAFFORD COUNTY. Notice is hereby given to the Unknown Proprietors and Owners of Land in the town of Sandbornton in said County, that a Direct Tax has been assessed, agreeably to an Act of Congress, and the Pieces and Lots of Land in said town, hereafter mentioned; and that the taxes became due and payable on the 8th day of January 1800, and unless they pay the taxes assessed on said lands to me the subscriber within sixty days so much of said lands will be sold at the dwelling house of Benjamin Colbey, innholder in said Sandbornton, on Monday the 9th day of February next, at 10 o'clock, A.M. as will pay said taxes with incidental charges.

Names Of Proprietors,	Quantity in Acres	Number	Division	Taxes dols. cts.
Love Chase,	100	54	2	0 42
Mr. Solly and March,	125	79	2	1 05
Josiah Sanborn,	100	unkno'n	2	84
John Sanborn,	200	40	2	2 52
Joseph Smith,	100	60	2	1 (?) 62
John Thomlinson,	50	61	2	63
William Thompson,	13	unkno'n	2	16 (?)

JOSEPH WOODMAN,
Collector of the 25th Collection District.
Sandbornton, Nov. 22, 1800.

Note: according to the "History and Bibliography of American Newspapers, 1690-1820," by Clarence S. Brigham, (American Antiquarian Society, Worcester, Mass., 1947) this paper was probably established 30 Aug. 1800. This source's inventory states that the New York Historical Society has the issues of 6 Dec. and 20 Dec. 1800, and the Library of Congress has the issue of 13 Dec. 1800.

Section 3.

Early Newspapers of Gilford, N.H.

Democratic Spy (1829-30)
The Strafford Republican (1831)

The Democratic Spy, Gilford, N.H.

The following items were extracted from a short-lived weekly newspaper published 1829-1830, by Hugh Moore, entitled *The Democratic Spy*. Though this paper is identified with Gilford, the paper was actually published in Sanbornton, according to "*American Newspapers, 1821-1936: A Union List of Files Available in the United States and Canada,*" 1937, by Winifred Gregory. That source indicates that the paper continued to publish into June of 1830. Six copies of this newspaper are located at the New Hampshire Historical Society in Concord, their issues bearing the dates of 21 Oct. 1829, 4 Nov. 1829, 30 Dec. 1829, 12 Jan. 1830, 19 Jan. 1830, and 9 March 1830. Due to time constraints, the first four issues in this group did not receive a full gleaning; only the marriages, deaths, and a few other items were transcribed. However, the issues of 19 Jan. and 9 Mar. 1830 were reviewed thoroughly, and all items of genealogical interest were abstracted.

The Democratic Spy

Vol. I (No. 1) Wednesday, 21 Oct. 1829.

===== MARRIED. =====

In Portland, Me. by the Rev. Mr. Rand, Mr. Paul Hall to Miss Sarah Leighton; Mr. Thomas Province to Miss Sarah F. Gooding.

In Dover, by Rev. Mr. Winslow, Mr. Thomas B. Twombly, to Miss Huldah T. Clark; by Rev. Mr. Otheman, Mr. William Howard, to Miss Mary Glidden, all of Dover.

In Exeter, Mr. Edmund Elliot to Miss Eliza Gilman.

In Meredith, Mr. Benjamin R. Gilman, to Miss Caroline Chase.—Mr. Warren Tucker, to Miss Irene Marsh.

===== DIED. =====

In Portsmouth, very suddenly, Mrs. Elizabeth, wife of Maj. Daniel Henderson, aged 66.

In Hancock, 8th inst. Mr. Isaac Fisk, of Stoddard, aged 34.

In Portsmouth, on Tuesday evening last, Mr. Thomas Furnald, of Nottingham, aged 44 years. He had been attending the market during the day, and in the evening sat down to supper at the Farmer's Hotel, in apparent health, and expired in about five minutes.

In Stratham, Miss Wingate, daughter of Hon. Paine Wingate.

In Boscawen, 28th ult. of consumption, Miss Martha Pritchard, aged 33.

In Augusta, on Thursday week, Enoch Lincoln, Governor of the state of Maine, aged about 40.

In this town, on Saturday last, widow Pottle.

Vol. I (No. 3) Wednesday, 4 Nov. 1829.

¶ [3a] ACCIDENT. Mr. Isaac Avery, of Gilmanton, in this County, a young man 21 years of age, was accidentally killed, in Charlestown, Mass. on Friday last, while blasting a rock. He was struck in the side by a fragment, an artery opened and he bled to death.

¶ [4d] INFORMATION WANTED. Mr. Isaac C. Goodwin, son of Mr. David Goodwin, of Barnstead, N.H. left the house of his father on the 27th of August last. He is about thirty three years old, light complexion, light blue eyes, height about six feet; had on the day he left a pair of tow pantaloons fustian color, considerably worn, a thin vest, a hat broken in at the top, and no shoes. His occupation has been that of a miller. Said Goodwin had been in a melancholy or deranged state of mind, and evaded company for several months previous to his leaving home. Barnstead Oct. 15, 1829.

Vol. I (No. 11) Wednesday, 30 Dec. 1829.

† [3c] Legal notice regarding Hannah P. Swasey of Gilmanton, widow, concerning her guardianship of Martha Ann Swasey, a minor under age 14; dated Gilford 2 Dec. 1829.

† [3d] Freedom notice for David Watson, son of Jonathan Watson; dated at Meredith, N.H. 23 Dec. 1829.

† [3d] Freedom notice regarding Stephen C. Philbrook, Thomas J. Philbrook and Moses C. Philbrook, all sons of David Philbrook; dated Sanbornton 25 Dec. 1829.

† [3d] Freedom notice of Amasa Small, eldest son of Ebenezer Small, "until he becomes of age." Dated at Alton 17 Dec. 1829. Witnessed by John Chesle and John R. Buzzell.

† [4d] Freedom notice of Jonathan Thurstain Thompson, son of Samuel Thompson; witnessed by Charles Prescott and Levi Thompson. The notice is not dated, nor is a location identified.

===== MARRIED. =====

In Charlestown, Ms. by Rev. L.S. Everett, Mr. George H. Jacobs to Miss Persis A. Teel, both of Charlestown.

The Democratic Spy (con't.)

In Deering, by Rev. Jabez Fisher, Mr. Luther Sumner of Roxbury, Ms. to Miss Elizabeth Ross.
In Barnstead, by Rev. Enos George, Mr. John Nutter, 4th, to Miss Hannah Nutter.

===== DIED. =====

In Durham, suddenly, Mr. John L. Blake, of Gilmanton, aged 33—a worthy and respectable individual.
In Alton, James P. Roberts, aged 39.
In Portsmouth, Hon. John Goddard, aged 73.
In Hampton Falls, Peter Tilton, Esq. aged 79.

Vol. I (No. 13) Tuesday, 12 Jan. 1830.

† [2d] Rev. Lewis E. Caswell, an evangelist, ordained at Meredith 31 Dec. 1829.
† [2d] Review of the first number of the *Plymouth Gazette*, published in Grafton County.
† [2d] Fire at the home of Mr. Zadock Bowman in Gilford, though the house is saved.
† [3d] Freedom notice of Joseph G. Bennett and Isaac Bennett, sons of John Bennett; dated at Gilford 11 Jan. 1830; witnessed by Smith Jewett and John Jewett.
† [4d] List of letters remaining at the Post Office, Gilford, N.H., 1 Jan. 1830, as compiled by F. Russell, Postmaster:

Ephraim Hoit	Joseph Bradbury
Enock Ollins	Emery Hackett, Gilmanton
Mrs. Rebecca G. Meheberle	William Saltmarsh
Mrs. Ann Libbey	Stephen Crosby
Mrs. Sally Rowe, Gilmanton	William Hinkley
Thomas Sargeant	Nathaniel Davis
Jacob Pollard	William Sewall
Miss Sally Sleeper	Miss Eliza Goss
Rebeccah Pickering	

===== MARRIED. =====

In Bristol, by Elder John Hill, Lieut. Wm. Lock, of Alexandria, to Miss Louisa Ferrin, of the former place.
In Bridgwater, on the 27th ult. Mr. Eliphalet Smith to Miss Sally Fisk.

===== DIED. =====

In Gilmanton, on Monday the 4th inst. Widow Elizabeth Cate, formerly of Greenland, N.H. aged about 93 years. Printers in Vermont are requested to notice the above.

Vol. I (No. 14) Tuesday, 19 Jan. 1830.

† [2d] Three daughters of Mr. Martinus Creiger, "of Nishayua," were overcome by fumes from burning charcoal in their rooms, though all of them survived. The event occurred on "the 13th ult;" The article was copied from the *Schenectady Cabinent*. ♦
† [3a] Lorenzo Dow, a preacher known as "the Wandering Jew," preached a sermon at Belchertown, Mass, and promised to return again in several weeks, but when the congregation gathered he did not appear. ♦
¶ [3c] A man, named Brown, was found dead, in Sandwich, one morning last week. He was unable to reach home, in consequence of being intoxicated, and perished with the cold.
† [3c] Freedom notice of Amasa Small, a minor son of Ebenezer Small of Alton, N.H., dated 17 Dec. 1829; witnessed by John Chesle and John R. Buzzell.
† [3d] D.V. Moulton adv. for an apprentice boy for the printing business; dated at Sanbornton, 8 Jan. 1830.
† [4b] Adv. by John P. Gass, "formerly of the Columbian Hotel at Concord, and recently from the Broadway House, one of the largest establishments in the City of New

The Democratic Spy (con't.)

York," now has "taken that splendid new Hotel, the Eagle Coffee House lately kept by Capt. William Richardson." Dated 28 Sept. 1829.
† [4b] David Burleigh adv. for a pair of steers found on his property; no town or date given.
† [4c] Lyman B. Walker offers reward for information on who poisoned his dog; one George P. Avery seems to be implicated; dated Gilford 9 Jan. 1830.
† [4c] Auction notice of the "Herriman Farm" at Plymouth; adv. placed by Rufus Parish; dated at Gilmanton 8 Dec. 1829.
† [4c] Stoves and other related metal wares for sale by Thomas J. Hill; dated Concord 9 Nov. 1829.
† [4d] Adv. for Richard Dame, Tailor, near Meredith Bridge; dated 26 Dec. 1829.
† [4d] Adv. by Charles Lane, agent for the N.H. Mutual Fire Insurance Company; dated at Sanbornton 3 Nov. 1829.

===== ¶ [3c] MARRIAGES. =====

In Bath, Mr. James H. Johnson, of Lisbon, to Miss Jane Hutchins.
In Chester, Mr. Hill Stevens, to Miss Roxana Mardin.
Another Revolutionary hero gone ! —In Hills, N.C. Charles Woods, of the revolutionary army, aged 81 years, to Miss Margaret Macklin, aged 15 !

===== ¶ [3c] DEATHS. =====

In Wakefield, Mr. John Horn, in the 92d year of his age.
In Salisbury, Dec. 29, Lieut. David Pettingill, aged 59.
In Antrim, the 5th ult. widow Sarah Sawyer aged 82.
In New Hampton, Mrs. Jane, widow of James Sanborn, aged 54.

Vol. I (No. 21) 9 March 1830.

† [1a] "An Indian Story," an extensive article regarding "Capt. Harmon and his Eastern rangers," who pursued and killed several Indians in June 1722, up the Kennebec River. Article copied from the *Essex Gazette*. ◆
† [1b-1e] Extensive political item concerning one Timothy Upham and Nathaniel Stoodley, accused of smuggling in the year 1810, with an affidavit given by one George Huntress, of Portsmouth, who sailed as master of the sloop Eliza, owned by Capt. Benning Morrill, from Portsmouth to Eastport. Articles also contained in [2b-2e]. ◆
† [3d] Wheeler Burley and William Burley offer land for sale in Gilmanton; dated there 2 March 1830.
† [3e] "Benjamin Brown, Joseph Brown, Josiah C. Philbrook and others, of Sandbornton, and Obadiah Elkins, Elijah Jackson, Asa Gile, and others, of Gilmanton, being situated near Union Bridge," form themselves into the United Free Baptist Society; dated at Sanbornton 2 March 1830.
† [3e] Freedom notice for Moses P. Moulton, son of Josiah Moulton, dated 4 March 1830, though no town is named.
¶ [4c] NOTICE. Ran away from the subscriber, the 3d inst. a boy by the name of Woodbry L. Crocket, thirteen years old, light complection, light hair, had on when he went away a light coloured napt hat, black coat. This is to forbid all persons harboring or trusting him on my account, as I shall pay no debts of his contracting after this date.
STEPHEN CROSBY.
Gilford, February 5, 1830.

† [4d] Extensive inventory of the goods for sale by W.M. Ladd, merchant at Meredith, dated "2d Mo. 1830." Location given as a "building recently occupied by E.S. Lawrence, 2d from the Bridge." An adv. also appears in [4e].
† [4d] Freedom notice for Isaac Buzzell, son of Isaac Buzzell, dated at Gilford 9 Feb. 1830. Witnessed by Ichabod Buzzell, Isaac D. Buzzell, Sally Small, and S. Buzzell.
† [4e] Notice published by "Johnatan Leavett," who forbids any person from purchasing a note "running to Levi R. Weeks," dated 1 March 1830, though no town is identified.

The Strafford Republican, Gilford, N.H.

Another short-lived weekly newspaper from Gilford, the *Strafford Republican*, commenced publication on 17 May 1831, and lasted only a brief while. The publisher was E.F. Lancaster. Only two issues have been located; those of the first and third issues, which are located at the New Hampshire Historical Society in Concord. According to the "*American Newspapers, 1821-1936: A Union List of Files Available in the United States and Canada*," 1937, by Winifred Gregory, this publication ended with the issue of 7 June 1831. According to that source, a copy of the second number of that publication, bearing the date of 24 May 1831, can be found at the American Antiquarian Society, Worcester, Mass.

Vol. I (No. 1) Tuesday, 17 May 1831

† [3a] Gruesome account of Josiah Randall, of Franklin, Vt., who murdered his wife, and a son about 14 years old "on Thursday night the 21st ult." Article copied from the *Burlington Sentinel*. ◆

† [3d] Fire at a house on Broad Street in Boston, killing several members of a family named Murphy, and supposedly mortally injured Mr. and Mrs. Sullivan. ◆

† [3d] Cases at the Superior Court of Judicature, held at Newport, N.H.:

    1) Joel Cobb for theft from a leather shop owned by Horace Weld, sentenced to five years at State Prison.
    2) William Mattocks for horse stealing, seven years hard labor.
    3) Harry White and Francis Wyman, larceny.
    4) Charles J. Patterson, assault and battery.

¶ [3d] A fine little boy, about 6 or 7 years old, son of Judge Nathaniel Williams, of this State, was recently killed by a hog, under circumstances of a most distressing nature. The little fellow, in the pursuit of his innocent sport, suddenly approached the bed of a sow with young pigs, and before he could make his escape, was attacked and destroyed by the affrighted and enraged animmal [sic].—*Nashville Banner*.

† [3e] Attempted escape of a prisoner named Welsh, at the prison in Catskill, N.Y. ◆

¶ [3e] *Violation of the Grave*. We are informed that the body of an old gentleman of the name of *Philbrook* was stolen from the Hopkinton graveyard on the 5th inst. and that it has not yet been found. Several persons have been apprehended on suspicion of having committed the offence. *Concord Journal*.

† [3e] Isaac C. Bradly adv. goods for sale at his *Concord Hat Store*; dated at Concord 9 May 1831.

===== ¶ [3e] **MARRIAGES**. =====

In Portsmouth, Mr. Joseph Parry to Miss Sophia Clapham, daughter of Thomas Clapham.—By Rev. Mr. King, Mr. Stephen Ladd, Jr. to Miss Dorothy Merrill, both of Brentwood.

In Hopkinton by Rev. Mr. Richardson, Mr. David Fox Eaton, of Barnstead, to Miss Eleanor Powers Chesley, of Gilmanton.

===== ¶ [3e] **DEATHS**. =====

In Hopkinton, May 1, Mr. Joseph Philbrick, aged about 80; and on the 5th May, his wife, aged nearly ninety years. (When the grave was opened for the purpose of interring the body of Mrs. Philbrick, it was discovered that the remains of her husband had been disinterred and carried away. The discovery, as might be expected, produced an excitement; search has been made, but the body has not been traced. A medical man has been arrested and his examination is to take place on Thursday.)

In Dover, Mr. William Hanson, aged 34 years.
In Durham, Mr. Francis Butler, aged 38 years.
   My home henceforth is in the skies.
   Miss Mary Ann Wiggin, 19 years ; Mr. Samuel Willey, aged 60 years.—He was taken with bleeding at the lungs and died in ten minutes after.
   In Wolfeborough, on the 1st of May, after a distressing illness of 18 months, which she bore with truly Christian fortitude and resignation, Mrs. Lydia, wife of Somuel [sic] Meder, Esq. aged 42 years.
   In Gilmanton, on the 3d instant Mrs. Elizabeth Badger, widow of the late Hon. Joseph Badger, jun. aged 83 years.

Vol. I (No. 3) Tuesday, 31 May 1831

¶ [2d] The powder works of Mr. Daniel Rogers, near Newburg, N.Y. blew up on Monday 16th and a man named Elihu Tudor was killed.

† [2e] Messrs. Brown, Willey, and Smallcorn arrested at a riot in Lowell, Mass., involving Yankees and Irish.

¶ [3b] *Replentish the Earth.*—The last North Star informs us that the wife of James Buckminster, of Franconia, N.H. and formerly of Walden in this state, has had NINE children at *three* births—three at the first, two at the next, and *four* at the last.—all boys, and all doing well ! ! They are named Abraham, Isaac, and Jacob; Elisha, Elihu, and Enoch, Noah, Samuel and Elijah.

† [3d] Mr. George Muir attacked and hit on the forehead with a rock, at Georgetown, Kentucky, inflicting an injury of which he later died. ♦

† [3e] Adv. by Ezra Allen, manufacturer of ploughs "at his shop nearly opposite the Merrimack County Bank." Dated at Concord 30 Jan. 1830.

† [3e] The copartnership of Simeon Chase and Lucius Harthan, a.k.a. Chase & Harthan, dissolved; dated at Meredith 28 May 1831.

† [3e] Freedom notice of James J. Dame, son of James Dame; dated at Gilford 20 May 1831, and witnessed by B.B. Allen.

===== ¶ [3e] MARRIAGES. =====

   In Wolfeborough, 12th inst. by Elder Hiram Holmes, Mr. Hezekiah Tibbetts to Mrs. Mary Edgerly, both of Wolfeborough.
   In Hopkinton, by the Rev. Mr. Putnam, of Dunbarton, Rev. Benjamin P. Stone, of Enosburgh, Vt. to Miss Apphia Farrington, of Hopkinton.
   In Keene, by Rev. Mr. Sullivan, Mr. Benjamin Cook, Preceptor of the Fitchburg Academy, to Miss Rebecca Harrington.
   In Portsmouth, Mr. James Pratt, to Mrs. Mary Smith;—on Sunday evening, by Elder Moses Howe, Mr. John Stockman to Miss Sarah White;—on Tuesday evening, by Elder Moses Howe, Mr. Seth Pratt, to Miss Rebecca W. Brooks.
   In New London, Mr. Rodney Jackson Bingham, to Miss Harriet Black, both of N.L.

===== ¶ [3e] DEATHS. =====

   In Concord, May 2, Mrs. Martha Garvin, wife of Mr. Chauncey Garvin, 22 years 5 mo., daughter of Mr. Joseph Parker;—May 24, Mr. Henry Fisk, 30, son of Mr. Ebenezer Fisk. He was an active, useful member of society, and an exemplary christian; and as he lived beloved, so he died lamented.—*Printers in Maine and New York are requested, &c.*
   In Dover, 13 May, Mrs. Mary Leighton, 75; wife of Jonathan L.—Miss Freelove Stone, daughter of Rev. E. Stone, of Brunswick, R.I. Her funeral was attended by nearly 1000 persons, and a sermon was delivered by Rev. E. Place.
   In Portsmouth, May 13, Capt. Oliver Chase, 60;—John G. Dow, 4, and Joseph Lowell, 20 months, children of Capt. E. Hook, both of throat distemper;—Lavinia B., 7, eldest daughter of Capt. John Davis.
   In Gilmanton, on the 3d inst. Mrs. Elizabeth Badger, widow of the late Hon. Joseph Badger, jun. aged 83 years.

Section 4.

Some Early Newspapers of Exeter, N.H.

Exeter Federal Miscellany (1799)
Political Banquet and Farmers Feast (1799)

Some Early Newspapers of Exeter, N.H.

Exeter Federal Miscellany
Political Banquet and Farmer's Feast

A weekly newspaper published at Exeter, N.H., by Henry Ranlet, which actually began under the title of *Ranlet's Federal Miscellany*, on 5 Dec. 1798. [212] A short while after, on 16 Jan. 1799, Ranlet changed the title to *Exeter Federal Miscellany*. The paper continued for about a year, with the title changing for a third time to the *Political Banquet and Farmer's Feast*. With each change in the title, the numbering system was continued on in sequence from the previous title's number. For this reason, and for the fact that these three titles were all published by Mr. Ranlet, all three titles are grouped together in this section. Few issues of this collection survive; none of *Ranlet's Federal Miscellany* have been located in New Hampshire, though a few issues are found in inventories outside of the state. The following is an imperfect inventory of surviving issues and their locations:

Title	Date	(Issue)	Location code
"Ranlet's Federal Miscellany."	12 Dec. 1798	(No. 2)	A.
	19 Dec. 1798	(No. 3)	A.
	26 Dec. 1798	(No. 4)	A.
	9 Jan. 1799	(No. 6)	C.
	16 Jan. 1799	(No. 7)	A.
	6 Feb. 1799	(No. 10)	A.
	13 Feb. 1799	(No. 11)	A., B.
	20 Feb. 1799	(No. 12)	F.
"Exeter Federal Miscellany."	17 Apr. 1799	(No. 20)	D.
	24 Apr. 1799	(No. 21)	B.
	28 May 1799	(No. 26)	B.
	2 July 1799	(No. 31)	E.
	20 Aug. 1799	(No. 38)	E.
	3 Sept. 1799.	(No. 40)	C., E.
	24 Sept. 1799	(No. 43)	B.
	8 Oct. 1799	(No. 45)	C.
"Political Banquet and Farmer's Feast."	5 Nov. 1799	(No. 49)	E.
	12 Nov. 1799	?	B.
	31 Dec. 1799.	?	B.

A = Harvard University
B = American Antiquarian Society
C = Library of Congress
D = New York Historical Society
E = Exeter Historical Society, Exeter, N.H.
F = Philips Exeter Academy, Exeter, N.H. (microfilm copy at N. H. State Library.)

Exeter Federal Miscellany

Vol. I (No. 12) Wednesday, 20 Feb. 1799

¶ [3d] DIED.] In the West Indies, Mr. Josiah We[scome?] aged about 21, and formerly an apprentice in this office.
At Portsmouth, Mr. James Shurburne, aged 20.--Mr. Stephen Ayers.
At Newbury-port, Deac. Enoch Titcomb, aged 70.
At Boston, Miss Nancy Loring, Æt. 21, eldest daughter of Mr. Joseph Loring.
Mrs. Rebecca Payne, Æt. 74.
At Salem, Mrs. Hannah Mansfield, wife of Mr. Matthew Mansfield.
In this town, Mrs. Lydia Nutter, wife of Mr. Mark Nutter, aged about 30.

† [3d] Legal notice concerning Joseph Peirce, Executor of estate of Daniel Rindge, late of Portsmouth, deceased, dated at Portsmouth 11 Feb. 1799. Notation made that "in the absence of said Joseph Peirce from Portsmouth, persons having business with him as Executor, are notified to apply to John Peirce, Esq."

† [4d] Public notice by Hawley Marshall and Henry Marshall regarding financial obligations of them and others, dated at Brentwood 13 Feb. 1799.

Vol. I (No. 31) Tuesday, 2 July 1799

===== ¶ [3c] DIED. =====

At Boston, Mrs. Mary Edes, aged 39, consort of Mr. Ebenezer Edes.
At Providence, Mr. R.G. Tillinghast, Distiller. He fell into a Vat in his Distill-house and perished.
At his seat in Virginia on the 4th inst. the Hon. Patrick Henry, Esquire, one of the lately appointed Commissioners for treating with the French Republic.
At St. Thomas, Capt. Patch, Mr. James Cunningham, Mr. Wm. Dana, the Captain, Supercargo, and passenger of the sch. Robert of Boston.
At New-Bedford, mrs. Susannah Duncan, wife of Capt. Thomas Duncan.
At Brookfield, mr. S. Hall.
— Braintree, master John Allen.
At Newburyport, mrs. Lydia Muzzey, aged 68, wife of Joseph Muzzey.
At Portsmouth, Mr. John Hooker, Æt. 76.—Mrs. Lydia Truesdell, Æt. 70.
At Dover, Col. Benj. Titcomb.
At Shrewsbury, Widow Lois Wheeler, Æt. 89.
At Holden, Mr. John Abbot, Æt. [61?].
At Standish, Dr. Isaac Thompson.
At New York, Mr. Stephen Wools, Æt. 70, Comedian.

† [3d] List of letters remaining at the Post Office, Exeter, N.H., 1 July 1799, as compiled by John W. Gilman, Postmaster:

Stephen Lamson, Exeter	John Philbrook, Exeter	Levi Gyles, Stratham.
Ephraim Robinson, Exeter	Josiah Dow, Epping	Joseph Kelley, Stratham.
Kinsly Lyford, Exeter	Joseph Smith, Jr., Epping	David Clifford, jr., Brentwood
Ebenezer Clifford, Exeter	Ruth Greenlief, Epping	Andrew Ward, Brentwood.
Daniel Jones, Exeter	Thomas Norris 3d, Epping	John Kimball, Poplin
Mary Carlton, Exeter	John Adams, Stratham	Joseph Dow, Hampton Falls.
William Cushing, Exeter	Phineas Merril, Stratham	Joseph Brown, Kensington
Samuel Marsh, Exeter	David Wiggin, Stratham	William Simpson, Greenland.
Josiah Folsom, Jr., Exeter	Timothy French, Stratham	
Jonathan Norris, Exeter	John French, Stratham	

Exeter Federal Miscellany (con't.)

¶ [3d] Whereas Mary, Wife of me the Subscriber, has Eloped from my bed and board, and has behaved herself very disorderly, this is therefore to forbid any person harbouring or trusting her on my account, as I am determined not to pay any debt she may contract after this date.

his
RHEUBEN X AUSTIN.
Stratham, June 28, 1799. mark

¶ [3d] *Take Notice.* All persons are hereby forbid trading with or trusting Marston Prescott, of Kensington, from this date if they would avoid the expence of the law.

JOSIAH PRESCOTT, } Guardians.
SIMON ROWE. }

Kensington, June 28, 1799.

† [3d] Josiah Prescott adv. for an apprentice in the shoemaking and tannery business; dated at Kensington 2 July 1799.
† [4b] Joseph S. Gilman adv. corn for sale at his store; dated Exeter 11 June 1799.
† [4b] Purington & Jones adv. that "they are erecting a Machine, for Carding all kinds of Wool, near the Great Bridge, in Exeter . . . " Dated at Exeter 10 June 1799.
† [4c] Legal notice regarding the estate of Col. Samuel Hobart, late of Kingston, deceased; Sarah Hobart, Adm'trix. Dated at Exeter 4 June 1799.
† [4d] Legal notice regarding the estate of Moses Lyford, late of Brentwood, deceased; Mehitable Lyford and Francis Lyford, Administrators; dated Brentwood 10 June 1799.
† [4d] Adv. of saddle bags found "In the road, about a mile this side of Esq. Coffin's of Epping; dated Exeter 25 June 1799.

Vol. I (No. 38) Tuesday, 20 Aug. 1799

† [1a] Adv. of a collection of hymms by Joshua Smith and Samuel Sleeper, published by Henry Ranlet at Exeter. Dated 22 July 1799.
† [1b] Samuel Elliot, *Collector of Revenue,* adv. a notice regarding inspections of carriages and granting of liquor licenses at the following locations: Mr. Hutchins' tavern, Exeter; Deacon Dearborn's tavern, Chester; Dr. Thom's tavern, Londonderry; Mr. Stickney's tavern, Concord; Mr. M'Clary's tavern, Epsom; and Mr. Butler's tavern, Nottingham.
† [1b] Daniel Kimball adv. an item found on the road from Exeter to Kingston; dated at Exeter — May 1799.
¶ [1b] Whereas I, Daniel Clay, through misrepresentation, was induced to post my wife Rhoda, in the Exeter Miscellany, of March last, now beg leave to inform the public, that I have taken her again to wife, after settling all our domestic broils in an amicable manner; so that every thing as usual, goes on like clock work.

[*Divorc'd like Scissars rent in twain,*
Each mourn'd the rivet out;
Now whet and rivetted again,
They'll make the old Sheers cut."]

Raymond, July 30.

¶ [3d] We hear from Gilmanton, that on Sunday afternoon the 11th inst. Mr. Caleb Bean and his Wife went into the field to taking hay, in order to secure it from an impending shower, when (painful to relate) a flash of lightning struck Mrs. Bean, and instantly killed her. Mr. Bean, being but a few paces from his wife, wast [sic] struck down, but receiving no injury, recovered in a few minutes, took up his wife and carried her into the house. Mrs. Bean was in the 19th year of her age, and has left a young child with her husband to lament the untimely end of parent and friend.
† [3d] Samuel Nay, Guardian to Josiah Bachelder of Raymond, *non compos mentis,* adv.

Exeter Federal Miscellany (con't.)

a notice regarding Bachelder's debts. Dated Raymond 13 Aug. 1799.

† [3d] Paragraph of some maritime news, which states that the schooner *Amity*, Capt. Samuel Fernald, "arrived here . . . in 15 days from St. Thomes [sic]." Presumably, "here" indicates Exeter, though it is not impossible that this news item was copied verbatim from a newspaper belonging to a seaport town. The paragraph also states that the schooner sailed "in company with Captains Hooper and Keene, in vessels belonging to this port . . . "

===== ¶ [3d] DIED. =====

At Portsmouth, after a short illness, Mr. John Wendell, jun. Merchant, aged 42.—Mr. John Underwood, aged 51.

On board the Schr. Amity of this port, Mr. Nathaniel Cotton, aged 23.

At Sullivan, while on a visit to see her Children, Mrs. Abigail Nims, of Keene, aged 80, wife of Mr. David Nims.—Her descendants are 81.

At Pembroke, Mr. Asaph Tracey, aged 75.

At Holliston, Col. Simeon Cutler, aged 49.

Near Newbury bar, on Thursday evening last, on board ————, Mr. Joseph Souther of Haverhill, mate, aged 2[0?], by the spliting of a swivel, discharged as an adieu gun, in compliment to some friends, who had come down from Port. He was mangled in an awful manner; but lived to reach town, where his case was instantly declared hopeless by the surgeon. He survived the accident about two hours in great misery, and then expired, leaving many who lament his loss.

Vol. I (No. 40) Tuesday, 3 Sept. 1799

† [1a] A notice stating that the copartnership of D. Prescott and F. Blake, both of Candia, is mutually dissolved. Signed by David Prescott, and dated at Candia, March 1799.

† [3c-d] Account of a fire at the home of Mr. Thomas Williams and wife, of Stratham, "on Monday last." The structure was described as a large double house, which was destroyed in the blaze, though some furniture was saved. Mr. Williams and his neighbors at the time were "all from home at work on the highways."

¶ [3d] LIGHTNING].—On [S]unday the 11th inst. a barn, 32 by 100 feet, belonging to Moses Baker, Esq. of Campton, was struck and consumed by lightning; together with its contents, which consisted of hay, grain, &c.

† [3d] Brief article describing the robbery of Mr. John Duncan, of New York, who lost a substantial sum. The event occurred "in the night of the 9th inst."

===== ¶ [3d] DIED. =====

At Bergen, (Norway) Joseph Surrington, aged 159. He retained his senses to the last hour of his long life. He was several times married, and left behind him a young widow. His eldest Son was 103, and his youngest 9 years old.

At Nottingham, Gen. Joseph Cilley, aged 65.

At Madbury, Mr. Benjamin Wingate, aged 18.

At Portsmouth, Mr. James Yates, aged 84.

At the Havanna, of the Yellow fever, Mr. Benjamin Chadbourn Leigh of Berwick, aged 22.

At St. Thomas, Capt. James Scott, jr. only son of James Scott, Esq. of Boston.

At Kingston, (Jam.) Wm. Brown, of Phelad [sic], aged 24, and Wm. Yeaton, of Durham, aged 20.   George Weeks, of Kittery, aged 31.

At sea, Mr. John Sheafe, jun. of Portsm. aged 22.

At Newmarkett, Dr. John Maustress, aged 61.

At Durham, Mr. Timothy Meservey.

At Kensington, Mrs. Mary Shaw, aged 87.

Sarah Clark has been sentenced to death, at Carlisle, Penn. for the murder of John Carothers, Esq.

Political Banquet and Farmer's Feast.

Vol. I (No. 49) Tuesday, 5 Nov. 1799

† [1a] Legal notice from Bradbury Cilley, Executor of estate of Joseph Cilley, Esq. deceased; dated at Nottingham 10 Oct. 1799.

† [1a] Public notice by Benjamin Boardman, Jr., dated at Exeter 14 Oct. 1799, on his "intending to close his business in this town by the first of December ensuing."

† [1a] Legal notice by Miriam Hoag, dated at Stratham 15 Oct. 1799, regarding the estate of Enos Hoag, late of Stratham, deceased.

† [1a] Letters remaining at the Post Office, Exeter, N.H., Oct. 1799, as compiled by J.W. Gilman, Postmaster:

Charles F. Blodget, Exeter	John Kimball, Exeter	Ede Robinson, Exeter
James Burly, "	Joseph Lamson, "	James Thurston 2, Exeter
Samuel Loud 2, "	William Meeds, "	Jacob Morril, Epping
William Cushing, "	Jacob Pearson, "	William Miltimore, Stratham
Fanny Johnson, "	W.P. Summers, "	George Parker, Greenland

† [1a] Partnership of Purington and Jones dissolved by mutual consent 21 Sept. 1799. No town is specified.

† [1a] Legal notice regarding Abigail Fellows, daughter of Joseph Fellows, late of Kingston, Gentleman, deceased, dated 14 Oct. 1799. The daughter inherited one half of his house and barn, and "one fifth part in value of the remainder of his Real Estate."

† [1b] Legal notice from Superior Court of Judicature, Rockingham County, in a petition for divorce of Betsey Dame and Mark Dame, who were married at Portsmouth, N.H. 10 Feb. 1791. Mark Dame was identified as a Taylor, and the wife claimed that he abandoned her 25 July 1796; that he "absented himself from her to parts unknown." Also, the divorce petition mentions "a certain tract of land and messuage thereon, situate in said Portsmouth, of which she was at the time of her said marriage, seized and possessed for the term of her life, and which the said Mark Dame now holds in her right may be restored to her." The notice is dated at Exeter 17 Sept. 1799.

† [3b] A paragraph describing the rescue of the crew of the schooner *Violet*, of Baltimore, John Conway, master, they having drifted at sea for fourteen days after their vessel had been upset by a water spout. Four of the crew had perished from hunger. They were rescued by an English vessel, which was bound for Jamaica. The news was relayed by Capt. Little "of the Boston frigate" in a letter dated 16 Sept.

† [3c] News of a fire at Nantucket, which claimed a shop owned by Isaac Folger and a barn owned by Sylvanus Coffin. The event occurred shortly before 25 Oct. 1799.

† [3d] Jonathan Melcher offers his house and barn for sale; the property was located in Kensington, "directly opposite Doctor Row's." Adv. Dated 4 Nov. 1799.

† [3d] Josiah Wyatt offers half a dollar reward for a strayed pig. The name of the town is illegible, but contains five or six letters. The adv. was dated 1 Nov.

===== ¶ [3d] MARRIED. =====

At Hopkinton, John Harris, Esq, attorney at Law, to Miss Mary Poor, of Candia.

Section 5.

Footnotes & Additions.

Footnotes.

The footnotes can be traced back to the news items that they relate to by noting the date contained within the brackets [ ] at the beginning of each footnote. Some of these footnotes contain information gathered from later dispatches, which may include additional names not found in the foregoing text. These additional names are included in the index. In some cases information regarding a particular news event was spread out over several weeks or months.

1   [18 April 1797] The issue of 9 May 1797 contains an extensive account of this event, and mentions that "they committed a most outrageous trespass, the last summer in the town of New Milford." Mr. Truman was "of Boston." ♦

2   [12 June 1797] This name is illegible on the microfilm; the second letter is missing. The space between the first and third letter is very small, so presumably the second letter was an "i". The fourth and fifth letters are faint, possibly "oh", so perhaps this name was *Bisoham*.

3   [19 June 1797] The issue of 26 June 1797 [3b] has this article duplicated, yet the dateline is Alexandria, *Georgia*.

4   [19 June 1797] The issue of 26 June 1797 [3b] has an extensive account of a fire which destroyed the house of Judge Bridgeman "in Hinsdale." This article seems to have been copied from a newspaper published at Brattleborough, Vt. on the 23d of June, 1797, and it refers to an article published "last week" of the fire "in Hinsdale." As Hinsdale, N.H. is just across the river from Brattleborough, Vt., it would seem more likely that this event occurred in the New Hampshire town by that name. As to the identity of the "consort of Judge Bridgeman," the latter article does not clarify, nor does it indicate if this "consort" died as a result of the fire. According to this second dispatch, Mrs. Richardson, the Judge's daughter, was killed in the fire, along with his nephew, John Trott, the nine year old son of Mr. Samuel Trott of Walpole. ♦

5   [3 July 1797] Was this Greenfield, *Mass.*?

6   [10 July 1797] An article in the issue of 17 July 1797 [3c] states that the two "M'Leans" were tried and executed in Canada. The sentence structure in this article is somewhat garbled, and the fate of Butterfield is not so clear. However, a short notice in the "Incidents at Home" in the issue of 7 August 1797 [3d] states that "the account, we gave to the publick, of the Canada plot is partially contradicted. The truth we are anxious to learn, and, when ascertained, will announce."

      An article in 14 Aug. 1797 [2d-3a], dated 11 July at Quebec, Canada, details the trial of David M'Lane for treason, and includes the plan for his barbaric execution. In this same issue, an extract of a letter was printed in [3b], under the dateline of Albany, 5 Aug., giving additional accounts concerning the "Canada plot." ♦

      The issue of 21 Aug. 1797 [3a-3b] contains extensive accounts of the trial and execution of David M'Lane; a brief account of his life states that he was "a merchant at Providence, and had failed in 1795. He was a young man and married. His brother is now confined at Montreal, whose trial will soon come on. It is expected he will share the same fate." ♦

7   [21 Aug. 1797] Presumably, the advertisement in the issue of 9 Oct. 1797 [3d], by *Nathaniel* Sikes, indicates that he was the one who lost his fulling mill. In this ad, he indicated that he was back in business after the repair of "his late losses." The ad also requests an "apprentice to the Clothier's Business." Notice dated at Walpole, 6 Oct. 1797.

8   [3 July 1798] This reference to an expected future article was indicated by the editor of the newspaper from which this article was copied, not from the editor of *The Farmer's Weekly Museum*.

9   [10 July 1798] The meaning of "M." is unknown.

10   [1 Oct. 1798] Is this a misprint of "Merrifield ?"

11   [25 Feb. 1799] Now the town of *Nelson*, New Hampshire.

12   [25 Feb. 1799] An advertisement in the issue of 8 July 1799 [3d] indicates that *Bellows & Stone* was still in business, as they "wish to purchase a number of likely shipping Horses, for which they will pay West India or English Goods . . . "

13   [8 April 1799] Berwick, Mass., *District of Maine*.

14   [29 April 1799] Note the Sawyer runaway in the issue of 22 April 1799. Were there two Sawyer women, or was the second adv. meant to be a correction to the first?

15   [6 May 1799] The issue of 20 May 1799 [3a] contains an account of the trial of John Fries at Philadelphia, and also includes a trial "of the following persons indicted for *Conspiracy, Rescue and Obstruction of Process*, viz.
Christian Ruth, Daniel Schwartz, sen. Daniel Schwartz, jun. Henry Stahler, Henry Schiffert, George Shaeffer."
The issue of 27 May 1799 [2d-3a] contains a further account of this trial.
The issue of 3 June 1799 [2d-3b] contains verdicts of "George Shaffer, Henry Stahler, Henry Schiffert, Christian Ruth, and Daniel Schwartz," who all belonged to the county of Northampton.
16   [6 May 1799] One line of the marriage record is obliterated on the microfilm. During the filming process, the original paper was folded over this section of print.
17   [17 June 1799] A misprint of *Harrisonburg* ?
17A [2 Sept. 1799] The name of "Glinden" was changed in subsequent adv. to read "Glidden."
18   [23 Sept. 1799] In this same paragraph, a severely injured man named *Whaling* is identified. The sentence structure seems to imply that the man Whaling was previously named in the list, though the only name close to Whaling is Whiting. Perhaps Whaling was a misprint of Whiting, or vice versa.
19   [23 Sept. 1799] Were *Whiting* and *Whaling* the same man? See also the previous footnote.
20   [4 Nov. 1799] With these two records blended together as they are, it is suggested that each event be verified through other sources, especially due to the fact that a "Kittery" record was catagorized under "Newhampshire."
21   [11 Nov. 1799] A misprint of *Belknap* ?
22   [25 Nov. 1799] This news item was contained under the collection of New York news.
23   [2 Dec. 1799] This item contained within the Philadelphia news.
24   [27 Jan. 1800] Probably Manchester, *Mass*.
25   [17 Feb. 1800] Though the article is dated at Portland, *Massachusetts*, it should read more precisely, *Massachusetts, District of Maine*.
26   [24 Feb. 1800] Presumably, this was Wells, Massachusetts, *District of Maine*.
27   [7 April 1800] As this article was contained under the news dated at Hartford, Conn., the casual designation of "Seabrook" may have referred to a place of fairly local prominence in the Connecticut area. Perhaps this article referred to *Saybrook*, Conn., but *Seabrook*, N.H. cannot be ruled out. Further research is advised.
28   [14 April 1800] A notice posted by Peter Bellows, dated at Charlestown 30 May 1800, appears in the issue of 2 June 1800 [3d], stating that the Superior Court in the Charlestown session "reversed the decree of the Judge of Probate appointing Samuel Bellows my Guardian, and repealed the letter of Guardianship."
29   [21 April 1800] The print in this section of the paper is in very poor condition. This surname appears to be six letters in length, and might be COTTON or COLTON.
30   [28 April 1800] The issue of 5 May 1800 [3d] contains a follow-up article concerning Charles Holt, "editor of a puny and factious paper in Newlondon . . . "
31   [28 April 1800] See also the notice concerning "Samuel Cofren," issue of 5 May 1800 [3d].
32   [5 May 1800] The issue of 12 May 1800 [2c-d] contains several accounts of these trials, including the conclusion of Conrad Marks' trial, he having been found innocent, but this is contradicted in a later article. Anthony Stahler was acquitted for treason.
Frederick Hainy and John Gettman were both found guilty of treason. Later in that same issue, contained in [3a-3b], the announcements of the death sentences for John Fries, Frederick Hainy, and John Gettman are given, "to be executed on the twenty third May instant, at the Cross Roads in Quaker Town." However these three men were pardoned by the President, according to a notice in the issue of 2 June 1800 [3b], contained under the New York news.
The issue of 19 May 1800 [2d-3c] contains extensive articles regarding the trials of those accused, and the sentences handed out. The names of several of those sentenced for the "insurrection in Northampton and Bucks counties" are given here: ◆

George Huber	Abram Samsell	Jacob Gable
——— Socks	Peter Hantsberger	Henry Smith
John Kline	Abram Shantz	Valentine Kuder
Daniel Kline	George Mumbower	Jacom [sic] Eyreman
Jacob Kline	Henry Mumbower	Michael Smyer
Adam Reisch	Peter Huger	Philip Ruth
William Gettman	Peter Gable	Conrad Marks
George Gettman	Daniel Gable	

33 [5 May 1800] The issue of 26 May 1800 [2c-2d] contains an account of the execution of "Peter Lacroix, Joseph Baker, and Joseph Berouse" at Philadelphia. ♦
34 [9 June 1800] Probably refers to Charlestown, *Mass.*
35 [23 June 1800] Probably *Danvers*, Mass.
36 [23 June 1800] Was this *Buxton, Maine* ? (then under jurisdiction of Massachusetts).
37 [14 July 1800] The print quality in this list and the duplicate in the next issue is very poor. The list which appears in the issue of 28 July 1800 is much more legible.
38 [14 July 1800]. Perhaps this should read *Chesterfield*, Cheshire County [N.H.]
39 [11 Aug. 1800] The name of Nathan Cram is omitted from this list, but appears on the one listed in the issue of 13 Jan. 1800.
40 [12 Jan. 1801] The tiny print used in the typeset, combined with the ancient use of a style of "s" which looks very similar to an "f ", makes this name impossible to ascertain. It was either CHASSIN or CHAFFIN.
41 [17 Feb. 1801] This age may have been a misprint, as the application of the title of *Mr.* to a teenager was not the custom of the time.
42 [31 March 1801] The issue of 28 April 1801 [1a] contains an advertisement by the proprietors of this paper for a new post rider, and stating that "Papers have been generally carried weekly from this office to Chester by Mr. Chandler."
43 [7 April 1801] After the word *Newlondon*, an abbreviated word, of one or two letters in length, probably appeared in the original, but the letter(s) here are illegible. Presumably, this was the abbreviation of whichever state this New London was located in.
44 [2 June 1801] The issue of 18 Aug. 1801 [3c-d] contains an extensive account of the Fairbanks' trial, where he was convicted of murder and sentenced to death. The issue of 25 Aug. 1801 [3b], in an article dated at Boston, states that he broke from jail and had fled; the issue of 1 Sept. 1801 [3d] states that he was captured at "Skeensborough," [New York—Ed.]. See also the article in 8 Sept. 1801 [3b-c] which gives an extensive account of his capture. Articles in 22 Sept. 1801 [3b] and 6 Oct. 1801 [2b] chronicle his execution. An advertisement appearing in 26 Jan. 1802 [1b] indicates that an account of his life was written, published, and offered for sale at the Walpole Bookstore.
45 [23 June 1801] In the issue of 30 June 1801 [3c], an erratum notation states that he was Member, not Speaker, of the House.
46 [7 July 1801] This brief item was contained in the news dated at New York
47 [7 July 1801] This surname has one or two letters missing. Perhaps the name was *Foster.*
48 [4 Aug. 1801] A misprint of *Dame* ?
49 [25 Aug. 1801] The article also contains a footnote, which states that Capt. John Pinkham of Nantucket brought the hull into port.
50 [1 Sept. 1801] The notice appearing the week previous gives his name as *Ornold* Clark.
51 [8 Sept. 1801] The printer numbered this issue as "X," obviously an error.
52 [15 Sept. 1801] North West Territory, now *Ohio.*
53 [17 Nov. 1801] A brief mention in this same issue [3c] states that "Lt. [Maley? or Malcy?], now a prisoner at Algeziras, in a letter to a friend at Newbury-Port, confirms the account of the inhumane treatment experienced by the crew of the Molly."
54 [19 Jan. 1802] Perhaps a misprint of *Lockwood* ?
55 [9 Feb. 1802] The title given here was perhaps a misprint. The age is questionable due to fading of the ink; the first digit is most likely a 3, while the second digit is very uncertain. One Lydia (Dickenson) Chipman, wife of Darius[5] Chipman of Rutland, Vermont, died between 1796 and 1803 (John Hale Chipman III, *A Chipman Genealogy,* [Norwell, Mass., 1970], pp. 44-45.)
55A [2 Mar. 1802] This adv. is dated at Alstead, 18 Feb. 1801 [sic].
56 [23 Mar. 1802] Presumably identical to "E. Alexander" in the 1797 and 1799 lists.
57 [23 Mar. 1802] Presumably identical to "M. Ashley" in the 1799 list.
58 [23 Mar. 1802] Presumably identical to "Capt. S. Hunt" in the 1797 and 1799 lists.
59 [23 Mar. 1802] Spelled *Palfrey* in the 1797 and 1799 lists; *Pulfrey* in the 1800 list.
60 [23 Mar. 1802] Presumably identical to "E. Stebbens" in the 1799 list.
61 [23 Mar. 1802] Spelled "Dwyer" in the 1799 list.
62 [23 Mar. 1802] Presumably identical to "J. Stebbens" in the 1799 list.
63 [23 Mar. 1802] Presumably identical to "J. Stoodley, jun." in the 1797 and 1799 lists.
64 [23 Mar. 1802] Presumably identical to "J. Stoodley, Esq." in the 1797 and 1799 lists.
65 [23 Mar. 1802] Presumably identical to "Sam. Willard" in the 1799 list.
66 [23 Mar. 1802] Not called "Esq." in the 1799 list.
67 [23 Mar. 1802] Perhaps identical to "T. Williams, jr." in the 1797 and 1799 lists.
68 [23 Mar. 1802] Presumably identical to "T. Williams, Esq." in the 1797 and 1799 lists.

69 [23 Mar. 1802] Perhaps identical to "Thomas Williams" in the 1800 list.
70 [27 April 1802] The marriage notices contained herein from Middlebury, Vt., between the parties of Campbell-Burham, Clark-Miller, and Griswold-Nichols, were later found to be a hoax. An apology from the editor in 18 May 1802 [3c] gives an explanation.
71 [27 April 1802] The marriage notices contained herein from Middlebury, Vt., between the parties of Campbell-Burham, Clark-Miller, and Griswold-Nichols, were later found to be a hoax. An apology from the editor in 18 May 1802 [3c] gives an explanation.
72 [27 April 1802] The marriage notices contained herein from Middlebury, Vt., between the parties of Campbell-Burham, Clark-Miller, and Griswold-Nichols, were later found to be a hoax. An apology from the editor in 18 May 1802 [3c] gives an explanation.
73 [27 April 1802] The issue of 4 May 1802 [3d] contains a few words of the deceased's character, and a religious reflection.
74 [4 May 1802] Probably a misprint of *Akerman*.
75 [4 May 1802] An article in 18 May 1802 [3c] briefly expands upon this news item, stating that the man's name was Nahum Day, and that he drowned on 24 April 1802. Mr. Day "was to have been married in a few days." This second article is contained in the news dated at Keene, N.H.
76 [3 Aug. 1802] The commissioners requested an extension of time, per the legal notice of 4 Oct. 1803 [3d].
77 ["6" Sept. 1802] In this issue, the printer inserted "erratum" on the third page, third column, stating that this date was an error; the correct date should have been 7 Sept.
78 ["6" Sept. 1802] Judging from the great lapse in time from the date of the adv. to the appearance in this newspaper, this place must have been far removed from Walpole. A check of a modern-day atlas indicates a town by this name in northern Pennsylvania, located near Tioga Point on the Susquehannah River. The first occurrence of this adv. appeared too late in print to be of any use to persons in northern New England; the adv. continued to be printed for several weeks after this initial appearance.
79 [12 Oct. 1802] The last portion of this surname, located near the left margin of the page, is illegible. This collection of newspapers was bound into a book with very tight binding, and was microfilmed in that condition.
80 ["3" Nov. 1802] Probably a misprint; presumably this date should have read 2 Nov. 1802.
81 [23 Nov. 1802] An article in 14 Dec. 1802 [3b] identifies this man as *Whitney*, who was convicted along with *Tibbets* for the murder of Stephen Gordon.
82 [7 Dec. 1802] The name of this locality is somewhat illegible, but resembles the word *Sununty*. As the record following this one is located at Savannah, perhaps the G. in the Ballie record is an abbreviation for *Georgia*.
83 [7 Dec. 1802] The North West Territories, organized by Congress in 1787, now comprise the states of Ohio, Michigan, Indiana, etc.
84 [11 Jan. 1803] A paragraph appended to this death notice, apparently copied from a Boston paper, describes the funeral rites given in honor of Rev. Thacher. The issue of 18 Jan. 1803 [4c-d] contains a biography of Thacher.
85 [18 Jan. 1803] Whether the fourth letter is *s* or *f* is impossible to ascertain.
86 [25 Jan. 1803] The issue of 8 Feb. 1804 [4c-d] contains an extensive description of this hermit's life. ♦
87 [1 Feb. 1803] The issue of 8 March 1803 [1c] also contains this delinquency notice, but indicates that some portion of the advertisement has been corrected.
88 [8 Feb. 1803] Presumably the printer mistakenly omitted a comma in this sentence; this should probably read Mr. Henry Hall, Merchant.
89 [29 Mar. 1803] See also a brief notice regarding Lyon in the issue of 26 April 1803 [2d]. The issue of 14 June 1803 [2c, 3b] states that Matthew Lyon is agent of the United States for furnishing supplies to the Western Army.
90 [12 Apr. 1803] Consult the original of 7 June 1803 [2d] for additional information.
91 [26 Apr. 1803] Consult the original of 24 May 1803 [3a] for additional information.
92 [24 May 1803] Now Natchez, Mississippi.
93 [7 June 1803] Presumably, this news article originated at Springfield, Mass., and thus the event probably occurred in nearby Enfield, Connecticut. The article is contained within Massachusetts news.
94 [21 June 1803] This spelling may have been a corruption of *Alfred*, located in Massachusetts, District of Maine. The news item was contained under the Boston news.
95 [28 June 1803] A misprint of *Carpenter*?
96 [26 July 1803] The issue of 19 July 1803 [3b] gives a brief account: "On Friday, a young man, at work at blowing rocks, on the Dedham turnpike road, was instantly killed by accidental explosion."
97 [9 Aug. 1803] Contained in the news under the Boston heading of 30 July.

98	[30 Aug. 1803] This issue of 11 Feb. 1804 [3c] contains a subsequent legal notice regarding the guardians petition to sell land.
99	[30 Aug. 1803] The first letter of this surname is faded—this name perhaps was *Gill*.
99A	[6 Sept. 1803] Presumably, this refers to Barnstable, *Mass.*, as this record was probably copied from a newspaper from that state.
100	[6 Sept. 1803] The remainder of this extensive list of deaths is illegible. When this page was photographed for the microfilm, the top half of the image was out of focus.
101	[13 Sept. 1803] See the testimony given in the issue of 27 Sept. 1803 [3a], where, on 27 Aug. 1803, John Hand, master of the sloop, John Albright, mate, and Mr. Joseph Hughes, passenger, testified in detail about the abduction of *David Kitchell*.
101A	[20 Sept. 1803] Though this article was contained under the Connecticut news, it probably related to the town of Southwick, *Mass.*
102	[18 Oct. 1803] The issue of 25 Oct. 1803 [3b-c] contains an extensive account of the murder and the trial, and also contains genealogical information about both families. Part of the text is illegible, as the camera was out of focus during the microfilming process.
103	[13 Dec. 1803] The remainder of this surname, consisting of two or three letters, is illegible.
104	[31 Dec. 1803] Why the printer designated this as Vol. X, and several subsequent issues, rather than continuing on with Vol. XI, is unknown. The issue of 10 March 1804 has a handwritten correction which states "Number should be 12 throughout the year." Beginning with the issue of 24 March 1804, the printer returned to the previous designation of Vol. XI. Beginning with the issue of 19 May 1804, the printer began using the correct designation, Vol. XII. However, another mistake began 9 Feb. 1805, when the number dropped back to XI, and continued on with that designation for several weeks.
105	[31 Dec. 1803] See the article in 7 Jan. 1804 [2d] for an article describing this event. Heald was 58 years old, and left a widow and son. The article was dated at Amherst, 20 Dec. 1803. ♦
106	[10 Mar. 1804] The Volume number has been corrected in handwriting, to read Vol. XII, and at the top of page, written "Number should be 12 throughout the year."
107	[28 Apr. 1804] The issue of 5 May 1804 [3d] has a correction to his age; it should read *61*, not 16.
108	[12 May 1804] Issue of 9 June 1804 [3b] gives an account of the escape from jail of most of these prisoners. Additionally, William F. Ayers and Ephraim Bailey escaped. This latter article also mentions that Robert Miller, James Brown, and ———— Morrill were convicted of forgery at Superior Court held at Plymouth, N.H., and belonged to the same gang of forgerers / counterfeiters convicted in the Hopkinton trials. ♦ The issue of 18 Aug. 1804 [3b] states that David Call was recaptured in northern N.H. The issue of 22 Sept. 1804 [2d] states that John Silver had been recaptured.
109	[26 May 1804] Much of this issue is illegible, due to the camera being out of focus during the microfilming process.
110	[23 June 1804] The issue of 9 March 1804 [4c] declares that this event occurred in Shutesbury, *Mass.*
111	[21 July 1804] This death notice could be interpreted two ways. This gentleman's name could have been *V. Ephraim Wheelock*, or, the *V.* used here was an abbreviation for Townsend, *Vermont*.
112	[15 Sept. 1804] Probably *Congregational* Church was intended here.
113	[22 Sept. 1804] Obviously a misprint; this should have read number *599*.
114	[20 Oct. 1804] Now the town of *Lisbon*, New Hampshire.
115	["31 Nov." 1804] Obviously, this date is a mistake. The first page has this error, but on the second page, last column, under the local heading of Walpole, the correct date is given: "Saturday, Dec. 1, 1804."
116	["31 Nov." 1804] This article, among others, is contained under the news from New York.
117	["31 Nov." 1804] A misprint of *Framingham*, (Mass.) ?
117A	[8 Dec. 1804] Compare this surname to the one in the marriage record from the previous week.
118	[12 Jan. 1805] Roland Cotten is named twice in this notice, he listed as delinquent on two parcels of land.
119	[19 Jan. 1805] This sentence regarding his age is presented here, just as it appeared in the original. An article in the issue of 23 Feb. 1805 [3c] mentions Kingsbery's time spent in the hospital, along with others infected with the disease. ♦
120	[2 Feb. 1805] See the correction herein, contained within the death notices in the issue of 23 March 1805 [3c].
121	[9 Feb. 1805] Beginning with this issue, the volume numbers were misprinted, as they were previously designated as *XII*.

122 [16 Feb. 1805] Articles in 29 June 1805 [3a] state that Stephen Arnold was tried and convicted, and sentenced for execution on 19 July. The name of the victim was Betsey Van Amburgh. However, an item in 10 Aug. 1805 [3a] states that Arnold received a reprieve from Governor Lewis. ◆

123 [2 Mar. 1805] The issue of 9 March 1805 [3b] contains an account of this event. ◆

124 [9 Mar. 1805] Benjamin Harris is also named in a separate notice at [3d] as having delinquent taxes for the year 1803.

125 [9 Mar. 1805] From the death notices in the issue of 23 June 1804, Pratt was said to have died in Shutesbury, Va.

126 [23 Mar. 1805] A footnote attached to this column reads: "The editor of the Observatory is informed that the mention of the above decease was not originally made in the Farmer's Museum.—It was inserted with others by the printer from a Boston paper."

127 [6 Apr. 1805] The volume number has been corrected over in pen, to read No. 13.

128 [6 Apr. 1805] One of these numbers is incorrect. If the individual number of descendants is correct, and tallied up, the total is 97, not 79.

129 [6 Apr. 1805] An assumption to this location would be the present town of Marietta, Ohio. However, it is unknown why this place was still designated as a territory, as Ohio was admitted to the union in 1803. Given the great length of time required for news to travel to distant locales, perhaps this event occurred when Ohio was still a territory.

130 [6 Apr. 1805] Presumably, the Hinsdale refered to in this article was Hinsdale, N.H. The "Reporter" may have been the newspaper published across the Connecticut River from Hinsdale, entitled the *Brattleboro'* (Vt.) *Reporter*.

131 [13 Apr. 1805] The issue of 6 Dec. 1805 [3b] contains a brief news update concerning Stanley Griswold, late editor of the Observatory, "now" residing in Michigan.

132 [27 Apr. 1805] The issue of 4 May 1805 [3a-b] contains an extensive account of these murders, and states that the son, J.P. Kendrick, suffered from insanity, as did his father and two brothers. ◆

133 [27 Apr. 1805] Compare this record carefully against the one reported in the deaths of 13 July 1805.

134 [11 May 1805] Another update appears in 15 June 1805 [2c], describing the rescue of those aboard the long boat, by several skippers: William Powars, ——— Dennis, both of Marblehead, John Powars, and Alexander Green. ◆

135 [11 May 1805] The issue of 15 June 1805 [2c] identifies this family as "Mr. *Ashby*, of Battle, near Beachyhead, Eng. his wife, 4 daughters, son in law, and grand child." ◆

136 [25 May 1805] When reviewing this issue on the microfilm, it was noticed that the third page of the issue of 19 Oct. 1805 is mixed in with the issue of 25 May 1805.

137 [13 July 1805] This event perhaps occurred in Charlestown, *Mass.*, rather that the town by that name in New Hampshire, as the record is clustered among several Massachusetts records. Further research advised.

138 [13 July 1805] Compare this death notice carefully to the one listed in the deaths of 27 April 1805.

139 [20 July 1805] The surname of this man consisted of four letters, but the second letter is missing. Probably this name was *Dole*, or *Dale*.

140 [17 Aug. 1805] This surname appears to have had four letters, but the second is missing. Perhaps the name was *Wade*.

141 [24 Aug. 1805] The issue of 31 Aug. 1805 [2d] contains additional information, including the charge that Butler disobeyed orders in "not cropping his hair." The article concludes with an "editorial" which blames the court-martial not on disobedience, but on a "political intolerance" of Federalists.

142 [21 Sept. 1805] The date set by the printer on the front page was 12 Sept. 1805, which was incorrect. The correction was written over in pen, and the correct date also appears under the Walpole head, third page. This mistake was admitted by the printer, in the issue of 28 Sept. 1805 [3d].

143 [5 Oct. 1805] The issue of 12 Oct. 1805 [1c-d] contains details of this crime, and the trial.◆ The issue of 28 Feb. 1806 [3a] states that Wheeler had escaped from jail, but was recaptured. The issue of Friday, 7 March 1806 [3b-c] gives an account of his execution "on Thursday last" at Lenox, Mass.

144 [12 Oct. 1805] The issue of 19 Oct. 1805 [2d-3a] contains another article on this case, which states that "Spring is an old offender, and partner with the notorious Stephen Burroughs in the Canada manufactory . . ."

145 [19 Oct. 1805] The issue of 29 Oct. 1805 [2a-b] contains a lengthy account of the kidnappings, and added that there was a third brother abducted, *Nathan Kemper*. ◆

146 [16 Nov. 1805] An article in 24 Jan. 1806 [3b] states that Eldridge was captured at Cooperstown, N.Y., and brought back to Charlestown, N.H. jail. The issue of 7 Nov.

1806 [3a] states that Eldridge was convicted, and sentenced. ♦

147 [23 Nov. 1805] The issue of 3 Dec. 1805 states that the two Irishmen, James Hilligan and Dominic Daly were arrested at Rye, N.Y. See the news item for that date included herein. The issue of 2 May 1806 [3c] has a brief paragraph regarding the case of the murder of Mr. Marcus Lyon; that item states that Daley and Hillighan were convicted and received sentences of execution.

148 [3 Dec. 1805] The issue of 20 Dec. 1805 [3a] has a similar news article, adding that "Clemmons had been for several weeks in a gloomy, melancholy mood, occasioned, it was supposed, by his great anxiety for the welfare of his numerous family." The issue of 27 Dec. 1805 [3a] states that Clemmons turned himself over to the authorities, 9 Nov. 1805. The issue of 1 Aug. 1806 [2c] states that Abel *Clements* was executed 3 June 1806.

149 [27 Dec. 1805] The issue of 3 Jan. 1806 [3c-d] contains an extensive account of the murders of Russell Freeman, Esq., and Capt. Joseph Starkweather. These two, along with Josiah Burnham, were prisoners of debt. ♦

150 [27 Dec. 1805] Perhaps an abbreviation for *printer*.

151 [3 Jan. 1806] Account of the trial of Peter Severance, of Chester, who was convicted of manslaughter of Mr. Witcher, of Boscawen, appears in the issue of 14 March 1806 [3b-c]. ♦

152 [17 Jan. 1806] A mistake appears on the third page of this issue, where the printer forgot to change the Walpole head from the previous week's issue. The correct date should have read Friday, January 17, 1806.

153 [24 Jan. 1806] The auction of Maj. Elisha Kingsbery's estate is advertised in the issue of 28 March 1806 [1b].

154 [24 Jan. 1806] Another legal notice regarding William Henry's estate appears in the issue of 21 Feb. 1806 [3d].

155 [14 Mar. 1806] The last letter of this surname is illegible. From the death notices of 4 April 1806, a Mr. Aaron Arms died at Deerfield, aged 57.

156 [21 Mar. 1806] The Vol. identification in the typeset reads "XIV," but it has been corrected by another hand to read "XII."

157 [28 Mar. 1806] As in the previous week's issue, the volume number was corrected to read "XII."

158 [9 May 1806] See the contradiction of his passing, in the death notices of 30 May 1806.

159 [16 May 1806] The bride's surname is illegible, but consists of three or four letters; the last letter appears to be a "d."

160 [23 May 1806] The issues for 23 May and 30 May 1806 have had their Vol. number "corrected" by another hand. The notation reads "13," but for the issue of 23 May, that "correction" is also scratched out.

161 [30 May 1806] The issues for 23 May and 30 May 1806 have had their Vol. number "corrected" by another hand. The notation reads "13," but for the issue of 23 May, that "correction" is also scratched out.

162 [13 June 1806] A brief paragraph in 18 July 1806 [3b] states that the Governor granted a reprieve for Burnham's execution until 12 Aug. 1806. The issue of 22 Aug. 1806 [2d-3a] contains a detailed account of Burnham's execution. ♦ Also in the issue of 22 Aug. 1806 [3d], an advertisement appears for "An Analysis or Outline of the Life and Character of Josiah Burnham," published at the Walpole (N.H.) Bookstore.

163 [13 June 1806] The issue of 20 June 1806 [2d] has an account of the dying words pronounced by Halligan and Daly. ♦

164 [20 June 1806] The issue of 4 July 1806 [3a] identifies this minister as Josiah N. Cannon.

165 [25 July 1806] The issue of 1 Aug. 1806 [2d] contains additional information regarding this tragedy. ♦

166 [8 Aug. 1806] Consult the issue of 15 Aug. 1806 [2d] for a detailed account of this event. ♦ The issue of 12 Dec. 1806 [2d-3a] contains an article detailing the status of the trial of Thomas Oliver Selfridge, Esq. Issue of 2 Jan. 1807 [2d] states that Selfridge was found Not Guilty. The issue of 23 Jan. 1807 [1d-2d] contains additional information regarding the trial.

167 [19 Sept. 1806] This date is obviously an error. The adv. was rewritten with the correct date of 13 Sept. 1806, and appears in the issue of 3 Oct. 1806 [1b].

168 [26 Sept. 1806] Misprint of *Moses* ?

169 [3 Oct. 1806] The issue of 17 Oct. 1806 [3c] contains an lengthy paragraph describing his death, which was caused by arsenic poisoning. Additional info can be found in the issue of 2 Jan. 1807 [3b]. The issue of 6 March 1807 [4a-d] contains the record of examination of the State of N.H. vs. Margery Fay. ♦

170 [10 Oct. 1806] The surname is illegible; the first letter may perhaps be an "S," and the name is comprised of about four letters.

171	[14 Nov. 1806] The bride's name in this record is not given. It is entirely possible that this was meant to be a death record, and the printer inserted it in the wrong place.
172	[14 Nov. 1806] Consult the issue of 21 Nov. 1806 [3c] for an extensive obituary of Edward Selfridge. ♦
173	[21 Nov. 1806] On the front page of this issue, in the header, the date appears as "Nov. 12, 1806." The number 12 has been scratched out, and the number 21 written above it. The correct date of 21 Nov. 1806 appears under the Walpole head on the second page of that issue.
174	[2 Jan. 1807] The issue of 23 Jan. 1807 [3c] contains a brief notice regarding the fate of the robber: "Johnson, the person who lately attempted to rob Mr. Pye, died last week in Albany jail, of the wound he received from Mr. Pye."
175	[16 Jan. 1807] Consult the issue of 9 Jan. 1807 [1d] for an article detailing the riots at New York. ♦
176	[16 Jan. 1807] The ages stated for the two daughters of Jonathan Stone are suspicious, given the wide spread of years between the two. Further research is advised.
177	[23 Jan. 1807] This issue was misnumbered; it should have read *No. 45*.
178	[13 Feb. 1807] Though the spelling of this locality is like that of the Massachusetts town, this record is squeezed between two New Hampshire towns, so probably this event occurred in *North Hampton, New Hampshire*.
179	[27 Feb. 1807] Obviously, the printer transposed this number; this issue should have been *No. 50*.
180	[27 Feb. 1807] This paragraph, along with another unrelated one, was copied from the *Middlebury Mercury*.
181	[20 Mar. 1807] Part of this line, consisting of about 4 words, is illegible in the original, as the paper was folded over during the microfilming process.
182	[27 Mar. 1807] An extensive biography of Rev. Samuel Stillman's life appears in this issue, columns [3a-c]. ♦
183	[24 Oct. 1808] Shortly before this newspaper suspended publication in March 1807, the last two issues published in that year were labelled as Vol. XV, Nos. 1 & 2. When the paper resumed publication in 1808, these two Vol./ No. sequences were used over again.
184	[24 Oct. 1808] Shortly before this newspaper suspended publication in March 1807, the last two issues published in that year were labelled as Vol. XV, Nos. 1 & 2. When the paper resumed publication in 1808, these two Vol./ No. sequences were used over again.
185	[28 Nov. 1808] A corruption of *Fitchburg* (Mass.) ?
186	[19 Dec. 1808] The fifth letter of this surname is uncertain, perhaps a "y" or a "v."
187	[26 Dec. 1808] Georgetown, *District of Columbia*.
188	[9 Jan. 1809] The casual statement "near the market," combined with the fact that no town is noted here, might imply that the event occurred locally in Walpole. However, many of these death notices were copied from other papers, and this event may have occurred in one of the coastal towns, such as Boston. Further research advised.
189	[27 Mar. 1809] Probably a misprint of *N.Y.*
190	[3 April 1809] The printer of the Walpole paper inserted in the heading that this article originated in Winchester, Maryland, however, this may have been an error. It is possible that the event occurred in Winchester, Virginia, as the article seems to suggest that Forrest was returning home, "a journey of 90 miles yet before him."
191	[10 April 1809] In the newspaper, the list of these names is presented alphabetically, with the surname given first, followed by the christian name. In the case of Mr. M'Crae, the name is oddly listed as "Crae, M' William."
192	[12 June 1809] The news item preceding this one was copied from a paper simply identified as *Cent.*, perhaps meaning the *Columbian Centinel* (Boston).
193	[28 Aug. 1809] Probably a misprint of *N.H.*
194	[11 Sept. 1809] The long lapse in the transmission of this article (25 Aug. to the time it was published, 11 Sept.) may imply that this event occurred a great distance from Walpole, Rather than Troy, N.H., this event may have occurred in Troy, *N.Y.*
195	[11 Sept. 1809] Some of this paragraph is illegible due to poor microfilm quality.
196	[20 Nov. 1809] Part of the column containing the death notices is torn.
197	[27 Nov. 1809] Page 1 of this issue was not microfilmed.
198	[27 Nov. 1809] Amos Avery is named twice in the list.
199	[19 March 1810] Georgetown, *District of Columbia*.
200	[19 March 1810] The issue of 26 March 1810 contains an obituary of Mrs. Prentiss which contains extensive lines of a religious nature.
201	[2 April 1810] The context of this name is unclear: perhaps this man's name was indeed "Maxwell Lot," but perhaps the property in question was simply refered to as *"the Maxwell lot."*

202 [2 April 1810] The issue of 26 March 1810, fourth page, also contains an extensive article describing symptoms and treatment of the Spotted Fever raging in Worcester County, Mass., written by three physicians from that area: Abraham Haskell, Mason Spooner, and Jacob Holmes. The article is dated at Petersham, 9 March 1810.
203 [2 April 1810] New Orleans Territory ?
204 [7 May 1810] This item is contained within a paragraph of news from Amherst, presumed to be N.H.
205 [18 June 1810] In the paragraph, the notice states that the delinquencies were for the years 1809 and 1810, though in the heading of the columns, the years stated are for 1808 and 1809.
206 [9 July 1810] A misprint of *Ezra* ?
207 [9 July 1810] In the issue of 9 Oct. 1809, one Alexander *Pukens* was a Commissioner to another estate in Claremont.
208 [9 July 1810] Either *Col.* was a locality in the District of Columbia, or, *Col.* was a misprint of *Con.* (Connecticut).
209 [3 Sept. 1810] An article in 24 Sept. 1810 [2b], dated at Lynchburg 31 Aug. 1810 states that this man was also known as "Creston." ◆
210 [1 Oct. 1810] The interpretation of the owners' names of this lot is unclear. Perhaps there was a Mr. Haven, along with William Craft & Co., as co-owners.
211 [8 Oct. 1810] The state given here was probably an error; more likely, this event occurred in Bath, *N.H.*

212 "*History and Bibliography of American Newspapers, 1690-1820*," by Clarence S. Brigham; American Antiquarian Society, Worcester, Mass. 1947.

ADDITIONS.

Vol. VII, No. 363, Monday, 17 March 1800:

† [3b] Article dated at Norwich, Conn., 27 Feb. describing a murder committed "on Sunday last in Preston, on the body of a child of Mr. Joseph Leonard, aged about 18 months, by a woman named Marcey Bump, who was supported by said town, at Mr. Eleazer Prentice's." ◆

Vol. X, No. 487, Tuesday, 3 Aug. 1802:

¶ [3a-b] Charlestown, July 16. Yesterday morning a young man, 18 or 19 years of age, by the name of Thompson, belonging to Marlow, but living with John Hubbard Esq. went into Connecticut river to bathe, and was unfortunately drowned. Having been in the water only about ten minutes before he was taken out, means were used for a considerable space to resuscitate him, but without effect.

Guide to using the Index to Persons.

The index to persons included herein contains a page number / line number combination for each of the approximately 20,000 names given. For example, the entry for *Henry Abbot* is given as 184~42, indicating that his record is found on page 184, line 42. The line numbers are approximate, but usually accurate to within one or two lines.

Many surnames with similar sounding names are grouped together under a phonetic arrangement, such as **AMES / EAMES / EMES**. However, the researcher should be aware that this system is far from perfect. Local dialects and lack of standardized spelling two centuries ago greatly impacted the written word. In compiling this list, many variations of surname spellings were found in the old newspapers, and thus a large number of similar surnames were grouped together. A few examples are noted here:

— The Walpole newspaper has a 1799 death notice of a comedian from New York City, Stephen *Woollis*, yet one of the Exeter newspapers included herein gave this man's name as Stephen *Wools*.

— In a 1797 delinquent tax list from Croydon, N.H., Thomas *Danney* and Luke *Drewry* were named in the list. The following year, their names appear as Thomas *Denny* and Luke *Drury*.

— In March 1804, the wife of Rev. Eli *Forbes* of Gloucester, Mass. died, while Rev. Eli *Fobes* died there in the following December.

— In an example of two records probably relating to the same man, one Mathew *Deekey* had a letter left at the Walpole, N.H. post office in 1809. In 1810, the daughter of Matthew *Dickey* of Walpole died of a fever.

Much of this index was computer-generated, and was compiled using a large database of surnames, now numbering about 7500; of this total, about 2200 surnames are variations of other spellings. The creation of this database was initiated during the research of my previous publications, *New England Vital Records from the Exeter News-Letter, 1831-1865,* (published in five volumes, by Picton Press of Camden, Maine). Although that publication primarily consists of information gathered from a newspaper printed at Exeter, and this latest book primarily pertains to a paper from Walpole, there is a significant overlap of the geographical distribution of vital records gathered from both sources, and thus the decision was made to group these names together. And in keeping these predominately New England surnames grouped together, some of the multiple spellings appear in this index, but are not relevant to any record located within this particular volume. For example, "**CAVERLY / CEVERLY / COVERLY,** Charles 99~27" appears in this index, however Charles is the only case of a person with any of the **CAVERLY** spellings to be found in this volume. The other two spellings were those which were gathered during the work on the *Exeter News-Letter* project.

In most cases, the selection of primary spellings for the surnames has remained consistent throughout my research, though a few have been changed here and there. The selection of one spelling over another does not necessarily indicate that the primary spelling selected was used any more frequently than any other of the secondary spellings; this system is used strictly to keep these similar names grouped together for the researcher's convenience. Though the surnames have been modified for the index, the original spelling was kept intact in the transcribed records included herein.

Many surnames of Scottish or Irish origin (McDonald, McNeal, McAllister, etc.) are indexed as if they were spelled with a "MAC" prefix. Likewise, names such as ST. JOHN or ST. CLAIR are indexed as if the "ST." portion were spelled out in full.

Most names located within the text portion of this volume are indexed; however, due to space restrictions, not all were indexed. Specifically excluded from the index were names of ministers who performed marriages, and in some cases, royalty and persons of nobility.

Index to Persons.

A.

ABBE, Charity 219~8 Daniel 284~34 John 219~8 Joshua 276~22 Shubael 160~33
ABBOT / ABBOTT / ABOTT, [Mr.] 308~55 [Mrs.] 269~18 Albert 329~17 Anna 231~44 Butler 314~28 Catharine (Thayer) 113~25 Curviah 285~45 Edward 101~25 Elmira 284~39 Fila 284~38, 284~39 Henry 184~42 Isaac 34~52, 38~2, 41~19, 74~33, 329~17 Jacob 110~38, 113~25 John 42~53, 193~56, 230~56, 243~57, 314~28, 361~34 John S. 177~26 Jonathan 201~24, 203~36 Maria 284~39 Mary 65~39 Mary (Badger) 218~4 Minerva 284~38 Nathan 86~45 Nehemiah 283~11 Rhoda (Bricket) 86~45 Sarah 103~21 Sophia (Moseley) 193~56 Stephen 218~4
ABBOTT see ABBOT
ABEEL see ABELL
ABEL see ABELL
ABELL / ABEL / ABEEL, Elijah 305~8
ABERCROMBIE, I. 258~50 Isaac 252~1, 322~27
ABERNETHY, John 50~20
ABOTT see ABBOT
ABRAHAM(S) see ABRAMS
ABRAM see ABRAMS
ABRAMS / ABRAHAMS / ABRAM / ABRAHAM, Betsy 126~42 Elizabeth 239~48 Henry 159~25, 183~29 Joseph 147~4 Martha (Hunt) 237~42 Mehitable (Welch) 75~46 Ralph 75~46 William 237~42
ACKERMAN see AKERMAN
ACKLEY see ECKLY
ADAMS, [children] 168~36, 178~12 [Mr.] 92~38, 178~12 [Mrs.] 202~58 [President] 3~40 Abigail 162~38, 279~37 Abraham 39~43 Alice 201~22 Alice (Wyman) 152~23 Andrew 15~3 Ann (Harrod) 194~40 Anna 78~17 Benjamin 34~37, 289~18 Benjamin B. 266~49 Betsey 168~33, 239~36 Caleb 150~48 Catharine 152~8 Catharine N. 250~29 Charles 79~47 Cornelius 223~9, 270~12, 271~6 Daniel 24~6, 27~35, 68~47 David 81~14, 309~55 E. 61~21 Ebenezer Thomas 166~32 Ephraim 6~33, 20~15, 81~44, 168~34, 181~36 Esther 320~15 Henry 273~51 Huldah 113~8 James 167~12 Joel 244~55 John 203~1, 361~44 Jonathan 82~53 Joseph 81~16, 102~43, 149~4 Knowles 49~21 Levi 212~17 Luther 74~35, 176~47 Marcy 224~46 Martha 3~40, 40~26 Mark (Fox) 175~24 Mary 134~31 Mary (Sampson) 194~1 Moses 78~18, 112~7 Nathaniel 134~28, 152~23, 272~12 Olive 114~9 Pat 40~26 Paul 96~50 Penelope 222~9 Polly 270~51 Rebecca 235~57 Rebecca (———) (Cargill) 96~50 Richard 161~33 Richard M. 58~50 Robert 232~26 S. 39~46, 233~18, 296~16 Samuel 152~9 Samuel F. 193~58 Sarah 41~1 Smith 47~1 Sukey 229~7 Susan (Foster) 273~52 Susannah (Pope) 112~7 Thankful 178~40 Thomas 40~11, 267~20 Thomas B. 194~40 William 78~24 Z.B. 175~24 Zabdiel 86~33, 134~31
ADKINS see ATKINS
ADKINSON see ATKINSON
ADSIT, Samuel 239~55
AHERMAN, Elizabeth (?) 118~14
AIKEN / AIKIN / AIKINS / AIKENS, James 143~40
AIKENS see AIKEN
AIKIN(S) see AIKEN
AINSWORTH / ENSWORTH, Laban 90~5 Laben 27~39 William 234~26
AIR see AYER
AITCHINSON, Andrew 154~32 Sally (Langdon) 154~32
AKERLY, Samuel 23~43

AKERMAN / ACKERMAN, Elizabeth (?) 118~14 Samuel 193~15
ALANZO, Francis 132~32
ALBERT see ELBERT
ALBERTSON, [Mr.] 119~45
ALBRA, John 81~42
ALBRIGHT, John 254~8, 370~9
ALCOCK, [Mr.] 241~2 Elizabeth 277~29 Robert 277~29
ALCOTT see OLCOTT
ALDEN, Ebenezer 262~43 Hannah (Pike) 92~34 Isaac 92~34 Lucinda 238~51 Mary 285~48 Noah 4~47 Thomas 53~7 Zenas 181~30
ALDER, Benjamin 106~4
ALDERMAN, Daniel 66~14
ALDEY, Ann (Tankesley) 208~36 Perrin 208~36
ALDRICH / ALDRIDGE, Caleb 20~50, 93~49 David 316~6 Diantha 136~40 Dianthe 81~17 Ezekiel 178~15 Israel 327~56 Jarept 101~40 Jonathan 13~47, 33~5 Joseph 93~49, 109~21 Luke 210~17 Mary 229~39 Sarah 231~48 Silas 316~10 Simeon 170~23
ALDRIDGE see ALDRICH
ALEAD, Eli 334~37
ALEN see ALLEN
ALEXANDER, [Mr.] 74~34, 81~15 Aaron 24~53 Abigail 225~19 Alexander 60~1 Asa 87~41 E. 368~54 Elisha 115~24, 143~5, 278~36 Giles 212~13 James 299~27 John 274~39 Jonathan 228~48 Mehitable 101~17 Nabby 87~41 Richard 332~35, 333~52 Sarah 189~39 Simeon 143~4, 278~38
ALEXIS, [Mr.] 148~41
ALFRED, John 78~36
ALLAIRE, Elizabeth 121~51 Peter A. 121~52
ALLAN see ALLEN
ALLD, William 211~40, 212~15
ALLEN / ALLAN / ALEN, [Mr.] 34~13, 221~56 [Mrs.] 93~17 A. 239~32 Aaron 16~21, 79~10, 90~2, 132~18, 159~13, 182~44, 295~27 Abel 89~47 Amasa 9~48, 25~25, 27~9, 31~4, 56~48, 71~45, 73~8, 85~41, 89~36, 115~8, 122~53, 134~20, 147~18, 169~12, 198~7, 207~42, 211~18, 218~53, 257~46, 306~27, 321~53 Asa 296~17 Asael 196~36 Caleb 68~48 Cary 245~36 Catharine (Salter) 79~10 Catharine 187~7 David 218~36 Dorothy 117~33 Dorothy (———) 91~18 Ebenezer 237~47 Edward 146~41 Elnathan 216~13 Esther 251~31 Ethan 140~12, 300~45 Ezra 357~24 Fanny 273~51 Freedom 103~23 Galen 20~13 George 302~50 George W. 257~10 Hannah (———) (Goldthwait) 194~44 Henry 302~50, 315~10 Holmes 84~26 Homes 314~46 Isaac 271~4, 275~16 Ithamer 100~5 James 1~18, 26~5, 75~26, 229~16, 284~11 Jane (Benton) 144~32 Jeremiah 291~22 John 96~16, 194~43, 361~29 Joram 303~14 Joseph 26~5, 55~23, 94~35, 117~33, 241~43, 315~11, 329~28 Joshua 296~1 Levi 110~10, 138~31, 182~44, 204~20, 236~35, 251~51, 251~52, 308~45, 311~49, 311~51, 321~7, 323~24 Lucy (Lawrence) 84~26 Lydia 168~45 Maria (Hinckley) 303~14 Mary 334~45 Mary (Morrill) 219~56 Mary H. (———) (Harrington) 196~37 Moses 141~21 Nabby (Flowers) 68~17 Nathan 235~35, 302~50, 312~41 Nehemiah 76~44 O. 239~32, 295~26, 303~34, 316~5, 320~14, 327~2, 333~41 Olive (Hoar) 307~3 Oliver 1~33, 144~32, 147~19, 169~12, 198~7, 218~53, 257~46, 306~27, 307~2, 309~40, 311~50 Pamela 140~12 Park 186~19 Paul 58~53 Peggy 205~57 Peter 144~17, 144~22 Polly 132~18 Polly (———) (Flagg) 259~2 Sally (Rice) 245~36 Samuel 39~38, 114~38, 248~15 Simeon 259~2 Solomon 68~17, 175~15 Sophia

273~50 Thomas 235~21, 236~14, 252~30 Timothy 226~39, 239~9 Ursula (M'Curdy) 96~16 Wilkes 219~55 William 123~10 William Pitt 129~8
ALLEY, Susan 295~1
ALLIBONE, William 5~18
ALLISON see ELLISON
ALLSOP, Ann 191~46 George 191~46
ALSTON, Benjamin 295~10
ALVERT, Pierre Antoine 248~46
ALVORD, Elijah 220~45 Melinda 205~55 Sarah (Wells) 220~46
AMAZEEN / AMAZINE, Abigail (———) 84~42 Lucretia 138~14
AMAZINE see AMAZEEN
AMES / EAMES / EMES, [Major] 33~20 Ambrose 211~15 Ann (Checkley) 99~51 Benjamin 291~26 Betsey 198~18 Betsy 57~12 David 26~44 Luther 198~18 Samuel 99~51 Sarah 274~42 Thomas 298~14
AMMIDOWN, Caleb 38~7
AMORY see EMERY
AMSBY see ORMSBEE
ANDERSON, [Capt.] 50~37 [family] 219~6 Ann 209~1 J. 64~31 James 288~47 John 219~6 Sally (———) 229~9 Thomas 198~21, 301~14
ANDRESS / ANDRUS / ANDROS, Hannah 240~33 Isabel 227~36 John 181~30 Roswell 227~34 Sarah 179~6 Theodore 208~48 Zephaniah 114~21
ANDREWS, [Mr.] 222~15 Catharine 117~10 Catharine (Budd) 175~26 Christen 135~44 Ebenezer T. 285~44 Edward 175~26 Eliza (Stevens) 245~34 Eliza (Weld) 285~44 Francis 75~22 Hannah (Cushing) 94~11 John 185~26, 191~51 Joseph 250~1 Loring 136~9, 219~13 Lucy 324~13 Philip 245~32 Rachel 256~36, 260~21 Sophia 275~46 Thomas 94~11
ANDROS see ANDRESS
ANDRUS see ANDRESS
ANEL, Robert 56~11
ANGEL see ANGELL
ANGELL / ANGEL, Ann 298~25 Esther 186~10 James 11~21
ANGER, Job 316~8
ANGIER / ANGIERS, [Mr.] 330~50 Samuel 178~57 Silas 300~51, 329~11
ANGIERS see ANGIER
ANNAN / ANNIN, Jos. 215~4
ANNIN see ANNAN
ANNIS see ENNIS
ANSLEY, John 123~11
ANSON, [Lord] 158~41, 246~50
ANTES, Henry 204~53
ANTHONY, Israel C. 64~18 Susannah 244~39
APPLETON, [child] 168~12 [Dr.] 168~11 [Mrs.] 168~11 Dorothy 57~16 Elizabeth 93~12 Elizabeth (Means) 74~52 Hannah (———) 144~31 Isaac 34~36, 232~26 Jesse 74~52 John 152~12 Maria Theresa (Gould) 238~44 Nathan 238~44 Nathaniel W. 245~33 Sarah 152~12 Sarah (Wildes) 245~33
APPLING, William 165~48
APTHORP, Charles Ward 5~33 James 54~28, 321~41
ARBUCKLE, John 43~30
ARCHER, Benjamin 95~29, 170~50 Margaret (Rider) 95~29 Starling 240~2
ARCHIBALD, Francis 100~4 Hulda 52~3
ARDEN, John 50~1 Mary 50~1 Thomas 212~31
ARDWAY see ORDWAY
ARMES / ARMS, [Mrs.] 201~39 Aaron 232~40, 235~14 Christopher 247~21 Ira 273~50 Jonathan 152~17, 249~25, 334~3 Lucinda 153~34 Sophia (Allen) 273~50 William 144~21
ARMINGTON, Benjamin 28~30
ARMISTEAD / ARNISTEAD, [Lieut.] 270~41 W. 311~26
ARMOUR, [Mr.] 12~12
ARMS see ARMES
ARMSBY see ORMSBEE
ARMSTRONG, [———] 89~15 Abigail 213~24, 215~28 Christian 214~35 Jonathan 117~11 Mary 297~16 Rebecca 64~29 Sally 61~22, 68~3, 93~48
ARNAUD, John Pascal 278~13
ARNEY, Ann (Francis) 167~2 William 167~1
ARNISTEAD see ARMISTEAD

ARNOLD, [Brig. Gen.] 97~3, 170~52 [Mrs.] 277~53 Benedict 113~50, 152~38 Christopher 277~53 David 124~15 Hannah 152~37 J. Rice 231~6 Margaret (Shippen) 170~52 Mary Maria 25~49 Mercy 186~11 Samuel 76~45, 170~35 Silas 174~29 Stephen 180~16, 232~2, 240~23, 371~1 William 145~20
ARNOT, Hugo 155~7 Lilias 155~7
ASHBY, [family] 371~36 [Mr.] 371~35
ASHLEY, [family] 192~13 [Mr.] 69~25 Benjamin 112~29 John 54~29, 57~29 M. 368~55 Margaret 181~48 Martin 80~9, 115~25 Oliver 1~45, 143~14 Polly (Wyman) 108~19 Sally (White) 112~29 Samuel 1~15, 80~11, 115~26, 143~13, 245~5 Timothy 108~19
ASHTON, [Mr.] 227~43
ASNER, James 196~9
ASPENWALL see ASPINWALL
ASPINALL see ASPINWALL
ASPINWALL / ASPINALL / ASPENWALL, Hannah 232~46
ATCHERSON, Alexander 121~46
ATHERTON, Amy 334~44 Charles H. 151~50 Hannah 109~22 Mary Anne (Tappan) 151~50 Rebecca 260~22
ATKER, Thomas 44~40
ATKINS / ADKINS, [boys?] 75~38 [Capt.] 75~34 George 1~46, 310~16 Giles 231~37 Jane 142~27 John 56~12, 142~28, 235~34, 261~31 Silas 123~10
ATKINSON / ADKINSON, B.(?) 20~27 Ichabod 154~10 John 127~55, 128~17, 326~16 Joseph 100~44 T. 151~47 Theodore 80~8, 80~10, 81~43, 115~27, 143~5, 320~36, 325~42, 325~47, 330~9 W.K. 12~18, 216~37 William K. 227~18
ATTWATER / ATWATER, Caleb 242~3 Charles 293~8 Clarissa (Storrs) 113~48 Diana (Lawrence) 242~3 Elisha 321~34 Jeremiah 96~7, 113~47 Noah 112~37 Reuben 9~40, 100~12
ATWATER see ATTWATER
ATWOOD, [children] 307~9 Amos 153~43 Anthony 45~27, 52~50 Elijah 197~56, 254~13 Joshua 122~16, 187~41, 193~22, 228~36, 307~8, 332~37 Mehitable 187~41, 193~22 Prince 74~16 William 332~37
AUSTIN, [Mr.] 311~28 Benjamin 90~12, 251~35 Catharine (Gerry) 260~25 Charles 251~35 Charlotte (Williams) 245~35 Daniel 133~29 Elizabeth 90~12 Hannah 162~25 Hezekiah 35~32 Horace 23~45 James T. 260~24 Jonathan 16~22 Mary 362~2 Rheuben 362~7 Stephen 56~42, 71~21, 221~56 W. 236~21 William 245~34
AVERHILL see AVERILL
AVERILL / AVERHILL / AVRILL, Asa 140~7 Eunice (Mahew) 92~28 Roger 238~10 William 92~27
AVERY, [Mr.] 273~7 Amos 313~48, 373~60 Ann 288~45 Christopher 43~34 George P. 355~6 Henry 43~33 Isaac 353~26 James 38~7 John 244~34, 264~16, 313~48 Oliver 231~3 Phebe 251~19 Polly 29~25 Rhoda 316~7 Samuel 29~26, 36~53, 212~25
AVRILL see AVERILL
AXTELL / EXTILL, Hannah 150~32 Joseph 310~32
AYER / AYRE / AIR / EYRE, [Mr.] 275~2 Catharine 19~28 Charles J. 105~20 Rebecca (Power) 105~20
AYERS / AYRES / EAYRS / EYARS / EAYERS, Charlotte 184~44 Elisha 23~15 Joseph 24~18 Mary 84~12, 146~42 Polly 110~27 Prudence 118~49 Sally 113~27 Samuel 33~4, 83~20 Stephen 361~5 William F. 370~35
AYLCOUGH, Samuel 184~5
AYLESWORTH, Sally 324~18
AYLWARD, [Capt.] 18~42
AYRE see AYER
AYRES see AYERS
AZUBY, Abraham 185~49, 199~16 Esther 199~16

B.

BABB, Elizabeth 100~46 Mary 266~7 Peter 60~4
BABBET see BABBETT
BABBETT / BABBET / BABBITT / BABBIT, Christopher 221~45 Nathan 93~4, 115~13, 129~10

BABBIT(T) see BABBETT
BABBRIDGE, Susanna 183~30
BABCOCK, [Mrs.] 238~1 Billens 32~12 Dolly 186~30 James 319~38 Joseph 141~18 Mary G. 120~40 Nancy 335~32 Nathaniel 277~14 Oliver 237~57, 259~23 Phebe 319~38 Rowse 93~17 Shubael 327~3 Smith W. 334~42 William 335~32
BABSON, Lydia 195~10
BACHE, Benjamin F. 27~25, 69~7 Margaret Harman 69~7
BACHELDER see BATCHELDER
BACHELDOR see BATCHELDER
BACHELLER see BATCHELDER
BACHELOR see BATCHELDER
BACHILOR see BATCHELDER
BACKHOUSE, Edward 274~8
BACKUS, Charles 156~3 Isaac 270~14, 271~12
BACON, [Mr.] 253~22 Benjamin 235~33 David 329~26 Dolly 116~14 Elias 316~50 Jeremiah 71~21, 320~39 Josiah 116~15 Margaret 292~9 Mary 97~19 Mary (Crocker) 118~15 Moses 272~21 Peirpont 85~11 Robert 118~15
BACOT, Mary 274~30
BADGER, [widow] 88~6 [Widow] 103~53 Daniel 239~6 Elizabeth 357~9 Elizabeth (Hall) 172~3 Elizabeth (Stanwood) 149~23 John 133~19, 149~23 Jonathan 172~3, 281~53 Joseph 291~5, 357~10 Lucinda 212~8 Mary 218~4 Samuel 2~54
BAEHR, Lewis 211~54
BAGLEY / BAGLY, Benjamin 196~15 Mary 160~29 Moses 241~32 Philip 311~39
BAGLY see BAGLEY
BAGNALE, William 48~53
BAILEY / BAYLEY / BAILY / BAILLIE / BALY, [Elder] 189~25 [Mr.] 296~18, 306~19 Aaron 81~22 Abigail 209~45 Benjamin 18~5 Cazneau 133~16 Christopher 299~36 David 155~53 Elizabeth 284~53 Ephraim 370~35 Hannah 178~49 Jacob 302~35 James 110~14 Jemima 264~28 Jether 2~47 Joseph 284~54 Kendal 144~23 Nathan 256~52 Prudence 302~35 Samuel Proctor 132~20 Samuel S. 182~15 Sarah 138~19 Susannah 298~33 Thankful 230~16 Theophilus 135~4 Thomas 50~7, 152~8
BAILLIE see BAILEY
BAILY see BAILEY
BAINBRIDGE, [Mr.] 141~23
BAKER, [Mr.] 153~13 [Mrs.] 109~9 [triplets] 109~9 Aaron 313~50 Ann 183~26 Anna 220~50 Betsey 98~30 Deborah 277~25 Ebenezer 250~13 Experience (———) 290~24 Henry 277~34 Hillel (?) 19~15 Isaac 37~5, 37~43, 53~55 Issachar 183~34 Jabez 191~34 Jane (Peters) 144~29 Joel 109~9 John Martin 144~29 Jonadab 89~51 Jonathan 315~12 Joseph 63~24, 276~40, 368~2 Moses 363~34 Nathaniel 151~36, 277~26 O. 325~46 Polly (———) (Robertson) 191~34 Sally 232~17 Samuel 238~58 Samuel Thompson 152~54 Sarah 238~57, 268~34 Silas 118~56 Thomas 16~54, 19~15, 90~5, 248~53 William 36~17, 278~52
BALCH see BELCH
BALDING see BAULDING
BALDWIN, [boy] 9~27, 309~28 [children] 29~19 [Mr.] 248~18 Abraham 282~5 Amos G. 258~47 Azubah (———) 196~36 Benjamin 284~55 Betsey 91~19 Dan 291~13, 313~9 Eleazer 106~3 Elizabeth 6~42 Hannah 265~20, 267~12 Henry 29~19 Isaac 182~18, 186~8, 309~28 James 233~10 Jed. 16~17 Jedediah 9~27 Loam. 279~44 Loammi 256~23 Lura (Calkins) 233~11 Moses 107~5 Philander 263~21 Rebecca 107~4 Roswell 116~40 Ruth 193~11 Thomas 82~49 William 124~11
BALES, Thomas 299~37
BALL (see also BULL, BELL), [Mr.] 133~31 [Mrs.] 173~43 Bulah 316~29 Eliphalet 173~43 Eusebius 1~47 Isaac 148~25 James 6~11 John 316~25 John B. 291~48 Jonas 274~35 Polly 21~42 Squire Bishop 148~25 Stephen 51~27 Susan (?) 83~49 William 326~28
BALLARD (see also BULLARD), Jeremiah 43~13 John 149~33, 220~44 Louisa (Paine) 220~44 Lucy 57~11 Margaret 229~25

BALLOCH see BULLOCK
BALLOCK see BULLOCK
BALLOU / BALLOW, James 195~19 Leonard 309~21 Tamson 195~18 William 334~42
BALLOW see BALLOU
BALOULE, Joseph 16~24
BALY see BAILEY
BANCKER, Abraham B. 230~27
BANCROFT, [Rev.] 199~3 Amos 75~45 Benjamin 169~33 Caleb 198~24 James 102~4 Nathaniel 256~38 Sally (Eastman) 256~38 Sarah (Bass) 75~46
BANFIELD / BANFILL / BANFIL / BENFIELD, John 84~47 Paul 329~23
BANFIL see BANFIELD
BANFILL see BANFIELD
BANGER, Goldsborough 89~10 Maria (Jay) 89~10
BANGS see BANKS
BANISTER see BANNISTER
BANKS / BANGS, [family] 190~43 Benjamin 196~48, 197~31 Edward 257~2 Hannah 257~2 John 248~21
BANNAKER, Benjamin 267~22
BANNISTER / BANISTER, Fanny 106~46 Patience 2~34 Solomon 2~34
BANSON see BENSON
BANTON / BENTON, [Dr.] 181~19 [Mr.] 65~24 Hannah 203~44 Jacob 6~38, 203~44 Jane 144~32
BAPTIST, John 59~38
BAR———, Alfred 153~33 Thede (Dickerman) 153~33
BARAL see BARRELL
BARBARIE, Ann (Van Tuyl) 143~27 John 143~26
BARBER / BARBOR / BARBOUR, [Dr.] 228~48 [Mrs.] 118~19 Chloe 243~11 Daniel 129~26, 243~12 Ebenezer 263~51 Elisha W. 70~3 Henry 75~1, 75~23 James 172~33 John 125~28 Susanna 212~21 Thomas 187~39 William 99~2
BARBOR see BARBER
BARBOUR see BARBER
BARCLAY see BARKLEY
BARDEN / BORDEN / BURDEN, Ebenezer 266~12 Remember 274~30
BARDSLY / BURDSLY, Evan 225~48, 227~53
BARGER see BURGER
BARK see BURKE
BARKER, Barnabas 1~39 Benjamin 145~43 Daniel 81~35 Eliza (Hazzard) 99~14 Elmira 129~33 Esther 251~24 Ezra 103~24 Jacob 99~14 John 145~39, 251~24 Josiah 146~36 Martha 226~7 Mary 291~25 Mary M. 256~42 Nathan 189~2 Sally 109~33 Thaddeus 34~31 William 28~54
BARKLEY / BARCLAY / BERKLEY, [children] 168~22 [widow] 168~22 Polly 245~24 Robert 168~21
BARLOW, Bradley 88~50 Helena 163~17 Joel 46~37
BARNAIRD see BARNARD
BARNARD / BERNARD / BARNAIRD, [Mrs.] 238~15 Abigail 296~22 Catharine 6~8 Ebenezer 46~9 Eliza 64~39 Elizabeth 175~32 George 310~18 J. 21~13 Jennison 116~25 Jinason 304~26 Johannes Christian 214~58 John 310~14 Jonathan 304~27, 321~17 Joseph 21~14, 27~9, 149~6, 230~10 Joshua 9~11 Levi 9~11, 177~52, 215~40 Lucy (Page) 177~53 Lucy (Stebbins) 197~20 Mary 230~10 Samuel 16~38 Theodore 197~20 Thomas 207~12 William 21~12
BARNE / BYRNE, John 101~21
BARNES / BARNS (see also BURNS), [Dr.] 217~24 [Mrs.] 217~24 [Rev.] 218~17 Abraham 269~40 Bill 139~36 David 6~12 Ezra 209~45 George 186~12 Jane 92~29 John 262~54, 328~49 Jonathan 2~21, 208~52 Lydia 49~45 Mary 67~25, 143~30 Rachel (Leonard) 218~16 Rebekah 6~12 Thomas 111~23, 184~33, 186~11 Zilpha 312~49
BARNET see BURNET
BARNEY / BURNEY / BIRNEY, Daniel 217~41 Jeffery A. 88~52 John 280~1 Nathaniel 301~24 Rebeccah 280~2 Samuel 121~50 Sarah (Ransom) 121~50
BARNHAM see BURNHAM
BARNS see BARNES
BARNUM see BURNHAM
BARNUN, Justus 58~18
BARON / BARRON / BARREN / BARRAN, Oliver 314~6 Samuel 20~34 Thomas 37~2 William 4~56, 81~20
BARR (see also BURR), Amos (?) 332~45 William

231~2
BARRALL see **BARRELL**
BARRAN see **BARON**
BARRE, Isaac 128~28 Nathaniel 318~40
BARRELL / BARRALL / BURRILL / BURRELL / BURILL / BARAL / BURRALL, Ebenezer 292~4 Elizabeth (———) 106~27 Jonathan 186~21 Joseph 95~37, 168~52 Polly 117~4 Reuben 209~21
BARREN see **BARON**
BARRET see **BARRETT**
BARRETT / BARET / BARRITT, [Mrs.] 327~36 Anny (Denison) 291~45 Benjamin 80~15, 115~28, 143~4, 278~32 Edward 328~45 Emerson 319~17 Francis 40~2 Hannah 154~2 J. 53~49, 270~30 Jaazaniah 104~7 James 265~33 John 138~46 Joseph 69~14, 295~5 Maria (Pallucar?) 40~2 Martha (Jones) 319~17 Mary 156~44 Oliver 80~13, 115~29, 143~12, 278~32 Polly 296~19 Rebecca 265~33 Samuel 327~37 Scena 295~5 Theodosia 110~26 Urban 328~45 William 160~27, 291~45
BARRIE see **BERRY**
BARRINGER, Charles C. 259~9
BARRINGTON, George 132~22 Lewis 163~44
BARRIOR, [Mr.] 148~39
BARRITT see **BARRETT**
BARRON see **BARON**
BARROW, John 48~53
BARROWS see **BURROUGHS**
BARRY see **BERRY**
BARSTOW, Caleb 61~53 Joseph 157~30 Samuel 107~8, 157~28
BARTER, Henry 348~13
BARTLATE see **BARTLETT**
BARTLET see **BARTLETT**
BARTLETT / BARTLET / BARTLATE, Anna 120~52 Artemas 164~48 Bathsheba 254~24, 257~13 Betsey (Huntoon) 230~45 Edmund 105~21 Giles 313~45, 331~40 J.B. 122~18 Jacob 316~53, 318~36 John 230~45 John H. 208~44 Love 236~51 Mary 274~27 Moses (?) 318~18 Naomi 217~20 Noah 274~27 Patience 318~18 Richard 208~52 Roger 184~43 W. 46~50 William 46~45, 71~26 Zilpha H. (Gerrish) 105~22
BARTON (see also **BURTON**), Benjamin 105~9, 307~47, 325~9 James 104~29 Peter 55~31 Rachel (———) 194~42 Siley 93~22
BARTOW, Samuel 183~22
BARTRAM, James 12~14
BASCOM see **BASCOMB**
BASCOMB / BASCOM, [Rev.] 199~3 Aaron 82~49 Ezekiel 199~17, 201~21 Ezekiel L. 232~9 Joseph 101~8 Reuben 68~32, 75~9 Ruth (Myers) 232~9 Sally 199~17, 201~21 Samuel 234~55 William 216~33
BASKIRK, Jacob V. (?) 74~3
BASS / BOSS / BUSS, [Rev.] 149~38 Ebenezer 95~41 Eliza (Bullard) 41~2 Findley 120~15 Frances 64~44 Hannah 99~1 Henry 41~2, 78~49 J. 64~44 Samuel 167~54 Sarah 75~46 Turell 25~47
BASSET see **BASSETT**
BASSETT / BASSET (see also **BISSET**), [Mrs.] 206~28 [Rev.] 206~29 Amos 275~45 Anner 24~18 Eunice (Pomeroy) 275~45 Hannah 222~29
BATCHELDER / BACHELOR / BACHELDER / BACHILOR / BACHELDOR / BACHELLER, Anna (Baker) 220~50 David 242~16 Elizabeth 292~11 Hannah 3~22 J.P. 311~8 Jethro 169~43 Jonathan 349~14 Joseph 292~11 Josiah 3~23, 135~13, 362~52 Mary (Montgomery) 333~19 Nancy (Rollings) 85~44 Nathan 85~44 Polly 117~54 Samuel 333~19 Thomas P. 220~50
BATCHELLE, A. 105~8
BATES, Clarissa 163~38 Elias 321~35 Ephraim 172~11 Harriet 200~36 Lucy (Turrill) 172~12 Merril 296~20 Merrill 304~28 Tarleton 228~54
BATTEAS, John 162~52
BAULDING / BALDING, Col 34~36 Moses 80~14
BAUMAN see **BOWMAN**
BAXTER, Benjamin 11~4, 14~38, 43~19, 89~28, 181~39, 289~18, 327~20 Charles 42~4 John 11~3 Margery Blanchard 73~15 Seth 207~22 Simon 36~8, 68~12, 316~13

BAY, John H. 77~43
BAYANT, Joseph 322~56
BAYLEY see **BAILEY**
BEACH, [family] 192~30 David 252~38 Gershom 230~7 Hannah (Baldwin) 265~20, 267~12 James 265~20, 267~12 John 296~6 Josiah 197~41 Julia 261~42 Sarah 216~20
BEACHAMP, Mary 110~55
BEAD see **BEEDE**
BEADLE(S) see **BEEDLE**
BEAKMAN / BEEKMAN, Christopher (?) 50~21
BEAL(E) see **BEALS**
BEALL see **BEALS**
BEALS / BEAL / BEALE / BEALL, Benjamin 24~44 Frances M. (Butler) 298~26 James D. 275~2 Jedidiah 193~8 Richard P. 298~26 Thomas 222~17
BEAMAN, [Mrs.] 4~52 Ephraim 189~5 Hannah 152~46 Nancy 99~48 Samuel 4~52
BEAN / BEANE, [child] 119~37 [Mrs.] 119~37, 362~46 Caleb 362~45 David 35~30 Durrel 348~13 James 45~18, 318~41 Nathaniel 170~46 Russel 119~37
BEANE see **BEAN**
BEARCE, [Mrs.] 173~43 Abigail 173~44 Alpheus 173~44 Jonathan 173~44 Sally 173~44
BEARD, Abijah 105~17 David 122~49 Sarah 105~12 Stephen 122~48
BEARDSLEE / BEARDSLEY, Ruggles 263~15
BEARDSLEY see **BEARDSLEE**
BEASLY, Frederick 173~42 Susan (Dayton) 173~41
BEATIS, John 162~52
BEATON, [Mrs.] 123~37
BEATTIE see **BEEDE**
BEATTY see **BEEDE**
BEBEE see **BEEBE**
BECK, [Mr.] 133~33 John 74~6
BECKET see **BECKETT**
BECKETT / BECKET, [Mr.] 147~54 [Mrs.] 147~54
BECKFORD see **BICKFORD**
BECKLEY see **BUCKLEY**
BECKMAN / BICKMAN, [Mr.] 208~24 Christopher (?) 50~21
BECKWITH, Andrew 77~55 Betsey 107~46 Byron 240~30 Candace (———) 240~30 Joseph 294~21 Merriam 295~13 Rebecca 197~19 Richard 299~5 Samuel 77~54
BEDDOES, Thomas 301~55
BEDE see **BEEDE**
BEDEE see **BEEDE**
BEDEL see **BEEDLE**
BEDFORD, Gunning 11~51 William 77~42
BEDORTHA, Eli 240~6
BEDWELL / BIDWELL, [Mr.&Mrs.] 151~41 Isaac 56~10, 68~49 Joseph 151~40 Mabel 74~4
BEEBE / BEBEE, Sophia (Gilbert) 250~31 Steward 250~31 Timothy 278~48 Zenas 216~19
BEEDE / BEDE / BEDEE / BEATTIE / BEAD / BEATTY, James 152~6 Nancy (Kimball) 179~35 Thomas 179~35 William 208~3
BEEDLE / BEADLES / BEADLE / BEDEL / BIDDLE, Abigail 111~7 Eben. 42~4 John 37~53 Sukey (Wilson) 37~53
BEEKMAN see **BEAKMAN**
BEERMAN, Robert 73~25
BEERS, Isaac 96~8, 208~46 Mary 208~46 William P. 335~9
BEGELOW see **BIGELOW**
BELCH / BALCH, Aron (Hovey) 146~31 David 97~4 Hanna (Whidden) 95~26 Hart (?) 294~40 Samuel 95~26 Thomas H. 146~31
BELCHER, Benjamin 217~51
BELDEN see **BELDING**
BELDING / BELDEN, Honor 98~56 Joshua 213~34 Martha 115~30, 143~7 Moses 115~31, 143~6, 278~38, 325~39 Thomas 239~53
BELKNAP, Jeremy 25~7 John 162~15, 183~24 Moses 183~28 Polly 149~20 Sarah (?) 53~10
BELL (see also **BALL, BULL**), Abednego 56~35 Joanna Smith 131~40 John 155~44, 271~2 Jonathan 59~26, 160~27, 298~40 Mary 2~36, 299~17 Mehetabel 333~30 Nancy (Hughes) 283~7 Patience 96~20 Persis (Thom) 155~44 Prudence 60~2 Samuel 237~2,

333~30 Shubael 283~7 Thomas 284~12 William 143~35
BELLINGS see **BILLINGS**
BELLOWS, [child] 309~31, 322~24 [Col.] 330~52 [Gen.] 51~46, 104~54 [Mr.] 121~7, 137~14, 170~5, 170~39, 195~39, 322~39, 335~28 Benjamin 16~55, 57~8, 89~43, 120~22, 128~22, 160~45 Betsy (Emes) 57~12 C. 316~10 Caleb 89~47, 127~52, 128~23, 157~33, 160~44, 324~13, 327~5, 333~46 Caleb Strong 157~32 Daniel 180~21 E. (Foster) 155~40 Edward 299~56 Eleanor (Sheldon) 180~21 Elizabeth (Davis) 305~55 Ellen 309~45 Frances 44~15 H. 320~18 Hannah 212~5 Harry 137~2 Hubard 316~9 J. 137~3, 241~55, 270~49, 332~54 John 8~27, 8~27, 57~12, 73~8, 74~29, 83~29, 89~36, 106~7, 130~56, 212~5, 220~40, 260~7 Joseph 12~39, 90~44, 93~2, 101~11, 122~34, 134~30, 140~40, 156~10, 161~49, 174~12, 177~36, 185~22, 203~19, 207~42, 222~1, 229~3, 229~5, 236~33, 309~31, 316~31 Josiah 31~5, 89~42, 299~56, 316~17 Josiah 2d 53~39, 222~21, 316~19 Lydia (Preston) 53~40 Martha 334~41 Martha (Lovell) 97~12 Mary (Adams) 134~31 Peter 62~7, 367~35 Rebecca 83~28 Roswell 93~9, 97~12 Sally 58~48 Salmon 310~40 Samuel 62~6, 221~15, 367~37 Solomon 172~1 Sophia 130~56 T. 241~55, 332~54 Theodore 249~19, 304~29, 305~55 Thomas 13~31, 44~9, 155~39, 305~46, 309~44, 322~24, 333~45 Thomas 2d 151~29, 236~33, 316~31, 324~29
BEMBRIDGE, [Mr.] 29~34
BEMIS, Calvin 310~1 Lucinda 168~17 Mary 99~24 Mehitable 282~13 Timothy 259~25, 262~4 William 36~54 Zeletes 304~29
BENDER, Abigail 60~2
BENEDICT, Benjamin 5~35 Ebenezer 58~18 Nathaniel 238~10, 244~37 Noble 301~16 Thaddeus 179~51, 180~33
BENENGER, Abraham 210~57
BENETT see **BENNETT**
BENFIELD see **BANFIELD**
BENGUDD, Gustavus Adol. 254~47
BENHAM see **BENTHAM**
BENICUE, Peter 42~11
BENJAMIN, Hannah (Swinnerton) 270~54 Jonathan 270~53
BENNET see **BENNETT**
BENNETT / BENNET / BENNIT / BENETT / BENNITT, Aaron 139~12, 309~46 Aron 295~30 Asaph 172~5 Ashur 255~13 Hannah (———) 190~21 Isaac 354~17 John 22~53, 50~10, 354~17 Joseph G. 354~17 Lydia (Elliot) 22~53 Mary 94~12 Robert 4~49 Sally (———) 115~50 Sarah (Simpson) 172~6 Sewall 295~31 Stephen 24~36, 139~15, 299~17 Tilton 33~36 William 203~12 William P. 302~23
BENNEY see **BINNEY**
BENNIT see **BENNETT**
BENNITT see **BENNETT**
BENNOIT, Peter 13~37
BENSON / BANSON, John (?) 160~43 Joshua 220~52
BENT, [Mr.] 249~8, 250~41 William 262~41
BENTHAM / BENHAM, Jesse 69~30
BENTLY, [Mrs.] 52~43 William 52~42
BENTON see **BANTON**
BERDEAUS, Peter Gilman 82~2
BERGE see **BURGE**
BERKLEY see **BARKLEY**
BERNARD see **BARNARD**
BEROUSE, Joseph 63~23, 368~2
BERREY see **BERRY**
BERRY / BARRY / BIRRI / BERREY / BARRIE, Abigail (Young) 152~1 Dorothy (———) (Emerson) 104~45 Dorothy (Churchill) 179~30 Enoch 70~23 Garret 317~11 Isaac 152~1 Jacob 75~48 Jer. 104~45 John 150~17, 164~9 Lavinia (Cutler) 75~48 Lucy 79~7 Samuel 179~29
BERWICK, [Deputy Sheriff] 8~8
BESBEE see **BISBEE**
BEST, [Mr.] 160~23 Catharine (Gray) 208~34 Peter B. 208~34
BETTS, Rachael 182~27
BICKFORD / BIGFORD / BECKFORD, Lydia 156~45, 183~40
BICKMAN see **BECKMAN**
BICKNACK, [Mrs.] 35~42
BICKNALL see **BICKNELL**
BICKNEL see **BICKNELL**
BICKNELL / BUCKNELL / BICKNEL / BICKNALL, Elijah 99~50 Ezra 179~16 Laura 233~13 Sally (Moore) 99~50
BIDDLE see **BEEDLE**
BIDWELL see **BEDWELL**
BIEGE, Hannah (Strong) 215~11 John 215~11
BIERLY, Jacob 228~29
BIGBEE see **BUGBEE**
BIGELOW / BIGLOW / BEGELOW, [Mr.] 275~39 Abigail 179~44 Abijah 159~48 Amos 288~17 Barna 287~35 Benjamin 97~20 Clarissa 268~54 Daniel 234~24, 265~49 Elisha 324~55 Ellen 319~40 Ezekiel R. 244~15 Hannah (Gardner) 159~49 Henry 213~7 Jabez 16~39 Levi 140~13, 296~41 Lewis 319~41 Lois (Griswold) 287~35 Lucy 201~14 Moses G. 298~13 Nabby 118~32 Nancy (Goodhue) 140~13 Sally 273~22 Tyler 268~53
BIGFORD see **BICKFORD**
BIGHAM, James 158~23
BIGLOW see **BIGELOW**
BIGSBEE see **BIXBY**
BIGSBY see **BIXBY**
BILL, [children] 149~13 [Mr.] 149~13
BILLING see **BILLINGS**
BILLINGS / BILLINS / BILLING / BELLINGS, Hester (Hill) 70~52 John 203~37, 305~42 John W. 209~4 Joseph 289~5 M. 162~45 Richard 16~23, 287~41 S. 38~54 Samuel 70~52 Thomas 277~27, 278~46 Winthrop 305~43
BILLINS see **BILLINGS**
BINGHAM, [Mrs.] 1~28, 91~31 Chester 221~16 Clarissa 148~50 Daniel 45~10 Deborah 221~16 Elizabeth 45~50 Hannah 61~25 Harriet (Black) 357~40 Isaac 17~50 J.H. 178~25, 237~21, 309~11, 320~21 James 72~51, 119~24, 146~24 James H. 288~10, 329~1 John 308~51 Polly 197~52 Ripley 45~51, 197~53 Rodney Jackson 357~40 Rosewell 73~25 Samuel 209~5 Simeon 151~18 Thomas 279~31 Walter 93~44, 215~49 William 91~31, 158~2 Zenas 316~15
BINNEY / BENNEY, Thomas 76~20, 218~38
BIRCH / BURTCH, Narcissa 159~47 William 107~21
BIRD, Elizabeth 226~40 Empson 286~50 John 229~41 Nath. 309~41 Nathan 230~33 Samuel 323~40 Seth 215~33
BIRDSEYE, Thaddeus 60~35
BIRGE see **BURGE**
BIRNEY see **BARNEY**
BIRRI see **BERRY**
BISBEE / BESBEE, Charity (Lathrop) 224~24 Ephraim W. 224~24 Reuben 129~25, 151~14
BISCO, [child] 248~3 [Mr.] 141~53 Abijah 103~20 D.W. 248~3, 320~19 Daniel W. 128~48, 131~22, 309~42
BISHOP, Abraham 157~53 Benjamin 68~18 Beriah 209~54 Betsey (Law) 157~53 Betsy (Chaplain) 68~18 Richard 241~58 Samuel 96~4
BISOHAM, Elizabeth (?) 5~38, 366~14
BISSEE see **BISSEY**
BISSEL see **BISSELL**
BISSELL / BISSEL, Ebenezer 159~25 George 301~17
BISSET, Russel 55~34
BISSEY / BISSEE, [Capt.] 49~50
BIXBY / BIGSBY / BIGSBEE, [boy] 73~40 [Mr.] 73~40 Betsey 285~56 Elijah 316~16 Joel 303~35 Manasseh 285~56 Moses 297~28
BLACK, Harriet 357~40 Mariot 93~51 Mary (Wadsworth) 218~6 Sally 50~3 William 218~5
BLACKINGTON, Tabitha 180~47
BLACKMAN, James 195~11 Rebecca 114~23 Samuel 217~42
BLACKSTOCK, Eliza (Maxwell) 98~25 William 98~24
BLAGUE, John 295~53
BLAIR, Catharine 160~51 Robert 56~9
BLAKE, [Mr.] 124~18, 158~10, 294~43 Abel 145~49, 199~14 Abigail 287~37 Ann 246~58 Bill 21~51,

95~15, 165~24, 309~46, 326~15 Caleb 112~41 Charles 123~29, 281~54 Elizabeth 164~12 Esther (Randal) 115~49 F. 363~26 Frances (Hunt) 123~29 Harriet 166~22 Increase 74~37, 150~5 J.W. 287~37 James 115~49 Jemima 6~56 Jemima (———) (Hart) 199~14 John 250~3 John (?) 60~36 John L. 354~6 John P. 269~49 Joseph 125~33 Joshua 133~22, 267~55 Nancy 215~12 Nathaniel 211~36 Obadiah 6~57, 328~48 Rebekah 150~2 Roxana 85~52 Sally 135~34, 145~48 Sally (Ellis) 269~49 Sarah (Staunton) 267~55 William 21~51
BLAKESLEE / BLAKESLY, [children?] 239~29 O. 239~28
BLAKESLY see **BLAKESLEE**
BLAKEY, Thomas 226~6
BLAKMER, [Mr.] 73~5
BLAMIRE, James 263~46
BLANCHARD / BLANCHER, [children] 261~17 [Mrs.] 261~16 Anna 40~23 Anstis 57~14 Augustus 20~17 Ebenezer 50~31 Isaac 122~35 James 20~34 John 21~44, 113~7 Jonas 218~9 Jonathan 20~27 Joseph 176~18 Nabby (Perry) 218~9 Nathan 261~15 Nathaniel 5~41, Samuel 231~45 Thomas 20~32 William 40~24, 326~21
BLANCHER see **BLANCHARD**
BLAZER, Catharine (Gayden) 146~27 William 146~27
BLEDSO, Jane 298~28
BLIGH see **BLY**
BLIMER, John (?) 245~46
BLISS, [Miss] 39~13 [Mr.] 16~6 Abigail (Rowland) 172~8 Asel 6~35 Azariah 99~55 Daniel 232~31 David 102~15 Delia 182~8 Elizabeth 125~16 Emily (Hitchcock) 101~14 Experience 217~18 Frances 64~8 George 172~8 Gurdon 39~12 Hubbard 101~14 John 146~37, 313~23 Joseph 87~2 Justin 217~19 Leonard 39~12 Louisa 321~30 Mary (———) 191~33 Mary (Worthington) 39~35 Oliver 190~28 Reuben 259~20 Samuel 185~32 Sarah 228~19 Stephen 231~8 Thomas 23~53, 43~53, 257~6
BLODGET see **BLODGETT**
BLODGETT / BLODGET, Charles F. 364~11 Hannah 148~52 John 44~6, 68~37 Samuel 225~38, 327~57
BLOOD, [widow] 106~36 Abel 106~36 Caleb 175~41 Elnathan 71~26, 320~35 Isaiah 189~6 Joshua 245~27 Nathan 244~56 Prudence 214~31
BLOODGOOD, Abraham 51~3, 281~26
BLOODWORTH, Samuel 324~38
BLOOM, Issac 140~21
BLOSS, Walter 22~17
BLOUNT, William 64~10
BLUNT, Charles 46~13 Sarah F. 317~52
BLY / BLIGH, Elisha 189~43 Samuel 189~44
BOARDMAN, [Mr.] 331~8 Benjamin 364~5 Daniel 88~45 Elijah 88~45 Esther 155~27 Fanny 108~29 Mary 155~16, 278~42 Sarah 64~5 Stephen 101~24
BOBEE, David 143~41
BODEN see **BOWDEN**
BODGE / BUDGE, [Elder] 202~37 Aaron B. 227~50 Benjamin 118~5
BODGLEY, Nancy 207~47
BODWELL, Abraham 268~44, 270~44
BOGG, Harry 144~17
BOGGS, [Mrs.] 249~51 James 249~51
BOICE see **BOYCE**
BOIES see **BOYCE**
BOIS see **BOYCE**
BOISE, [Rev.] 188~56 Caroline (Cogswell) 188~56
BOLE, Thomas 44~6
BOLES see **BOWLES**
BOLLES, David 279~36
BOLTER, John 76~30
BOLTON, Cynthia (Chamberlin) 261~39 Elias 62~35 John 261~39 Matthew 312~10
BOLTWOOD, Ebenezer 165~14
BOMAN see **BOWMAN**
BONAPARTE, E. (Patterson) 155~42 Jerome 155~41, 220~20
BOND, [Mrs.] 292~52 Charles 303~37 Elizabeth 256~49 John 75~4, 156~54 John G. 122~38 Mary 75~4, 224~41, 255~57 Sally (Newcomb) 122~38 Samuel 292~51 Thaddeus 218~24 Thomas 195~2

William 318~50
BONER see **BONNER**
BONEY see **BONNEY**
BONNEL see **BONNELL**
BONNELL / BONNEL, Benjamin 30~12 Isaac 272~33
BONNER / BONER, Samuel 30~35
BONNEY / BONNY / BONEY, [children] 294~11 [Mr.] 7~44, 294~10 Hannah 295~29 Peter 19~48 West 15~12, 56~8
BONNY see **BONNEY**
BONTICOU, Susannah 50~27
BOOGE, Amos M. 257~11
BOOKER, John (?) 3~23
BOOMIS, Abdiel (?) 69~11
BOOTH / BOOTHE, [Mr.] 255~37, 319~30 [Mrs.] 255~39 Freegrace 190~6 George 119~7 Henry 118~11 Jonathan 303~38 Lucinda (Jenison) 314~39 Prosper 314~39
BOOTHE see **BOOTH**
BOOTMAN, Mary 138~19
BORDEN see **BARDEN**
BORWELL, U. 141~20
BOSS see **BASS**
BOSTWICK, [Mrs.] 91~11 Arthur 91~12 Erastus 88~51 Joseph 266~1
BOSTWITH, Robert 140~11 Sybil (Geer) 140~11
BOSWELL see **BUSWELL**
BOSWORTH / BOZWORTH, [Mr.] 305~36 Lewis 310~52 Mehitable 131~43
BOTANG, Frances 35~51
BOTH, Adam 25~51
BOUCHER, Jean Baptiste 72~55
BOUDINOT, Elias 285~4 Hannah 285~3
BOUGHTON see **BOUTON**
BOUKER, John (?) 3~23
BOULANGER, Joseph 63~24
BOURDETT, Stephen 67~28
BOURNE, [Mrs.] 243~41 Abigail (———) (Parker) 259~1 Abner 243~39 Ansel 259~1 Charles 317~2 Meletiah 57~12 Ruth (Lambert) 57~13 Shearjashub 233~26
BOUTELL see **BOUTELLE**
BOUTELLE / BOUTELL / BOWTELL, [Mrs.] 3~43 Amos 164~10 Caleb 3~43 Josiah 36~38 Timothy 324~44
BOUTON / BOUGHTON, [boy] 34~20 Lydia (Shove) 260~54 Thomas 34~20
BOW, Thomas R. 316~12
BOWDEN / BODEN, [Capt.] 348~16
BOWDISH see **BOWDITCH**
BOWDITCH / BOWDISH, Joseph 64~33 Mary 224~36
BOWEN, [Mr.] 135~10 Charles 11~5, 312~37, 321~51, 331~12 E. (Leonard) 91~23 Elizabeth 4~49 Jabez 91~23 Mary 92~17 Nath. A. 151~20 Nathan 4~50 Nathaniel A. 129~27 Oliver 71~34 Sarah 38~53 Thomas B. 206~6
BOWER, [Mrs.] 109~11 [triplets] 109~11 Aaron 109~10
BOWERS, Bradley 37~54 Elizabeth 62~17 Fanny (Lane) 37~54 Mr. 3~32
BOWESING, [Mr.] 255~40
BOWIE, [Lieut.] 303~23 John F. (?) 207~39
BOWKER, Bartlett 290~30 Benjamin 67~57 Hannah (Carpenter) 290~30 John 279~36 Lucy (———) 156~34 Stephen 65~28, 89~44, 120~19
BOWLES / BOLES, [Gen.] 227~26 [Mr.?] 207~49 [Mr.] 176~52, 216~29 H. 133~14 Samuel 131~42, 134~33 Thomas 68~39
BOWMAN / BAUMAN / BOMAN, Jonathan 167~27 Joseph 240~13, 242~17 Lovell 210~23 Phila 304~30 S. 152~14 Samuel 321~15 Sibil 284~17 Thaddeus 284~17 Zadock 354~16
BOWTELL see **BOUTELLE**
BOYCE / BOYES / BOICE / BOIES / BOIS, [infant] 41~18 [Mr.] 41~15, 221~11 [Mrs.] 41~15 John 51~31, 76~57 Margaret 51~31 Mercy (Hichborn) 76~58 Thomas 299~24 William 35~49, 35~52
BOYD, Abigail 117~31 Adam P. 17~19 Hugh 30~34 James 154~47 Lucy 32~15 R. 201~54 William 57~20, 133~29, 310~13
BOYDELL, Alderman 182~4
BOYDON see **BOYNTON**
BOYER, Charlotte 168~53

BOYES see BOYCE
BOYINGTON, Richard 126~47
BOYLER, John 73~36
BOYLESTON see BOYLSTON
BOYLSTON / BOYLESTON, Mary (Mosely) 330~30 Richard 330~29 Thomas 38~49
BOYNTON / BOYTON / BOYDON, Amozoel (?) 273~14 Polly 4~36 Richard 273~15, 350~6
BOYSON, E.C. 10~25
BOYTON see BOYNTON
BOZWORTH see BOSWORTH
BRACE, David 4~48 Lucy 202~19, 202~56
BRACKEN, Thomas 48~24
BRACKET see BRACKETT
BRACKETT / BRACKET (see also BRICKETT), [Dr.] 124~34 Hannah 193~7 Joshua 193~8 Mary 217~25 Moses 217~25
BRADBRAY see BRADBURY
BRADBURY / BRADBRAY, Barnabas 35~45 Joseph 354~21 Mehitable (Bradley) 35~45 Theophilus 149~48
BRADFORD, [Capt.] 73~35 Benjamin 59~31 Eben. 243~3 Elizabeth Green 243~2 Ephraim P. 256~42 Ephraim Putnam 232~6 Hitty (Hinckley) 64~26 J.H. 220~49 John 142~47 Lemuel 64~26 Mary 221~25 Mary M. (Barker) 256~42 Moses 142~47 Sally (Ralston) 220~50 Samuel 304~24 Thomas 221~25
BRADISH, Abigail 167~22
BRADLAY see BRADLEY
BRADLEY / BRADLAY / BRADLY, [Mrs.] 110~35 Abigail (Hildreth) 131~34 Abraham 96~7 Dudley 44~23 Enoch 131~34 F. 211~10 Francis 299~36 Isaac C. 356~35 John 77~42 Malinda (Wills?) 150~9 Mehitable 35~45 Rachael 184~41 S.R. 110~35 Sally (Richards) 129~30 Stephen 142~38 Stephen R. 9~41, 150~8 William 135~4 William Czar 129~30
BRADLY see BRADLEY
BRADSHAW, Elizabeth 203~26 John 244~23
BRADSTREET, [Gov.] 260~39 Nathanile 236~11 Sarah 114~24
BRADT, A. 8~14
BRAGDEN see BRAGDON
BRAGDON / BRAGDEN / BRIGDEN, Catharine 120~41 Samuel 229~25
BRAGG, Henry 170~43 Luther 167~15 Mary 95~38 Polly (Felt) 170~44 Timothy 1~37
BRAIGE, Martha (?) 102~40
BRAINARD see BRAINERD
BRAINER see BRAINERD
BRAINERD / BRAINARD / BRAINER, Elijah 230~30 Jabez 119~26, 243~58
BRAITHWAITE, Richard 213~26
BRAMBLE, William 200~19
BRANCH, Daniel 170~34
BRAND, [children] 192~34 David 192~34
BRANDEGEE / BRENDEGEE, Jacob 36~9, 43~17
BRANDEL, [children] 106~20 [Mr.] 106~18 [Mrs.] 106~20
BRANTON, Cader 59~40
BRASS, Andrew 299~36
BRAXTON, Tylor 293~27
BRAY, Frances (Eliot) 226~33 John 152~49 Joseph 226~33 Sarah 38~56
BRAYTON, Isaac 306~6
BRAZER see BRAZIER
BRAZIER / BRAZER, Henry 165~51 James 211~53
BREAKER, George 158~20
BREASLEY, Joseph 180~53
BRECK, [Miss] 314~41 [Mr.] 332~23 Clarissa (Allen) 187~7 Edward 154~12 John 187~7 Samuel 314~42 William 58~25
BRECKENRIDGE, [Mr.] 137~35
BREED, Allen 67~21 Hannah 142~42 William 142~42
BREESE see BREEZE
BREEZE / BREESE, John 39~31, 40~7
BREISH / BRIECH, A. 38~16 Adam 63~16
BRELLAN, John 295~28
BRENDEGEE see BRANDEGEE
BRETT / BRIT / BRITT, Betsey (Robinson) 244~18 Seth 244~18
BRETTON see BRITTON
BREWER, Ebenezer 330~19 Eleanor 265~23, 269~52

Henry 155~12 J. 39~45 James 28~55 John 265~24, 269~53 Lucy 155~12 Lucy (?) 292~38 Luey (?) 292~38 Sally 120~40 Thomas 191~14
BREWSTER, [Gen.] 98~55 Abigail 44~44 Caleb 164~9 Ebenezer 59~49, 167~20 Edmund 107~37, 145~5, 233~37, 233~38 Hannah 98~55, 167~20 Jerusha 119~16 Mary (Jones) 69~2 Moses 292~56 Oliver 69~2 Peleg 91~32 Sally 92~31, 200~49
BRIANT see BRYANT
BRIARD / BRIER, Oliver 133~23
BRICKET see BRICKETT
BRICKETT / BRICKET (see also BRACKETT), Rhoda 86~45
BRIDGE, [infant] 299~29 Ann (———) 195~11 Eben. 20~30 Ebenezer 81~48, 154~25 Experience 154~25 Irene (Morse) 232~10 John 260~19 Joseph 299~29, 309~14, 322~36, 335~29 Josiah 94~18, 232~10 Mary 260~20 Matthew 195~13 William 184~29
BRIDGEMAN see BRIDGMAN
BRIDGET, Peter 159~1
BRIDGMAN / BRIDGEMAN, [Judge] 6~13, 366~18 [Mrs.] 6~13, 366~23 John 179~50
BRIDGSTOCK, William 20~43
BRIECH see BREISH
BRIER see BRIARD
BRIERLY, Benjamin 133~16
BRIGDEN see BRAGDON
BRIGGS, [children] 71~54 [widow] 71~54 Abial 74~18 Abiel 6~37 Asa 6~9 Betsey (Hudson) 54~19 Betsey (Warren) 270~52 Dameris 112~38 Elisha 27~42, 98~31, 149~42 Jehosaphat 270~52 Joseph 169~34 Josiah 71~52 Nathan 143~42 Prudence 271~30 Richard 301~40 Samuel 149~33 Silas 134~25 William 54~19, 127~54, 134~51, 137~22, 186~44, 206~55, 249~28, 254~54, 278~22, 293~10, 319~31
BRIGHAM, [Widow] 153~24 Antipas 37~51 Josiah 322~51 Julia (Whitney) 37~51 Lewis 138~54 Nabby 11~14 Susannah (———) (Hayward) 138~54
BRIGHT, [Mr.] 308~4 George 206~30 Rachel 252~31
BRIMMER, Herman 75~54 Martin 167~54
BRINLEY, Catharine (Putnam) 192~46 George 192~46, 214~33, 301~3
BRISK, Samuel 61~42
BRISTOL, Simeon 218~14
BRIT see BRETT
BRITON see BRITTON
BRITSON, George 39~9
BRITT see BRETT
BRITTON / BRITON / BRITTUN / BRETTON, Asa 124~15 Asahel (?) 24~42 Benjamin 255~9 James 66~13 John 303~39 Joshua 143~32 Jotham 56~7 Phillip 27~48 Relief (Durant) 255~9 Seth 24~38, 48~9 William 129~10
BRITTUN see BRITTON
BROAD, Aaron 108~19 Sabra (Sanderson) 108~20
BROADERS, Priscilla 99~2
BROADHEAD / BRODHEAD, John 98~48 Luke 247~37 Mary (Dodge) 98~49
BROCHWAY see BROCKWAY
BROCK, Walter 56~17
BROCKINS, Johnson 46~57
BROCKWAY / BROCHWAY, Christiana (Chapel) 249~32 Christopher 249~32 Diodate 164~50 John 114~39, 198~41 Woolston 333~53
BRODHEAD see BROADHEAD
BRONSON / BRUNSON, [Mrs.] 72~44 David 270~9
BROOKLINE, (———) 33~33
BROOKS, [Messrs.] 318~14 [Mr.] 10~42, 24~50, 50~57, 322~14 Amy 147~7 Benjamin 319~8 Catharine 4~28 Daniel 275~38, 332~14, 332~14 David S. 195~25 Eleazer 268~35 Eliza 110~34 Esther 202~28 James 4~28, 120~39 Job F. 14~15, 68~10, 74~36, 129~10 John 28~48, 33~50, 116~39, 244~45, 281~18 John Drury 244~45 Lucinda (Hatch) 260~27 Mary 38~44, 319~7 Moses D. 153~43 Nancy (Redington) 281~19 Nathaniel 225~8 Polly (Caldwell) 120~39 Rebecca 312~3 Rebecca W. 357~39 Sally 54~18 Seth 239~12 Simeon 106~40 Simon 207~8, 332~56 Thomas D. 260~26 Timothy 239~12
BROTON see BROUGHTON
BROTTON see BROUGHTON

BROUGHTON / BROTTON / BROTON, Benjamin 313~45, 331~40 Lydia 259~11
BROWN / BROWNE, [child] 79~54 [children] 5~7 [Mr.] 5~6, 16~43, 354~46, 357~15 [Mrs.] 5~7, 279~11 [Rev.] 261~22 Aaron 157~14 Abel 328~13 Abigail 130~8, 225~8 Abishai 39~33 Abraham 318~30 Amos 86~46, 265~16 Andrew 281~26 Arch 17~48 Augustus 19~50 Benjamin 5~27, 296~12, 355~36 Bowes 79~51 C.B. 171~30 Charles B. 319~9 Clark 316~18, 331~33 Daniel 10~41, 272~10 David 20~23, 22~22, 81~47, 89~22 Deborah 10~40 Dorcas 113~7 E. 126~39 Ebenezer 1~30 Edward 176~25 Elias 259~15 Elijah 205~5 Elisha 296~23 Elizabeth (Linn) 171~30 Elizabeth (Temple) 140~17 Ellen 44~16 Ephraim 267~15 Francis 12~41, 121~44 Hannah (Warren) 79~50 Harry 321~16 James 108~13, 370~36 James N. 260~10 Jno. 68~22 John 48~53, 52~27, 150~32, 177~16, 252~19, 254~25, 281~4, 297~25, 315~4, 334~41 John B. 286~52 Jonas 32~54 Jonathan 260~38, 262~6 Joseph 59~55, 90~9, 129~17, 321~48, 355~36, 361~45 Joseph 2d 130~21 Kyseba (———) 152~26 Levi 140~16, 318~49, 326~12 Lucy 326~13 Lucy (Ridley) 176~25 Luke 90~33 Mary 84~41, 157~13, 191~49, 211~57, 299~18 Mary (Huntington) 267~15 Mary (Steele) 96~17 Micah 23~53 Moses 46~44, 85~46, 258~33 Nancy (Eastman) 86~46 Nathaniel 108~6, 327~4 Nicholas 96~17 Obadiah 191~49 Oliver 328~13 Peggy (Shepard) 79~44 Peter 211~1 Philip 243~49 Phineas 190~54 Rebecca 175~32 Reuben 221~56, 309~43 Robert 7~14 Sam'l 240~4 Samuel 34~35, 124~27, 175~31, 178~45, 183~33, 222~7, 299~18 Sarah 1~30 Sarah (Tuft) 286~52 Simeon 296~21, 321~15 Spencer 81~45 Stephen 191~44, 219~5, 235~20 Stephen Rowe 225~31 Susannah 91~30 Susannah (Sumner) 85~46 Thomas 69~10, 95~39, 175~33, 179~17, 179~53, 214~15 Titus 316~11 William 4~7, 79~44, 117~55, 314~49, 363~48
BROWNE see BROWN
BROWNELL, [Capt.] 262~54 Nancy 105~21
BROWNIN / BROWNING, Abigail (Putnam) 190~46 William 190~47, 265~50
BROWNING see BROWNIN
BROWNLOW, John 17~55
BRUCE, John 294~34 Roger 297~21 Stephen 265~48 Zeriah 297~21
BRUM, [Capt.] 208~21
BRUMBLY, Christopher 240~15
BRUNSON see BRONSON
BRUSH, Elkanah 285~21 Lucretia (———) (Strong) 285~21
BRYAN, Nathan 23~41
BRYANT / BRIANT, Annas (Spalding) 172~53 Israel 325~31 Jacob 194~6 Josiah 148~5 Sally (Withington) 148~5 Sukey 232~14 William 89~33, 172~53, 295~46
BUCHAN, William 191~8
BUCHANAN, [Judge] 301~33 David 99~36 Robert 99~36
BUCK, [Lieut.] 153~11 Daniel 216~42, 219~50, 236~29, 264~22 Ebenezer 224~40 John 147~6 Julia (Mitchell) 216~43 Samuel 152~32 William 189~52, 218~38
BUCKELIN see BUCKLIN
BUCKINGHAM, [Mrs.] 135~47 Catharine (Putnam) 224~25 Ebenezer 224~26 John 135~47 Joseph T. 205~55 Melinda (Alvord) 205~55
BUCKLAND see BUCKLIN
BUCKLEY / BECKLEY, Amelia (Daggett) 121~48 Hosea 285~22 Joanna 110~33 John 121~48 Lydia (Pierson) 285~22
BUCKLIN / BUCKELIN / BUCKLAND, A. 276~48 Daniel 194~18 Jeremiah 288~25 Jonathan 231~5 Sylvester F. 284~29 William 249~50
BUCKMAN, David 21~51, 95~15, 185~37, 243~50 Edward 28~22 Lydia 280~22
BUCKMINSTER, [Mrs.] 357~17 [Rev.] 197~45 Abraham 357~20 Elihu 357~20 Elijah 357~21 Elisha 357~20 Enoch 357~21 Isaac 357~20 Jacob 357~20 James 357~17 Joseph Stevens 179~26 Mary 197~45, 200~53 Noah 357~21 Samuel 357~21
BUCKNAM see BUCKNUM

BUCKNELL see BICKNELL
BUCKNUM / BUCKNAM, Asa 215~38
BUCKSTON see BUXTON
BUDD, Catharine 175~26
BUDGE see BODGE
BUDINOT, [Judge] 162~40 Rachel 162~40
BUEL see BUELL
BUELL / BUEL, (———) (Metcalf) 77~12 [children] 247~47 [Mr.] 32~6 [Mrs.] 247~47 Aaron 62~29 Amy 62~29 Benjamin 324~39 Charles 238~51 Enos 247~45 James 95~32 Jane 329~45 John H. 77~11 Josiah 44~6 Lucinda (Alden) 238~51 Meigs 314~36, 322~38 Phebe 323~31 Solomon 95~33
BUFFUM, Joseph 51~7, 67~10, 74~38, 93~4, 115~13
BUGBEE / BIGBEE / BUGBEY, Alpheus 63~56 Betsey 321~16 Eliza 207~30 Ruth 316~57 Samuel 304~30
BUGBEY see BUGBEE
BULFINCH, Abigail 155~55 Thomas 114~18
BULKELEY see BULKLEY
BULKLEY / BULKELEY, Daniel 6~44 Roger 200~25
BULL (see also BALL, BELL), David 314~15 Hannah 293~38 Jonathan 314~15 Joshua 293~42 Nancy 293~37 Rebecca 293~40 William 51~26
BULLARD (see also BALLARD), (———) 71~41 [Brother] 65~50 [Major] 70~48, 156~40 A. 109~17 Asa 64~55, 120~5, 175~42 Eleazer 47~11 Eliza 41~2 Isaac 36~10 Maria 24~16 Samuel 146~24 Simon 43~14
BULLOCK / BALLOCK / BALLOCH, [Mrs.] 183~31 [Widow] 171~1 James 66~28, 144~25 M. 66~29 Timothy 20~6 William 13~28
BULLY, William M. 333~43
BUMP, Marcey 374~29
BUMSTEAD, [Mr.] 135~11 Jeremiah 92~3 Sarah (Crosswell) 92~3
BUN, Ira 21~45
BUNDY, [children] 326~48 Asahel 267~16 Elias 243~23, 325~55, 326~44, 328~6 Esther 140~17 Henry 254~35 Martha 326~10, 328~6 Martha (———) (Isham) 326~44 Nathan 56~18, 87~20, 90~6, 135~30, 330~54 Philip 287~2 Philip P. 254~35 Sibel 267~16 Susan 243~22, 320~17
BUNKER, [Capt.] 75~36, 313~4
BURBANK, [Mr.] 162~24, 330~51 Abraham 288~50 David 230~21 Eben 131~43 Elias 303~36, 333~44 Hannah 184~30 Isaac 304~26 Laura 157~4 Sarah 288~51 Susannah 278~39
BURDEN see BARDEN
BURDITT, [Mrs.] 135~11 Sarah 245~53
BURDSLY see BARDSLY
BURFORD, [Col.] 247~35
BURGE / BERGE / BIRGE, Caleb 283~39 David 20~33 Dyer 307~44 John 239~9 Nathaniel 310~20
BURGER / BARGER, [children] 196~19 [Mr.] 67~43, 196~18 [Mrs.] 196~19
BURGES see BURGESS
BURGESS / BURGES, John 199~32
BURILL see BARRELL
BURK see BURKE
BURKE / BURK / BARK, [girl] 47~14 Betsey (Elbert) 41~39 Edanus 118~28 Edmund 10~2 Elijah 47~14 Hannah 125~2 Jacob 150~39 John 269~14 Joseph 140~4 M. 41~39 Polly (Crague) 183~45 Rachel 269~14 Silas 127~35 Solomon W. 183~44 Thomas 301~34
BURKET see BURKITT
BURKITT / BURKET, Thomas 239~45
BURLEIGH / BURLEY / BURLY, David 355~5 Henry 133~44 James 364~12 Wheeler 355~34 William 355~34
BURLEY see BURLEIGH
BURLING, Eliza (Earl) 54~14 Joseph 210~54 W.S. 54~14
BURLINGAME, [infant] 171~22 Amasa 171~21 Eliza 171~21
BURLY see BURLEIGH
BURNAP, Asa W. 88~5, 292~21 John 175~48, 233~12 Polly (Peak) 233~12
BURNES see BURNS
BURNET / BURNETT / BARNET, [Deacon] 171~33 Abel 96~7 John 199~55 Matthias 248~49 Oliver

318~11
BURNETT see **BURNET**
BURNEY see **BARNEY**
BURNHAM / BARNUM / BARNHAM, Abraham 317~53 B. (———) (Pitman) 66~38 Frederick 179~38, 185~45 Hannah (Mason) 179~38, 185~45 J. 66~38 Joseph 10~7, 85~24 Josiah 223~2, 243~44, 372~15 Lucy (Smith) 36~27 Mary (White) 317~53 Miriam 10~7 Simeon 36~27 Stephen 87~46
BURNS / BURNES (see also **BARNES**), [Capt.] 27~14 David 334~43
BURPEE / BURPY, Samuel 305~38
BURPY see **BURPEE**
BURR (see also **BARR**), [Col.] 209~29 [Mr.] 178~29 [widow] 325~48 E. 107~32 Ebenezer 122~17 Elisha 12~48 Eunice 209~4 Eunis (Turner) 56~39 Laban 314~24, 316~12, 334~31 Martha (Gardner) 12~47 Martin 56~38 Mary 289~2 Prudence 314~23 Samuel 56~6, 61~24, 68~50 William 77~17
BURRALL see **BARRELL**
BURRELL see **BARRELL**
BURRILL see **BARRELL**
BURROUGHS / BURROWS / BARROWS, [Col.] 142~25 [Dr.] 320~5 [Miss] 142~24 [Mr.] 112~3, 208~30 Asa 310~17 Benjamin 49~54 Caleb T. 138~9 E. 104~41 Elijah 150~26, 241~5 G. 326~19 Jesse 320~16 Joel 274~46 John 321~14 Lemuel 286~48 Sally 49~54 Samuel 105~11, 327~13 Stephen 255~44, 371~61 William W. 186~27
BURROWS see **BURROUGHS**
BURSA, Joseph (?) 63~23
BURT / BURTT, [Judge] 43~2 [Mr.] 103~17 Alvin 61~23, 81~18 Anne 189~50 Benjamin 215~26 Clarissa 183~42 George 42~45 Gideon 153~31 Hannah 181~49 Hannah (Gage) 103~17 Israel 182~10 James 78~43, 215~3 Joseph 1~21, 19~18, 20~50, 21~21, 67~10, 94~36, 95~20, 119~50, 124~23, 180~23 Leonard 54~32 Moses 44~10, 264~2 Ross 264~2 Susannah 54~31 Sylvester 236~28
BURTCH see **BIRCH**
BURTON (see also **BARTON**), [Mrs.] 218~40 Asa 218~40 Betsey (Safford) 233~9 Jacob 233~8 Joseph 212~11 Polly (Hodgman) 212~11
BURTT see **BURT**
BUSBY / BUSHBY, [Mr.] 239~26
BUSH, Ellis 79~8 Martha 256~35
BUSH———, Martha 128~44
BUSHBY see **BUSBY**
BUSHNELL, John 228~32, 228~33
BUSS see **BASS**
BUSSEY, Eliza 152~44
BUSWELL / BOSWELL, [child] 308~31 [Mrs.] 308~30 James 4~55 John 202~1 Mary 244~28 Richard 308~24 William 45~17, 60~45, 65~34, 318~43
BUTLER, [boy] 95~13 [Lt. Col.] 216~54 [Mr.] 362~32 Benjamin 178~52 Daniel 268~11, 268~12 David 227~52 Edward 142~34 Frances M. 298~26 Francis 90~11, 357~2 John 77~20 Lois 80~12, 115~32, 143~13, 278~33 Mary 284~11 P. Wentworth 66~41 Simeon 241~49 Theodore 177~28 Thomas 95~13, 207~41 Zebediah 259~22
BUTMAN, [child] 179~6 Joseph 77~14 Olive (Heldrith) 245~38 William 179~6, 245~38
BUTT, Joshua 52~19 Polly 246~31
BUTTERFIELD, [child] 156~27 [Mr.] 156~27, 366~30 Abraham 75~47 Amos 25~33, 143~47, 143~54, 152~26 Anna 143~47 Ben. 20~18 Benjamin 173~8, 176~21 Caleb 28~17 Hannah 93~6, 189~16 Isaac 36~18, 36~43, 68~4, 77~2, 87~18, 91~37, 93~3, 95~52, 115~12, 119~53, 141~56 Jonas 19~46, 28~16 Lusena (———) (Brown) 152~26 M. 324~6 Martin 87~19, 119~49, 127~37, 131~10, 296~53 Mary (Cordia) 75~47 Nat. 20~24 Nathaniel 81~46 Parker 310~12, 316~14 Ralph 81~21, 124~47 Thomas 6~52 Timothy 81~19 Warren 77~2 Willard 93~50, 95~51, 119~53, 141~56 William 14~37
BUTTERS, Abigail (Jaquith) 105~38
BUTTLES, Levi 207~53
BUXTON / BUCKSTON, [Mr.] 11~14 [Mrs.] 330~45 Jonathan 330~45
BUZELL / BUZWELL / BUZZELL / BUZZEL, Ichabod

355~52 Isaac 355~51 Isaac D. 355~52 John R. 353~46, 354~50 S. 355~52
BUZWELL see **BUZELL**
BUZZEL see **BUZELL**
BUZZELL see **BUZELL**
BYAM, Ben. 20~15 John 20~17
BYEARD, [Mr.] 216~27
BYINGTON, Abraham 70~49
BYLES, [Rev.] 142~45 Mather 142~45
BYRNE see **BARNE**
BYTES, [Rev.] 47~31 Anna 47~31

C.

CAADY see **CADY**
CAAL see **CALL**
CABOT / CABOTT, Alice 155~31 Elizabeth 105~24 Sally 290~8 Samuel 292~2 Sarah 292~1
CABOTT see **CABOT**
CADE see **CADY**
CADET, Amons 2~41
CADWELL see **CALDWELL**
CADY / CATY / CAADY / CADE (see also **CATE**), [Mrs.] 181~2 Albe 256~46 Betsey 135~34 George 198~36 Isaac 51~33 Lyman 11~22 Sarah 68~52 Sarah (Warner) 256~46 Thomas 181~2
CAFFIN see **COFFIN**
CAHOON see **CALHOUN**
CAIN see **KAIN**
CALDWELL / CADWELL, [Lieut.] 176~45 [Mrs.] 209~12 Alice 260~47 Charlotte B. 226~49 Daniel 44~11 Deborah 262~49 George 28~29 John 30~34, 172~31, 282~14 John William 162~44 Mittia 317~48 Polly 120~39 Seth 194~13 Thomas 286~45 William 202~41, 209~12, 226~49, 244~53
CALEF / CALFE, Betsey 99~7 John 285~52
CALFE see **CALEF**
CALHOUN / CAHOON / COHOON, John 90~39
CALKINS see **CAULKINS**
CALL / CAAL, David 92~44, 160~42, 370~39 Hannah (Eastman) 269~56 Nathan 269~56 Phineas 68~53 Timothy 160~42, 164~54
CALLAGHAN see **CALLAHAN**
CALLAHAN / CALLAGHAN, Capt. 12~10 John 221~36
CALLENDAR see **CALLENDER**
CALLENDER / CALLENDAR, James Thompson 146~46 John 217~41
CALLEY see **COLLEY**
CALVER see **CULVER**
CALVERT, George 326~26
CALVETT, Joseph Peters 156~50 Margaret Williams 156~49
CAMBDEN see **CAMDEN**
CAMBELL see **CAMPBELL**
CAMBRIDGE, Harriot 289~31
CAMDEN / CAMBDEN, [Mr.] 192~37, 193~2
CAMELFORD, [Lord] 160~22
CAMPBELL / CAMBELL, [child] 163~27 [Mrs.] 34~8, 162~36 Abigail (Coburn) 295~3 Alexander 165~13 Betsey 316~35 Betsey (Sedgwick) 177~46 C. (M'Donald) 138~15 Collin Lina 191~38 Dan 295~3 Daniel 117~45, 163~27, 177~46 Edward R. 88~3, 134~26 James 137~30, 165~31, 213~17, 273~15, 306~50, 316~20, 331~50, 333~47 John 52~28, 90~33, 113~1 Mathew 138~15 Michael 20~44 Sarah 147~48
CAMPTON / KEMPTON, Thomas 228~23
CANEY see **KENNEY**
CANNEY see **KENNEY**
CANNON, Almira (Smith) 259~1 John 182~55 Josiah 258~57 Josiah N. 372~49 Josiah W. 244~13
CANTILLON, Richard D. 232~33
CANTINE, Moses 323~42
CANTISBEER, William P. 335~48
CAPERHAUM, Sally (Black) 50~3 Thomas 50~3
CAPRON, Jonathan 89~53 Joseph 199~47 Lois 297~48 Sally 199~47
CARD, John R. 189~48

CAREW, Richard H. 228~9
CAREY see CURREY
CARGILL, Rebecca (———) 96~50 William 38~5
CARL see CARLL
CARLE see CARLL
CARLETON see CARLTON
CARLISLE / CARLYLE, Alice (———) 220~46 D. 94~24, 102~18 David 1~17, 6~30, 11~11, 13~38, 14~41, 16~20, 19~36, 21~11, 24~35, 30~16 John 4~2, 10~19, 30~17, 127~31, 316~22 Mary 242~7 Sally 200~34 Samuel 166~7, 220~47 T. 94~24, 102~18
CARLL / CARYL / CARLE / CARL (see also CARROLL), [Mr.] 5~4 Amos 86~25 B. 61~26 Benjamin 86~25 Jonathan 251~29 Rufus 32~14
CARLTON / CARLETON, [Col.] 265~39 Asa 139~42 Charles C. 168~47 Dean 111~11, 321~17 Dorcas (Perry) 139~43 Elizbeth 209~7 James 286~54 Joanna 84~32 John 160~18 Judith 160~17 Mary 361~44 Willard 84~33, 215~46 William 204~50, 209~8
CARLYLE see CARLISLE
CARNES see KARNS
CARNEY / CORNEY, [Mr.] 195~53 Mary 125~10
CAROL see CARROLL
CAROTHERS see CARRUTHERS
CARPENDEE, Catharine (Parsells) 143~29 John G. (?) 143~29
CARPENTER, [———] 43~20 [Capt.] 127~51, 310~4 [Dr.] 181~19 [Miss] 160~14 [Mr.] 252~12, 255~45 [Mrs.] 6~42, 141~54, 299~16 Amasa 89~50 Asa 299~16 Betsey (Patridge) 179~39 Charity 114~10 D. 290~30 Dan 179~39 Davis 73~10, 90~9, 113~44, 130~36, 141~55, 156~34, 327~8 Desire (Hall) 287~33 E. 308~48 Eber 139~42, 281~16, 305~1, 328~33, 332~18 Elijah 316~24 Elizabeth (Welch) 163~40 Ephraim 20~56, 21~1, 81~31, 149~43, 252~24 Ezra 328~9 Hannah 290~30 Isaiah H. 163~40, 194~3 Jerusha 321~20, 334~40 Jesse 316~21 John 273~37 Joseph 6~43 Judith (Greene) 139~42 Lucy (———) (Bowker) 156~34 Oliver 231~6 Polly 149~42 Rebecca 114~11 Roswell 217~42 Vine 287~33 William B. 217~42 Zachariah 316~23
CARR, [brothers] 124~29 [children] 124~31 [wives] 124~31 Archibald 5~50 Benjamin 259~21 Elmira (Barker) 129~33 Joseph 129~32 Nathan 320~34 Robert 320~37
CARRIER see CURRIER
CARRIGAIN / CORRIGAN, Philip 252~44
CARROBIE, Dennis 223~15
CARROLL / CAROL (see also CARLL), Lawson 117~31 Olive 117~31
CARRUTHERS / CAROTHERS, [family] 24~26 [Mrs.] 24~26 John 24~25, 363~54
CARSON see CORSON
CARSWELL see CASWELL
CARTER, [children] 193~52 [Mrs.] 193~52 Benjamin 130~35, 252~43 Betsey 92~32 Charity 148~24 D. 233~6 David 138~23, 155~3, 177~39, 182~46, 185~33, 222~9, 226~22, 260~5, 275~42, 290~18 Ephraim 23~8 Jacob 177~30, 178~51 James 30~13, 59~29 Jeremiah 97~16 John 75~32, 193~48 Jonah 304~41 Joseph 172~4 Josiah 28~7 Margaret (Taylor) 172~4 Mary 297~28 Mrs. 30~13 Nabby 32~15 Phebe 43~24 Polly 202~36 Samuel 148~24, 179~17 Seth 249~7, 250~40 Sophia 35~44
CARTWRIGHT, [Judge] 169~55
CARVER, Reuben 64~6 Sarah (———) (Kelsa) 64~6
CARY see CURREY
CARYL see CARLL
CASE, Daniel 2d 71~5 Elizabeth 71~6 Hugh 71~2 Irene 268~52 Joseph 167~31 Loyal 283~21 Silas 306~8
CASEY / KASEY, [Mr.] 18~42 Mary 282~2
CASS, Daniel 30~19 Luke 56~36 Nathan 138~51 Sarah 68~51, 82~41
CASTLETON, Rhoda 316~51
CASWELL / CARSWELL, [Mrs.] 67~23 Asa 83~48 Asenath (Morgan) 83~48 Ezra 67~24 John M. 87~21 Lewis E. 354~21
CATE (see also CADY), Elizabeth 354~35 George 133~11
CATLIN, Alexander 78~38 Daniel 167~13 Seth 115~33,
143~7
CATY see CADY
CAULKINS / CALKINS, Aquila 238~23 Jedidiah 191~43 Lura 233~11 Samuel 97~18 Simon 228~20
CAVANAUGH / KAVANAGH, Bridget 198~13
CAVENEAU, Mary 281~22
CAVERLY / CEVERLY / COVERLY, Charles 99~27
CAWLEY see COLLEY
CAYWOOD, Abigail 210~57
CEVERLY see CAVERLY
CHACE see CHASE
CHADBORNE see CHADBOURNE
CHADBOURN see CHADBOURNE
CHADBOURNE / CHADBOURN / CHADBORNE, Ann (Hale) 267~35 Benjamin 36~29 Humphrey 23~48 Jonathan 267~35 Thomas 319~24
CHADWICK, [Mr.] 52~48, 216~34 Ebenezer 133~36 Elizabeth 144~39 John 2~33
CHAFEE / CHAFFE, Calvin 127~32 Constant (?) 240~14
CHAFFE see CHAFEE
CHAFFIN, John 106~4 Sally 327~7
CHAMBERLAIN / CHAMBERLIN / CHAMBERLINE, Abigail (Mellendy) 229~8 Anna 160~53 Benjamin 258~19 Betsey 265~27 Calvin 62~4, 128~26 Cynthia 261~39 Ebenezer 258~19 Elizabeth 163~23 Esther 112~9 J.C. 1~18, 285~40 James 168~47 Joanna 198~22 Job 10~35 John 6~37, 48~11, 319~13, 319~23, 327~27 John C. 18~31, 47~52, 60~49, 123~1, 178~26, 190~13, 199~53 Joseph 74~8 Kezia 143~32 Laban 229~8 Lydia 232~47, 327~22 Lydia (Ripley) 319~13 Olive 99~27 Polly 62~16 Sally 123~31 Samuel 310~19 William 62~5
CHAMBERLIN see CHAMBERLAIN
CHAMBERLINE see CHAMBERLAIN
CHAMBERS, James 194~14 Mary 321~32
CHAMPION, Henry 200~23 Judah 256~15
CHAMPLAIN, Gibbons M. 200~23
CHAMPLIN, Christopher 191~50, 194~18 George 252~50 Jabez 178~48 Mary 106~26 Ruth 252~50
CHAMPNEY, Benjamin 312~3 Caleb 129~3 Caleb D. 110~48 Ebenezer 333~29 Hannah (Lombard) 110~48 Jabez 177~14 Rebecca (Brooks) 312~3 Richard 335~20 Sarah 196~52 Thankful 252~55
CHANDLER, [Mr.] 86~23, 275~39, 368~18 [Mrs.] 260~37 Abijah 17~44 Asa 296~25, 334~45 Benjamin 25~8 C.W. 281~52 Chancy C. 68~5 Charles 21~35, 22~28 Clare 162~15 Daniel 11~6, 17~43 Eliza (———) 223~12 Eliza (Davis) (Dana) 129~31 Elizabeth (Greene) 66~40 Gardner 22~1 Isaac 318~5 James 12~20, 260~37 John 22~13, 66~39, 78~27 Nathaniel 52~56, 86~35 Perly 25~17 Sally 82~48, 185~46 Salmon 24~47 Samuel 22~28, 232~27 Thomas 129~31 Thomas L. 87~5 Timothy 308~53 Welthy (Lummas) 52~56 Willard 54~40
CHANDLERS, [Mr.] 5~4
CHANNEY see CHENEY
CHANNING, Francis D. 269~47 Susan (Higginson) 269~47
CHAPE see CHAPPE
CHAPEL see CHAPPELL
CHAPEN see CHAPIN
CHAPIN / CHAPEN, Abigail 301~42 Ann 64~11 Ebenezer 184~25 Edward 238~20 Eliphalet 275~55 Ellis (Bush) 79~8 Eunice 238~19 Gordon 283~18 John 5~54 Oliver 79~7, 343~43 Perez 310~19 Phinehas 69~56 Seth 231~10 Stephen 199~49
CHAPLAIN see CHAPLIN
CHAPLIN / CHAPLAIN, [Mr.] 226~16 Betsy 68~18 Daniel 18~35 Esther 263~55, 266~4 Jeremiah 238~45 Mary 182~41 Mercy (O'Brien) 238~46 Sally 334~46 William 263~56, 266~4
CHAPMAN / CHATMAN, [Mr.] 121~45, 137~35, 172~47, 195~37, 228~48, 328~57 Abigail (———) 285~49 Amos 301~17 Augustus 117~25, 164~20 Daniel 27~1, 203~17 David 237~20 Hannah 35~51, 36~33, 254~11 Henry L. 284~57 James 254~11 Jonathan 176~34 Joseph 117~25 Lydia 112~13 Nancy 100~38 Norman 194~42 Persis 294~55 Rachel (———) (Barton) 194~42 T. 37~25
CHAPONE, [Mrs.] 118~51
CHAPPE / CHAPE, [Mons.] 203~4 Claude 195~51

CHAPPEL see **CHAPPELL**
CHAPPELL / CHAPPEL / CHAPEL, Christiana 249~32 Elizabeth 289~39 Stephen 289~39
CHARDALL, William 13~6
CHARLTON, Thomas 299~37
CHARTER, Fanny 273~23 Lovina (Trowbridge) 220~49 Nathaniel 220~48, 273~23, 282~25 Nathaniel Trowbridge 282~24
CHASE / CHACE / CHASSE, [Capt.] 46~48, 46~56, 47~3 [Mr.] 324~24, 329~11, 330~51, 333~38 [widow] 263~1 Aaron 96~46, 285~14, 298~20 Abner 45~11 Bradford 181~42 Caleb 14~5, 284~9, 291~40 Caroline 353~9 Catharine (Clap) 273~49 Constant (?) 240~14 Daniel 13~44, 32~54, 83~14, 83~18, 185~38, 320~27, 325~16, 328~32 Daniel M. 331~18 David 43~19 Deborah 265~52 Dudley 254~2 Dudly 32~55 Eliza 170~41 Eunice (Dana) 332~30 Francis 257~7 Gratia 243~4 Hannah 137~12 Harriot 74~51 Harvey 297~9, 304~6, 317~44, 332~30 Ith. 291~40 Ithamar 303~6, 331~48 Jacob 221~54 James 101~22, 348~9 Jeremiah S. 318~35 John 140~38, 143~42, 331~18 Jonathan 25~42, 33~35, 58~24, 77~52, 83~22, 84~7, 263~1, 331~48 Lebeus 325~23 Love 350~25 Lucy (Hyde) 289~32 March 73~50, 83~16, 98~17, 114~41, 128~25, 325~15 Marsh 32~56 Mary 298~35 Moodey 83~16 Moody 88~25 Moses 32~55, 51~32, 82~38, 83~15 Nathaniel 284~10 Oliver 357~50 Paul 289~32 Peter S. 258~11 Roger 273~49 Sally 171~26, 172~14 Salmon 254~2 Samuel 32~53, 33~3, 73~49, 83~13, 83~19, 98~16, 114~40, 128~24, 170~41, 298~20 Sarah 58~27 Simeon 357~26 Solomon 13~48, 33~6, 83~19, 298~36, 325~18 Stephen 73~10, 89~54, 147~39, 189~2, 189~53, 325~27 T. 263~35 Thomas 277~23
CHASSE see **CHASE**
CHASSIN, David (?) 82~40
CHATMAN see **CHAPMAN**
CHATTERTON, Clarry 162~19 Joseph 162~11
CHAUNCEY, Charles 221~21 Lucy 221~20
CHECKLEY, Ann 99~51 John Webb 52~3
CHEENEY see **CHENEY**
CHEETHAM, James 335~10
CHEEVER / CHEVER, Abigail 291~3 Ann 38~51 Hannah (Clark) 64~40 Joshua 291~4 Mary 173~54 Samuel 64~39 William 78~25
CHENE see **CHENEY**
CHENEY / CHEENEY / CHANNEY / CHENE, [Mr.] 324~8 [Widow] 230~43 Abner 18~14, 20~56 Alpheus 107~19 Daniel 304~40 Ebenezer 18~16 Elizabeth 173~55 John 93~52 Laura 310~20, 321~18 Rebeckah 141~2 Samuel 89~6 Timothy 280~55 Triphene (Hatch) 86~31 William 86~31, 125~18, 141~2, 316~56, 334~46
CHERRY, Moses 207~47 Nancy (Bodgley) 207~47
CHESLE see **CHESLEY**
CHESLEY / CHESLY / CHESLE, Eleanor Powers 356~41 Hannah 210~31 John 353~46, 354~50 Sophia 203~28
CHESLY see **CHESLEY**
CHESTER, John 244~20, 313~22 Mary 244~19 William 48~51
CHESTNUT, [children] 99~40 [Mrs.] 99~40
CHEVER see **CHEEVER**
CHICK, [Mr.] 234~28
CHICKEREN see **CHICKERING**
CHICKERING / CHICKEREN, Betsey (White) 234~4 Joseph 234~4
CHIDESTER, Moses 28~27
CHILD, James 211~35 Mehitabel 178~15
CHILDERS, John 144~3
CHILDS / CHILES, [Mr.] 39~45 Amzi 260~45 James 260~45 Josiah 265~52 Levi 114~6 Patty 167~19
CHILES see **CHILDS**
CHILLSON see **CHILSON**
CHILSON / CHILLSON, Abigail 188~54
CHIPMAN, [Capt.] 60~17, 348~23 [Mr.] 105~6 Charity 321~45 Darius 368~50 Elizabeth 271~14 Fanny 224~23 G.D. 321~45 Lydia 112~39 Lydia (Dickenson) 368~50 Mary 194~3
CHISHOLM, widow 217~40
CHITTENDEN, [Gov.] 314~12 Bethuel 314~8 Medad 314~21
CHOAT see **CHOATE**
CHOATE / CHOAT, Amos 118~43 Jacob 48~58 Lucy (Smith) 118~43 Mary 286~44 Samuel 24~43, 27~44
CHOATHE, John 13~4
CHRISTIE / CHRISTY, Nancy 268~57
CHRISTY see **CHRISTIE**
CHURCH, [Mr.] 247~3 Abigail 27~46 Asa 247~1 Benjamin 247~1 Caleb 274~11 Charles 56~17, 124~17, 183~13 Deborah 23~8 Eber 309~12 John 239~47 John H. 238~13 Jonathan 166~25 Sally 219~22 Samuel 86~9 Thankful 238~13
CHURCHELL see **CHURCHILL**
CHURCHILL / CHURCHELL, David 144~48 Dorothy 179~30 Jesse 122~19
CHURCHMAN, John 216~8
CIER, Anna 118~22
CILLEY, Bradbury 176~10, 364~3 Joseph 363~42, 364~3
CIMBAL (see also **KIMBALL**), Thomas 11~18
CLAGGET see **CLAGGETT**
CLAGGETT / CLAGGET, Gustavus A. 324~38 Wiseman 20~25
CLAIBORNE, [child] 169~39 [Gov.] 169~34, 169~39 [Mrs.] 187~20 Ann (Driver) 210~26 Buller 167~18 Clarice (Duralde) 269~51 Ferdinand L. 130~4 John 284~3 Magdaline (Hutchins) 130~5 Thomas 210~26 William 311~27 William C.C. 269~51
CLANDINNAN see **CLENDENIN**
CLAP see **CLAPP**
CLAPHAM, Sophia 356~38 Thomas 356~38
CLAPP / CLAP, Abner 42~6 Bathsheba 102~8 Bela 182~36 Beriah 11~13 Catharine 273~49 Ebenezer 145~13 Elizabeth 145~12 Elizabeth (Gilbert) 182~36 Hophni 286~3 Nancy 225~3 Oliver 32~16 Otis 253~23
CLARE, Marsh 72~13 Mary L. (Fallon) 72~13
CLARECK, William 288~52
CLARK / CLARKE / CLERK, [infant] 301~9 [Mr.] 134~45, 204~44 [Mrs.] 165~39, 196~43 [woman] 301~7 Achsah 1~19 Alex. 20~23 Allen 124~56 Arnold 98~36, 224~45 Arnold (?) 126~1, 368~40 Augustine 117~46 Benjamin 34~38, 206~57, 226~28, 307~27 Betsey 91~8 Catharine 239~5, 241~29 Catherine 103~54 Clarissa 262~29 Danforth 1~21, 48~2, 119~52 Daniel 176~28 David 303~40 Ebenezer 229~20 Elinor 286~34 Eliza 171~46 Elizabeth 23~45, 40~12 Eunice 271~16 George 306~18 Greenleaf 77~45 Hannah 64~40, 113~34, 300~22 Huldah T. 353~6 Isaac Bowers 72~19 Isabel 290~7 Ithamar 111~42 James 131~37 Jedidiah 155~26 Joel 251~17 John 23~30, 84~1, 93~27, 98~29, 191~14, 251~24 John Pitman 160~48 Jonas 183~44, 202~52, 220~55 Jonathan 71~24, 77~45, 87~22, 133~44 Josiah 200~23, 286~4 Judah 200~17 Mary 179~42, 180~46, 202~51 Mary (Jacobs) 124~56 Mary (Pitman) 160~48 Mehitable 114~44 Mosely 226~41 Moses 294~30 Nancy 226~32 Nancy (Gould) 41~4 Nathaniel 32~28, 220~13 Ornal 126~1 Ornold 368~40 Peleg 154~10 Peter 171~47, 176~42 Polly 226~41 Rebecca 152~49 Rebecca P. (Hull) 194~47 Richard 316~36 Roger 82~46 Rosanna 134~2 Sally 179~37 Sally (Lake) 183~44, Sally (Thornton) 316~36 Samuel 140~32, 194~47, 296~24, 304~25, 322~34, 334~43 Sarah 2~13, 24~24, 110~11, 322~17, 363~54 Selah 271~17, 271~14 Stephen 79~40, 155~25 Susannah 93~20, 231~3 T. 227~3 Tevasia 116~47 Theo. 310~38, 320~26 Theophilus 93~43 Timothy 145~10, 203~2 Willard 41~4 William 205~48 Winlock 321~43
CLARKE see **CLARK**
CLARKSON, Matilda (———) (Odiorne) 127~14 William 127~13
CLAVES see **CLEAVES**
CLAY, Daniel 362~36 Joseph 177~10 Rhoda 362~37 Samuel 32~27, 47~23 Stephen 292~5
CLAYLAND, Thomas E. 15~21
CLAYPOOLE, Elizabeth 194~15
CLAYTON, Elizabeth 195~46
CLEAVELAND see **CLEVELAND**
CLEAVES / CLAVES, Sophia 208~15
CLEMENS see **CLEMENTS**
CLEMENT, [Mrs.] 231~4 Charles 64~7 David 3d 225~36

David Smith 225~36 Dolly (Quincy) 64~7 Isaac 225~35, 325~47 Isaac Langdon 225~35 Jere. 44~5 John 171~35 Joshua 108~14
CLEMENTS / CLEMENS / CLEMMONS, [children] 220~25 [Mrs.] 220~25 Abel 220~22, 372~11 Jeremiah 68~43 Lydia 229~43 Nathan 318~6
CLEMMONS see CLEMENTS
CLENDENIN / CLINDENIN / CLANDINNAN, Alexander 30~35
CLERK see CLARK
CLETTER, William 329~25
CLEVELAND / CLEAVELAND, [children] 113~20 Axa 35~43 Ebenezer 202~42 John 39~32 Martha (Bush) 256~35 Moses 268~14, 269~26 Samuel 113~19, 269~13 William P. 256~34
CLEVERLY, John 96~25 Stephen 245~47
CLIFFORD, Benjamin 81~50 David 361~41 Ebenezer 361~42 Edward 81~49 Joseph 240~1
CLIFT, Amos (?) 254~12
CLINDENIN see CLENDENIN
CLINGAN, Sarah (———) (Derby) 148~46 Wm. 148~45
CLINTON, [children] 149~12 [Gov.] 152~29 [Rev.] 149~12 Catharine (———) 60~32 Elizabeth 152~28 George 310~55 Mary 225~20
CLIST, Amos (?) 254~12
CLOSEN, Rozel 21~42
CLOUGE, Thomas 86~6
CLOUGH (see also CLOW, CLUFF), [Mr.] 248~16, 349~5 Benj. 151~22 Cornelius 45~18, 318~42 Ebenezer 204~56 Huldah 99~13 Nathan 174~3 Sarah 39~28 Thomas 151~46
CLOUS, Catharine 41~21
CLOUSTON, Louise (?) 269~12
CLOW (see also CLOUGH, CLUFF), Rebecca 199~26
CLOYES / CLOYS, Benjamin 81~36 Ruthy 53~37
CLOYS see CLOYES
COATES see COTES
COATS see COTES
COBB, [Mr.] 229~1, 319~30, 320~21 Abner 135~22 Benjamin 50~50 Ebenezer 109~37 George 185~46, 233~2 Jerusha 293~21 Joel 356~20 Joseph 293~12, 314~54, 329~8 Meriam 298~34, 301~20 Nehemiah 190~56 Sally (Chandler) 185~46 Samuel 34~24, 76~22, 234~21 Tisdale 1~51
COBBETT, William 60~20, 77~5
COBIN see CORBIN
COBLETH, Mary 271~20
COBURN see COLBURN
COCHRAN / COCHRANE, [Mr.] 141~22 Alex. 1~27 George 333~49 James 251~57, 297~40, 306~53, 316~21, 321~55 John 198~17 Letitia 181~56 Thomas 212~2
COCHRANE see COCHRAN
COCKE, John P. 255~14 Samuel 158~26
CODDING, Lydia 109~34
CODMAN, Isaac 213~36 Richard 228~19
COE, [Rev.] 41~33 David 276~35 Eliza H. 193~13 Jonas 193~14
COFERAN see COFRIN
COFFIN / CAFFIN, [Esq.] 362~23 Abner 113~51 Ann (———) (Waters) 102~7 Charles 102~7 David 82~6 Elizabeth 102~27 John (?) 145~46 Nancy (Morland) 99~46 Peter 133~41 Polly (Butt) 246~31 Reuben 246~31 Shubael 149~5 Stephen 99~46 Susan 249~37 Susannah (Graves) 85~47 Sylvanus 51~41, 364~35 Tristram 262~6 William 85~47
COFFRIN see COFRIN
COFRAN see COFRIN
COFREN see COFRIN
COFRIN / COFRAN / COFERAN / COFFRIN / COFREN, Samuel 62~47, 63~53, 367~43
COGGSWELL see COGSWELL
COGSWELL / COGGSWELL / GOGSWELL, Caroline 188~56 David 231~49 James 274~11 Mason F. 320~42 Thomas 335~21
COHEN, Isaac 224~43 Jacob 289~4
COHOON see CALHOUN
COIN, Shubal 67~38
COKE, Thomas 202~48
COLBEE see COLBY
COLBERT, Abigail (Stoodley) 97~11 Jabez 97~11

COLBEY see COLBY
COLBURN / COBURN, Abigail 295~3 Asa 325~30 Ezekiel 22~25, 22~28, 40~47 Josiah 160~17 Judith (Carleton) 160~17 Patience 207~8 Thaddeus 303~48
COLBY / COLBEE / COLBEY, [Mr.] 216~28 [Rev.] 41~34 Archelaus 153~7 Benjamin 350~21 Jemima 153~7 Levi 309~47 Molly 293~16 Nehemiah 134~34 Peter 293~16 Simeon 90~33
COLCORD / COLKET / GOLCORD, Samuel 45~17 Thomas 36~19
COLDEN, Cadwalader R. 54~5
COLE, [Mr.] 39~45 [Mrs.] 123~32 Abel 296~52 Arethusa 159~41 Benoni 28~41 Chloe 159~40 Daniel 43~23 Ebenezer 79~2, 286~30 Editha 181~4 Edward 228~18 Elizabeth 228~18 Eunice 297~30 Ezekiel 53~51 Isaac 144~11 Isaiah M. 202~13 John 134~27 Jonathan 181~4 Levi 159~44 Nathaniel 286~26 Olive B. (Munroe) 202~13 Persis 159~41 Phebe (Carter) 43~24 Sally (Putnam) 286~27 Walter Kerr 276~21 Webster 243~49 William 144~12
COLEMAN / COLMAN, (———) 133~31 [Mr.] 252~13 Alice (Fitch) 166~50 Benjamin 24~15 Eliphalet B. 166~50 William 97~20
COLESWORTHY, Anna (Collins) 92~4 Daniel P. 92~3
COLIN, [Mr.] 176~56
COLKET see COLCORD
COLLET, Robert 76~34
COLLEY / CALLEY / CAWLEY / COLY, Lucinda 53~1 William 13~11
COLLIER see COLLYER
COLLIN, John (?) 145~46
COLLINS, [Capt.] 333~2 [Gov.] 51~52 [Mrs.] 212~31 Ann 286~46 Anna 92~4 Eunice (French) 155~49 Isaac 212~32 James 155~49 John 78~36 Lucy 105~29 Mary 51~51 Peter 321~38 Ruth 160~47 Samuel 275~22, 277~18 Zachariah 105~30
COLLYER / COLLIER, Daniel 171~38 Jennet 265~45 Mary Bouel 211~25
COLMAN see COLEMAN
COLSON, Mary 173~46
COLT, Christopher 121~43 Joshua 27~28
COLTON, Ashley 26~44 Edward (?) 62~18 Hannah (Seward) (?) 62~18
COLVER see CULVER
COLVERT / COVERT, Harris 308~49
COLY see COLLEY
COMB / COMBE, Daniel 48~52 John 257~58
COMBE see COMB
COMBS see COOMBS
COMERFORD, F. 59~23
COMFORT, [Rev.] 51~4
COMING see CUMMINGS
COMINGS see CUMMINGS
COMISAU, Nicholas 269~4
COMMING see CUMMINGS
COMPTON, William 18~2
CONANT, Elizabeth S. 24~16 Ezra 172~30, 229~37 John 68~22 Jonathan 171~19 Sarah 108~30 Shubael 251~54, 276~56, 296~43, 316~6
CONDE see CONDI
CONDI / CONDE / CONDY, Gideon 182~23 Sally 299~24
CONDON / CONGDON, John 274~56 Philip 274~56 Stephen 206~39
CONDWAY see CONWAY
CONDY see CONDI
CONE, Daniel 321~19 Daniel H. 235~35 Gilbert 200~21 Samuel 54~32, 118~4
CONEY see KENNEY
CONGDON see CONDON
CONGER, [infant] 213~22 Sarah 213~21
CONKLIN, Jonathan 125~9 Titus 123~8 William 144~8
CONLEY see CONNERLY
CONNEL / CONNELL, Charles M. 231~35
CONNELL see CONNEL
CONNELLY see CONNERLY
CONNER / CONNOR, Benjamin 80~22 Elizabeth 118~16
CONNERLY / CONNOLY / CONNELLY / CONLEY, Benjamin 319~5 Mary 23~5
CONNET, Benjamin 138~30

CONNEY see KENNEY
CONNOLY see CONNERLY
CONNOR see CONNER
CONROW, Andrew 7~14
CONSTABLE, [children] 263~26 Francis 263~25
CONVERS see CONVERSE
CONVERSE / CONVERS, [children] 40~21 [Mrs.] 40~21 Israel 242~17 James 111~10 John 40~18 Lyman 172~13 Mary 96~51 Polly (Kent) 172~13
CONWAY / CONDWAY, John 52~23, 364~30 Patrick 299~19
CONYNE, Casparus 186~9
COOK / COOKE, [Mr.] 167~3, 285~12 [widow] 49~35 Aaron 216~52 Abigail 121~22 Abigail (Hubbard) 165~6 Abigail (Sparhawk) 212~6 Amos 76~45 Andrew 212~6 Benjamin 357~35 Betsey (Baldwin) 91~19 Duncan 166~41 Edward 101~52 Ezekiel 144~21 George 323~49 Godfrey 165~6 Hannah 239~46 John 91~19, 106~51, 169~49 Jonathan 196~4 Lucy 255~28 Luther 52~52 Mary 49~3, 104~51 Noah 104~52, 153~37 Rebecca (———) (Halwell) 106~54 Rebecca (Harrington) 357~36 Sally 151~55 Samuel 307~30 Sibyl 200~24 Susan 64~38 Susannah (Woods) 143~32 Sybel 184~47 Thomas 111~9 William 143~31
COOKE see COOK
COOKLEY, [Mr.] 252~48
COOKSON, Samuel 232~36
COOLBROTH, [Mr.] 224~10
COOLEDGE see COOLIDGE
COOLER, Robert 195~55
COOLEY / COOLY, [Colonel] 104~1 D. 324~40 Joseph 225~46
COOLIDGE / COOLEDGE, [child] 273~26 [widow] 273~26 Daniel 253~6, 312~23 Louisa (———) (Patterson) 117~28 Luther 117~28 Philip 163~24 William 74~39, 89~49, 101~41, 109~23
COOLY see COOLEY
COOMBS / COMBS / COONS, [children] 114~5 [Mr.] 291~55 Oliver 114~3 Orpah 114~2
COONS see COOMBS
COOPER, [brothers] 35~24 [Miss] 35~22 [Mr.] 148~14, 241~35 Alling 190~36 Barna 182~3 Caleb 317~21 Elijah 85~51 Eliza (Gale) 75~51 George 170~22 Horatio 75~51 Huldah 238~49 Jemima 268~55 Joel 85~51 John 207~54, 208~12, 230~26 Lois Sanger 238~49 Louis S. 277~2 Mary 182~3 Nabby 98~50 Nathaniel 62~13 Sally 88~7, 286~28 Shearman 6~34, 16~29 Thomas 63~18 William 314~47, 334~40
COPELAND, Daniel 323~38 Jacob 1~2 Nabby 323~38 Russel 323~38
COPEMAN, John 208~41
COPPLE / KOPPLE / KAPPLE / KEPPLE, Adam 13~13 George Henry 126~45 John 94~16
CORBIN / COBIN, Abigail 169~36 Abigail (Hurd) 269~55 Asa 269~55 Ebenezer 82~39 Ezra 295~47 James 93~41, 205~41 Nathaniel 296~9 William 305~35
CORDIA, Mary 75~47
CORDIS (see also CURTIS), Joseph 179~15
CORDWELL, Hannah 231~37
COREY see CURREY
CORNEY see CARNEY
CORNING, Richard 57~20
CORRIE see CURREY
CORRIGAN see CARRIGAIN
CORSON / CARSON / COURSON / CURSON, George 59~43 Robert 203~33
CORY see CURREY
COSET see COSSIT
COSSET see COSSIT
COSSETT see COSSIT
COSSIT / COSET / COSSIT / COSSETT / COSSET, Ambros 44~5 Ambrose 68~38, 310~36 Ambrous 70~5 Ranna 35~13
COTES / COATES / COUTTS / COATS, [Capt.] 67~41 Betsey 286~35 Henry 106~31
COTRON, [Capt.] 61~12
COTTELL see COTTLE
COTTEN see COTTON
COTTERIC, [———] 89~16

COTTINEAU, D.N. 288~18
COTTLE / COTTELL, Rachel 228~24 Susanna 245~36
COTTON / COTTEN, [Mr.] 112~51 Catharine 155~28 Edward (?) 62~18 Hannah (Seward) (?) 62~18 Nathaniel 363~13 Roland 176~19, 370~59 Samuel 272~13 Solomon 207~18 Thomas 65~12
COTTRELL, D. 258~42 David 168~42
COUCH, Ebenezer 2~55 James 101~17 Mehitable (Alexander) 101~17
COUDREY, Catharine 260~50 John 260~50
COUES see COULES
COULES / COWLES / COUES / COWES, Jacob G. 53~10 Joseph 239~46 Timothy 292~6
COURSON see CORSON
COURTNEY, H. R. 148~12
COUTTS see COTES
COVELL, Samuel 271~3
COVERLY see CAVERLY
COVERT see COLVERT
COWDEN / COWDIN, [Capt.] 286~5 Betsey (Goodridge) 219~57 Mary 286~5 Samuel 219~56
COWDERY, Jonathan 205~30
COWDIN see COWDEN
COWEL see COWELL
COWELL / COWEL, Charles 129~23 Hannah 310~54 William 12~10
COWES see COULES
COWLES see COULES
COWPER, William 68~21
COX / COXE, [Mrs.] 100~9 D.W. 224~17 Elizabeth (Motty) 237~43 Francis 17~27 Isaac 198~10 James 335~16 John S. H. 144~30 Lydia 291~18 Nancy (Lewis) 144~30 Phebe (Harslet) 92~30 Rebecca 231~13 Samuel 255~56 Sarah Rebecca 300~16 Tench 231~14, 300~16 William 92~30 William J. 263~48
COXE see COX
CRADDICK, [children] 49~18 [Mrs.] 49~18
CRAFT, Royal 21~25 Royal (?) 134~47 William 374~19 William (?) 334~14
CRAFTS / KRAFFTZS, [Lieut.] 122~40 Dolly (Herrman) 122~41 Eben. 247~31 Harriet P. (Poaug) 335~31 John 89~44 Royal 332~49 Sarah H. (Spooner) 247~31 Wm. 335~31
CRAGGIN see CRAGIN
CRAGIN / CREGAN / CRAGGIN, Francis 301~22 John 6~15 Sibbil 301~21
CRAGUE see CRAIG
CRAIG / CRAIGE / CRAGUE, Polly 183~45 Thomas 20~24, 295~32
CRAIGE see CRAIG
CRAIN see CRANE
CRAM, Achsah 202~4 Jacob 166~52 Jonathan 3d 327~43 Jonathan W. 327~44 Mary (Poor) 166~52 Nathan 56~42, 368~9 Samuel 202~8
CRAMPTON, Harry 58~9
CRANCH, Joseph 268~16
CRANDAL see CRANDALL
CRANDALL / CRANDLE / CRANDAL, [Miss] 288~3 Azel 288~3 Edward 5~12, 74~40 Jabesh 159~4 Joseph (?) 158~55
CRANDLE see CRANDALL
CRANE / CRAIN, [children] 86~17 [Mrs.] 86~17 Bathsheba 265~53, 275~19 Caroline 97~1 Elishama 292~7 H. 61~54 Jerusha 116~3 John 210~46 Joshua 114~48 R. 193~42 Sabra 103~14 Sally (Giddings) 114~48 Sam. 44~6 Susannah 97~2 Thomas 86~13, 169~6 Vose 171~37
CRARY, Ezra 14~51 Sarah 186~19
CRAST, Royal (?) 134~47
CRATER, Frederick 208~7
CRAVEN, [Mrs.] 19~1 Joseph 19~1
CRAW, Roswell 233~10 Sally (Hammond) 233~10
CRAWFORD / CROFFORD, (———) 72~45 Ebenezer 231~22 Jane 227~32 Joseph 4~30 Kesiah 229~56 Rebecca 148~7, 149~22 William H. 125~55
CREASY see CRESSEY
CREGAN see CRAGIN
CREGMILES, [Mr.] 81~2
CREHORE, Ann 1~37 E. 334~49 Ebenezer 13~23, 89~40 Sarah (Clarke) 322~17 William 1~38, 322~17

The Farmer's Weekly Museum, Walpole, N.H. 389

CREIGER, [girls] 354~40 Martinus 354~40
CRESSEY / CREASY / CRESSY, Mary 131~36
CRESSY see CRESSEY
CRESTON, [Mr.] 374~17
CRICK, [Mr.] 246~47
CRIMES, Henry 161~35
CRISPEEN / CRISPIN, James 77~42
CRISPIN see CRISPEEN
CRISTIE see CRISTY
CRISTY / CRISTIE, Esther (Mosely) 37~54 James 37~53 Peter 4~52 Rebecca 166~32
CROCKER / CROOKER, Andrew S. 24~7 Asa 200~21 Bathsheba 152~50 Doddridge 255~36 Isaac 200~20 John 244~34 Maria 249~35 Mary 118~15 Robert 291~22
CROCKET see CROCKETT
CROCKETT / CROCKET, Woodbry L. 355~42
CROFFORD see CRAWFORD
CROMBIE, Benjamin 56~38 Betsey (———) (Grave?) 56~38
CROOK see CROOKS
CROOKER see CROCKER
CROOKS / CROOK, Richardson 110~21
CROSBEY see CROSBY
CROSBIE see CROSBY
CROSBY / CROSBEY / CROSBIE, Aaron 82~27 Daniel 174~33 Harriot (Chase) 74~51 Henry 146~14 John 312~45 Josiah 303~41, 316~7 Lovina 204~30 Oliver 74~51 Ruth 146~15 S. 11~2, 101~51 Samuel 1~44, 4~6, 9~13, 17~41, 24~9, 24~49, 36~16, 45~24, 65~3, 68~46, 71~47, 82~37, 109~15, 115~10, 116~24, 122~15, 126~11, 127~53, 134~52, 146~14, 186~44, 206~54 Stephen 354~24, 355~46 Thankful 115~1 William 43~9
CROSFIELD, Eugenia (Frink) 330~28 James 330~28
CROSS, [triplets] 273~43 [twins] 273~42 Catharine 273~41 David 79~5 Elizabeth 247~56 Ephraim 273~41 John 46~18 Nathaniel 163~34 Olive (Kimball) 79~5 Stephen 295~56 Thomas 66~22 Thomas (?) 63~27
CROSSETT see CROSUT
CROSSMAN, Josiah 91~22 Marsa (Hodges) 91~22
CROSSWELL / CROSWELL, Caleb 261~53 Sarah 92~3
CROSUT / CROSSETT, [Mrs.] 12~35 Benjamin 12~34 Samuel 215~3 Sarah 218~21
CROSWELL see CROSSWELL
CROWELL, [Mrs.] 278~8 Christopher 206~36
CROWNINGSHIELD see CROWNINSHIELD
CROWNINSHIELD / CROWNINGSHIELD, Benjamin 155~16 Mary 134~4 Mary (Boardman) 155~16
CRUGER, Anna (———) (Heywood) 51~50 Nicholas 51~49
CRUINFEATHER, Stephen 260~16
CRUSOE, Robinson 3~6
CULLEN, [Lord Viscount] 126~49
CULLER, [Mrs.] 94~33 John 94~33
CULTURE, [Miss] 181~45
CULVER / CALVER / COLVER, [boy] 238~34 Francis 238~34 Stephen 37~16 Zebulon 272~42
CUMINGS see CUMMINGS
CUMMING see CUMMINGS
CUMMINGS / COMING / CUMMINS / CUMMING / COMINGS / CUMINGS / COMMING, Amos 68~6 Asa 274~14 Benjamin 117~41, 303~7 Betsey 275~47 Catherine (Kelchre) 124~55 Eleazer 244~55 Ellen 326~23 Isaac 89~45 John 124~55 Leonard 331~48 Lot 289~17 Mary (Putnam) 154~31 Moses 100~48 Nathaniel 8~18, 154~31 Samuel 20~22, 83~16 Sarah 55~14, 209~56 Stephen 3~21
CUMMINS see CUMMINGS
CUNNINGHAM, Abigail 110~22 Andrew 300~14 Esther 327~6 Isaac 295~33 James 235~7, 254~56, 306~17, 361~25 Johama 42~5 Mary 300~13 Richard 310~43 Sally M. 235~7 Sarah Athorp (Morton) 310~44
CURREY / CAREY / COREY / CORY / KURY / CURRY / CURRIE / CORRIE / CARY, [Dr.] 295~52 [Mrs.] 126~50, 160~34, 295~52 Eliot 119~24 Elliot 327~18 James 216~52 Jane 297~54 Jonathan 126~50 Joseph 142~37 Joshua 307~48 Lockwood 96~29 Lucius 158~25 Mary 92~16 Nathaniel 196~21 Richard 272~38 Samuel 284~45, 288~40 Sarah 284~45 Sukey 151~24 William 96~31

CURRIE see CURREY
CURRIER / CARRIER, Charlotte (Story) 218~8 Delia 75~17 Ezra 93~34 Gideon 93~34 John 49~46 John 3d 277~40 Joseph 221~7 Moses 46~57, 218~8 Nancy (Pickerman) 277~40
CURRY see CURREY
CURSON see CORSON
CURTICE see CURTIS
CURTIS / CURTICE / CURTISS (see also CORDIS), [Mr.] 155~4, 169~30, 233~26 [Mrs.] 13~16 Abel 179~34 Abigail 208~9 Benjamin 125~1 Bethiah (Parker) 69~5 Betsey 125~1 David 262~39, 263~54 Ephraim 55~21 Jenny (M'Cullough) 163~20 John 13~15, 282~3 Joseph 69~5, 156~37 Joseph S. 277~19 Joshua 314~6 Lucia 255~7 Lucy (Morey?) 179~34 Marlborough 133~4 Mary 68~23, 127~43 Nancy (Stowel) 282~3 Nathaniel 226~46 Noah 163~19 Philip 15~25 Relief 140~10 Samuel 312~24 Simeon 62~21 Thomas 151~19 Tirzah 277~18 William 13~5 Zebina 80~20, 255~8
CURTISS see CURTIS
CURWIN, Theophilus 85~38
CUSHING, Abigail 269~48 Ann (Avery) 288~45 Ann (Sheafe) 187~6 Anna 260~44 Benjamin 294~24 Caleb 2~28, 263~54 Catharine (Willard) 98~22 Catharine S.P. (Orne) 187~48 Charles 187~6 Elizabeth 173~4 George R. 98~22 Hannah 94~11 Jacob 260~45 Joseph 170~12 Joshua 227~42, 288~45 Josiah 259~18 Mary 71~35, 294~23 N. 269~36 Nathan 269~49 Rachel (Andrews) 256~36, 260~21 Rebecca (Edmunds) 170~13 Ruth 259~17 Sally 41~3 Sarah 202~54 Stephen 173~5 Thomas 43~48 Thomas C. 256~36, 260~20 William 223~26, 335~21, 361~45, 364~14
CUSHMAN, Joshua 101~13 Lucy (Jones) 101~13 Polycarpus 15~26
CUTLER / CUTTLER, [child] 330~46 Anna (Woodward) 188~52 Experience (Graves) 260~23 Isaac 274~7 James 260~23 John 217~40 John L. 248~55 Jonathan 323~31, 330~46 Joseph 93~14, 172~27, 269~28 Lavinia 75~48 Nancy 95~28 Phebe (Buel) 323~31 Phebe (Ward) 93~14 Samuel 68~9, 248~55 Simeon 363~17 William 71~34 Younglove 188~52
CUTTER, [Mr.] 82~22 Benjamin 27~21, 271~32, 274~28 Daniel 268~52 Ephraim 309~48 Hannah (Webber) 181~42 James 40~10 Moses 181~41 Nathan 288~32 Polly 271~32 Sally (Jones) 268~53
CUTTIN see CUTTING
CUTTING / CUTTIN, Benjamin 100~48 Elizabeth 95~35 Fanny (Hatch) 290~29 John 86~9, 268~45 Jonas 76~18 Joseph 290~29 Mary (Hunter) 250~30 Sally 238~50, 289~33 Sewall 250~30 Zebulon 76~15, 86~8
CUTTLER see CUTLER
CUTTS, [Mrs.] 133~12 Charles 327~51 Edward 272~9 George 133~9, 272~10 Richard 159~22 Samuel 92~18
CUYLER, [Col.] 216~22 [Mrs.] 224~4 Abraham 319~19 Cornelius 278~43 Henry 216~23 Jacob I. 224~2

D.

D'FOREST see de FOREST
D'WOLF see De WOLF
DAGGETT / DOGGETT, Abigail 149~5 Amelia 121~48 Henry 121~49 John 301~11 Nathan 164~3 Simeon 327~10 Zeruah (Graves) 164~4
DAILEY / DALEY / DAILY / DALY, [Mr.] 240~20 Dominic 220~36, 372~3, 372~48 Dominick 239~24, 243~55
DAILY see DAILEY
DAKIN, James 57~20
DALAND see DELAND
DALE, James (?) 202~35
DALEY see DAILEY
DALL / DOLL, Joseph 200~46 Susan (?) 83~49
DALLAS, [Mr.] 63~7
DALTON / DOLTON, Margaret 219~16, 221~43
DALY see DAILEY
DAM, John 69~45
DAME, Betsey 364~22 Edward 101~42 George 95~47

James 357~28 James J. 357~28 Mark 364~22 Richard 355~12 Timothy 150~19
DAMON / DEMON, [Mrs.] 191~4 Abigail 231~38 Elias 212~13, 328~15 Noah 82~42
DANA, [Mr.] 256~20 [Rev.] 230~25, 274~20 Anna 193~19 Dexter 51~19 Eliza (Davis) 129~31 Eunice 332~30 Isaac 183~3 Isabella C. 213~29 J. 213~30 John 74~42 John C. 61~29 Josiah 2~23, 102~38, 220~7 Mittia (Caldwell) 317~48 S.B. 317~48 Sally (Windship) 51~19 Sarah 220~7 Thomas 133~55 William 361~25
DANDRIDGE, Bartholomew 125~31
DANEY / DANY / DANNEY / DANIE / DENNY, George 133~17 Thomas 14~11, 32~54
DANFORTH, (———) 73~11 [Dr.] 212~57 David 16~26, 71~23 Elizabeth (Bowers) 62~17 Israel 133~55 Jacob 226~23 Job 100~1 Jonathan 281~29 Lucy 111~43 Thomas 62~17
DANIE *see* **DANEY**
DANIELS, [Mr.] 39~51 Abigail (Leach) 152~45 Benjamin 152~45 Clement 27~38 Eben. 194~35 Ebenezer 204~32 Elizabeth (Hill) 184~20 George 184~20 John 42~3 Joseph 322~57 Patty (Mann) 204~32
DANNET *see* **DENNETT**
DANNEY *see* **DANEY**
DANY *see* **DANEY**
DARAH *see* **DARRAH**
DARBY *see* **DERBY**
DARLEY, Lewis 186~55
DARLING / DAWLING (*see also* **DOWLING**), [children] 43~45 [Mrs.] 43~45 Eli 55~30 George 43~40 Jos. 294~19 Keziah 119~9 Otis 119~12
DARRAH / DARAH / DARRUH, Joseph 101~53
DARROW, Elizabeth 239~47 George 213~20
DARRUH *see* **DARRAH**
DARSEE *see* **DORSEY**
DART, Eliphalet 316~9
DARWIN *see* **DERWIN**
DASCOMB / DASCOMBE, Daniel 224~42
DASCOMBE *see* **DASCOMB**
DAVENPORT, Elijah 183~48 Isaac 36~32, 221~55 James 9~25 Sophia 155~13 Susan (Ward) 183~48
DAVERSON *see* **DAVIDSON**
DAVID, Jonathan 43~49 Mary (Amory) 43~49
DAVIDSON / DAVERSON / DAVISON / DAVISSON / DEVERSON, [Mr.] 193~37 [Mrs.] 242~56 [Rev.] 242~56 Abigail (Prouter) 147~21 Henry 123~8 James 26~12, 81~51 John 147~21
DAVIES, Elizabeth 195~16 William 225~25
DAVIS, Aaron 53~14 Abigail 208~4 Amasa 43~22 Ann (———) 109~33 Benjamin 333~50 Caleb 7~48 Charles 152~44 Daniel 38~54, 323~56 Edward 91~1, 150~16 Elijah 187~2 Eliphalet 166~30, 167~14 Eliza 129~31 Eliza (Bussey) 152~44 Elizabeth 305~55 Elizabeth (Pitman) 65~40 Elnathan 178~45 Ephraim 265~17 Hannah (Moore) 43~22 Henry 127~46, 175~14 Isaac P. 231~28 Jeremiah 80~17 John 32~20, 53~14, 72~22, 95~28, 328~16, 357~52 Jona. 296~26 Jonathan 303~43 Joshua 3~34, 30~3 Lavinia B. 357~51 Levi 46~5 Mary 46~5 Moses 76~11 N. 112~46 Nancy (Cutler) 95~28 Nancy (Fuller) 76~11 Nathaniel 354~26 Paul 211~17 Peter 68~55 Philip 61~28, 85~21, 98~46, 120~36 Rhoda 37~56, 301~1 Robert 3~34, 30~3, 129~32 Ruth 286~48 Sally 187~2, 260~18 Samuel 65~39, 103~53, 187~2 Sarah 126~28 Solomon 1~48, 6~39, 56~24, 74~43, 89~54 Theodore 166~34 Thomas 178~35 Timothy 286~21 W.R. 58~4
DAVISON *see* **DAVIDSON**
DAVISSON *see* **DAVIDSON**
DAWES, Thomas 288~51
DAWLING *see* **DARLING**
DAWSON, Abigail 53~48
DAY / DEY, [children?] 22~7 [Mr.] 118~34, 369~16 Alpha (?) 101~25 Aspha (?) 101~25 Benjamin 117~19 Calvin 310~21 Hannah 69~12 James 272~11 Jeremiah 195~8, 202~38, 236~56, 260~47 John 22~3 Lucy 67~6 Martha 236~56 Mary 22~3 Nathaniel 251~17 Standish 47~35 Vincent 167~25
DAYTON, Jonathan 173~42 Susan 173~41
DEAN / DEEN / DEANE, [Mrs.] 297~30 Aaron 172~49 Abia 172~41 Abiathar 109~24 Abigail 172~43 Abigail (?) 207~29 Benjamin 322~57 Cyrus B. 283~30, 285~8 Ezra 272~44 Frances (———) 114~46 George 305~48 John 54~43 Jonathan 211~37 Joseph 158~25 Lemuel 172~41, 172~42 Luther 303~18 Nancy H. (Grubb) 121~16 Nath. 133~24 Nathan 172~42 Phebe 309~24 Polly 109~25 Sally (———) (Harris) 54~43 Thomas 121~16 William 46~31, 297~30
DEANE *see* **DEAN**
DEARBORN / DURBIN / DEARBORNE / DURBERN, [Deacon] 362~31 [Gen.] 48~20 John 334~13 John S. 244~30 Levi 121~54 Mary 239~58, 244~30 Samuel 60~46
DEARBORNE *see* **DEARBORN**
DEARING *see* **DEERING**
DEBALL, Levi 240~42
DEBLOIS, Charles 261~11 Stephen 184~46
de CAESTRO, Mary Ann 54~37
DECATUR, [Lieut.] 176~45 Stephen 285~55
de CORDOVA, Joshua His 15~18
DEEKEY *see* **DICKEY**
DEELY, Abigail 309~45
DEEN *see* **DEAN**
DEERING / DEARING, Dorothy 100~45 Eunice 231~45 Mary 87~42
de FOREST / D'FOREST, Hannah (Hitchcock) 135~32 Isaac 132~5 Jude Mills 135~32
de GRASSE, [Count] 86~49 Adelle 86~48
DEHART, [Mr.] 184~36
de HEART, William 95~40
DELADERNIA, Anne Maria 117~51
DELAND / DALAND, [Mrs.] 280~56 Eunice 94~20 Rufus 280~57 Thorndike 236~45
DELANEY / DELANY / DULANY, Daniel 2~53 William 218~29
DELANO / DELENO, Amasa 144~31 Cynthia 113~46 Gideon 305~14 Hannah (———) 284~48 Hannah (———) (Appleton) 144~31 Judah 99~22 Thomas 263~53
DELANY *see* **DELANEY**
DELARY, Sharp 41~5
DELAWARE, John 328~27
DELENO *see* **DELANO**
DEMICK *see* **DIMICK**
DEMING, [Mr.] 222~13 Gideon 185~56 Henry 265~48 Julius 251~49 Mary 265~47
DEMON *see* **DAMON**
DEMOND, Joseph 107~48 Josiah 261~42 Julia (Beach) 261~42 Sally (Gage) 107~48
DEMORASCI, Francisco 310~21
DENCH, Lawson 126~9 Mary (Stoddard) 126~9
de NEUSVILLE, Anna 54~17
DENISON *see* **DENNISON**
DENISTON, Minerva 268~50
DENLO, Enos 118~54
DENNA, Thomas 83~14
DENNET *see* **DENNETT**
DENNETT / DENNET / DANNET, John 97~21 Polly 118~13 Thomas 171~48
DENNIS, [Mr.] 371~33 [widow] 217~2 John 242~6 254~4, 274~5 Mary (Carlisle) 242~7 Richard 167~17, 182~55
DENNISON / DENISON, [Capt.] 38~43 Abel 121~49 Anny 291~45 Benj. B. 46~54 E. (Hide) 38~44 George 219~44, 291~45 John 312~35 Mary 209~13 Mary (Whetmore) 121~49
DENNY *see* **DANEY**
DENSMORE *see* **DINSMOOR**
DEO, [girl] 101~35 [Mrs.] 101~34 Josiah 101~34
DEPEYSTER, Helen 102~42
DEPUI, Samuel 198~44
DERBY / DARBY, [children] 164~32 Auphe 164~31 Auphea 313~11 E.H. 105~23 Elias Hasket 47~33 Elizabeth 38~1 Lucy 192~45 Margaret 125~26 Martha 148~46 Thomas 164~35, 313~14
DERRY, Peter 95~23
DERWIN / DARWIN, [Dr.] 120~45 John 207~15
DESBRISAY, Anna (Bytes) (?) 47~31 Thomas (?) 47~30
DESBROSSES, Elizabeth 40~3
DESH, Philip 63~4

DEVELIN / DEVLIN, Charles 30~34
DEVENS, Abigail (Adams) 162~38 David 162~37
DEVERSON see DAVIDSON
DEVIL (see also DIVOL, DUVAL), George 206~1 Rebecca 206~2
DEVLIN see DEVELIN
DEVOE, Richard 257~38
DEW see DOE
DEWAR / DUER, Catherine (————) 101~15 William 38~2, 40~6, 101~15
DEWEES, Joseph 53~4
de WEISSENFELS, Frederick H. Baron 259~5
DEWERS, Eliza (MacKean) 39~25 Samuel 39~25
DEWEY, [Mrs.] 163~43, 246~43 Chester 334~55 Elenor 247~30 Israel 246~43 Josiah 194~51 Sarah 334~56 Sarah (Dewey) 334~56
DEWING, Lucy 269~16
de WITT / De WITT, [boy] 129~38 [Mr.] 309~2 [Mrs.] 129~38 Margaretta 155~9 Peter 50~28
De WOLF / D'WOLF, Lyman 335~45 Stephen 270~10
DEXTER, [Lord] 240~8, 263~57 David 32~23, 119~5, 320~26 Mehitable 100~8 Mehitable (Hoyt) 67~16 Paul 289~41 Sally 266~43 Samuel Lord 67~15 Stephen 32~23, 57~41, 70~10 T. 242~50 Timothy 240~8, 263~57
DEY see DAY
DIBBLE, [Miss] 205~20 [Mr.] 205~17
DICKENS / DICKINS, Ashbury 155~6 Lilias (Arnot) 155~7
DICKENSON see DICKINSON
DICKERMAN, Abigail (Lord) 152~25 Peter 152~25 Thede 153~33
DICKERSAN see DICKERSON
DICKERSON / DICKERSAN, Azariah 90~42, 120~2 Elihu 81~37 Nathaniel 143~9 Samuel 143~12 Silas 276~45
DICKEY / DICKIE / DEEKEY, [children] 163~27 [girl] 322~2 James 163~27, 200~8, 205~45 James 2d 217~53 Matthew 309~49, 322~2 Robert 67~32
DICKIE see DICKEY
DICKINS see DICKENS
DICKINSON / DICKENSON, (————) 71~42 Charles 247~34, 328~14 Clarissa (Clark) 262~29 E. 258~50 Elijah 252~1 John 209~33 Medad 322~28 Nathaniel 9~23, 115~34 Parry 262~28 Pliny 182~33, 324~29 S.F. 258~50 Samuel 80~18, 115~35 Samuel F. 252~2, 322~27 Sidney 162~38 Silas 205~43 Thankful 131~39
DICKMAN, [child] 99~56 Thomas 99~56, 211~14
DICKSON see DIXON
DIKE, Anna 230~53 Betsey (Huntoon) 257~52 John 230~53 Noah 257~52
DILL / DILLE, [Mrs.] 60~8 George 180~56 James 26~29, 69~45 John 40~16 Nathaniel 78~34 Samuel 60~8
DILLE see DILL
DILLEN / DILLON, Arthur Richard 256~48 Mary 137~32
DILLON see DILLEN
DIMICK / DIMMICK / DEMICK / DIMMOCK, Theoda 184~31
DIMMICK see DIMICK
DIMMOCK see DIMICK
DINGLEY, Thomas 262~2
DINSMOOR / DINSMORE / DENSMORE / DINSMOORE, Abel 150~53 John 153~18, 318~50 Mary (Gordon) 253~42 Olive (Wardner) 153~18 Phineas 326~42 Silas 253~41
DINSMOORE see DINSMOOR
DINSMORE see DINSMOOR
DISK, Philip 39~8
DIVERS, Charity (Onion) 156~24 John 156~24
DIVOL (see also DEVIL, DUVAL), Sarah 98~54 William 56~11, 68~54
DIX, [Dr.] 218~45 [Mr.] 294~43 Jonas 49~12 Jonathan 176~32 Samuel 79~52
DIXEN see DIXON
DIXON / DICKSON / DIXEN, [Capt.] 44~34 Achibald 148~12 Archimedes 51~29 Daniel 253~54 David 213~18 George 126~31 John 197~34 Lucy 262~47 Margaret 186~25 Polly 260~29 Simon (?) 260~30 Stephen 50~8 Timon (?) 260~30 William 264~9
DOAK, Benjamin 180~7

DOAN see DOANE
DOANE / DOAN, [Capt.] 61~13 Isaiah 191~15 Joseph 245~44
DOBELL see DOBLE
DOBLE / DOBELL, Lucy 144~30
DODD, Bethuel 160~36 John 293~43, 293~44 Josiah 293~45 Lydia 286~49 Mary 293~44
DODGE, Barnabas 106~44 John 23~47, 289~16 Joseph 257~45 Joshua 288~41 Josiah 48~10 Mary 98~49, 145~22 Nathaniel 33~32 Oliver 124~26 Peggy 106~44 R. 325~41 Rachel 216~47 Sally (Williams) 124~26 Shadrack 94~30 Solomon 41~5 William 152~35
DODRILL, William 213~27
DOE / DEW, Robert 171~37 Samuel 93~20
DOGGETT see DAGGETT
DOGORN, [Mrs.] 329~52 John 329~52
DOLBEER / DOLBER / DOLEBEAR, George 186~31
DOLBER see DOLBEER
DOLE, James 260~17 James (?) 202~35 Jane (M'Creedy) 260~17 Lydia (Nelson) 68~18 Peabody 68~18 Sally 306~7
DOLEBEAR see DOLBEER
DOLF, Anna (Spalding) 285~50 Giles 285~50
DOLL see DALL
DOLLIVER see DOLVER
DOLTON see DALTON
DOLVER / DOLLIVER, Peter 230~17
DOME, George 96~25
DONAHOE / DONAHUE / DUNIHUE, [Capt.] 254~41 Alexander 233~46 Thomas 254~50
DONAHUE see DONAHOE
DONCASTER, J.P. 301~25
DONEY, Loudon 8~34
DOODY see DOTY
DOOLITTLE, Charles 143~3 Ephraim 282~15 Isaiah 278~39 Joel 134~49, 312~50 John 134~49 Lucius 115~36, 325~43 O. 304~18 Olive 143~2 Oliver 80~16, 115~37, 278~31, 325~46 Otis 32~13 Polly 5~39 Sally (Fitch) 312~50
DOOR see DORR
DORE see DORR
DOROTHY, Joseph 137~44, 168~13
DORR / DORE / DOOR, E. 264~55 Eliza (Smith) 126~43 George 56~19 Gridley 313~18 Jonathan 126~43 Joseph 34~14, 56~18, 284~50 Lucy (Fox) 151~54 Lydia 62~21 Lydia (Allen) 168~45 Moses 56~20 Roxilana (Kimball) 313~18 Samuel 151~54 Sullivan 168~45
DORSEY / DARSEE, [Mr.] 176~45 Job (?) 332~42 John 54~51 William 130~16
DOTY / DOUGHTY / DOUTY / DOODY, [Mrs.] 185~25 Daniel 185~24 Elihu 76~28
DOUBLEDAY, [children] 227~39 Elisha 227~38
DOUGHTY see DOTY
DOUGLAS / DOUGLASS / DUGLASS, Barnard 275~47 Betsey (Cummings) 275~47 Mary 257~14 Temperance 214~27 Thomas 69~46 Thomas J. 214~28 Thomas L. 257~14
DOUGLASS see DOUGLAS
DOUTY see DOTY
DOW / DOWE, [children] 88~28 Asenath (Smart) 288~14 Betsey 301~48 Elizabeth 163~42 Hannah 257~8 Jonathan 140~43 Joseph 361~44 Josiah 361~40 Lorenzo 174~7, 287~25, 290~2, 354~43 Lucy 140~42 Noah 349~35 Peter (?) 246~42 Thomas 88~28 Zebadiah B. 288~14
DOWE see DOW
DOWIE, George 180~30
DOWING see DOWNING
DOWLIN see DOWLING
DOWLING / DOWLIN (see also DARLING), [Mr.] 252~52 Susannah 252~51
DOWN / DOWNE, George 145~4 Richard 101~26 William 142~43
DOWNE see DOWN
DOWNER, George 264~17 John 1~49
DOWNES see DOWNS
DOWNING / DOWING, Daniel 181~37 Ichabod 254~12 John 83~20, 325~21
DOWNS / DOWNES, Charlotte 40~1 Harriet 156~13
DOWRY, Thomas 314~45

DOWST, William 95~54
DOWZICK, Gosper 301~18
DOYLE, [Mr.] 135~11   Martha (Thompson) 183~52   Martin 183~52   Polly 20~6   Thomas 189~7
DRAKE, Asaph 28~23   Ethan 209~6   John 75~20   Nathaniel 232~37   Polly (Dreggs) 124~12   Sarda 124~12
DRAPER, Eliza (Paine) 312~4   Nathaniel 291~13, 313~9   Ursula M. 284~47   William 312~4
DREGGS, Polly 124~12
DREW, Abigail 200~33   Silas 83~41   T.C. 327~11   Thomas 138~31   Thomas C. 11~42, 31~5, 40~44, 159~10
DREWRY see DRURY
DRIFT, Emmanuel 59~16
DRINKER, [Mr.&Mrs.] 12~4   Edward 12~2   John 72~18
DRINKWATER, Stephen 200~24
DRISCO, Sarah 184~32
DRIVER, Ann 210~26
DROWN / DROWNE, Catharine 276~34   Cyrene 165~50   John 67~35
DROWNE see DROWN
DROYSE, James 278~33
DRUARY see DRURY
DRUMMOND, [Capt.] 256~9
DRURY / DRUARY / DREWRY, [child?] 290~15   David 71~44   Ephraim (?) 290~15   Luke 13~53, 33~2, 83~20, 325~25   Manoah 90~4   Polly 181~42   Sally 317~19   Sampson 303~42   Sarah 228~27
DRYEN, Jas. 304~21
DUANE, Margaret Harman (Bache) 69~7   William 69~7
DUBBS, Phebe 200~34
DUBOIS, Betsey (Ryall) 102~28   Nicholas 102~28
DUCHE, Jacob 17~18, 41~42   Sophia 41~41
DUCHEMIN, Peter 208~21
DUDLEY / DUDLY, Chester 222~47   Daniel 76~16   Jeremiah 11~7, 74~41   John 196~4, 196~53, 199~21   Josiah 1~50   M. 61~27   Moses 200~34   Sally (Carlisle) 200~34   Samuel 33~5   William 219~18, 222~47   Zurviah 215~14
DUDLY see DUDLEY
DUER see DEWAR
DUGAN, Eliza (Chase) 170~41   George 170~41
DUGLASS see DOUGLAS
DUHALL, Louis Etienne 12~25
DUKEHAM, [Mr.] 112~51
DULANY see DELANEY
DUMBOLTON, Nat. 21~43
DUMMER, Gorham 178~39   Richard 239~56
DUMONT, William 240~32
DUNBAR, Abel 35~27   Elijah 267~9   Ezekiel 138~42   George 256~52   Rachel (White) 267~10   Sarah 80~22   Sophia 185~43
DUNCAN / DUNKIN, [Admiral] 167~30   [Mr.] 18~26   Abel 251~27, 281~51   Charles 306~35, 328~56   George 159~51   George W. 152~22   Isaac 44~38   John 44~38, 45~48, 55~1, 246~23, 285~40, 363~36   Jonathan 184~17   Joseph 144~3   Margaret (Weeks) 152~22   Mary 227~21   Robert 72~10, 259~31   Stephen 144~4   Susannah 361~27   Thomas 361~27   William 180~45
DUNCHE, Hugh 333~51
DUNHAM, [family] 140~56   Abijah 186~55   Alpheus 140~43   Asa 140~56   Elisha 178~2   Grace (Learned) 140~43   Josiah 329~40   Solomon 68~33
DUNIHUE see DONAHOE
DUNING see DUNNING
DUNKIN see DUNCAN
DUNLAP, Andrew 164~7   James 64~13, 292~16   John 28~28
DUNN, Gershom 215~34   Mary 212~48
DUNNING / DUNING, John 34~19   Mary (O'Brien) 137~26   Robert 137~26
DUNSHEE, Thomas 6~36
DUNSTER, Jason 186~12
DUNTON, [boy] 236~22   Ebenezer 310~51   James 236~22   William 7~3
DUPARR, Abigail 67~14
DUPRAY / DUPRE, Elizabeth 50~17
DUPRE see DUPRAY
DURALDE, Clarice 269~51   Martin 269~52
DURANT, Relief 255~9   Samuel 256~18
DURBERN see DEARBORN

DURBIN see DEARBORN
DURKEE, Asa 145~42   Jirah 294~9   Moses P. 268~46
DUSAN, Dorothy 183~25
DUSTAN see DUSTIN
DUSTEN see DUSTIN
DUSTIN / DUSTON / DUSTAN / DUSTEN, [child] 201~7   [Mr.] 308~55   Caleb 275~23   Mary 275~23   Melinda 245~41   Moody 58~25, 245~41, 310~15   Moses 201~7   Peter 309~44   Timothy 20~29
DUSTON see DUSTIN
DUTTEN see DUTTON
DUTTON / DUTTEN, Aaron 275~5   Abigail (Smith) 297~48   Betsey 200~51   George 262~14   Jesse 261~24   John 176~22, 182~28   Oliver 325~33   Salmon 60~24, 79~39, 80~39, 108~15   William 151~16, 297~48
DUVAL / DUVALL (see also DEVIL, DIVOL), Benjamin 155~22   Dorothy (———) (Allen) 91~18   Marcea H. 91~18
DUVALL see DUVAL
DWIGHT, Clarissa (Strong) 301~47   Daniel 131~9   Elihu 103~16   H. 217~52   Henry W. 167~53   J. 217~52   Jonathan 152~7   Josiah 133~20   Lydia (White) 103~16   Mary (Edwards) 280~51   Nancy 94~8   Timothy 36~2, 280~51, 301~46
DWINEL see DWINNELS
DWINEL(L) see DWINNELS
DWINNELS / DWINNEL / DWINNIELS / DWINNELL / DWINEL, Israel 100~20   Jonathan 89~56   Sally (Hayward) 104~46   Simeon 104~46
DWINNIELS see DWINNELS
DWYER / DWYRE, James 115~38, 143~2
DWYRE see DWYER
DYER, [Mr.] 200~55   Charles 279~33, 280~37   Elisha 104~9   Ezra 110~48   Frances (Jones) 104~9   Nancy (Jennings) 110~49   Oliver 295~13

E.

EACKER / EAKER, George I. 107~16   Simon 253~32
EAGER, Asher 310~50   Nahum 180~46
EAKER see EACKER
EALE, Benjamin 183~12
EAMES see AMES
EARL / EARLE, [boy] 179~22   [children?] 22~7   Deborah 176~30   Eliza 54~14   George 251~26   Joseph 179~22   Ralph 287~41   Robert 221~8   Sally 22~5   Sarah 22~7   William 177~6, 182~20
EARLE see EARL
EARLS, Stephen 258~44
EASTEN / EASTON, Catharine 2~29   Timothy 2~29
EASTERBROOKS see ESTABROOK
EASTMAN, Abiel 174~5   Hannah 269~56   Hepzibah (———) 313~17   John 167~23   Moses 134~16, 183~13, 267~39   Nancy 86~46   Sally 256~38   Stephen 268~47   Sukey 267~39   William 76~17
EASTON see EASTEN
EASTY see ESTEY
EATEN see EATON
EATON / EATEN / HEATON, [Mr.] 330~52   [widow] 311~49   Aaron 121~21   Asa 205~38   Azubah (———) (Grout) 276~18   Calvin 236~35, 251~51, 292~37, 299~8, 311~48   Clarissa 278~41   Comfort 311~49   Daniel 133~29   David 252~26   David Fox 356~40   Ebenezer 90~7, 209~14, 236~35, 251~50, 261~23, 298~37   Eleanor Powers (Chesley) 356~41   Elizabeth 102~35   Florella 298~36   Ira 296~50   Isaiah 146~16, 169~37, 169~44, 204~27, 206~46, 224~29, 276~17, 278~41, 296~51   Jonas 320~4   Jonathan 140~34, 252~27   Joseph 56~25, 89~50, 180~34, 184~40, 222~21   Josiah 281~12, 306~38, 311~49   Mary 184~41   Moses 148~28   Nathaniel 178~50   Noah 89~54   Polly 295~34   Priscilla 169~37, 169~44, 224~29   Samuel 90~7   Seth 6~14   Sophronia 298~36   Timothy 218~35   William 130~23
EAYERS see AYERS
EAYRS see AYERS
EBANKS, [family] 201~30

EBERHEART / EVERHARD / EVERBARDT, John 37~13, 63~15
ECCLESTON / EGLESTON, [children] 3~32 [Mr.] 3~31 Elizabeth 98~28
ECKLEY see ECKLY
ECKLY / ACKLEY / ECKLEY, [Rev.] 193~29 David 193~28
EDDY, Ann (Angell) 298~25 Benj. 104~43 Charles 158~24 Gibbs W. 200~54 John 193~29 Mary (Vose) 137~27 Samuel 298~25 Solomon 137~27
EDES, Benjamin 154~5 Catharine C. (May) 204~33 Ebenezer 361~20 Henry 203~16, 204~33 Mary 361~20
EDGAR, David 185~2
EDGARTON, [Capt.] 233~42 Benjamin 236~53 Samuel 316~8
EDGELL, Levi 73~2
EDGERLEY see EDGERLY
EDGERLY / EDGERLEY, Mary (———) 357~31
EDGERTON, [Mr.] 327~8 Cybele 100~37 Daniel 302~19 Erastus 302~19 Jabez 231~36 James 320~17 Samuel 327~4
EDMANDS see EDMUNDS
EDMISTER, Sarah 159~12
EDMONDS see EDMUNDS
EDMUNDS / EDMANDS / EDMONDS, [Mrs.] 79~26 Ann 175~41 Rebecca 170~13
EDSON, Betsey (Weatherby) 51~24 Lydia 257~15, 278~53 Obed 131~13 Timothy 51~23
EDWARDS, [Capt.] 65~26 [Col.] 155~25 [Mr.] 226~15, 279~24 [Mrs.] 135~14 Abigail 183~25 Daniel 8~21 Elizabeth (———) Wright 47~29 Enoch 118~53 Jabez 216~2 John 117~4, 155~55 John Starke 58~40 Jonathan 97~16, 280~52 Katharine 140~24 Louisa (Morris) 279~24 Lydia 114~14 Margaret 206~34 Mary 280~51 Medard 255~26 Noah 47~29 Pierpont 58~39 Polly (Baral) 117~4 Richard 275~53, 277~24 Samuel 140~24 Sophia (Simonds) 216~2 Thomas 28~32, 64~3, 73~10, 74~29, 85~58, 250~17, 252~33 William 206~34
EELS / ELLS, Abigail (Turner) 56~39 J. 180~43 Nathaniel 50~27, 56~39
EGERTON (see also EDGERTON), James 29~13, 279~13, 321~26
EGLESTON see ECCLESTON
ELBERT / ALBERT, [Gen.] 41~40 [Sergeant] 304~53 Betsey 41~39
ELDERKIN, Anna 162~42 Joshua B. 111~8
ELDREDGE see ELDRIDGE
ELDRICH see ELDRIDGE
ELDRIDGE/ELDREDGE/ELDRICH, Amos 131~16 Elijah 327~12 Elisha 47~58, 320~20 Nathan 218~53
ELIOT / ELLIOT / ELIOTT / ELLIOTT, [Mr.] 66~55 [Rev.] 128~11 Abigail 64~13, 120~43 Amos 147~21 Andrew 214~18 Daniel 309~3 Edmund 353~8 Eliza (Gilman) 353~8 Fanny (Foster) 200~41 Fanny A. 251~20 Frances 226~33 James 5~2, 140~42, 335~24 Lucy (Dow) 140~42 Lydia 22~53 Mary 71~31 Peggy (Willey) 147~22 Ralph Emms 268~24 S. 236~20 Samuel 200~40, 251~20, 362~29 Sarah 178~5 Simon 178~5 Susan 118~41
ELIOTT see ELIOT
ELKINS, Elizabeth 282~16 Harvey 55~5 Henry 286~15 Jonathan 282~16 Obadiah 355~37
ELLENWOOD / ELLINGWOOD, (———) 327~20 [Mr.] 289~16
ELLERSON see ELLISON
ELLINGWOOD see ELLENWOOD
ELLIOT(T) see ELIOT
ELLIS, [Mrs.] 239~26 Asa 249~18 Benjamin 260~15 C. 18~33 Caleb 90~27 Ferdinand 270~43 Hannah 260~14 Jennings 328~30 Jeremiah 116~26, 334~39 John 6~33, 16~25, 217~3, 218~15, 218~32 Joseph 28~27, 36~20, 138~48 Joshua 134~2 Lydia 204~51 Rebecca 136~44 Rosanna (Clark) 134~2 Sally 269~49 Sally (Graham) 260~16 Stephen 230~12 Ziba 116~27
ELLISON / ELLERSON / ALLISON, James 158~22 John 138~50 Robert 93~21
ELLS see EELS
ELLSWORTH / ELSWORTH, Betsey (Harrison) 92~5 Nathaniel 92~5 Verdine 326~31
ELMAR see ELMER

ELMER / ELMAR, Eli 190~35, 194~22
ELMSLEY, John 194~28
ELSWORTH see ELLSWORTH
ELWELL, Jonathan 146~38 Robert 188~3 Thomas 142~35
ELWIN see ELWYN
ELWYN / ELWIN, Francis 231~16
ELY, [Mr.] 237~16 Ezra Stiles 263~30 Isaac 159~17 Isaac H. 36~21, 81~38, 206~58, 285~42, 311~53
EMERSON / EMMERSON, [child] 161~54 [Mrs.] 4~55, 161~53 B. Dudley 233~52 Brown 265~21 Bulkeley 147~55 C. 111~37, 112~12 Charles 313~46, 331~41 Daniel 102~38, 103~26 Dorothy (———) 104~45 Edward 262~3 Eleanor 286~43 Hezekiah 101~54, 122~20, 215~56, 263~2 John 33~22 Joseph 162~45, 286~43 Mary (Hopkins) 265~21 Nancy 112~31, 162~44 Nathaniel 157~17, 163~9, 190~13, 237~22 Persis (Harden) 62~39 Reuben 62~39 Richard 316~12 Robert 331~36 Samuel 4~55 Solomon 78~26
EMERY / AMORY, Abigail 131~41 Daniel 90~4 Francis 165~4 John 56~19 Joseph 286~17 Joshua 87~24 Mary 43~49 Philip 306~17 Rhoda 303~12 Sally (Kirkland) 165~4 Samuel 61~39, 87~25 Stephen 106~32 Thomas 43~50 William 286~2
EMES see AMES
EMLY, Cyrus 91~4
EMMERSON see EMERSON
EMMONS, [Mr.] 296~39 Abner 134~18 Martha 177~16 Mary 231~38 Rachel 233~25 Samuel 231~27, 271~6
ENDICOTT, Elizabeth 308~36 Jacob 148~6 Joseph 273~13 Ruthy (Hawkes) 148~6
ENGLAND, [Gen.] 261~36 [Miss] 261~36 Poole 261~36
ENGLESBY, Abigail 303~20
ENGLISH, Anna 39~37 Charles 299~37
ENNIS / ANNIS, [Mr.] 136~7
ENSIGN, Moses 191~42
ENSWORTH see AINSWORTH
EPES / EPPES, [Mrs.] 160~55 Samuel 154~40
EPPES see EPES
ERNST, John F. 221~26
ESTABROOK / ESTABROOKS / EASTERBROOKS / ESTERBROOKS / ESTERBROOK, [Mr.] 87~23 [Mrs.] 320~48 Charles 35~49 Daniel 320~47 Mary 60~38 Moses 20~24 N. 74~45 Nat. 20~50 Nathan 30~15 Patience 74~44, 93~53
ESTABROOKS see ESTABROOK
ESTERBROOK(S) see ESTABROOK
ESTEY / ESTY / EASTY, David 333~42 Edward 28~18, 122~54 Esther 208~13 Reuben 7~49 Sally (Blake) 135~34 Stephen 89~55 William 135~34
ESTHEREDGE / ETHERIDGE, Samuel 88~37
ESTY see ESTEY
ETHERIDGE see ESTHEREDGE
EULEN, Susannah 142~27
EUNSON, Betsey 138~13 James 293~27
EUSTACE see EUSTIS
EUSTIS / EUSTACE, [Gen.] 214~39 Benjamin 161~4 Caroline (Langdon) 334~57 John Skey 210~40 William 334~57
EUSTON see HOUSTON
EVANS, [Major] 11~8 [Mr.] 3~52, 148~14 Abiel 88~8 Ann (Penhallow) 323~29 Asa 188~46 Elizabeth 160~15 George 172~28, 186~22 Gilbert 16~40, 43~18 Jonathan 252~53 Margaret 299~27 Mary 91~28 Nathaniel 259~39, 309~47 Peter 198~5 Richard 133~21, 323~29 William 80~26
EVE, [Mrs.] 209~23
EVELETH, Elizabeth (———) (Burill) 106~27 John 106~27 Stephen 273~20
EVERBARDT see EBERHEART
EVERETT, [children] 119~44 David 57~16 Dorothy (Appleton) 57~16 John 36~31 Melatiah 218~7 Nancy (Shaw) 218~7 Richard C. 48~58 Sylvester 333~53 William 119~42
EVERHARD see EBERHEART
EVERISH, Joseph 88~54
EWEN see EWINS
EWENS see EWINS
EWES see HUSE

EWING, [Capt.] 12~11 Hannah 236~7 James 236~6, 244~22 John 236~7
EWINS / EWENS / EWEN / HEWINS, Alex. 133~43 Josiah 81~52 Peter 81~52
EXLEY, John 155~23
EXTILL see AXTELL
EYARS see AYERS
EYRE see AYER
EYREMAN, Jacob 63~5   Jacob (?) 367~60   Jacom 367~60
EZELL, Avris (?) 50~12

F.

FACEY, Robert 77~27
FAGER, Nahum 179~43
FAIRBANK see FAIRBANKS
FAIRBANKS / FAIRBANK, Daniel 209~19   E. 112~45 Jason 90~36, 112~46, 178~30 Jones 56~21 Josiah 84~46 Luke 209~19 Moses 306~40 Stephen 112~49 Uri 303~46 Willard 332~56
FAIRCHILD, [Mrs.] 232~4 [triplets] 232~5 Aaron 232~4 Patty 242~37 Zachariah 242~38
FAIRFAX, Brian Lord 125~34 Bryan 202~39 Jane 202~39
FAIRFIELD, Samuel 147~2
FAIRWEATHER see FAYERWEATHER
FALCONER see FAULKNER
FALEE see FARLEY
FALES, Eliza 178~32 Elizabeth 90~35 Nathaniel 183~12 Nehemiah 246~8 Samuel 68~8
FALEY see FARLEY
FALFETT, Jonathan 21~19
FALHAFFER, Job 18~6
FALL, Elizabeth 234~23
FALLING, John 250~43
FALLON see FOLLEN
FANNIN / FANNING / FANNON, N. 216~50
FANNING see FANNIN
FANNON see FANNIN
FAR see FARR
FAREWELL see FARWELL
FARGUAHASON, Francis 254~49
FARLEY / FALEY / FALEE, Abel 182~57, 185~31 John D. 54~43 Joseph 21~18 Lucretia (Gardner) 216~44 Mark 216~44 Mary (Swett) 54~44 Stephen 296~47
FARMER, Jacob 20~21 Jehiel 332~25 John 226~40, 329~25 Joseph 332~26 Polly 146~28
FARNAM see FARNHAM
FARNHAM / FARNUM / FARNAM, Daniel 6~25 Elizabeth 35~52 James 161~12 Jared 16~32 K. 24~39 M. 125~18 Roger 109~26, 116~41 Sibyl 6~25
FARNSWORTH / FARNWORTH, [Mr.] 315~1 Asenath (Waters) 71~32 Catherine (Wells) 189~35 Daniel 252~4 David 330~6 Ebenezer 22~51 Esther 9~46 John 10~17 Jonathan 265~12 Joseph 71~32, 139~41, 164~21, 183~29 Patty (Proctor) 252~4 Patty (Shepard) 139~41 Simeon 9~46, 187~37 Thomas 189~35 Zacheus 90~8
FARNUM see FARNHAM
FARNWORTH see FARNSWORTH
FARR / FAR, Aaron 48~5 Abel 225~37 Daniel 39~22 Isaac 316~11, 329~16 Jonathan 11~12 S. 81~8
FARRA / FARRAH, [Mr.] 294~51 John 295~55
FARRAH see FARRA
FARRAND see FERREN
FARRAR, Josiah 289~52 Luther 265~25 Marcy A. (Whiting) 265~25 Phineas 89~43 Rebecca 173~33
FARRELL, John C. 107~35
FARRIER, [Capt.] 67~47 Mary 234~30
FARRIN see FERREN
FARRINGTON, Apphia 357~34 Elijah 203~57 Elizabeth 203~57 Moses 203~56 R. 112~45 William 285~4
FARRIS see FARRISS
FARRISS / FERRISS / FARRIS, [children?] 239~51 [Mrs.?] 239~51 Andrew 179~13 Jerusha 182~51 John 254~49 Walter (?) 239~49
FARVELL, Ephraim 71~22

FARWELL / FAREWELL, [Mr.] 196~22 Betsey (Carter) 92~32 Ephraim 5~16, 265~17 Fanny (York) 275~13 Henry 156~4   J. 145~8 Jane 274~36 Leonard 275~13 Levi 92~32 Nicholas 145~8 Oliver 20~30 Samuel 91~16 William 133~49, 138~43
FASSET see FOSSETT
FASSETT, Asa 169~6 Margaret 169~5
FAULCONER see FAULKNER
FAULKNER / FAULCONER / FALCONER, Daniel 216~17, 216~17 Francis 207~21 Nathaniel 267~30, 269~4 William 208~51
FAUNCE, Thomas 275~51
FAXON, Azariah 5~15, 6~31, 10~43, 71~22 James 10~43, 320~30, 330~5 Sukey 52~57
FAY, [Capt.] 57~36 Benjamin 259~28 Dinah 186~6 Galen H. 298~41 Gersham 234~15 Hannah 234~15 Hollon 124~22 John 290~13, 315~3 Jonathan 62~42 Joseph 152~14, 320~21 Josiah 43~2 Levi 183~17 Lydia (———) (Smith) 194~4 Margery 372~64 Margery (Newton) 75~49 Mary 293~23 Mary (Putnam) 37~52 Nahum 37~52 Nahunt 167~25 Nath. 316~15 Nathan 33~51, 58~45, 75~49, 259~28 Polly 2~38 Warren 284~28 William 194~4
FAYERWEATHER / FAIRWEATHER, Thomas 180~57
FEALCH see FELCH
FELCH / FEALCH / FELTCH, C. 305~51, 324~5 Cheever 303~10, 324~29 Mary 261~1 Mary (Hale) 303~11 Nathan 312~30 Walton 281~44
FELLOWES see FELLOWS
FELLOWS / FELLOWES, [Mrs.] 2~36 [widow] 238~17 Abigail 364~18 Adonijah 2~37 Ezra 203~40 Gustavus 293~6 Isaac 235~15, 238~17 Joseph 364~18 Nathaniel 241~22
FELT, Aaron 34~35 Abner 10~49, 68~13, 74~46 Chloe 200~46 Eliphalet 3~53, 190~58 John 190~58 Mary (———) (Gilmore) 297~47 Peter 297~47 Polly 170~44
FELTCH see FELCH
FELTON, [children] 71~14   [Mrs.] 71~14   Ann (Richards) 38~47 Asa 71~11 Isaac 38~46 James 180~6 Nathaniel 280~41
FENLY / FENNELLY, Eliza (Hilt) 75~45 Robert 75~45
FENN, Nancy 214~11 Nathan 38~55
FENNELLY see FENLY
FENNER, Arthur 217~11 John 231~7
FENNO, Catharine N. (Adams) 250~29 Fanny 67~12 Harriet 83~33 John 83~34 John Ward 115~54 Reuben 62~44, 67~9 Samuel 252~32 William 250~29
FENTON / FINTEN, Gamaliel 19~34 Lese (Harrington) 84~29 Martha 148~9 Richard W. 84~29 Roger 28~53, 56~22, 74~47, 93~54, 156~10, 309~51
FERGESAN see FERGUSON
FERGUSON / FURGUSON / FERGESAN, Henry 176~21
FERNALD / FIRNALD / FURNALD / FURNAL, Dennis 208~44 Edward 266~6 Samuel 363~5 Thomas 353~15
FERRE see FERRY
FERREN / FARRIN / FERRIN / FARRAND, [Rev.] 19~32 Daniel 57~31, 61~41, 69~39 David 68~9 Louisa 354~31 Phineas 106~47 Polly (Spencer) 106~47
FERRIN see FERREN
FERRISS see FARRISS
FERRITER, Nicholas 37~56
FERRY / FERRE, Aura 220~3 Joseph 267~33 Mabel 267~33
FESSENDEN, [Mr.] 75~12, 105~6 [Rev.] 182~33 Elizabeth Clement 201~37 Fanny 177~42 Hannah 125~11 Martha 116~49 Samuel 118~7 Thomas 19~45, 118~8 Thomas G. 311~22 Timothy 186~2 W. 311~23 William 11~15, 201~38, 334~16
FFROST see FROST
FIARS, Joanna 92~18
FIELD, [Rev.] 276~13 Ann 50~20 Anna 27~54 Daniel 16~37 David 80~9, 143~4, 304~17 George 80~8, 115~39 Hannah 187~28 John 36~11 Lilley 51~29 M. 65~51 Martin 40~48, 88~4 Moses 179~54 Richard 185~36 Rufus 143~10 Seth 80~10, 115~40 Spencer 107~7 Thomas 66~21, 93~40 Waighstell 27~53 Zechariah 57~45
FIELDS / FILLS, Henry 201~11 Thankful 138~38 Thomas 138~38
FIFE, Silas 90~3
FIFIELD, Edward 60~45, 65~36

FILER, [Mr.] 259~44
FILLS see FIELDS
FILLY, Jonathan 190~31
FINCH, Ann (———) (Wicley) 106~56 Richard 106~55
FINDLAY see FINLEY
FINLAY see FINLEY
FINLEY / FINLAY / FINDLAY, Charles 73~39 James 68~27 Samuel 41~53, 45~30, 205~45, 217~53
FINNEY, Abigail 277~43
FINNICK, Patrick 210~55
FINS, Hannah 273~12
FINSON, Thomas 279~38
FINTEN see FENTON
FIRBUSH see FURBUSH
FIRNALD see FERNALD
FISH, Alexander 164~2 Alvin 98~56 Anna 86~39 Anna (Hardy) 87~31 David 86~42, 87~32, 304~41 Elijah 218~41 Isaac 109~33 Jonathan 17~46 Nancy (Stone) 260~22 Polly 75~52, 321~27 Sally (Barker) 109~33 Samuel 260~21 Sarah (Stillman) 146~39
FISHER, [Mr.] 42~36, 324~24 Aaron 301~53 Asa 68~7 Betsey 266~11, 267~36 Henry 49~7 Isaac 116~34 Jabez 262~42 Jabez Pond 307~45 John 70~20, 207~31 Jonathan 70~9, 235~56 Joseph 10~24 Lucy 272~48 Nathaniel 75~8 Orison 118~5 Polly 70~20 Rebecca (Adams) 235~57 Sally 49~7 Samuel 239~56, 243~12 Thomas 266~11, 267~37 Timothy 88~3, 106~3
FISK / FISKE, [Mr.] 118~23 [Rev.] 295~54 Abigail 41~23 David 41~24, 61~39 Ebenezer 357~43 Eleanor 78~6 Elijah 221~39 Elisha 202~53 George 328~30 Hannah (———) 107~47 Henry 357~43 Ichabod E. 78~6 Isaac 353~14 John 26~47 Jonathan 184~34, 284~10 Lucy 183~47 Lydia 202~53 Mary 41~24 Meriam 74~20 Moses 54~56 Naomi 99~54 Nathaniel 1~22, 67~10 Olive 103~21 Oliver 62~37 Sally 354~33 Samuel 26~49, 58~25, 296~47 Sarah 295~53 Stephen 74~24 William 226~9, 310~22
FISKE see FISK
FITCH, Alice 166~50 Apollos 100~37 Charles 70~37, 70~42 Cybele (Edgerton) 100~37 Eleazer 1~33 Ephraim 73~26 Frances (Gage) 78~22 Grata 203~42 Henry 51~45, 68~11, 70~42, 78~22 Jabez 277~16 Jabez G. 244~27 James 112~55, 218~20 Joseph 36~26 Olive 216~3 Sally 312~50 Sally (Knap) 36~26 Samuel 81~54 Speedy 244~27 Stephen 231~48, 244~28 William 3~14, 67~49, 170~25 Zebediah 16~9 Zeruviah 1~32
FITTS / FITZ, Mary 265~51 Sarah 183~46
FITZ see FITTS
FITZBURG, John 301~4
FITZGERALD, [Mrs.] 266~7 Thomas 59~36
FITZPATRICK, James 212~45
FLAGG, Asa 201~23 Joshua 110~52 Polly 91~26 Polly (———) 259~2 Rebecca 109~35, 274~22 Richard 54~30 Rufus 186~14
FLAMAGAN, John 307~42
FLANDERS, Anna 294~29 Ezekiel 264~19 Moses 325~48
FLANKINGTON, [Mr.] 247~50 [Mrs.] 247~49
FLEET, Anne 152~52 John 234~18 Thomas 1~35
FLEMING / FLEMMING / FLEMINGS, Alice 234~14 George 106~14
FLEMINGS see FLEMING
FLEMMING see FLEMING
FLETCHER, Asa 181~50 Asaph 181~52 Ebenezer 35~28 Ephraim 211~21 James 296~27 Jonathan 9~57, 101~43 Joseph 214~21 Josiah 181~51 Luther 181~50 Meriam 333~54 Peter 67~56, 100~34, 106~3, 296~28, 303~45 Rachel (Scott) 232~12 Rebecca 100~36 Rebekah 101~51 Robert 20~21, 24~8, 312~13 Russell 232~12 Salome 181~50
FLINT, [Mr.] 233~12, 241~2, 323~2 James 267~4 John 138~31, 265~15, 332~6, 334~48 Joshua 31~15 Lydia 303~44 Mary 85~45 Olive (Smith) 233~13
FLOOD, Joseph 141~28
FLOWER / FLOWERS, Alford 142~29 Harriot (Leonard) 142~30 Nabby 68~17
FLOWERS see FLOWER
FLOYD, Ben. H. 303~47 Benjamin M. 116~42 Ebenezer 312~9 Hannah 216~57 Horace 89~51
FOBES see FORBES
FOGG, Jeremiah 286~18

FOLGER / FOLGIER, George 299~21 Isaac 51~40, 364~34 Robert 16~48
FOLGIER see FOLGER
FOLKENHAN, Elizabeth 14~34
FOLLEN / FALLON, Jones 72~14 Mary L. 72~13
FOLLETT / FOLLET, John 57~46 Levi 105~8
FOLSOM, (———) 133~46 Abraham 24~53 Josiah 57~23, 361~47 N.B. 133~17 Nathan B. 133~28
FONDA, David 207~27
FONERDEN, Ann 228~5
FONTANA, [Mr.] 155~54
FOOT / FOOTE, David Y. 200~26 John 141~30 Noah B. 200~12 Samuel 46~54 Sophia 200~25
FOOTE see FOOT
FOOTMAN, Jonathan 203~27 Sally (Hodgdon) 203~27
FORBER see FURBER
FORBES / FOBES, (———) 71~43 [Governour] 7~27 Daniel 292~56 Eli 158~5, 173~53 Esther (Chamberlain) 112~9 Jane 16~38 Jonathan 21~17, 112~9, 198~20 Joshua 271~25 Jotham 271~25 Lucy 158~5 Thomas 170~36
FORBLE, Edward 229~56 Kesiah (Crofford) 229~56
FORD, David 233~11 Hannah 90~12 Joseph 310~23 Sally (Lyman) 233~11 William 78~33
FORDMAN, Samuel 200~58
FORLAR, William 142~38
FORMAN, Mary 199~19 William 199~20
FORREST, [children] 294~48 [Mrs.] 294~48 Uriah 203~32 William 294~46
FORRESTER / FORSTER, Robert 50~19
FORSTER see FORRESTER
FORTESCUE, [Capt.] 246~56
FORWARD, [Rev.] 254~2 Eunice 297~22 Justus 297~23 Pamela 254~1
FOSDIC / FOSDICK, Charlotte 40~11 Thomas 100~9
FOSDICK see FOSDIC
FOSICK, Nathaniel F. 141~51
FOSKETT, Susanna 189~41
FOSS, Joshua 298~6, 298~42, 301~18
FOSSETT / FASSET, Adonijah 87~26
FOSTER, [Lieut.] 270~41 [Mr.?] 234~1 Abiel 231~40 Abigail 111~2, 233~55 Abijah 330~23 Alice (———) (Carlisle) 220~46 Benjamin 104~53 Bossenger 191~12, 192~49 Dan 65~52, 312~54, 334~2 David 17~24 David M. 1~22 F. 155~40 Elizabeth (?) 94~21 Fanny 200~41 G.W. 322~51 Henry 32~17, 56~20, 269~44 Hepzebeth 309~50 Isaac 39~49 Israel 81~42 Issac 244~1 Jacob 30~51, 241~32 James 59~13, 133~24, 250~29 James (?) 269~18 Joel 138~18 John 278~15 John M. 220~46 Joshua 191~52 Lucy (———) 104~10 Lydia 102~35 Nathan 262~10, 263~47 Priscilla 138~18 Rachel 153~26 Rebecca 2~36 Samuel 333~42 Sarah (Porter) 250~29 Susan 273~52 Whitfield 150~28
FOULTON see FULTON
FOUNTAIN, Hannah 163~18
FOWLER, [children] 149~13, 228~52 [Mrs.] 228~53 Bancroft 196~28, 255~7 Charles 21~20 Cheever 89~45 John 191~48, 195~28 Joshua 328~17 Lucia (Curtis) 255~7 Saul 149~13 William 228~52
FOX, Charles 205~57 Eliphalet 34~53, 89~49, 93~55, 316~14 Elisha 63~44 Eliza 200~32, 263~12 Joseph 25~27, 25~28, 175~25 Justus 180~52 Lucy 151~54 Martha 175~24 Nancy 118~42 Peggy (Allen) 205~57
FOXCRAFT see FOXCROFT
FOXCROFT / FOXCRAFT, [Mr.] 256~20 Abigail (Hammond) 313~19 Eliza 98~51 Frances 181~54 J.E. 313~19 Martha B. 216~40 Samuel 282~9
FOY / FOYE, Robert 231~37
FOYE see FOY
FRANCES see FRANCIS
FRANCIS / FRANCES, [boys] 22~45 [child] 261~19 [girl] 22~47 [Mrs.] 22~46 Ann 167~2 David 224~49 Ebenezer 53~1 Elizabeth 264~29 Elizabeth (Thorndike) 53~2 Evan 22~43 Francis 78~36 James 261~19 Nathaniel 274~25 Phebe 274~24 Tench 64~46
FRANCK, Mary 221~37
FRANKLIN, [Dr.] 196~44 John 99~57, 126~35
FRASER see FRAZIER
FRASURE see FRAZIER
FRAZER see FRAZIER

FRAZIER / FRAZER / FRASER / FRASURE, [Major General] 199~33 James Priolare 6~19 John 120~15 Mary 191~2 Moses 64~10 Nathan 65~1 Simeon 303~48 Simon 221~6
FREDENBURG, [Miss] 239~34
FREELAND, James 124~45
FREEMAN, [children] 242~31 [Lt. Col.] 207~41 [Mr.] 58~32, 243~45 [Mrs.] 242~31, 293~35 Comfort 271~21 Constant 229~26 Daniel 242~31 Deborah 189~5 Dummer 322~41 James 90~46, 230~37, 288~41 Jonah 251~5 Jonathan 11~38, 72~7, 152~19 Mary 184~42, 254~3 Mary (Whitehouse) 152~19 Phebe 232~38 Randolph 33~34 Russell 223~3, 372~14 Ruth 224~37 Sam 219~31 Samuel 293~35
FRELINGHUYSEN, Frederick 159~53
FRENCH, Abby (Winch) 270~55 Abel 165~22, 267~48 Andrew 60~53, 73~48, 116~21, 132~48 Ben. 20~19 Benjamin 231~42 Daniel 269~19 Edmund 289~4 Elkanah 284~20 Eunice 155~49 Fanny (Allen) 273~51 Frederick 82~7 Hannah 266~8 Hannah M. 323~39 Isaac 270~55 Jabez 266~8, 266~9 Jeremiah 92~50 John 103~9, 165~21, 273~50, 361~48 Jonathan 173~32, 307~9 Militiah 170~43 Nathaniel 45~21, 60~46, 65~34, 318~40 Rebecca 210~7, 269~19 Rebecca (Farrar) 173~33 Sally 70~21 Samuel 20~28, 81~53 Timothy 361~47 Zadock 323~39
FRERO, Sarah 163~23, 163~44
FRIES, John 37~13, 39~7, 63~4, 367~1, 367~50
FRINK, Alexander Steward 50~13 Bela 293~53 Elijah 138~43 Eugenia 330~28 John 217~15 Peter 11~12 William Blodget 50~24
FRITH, Joseph 261~54
FRITZ, Henry 271~35
FROBISHER, William 114~54
FROST / FFROST, Gideon 202~48 Jacob 234~23 Jesse 278~49 Joseph 233~5 Mary 217~1 Sarah 202~47 Susan (Coffin) 249~37 Timothy 249~37
FROTHINGHAM, [Rev.] 167~38 Benjamin 308~20 Ebenezer 15~1 John 133~18 Mildred 183~24
FRY see **FRYE**
FRYE / FRY, Betsy 65~42 Ebenezer 32~37 James 174~31 Jonathan 221~8 Sarah (Earl) 221~7
FUDGE, Hannah 99~3
FUDGER, John G. 112~32
FULERTON see **FULLERTON**
FULLER, [Capt.] 128~38, 261~35 [family] 128~38 [Mrs.] 228~30, 298~39 Abigail (Learned) 99~49 Alfred 194~49 Bartholomew 258~43 Caleb 76~12 Elisha 305~12 Ester 293~30 Hannah 178~17 John 83~4, 227~46 Josiah 16~31 Levi 326~49, 328~9 Lucena (Wyllys) 194~49 Nancy 76~11 Nathan 204~20 Nathaniel 68~24 Noah 293~30, 298~39 Oliver 99~49 Oliver W. 269~36 Sarah 299~53 Simeon 214~34 Thomas 37~3 Timothy 202~20
FULLERTON / FULERTON, Catharine 171~40 H. 39~46 Henry 274~57 Martha (Thompson) (Gregory) 262~26 Thomas S. 8~15, 16~41 Walter 262~25
FULMER, Elizabeth 198~43
FULTON / FOULTON, [children] 211~43 [Mrs.] 211~43 Henry 41~48 John 211~43
FURBER / FORBER, Theodore 133~41
FURBISH see **FURBUSH**
FURBUSH / FURBISH / FIRBUSH, Sarah 156~54
FURGUSON see **FERGUSON**
FURLONG, Lawrence 243~13
FURNACE see **FURNESS**
FURNAL see **FERNALD**
FURNALD see **FERNALD**
FURNESS / FURNISS / FURNACE, [Mrs.] 133~20
FURNISS see **FURNESS**
FUSHAM, Bathsheba (———) (Leach) 201~16 Phinehas 201~15

G.

GABLE, Daniel 63~12, 367~64 Jacob 63~12, 367~57 Peter 63~12, 367~63

GAFFIELD see **GARFIELD**
GAGE, [Capt.] 193~41 Asa 42~28 Betsey (Merriam) 147~23 Frances 78~22 Hannah 103~17 John 147~23 Moses 125~32 Rebecca 236~52 Sally 107~48, 107~48 Sally (Hooper) 96~53 Samuel 70~38 Thaddeus 92~49 William 96~53
GAINE, Hugh 193~16, 197~10
GAINES / GAINS, George 298~45 John 133~36
GAINS see **GAINES**
GALBRAITH, Andrew 235~12
GALE, [girl] 4~19 [Mr.] 4~19 Amos 181~34 Betsey 184~30 Eliza 75~51 Elizabeth 114~19 Harriet (Bates) 200~36 James 200~34 Phebe (Dubbs) 200~34 Thaddeus 200~35
GALLAT see **GELLET**
GALLESPIE see **GILLESPIE**
GALLET, M. France 193~18
GALLOP, William 142~48
GALLOWAY, Abigail 268~16 Joseph 152~36
GALT see **GAULT**
GALUSHA, [Judge] 300~25
GAMOTH, Reo 304~56
GANO, John 166~31
GANSEVOORT, Eliza 262~27 L. 262~28
GARDER, Rachel 195~15
GARDIE, [Madam] 26~11 [Monsieur] 26~11
GARDINER / GARDNER, [Capt.] 254~43, 257~40 [Lt. Gen.] 234~38 Andrew 65~19 Caleb 51~51 Francis 159~49, 169~15, 186~41, 199~57, 216~44, 249~36, 333~43 George 105~33 Hannah 159~48, 186~34, 217~1 Huldah 260~40 Isaac S. 92~8 James 254~47 Jane 110~11 Joanna 307~6 John 42~5 Joseph 217~2, 236~9 Lucretia 216~44 Martha 12~7 Mary 107~7, 182~39 Mary (Collins) 51~51 Mercy 249~34 Nancy 249~36 Noah 77~40 Peleg 12~48 Peyton Randolph 165~12 R. 213~4 Samuel 105~32 Sarah 290~35 Sarah (Spooner) 92~8 Thomas 177~17 Weld 105~32 William 239~1
GARDNER see **GARDINER**
GAREY see **GEARY**
GARFIELD / GAFFIELD, Jane (———) 294~57 John 22~32 Samuel 2~50
GARLAND, Amos 79~30 Olive (Jenness) 79~30 William 133~38
GARNSEY see **GUERNSEY**
GARRISON, Phebe 158~16
GARRY see **GEARY**
GARTHRIGHT, Elvey 75~30
GARVIN / GURVIN, Chauncey 357~42 Martha (Parker) 357~42
GARY see **GEARY**
GASKILL, Samuel 68~56
GASS see **GOSS**
GASTON see **GUSTIN**
GATCHELL see **GETCHELL**
GATES, Ira 276~9 Isaac 36~12 Jonathan 283~20 Josiah 5~56, 134~28 Lemuel 264~36 Levi 89~47 Nathan 80~4 William 208~17
GAULT / GALT, Ann 232~29
GAVET see **GAVETT**
GAVETT / GAVETTE / GAVITT / GAVET, Abigail (Duparr) 67~14 James 67~14 Jonathan 251~5 Joseph 133~39
GAVITT see **GAVETT**
GAY / GOY / GUY, [Mr.] 24~46 Bunker 115~41, 143~9, 278~35, 325~44 David 304~31 Ebenezer 72~14, 83~24 Henry 39~3 Jane (———) 98~23 John 108~26 L.D. 39~46 Martin 291~2 Mary Alline (Otis) 72~15 Nathaniel 258~22 S. 112~46 Sarah 108~26 William 39~3
GAYDEN, Catharine 146~27
GAYLORD, Chester 162~7 Sidney (Dickinson) 162~8
GAYOSO, [Gov.] 47~32, 226~31 [widow] 226~30
GEAR / GEEAR / GEER / GERE, Frederick W. 8~49 Jemima 137~32 Shubael 115~5 Sybil 140~11 William 206~43
GEARFIELD, Nat. 20~32
GEARY / GERRY / GARRY / GURREY / GARY / GAREY, Catharine 260~25 Elbridge 260~25 Loved 16~22 Seth 16~21, 21~14
GEDDES, [Mr.] 253~24
GEE, [Mr.] 148~41 Debroah 297~19 Solomon 81~43, 165~37

GEEAR see GEAR
GEER see GEAR
GELLET / GILLET / GALLAT, [Rev.] 6~45 [Widow] 2~28 Anne 200~27 Augustus 32~18 Eliphalet 199~12 Ely 200~13, 200~17 Irene 6~45 Mary (Gurley) 199~12 Patty 200~25 Phebe 2d 200~18 Solomon L. 200~26 Zenas 50~22
GEOFFRAY see JEFFERY
GEORGE, David 268~2, 275~14 Enos 203~27 Jean 183~31 Lemuel 180~31 Mary 275~14 Paul 254~43 Paul P. 254~51 Sophia (Chesley) 203~28 Thomas 32~3 Timothy 116~33
GERALD / GEROULD, Samuel 68~11
GERE see GEAR
GERMAN / JERMAIN, Rebecca 280~29 W. 38~16
GEROULD see GERALD
GERRISH, Enoch 92~13, 233~50 Samuel 1~36 William 6~26 Zilpha H. 105~22
GERRY see GEARY
GETCHELL / GATCHELL / GITCHELL, [children] 148~36 [Mrs.] 148~46 Daniel 148~35
GETMAN / GETTMAN, G. 38~16 George 63~16, 367~64 John 38~17, 39~8, 367~48, 367~50 William 63~16, 367~63
GETTMAN see GETMAN
GEYER, F.W. 32~9, 44~41, 314~54 Frederic W. 27~20 Frederick W. 28~6 Frederick William 46~15, 114~53 John J. 287~42 Peter 155~14 Polly (Sancry) 155~14 Susan 114~53
GIBAUT, John 207~51
GIBSON, [children?] 75~37 [Mr.] 75~37 [Mrs.] 75~37 Ann (Seavey) 280~54 Elizabeth 156~2 Frances 171~39 Gabriel B. 61~37 John 105~46, 163~10, 323~3 Sukey 286~26 William 75~19, 151~14, 151~18
GIDDINGE see GIDDINGS
GIDDINGS / GIDINS / GIDDINGE, Ann 127~12 Anna 225~41 Eliphalet 225~42 John 211~33 Joshua 279~32 Nathaniel 225~40 Sally 114~48
GIDEONS, [Capt.] 245~40 Mary 245~39
GIDINS see GIDDINGS
GIDNEY, Joshua 52~40
GIFFORD, [widow] 216~11 John 216~11
GILBERT, [Capt.] 14~49 [Judge] 250~32 Calvin 110~26 Charles 187~54 David 95~22, 103~55 Elizabeth 182~36 Frederick 129~1 Maria (———) 155~48 Moses 95~21 Sophia 250~31 Theodosia (Barret) 110~26 Thomas 6~14 Wheat 111~37 Whitman 292~57
GILCHREAST see GILCHRIST
GILCHRIST / GILCHREAST, Elizabeth 225~25 James 212~45
GILE, Asa 355~37 Richard 278~26
GILES / JILES / GYLES, [family] 192~31 [Mr.] 272~18 Anna 83~38 Frances Ann (Gwynn) 319~16 Hannah 207~54 James L. 133~14 John 213~52 Levi 361~39 Nabby 65~41 Samuel 278~19 William B. 319~15
GILKEY, William 316~49
GILL / GUILL, Betsey 153~46 David 148~27 John 111~12 Sarah 148~27 Susannah 99~47
GILLESPIE / GALLESPIE, James 178~34
GILLET see GELLET
GILLEY, John 305~20
GILLINGHAM, Elizabeth 127~39
GILLMORE see GILMORE
GILMAN, [Gov.] 156~15, 260~36 Allen 265~23, 269~52 Bartholomew 12~44 Benjamin R. 353~9 Caroline (Chase) 353~9 Charles Frederick 288~33 Constantine 53~31, 113~16 Daniel 156~15 David 81~24 Dorothea F. 324~54 Eleanor (Brewer) 265~23, 269~52 Eliza 84~28, 353~8 Elizabeth 187~56 Frederick 23~9 Hannah 99~26 Henry 188~58 J.W. 364~10 John 36~53 John T. 80~23, 286~15, 324~35 John W. 361~38 Joseph 56~23, 243~15 Joseph S. 362~16 Joshua 56~31 Nancy (Wiggin) 188~58 Nicholas 80~45, 288~34 Peter 234~37 Polly 199~18 Sally 144~19, 332~43 Tristram 298~3, 332~43 William 160~42, 266~51
GILMORE / GILLMORE, [Mr.] 195~33 Andrew 254~25 Apollo 81~40 Apollos 48~3, 89~53, 165~2 David 202~29 J. 239~18 John 79~3 Jon. 20~25 Mary (———) 297~47 Nathaniel 225~57 Roger 90~6 Sally

202~28
GILPATRICK, Joseph 42~50
GILSON, Amelia 232~13 Michael 9~40 Sukey (Briant) 232~14
GIRNEY see GURNEY
GITCHELL see GETCHELL
GITTEAU, Joshua 50~26
GLEASON / GLEESON, Amos 194~2 Lucy (Hall) 194~2 Ruthy (Cloyes) 53~37 Thaddeus 81~35, 81~41, 133~52 Thomas 298~13 William 53~36
GLEEN, Cornelius 321~42
GLEESON see GLEASON
GLENN / GLEN / GLINN / GLYNN, John 231~50 Mary 260~31
GLIDDEN / GLIDEN / GLIDDIN, Jacob 111~15 Jonathan 36~23, 60~43, 86~5, 296~29 Mary 353~7 Polly (Prouty) 225~2 Thomas 151~23 Willard 225~2
GLIDDIN see GLIDDEN
GLIDEN see GLIDDEN
GLINDEN, Jonathan 45~56
GLINN see GLENN
GLOSSON, Nathan F. 27~45
GLOVER, Edward 167~23 Ichabod 276~55 James 215~4 Jonathan 175~33 Josiah 154~23
GLYNN see GLENN
GODDARD, [children] 295~19 [Mrs.] 295~19 Archelaus 93~13 Betsey (Low) 93~13 Edward 7~1 Hannah 268~30 John 268~30, 354~9 Jonathan 133~22 Mary (Storer) 225~51, 271~22 Rebecca 106~22 Samuel 254~15 Silas 292~8, 295~17 Simon 295~18 William 225~51, 271~22
GODFREY, Isaac 318~42 Mary (Jenison) 100~39 Solomon 100~39, 114~6
GODWIN, Burgo (?) 322~49
GOFF, [child] 111~50 Anthony 148~9 Esther 283~19 Martha (Finten) 148~9 S. 111~50
GOGGIN, Jacob 152~52
GOGSWELL see COGSWELL
GOING see GOWING
GOINGS see GOWING
GOLCORD see COLCORD
GOLD see GOULD
GOLDSBOROUGH, H. 50~36
GOLDSBURY, Sally (Jones) 299~52 Samuel 299~52
GOLDSMITH, John 74~49, 82~43 Josiah 6~32
GOLDTHWAIT see GOLDTHWAITE
GOLDTHWAITE / GOLDTHWAIT, Hannah (———) 59~52, 194~44 Sarah 229~39 Susanna 180~25 Thomas 43~12
GOOCH / GOOGE, William 186~52
GOOD, Asahel 93~56
GOODALE / GOODALL / GOODELL, [Mr.] 229~34, 312~28 Anne 278~1 Bartholomew 98~41 Emma 252~44 Enos 316~13 Henry 182~11 Nathan 252~34 Oliver 81~23 Sarah 98~40, 319~44 Solomon 69~47 Speedy 137~43
GOODALL see GOODALE
GOODELL see GOODALE
GOODENOUGH see GOODENOW
GOODENOW / GOODENOUGH / GOODNOW, Asel 234~17 Caleb 70~39 Fanny 123~28, 234~17 Nahum 174~4 Rebeckah (———) 260~26 Rebekah (———) 57~15 Sally 208~53 Sally C. 310~16 Sterling 211~12 William 294~40
GOODHUE, [Dr.] 142~16 Ann (Willard) 172~51 Benjamin 172~51 Ebenezer 103~6 Francis 28~55, 326~52, 326~53 Joseph 65~19, 107~31 Nancy 140~13 Rebecca 230~31 Rebekah 231~4 William 38~50, 277~14
GOODING, Daniel 250~15 Mercy 184~44 Sarah F. 353~5
GOODMAN, Asa 200~53
GOODNOW see GOODENOW
GOODRICH / GOODRIDGE, [Miss] 296~46 Abigail 292~5 Amos 236~48 Ansel 147~3 Asael 106~6 Asahel 93~56 Betsey 219~57 Chauncey 187~17 Eliphalet 240~14 Elizur 96~3 Jeremiah 67~31 Josiah 142~33, 231~46 Levi 32~4 Lucy 233~10 Mary Ann 187~16 Millicent 236~47 S. 258~42 Sewall 295~7 Thuril 137~31
GOODRIDGE see GOODRICH
GOODWILLIE, Polly 249~41

GOODWIN, [Mr.] 99~29 Abigail 69~57 Charles 68~24 Comfort 318~3 David 353~30 Elizabeth 318~3 Frances 182~35 Isaac C. 353~30 Israel 70~1 John 102~26 Mary 270~25 Mary (Munroe) 102~26 Molly 69~57 Nathan 270~25 Rhode 69~57 Ruth 69~57 Sarah 251~18 Theophilus 70~1 Thomas 6~46 William 196~48 Willson 49~9
GOOGE see GOOCH
GOOGINS see GOOKIN
GOOKIN / GOOKINS / GOOGINS, Samuel 165~42 Sarah 165~43
GOOKINS see GOOKIN
GOOLD see GOULD
GOOSS, Adam 173~9
GORBET, [Mr.] 291~54
GORDAN see GORDON
GORDON / GORDAN, [Mr.] 133~24 [Mrs.] 256~43 D. 48~52 Elizabeth 99~21 James 176~56, 189~28 John 79~15 Mary 253~42 Mercy 177~25 Nancy (Pitcher) 176~57 Samuel 136~26 Stephen 369~34 William 119~27, 256~44
GORE, John 120~40 Mary G. (Babcock) 120~40
GORHAM, Edward 283~48 Lucy 283~47 Mary 65~17 William 164~18
GORTON, [children] 21~54 Betsy 21~53 Jonathan 21~54 Lydia 288~28
GOSLIN, [Mr.] 261~12
GOSS / GASS, Elenor 289~32 Eliza 354~28 John 76~50 John P. 354~53
GOULD / GOLD / GOOLD, Asa 23~47 Benjamin 303~49 Betsey 210~27 Betsy (———) (Keyes) 230~1 Daniel 27~45 Eben. 20~22 Gideon 304~56 Henry 229~57 Isaiah (Eaton) 278~41 John 129~27 Jonathan 69~46, 82~46 Josiah 123~9 Lucy 255~56 Maria Theresa 238~44 Nancy 41~4 Nathan 309~42 Nathaniel 207~4, 273~31, 278~41 Reuben 20~18 Sally 299~14 T. 62~20 Thomas 238~45 Wales 328~18 William 207~23
GOUVERNEUR / GOUVERNER, [Miss] 38~46 Nicholas 123~53
GOVE, [Mrs.] 193~34 Abner 193~34 Hannah Langdon 186~5 Jesse 289~24 Sophia (Ingersol) 289~24
GOWING / GOING / GOINGS, Esther 65~10, 65~38 James 202~27
GOY see GAY
GRACIE see GRACY
GRACY / GRACIE, George 226~11
GRAFF, C. 230~16 William 305~10
GRAFTON, [Rev.] 162~10 Hannah (Parker) 219~55 Joseph 219~54 Sally 162~10
GRAGG see GREGG
GRAHAM / GRAHAME / GRAM, [Mr. & Mrs.] 130~53 A. 236~43 Archibald 237~6 David 195~33 Hans 161~1 Hans (?) 269~27 Jane (?) 269~26 John 195~34, 289~19 John A. 224~29 Nancy 309~53 Priscilla (Eaton) 224~29 Sally 260~16 Samuel 27~32 William 68~10
GRAHAME see GRAHAM
GRAM see GRAHAM
GRANDEY, Benjamin 65~42 Susannah (Leet) 65~42
GRANGE, [Mrs.] 192~32
GRANGER, [Mr.] 191~21 Amelia 61~30 Gideon 77~18, 213~5
GRANNIS / GRANNISS, Edward 232~23 Melinda (Dustin) 245~41 Timothy 14~53 William 245~40
GRANNISS see GRANNIS
GRANT, [Mr.] 75~12, 322~36 Asa 299~5 James 86~46 John 123~11, 248~30 Joshua 332~44 Mary 332~8 Mercy (Tetherly) 86~47 Nathaniel 248~30 Ruth 116~25 Samuel 25~30, 27~9, 30~28, 31~7, 73~10, 128~23, 131~22, 210~42, 285~38, 293~50, 302~27, 309~52, 327~10, 332~8
GRATTAN see GROTON
GRAUPNER, [Mr.] 39~45
GRAVE, Betsey 56~38
GRAVES / GRIEVES / GREAVES, [Lord] 117~13 [Mr.] 47~42 [Mrs.] 157~10 [Rev.] 254~1 Amos 227~18, 333~38 Daniel 36~22 Darius 227~18, 327~9 Elizabeth (Sylvester) 49~55 Experience 260~23 Ezekiel 28~16 John 30~37, 227~17 Lydia 30~40 Nathaniel 167~36 Orange 48~5, 90~50, 136~49, 159~7 Pamela (Forward) 254~1 Phineas 239~54 Rufus 3~13, 34~11 Samuel 49~55 Samuel 2d 227~16 Susannah 85~47 widow 323~45 Zeruah 164~4
GRAY / GREY, (———) 72~45 [Mrs.] 100~10 Catharine 208~34 Edward 189~8 Helen 323~12 John 110~44, 194~10 Lydia 100~1 Mary (Brooks) 38~44 Phebe 6~36 Robert 53~11, 100~10, 123~10 Samuel 38~44, 163~49 Sarah (Fitts) 183~46 Simeon 183~46 William 224~40
GREAVES see GRAVES
GREELE see GREELEY
GREELEY / GREELE / GREELY, [Mrs.] 58~51 Frances 86~50 Jonathan 20~31
GREELY see GREELEY
GREEN / GREENE, [Mr.] 10~42, 27~20 Abigail 139~2 Alexander 371~34 Andrew 44~17 Benjamin 66~40 Bethiah (Hopkins) 92~4 Daniel 15~6 David 92~4 Ebenezer 122~45 Elizabeth 66~40 Hannah 221~3 Isaac 57~7, 229~33 Joel 224~24 John 53~11, 95~37 Joseph 108~17, 154~45 Josiah 240~26 Judith 139~42 Levi 25~34, 71~15, 295~35, 316~17 Lucy (Horton) 224~25 Lucy (Merriam) 265~28 Lydia 10~27 Nathaniel 240~34 Philip 143~41 Rebecca 65~46, 232~22 Sally F. 87~46 Samuel 131~48, 349~42 Sarah 195~16 T.K. 74~48 Tabitha 36~34, 163~46 Thomas 164~23 Thomas K. 33~41, 41~55, 87~27 Thomas R. 14~15 Timothy 232~22 Ushall 12~27 William 39~38, 40~5, 143~41 William E. 265~28
GREENE see GREEN
GREENLEAF / GREENLIEF, Clarina P. 107~45 Daniel 62~16 Enoch 176~29 Gardner 286~42 Israel 140~2 Mary 131~36 Polly (Chamberlain) 62~16 Richard 285~28 Ruth 361~42 Stephen 88~8 Thomas 27~26 Timothy 106~4 William 146~37
GREENLIEF see GREENLEAF
GREENMAN, Hannah 287~38
GREENO see GREENOUGH
GREENOUGH / GREENO, Daniel 280~56 Sally 216~46 Violet 155~56 William 173~53, 214~19
GREENWOOD, [Mrs.] 133~32 Elizabeth V. 112~26 Nathaniel 112~27
GREGG / GRIGG / GRAGG, [Mr.] 164~49 Aaron 175~34 Joseph 138~50
GREGORY, George 158~40, 183~30 Martha (Thompson) 262~26 Nathaniel 289~1 Sally (Cutting) 289~33 William 289~32
GREW / GROW, Henry 122~31, 296~12 John 328~16 Susannah 296~11 Susannah (Pittman) 122~31
GREY see GRAY
GRIDLEY, Joseph 178~9 Samuel 57~19 Sarah 178~10
GRIEVES see GRAVES
GRIFFIN / GRIFIN, Allen 309~2 Asa 327~29 David 31~18, 309~41 John 93~16 Kezia 155~18 Moses 123~1 Samuel 120~19
GRIFFITH see GRIFFITHS
GRIFFITHS / GRIFFITH, [Mr.] 11~29, 266~35 John 234~29 Ralph 154~34 Robert 214~57
GRIFIN see GRIFFIN
GRIGG see GREGG
GRIGGS, Gideon 28~46
GRINDAL see GRINDALL
GRINDALL / GRINDEL / GRINDAL / GRINNELL, Charlotte 310~24
GRINDEL see GRINDALL
GRINGER, John 286~50
GRINNELL see GRINDALL
GRISWOLD / GRISWOULD, [child] 152~39 [Mr.] 112~3 Asel 26~24 Daniel 304~31 David H. 117~48 Elisha 116~43 Ethan 50~32 Gaylord 293~32 Gilbert 48~4, 174~13, 222~2, 275~10, 281~9, 283~41, 309~55 H. 272~42 Jeremiah 192~45 Joseph 234~19 Josiah 56~24, 152~39, 227~17 Lois 287~35 Lucy (Darby) 192~45 Mary 316~48 Matthew 39~34 Samuel 282~8 Shubael 281~23 Stanley 188~43, 256~12, 322~30, 371~26 Stephen 81~25, 89~51
GRISWOULD see GRISWOLD
GROCHAN, Adelle (de Grasse) 86~48 John 86~48
GROESBECK, Garret 281~27
GROMET, [Mrs.] 253~20 John 253~20
GROOM, George 78~35 William 272~47
GROSS, [Mrs.] 207~33 [Rev.] 207~33, 214~1 Esther

(Hilliard) 293~22 Gilbert 293~21 Phebe 255~27 Thomas 213~58
GROSVENOR, Ebenezer 171~46   Eliza 131~31   Eliza (Clark) 171~46
GROTON / GRATTAN, [Col.] 85~52 Lucia C. 85~52
GROUARD, James 252~55
GROUT, [child] 128~32 [Major] 256~25 [widow] 128~32 Andrew 138~49, 256~21 Azubah 132~9, 142~2 Azubah (———) 276~18 Daniel 11~45, 103~15, 128~31, 132~9, 306~11 Elijah 227~54 Hannah (Stebbins) 147~47 Jehasophat 259~25 John 147~47 Jon. 1~45 Jonathan 81~29, 136~13, 226~25 Lucinda (Slader) 234~44 Lucinda (Slader?) 146~56 Mindwell 103~15 Nancy 142~2 Nathaniel 146~56, 234~45 Thomas 173~4 William 292~33
GROVE, Jno. 11~9
GROVER, Benjamin 72~55 Hannah 147~6 James 195~7
GROW see **GREW**
GROWER, Joseph 59~18
GRUBB, Nancy H. 121~16
GRUBER, Gabriel 201~27
GUERNSEY / GARNSEY / GURNSEY, Amos 183~14 Eldad 1~23 James 151~13
GUEST, Betsey 128~13
GUILD, Jesse 3~15 Joseph 303~50 Rufus 3~15, 81~39 Samuel 3~15
GUILE, William 309~54
GUILL see **GILL**
GULLION, Patrick 219~24
GUNDY, Joseph 140~53
GUNN, James 6~2, 99~1 Mary Jane 6~2
GUNNISON, Samuel 241~12 William 316~55
GURLEY see **GURLY**
GURLY / GURLEY, Grace (Stackpole) 71~32 John W. 71~31 Mary 199~12
GURNEY / GIRNEY, [Mrs.] 190~10 [Rev.] 190~10
GURNSEY see **GUERNSEY**
GURREY see **GEARY**
GURVIN see **GARVIN**
GUSTIN / GASTON, [child] 263~52 Mary 263~52 Rufus 263~52
GUY see **GAY**
GWIN / GWYNN, Frances Ann 319~16 Thomas Peyton 319~16
GWYNN see **GWIN**
GYLES see **GILES**

H.

H———, A——— 201~5
HACKET see **HACKETT**
HACKETT / HACKET / HAGGETT / HAGGET, Emery 354~22 Isaiah 309~53 W. 286~34
HACKWOOD, Samuel 314~19
HADLEY, George 230~57, 232~25 Jacob 140~33 Joshua 294~34 Lydia 230~57, 232~25 Timothy 132~38
HADLOCK, Patty 249~39
HAGAR / HAGER, [family] 332~21 Amos 307~46 Jane (Atkins) 142~27 Joel 194~51 Peter 63~12 Sarah 99~21 Uriah 142~27
HAGARTY, [Mr.] 50~57 John 296~4
HAGEMAN, Ellen 173~30
HAGER see **HAGAR**
HAGGET(T) see **HACKETT**
HAGINS see **HIGGINS**
HAGUE, [Lieut.] 303~23
HAIL(E) see **HALE**
HAINES / HAYNES / HAYNE / HAINS, [widow] 290~47 Abigail 303~51 Betsey 99~54 John 70~53, 290~43 Mary (Hall) 70~53 Samuel 162~17
HAINEY see **HANEY**
HAINS see **HAINES**
HAINY see **HANEY**
HAIR see **HARE**
HALE / HAILE / HAIL, [Col.] 148~22 Abel 46~56, 47~2 Ambrose 111~40 Amos 110~20 Ann 267~35 Asa 305~51 Bezaleel 177~26 Dorcas 207~10 Dorothy 161~37 Hannah (Swazey) 113~5 Israel 172~5   J.R. 74~33 Jno. R. 16~23 John 118~18 Jonathan R. 24~41, 24~54, 68~58 Joseph 113~5 Joshua 27~40, 42~24, 65~54, 89~40 Lois (Smith) 289~29 Lucy 111~40 Mary 303~11 Mary (———) (Porter) 190~20 Mary (Wood) 172~5 Moses 68~12, 97~5, 118~18, 129~23, 141~41, 143~56, 178~25, 190~20, 241~6, 292~25 Rachel 271~33 Richard 261~4 Richard Page 97~5 Robert 1~25 Salma 297~44 Salmon 289~29 Samuel 267~36 Stephen 115~51 Sukey (Waldron) 115~51 Thomas 14~40, 289~17 Timothy 94~15 William 291~4 Zacheus 310~26
HALEY, Mary 225~23
HALL, [boy] 107~25, 218~46 [Capt.] 246~49 [child] 329~47 [Dr.] 211~34 [Judge] 216~38 [Mr.] 135~14, 293~13, 297~42, 330~25 [Mrs.] 3~40, 126~26, 128~7   A.   161~21 Abigail 80~13, 143~11, 325~49 Abijah 241~53 Abraham 189~51 Alexander 82~17 Andrew 191~15 Anna 209~47 Atherton 158~46, 287~43 Augustus 61~33 Benjamin 80~12, 115~42, 115~43, 143~2, 143~8, 278~31, 325~50 Betsey (Stone) 270~54 Betsy 335~5 Calvin 61~50 Chloe 74~35 Cornelia 186~36 Cyrus 238~49 David 189~13, 204~22, 251~52 Delia 40~3 Desire 287~33 Dorcas 79~6   E.A. 74~37 Ebenezer 60~3, 64~33, 191~43 Ed. 325~49 Edward 13~41, 32~49, 35~30, 55~33, 241~53, 304~3, 332~21 Elihu 333~44 Elijah 92~55, 94~2, 245~6 Elijah A. 81~16, 87~28 Elisha 30~38, 227~18 Elisha 2d 212~8 Eliza (Fox) 200~32 Elizabeth 101~21, 172~3 Emerson 83~9 Ephraim 248~51 Fitch 296~2 Frederick 111~27 George 265~47 George H. 90~34 Henry 369~49 Henry (?) 136~41 Hezekiah 280~14 Horace 127~54, 134~51, 186~45, 206~55, 206~57, 226~28 Horatio Gates 50~15 Hulda 294~27 Isaac 221~32, 280~14 Jairus 218~46   James 28~19, 68~57, 107~25, 272~49, 310~23, 332~55 Jerusha (Kilborn) 136~41 Job W. 123~8 John 80~24, 172~7, 232~47, 329~47 John W. 56~12 Jonathan 30~38, 68~13, 126~26 Jonathan P. 209~41 Joseph 166~13 Joshua 94~3 Loisa (Morgan) 172~7 Lot 300~4, 305~44 Lucinda (Badger) 212~8 Lucy 194~2 Lydia 204~24, 251~53 Mary 70~53 Mary (Deming) 265~47 Matthew 274~2 Miles 11~47, 254~48 Moody 323~49 Moses 147~38 Nath. 304~19 Nathaniel 25~42, 82~38, 98~17, 114~41, 133~51, 325~29 Obed 200~32 Oliver 10~16, 16~7, 127~54, 134~51, 183~6, 186~44, 206~55 Paul 353~4 Polly 249~39, 305~45 Prescott 281~54 Ralph 289~21 Richard 195~9 Roxina 172~5 Ruth 158~45 S. 361~28 Sally (Cutting) 238~50 Sally (Hardy) 102~6 Samuel 113~31, 228~25 Sarah (Leighton) 353~4 Seth 61~32, 81~15, 101~45, 189~23, 195~40 Simeon G. 102~6 Solon 272~49 Stephen 321~36 Susannah 60~3 Thomas 166~30, 166~35, 294~27 Timothy 161~20   W.B. 307~19 Willard P. 270~54 William 7~29, 61~31, 93~7, 98~14, 206~49 William T. 145~2
HALLADAY see **HOLLIDAY**
HALLAM, Lewis 284~52
HALLECK / HALLOCK, [children] 257~30   Henry 257~30 Sarah 257~30
HALLEGAN / HALLIGAN / HALLIGHAN / HILLIGAN, James 220~55, 239~24, 240~20, 243~55, 372~2, 372~48
HALLEY see **HAWLEY**
HALLIG(H)AN see **HALLEGAN**
HALLMAN see **HOLMAN**
HALLOCK see **HALLECK**
HALLOWELL / HALWELL, Charles 39~28 Lois (———) (Miller) 39~28 Rebecca (———) 106~54
HALWELL see **HALLOWELL**
HAM / HAMM, Conrad W. 179~4 George 327~45 George Washington 327~46 John 224~41 Samuel 268~4 William 140~38
HAMANT see **HAMET**
HAMBLEN see **HAMLIN**
HAMBLIN see **HAMLIN**
HAMET / HAMANT, [Mrs.] 156~16 Peter 156~17 Samuel 156~16
HAMILTON, (———) 133~46 [boy] 148~39 [Dr.] 67~4 [Gen.] 107~17, 172~18 [Mr.] 178~29,

194~36, 227~2 Alexander 145~30 Charity (Carpenter) 114~10 Comfort 114~10 Dolly 247~41 George L. 59~54 James 30~36 John 247~42 Joseph 186~9 Joshua 247~41 P. 107~17 Samuel 17~43 Sarah 271~31
HAMINGWAY see HEMINWAY
HAMLIN / HAMBLIN / HAMBLEN, [Capt.] 256~25 [children] 203~9 [widow] 203~9 Joseph 110~19
HAMM see HAM
HAMMATT see HAMMETT
HAMMEKEN, Eliza (Ogden) 199~11 George 199~10
HAMMETT / HAMMET / HAMMATT, Benjamin 189~10
HAMMOND, [child?] 45~2 [Mrs.] 45~3 Abel 45~1, 227~37 Abigail 313~19 Benjamin 307~17 David 45~1 Dorothy 225~12 Experience (Stanley) 235~8 Hannah 182~16 James D. 179~16 John 192~10, 221~19 Josiah 235~8 Mary 230~17 Moses 225~12 Sally 233~10
HAMPSON, [Mr.] 112~51
HAMPTON, [Dr.] 199~44 Richard 175~43
HAMTRAMCK, John F. 141~11
HANAFORD / HANFORD / HANNAFORD / HUNEFORD / HANNIFORD, [Widow] 273~18
HANCHETT, [child] 149~15 Thomas 149~15
HANCOCK, [children] 141~38 [widow] 141~38 John 170~19, 178~55 William 141~36
HANCOCKS, George 26~14
HAND, [Capt.] 148~34 John 370~9
HANDERSON see HENDERSON
HANDLEY / HANLEY / HENLEY, Rebecca 172~9
HANDY / HENDEE, Hast. 231~32 Josiah 103~11
HANEY / HAINEY / HEANY / HAINY, Fred. 38~17 Frederick 39~7, 367~48, 367~50
HANFORD see HANAFORD
HANLEY see HANDLEY
HANNA see HANNAH
HANNAFORD see HANAFORD
HANNAH / HANNA, John A. 206~19
HANNARS see HANNAS
HANNAS / HANNARS, John 78~11 Nancy 316~52
HANNIFORD see HANAFORD
HANSCAM see HANSCOM
HANSCOM / HANSCOMB / HANSCAM, [Mrs.] 38~38 James 38~30
HANSCOMB see HANSCOM
HANSEN see HANSON
HANSON / HANSEN, Alexander Contee 228~14 William 357~1
HANTSBERGER, Peter 367~58
HAPGOOD, Solomon 8~50
HARBACK, Polly 236~44
HARD see HURD
HARDEIN see HARDING
HARDEN see HARDING
HARDENBERGH, Elias 157~40
HARDEY see HARDY
HARDIN see HARDING
HARDING / HARDEN / HARDEIN / HARDIN, Hezekiah 50~2 Jonathan 142~25 Joshua 1~36 Persis 62~39 Persis (Stevens) 142~15 Polly 334~30 Polly (Howard) 324~17 Sally (Seamons) 50~2 Stephen 281~6 Willard 324~17
HARDWICK see HARDWICKE
HARDWICKE / HARDWICK, Martha 291~30
HARDY / HARTY / HARDEY, [Mr.] 201~53, 225~15, 226~2, 269~31 Anna 87~32 Daniel 92~9 Hannah (Marston) 92~9 John 20~33 Jonathan 20~31 Mary 133~32 Polly (Belknap) 149~20 R. 331~42 Rebecca 313~47 S. 149~20 Sally 102~6 Samuel 296~32
HARE / HAIR, [Mrs.] 149~16
HARFORD see HARTFORD
HARGILL, [child] 63~42 William 63~42
HARLEY see HURLEY
HARLIUN, Joseph 175~21 Sally (la Croix) 175~21
HARLOW, Avery 205~10 David 310~24
HARMAN see HARMON
HARMAR, [Gen.] 249~44 Charles 249~44
HARMON / HARMAN / HORMAN, [Capt.] 355~27 Daniel 202~19 Ebenezer 275~56
HARN see HORN

HARNES / HARNS, David 2~30
HARNS see HARNES
HAROLD see HARROLD
HARP, [Messrs.] 47~40 William 147~3
HARPER, John 36~50
HARRAT / HARROD / HEROD, [Capt.] 141~45 Ann 194~40 Mary 176~28
HARRIMAN / HERRIMAN, [————] 355~8 Sarah (————) (Silver) 103~13 Stephen 103~13
HARRINGTON / HERRINGTON / HERINGTON, [Mr.] 127~1 Ann (————) (Bridge) 195~11 Antipas 136~20 Asa 304~27, 316~48 Clarissa 268~31 Eli 132~54, 289~19 Elizabeth (————) (Renous) 73~14 Ephraim 140~34 Grace 216~13 Henry W. 298~43 Isaac 203~36 John 268~31 Jonathan 160~16 Joseph 268~31 Leonard 28~21 Lese 84~29 Lucy (Hunewell) 160~16 Lydia 284~16 Mary H. 196~37 Meriam 85~50 Philorus 268~31 Rebecca 357~36 Robert 73~14 Ruth 229~20 Samuel 284~16 Susannah 132~54 Timothy 114~55, 195~12
HARRIS, [Mr.] 54~6 Abel 133~10, 272~18 Abigail (Chapin) 301~42 Abner 27~3 Benjamin 183~11, 371~6 Bridget 10~6 Elizabeth (————) (Hempstead) 218~3 Ephraim 291~18 Helen Lucinda 219~20 Isam 193~44 James 110~9 James B. 144~16, 144~25 Jeremiah 2~57 Job 133~38 John 2~50, 53~35, 169~2, 325~47, 364~41 Joseph 185~44 Lucretia (Lord) 185~44 Lydia (Cox) 291~18 Mary (Poor) 53~35, 364~41 Paul 201~24 Preserved 4~31 Robert 272~8, 308~54 Sally (————) 54~43 Samuel 215~44, 329~13 Thomas 219~20, 301~42 Timothy 7~40 Walter 266~37 William 218~3 William M. 317~21
HARRISON, [Capt.] 114~34 Betsey 92~5 Elihu 240~33 John 102~34, 165~38 William 204~37
HARROD see HARRAT
HARROLD / HERRALD / HAROLD, Elizabeth (Conner) 118~16 Joseph 118~16
HARRY, Thomas 155~28
HARSLET see HAZLITT
HART / HERT, [Mrs.] 18~44, 64~13, 133~10 Abner 92~2 Alcis E. 191~42 Almira (Thompson) 92~2 Bliss 288~39 Delia Maria 202~34 Elizabeth 184~54 Emma 307~56 Esther 277~22 Ichabod W. 304~36 Jemima (————) 199~14 Joseph B. 335~46 Josiah 2~48, 8~52, 13~32, 209~43 Levi 284~52 Mathew 18~45 Richard P. 202~35 Ruth 114~45 Samuel 128~54 Solomon 196~1 Theodore 316~40 William 133~31
HARTFORD / HARFORD, Joseph 95~10 Joshua 101~22
HARTHAN, Lucius 357~26
HARTHAWAY see HATHAWAY
HARTLEY, Thomas 78~34
HARTLINE, John Adam 243~37
HARTSHORN, Abigail 293~33 Mary 282~12 Thomas 293~34
HARTSTENE, Joachim 146~43
HARTUNG, [Mrs.] 41~17 Godfrey 41~14
HARTUPIE, Catharine 49~56
HARTWELL / HEARTWELL, [Mr.] 121~45, 172~47, 195~37, 237~20 Amos 307~41 Elizabeth 215~28 Ephraim 233~6 George 167~58 Joseph 82~50
HARTY see HARDY
HARVEY / HERVEY / HERVY / HORVEY, Asahel 101~44 Ebenezer 87~29, 289~51 Ezra 231~21 James 211~54, 306~18 Joshua 137~53, 282~9 Mary 169~7 Mat. 183~12 Matt. 38~2 Nathan 191~13 Rebecca 166~33 Rebecca (Plummer) 152~21 Robert 152~21 Timothy 89~40 William 259~15
HARWOOD, Clark 95~20 David 283~16 Elizabeth 323~51 James 137~47 John 323~51 Polly 137~47 Rebecca 283~17
HASBROOK, Jonathan 105~3
HASELTINE / HAZELTON / HASELTON / HESSELTINE / HASSELTINE / HAZELTINE, [Rev.] 41~33 David 100~37 Jane 319~35 John 218~28, 319~35 Lucy 218~27 Mary (Ward) 100~37 Richard 43~23 Ruth 249~41
HASELTON see HASELTINE
HASHAM, Mayhew 8~3
HASKELL / HASKEL, [widow] 51~9 Abraham 374~3 Caleb 118~41 Daniel 322~33 Elizabeth 120~42 Hannah 35~50 Huldah 252~39 John 211~40 Josiah 53~21

Levi 51~6 Nancy (Fox) 118~42 Roger 301~13 William 238~16
HASKINS / HOSKINS, Eliza (Foxcroft) 98~51 Thomas 98~51
HASLET see HAZLITT
HASSELTINE see HASELTINE
HASTINGS, [Dr.] 181~19   C. 285~30 Elizabeth (——) (Jackson) 64~28 Esther (Woodward) 232~15 J. 258~50 John 68~47, 81~37, 171~49, 213~47, 252~2 Jonathan 33~26 Joseph 245~11 Josiah 3~12 Lemuel 136~17 Louisa 307~21 Mary 183~26 Moses W. 134~53 Moses Willard 146~21 Nathan 232~15 Oliver 33~26, 111~16, 157~44, 333~35 Seth 285~30 Susannah 118~48 Sylvanus 274~50 Thomas 64~28 Willard 8~24 William 89~14
HASTY, [Mr.] 133~33
HASWELL, Anthony J. 308~22   J.M. 78~35 Lucy 308~22
HATCH, Abigail 327~14 Alpheus 272~29 Ann 117~50 Asa 208~10, 209~13 Azel 288~11, 325~1, 327~15 Eliza 280~30 Fanny 290~29 Ichabod 325~1 Israel 249~11 Joel 171~56 Joseph 115~3 Lucinda 260~27 Lucy (Andrews) 324~15 Narcissa (Birch) 159~47 Perses 139~46 Phinehas 139~46 Reuben 280~31, 324~15 Sally (Hutchinson) 272~30 Sarah 179~8 Seth 186~53 Triphene 86~31 Urial C. 110~22 Uriel C. 153~42, 159~47
HATHAWAY / HARTHAWAY / HATHWAY, [boys] 34~22 [Mr.] 34~23 Ebenezer 273~11
HATHORNE see HAWTHORN
HATHWAY see HATHAWAY
HAUER, John 17~27
HAUGHTON see HOUGHTON
HAVEN, [Dr.] 320~34 [Mr.?] 334~14 [Mr.] 374~19 Henry 133~25   J. 133~42, 133~42, 325~44 James 331~16 Jason 141~16 John 272~15 Margaret 233~17 Mehetable 331~16 N.A. 133~42 Nathaniel A. 272~14 Samuel 133~23, 232~36, 233~17 Susanna 265~52
HAVENS / HEVINS, [family] 333~11 James 143~7 Jonathan N. 53~8 Stratton 333~10
HAWARD see HAYWARD
HAWELL see HOWELL
HAWES / HAWS / HOWES, Edmand 320~5   Hilkiah 225~17 Jonathan 105~28
HAWK / HAWKE, [Lord] 195·-51 Jonathan 80~17 Moses 80~18, 115~44
HAWKE see HAWK
HAWKES see HAWKS
HAWKIN see HAWKINS
HAWKINS / HAWKIN, Clarina B. 213~13 Daniel 17~42, 21~23, 28~9 Ephraim 28~9
HAWKS / HAWKES, John 143~10 Moses 143~11, 278~37, 304~21 Ruthy 148~6
HAWLEY / HOLLY / HALLEY / HOLLEY, Horace 213~7, 293~9 Joseph 271~19 Marcy 271~19 Sarah 179~52 Tamar 191~2
HAWS see HAWES
HAWTHORN / HATHORNE, Eliza (Manning) 96~51 Nathaniel 96~50
HAY, Eliza (Monroe) 283~45 George 283~45 Udney 257~16
HAYDEN / HEYDEN, [Mr.] 135~14 Anna (Williams) 76~57 Charles 76~57 Frances 262~30 Lebah 300~53 Lettia 230~16 Nathaniel 155~28 Sarah (Oliver) 300~53 William 146~38
HAYDOCK, James 213~18
HAYES / HAYS, [Miss] 297~2 Harriot 324~28 Joseph 136~26   M.M. 194~10 Polly 83~39 Samuel 110~32
HAYNE see HAINES
HAYNES see HAINES
HAYS see HAYES
HAYWARD / HAWARD / HEYWOOD / HAYWOOD, [child] 163~26 [children] 153~26 [Mr.] 39~51, 135~8 Amaziah 153~26 Anna 51~50 Barza 229~7 Benjamin 90~8 Calvin 236~30 Charles 238~24 Daniel 51~50 Hercules 74~36 Isaiah 55~31 Jacob 163~26 James 4~37 Lemuel 321~19 Levi 87~54, 104~6, 215~46 Otis 16~49 Sally 104~46 Samuel 136~43 Sukey (Adams) 229~7 Susannah (——) 138~54 William 47~55, 136~16, 137~22

HAYWOOD see HAYWARD
HAZARD / HAZZARD, Eliza 99~14 John 13~12 Nathaniel 24~13 Patrick 182~13
HAZELTINE see HASELTINE
HAZELTON see HASELTINE
HAZLET see HAZLITT
HAZLETT see HAZLITT
HAZLITT / HASLET / HAZLETT / HARSLET / HAZLET, Enoch 313~6 Nancy 65~45 Phebe 92~30 Rebecca (Crawford) 148~7, 149~22 William 2~6, 148~7, 149~21
HAZZARD see HAZARD
HEAD, Isaac 177~50 John 172~54 Sally (Ross) 172~54
HEALD, Amos 114~13, 300~44 David 72~51, 157~49 E. 283~37 Elizabeth 181~20 John 105~50 Joseph 154~47 Josiah 181~21 Lydia 105~50 Lydia (Edwards) 114~14
HEALEY / HEALY, Jesse 8~24, 109~15, 304~33, 314~37 John 331~15 Joseph 122~21
HEALY see HEALEY
HEAMES, [Mr.] 85~2 [Mrs.] 85~1
HEANY see HANEY
HEARD see HURD
HEARSEE see HERSEY
HEARSEY see HERSEY
HEARTWELL see HARTWELL
HEATH, [Mr.] 160~43 John 160~30 Robert 80~25
HEATON see EATON
HEBARD see HUBBARD
HEBBARD see HUBBARD
HEBBERD see HUBBARD
HEDGE, A. 5~52 Abraham 82~51, 103~56, 298~38 Lemuel 97~57 Samuel 217~48
HEILEMAN see HEILMAN
HEILMAN / HEILEMAN, Amelia 97~13 John F. 97~14
HEINEMAN, Sarah 289~27
HEISTER, Catharine 204~41   D. 158~6
HELDRITH see HILDRETH
HELPMAN, Thankful 65~17
HELYER, Joseph 160~31
HEMENWAY see HEMINWAY
HEMINGWAY see HEMINWAY
HEMINWAY / HAMINGWAY / HEMINGWAY / HEMENWAY, Samuel 307~39
HEMPSTED / HEMPSTED, Elizabeth (——) 218~3 Joshua 25/~3, 259~13
HEMPSTED see HEMPSTEAD
HENDEE see HANDY
HENDERSON / HANDERSON, [Mr.] 27~16 Beersheba 74~2 Daniel 353~12 Elizabeth 353~12 Gideon 91~53 James 133~27, 236~63 John 319~34 Thomas 83~40
HENIDALE, Frances (——) (Lyman) 220~2 Theodore 220~2
HENLEY see HANDLEY
HENMAN see HINMAN
HENNIKER, [Lord] 143~40
HENRY, [Capt.] 289~1 [child] 320~5 [children] 319~22 [Landlord] 23~18 [Lieut.] 256~11 [Mr.] 7~44 [Mrs.] 288~56, 319~22 David 309~45 Hugh 81~17, 131~24 Isaac 59~44 James 180~39, 261~50, 266~28 John 41~40 Joseph 249~39 Mathew 165~42 Michael D. 42~1 Patrick 361~23 Patty (Hadlock) 249~39 Robert 81~36   S. 320~5 Sophia (Duche) 41~41 William 25~2, 55~11, 137~24, 206~56, 207~19, 226~27, 239~31, 244~14, 256~24, 319~22
HENSHAW, Phebe 284~55 Samuel 293~36 William 284~55
HERBERT, Sally 320~22
HERD see HURD
HERICK see HERRICK
HERINGTON see HARRINGTON
HERLEY see HURLEY
HERMAN / HERRMAN, Dolly 122~41
HEROD see HARRAT
HERRALD see HARROLD
HERRECK see HERRICK
HERRICK / HERICK / HERRECK, [children] 114~29 [Mrs.] 114~27 Asa 4~54 Ebenezer 129~4 John 4~54, 6~15 Jonathan 183~11 Joseph 2~12 Mary 270~26 Rufus 114~27
HERRIMAN see HARRIMAN

HERRINGTON see HARRINGTON
HERRMAN see HERMAN
HERSCHELL, [Dr.] 88~14
HERSEY / HEARSEY / HEARSEE, Abigail 291~16 Nancy 89~17
HERT see HART
HERVEY see HARVEY
HERVY see HARVEY
HESSELTINE see HASELTINE
HETHERINGTON, Margaret 167~49
HEVINS see HAVENS
HEWES see HUSE
HEWINS see EWINS
HEWIT see HEWITT
HEWITT / HEWIT, Aaron 258~16 John 126~56 Joseph D. 288~6
HEWSTER, Abigail 38~51
HEYDEN see HAYDEN
HEYWOOD see HAYWARD
HIBBARD see HUBBARD
HIBBERD see HUBBARD
HIBBERT see HUBBARD
HICHBORN, Mercy 76~58
HICKES see HICKS
HICKOK / HICKOX, Amos 186~3 Jeremiah 294~26 William 18~8
HICKOX see HICKOK
HICKS / HIX / HICKES, Jacob 297~19 John 36~30 William 193~37
HIDE see HYDE
HIERNE, [Judge] 88~42
HIGBEE see HIGBY
HIGBY / HIGBEE, [Mrs.] 243~20 [Rev.] 243~20 Abigail 268~13 Jeremiah 1~19, 100~50, 290~40, 316~19 Lemuel 268~13 Lydia 100~50 Miner 321~32
HIGGENS see HIGGINS
HIGGINS / HIGGENS / HAGINS, Isaac 73~44 John 78~33 Ruth 73~44 Seth 5~37 Susannah 207~28
HIGGINSON / HIGINSON, Elizabeth 3~22 Stephen 269~47 Susan 269~47
HIGHLAND, John 59~24
HIGINSON see HIGGINSON
HIGLEY / HIGLY, Brewster 193~11
HIGLY see HIGLEY
HILBURT see HURLBURT
HILDRETH / HILDRITH / HELDRITH, Abigail 131~34 E. 81~8 Ephraim 275~26 James 215~3 Josiah 275~25 Olive 245~38 P.G. 215~4 William 310~41
HILDRITH see HILDRETH
HILDROP see HILDRUP
HILDRUP / HILDROP, [Capt.] 143~43
HILL, [Mr.] 259~44, 309~52 [Mrs.?] 147~55 Abner 264~45 Alexander 224~37 Benjamin 272~8 Eliza 309~44 Elizabeth 184~20 Francis 46~57 Goodwin 48~53 Hester 70~52 Israel 326~42 Jane 230~55 Jeremiah 96~22 Jesse 326~42 John 10~34, 159~38, 210~11, 231~32, 250~14 Jonathan 262~37 Joseph 23~51 Laura 317~54 Naomi 80~41 Samuel 133~44, 160~30 Thomas J. 355~10 Tower 8~23
HILLARD see HILLIARD
HILLER, John 179~55
HILLIARD / HILLARD, Benjamin 172~4 Esther 293~22 John 196~3 Roxina (Hall) 172~5
HILLIGAN see HALLEGAN
HILLS, Abijah 160~26 Ebenezer 8~18 Samuel 300~50, 333~54
HILLVER, James (?) 287~20
HILLYER, James (?) 287~20
HILT, Eliza 75~45
HILTON, [Mrs.] 20~40 John 20~41 Matthew 160~8 Simon 160~7 William 196~5
HIMES / HYMES (see also HINES), Abigail 66~47 Amos 178~53 Mary 236~2 Walter 39~50, 55~26, 66~50
HINCKLEY / HINKLEY, [Lt.] 139~26 [Mrs.] 126~24, 139~26 Elizabeth 103~28 Hitty 64~26 Maria 303~14 Martha (Prince) 305~3 O. 303~14 Samuel 126~25, 305~3 Sophia 283~6 William 354~25
HINDMAN, [Mrs.] 2~9
HINDS see HINES
HINES / HYNES / HINDS (see also HIMES), [Mr.] 117~24 Joseph 208~14 Joseph B. 316~54 Justin 281~48, 295~36 Loretho 327~11 Thomas 187~13
HINKLEY see HINCKLEY
HINMAN / HENMAN, [children] 229~23 Anna 229~22 Thomas 268~17
HINTON, Polly 210~5
HITCHCOCK, Benjamin 58~18 Daniel 323~34 Ebenezer 25~3 Eldad 66~4, 73~3 Emily 101~14 Gad 148~51 Hannah 135~32 Lemuel 151~17 Martha 84~47 Noah 42~6
HITCHINGS see HUTCHINS
HITSELL, Joseph 73~32
HIX see HICKS
HOADLEY, Ithiel 328~25 Jehiel 321~35
HOAG / HOGG, [Mr.] 35~38 David 43~12 Enos 364~8 Huldah 303~58 Huldah (Winter) 286~27 James 173~40 Jerusha 297~47 John 94~32 Joseph 244~46 Miriam 364~7 Robert 286~27 Samuel 81~45 Simpson 244~46 William 82~9, 244~46
HOAR see HORR
HOARE see HORR
HOBART, David 41~8 Dudley B. 227~31 John S. 180~55 Mary 113~14 Samuel 362~19 Sarah 362~20
HOBBS, John 135~38
HOBSON / HOPSON, Anna 233~9
HOCHSTRASSES, Jacob 289~35
HOCOLM see HOLCOLM
HODGDEN see HODGDON
HODGDON / HODSDON / HODGDEN, Caleb 79~14 Sally 203~27 Shadrach 202~18
HODGE, Abraham 208~6 Hannah 226~36 Henry 252~31 Jane 144~33 Mary (Johnson) 188~57 Michael 188~57 Sarah 252~30
HODGES, Chatfield 30~12 John 44~16 Judith 323~7 Margaret 323~7 Marsa 91~22
HODGKINS, Aaron 89~56, 308~45 Luther 268~42
HODGKINSON, Frances 151~8 John 212~28
HODGMAN, Polly 212~11 Willard L. 310~22
HODGSON, [Mr.] 48~43
HODSDON see HODGDON
HOFFMAN / HUFMAN / HOOFMAN / HUFFMAN, [children] 101~35 Frederick 32~4 John 120~14 Peter 333~29 Samuel 48~51 Zachariah 101~34
HOGAN, [children] 205~2 John 205~2, 209~50
HOGEBOOM, Lawrence 189~7
HOGG see HOAG
HOISINGNON see HOISINGTON
HOISINGTON / HOISINGNON, Ebenezer 215~2
HOIT see HOYT
HOITT see HOYT
HOLAND see HOLLAND
HOLBROOK, [Mr.] 91~7 Benjamin 235~9 Betsey (Shearley) 235~9 Daniel 280~46 Elihu 235~18 Elijah 21~13 Esther 280~45 Hannah 91~33 Mary 235~18 Phineas 175~6 Stephen 21~24 William 295~38
HOLCOLM / HOCOLM / HOLCOMB, Silas 263~50
HOLCOMB see HOLCOLM
HOLCROFT, Thomas 300~19
HOLDEN, [Mrs.] 221~48 Asa 81~40 Elijah G. 296~17 Eliza 304~35 J. 40~50 John 79~34 Joseph 212~34 Julius S. 334~38 Justinian 105~28 Nathan 247~2 Nathaniel 239~30, 244~14, 256~26 Sawtell 49~3 Timothy 227~56, 244~2
HOLEMAN see HOLMAN
HOLGATE, [child] 63~50 [Mr.] 63~49 [Mrs.] 63~50
HOLLAND / HOLAND, Abraham 84~23, 112~1, 269~45, 281~53, 309~30 Antipas 32~53 Hannah 190~55 John 14~10, 33~7, 83~17, 156~36 Thomas 95~43
HOLLENBACK, Samuel 237~13
HOLLEY see HAWLEY
HOLLIDAY / HALLADAY, John 241~23
HOLLINGSWORTH, [Mr.] 221~12 Henry 150~52
HOLLIS, David 100~3 Thomas Brand 172~16
HOLLISTER, Benjamin 104~33 Clarissa (Hurlburt) 219~57 Jesse 219~57
HOLLOWAY / HOLWAY, Martha 190~26 Nathaniel 1~46
HOLLY see HAWLEY
HOLMAN / HOLEMAN / HALLMAN, Abraham 195~52 Edward 59~33 Smith 296~35 Stephen 21~29 Sullivan 71~37

HOLMER see HOMER
HOLMES / HOMES, [Mr.] 19~42 Andrew H. 321~56 Benjamin 267~56 Calvin 109~28 Charles 90~55 Jacob 374~4 John 244~17 Joseph 316~42 Lathrop 97~39 Lemuel 16~27, 109~27 Margaret 134~4 Nancy (Rand) 267~56 Oliver 72~52, 261~4, 262~58 Parley 310~25 Perley 316~53 Sally (Town) 244~18 Sarah (Sumner?) 97~42 Thomas 83~2 Uriel 314~3
HOLT, Anna 106~46 Bethiah 179~47 Charles 49~27, 62~32, 367~42 Ebenezer 3~27 Sally 140~15 Sarah 192~54 Thomas 291~38
HOLTEN see HOLTON
HOLTHUYSEN, J.C. 204~57
HOLTON / HOLTEN, Joel 76~19 John 110~20 Jonathan 8~17, 25~1, 153~53 Luther 292~53 Nancy (Pope) 153~54 Nathaniel 61~38 Timothy 130~31 Worthington 61~37
HOLWAY see HOLLOWAY
HOLYOKE, Edward 172~25 Elizur 236~45
HOMANS, [Major] 227~22 Phebe 227~22
HOMER / HOLMER, [Mr.] 312~28 Michael 274~55 William 274~55
HOMES see HOLMES
HONEY, Rebekah (Huntoon) 230~46 Solomon 230~45
HOOD, [Admiral Lord] 334~54 Charlotte (Nelson) 334~54 Mary 174~33 Samuel 334~54
HOOFMAN see HOFFMAN
HOOK see HOOKE
HOOKE / HOOK, E. 357~51 John G. Dow 357~50 Joseph Lowell 357~50
HOOKER, John 174~23, 361~31 John Worthington 174~22 Lucretia 177~15 Thomas 186~38
HOOKEY, Lucretia 178~48
HOOPER, [Capt.] 363~8 [child] 292~37 Asa 316~50 Benjamin 274~16 Elisha 141~8 James 292~37 Jemima (Ormsby) 141~9 Levi 30~38, 263~4 Lydia 274~16 Sally 96~53
HOOTEN see HOOTON
HOOTON / HOOTEN, John 124~37, 135~14
HOPE, William 116~12
HOPKIN see HOPKINS
HOPKINS / HOPKIN, [Rev.] 328~34 [widow] 113~29 Asa 222~30 Bethiah 92~4 Caleb 47~35 Daniel 265~22 James 140~30, 163~9 John 282~7 John E. 230~52 Lemuel 45~42 Mary 265~21 Nancy (Brownell) 105~21 Nicholas 161~4 Rebecca 94~10 Samuel 155~30 Stephen 105~21 Susan 294~14
HOPKINSON, [Mr.&Mrs.] 9~8 [Mr.] 63~8 Mary 170~49 Parker 8~42, 9~8 Samuel 46~56
HOPPIN, [boys] 195~29 Aaron 195~29
HOPSON see HOBSON
HORE see HORR
HORMAN see HARMON
HORN / HORNE / HARN (see also ORNE), Betsey (Marsh) 51~21 Cecelia 35~53 Eliza 101~2 John 355~21 Robert 51~22 William 101~3
HORNBECK, Isaac 204~6
HORNBY, Maria 29~36
HORNE see HORN
HORNELL, George 324~41 William D. 324~41
HORR / HOARE / HORE / HOAR, Ann 184~54 Deborah 296~34, 304~32, 310~27 Esther (Kendall) 269~50 John 269~50 Lucy 166~25 Olive 307~3 Peter 20~2 Sally 4~26 Samuel 111~14
HORROCKS, Alice 215~10
HORSWILL, [Mr.] 16~6 John W. 23~53
HORTON, David 153~34 Lucinda (Arms) 153~34 Lucy 224~25
HORVEY see HARVEY
HOSFORD, Sarah 208~4
HOSKINS see HASKINS
HOSLEY, David 124~7 James 301~20
HOSMER / HOSMORE, Jonas 308~45 Nancy (Chapman) 100~38 Oliver 244~56 Robert 100~38
HOSMORE see HOSMER
HOTCHKISS, [Mr.] 170~47 Enoch 264~47
HOUGH see HOWE
HOUGHTON / HAUGHTON, [Miss] 281~20 [Mr.] 3~1 Abel 151~13 Abigail 177~25, 183~39 Abigail (?) 177~26 Adonijah 93~57 Amasa 296~16 Benjamin 214~36 Betsey (Leonard) 323~30 Enoch 71~25 Isabel (Clark) 290~7 John 89~53 Jonathan 329~51 Joseph 170~51 Obediah 111~48 Peter 290~7 Wheelock 323~30
HOULE, Judith 104~22 Laurent 104~22
HOUSAN, [girl] 103~40 John 103~40
HOUSE, [Capt.] 296~38 Cynthia 200~31 Deborah 188~51 Enoch 4~32 G. 300~21 Job 223~21 John 202~56 Levi 86~29 Mary 267~13 Nabby (Torry) 86~29 Olive 86~30 Susan 211~24
HOUSER, Elias 158~20
HOUSTON / EUSTON / HUSTON, Alexander 260~10 Harriet 153~47 James 130~13
HOVEY, [Rev.] 232~56 Aron 146~31 Erin (?) 146~31 Fanny 40~8 Francis 119~1 Hannah (Lewis) 119~1 I. 40~9 Joshua 144~18 Samuel 252~37
HOW see HOWE
HOWARD, [———] 325~26 [Deacon] 282~20 [Mr.] 318~5 Aaron 158~56 Alexander 158~56 Ame 236~45 Betsey (Prince) 92~27 Daniel 304~42 Hannah 31~14 Isaiah 222~32 Mary (Glidden) 353~7 Nathan 289~12 Polly 307~53, 324~17 Robinson 212~48 S. 134~36 Samuel 92~27, 103~57 Simeon 165~16 Thomas 219~11 William 49~44, 179~18, 353~7 Zachariah 258~20
HOWE / HOW / HOUGH, [child] 203~3 [Mr.] 205~35 Adams 247~16 Adonijah 74~56 Caleb 188~23 Daniel 273~9 Earl 50~5 Eli 169~36 Eliphalet 247~16 Elizabeth 282~13 Elizabeth (Clap) 145~12 Eunice (———) (Russell) 109~32 Geo. 24~6 George 217~45, 286~16, 311~17, 312~23 Gershom 85~53 Gilbert 81~44 Hannah 214~21, 245~53 Issac 287~22 J. 231~26 James 17~23, 94~19, 145~12 John 69~15, 184~7 Joseph 112~31, 321~18 Kezia 287~21 Margaret 193~20 Martin 109~32 Mary 69~14, 99~1, 112~28 Mehitable 256~3 Nehemiah 39~39 Phebe 98~29 Salah 33~37 Sally 23~11, 160~50 Sampson 3~3 Samuel 129~9 Sarah 239~11 Simon 24~46, 255~57 Thomas 74~34, 185~27 William 203~3, 205~34
HOWELL / HAWELL, George 301~36 Joshua 5~32 Silas W. 214~25 William 59~42
HOWES see HAWES
HOWLAND, [Capt.] 42~19 Charles 79~1, 81~14 Daniel 281~40 John 172~38
HOXCY see HOXEY
HOXEY / HOXSE / HOXCY, Gideon 195~5 John 9~5, 59~27
HOXSE see HOXEY
HOY see HOYE
HOYE / HOY, John 212~25
HOYT / HOIT / HOITT, [Mr. & Mrs.] 197~51 Ephraim 354~21 James 309~48 John 197~47 Mehitable 67~16 Reuben 80~4, 311~12, 334~7 Reubin 286~11
HOZEY, [girl] 208~24 Isaac 208~24
HUBBARD / HIBBARD / HIBBERD / HEBBERD / HEBBARD / HIBBERT / HEBARD, [Capt.] 114~36 [Col.] 304~54, [Mr.] 5~30, 22~10 Abel 65~6 Abigail 165~6 Abigail Mehitable (Lester) 300~57 Arethusa 244~29 Caroline (Jones) 153~37 Daniel 193~10 David 73~19 Elisha 247~44 Ezra 243~17 Fanny 139~44 Henry 253~38, 267~46, 267~49, 277~3, 318~50 Isaac 7~55, 153~38 John 4~5, 21~3, 28~15, 32~11, 36~7, 41~35, 44~43, 55~29, 90~9, 99~11, 111~52, 112~23, 120~18, 165~20, 178~28, 242~33, 253~37, 267~45, 277~1, 330~37, 374~32 Jonathan 31~16, 32~21, 328~17 Mary 92~38 Nabby 307~52 Prudence 253~38, 277~3 Reuben 300~57 Roswell 276~15 Russel 66~14 Sally 243~17 Sally (Wilson) 276~15 Salmon 70~17 Thomas 32~19
HUBBEL see HUBBELL
HUBBELL / HUBBEL, Aaron 3~25 Sally 3~25 Walter 150~16
HUBER, George 367~57 Henry 63~10 Jacob 37~14, 38~17 John 38~17, 63~15 M. 189~45
HUBERT, Jean Francois 15~19
HUCKING see HUCKINGS
HUCKINGS / HUCKING / HUCKINS / HUGGINS / HUNKING / HUNKIN / HUNKINS, David 293~21 Jerusha (Cobb) 293~21 Jonathan 289~35 Nath. 117~41 Nathaniel 173~31 Sally (Stone) 173~31 Samuel 303~5

HUCKINS see HUCKINGS
HUDSON, Benjamin 213~37 Betsey 54~19 Eleazer 53~50 Eliz. 125~19 Henry 221~33 Maria (Trumball) 221~33 Mary 288~20, 314~1 Thomas 288~20
HUESTEAD, [Mr.] 144~48
HUFFMAN see HOFFMAN
HUFMAN see HOFFMAN
HUGER, [Lieut.] 54~24 Peter 367~62
HUGG, Samuel 186~29
HUGGINS see HUCKINGS
HUGHES see HUSE
HUGUEL, Noel 278~14
HULL, [Capt.] 289~45 [Dr.] 217~13 [Gov.] 194~48 Comfort 264~28 James 184~41 John 109~34 Lydia (Codding) 109~34 Rebecca P. 194~47
HUMASON, Timothy 167~13
HUMPHERWILLE, Ebenezer 113~30
HUMPHREY, Bela 197~19, 197~52 Benjamin 197~1 Clarisa 241~12 Ireana (Lastis) 317~18 Manly 317~17 Polly (Bingham) 197~52 Rebecca (Beckwith) 197~19 Samuel 241~13
HUMPHREYS see HUMPHRIES
HUMPHRIES / HUMPHREYS, [Col.] 188~19 Daniel 23~52 David 36~41 Mary 23~51
HUNDSBERG, Peter 63~11
HUNEFORD see HANAFORD
HUNEWELL see HUNNEWELL
HUNEWILL see HUNNEWELL
HUNGERFORD, Green 287~19
HUNKIN see HUCKINGS
HUNKING see HUCKINGS
HUNKINS see HUCKINGS
HUNNEWELL / HUNEWELL / HUNEWILL, Eunice 230~54 Lucy 160~16 Phebe 230~52 Richard 221~31 Susan (Cook) 64~38 Walter 64~38 Zerub 149~2
HUNT, [———] 71~42, 136~16 [Col.] 268~37 [Mr.] 300~40 [Mrs.] 39~46, 195~42, 268~37 Abigail 99~20, 100~1 Alph. M. 315~5 Arad 115~45, 143~11, 278~33 Asahel 55~21, 79~42, 157~7, 206~43, 246~27, 311~45, 315~6 Caleb 50~55, 57~3, 116~26, 296~33 Clifford 335~42 Ebenezer 128~51, 148~26 Eliphalet 67~21, 233~9 Elisha 115~46, 304~19 Ellen 96~15 Ephraim 217~8 Experience 232~40 Frances 123~29 Frederick 194~16 Hadock 135~4 Hannah 39~44 J. 195~42 James 256~28 Joel 264~47 John 80~16, 83~36, 115~24, 115~47, 143~15, 325~45 Jonathan 80~11, 115~25, 123~30, 143~10, 278~30 Josiah 200~44 Lewis 315~5 Lucy (Goodrich) 233~10 Martha 237~42 Polly (Wilder) 272~30 Prudence 301~15 Roswell 312~38 Rowell 109~15, 275~6 Ruth 83~36 S. 304~20, 304~20, 368~56 Sally 128~50 Sampson 124~5 Samuel 45~39, 56~13, 80~14, 80~15, 115~26, 115~27, 136~15, 143~9, 158~13, 228~37, 272~30, 278~33 Sarah 148~26 Simeon 101~55 Thomas 284~2 William 140~26, 170~35 Zebulun 201~10
HUNTER, [Maj. Gen.] 234~39 [Mr.] 27~17 Amy 83~38 Elizabeth (Desbrosses?) 40~3 George 7~8 John 40~3 Mary 250~30 Peter 209~56 William 127~7
HUNTING, Jesse 33~48 Jonathan 309~43
HUNTINGDON / HUNTINGTON, [Rev.] 256~16 Anna 118~45 Benjamin 79~15 Dan 310~9 Daniel 222~31 Eliphalet 226~32 Enoch 155~9, 305~6 G. 65~51 Gurdon 27~7, 41~50, 87~30, 116~37, 164~13, 165~30, 199~56 Jerusha 113~4 John 157~3 Joshua 300~55 Laura (Burbank) 157~4 Margaretta (Dewitt) 155~9 Mary 267~15, 297~31 Nancy (Clark) 226~32 Roxelana 305~10 Samuel 2~57, 297~32, 305~11 Solomon 295~6 Susan (Mansfield) 300~55 William 55~3
HUNTINGTON see HUNTINGDON
HUNTLEY / HUNTLY, [Col.] 136~10 [girl] 297~53 [Widow] 289~38 David 305~49 Elijah 297~53 Elisha 30~47, 37~5, 37~43, 89~37, 157~49, 289~14, 327~19, 332~18 Lewmon 312~41 Nathan 29~10, 30~48 Rufus 95~24, 98~37
HUNTLY see HUNTLEY
HUNTON see HUNTOON
HUNTOON / HUNTOONE / HUNTON, Benjamin 45~21, 60~45, 65~34 Betsey 230~45, 257~52 Charles 45~56, 304~40 James 296~30 Joseph 29~11 Louisa 296~31 Nathaniel 45~55, 101~52 Philip 45~20, 129~28 Rebekah 230~46
HUNTOONE see HUNTOON
HUNTRESS, George 355~31
HURD / HEARD / HERD / HARD, [boy] 201~47 Abigail 269~55 Abigail (Willcox) 269~56 Edmund 304~56 Elizabeth 239~7 Joanna 114~17 Joseph 85~45 Mary (Flint) 85~45 Rachel 69~15 Samuel 75~9, 101~8 Shubael 69~16 Stephen 111~34, 269~55 Uzzel 285~14
HURLBURT / HILBURT, Clarissa 219~57 Isaac 82~32 Phebe 79~25 Thaddeus 69~49 William 246~7
HURLEY / HARLEY / HERLEY, Mary 48~43
HUSE / HUGHES / HEWES / EWES, Hannah 107~2 James 143~21 Joseph 234~40, 370~9 Nancy 283~7 Victor 258~8
HUSSEY, Joseph 74~7
HUSTON see HOUSTON
HUTCHESON see HUTCHINSON
HUTCHINGS see HUTCHINS
HUTCHINS / HUTCHINGS / HITCHINGS, [Col.] 130~5 [Mr.] 362~30 [Mrs.] 186~8 Betsey 242~2 David 51~7 Elizabeth 91~35 Ezebon 209~20 Jane 355~16 John S. 11~16 Joseph 161~12 Magdaline 130~5 Matilda 153~51 Rachel 272~28 Sally 238~47 William 93~4, 115~13, 292~54
HUTCHINSON / HUTCHESON, [Mr.] 137~4, 157~37, 204~25, 224~53, 324~7 Aaron 48~57 Ann 84~44 Jerusha C. 333~49 Phineas 151~21 S. 275~40 Sally 272~30 Samuel 21~15, 113~40, 241~8, 245~1, 249~30, 253~39, 254~53, 258~52, 262~15, 272~52, 272~53, 277~35, 292~27, 295~37, 296~44, 300~38, 303~31, 309~7, 314~35, 315~22, 316~18, 327~12, 330~26, 332~17
HUTTLESON, Peleg 92~15
HUTTON, George 240~2
HUXHAM, Jane 163~16
HUXLEY, Mary 117~54
HYDE / HIDE, Benjamin 15~7 C. 247~39 Charles 137~52 David 220~15 E. 38~44 Elizabeth 247~39 Ezra 50~26 Lucy 289~32 Matthew 260~48 Rebekah 24~19 Sarah 50~25
HYMES see HIMES
HYNES see HINES
HYOT, James 13~9

I.

IDE, James 142~12
ILBERY, James 192~35
INCHES, [Miss] 39~44
INGALLS / INGALS / INGOLS / INGLES / INGOLL, [Capt.] 67~46 Ira 297~47 Jane (———) 169~14 Jerusha (Hogg) 297~47 John 146~54, 295~40, 316~22 Jonathan 113~33 Josiah 297~48 Lois (Capron) 297~48 Lucy 178~16 Simeon 82~9 Theophilus 103~37
INGALS see INGALLS
INGERSOL see INGERSOLL
INGERSOLL / INGERSOL, [Major] 202~57 George 203~45 Mary 286~1, 286~53 Sophia 289~24
INGLES see INGALLS
INGOLL see INGALLS
INGOLS see INGALLS
INGRAHAM / INGRAM, Daniel 91~29 Duncan 199~22
INGRAM see INGRAHAM
INNES / INNIS, Alexander 152~9 Isabella 39~24 James 26~37 John 35~50, 77~15 William 39~24
INNIS see INNES
IREDELL, James 54~22
IRELAND, [Mrs.] 35~2 George 71~36 Thomas 13~8 William 35~2
IRVINE, William 166~11
ISAACS, Isaac 123~11 Ralph 54~27
ISHAM, Benjamin 326~46 Esther 254~13 Firah 216~41 Griswold 200~19 John 200~27 Joseph 200~22 Martha 326~46 Sally (Starr) 216~41 Timothy 200~27
ISRAEL / ISRAELS, [Mr.] 148~42 John 264~24

ISRAELS see ISRAEL
IVES, [Mr.] 71~4   Aner 216~18   E. 204~13   Jesse 226~2
IZARD, [Mr.] 176~46   Ralph 162~11

J.

JABINS, Ephraim 59~30
JACKSON, [child] 211~50 [Gen.] 122~51, 247~34 [Major] 224~17 [Mr.] 299~41 [Mrs.] 42~13, 126~45, 299~41   Charles 107~52   Clement 133~37   Daniel 211~48, 243~16   David 102~11   Deborah (Nowell) 145~16   Ebenezer 318~16   Eleazer 48~15, 56~25, 317~45   Elijah 355~37   Elizabeth (———) 64~28   Elizabeth (Cabot) 105~24   George 220~23   Hannah 75~21   Henry 271~15, 289~5   J. 105~23   James 39~9, 235~11   Job 145~15   John 286~31   Johnson 44~14   Jonathan 79~16   Lavina 295~2   Mary 91~28, 147~52   Michael 318~17   Mungo 195~58   Polly (Merrill) 67~15   Polly (Nowell) 44~14   Robert 66~44   Ruth 318~4, 318~16   Samuel 262~3   Samuel Stillman 67~14   Treadwell 42~13   William 6~7, 168~48, 296~18
JACOBS, Abel 35~9   Ariel 81~7   Calvin 324~48   George H. 353~51   John 82~52   Loring 122~30   Mary 124~56, 146~42   Mary (Simmons) 122~30   Paul 194~43   Persis A. (Teel) 353~51   Prudence (———) (Stow) 194~43   Saranus 324~48   Warren 244~9
JACQUES see JAQUES
JACQUITH see JAQUETH
JAFFREY see JEFFERY
JAMES, Ann 113~8   George 102~26   Sally 184~54   Susannah (Mollett) 102~27
JAMESON / JAMIESON, Gabriel 49~53   Sally (Thompson) 49~53
JAMIESON see JAMESON
JANES, Henry 196~7   Naomi 79~27
JANNEY see JENNEY
JANS, Abraham 63~11
JAQUES / JACQUES, [Mrs.] 190~55
JAQUETH / JAQUITH / JACQUITH, Abigail 105~38   Abraham 105~39   Adford 105~41   Anna (Holt) 106~46   Benjamin 105~41   Ebenezer 5~15, 105~41, 221~50   Elizabeth 105~42   Hannah 5~42   James 151~26   John 105~41   Josiah 106~46   Mary 105~42   Sarah 105~39   Spencer (?) 99~53
JAQUISH, Spencer 99~53
JAQUITH see JAQUETH
JARMAN, Matthew 50~13
JARREL / JERREL, Joanna 257~9   Thomas Fitch 169~50
JARVIS / JERVIS, [Capt.] 187~51   Betsy 104~11   Charles 259~9   James 59~5, 226~17   John 39~43   Jonathan 161~34   Lenoard 3d 123~9   Nathaniel 100~3   Walter (?) 240~39
JAY, [Gov.] 89~11   John 120~49   Maria 89~10   Sarah (Livingston) 120~48
JAYNE, Peter 257~5
JEFFERDS / JEFFERS, Joseph 275~32
JEFFERS see JEFFERDS
JEFFERY / JEFFREY / JAFFREY / GEOFFRAY / JEFFRIES / JEFFRY, Benjamin 267~32   George 20~33, 82~8, 110~30, 111~54   John 111~53   Maria (Uniacke) 196~35   Salona 35~52   Sarah 50~29   Thomas N. 196~34
JEFFREY see JEFFERY
JEFFRIES see JEFFERY
JEFFRY see JEFFERY
JENCKS see JENKS
JENESEE, Stephen Arthur 151~25
JENISON see JENNISON
JENKINS / JUNKINS, [Mrs.] 133~33   Robert 10~26   Samuel 206~21   William 26~3
JENKS / JENCKS, Betsey (Russell) 51~20   Clarina P. (Greenleaf) 107~45   Eleazer A. 107~44   Hannah (———) (Bennit) 190~21   Henry 146~36   Joseph 190~21   Lavina (Jackson) 295~2   Oliver 295~2   Samuel 92~14   William 51~20, 224~52
JENNESS, James 258~33   Mary (George) 275~14   Nancy 87~47   Olive 79~30   Samuel 277~20   William 275~13

JENNEY / JENNY / JANNEY, Isaac 204~38   Nathaniel 290~8   Sally (Cabot) 290~8
JENNINGS / JENNINS, [Mr.] 275~2   Benjamin 74~7   Daniel 190~57   Isaac 306~21   Nancy 110~49   Richard 219~21
JENNINS see JENNINGS
JENNISON / JENISON, [child] 235~20   John 53~30, 168~24, 190~15   John F. 143~31   Jonathan 90~5, 320~23   Lucinda 314~39   Martin 43~11   Mary 100~39   Nancy (Rand) 143~31   Sarah (Fiske) 295~53   Thomas 94~4, 101~46, 235~20   William 190~15, 333~45, 334~52
JENNY see JENNEY
JERMAIN see GERMAN
JEROME, Amarilla 209~55   Amasa 168~56   Lucy (Treadwell) 168~55
JERREL see JARREL
JERVIS see JARVIS
JEUDEVINE / JUDIVINE / JEUDWINE, Cornelius 326~51   Hannah (Powers) 276~16   Joseph 276~16   Luther 315~21   William 14~30
JEUDWINE see JEUDEVINE
JEWET see JEWETT
JEWETT / JEWET, [girl] 4~19 [Mr.] 4~19   Caleb 118~19   David 217~50   Eleazer 295~39   George 4~33   Jacob C. 215~55   James 24~7   Jesse 173~35   John 80~24, 354~18   Joshua 173~35   Mark 306~19   Smith 354~18   Solomon 270~23
JILES see GILES
JOCELYN see JOSSELYN
JOFES, Isaac 226~47
JOHNS, John 211~32
JOHNSON / JOHNSTON, [boy] 125~50, 161~8 [Capt.] 47~46, 129~50 [children] 13~32, 19~21, 234~51 [Landlord] 20~9 [Mr.] 40~45, 46~38, 54~1, 137~5, 166~40, 373~10 [Mrs.] 19~21, 234~51, 259~24 [Rev.] 258~57   Abel 147~40   Abner 161~8   Abraham 4~11, 153~22   Alfred 213~8, 215~6   Almon 8~53, 328~18   Amos 261~32, 261~33, 310~29, 321~21   Anne 231~30   Augustus 115~49   Caleb 3~4, 5~55, 9~15, 11~42, 17~12, 103~4   Calvin 233~11   Charles 254~48   Charlotte 8~53   Christian 162~53   Clarissa 8~53   Convers 55~3   Daniel 114~21   David 54~30   Ebenezer 207~32   Elizabeth 259~11, 260~49   Fanny 364~15   Frances 190~24   Francis 301~27   G. 259~11   George 13~10   Gordon 260~49   Guy 39~13   Hagar 259~10   Hannah (?) 332~36   Hisley (?) 8~53   Ira 255~43, 264~14   Izal 204~55   James 67~54, 120~51, 195~36, 201~12, 220~5, 237~18, 288~57   James H. 355~16   Jane (Hutchins) 355~16   Jedediah 16~40   Jerusha (Randal) 115~50   Jesse 133~54   Job 2~48, 8~53, 13~32, 209~42   John 318~21, 327~13, 332~36   John M. 215~30   Joseph 210~19   Joshua 118~47   Jotham 28~7, 131~32   Lewis 303~52   Lucy 258~56   Luke 234~51   Mary 188~57, 297~18   Matthew 141~25   McNicholas (?) 132~21   Micah 72~17   Moses 16~10, 17~11, 20~1, 22~50, 25~26, 26~41, 33~8, 33~11, 42~23, 45~36, 46~33, 54~10, 55~6, 56~46, 64~53, 190~24   Oliver 7~43, 15~15, 19~18, 20~3, 119~54   Polly 8~53   Richard 297~18   Sabin 170~8   Samuel 8~53, 48~14, 48~23, 74~38, 125~50, 259~24   Sarah 48~25, 168~48, 238~15   Sherman 180~18   Stephen 78~50, 89~48, 120~17, 129~16, 153~14, 308~45   Susannah (Tufts) 131~32   Sylvanus 159~28   Temper (Morse) 233~12   Unity 141~27   William 48~51, 159~27, 240~18
JOHNSTON see JOHNSON
JOHONNET see JOHONNOT
JOHONNOT / JOHONNET, Andrew 158~6   Moses 306~18   Peter 312~12
JOICE see JOYCE
JOINER, William 224~20
JOLLEY / JOLLY, [Mr.] 166~23   Mary (Musgrove) 166~23
JOLLIER, Frances 267~29, 269~6
JOLLY see JOLLEY
JONES, [child] 190~1 [Col.] 29~21 [Dr.] 332~42 [Major] 318~6 [Mr.] 131~39, 176~32, 255~11, 362~17, 364~16 [Mrs.] 122~4, 193~25   Abigail 293~29   Ann (———) (Pope) 245~32   Ann (Joyse) 98~51   Benjamin 116~27, 177~5, 193~26, 313~29

Betsy (Abrams) 126~42 Caroline 153~37 Daniel 6~10, 143~5, 361~43 Darius 280~30 David S. 93~31 Dinah 154~13 Edw. 145~35 Edward 145~34, 210~10, 245~32 Elias 80~8, 115~28, 278~34 Eliza (Hatch) 280~30 Elizabeth 236~43 Ephraim 236~44 Eunice 85~43 Ezra 70~9, 153~38 Frances 104~9 Gabriel 122~2, 267~26 Henry 113~26 John 332~41 John R. 210~53 John W. 98~50 Jonas 293~29 Jonathan 319~25 Joseph 124~24, 190~1, 220~6, 282~18, 350~13 Josiah 115~29, 143~6, 299~2, 304~18, 325~41 Laura 10~29 Lewis 265~31 Lews 311~38 Lucy 101~13 Lydia 6~10 Martha 319~17 Mary 69~2 Mary (Richardson) (Baldwin) 29~17 Nathaniel 150~24 Nehemiah 221~54 Noah 103~54 Noble Wimberly 180~44 Perez 213~9 Rice 292~15 Richard H. 151~29, 168~6 Sally 268~53, 299~52 Sally (Eyars) 113~27 Samuel 81~46, 122~3, 133~39, 163~31 Samuel Paul 175~36 Sarah 184~28 Thomas 167~37, 210~56 Timothy 126~42 William 133~40, 184~28, 289~7, 302~14
JONSTONE, [Mrs.] 335~13
JORDAN / JORDON / JOURDON / JOURDAN, Charles 150~34 Putnam 120~40 Sally (Brewer) 120~40
JORDON see JORDAN
JOSES, Isaac (?) 226~47
JOSEY, Mathias (?) 78~33
JOSLIN see JOSSELYN
JOSLYN see JOSSELYN
JOSSELYN / JOSLIN / JOCELIN / JOSLYN, Amasa 264~53 Daniel 16~26 Job 44~27 Mary 185~54 Peter 300~3 Samuel 44~12
JOURDAN see JORDAN
JOURDON see JORDAN
JOURNEY, (———) (Cole) 123~32 [Mr.] 123~32
JOY, Anna 36~33 David 294~39 Eliza 294~39 Franklin 294~38 Jacob 187~44 Kesia 294~38 Mary 294~38 Mary (Eliot) 71~31 Melzer 71~31 Obadiah 83~3 W. 294~38
JOYCE / JOICE / JOYSE, Ann 98~51
JOYSE see JOYCE
JUDD, John 6~23 Rebecca 207~20, 208~16 Reuben 262~49 William 171~34, 172~19
JUDIVINE see JEUDEVINE
JUDKINS, David 310~28, 321~26 John 45~18 Samuel 45~19
JULIAN / JULIEN, [Mons.] 200~55
JULIEN see JULIAN
JUNKINS see JENKINS

K.

KAIN / KANE / CAIN (see also KEEN), Elitheia 243~14 John 246~4 Sybil 246~4
KANADY see KENNEDY
KANE see KAIN
KAPPLE see COPPLE
KARNS / KERNS / CARNES, Burrill 213~29 Dolly (———) (Wellman) 35~44 Nathaniel W. 35~43
KASEY see CASEY
KASSOEN / KASSON, Ambrose 317~54 Laura (Hill) 317~54
KASSON see KASSOEN
KATEN, Sarah S. 170~14
KAVANAGH see CAVANAUGH
KAY / KEAY / KEY, Ch. 38~3 Charles 63~26
KEAY see KAY
KEAYS see KYES
KECKWITH, [Capt.] 29~37
KEDER see KIDDER
KEELS, (———) 72~45
KEEN / KEENE (see also KAIN), [Capt.] 363~8
KEENE see KEEN
KEEP, Imla 285~10
KEISER / KYSER, John 38~18 Peter 38~18
KEITH, Hannah 275~20 Isaac S. 163~16 Jane (Huxham) 163~16 William 236~52
KELCHRE, Catherine 124~55
KELKNAP, Sarah (?) 53~10

KELLAM see KILHAM
KELLECUTT, Reuben 20~16
KELLEY / KELLY, Elizabeth (———) 151~53 Jeremiah 313~49 John 348~9 Joseph 3~18, 361~40 Levi Israel W. 100~36 Melon 228~44 Rebecca (Fletcher) 100~36 Richard 70~47
KELLOG see KELLOGG
KELLOGG / KELLOG, Enos 11~3, 17~42 Gardner 185~1 Jabez 238~46 Martin 206~49 Moses 244~12 Ruby (Utley) 238~47 Thankful 185~1
KELLY see KELLEY
KELSA, Sarah (———) 64~6
KELSEY, Jeremiah 331~44
KELTON / KILTON, Elizabeth 167~22
KEMBALL see KIMBALL
KEMBLE see KIMBALL
KEMP / KEMPT, [Capt.] 39~18 Aaron 312~22 David 296~19 James 201~36 Lawrence 216~14, 217~30 Polly 310~15
KEMPER, Daniel 254~51 Nathan 371~64 Reuben 214~51 Samuel 214~51
KEMPT see KEMP
KEMPTON see CAMPTON
KENARD see KENNARD
KENDAL see KENDALL
KENDALE see KENDALL
KENDALL / KENDALE / KENDAL, Benjamin 185~52 Catharine 102~37 Esther 269~50 Jesse 4~34 Reuben 156~26 Seth 258~25
KENDRICK / KENRICK / KINDRECK, [widow] 190~7 Benjamin 146~16, 206~46 J.P. 371~28 John 186~34, 212~19 John Penuel 195~21
KENEDY see KENNEDY
KENERSON see KENNISTON
KENISON see KENNISTON
KENISTON see KENNISTON
KENNARD / KENARD, Michael 65~40 Nabby (Mason) 65~40
KENNEAR / KINNEAR / KINNER, Ruth 184~21
KENNEDY / KENEDY / KANADY, [Mr.] 148~41, 180~12 Jacob 316~54 James 302~15 Nath. 298~15 Robert 192~32 Sarah 93~18
KENNERSON see KENNISTON
KENNEY / KENNY / KINNEY / CANNEY / CANEY / CONNEY / CONEY, [Mr.] 39~45, 281~33 [Mrs.] 101~22 Edward 1~20 Elizabeth 281~33 Hannah 260~40 P.M. 260~41 Patrick Moore 272~47 Thomas 144~18
KENNISON see KENNISTON
KENNISTON / KENISTON / KENNISON / KENERSON / KINNISTON / KINNERSON / KENNERSON / KENISON, Thomas 47~1
KENNY see KENNEY
KENRICK see KENDRICK
KENSINGTON, [Lord] 124~36
KENT, [child] 149~15 [Mrs.] 149~16 Ezra 149~15, 149~16 Israel 316~21 Joseph 124~40 Polly 172~13 Rachel 200~45 William A. 11~39
KENTHOUGH, Benjamin 104~10 Lucy (———) (Foster) 104~10
KEPPLE see COPPLE
KER see KERR
KERBY / KIRBY, Azubah 189~52 E. 178~53 Ephraim 173~38 Ruth 178~52, 185~51
KERN, George 27~15
KERNS see KARNS
KERR / KER, David 185~48 Nathaniel 178~56
KERSEY, Joseph 269~36 William 64~49
KETCHAM, Jonas 179~53
KETTRIDGE see KITTREDGE
KEY see KAY
KEYES see KYES
KEYS see KYES
KIARNEY, Philip P. 25~19
KIBBE see KIBBEY
KIBBEY / KIBBE, Elisha 110~27 Polly (Ayres) 110~27
KIDD, [girls] 34~50 [Mrs.] 34~49 Charles 34~48
KIDDER / KEDER, Deborah 295~41 Elizabeth 182~39 Ezra 226~26 Fanny (Hubbard) 139~44 Gideon 139~43 Isaac 160~25 Isaiah 320~38 John 204~28 Samuel 309~49

KIDNEY, James 23~22
KILBORN see KILBURN
KILBOURN(E) see KILBURN
KILBURN / KILBOURNE / KILBORN / KILBOURN, [Mrs.] 229~30 Abigail 84~13 Appleton 184~58 Elijah 23~17 Ezra 101~54 Hezekiah 274~35 James 208~47 Jerusha 136~41 John 28~22 Joseph 260~37 Leurenda 98~28 Roxana 272~29 Solomon 252~38 Theral 231~47 William 229~28
KILHAM / KILLUM / KILLOM / KILLAM / KELLAM, Joseph 234~14
KILLAM see KILHAM
KILLEN, William 216~15, 217~14
KILLOM see KILHAM
KILLUM see KILHAM
KILTON see KELTON
KIMBALL / KEMBALL / KEMBLE (see also CIMBAL), [widow] 177~29 Amos 56~27 Barnard 94~5 Benjamin 162~1 Betsey 20~37 Daniel 143~51, 295~50, 303~6, 323~49, 362~34 David T. 261~29 Eliphaelt 194~30 Fanny (Stimpson) 152~2 George 68~48, 138~14, 316~23 Jabez 187~40 Jeremiah 285~29 John 6~55, 361~43, 364~11 Joseph 47~49, 57~15, 152~2 Lydia 258~24 Martha 231~15 Mary 193~12 Nabby 179~36 Nancy 179~35 Olive 79~5 Rebekah (———) (Goodenow) 57~15 Roxilana 313~18 Ruth 2~32 Stephen 20~37, 286~16, 311~17 Steven 334~11 Sukey 334~39 Thomas 45~34, 60~56 Thomas H. 60~55
KIMBERLEY, William 1~9
KIMPSTON, John 213~16
KINDRECK see KENDRICK
KING, [Mrs.] 229~36 Benjamin 105~7 Daniel 176~35 David 135~5 Eliza (Sharp) 87~44 Elizabeth 235~15 Erastus 185~4 Henry 87~43 James 229~36 John A. 317~49 Jonathan 289~3 Joseph 87~14, 185~3 Lucy 289~2 Mary (Ray) 317~49 Mary A. 274~13 Richard 88~5 Rufus 317~49 Samuel 20~20 Seth 150~30 Susannah 64~40 Thomas 92~14
KINGMAN, David 195~9 Ezra 4~35, 12~16 Nathan 12~15 Susannah 4~34
KINGSBERY see KINGSBURY
KINGSBURY / KINGSBERY / KINSBURY, [child] 322~4 [Mr.] 124~18, 158~10, 198~34 Abraham 289~30 Absalom 191~54, 194~37, 214~3, 265~13, 318~44 Cyrus 208~10, 309~11 E. 298~22, 311~54 Elisha 1~20, 21~51, 26~21, 41~37, 95~15, 124~21, 132~35, 165~24, 166~9, 177~21, 178~24, 214~5, 222~19, 224~56, 226~21, 262~20, 372~23 Ephraim 125~17, 194~38, 214~3, 237~23, 265~13, 278~22, 316~20, 318~45 Joel 114~9 Jonathan 262~43 Joseph 246~5, 246~45, 286~33 Leonard 125~17 Margaret 234~41 Olive (Adams) 114~9 Oliver 314~4 Priscilla 182~41 Rebecca (?) 318~45 Sally (Palmer) 289~30 Samuel 29~13, 81~41, 312~19, 322~4 Sanford 58~28, 70~5, 77~51, 84~7 Sarah 286~32 Simeon 270~24 Submit (———) 196~22
KINGSLEY / KINGSLY, Alpha 83~3 Hains 255~25 Polly 270~52
KINGSLY see KINGSLEY
KINNEAR see KENNEAR
KINNER see KENNEAR
KINNERSON see KENNISTON
KINNEY see KENNEY
KINNISTON see KENNISTON
KINSBURY see KINGSBURY
KINSMAN, [Dr.] 19~31 [Mrs.] 19~31 Aaron 286~18, 334~12 Nathaniel 286~53
KIP, Leonard 197~42
KIRBY see KERBY
KIRKLAND, [Rev.] 165~5 George 254~43 Sally 165~4 William 276~34
KIRKWOOD, James 212~48
KIRTLAND, Billious 219~12
KITCHEL / KITCHELL, Abraham 276~20 David 370~10
KITCHELL see KITCHEL
KITFIELD, [Mrs.] 23~27 Edward 23~27
KITTERA, John Wilkes 92~41
KITTERIDGE see KITTREDGE
KITTREDGE / KITTRIDGE / KITTERIDGE / KETTRIDGE, [Dr.] 112~53, 183~17, 330~53 [Mrs.] 80~46 Ebenezer Eaton 183~15 Elijah 317~36 Elizabeth 87~38 Francis 267~16 James 208~48 Jesse 24~41, 144~1, 295~42 Jessemiah 69~50 Jesseniah 69~51, 299~9, 306~37 John 168~51, 242~4 Mary (Plummer) 242~5 Roswell 183~14 Sibel (Bundy) 267~16 Stephen 87~38, 183~14 Sukey 183~14
KITTRIDGE see KITTREDGE
KITTS, Michael 245~9
KLEIN see KLINE
KLIEN see KLINE
KLINE / KLIEN / KLEIN, D. 38~17 Daniel 63~15, 367~60 Jacob 38~16, 39~8, 63~4, 367~61 John 38~16, 63~15, 63~15, 367~59
KNAP see KNAPP
KNAPP / KNAP, [girl] 259~47 Ebenezer 171~28, 259~47 Irene (Wright) 171~28 James 87~19, 113~42 Jno. 116~28 Joshua 101~53, 116~28 Sally 36~26 William 116~28
KNEELAND, [child] 228~41 Abner 216~36, 228~41, 243~7, 302~32, 303~53, 304~24, 320~18, 321~13 Eliza 149~24 Waitstill (Ormsbee) 228~39 William 211~55
KNIGHT, [Judge] 178~48 [Mr.] 23~34, 229~28 [sisters] 23~34 Artemas 296~8 Daniel 52~5 Elijah 21~43 Elizabeth 92~46 Enos 163~24 Jonathan 291~30 Joshua 9~3 Mary 95~38 Rhodolphus 297~33 Samuel 178~47
KNIGHTS, Elijah 87~18 Samuel 164~10
KNOTT see NOTT
KNOULTON see KNOWLTON
KNOWLTON / KNOULTON, [Mr.] 236~18 Ezekiel 262~57 Luther 333~46 Sally 23~46
KNOX, [Gen.] 18~36, 266~22 John 192~53 Julia Wadsworth 18~36 Ruth 129~3 Samuel 192~53 Thomas 179~46
KOESTER, Becksmith 204~39
KOLLOCK, Henrietta 181~44 Henry 162~35
KOPPLE see COPPLE
KRAFFTZS see CRAFTS
KRIST, [Mrs.] 208~24
KROUCHER, [Mr.] 69~21
KUDER, V. 38~16 Valentine 39~8, 63~13, 367~59
KUGLER, Polly 38~42
KURY see CURREY
KYES / KEYES / KEYS / KEAYS, Amos 217~55, 246~22, 274~45, 292~34 Betsey (———) 230~1 Catharine 105~47 Eber 58~7 Eleazer W. 140~11 John 316~49 Metalda 244~1 Mezalda 292~33 Pamela (Allen) 140~12 Polly 274~45
KYSER see KEISER

L.

L'ESTRANGE, Joseph 195~56
LABEREE see LABREE
LABREE / LABEREE, Benjamin 227~56 Peter 136~17
LACOCK, Samuel 202~32
LACROIX see la CROIX
la CROIX / La CROIX / LACROIX, Peter 63~23, 368~2 Sally 175~21
LAD see LADD
LADD / LAD, Daniel 45~21, 181~49 Dorothy (Merrill) 356~39 Eliphalet 133~34, 231~43 Ezekiel 310~53 Hannah (Burt) 181~49 Henry 133~34 James 316~55 John 45~19 Noah 151~45 Samuel 277~25 Simeon 80~25, 286~15, 286~17, 311~19, 334~11, 334~13 Stephen 356~39 W.M. 355~48
LADER, Thomas 45~30
LAFLIN see LAUGHLIN
LAIDLIE / LEDLIE, Abigail (Kilbourne) 84~13 James 254~41 Samuel 84~13 William 75~41, 77~33, 92~23
LAIGHT, Eliza 321~3
LAIGHTON see LEIGHTON
LAINE see LANE
LAKE / LEAK / LEAKE / LEEK, [children] 238~32 [Mrs.] 238~32 Benjamin 238~30 Elisha 274~15, 277~10 Hannah (Bark) 125~2 Henry 211~55 Nicholas

125~2 Sally 183~44
LAKIN / LUKIN, Agnes 29~39 Peter 111~51 William 29~39
LAMB / LAMM, [Capt.] 246~33 Betsey 183~51 George 40~6 John 67~19 Mark 76~33 Obadiah 66~3 Robert 75~19 William 187~36
LAMBERT / LUMBERT, Ann 255~26, 255~55 Daniel 308~2 John 170~34 Ruth 57~13
LAMBERTON, Elizabeth 303~13
LAMBSON see LAMSON
LAMM see LAMB
la MOUCHE, Antoine Robert 214~13
LAMPHEAR see LAMPHIER
LAMPHERE see LAMPHIER
LAMPHIER / LAMPHEAR / LANPHEAR / LAMPHERE / LANPHIER, [mother] 266~54 [Mr.] 277~37 [Mrs.] 266~55 George 266~54 William 224~55
LAMPREY, Morrise 313~28
LAMPSON see LAMSON
LAMSON / LAMPSON / LAMBSON, [boy] 131~19 [Mr.] 131~20, 226~16, 286~15, 311~19 Benjamin 80~29 Elizabeth 90~13 John 11~4, 282~23 Joseph 364~12 Stephen 361~39
LANCASTER, Betsey (Miller) 87~43   E.F. 356~4 Moses P. 87~42 William 216~7
LANCKTON see LANGDON
LANCTON see LANGDON
LANDER, [Capt.] 52~48
LANE / LAYN / LAINE, [boy] 90~18 [girl] 90~17 Angelica (Van Rensselaer) 205~52 Betsey 65~9 Charles 355~13 Derick 205~52 Elizabeth (Appleton) 93~12 Ephraim 41~36, 109~29, 121~3, 204~23 Esther 183~32 Fanny 37~54 George 177~7 Ira 204~19 Jedidiah 197~2 Jesse 6~35, 75~9, 86~9, 90~17, 101~8 Lydia 99~28, 99~57 Samuel 1~10, 277~21 Thomas 93~12 William 211~31
LANFORD see LANGFORD
LANG, Betsey 37~46 Jacob 69~47 Richard 183~5 Stephen 37~49
LANGDON / LANGTON / LANCTON / LANCKTON / LANKTON, [Gov.] 319~2 [Mr.] 156~27 [Rev.] 41~32 Abigail 167~14 Caroline 334~57 Israel 92~15 John 133~30, 240~36, 283~42 Levi 28~17 Sally 154~32 Samuel 15~27 Thomas 120~30 Woodbury 177~56, 319~3, 334~58
LANGFORD / LANFORD / LANKFORD, Jesse 321~21 Sarah 61~56
LANGLEY / LANGLY, Charles 12~13   J. 124~30
LANGLY see LANGLEY
LANGTON see LANGDON
LANGWORTHY, James 92~37 Jonathan 92~37
LANKFORD see LANGFORD
LANKSFORD, Jesse 116~30, 133~56
LANKTON see LANGDON
LANMAN, James 180~26 Susanna (Goldthwait) 180~25
LANPHEAR see LAMPHIER
LANPHIER see LAMPHIER
LANSING, Abraham D. 214~25   Jane 275~35   S. 275~35
LAPHAM / LAPPIN, Abner 242~23 Luther 185~43, 250~19 Samuel 250~20 Sophia (Dunbar) 185~43
LAPPIN see LAPHAM
LARABEE see LARRABEE
LARCOM, David 120~42 Elizabeth (Haskell) 120~42 Mary 116~28
LARKIN, [boy] 314~30 [children] 236~13 [girls] 314~30 [Mrs.] 236~12 Abel 314~29 Benjamin 152~34 E. 213~4 Ebenezer 112~28 Isaac 15~4 Mary (Howe) 112~28 Patrick 236~12 Samuel 133~16 T. 314~30
LARNED see LEARNED
LARRABEE / LARABEE, James 92~41
LASELL see LASELLE
LASELLE / LASELL / LAZELL, G. 262~7 John R. 335~16 Margaret 262~7
LASH, Mary 117~49
LASHER, John 232~20
LASKEY, [boy] 161~30 Jonathan 161~30
LASSLY see LESLIE
LASTIS, Ireana 317~18
La TAPPY, L. 314~45

LATHAM, Lucy 95~35 Simeon 10~21
LATHROP see LOTHROP
LATIMER see LATTEMER
LATTEMER / LATIMER, Elizabeth 5~36
LAUGHLIN / LAFLIN, John 156~3
LAUGHTON, John 312~31
LAURENCELLE, [woman] 187~24
LAURENS see LAWRENCE
LAW, Betsey 157~53 Richard 192~29, 228~20
LAWRANCE see LAWRENCE
LAWRENCE / LAURENS / LAWRANCE, [child] 264~50 [Dr.] 190~8 [Mrs.] 213~45 Ama (Rice) 228~7 Bigelow 242~4 Charles 176~18 David 284~18 Diana 242~3   E.S. 355~49 Harry 213~44 Jonathan 158~21, 248~1 Lucy 84~26 Lucy (Bigelow) 201~14 Luther 201~14 Oliver 2~35, 3~27 Parker 335~51 Philemon 264~50   William 51~3, 156~44, 270~3, 320~31 Zacheriah 228~6
LAWREY see LAWRY
LAWRY / LOWRIE / LOWERY / LOWRY / LAWREY / LOUGHRY, [Mr.] 27~18 William 30~36
LAWS, George 297~20
LAWSON, [Lieut.] 136~3   Edward 213~24   John 260~18 Richard 152~13 Robert 189~47 Sally (Davis) 260~18
LAWTON, Josiah 280~9 Lewis 280~9
LAYCOUNT, [Mrs.] 99~55
LAYN see LANE
LAZELL see LASELLE
LaCROIX see laCROIX
LEACH / LEETCH / LECH / LEICH / LEECH, [Mrs.] 203~41 Abigail 152~45 Asa 258~21 Bathsheba (———) 201~16 Jane 109~35 John 48~51, 160~3 Joseph 109~35 Molineux 100~2 Rebecca (Flagg) 109~35 Thomas 160~2
LEAK see LAKE
LEAKE see LAKE
LEALAND see LELAND
LEAMAN see LEEMAN
LEAMING, Jonathan 295~52
LEAR, Benjamin 135~39
LEARNARD see LEARNED
LEARNED / LEARNARD / LARNED, Abigail 99~49 Daniel 17~50 Erastus 182~31 Grace 140~43 Jonathan 328~50 Joseph D. 305~15 Joshua 33~45 Mary 305~15 Samuel 33~47 Sarah 33~45
LEARNING, Jeremiah 168~54
LEASH, James 17~44
LEATE see LEETE
LEATHERS / LEITHERS, Ezekiel 96~24   Isaac 203~12 John 193~10
LEAVE see LEAVY
LEAVETT see LEAVITT
LEAVITT / LEVETT / LEAVETT, D. 65~51 David 112~55, 276~24 Dudley 349~5 Edmond 80~27   G. 272~16 Hannah (———) (Shannon) 148~44 Hooker 288~44 Jemima (Loomis) 83~25 Joanna (?) 92~7 John 148~44 Jonathan 355~53 Joseph 117~13 Nancy (Munn) 288~44 Thaddeus 83~25
LEAVY / LEAVE / LEVY, Benjamin 113~29
LEBAY, Sally 64~41
LECH see LEACH
LEDLIE see LAIDLIE
LEDYARD, Benjamin 153~35 Isaac 148~55
LEE / LEIGH, [Mr.] 217~40 [Mrs.] 255~52   Aaron 246~6 Abigail 171~39, 219~9 Abigail (Smith) 105~24 Abner 313~29 Andrew 105~24 Benjamin Chadbourn 363~45 Chauncey 219~10 Edmond 321~20 Elizabeth 151~4, 200~49 Elizabeth (Tucker) 230~42 Ezekiel 173~3 Francis Lightfoot 2~4 George 87~11 Gideon 133~50 James 111~20 Jane 213~36 Jason 321~3 John 146~35 Jonathan 4~4, 21~16, 24~38, 68~14 Joseph 3~1, 111~31, 217~4, 227~29 Lucy 227~29 Mary 217~4, 239~35 Mehitable 301~22, 302~13 Nathaniel 230~41 Samuel 227~28, 312~43 Thomas 5~20, 211~37, 213~36 William 155~21 Woodes 244~56 Zebulon 265~3
LEECH see LEACH
LEEDS, Patience 160~26 William 232~30
LEEK see LAKE
LEEMAN / LEAMAN, John 143~43

LEET see LEETE
LEETCH see LEACH
LEETE / LEET / LEATE, [children] 192~33 [Mrs.] 192~33 Sarah 227~32 Susannah 65~42
LEFAVOR / LEFAVOUR / LEFEVRE, Stephen 9~55
LEFAVOUR see LEFAVOR
LEFEVRE see LEFAVOR
LEFFINGWELL, Christopher 174~29 Fanny 131~55, 174~28 Samuel 3~18
LEGATE, Deborah 107~6 Thomas 107~7, 280~53
LEGAUX, Peter 74~15
LEGGETT, [children] 121~38 Thomas 121~37
LEICH see LEACH
LEIGH see LEE
LEIGHTON / LAIGHTON, Deborah (Seavey) 95~27 Jonathan 357~47 Mark 95~27 Mary 357~47 Samuel 116~1 Sarah 353~4
LEITHERS see LEATHERS
LELAND / LEALAND, [child] 153~25 [Mrs.] 51~34, 153~24, 153~25 Aaron 5~44, 49~13, 51~35, 300~45 Benjamin 325~19 Daniel 153~25 Hepsebah 199~25 John 199~25, 310~25 Joshua 329~27 Phineas 3~41, 153~25 Phinehas 83~17 Solomon 13~46, 33~4, 83~19, 325~28
LEMAN see LEMON
Le MERCIER, Mary 98~21
LEMON / LEMAN, John 275~1
LENNOX / LENOX, George 194~54 Hugh 274~33 William 143~46
LENOX see LENNOX
LEOMIS see LOOMIS
LEONARD / LEONARDS, [child] 374~27 [Mr.] 3~52 Abigail 38~52 Apollos 35~53 Apollos B. 105~26 Betsey 323~30 Daniel 186~2, 214~11 E. 91~23 Ezra 172~46 G. 91~24 George 218~17 H. 15~12, 33~24 Harriot 142~30 Lucinda 267~11 Joseph 374~27 Mary 96~56 Mary G. 160~24 Nancy (Fenn) 214~11 Peggy 169~15 Rachel 218~16 Rhoda 186~1 Sally (Fisher) 49~7 Samuel 289~37 Sukey 120~25 Wesley 186~1 William 254~26 Zenas Lockwood 49~6
LEONARDS see LEONARD
LEOWENSTERN, Ferdinand 14~33
Le PORTEVINE, Jane 173~46
LESLIE / LASSLY, Archibald 256~10 George 75~2 James 81~47 Jane Livermore 111~47
LESTER, Abigail Mehitable 300~57
LEVALLEY, John 286~37
LEVERETT, Benjamin 133~38
LEVETT see LEAVITT
LEVIUS, Peter 20~29
LEVY see LEAVY
LEWIN, (——) 72~45
LEWIS, [Gov.] 314~22 [Lieut.] 65~26 [Miss] 247~35 [Mr.] 63~7, 105~51, 148~41 A. 160~11 Abner 160~10 Benjamin 202~22 Caleb 130~33 Charles 59~37 Daniel 291~37 Daniel Taylor 112~26 David 112~40 Eliza 57~21 Elizabeth V. (Greenwood) 112~26 Experience 225~20 Francis 136~21 Hannah 54~47, 119~1 Jacob Azott 105~49 James 24~42, 61~22 John 175~32, 180~36 Lydia 97~21 Lyman 181~48 271~31 M.G. 187~20 Margaret (Ashley) 181~48 Mary 5~19 Mordecai 35~53 Nancy 144~30 Rebecca (Brown) 175~32 Rebecca B. 137~28 Sally 153~48 Susanna 207~46 Thomas 5~19, 119~2, 299~23 William 151~15
LIBBEE see LIBBEY
LIBBEY / LIBBY / LIBBEE, [Mr.] 135~14, 180~6 Ann 354~24 Daniel 96~26, 165~40 Hannah (——) (Watson) 177~44 James 57~53, 348~26 Jeremiah 111~53, 133~35, 272~8 Lydia 83~19 Roger 177~44
LIBBY see LIBBEY
LIGHTFOOT, Francis 222~37 Henry Benskin 220~11, 222~35 Nicholas 222~41 William 59~7, 222~41
LILLIBRIDGE, Charlotte 178~50
LILLIE see LILLY
LILLY / LILLIE, Daniel 284~12 Nabby 96~23
LIMINGTON, James 144~8
LINCOLN, Abiather 48~12 Amos 102~36 Benjamin 323~43 Elkenah 26~35 Enoch 353~21 Jane 64~27 Mordecai 296~2 Nancy Thorndike 158~3 Perez 206~42, 212~1 Susannah (Gill) 99~47 Welcome 99~47

William 89~41
LINDERMAN, Dorothy 213~35, 214~18
LINDSAY see LINDSEY
LINDSEY / LINSAY / LINDSAY, [Mr.] 50~37 Benjamin 113~26 Elizabeth (Woods) 113~26 Robert 204~39
LINN see LYNN
LINSAY see LINDSEY
LINSLEY, John 195~33
LION see LYON
LIPPINCOTT, [Mr.] 254~42
LISCAN see LISCOMB
LISCOMB / LISCAN / LUSCOMB, Harriet 50~11
LISLE see LYLE
LISLET, Elizabeth 305~6 Moreau 305~7
LITHGOW, Robert 131~42
LITTLE, Benjamin 295~11 Betsey 335~34 Daniel 103~27 Edmund 149~3 George 140~33 Jane 97~10 John 135~27 John P. 214~10 Jonathan 130~32 Mary F. (Prescott) 214~10 Samuel 36~31 Sarah 231~51 Stephen 133~35, 272~10 W. 335~34 Walter 81~6
LITTLEFIELD, Edmond 258~22
LITTLEHALE, Hannah (——) 268~55
LITTLEJOHN, Duncan 174~25
LITTLEPAGE, Lewis 125~6
LIVELY, Dominick 211~53
LIVERMORE, Arthur 321~29, 327~53 Daniel 47~20 E. 41~8 Edward St. Loe 39~25 George William 196~56 Jane 113~12 Jonathan 307~8 Louisa (Bliss) 321~30 Samuel 113~13 Sarah Crese Stackpole 39~26
LIVINGSTON / LIVINGSTONE, [Gov.] 120~50 Albert 258~12 Brockholst 281~28 Edward 88~41, 201~16 J. 202~11 Joana 218~2 John 27~7, 56~26, 120~1, 276~37, 295~43, 316~24 Louisa C. 281~28 Peter R. 218~2 Robert H. 166~31 Sarah 120~48 Walter 4~43
LIVINGSTONE see LIVINGSTON
LLEWELLYN, Morris 39~9
LLOYD, [Major] 221~30 James 314~41 Sarah 221~30 T. 250~34 Thomas 309~19
LOCK see LOCKE
LOCKE / LOCK / LOOK, Abigail (——) (Amazeen) 84~42 Anna 228~38 Edward 27~40 Elizabeth 177~29 228~38 Hall Jackson 84~42 Jacob 79~10, 140~17 John 37~3, 61~40, 82~50 Jonathan 324~26, 330~33 Joseph 87~20, 145~19 Louisa (Ferrin) 354~31 Nathaniel 58~31 Polly (Muzzy) 140~18 William 48~7, 354~31
LOCKWOOD, [Mrs.] 35~48, 52~34 A. 296~20 Abigail (Chillson) 188~54 Abraham 304~32 Abraham 2d 304~33 Benoni 316~51, 328~19 Daniel 188~54 John 49~12 Joseph 53~6, 111~17
LOGAN, [Rev.] 197~43 John 59~35, 174~32 Sheldon 103~24, 104~49
LOILER, Robert 285~2
LOMBARD / LOMBARE, Aaron 89~42 Cornelia (Hall) 189~36 Hannah 110~48 Martha 191~44 Roswell 189~36 Stephen 191~22
LOMBARE see LOMBARD
LOMIS see LOOMIS
LONG, (——) 133~46 Henry 269~6 John 179~45, 211~57 Joseph 176~31 Richard 46~57 William 65~53, 318~43
LONGLEY, Benjamin 73~11, 235~17 Edward 235~16 John 48~8 Robert 170~51
LONGSTREET, John 176~27
LOOK see LOCKE
LOOMIS / LUMMUS / LUMMAS / LOMIS / LEOMIS, Abdiel 69~11 Abijah 204~43 Amasa 196~54 Horace 194~3 Jemima 83~25 Lydia 140~14 Margaret 197~33 Mary (Chipman) 194~3 Priscilla 196~54, 197~32 Samuel 309~50 Welthy 52~56 Zacheus Hale 76~36
LOOTZ, Leonard 296~3
LOPEZ, Catharine 264~43
LORD, Abigail 157~45, 155~11 Benjamin 281~24 Ellice 126~3 George 126~6 Hezekiah 248~52 John 69~37 John (?) 171~26 Joseph 150~14 Jotham 95~23 Lucretia 185~44 Lynde 93~16 Nathaniel 248~52 Sally (Chase) (?) 171~26 Samuel 69~37, 288~30 Sarah 173~2
LORING, Caleb 123~10 Edward 86~50 Elijah 135~11 Frances (Greely) 86~50 Israel 64~41 Jonathan 60~37

Joseph 40~9, 361~7 Mary 53~48 Nancy 361~7 Sally (Lebay) 64~41
LORKWOOD, Joseph 111~17
LORNAX, Thomas Lumford 197~33
LORNING, Frances (———) (Dean) 114~46 Israel 114~45
LOT see **LOTT**
LOTHROP / LATHROP, [Rev.] 271~7, 290~34 Abigail 275~54 Benjamin 165~41 Charity 224~24 Dorcas 190~33 Dwight 232~8 Ebenezer 266~38, 271~7 Elijah 190~33, 229~10 Elizabeth 290~34 Lora (Stebbins) 232~8 Peggy (———) (Palmer) 229~10 Roswell 252~37 Rufus 209~45 Solomon 333~36 Thatcher 275~55 William 101~30
LOTT / LOT, Abraham 58~5 Maxwell (?) 320~39
LOTTY, Daniel 241~34
LOUD see **LOWD**
LOUDON, [Dr.] 91~2 John 239~23
LOUGHRY see **LAWRY**
LOVE, [Mr.] 53~57
LOVEJOY / LOVJOY, Benja (?) (Woodbridge) 153~50 Hannah 182~42, 223~17 Nathaniel 153~50
LOVEL see **LOVELL**
LOVELAND, Eunice 332~45 Polly 272~31
LOVELL / LOVEL, Betsey 41~20 Enos 258~42 Hannah 292~8 Helen 124~37 Irena 165~35 John 94~6, 101~47 Martha 97~12, 157~46 N. 311~9 Noah 146~3, 238~50 Oliver 74~39, 165~34 Phebe (Putnam) 238~50 Thomas 292~8 Timothy 61~34, 133~53 Vriling 36~13 Vryling 157~46
LOVEREN see **LOVERING**
LOVERIN see **LOVERING**
LOVERING / LOVERIN / LOVEREN / LOVRING, [Mr.] 141~47 Alice Winchester 75~15 Ebenezer 273~19 Thomas 279~10
LOVET see **LOVETT**
LOVETT / LOVET, [children] 217~22, 217~24 [widow] 217~21 Abigail (Elliot) 120~43 Alexander 41~3 Hannah 217~23 Hannah (Williston) 41~3 Israel 120~42 Joanna (?) 92~7 John 6~8, 217~22 William 94~17, 217~21
LOVJOY see **LOVEJOY**
LOVRING see **LOVERING**
LOW see **LOWE**
LOWD / LOUD, Samuel 364~13
LOWDER, Ann 94~16
LOWE / LOW, Betsey 93~13 John 301~28 John (?) 172~14 Joseph 155~23 Peter (?) 246~3 Sally (Chase) (?) 172~14 Sarah 40~11, 183~27
LOWEL see **LOWELL**
LOWELL / LOWEL, Charles 224~51, 261~40 Elizabeth 215~30 Harriot (Spence) 261~40 John 119~30 Mary 37~55 Olive 132~50 Samuel 132~50, 144~19
LOWERY see **LAWRY**
LOWRIE see **LAWRY**
LOWRY see **LAWRY**
LOWTHER, Henrietta 92~10
LUCAR, Catharine (———) (Clinton) 60~32 John 60~31 Mary 60~28
LUCAS / LUCKIS, Abigail 297~29 H. 163~47 Paul 265~56 Samuel 297~29
LUCKET, John M. 177~56
LUCKIS see **LUCAS**
LUDDEN, [Mr.] 26~32
LUDLOW, Gabriel W. 182~6 George D. 286~40
LUEY, Sally 117~42 William 117~40
LUFF, Rachel 192~19
LUKIN see **LAKIN**
LULL, [boy] 7~40 Jesse 111~18 Peggy 280~57 Richard 7~39 Thomas 117~8 Timothy 280~58
LUMBERT see **LAMBERT**
LUMMAS see **LOOMIS**
LUMMUS see **LOOMIS**
LUND, Jonathan 32~18
LUNT, Daniel 263~55 Joseph 47~20, 80~28, 334~14 Margaret 263~55 Sarah 42~52
LUNZIES, [infants] 218~52 [Mr.] 218~52 [widow] 218~52
LUPAZZOLO, [Mr.] 124~50
LUPTON, [children] 189~21 Asa 189~21
LUSCOMB see **LISCOMB**
LUTHER, Betsey (Parkman) 263~35 Jabez 263~35

LUTWYCHE, Ed. G. 20~27
LUYSTER, Matthias 155~22
LYDE, George 158~18
LYFORD, Francis 362~22 Kinsly 361~41 Mehitable 362~22 Moses 362~21
LYLE / LISLE / LYLES, [Mrs.] 291~9 Enoch M. 207~38, 207~49 Harriet (Huston) 153~47 James 252~49 John 232~19, 291~8 Thomas 153~47
LYLES see **LYLE**
LYMAN, Abigail 184~35 Abigail (Ripley) 170~16 Cornelius 192~50 Elias 11~5, 20~54, 36~46 Elihu 56~14 Eliphalet 170~16 Elisha 61~21 Erastus 272~27 Eunice 103~22 Frances (———) 220~2 Frances (Goodwin) 182~35 Gad 80~9, 115~30, 143~16 Isaac 234~5, 319~49 J. 142~36 Jane 98~33 Jonathan H. 283~6 Joseph 169~18, 217~20 Justin 20~54, 36~46, 182~35 Lucretia (Pickering) 234~5 Mary 142~23, 217~19 Mary (Warren) 141~5 Naomi (Janes) 79~27 Phenious 143~6 Phin. 304~17 Phineas 278~34 Phinehas 80~10, 325~40 Rachel (Hutchins) 272~28 Sally 233~11, 286~2 Samuel 121~18 Seth 103~22 Solomon 286~3 Sophia (Hinckley) 283~6 Sylvester 79~27 Theodore 250~21 William 142~36
LYNDES see **LYNES**
LYNDS see **LYNES**
LYNES / LYNDES / LYNDS, Rebecca 118~55
LYNN / LINN, [Rev.] 171~31 Elizabeth 171~30 John 114~51 John Blair 166~27
LYON / LION, [Widow] 246~44 Abigail 107~45 Baxter 193~46 Benjamin 61~45 Betsey (Lamb) 183~51 Daniel 183~11 David 48~13 Eli 182~50 Isaac 218~19 John 24~43, 143~52 Josiah 256~55 Marcus 219~44, 239~25, 372~5 Matthew 28~36, 138~5, 369~51 Robert 205~45 Thomas 183~51 William 189~12
LYONS, David 151~4 Peter 307~16 Robert 217~53 William 41~53, 45~29, 51~14, 87~53

M.

M'..... see Mac .....
MACAFEE, [Mrs.] 240~45
MacALLISTER / MacOLLISTER / McALLISTER / M'COLLISTER / M'COLLESTER, Francis 272~19 Jannet 299~19 Richard 81~50
MacALPIN / M'ALPIN, Robert 167~16
MacBEATH / M'BEATH, Andrew 57~51 Martha 57~50
M'BRIDE, Daniel 194~9
M'BRIEN, Rebecca 209~49
M'CABE, B. 54~51
MacCARNEY / M'CARNEY, Martha 252~32
MacCARREL / M'CARREL, John 7~14
MacCARTNEY / M'CARTNEY, Olive (Swanzey) 143~25 Reynal 143~25
MACCARTY see **MacCARTY**
MacCARTY / MACCARTY / M'CARTY, Edward 219~24 Lucretia 317~21 Martha 152~33 Mary 108~21 Thaddeus 108~21, 132~20
MacCAULEY / M'AULEY, Mary (Magossin) 253~43 Thomas 253~43
MacCHRISTIE / M'CHRISTIE, John 218~13
MacCLANEN / Mc'CLANEN, James 33~2
MacCLARY see **MacCLEARY**
MacCLEARY / MacCLARY / M'CLARY / M'CLEARY, [Mr.] 362~32 John 94~15 Mary 165~14 Michael 11~39 Robert 133~37, 155~13 Sophia (Davenport) 155~13
MacCLINTOCK / McLINTOCK / M'CLINTOCK, [———] 77~55 [Capt.] 133~15 [Rev.] 160~26 Aaron 64~32 Samuel 160~53 William 280~26, 329~42
MacCLURE / M'CLURE / M'CLUER / McLURE, [General] 173~40 [Maj. Gen.] 174~27 Elizabeth 208~39 James 205~47, 311~18
MacCLYMENT / M'CLYMENT, James 118~45
MacCOBB / M'COBB, Mary (Langdon) 240~36
MacCOLLUM see **MacCULLUM**
MacCONNELL / M'CONNELL, Charles 232~45
MacCORKLE / M'CORKLE / M'CORCLE, [Mr.] 250~23

James Ray 246~36
MacCORMICK / M'CORMICK, Christopher 59~19 James 187~3
MacCOWAN / M'COWAN, Cady 198~23
MacCRACKEN / M'CRACKEN, (———) 72~46 J. 94~10 Rebecca (Hopkins) 94~10
MacCREEDY / M'CREEDY, Jane 260~17
MacCROSKY / M'CROSKY, [Rev.] 145~26
MacCULLER, William 229~52
MacCULLOUGH / M'CULLOUGH, Jenny 163~20
MacCULLUM / M'COLLOM / MacCOLLUM, Archibald 331~10 Martha 333~48 Rebecca 331~11
MacCUMMING / M'CUMMING, Bryce 202~16
MacCURDY / M'CURDY / M'CURDAY / M'CORDY, Elizabeth 289~53 Hugh 187~12 James 21~22, 87~21 John 181~38, 220~11, 289~21 Samuel 289~53 Ursula 96~16
MacDANIELS / M'DANIELS, Peletiah 304~54
MacDONALD / M'DONALD, [child] 29~56 [Mrs.] 29~56 C. 138~15 James 29~56
MACDONOGH see MacDONOGH
MacDONOGH / MACDONOGH, Thomas 179~1
MacDOUGALL / M'DOUGLE, John 138~4 Mary 138~3
MacDOWELL / McDOWELL / M'DOWELL, [Mrs.] 48~43 Esther 138~28 John 138~29, 181~44 Joseph 100~42
MacELLORY / M'ELLORY, Elizbaeth 40~10
MacEWEN / M'EWEN, Abel 265~8
MacFALL / M'FALL, Judith (———) (Perkins) 301~44 William 301~43
MacFARLAN see MacFARLAND
MacFARLAND / MacFARLAN / M'FARLAND / M'FARLIN / M'FARLAN / M'PHARLAND, [Mr.] 46~38, 56~6 Asa 53~52, 94~8, 100~43, 149~24 Betsey 211~31 Clarissa 53~52 Eliza (Kneeland) 149~24 John 253~33 M. 306~5 Nancy 100~43 Nancy (Dwight) 94~8 William 178~46
MacFEE / M'FEE, [Mrs.] 221~22 Daniel 20~26
MacFOOT / M'FOOT, [Mr.] 194~36
MacGAHAGAN / M'GAHAGAN, Lewis 239~22
MacGAW / M'GAW, Jacob 329~35
MacGEE / MAGEE, James 84~31
MacGINNESS / MAGINNIS, Samuel Jameson 218~28
MacGIRK / M'GIRK, [Mrs.] 131~7 James 131~7
MacGLOUGHLAN / M'GLOUGHLAN, Thomas 19~49
MacGREGOR / M'GREGOR / M'GREGORE / McGREGORY, [Mrs.] 251~21 [Rev.] 251~22 David 20~19 James 20~20, 32~30, 80~22, 81~49, 108~13
MacGUER see MacGUIRE
MacGUIRE / MacGUER / M'GUIRE, Edward 268~24
MacILVAINE / M'ILVAINE, William 260~30
MacINTIRE / M'INTIRE / McINTIRE, [Mr.] 180~9, 210~47 Charles 289~26 Joseph 335~46 Neil 133~13 Sarah 307~48 Sarah (Heineman) 289~27
MacINTOSH / MACKINTOSH / M'INTOSH, [Lt. Col.] 267~19 Donald 148~49 Duncan 265~41 Lachlan 228~10
MACK, David 309~50 Elisha 87~23, 93~49 Eruel 87~22 Joel 222~30 Ruel 109~21 William 304~37
MACKALL see MICKELL
MACKANESS, Thomas Thornton 211~1
MACKAY see MacKAY
MacKAY / MACKAY / MACKEY, Alexander 107~54 Andrew 312~11 Joshua 214~57 Mungo 64~31 Robert 203~31
MacKEAN / MacKEON / M'KEAN, Eliza 39~25 Robert 121~19
MacKEE / M'KEE, William 78~33
MacKELLER / M'KELLAR, [Mr.] 27~17
MacKENNON / M'KENNON / M'KENNAN, [Mr.] 48~42 W. 48~52 William 301~26
MACKENZIE see MacKENZINE
MacKENZIE see MacKENZINE
MacKENZINE / MacKENZIE / McKENZIE / M'KENZIE / MACKENZIE, Alexander 111~19 Elizabeth 156~22 Joseph 19~3 Polly 155~31
MacKEON see MacKEAN
MACKEY see MacKAY
MACKINTOSH see MacINTOSH
MACKLIN, Margaret 355~19
MacKNIGHT / M'KNIGHT, [Capt.] 136~3

MacLANATHAN / M'LANATHAN, John 107~5 Rebecca (Baldwin) 107~4
MacLANE / MacLEAN / M'LEAN / M'LANE, [brothers] 366~29 [Capt.] 10~33 [Messrs.] 6~52 David 366~35 John 190~28, 217~1 Sally 217~12
MacLAUGHLIN / M'LAUTHLIN, Elenor 14~20 Thomas 14~21
MacLEAN see MacLANE
MacLELLAN / M'LELLAN, S.R. 315~19
MacLEOD / M'LEOD, [Capt.] 299~35
MacMANAS / M'MANUS, Charles 17~27
MacMILLEN / M'MILLEN / M'MILLIN / M'MILLION, (———) 72~45 Ann 184~43 Catherine 221~7 John 136~32, 221~6
MacMURRAY / McMURRAY, Samuel 11~20
MacNARY / M'NAIRY, Nathaniel A. 209~31
MacNEAL / MacNEIL / MacNEILL / MacNEALE / Mc'NEIL / M'NEAL / McNEIL / M'NEILL / M'NEIL, Archibald 284~ Elizabeth 145~15 Hopestill 245~17 John 72~52 Thomas 22~38
MacNEALE see MacNEAL
MacNEIL see MacNEAL
MacNEILL see MacNEAL
MacNORVELL / M'NORVELL, Mackay 233~15
MacOLLISTER see MacALLISTER
MACPHERSON see MacPHERSON
MacPHERSON / M'PHERSON / MACPHERSON / McPHERSON, [Gen.] 255~39 [Miss] 255~37 Daniel 123~10 E.M. 255~36 Elizabeth 267~8 Elizabeth (White) 138~11 William 138~11
MacQUAY / M'QUAY, [Capt.] 21~7
McQUEEN / M'QUEEN, Lewis 140~31
MacRAE / MacREA / M'REA / M'CRAE, Mary (Champlin) 106~26 William 85~32, 106~25, 296~21, 373~50
MacREA see MacRAE
MADISON, James 86~54, 322~32
MAFFAY see MOFFAY
MAFFIT / MOFFATT, Daniel 99~13 Huldah (Clough) 99~13
MAGEE see MacGEE
MAGINNIS see MacGINNESS
MAGOSSIN, Joseph 234~39 Mary 253~43
MAGRUDER, Philip 93~21
MAHEW, Eunice 92~28
MAHON, Bernard 137~19
MAHONEY / MAHONY, Mary 162~12
MAHONY see MAHONEY
MAHURIN, Ephraim 93~48
MAIN / MAINE / MAYNE, [Mrs.] 217~12 Isaac 175~9
MAINE see MAIN
MAITLAND, James 208~5
MAJOR, Francis 192~38, 193~2
MAKAHALY, Michael 128~55
MAKENS, Anna 101~30
MAKEPEACE, Rebecca (———) (Vose) 200~42 Royal 200~41
MALCOMSON, James 168~50
MALEY, [Capt.] 348~18 [Lt.] 368~44 Lydia 127~13
MALLEN see MELLEN
MALLET see MICKELL
MALLON see MELLEN
MALLOON see MELOON
MALLORY, David 208~51
MALON see MELLEN
MALOON see MELOON
MAN see MANN
MANARD see MANERD
MANCIUS, Withelmus 284~14
MANERD / MANARD / MAYNARD, [children] 303~4 [Mrs.] 303~3 Artemas 283~17 Daniel 225~55 David 302~55 Holland 172~30 J. 313~51 John 35~44, 297~40 Lemuel 310~26 Persis 172~29 Phineas 299~57 Sophia (Carter) 35~44 Trobridge 98~31 Warban 50~51
MANLY, David 333~47 Dorcas (Hale) 207~10 Ira 207~10
MANN / MAN / MUNN, [children] 291~36 [Miss] 243~7 [Mrs.] 124~33 [Rev.] 243~8 Abijah 294~28 Alexander 291~35 Alice 262~39 Anna 108~27 John 191~20, 292~40, 294~28 John 3d 290~26 Larnard 127~20, 136~47, 307~26, 312~18, 317~35 Learnard

296~56 Lewis 287~6 Louisa (Weld) 287~6 Lydia 292~40 Martha (Phelps) 290~26 Moses 71~25, 221~53 Nancy 288~44 Patty 204~32 Rufus 305~47
MANNA, Emmanuel 59~14
MANNERS, Mary (Rush) 155~47 Thomas 155~46
MANNING, Eliza 96~51 Joel 209~6 John 34~7 Josiah 273~12 Laurence 178~6 Lucy 168~44
MANNIS, Andrew 177~42 Fanny (Fessenden) 177~42
MANSFIELD, Achilles 300~56 Elizabeth 38~45 Hannah 361~9 Matthew 77~14, 361~9 Susan 300~55
MANSON / MUNSON / MONSON, Maria 165~8 Samuel 56~28 Seth 266~57
MANTER / MANTOR, Daniel 286~42
MANTON, Francis 226~8
MANTOR see MANTER
MANWARING, Hannah 254~11 Joseph 254~14
MAPLES, Thomas 209~16
MARBLE, Antipas 90~26 Joseph 206~33 Patience 211~39
MARCEY / MARCY / MORSEY / MARSEY / MERCY / MERCEY, Abel 24~17 Reuben 228~31 Samuel 151~23 Willard 115~17 Woodbury 328~4, 331~2
MARCH / MURCH, [Mr.] 320~34, 330~11, 350~26 [Mrs.] 158~31 Daniel 325~20 John 24~47, 244~49, 302~34, 308~44, 311~51 Joshua 81~18 Samuel 1~23, 170~21
MARCHAND see MARCHANT
MARCHANT / MARCHAND / MERCHANT, David 307~18 Henry Hall (?) 136~41 Jerusha (Kilborn) (?) 136~41
MARCY see MARCEY
MARDEEN, James 69~48
MARDEN / MARDIN, Jonathan 23~52 Roxana 355~17
MARDENBROUGH, [Miss] 189~29 Christopher 189~29
MARDIN see MARDEN
MARK, Philip 138~17
MARKHAM see MARKUM
MARKLIN, Charles 10~2
MARKS, [Lieut.] 64~50 Conrad 39~7, 63~4, 367~46, 367~63 William 301~19
MARKUM / MARKHAM, Daniel 316~7 Lucy 317~17
MARR, Eleanor 92~35 James 68~15
MARRIAN see MERRIAM
MARRICK see MERRICK
MARRY see MERRY
MARSEY see MARCEY
MARSH / MASH, [children] 230~13 [Mr.] 44~30 Asa 301~1 Benjamin 189~4 Betsey 51~22, 189~3 Daniel 1~25, 102~39, 247~23, 295~27, 309~47, 316~9 David 230~13 Ebenezer Grant 152~53 Elisha 93~24 Enoch 230~12 Farnham 196~14 Irene 353~10 James 82~47 John 82~39, 174~5, 303~55 Joseph 51~23 Josiah 44~51 Lucy 243~18 Rebecca 207~52 Rhoda (Davis) 301~1 Sally 289~31 Samuel 83~8, 127~44, 325~8, 361~46 Zebulon 231~43
MARSHALL, Charles 252~42 Christopher 169~7 Elizabeth (Lamberton) 303~13 Ethan 165~39 Hawley 361~15 Henry 361~15 Moses 303~12 Susannah 179~47 William 215~22
MARSTIN see MARSTON
MARSTON / MASTON / MARSTIN, [Miss] 72~56 Hannah 92~9 Jacob 44~42 William 3~44
MARTEN see MARTIN
MARTIN / MARTYN / MARTEN, [Mrs.] 98~24 Aaron 74~17 Alexander 96~18 Betsey (Adams) 239~36 Charles 253~32 Christopher 9~18 Daniel 239~36, 328~21 Isaiah 189~22 John D. 206~25 Josephus 261~58 Julia 206~25 Mary 299~23 Mary (Rogers) 96~18 Peter 106~3 Polly 150~28 Rachel 197~35 Stephen 221~35 Thomas 182~15
MARTINDALE, Elias 325~26
MARTYN see MARTIN
MARVIN, [Mr.] 8~12 [widow] 310~34 Carolina 294~2, 333~42 Giles 106~41, 207~7 John 294~1, 310~33 Patience 106~40 William 316~16
MASH see MARSH
MASON, [children] 232~55 [Mr.] 125~37, 145~54, 160~14 [Mrs.] 183~27 [widow] 232~55, 321~8 Ann 110~33 Asa 135~41 Ebenezer 129~7, 135~42 Elijah 89~42, 321~6, 323~23 Experience (———)

(Baker) 290~24 Hannah 179~38, 185~45, 320~16, 321~7, 323~24 Henry 48~53 Jeremiah 53~38 Job 95~46 John 60~47, 65~35, 95~46, 294~22 Jonas 89~5 Joseph 232~54, 303~54, 303~56 Lorany 92~33 Lucy 303~35, 333~48 Lydia 148~27 Mary (Means) 53~39 Nabby 65~40 Russel 68~49 Sadey 168~20 Sam 141~34 Simeon 290~24 Thaddeus 118~53 Thomas 95~38, 148~28 William 186~18
MASSAY see MASSEY
MASSEY / MASSAY / MESSEY, Ebenezer 49~9 Elizabeth (Mansfield) (?) 38~45 Nathaniel 38~45
MASSON, Francis 226~37
MASTEN, [Mr.] 76~27
MASTERS, Elizabeth (———) (Osborn) 261~38 James 261~38 Jonathan 158~42
MASTON see MARSTON
MATHER, Benjamin 200~20 Gibbons P. 200~29 John 264~21, 276~48 Sally (———) (Anderson) 229~9 Samuel 229~9, 287~22, 297~26
MATHES, Benjamin 256~39 Comfort (Smart) 256~39
MATHEWS see MATTHEWS
MATHEWSON see MATTHEWSON
MATSON / MATTESON, Aaron 37~5 David 238~38 Epaphras 56~7
MATTESON see MATSON
MATTHEWS / MATHEWS, Charlotte (Walsh) 332~32 George 59~34 James 332~32
MATTHEWSON / MATHEWSON, Othniel 265~44
MATTOCKS, Samuel 156~43 William 356~22
MATTOON, [Gen.] 155~35 Charles 207~5
MAULLING, James 147~5
MAUSTRESS, John 363~51
MAWPER, Amey (?) 203~35
MAXFIELD, [infant] 30~13 [Mr.] 209~37 [Mrs.] 209~39 Abigail 30~13
MAXSON, Martha 170~48
MAXWELL, (———) 320~39 Eliza 98~25 Elizabeth 191~16 Joseph 249~2, 250~40 Robert 15~10 William 81~3
MAY, Catharine C. 204~33 Eleazer 16~36, 21~41, 28~25, 36~52, 49~40, 61~36, 69~44, 82~45, 88~2, 103~51, 110~18, 134~24, 140~49, 275~39 Ephraim 5~20 Hezek. 152~43 Lemuel 220~56 Margaret (White) 152~43
MAYER see MEYER
MAYHEW, Zachariah 241~19, 245~50
MAYNARD see MANERD
MAYNE see MAIN
MAYO, Benjamin 5~23 Catharine 147~4 Samuel 104~20
Mc' . . . . . see Mac . . . . .
Mc . . . . . see Mac . . . . .
MEACHAM / MEACHEM, James 51~12
MEACHEM see MEACHAM
MEAD / MEADE, [Mr.] 324~24 Anna 202~18 Betsey (Gould) 210~27 David 140~17 Esther (Bundy) 140~17 Harriot 181~16 Moses 150~25, 309~48 Richard Kidder 184~49 Samuel 26~21, 181~15, 309~46 Stephen 244~51 Truman 210~27
MEADE see MEAD
MEADER / MEEDER / MEDER, Lydia 357~7 Samuel 357~7
MEADS / MEEDS, Ephraim 295~28 William 364~13
MEANS, Elizabeth 74~52 Jane 218~35 Mary 53~39 Robert 218~35 Thomas 327~47
MEARS, James 162~16
MEASE, John 10~4
MEDCALF see METCALF
MEDER see MEADER
MEECH, Esther 28~28
MEEDER see MEADER
MEEDS see MEADS
MEHEBERLE, Rebecca G. 354~23
MEIER see MEYER
MEIGGS see MEIGS
MEIGS / MEIGGS, Josiah 85~6 Mehitable 289~28 Nathan 329~49
MEINZES see MENZIES
MEIRCKIN, Rebecca 312~7
MELBECKE, [Lieut.] 38~13
MELCHER, Arthur 118~13 Elizabeth (Akerman) 118~14 John 91~26, 133~43 Jonathan 364~36 Polly (Flagg)

91~26 Tobias 228~25
MELENDY / MELLENDY, Abigail 229~8 Daniel 294~13 Ebenezer 194~42 Rhoda (Emery) 303~12 Sally (Powers) 294~13 Sibley 303~12 Sybil (———) (Willard) 194~43
MELIN *see* **MELLEN**
MELLAN *see* **MELLEN**
MELLEN / MALLEN / MULLEN / MULLIN / MILLEN / MELLAN / MELIN / MALLON / MALON, John 5~46, 112~16 Peter 221~22 Rebecca 112~16 Sophia 219~2 Thomas 217~31
MELLENDY *see* **MELENDY**
MELLENS, Rebeker 327~15
MELLER *see* **MILLER**
MELLISH, Samuel 217~34 Stephen 56~27, 61~23
MELLOON *see* **MELOON**
MELLUS, John (?) 154~11
MELOON / MALOON / MELLOON / MALLOON, Rachel 170~46
MELVILL *see* **MELVILLE**
MELVILLE / MELVILL, Allan 311~2
MELVIN, Josiah 34~30
MENDELL / MONDELL, James 305~48 Paul 274~32, 310~53
MENDUM, Mary (———) 98~20
MENTGES, Artchibald 39~10
MENTHER, Francis 220~53
MENZIES / MEINZES, Hannah 98~24
MERCER *see* **MERCIER**
MERCEREAU, John 75~20
MERCEY *see* **MARCEY**
MERCHANT *see* **MARCHANT**
MERCHAUD, Coste 295~29
MERCIER / MERCER, [Mr.] 256~10 James 265~4
MERCKELL, [Mr.] 39~44
MERCY *see* **MARCEY**
MEREDITH, Jonathan 10~39 Mary 286~39
MERIAM *see* **MERRIAM**
MERRFEILD *see* **MERRIFIELD**
MERRIAM / MERIAM / MARRIAN / MIRIAM, [widow] 151~6 Amos 168~20 Betsey 147~23 Hannah 53~12 Hezekiah 151~6 Isaac 151~22 Joseph 5~22, 13~55, 83~21, 325~22 Lucy 265~28 Nathan 73~9, 73~12
MERRICK / MARRICK / MIRRICK / MIRIC / MIRICK / MYRIC / MYRYCK, [Dr.] 39~13 [girl] 243~53 [Miss] 39~13 [Mr.] 324~25 Edward 170~54 Lois 112~8 Parnel M. 74~4 Phineas 243~53 Samuel 271~20
MERRIFIELD / MERRFEILD, Benjamin 27~47, 89~48 Preston 300~47 Silas 316~8, 333~49
MERRIL *see* **MERRILL**
MERRILL / MERRIL, Abel 10~28 Dorothy 356~39 John 10~28 Mary 3~26, 314~44 Mary (?) 207~19 Mary (Robinson) 210~28 Orsamus C. 210~28 Peter 124~10 Phineas 361~45 Polly 67~15 Thomas A. 224~51
MERRIMAN / MERRYMAN, Egra (?) 328~19 Ezra (?) 328~19
MERRITT / MIRRITT, [family] 192~15 [Mr. & Mrs.] 192~29
MERRY / MARRY, Samuel 305~8 Sarah Maria (Taylor) 143~26 Thomas H. 143~26
MERRYMAN *see* **MERRIMAN**
MERWIN, Samuel 180~18
MESERVE / MESERVEY / MESSERVE, Lemuel 257~42 Samuel 171~10 Timothy 363~52
MESERVEY *see* **MESERVE**
MESIER, Mary (Van Wyck) 79~9 Peter A. 79~9
MESK, Mercy (Nichols) 148~4 Thomas 148~4
MESSENGER *see* **MESSINGER**
MESSENNIER, Henry 137~52
MESSER, Asa 248~49 Lydia 131~25 Theodore 131~28
MESSERVE *see* **MESERVE**
MESSEY *see* **MASSEY**
MESSINGER / MESSENGER, Mary (Brown) 84~41 Roswell 84~41
METCALF / MEDCALF, [family] 192~14 [Mrs.] 77~12 Anna 291~30 James 149~34 John 251~58 Joseph 238~47 Julia (Tracy) 313~54 Sally (Hutchins) 238~47 Silas 117~8 Theron 313~54
METTLER, [Mr.] 274~6
MEYER / MAYER / MEIER / MEYERS / MYERS, [Capt.]

282~6 John H. 258~9 Mary A. 257~51 Ruth 232~9 William 214~32
MEYERS *see* **MEYER**
MICKELL / MIGHILL / MACKALL, Walter 158~23
MICOW, [Mrs.] 164~39 Lewis 164~39
MIDDLETON, Henry 29~7
MIFFLIN, [Gen.] 57~37
MIGHILL *see* **MICKELL**
MILES, [Mr.] 27~20, 167~56 Asa 189~40 Rebecca 190~40
MILIKEN *see* **MULLIKEN**
MILLARD *see* **MILLIARD**
MILLEN *see* **MELLEN**
MILLER / MELLER, [children] 162~32 [Dr.] 195~45 [Mr.] 35~42, 72~41 [Mrs.] 52~39, 72~42, 162~32 [Rev.] 240~44 Andrew 178~22 Asher 284~31 Betsey 87~43 Christopher 126~20 Hannah 10~27 Irene 117~47 James 24~44, 54~26, 84~46 Jeremiah 2~56 John 105~46, 182~5 John C. 208~56 Lois (———) 39~28 Maria 211~53 Mary 240~43 Mathew 298~16 Matthew 78~46 Moses 176~51, 317~19 Phebe 327~11 Phillip 162~31 Phineas 155~51 Rebecca 320~15, 327~14 Rebeckah 309~49 Robert 23~50, 304~57, 370~36 S. 117~47 Sally (Drury) 317~19 Sardis 5~9 Toby 255~22 William 46~10, 118~6
MILLET *see* **MILLETT**
MILLETT / MILLET / MALLET, John 180~7
MILLIARD / MILLARD, [Mr.] 100~32
MILLICAN *see* **MULLIKEN**
MILLIKEN *see* **MULLIKEN**
MILLS, [Mr.] 71~4 [Mrs.] 201~28 Ebenezer 46~10 Edmund 58~8 Elijah H. 128~50, 166~21 Florella 332~29 Hannah 228~30 Harriet (Blake) 166~22 James 328~20 Joseph 270~11 Joseph L. 247~24, 252~18 Polly 58~7 Rebecca 99~20 Sally (Hunt) 128~50 Samuel 268~48 Sarah 270~11 William 21~15 Zachariah 96~22
MILTEMERS *see* **MILTIMORE**
MILTEMORE *see* **MILTIMORE**
MILTIMORE / MILTEMORE / MILTEMERS, James 20~22 John 76~46 William 364~14
MINARD, William 96~13
MINER / MINOR, Andrew 283~20 E. 108~3 John 196~2 Nathan 216~20 Oliver 247~48, 295~49 Philenda 282~17 Richard 209~18 Roswell 282~18 Sarah 196~2 Timothy 9~50, 146~24 Turner 118~46
MINIS, Abraham 100~8
MINNS, Nancy 142~29
MINOR *see* **MINER**
MINOT, George Richards 110~23 Mary 110~9 Timothy 110~10
MIRIAM *see* **MERRIAM**
MIRIC(K) *see* **MERRICK**
MIRRICK *see* **MERRICK**
MIRRITT *see* **MERRITT**
MITCHEL *see* **MITCHELL**
MITCHELL / MITCHEL, [Dr.] 205~31 [infant] 149~11 [Mr. & Mrs.] 192~21 [Mrs.] 149~11 Andrew 196~32 Asaph 223~7 David B. 127~8 Elizabeth 40~4 J. 39~45 James 94~38, 94~39 John 20~51, 304~50, 332~38 Julia 216~43 Justus 233~29, 234~25 Mary (Uniacke) 196~33 Mehitabel 247~44 Nancy 79~45 Nancy (Mitchell) 79~45 Phebe 20~52 S.M. 216~43 Stephen 94~39, 332~38 T. 138~48 Thomas 79~45 William 312~21 William Alton 149~9
MITCHELSON, Eliphalet 255~55
MIX, Sarah 292~6
MOFFATT *see* **MAFFIT**
MOFFAY / MAFFAY, Elizabeth (Mansfield) (?) 38~45 Joseph 12~9 Nathaniel (?) 38~45
MOIS, Abraham 218~12
MOLINEUX *see* **MULNEAUX**
MOLLETT, Susannah 102~27
MOLYNEAUX *see* **MULNEAUX**
MONDELL *see* **MENDELL**
MONGER / MUNGER, [Mrs.] 216~30 Billy 265~57 Elisha S. 186~22
MONK, [Judge] 282~26 [Mr.] 282~26 Abigail 251~4
MONRO *see* **MUNROE**
MONROE *see* **MUNROE**
MONROW(E) *see* **MUNROE**

MONSON see MANSON
MONTAGUE, Ebenezer 302~12 Jane (Little) 97~10 Lydia 200~54, 202~50 William 97~10 Zebina 292~7
MONTGOMERY, James 52~27 John 297~14, 333~20 Maria (Nicholson) 297~15 Mary 333~19
MONTVILLE, Thomas Dewall 6~21
MOODY, Benjamin 102~27 Daniel 24~45, 268~15 Elizabeth 251~4 Elizabeth (Coffin) 102~27 Mabel 268~15 Stephen 349~30
MOOERS / MORES / MOORS, Aaron 253~4 Thomas 14~14
MOON, Peleg 131~16
MOONEY, John 244~51
MOOR see MOORE
MOORE / MORE / MOOR, (——) 161~23 [boy] 174~10 [Dr.] 181~19 [Mr.] 14~28, 56~6, 111~46 [Mrs.] 30~13 Abraham 94~20 Alph. 21~24 Alpheus 32~19, 56~21, 139~50 Ann (Odiorne) 166~51 Benjamin 270~13 Daniel 116~34 David 298~5 Delia (Hall) 40~3 Hannah 43~22 Henry 166~51 Hugh 352~3 J. 174~10 James 118~26, 129~36 John 185~37, 187~48, 291~28 Jonathan 107~31, 281~50 Philip 40~2 Polly 24~19 Polly (Fish) 75~52 Sally 99~50 Sally M. (Rand) 131~33 Samuel 3~47, 25~7 Solomon 142~32 Thomas 6~34, 132~29, 153~10, 251~23 Tristrim 30~34 Willard 21~45, 75~51, 112~54 William 99~22, 103~23, 131~33, 162~56
MOOREHEAD see MOORHEAD
MOORHEAD / MOOREHEAD, [child] 136~33 John 136~31 Thomas 299~32
MOORHOUSE see MOREHOUSE
MOORS see MOOERS
MORAN / MORAND, Joshua 249~40 Sally (Pierce) 249~40
MORAND see MORAN
MORE see MOORE
MOREHOUSE / MOORHOUSE, Ralph Alexander 273~52
MOREL see MORRILL
MORES see MOOERS
MOREVELL, John 211~54
MOREY / MOWRY, Augustus 102~1 Lucy (?) 179~34
MORGAN, [child] 156~18 [Mr.] 76~4, 156~18 Ann 318~10 Asaph 210~22 Asenath 83~48 Benjamin 28~26 Charles 215~23 Daniel 123~56 Hannah (Stebbins) 268~56 Isaac 84~9 Jacob 129~2 Jesse 268~55 John 249~41, 288~29 Loisa 172~7 Lucas 280~42 Lucinda 157~23 Mary 182~7 Quartus 65~55, 157~24, 229~53, 318~56 Robert W. 137~30 Ruth (Haseltine) 249~41 Samuel 276~25 Sophia 280~41 Stephen 6~22 Thomas 93~28 Violet 102~9 William 202~34 William A. 200~24
MORISON see MORRISON
MORLAND, George 184~4 Nancy 99~46
MORONA, Jemima (?) 162~41
MORREL(L) see MORRILL
MORRET, John 50~30
MORRICE see MORRIS
MORRIL see MORRILL
MORRILL / MORRELL / MORREL / MOREL / MORRIL, [Gunner] 148~38 [Mr.] 370~36 Benning 355~32 David 42~51 David Lawrence 121~9 Henrietta (——) 143~28 Jacob 364~13 John 143~29 Mary 219~56 Mary (?) 207~19 Mrs. 163~2 Samuel 322~10
MORRIS / MORRICE, [Gen.] 270~32 [Miss] 245~49 Abbey 283~49 Andrew 130~24 Benjamin W. 158~11 David 114~35 Ellen (Hunt) 96~15 James 283~50 L.R. 279~25 Lewis 146~8 Lewis R. 96~15, 146~7, 288~31 Louisa 279~24 Martha 146~8, 288~31 Richard 322~50 Robert 241~26 Samuel 114~52
MORRISET, [Widow] 238~36
MORRISON / MORISON, [Mrs.] 62~22 Abraham 27~37 Alexander 140~36 George 106~14 George W. 305~33 Jane 50~14, 320~24 John 89~17 Noah 88~30 Robert 122~8 Samuel 1~24, 289~16
MORSE / MORSS, [Mrs.] 92~44, 189~11 [Private] 119~43 [Rev.] 189~11 A. 232~10 Asa 277~2 David 212~15 Ebenezer 40~42, 110~32 Ebenezer 2d 208~38 Eliza (Barnard) 64~39 Esther 212~14 Farnum 277~2 Hannah 221~44 Irene 232~10 J. 92~45 Jedidiah 88~36 Martha 67~17 Micah 215~56 Moody 211~39 Sally (Goodenough) 208~38 Samuel 64~39 Solomon 65~1 Stephen 321~22 Stephen 3d 327~44 Stephen B. 327~45 Temper 233~12
MORSEY see MARCEY
MORSS see MORSE
MORTON / MOURTON, Abner 56~8, 65~3 C.W.A. 293~28 Nathaniel 36~30 Perez 310~44 Perez (?) 293~28 Sarah Athorp 310~44 Washington 93~31
MOSEL(E)Y see MOSLEY
MOSES, Abel 73~20 Benjamin 146~41 D. 331~44 Daniel 313~49 Joseph 289~44 Nancy 161~23
MOSHER / MOZIER / MOSIER, Charles 77~43
MOSIER see MOSHER
MOSLEY / MOSELY / MOZELY / MOSELEY, [Mr.] 14~48 Ebenezer 193~57 Elizabeth Green (Bradford) 243~2 Esther 37~54 Isaac 242~10 Mary 330~30 Mason 253~18 Sophia 193~56 William 283~12
MOSMENT, M. 252~44
MOSS, Reuben 292~39
MOTLEY, Isaac 265~56
MOTT, Elizabeth 206~29 Jesse 206~29 Samuel 68~3, 184~34, 186~2
MOTTEY see MOTTY
MOTTY / MOTTEY, Elizabeth 237~43 Joseph 237~44 Mehitable 91~32
MOULDEN see MOULTON
MOULTON / MOULDEN, D.V. 354~51 Daniel 45~16, 151~47, 272~28 Dolly 95~30 Job 136~38 John 151~47, 318~41 Josiah 355~40 Lydia 255~23 Moses P. 355~40 Patience 136~37 Roxana (Kilbourn) 272~29
MOULTRIE, William 215~35
MOURTON see MORTON
MOWDOCK, Benjamin 261~2
MOWER, Nathaniel 218~44 Thomas 260~34
MOWRY see MOREY
MOZELY see MOSLEY
MOZIER see MOSHER
MUDGET see MUDGETT
MUDGETT / MUDGET, Benjamin 281~35
MUHLENBERG, Frederick Augustus 92~40
MUIR, George 357~22 Thomas 38~48
MULLEN see MELLEN
MULLICAN see MULLIKEN
MULLIGAN see MULLIKEN
MULLIKEN / MULLICAN / MULLIGAN / MILLIKEN / MILLICAN / MILIKEN, (——) 70~14
MULLIN see MELLEN
MULNEAUX / MOLINEUX / MOLYNEAUX, Robert 271~32, 274~41, 287~40
MULVANEY, Sarah 201~26
MUMBOWER, George 63~12, 367~60 Henry 63~12, 367~61
MUMFORD, David 267~30 Paul 206~20 Polly 181~47 Sarah 303~24 William 150~20, 303~25
MUNGER see MONGER
MUNN see MANN
MUNRO see MUNROE
MUNROE / MONROE / MONRO / MUNRO / MONROWE / MONROW, [Mrs.] 104~50 [Rev.] 89~17 Edmund 156~13 Eliza 283~45 Harriet (Downes) 156~13 Isaac 109~30 James 283~46 Mary 102~26 Olive B. 202~13 Oliver 139~2 Philip 275~40 Sally 196~39 Solomon 269~36 William 196~40
MUNSEL see MUNSELL
MUNSELL / MUNSEL, Jabez 121~9 James 53~55
MUNSON see MANSON
MUNTZENBECHER, John 269~28
MURCH see MARCH
MURDOCH see MURDOCK
MURDOCK / MURDOCH, [Rev.] 123~15 George 195~1 James 123~14 Jasper 21~38 John 118~48 Mary 230~54 William 77~44
MURDOUGH / MURTAUGH, Robert 327~42
MURGATROYD, S. 38~46
MURIR, Peter 255~20
MURPHEY see MURPHY
MURPHY / MURPHEY, [family] 356~17 Arthur 208~15 William 171~38
MURRAY / MURRY, J.B. 19~54 John 197~8, 197~26, 210~34, 283~14 Nancy 51~54 Robert Lithgow 197~7 William Vans 154~38

MURRY see MURRAY
MURTAUGH see MURDOUGH
MUSCISSIAN, Ramadow 181~45
MUSGROVE, Mary 166~23 William 59~28
MUSSEY / MUZZEY / MUZZY, Benjamin 169~14, 311~42, 316~6 Harriot 311~42 James 312~13 Jane (———) (Ingalls) 169~14 Jonathan 28~45 Joseph 296~22, 361~30 Lydia 361~30 Polly 140~18 Thomas 266~9
MUTTON, [Miss] 167~3
MUZZEY see MUSSEY
MUZZY see MUSSEY
MYCOT, Eli 58~17
MYERS see MEYER
MYNDERSE, Marte 240~2   W. 215~4
MYRIC(K) see MERRICK

N.

NASH, Abigail 150~31 Abraham 123~25 Judah 186~13 Nancy 123~22 Thomas 58~14, 75~27
NAY, Samuel 362~52
NAYLOR, [Mrs.] 184~39
NEAL / NEALE / NEIL / NEILE / NIELL / NEILL, Charles 272~15   H. 277~19 Hannah 89~18 Hubartus 273~20 Jackson 281~39 James 320~17 James Armstrong 196~27 John 231~12 Polly 281~39 William 111~8, 133~53, 260~4, 263~30, 312~42
NEALE see NEAL
NEAT, Hannah (?) 89~18
NEEDHAM, Thomas 163~47
NEGUS, Joel 319~39 John 319~39 Mary 319~39 Mehitable 319~39
NEIL see NEAL
NEILE see NEAL
NEILL see NEAL
NELSON, [boy] 103~35 [Lord] 120~48 [Mrs.] 133~26 [Rev.] 120~47 Amos 256~51 Catherine (———) (Duer) 101~15 Charlotte 334~54 Elizabeth 121~12 James 231~41 John 133~39 Levi 173~26 Lydia 68~18 Oliver 103~35 Samuel 149~26 Sarah 70~39 William 101~15, 234~24
NESMITH, John 231~42
NETTLES, Joshua 182~54
NEUSWANGER, Christopher 274~8
NEVENS see NEVINS
NEVERS, Joseph 327~5
NEVIN see NEVINS
NEVINS / NEVIN / NEVENS / NIVAN, Hannah (Wood) 291~48 James 20~28, 21~48, 80~11, 115~31, 278~37, 325~39, 325~40 Samuel 291~48
NEW, Sarah 160~54
NEWALL see NEWELL
NEWBY, Ann 277~44 Robert 277~46
NEWCOMB, Daniel 33~20, 59~52, 90~3, 91~54, 116~53, 122~39, 123~19, 155~2, 300~7 Elizabeth 217~31 Hannah (———) (Goldthwait) 59~52 Joanna (Gardner) 307~6 Mary (Lyman) 142~23 Mary (Warren) (Lyman) 141~5   R.E. 142~23 Richard E. 141~5 Sally 122~38 Seth 307~6 Silas 43~9, 56~29
NEWEL see NEWELL
NEWELL / NEWEL / NEWHALL / NEWALL, (———) 133~20 [Mr.] 144~55 Abijah 280~43 David 120~25 Gordon 197~22 John 1~12, 11~16 Joseph 246~29 Lemuel 134~8 Mary 160~31 Mary (Reynolds) 246~29 Moses 58~33 Nancy (Prentiss) 197~22 Norman 260~8 Robert 323~36, 327~43 Sukey (Leonard) 120~25 Thomas 335~43 Timothy 38~1 Zenas 7~5, 22~39
NEWHALL see NEWELL
NEWTON, [Miss] 101~5 Abigail 218~31 Abigail (Lyon) 107~45 Ann 50~52 Betsey (Beckwith) 107~46 Christopher 235~4 Cyrus 103~14 David 233~8 Eliza (Partridge) 233~8 Erastus 89~26, 107~46 Hannah 292~47 Hepzibah (———) (Eastman) 313~17 Hubbard 107~45 Isaac 44~2, 313~17 Israel 217~57 Jonas 28~18, 64~34, 66~32 Margery 75~49 Mary 66~34 Paul 5~21 Phinehas 284~11 Roger 218~31 Sabra

(Crane) 103~14 Sylvester 321~23
NEWTUS, [Capt.] 126~33
NICE, John 249~47
NICHOLAS, C. 117~5 Lydia (Pope) 117~5
NICHOLLS see NICHOLS
NICHOLS / NICHOLLS / NICKELS / NICKLES / NICOLLS / NICOLL / NICKOLS, [child] 191~4 [children] 105~55 [Col.] 38~19 [girl] 266~15 [Mr.] 121~41, 210~14 [widow] 324~11 Alpheus 312~41, 324~11 Asa 312~40, 324~10 Benjamin 103~57 Calvin 232~14 David 216~10 Desire 151~5 Dorothea F. (Gilman) 324~34 Ebenezer 261~58 Esther (Gowing) 65~10, 65~38   G.W. 295~30 George 72~30, 106~45, 191~4 George W. 303~36 Ichabod 324~34 Isaac 168~53 Israel 65~10, 65~38   J. 117~49 Jane (Hodge) 144~33 John 84~17, 313~3 John H. 192~39, 194~35 Levi 82~40, 83~2, 116~31, 297~54 Lewis 212~32 Mary 105~53 Mercy 148~4 Moses 72~28, 72~36 Nathaniel 105~54 Polly 117~48 Robert 207~52 Ruth 268~27 Sally (———) (Peirce) 106~45 Samuel 113~37, 119~23, 254~28 Sarah (?) 261~57 Seran (?) 261~57   T. 266~15 Thomas 102~24, 144~33, 225~13
NICHOLSON, Benjamin 106~14 James 166~27 John 333~27 John B. 184~35 Maria 297~15
NICKELS see NICHOLS
NICKLES see NICHOLS
NICKLIN, Philip 266~34
NICKOLS see NICHOLS
NICOLL see NICHOLS
NICOLLS see NICHOLS
NIELL see NEAL
NIGHTINGALE, John C. 261~45
NIHEN, [Capt.] 201~3
NILES, Almira (Willy) 84~14 Isaac 84~13 Peter 308~14 S. 118~20 Sarah 118~20 Silas 16~28
NIMS, Abigail 363~14 Alpheus 162~16 Amasa 155~43 David 145~49, 363~15 Nancy (Quin) 155~43
NIVAN see NEVINS
NIXON, John 289~43
NOATHRUT, Betsey 257~50
NOBLE, [child] 149~14 [Mr.] 133~37 Joseph 193~20 Margaret 227~33 Timothy 149~14
NODINE, [Mr.] 84~53 Andrew 118~26
NOEL see NOWELL
NOEYS see NOYES
NOLL see NOWELL
NORMAN, [Mr.] 96~48 John 255~22
NORRIS, Elijah 74~40 James 247~25 John 158~13, 288~27 Jonathan 361~48 Nealleay 333~55 Thomas 3d 361~43
NORTH, Joseph 254~7 Phineas 329~30
NORTHEY, Edward 134~34
NORTHORP see NORTHROP
NORTHROP / NORTHORP, [Miss] 12~34 James 12~33
NORTON, [Mrs.] 189~3 Abigail 256~55 Catharine 146~30 David 125~19 Joseph 47~1 Lucy (Smith) 255~8 Mary 73~18 Rufus 255~8 Thomas 206~44
NORWOOD, N. 202~30
NOTT / NUTT / KNOTT, [Rev.] 173~24 Joseph 108~2 Sarah 91~34
NOTTAGE, Jane 97~19
NOURS see NOURSE
NOURSE / NOURS (see also NURSE), Philip 29~12 Rebecca (Carpenter) 114~11 Silas 114~11
NOWELL / NOLL / NOEL, Deborah 145~16 Experience 191~36 Polly 44~14
NOYCE see NOYES
NOYES / NOYSE / NOEYS / NOYCE, Daniel 108~11, 286~12 Ebenezer 225~18 Hannah 96~24 Jane 217~30 Jeremiah 258~56 Jeremiah (Noyes) 258~56 John 6~38, 23~24, 229~27 Joseph 117~10, 308~56 Moses 209~21 Nathan 288~47 Stephen 19~13 Tabitha 229~27 Ward 288~50 William 10~12
NOYSE see NOYES
NURSE, John 296~23 Stephen 161~14
NUTT see NOTT
NUTTER, [Mr.] 133~45 [Mrs.] 133~30 Hannah 354~4 John 4th 354~4 Lydia 361~10 Mark 361~10
NUTTING, Marsa 39~33 Samuel 116~39

NYE, George 111~7 Jonathan 187~26 Lois (Marrick) 112~8 Stephen 112~8

O.

O'BRIEN see O'BRYAN
O'BRYAN / O'BRIEN, [Mr.] 108~24 Mary 137~26 Mercy 238~46
O'DANIEL, Charity 102~23
O'HARA / O'HARRA, [children] 260~1 Charles 118~25 Oliver 259~58
O'HARRA see O'HARA
O'REILLY / O'RILEY, Thomas 123~7
O'RILEY see O'REILLY
OAKES / OAKS, [Mr.] 44~30 [Mrs.] 101~24, 102~11 Nancy 328~27
OAKLEY / OAKLY, Laban 185~26
OAKLY see OAKLEY
OAKMAN, [Widow] 202~51
OAKS see OAKES
OBER, Benjmain 167~55
OBIE, John 222~31
ODELL, Hannah 146~29
ODION see ODIORNE
ODIORNE / ORDIORNE / ODION, Ann 166~51 George B. 184~20 Jotham 176~16 Matilda (———) 127~14 Olive (Thomas) 91~26 Ruth (Kinnear) 184~21 Samuel 91~25
ODLIN, Abigail 105~31
OGDEN, Elias 189~48 Eliza 199~11 Samuel 182~17
OGILVIE, [Lieut.] 253~29
OGLE, Benjamin 306~4
OLCOT see OLCOTT
OLCOTT / OLCOT / ALCOTT, Anne 277~50 George 334~3 Lucretia 146~10 Mills 21~38 Pelatiah Mills 83~26 Rhoderick 97~17 Sarah (Porter) 83~26 Simeon 159~16, 163~35 Theophilus 61~24, 146~10
OLDEN, John 53~4
OLDS, Damaris 184~25 Robert 131~20
OLIN / OLLINS, Deborah (Pope) 117~6 Enock 354~22 G. 117~6 Henry 324~18 Sally (Aylesworth) 324~18
OLIVE, John 14~29
OLIVER, Ann H. 84~11 Daniel 183~4, 297~13, 300~54 Edward Brattle 2~32 Elizabeth 297~12 Luther 56~29 Sarah 300~53 Stephen 113~9
OLLINS see OLIN
OLMSTEAD see OLMSTED
OLMSTED / OLMSTEAD, Nathaniel 209~3
OLNEY, Christopher 294~22 Christopher A. 255~5 Daniel 123~9 Phebe (Trumbull) 255~6
OLYPHANT, David 198~19
ONDERDONK, Andrew 11~24
ONION, Charity 156~24 Ichabod 109~22
ORCOTT / ORCUTT, John S. 77~54
ORCUTT see ORCOTT
ORDIORNE see ODIORNE
ORDWAY / ORWAY / ARDWAY, Ann 32~31, 80~29, 108~13, 311~19 Jeremiah 299~3
ORMSBEE / ORMSBY / ORMSBURY / ARMSBY / AMSBY, Chloe (Barber) 243~11 Christopher 74~17, 228~40 Gideon 243~11 Jemima 141~9 Phebe 242~34 Stephen 242~35 Waitstill 228~39
ORMSBURY see ORMSBEE
ORMSBY see ORMSBEE
ORN see ORNE
ORNE / ORN (see also HORN), [Capt.] 264~11 Azor 38~8 Catharine Sewall Pynchon 43~48 Isaiah 285~26, 286~51 Joshua 234~34 Mary 38~8
ORR, [Mr.] 137~5, 166~40 Agnes 64~41 John 51~31, 251~22 Mary 164~24 Noble 141~39, 153~14
ORVIS, Elizabeth 266~42 Lucy 221~1
ORWAY see ORDWAY
OSBORN see OSBORNE
OSBORNE / OSBORN / OSBOURNE / OSBURN, Abraham 221~40 Alexander 142~33 Ann H. (Oliver) 84~11 Elizabeth (———) 261~38 John P. 84~11 Selleck 251~47

OSBOURNE see OSBORNE
OSBURN see OSBORNE
OSGOOD, Joshua 36~14, 43~13 Kendall 99~21 Mary 267~7 Mary S. 301~46 Samuel 301~45 Thaddeus 329~19 widow 217~33
OSTRANDER, Peter 50~57
OTHEMAN, Mary 117~32
OTIS, Abigail (Cushing) 269~48 Charlotte (Downes) 40~1 Cushing 269~48 James 335~53 Joseph 335~52 Mary Alline 72~15 Thomas 40~1, 148~21
OVENSHIRE, James 267~7 Mary 267~18 Mary (Osgood) 267~7
OVERLOCKE, Widow 251~30
OVERTON, Thomas J. 209~30, 209~32
OWEN, [child] 149~15 John 23~6, 107~54 Samuel 149~15
OZIER, Mary 252~33

P.

PACKARD / PACKERD, Agnes (Orr) 64~41 Daniel 64~41 Hezehiah 127~19 Joseph 310~27 Nathaniel 309~19 Th. 330~9 Thomas 320~35
PACKER see PECKER
PACKERD see PACKARD
PADDLEFORD, Patience (Moulton) 136~37 Philip 22~55 Seth 136~37
PADDOCK, James 298~37
PAGAN / PEGIN, Abigail (Drew) 200~33 Robert 19~7 William 200~33
PAGE / PAIGE, [Col.] 124~19 Abel 312~49 Benjamin 350~5 Cynthia 212~9 Daniel 93~18 Elijah 32~45, 48~6, 56~31 Enoch 101~49 Hannah (Straw) 230~3 Jeremiah 244~33 John 77~43, 110~38, 284~4 Lucy 177~53 Maria (Crocker) 249~35 Mary 322~21 Mary (Boardman) 278~42 Peter 56~9 Phineas 5~25 Richard 230~2 Sally 5~25 Samuel 44~23 Sarah 350~8 Seneca 308~49 Sherman 249~34 William 16~33, 19~7, 32~6, 33~38, 55~1, 55~18, 56~32, 61~38, 79~22, 79~40, 86~19, 111~26, 128~17, 132~41, 177~54, 184~18, 212~10, 278~42, 322~21 William (2d column) 56~32 Zilpha (Barnes) 312~49
PAIGE see PAGE
PAIN see PAINE
PAINE / PAYNE / PAIN / PANE, [child] 192~17 [Judge] 135~45 [Major] 220~45 [Miss] 159~23 [Mrs.] 192~17 Charles 41~3 Elisha 113~11 Eliza 312~4 Harriet 116~9, 117~2 Isaac 192~17 Jabez 49~48, 82~53, 88~4 James 270~2 Jonathan 245~48 Joshua 57~22 Louisa 220~44 Lucy (Dobell) 144~30 Martha 245~47 Nancy Leonard 135~45 Noah 272~34 Rebecca 361~3 Robert Treat 138~2 Sally (Cushing) 41~3 Samuel 325~24 Solomon 4~44 Thomas 101~23, 138~1 Unice 4~44 William 116~10, 144~30, 179~13
PAINTER, [Judge] 117~46 [Mr.] 272~5 Dolly Burnham 117~46
PALCO, Joseph (?) 206~31
PALEY, [Dr.] 206~4
PALFREY / PULFRY / POLFREY, John 167~21 William 80~13, 115~33, 143~3, 325~48
PALLUCAR, Maria F.(?) 40~2
PALMER, Aaron 280~20 Benjamin 165~21 Ebenezer 48~6, 155~56 Elihu 236~39 Eliphalet 321~37 Elizabeth (Allaire) 121~51 Galen 307~53 Humphrey 277~16, 277~42 J.H. 140~13 John 36~54 Joseph 242~29 Lydia (Lomis) 140~14 Peggy (———) 229~10 Polly (Howard) 307~53 Sally 289~30 Samuel 71~6, 121~51 Sarah 242~29, 245~50 Seth 165~41 Stephen 236~10 Susannah (Burbank) 278~39
PALSY, Robert 189~41
PANE see PAINE
PARHAM see PERHAM
PARISH, E. 88~36 Rufus 355~8
PARK, Hannah 206~12 James 144~6 John 179~36 Jonas 82~3 Mungo 248~36 Nabby (Kimball) 179~36 William 16~29, 71~35, 144~6
PARKER, [Landlord] 129~21 Abel 129~21 Abiah 133~50

Abigail (———) 259~1 Abigail (Watson) 64~6 Amos 194~45, 334~35 Anson 52~8 Benjamin 71~9 Bethiah 69~5 Betsy (Frye) 65~42 C. 167~28 Catharine (Brigden) 120~41 Daniel 186~56 David 304~38 Dorothy 61~28 E. 107~32 Ebenezer 176~20 Elizabeth 14~41, 102~41, 328~21 Elizabeth (Whitney) 194~45 Frederick 270~20, 271~23 George 364~15 Hannah 36~24, 219~55 Hannah (Chesly) 210~31 Hyde 234~33 Isaac 231~53 Isaiah 233~41 Jacob 133~52 James 68~4, 327~48 Jeremiah 223~25 John 20~32 John Rowe 120~41 Joseph 3~41, 104~52, 357~43 Luther Calender 272~19 Lyman 106~11 Martha 223~25, 357~42 Moses 20~23, 313~34 Nathaniel 100~10 Pearl 327~3 Peter 50~6, 167~29 Phineas 61~48 Phinehas 9~45, 45~32, 74~41 Polly 105~31 Robert 210~31 Roland 231~53 Rowland 233~41 Sally 71~8 Samuel 173~46, 227~33, 228~26 Sophia 177~24 Stephen 3~51, 293~53 Thomas 221~53 Timothy 5~36, 103~52 Warren 65~41 William 101~20, 102~41 William B. 64~5
PARKHURST, [Mrs.] 316~43 Betsy (Hall) 335~5 Elisha 335~5 Joseph 316~43
PARKINS see PERKINS
PARKMAN, Abigail 7~47 Betsey 263~35 Elias 7~47 Hannah 99~25 Robert B. 16~32
PARKS, Aaron 296~26 Ameriah 40~36 Anna 40~37 Arthur 254~6, 258~2 Cady 142~20, 177~34, 306~43, 309~4, 316~10 Charles 86~53 Elisha 103~15 Elizabeth 328~22 Josiah 56~30 Mindwell (Grout) 103~15 Nathan 111~10 Paul 43~36 Rebecca 147~7 Sally 178~16 Timothy 106~10 Warham 86~55
PARMELE see PARMELEE
PARMELEE / PARMELE, [Mr.] 28~38, 88~38 Daniel 296~48 Eben. 113~30 Sible 161~7
PARMENTER / PARMERTER, Electa 327~12 Joseph 28~31, 37~2
PARMER, Betsey 303~37
PARMERTER see PARMENTER
PARR, [Mr.] 183~39
PARRINGTON, William 194~55
PARROT see PARROTT
PARROTT / PARROT, Hannah (Parker) 36~24 John F. 36~24
PARRY see PERRY
PARSELLS, Catharine 143~29
PARSHLEY / PARSLEY, John 116~47 Tevasia (Clarke) 116~47
PARSLEY see PARSHLEY
PARSON / PORSON, [children] 213~48 [Mrs.] 213~48 Jabez 16~25 Nathaniel 213~46 Richard 287~23
PARSONS / PERSONS, [Chief Justice] 307~5 [Rev.] 13~45, 33~3, 325~17 Benjamin 179~42 Elisha 79~25 Eliza 307~4 Ezekiel 301~38 Hosea 52~58 Jabish 25~2 Joseph 220~9, 255~28 Mehitable 125~28 Moses 97~2 Nathaniel 213~33 Oliver 140~26 Phebe 177~16 Phebe (Hurlburt) 79~25 Rachel 322~45 Sally (Upham) 53~1 Sarah 182~8 Silas 276~12
PARTRIDGE / PATRIDGE, [Mr.] 127~10 [Mrs.] 228~26 Asa 149~51, 208~26, 309~5 Betsey 179~39 Cyrus 272~30 Eli 43~14, 61~27 Elisha 55~31 Eliza 233~4 John 239~10 Moses 172~34 Nathaniel 61~26, 93~51 Polly (Loveland) 272~21 Robert 169~42 Samuel 115~34, 143~14, 278~32, 325~42 Sheffield 101~48, 109~24
PASCO, Joseph (?) 206~31
PASTEUR, Thomas 259~7
PASTONA, John 54~36
PATCH, [Capt.] 361~25 John 80~23 Nathaniel 106~31 Samuel 81~9 Simeon 81~10
PATERSON see PATTERSON
PATON see PATTEN
PATRIDGE see PARTRIDGE
PATSON, Mary D. 296~25
PATTE see PETTEE
PATTEE see PETTEE
PATTEN / PATTON / PATON, Nathaniel 323~34 Sarah 323~34 Thomas 179~49
PATTERSON / PATERSON, [Mr.] 27~17 Benjamin 143~30 Charles J. 356~24 E. 155~42 James 163~22, 224~25 John 74~12, 142~26, 227~37

Louisa (———) 117~28 Mary (Barnes) 143~30 Matthew 280~50 Robert 220~20, 285~26 Sally (Stearns) 224~25 Susannah (Eulen) 142~27 William 190~29, 253~57, 257~23, 265~32, 284~13
PATTON see PATTEN
PAUL, [boy] 304~49 A. 231~30 Alpheus 309~51 Anne (Johnson) 231~30 Eben. 147~56 Elizabeth (Nelson) 121~12 James 184~53 John 121~12, 317~50 Joshua 184~24 Luke 286~28 Mary (———) 317~50 Noah 52~5 Sally (Cooper) 286~28 Stephen 304~49 Thomas 269~43
PAYMENT, Joseph 56~10
PAYNE see PAINE
PAYSON, [children] 239~44 [widow] 239~44 John 239~42, 241~30 Joseph 97~20 Philips 279~3, 302~14 Phillips 256~22, 258~52
PAYTON, Randolph (?) 33~34
PEABODY, [children] 227~9 [Mrs.] 227~9 Andrew 227~8 Elizabeth (Willes) 171~29 Isaac 274~58 Jacob 168~42 Lucy (Manning) 168~44 Polly (Reed) 36~28 Thomas 36~27, 171~28
PEAK, Catharine (Clous) 41~21 Chester 96~32 John 123~12 Philip 41~21 Polly 233~12 Sally (Lewis) (?) 153~48 Samuel A. (?) 153~48
PEALERT, W.J. 253~46
PEARCE see PIERCE
PEARSE see PIERCE
PEARSON / PEARSONS / PEIRSON / PIERSON / PERSON, Elizabeth 117~32 George 192~31 Jacob 364~14 Lydia 285~22 Margaret 92~5 Moses 189~18 Oliver 242~38, 304~4 Patty (Fairchild) 242~37 Richard 190~48 Samuel 46~57 William 299~38
PEARSONS see PEARSON
PEAS see PEASE
PEASE / PEAS, [Mr.] 155~17 Aaron 236~54 Augustus 9~17 Elijah 36~8, 43~11 Elizabeth (Walker) 102~29 Enoch 102~28 Ezekiel 1~26 Isaac 328~20 Josiah 32~56 Kezia (Griffin) 155~18 T. 39~45
PECK, David 271~6 Eliza (Gilman) 84~28 John 84~28 Lucy 200~51 Lydia 24~17 Pascal Paoli 214~44 Sally (Lewis) (?) 153~48 Samuel A. (?) 153~48 T. 14~56 William 214~45
PECKENS / PUKENS, Alexander 310~37, 328~30, 374~12
PECKER / PACKER, [Miss] 278~36 [Mrs.] 115~32, 143~3 Thomas 71~26
PECKHAM, [Mrs.] 207~24 George 207~24
PEDRICK, [Capt.] 51~43
PEEBLE, John 153~36
PEGIN see PAGAN
PEIRCE see PIERCE
PEIRSE see PIERCE
PEIRSON see PEARSON
PELOT, (———) 72~45
PELOUZE, Edmond 116~29
PELS, Daniel 334~19
PEMBERTON, Asa 74~42
PENDLETON, [Mr.] 149~33 Edmond 152~5 John 254~4
PENHALLOW, Ann 323~29 B. 133~32 H. 133~32 John 89~48, 133~26, 294~24 Samuel 191~39
PENKHAM see PINKHAM
PENNEY / PENNY / PINNEY, [Mr.] 126~33
PENNIMAN / PENNYMAN, Clarissa (Bates) 163~38 Cynthia (Stimpson) 66~8 Joshua 163~38 Mary 215~27 O. 215~27 Olive (Fitch) 216~3 Peter 204~43 Ruth 176~30 Silas 66~8 Sylvanus F. 216~3 Thomas 18~33, 215~13 Zurviah (Dudley) 215~14
PENNINGTON, Aaron 57~18 Isaac 140~20
PENNY see PENNEY
PENNYMAN see PENNIMAN
PEPOON, S. 162~43
PERCIVAL, James 276~35
PERFETT, Peter 110~19
PERHAM / PARHAM, [boy] 99~39 Joel 99~38 Stephen 254~9
PERIE see PERRY
PERIN see PERRIN
PERKINS / PARKINS / PURKENS, [Mr.] 171~5 [Mrs.] 25~23, 171~7 Abram 167~19 Ann D. (Powell) 78~21 Betsy (Jarvis) 104~11 Charles 64~54 Chloe 61~25

Cyrus 129~26   David 186~32   Dorcas 317~22   Dudley 119~47   E. 181~47   Elisha 47~33   Isaac 152~32   Jabez 104~10   Jacob 79~7   James 116~16, 161~13, 221~4   John 22~19, 92~56, 334~30   John A. 3~49   Joseph 44~20   Judith (———) 301~44   Lucy (Berry) 79~7   Mary 239~41, 318~7   Polly (Mumford) 181~47   Rebecca Sumner 116~15   Richard 239~41, 322~42   Thomas 78~20   Vina 191~1   William 196~15   Zeb 335~49
PERKITT / PURKITT, Eunice 108~29
PERRIN / PERIN, Daniel 27~36, 60~48, 278~21   Rebecca (?) 278~20   Rebeka 60~51   Thomas 240~46
PERRY / PARRY / PERIE, [Mr.] 320~8   [Mrs.] 320~6   Aaron P. 293~23   Benjamin 52~46   Dorcas 139~43   Edward 10~54, 82~5, 133~21, 160~47   James 197~24   John 273~13   John H. 222~25   Joseph 141~22, 356~38   Mary (Fay) 293~23   Mercy 19~14   Nabby 218~9   Nathan 231~4   Richard 133~25   Ruth (Collins) 160~47   Sophia (Clapham) 356~38   Thomas 185~37
PERSON see PEARSON
PERSONS see PARSONS
PETEGREW / PETTIGREW / PETIGREW / PETTIGEW, Mary (Alden) 285~48   William 285~48
PETER see PETERS
PETERS / PETER, [Judge] 38~19   Jane 144~29   John 86~55, 170~47, 205~32   Joseph 62~41   Lemuel 25~1   Robert 270~3   Ziba 200~22
PETERSON, Benjamin 70~4   Peter 63~23
PETIGREW see PETEGREW
PETIT / PETTIT, Charles 257~58
PETTEE / PATTEE / PATTE / PETTY / PITTY, David 140~33   Elisha 68~52   Joseph 120~51
PETTENGILL see PETTINGILL
PETTIGEW see PETEGREW
PETTIGREW see PETEGREW
PETTINGAIL see PETTINGILL
PETTINGALE see PETTINGILL
PETTINGALL see PETTINGILL
PETTINGELL see PETTINGILL
PETTINGILL / PETTINGELL / PETTENGILL / PETTINGALE / PETTINGALL / PETTINGAIL, Benj. 225~14   David 355~22   Eunice 98~53   Joshua 160~25   Matt. 32~38   Peter 110~22
PETTIT see PETIT
PETTY see PETTEE
PHELAN, [Capt.] 255~41
PHELPS, [children] 191~27   [Mrs.] 17~31, 38~26, 165~39, 191~24   Aaron 164~11   Abel 208~27, 231~52   Abner 297~22   Barnabas 134~21, 138~34   Bethiah 98~53   Daniel 17~31   Elijah 16~28   Eliphalet 276~33   Elkanah 57~5   Esther 225~56   Eunice (Forward) 297~22   J. 191~28   Joshua 127~9, 265~10, 293~55   Levi 146~5   Martha 290~26   Nathan 231~52   Oliver 33~47, 294~25   Peter 91~20   Roger 191~25   Seth 68~50   Sukey (Stickney) 91~20
PHENIX, [Mrs.] 229~21
PHILBRICK / PHILBROOK, [Mr.] 356~32   [Mrs.] 356~43   David 353~44   Jedediah 35~28   John 285~36, 361~39   Joseph 356~43   Josiah C. 355~36   Moses C. 353~44   Stephen C. 353~43   Thomas J. 353~43
PHILBROOK see PHILBRICK
PHILIPS see PHILLIPS
PHILLIPS / PHILIPS, [———] 72~46   [Capt.] 272~17   [child] 158~34   [children] 102~36   [Mr.] 102~36, 325~53   [Mrs.] 325~53   Aaron 98~11   Amos 125~14, 142~1, 158~34   Barnard 329~30   Benjamin 335~15   Benjamin H. 141~24   Bethiah 98~6   Eliza 272~27   George Washington 168~17   James 84~27   Jonathan 94~44, 214~8   Lucinda (Bemis) 168~17   Mary (Tilden) 84~27   Pierce 227~44   Rebecca (Salisbury) 214~8   Samuel 94~45, 113~15   Walter 335~14   William 254~18
PHIPPEN, Nathaniel 293~34
PHIPPS, Samuel D. 51~30
PICKERING / PICKING, [Judge] 133~25, 223~24   Abigail (Sheafe) 223~23   Ephraim 135~37, 304~48   John 189~57   Joseph W. 244~47   Lucretia 234~5   Nicholas 288~26   Rebeccah 354~29   Samuel 207~44
PICKERMAN, Nancy 277~40
PICKET see PICKETT
PICKETT / PICKET, Sarah 160~28
PICKING see PICKERING

PICO, Joshua 274~21
PIERCE / PEIRSE / PEIRCE / PEARCE / PEARSE, [child] 128~8, 274~48   [Miss] 126~15   [Mr.] 292~25, 294~4, 349~44   Abigail 70~37   Abigail (Brewster) 44~44   Arvin 320~18   Benjamin 334~38   Benjamin Franklin 18~8   Charles 133~15   D. 133~13   Daniel 41~44   Ebenezer 176~20   Ezra 19~47, 119~50   Hannah (———) (Littlehale) 268~55   Harriet 54~45   Jacob 75~43, 168~13, 328~38   Jeremiah 230~51   John 28~26, 34~43, 35~11, 119~33, 133~9, 361~14   Jos. 20~16   Joseph 34~41, 320~37, 361~11   Joshua 320~36, 330~10   Josiah 265~53   Levi 76~40   Loisia 327~16   Mary 328~37   N.S. 133~19   Nathaniel S. 216~45   Oliver 20~19   Peter 56~42, 71~20, 71~26, 133~12, 133~28, 221~54, 320~37, 330~10   Proctor 211~16   Rebecca 249~40   Sally 249~40   Sally (———) 106~45   Sally (Greenough) 216~46   Samuel 133~15, 144~1, 176~27   Sarah 126~15   Seth 297~20   Silas 268~54   Stephen 133~11   Thomas 260~33   Timothy 99~17   W. 133~19   Warren 166~45   Washington 272~15   William 12~38, 20~17, 44~44, 89~45, 101~40, 103~3, 109~23, 128~8, 149~53, 256~50, 274~48, 292~54, 306~52, 323~21, 331~51   William H. 324~49
PIERPONT see PIERREPONT
PIERREPOINT see PIERREPONT
PIERREPONT / PIERPONT / PIERREPOINT, Joseph 238~53
PIERSON see PEARSON
PIGGOTT / PIGOT, [Capt.] 75~27
PIGOT see PIGGOTT
PIKE, [Mr.] 19~20   [Mrs.] 308~38   Daniel 286~38   Ebenezer 308~38   Elizabeth 260~43   Hannah 92~34   John 76~16   Richard 64~5   Samuel 71~36   Sarah (Boardman) 64~5
PILLOR, John 118~5
PILLSBURY see PILSBURY
PILSBURY / PILLSBURY, [children] 100~30   [Mr.] 201~56   [Mrs.] 100~30   Levi 93~39   Miriam 94~29   Susannah 208~53   Thomas 100~28
PINCKNEY, Mary 167~12
PINEVERET, John 218~18
PINGLE, Henry (?) 218~30
PINGREE / PINGRY, John 134~17   William 134~18
PINGRY see PINGREE
PINKERTON, John 82~10   William 10~24
PINKHAM / PENKHAM, Daniel 242~12   John 368~38
PINNEY see PENNEY
PINNOCK, Joseph 25~12
PINTARD, Samuel 189~49
PINTO, Jacob 228~34
PIPER, [Mrs.] 111~42   Asa 111~42   Nathaniel 349~40   Simon 90~2   Stephen 4~37
PISHEN see PUSHON
PITCHER, Nancy 176~57
PITKIN, [Gov.] 239~4   George 239~2   John 154~14   Thomas W. 107~20
PITMAN / PITTMAN, B. (———) 66~38   Elizabeth 65~40   John 301~23   Mary 160~48   Susannah 122~31
PITT, William 234~7
PITTMAN see PITMAN
PITTY see PETTEE
PLACE, Eleanor (Powers) 229~57   Samuel 60~4   Stephen 111~9   Warden 229~56
PLAISTED, Samuel 272~46
PLANT, [Mrs.] 234~22   Samuel 325~43
PLAT see PLATT
PLATT / PLATTS / PLAT, John Sweat 32~41
PLATTS see PLATT
PLAYFAIR, [Dr.] 191~6
PLEIFFER, Joseph 160~35
PLOUGHRIGHT, Robert 12~8
PLUMB, Mary 238~16
PLUMER see PLUMMER
PLUMER see PLUMMER
PLUMMER / PLUMER / PLUMBER, [Mr.] 235~30   David 96~20   Elizabeth 231~49   Lyman 250~17   Mary 186~32, 242~5   Rebecca 152~21   Seth 96~23   Sophia 95~39   William 23~9, 23~49
POAUG, Harriet P. 335~31
POINDEXTER, [Mr.] 283~32   Eliza 116~46   James

222~42 Lightfoot 222~41
POLACK see **POLLOCK**
POLFREY see **PALFREY**
POLLARD, [widow] 135~11 Jacob 354~27 Othello 135~11 Robert 54~8
POLLEY see **POLLY**
POLLOCK / POLACK, [Justice] 278~12 Charlotte 278~2, 281~3 Coshman 23~5 James 278~12
POLLY / POLLEY, Simeon 268~17
POMEROY / POMROY, [Dr.] 238~32 [Major] 161~53 [Mrs.] 98~32, 161~52 Arabella 106~31 Eben 143~15 Eleazer 278~31, 325~41 Eunice 275~45 James 263~6 Med. 304~19 Medad 80~14, 115~35, 143~14, 278~34, 325~44 Olive (House) 86~30 Pliny 170~49 Quartus 152~4 Ralph 275~46 Seth 86~29, 98~33 Timothy 131~48
POMPEY, (———) 118~49
POMROY see **POMEROY**
POND, [Mrs.] 264~48 Ezra 155~24 Joab 43~10, 264~48
POOL see **POOLE**
POOLE / POOL, [child] 133~5 [widow] 133~5 David 133~4 Elias 133~3 J. 325~50 John 231~17 Samuel 4~46
POOR / POORE, Mary 53~35, 166~52, 364~41 Nathan 230~24 Simeon 62~22
POORE see **POOR**
POPE, [Mrs.] 106~52, 148~13 Ann 335~2 Ann (———) 245~32 Deborah 117~6 Hannah 185~55 John 112~8 Lydia 117~5 Nancy 153~54 Nathaniel 295~15 Samuel 97~19 Sarah 38~51 Susannah 112~7 William 245~33
PORSON see **PARSON**
PORTER, [Capt.] 16~14, 235~25, 250~9 [Col.] 83~27 [Dr.] 231~21 Abner 309~16 Asa 82~4 Benjamin 69~41 David 213~9 Eleazer 5~39 Ethel 1~34 Hannah 221~32 Henry 57~44 Isaiah 309~16 John 116~13, 244~36, 271~26 Mary (———) 190~20 Mary (Swett) 335~3 Matthew 334~44 Mehitable (Meigs) 289~28 Moses 122~44 Noah 186~3, 199~52, 268~43, 289~28 Oliver 250~13 Reuben 335~3 S. 258~50 Samuel 252~1, 322~27 Sarah 83~26, 250~29 Simeon (?) 231~40
POST, Cornelius 151~5 Frances (Hayden) 262~30 Joseph O. 209~53 Otis 209~53 Sala 262~30
POTTER, Barrett 306~1 Edward 12~12 Isaiah 213~58 Job 268~26 Joel B. 261~48 John 52~53 Mary 268~26 Moses 27~11, 333~56 Nancy (Storor) 306~1 P. 106~53 Sibyl (———) 148~46 Simeon 245~17 Simeon (?) 231~40
POTTLE, [widow] 353~23
POTTS, John 99~37
POULSON, Zachariah 156~28
POWARS see **POWERS**
POWEL see **POWELL**
POWELL / POWEL, [Mr.] 252~47 Ann D. 78~21 Jeremiah D. 235~13 John 64~40 Pardon 321~42 Sarah 235~12 Silas 228~49 Susan 242~11 Susannah (King) 64~40 William 59~17, 182~16
POWER see **POWERS**
POWERS / POWER / POWARS, Abijah 304~3 Abraham 21~44 Amasa 215~31 Asahel 111~13 Benjamin 315~4 David 332~22 Eleanor 229~57 Elizabeth (M'Clure) 208~39 Ezekiel 286~30 Gideon 273~19 Hannah 276~16 Huldah (Cooper) 238~49 James 238~48 John 371~34 Lois Sanger (Cooper) 238~49 Louis S. (Cooper) 277~7 Lucy (Stoddard) 291~47 Nicholas 230~32 Peter 238~49, 277~7 Rachel 303~16 Rebecca 105~20, 132~6 Sally 294~13 Samuel 35~28, 268~46 Simon 51~11 Stephen 20~29, 303~16, 315~24 Sukey 238~48 Thankful 290~11 Timothy 235~48 Titus 9~22 Walter 208~39 William 291~47, 371~33
POWNALL, Thomas 195~43
POYNTELL, William 255~48
POYNTZ, Antonio 59~32
POZER, George 267~20
PRATT, [children] 155~32, 293~45 [Mr.] 34~4, 134~45, 242~26 Allen 93~50 Betsey 100~3 Caleb 117~49 Daniel 242~27, 242~28 David 259~20 Ebenezer 155~32, 184~12 Ephraim 139~53, 162~14, 183~23 Eunice 315~25 James 357~37 John 275~30 Joseph 293~46 Joshua 115~56 Kimball 67~16 Luther 222~42 Lightfoot 222~41

11~48 Margaret 112~38 Martha (Morse) 67~17 Mary 299~25 Mary (———) (Smith) 357~37 Mary (Lash) 117~49 Nathan 315~26 Noah 274~40 Nymphus 196~37 Rebecca W. (Brooks) 357~39 Samuel 9~40, 11~41, 24~54 Sarah (Thayer) 92~11 Seth 357~39 Submit (———) (Kingsbury) 196~37 Thomas 92~11
PRAY, [Capt.] 77~41 Samuel 313~7
PREBLE, [Brig. Gen.] 209~10 Abigail (Torrey) 78~20 Ebenezer 78~20 Edward 87~42, 209~10 Mary (Deering) 87~42 Mehitable 209~9
PRECY see **PRESSEY**
PREIST see **PRIEST**
PRENOUVEAU, Charles 104~21
PRENTICE see **PRENTISS**
PRENTISS / PRENTICE, [Major] 330~53 [Mrs.] 373~62 Anna 319~26 Caleb 234~16 Charles 171~53, 196~47 Chloe (Wells) 115~52 Clarinda 196~47 Diantha (Aldrich) 136~40 Eleazer 221~34, 374~29 Henry 168~16, 328~26 James 219~2, 295~33, 320~19 John 68~53, 90~34, 136~40, 165~21, 178~25, 319~26 Joshua 162~13 Josiah 41~31 Levi 12~42, 17~3, 35~18, 44~3, 85~15 Martha 254~32 Mary 162~13 Nancy 197~22 Nathaniel 47~23, 244~55 Nathaniel S. 254~32 Sally (Whipple) 168~16 Samuel 115~51, 186~39 Sartile 316~13 Sophia (Mellen) 219~2 Stephen 14~35 Tabitha 327~6, 333~45 William 234~16
PRESCOTT, Benjamin 73~8, 73~11, 233~4 Charles 353~48 D. 363~26 David 363~27 Frances (Johnson) 190~24 Joseph 314~46 Josiah 362~11, 362~14 Marston 362~9 Mary F. 214~10 Oliver 171~2 Samuel 190~23 Vashti 182~40
PRESLEY / PRESLY, (———) 72~45
PRESLY see **PRESLEY**
PRESSEY / PRESSY / PRECY, Betsey 36~35
PRESSY see **PRESSEY**
PRESTON, Esther (Taylor) 177~51 Hannah 226~7 Isaac 242~54 John 137~2 Lydia 53~40 Samuel 177~51
PRICE, Dorothea 253~54 Ebenezer 167~39 George 53~45
PRICHARD / PRITCHARD, Charles 180~27 Charlotte (Pursuivance) 180~27 Martha 353~20
PRIEST / PREIST, Thomas 74~6
PRINCE, [boy] 137~41 [children] 295~23 [girl] 137~41 [Rev.] 270~20 [widow] 295~23 Betsey 92~27 David C. 295~21 John 105~22, 305~4 Joseph 75~54, 137~39 Martha 305~3 Martha (Derby) 105~22 Mary 270~19 Nath. 296~27 Samuel 79~28 Sarah (Stickney) 79~28
PRINGLE, Henry (?) 218~30
PRIOR, John 64~23
PRITCHARD see **PRICHARD**
PROCTER see **PROCTOR**
PROCTOR / PROCTER, Benjamin 65~9 Betsey (Lane) 65~9 John 97~6, 265~6 Lucy 243~6 Mary 174~34 Patty 252~4 Thomas 234~43
PROUDSIT, James 132~4
PROUTER, Abigail 147~21
PROUTY, Isaac 24~40 Lucinda 139~47 Martha (Taft) 150~11 Polly 225~2 Samuel 267~48 Thomas 150~12
PROVINCE, Sarah F. (Gooding) 353~5 Thomas 353~5
PROVOST, John 54~4
PROWNING, Nancy 210~56
PRUDEN, Nehemiah 148~46 Sibyl (———) (Potter) 148~46
PRUYN, Sally 299~50
PUFFER, [Rev.] 199~6 Nathan 174~4
PUKENS see **PECKENS**
PULCIFER / PULSIFER, L. 220~41 S. 220~41
PULFRY see **PALFREY**
PULLEN, John 169~9
PULSIFER see **PULCIFER**
PULTENEY see **PULTNEY**
PULTNEY / PULTENEY, William 204~35, 206~32
PURINGTON see **PURINTON**
PURINTON / PURINGTON, [children] 248~8 [Mr.] 362~17, 364~16 [Mrs.] 248~8 Content 36~26 James 248~8
PURKENS see **PERKINS**
PURKITT see **PERKITT**
PURSUIVANCE, Charlotte 180~27
PURVIANCE, Robert 262~36

PUSHON / PISHEN, Ellis 333~48
PUTMAN, Daniel 13~52 John 304~35 Lucy 304~25
PUTNAM, [General] 188~19 [Mrs.] 284~13 Abigail 190~46 Andrew 295~9 Bayley 310~31 Catharine 192~46, 224~26 Daniel 88~7, 301~15 David 192~47, 310~30, 334~36 Elijah 29~15, 295~32 Elisha 150~45 Elizabeth 169~36 Hannah 328~22 Henry 269~11 Israel 269~38, 284~13 Jesse 19~53 John 96~51, 134~27, 140~35, 327~14 Joseph 256~3 Mary 37~52, 154~31 Mary (Converse) 96~51 Miles 69~49 Phebe 238~50 Rachel (———) 216~5 Rufus 190~47, 224~27 Sally 286~27 Samuel 286~26 Seth 106~4 Sukey (Gibson) 286~26
PYE, [Mr.] 373~10 John 272~2
PYNCHON, Catharine 152~33

Q.

QUAILS see QUALES
QUALES / QUAILS, Charles 294~35
QUARTERMAN, John 183~21
QUIGLEY, [Mrs.] 7~36 John 7~36
QUIMBY / QUINBY, J. 311~13 Jacob 80~24 John 334~8
QUIN see QUINN
QUINBY see QUIMBY
QUINCE see QUINCY
QUINCY / QUINCE, Dolly 64~7 Marcus 104~4 Peter 60~22
QUINER, Henry 192~6
QUINN / QUIN, Allen 152~48 Henry 203~5 John 30~35 Nancy 155~43
QUINTON, Samuel 53~32
QUIRK, Elizabeth 187~29

R.

RABY see ROBIE
RACKLIFF / RADCLIFF / RADCLIFFE / RATCLIFF / RACKLYEFT, [girl] 22~48 Stephen 22~48
RACKLYEFT see RACKLIFF
RADCLIFF see RACKLIFF
RADCLIFFE see RACKLIFF
RALSTON / ROULSTONE / RALSTONE / ROLSTON, Alexander 34~37, 43~46, 90~4, 320~46 Elizabeth 317~13 George 191~47 J. 185~28 James 11~6, 17~45 Sally 220~50
RALSTONE see RALSTON
RAMDELL see RAMSDEL
RAMSAY see RAMSEY
RAMSDEL / RAMSDELL / RAMDELL, [Mr.] 92~17, 196~57
RAMSDELL see RAMSDEL
RAMSEY / RAMSAY, Ephraim 110~29 James 224~38, 289~22 Mary 81~7 William 13~29, 36~9, 87~24, 101~41, 109~25
RAMSON, Harris 142~8
RAN, [Capt.?] 202~55
RAND, [Mr.] 57~55, 348~30 Jane 2~31 Nancy 143~31, 267~56 Robert 261~33 Sally M. 131~33 Thomas 14~19
RANDAL see RANDALL
RANDALL / RANDELL / RENDELL / WRENDALL / RANDAL / RENDALL, [boy] 356~14 [Mr.] 176~10 [Mrs.] 228~26, 356~14 Amos 50~42, 316~52 Elijah 50~39 Elisha 67~22 Esther 115~49 Hannah (Field) 187~28 Isaac 11~13, 21~51, 95~15, 151~27, 165~26 Jerusha 115~50 Job 272~45 Josiah 356~14 Merrel 88~7 Polly (Kingsley) 270~52 Robert 99~9, 210~36 Simeon 304~36 Simon 321~24 Stetson 270~51 Thomas 187~28
RANDELL see RANDALL
RANDLETT see RUNDLETT

RANDOLPH, Edmund 321~2 Edward 214~54 Elizabeth 321~2 John 233~16
RANLET see RUNDLETT
RANNA, Joel 109~26
RANNEY see RENNIE
RANNY see RENNIE
RANSOM / RANSON, [child] 240~54 [Mrs.] 240~54 Elanar 88~6 Joshua 259~12 Molly 91~33 Robert 240~48 Sarah 121~50
RANSON see RANSOM
RANTOUL, Joanna (Lovett?) 92~7 Robert 92~7
RATCLIFF see RACKLIFF
RATSTRAW, John G. 250~16
RAWLEY, Stephen 164~24
RAWLINGS see ROLLINS
RAWN, David 203~30
RAWSON / ROWSON, [children] 148~48 [Dr.] 215~48 Bailey 69~48 Desire (———) 104~47 Ebenezer 13~51 Grindall 180~42 Joseph 148~48 Levi 77~17, 241~24 Nathaniel 146~43 Thankful 241~23
RAY / WRAY, Catharine 256~53 George 256~54 Mary 317~49 Thomas 119~6
RAYENHILL, Joseph 144~4
RAYMOND, John 94~32 Joshua 236~52 Josiah 36~17 William 30~43
RAYNER see REYNOR
REA / RHEA, Elizabeth 155~29
READ see REED
READE see REED
READING / REDING / REDDING, [Mr.] 279~7 [Mrs.] 1~54 Ed. 1~54
REBIS, [child] 106~38 [Mr.] 106~37
RECORD, [girl] 259~42 John 259~42
REDDING see READING
REDDINGTON / REDINGTON, [Mr.] 112~3, 329~10 I. 135~29 Isaac 2~26, 11~46, 25~39, 31~2, 45~35, 89~41, 113~22, 121~6, 145~5, 158~51, 158~54, 165~31, 179~27, 204~23, 207~2, 233~36, 234~56, 249~27, 258~49, 278~23, 294~4, 297~7, 299~48, 306~45, 318~53, 330~55 Mary 137~9 Nancy 281~19 Sukey 46~21 T. 135~29 Thomas 2~26, 25~39, 31~2, 42~24, 45~35, 89~41, 113~22, 121~6, 145~5, 158~51, 179~27, 207~3, 233~36, 306~40
REDFIELD, [Mrs.] 211~9 Ambrose 106~3 Bela 211~9 Charles 320~51 Hannah 88~11 Heman 320~25, 320~50 Sophia 320~49 Tryphena (Sims) 88~12 Zina 88~11
REDING see READING
REDINGTON see REDDINGTON
REDMAN, Elizabeth 131~2 Jonathan 131~3 Kitty 131~2
REED / READ / READE / REID, [Capt.] 259~45 [Miss] 263~51 [Mr.] 220~39 Alpheus 33~17 Charlotte 21~21 Cheney 2~34 Chester 103~9 Daniel 33~4 David 77~42, 177~31 Ebenezer 263~51, 265~55 Elizabeth 285~11 Hephzibah 1~26 Hepzibah 36~18, 68~54 Howard 10~55, 310~12 Jacob 206~22 James 4~33, 46~24, 278~51 Joel 33~13 John 26~6, 78~55, 81~51, 154~19 Jonas 238~14 Joseph 102~14, 176~20 Kincaid 25~34 Leonard 327~7 Mary 265~55 Micah 33~19, 124~15 Nancy 2~33 Peter 60~24 Phinehas 285~31 Polly 36~28, 295~36 Priscilla 196~41 Robert 198~37 Sampson 121~19 Samuel 191~13 Sarah 292~3 Thomas 33~19, 176~19 William 47~57, 48~1, 317~12
REES / RHEES, Herbert 145~36 Morgan J. 174~27
REEVE, Aaron Burr 287~7 Annabella (Sheldon) 287~7 Sarah 2~56 Tappan 2~56
REID see REED
REIDLE, James 7~9
REISCH, Adam 367~62
RELLIEUX, Michael 320~55
REMINGTON, Anne 211~33
RENDALL see RANDALL
RENDELL see RANDALL
RENICK, Seymour 71~28
RENNEY see RENNIE
RENNIE / RENNEY / RANNEY / RANNY (see also RUNEY), Benjamin 331~54 Desire (———) (Rowson) 104~47 Ephraim 66~4 Joel 76~23, 305~45 Stephen 156~4 Thomas 104~47 Waitstill 61~43
RENOUS, Elizabeth (———) 73~14

REVERE, John 95~45 Silence 90~11
REYNAL see REYNOLDS
REYNOLD see REYNOLDS
REYNOLDS / RUNNALS / RUNNELS / RUNELS / REYNOLS / REYNOLD / REYNAL, [Miss] 144~35, 185~10 Ellen (Hageman) 173~30 Gamaliel 194~11 George (. . .) 173~29 James 77~41 Jean Baptiste 191~40 John 197~28 Joseph 185~8 Mary 246~29 S. 179~22 Zadock 211~44
REYNOLS see REYNOLDS
REYNOR / RAYNER, Thomas 169~1
RHEA see REA
RHEES see REES
RHOADES see RHODES
RHOADS see RHODES
RHODES / RHOADES / RODES / RHOADS, Alexander 197~39 James 248~51 Samuel 101~42 Solomon 214~16 William 111~13, 116~31, 137~20, 138~44, 144~24
RICE, [children] 165~17 [Mr.] 241~37 [Mrs.] 107~32, 183~21 Abel 167~44, 280~21 Adonijah 114~50 Ama 228~7 Amos 270~22, 270~23 Asaph 49~41 Benjamin 168~50 David 33~13 Francis 78~36 Henry 293~12, 304~11, 312~33 Hezekiah 70~9 Huldah 47~27 J. 324~23 James 47~27 John 28~30, 142~42, 270~22, 270~53 Lemuel 242~13 Luke 242~14 Lydia 167~41, 280~22 Mehitable 198~19 Nabby (Smith) 270~53 Nahum 82~41 Phinehas 164~28, 165~17 Sally 151~24, 245~36 Samuel 222~3 Stephen 241~45, 329~7 Stephen (?) 313~51 William 133~12
RICH, Benjamin 318~25 Betsey (Marsh) 189~3 Jacob 198~3 Josiah 56~13 Thomas 253~4
RICHARDS, [Mrs.] 148~20 Alice Winchester (Lovring) 75~15 Ann 38~47 Archibald M'Curdey 283~42 Edward 116~30 Joel 93~41, 310~37 Joseph 75~15 Mary 184~27, 190~56 Sally 129~30 Thomas 184~28 W.M. 182~25 William 148~19
RICHARDSON, [boy] 91~14 [Mr.] 221~45 [Mrs.] 366~25 Addison 57~13 Anstis (Blanchard) 57~14 Betsey 156~1 Easter 295~7 Eunice 128~5 Ezekiel 156~1 James 83~15, 91~14, 289~3 Jason 216~9 Jeffry 217~35 Jephthah 262~9 Jesse 252~15 Joel 250~10 John 249~16 Josiah 89~52 Juda 306~6 Mary 29~18 Mary Ann 110~51 Nathaniel 176~19, 259~22 Peggy 221~2 Phebe 127~45 Samuel 155~26, 221~3 Susannah 257~17 Thomas 64~12, 306~7 William 289~18, 355~3
RICHES, John 50~20
RICHIE, Robert 64~21
RICHMOND, [Capt.] 259~39
RICKER, John 304~56
RICKETSON, [Dr.] 320~43
RIDDLE, [Mr.] 110~53 Isaac 162~48
RIDER see RYDER
RIDG see RIDGE
RIDGE / RIDG, William 64~22
RIDLEY, Lucy 176~25
RIGHT see WRIGHT
RIMES see RINES
RINDGE / RINGE, Daniel 34~40, 361~11 John 272~16, 320~35, 330~12 Thomas 335~47
RINES / RYMES / RIMES, [Mr.] 133~35 C. 272~17 Christopher 272~12
RINGE see RINDGE
RIPLEY, [Mr.] 245~35 Abigail 170~16 Calvin 58~48, 89~46 Daniel 30~20 Florella (Mills) 332~29 James 117~41, 291~40, 332~29 Laura 323~28 Lydia 319~13 Mary 154~43 Noah 193~17 Sally 193~17 Sally (Bellows) 58~48 Susanna (Cottle) 245~36 Sylvanus 170~17
RISLEY / WRISLEY, Anna 236~54 John 236~55
RISQUE, J. 222~17
RITCHIE, Duncan 207~32 Jane (Leach) 109~35 William 109~34
ROACH, George 301~55 James 98~20 Joseph 193~21 Mary (———) (Mendum) 98~20
ROBARDS see ROBERTS
ROBB, [girl] 173~20 [Widow] 173~18
ROBBINS / ROBINS, [Mr.] 73~41, 180~12 Chandler 43~26 Daniel 180~58 David 111~55 Jasiah 48~13

Jeremiah 309~51 John 5~37, 56~22 Jonathan 58~15, 75~28 Josiah 309~10 Lydia 93~53 Nancy 167~21 Nathan 58~15 Richard 201~20 Samuel P. 229~51 Samuel Prince 236~27 Silas 332~56 Solomon 72~47, 320~19 Thomas 172~25
ROBERSON / ROBESON, Betsey 282~22 I. 48~7 James 48~4 Jno. 48~7 Jonas 282~22
ROBERTS / ROBARDS, [children] 123~51 [Col.] 100~5 [Mrs.] 123~51 Alpheus 313~21 David 323~55 James 105~3 James P. 354~8 John 88~23 Josiah 123~11 Richard Brooke 2~7 Thomas 123~43 William 135~4, 150~30
ROBERTSON, Alexander 273~55 Christopher 161~2 James 29~2, 98~23 Jane (———) (Gay) 98~23 Patrick 3~39 Polly (———) 191~34 Sally (Baker) 232~17 Timothy 95~44 William 232~16
ROBESHAW, Alvin 93~52
ROBESON see ROBERSON
ROBEY see ROBIE
ROBIE / ROBY / ROBEY / RABY / RUBY, (———) 33~33 [Mr.] 155~4, 169~30 Charles 132~39 Jane 270~28 Joseph 140~10, 199~53, 270~28 Margaret 129~34 Mary 260~38 Relief 270~27 Relief (Curtis) 140~10 S.S. 43~15 William 20~30
ROBINS see ROBBINS
ROBINSON, [Capt.] 16~2, 191~46 [Dr.] 191~5 Andrew 216~54 Bethiah 275~20 Betsey 244~18 Ede 364~11 Elijah 95~22 Eliphalet 328~29 Ephraim 361~40 George 110~40 Hannah 309~52 James 110~40, 220~10 John 27~16, 59~8, 174~24 Jonathan 19~25, 210~29 Joseph 250~16 Mary 210~28 269~27 Samuel 50~16, 95~36 Susanna 183~22 Thomas 104~20 Timothy 190~26
ROBITAILIE, M. 212~26
ROBUT, Peter 322~49
ROBY see ROBIE
ROCKWELL, [Mr.] 276~48 Amariah 60~52, 73~47, 116~21, 132~48 Benjamin 146~39 Earl 308~23 Francis 191~1 Samuel 287~8 Sarah Ann (Spencer) 287~8 Stephen 200~50
ROCKWOOD, Elisha 283~38 Thomas 115~36 Timothy 233~25
RODES see RHODES
RODGERS see ROGERS
RODMAN, Harriot (Fenno) 03~33 John 83~33
ROGERS / RODGERS, [boy] 99~32 Abner 328~23 Clarissa 89~5 D.R. 133~21 Daniel 80~25, 227~22, 357~13 Evan 290~53 George W. 203~52 George Whitefield 203~51 James 20~18, 56~28, 59~25, 61~30, 246~23 Jean 37~41 John 24~8, 37~42, 50~20, 268~50 Jonathan 37~42, 321~13 Joseph 296~24 Mary 96~48, 288~28 Mary (Pierce) 328~37 Minerva (Deniston) 268~50 Penuel B. 231~27 Phebe (Homans) 227~22 R.C. 313~48, 331~37 Rebecca 165~50 Richard C. 313~42 Samuel 162~12, 313~41 Sophia 6~5 Timothy 328~37 Timothy F. 310~8 William 99~52, 165~50
ROHE see ROWE
ROLES / ROWLES, [brothers] 52~21 Moses 293~3
ROLEY see ROLLEY
ROLF / ROLFE / ROLPH, Susannah 219~26
ROLFE see ROLF
ROLLEY / ROLEY, John 7~15 Joseph 312~39
ROLLINGS see ROLLINS
ROLLINS / ROWLINS / ROLLONS / ROLLINGS / RAWLINGS, [Mrs.] 101~23 Ebenezer 146~28 Moses 301~5 Nancy 85~44 Polly (Farmer) 146~28
ROLLONS see ROLLINS
ROLPH see ROLF
ROLSTON see RALSTON
ROMEYN, D. 160~29 John B. 173~23
ROMNEY see RUMNEY
RONEY see RUNEY
ROOSA, [Miss] 175~52 Johanne I. 175~51
ROOT, [child] 149~14 [Judge] 95~34 [Mr.] 149~14 [Mrs.] 100~44 Andrew 203~3 David 266~48 Eli 170~20 Eliza (Stockton) 262~31 Erastus 262~30 Joseph 131~48 Lucretia (Star) 256~41 Susannah 190~30 William 256~41
ROPES, Benjamin 97~54 Samuel 97~54
ROSBOROUGH, William 324~37

ROSCOE, William 218~21
ROSE, Elizabeth 255~24 Harriet (Paine) 116~9, 117~2 Jos. W. 116~9 Joseph 117~1 Philip 60~36 Stephen 320~56
ROSEBOOM, Myndert 238~56
ROSS, [Mr.] 63~8 Eliza (Gansevoort) 262~27 Elizabeth 83~39, 354~3 Hannah 117~51 Joshua 84~12 Mark 301~44 Mary (Eayrs) 84~12 Sally 172~54 Theodore 262~27 Thomas 281~23
ROTHERAM, [Dr.] 191~7
ROULSTONE see RALSTON
ROUNDY / ROUNDYE, [Mr.] 142~17 Robert 7~51
ROUNDYE see ROUNDY
ROUNSEVEL, Joseph 5~14
ROUSEAU see ROUSSEAU
ROUSSEAU / ROUSEAU, Martha 296~7
ROUSSELET, [Mrs.] 38~6
ROW see ROWE
ROWAN, Eliza (———) (Chandler) 223~12 Elizabeth 263~50 James 223~12 Mary H. 91~34
ROWE / ROW / ROHE, (———) 133~14 [Dr.] 364~37 Hannah 201~34 James 218~23 John 95~44, 165~47, 201~34 Joseph 171~13 Sally 354~25 Simon 362~12 Stephen 225~30
ROWEL see ROWELL
ROWELL / ROWEL, [children] 94~51 [Mrs.] 94~51 Eliphalet 94~47 Hannah (Chase) 137~12 Joseph 137~12 Moses 74~5 William 80~26, 311~18, 334~12
ROWLAND / ROWLIN, Abigail 172~8 Ann (Giddings) 127~12 Augustus 64~7 Frances (Bliss) 64~8 William F. 127~12
ROWLES see ROLES
ROWLEY, Issachar 227~50 Samuel H.G. 294~14 Susan (Hopkins) 294~14
ROWLIN see ROWLAND
ROWLINS see ROLLINS
ROWSEL see RUSSELL
ROWSON see RAWSON
ROYCE / ROYS, Abner 88~40 Hezekiah 70~5 Jon. 293~53 Jonathan 6~40, 30~5, 70~46, 181~37, 241~5, 294~2, 310~34
ROYS see ROYCE
ROYSTER, Jethro 202~30
ROZIER, I.A.B. 46~8
RUBY see ROBIE
RUFF, Daniel 323~41
RUGG, Electa 277~8 Elijah 327~35 Jane 316~11 Lucinda 93~54 Ora 13~22
RUGGLES, Ebenezer 28~23, 32~20, 81~19 Edward 61~29 Eliza 78~19 Elizabeth 166~53 John 16~27, 293~33 Joseph 3d 74~8 Lucy 293~33 Nathaniel 247~40 Samuel 300~40
RUMNEY / ROMNEY, Abigail 24~15
RUNDLET see RUNDLETT
RUNDLETT / RUNDLET / RANLET / RANDLETT / RUNLET, Charles 147~52 Elizabeth 267~34 Henry 267~34, 360~4 James 133~22 John 78~36, 168~49 Jonathan 161~38
RUNELS see REYNOLDS
RUNEY / RONEY (see also RENNIE), Hannah 161~3 John 160~35
RUNLET see RUNDLETT
RUNNALS see REYNOLDS
RUNNELS see REYNOLDS
RUSH, [Dr.] 155~47 Mary 155~47
RUSSEL see RUSSELL
RUSSELL / RUSSEL / ROWSEL, [Miss] 29~34 [Mr.] 42~39 Aquilla 295~35 Benjamin 147~48 Betsey 51~20 Caleb 200~48 Elias 53~1 Elijah 348~3 Eliza 180~26 Eunice 173~54 Eunice (———) 109~32 Ezekiel 262~38 F. 354~20 Flint 287~2 James 151~15, 250~2, 281~20 John 254~19, 294~7 Jonathan 123~9 Joseph 96~41, 123~7, 327~4 Levi 210~30 Lucinda (Colley) 53~1 Martha 181~1 Mary 250~1 Sarah 262~37 Sarah (Campbell) 147~48 Sarah (Wentworth) 210~30 Simeon 27~39 Stephen 67~25, 207~50 Thomas 20~8, 86~53, 295~34 Zacheriah 6~4
RUST, Enoch 158~5 Mary 314~20 Stephen 105~4 Wallis 333~25
RUTH, Christian 367~4, 367~8 Philip 367~62
RUTLEDGE, [Gov.] 58~4 John 73~19, 255~36

RYALL see RYLE
RYAN / RYON, Ann (———) (Davis) 109~33 James 266~6 William 109~33
RYDER / RIDER, [children] 257~20 David 214~29 Fidela 208~11 Margaret 95~29 Peter 257~19 Rhoda 257~19
RYLE / RYALL, Betsey 102~28
RYMES see RINES
RYON see RYAN

S.

SABIN / SABINE, John 186~40 Levi 284~24 Mary 62~23 Noah 62~24, 76~37, 273~34 Noah 3d 48~2 Thomas 181~39
SABINE see SABIN
SAFFORD, Anna (Hopson) 233~9 Betsey 233~9 Daniel 68~55 Nathan 233~9
SAGE, Benjamin 201~42 Comfort 35~46 John 230~27 Sally 35~47 Sylvester 278~40
ST. CLAIR, John 213~52
ST. JOHN, Abigail 212~22 Allen Rice 212~22 Elizabeth 212~21 Silas 212~22 William B. 221~5
SALISBURY / SALSBURY / SILSBURY, [Mr.] 51~4 Betsey (Cady) 135~34 John 89~35, 129~22 Lydia (Thurber) 269~54 Nancy (Gardner) 249~36 Rebecca 214~8 Richard 269~53 Samuel 214~9, 249~35 Sarah 214~9 Seth 135~33 William 104~38
SALLY / SOLLY, [Mr.] 320~34, 330~11, 350~26
SALMON, George 156~53
SALSBURY see SALISBURY
SALTER, [Capt.] 248~22 Catharine 79~10 Elizabeth 207~18 James 154~41 Perkins 250~58 Richard 97~18, 250~58 Samuel 36~4, 122~36 Sarah 193~9 Thomas 172~26
SALTMARSH, William 354~23
SALTONSTALL, Hannah 210~55
SAMMES / SAMMES, Isaac 250~21
SAMMES see SAMMAS
SAMPSON / SAMSON, [Mr.] 334~13 Charles 158~4 Ezra 194~1 Mary 194~1 Philemon 180~35 Silvanus 43~15 Sylvanus 36~10 West W. 56~34
SAMSEL / SAMSELL, Abraham 63~11 Abram 367~57
SAMSELL see SAMSEL
SAMSON see SAMPSON
SANBORN / SANDBORN, Benjamin 249~39 Ebenezer 156~36 James 355~24 Jane 355~24 John 350~28 Josiah 350~27 Polly (Hall) 249~39
SANCRY, Polly 155~14
SANDBORN see SANBORN
SANDERS see SAUNDERS
SANDERSON / SAUNDERSON, Abel 163~11 Betsey (Gill) 153~46 David 10~8, 32~16, 122~23 Davis 194~12 Eli 163~13 Elizabeth 99~19 Isaac 153~46 Lucretia 10~8 Sabra 108~20
SANDFORD see SANFORD
SANDS, Juliana 69~22 Juliana Elmore 62~12 Juliana Gilmore 56~54
SANFORD / SANDFORD, Aaron 310~52 E. 259~49 Mary (?) 276~25 Peleg 68~6 Rebecca 4~46 Zechariah 275~57
SANGER, James 191~45
SANLORD, Mary (?) 276~25
SARGEANT see SARGENT
SARGENT / SARGEANT / SARJEANT / SERGENT, [Mr.] 140~46 Abigail 111~39 Betty 286~6 Daniel 230~55 Dinah 229~32 Helena (Barlow) 163~17 Jabez 54~39 Jonathan 232~48 Joseph 304~13 Mary 179~48 Orlando 286~6 Thomas 163~17, 354~26
SARJEANT see SARGENT
SARTELL see SAWTELL
SARTWELL, Asa 146~22, 186~42 Clarissa 146~20, 186~42, 310~44 Cynthia 146~20, 186~42 Eliab 296~49, 320~20 Fanny 146~20, 186~43 John 267~48, 303~42 Lucy 146~20, 186~43 Obadiah 327~9 Reuben 304~37
SAUNDERS / SANDERS, [Mr.] 53~28 [Rev.] 78~41

David 56~33 Edward 290~34 Robert 198~15
SAUNDERSON see **SANDERSON**
SAVAGE, Ann 264~44 Edward 215~3 Littleton 182~4 Samuel Phillips 15~5
SAVARY see **SAVORY**
SAVERY see **SAVORY**
SAVILS, William 217~32
SAVORY / SAVARY / SAVERY, Moses 13~20 William 163~45
SAWERS, Elizabeth (M'Pherson) 267~8 John 267~8
SAWTELL / SARTELL / SAWTELLE, Joel 115~50 Mary 262~59 Sally (———) (Bennett) 115~50
SAWTELLE see **SAWTELL**
SAWYER / SOHIER, [women] 366~59 Aaron 210~6, 210~45 Caroline 37~43 Edward 258~24 Hannah 107~50 Jonathan 138~44, 313~33 Jotham 183~46 Lucy (Fisk) 183~47 Mary 37~6 Moses 121~10 Nathaniel 284~19 Sally 179~49 Sarah 355~23 Susannah 219~21
SAX / SOCKS, [Mr.] 367~58 Christopher 63~15
SAXTON see **SEXTON**
SAYERS see **SAYRE**
SAYRE / SAYERS, Daniel 215~4 Ephraim 67~1
SAYWARD / SEAWARD, Samuel 176~16
SCARBOROUGH, Elizabeth (Dudley) 219~18
SCHEILLEY, Margaret 228~11
SCHIFFERT / SHIFFERT, H. 38~18 Henry 367~5, 367~8
SCHILLINGER, [Miss] 135~18
SCHMIDT / SCHMIT, Anthony 279~30 Daniel 196~18 Dorothy 148~18
SCHMIT see **SCHMIDT**
SCHOFIELD see **SKOLFIELD**
SCHOTT see **SCOTT**
SCHROEDER, Mary (———) (Paul) 317~50 Nicholas 317~50
SCHULLEY see **SCULLY**
SCHUSTER, Jacob 63~27
SCHUYLER, Catharine (Van Rensselaer) 255~3 Diana 218~20 John A. 255~2 Philip 171~33, 172~17 Simon 157~42
SCHWARTZ, Daniel 367~4, 367~8
SCILLY see **SCULLY**
SCOBIE, James 212~53 John 127~12 Lydia (Maley) 127~13
SCOFIELD see **SKOLFIELD**
SCOLLAY see **SCULLY**
SCOTT / SCHOTT, [Mr.] 19~41 [widow] 188~6 Abel 188~4 Alexander 321~39 Cynthia 188~8 Ebenezer 172~29 Freeman 188~4 George 23~23 Gustavus 84~16 Hannah (Meinzes) 98~24 Harriet (Pearce) 54~45 James 303~20, 363~47 John 54~44, 66~43 John P. 98~24 Jonathan 270~44, 275~44 Martin 192~42 Polly 188~7 Rachel 232~12 Reuben 188~5 Ruby 188~6 Samuel 81~20 Sarah 188~5 Thomas 188~8 Timothy 289~21 William 122~1
SCOVEL see **SCOVILLE**
SCOVIL see **SCOVILLE**
SCOVILL see **SCOVILLE**
SCOVILLE / SCOVIL / SCOVEL / SCOVILL, Henery 28~20 Henry 32~17, 316~15 John 181~12
SCRANTON, Erastus 204~21
SCRIBNER, Ebenezer 289~50 Elizabeth 289~51 Thomas 45~19, 60~46, 65~35
SCRIPTER see **SCRIPTURE**
SCRIPTOR see **SCRIPTURE**
SCRIPTURE / SCRIPTER / SCRIPTOR, Asahel 235~57 Azuba (Tenney) 235~57 James 34~39, 328~47 Jero. 142~6 Oliver 34~38
SCUDDER, Daniel 106~43 Jesse 332~40 Robert 253~56 Sally (Weld) 106~43 Sarah 335~44
SCULLY / SCOLLAY / SCILLY / SCHULLEY , Mercy 57~19 William 294~23
SEAGRAVES, Joseph 82~48
SEAMAN see **SEAMANS**
SEAMANS / SEAMAN / SEAMONS, Aaron 300~45 Sally 50~2
SEAMONS see **SEAMANS**
SEARL see **SEARLE**
SEARLE / SEARL / SEARLS / SURREL, [children] 147~32 Boaz 16~37 Gideon 271~17 James 8~29 Mary 271~18 Nabby (Giles) 65~41 Nathaniel 271~18 Uriah 65~41,
321~22 Zenas 147~25
SEARLS see **SEARLE**
SEARS, [Mrs.] 18~24 Freeman 225~48 William S. 18~23
SEATON see **SETON**
SEAVER / SEVER, [child] 154~44 [Mr.] 154~44, 306~45, 329~10, 330~55 Elizabeth Grafton 131~41 Peter Johonnot 167~57 William 303~26
SEAVEY / SEVEY / SEAVY, [Mr.] 133~34 [Mrs.] 133~19 Amos 281~36 Ann 280~54 Deborah 95~27 Paul 87~47 Stephen 280~54
SEAVY see **SEAVEY**
SEAWARD see **SAYWARD**
SEDEN, Ezra 289~22
SEDGWICK, Betsey 177~46 Frances P. 89~2 Gad 122~22 Theodore 89~3
SEEDS, Thomas 258~14
SEELEY / SEELY, Obadiah 11~31
SEELY see **SEELEY**
SELDEN, Ezra 181~36 Joseph 296~30
SELFRIDGE, Edward 265~50 Thomas O. 251~37 Thomas Oliver 372~55
SELKIRK, Alexander 3~6 John 3~9
SELLECK, Frederick 213~21
SELMAN, Archibald 264~5
SENEY, Horatio 119~39
SENF, Christian 257~55
SENIER see **SENIOR**
SENIOR / SENIER, Ebenezer 119~3
SEREVEN, Thomas 162~14
SERGENT see **SARGENT**
SERVICE, John 30~34
SESSION / SESSIONS, Alexander 319~47 Amasa 38~50 Darius 298~32, 301~12 Joseph 319~45
SESSIONS see **SESSION**
SETON / SEATON, Andrew 27~42 Christopher 66~40 Harriot 317~7 P. Wentworth (Butler) 66~41 William 23~43, 317~7 William M. 158~18
SEVER see **SEAVER**
SEVERANCE / SEVRENS / SEVERENCE / SEVERNS, [Mrs.] 96~55 Catharine 321~37 Ebenezer 153~18 Mary 154~11 Peter 224~14 Sarah (Wardner) 153~18 Thankful 271~24
SEVERENCE see **SEVERANCE**
SEVERNS see **SEVERANCE**
SEVEY see **SEAVEY**
SEVRENS see **SEVERANCE**
SEWALL, John 196~49, 199~39 John B. 133~27 Jonathan M. 284~42 Rebecca B. (Lewis) 137~28 Stephen 164~6 William 354~27 William H. 137~28
SEWARD, Hannah 62~18 Sukey (Faxon) 52~57 Thomas 52~57
SEWELL see **SEWALL**
SEXTON / SAXTON, David 75~3 James 200~22 Mary 244~24 Persis 323~15 Phinehas 323~16 Rebecca 203~43 William 272~46
SEYMORE / SEYMOUR, [Mrs.] 35~48 David 138~45 John 291~31 Matthew 227~46
SEYMOUR see **SEYMORE**
SHACKFORD, Eleanor 183~23
SHAEFER see **SHAFFER**
SHAEFFER see **SHAFFER**
SHAFFER / SHAEFER / SHAEFFER, David 39~8 George 367~5, 367~7
SHANNON / SHANON, Hannah (———) 148~44 James 50~53 John L. 317~52 Mary (Tebbetts) 98~26 Richard C. 98~26 Sarah F. (Blunt) 317~52
SHANON see **SHANNON**
SHANTZ, Abraham 63~11 Abram 367~59
SHAPLEIGH / SHEPLEY / SHAPLEY / SHIPLIE / SHIPLEY, [Mr.] 312~38, 319~32 Alexander 111~2 J. 133~45, 306~51, 313~39, 331~51 Jabez 101~43 James 252~56 Josiah 292~48, 296~57, 318~51, 326~13, 326~55, 334~4 Polly 29~30 Richard 77~42 Thankful (Champney) 252~55
SHAPLEY see **SHAPLEIGH**
SHARMAN see **SHERMAN**
SHARON, David 87~25
SHARP see **SHARPE**
SHARPE / SHARP, [Lieut.] 47~46 Daniel 300~37 Eliza

87~44 Grace 212~47
SHATSWELL, Thomas 317~22
SHATTUCK, Mary 39~37 Mary (Wallace) 245~37 Moses 321~24 Nathaniel 245~37 Samuel 328~23
SHAVER, Barbara 205~37 Peter 205~36
SHAW, Abiather 48~15, 322~13 Dan 191~33 Dan. 194~16 Daniel 25~5 David 30~36 J. 32~3 Jacob 98~37, 144~20 James 167~16, 182~55 Joanna 153~35 Joshua 295~12 Judy P. 287~32 Mary 363~53 Mary (———) (Bliss) 191~33 Nancy 218~7 Oakes 278~50 Oaks 280~39 Royal 106~23 Sally 52~58 Sarah 47~36 William 30~36, 213~49
SHEAD see SHED
SHEAF / SHEAFE / SHEAFFE, Abigail 213~27, 223~23 Ann 160~32, 187~6 Jacob 121~14, 133~28, 213~28, 223~24 James 70~19 John 363~50 Olive 121~14 Polly (Fisher) 70~20
SHEAFE see SHEAF
SHEAFFE see SHEAF
SHEARLEY see SHIRLEY
SHED / SHEDD / SHEAD, (———) (Martin) 98~24 Ebenezer 106~46 Fanny (Bannister) 106~46 Joseph 98~23 Thomas 231~39
SHEDD see SHED
SHELDEN see SHELTON
SHELDON see SHELTON
SHELLEY, Azel 34~39
SHELTON / SHELDON / SHELDEN, [Mr.] 82~17 [Mrs.] 82~18 Abraham 34~36 Annabella 287~7 Benjamin 151~7 Eleanor 180~21 Elizabeth 237~1 Jeremiah 82~19 John 256~56 Judea 82~18 Lydia 274~34 Nathaniel 82~17 Polly 82~17 Sally (Holt) 140~15 Thomas 100~31 William 82~19, 140~14
SHEPARD / SHEPHARD / SHEPHERD / SHEPERD / SHEPPARD, [Gen.] 123~1, 127~21, 136~48, 330~52 [General] 4~41, 178~27 [Mr.] 137~4, 157~37, 204~25, 224~53, 258~53, 277~35, 324~7 Amos 45~8, 62~13, 113~40, 157~49, 190~13, 214~6, 222~20, 237~23, 241~8, 262~23, 272~53, 297~8, 303~44, 326~41, 333~52 Ann (———) (Watson) 106~49 Betsey (Dow) 301~48 Betsey (Hutchins) 242~2 Charles 301~48 Eliza (Phillips) 272~27 Henrietta (Tryon) 249~55, 254~30 I. 140~1 Isaac 182~9 James 2d 272~27 John 2~9, 59~46, 108~27, 198~50, 249~55, 254~31, 298~34, 301~20 Jonathan 327~46 Joshua 60~50, 165~44 Jotham 43~10 Levi 218~15, 242~2 Lucy (Gorham) 283~47 Lydia 1~31 Oliver 60~49, 66~33, 241~3 Patty 139~41 Peggy 79~44 R. 106~48 R.D. 283~47 Samuel 349~13 Simeon 180~3 Sybil 141~20 Timothy 1~32, 105~26
SHEPARDSON / SHEPHARDSON, Harriot (Cambridge) 289~31 Stephen 240~38 William 200~17, 200~29, 289~30
SHEPERD see SHEPARD
SHEPHARD see SHEPARD
SHEPHARDSON see SHEPARDSON
SHEPHERD see SHEPARD
SHEPLEY see SHAPLEIGH
SHEPPARD see SHEPARD
SHERBERN see SHERBURNE
SHERBURN see SHERBURNE
SHERBURNE / SHERBURN / SHURBURNE / SHERBERN, Dorcas (Hall) 79~6 James 361~5 John 1~40, 45~16, 151~46, 318~40 Joseph 79~6 Margaret 17~22 Nathaniel 224~46 Samuel 280~58 Thomas 115~55
SHERIDAN, Charles Francis 252~40 Richard Briasley 252~40 Upton 58~5
SHERILL, Jacob 113~4 Jerusha (Huntington) 113~4
SHERMAN / SHERMON / SHARMAN, [child] 12~36 [Mr.] 298~45 [Mrs.] 12~36 Eliza (Poindexter) 116~46 Ephraim 14~7, 33~6, 83~15, 83~22, 316~16 Michael 116~45 Roger 236~57
SHERMON see SHERMAN
SHERWIN, David 20~4
SHIFFERT see SCHIFFERT
SHILABER see SHILLABER
SHILLABER / SHILABER, William 172~24
SHIMMIN, Thomas 154~24
SHINCKLE, Frederick 323~33
SHIPLEY see SHAPLEIGH
SHIPLIE see SHAPLEIGH

SHIPMAN, [Mrs.] 121~23 Alvan 243~50 Elias 96~7 Nathaniel 211~36
SHIPPEN, Edward 170~53, 238~54 John 212~35 Margaret 170~52
SHIRLEY / SHIRLY / SHEARLEY, A. 59~20 Betsey 235~9
SHIRLY see SHIRLEY
SHIRTLEFF see SHIRTLIFF
SHIRTLIFF / SHIRTLEFF / SHURTLUFF / SHURTLEFF, Ann (Pope) 335~2 Asahel 109~27 Roswell 66~26, 61~32, 335~1 Sarah 295~56
SHITZ, Francis 17~28 Peter 17~29
SHOEMAKER, John 280~33
SHORES, Daniel 118~13 Hannah 136~21 Polly (Dennett) 118~13
SHOREY / SHORY, [infant] 144~54 [Mrs.] 144~53 Miles 144~52
SHORT, John 196~52
SHORY see SHOREY
SHOVE, Daniel 238~40 Lydia 260~54 Seth 260~56
SHREEVE see SHREEVES
SHREEVES / SHREEVE, John 4~9
SHULTS see SHULTZ
SHULTZ / SHULTS, [Mr.] 148~39
SHURBURNE see SHERBURNE
SHURTLEFF see SHIRTLIFF
SHURTLUFF see SHIRTLIFF
SHUTE, Daniel 127~48
SHUTER, Joseph 259~52
SHUTTLEWORTH, Samuel 297~38
SIBLEY, [Miss] 219~41 Asa 28~20, 90~3, 165~32, 229~1 Ebenezer 219~40 Joseph 178~17 Samuel 100~11
SIGOURNEY, Charles 119~20, 130~19
SIKES / SYKES, [Mr.] 8~48 Charlotte 156~12 John 210~54 Nathaniel 55~36, 69~18, 83~5, 90~50, 136~49, 159~7, 210~24, 366~44 Polly 69~17 Reuben 178~11
SILL, William 204~48
SILSBEE / SILSBY, Benjamin 29~50 Eliphaz 128~52, 133~58 Esther 133~57 Lasell 133~57 Lazel 81~53 Mary (Crowninshield) 134~4 Nathaniel 134~4 Woodward A. 81~52
SILSBURY see SALISBURY
SILSBY see SILSBEE
SILVER, John 160~42, 370~40 Sarah (———) 103~13
SILVEY, Jer. 279~34
SIM see SIMES
SIMES / SIMS / SIM / SYMMES / SIMMS / SYMS, [Mrs.] 133~45 Andrew 2~31 B. 133~18 H. 133~18 Joshua Gee 58~6 Mark 272~16 Thomas 134~33 Tryphena 88~12 William 133~18, 143~8, 278~36
SIMMONS see SIMONS
SIMMS see SIMES
SIMON, Dick 28~32 John 9~16
SIMONDS see SIMONS
SIMONS / SIMONDS / SIMMONS / SYMONDS, [———] 72~45 [Col.] 302~25 Alvin 87~29 Benjamin C. 324~39 Charity 293~23 Charity (Simons) 293~23 Charles W. 36~25 Content (Purington) 36~26 Elisha 333~54 Ephraim 94~14 Hannah 219~32 Hebry 248~5 Huldy (Yeomans) 312~42 Job 11~7 John 321~23 Joseph 11~8 Mary 122~30 Moses 248~5 S. 39~32 Samuel 269~17 Sophia 216~2 William 61~40, 311~2
SIMPSON, [Mr.] 102~22 Allese 102~21 Charles 10~26 David 231~44 Elizabeth 203~41, 207~25 John 93~19, 299~34 Michael 203~42 Sarah 172~6 William 225~44, 361~46
SIMS see SIMES
SINCLAIR see SINKLER
SINCLAIRE see SINKLER
SINGLETARY, Amos 268~18
SINGLETON, (———) 72~45 John 50~12 William 238~5
SINKLER / SINCLAIR / SINCLAIRE, David 204~58 John 69~53
SISCHO, Samuel 334~32
SISK, D. 112~45
SISSON, Sylvanus 83~51
SKEELS, Truman 220~30
SKELTON, Ama (Willard) 283~51 Thomas 283~51, 284~29

SKEPER, (———) 133~14
SKERRET / SKERRETT, Maria 126~22 Nathan 170~8
SKERRETT see SKERRET
SKILLIN see SKILLING
SKILLING / SKILLIN / SKILLINGS, John 58~6 Samuel 36~35 Sarah 210~55
SKILLINGS see SKILLING
SKILLMAN, [Mr.] 240~19
SKINNER, [Alderman] 234~33 Abigail 242~24 Benajah 261~6 I. Lord 200~29 John 132~31 Mary 184~49 Samuel 101~44, 109~28 Sarah 36~33 Sylvester 10~36 Timothy 93~56, 242~25 William 117~32
SKINNOW, Sarah 185~55
SKIPWITH, P. 218~13
SKOLFIELD / SCOFIELD / SCHOFIELD, Luther 296~33 Philo 314~18 Thomas 26~1
SLADE / SLAID, [Mr.] 205~12 Experience 286~47 John 2~1 Samuel 2~1, 43~8 William 12~23, 241~5
SLADER see SLATER
SLAID see SLADE
SLATER / SLADER, Edward 292~33, 313~38 Lucinda 234~44 Lucinda (?) 146~56 Thomas 41~53, 234~45, 244~1
SLEEPER, Jonathan F. 175~47 Moses 86~6 Sally 354~28 Samuel 362~27
SLIDELL, John 190~52
SLOAN, Isaac 238~6
SLOCUM see SLOCUMB
SLOCUMB / SLOCUM, Mary 106~26
SLOSSON, William 291~53
SLOWMAN, George 192~18
SMALL, Alexander 219~4 Amasa 353~45, 354~49 Benjamin 268~27, 269~18 Daniel 248~5 Ebenezer 353~45, 354~49 Sally 355~52 William 59~41
SMALLCORN, [Mr.] 357~15
SMART, Asenath 288~14 Benjamin 96~43 Comfort 256~39 Francis 149~57 Stickney 149~56
SMEAD, Azor 162~42 Bathsheba 178~8 David 271~24
SMILEE see SMILEY
SMILEY / SMILEE / SMILIE, [Rev.] 101~37 David 320~38 Robinson 321~25
SMILIE see SMILEY
SMISSAERT, Gilbert I.E. 192~12
SMITH / SMYTH, [boy] 95~13, 130~42, 283~23 [children] 4~12, 157~21, 175~3, 332~53 [Col.] 87~28 [Deacon] 262~40 [Dr.] 240~3 [infant] 253~26 [Miss] 95~56 [Mr.& Mrs.] 253~26 [Mr.] 134~44, 227~2, 254~44 [Mrs.] 175~3, 324~45 [Rev.] 41~32 [widow] 332~53 Abigail 105~24, 262~40, 297~48 Abner 126~1 Almira 259~1 Amasa 267~44 Ann 30~13 Anna 329~34 Arethusa 157~19 Ashbel 196~36 Azubah (———) (Baldwin) 196~36 Benjamin 92~13, 303~40 Benoni 274~26 Caleb 211~56 Catherine 101~21 Catherine 83~41 Chancey 296~32 Charles 102~13 Chloe 319~24 Cornelius 63~47 Cushman 19~23, 74~45, 175~17, 236~31 D. 201~54 Darius 70~44, 73~23 David 24~13, 79~19, 157~9, 284~56 Dorcas (Stone) 274~23 Dorothy 245~31 E. 324~45 Ebenezer 49~1, 286~46 Edward 99~19, 99~26, 182~14, 221~29 Elihu 106~26 Elihu H. 27~50 Elihu Hubbard 37~10 Eliphalet 354~33 Eliza 126~43 Elizabeth 49~52, 130~43 Elizabeth (Ruggles) 166~53 Ephraim 110~21 Esquire 8~10 Fanny (Chipman) 224~23 Fessenden 215~44 George 82~55 Gerard 224~24 Hannah 280~57 Hasadiah 319~29 Henry 63~13, 196~29, 367~58 Hezekiah 178~58 Hugh 116~32, 328~24 Huldah 295~3 I. 51~1 Isaac 36~19, 125~26, 129~28, 133~27, 257~44, 327~55 Israel 215~4, 290~37, 295~38, 295~39 J.K. 329~35 Jacob 146~9 James 115~16, 218~34, 278~27, 303~39, 310~56, 321~10, 334~26 Jeffrey 175~2 Jeremiah 50~22, 283~23 Jerusha 330~21 Jesse 7~20 Joel 112~20, 130~42, 151~20 John 4~12, 13~25, 59~9, 77~43, 93~23, 120~15, 161~37, 179~16, 179~17, 258~16, 292~48, 298~47, 316~41 Jonathan 52~30, 80~26 Jos. 281~14 Joseph 96~30, 158~48, 209~5, 262~16, 303~38, 326~35, 350~29, 361~41 Joseph L. 256~14 Joshua 78~2, 303~19, 323~19, 362~27 Latham 145~31 Levi 79~20 Lois 289~29 Lucy 36~27, 46~30, 118~43, 255~8 Lucy (Willard) 203~22 Lydia (———) 194~4 Lyman 260~42 Martha 146~10 Mary 57~21, 275~23, 309~53 Mary (———) 357~37 Mary (Slocum) 106~26 Mary Ann 100~4 Mehitable 312~52 Mercy 295~40, 333~51 Moses 11~18, 21~20, 43~16, 48~3, 61~31 N. 325~45 Nabby 270~53 Nancy (Blake) 215~12 Nathan 74~43, 95~12, 116~40, 144~47 Nathaniel 122~16, 137~43, 166~19, 322~28 Nathaniel R. 166~46 Nehemiah 149~3 Noah 215~12, 319~24 Olive 233~13 P. Stephen 166~53 Pardon 42~32 Pascal N. 213~19 Peter 13~36, 203~20 Peyton B. 316~41 Philip 11~17, 59~39 Ralph 126~43 Rebecca (Stevens) 277~39 Reuben 167~18 Richard 262~2 Robert 59~15, 107~3, 120~15, 154~8, 239~55, 268~41 Roger 208~41 Roswell C. 58~35 Ruth 306~10 Sally 323~20 Sally (Fisk) 354~33 Samuel 56~2, 179~20, 219~43, 332~51 Sarah 65~46 Silas 302~13 Simeon 16~30, 249~5, 295~37 Simon 244~5, 250~42 Speedy (Goodell) 137~43 Stephen 24~37, 262~41 Sukey 23~11 Susannah 297~51 Sylvester 277~39, 316~17, 327~15, 328~8, 333~44 Thomas 12~43, 18~28, 108~30, 157~20, 164~5, 226~35, 272~21, 296~10, 335~42 Timothy Treadwell 152~54 William 77~24, 231~11 William D. 224~23 William Green 328~44 William P. 103~19
SMOLLET, [Dr.] 300~10
SMYER, John 38~17 Michael 367~61
SMYTH see SMITH
SNELL, Benjamin 267~2
SNELLING, Joseph 272~46 Samuel G. 295~1 Susan (Alley) 295~1
SNOW, Abigail 189~9 Benjamin 180~23, 233~38 Daniel 189~9, 242~18 James 186~56 John 77~9, 275~38 Marcy 180~24 Thomas 169~1
SNOWDEN see SNOWDON
SNOWDON / SNOWDEN, Gilbert 2~8 Isaac 317~8
SNYDER, [Gov.] 321~2 [Mrs.] 321~2
SOAMES / SOMES, Benjamin 179~48 Jane 143~31
SOCKS see SAX
SOHIER see SAWYER
SOLEY, John 172~9 Rebecca (Henley) 172~9
SOLLY see SALLY
SOMERS see SUMMERS
SOMES see SOAMES
SON, Francisco 236~42, 237~5
SOPER, Amasa 197~55
SOTHOD, (———) (———) (Speck) 69~4 [Capt.] 69~4
SOTRIDGE, [Dr.] 199~44 [Miss] 199~46
SOUTHACK see SOUTHWICK
SOUTHARD / SOUTHER / SOUTHWORD / SOUTHWORTH, [Mr.] 159~20, 196~29, 297~45, 315~16 A. 156~40, 178~30 Asher 4~25, 205~49, 233~1, 299~10, 308~46, 334~50 Ashur 78~52 G.S. 178~44 Hannah (Wilcox) 316~36 James 316~35 John 172~29 Joseph 363~18 Sally 178~44 Sally (Hore) 4~26
SOUTHER see SOUTHARD
SOUTHERLAND see SUTHERLAND
SOUTHGATE, John 256~56
SOUTHICK see SOUTHWICK
SOUTHWICK / SOUTHICK / SOUTHACK, J. 32~3 Jane (Barnes) 92~29 John 92~29 Solomon 16~45 William 166~5
SOUTHWORD see SOUTHARD
SOUTHWORTH see SOUTHARD
SOWERS, [Mr.] 221~56
SPAFFORD see SPOFFORD
SPAIGHT, Richard Dobbs 128~41
SPALDEN see SPALDING
SPALDING / SPAULDING / SPALDEN, [Dr.] 181~19 Abel 92~39, 147~41, 297~53 Amos 80~4, 142~54 Andrew 239~11 Anna 285~50 Annas 147~45 Bery 89~55 Betsey 147~43 Bezaleel 34~35 Charles 47~49 Daniel 214~20 Ebenezer 56~43, 71~25, 85~43 Elizabeth 92~39 Elizabeth (Bradshaw) 203~26 Eunice (Jones) 85~43 Hannah (Woods) 285~50 John 289~20 Jonas 285~49 Jonathan 246~23, 325~34 Joseph 176~17 Joshua 147~43, 203~26 Lebbeus 147~44 Lovell 147~43 Lyman 17~14, 43~8, 137~15, 228~58 Matthias 260~22 Moses 294~55 Nancy 147~45 Persis (Chapman) 294~55 Philip 314~32 Rebecca (Atherton) 260~22 Reuben 202~29, 294~32 Sally 214~20 Samuel

147~44 Susanna 294~33 Zebina 147~43
SPARHAWK, [Mr.] 322~36 Abigail 212~6 Elizabeth
221~36 Elizabeth (M'Kenzie) 156~22 George 66~36,
132~17, 303~41 Hannah (Whitney) 79~32 Henry
278~55 John 207~35 John S. 44~36 Jonathan H.
127~17 Mary 303~43 O. 320~22 Oliver 31~5,
79~31, 309~54, 316~14, 327~5 Polly (Allen) 132~18
Samuel 23~44, 156~22, 293~50, 302~27 Thomas
6~31, 24~36, 44~37, 130~46, 132~47, 204~23,
264~43, 278~55
SPAULDING see SPALDING
SPEAR, [children] 187~2 [Mr.] 187~2 Betsey 278~3
David 278~4 Mary 278~4 Samuel 118~32
SPECK, [Mrs.] 69~4
SPENCE, Anna 28~21 Harriot 261~40
SPENCER, Aaron 296~29 Abraham 82~47 Alexander
116~49 Benjamin 322~11 David 181~3 Emily 139~22
Ephraim 103~52 Esther 310~48 Hannah 287~19 Joel
287~20 John 244~31, 249~38 Levi 151~17, 321~25
Norman 177~6 Polly 106~47 Polly (Thurston) 249~38
Sarah Ann 287~8
SPERRY, Henry 307~30
SPIERES, Henry 52~19
SPILLARD see SPILLER
SPILLER / SPILLARD, W. 69~12
SPINNER, Kitty 335~6
SPOFFORD / SPAFFORD, Amos 226~1 John 136~17
SPOONER, [Mrs.] 278~9 Alden 280~28 Amelia (Grout)
232~13 Daniel 168~5, 267~5 Eliakim 232~12
Jeduthun 278~10 Judah P. 278~45 Mason 374~3 Pe-
ter 250~18 Polly 230~34 R. 118~41 Rebecca
(Jermain) 280~29 Sarah 92~8 Sarah H. 247~31 Susan
(Elliot) 118~41
SPOTSWOOD, William 190~51
SPRAGUE, [Judge] 140~23 [Mrs.] 203~17 Charles
92~5 George 200~57, 201~25, 201~26 John 5~21,
74~55, 211~30, 319~20 Margaret (Pearson) 92~5
Peleg 27~44, 62~44 Samuel 133~13 Samuel John
211~29 Sarah 140~22
SPRIGG, Thomas 317~6
SPRIGGS, George 58~50
SPRING, (———) 133~46 [Rev.] 300~15 Samuel
213~51 Walton 300~14
SPRINKLE, [children] 277~33 Michael 277~32
SPROAT, Ebenezer 186~23
SQUIRE, Sarah 40~5
SQUIRES, [Mrs.] 208~14 Samuel 208~13
ST. CLAIR see S(AIN)T CLAIR
ST. JOHN see S(AIN)T JOHN
STACEY see STACY
STACKPOLE / STAGPOLE, Aaron 232~35 Grace 71~32
Sarah Crese 39~26 William 39~27
STACY / STACEY, [children] 97~47 James 97~47 Nym-
phas 177~28 William 20~16
STAFFORD, Elizabeth 150~40
STAGG, John 148~18
STAGPOLE see STACKPOLE
STAHLER (see also STEKLER), Anthony 39~7, 63~4,
367~47 Henry 367~4, 367~7
STALCUP, Peter 308~51
STALNEAKER, A. 38~18
STANDLY see STANLEY
STANDWOOD see STANWOOD
STANFORD / STANIFORD, Daniel 254~52 James 77~43
Jeremiah 94~18
STANIFORD see STANFORD
STANLEY / STANDLY / STANLY, Edward 142~26 Esther
(Waters) 142~26 Experience 235~8 Jacob 142~36
John 128~42 Rebecca B. (Taylor) 203~39 Tayle
(Taylor) 203~39
STANLY see STANLEY
STANSBURY, Joseph 313~32
STANTON / STAUNTON, Joshua 269~9 Sarah 267~55
William 225~21
STANWOOD / STANDWOOD, Elizabeth 149~23 Isaac
133~36
STAPLES, Ebenezer 247~40 John 157~25, 272~14
STAR see STARR
STARK, Anna 255~25 Samuel 296~9
STARKS, [Mr.] 46~48
STARKWEATHER, [Mr.] 243~44 Joseph 223~4, 372~14

STARLING see STERLING
STARR / STAR, [Mr.] 169~25 Daniel 2~17 Elijah
252~36 Ezra 195~10 Jonathan 216~42 Lucretia
256~41 Richard 188~3 Sally 216~41 Samuel 260~9
Thomas 239~54 Timothy 2~55
STAUNTON see STANTON
STEARNS / STERNES / STERNS, [family] 9~37 [Mr.]
327~8 [Mrs.] 103~25 Aaron 25~55 Abram 26~9,
30~54 Amos 93~55 Ben. 296~31 Calvin 287~17
Charles 286~7 David 47~8 Deborah 287~17 Eben
169~29 Eben. 30~54 Ebenezer 26~9, 87~27, 296~28
Elizabeth 197~36 Elizabeth (———) (Kelley) 151~53
Ephraim 247~7 Jesse 72~26, 151~16 John 169~29
Jonathan 23~20 Joseph S. 8~56 Mary Ann 275~49
Reuben 268~23 Sally 9~31, 224~25 Samuel 103~25,
151~52, 281~52, 307~19 Sarah 298~5 Silas 177~15
Susan 286~6 Thomas 298~12 William 65~54 William J.
298~5
STEBBENS / STEBBINS / STEBBIN, Asa 49~34 E.
368~58 Edward 266~42 Elia. 304~17 Eliakim 80~16
Elijah 80~15, 115~37, 143~16, 287~35 Elikim 325~40
Elizabeth 194~20 Hannah 147~47, 268~56 J.
368~60 Joel 69~11 Joseph 115~38, 143~15 Lora
232~8 Lucy 197~20 Moses 96~55 Rufus 95~42 Selah
239~7 Sophia 242~25 Stephen W. 242~26 T.
163~46 Thomas 141~50, 163~6 Zebina 141~49
STEBBIN see STEBBENS
STEBBINS see STEBBENS
STEDMAN, David 219~23 Margaret 146~44
STEEL see STEELE
STEELE / STEEL, Alexander 164~6 Jonathan 82~42,
277~23 Joseph 132~14 Lois 309~55 Margery Sullivan
277~22 Mary 96~17 Sally 132~11 Timothy 245~51
William 225~32
STEGALL, [child] 53~57 [Mrs.] 53~57 Moses 53~57
STEKLER (see also STAHLER), Henry 38~18
STEPHENS see STEVENS
STEPHENSON see STEVENSON
STERLING / STIRLING / STARLING, Eunice 284~51,
286~47 Moses 314~44 William 204~10, 204~47
STERNE, [Dr.] 181~17 Thomas 70~7 William 159~19,
170~5
STERNES see STEARNS
STERNS see STEARNS
STERRY, Elizabeth 110~32 Robert 187~21
STETSON, [Mr.] 24~46 [Mrs.] 164~8 Joshua 101~46
Samuel 164~7 Snow 164~16
STEVEN see STEVENS
STEVENINGHAM, John 317~6
STEVENS / STEPHENS / STEVEN, [boy] 253~1 [Dr.]
348~25 [Mr.] 28~38, 88~38, 253~1 Abigail (———)
(Weatherby) 138~54 Calvin 264~49, 266~5 Daniel
244~29 Ebenezer 29~10, 45~16 Edward 48~10,
60~11, 97~27 Eliza 245~34 Enoch 328~14 Enos
315~12 Fanny 122~12 Henry 68~42 Hepzibeth 288~54
Hill 355~17 Jacob 144~22 Job 46~31 Josiah 36~20,
47~17, 57~41, 72~53, 111~14, 163~48 Levi 266~6
Levy 73~26 Linus 296~47 Lovel 21~19 Lucretia
122~11 Martin 310~13 Mary 153~27 Mary (Sumner?)
97~46 Persis 142~25 Rachel 122~12 Rebecca 277~29
Roxana (Mardin) 355~17 Roxy 122~12 S. 325~49
Samuel 30~27, 136~15, 159~16, 208~2, 304~56
Sarah 97~37, 122~12 Silsby 138~54 Simon 136~18
Sylvester 67~22 William 307~13 Ziba 127~30
STEVENSON / STEPHENSON, Benajah 239~8 John
220~14 Joshua 41~43 Thomas 59~10 William 5~44,
11~9, 44~24
STEWARD see STEWART
STEWART / STUART / STEWARD, [Mr.] 211~54,
297~42, 320~21 Archibald 184~55 Bryan 1~8
Ebenezer 109~5 H. 312~11 Jacob 17~45 James C.
172~34 John 27~38, 160~41, 183~32, 272~21 John
D. 120~14 Joseph S. 229~24 Martha 234~20 Polly
22~47 Silas 109~6 Stephen 219~51, 333~50, 334~15
Thomas 228~55, 259~35
STEYLES see STILES
STICKNEY, [Mr.] 362~32 David 49~49, 216~4 Eliza
186~7 John 177~30 Jonathan 77~49, 118~50 Rachel
(———) (Putnam) 216~5 Sarah 79~28 Sukey 91~20
Thomas 285~28, 290~36, 290~54
STIELS see STILES

STILES / STYLES / STEYLES / STIELS, [children] 149~14 [Mrs.] 104~15, 320~46 [Pres.] 104~15 Hepsibah (Towner) 270~56 Jeremiah 80~46, 320~46 John W. 108~20 Mary (Maccarty) 108~21 Samuel 270~56 Shubael 149~14 Z. 149~44
STILLE, [Capt.] 226~30
STILLMAN, Allen 146~40 Benjamin 310~46 George 171~45 Harriot (Trumbull) 310~47 John 222~28 Samuel 222~28, 282~10, 373~26 Sarah 146~39
STILWELL, [child] 217~5 [Mrs.] 217~5 Samuel 217~7
STIMPSON see **STINSON**
STIMSON see **STINSON**
STINSON / STIMSON / STIMPSON, [Mr.] 176~6 Cynthia 66~8 Fanny 152~2 James 275~46 John 17~4, 130~13 Nabby 67~24 Sarah 168~52 Sophia (Andrews) 275~46 Thomas 217~33
STIRLING see **STERLING**
STOCK, C. 38~16
STOCKBRIDGE, Charles 270~16 John 1~7 Polly 1~4 Stephen 118~50
STOCKLEY, Charles 191~11
STOCKMAN, John 357~38 Sarah (White) 357~38
STOCKTON, Charles W. 262~31 Eliza 262~31
STOCKWELL / STORKWELL, Abel 74~44, 219~38 David 325~46 Hewet 218~41 Hewett 221~39 William 318~18
STODARD see **STODDARD**
STODDAR see **STODDARD**
STODDARD / STODDART / STODARD / STODDERT / STODDAR, [Col.] 176~16 [Mr.] 224~19 John 321~27 Lemuel 243~24 Lucretia 25~8 Lucy 291~47 Mary 126~9 Polly 38~43 Rebecca 114~20 Sampson 20~15, 20~25, 82~11 Sarah 224~39 Thomas 334~34 Vryling 20~26
STODDART see **STODDARD**
STODDERT see **STODDARD**
STOKES, Maria Jane 64~42 Mary 127~42
STOLE, David D. 17~48
STONE, [girl] 153~3 [Mr. & Mrs.] 296~39 [Mr.] 137~14, 170~6, 170~39, 195~39, 322~39, 335~28 [Mrs.] 153~3 Abel 84~35 Abigail 183~28 Abigail (Brown) 130~8 Amos 116~33, 129~22 Amy 138~53 Apphia (Farrington) 357~34 Benjamin 88~9 Benjamin P. 357~33 Betsey 270~54 Caleb 130~8 Calvin 320~20 Chary 274~23 David 44~15, 48~17, 53~33, 58~42, 60~7, 66~31, 76~40, 93~9, 147~10, 153~2, 212~4, 218~58, 222~21, 229~4, 233~54, 255~47, 275~10, 279~15, 291~13, 292~30, 297~31, 313~9 Dorcas 274~23 E. 357~48 Ebenezer 81~22 Elizabeth 245~10 Elizabeth (————) 220~1 Enoch 84~35 Ephraim 305~40 Frances 147~10, 153~1 Frances (Bellows) 44~15 Freelove 357~47 Gregory 331~4 Hannah (Bellows) 212~5 Isaiah 227~15 John 47~1, 154~15 John Hoskins 169~3 Jonas 168~55, 240~43, 295~14 Jonathan 216~13, 274~24, 274~25, 373~14 Kesia 24~39 Maria 305~54 Martha 240~43 Mary (Huntington) 297~31 Micah 99~14 Nancy 260~22 Nathan 281~54 Polly 47~9 Sally 173~31 Samuel 1~47, 21~48, 106~5, 220~29 Sarah (Wood) 99~15 Shubael 145~39
STOODLEY / STUDLEY, Abigail 97~11 J. 368~61, 368~62 James 115~39, 115~40, 278~30, 325~43, 325~45 Nathaniel 355~30
STOPFORD, [Dr.] 187~50
STORER / STOROR, Catherine 219~22 Charles 317~29, 326~16 E. 280~16 Ebenezer 274~22 George 53~23 Mary 225~51, 271~22 Nancy 306~1 W. 201~54 Woodbury 225~52, 271~23, 306~2
STOREY see **STORY**
STORKE, Catharine 206~12 William 206~13
STORKWELL see **STOCKWELL**
STOROR see **STORER**
STORRS, Clarissa 113~48 Experience 21~23, 43~17, 56~23, 74~46, 101~45 J. 53~9 Sarah 186~32
STORY / STOREY, Abraham B. 181~55 Charles 273~56 Charlotte 218~8 Daniel 188~1 Elisha 213~21 Isaac 28~19 John 242~30 Jonathan B. 202~36 Letitia (Cochran) 181~56 Lydia 147~53 Polly 94~14 William 138~36
STOUGHTON, Anna (de Neusville) 54~17 Don Juan 54~16 John 303~17
STOUT, Elizabeth (Evans) 160~15 Phebe 214~24 Robert 160~15

STOW see **STOWE**
STOWE / STOW, Abner 111~28 Amos 304~39 Dinah 95~42 John 325~14 Jonah 70~55 Prudence (————) 194~43
STOWEL see **STOWELL**
STOWELL / STOWEL, Benjamin 147~8 Cornelius 155~52 Elenor (Goss) 289~32 Ezra 334~47 Ira 289~31 Jacob 267~37 Jerusha 101~20 Joseph 81~21 Nancy 282~3 Thomas 54~29
STRACHAN, Walter 314~13
STRANTON, John 114~45 Ruth (Hart) 114~45
STRAP, Hugh 300~9
STRATTEN see **STRATTON**
STRATTON / STRATTEN, [Mr.] 45~32 Asa 131~46 Charles 267~41 John 162~11 Jonas 221~55 Mary 267~41
STRAW, Hannah 230~3 Joseph 316~56 Sally (Gould) 299~14 Sargent 299~14
STREET, Jostin Washington 132~1 Nancy (Whidden) 132~1 Nicholas 262~46, 263~49
STREETER, Asil 87~26 Elijah 271~34 Jesse 46~19, 328~8 Sebastian 283~2 Zebulon 271~34, 283~22
STRICKER, Adam 217~29
STRICKLAND, [children] 63~38 [Mrs.] 63~37 Stephen 63~30
STROAD, John 24~37
STROG, Jonathan 3~24
STRONG, [boy] 226~9 [Gov.] 72~20, 126~25 [Mr.] 100~16 [Rev.] 259~53 Aaron 226~10 Asahel 220~2 Ashbel 294~25 Aura (Ferry) 220~3 Bela 140~25 Caleb 301~47 Clarissa 301~47 Daniel 181~2 David 102~43 Electa 274~37 Elisha 329~48 Elnathan 274~12 Hannah 215~11 Henry 170~43 Jedadiah 127~44 Job 271~16 John M'Curdy 259~32 Jonathan 154~23 Joseph 135~43, 245~26 Joseph C. 16~13 Lois (?) 218~37 Louise (?) 218~37 Lucretia (————) 285~21 Milatiah (French) 170~43 Oliver 218~37 Phebe 110~31 Phillip 72~20 Return 282~30 Simeon 223~19 Tertius 121~18
STROTHER, George 177~57
STUART see **STEWART**
STUDLEY see **STOODLEY**
STUMP, Herman 102~33
STURDEVANT / STURDIVANT / STURTEVANT, Cornelius 27~41, 40~46 Earl 98~21 Eliab 192~30 Isaac 247~57 Mary (Le Mercier) 98~21
STURDIVANT see **STURDEVANT**
STURGES see **STURGIS**
STURGIS / STURGES, [Rev.] 238~42 John 41~9
STURTEVANT see **STURDEVANT**
STUYVESANT, Petres 215~26
STYLES see **STILES**
SULLIVAN, [Mr.& Mrs.] 356~18 Catharine (Blair) 160~51 George 290~27 Humphrey 4~41 James 287~10 John 77~42, 160~51 Sarah Bowdoin (Winthrop) 290~27 William Bant 270~21
SUMMERS / SOMERS, [Capt.] 176~45 Alvan 215~43 W.P. 364~15
SUMNER, Benjamin 39~27 David H. 216~40 Ebenezer 92~10 Elizabeth (Ross) 354~3 F.A. 138~41, 144~15, 296~15, 310~11, 315~12, 316~47, 321~12, 328~12, 334~29 Fred. A. 284~41, 304~23 Frederick A. 129~20, 133~48, 256~27 George W. 153~51 Henrietta (Lowther) 92~10 Increase 42~7 Luther 354~2 M. 199~5 Martha B. (Foxcroft) 216~40 Mary 97~3 Mary (?) 47~46 Matilda (Hutchins) 153~51 Nancy 97~46 Samuel 199~1 Sarah (?) 97~42 Sarah (Clough) 39~28 Susannah 85~46
SURREL see **SEARLE**
SURRINGTON, Joseph 37~31, 363~39
SUTHERLAND / SOUTHERLAND, David 216~35 John 308~7
SUTTON, Andrew 158~16 Charles Manners 187~49 Phebe (Garrison) 158~16
SWADDLE, Hannah 276~36
SWAIN, William 16~52
SWAN, [family] 279~6 [infant?] 290~15 [Lieut.] 66~55 Aaron 170~7 Abigail 4~29 Caleb 316~39 Charles 279~6 Edward 202~25 Ellis 277~43 George 4~29 Samuel 256~22, 279~3 Thomas (?) 290~15 Timothy 229~45

SWANSON, William 199~20
SWANZEY, Olive 143~25
SWARTOUT / SWARTWOUT, Abraham 53~7   Jno. 215~3
SWARTWOUT see SWARTOUT
SWARTZ, D. 38~17
SWASELY, Margaret 262~7
SWASEY / SWAZEY, Hannah 113~5   Hannah P. 353~39   Joseph 38~43, 156~31   Margaret 279~18   Martha Ann 353~40   Polly (Stoddard) 38~43
SWAZEY see SWASEY
SWEAT see SWETT
SWEATT see SWETT
SWEENEY, Edward 132~23   Nancy 211~55
SWEET (see also SWETT), Benjamin 133~40   John 108~13
SWEETSER / SWEETZER, [———] 177~40   Eliza D. 50~45   John 110~30, 197~16   Joseph 10~45, 28~50   Philip 103~7   Phillip 138~24   Phillips 89~44, 128~1, 185~34, 275~43, 290~19   William 72~52
SWEETZER see SWEETSER
SWEITZER, Henry 38~42   Polly (Kugler) 38~42
SWETLAND, Sarah 207~25
SWETT / SWEAT / SWEATT (see also SWEET), Benjamin 221~53, 320~36, 330~11   John 311~16   Josiah 291~12, 313~8   Mary 54~44, 335~3
SWIFT, Aner 277~52   Earl 323~28   Ebenezer 178~6   Ephraim G. 335~27   Heman 161~6   Huldah 277~51   Job 169~35   Joseph 274~1   Laura (Ripley) 323~28   Nathaniel 277~52   Patience 284~51   Sarah 161~5   Seth 278~51, 279~58   Socrates 56~33
SWINATON / SWINERTON / SWINNERTON, Hannah 270~54
SWINERTON see SWINATON
SWINFIELD, Robert 218~11
SWINNERTON see SWINATON
SYKES see SIKES
SYLVESTER, Elizabeth 49~55   Israel 193~55   Peter 86~36   Sarah (———) (Totman) 193~55   William 35~50, 36~32
SYMMES see SIMES
SYMONDS see SIMONS
SYMS see SIMES

T.

TABER see TABOR
TABOLE, Richard 214~57
TABOR / TABER / TUBER, Elnathan 152~11   Eunice 216~10   George 107~53   Jeremiah 217~3, 218~22   William 120~14
TADERHORST, George F. 173~50
TAFT, Aaron 134~25   Amariah 150~11   Bezaleel 300~23   Lovice 240~40   Martha 150~11   Sarah 300~23   Willard 240~41
TAIT see TATE
TALBERT / TALBOT, [Mr.] 164~47   Daniel 162~51   Philo 281~1   Ruth 230~19   Sally 162~50   Thomas 230~19
TALBOT see TALBERT
TALCOT / TALCOTT, Jesse 229~49   Matthew 127~43   Samuel 1~32
TALCOTT see TALCOT
TALLMADGE / TALMADGE, Benjamin 197~41   Elizabeth (Clinton) 152~28   Mary 197~40   Matthias B. 152~28
TALLMAN / TOLMAN, Thomas 28~55
TALMADGE see TALLMADGE
TANKESLEY, Ann (———) 208~36
TANT, John 262~8
TAPLEY, Gilbert 241~21
TAPPAN / TOPPAN, [Capt.] 67~46   Caleb 245~49   Christopher 96~21   John 192~34, 214~8, 326~32   Mary Anne 151~50   Sarah 41~9, 96~21   Sarah (Salisbury) 214~9   William 16~16
TARBELL, John 173~3, 174~32
TARBOX, Mary 217~16
TARE, Mary 182~6
TARLETON see TARLTON

TARLOW, Mary 122~3
TARLTON / TARLETON, William 298~22, 311~54
TATE / TAIT, [Mr.] 255~39
TATSON, John 17~15
TATUM, Zachariah 43~31
TAYLOR, [children] 161~42   [daughters] 209~52   [Major] 58~20   [Mrs.] 161~42, 226~1, 273~52   Abigail 277~54   Adam 243~13   Allen 7~26   Arthur 90~7   Benjamin 7~46   Calvin 278~47   David 98~57, 137~9, 161~41, 245~27, 299~47, 329~5   Dorothy (Smith) 245~31   Elisha 230~43   Elizabeth 110~34, 256~45   Esther 177~51   Hannah (———) (Delano) 284~48   Henry 105~30   Hezekiah 40~38   Horace 41~37   James 14~6   John 107~55   Joseph 259~7, 327~7   Joshua 245~31, 284~48   Josiah 252~41   Lewis 77~44   Major 215~33   Margaret 172~4   Mary (Redington) 137~9   Moses 203~40, 209~52   Nathaniel 80~47, 239~39   Oliver 107~33   Osgood 108~9   Patty 203~39   Polly 316~19   Sally 102~14   Samuel 122~27   Sarah Maria 143~26   Simon 1~27   Thankful 1~48   Thomas 66~33   William Henry 273~53
TEBBETS / TIBBOTS / TIBBOTTS / TIBBITS / TEBBOTS / TEBBETT / TEBBETTS / TIBBITTS / TIBBETS / TIBBETTS, Catharine 181~6   George 131~15, 369~34   Hezekiah 357~31   John 328~1   John Gerrish 328~2   Mary 98~26   Mary (———) (Edgerly) 357~31   Samuel 272~21
TEBBETT see TEBBETS
TEBBETTS see TEBBETS
TEBBOTS see TEBBETS
TEEL, Persis A. 353~51
TEELOCK, [Mrs.] 301~45
TELFORD, Wm. 216~21
TEMPLE, [Mr.] 192~23   Archelaus 75~56   Clarina B. (Hawkins) 213~13   Ebenezer 28~50, 221~55   Elizabeth 140~17   Hannah (Redfield) 88~11   Isaac 26~34, 71~49, 333~53   James B. 192~33   John 88~11, 106~2, 130~38   Lucy 75~50   Prudence 220~8   Robert 213~13   Ruth 93~57
Ten EYCK, Axa (Cleaveland) 35~43   Jacob 35~42   Josias 219~17
TENNEY / TENNY, Azuba 235~57   Hannah 116~17   William 89~46, 89~52, 246~6
TENNY see TENNEY
TETHERLY see TETHERLY
TETHERLY / TETHERLEY, Mercy 86~47
THACHER see THATCHER
THAMPSON see THOMPSON
THARP see THORPE
THATCHER / THACHER, [Rev.] 111~38, 369~41   Daniel 334~21   David 78~26   Enoch 233~13   Gamaliel 190~34   John 237~15   Joseph 96~36   Josiah 112~14   Laura (Bicknell) 233~13   Peter 134~37, 237~16   Sarah 111~38
THAXTER, Anna 40~8   Benjamin 201~25, 202~24   Joseph 283~10
THAYER, Abagail (Treat) 54~42   Alpheus 314~4   Asa 296~13   Catharine 113~25   Cotton 54~42   Ebenezer 291~22   Martha 291~21   Mary 314~4   Rachel 141~7   Richard 274~58   Rufus 76~45   Sarah 35~41, 79~34, 92~11   Stephen 35~41   Timothy 219~34
THEOBALD, Philip 308~32
THING / THYNG, Betsey (Calfe) 99~7   John 99~6
THISSEL see THISTLE
THISTLE / THISSEL, John 114~44   Mehitable (Clarke) 114~44
THOM, [Dr.] 362~31   Eliza 299~13   Persis 155~44
THOMAS / THOMES, [children] 202~23   [Mr.] 202~23, 222~15   [Mrs.] 51~55   A. 116~36, 172~56   Abigail (———) (Chapman) 285~49   Alex. 74~32, 93~47   Alexander 22~36, 43~7, 56~16, 61~20, 81~13, 87~17, 101~39, 109~20, 304~30, 306~23, 306~47, 310~3   Ann (Fonerden) 228~5   Aram 285~49   Dudley 28~31   E.S. 228~4   Ebenezer 185~29   Edward 241~28   Elenora 148~23   Elias 270~51   Frederick 288~49   Hannah (Beaman) 152~46   Isaac 202~38   Isaiah 4~23, 19~40, 22~34, 306~23, 335~25, 336~18   Jabez 281~41   James 171~35, 183~35, 232~33   John 46~41, 148~23, 177~27, 181~17, 211~30, 211~54, 232~11   John P. 134~3   Joshua 297~16   Lucy (Turner) 232~11   Margaret (Holmes) 134~4   Mary 234~42, 271~11   Mary

(Armstrong) 297~16 Mary (Weld) 4~23 Olive 91~25 Polly (Adams) 270~51 Robert B. 152~46 Sally (———) 36~25 Sarah 321~40 Thomas 155~21 Thomas K. 306~24 William 187~53, 272~14
THOMES see **THOMAS**
THOMLINSON see **TOMLINSON**
THOMPSON / THOMSON / TOMPSON / THAMPSON, (———) (Burrows) 142~24 [boy] 299~45 [brothers] 144~10 [children] 161~46 [Judge] 262~26 [Mr.] 320~9, 374~32 [Mrs.] 161~45 [Vice Admiral] 39~29 Almira 92~2 Benjamin 61~33 Charles 309~23 David 49~10, 77~54, 234~58, 268~51, 276~31 Ebenezer 223~22, 272~13 Enoch 133~9 Hannah 47~34, 321~33 Henry 250~14 Humphrey 161~44 I. 215~54, 312~47 Ignatus 213~58, 221~14 Irene (Case) 268~52 Isaac 312~46, 361~35 Isaac S. 42~53 J.P. 301~6 Jacob 10~4 James 84~31, 142~24 John 61~41, 207~57, 211~38, 212~20, 266~50, 320~53 Jonathan 25~3 Jonathan Thurstain 353~47 Joseph 180~2 Levi 353~48 Margaret 301~6 Martha 183~52 Mary 316~18 Moses 299~45 Rachael 111~39 Richard 267~38 Sally 49~53 Samuel 121~2, 133~23, 353~47 Thomas 32~34, 80~27, 134~14, 202~33, 245~6 William 20~28, 34~37, 277~56, 350~31
THOMSON see **THOMPSON**
THORBURN, Eleanor (Marr) 92~35 John 92~35
THORNDICK, [Mr.] 66~18
THORNDIKE, Elizabeth 53~2 Freeborn 265~22
THORNLEY, Robert 208~5
THORNTON, Betsey (Campbell) 316~35 Elizabeth 162~30 Jesse 316~35 Matthew 20~20, 82~12, 145~18, 176~17 Sally 316~36 Stephen 47~26, 162~21 William 112~17
THORPE / THARP, John 54~33
THOUSAR, Bartemous 264~45
THRALL, Moses 229~40
THROOP, Benjamin 102~12
THURBER / THURBUR, Barnabas 95~21 Daniel 45~5 Edward 305~9 Hezekiah 45~5 Lydia 269~54 Samuel W. 29~8
THURBUR see **THURBER**
THURLO see **THURLOW**
THURLOW / THURLO, John 192~49 Mary 152~31 Rebecca 25~49
THURSBY, Thomas 140~20
THURSTON, Benj. 151~21 Elizabeth 260~44 Gardner 126~46 James 364~12 Martha 41~6 Moses 64~12, 82~52, 151~19 Polly 249~38 Sally (French) 70~21 Samuel 70~21
THWING, James 269~13 Martha 269~12 Samuel 154~25
THYNG see **THING**
TIBBET(T)S see **TEBBETS**
TIBBIT(T)S see **TEBBETS**
TIBBOT(T)S see **TEBBETS**
TICKNER / TICKNOR, [children] 226~43 [widow] 226~43 Benajah 226~43
TICKNOR see **TICKNER**
TIFFANY, Amasa 303~49 Sally 303~50
TILDEN, Abigail (Hearsee) 291~16 James 72~19 Lyman 291~16 Mary 84~27 Zeruvia 252~38
TILESTON, [Mr.] 221~12 Edmund 142~28 Ezekiel 39~36 Hannah 99~24 Nancy (Minns) 142~29 Nathaniel 15~6 William 331~8
TILGHMAN, James 301~11
TILLINGHAST, Daniel 259~16 J. 65~16 Nicholas 262~5 R.G. 361~21
TILLMAN, Christopher 69~27 Jack 69~26
TILLSON, Elisha 74~2
TILTON, [Dr.] 67~41 Increase 318~11 Mary (Lucar) 60~28 Nehemiah 286~16 Peter 354~10 Thomas 60~27
TINGLEY, Margaret 220~12
TINKER, Amos 102~8 Bathsheba (Clap) 102~8 Charlotte (Sikes) 156~12 Joel 156~12
TINKHAM, Amos 297~38 Joseph 131~47
TIRRELL see **TYRRELL**
TISDALE, [Mrs.] 98~31 Triphene 176~24
TISLOT, Legyard (?) 335~17
TITCOMB, Abigail (Whitney) 146~30 Anne Maria (Deladernia) 117~51 Benjamin 42~51, 98~5, 361~32 Enoch 146~29, 361~6 Pearsons 117~51 Samuel 145~48, 248~4
TITFORD, Ann 333~13 Elsia 333~13 Isaac 333~14
TITTERMAFY, [R.?] 182~24
TITUS, James 8~4, 24~30
TOBEY see **TOBY**
TOBY / TOBEY, Joseph 109~18
TODD, [———] 22~46 [Mr.] 35~17, 332~12 [Mrs.] 27~26 Charlotte 27~26 James 224~35 Moses 33~22 Nathaniel 243~2 Sally 332~11 Sally (Shaw) 52~58 Samuel 52~58, 268~36 William 27~52, 57~8, 110~16, 123~8
TOLLEY, William 100~3
TOLMAN see **TALLMAN**
TOMLINSON / THOMLINSON, [Rev.] 335~46 D. 335~45 John 350~30
TOMPKINS, James 252~49 Michael 267~2
TOMPSON see **THOMPSON**
TOOD, James 333~26
TOOKE see **TUKEY**
TOOPE / TUPE, Elizabeth 213~30 James 46~41
TOPPAN see **TAPPAN**
TORRENCE, Robert 179~37 Sally (Clark) 179~37
TORREY / TORRY, Abigail 78~20 Erastus 243~4 Gratia (Chase) 243~4 Hannah 214~34 Jesse 227~49 John 268~33 Lydia 251~24 Nabby 86~29 Nathaniel 37~55
TORRY see **TORREY**
TOSCAN, John J. 195~14, 196~5
TOTMAN, Jabez 282~15 Sarah (———) 193~55
TOTTEN, Maria (Stone) 305~54 Noah 305~54
TOTTY, [Rear Adm.] 126~49
TOWER / TOWRE, Betsey 103~21 Enoch 150~42 Isaac 68~56, 304~38, 334~33
TOWN see **TOWNE**
TOWNE / TOWN, Amos 114~12 Betsy (Wright) 114~12 Eliza 288~26 Gardiner 68~15, 74~48 Gardner 176~14 Joseph 331~43 Moses 332~23 Sally 244~18 Sarah 184~33 William 181~36, 197~54, 204~26, 281~52
TOWNER, Asa Lyman 101~7 Ephraim 68~14 Hepsibah 270~56 Shaler 93~41, 334~37
TOWNS, William 289~17
TOWNSEND, [boy] 93~35 David 53~49 James 93~22, 175~11 Jeremiah 206~31, 207~30 Phila 117~11 Robert 269~11 Samuel 102~37 Timothy 93~35
TOWNSLEY, N. 253~36, 334~49 Nicanor 7~28, 147~38, 299~9
TOWRE see **TOWER**
TRACEY see **TRACY**
TRACY / TRACEY / TRICE, [Mrs.] 192~16, 202~24 Amy 261~8 Andrew 147~40 Asaph 363~16 Henry L. 5~40 James 192~16 Julia 313~54 Samuel 261~8 Simeon 267~2 Thomas 192~36, 273~6 Timothy 202~24 Uria 313~55
TRASK, Ezra 305~47 Francis 179~18 I.E. 74~47 Israel E. 52~15, 62~53 John 140~34 Jonathan 77~16 Mary 286~34 Retire 81~54 Sophia 77~16 Thomas 309~20
TREADWELL / TREDWELL, [Gov.] 168~56 Alexander (...) 332~3 Carolina (...) (Williams) 332~4 D. 133~11 Hannah (Austin) 162~5 Jacob 76~33 John 162~5 Lucy 168~55 Phebe 218~16, 225~57 W. 133~11
TREAT, Abagail 54~42 Elizabeth 313~27 Joseph 313~28 Mary 94~17 Samuel 240~6
TREDICK, William 257~9
TREDWELL see **TREADWELL**
TREFETHEN / TREFETHEREN, [boy] 304~51 Abigail 65~45
TREFETHEREN see **TREFETHEN**
TREVETT, Russell 127~42
TREZEVANT, [Judge] 143~28 Henrietta (———) (Morel) 143~28
TRICE see **TRACY**
TRICKEY / TRICKY, Benjamin 203~14
TRICKY see **TRICKEY**
TRIPP, Lot 185~57
TRIST, Clarissa (Burt) 183~42 Moses 183~42
TROOP, Benjamin 101~24
TROTT, John 366~26 Peter 218~18 Samuel 219~27, 366~1
TROW (see also **TRUE**), B. 129~41 Bartholomew

259~19
TROWBRIDGE, Clement 81~23, 94~2, 129~12 David 220~49 James 249~49 John 160~49 Justus 321~33 Lovina 220~49 Lydia 113~31 Rebecca 51~21 Sally (Howe) 160~50
TRUDEAU, [Mademoiselle] 322~18
TRUE (see also TROW), Benjamin 20~36, 155~48 Betsey (Kimball) 20~37 Daniel 215~57 Henry 261~29 Joseph 322~9 Maria (———) (Gilbert) 155~48
TRUESDELL see TRUSDELL
TRUFANT, John 264~17
TRUMAN, [Mr.] 2~20 Mr. 366~10
TRUMBUL see TRUMBULL
TRUMBULL / TRUMBUL, [Gov.] 221~34, 310~47 Harriot 310~47 John 35~35, 247~29 Jonathan 307~10 Julia Anna 247~28 Maria 221~33 Phebe 255~6 Sarah 187~55 T. 255~6
TRUSDELL / TRUSSELL / TRUSELL / TRUESDELL, Lydia 361~31 Mary 194~30
TRUSELL see TRUSDELL
TRUSSELL see TRUSDELL
TRUXTON, Thomas 59~3
TRYON, [Judge] 254~30 Henrietta 249~55, 254~30 John 249~56
TUBBS, William 56~34
TUBER see TABOR
TUCK / TUCKE, Joseph 94~53
TUCKE see TUCK
TUCKER, [Mr.] 248~57 [Mrs.] 118~6 Alanson 299~13 Andrew 313~30 Benjamin 258~18, 259~27 Ebenezer 114~23 Elisha 145~19 Eliza (Thom) 299~13 Elizabeth 230~42 Ephraim 25~6 George 143~22, 199~28 Irene (Marsh) 353~10 Isaac 51~26 John 234~32, 234~49, 246~48 Joseph 114~32 Mary (Abbot) 65~39 Moses 89~50 Richard 65~39 Samuel 14~47 Timothy 170~9 Warren 353~9
TUCKERMAN, Elizabeth 209~8 Joseph 284~45 Judy P. (Shaw) 287~32 Sarah (Cary) 284~45 William 287~32
TUDOR, Elihu 357~14 John Henry 113~9 William 113~10
TUELL, Ruth 267~31
TUFFT see TUFTS
TUFT see TUFTS
TUFTS / TUFFTS / TUFT / TUFFT, B. 286~52 Hall 99~23 Mary 43~27, 288~55 Sally 10~27 Sarah 286~52 Simond 180~38 Susannah 131~32 Tabitha 234~18 Walter 249~49
TUFTTS see TUFTS
TUKEY / TOOKE, John Horn 287~24
TUNBRIDGE, Benjamin 207~50
TUPE see TOOPE
TURELL see TYRRELL
TURNBULL, Andrew 25~20
TURNER, (———) 72~44 Abigail 56~39 Andrew 260~41 Daniel 286~41, 320~23 David 303~46 Deborah 174~31 Delia (Currier) 75~17 Edward 117~18 Eunis 56~39 Gregory 191~9 Israel 117~12 Joel 79~28 John 173~29 Joseph 172~11, 195~13 Levi 75~17 Lucy 232~11, 296~5, 297~26 Nabby (Cooper) 98~50 Rebecca 117~17 Sally (Tuttle) 172~11 Samuel 214~14, 292~55, 295~41, 320~41, 320~24, 331~53 Seth 228~28 Stephen 98~50
TURRELL see TYRRELL
TURRILL see TYRRELL
TUTE, Amos 188~28 Jemima 188~17
TUTHILL see TUTTLE
TUTTLE / TUTHILL, [child] 184~9 [children] 327~25 [widow] 272~15 Curviah (Abbot) 285~45 Cynthia (Page) 212~9 D. 258~42 Daniel 217~10, 303~21, 327~23 David 203~13 David D. 30~12 Hugh H. 328~49 Jesse C. 285~45 John 1~24 Leverett 157~51, 166~48, 182~47, 212~9, 213~9, 279~17, 318~28 Mary 303~20 Nancy 138~20 Rebecca 227~30 Rebecca (Trowbridge) 51~21 Sally 172~11, 327~22 Sampson 51~21 Samuel 138~20, 184~9, 303~45 Simon 259~17 William 303~47
TUVNER, Ed. 131~31 Mary (West) 131~32
TWIMAN, Elizabeth 166~34
TWISS, Hannah 207~20 Jona. 122~18
TWISTUM, Simon 311~24
TWOMBLEY see TWOMBLY

TWOMBLY / TWOMBLEY, Huldah T. (Clark) 353~6 Thomas B. 353~6
TYLER, Asahel 238~9 Benjamin 262~22 Daniel 116~1 David 148~50 Dean 132~23 James 1~53 John 46~54 Joseph 245~39 Lorany (Mason) 92~33 Mary (Gideons) 245~39 Solomon 92~33 Vashty 238~9
TYNG, D.A. 285~25 Sarah 285~25
TYRRELL / TURRELL / TIRRELL / TURRILL / TURELL, John 335~42 Lucy 172~12

U.

UNDERHILL, [Mr.] 302~24 Updike 7~34
UNDERWOOD, James 334~32 John 211~57, 363~12 Peter 271~11 Russel 49~42, 213~51
UNIACKE, Maria 196~35 Mary 196~33 R.J. 196~33
UNZER, John Augustus 43~25
UPDIKE, Richard 184~56
UPHAM, [Rev.] 41~33 George B. 18~32, 227~21 Hannah 100~45 Joshua 298~56 Martha 98~54 Mary (Duncan) 227~21 Sally 53~1 Susannah 117~37 Timothy 355~30
UPSHAW, James 249~48
UPTON, Mary 282~12
URAN / URANN, Joshua 275~1
URANN see URAN
USTIC, [Rev.] 141~19
UTLEY, [Dr.] 200~12 Ruby 238~47

V.

VACKERY see VICKERY
VAIN, [boys] 208~50 John M. 208~50
VALENTINE, Isaac 239~34
VALLIER, John 193~44
Van ALLEN / Van ALEN, [family] 258~30 John E. 281~31 Peter 213~22 Peter L. 125~54, 258~28
Van AMBERG / Van AMBURGH, Betsey 232~3, 371~3
Van BIBBER, Abraham 209~50
Van BLARCUM, James 266~50
VANCE / VANS, William 4~48
Van Der ZEE, Harman 126~53
Van EPT, Charles H. 206~27
VANERD see VENNARD
Van HOOK, A——— 27~27
VANHORN, Abraham 267~32, 268~14
Van INWAGEN, [Mrs.] 11~35 David 11~35
VANKIRK, Andrew 49~55 Catharine (Hartupie) 49~56
VANN, James 250~43
Van NESS, Garret B. 262~45 Peter 175~45
Van RENSSELAER, [Mrs.] 87~49 Angelica 205~52 Catharine 155~3 Henry I. 205~53 John R. 205~53 Robert 255~4 Sol. 244~3 Stephen 257~21
VANS see VANCE
Van SCHAACK, Henry C. 2~10
Van TUYL, Andrew 143~27 Ann 143~27
Van VALKENBURGH / Van VOLKENBURGH, Anna 256~32 Barney 256~54 Henry 256~51 Isaac P. 24~14
Van VECHTEN / Van VECKTEN, Lucas 110~51
Van VOLKENBURGH see Van VALKENBURGH
Van WYCK, Mary 79~9
Van ZANDT / Van ZANT, [Mr.] 54~6 Garrit 249~54 Wynant 23~21
VARGASON, Elizabeth 133~51
VARICK / VARRICK, Abraham 42~2 Terentie 42~2
VARNEY, Joshua 49~47
VARNUM, [Mr.] 99~55 Deidamia 129~24 Ebenezer 187~46
VARRICK see VARICK
VASSA, Gustavus 9~20
VASSAL, John 14~55
VAUGHAN, (———) 72~45 Dorothea 97~1 Mary 50~30
VEASEY / VEAZEY / VESEY / VEAZIE, Mary (Miller)

240~43 Samuel 272~24, 292~1
VEAZEY see VEASEY
VEAZIE see VEASEY
VENNAR see VENNARD
VENNARD / VENNAR / VENNER / VANERD, John 158~24
VENNER see VENNARD
VENSON / VINSON, Joseph 33~2, 83~18
VERNON, William 274~15
VERPLANK, William B. 177~4
VERY, Ephraim 191~11 Luther 30~45, 35~40
VESEY see VEASEY
VESPASIAN, Titus 258~26
VICKERY / VACKERY, Elizabeth 220~57
VILAS, [Mrs.] 176~39 Lovina (Crosby) 204~30 Nathan 303~51 Nathaniel 51~47, 92~22, 204~30, 312~19
VILLENEUVE, [family] 187~22
VILLIERS, [Mrs.] 149~30 Thomas Clarendon 149~28
VILLOP, Thomas 254~50
VINCENT / VISCENT (?), Alpheus 77~43
VINSON see VENSON
VINTON, Daniel 295~2 Elizabeth (Oliver) 297~12 Huldah (Smith) 295~3 John 297~10 Thomas 297~12
VISCENT see VINCENT
Von HAGEN, Lucy (Ballard) 57~11   P.A. 57~11
Von MULLER, Johannes 307~13
Von VLECK, Arent 299~50 Sally (Pruyn) 299~50
VOSE, Betsey (Lovell) 41~20 Bill 301~11 Elijah 301~10 Esther 170~23 George 207~46 Joseph 308~35 Joshua 41~20 Lucy 6~9 Mary 137~27 Peter 136~21 R. 230~38 Rebecca (———) 200~42 Rebecca (Bellows) 83~28 Robert 152~34 Roger 19~37, 83~28, 306~25, 309~42 Solomon 57~47, 308~35 Susanna (Lewis) 207~46
VOYER, James 76~48

W.

WABURTON / WARBURTON, [Mr.] 276~48
WACKERHAGEN, Augustus 257~51 Mary A. (Mayer) 257~51
WADE, Abner 154~39 Nehemiah 207~17 William 53~47
WADKINS see WATKINS
WADSWORTH, [Lieut.] 176~45 [Mr.] 8~37 [Rev.] 218~6 Eliza 125~20 Jeremiah 160~56 Mary 218~6 Peleg 125~20, 176~46 Rebecca 274~26 Seth 257~39 Susannah 187~57
WADWELL see WARDWELL
WAELDIN see WALDEN
WAGNER, [children] 196~20 [Mrs.] 196~19 Jacob 196~19
WAIN / WAINE, Edward 6~24
WAINE see WAIN
WAIT see WAITE
WAITE / WAIT, Amelia (Heileman) 97~13 Amy (Stone) 138~53 Hannah 226~8 Jason 252~6 John 32~12, 138~53 Marmaduke 97~12 Nancy (Christy) 268~57 William 14~13, 32~55, 268~57
WAKEFIELD, Gilbert 106~30 Joel 303~19 Mary 232~29
WALBACK / WALBECK, [Capt.] 304~47
WALBECK see WALBACK
WALCH see WELCH
WALCOT(T) see WOLCOTT
WALCUTT see WOLCOTT
WALDEN / WALDON / WELDEN / WAELDIN / WELDON (see also WALTON), Isaac 13~7 Jacob 133~17 John 209~19, 231~44 William 125~44
WALDO, Daniel 218~45, 287~18 Edward 56~30 Elijah 327~10 Elisha H. 97~22 Jeduthan 317~17 Lucy (Markham) 317~17 Nathan 234~54
WALDON see WALDEN
WALDRON, Ann 273~18 Daniel 121~14 Olive (Sheafe) 121~14 Sukey 115~51
WALES, [Mr.] 263~33 Betsey (Noathrut) 257~50 Elijah 257~49 Peter T. 301~23 Roger 273~16
WALKAR see WALKER
WALKER / WALKAR, [Capt.] 313~3 [Mr.] 178~54

[Mrs.] 151~38 [son] 151~39 Abel 4~21, 20~56, 25~45, 29~13, 55~21, 206~57, 226~28 Asa 185~39, 279~13, 323~37 Beulah 300~21 Charles C. 218~25 David 102~9 Dorcas 267~14 Eliza (Russell) 180~26 Elizabeth 102~29 Jabez 12~22 Jesse 21~18 Jimna 328~24 John 334~31 Joseph 92~30 Joseph G. 323~37 Leonard 328~25 Lovell 180~26 Lyman B. 355~6 Rebekah 87~49 Reuben 15~7 Sally (Brewster) 92~35 Samuel 68~7, 74~5, 212~1 Seth 136~18, 151~37 Theodorick 222~55 Thomas 238~7 Timothy 299~22, 300~15 Violet (Morgan) 102~9 William 250~18, 272~9
WALKINSHAW, Gavon 78~35
WALL / WHALL, Humphrey 91~4 James 100~4 John 260~13, 274~32 Margaret 188~39 Maria Jane (Stokes) 64~42 Patrick 188~39 William 64~42
WALLACE / WALLIS, [Capt.] 41~1 [child] 160~36 Isabella 40~10 James 160~37 John 128~55, 138~47 Joseph 311~5 Mary 245~37 Sarah (Adams) 41~1 Thomas 154~27, 292~32, 311~4
WALLANCE, James 30~35
WALLINGFORD, Abigail 200~52 David 146~4
WALLIS see WALLACE
WALNUT, Mary 267~30
WALSH see WELCH
WALTON / WELTON (see also WALDEN), [child] 264~34 [Mrs.] 264~34 John 264~30
WANUP, [Mr.] 91~51
WARBURTON see WABURTON
WARD, [boy] 208~43 [infant] 309~27 Abigail 49~30 Andrew 272~43, 361~42 Artemas 79~13 Benjamin 252~54 Betsey 49~30 David 293~24 Ebenezer B. 202~50 Elisha 309~28 Ephraim 183~49 George C. 86~5 Henry 15~23 John 130~10 Josiah 208~43 Mary 100~37 Mary (Bennett) 94~12 Nathan 163~42 Phebe 93~14 Phinehas 286~43 Richard 48~14 Roswell 310~29 Samuel 49~31 Susan 183~48 Walter 56~35 William 50~52, 94~12
WARDEN see WORDEN
WARDNER, Olive 153~18 Sarah 153~18 Shubel 304~28
WARDWELL / WADWELL, Benjamin 95~30 Church 256~18 Dolly (Moulton) 95~30 Margaret 100~12
WARE / WEIR / WEAR / WEARE / WIER / WYER, B. (?) 272~11 Fanny 79~11 Henry 202~52 J.(?) 272~12 James 140~46 John 57~21, 201~36 Martha 191~53 Mary (Clark) 202~51 Mesheck 318~42 Nathaniel 133~26 Robert 159~26 Samuel 120~10
WAREN see WARREN
WARES see WIRES
WARNER / WARRENER / WERNER, [Capt.] 28~46 [child] 300~27 [girl] 217~14 [Mrs.] 133~40, 133~41, 254~29 Caleb 196~41, 300~28 Catherine 39~13 Daniel 72~52, 195~17 David 204~14, 204~14 Elizabeth 25~5 Elizabeth (———) (Stone) 220~1 Gideon 66~6 Ichabod 117~22 James M. 144~16 John A. 107~42 Lemuel 220~1 Lupron 254~29 Lydia 215~31 Mary 99~25 Moses 9~17 Oliver 115~41, 325~39 Priscilla (Reed) 196~41 Samuel 246~16 Sarah 256~46 Thomas 310~37, 320~26
WARREN / WAREN, [Gen.] 141~6 [Major Gen.] 164~23 Agrippa 99~44 Betsey 270~52 Cornelius 211~19, 228~1, 234~46, 241~4, 292~24 Elizabeth 164~21, 303~22 Hannah 79~50 Isaac 303~22 James 286~38 Jonas 327~49 Joseph 3~20, 176~22, 300~13 Lazarus 48~8 Levi 27~37, 102~52, 198~8 Lucy (Proctor) 243~6 Mary 135~44, 141~5 Peter 284~57 Polly 125~22 R. 59~22 Richard H. 3~20 Samuel 218~33, 243~5 Silas 33~7 Thomas 293~31 Zenas 333~52
WARRENER see WARNER
WARTON see WHARTON
WASHBURN, [Mr.] 108~7 [Mrs.] 102~40 Cyrus 229~32 Electa 229~31 Joseph 228~35 Josiah 297~52 Mary 170~24 N. Wetmore 11~40, 62~2 Phebe 297~52
WASHINGTON, [Pres.] 291~1 George Stepton 290~54 William Henry 144~37
WATERMAN, Elijah 200~28, 226~20 Elizabeth (McNeil) 145~15 Hannah (Fountain) 163~18 James 163~18 Judith 240~7 Richard 10~5 Thomas 145~14
WATERS, Ann (———) 102~7 Asenath 71~32 Charles

64~14 Ebenezer 14~3, 83~18 Esther 142~26 John 48~9 Lucretia (Amazeen) 138~14 Nicholson 166~26 Samuel 138~13
WATHERTON, Joseph 19~23
WATKINS / WADKINS, [boy] 254~34 [Widow] 254~34 Alex. 165~31 Alexander 25~31, 28~11, 28~52, 89~55, 132~45, 141~40 Alpheus 81~38 B.G. 23~53 Charles 102~34 Edward 24~45, 254~35 John 190~2 Robert 122~51 William 299~9, 334~49
WATROUS, John R. 200~11
WATSON, [child] 136~33 Abigail 64~6 Ann (———) 106~49 B.M. 307~4 David 353~41 Ebenezer 89~2 Eliza (Parsons) 307~4 Elizabeth 108~28 Elizabeth (Smith) 49~52 Frances P. (Sedgwick) 89~2 Hannah 51~27 Hannah (———) 177~44 James 243~10, 265~40 John 75~26, 108~28, 136~30, 141~31 Jonathan 129~25, 353~41 Marston 72~18, 73~17 Oliver 176~29 Priscilla 152~11 Seth 139~32 William 49~52, 219~19
WATT, George 67~3
WATTS / WHATS, Betsey 333~32 Calvin 160~20 Edward 42~50 Isaac 299~23 John 48~27 Prince 236~46 Samuel 129~3 Susan (House) 211~24 William 211~23, 244~26
WAUGH, Nancy 211~6
WAY, Abigail 234~20 John 111~41, 296~35
WAYLAND / WHALON / WHALAN / WHELEN / WILLEN / WILON, [Capt.] 53~27, 63~25 Israel 266~36 James 73~15 Margery Blanchard (Baxter) 73~15 Solomon [Wilson?] 43~16
WEALD see WELD
WEANE, B. (?) 272~11 J. (?) 272~12
WEAR see WARE
WEARE see WARE
WEATHERBE see WEATHERBY
WEATHERBEE see WEATHERBY
WEATHERBY / WETHERBEE / WETHERBE / WEATHERBEE / WEATHERBY / WITHERBE, (———) 136~16 [Capt.] 136~18 Abigail (———) 138~54 Abigail (Wright) 285~47 Betsey 51~24 Edmund 285~47 Hannah (Ross) 117~51 Isaac 138~36 Jason 7~12, 199~53 Samuel 51~24, 117~50 Thomas 91~4, 274~46
WEATHERINGTON, John 71~25
WEATHERS, William 143~17
WEATHERSTINE, William 50~18
WEAVER, [Dr.] 169~24 Henry 129~34 Joseph 335~6 Kitty (Spinner) 335~6 Margaret (Ruby) 129~34
WEBB, Calvin 65~54 Daniel 164~21 Eliphalet 191~3 Esther 239~47 George W. 239~35 Jahiel 40~29 Mary (Lee) 239~35 Sarah 85~53
WEBBER, [Rev. Pres.] 300~18 Catherine 19~13 Christopher 113~53, 129~14 George 300~18 Hannah 181~42 Lucy 131~51 Norman 129~15
WEBSTER, [Mrs.] 181~17, 208~47 Daniel 27~43, 143~55 Ebenezer 236~50, 241~31 Elizabeth 232~48 Gideon 73~3 John 45~20, 86~6, 151~47 Jonathan 289~20 Matthew 279~40 Moses 32~36, 80~28 Nathan 212~37 Rebecca (Meirckin) 312~7 S.P. 298~22, 311~54 Sarah 236~50 W. True 289~20 William H. 312~6
WEDERSTRAND, P.C. 59~21
WEED, Anna 131~37, 199~19 David 22~51, 137~45 Deborah (House) 188~51 Joseph 188~50 William 137~45
WEEKES see WEEKS
WEEKS / WEEKES, Benjamin 333~28 Bracket 225~33 Daniel 272~9 George 363~49 John 17~20, 326~32 Jonathan 190~27 Joshua W. 170~19 Levi 56~55, 62~11 Levi R. 355~54 Margaret 152~22 Nabby (Hubbard) 307~52 William 264~9, 307~51, 319~20, 333~28
WEEMS, [Dr.] 148~40 George 286~50
WEIDEMEYER, George 196~18
WEIR see WARE
WELCH / WALSH / WALCH / WELSH, [Mr.] 356~30 [Rev.] 261~44 Abby 289~48 Catharine 6~6 Charles 332~32 Elizabeth 163~40 Enoch 230~15 George W. 308~52 Hezekiah 64~32 James 6~6 John 249~11 Keyron 133~30 Mehitable 75~46 Sally 289~48 Samuel 269~3, 289~47 Thomas 186~46 William 214~31
WELD / WEALD, [Mr.] 330~25 Benjamin 61~55 Betsy 61~55 Chloe 251~19 Daniel 66~38 Edward 292~2 Elias 194~17 Eliza 285~44 Hannah 167~21 Hannah (Williams) 66~39 Horace 356~20 Joseph W. 313~6 Louisa 287~6 Mary 4~23 Sally 106~43
WELDEN see WALDEN
WELDON see WALDEN
WELIS see WILLIS
WELLES see WELLS
WELLINGTON, [widow] 288~12 Abigail 317~33 Edmond 316~22 Palsgrave 288~9, 317~32 Quincy 288~9, 288~32, 296~55, 307~25, 310~6, 317~34
WELLMAN, [widow] 291~41 Dolly (———) 35~44 James 288~30, 291~39, 323~48, 325~13 Lemuel 47~49 Oliver K. 284~47 Ursula M. (Draper) 284~47
WELLS / WELLES, (———) 72~46, 103~8 (———) (Edmonds) 79~26 [Mrs.] 58~34, 335~44 Abigail 276~1 Allen 198~34 Archibald 273~11 Arnold 125~21, 164~22 Ashbel 276~3 Catherine 189~35 Chloe 115~52 David 54~27, 58~51, 79~25, 90~49, 294~3 Eleazer 200~50 Elizabeth (Warren) 164~21 Erastus 276~4 George 146~33, 255~16 Hannah 277~17 Horace 233~5 James 288~15 James A. 276~2 John 241~41 Martha 98~32 Nathaniel 58~34 Obadiah 65~5 Obediah 334~3 Rebecca 239~6 Rocksiney 99~18 Rowell 88~49 Rufus 143~13 Sally (Wilder) 288~15 Samuel 50~50, 91~29, 92~16 Sarah 220~46 Thomas 116~54, 123~20, 198~35, 319~51 Titus 123~9 Ursula 147~5 William 142~37
WELSH see WELCH
WELTON see WALTON
WENDAL see WENDALL
WENDALL / WENDELL / WENDAL, George 272~17 Jacob 272~13 John 80~28, 363~11 Philip 288~24
WENDELL see WENDALL
WENTWORTH, [boy] 308~12 [Lady] 310~45 [Major] 82~13 B. 151~48 Ben. 318~41 Benning 45~17, 60~47, 65~35, 322~44 Benning William Bentick 322~43 C.M. 81~7 John 20~26, 310~43 Joseph 228~22 Samuel 308~12 Sarah 210~30 Thomas 182~14
WERNER see WARNER
WERSING, John Casper 107~38
WESCOME, Josiah 361~3
WESSON, Ephraim 334~33 James 311~38 William B. 219~47
WEST, [Dr.] 291~56 [Mrs.] 326~36 [Rev.] 167~53, 318~15, 335~27 B. 18~32 Benjamin 96~41, 104~41, 147~51, 256~43, 295~12, 296~6 Eber 130~15 Elenor (Dewey) 247~30 Elizabeth 167~52 Gersham 130~15 James 204~36 Jeremiah 176~37, 263~49, 264~25 John 109~2, 125~40, 222~15 Julia 291~56 Mary 131~32, 147~51 Oliver 235~14 Patty 176~37 Samuel 8~54, 36~11, 47~1, 64~1, 70~15, 85~57, 119~50, 120~6, 138~42, 318~15 Samuel S. 36~21, 304~39, 334~36 Stephen 247~30 Thankful 235~14
WESTERN see WESTON
WESTGATE, George 1~49 John 1~50
WESTON / WESTERN / WHISTON / WHESTONE, [Capt.] 168~10 [family] 52~34 Abraham 94~48 Ebenezer 224~38 Joseph 65~31 Richard 238~25
WESWILL see WISWALL
WETHERBE(E) see WEATHERBY
WETHEREL see WETHERELL
WETHERELL / WITHERELL / WETHEREL, Frances (Foxcraft) 181~54 Mary (Casey) 282~2 Medcalf 181~54 Naphtali 282~2
WETHERLY, Malinda 225~16
WETMORE see WHITTEMORE
WHALAN see WAYLAND
WHALING, [Mr.] 47~2
WHALL see WALL
WHALON see WAYLAND
WHARTON / WARTON, [Dr.] 65~12 Chamless 135~40 William 179~4
WHATCOAT, Richard 249~45
WHATS see WATTS
WHEATON (see also WHIDDEN), [Capt.] 42~15 [child] 18~13 [Miss] 135~18 Ephraim 131~44 Isaac 135~17 Oliver 18~13 William 112~11
WHEATOR, John 11~17

WHEELER / WHELER, [boy] 275~33 [Mr.] 103~31 [Mrs.] 275~33 [widow] 229~24, 254~16 Aaron 244~55 Abigail 50~47 Abijah 6~32, 133~49 Amos 270~24 Asa 60~25, 80~38, 108~15 Benjamin 107~13 Bennett 238~56 Betty 212~41 Carler 243~19 D.G. 131~31 Daniel 98~15, 206~49 Daniel G. 50~45, 67~20 Daniel Greenleaf 225~3 David 152~51 Dexter 329~50 Ebenezer 86~35 Eliza 67~20 Eliza (Grosvenor) 131~31 Eliza D. (Sweetser) 50~45 Ephraim 212~40, 228~33, 229~23 George 264~16 Hannah (Odell) 146~29 Ira A. 334~34 J.B. 7~29 John 51~7, 52~46 John B. 93~7, 98~14 Joseph 94~5 Lois 42~53, 361~33 Lucy 71~15 Mary 125~10 Moses 136~15, 136~16, 202~25 Nancy (Clap) 225~3 Obadiah 190~31 Polly 243~19 Seth 176~17 Simeon 334~35 Susannah 270~12 Thankful 170~51 Thomas 171~40 William D. 316~21 William Neavens 146~28
WHEELOCK, [Pres.] 181~31 Daniel 76~54 Ephraim 163~43, 370~46 Fanny (Goodenow) 123~28 Gershom 228~27 John 267~10 Jonathan 196~39 Lucinda (Leonard) 267~11 Rachel 200~48 Sally (Munroe) 196~39 Samuel 123~28 V. Ephraim 370~46 V. Ephraim (?) 163~43
WHEELWRIGHT, Ebenezer 36~23
WHELEN see WAYLAND
WHELER see WHEELER
WHESTONE see WESTON
WHETMORE see WHITTEMORE
WHETON see WHIDDEN
WHICHER see WITCHER
WHIDDEN / WIDDEN / WHITTEN / WHITTON / WHITTING / WHITEN / WHITING / WHIDON / WHETON (see also WHEATON), Abbey (Morris) 283~49 Abijah 76~13 Betsey (Chamberlain) 265~27 Daniel 127~28 Fanny (Leffingwell) 131~55, 174~28 George 46~7, 131~15 Hanna 95~26 Jeremiah 154~9, 154~14 John 46~56, 332~39, 333~22 John M. 283~2, 283~49 L. 112~45 Lucy 80~30 Marcy A. 265~25 Maria 46~7 Mary 44~46 Nancy 132~1 Peter 225~26 Ruth 127~23 Samuel 22~26, 44~47, 81~24, 94~6, 109~29, 131~54, 174~28, 187~40, 265~27 Sarah 195~53, 197~35, 258~23 Thomas 57~35, 80~34, 108~28 William 70~8
WHIDON see WHIDDEN
WHILEY see WILLEY
WHIPPLE, [child] 153~24 [Mrs.] 153~22 Benjamin 4~51 Daniel 11~44, 43~20, 52~54, 90~8, 122~24, 128~35, 138~32 Elizabeth 234~22 Hepzibah 4~51 Jacob 77~53 James 14~9, 83~13, 138~47, 153~23, 296~34 John 14~4, 83~14, 152~5 Joseph 33~5, 83~21 Josiah 153~23 Martha 11~45, 12~51 Moses 32~56, 83~17 Nathaniel 153~24 Plato 57~27 Sally 168~16 Stephen 122~20 Thomas 120~21, 268~46, 303~57
WHISTON see WESTON
WHITAKER see WHITTAKER
WHITCHER see WITCHER
WHITCOMB / WHITCOMBE, Asa 229~19 Dorothy 180~48 E. 78~19 Eliza (Ruggles) 78~19 Israel 89~56, 153~28 Jacob 129~24 Lucretia 179~50 Peris 138~49
WHITCOMBE see WHITCOMB
WHITE / WITE / WIGHT, [Bishop] 138~12 [Capt.] 91~46 [Dr.] 69~6 B. 41~51 Betsey 234~4 Buckminster 267~47 Daniel 186~14, 249~40 Ebenezer 177~36 Elisha 116~41 Elizabeth 138~11 Esther 165~23 George 139~5 Hannah 111~29 Harry 356~23 Hepzibah 155~29 Hosea 5~8 Isaac 252~57, 255~27 Jacob 277~15, 278~44 James Shafter 78~47 Job 280~50 John 36~22, 58~52, 94~3, 116~42, 156~26, 165~22, 284~19, 291~25 Joseph 247~5, 316~20, 327~8 Josiah 78~14, 246~23, 309~54 Jotham 122~21, 290~10 Lydia 103~16 Margaret 152~43 Mary 99~22, 317~53 Moses 137~53 Nathaniel 133~10, 260~35, 298~41, 299~26 Oliver 176~38, 179~58 Peregrine 164~25 Peregrine 109~39 Philip 80~27 Phillip 7~50 Preserved 124~33 Rachel 267~10 Rachel (Thayer) 141~7 Rebecca (Pierce) 249~40 Robert 59~48 Ruth 7~49 Sally 112~29 Sarah 357~38 Sewall 16~30 Thomas 7~31, 10~17, 31~16, 67~35, 141~7, 159~53 William 187~53

WHITECAKE, Catharine (Wise) 148~3 John Walton 148~3
WHITEFIELD, [Rev.] 264~32
WHITEHEAD, Sarah 166~12
WHITEHOUSE, Mary 152~19
WHITELAW, James 16~4
WHITEMAN / WIGHTMAN, [child] 328~53 Henry 195~5 Israel 328~53
WHITEMORE see WHITTEMORE
WHITEN see WHIDDEN
WHITHAM see WITHAM
WHITMORE see WHITTEMORE
WHITING see WHIDDEN
WHITLOCK, [Mrs.] 75~32
WHITMAN, Abel 307~40 Darius 101~55 Edward 212~34 Polly 129~53 S.R. 272~25, 284~37, 298~16, 311~46, 315~15 Stephen R. 166~39, 215~7, 241~52, 262~19, 275~40
WHITMARSH, Samuel 232~28
WHITMORE see WHITTEMORE
WHITNEY, [children] 18~17 [Mr.] 82~34, 121~7, 306~19 [Mrs.] 82~35, 194~17 [Rev.] 199~4 Abel 280~44 Abigail 146~30 Anna (Adams) 78~17 Asa 18~20 Asahel 270~46 Aseneth 18~17 Benjamin 145~32, 314~3 Caleb 103~56 Clarissa (Wolcott) 120~8 Cyrus 328~26 Daniel 102~37 Ebenezer 259~20 Eli 284~31 Elisha 280~40 Elizabeth 194~45 Ephraim 96~56 George 369~33 Hannah 61~42, 79~32 Jane (———) (Gaffield) 294~57 Jane (Lincoln) 64~27 John 11~15 Joseph 321~14 Joshua 68~57 Josiah 71~40, 83~41, 181~38 Julia 37~51 Lemuel 310~30 Lydia 216~15 Nathan 254~3 Nicholas B. 78~17 Oliver 16~31 Peter 64~27 Phineas 194~46 Phinehas 216~16, 294~57 Richard 257~18 Samuel 61~34 Silas 168~30 W.H. 120~8 William 194~14
WHITTAKER / WHITAKER, [boy] 232~52 Ezra 232~52
WHITTLESEY see WHITTLESEY
WHITTEMORE / WHITEMORE / WETMORE / WHITMORE / WHETMORE / WHITIMORE, [Mrs.] 206~26 [Widow] 276~6 Alice 37~56 Daniel 181~37 David 276~50 Elizabeth 52~4 Joseph 194~12, 195~18, 203~38, 206~26 Josiah 111~16 Mary 121~49, 124~38, 203~37 Nathan 7~17, 176~18 Richard 142~46 Samuel 60~37, 248~50 William 320~38
WHITTEN see WHIDDEN
WHITTER / WHITTIER / WITTER, Amos 283~9
WHITTIER see WHITTER
WHITTING see WHIDDEN
WHITTINGTON, William 41~6
WHITTLE, Alice (Horrocks) 215~10 Electa (Rugg) 277~8 James 215~9 Samuel 136~51, 144~13, 185~23 William 256~50, 263~32, 277~7
WHITTLESEY / WHITTELSEY, [boy?] 237~8 Azariah 237~8 Newton 122~22, 286~23, 303~6
WHITTON see WHIDDEN
WHITWELL, Benjamin 140~22 Samuel 92~18 Sarah (Sprague) 140~22 William 77~15
WIBIRD, Anthony 66~44, 70~38
WICHER see WITCHER
WICKHAM, Joseph 229~40
WICLEY, Ann (———) 106~56
WIDDEN see WHIDDEN
WIER see WARE
WIGGIN / WIGGINS, David 361~46 Jonathan 317~23 Mary Ann 357~4 Nancy 188~58
WIGGINS see WIGGIN
WIGGLESWORTH, [Dr.] 131~49
WIGHT see WHITE
WIGHTMAN see WHITEMAN
WILBAR see WILBUR
WILBOUR see WILBUR
WILBUR / WILBAR / WILBOUR, Abijah 65~15 David 307~38
WILCOCKS see WILCOX
WILCOX / WILLCOX / WILCOCKS, [child] 92~51 [Mr.] 150~25, 324~26 Abel 277~49 Abigail 269~56 Alexander 97~4 Asa 55~9, 236~30, 328~9 Benjamin 301~31 Comfort 133~54, 310~18 Gaylord 328~9 Hannah 316~36 Jacob 92~51 Jesse 36~13, 49~43, 68~34, 75~10, 85~16, 86~10, 90~27, 101~9, 214~2, 246~25, 267~50, 302~29, 314~57, 318~26 John

215~53 Phebe 221~2 Uriah 68~32 William 205~7, 221~1
WILD / WILDE / WYLDE, Greela 23~49 John 232~32
WILDE see **WILD**
WILDER, Abel 245~13 Abijah 288~15 David 47~8 Ephraim 180~34 Henry 111~1 Jerathmeel 5~22 John 162~18, 311~41 Jonathan 201~21 Joseph 257~16 Mary 101~27, 311~40 Nancy (Beaman) 99~48 Polly 272~30 Sally 288~15 Sarah 165~38 Thomas 36~12, 55~24 William 99~48
WILDES / WILDS, Sarah 245~33
WILDS see **WILDES**
WILEY see **WILLEY**
WILKES, Israel 221~38 Joseph 207~55
WILKINS, Benjamin 154~41, 155~24
WILKINSON, Benjamin 152~10, 298~52 James 322~18
WILLARD / WILLIARD, [boy] 37~38 [Col.] 254~54 [Dr.] 189~28 [girl] 37~37 [Pres.] 205~6 Aaron 78~1 Abijah 172~52 Ama 283~51 Ann 172~51 Bial 189~8 Catharine 98~22 Charles 92~53 Daniel 67~19 Edah 303~54 Elizabeth (Taylor) 256~45 Emma (Hart) 307~56 Esther 174~15, 235~37, 237~30 George 295~42, 303~55 Hannah (———) (Fisk) 107~47 Isaac 225~13 Jacob S. 205~6 Jesse 289~19, 327~20 Joanna 116~6, 132~52 Joannah 159~6 John 22~33, 104~40, 107~47, 233~53, 279~43, 307~55, 312~38 Jonathan 160~31, 174~19, 235~46, 237~24, 237~33 Joseph 41~7, 168~1, 169~18, 278~20, 279~54, 310~17, 318~45 Joshua 298~12 Josiah 34~26, 55~20, 90~6, 95~36, 189~9 Lockhart 73~8, 89~36, 260~56 Lucy 203~22 Marcian 7~22 Martha 225~19 Mindwell 9~42 Moses 32~14, 60~42, 65~29, 86~2, 144~20 Oliver 144~23 Peter 235~42, 237~39 Phinehas 12~21 Prentice 9~39 Prentiss 2~12 Rebecca (Kingsbury?) 318~45 Rebecca (Perrin?) 278~20 Rebeckah (———) (Goodenow) 260~26 Roswell 248~33, 256~45 Ruel 242~18 Sam. 368~63 Samp. 304~18 Sampson 278~30 Samson 115~42 Samuel 109~3, 109~14, 116~6, 132~52, 159~5, 279~56 Simon 16~24, 37~37 Sybil (———) 194~43
WILLARDS, John 56~14
WILLCOX see **WILCOX**
WILLCUTT see **WOLCOTT**
WILLEN see **WAYLAND**
WILLES see **WILLIS**
WILLET / WILLETT / WILLETTS / WILLETS, [Mr.] 259~44
WILLETS see **WILLET**
WILLETT see **WILLET**
WILLETTS see **WILLET**
WILLEY / WILEY / WILLY / WHILEY, [Mr.] 357~15 Allen 134~21, 138~34 Almira 84~14 Barnabas 89~41 Benjamin 215~56 David 21~17, 119~24 Josiah 95~40 Nathan 310~4 Patience 80~45 Peggy 147~22 Samuel 357~4
WILLIAM see **WILLIAMS**
WILLIAMER / WILMER, Ann Eleanor 114~16 John L. 41~44
WILLIAMS / WILLIAM, [boy] 103~43, 261~26, 356~25 [children] 130~27 [Mr.] 51~2, 250~49, 305~7 [Mrs.] 130~27, 265~31 [Rev.] 279~53 Abigail (Lord) 155~11 Ann 180~37 Anna 76~57 Arter 5~10 B. 134~8 Benjamin 54~38 Carolina (...) 332~4 Charles 328~28 Charles W. 155~11 Charlotte 245~35 Cynthia (Delano) 113~46 Cynthia (House) 200~31 Daniel 10~51, 36~14, 113~46 David 204~17 Delia 41~31 E. 115~43, 115~44 Ebenezer 250~15 Elijah 64~29, 80~18, 143~12 Eliphalet 109~13, 145~47 Elisha 261~26 Elisha O. 224~43 Enoch 243~36 Eunice 101~26 Frederick 86~12 George 6~7, 17~8 Hannah 66~39 Henry 17~9 Isaac 46~31, 49~24 Israel 103~43 J. 200~27 James 192~22 John 17~9, 59~11, 123~30, 130~27, 143~8, 183~3, 238~48, 250~22, 251~21, 253~55, 268~28, 303~21, 309~43 John P. 216~47 Jonathan 11~28, 123~8 Joseph 23~6, 23~46, 120~15, 245~52 Levi 68~5 Lydia 184~55 Margaret 156~49 Matilda 222~26 Mercy (Gardner) 249~34 Nathaniel 356~25 Nehemiah 243~35 Othniel 5~11 Phineas 72~51 Polly 286~33 Rachel (Dodge) 216~47 Rebecca (Armstrong) 42~29 Richard 180~57 Robert 180~37 Roger 294~17 Roswell 249~33 Sally 124~26 Sally (Chamberlain) 123~31 Samuel 46~54,

67~23, 256~57, 256~58, 286~34 Samuel P. 273~47 Smith 272~21 Solomon 200~31, 335~36 Sukey (Powers) 238~48 T. 115~47, 368~65 Thomas 41~30, 80~17, 115~45, 115~46, 192~25, 291~23, 363~29, 369~1 Timothy 17~10 Urania 273~16 William 90~2, 105~8, 186~54
WILLIAMSON, [Mrs.] 131~38 Abner 36~25 J.B. 131~38 Johannes 20~43 John B. 118~24 Sally (———) (Thomas) 36~25
WILLIARD see **WILLARD**
WILLINGTON, [Col.] 139~20 Ebenezer 108~26 Elizabeth 236~10 John 103~55 Josiah 327~3
WILLIS / WILLES / WYLLYS / WELIS (see also **WILLS**), Caleb 319~40 Clarissa 319~40 Ebenezer 244~19 Eliakim 86~56 Elizabeth 171~29 John 122~1 Jonathan 231~47 Joseph 22~46 Lathrop 176~24 Lucena 194~49 Mary (Chester) 244~19 Silas 227~34 Thomas 231~12 Triphene (Tisdale) 176~24
WILLISTON, Hannah 41~3 Marshfield 214~28
WILLOBY / WILLOUGHBY, Azubah 281~2 John 281~2 Zerah 21~25
WILLOUGHBY see **WILLOBY**
WILLS (see also **WILLIS**), (———) 72~44 Malinda (?) 150~9 Moses 138~46 Nath. 138~46
WILLSON see **WILSON**
WILLY see **WILLEY**
WILMER see **WILLIAMER**
WILMOT, John 318~12
WILON see **WAYLAND**
WILSON / WILLSON / WOOLSON, [Mr.] 102~47, 327~32 Archelaus 122~43 Betsey 333~31 Betsey (Little) 335~34 Cyrus Baldwin 114~46 Ebenezer 320~22 Ephraim 113~11 George 267~13 James 21~16, 27~23, 335~33 Jane (Somes) 143~31 Jane Livermore (Lassly) 114~47 John 59~12, 160~43 John 3d 270~47 Jonathan 311~16 Joseph 111~15, 116~32, 122~19, 138~45, 151~25, 328~15 Lewis F. 177~12 Mary (House) 267~13 Moses 143~30 Rebecca (Goddard) 106~28 Sally 236~48, 276~15 Solomon 54~39 Solomon (?) 43~16 Sukey 37~53 William 43~47, 106~27, 236~49, 333~31, 333~47
WINANS, Mary 52~2 William Walton 52~56
WINCH, Abby 270~55
WINCHESTER, Elhanan 3~19, 19~9, 31~6 James 238~7 Jonathan 43~18 Maria 19~9, 21~22, 27~55
WINDSHIP see **WINSHIP**
WING, [Mrs.] 221~19 David 257~16
WINGATE, [Miss] 353~19 Benjamin 363~43 Paine 353~19
WINKLEY, [Mrs.] 133~43
WINN, Caleb 7~23 Custeen 50~11
WINSE, Abijah 144~24
WINSHIP / WINDSHIP, Anna 231~8 Jonathan 90~25 Sally 51~19
WINSLOW, Isaac 244~35 John 83~49 Josiah 135~7 Luther 83~4 Mary 75~21 Samuel 151~47 Susan (Ball?) 83~49
WINSTON, James William 92~43
WINTER, Daniel 303~58 Ebenezer 13~40, 304~3 Fila 303~58 Garey 304~1 Huldah 286~27 Jasper 303~58 Thaddeus 304~1
WINTHROP, John 58~33 Sarah Bowdoin 290~27 Thomas L. 290~28
WIRES / WARES, [children] 308~30 [Mrs.] 308~30 John H. 123~17, 142~21, 273~1 Samuel 24~40, 123~17, 124~14, 272~56 William 308~24
WISCHAM, William 209~48
WISE, [children] 241~15 Catharine 148~3 Hannah 241~14 John 241~15, 275~48 Mary Ann (Stearns) 275~49
WISEMAN, Joseph 206~23
WISWAL see **WISWALL**
WISWALL / WISWELL / WISWAL / WESWILL, [Mr.] 272~20 John 28~29 Joseph 134~26 Moses 21~12 Nabby 262~44 Noah 37~4, 82~51
WISWELL see **WISWALL**
WITCHER / WHITCHER / WHICHER / WICHER, [Mr.] 372~18 Benjamin 224~15
WITE see **WHITE**
WITHAM / WHITHAM, Theodore 304~55
WITHERBE see **WEATHERBY**

WITHERELL see WETHERELL
WITHINGTON see WORTHINGTON
WITTER see WHITTER
WOLCOTT / WALCOT / WILLCUTT / WALCOTT / WALCUTT, [Mr.] 220~38 Arodi 197~32 Clarissa 120~8 Elizabeth 214~26 Jesse 62~20, 62~42 Josiah 112~37 Lydia 196~55 Mary 55~15 Oliver 15~2, 214~27 Roger 55~15, 320~15 William 42~3
WOLF / WOLFE, [Dr.] 207~26 Arthur 213~15
WOLFE see WOLF
WOLLAGE, Elijah 94~4
WOOD, [infant] 40~35 [Rev.] 41~51 Abel 6~48 Abiel 170~14 Abraham 101~47 Anna (Parks) 40~32 Benjamin 13~50, 32~53 Benjamin L. 40~32 Daniel 287~21 Darius 289~31 David 7~48 Dorcas 310~54 Eleazer 192~20 Elizabeth 23~7, 131~47 Hannah 291~48 Jesse 248~28, 266~47 John 303~56 Joshua 38~52, 68~8, 68~58, 327~16 Mary 6~47, 172~5 Nathan 160~35 Robert H. 265~38 Ruth 164~11 Sally (Marsh) 289~31 Sarah 99~15 Sarah S. (Katen) 170~14 Thomas 72~57 William H. 318~8
WOODBERRY see WOODBURY
WOODBRIDGE, Benja (?) (———) 153~50 Enoch 66~46, 193~12 Fanny 226~47 John 328~34 Julia Anna (Trumbull) 247~28 Mary 208~46 Nancy 66~45 Nathaniel S. 200~18 Nathaniel Shaw 6~43 Ruggles 28~2 Timothy 288~24 William 247~28
WOODBURY / WOODBERRY, Andrew 133~56 Judith 153~20 Samuel 3~21
WOODCOCK, Ann (Hatch) 117~50 Elizabeth 56~51 Joseph 117~50 Nathaniel 299~53 Sarah (Fuller) 299~53
WOODFORD, Susanna 197~37 William 197~37
WOODHULL, Nathan 319~34
WOODMAN, [Mr.] 201~53 Catharine (Norton) 146~30 Joseph 297~32, 350~32 William R. 146~30
WOODRUFF, [brothers] 142~44 [families] 142~44 [Mrs.] 216~31 John 37~23 Joseph 50~49 Nathaniel 280~49
WOODS, [boy] 146~1 [daughters] 170~27 [Mrs.] 156~2 Abiah 113~32 Abigail (Wheeler) 50~47 Amy 273~17, 274~37 Benjamin 170~27 Betsey 43~23 Charles 355~18 Ebenezer 14~1, 170~27 Elizabeth 113~26 Ephraim 5~23 Hannah 285~50 John 2~10, 156~2 Jonathan 170~25 Leonard 50~46 Margaret (Macklin) 355~19 Nathaniel 102~3 Nathaniel W. 170~26 Susannah 143~32
WOODWARD, Anna 188~52 Betsey (Curtis) 125~1 Bezaleel 165~45 Esther 232~15 James W. 166~17 John 282~7 Jonas 221~44 Joseph 194~27 Moses H. 178~11 Park 288~29 Samuel 320~41 William 124~56
WOODWORTH, [boy] 73~28 [girl] 73~27 Ellen (Cummings) 326~23 Isaac 32~15 Jonathan 326~23 Joshua 73~27 Oliver 150~49 Robert 292~17
WOOLLEY, Lydia 187~47
WOOLLIS / WOOLS, Stephen 42~54, 361~36
WOOLS see WOOLLIS
WOOLSON see WILSON
WORCESTER / WORSTER, [Rev.] 274~19 [widow] 312~18 Arad 317~37 Benjamin 206~41 John 312~17 Joseph 27~36
WORDEN / WARDEN, [child] 131~52 [Mr.] 131~52 Elizabeth 294~23
WORKMAN, Phebe 299~18
WORMELEY see WORMLEY
WORMLEY / WORMELEY / WORMLY, Ralph 230~14, 231~11
WORMLY see WORMLEY
WORSTER see WORCESTER
WORTHINGTON / WITHINGTON, Jeffry 200~28 Joel 200~26 John 39~35 John G. 2~5 Mary 39~35 Sally 148~5 Sarah 175~40
WRAY see RAY
WRENDALL see RANDALL
WRIGHT / RIGHT, [child] 139~9 [children] 197~6 [Mr.] 201~53, 276~49 [Mrs.] 139~9 [widow] 197~15 Aaron 1~40, 104~14, 274~28 Abigail 285~47 Betsy 114~12 Chester 307~43 Daniel 241~50 Deliverance 40~40 Dorcas (Walker) 267~14 E. 315~14 Ebenezer 47~48, 197~3 Elijah 297~33, 298~46 Elizabeth 92~43 Elizabeth (———) 47~29 Elizabeth (Quirk)

187~29 Esther 264~27 Fanny 147~13 George 189~31 Irene (———) 171~28 J. 224~32 Jacob 267~14, 332~41 James 114~12 John 40~41, 187~29 John Crafts 211~24 Joseph 15~17 Josiah 240~1 Judah 239~57 L. 53~13 Martha 47~51 Mary (Hudson) 314~1 Mary Bouel (Collier) 211~25 Nathaniel H. 314~1 Oliver 89~46, 89~49 Phineas 135~36 Roxana 147~13 Samuel 234~41 Sarah 274~28 Stephen 176~13, 305~13 Susan 303~53 Susannah 210~56 Timothy 152~55 Ursula 118~7 Zaccheus 94~28
WRISLEY see RISLEY
WYATT, [Mr.] 214~19 Josiah 364~38
WYCOFF, Mary 5~33
WYER see WARE
WYLDE see WILD
WYLLYS see WILLIS
WYMAN, [Mr.] 328~57 [widow] 293~54 Alice 152~23 Betsey 202~20 David 151~55 Francis 323~3, 356~23 Isaac 131~40 Jacob 185~57 Mary 320~16 Polly 108~19 Sally (Cook) 151~55 Sarah 287~18 Thomas 127~45 William 78~55, 88~53, 291~20, 293~52
WYTHE, [Chancellor] 246~9 George 245~11

Y.

YANARDI, [Mr.] 54~21
YARD, Theodosia 199~18
YARRINGTON, Zipporam 208~45
YATES, [Mrs.] 265~46 Andrew 109~12, 268~11 Charles 291~2 James 363~44 Mary 268~10 Robert 100~41
YEATEN see YEATON
YEATON / YEATEN / YUATON (?), John 269~19 Lucy (Chauncey) 221~20 William 38~6, 221~20, 363~48
YELL, [girl] 104~25 [Mr.] 104~25
YELLOTT, Jeremiah 182~3
YEOMANS, Huldy 312~2 Joseph 104~16 Judith (Woodbury) 153~20 Ralph 200~28 Stephen 153~20
YORK, Fanny 275~13
YORKUS, Polly 39~44
YOUNG, [Dr.] 281~4 [Mr.] 8~7 [Mrs.] 285~34 Abigail 152~1 Andrew 2~44 Betsy 126~48 David 285~34 Joab 22~24, 40~48 John 80~41 Joseph 318~48 Levi 203~11 Naomi (Hill) 80~41 Nehemiah 262~55 Polly (Goodwillie) 249~41 Samuel 39~9, 78~34 Thomas 159~51, 249~41 William 212~33
YOUNGLOVE, John 250~25
YUATON see YEATON

Z.

ZANDT, [Mr.] 126~54
ZEISBERGER, David 287~38
ZINGLER, Christopher 160~33

Others.

INDIANS, Drunken Joe 127~5 Martha 199~23 Orono 87~49 Zacarah 199~23
SLAVES, [———] 51~3 Anthony 183~37 Archy 197~16 Beaufort 66~27 Dennis 195~27 Frank 4~7 George 195~27 Jack 326~27 Jonah Freeman 251~5 Kate 195~28 Ned 195~28 Phil 39~53 Pompey 165~13, 183~36 Sylvia 196~1 York & Ruf 244~3
———, Horatio 260~14 Ithamar 161~24 old woman 201~5 Unknowns 46~28, 95~50, 245~21, 330~3

www.ingramcontent.com/pod-product-compliance
Lightning Source LLC
Chambersburg PA
CBHW050325230426
43663CB00010B/1743